THIRD EDITION

Human Sexuality
Diversity in Contemporary America

BRYAN STRONG
University of California, Santa Cruz

CHRISTINE DeVAULT
Cabrillo College

BARBARA WERNER SAYAD
California State University, Monterey Bay

Mayfield Publishing Company
Mountain View, California
London • Toronto

Library of Congress Cataloging-in-Publication Data
Strong, Bryan.
    Human sexuality : diversity in contemporary America / Bryan
Strong, Christine DeVault, Barbara Werner Sayad. —3rd. ed.
      p.   cm.
    Includes bibliographical references and index.
    ISBN 0-7674-0045-3
    1. Sex.   2. Sex customs.   3. Hygiene, Sexual.   I. DeVault,
Christine.   II. Sayad, Barbara Werner.   III. Title.
HQ21.S8126   1998
306.7—dc21   93-38846
                                         CIP

Manufactured in the United States of America
10   9   8   7   6   5   4   3   2   1

Mayfield Publishing Company
1280 Villa Street
Mountain View, CA 94041

Sponsoring editor, Franklin Graham; production editor, Melissa Kreischer; developmental editors, Kate Engelberg and Megan Rundel; manuscript editor, Beverley J. DeWitt; art director, Jeanne M. Schreiber; design manager and cover designer, Susan Breitbard; text designer, Anne Flanagan; cover art, © Diane Fenster; art manager, Robin Mouat; illustrators, John & Judy Waller; photo researcher, Brian Pecko; manufacturing manager, Randy Hurst. The text was set in 9.5/12 Palatino by GTS Graphics, Inc., and printed on acid-free 45# Chromatone LG by Banta Book Group.

Brief Contents

Contents

3

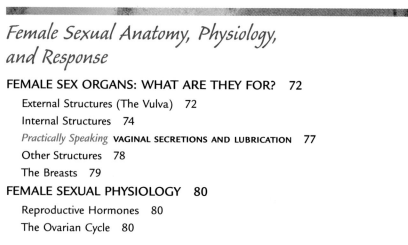

Female Sexual Anatomy, Physiology, and Response   *71*

4

Male Sexual Anatomy, Physiology, and Response   97

5

Gender and Gender Roles   114

6

Sexuality Over the Life Span

7

Love, Intimacy, and Sexuality   *202*

8

Communicating About Sex

9

Sexual Expression

10

Atypical and Paraphilic Sexual Behavior   286

11

Contraception and Birth Control   309

12

Conception, Pregnancy, and Childbirth   354

13

The Sexual Body in Health and Illness 394

16

HIV and AIDS   488

17

Sexual Coercion: Harassment, Aggression, and Abuse 523

18

To my children—Gabe, Will, and Maria. I'm proud of the loving young adults you've become.

—C.D.

To my family—my husband, Bob, and my children, Sarah, Elizabeth, and Sam—whose love is a never-ending source of joy and inspiration.

—B.W.S.

Preface

WE WROTE THIS textbook to make the study and teaching of human sexuality a meaningful and rewarding experience for both students and instructors. We present the study of human sexuality in such a manner as to enlarge both the student's personal and intellectual understanding. A personal approach does not exclude scholarship; nor does scholarship exclude personal understanding. Instead, scholarship allows the student to see beyond his or her own experience; and personal exploration breathes life into academic research.

The primary goal of this textbook is to integrate the personal and intellectual foundations of human sexuality. This goal led us to ask two fundamental questions. First, if we were college students, what would we want and need to know and understand about human sexuality? Second, what do we, as instructors and researchers, believe is important for an educated person to know about human sexuality? With these questions in mind, we formulated the structure and direction of this textbook. There are six important aspects to this textbook, described below.

Popular Culture   As we thought about the context in which students would read this textbook, we were struck by how powerful popular culture is in shaping attitudes, beliefs, and ideas about sexuality. In contemporary America, Dr. Ruth, Abigail van Buren, Oprah, Dr. Drew, and Demi Moore, Leonardo DiCaprio, Antonio Banderas, RuPaul, and Madonna, are among the most significant sources of sexual information, ideas, stereotypes, and values. It is important that students think about the depictions of sexuality in popular culture and critically evaluate their impact on our lives. Just as any research finding on human sexuality is subject to critical thought, so too is every image given to us by our popular culture.

Ethnic Diversity   As we looked at the demographic composition of our classes, colleges, and universities, we were struck by their increasing ethnic diversity. This diversity reflects the diversity of our nation, in which over 20% of Americans are from African American, Latino, Asian American, Native American, or other ethnic descent. To reflect this diversity, we have integrated scholarship on ethnicity and sexuality as much as possible. This scholarship, however, is limited, and much of it is problem oriented. But we believe it is important in our ethnically diverse society to expand the study of human sexuality to include all distinct ethnic groups.

Integration of Gay/Lesbian/Bisexual Research   As we considered the subject of sexual orientation, we decided that it is important to integrate gay/lesbian/bisexual research into the text rather than segregate these issues into a separate chapter. There are no compelling intellectual reasons to segregate research on gay, lesbian, and bisexual men and women from general discussions per se of communication, love, cohabitation, sexual expression, and so on. Such segregation implies differences where none may exist. It distorts our common humanity and relegates gay men, lesbians, and bisexuals to a "special" category. Such segregation, we believe, unintentionally encourages continued stigmatization.

HIV/AIDS Crisis   We are acutely aware of the HIV/AIDS epidemic. Because of its severity, we have devoted a chapter to examining its various aspects, including not only the biological and health aspects but also the personal, social, and psychological aspects. This chapter, along with the one on sexually transmitted diseases, has been thoroughly updated for this edition.

Research Based   We are deeply committed to scholarship and to presenting cutting-edge research in the field of human sexuality. In writing this book we carefully evaluated the current literature, using bibliographic databases and communicating with scholars around the country. We include what we believe to be the most up-to-date, important, and interesting research findings available. Our own research on love and sexuality continues to remind us of the joys (and limits) of research.

Teaching Support   We want to provide as much support as we can to the instructor teaching human sexuality. We believe a textbook's effectiveness as a teaching tool is dramatically increased when the text is systematically integrated with supplementary instructional material. We have developed a comprehensive, integrated teaching package that dovetails with the text and with classroom needs. Included in this package (described in detail below) are an instructor's resource book, a printed test bank, corresponding computerized test bank, a student study guide, supplemental videos, and a student guide to Internet resources.

Changes to This Edition

One of our objectives in preparing this text was to combine *Human Sexuality,* second edition, and *Core Concepts in Human Sexuality,* thereby offering the best of both books in a lower-cost, paperback edition. The result is a book whose length is midway between that of the two previous editions. For this, the third edition of *Human Sexuality,* we brought together both texts on a line-by-line and paragraph-by-paragraph basis, took the best of each, added new material where appropriate, and updated the text throughout. We have combined Chapters 6 and 7 of *Human Sexuality* into one chapter, now titled "Sex Over the Life Span." We also revised the pedagogy, eliminating the chapter-opening self-quizzes, removing the running glossary, and creating new titles for boxes, which we feel give a better idea of the focus of each one.

Additionally, we gathered some of the more practical and applied information from the text and included it, along with new material, in a Resource Center at the end of the book. The Resource Center also contains an expanded directory of organizations, hotlines, and World Wide Web sites, grouped by topic, which students can explore on their own.

We have addressed many new topics and issues in this edition and expanded coverage of numerous others. New and expanded topics include contemporary approaches in the treatment of sexual ambiguities, the business of cybersex, celibacy as a choice, friendship and its relationship to love, pros and cons of home tests for STDs (including HIV), and the transgender phenomenon. Another key change in this book is the use of color throughout and the inclusion of many new and striking photographs. A revised design helps to increase the visual appeal of the book.

PEDAGOGICAL AIDS

Human Sexuality is written in an accessible style at a level appropriate for most undergraduates. To support both teaching and learning, we have incorporated several learning aids in the text. Each chapter begins with a **chapter outline,** designed to give the student an overview of topics discussed in the chapter. Reinforcing the outline is an **"In this chapter"** paragraph, describing the chapter's contents.

Providing students with greater understanding of particular timely, high-interest topics are boxes called **"Think About It."** Sample titles include "My Genes Made Me Do It: Sociobiology, Evolutionary Psychology, and the Mysteries of Love," "Bisexuality: The Nature of Dual Attraction," "Body Play: Tattooing and Piercing," and "Gay and Lesbian Parents." Also featured are boxes called **"Practically Speaking."** These boxes give students the opportunity to reflect on their personal attitudes, beliefs, and behaviors and to evaluate their own experiences in light of knowledge gained through reading the chapter. Sample titles include "Touch: Overcoming Differences,"and "Guidelines for Choosing a Contraceptive Method."

Important **key terms** are printed in boldface type and defined in context as well as in the glossary. Appearing at the ends of chapters are chapter **summaries,** designed to assist students in understanding main ideas and in reviewing chapter material. An annotated listing of **suggested reading** is included at the end of every chapter as well, providing the student with sources of additional information and resources for research projects. Together, these pedagogical aids support and facilitate effective teaching and successful learning.

INTEGRATED TEACHING PACKAGE

As noted above, *Human Sexuality* includes a teaching package designed to increase the text's effectiveness as a teaching tool. At the heart of this package is the **Resource Book.** Developed by Bryan Strong and Barbara W. Sayad, this book begins with general concepts and strategies for teaching human sexuality. We offer suggestions on issues such as setting the ground rules for creating a supportive classroom environment, guidelines for integrating ethnicity, popular culture, gay men, lesbians, and bisexuals into the course, and using the computer in research. Also in this section are suggested background readings, bibliographies, films and videos, and lists of transparency masters and student worksheets. We then provide the following resources for each chapter: outline, learning objectives, discussion questions, activities, list of films and videos, bibliography, worksheets, handouts, and transparency masters.

A **computerized test bank** of over 2,000 test items has been prepared by Roy O. Darby III, University of South Carolina, Beaufort. He brings substantial experience in teaching and in testing and measurement to this element of the package. Each chapter contains approximately 130 test items, including multiple choice questions, true-false questions, fill-in questions tied to key terms, short-answer questions, and essay questions. The test bank can be used with either IBM or Macintosh computers. The test bank is also printed and bound into one volume.

A student **study guide** has been prepared by Bobbi Mitzenmacher, California State University, Long Beach, and Barbara Sayad. The study guide contains detailed learning objectives, key terms, practice tests, activities, personal involvement assessments, and a step-by-step guide to preparing a personal and meaningful gender identity paper.

Videotapes are available that give instructors the opportunity to illustrate and extend coverage of the most current and compelling topics treated in the text. The **Mayfield Relationships and Intimacy Videotape,** which has been developed to accompany this text, comprises 13 10- to 15-minute video segments on subjects such as gender roles, the effect of AIDS on women, and date rape. Other videotapes on a wide range of topics are also available.

A new resource for students is the **Mayfield Quick View Guide to the Internet for Students of Intimate Relationships, Sexuality, and Marriage and the Family** by M. Paz Galupo, Towson University, Jennifer Campbell, and Michael Keene, both of the University of Tennessee, Knoxville. This short text introduces students to the Internet and provides them with extensive resources for using the Internet in the study of human sexuality. The guide can be shrinkwrapped with *Human Sexuality* at no additional cost to the student. We also will offer PowerPoint lecture outlines for this edition which can be customized to fit your course and can be printed as color transparencies.

For information on any component of the teaching package, instructors should contact their Mayfield representative or call (800) 433-1279.

ACKNOWLEDGMENTS

Many people contributed to the creation and development of this book. We are grateful, first of all, for the kind assistance of the reference staff at California State University, Monterey Bay.

Ruth Gunn Mota of International Health Programs has provided valuable information about HIV and AIDS, as have the staff of the Santa Cruz AIDS Project. They are deeply committed to increasing AIDS awareness among students and members of the community, as are a number of people living with AIDS in our community. We applaud their work.

Our friend and colleague Art Aron, one of the leading researchers in the social psychology of love, assisted us in developing Chapter 7, "Love, Intimacy, and Sexuality." Terence Crowley, professor of library science at San

Jose State University, continues to assist us—and entertain us—when we have difficult questions to research. Pepper Schwartz at the University of Washington has shared her ideas with us about the relationship between sex research and its popularization in the media. Fran Bussard, formerly of California State University, Chico, is an ever-thoughtful friend who provides ongoing insight into human relationships. Julie Rogers contributed greatly to the development of the instructor's manual. Special thanks to William Yarber of Indiana University for allowing us to use his health assessment instruments.

Of those at Mayfield Publishing Company, we particularly wish to acknowledge Frank Graham, our editor, and thank him for his inspiration, knowledge, and hard work. We also wish to thank Kate Engelberg, managing developmental editor, for her insights, sensitivity, patience, and professionalism. Megan Rundel, our developmental editor, was a source of insight and support as we revised the manuscript. Thanks to our production editor, Melissa Kreischer, who did outstanding work in managing the production process, keeping the book on schedule, and working closely with us from the first edition developing the photo program. We appreciate the conscientious editing and help of our manuscript editor, Bev DeWitt. Thanks to Susan Breitbard, design manager; Robin Mouat, art manager; Brian Pecko, photo researcher; Martha Granahan, permissions editor; and Susan Shook, supplements editor. Linda Toy, vice president, production, was a source of encouragement in producing the book. Dick Greenberg, president of Mayfield, also offered support and encouragement; it has been a pleasure working with him.

Author's Note

It was a pleasure and a privilege to co-author Human Sexuality *with Bryan Strong, my husband, beginning with its first edition. Our work on the book was exciting and challenging—and tinged with bittersweetness, as Bryan was diagnosed with malignant melanoma in May of 1993. He died on August 10, 1996. Through his teaching and writing, Bryan touched the lives of thousands of students, both known and unknown to him. In the third edition of the text, my co-author, Barbara Sayad, and I have endeavored to keep Bryan's legacy alive by continuing his commitment to rigorous research and scholarship as well as maintaining the sensitivity, accessibility, and essential humanity that have distinguished* Human Sexuality *since its inception.*

Our editor, Frank Graham, the staff at Mayfield, and Barbara Sayad have been unstintingly supportive and gracious to me throughout difficult times. I am deeply grateful to them all.

Christine DeVault

Prologue

*B*EING SEXUAL IS an essential part of being human. Through our sexuality, we are able to connect with others on the most intimate levels, revealing ourselves and creating strong bonds. Sexuality is a source of great pleasure and profound satisfaction. It is the means by which we reproduce—bringing new life into the world, and transforming ourselves into mothers and fathers. Paradoxically, sexuality can also be a source of guilt and confusion, a pathway to infection, and a means of exploitation and aggression. Examining the multiple aspects of human sexuality will help you understand your own sexuality and that of others. It will provide the basis for enriching your relationships.

Throughout our lives, we make sexual choices based on our experience, attitudes, values, and knowledge. The decisions many of us may face include whether to become or keep on being sexually active; whether to establish, continue, or end an intimate relationship; whether to practice safer sex consistently; and how to resolve conflicts, if they exist, between our values and our sexual desires, feelings, and behaviors. The choices we make may vary at different times in our lives. Our sexuality changes and evolves as we ourselves change.

STUDYING HUMAN SEXUALITY

Students begin studying sexuality for many reasons: to gain insight into their sexuality and relationships, to explore personal sexual issues, to dispel anxieties and doubts, to resolve traumatic sexual experiences, to prepare for the helping professions, or to increase their general knowledge. Many students find the study of sexuality empowering. They discover their ability to make intelligent sexual choices based on their own needs, desires, and values rather than on guilt, ignorance, pressure, fear, or conformity.

The study of human sexuality differs from the study of accounting, plant biology, and medieval history because human sexuality is surrounded by a vast array of taboos, fears, prejudices, and hypocrisy. For many Americans, sexuality creates feelings of stress. It is linked not only with intimacy and pleasure, but also with stress, guilt, and discomfort. As a result, you may find yourself confronted with society's mixed feelings about sexuality as you study it. You may find, for example, that others perceive you as somehow "different" for taking a course in human sexuality. Some may feel threatened in a vague, undefined way. Parents, partners, or spouses (not to mention your own children, if you are a parent) may wonder why you want to take a "sex class"; they may want to know why you don't take something more "serious"—as if sexuality were not one of the most important issues we face as individuals and as a society. Sometimes this uneasiness manifests itself in humor, one of the ways in which we deal with ambivalent feelings: "You mean you have to take a *class* on sex?" "Are there labs?" "Why don't you let me show you?"

Ironically, despite societal ambivalence, you may quickly find that your human sexuality textbook becomes the most popular book in your dormitory or apartment. "I can never find my textbook when I need it," one of our students complained. "My roommates are always reading it. And they're not even taking the course!" Another student observed: "My friends used to kid me about taking the class, but now the first thing they ask when they see me is what we discussed in class." "People borrow my book so often without asking," wrote one student, "that I hide it now."

What these responses signify is simple: Despite their ambivalence, people *want* to learn about human sexuality. On some level, they understand that what they have learned may have been haphazard, unreliable, stereotypical, incomplete, unrealistic, irrelevant—or dishonest. As adults, they are ready to move beyond "sperm meets egg" stories.

As you study human sexuality, you will discover yourself exploring areas not ordinarily discussed in other classes. Sometimes they are rarely talked about even among friends. They may be prohibited by parental or religious teaching. The more an area is judged to be in some way "bad" or "immoral," the less likely it is to be discussed. Ordinary behaviors such as masturbation and sexual fantasies are often the source of considerable guilt. But in your human sexuality course, they will be examined objectively. You may be surprised to discover, in fact, that part of your learning consists in *unlearning* myths, half-truths, factual errors, and distortions you learned earlier.

You may feel uncomfortable when you go to the first class meetings. That's not at all uncommon. When I (Bryan Strong) went to the first day of my human sexuality class as a student in 1970, I felt embarrassed, out of place. The class was in a darkened auditorium, which gave me the uncomfortable sense I was in an adult movie house. Because I was nervous, I went with a friend; I slouched low in my seat. In retrospect, these feelings are not surprising. Sexuality may be the most tabooed subject we study as undergraduates. (Highly respected sex researchers have been investigated by the FBI because of their research.) Your comfort level in class will probably increase as you recognize that you and your fellow students have a common purpose in learning about sexuality. Your sense of ease may also increase as you and your classmates get to know each other and discuss sexuality, both inside and outside class.

You may find that as you become used to using the accepted sexual vocabulary, you become more comfortable discussing various topics. Perhaps you may find that you have never before used the words "masturbation," "sexual intercourse," "vulva," "penis," "heterosexuality," or "homosexuality" in a class setting (or any kind of setting, for that matter). But after a while, they may become second nature to you. You may discover that discussing sex academically becomes as easy as discussing geography, accounting, or literature. You may even find yourself, as many students do, telling your friends what you learned in class while on a bus or in a restaurant, as other passengers or diners gasp in shock or lean toward you to hear better!

Studying sexuality requires respect for your fellow students. You'll discover that the experiences and values of your classmates vary greatly. Some students have little sexual experience, while others have substantial experience; some students hold liberal sexual values, while others hold conservative ones. Some students are gay, lesbian, or bisexual, while the majority are heterosexual. Most students are young, others middle-aged, some old—each in a different stage of life and with different development tasks before them. Furthermore, the presence of students from any of the more than 124 ethnic groups in the United States reminds us that there is no single behavioral, attitudinal, value, or belief system that encompasses sexuality in contemporary America.

Because of America's diversity in terms of experience, values, orientation, age, and ethnicity, the study of sexuality calls for us to be open-minded: to be receptive to new ideas and to differentness; to seek to understand what we have not understood before; to reexamine old assumptions, ideas, and beliefs; to encompass the humanity in each of us. In our quest for knowledge and understanding, we need to be intellectually curious. As writer Joan Nestle observes, "Curiosity builds bridges. . . . Curiosity is not trivial; it is the respect one life pays to another."

THE AUTHORS' PERSPECTIVE

We developed this textbook along several themes, which we believe will help you better understand your sexuality and that of others.

Biopsychosocial Orientation

Although we are creatures rooted in biology, hormones and the desire to reproduce are not the only important factors shaping our sexuality. We believe that the most significant factor is the interplay between our biology, our individual personality, and social factors. As a result, we use a biopsychosocial perspective in explaining human sexuality. This perspective emphasizes the roles of biology (being male or female, the influence of genetics, the role of hormones), of psychological factors (such as motivation, emotions, and attitudes), and of social learning (the process of learning from others and society). We look at how sexuality is shaped in our culture; we examine how it differs in different historical periods and between different ethnic groups in our culture. We also examine how sexuality takes different forms in other cultures throughout the world.

In addition, because we want students to apply the concepts presented in this book to their own lives, we have presented information and ideas in ways that encourage students to become proactive in their own sexual well-being. We have highlighted sexual health-related topics in boxes called "Think About It" and asked questions that prompt students to examine their own values and the ways they express their sexuality in boxes called "Practically Speaking."

Sex as Intimacy

We believe that sex in our culture is basically an expressive and intimate activity. It is a vehicle for expressing feelings, whether positive or negative. It is also a means for establishing and maintaining intimacy. Sex is also important as a means of reproduction, but because of the widespread use of birth control, reproduction has become increasingly a matter of choice.

Gender Roles

Gender roles are societal expectations of how women and men are expected to behave in a particular culture. Among other things, gender roles tell us how we are to act sexually. Although women and men differ, we believe most differences are rooted more in social learning than in biology.

Traditionally, our gender roles have viewed men and women as "opposite" sexes. Men were active, women passive; men were sexually aggressive, women sexually receptive; men sought sex, women sought love. Research, however, suggests that we are more alike than different as men and women. To reflect our commonalities rather than our differences, we refer not to the "opposite" sex, but to the "other" sex.

Sexuality and Popular Culture

Much of what we learn about sexuality from popular culture and the media—from so-called sex experts, magazine articles, how-to-do-it books, and TV and the movies—is wrong, half-true, or stereotypical. Prejudice may masquerade as fact. Scholarly research may also be flawed for various reasons. Throughout the textbook, we look at how we can evaluate what we read and see, both in popular culture and in scholarly research. We compare scholarly findings to sexual myths and beliefs, including research about gay men and lesbians and ethnic groups.

Homosexuality as a Normal Sexual Variation

We recognize the normalcy of gay and lesbian sexual orientations. Gay men and lesbians have been subjected to discrimination, prejudice, and injustice for centuries because of their orientation. But as society has become more enlightened, it has discovered that lesbians and gay men do not differ from heterosexuals in any significant aspect except in their choice of sexual partners. In 1972, the American Psychiatric Association removed homosexuality from its list of mental disorders. Today, the major professional psychological, sociological, and health associations in the United States regard homosexuality as a normal sexual variation. For this reason, we have integrated discussions of lesbians and gay men throughout the book.

The Significance of Ethnicity

Until recently, Americans have ignored ethnicity as a factor in studying human sexuality. We have acted as if being White, African American, Latino, Asian American, or Native American made no difference in terms of sexual attitudes, behaviors, and values. But there are important differences, and we

Students begin the study of human sexuality for a multitude of reasons. When we asked our students to tell us what they wanted to learn in our class, their answers emphasized the personal dimension of learning. The student responses below are representative.

- My biggest issue is setting my own sexual guidelines, rather than accepting those of others, such as my friends, society, etc. —*a 20-year-old woman*

- I want to know the difference between sex and love. When I have sex with a woman, I think I'm in love with her, or at least want to be. Am I kidding myself? —*a 21-year-old man*

- I have a hard time telling my boyfriend what I want him to do. I get embarrassed and end up not getting what I need. —*a 19-year-old woman*

- I lost my virginity last week. What do you do when you sleep with someone for the first time? —*an 18-year-old man*

- I recently separated from my husband and am beginning to date again. I'd like to know what the proper sexual etiquette is today. Such as, do you kiss or have sex on the first date . . . or what? —*a 37-year-old woman*

- I'm gay, but my family would disown me if they found out. What can I do to make my parents understand that it's OK to be gay? —*a 20-year-old man*

- My parents continue to hassle me about sex. They want me to be a virgin when I marry (which is next to impossible, since I lost my virginity when I was

16). Any suggestions on how to raise parents? —*a 19-year-old woman*

- Is it wrong to masturbate if you have a regular partner? —*a 22-year-old man*

- Why do women get called "sluts" if they have more than one partner, and it doesn't matter for guys? In fact, the more women they "have," the more points they get. —*an 18-year-old woman*

- How do I know if I'm normal? What is normal? And why do I care? —*a 21-year-old man*

- I'm a sexy 70-year-old. How come young people think sex stops when you're over 40? We don't spend all day just knitting, you know. —*a 70-year-old woman*

Some of these questions relate to facts, some concern attitudes or relationships, and still others concern values. But all of them are within the domain of human sexuality. As you study human sexuality, you may find answers to many of these questions, as well as those of your own. You will also find that your class will raise questions the textbook or instructor cannot answer. Part of the reason we cannot answer all your questions is that there is insufficient research available to give an adequate response. But part of the reason also may be that it is not the domain of social science to answer questions of value. As social scientists, it is our role to provide you with knowledge, analytical skills, and insights for making your own moral evaluations. It is you who are ultimately responsible for determining your sexual value system.

discuss these throughout the textbook. It is important to examine these differences within their cultural context. Ethnic differences, therefore, should not be interpreted as "good" or "bad," "healthy" or "deficient," but as reflections of culture. Our understanding of the role of ethnicity, however, is limited because ethnic research is only now beginning to emerge.

* * *

Over the years, we have asked our students to briefly state what they learned or gained in our human sexuality class. Here are some of their answers.

I learned to value the exploration of my sexuality much more. I learned that sexuality comes in many forms, and I'm one of them. The class gave me a forum or safe place to explore sexuality, especially since I have not yet had a fully sexual relationship

I found the psychological, historical, and anthropological elements of sexuality we discussed to be valuable. I see homosexuality in a totally new light.

I learned that being sexual is OK, that basically we are all sexual beings and that it is normal to want to have sex. I am no longer afraid to talk about sex with my boyfriend.

The information about AIDS cleared up many misconceptions and fears I had. I will always practice safer sex from now on.

The class has helped me come to terms with things that have happened over the last few months that are disturbing to me.

I have paid more attention to the erotic nature of things, not just the physical aspects of sex.

We believe that the knowledge you gain from studying human sexuality will be something you will carry with you the rest of your life. We hope it will help you understand and appreciate not only yourself but those who differ from you, and that it will enrich, expand, and enliven your experiences and your relationships.

1

Perspectives on Human Sexuality

*S*EXUALITY WAS ONCE HIDDEN from view in our culture: Fig leaves covered the "private parts" of nudes; poultry breasts were renamed "white meat"; censors prohibited the publication of the works of D. H. Lawrence, James Joyce, and Henry Miller; and homosexuality was called "the love that dares not speak its name." But over the past few generations, sexuality has become more open. In recent years, popular culture and the media have transformed what we "know" about sexuality. Not only is sexuality *not* hidden from view, it often seems to surround us.

In this chapter, we examine popular culture and the media to see how they shape our ideas about sexuality. Then we look at how sexuality has been treated in different cultures and at different times in history. Finally, we examine how society defines various aspects of our sexuality as natural or normal.

SEXUALITY, POPULAR CULTURE, AND THE MEDIA

Much of sexuality is influenced and shaped by popular culture, especially the mass media. Popular culture presents us with myriad images of what it means to be sexual. But what kind of sexuality do the media portray—for our consumption? What messages do the media send about sex to children, adolescents, adults, and the aged? To men? To women? To Whites, African Americans, Latinos, Asian Americans, and other ethnic groups? Perhaps as important as what the media portray sexually is what is not portrayed—masturbation, condom use, and erotic marital interactions, for example.

Images of sexuality permeate our society, sexualizing our environment. Think about the sexual images you see or hear in a 24-hour period. What messages do they communicate about sexuality?

Media Portrayals of Sexuality

Media depictions of sexuality are not as obvious and straightforward as we may initially think. On television, for example, we are usually presented with visual images that suggest but do not show sexual activities other than kissing. In the movies, a wider range of sexual behaviors is shown more explicitly. "Steamy " sex scenes and female nudity (often combined with violence) are part of the Hollywood formula for success. ("How can we put more tits and c— [sic] into this movie?" the director of *Basic Instinct* reportedly asked, upon walking onto the set [Zevin, 1992].)

The music industry is awash with sexual images. Contemporary pop music, from rock 'n' roll to hip hop, bursts with lyrics about sexuality mixed with love, rejection, violence, and loneliness. Heavy metal often reinforces negative attitudes toward women (St. Lawrence & Joyner, 1991). Popular music is transmitted through CD or cassette players or through television and radio. MTV, VH1, and music video programs televise videos filled with sexually suggestive lyrics, images, and dance. Because of censorship issues, the most overtly sexual music is not played on radio, except for some college stations. Disk jockeys, "shock jocks" such as Howard Stern, weather reporters, and sportscasters make numerous sexual references.

Magazines, tabloids, and books contribute to the sexualization of our environment. Popular novels, romances, and self-help books help disseminate popular ideas and values about sexuality. Supermarket tabloid headlines exploit the unusual ("Woman with Two Vaginas Has Multiple Lovers") or sensational ("Televangelist's Love Tryst Exposed").

Men's magazines have been singled out for their sexual sell. *Playboy* and *Penthouse*, with their Playmates of the Month, Pets of the Month, and other nude pictorials, are among the most popular magazines in the world. *Playboy* sells about 10 million issues monthly, including 2 million to women (Martin, 1992). (One-quarter of the top 40 best-selling videocassettes are usually produced by *Playboy* and *Penthouse*.) *Sports Illustrated*'s annual swimsuit edition sells over 5 million copies, twice as many as its other issues. But it would be a mistake to think that only male-oriented magazines focus on sex.

Women's magazines, such as *Cosmopolitan* and *Redbook*, have their own sexual content. These magazines feature romantically staged photographs of lovers to illustrate stories with such titles as "Sizzling Sex Secrets of the World's Sexiest Women," "Making Love Last: If Your Partner Is a Premature Ejaculator," and "Turn on Your Man with Your Breasts (Even If They Are Small)." Katherine McMahon (1990) found that almost all the articles she surveyed over a 12-year period in *Cosmopolitan* magazine dealt directly or indirectly with sex. Preadolescents and young teens are not exempt from sexual images and articles in magazines such as *Seventeen* and *YM*.

Advertising in all media uses the sexual sell, promising sex, romance, popularity, and fulfillment provided the consumer purchases the right soap, perfume, cigarettes, alcohol, toothpaste, jeans, or automobile. An advertisement for Infiniti, for example, claims: "It's not a car. It's an aphrodisiac." In reality, not only does one *not* become "sexy" or popular by consuming a certain product, but the product may actually be detrimental to one's sexual well-being, as in the case of smoking or alcohol consumption.

Media images of sexuality permeate a variety of areas in people's lives. They can produce sexual arousal and emotional reactions, increase sexual

Shock jocks such as Howard Stern are popular media personalities whose programs are filled with sexual references and innuendos. What messages do they suggest about sexuality? Men? Women? Homosexuality?

Women's magazines, such as Cosmopolitan, Redbook, *and* Mademoiselle, *use sex to sell their publications. How do these magazines differ from men's magazines, such as* Playboy *and* Penthouse, *in their treatment of sexuality?*

Sexual images are used to sell products. What ideas are conveyed by this advertisement? How does its appeal differ according to whether one is male or female?

behaviors, and be a source of sex information for both men and women (Davis & Bauserman, 1993; Duncan & Donnelly, 1991). In their analysis of the impact of sexually explicit materials on individuals' attitudes and behaviors, researchers Davis and Bauserman (1993) suggest that sex in the media is a form of persuasive communication because of its clear impact on those who view it.

Mass-media depictions of sexuality are meant to entertain, not to inform. As a result, the media do not present us with "real" depictions of sexuality. Sexual activities, for example, are usually not explicitly acted out or described in mainstream media. The various media present the social *context* of sexuality (Smith, 1991); that is, the programs, plots, movies, stories, articles, newscasts, and vignettes tell us *what* behaviors are appropriate (e.g., kissing or sexual intercourse), *with whom* they are appropriate (e.g., girlfriend/boyfriend, partner, between heterosexuals), and *why* they are appropriate (e.g., attraction, love, loneliness, exploitation). Furthermore, it is probable that regular consumers of media sex are likely to believe that sex acts in various forms happen more frequently than they actually do—that there are, for example, more affairs outside marriage, as well as more rape and prostitution (Greenberg, 1994).

Television

The vast wasteland of TV is not interested in producing a better mousetrap but in producing a worse mouse.

—*Laurence Coughlin*

Television is the most pervasive and influential medium affecting our views of sexuality. The visual depiction of explicit sexual behavior on network television, however, is limited. We generally see nothing more than kissing and occasional fondling—and only between heterosexuals. Other sexual behaviors, such as coitus or oral sex, may be suggested through words ("Oh, it feels so good") or visual or sound cues (close-ups of faces tensing during orgasm or music from Ravel's *Bolero* playing on the soundtrack). Sexual behavior is never overtly depicted, as it is in sexually oriented films. References to masturbation are rarely made; when they are, they are usually negative and consigned to an adolescent context, suggesting that such behavior

Television is one of the most pervasive media affecting our views of sexuality. What ideas and images about sexuality do your favorite programs convey?

is "immature." The popular comedy show "Seinfeld" was the first program to deal openly with masturbation. Female breasts may be shown, but usually in tight garments, with suggestive cleavages or nipples outlined through clothing; nipples themselves are taboo. In most cases TV talks about sex rather than depicts it (Greenberg, 1994).

Television helps form our sexual perceptions through its depiction of stereotypes and its reinforcement of **norms,** which are cultural rules or standards. Television shapes our perceptions differently, however, depending on the TV genre (the type of program). There are six major TV genres in which sexual stereotyping and norms are especially influential: situation comedies, soap operas, crime/action-adventure programs, made-for-TV movies, commercials, and music videos.

New content-based ratings for sex, violence, and language have begun to appear at the opening of many television programs. The labels are being used by most cable and broadcast networks, in addition to the age-related labels (such as TV-14 or Y-7) that were introduced in 1997 ("New Ratings . . . ," 1997). These new ratings are:

- S (sexual situations)
- L (coarse language)
- V (violence)
- D (suggestive dialogue)

Some shows will not need these new ratings; others will add such alphabet-soup labels as TV-14, L, V. The verdict is still out on the effectiveness and accuracy of these labels.

Situation Comedies   Sex in situation comedies? When asked, most people think there is none. After all, sitcoms usually deal with families or family-like relationships; children are often the major characters. Because they are family-oriented, sitcoms do not explicitly depict sex (Smith, 1991; Taylor, 1989). Instead, they deal with sexuality in the form of taboos centering around marital or family issues. The taboos are mild, such as the taboo

Television situation comedies, such as "Dharma and Greg," frequently use sexual themes. What are some of the sexual themes or ideas of the most popular sitcoms? Do they differ according to ethnicity?

against a married person flirting with another man or woman. If a sitcom were to deal with a major taboo, such as incest, the program would go beyond the genre's normal boundaries; it would not be funny.

In sitcoms, the formula is to put characters in situations in which they unknowingly violate conventional social rules, thereby creating chaos. The chaos, however, is resolved by the show's end, and everyone "lives happily ever after" until the next episode. Thus, a married man can be getting an eyelash out of his sister-in-law's eye when his wife comes home early and becomes jealous, suspecting her husband and sister of kissing. While the laugh track plays, the husband tries to explain that "she had something in her eye."

Sitcoms are sexually stereotypical. Their range of sexual standards and implied behaviors is limited, although the sexual references have increased considerably since the days of "I Love Lucy" (Cantor, 1991). Despite the increase in sexual references, sitcoms barely touch on the variety of values and behaviors found in the real world. Billy Crystal's breakthrough gay character in "Soap," Martin Mull's in "Roseanne," and Ellen DeGeneres's in "Ellen" are examples of gay characters in mainstream sitcoms, but they remain the exception. Conservative advocacy groups continue to oppose depictions of gay men and lesbians as normal. Although sitcoms have a limited range, they are nevertheless affirming of connectedness and family values. They provide a context of intimacy for sexuality. Whatever transgression occurs, it is forgotten by the next episode.

Soap Operas   Soap operas are one of the most popular TV genres. One soap, "Days of Our Lives," is among the top ten most-watched television programs among college students (Cary, 1992). Although sexual transgressions are soon forgotten in sitcoms, they are never forgotten in soap operas. Transgressions are the lifeblood of soaps: jealousy and revenge are ever-present. Most characters are now, or once were, involved with each other. The ghosts of past loves haunt the mansions and townhouses; each relationship carries a heavy history with it. Infidelity, pregnancy alarms, wild affairs, betrayals, and jealousy punctuate every episode. Depictions of sexual behavior are fairly frequent.

Soap operas, including prime-time soaps such as "Melrose Place," offer distinct visions of sexuality. Sexuality is portrayed as intense and inspiring jealousy. Women are the primary audience. Why?

In recent years, *telenovelas,* Spanish-speaking soaps such as "Cañaveral de Pasiones" ("Canefield of Passion"), "Te Sigo Amando" ("I Still Love You"), and "Pueblo Chico, Infierno Grande" ("Small Town, Big Hell") from Latin America, have become increasingly popular among the Latino population. The content and messages of Latino soaps, however, do not differ significantly from those of soaps produced in the United States. They differ mainly in presenting fewer scenes suggestive of sexual activities, such as characters in bed.

The most explicit nudity is seen on the soaps: frontal shots of nude male torsos (genitals are not shown) and back shots of nude female torsos (to avoid the taboo naked female breast). Characters lounge in bed, wrapped in sheets; they are either about to engage in sex or are basking in its pleasurable aftermath. At the same time, no one seems to use contraception or take measures to prevent sexually transmitted diseases (STDs). By the odds, one would expect many pregnancies and an epidemic of STDs (Lowry & Towles, 1989).

Bradley Greenberg (1994), a leading media researcher, found that there were 3.7 sexual acts or references (including prolonged kissing, hugging, and intercourse) per hour in daytime soaps. "All My Children" had the most, averaging 5.2 per episode. Almost two-thirds of sexual references were to intercourse; this was followed in frequency by long, passionate kissing. Only kissing was visually depicted, however; sexual intercourse was usually discussed rather than shown. Most sexual interactions were between unmarried people; only about one-fourth of the couples who had sex were married to each other.

According to Greenberg (1994), the attitudes of soap characters toward sex are surprisingly negative. Those who were not participating in a sexual activity expressed disapproval when they learned of it. Seventy-four percent thought the sexual activity was dishonest, exploitative, or meaningless. They were especially negative about marital intercourse. Ninety-four percent, in fact, found fault with it. Among the characters participating in the sexual activities, only a slim majority expressed positive feelings about them. Many—whether married or unmarried—felt used or exploited.

Although there is also intimacy in the world of soaps, it is intense, unstable, and desperate. Relationships are usually stormy and short-lived, setting the scene for jealousy and revenge in subsequent episodes. There is no satisfaction or fulfillment in most soap relationships. Despite the genre's focus on sex, TV soaps give a clear message that sex is guilt-ridden, unsatisfying, and exploitative.

Crime/Action-Adventure Programs   In crime and action-adventure programs, there are few intimate relationships. Instead, relationships are fundamentally sexual, based on attraction. They are the backdrop to crime and adventure, which form the main plot of the story. The basic theme of a crime program is disorder (a crime) that must be resolved so that order can be restored. Often the disorder is caused by a sexual act or a sexually related issue, such as prostitution, pornography, rape, cross-dressing, sexual blackmail, or seduction for criminal purposes. As such, we see the underside of sex. Plots involve police searching for female killers who turn out to be cross-dressers, prostitutes who are murdered by sociopaths, runaways lured into pornography, and so on. Detectives and police go undercover, leading the audience into the underworld of prostitutes, pimps, and johns.

The detectives live isolated, emotional lives. Their involvements are ephemeral, usually not lasting beyond a single episode. Often their love interests are murdered; other times, the women themselves prove to be criminals. Detectives are portrayed as loners. The only intimacy they may find is with their detective partners or with secretaries (Clark, 1992). Marital intercourse is virtually nonexistent. Most sexual intercourse takes place between unmarried people or between men and prostitutes (Greenberg, 1994).

Made-for-TV Movies   Made-for-TV movies focus on "problem" themes. In contrast to most series, TV movies revolve around more controversial topics. When plots center on sexuality, they generally focus on sex as a social issue rather than sex as intimacy. Their plots feature such issues as adolescent pregnancy, extramarital affairs, rape, sexual harassment, and AIDS. (TV movies about AIDS have introduced, for the first time, nonstereotypical gay and lesbian characters who display a full range of human emotions.) Most sexual topics lend themselves easily to sensationalism, which TV often exploits because TV seeks to entertain rather than inform.

TV movies in which rape occurs often place rape within the context of entertainment. Such movies may use gratuitous sexual aggression as a means of "hooking" an audience. In the process, these movies may distort the seriousness of rape. Rape movies may present misleading stereotypes, such as a woman being sexually provocative, "deserving" to be raped or "leading the man on." By using a certain type of music, they make rape seem titillating. Although most rapists are known to the victim, TV films generally depict rapists as strangers. And although most rapes take place between members of the same ethnic group, rape movies on TV disproportionately depict African American men preying on White women (South & Felson, 1990).

Commercials   Commercials form a unique genre of TV programming. Although they are not part of the television program per se, because they are inserted before, after, and during the program, they become a free-floating part of it. In television commercials, advertisers may manipulate sexual images to sell products. The most sexually explicit commercials generally advertise jeans, beer, and perfume.

These commercials present a story told visually through a series of brief scenes or images. They do not pretend to explain the practical benefits of their product, such as cost or effectiveness. Instead, they offer the consumer an image or attitude. Directed especially toward adolescents and young adults, these commercials play upon fantasies of attractiveness, sexual success, and fun. Consumers are led to believe that they can acquire these attributes by using a particular product. However, research indicates that consumers tend to be offended by strong, overtly sexual ads (Latour & Henthorne, 1994).

Other TV Genres   Sex is present in other TV genres, too. Game shows often play on sexual themes, either suggestively ("The Newlywed Game") or explicitly ("Singled Out"). Among the staples of daytime talk shows, including "Oprah," "Jerry Springer," "Ricki Lake," and "Cristina," are unconventional guests and topics, such as women married to gay men or transsexuals, so-called sex addicts, and polygamists. Such talk shows use unconventional sexuality to provoke viewer interest. Although their prime purpose remains entertainment, talk shows can provide firsthand accounts of atypical sexual behavior that differs from the more common forms of sexual expression. These shows reveal the diversity of human sexuality, as well as give its participants a human face. As critic Walter Goodman (1992) observes: "They carry a gospel of tolerance, preaching openness for the unusual and encouraging greater acceptance of groups and behavior that have long been the objects of ignorance and fear." A few syndicated programs, such as "Loveline," offer more thoughtful (though still entertaining) discussions of sexuality from a nonjudgmental perspective.

News programs continually report rapes, child sexual abuse, pornography, sex therapies, and opinion polls on sexuality. TV news magazines examine various sexual issues "in depth" (for example, they devote more time, not thought). Both types of news programs usually deal with atypical or controversial aspects of sexuality.

In addition to mainstream television broadcasting, religious television networks and programs have wide appeal. Religious programming, such as "The 700 Club," broadcasts Christian fundamentalist visions of sex, sin, and morality (Shepard 1989; Wills 1989, 1990). These programs stress conservative family themes, such as adolescent chastity, opposition to sex education based on choice rather than abstinence, pro-life appeals, and homophobia.

> Of the delights of this world man cares most for sexual intercourse, yet he has left it out of his heaven.
>
> —*Mark Twain (1835–1910)*

Music and Music Videos

MTV, VH1, and music-video programs such as "Sex Appeal" are some of the most popular programs among adolescents and young adults. Most viewers, however, do not watch music videos for longer than 15 minutes at a time because they are repetitive.

Unlike audio-recorded music, music videos play upon the eye as well as the ear. Some productions, such as those of Michael Jackson and Madonna, are exceptionally artistic. Cindy Lauper's "Girls Just Want to Have Fun" was a breakthrough video with its affirmation of female freedom (Lewis, 1992). More recently, young female artists such as Jewell, Fiona Apple, Tori Amos, Shawn Colvin, and Sarah McLachlan have brought vigor, empathy, and individualism to the young music audience. Their music videos reflect their confidence, sensuality, and spirituality (Farley, 1997).

A few new music groups and individuals have broken ground by expressing their views about alternative sexual orientations. The lead singer of the group Marilyn Manson is bisexual, and the members of The Pansey Division are gay and use the pink triangle as their symbol. Lesbian musicians k. d. lang and Melissa Etheridge have a strong following among gays and lesbians. All of this music is slowly finding its way to mainstream audiences.

Most music videos are of average quality, relying on flashing visual images to sustain audience interest. Because TV prohibits the explicit depiction of sexual acts, music videos use sexual innuendos and suggestiveness to impart sexual meaning. Kissing, hugging, and suggestive behavior occur at twice the rate as in conventional TV shows. Interestingly, almost 25% of the videos in one study depicted considerable lesbian or gay exchanges. All

Sexuality is an ever-present theme in rock and rap. What image are the Red Hot Chili Peppers communicating about themselves, their music, and their fans?

but one, however, limited the activities to nonintimate touching or flirtation (Greenberg, 1994).

Hollywood Films

American motion pictures follow different rules from those of television regarding sexuality. Movies generally are permitted greater license in graphically depicting sexual behavior. But films are still limited by censorship. Like television, films tend to depict sexual stereotypes and to adhere to mainstream sexual norms.

Mainstream Films   From their very inception, motion pictures have dealt with sexuality. In 1896, a film entitled *The Kiss* outraged moral guardians when it showed a couple stealing a quick kiss. "Absolutely disgusting," complained one critic. "The performance comes near being indecent in its emphasized indecency. Such things call for police action" (quoted in Webb, 1983). Today, by contrast, film critics use "sexy," a word independent of artistic value, to praise a film. "Sexy" films are movies in which the requisite "sex scenes" are sufficiently titillating to overcome their lack of aesthetic merit. *Basic Instinct,* for example, was most noted for its "hot" sex scenes involving Sharon Stone, who subsequently achieved stardom based on her "sexiness" rather than her acting ability. Interestingly, sex scenes do not create equally famous male stars.

In Hollywood films of the 1990s, there is considerable female nudity, especially above the waist. But men are never filmed nude in the same manner as women. Men are generally clothed or partially covered; if they are fully nude, the scene takes place at night, the scene is blurred, or we see only their backsides. Except on rare occasions, the penis is never visible; if it is visible, it is limp, not erect, according to one film director (Toback, 1992). Even when the central theme of the movie involves male genitals, as in *Boogie Nights* and *The Full Monty,* the erect penis is not shown. In *Basic Instinct,* the director reported that the motion picture ratings board permitted him to show the penis of a murdered man "because it was dead" (Andrews, 1992). (In the more liberal European version of the film, however, a scene reveals Michael Douglas's penis in a frontal nude shot; the shot was cut for the American release.) A film psychologist notes: "People have gotten accustomed to wanting to see women nude. They don't think a nude woman looks vulnerable anymore. When a man is uncovered . . . the reaction is that he is extremely vulnerable" (Andrews, 1992).

Although movies today show more naked flesh, the old war-between-the-sexes theme continues with a significant variation. In today's film comedies and dramas, men pursue women and women resist, as they did before. What is new, however, is that the man's persistence awakens the woman's sexual desire. They fall in love, make love (or vice versa), and have passionate sex happily ever after. In these films, sex takes place outside of marriage (usually before marriage), reflecting the widespread acceptance of nonmarital intercourse. Such scenarios reflect traditional male/female stereotypes of the active man and passive woman. At the same time, however, they validate premarital sexual intercourse as a social norm.

Shots suggesting sexual intercourse and oral sex are commonplace in today's films. But scenes of sexual intercourse are generally filmed from a male perspective; the camera explores the woman's body and her reaction (Andrews, 1992). Even family-centered films, such as *Liar, Liar* (1997), have scenes intimating sex. But other common forms of sexual behavior, such as masturbation, are virtually absent from contemporary films.

Dangerous men and dangerous women are depicted differently in movies. As film critic Jerome Weeks (1993) notes:

> Masculine menace on screen and stage is usually seen as a generalized threat: Anyone would fear this particular male because he's a master of violence or dangerously out of control. But if female performers are dangerous, they're dangerous only "to men." It's practically unheard of for a female character to be intimidating in any terms that are not sexual. If they're killers, they kill their husbands, lovers, or the patsies they need and therefore seduce.

Violence among men, however, is portrayed. The horrifying rape of the character Marselles in *Pulp Fiction* (1994) interweaves violence and aggression with sex. Only a few female stars, such as Demi Moore in *G.I. Jane,* Linda

In recent years, movies such as Chasing Amy *have presented their lesbian, bisexual, and gay characters as fully realized human beings.*

Hamilton in *The Terminator* movies, and Sigourney Weaver in the *Alien* movies, dispense aggression and violence with the ease of a Clint Eastwood, Arnold Schwartzenegger, or Jean-Claude van Damme.

Gay Men and Lesbians in Film   Gay men and lesbians are generally absent from mainstream films. When gay men and lesbians do appear, they are consistently defined in terms of their sexual orientation, as if there was nothing more to their lives than sexuality. Gay men are generally stereotyped as effeminate, flighty, or "arty," or they may be closeted, as Kevin Kline was in *In & Out.* Lesbians are often stereotyped as humorless, mannish, or "butch." They are often excluded from the usual female norms of attractiveness in the media (Rothblum, 1994).

If gay men and lesbians are not seen as effeminate or butch, they are portrayed as sinister beings. Their sexual orientation is symptomatic of a dangerous pathology. In *The Silence of the Lambs*, the killer is a gay cross-dresser. Violent women are often depicted as lesbians or as having lesbian tendencies (Hart, 1994). And one film critic (Weir, 1992) notes:

> In Hollywood movies, heterosexuals are never defined as evil or irrelevant simply *because* of their sexuality. Whether they act nobly or ignominiously, other aspects of their personalities are brought to bear. Gay men and lesbians, on the other hand, are consistently characterized solely in terms of their homosexuality—when they are depicted at all. What's more, in American movies, homosexuality seems invariably to signal that a character is either sinister or irrelevant.

In recent years, gay and lesbian films have been increasingly integrating their characters' gayness into a wider focus. The poignant *Torch Song Trilogy* (1989), based on the Tony award-winning play about a gay female impersonator, and *Boys on the Side* (1995), an insightful love story, are not as much films about being gay or lesbian as they are about being human. Foreign films, by contrast, often treat gay men and lesbians more realistically than American films do. *The Crying Game* (1992), *Four Weddings and a Funeral* (1994), and *The Full Monty* (1997) all include gay themes, but the films are not about homosexuality per se. Instead, they touch on universal themes, such as love, loyalty, and self-discovery. Film historian Vito Russo (1987) observed:

> The fact they are movies about self-identified gays often confuses people into thinking that they are films by gays about homosexuality. This confusion will end when gayness is no longer a controversial topic. As Quentin Crisp has said, "Homosexuality won't be accepted until it is completely seen as boring—a mundane, inconsequential part of everyday life."

There is no more need to identify *Jeffrey* as being about gay men than there is to identify *Titanic* as being about heterosexuals.

Computer Sex and Dial-a-Porn

In recent years, computer networks and telephone media have created new ways of conveying or creating sexual fantasies. As a result of technological developments, we now have cybersex and dial-a-porn.

Cybersex   Cybersex involves expressions of sexuality (such as fantasies, talking about sex, and masturbation) while responding to images or words on a computer. It also includes online information about sex education and self-help groups. There is no question that the Internet is revolutionizing the way we think about sexuality. What is contributing to the popularity of cybersex is access, affordability, and anonymity. Using a computer on the Internet, for example, a person called "Hot Dog" can enter a "place" called "Hot Tub" and soak for a couple of hours with "Bubbles," "Sexy Lady" (a transvestite), and others who pop in and out. "Hot Dog" flirts with everyone; he describes himself, tells his fantasies, has kinky sex with "Sexy Lady" and a dozen others. "Hot Dog" is actually a woman but doesn't tell anyone. Every now and then, "Hot Dog" goes private and exchanges fantasies. None of this happens in the physical world. "Hot Tub" is a chat room on a computer network. People at different locations, linked by the network, type their fantasies on their keyboards, and those fantasies almost immediately appear on one another's computer screens. There are about 70,000 sex-related Web sites, accounting for a sizable chunk of the $4 billion U.S. adult-entertainment industry (Swartz, 1998).

Three of the top ten computer bulletin boards are dedicated to sexually explicit discussions. One network allows subscribers to interact with computer-animated graphic sex games. Users configure the appearance of their cartoonlike characters and engage in a variety of situations with characters controlled by other subscribers. When the characters have sex, only their faces are visible on the screen. The users, however, are able to see their partner's face, and they can control the expression on their own character's face.

In the first comprehensive survey of sexual habits in cyberspace, it was found that "erotic pursuits" are among the most frequent uses of the Internet and that "sex" is the most frequently searched word online ("Sex Called a Big Deal," 1998). One such site is marketed by ex-stripper Damni Ashe and receives 1.5 million "hits" a day. Not only can you conduct discussions or fantasies; you can also transfer to your own computer text files describing endless sexual encounters. There are also personal ads and shopping places

Cybersex—fantasy sex using computers—is a popular activity among many Internet users.

where you can order whips and chains. Hundreds of computer software programs that are animated and X-rated, such as "Leisure Suit Larry," are available.

As Gerard Van der Leun (1995) writes of cybersex on the Internet:

> A maze of steamy places that don't exist makes up the warp and woof of sex on the Net today. . . . [O]nline sex is as wild and far-ranging as the human imagination . . . But remember that cybersex has been going on since humans received the gift of imagination. Cybersex is, at bottom, simply old sexual fantasies in a new electronic bottle.

Computers are also used to create virtual reality (VR) sex. Jaron Lanier, who coined the term "virtual reality," is working on VR technology that will allow cable TV subscribers to use goggles, gloves, and body sensors to create their own sexual virtual reality.

Because of the high volume of sexual discussions and material available on computer networks, there is an increasing demand for censorship. In 1996, Congress passed the Communications Decency Act to make it an offense to use computer networks to transmit "obscene" materials or place "indecent" words or images where children might see or read them. Opponents have decried this legislation as a violation of freedom of speech. (For further discussion of this issue, see Chapter 18.)

Dial-a-Porn　Millions of individuals have called 900-number telephone sex lines. Advertisements for phone sex calls appear in most sexually oriented magazines; they depict nude or seminude women and men in sexually suggestive poses. For fees ranging from $3 to $15 a minute, a person can call a phone line and have a woman or man "talk dirty" with him or her. An analysis of dial-a-porn recordings found that subservience of the male to the female and reciprocal sex acts were the most common themes. In this survey, there were no violent themes, such as rape or bondage (Glascock & LaRose, 1993). Fantasy phone sex also caters to "specialty" interests, such as domination and submission, transvestism, and transsexualism.

Anonymous telephone sex provides the caller with pseudo-intimacy. Through the voice, the caller receives a sense of physical closeness. Because the phone worker is paid to respond to the caller's fantasies, the caller can move the conversation in the direction desired. The worker gives the caller the illusion that his or her fantasies are being fulfilled.

Although the ads depict the fantasy phone worker as highly erotic, the calls are often forwarded to the worker's home phone. At home, the worker is probably pursuing mundane tasks, such as washing dishes, changing a baby's diaper, or studying for an accounting exam. Sometimes the workers become involved in the fantasy, but more often they only half-listen while doing other tasks.

SEXUALITY ACROSS CULTURES AND TIMES

What we have learned to call "natural" in our culture may be viewed as unnatural in other cultures. Few Americans would disagree about the erotic potential of kissing. But other cultures perceive kissing as the exchange of saliva. To the Mehinaku of the Amazonian rain forests, for example, "kissing" is a disgusting sexual abnormality. No Mehinaku engages in it (Gregor, 1985). The fact that Whites press their lips against each other, salivate, *and* become sexually excited merely confirms their "strangeness" to the Mehinaku.

Culture takes our **sexual impulses**—our incitements or inclinations to act sexually—and molds and shapes them, sometimes celebrating sexuality, other times condemning it. Sexuality can be viewed as a means of spiritual enlightenment, as in the Hindu tradition, where the gods themselves engage in sexual activities; it can also be at war with the divine, as in the Judeo-Christian tradition, where the flesh is the snare of the devil (Parrinder, 1980).

Among the variety of factors that shape how we feel and behave sexually, culture is the most powerful. A brief exploration of sexual themes across cultures and times will give you a sense of the diverse shapes and meanings human beings have given to sexuality.

Sexual Impulse

All cultures assume that adults have the *potential* for becoming sexually aroused and for engaging in sexual intercourse for the purpose of reproduction (Davenport, 1987). But cultures differ considerably in terms of how strong they believe sexual impulses are. These beliefs, in turn, affect the level of desire expressed in each culture.

The Mangaia   Among the Mangaia in Polynesia, both sexes, beginning in early adolescence, experience high levels of sexual desire (Marshall, 1971). Around age 13 or 14, following a circumcision ritual, boys are given instruction in the ways of pleasing a girl: erotic kissing, cunnilingus, breast fondling and sucking, and techniques for bringing a partner to multiple orgasm. After two weeks, an older, sexually experienced woman has sexual intercourse with the boy to instruct him further on how to sexually satisfy a woman. Girls the same age are instructed by older women on how to be orgasmic: how to thrust their hips and rhythmically move their vulvas in order to have multiple orgasms. A girl finally learns to be orgasmic through the efforts of a "good man." If the woman's partner fails to satisfy her, she is likely to

The sensual movements of Latin American dancing have become popular in American culture. These dancers are celebrating their culture in a Latin American heritage festival.

leave him; she may also ruin his reputation with other women by denouncing his lack of skill. Young men and women are expected to have many sexual experiences prior to marriage.

This adolescent paradise, however, does not last forever. Mangaian culture believes sexuality is strongest during youth. As a result, when they leave young adulthood, youths experience a rapid decline in sexual desire and activity. They cease to be aroused as passionately as they once were. They attribute this swift decline to the workings of nature and settle into a sexually contented adulthood.

The Dani   In contrast to the Mangaia, the New Guinean Dani show little interest in sexuality. To them, sex is a relatively unimportant aspect of life. The Dani express no concern about sexual techniques or enhancing erotic pleasure. Sexual affairs and jealousy are rare. As their only sexual concern is reproduction, sexual intercourse is performed quickly, ending with male orgasm. Female orgasm appears to be unknown to them. Following childbirth, both mothers and fathers go through five years of sexual abstinence. The Dani are an extreme example in which culture rather than biology shapes sexual impulses.

Victorian Americans   In the nineteenth century, White middle-class Americans believed that women had little sexual desire. If they experienced desire at all, it was "reproductive desire," the wish to have children. Reproduction entailed the unfortunate "necessity" of engaging in sexual intercourse. A leading reformer (Alcott, 1868) wrote that in her "natural state" a woman never makes advances based on sexual desires, for the "very plain reason that she does not feel them." Those women who did feel desire were "a few exceptions amounting in all probability to diseased cases." Such women were classified by a prominent physician as suffering from "Nymphomania, or Furor Uterinus" (Bostwick, 1860).

Although women were viewed as asexual, men were believed to be driven by raging sexual appetites. Men, driven by lust, sought to satisfy their desires on innocent women. Both men and women believed that male sexuality was dangerous, uncontrolled, and animal-like. It was part of a woman's duty to tame unruly male sexual impulses.

The polar beliefs about the nature of male and female sexuality created destructive antagonisms between angelic women and demonic men. These beliefs provided the rationale for a "war between the sexes." They also led to the separation of sex from love. Intimacy and love had nothing to do with male sexuality. In fact, male lust always lingered in the background of married life, threatening to destroy love by its overbearing demands.

Although almost 100 years have passed since the end of the Victorian era, many Victorian sexual beliefs and attitudes continue to influence us. Some of these include the belief that men are "naturally" sexually aggressive and women sexually passive, the sexual double standard, and the value placed on women being sexually "inexperienced."

Sexual Orientation

Sexual orientation is the pattern of sexual and emotional attraction based on the gender of one's partner. **Heterosexuality** refers to sexual relationships between men and women. **Homosexuality** refers to same-sex sexual relationships. In contemporary American culture, heterosexuality is the only sexual orientation receiving full social legitimacy. Although same-sex relationships are relatively common, they do not receive general social acceptance. Some other cultures, however, view same-sex relationships as normal, acceptable, or preferable. Marriage between members of the same sex is recognized in 15–20 cultures throughout the world (Gregersen, 1986). (As this book is in production, the Hawaiian Supreme Court is reviewing a lower court decision legalizing same-sex marriages.)

Ancient Greece   In ancient Greece, the birthplace of European culture, the Greeks accepted same-sex relationships as naturally as Americans today accept heterosexuality. For the Greeks, same-sex relationships between men represented the highest form of love.

The male-male relationship was based on love and reciprocity; sexuality was only one component of it. In this relationship, the code of conduct called for the older man to initiate the relationship. The youth initially resisted; only after the older man courted the young man with gifts and words of love would the youth reciprocate. The two men formed a close, emotional bond. The older man was also the youth's mentor as well as his lover. He introduced the youth to men who would be useful for his advancement later; he assisted him in learning his duties as a citizen. As the youth entered adulthood, the erotic bond between the two evolved into a deep friendship. After the youth became an adult, he married a woman and later initiated a relationship with an adolescent boy.

Greek male-male relationships, however, were not substitutes for male-female marriage. The Greeks discouraged exclusive male-male relationships

In ancient Greece, the highest form of love was that expressed between males.

because marriage and children were required to continue the family. Men regarded their wives primarily as domestics and the bearers of children (Keuls, 1985). (The Greek word for woman, *gyne,* translates literally as "childbearer.") Husbands did not turn to their wives for sexual pleasure but to *hetaerae* (hi-TIR-ee), highly regarded courtesans who were usually educated slaves.

The Sambians of New Guinea   Among Sambian males of New Guinea, sexual orientation is very malleable (Herdt, 1987). Young boys begin sexual activities with older boys, move to sexual activities with both sexes during adolescence, and engage in exclusively male-female activities in adulthood. Sambians believe that a boy can grow into a man only by the ingestion of semen, which is, they say, like mother's milk. At age 7 or 8, boys begin their sexual activities with older boys; as they get older, they seek multiple partners to accelerate their growth into manhood. At adolescence, their role changes, and they must provide semen to boys to enable them to develop. At first they worry about their own loss of semen, but they are taught to drink tree sap, which magically replenishes their semen. During adolescence, boys are betrothed to preadolescent girls, with whom they engage in sexual activities. When the girls mature, the boys give up their sexual involvement with other males. They become fully involved with adult women, losing their desire for men. They become sexually interested only in women from then on.

Gender

Although sexual impulses and orientation may be influenced by culture, it is difficult to imagine that culture has anything to do with **gender,** the characteristics associated with being male or female. There are, after all, only two sexes: male and female. These appear solidly rooted in our biological nature. But is being male or female *really* biological? The answer is yes *and* no. Having male or female genitals is anatomical. But the possession of a penis does not *always* make a person a man, nor does the possession of a vulva and vagina *always* make a person a woman. Men who consider themselves women, "women with penises," are accepted or honored in many cultures throughout the world (Bullough, 1991).

Transsexuals   Within the United States there are approximately 15,000 **transsexuals,** people whose genitals and identities as men or women are discordant. In transsexuality, a person with a penis, for example, identifies as a woman, or a person with a vulva and vagina identifies as a man.

In order to make their genitals congruent with their gender identity, many transsexuals have their genitals surgically altered. If being male or female depends on genitals, then postsurgical transsexuals have changed their sex—men have become women and women have become men. But defining sex in terms of genitals presents problems, as has been shown in the world of sports. In the 1970s, Renee Richards, whose genitals had been surgically transformed from male to female, began competing on the women's professional tennis circuit. Protests began immediately. Although Ms. Richards's genitals were female, her body and musculature were male. Despite the surgery, she remained genetically male because her sex chromosomes were male. Her critics insisted that genetics, not genitals, defines a person's sex; anatomy can be changed, but chromosomes cannot. Richards, however, maintained that she was a woman by any common definition of the word. (Issues of sex, gender, and biology are discussed in Chapter 5.)

Two-Spirit   Most Americans consider transsexuality problematical at best. But this is not necessarily true in all cultures. In some cultures, an anatomical man identifying as a woman might be considered a "man-woman" and be accorded high status and special privileges. He would be identified as a **two-spirit,** a man who assumes female dress, gender role, and status. Two-spirit is regarded as a third gender (Callendar et al., 1983). It is neither transsexuality, transvestism (wearing the clothes, or passing as a member, of the other sex), nor a form of same-sex relationship (Callendar & Kochems, 1985; Forgey, 1975; Roscoe, 1991). Two-spirit is found in numerous cultures throughout the world, including Native American, Filipino, Lapp, and Indian cultures. In Indian culture, the third gender is known as the *hijra*. Regarded as sacred, they perform as dancers or musicians at weddings and religious ceremonies as well as provide blessings for health, prosperity, and fertility (Nanda, 1990). It is almost always men who become two-spirits, although there are a few cases of women assuming male roles in a similar fashion (Blackwood, 1984). Two-spirits are often considered shamans, individuals who possess great spiritual power.

Among the Zuni of New Mexico, two-spirits are considered a third sex (Roscoe, 1991). Despite the existence of transsexuals and pseudohermaphrodites (individuals with two testes or two ovaries but an ambiguous genital appearance), Western beliefs about gender focus on gender as biological. The Zuni, by contrast, believe that gender is socially acquired.

Two-spirits were suppressed by missionaries and the government as "unnatural" or "perverts." Their ruthless repression led anthropologists to believe that two-spirits had been driven out of existence in Native American cultures. But there is evidence that two-spirits continue to hold ceremonial and social roles in some tribes, such as the Lakota Sioux. Understand-

In some cultures, men who dress or identify as women are considered shamans. We'wha was a Zuni man-woman who lived in the nineteenth century.

ably, two-spirit activities are kept secret from outsiders for fear of reprisals (Williams, 1985). Among gay and lesbian Native Americans, the two-spirit provides historical continuity with their traditions (Roscoe, 1991).

SOCIETAL NORMS AND SEXUALITY

The immense diversity of sexual behaviors across cultures and times immediately calls into question the appropriateness of labeling these behaviors as *inherently* natural or unnatural, normal or abnormal. Too often we give such labels to sexual behaviors without thinking about the basis on which we make those judgments. Such categories discourage knowledge and understanding because they are value judgments, evaluations of right and wrong. As such, they are not objective descriptions about behaviors but statements of how we feel about those behaviors.

Natural Sex

How do we decide if a sexual behavior is natural or unnatural? To make this decision, we must have some standard of nature against which to compare the behavior. But what is "nature"? On the abstract level, nature is the essence of all things in the universe. Or, personified as Nature, it is the force regulating the universe. These definitions, however, do not give us much information for deciding what is natural or unnatural.

When we asked our students to identify their criteria for determining which sexual behaviors they considered "natural" or "unnatural," we received a variety of responses. These included the following:

If a person feels something instinctive, I believe it is a natural feeling.

Natural and unnatural have to do with the laws of nature. What these parts were intended for.

I decide by my gut instincts.

I think all sexual activity is natural as long as it doesn't hurt yourself or anyone else.

Everything possible is natural. Everything natural is normal. If it is natural and normal, it is moral.

When we label sexual behavior as "natural" or "unnatural," we are actually indicating whether the behavior conforms to our culture's sexual norms. Our sexual norms appear natural because we have internalized them since infancy. These norms are part of the cultural air we breathe, and, like the air, they are invisible. We have learned our culture's rules so well that they have become a "natural" part of our personality, a "second nature" to us. They seem "instinctive."

Normal Sex

Closely related to the idea that sexual behavior is natural or unnatural is the belief that sexuality is either normal or abnormal. More often than not, describing behavior as "normal" or "abnormal" is merely another way of

THE QUESTION, "AM I NORMAL?" seems to haunt many people. For some, it causes a great deal of unnecessary fear, guilt, and anxiety. For others, it provides the motivation to study the literature, consult with a trusted friend or therapist, or take a course in sexuality.

What is normal? We commonly use several criteria in deciding whether to label different sexual behaviors "normal" or "abnormal." According to professor and psychologist Leonore Tiefer (1995), these criteria are subjective, statistical, idealistic, cultural, and clinical. Regardless of what criteria we use, they ultimately reflect societal norms.

- *Subjectively "normal" behavior.* According to this definition, normalcy is any behavior that is similar to one's own. Though most of us use this definition, few of us will admit it.

- *Statistically "normal" behavior.* According to this definition, whatever behaviors are more common are normal; less common ones are abnormal. However, the fact that a behavior is not widely practiced does not make it abnormal except in a statistical sense. Fellatio (fel-AY-she-o) (oral stimulation of the penis) and cunnilingus (cun-i-LIN-gus) (oral stimulation of the female genitals), for example, are widely practiced today because they have become "acceptable" behaviors. But a generation ago, oral sex was tabooed as something "dirty" or "shameful."

- *Idealistically "normal" behavior.* Taking an ideal for a norm, individuals who use this approach measure all deviations against perfection. They may try to model their behavior after Christ or Gandhi. Using idealized behavior as a norm can easily lead to feelings of guilt, shame, and anxiety.

- *Culturally "normal" behavior.* This is probably the standard most of us use most of the time: we accept as normal what our culture defines as normal. This measure explains why our notions of normalcy do not always agree with those of people from other countries, religions, cultures, and historical periods. Men who kiss in public may be normal in one place but abnormal in another. It is common for deviant behavior to be perceived as dangerous and frightening in a culture that rejects it.

- *Clinically "normal" behavior.* The clinical standard uses scientific data about health and illness to make judgments. For example, the presence of the syphilis bacterium in body tissues or blood is considered abnormal because it indicates that a person has a sexually transmitted disease. Regardless of time or place, clinical definitions should stand the test of time. The four criteria mentioned above are all somewhat arbitrary—that is, they depend on individual or group opinion—but the clinical criterion has more objectivity.

These five criteria form the basis of what we usually consider normal behavior. Often, the different definitions and interpretations of "normal" conflict with one another. How does a person determine whether he or she is normal if subjectively "normal" behavior—what that person actually does—is inconsistent with his or her ideals? Such dilemmas are commonplace and lead many people to question their normalcy. However, they should not question their normalcy so much as their *concept* of normalcy.

Source: Tiefer, 1995.

making value judgments. Although "normal" has often been used to imply "healthy" or "moral" behavior, among social scientists it is used strictly as a statistical term. For them, **normal sexual behavior** is behavior that conforms to a group's average or median patterns of behavior. Normality has nothing to do with moral or psychological deviance.

Ironically, although we may feel pressure to behave like the average person (the statistical norm), most of us don't actually know how others behave sexually. People don't ordinarily reveal much about their sexual activities. If they do, they generally reveal only their most conformist sexual behaviors, such as sexual intercourse. They rarely disclose their masturbatory activities, their sexual fantasies, their anxieties or feelings of guilt. All that most people present of themselves—unless you know them well—is the conventional self that masks their actual sexual feelings, attitudes, and behaviors.

The only guidelines most of us have for determining our normality are given to us by our friends, partners, and parents (who usually present conventional sexual images of themselves) through stereotypes, media images, religious teachings, customs, and cultural norms. None of these, however, tells us much about how people *actually* behave. Because we don't know how people really behave, it is easy for us to imagine that we are abnormal if we differ from our cultural norms and stereotypes. We wonder if our desires, fantasies, and activities are normal: Is it normal to fantasize? To masturbate? To enjoy erotica? To be attracted to someone of the same sex? Some of us believe that everyone else is "normal" and that only we are "sick" or "abnormal."

Because culture determines what is normal, there is a vast range of normal behaviors across different cultures. What is considered the normal sexual urge for the Dani would send most of us into therapy for treatment of low sexual desire. And the idea of teaching sexual skills to early adolescents, as the Mangaia do, would horrify most American parents.

> Morality is the custom of one's country and the current feelings of one's peers. Cannibalism is moral in a cannibal country.
>
> —*Samuel Butler (1612–1680)*

Sexual Behavior and Variations

Sex researchers have generally rejected the traditional sexual dichotomies of natural/unnatural, normal/abnormal, moral/immoral, and good/bad. Regarding the word "abnormal," Ira Reiss (1989) writes:

> We need to be aware that people will use those labels to put distance between themselves and others they dislike. In doing so, these people are not making a scientific diagnosis but are simply affirming their support of certain shared concepts of proper sexuality.

Instead of classifying behavior into what are essentially moralistic normal/abnormal and natural/unnatural categories, researchers view human sexuality as characterized by **sexual variation**—that is, sexual variety and diversity. As human beings, we vary enormously in terms of our sexual orientation, our desires, our fantasies, our attitudes, and our behaviors. Kinsey (1948) succinctly stated the matter like this: "The world is not to be divided into sheep and goats."

Researchers believe that the best way to understand our sexual diversity is to view our activities as existing on a continuum. On this continuum, the frequency with which individuals engage in different sexual activities, such as sexual intercourse, masturbation, and oral sex, ranges from never to always. Significantly, there is no point on the continuum that marks normal or abnormal behavior. In fact, the difference between one individual and the next on the continuum is minimal (Kinsey, Pomeroy & Martin, 1948, Kinsey, Pomeroy, Martin & Gebhard, 1953). The most that can be said of a person is that his or her behaviors are more or less typical or atypical of the group average. Furthermore, nothing can be inferred about an individual whose behavior differs significantly from the group average except that his or her behavior is atypical. The individual who differs is not sick, abnormal, or perverse; rather, he or she is a sexual nonconformist (Reiss, 1986, 1989). Except for engaging in sexually atypical behavior, a person may be indistinguishable from any other person.

Many activities that are usually thought of as **deviant sexual behavior**—activities diverging from the norm, such as exhibitionism, voyeurism, and fetishism—exist in most of us to some degree or another. We may delight

My Genes Made Me Do It: Sociobiology, Evolutionary Psychology, and the Mysteries of Love

DO YOU EVER WONDER why you do what you do or feel as you feel—especially when it comes to matters like attraction, relationships, and sex? Do you wonder why the object of your affection behaves in such inexplicable ways—why he or she flies into a jealous rage for "no reason"? Or why your friend always seems to fall for the "wrong" person? Sometimes the answers may be obvious, but at other times they are obscure. Our motivations come from a variety of sources, among them, personality traits, past experiences, peer pressure, and familial and cultural influences. Many of our feelings probably result from a complex yet subtle blending of these influences—combined with innate responses programmed into our genes. Our sexual urges and responses are largely governed by hormones, tiny chemical structures that perform a number of functions, including that of "messenger," triggering diverse actions and reactions in the brain and various parts of the body. Our genetic makeup has been passed down to us from our early primate ancestors—both human and nonhuman. We share 98–99% of our genetic material with our closest primate cousins, the chimpanzees and bonobos (Blum, 1997).

Our growing understanding of the biological bases of behavior comes largely from the field of sociobiology and its offshoot, evolutionary psychology. Sociobiologists base their study of human behavior on Charles Darwin's theory of evolution. According to Darwin's theory, evolution favors certain physical traits that enable a species to survive, such as, for early humans, the ability to walk upright. According to sociobiology, evolution also favors certain genetically based behaviors or "reproductive strategies" that enhance an individual's ability to pass along his or her genes and ensure their survival (Symons, 1979). Thus, sociobiology finds biological explanations for phenomena such as male dominance, the sexual double standard, and maternal behavior.

An example of a sociobiological explanation for behavior can be found when we look at the apparently different attitudes that men and women have about the roles of sex and love. From a sociobiological perspective, males, who are consistently fertile from early adolescence on, seek to impregnate as many females as possible to ensure genetic success. Females, however, ovulate only once a month. For them, a single act of intercourse can result in pregnancy, childbirth, and years of child rearing. Thus it is important to females to find a partner on whom they can rely for protection and support over the long course of child rearing. In this way, they help ensure that the carriers of their genes (their children) will reach adulthood and pass along their parents' genetic legacy. The bonds of love are what keep the male around.

Or, in other words, females trade sex for love and males trade love for sex.

Evolutionary psychologists seek to explain the biological bases of love and other emotions such as hope, anger, jealousy, fear, and grief. We may wonder why Mother Nature made us so emotional when emotion so often leads us to disaster. But, Mr. Spock notwithstanding, there are good reasons (evolutionarily speaking) for having emotions. Even though in the short term emotions can get us into trouble—if we act impulsively rather than rationally—over the long term our emotions have helped our genes survive and replicate (Pinker, 1997). Emotions exist to motivate us to do things that serve (or once served) the best interests of our genetic material—things like fleeing, fighting, or forming close relationships to protect our "genetic investment" (offspring).

Critics of sociobiology argue that inferences from animal behavior may not be applicable to human beings; they feel that sociobiologists base their assumptions about human behavior (such as men wanting sex versus women wanting love) more on cultural stereotypes than on actual behavior. Sociobiologists reply that they report what they observe in nature and suggest connections to human behavior (humans are part of nature, after all) but do not make judgments about the meaning or morality of their observations. In fact, we must take care not to assume that because something is "natural," it is appropriate, moral, or the right thing to do. Thinking that confuses the "natural" with the "good" is called the naturalistic fallacy. This fallacy can be used to justify all sorts of antisocial or just plain rude behavior. For example, a man could use this sort of reasoning to justify extramarital affairs ("My genes made me do it"). In reality, our genes don't "make" us do anything. As social beings, we are still expected to learn to think before we act and to take the feelings and needs of others into account. This process, in fact, has a name: It's called "growing up."

As you study human sexuality, the authors of this textbook hope that the information you gain will help you integrate your own feelings and experiences with the information and advice you get from family, friends, lovers, and society. In the text, we take what might be called a "bio-psycho-social" approach to our subject, recognizing that the sexual self is produced by the interconnections of body, mind, and culture. As you continue your study, remember that although our culture and ways of thinking (what we might call the "software" of the mind) have been created by humans, our bodies and brains (the "hardware" of the mind) are the products of evolution. They've been developing over a long, long time.

Kissing is "natural" and "normal" in our culture. It is an expression of intimacy, love, and passion for young and old, heterosexuals, gay men, and lesbians.

in displaying our bodies on the beach or in "dirty dancing" in crowded clubs (exhibitionism). We may like watching ourselves make love, viewing erotic videos, or seeing our partner undress (voyeurism). Or we may enjoy kissing our lover's photograph, keeping a lock of hair, or sleeping with an article of his or her clothing (fetishism). Most of the time these feelings or activities are only one aspect of our sexual selves; they are not especially significant in our overall sexuality. Such atypical behaviors represent nothing more than sexual nonconformity when they occur between mutually consenting adults and do not cause distress (Reiss, 1989).

The rejection of natural/unnatural, normal/abnormal, and moral/ immoral categories by sex researchers does not mean that standards for

The fact of the matter is that the prime responsibility of a woman probably is to be on earth long enough to find the best mate possible for herself, and conceive children who will improve the species.

—*Norman Mailer*

evaluating sexual behavior do not exist. There are many sexual behaviors that are harmful to oneself (e.g., masturbatory asphyxia: suffocating or hanging oneself during masturbation to increase sexual arousal) and to others (e.g., rape, child molestation, exhibitionism, and obscene phone calling). Current psychological standards for determining the harmfulness of sexual behaviors center around the issues of coercion, grave potential for inflicting harm on oneself or others, and personal distress. (These issues are discussed in greater detail in Chapter 10.)

We, the authors, believe that the basic standard for judging various sexual activities is whether they are between consenting adults and whether they cause harm. Normality and naturalness are not useful terms for evaluating sexual behavior, especially variations, because they are usually nothing more than moral judgments. What people consider "normal" is often statistically common sexual behavior, which is then defined as good or healthy. But for many forms of sexual behavior, a large percentage of people will not conform to the average. There is a great deal of variation, for example, in the extent to which people eroticize boxer shorts and lacy underwear. Who determines at what point on the continuum that interest in undergarments is no longer acceptable? The individual? His or her peer group? Religion? Society? As Suzanna Rose and Victoria Sork (1984) note: "Because everyone's sexuality does not completely overlap with the norm, the only liberating approach to sexuality is to envision it from the perspective of variation."

As social scientists, sex researchers have a mandate to *describe* sexual behavior, not evaluate it as good or bad, moral or immoral. It is up to the individual to evaluate the ethical or moral aspect of sexual behavior in accordance with his or her ethical or religious values. At the same time, however, understanding diverse sexual attitudes, motives, behaviors, and values will help deepen the individual's own value system.

▪ Popular culture both encourages and discourages sexuality. It promotes stereotypical sexual interactions between men and women that fail to touch on the deeper significance sexuality holds for us. Marital love and sexuality are infrequently depicted, in contrast to casual or nonmarital sex. (By ignoring marital sex, popular culture implies that marriage is a sexual wasteland. Yet it is within marriage that the overwhelming majority of sexual interactions between men and women take place.) The media ignore or disparage the wide array of sexual behaviors and choices, from masturbation to gay and lesbian relationships, that are significant in many people's lives. They discourage the linking of sex and intimacy, contraceptive responsibility, and the acknowledgment of STD risks.

What is clear from examining other cultures is that sexual behaviors and norms vary from culture to culture and, within our own society, from one time to another. The variety of sexual behaviors even within our own culture testifies to diversity not only between cultures but within cultures as well. Understanding diversity allows us to acknowledge that there is no such thing as inherently "normal" or "natural" sexual behavior. Rather, sexual behavior is strongly influenced by culture—including our own.

SUMMARY

Sexuality, Popular Culture, and the Media

- Popular culture, especially the media, strongly influences our sexuality through the depiction of sexual stereotypes and *norms*. Mainstream media do not explicitly depict sexual behavior.

- Each television genre depicts sexuality according to its formula. Situation comedies focus on the violation of minor taboos centering on marital and family issues. Soap operas deal with sexual transgressions, jealousy, and power linked to sex. Crime/action-adventure programs depict relationships that are based on attraction and are short-lived; detective heroes form close relationships primarily with their detective partners or secretaries. Made-for-TV movies focus on "problem" themes, such as rape or adolescent pregnancy. TV commercials may promote a product by suggesting that consuming the product will lead to attractiveness or sexual success.

- Many popular music videos rely on suggestiveness and innuendo to depict sexuality. Women are usually portrayed as sex objects.

- Although Hollywood films depict sexual behavior more graphically than television does, sex scenes are often gratuitous. Sexuality tends to be stereotypical. Gay men and lesbians have generally been absent from films except in stereotypical roles. More recently, a few nonstereotypical gay and lesbian characters have been introduced.

- Computer networks and telephone media have created "cybersex," providing new ways of conveying sexual fantasies. The legal debate concerning the transmittal of these materials continues.

Sexuality Across Cultures and Times

- The most powerful force shaping human sexuality is culture. Culture molds and shapes our *sexual impulses.*

- The Mangaia of Polynesia and the Dani of New Guinea represent cultures at the opposite ends of a continuum, with the Mangaia having an elaborate social and cultural framework for instructing adolescents in sexual technique and the Dani downplaying the importance of sex.

- Middle-class Americans in the nineteenth century believed that men had strong sexual drives but that women had little sexual desire. Because sexuality was considered animalistic, the Victorians separated sex and love.

- In ancient Greece, same-sex relationships between men represented the highest form of love. Among the Sambians of New Guinea, boys have sexual relations with older boys, believing that the ingestion of semen is required for growth. When the girls to whom they are betrothed reach puberty, adolescent boys cease these same-sex sexual relations.

- A *transsexual* has the genitals of one sex but identifies as a member of the other sex.

- A *two-spirit* is a person of one sex who identifies with the other sex; in some cultures, such as the Zuni, a two-spirit is considered a third gender and is believed to possess great spiritual power.

Societal Norms and Sexuality

- Sexuality tends to be evaluated according to categories of natural/unnatural, normal/abnormal, and moral/immoral. These terms are value judgments, reflecting social norms rather than any quality inherent in the behavior itself.

- There is no commonly accepted definition of natural sexual behavior. *Normal sexual behavior* is what a culture defines as normal. We commonly use five criteria to categorize sexual behavior as normal or abnormal: subjectively normal, statistically normal, idealistically normal, culturally normal, and clinically normal.

- Human sexuality is characterized by *sexual variation*. Researchers believe that the best way to examine sexual behavior is by using a continuum. Many activities that are considered *deviant sexual behavior* exist in most of us to some degree or another. These include exhibitionism, voyeurism, and fetishism.

- Behaviors are not abnormal or unnatural; rather they are more or less typical or atypical of the group average. Those whose behaviors are atypical may be regarded as sexual nonconformists rather than as abnormal or perverse.

SUGGESTED READING

Bullough, Vern. (1976). *Sexual Variance in Society and History.* New York: Wiley. A thorough examination of attitudes toward sexuality in Western and non-Western cultures.

D'Emilio, John, & Freedman, Estelle. (1988). *Intimate Matters: A History of Sexuality in America.* New York: Harper & Row. An important study of American sexuality, especially in the nineteenth century.

Dines, Gail, & Humez, Jean (Eds.). (1995). *Gender, Race, and Class in the Media.* Thousand Oaks, CA: Sage. An excellent introduction to popular culture and the media.

Francoeur, Robert T. (Ed.). (1996). *Taking Sides: Clashing Views on Controversial Issues in Human Sexuality* (5th ed.). Madison, WI: Dushkin Publishing Group/Brown & Benchmark. Point-counterpoint discussions that help readers clarify their personal values and identify what society's are or should be.

Pally, Marcia. (1994). *Sex and Sensibility: The Vanity of Bonfires.* Hopewell, NJ: Ecco Press. A comprehensive survey of information on the effects of sexually explicit materials and the implications relating to censorship.

Suggs, David N., & Miracle, Andrew (Eds.). (1993). *Culture and Human Sexuality.* Pacific Grove, CA: Brooks/Cole. A collection of essays on sexuality in diverse cultures throughout the world.

2
Studying Human Sexuality

AN IMPORTANT DISCOVERY about orgasm was announced today by Harvard researchers. . . . But first, a message from. . . ." So begins a commercial lead-in on the ten o'clock news report, reminding us that sex research is often part of both news and entertainment. In fact, most of us learn about the results of sex research from TV and magazines rather than from scholarly journals and books. After all, the mass media are more entertaining than most scholarly research. And unless we are studying human sexuality, few of us have the time to read the scholarly journals in which scientific research is regularly published.

But how accurate is what the mass media tell us about sex and sex research? In this chapter, we discuss the dissemination of sex information by the various media. Then we look at the critical-thinking skills that help us evaluate how we discuss and think about sexuality. When are we making objective statements? When are we reflecting biases or opinions? Next, we examine sex research methods because they are critical to the scientific study of human sexuality. Then, we look at the leading sex researchers to see how they have influenced our understanding of sexuality. Finally, we examine feminist, gay and lesbian, and ethnic sex research to see how they enrich our knowledge of sexuality.

SEX, ADVICE COLUMNISTS, AND POP PSYCHOLOGY

As we saw in Chapter 1, the mass media convey seemingly endless sexual images. But in addition to the various television, film, and advertising genres, there is another genre that we might call the sex information/advice genre, which transmits *information* rather than images. The **sex information/advice genre** is a media genre that transmits information and norms about sexuality to a mass audience to both inform and entertain in a simplified manner. For most college students, as well as many others, the sex information/advice genre is a major source of their knowledge about sex.

This genre is ostensibly concerned with transmitting information that is factual and accurate. In newspapers, it is represented by such popular national columnists as Abigail Van Buren (whose column, "Dear Abby," is now written by a man), Ann Landers, Beth Winship, and Pat Califia. Sexual self-help and pop sex books written by "experts" frequent the best-seller lists.

Information and Advice as Entertainment

Newspaper columns, magazine articles, TV programs, and syndicated radio programs share several features. First, their primary purpose is to sell newspapers and magazines or to raise program ratings. This goal is in marked contrast to that of scholarly research, whose primary purpose is to pursue knowledge. Even the inclusion of survey questionnaires in magazines asking readers to respond about their sexual attitudes or behaviors is ultimately designed to promote sales. We fill out the questionnaires for fun, much as we would crossword puzzles or anagrams. Then we buy the subsequent issue or watch a later program to see how we compare to others.

Second, the media must entertain while disseminating information and advice about sexuality. The success of media personalities such as Ruth Westheimer, Laura Schlessinger, and Adam Carolla and Dr. Drew Pinsky of "Loveline" does not rest as much on their expertise as it does on their ability to present information as entertainment. Because the genre seeks to entertain, sex information and advice must be simplified. Complex explanations and analyses must be avoided because they would interfere with the entertainment purpose. Furthermore, the genre relies on high-interest or bizarre material to attract readers or viewers. Consequently, we are more likely to read, hear, or view stories about increasing sexual attractiveness or unusual sexual practices than stories about new research methods or the process of sexual stereotyping.

Third, the genre focuses on how-to information or on morality. The how-to material tells us how to improve our sex lives. Advice columnists often give advice on issues of sexual morality. "Is it all right to have sex without commitment?" "Yes, if you love him/her" or "No, casual sex is empty," and so on. Advice columnists act as moral arbiters, much as ministers, priests, and rabbis.

The line between media sex experts and advice columnists is often blurred. Ruth Westheimer, for example, mixes information and normative judgments. In a discussion of oral sex and ice cream cones, for example, not only does Westheimer suggest ways to engage in oral sex, but she also implies two contradictory norms: (1) Oral sex is a matter of individual choice, and (2) a woman should do what a man wants. The popular radio talk show host Laura Schlessinger has also become famous for the advice she dispenses, much of which is based strictly on her personal values and morals.

Fourth, the genre uses the trappings of social science and psychiatry without their substance. Writers and columnists interview social scientists and therapists to give an aura of scientific authority to their material. They rely especially heavily on therapists whose background is clinical rather than academic. Because clinicians tend to deal with people with problems, they often see sexuality as problematical.

Popular advice personalities, such as Adam Carolla and Dr. Drew Pinsky of "Loveline," dispense information while they entertain.

The Use and Abuse of Statistics

To reinforce their authority, the media also incorporate statistics, which are key features of social science research. But as Susan Faludi (1991) notes:

> The statistics that the popular culture chooses to promote most heavily are the very statistics we should view with the most caution. They may well be in wide circulation not because they are true but because they support widely held media preconceptions.

AFTER YOU HAVE READ several sex books and watched several sex experts on television, you discover that they tend to be repetitive. There are two main reasons for their repetitiveness. First, the media repeatedly report more-or-less the same stories because there is relatively little new in the world of sex or sexual science. Scientific research is painstakingly slow, and the results are tedious to produce. Research results rarely change the way we view a topic; usually they flesh out what we already know. Although research is seldom revolutionary, the media must nevertheless continually produce new stories to fill their pages and programs. Consequently, they report similar material in different guises: as interviews, survey results, and first-person stories, for example.

Second, the media are repetitive because their scope is narrow. There are only so many ways how-to books can tell you how to do it. Similarly, the personal and moral dilemmas most of us face are remarkably similar: Am I normal? Should I have an affair? Is sex without love moral?

With the media awash with sex information and advice, how can we evaluate what is presented to us? Here are some guidelines:

- *Be skeptical.* Remember, much of what you read or see is meant to entertain you. If it seems superficial, it probably is.

- *Search for biases, stereotypes, and lack of objectivity.* Information is often distorted by points of view. Is there any reason to suspect bias in the selection of subjects? What conflicting information may have been omitted? How are women and ethnicity portrayed?

- *Look for moralizing.* Many times what passes as fact is really disguised moral judgment. What are the underlying values of the article or program?

- *Go to the original source or sources.* The media always simplify. Find out for yourself what the studies really reported. What were the backgrounds and credentials of the people or organizations who conducted the research? How large were the samples? How valid were the methodologies used in the studies? What were their strengths and limitations?

- *Seek additional information.* The whole story is probably not told. Look for additional information in scholarly books and journals, reference books, or textbooks.

Keeping questions like these in mind will help you steer a course between blind acceptance and offhand dismissal of a study.

Even such renowned sex researchers as William Masters and Virginia Johnson could sometimes be guilty of "statistical excess." Without a shred of evidence, for example, they made the oft-quoted claim that "half of American marriages are sexual disaster areas" (Masters & Johnson, 1974). The media unquestioningly repeated this statistic for years because it reinforced the popular conception that sex and marriage don't mix. In the 1980s, the media also popularized the G-spot, a supposedly highly erotic area within the vagina, supported by questionable scientific evidence. The media publicized the G-spot as an incontrovertible fact, while its existence and significance continue to be disputed among sex researchers (Tavris, 1992). (The G-spot is discussed further in Chapter 3.) A few years later, the media promoted the idea of a possible infertility "epidemic" occurring because of a decline in male sperm counts. Just two years later, a different group of scientists discounted this theory, claiming "unaccounted-for regional differences" (Fisch, Goluboff, Olson, Feldshuh, Broder, & Barad, 1996).

The media frequently quote or describe social science research, but they may do so in an oversimplified or distorted manner. Scholars tend to qualify their findings as tentative or limited to a certain group. They are very cautious about making generalizations. By contrast, the media tend to make results sound more certain and generalizable. The media may report, for example, a study finding that premarital sexual intercourse generally results in feelings of guilt, although a later study finds no relationship between the two. On what basis do you decide which study to believe? Many of us think all studies are equal, that one is as good as another as long as they are conducted by experts who presumably know what they are doing. But all studies are not necessarily comparable or equally well done. One study may have drawn its sample from the fundamentalist Bob Jones University, while the other may have drawn its sample from the more liberal Harvard University. In one case, information may have been drawn from a clinical study of students being treated for depression, while the other may have been based on a cross section of nondepressed students. Often such critical information about studies is missing in media research accounts.

THINKING CRITICALLY ABOUT SEX

Although each of us has his or her own perspective, values, and beliefs regarding sexuality, as students, instructors, and researchers, we are committed to the scientific study of sexuality. Basic to any scientific study is a fundamental commitment to **objectivity,** the observation of things as they exist in reality as opposed to our feelings or beliefs about them. Objectivity calls for us to suspend the beliefs, biases, or prejudices we have about a subject in order to understand it.

> He who knows nothing doubts nothing.
>
> —*French proverb*

Objectivity is not always easy, for sexuality is the focal point of powerful emotions, moral ambivalence, anxiety, and fear. We experience sex very subjectively. But whether we find it easy or difficult to be objective, objectivity is the prerequisite for studying sexuality.

Most of us think about sex, but thinking about it critically requires us to think with logic and objectivity. We make common errors when discussing sexuality that inhibit our understanding and comprehension. Some of these mistakes are discussed in the following sections.

Value Judgments Versus Objectivity

For many of, us objectivity about sex is difficult because our culture has traditionally viewed sexuality in moral terms: Sex is moral or immoral, right or wrong, good or bad. When examining sexuality, we tend, therefore, to make **value judgments,** evaluations based on moral or ethical standards rather than objective ones. Unfortunately, value judgments are often blinders to understanding. They do not tell us about motivations, how frequently a behavior is practiced, or how its participants feel. Value judgments do not tell us anything about sexuality except how we ourselves feel. In studying human sexuality, then, we need to put aside value judgments as incompatible with the pursuit of knowledge.

> Morality is simply the attitude we adopt towards people we personally dislike.
>
> —*Oscar Wilde (1854–1900)*

How can we tell the difference between a value judgment and an objective statement? Examine the following two statements. Which is a value judgment? Which is an objective statement?

1. College students should not have sexual intercourse.
2. The majority of students have sexual intercourse sometime during their college careers.

The first statement is a value judgment; the second is an objective statement. There is a simple rule of thumb for telling the difference between the two: Value judgments imply how a person *ought* to behave, whereas objective statements describe how people *actually* behave. The first statement is a value judgment because it makes a judgment about sexual behavior. The second is an objective statement because it describes how people act.

There is a second difference between value judgments and objective statements: Value judgments cannot be empirically validated; objective statements can be validated. The truth or accuracy of an objective statement can be measured and tested. Despite claims of universality, however, standards of objectivity are generally regarded by social scientists as culturally relative. (**Cultural relativity** is an important anthropological concept meaning that the positive or negative appropriateness of any custom or activity must be evaluated in terms of how it fits in with the culture as a whole.)

Opinions, Biases, and Stereotypes

Value judgments obscure our search for understanding. Opinions, biases, and stereotypes also interfere with the pursuit of knowledge.

Opinions   An **opinion** is an unsubstantiated belief or conclusion about what seems to be true according to an individual's personal thoughts. Opinions are not based on positive knowledge or concrete evidence. Because opinions are unsubstantiated, they often reflect the opinion-holder's personal values or biases.

Biases   A **bias** is a personal leaning or inclination. Biases lead us to select information that supports our views or beliefs while ignoring information that does not. We need not be victims, however, of our biases. We can make a concerted effort to discover what they are and overcome them. To avoid personal bias, scholars apply the objective methods of social science research.

Stereotypes   A **stereotype** is a set of simplistic, rigidly held, overgeneralized beliefs about an individual, a group of people, an idea, and so on. Stereotypical beliefs are resistant to change. Although men may think that their perceptions of women have changed, research indicates that they continue to hold the same stereotypical beliefs about women today as they did 25 years ago (Bergen & Williams, 1991). Furthermore, stereotypes—especially sexual ones—are often negative.

Common sexual stereotypes include the following:

- Men are "animals."
- "Nice" women are not interested in sex.
- Virgins are uptight and asexual.
- Gay men are child molesters.
- Lesbians hate men.
- African Americans are sexually uninhibited.
- Latino men are macho.

Psychologists believe that stereotypes structure knowledge. They affect the ways in which we process information: what we see, what we notice,

> Ignorance is like a delicate exotic fruit; touch it and the bloom is gone.
>
> —*Oscar Wilde*

what we remember, and how we explain things. Or, as humorist Ashleigh Brilliant said, "Seeing is believing. I wouldn't have seen it if I hadn't believed it." A stereotype is a type of **schema,** a way in which we organize knowledge in our thought processes. Schemas help us channel or filter the mass of information we receive so that we can make sense of it. They determine what we will regard as important. Although these mental plans are useful, they can also create blind spots. With stereotypes, we see what we expect to see and ignore what we don't expect to see.

Sociologists point out that sexual stereotyping is often used to justify discrimination. Targets of stereotypes are usually members of subordinate social groups, such as women, those with limited economic resources, and members of ethnic groups. As we will see, sexual stereotyping is especially powerful in stigmatizing African Americans, Latinos, and gay men and lesbians.

We all have opinions and biases; most of us to varying degrees think stereotypically. But the commitment to objectivity requires us to become aware of our opinions, biases, and stereotypes and to put them aside in the pursuit of knowledge.

Confusing Attitudes and Behavior

An **attitude** is a predisposition a person has to act, think, or feel in certain ways toward particular things. A **behavior** is the way a person acts. There are two problems we commonly experience when discussing sexual attitudes and behavior: (1) We fail to identify whether we are discussing attitudes or behavior, and (2) we assume attitudes reflect behavior and vice versa.

Failure to identify whether we are discussing attitudes or behavior can lead to confusion and an endless round of disagreement. Imagine, for example, two friends discussing premarital sex without either specifying whether he or she is talking about attitudes or behavior. One says, "Everyone I know accepts premarital sex." The other disagrees: "That's not so. Almost all our friends are virgins." The fact is, both may be correct. But the first person is talking about *attitudes* about premarital sex, whereas the second is talking about actual premarital sexual *behavior.* The two may never find agreement because they are talking about different things.

There is often a discrepancy between attitudes and behavior. As a result, we cannot infer a person's behavior from his or her attitudes about sexuality, or vice versa. A person may disapprove of premarital sexual intercourse, for example, but nevertheless engage in it. A woman may oppose abortion but may terminate her own pregnancy.

Common Fallacies: Egocentric and Ethnocentric Thinking

A **fallacy** is an error in reasoning that affects our understanding of a subject. Fallacies distort our thinking, leading us to false or erroneous conclusions. In the field of sexuality, egocentric and ethnocentric fallacies are common.

The Egocentric Fallacy   The **egocentric fallacy** is the mistaken belief that one's own personal experience and values are held by others in general. On the basis of our belief in this false consensus, we use our own beliefs and values to explain the attitudes, motivations, and behaviors of others. Of

Ethnocentrism views one's own culture or ethnic group as superior to that of others. Although child marriage is prohibited in our society, it is acceptable in many cultures throughout the world, including India. Such marriages generally do not include cohabitation or sexual relations until the couple is old enough in the eyes of their society.

course, our own experiences and values are important; they are the source of personal strength and knowledge. They are often valuable in giving us insight into others. But we cannot necessarily generalize from our own experience to that of others. Our own personal experiences are limited and may be unrepresentative; sometimes they are merely opinions or disguised value judgments.

The Ethnocentric Fallacy   The **ethnocentric fallacy,** also known as **ethnocentrism,** is the belief that one's own ethnic group, nation, or culture is innately superior to others. Ethnocentrism is reinforced by opinions, biases, and stereotypes about other groups and cultures. As members of a group, we tend to share similar values and attitudes with other group members. But the mere fact that we share these beliefs with others is not sufficient proof of their truth.

Ethnocentrism has been increasingly evident as a reaction to the increased awareness of **ethnicity,** ethnic affiliation or identity. For many Americans, a significant part of their sense of self comes from identification with their ethnic group. An **ethnic group** is a group of people distinct from other groups because of cultural characteristics, such as language, religion, and customs, that are transmitted from one generation to another. Contemporary Ameri-

All universal judgments are weak, loose, and dangerous.

—*Michel de Montaigne (1533–1595)*

can ethnic groups include African Americans, Latinos (Hispanics), Native Americans, Japanese Americans, and Chinese Americans.

Although there has been little research on ethnicity and sexuality until recently, evidence suggests that there is significant ethnic variation in terms of sexual attitudes and behavior (Cortese, 1989; Staples, 1991; Staples & Johnson, 1993). For example, it appears that Whites are less sexually permissive than African Americans, and Latinos are less permissive than either Whites or African Americans. From a White ethnocentric viewpoint, the greater acceptance of premarital sex among African Americans may be evidence that Blacks are "promiscuous." From an African American point of view, Whites may be viewed as sexually "uptight." Latinos may see both groups as "immoral."

Ethnocentrism is also expressed in stereotyping other cultures as "primitive," "innocent," "inferior," or "not as advanced." We may view the behavior of other peoples as strange, exotic, unusual, or bizarre, but to them it is normal. Their attitudes, behaviors, values, and beliefs form a unified sexual system, which makes sense within their culture. In fact, we engage in many activities that appear peculiar to those outside our culture. For example, Amazonian people do not understand why young men or women would masturbate. As a Mehinaku youth asked incredulously: "Having sex with the hand? Why would anyone bother? There are plenty of women around" (Gregor, 1985).

SEX RESEARCH METHODS

One of the key factors that distinguishes the findings of social science from beliefs, prejudice, bias—and pop psychology—is its commitment to the scientific method. The **scientific method** is the method by which a hypothesis is formed from impartially gathered data and tested empirically. The scientific method relies on **induction**—that is, forming arguments whose premises are intended to provide some support, but not conclusive support, for their conclusions. The scientific method seeks to describe the world rather than evaluate or judge it.

Although sex researchers use the same methodology as other social scientists, they are constrained by ethical concerns and taboos that those in other fields do not experience. Because of the taboos surrounding sexuality, some traditional research methods are inappropriate.

Sex research, like most social science research, uses different methodological approaches. These include the following:

- Clinical research
- Survey research: questionnaires and interviews
- Observational research
- Experimental research

Research Concerns

Researchers face two general concerns in conducting their work. The first concern is ethical, centering around the use of human beings as subjects. The second concern is methodological, regarding sampling techniques and their accuracy. Without a representative sample, the conclusions drawn by these methodologies are limited.

Ethical Issues Ethics are important in any scientific endeavor. They are especially important in such an emotional and value-laden subject as sexuality. Among the most important ethical issues are informed consent, protection from harm, confidentiality, and the use of deception.

Informed consent is the full disclosure to an individual of the purpose, potential risks, and benefits of participating in a research project. The potential participant must be at least age 18 and without mental impairment. Under informed consent, people are free to decide whether to participate in a project without coercion or deceit. Once a study begins, participants have the right to withdraw at any time without penalty.

Each research participant is entitled to protection from harm. Some sex research, such as the viewing of explicit films to measure physiological responses, may cause some people psychological distress. The identity of research subjects is to be confidential. Because of the highly charged nature of sexuality, participants need to be guaranteed anonymity.

Of all the ethical issues surrounding research, the use of deception is the most problematic. Sometimes it is necessary to deceive subjects in order for the experiment to work. If participants in a study on the role of attractiveness at first meetings knew they were being studied in terms of their response to attractive people rather than, say, opening lines, their responses might be different. The issue of deception is generally resolved by requiring that the researcher debrief participants following the experiment. During the debriefing, the deception is revealed and its necessity explained. Participants are given the opportunity to ask questions. They may also request that their data be removed from the study and destroyed.

Most colleges and universities have review boards or human subject committees to make sure that research follows ethical guidelines. Proposed research is submitted to the committee before the project begins. If the committee believes the research poses ethical problems, the project will not be approved until the problems are corrected.

Sampling In each research approach, the choice of a sample—a portion of a larger group of people observed or studied—is critical. To be useful, a sample should be a **random sample**—that is, a sample collected in an unbiased way. Further, the sample should be a **representative sample,** a small group representing the larger group in terms of age, sex, ethnicity, socioeconomic status, orientation, and so on. Samples that are not representative of the larger group are known as **biased samples.** Using samples is important. It would be impossible, for example, to study the sexual behaviors of all college students in the United States. But we can select a representative sample of college students from various schools and infer from their behavior how other college students behave. Using the same sample to infer the sexual behavior of Americans in general, however, would be using a biased sample. We cannot infer the sexual activities of Americans from studying college students because the college-student sample is biased in terms of age (young), education (college), socioeconomic status (middle class), and ethnicity (White) (Strassberg & Lowe, 1995).

Most samples in sex research are limited for several reasons:

1. They depend on volunteers or clients. Because these samples are generally self-selected, we cannot assume that they are representative of the population as a whole. Volunteers for sex research are generally more sexually experienced, more liberal, and less religious than the population as a whole. They are generally more positive about their sexuality than nonvolunteers (Strassberg & Lowe, 1995).

2. Most sex research takes place in a university or college setting with student volunteers. College students, however, are generally in late adolescence or early adulthood and are single; they are at the beginning of their sexual lives. Is the value they place on sexuality in marriage, for example, likely to be the same as that that older, married adults give it?

3. Ethnic groups are generally underrepresented. Representative samples of African Americans, Latinos, Native Americans, and some Asian Americans are not easily found because these groups are underrepresented at the colleges and universities where subjects are generally recruited.

4. The study of gay men and lesbians presents unique sampling problems. Are gay men and lesbians who have come out (publicly identified themselves as gay or lesbian) different from those who have not? How does one find and recruit subjects who have not come out?

Because these factors limit most studies, one must be careful in making generalizations from studies.

Clinical Research

Clinical research is the in-depth examination of an individual or group that comes to a psychiatrist, psychologist, or social worker for assistance with psychological or medical problems or disorders. Clinical research is descriptive. Inferences of cause and effect cannot be drawn from it. The individual is interviewed and treated for a specific problem. At the same time the person is being treated, he or she is being studied. In their evaluations, clinicians attempt to determine the causes of a disorder and how it may be treated. They may also try to infer from dysfunctional people how healthy people develop.

Clinical research focuses largely on what is considered deviant, abnormal, inadequate, or unhealthy sexual behavior, such as transsexuality (individuals who feel they are trapped in bodies of the wrong sex) and sexual dysfunctions (such as lack of desire, premature ejaculation, erectile difficulties, or lack or orgasm).

A major limitation of clinical research is its emphasis on unhealthy or **pathological behavior** (diseased behavior). Such an emphasis makes clinical research dependent on cultural definitions of what is "unhealthy" or "pathological." These definitions, however, change. In the nineteenth century, for example, masturbation was considered pathological. Physicians and clinicians went to great lengths to root it out. In the case of women, surgeons sometimes removed the clitoris.

In evaluating clinical research, we should ask several questions (Gagnon, 1977). First, on what basis is a condition defined as healthy or unhealthy? For example, are the bases for classifying homosexuality and masturbation as healthy or unhealthy behaviors scientific, cultural, or moral? Second, can inferences gathered from the behavior of patients be applied to others? For example, if we learn that male-to-female transsexuals tended to play with dolls when they were young, should we discourage male children from playing with dolls? Third, how do we know that the people we are studying are representative of the group with which we are identifying them? Most of what we know about the psychological makeup of rapists comes from the study of imprisoned rapists. But are imprisoned rapists representative of all rapists?

Survey Research

Survey research is a method used to gather information from a small group and to make inferences about a larger group. The survey method uses questionnaires or interviews to gather information. Questionnaires offer anonymity, may be completed fairly quickly, and are relatively inexpensive to administer; however, they usually do not allow an in-depth response. A person must respond with a short answer or a limited choice. Interview techniques avoid some of the shortcomings of questionnaires, as interviewers are able to probe in greater depth and follow paths suggested by the subject.

Although surveys are important sources of information, the method has several limitations. First, people tend to be poor reporters of their own sexual behavior. Men may exaggerate their number of sexual partners; women may minimize their casual encounters. Members of both sexes generally underreport experiences considered deviant or immoral, such as same-sex experiences, bondage, and so on. Second, interviewers may allow their own preconceptions to influence the way in which they frame questions and to bias their interpretations of responses as well. Third, some respondents may feel uncomfortable about revealing information—such as masturbation or incestuous experiences—in a face-to-face interview. Fourth, the interviewer's gender may also influence how comfortable respondents are in disclosing information about themselves. Finally, some ethnic groups, because of their cultural values, may be reluctant to reveal sexual information about themselves. Some findings suggest, however, that African Americans and Latinos are willing to participate in research and to answer sensitive questions (Jackson, 1991; Marin & Marin, 1989, 1991).

Observational Research

Observational research is a method by which a researcher unobtrusively observes and makes systematic notes about people's behavior without trying to manipulate it. The observer does not want his or her presence to affect the subject's behavior. But because sexual behavior is regarded as significantly different from other behaviors, there are serious ethical concerns involved in observing people's sexual behavior without their knowledge and consent. (Even with their knowledge and consent, such observation may be considered voyeuristic and subject to criminal prosecution.) Because researchers cannot observe sexual behavior as they might observe flirting at a

Discovery consists of seeing what everybody has seen and thinking what nobody has thought.

—*Albert Szent-Gyorgyi (1893–1986)*

Participant observation is an important means by which anthropologists gain information about other cultures.

party, dance, or bar, such observations usually take place in a laboratory setting. In such instances, the setting is not a natural environment; participants are aware that their behavior is under observation.

Participant observation, in which the researcher participates in the behaviors he or she is studying, is an important method of observational research. A researcher may study prostitution by becoming a customer (Snyder, 1974); swinging, by exchanging partners in a group of swingers (Bartell, 1970); anonymous sex between men in public restrooms by posing as a lookout (Humphreys, 1975). There are several questions raised by such participant observation. First of all, how does the observer's participation affect the interactions being studied? For example, does a prostitute respond differently to a researcher as he or she tries to obtain information? If the observer participates, how does this affect his or her objectivity? If observers are involved in swinging, for example, are they more likely to report favorably on swinging? And what are the researcher's ethical responsibilities regarding informing those he or she is studying?

Participant observation is also the most important method used by anthropologists in studying other cultures (Frayser, 1994). Anthropologists may spend considerable time securing the trust of group members so that they reveal their group's beliefs and behaviors, including their sexual beliefs and behaviors. Because cultural differences can be great, researchers must avoid moral judgments. Anthropologists often find that their gender affects their ability to gather information. Male anthropologists rarely observe childbirth or menstrual rituals; female anthropologists are usually excluded from male initiation ceremonies. However, despite limitations, anthropologists

The Kinsey Institute/Roper Organization National Sex Knowledge Test

THIS SELF-ASSESSMENT WAS GIVEN to a representative sample of Americans in 1990. It was found that the average American knows little about sexuality, contraception, or STDs. Worse, what the average American believes about these subjects is often incorrect.

Circle one answer after reading each question carefully. If you have trouble or want advice about any of these issues, look them up in the text and/or discuss them with a professional.

1. **Nowadays, what do you think is the age at which the *average or typical* American *first* has sexual intercourse?**

   a. 11 or younger
   b. 12
   c. 13
   d. 14
   e. 15
   f. 16
   g. 17
   h. 18
   i. 19
   j. 20
   k. 21 or older
   l. Don't know

2. **Out of every ten married American men, how many would you estimate have had an extramarital affair—that is, have been sexually unfaithful to their wives?**

   a. Less than one out of ten
   b. One out of ten (10%)
   c. Two out of ten (20%)
   d. Three out of ten (30%)
   e. Four out of ten (40%)
   f. Five out of ten (50%)
   g. Six out of ten (60%)
   h. Seven out of ten (70%)
   i. Eight out of ten (80%)
   j. Nine out of ten (90%)
   k. More than nine out of ten
   l. Don't know

3. **Out of every ten American women, how many would you estimate have had anal (rectal) intercourse?**

   a. Less than one out of ten
   b. One out of ten (10%)
   c. Two out of ten (20%)
   d. Three out of ten (30%)
   e. Four out of ten (40%)
   f. Five out of ten (50%)
   g. Six out of ten (60%)
   h. Seven out of ten (70%)
   i. Eight out of ten (80%)
   j. Nine out of ten (90%)
   k. More than nine out of ten
   l. Don't know

4. **A person can get AIDS by having anal (rectal) intercourse even if neither partner is infected with the AIDS virus.**

   True   False   Don't know

5. **There are over-the-counter spermicides people can buy at the drugstore that will kill the AIDS virus.**

   True   False   Don't know

6. **Petroleum jelly, Vaseline Intensive Care, baby oil, and Nivea are *not* good lubricants to use with a condom or diaphragm.**

   True   False   Don't know

7. **More than one out of four (25%) of American men have had a sexual experience with another male during either their teens or adult years.**

   True   False   Don't know

8. **It is usually difficult to tell whether people *are or are not* homosexual just by their appearance or gestures.**

   True   False   Don't know

9. **A woman or teenage girl can get pregnant during her menstrual flow (her "period").**

   True   False   Don't know

10. **A woman or teenage girl can get pregnant even if a man withdraws his penis before he ejaculates (before he "comes").**

    True   False   Don't know

11. **Unless they are having sex, women do not need to have regular gynecological examinations.**

    True   False   Don't know

12. **Teenage boys should examine their testicles ("balls") regularly just as women self-examine their breasts for lumps.**

    True   False   Don't know

may be able to gather information about sexuality that shows how it is integrated into a culture.

Experimental Research

Experimental research is the systematic manipulation of an individual or the environment to learn the effect of such manipulation on behavior. It enables researchers to isolate a single factor under controlled circumstances

13. **Problems with erection are most often started by a physical problem.**

    True   False   Don't know

14. **Almost all erection problems can be successfully treated.**

    True   False   Don't know

15. **Menopause, or change of life as it is often called, does *not* cause most women to lose interest in having sex.**

    True   False   Don't know

16. **Out of every ten American women, how many would you estimate have masturbated either as children or after they were grown up?**

    a. Less than one out of ten
    b. One out of ten (10%)
    c. Two out of ten (20%)

d. Three out of ten (30%)
e. Four out of ten (40%)
f. Five out of ten (50%)
g. Six out of ten (60%)
h. Seven out of ten (70%)
i. Eight out of ten (80%)
j. Nine out of ten (90%)
k. More than nine out of ten
l. Don't know

17. **What do you think is the length of the average man's erect penis?**

    a. 2 inches
    b. 3 inches
    c. 4 inches
    d. 5 inches
    e. 6 inches
    f. 7 inches
    g. 8 inches
    h. 9 inches
    i. 10 inches
    j. 11 inches
    k. 12 inches
    l. Don't know

18. **Most women prefer a sexual partner with a larger-than-average penis.**

    True   False   Don't know

Scoring the Test

Each question is worth one point. So, the total possible number of points you can get is 18. Using this chart, score each item and then add up your total number of points. When a range of possible answers is correct, according to currently available research data, all respondents choosing one of the answers in the correct range are given a point.

Question number	Give yourself a point if you circled any of the following answers	Circle the number of points you received		Question number	Give yourself a point if you circled any of the following answers	Circle the number of points you received	
1	f,g	0	1	11	False	0	1
2	d,e	0	1	12	True	0	1
3	d,e	0	1	13	True	0	1
4	False	0	1	14	True	0	1
5	(any answer, everyone gets a point as explained in discussion of question)		1	15	True	0	1
6	True	0	1	16	g,h,i	0	1
7	True	0	1	17	d,e,f	0	1
8	True	0	1	18	False	0	1
9	True	0	1				
10	True	0	1		Total Number of Points: _____		

Source: Reinisch, J. *The New Kinsey Report*, New York: St. Martin's Press, 1990, pp. 3–5.

to determine its influence. Researchers are able to control their experiments by using **variables,** aspects or factors that can be manipulated in experiments. There are two types of variables: independent variables and dependent variables. **Independent variables** are factors that can be manipulated or changed by the experimenter; **dependent variables** are factors that are likely to be affected by changes in the independent variable.

Because it controls variables, experimental research differs from the previous methods we have examined. Clinical studies, surveys, and observational research are correlational in nature. **Correlational studies** measure two or more naturally occurring variables to determine their relationship to each other. Because these studies do not manipulate the variables, they cannot tell us which variable *causes* the other to change. But experimental studies manipulate the independent variables, so researchers *can* reasonably determine what variables cause the other variables to change.

Much experimental research on sexuality depends on measuring physiological responses. These responses are usually measured by **plethysmographs,** devices attached to the genitals to measure physiological response. Researchers use either a penile plethysmograph or a **strain gauge** (a device resembling a rubber band) for men and a vaginal plethysmograph for women. Both the penile plethysmograph and strain gauge are placed around the penis; they measure changes in the circumference of the penis that accompany sexual arousal. The vaginal plethysmograph is about the size of a menstrual tampon and is inserted into the vagina like a tampon. The vaginal plethysmograph measures the amount of blood within the vaginal walls, which increases as a woman becomes aroused.

Suppose researchers want to study the influence of alcohol on sexual response. They would use a plethysmograph to measure sexual response, the dependent variable. In this study, the independent variables would be the levels of alcohol consumption: no alcohol consumption, moderate alcohol consumption (1–3 drinks), and high alcohol consumption (3+ drinks). In addition, extraneous variables, such as body mass and tolerance to alcohol, need to be controlled. In such an experiment, subjects may view an erotic film. To get a baseline measurement, researchers measure the genitals' physiological patterns in an unaroused state before participants view the film or take a drink. Then they measure sexual arousal (dependent variable) to erotica as they increase the levels of alcohol consumption (independent variables).

Good experiments are difficult to design because the experimental situation must resemble the real world. There are four important concerns about experimental research. (1) To what degree does the experiment replicate the complexities and settings of real-life sexuality? Does a laboratory setting radically alter responses? (2) Do the devices used to measure sexual response affect the subject's sexual responsiveness? (3) The measuring devices measure only genital response, whereas overall sexual response includes increased heart rate, muscle tension, changed brain-wave patterns, sexual fantasies and thoughts, and so on. (4) Can the results from the experiment be generalized to nonlaboratory conditions? Because there are so many variables outside controlled laboratory conditions, many researchers believe that experimental findings are highly limited in their applicability to the real world.

THE SEX RESEARCHERS

It was not until the nineteenth century that Western sexuality began to be studied using a scientific framework. Prior to that time, sexuality was claimed by religion rather than science; sex was the subject of moral rather than scientific scrutiny. From the earliest Christian era, treatises, canon law, and papal bulls, as well as sermons and confessions, catalogued the sins of the flesh. Reflecting this Christian tradition, the early students of sexuality were concerned with the excesses and deviances of sexuality rather than its healthy functioning. They were fascinated by what they considered the pathologies of sex, such as fetishism, sadism, masturbation, and homosexuality—the very behaviors that religion condemned as sinful. Alfred Kinsey ironically noted that nineteenth-century researchers created "scientific classifications . . . nearly identical with theological classifications and with moral pronouncements . . . of the fifteenth century" (Kinsey et al., 1948).

But as we will see, there has been a liberalizing trend in our thinking about sexuality. Both Richard von Krafft-Ebing and Sigmund Freud viewed sexuality as inherently dangerous and needing repression. But Havelock Ellis, Alfred Kinsey, William Masters and Virginia Johnson, and a number of more recent researchers have viewed sexuality more positively; in fact, historian Paul Robinson (1976) regards these later researchers as modernists ("sexual enthusiasts," he calls them). Three themes are evident in their work. First, they believe that sexual expression is essential to an individual's well-being. Second, they seek to broaden the range of legitimate sexual activity, including homosexuality. Third, they believe that female sexuality is the equal of male sexuality.

As much as possible, sex researchers attempt to examine sexuality objectively. But, as with all of us, many of their views are intertwined with the beliefs and values of their times. This is especially apparent among the early sex researchers.

Richard von Krafft-Ebing (1840–1902)

Richard von Krafft-Ebing, a Viennese professor of psychiatry, was probably the most influential of the early researchers. In 1886, he published his most famous work, *Psychopathia Sexualis,* a collection of case histories of fetishists, sadists, masochists, and homosexuals. (He invented the words "sadomasochism" and "transvestite.")

Krafft-Ebing traced variations in Victorian sexuality to "hereditary taint," to "moral degeneracy," and, in particular, to masturbation. He intermingled descriptions of fetishists who became sexually excited by kid gloves with those of sadists who disemboweled their victims. For Krafft-Ebing, the origins of fetishism and murderous sadism, as well as most variations, lay in masturbation, the sexual sin of the nineteenth century.

In our time, Krafft-Ebing's theories on the origins, nature, and dangers of sexual aberrations are little more than amusing stories or strange curiosities. Much of what he considered degeneracy, such as masturbation, is today considered normal sexual behavior. His *Psychopathia Sexualis,* however, brought to public attention and discussion an immense range of sexual behaviors that had never before been documented in a dispassionate, if erroneous, manner. A darkened region of sexual behavior was brought into the open for public examination.

Richard von Krafft-Ebing (1840–1902) viewed most sexual behavior other than marital coitus as a sign of pathology.

Sigmund Freud (1856–1939)

Few people have had as dramatic an impact on the way we think about the world as the Viennese physician Sigmund Freud. In his attempt to understand the **neuroses,** psychological disorders characterized by anxiety or

Sigmund Freud (1856–1939) was the founder of psychoanalysis and one of the most influential European thinkers of the first half of the twentieth century. Freud viewed sexuality with suspicion.

tension, plaguing his patients, Freud explored the unknown territory of the unconscious. If unconscious motives were brought to consciousness, Freud believed, a person could change his or her behavior. But, he believed, **repression,** a psychological mechanism that keeps people from becoming aware of hidden memories and motives because they arouse guilt, prevents such knowledge.

To explore the unconscious, Freud used various techniques; in particular, he analyzed the meaning of dreams. His journeys into the mind led to the development of **psychoanalysis,** a psychological system that traces behavior to unconscious desires. He fled Vienna when Hitler annexed Austria in 1938 and died a year later in England.

The Theory of Personality   Freud's clinical work led him to develop a theory of personality in which sexuality played a critical role. (For a concise discussion of Freudian psychology, see Hall, 1980.) According to Freud's theory, personality consists of three parts: the id, the ego, and the superego. The **id** represents the instincts and is driven by the **libido,** which seeks pleasure, especially sexual pleasure. The libido, or sexual drive, pursues pleasure regardless of the cost; it follows what Freud called the **pleasure principle,** the idea that organisms seek pleasure and avoid pain. The **ego,** however, deals with reality. It acts as an intermediary between the demands of the id and those of society. It is governed by the **reality principle,** the control the external world exerts on the organism, which postpones pleasure. The **superego** acts as the individual's conscience or **moral principle.** It is an internalization of society's demands, which the individual learns from birth. These various elements are in constant conflict with each other. The id is constantly seeking gratification; the superego is constantly seeking to repress the id. The outcomes of these conflicts, which occur at different stages of development, often determine adult behavior.

The Theory of Psychosexual Development   Freud believed that sexuality begins at birth. His belief in infant and child sexuality set him apart from other researchers. Freud described five stages in psychosexual development. The first stage is the **oral stage,** lasting from birth to age 1. During this time, the infant's eroticism is focused on the mouth; thumb-sucking produces an erotic pleasure. Freud believed the "most striking character of this sexual activity . . . is that the child gratifies himself on his own body; . . . he is auto-erotic" (Freud, 1938). The second stage, between ages 1 and 3, is the **anal stage.** The child's erotic activities continue to be autoerotic, but the region of pleasure shifts to the anus. From age 3 through 5, the child is in the **phallic stage,** in which he or she exhibits interest in the genitals. At age 6, children enter a **latency stage,** in which their sexual impulses are no longer active. At puberty, they enter the **genital stage,** at which point the adolescent becomes interested in genital sexual activities, especially sexual intercourse.

The phallic stage is the critical stage in both male and female development. The boy develops sexual desires for his mother, leading to the **Oedipal complex.** He simultaneously desires his mother and fears his father. This fear leads to **castration anxiety,** the belief that the father will cut off his penis because of jealousy. Girls follow a more complex development, according to Freud. A girl develops an **Electra complex,** desiring her father while fearing her mother. Upon discovering that she does not have a penis, she feels deprived and develops **penis envy.** By age 6, both boys and girls resolve their Oedipal and Electra complexes by relinquishing their desires for the parent of the other sex and identifying with their same-sex parent. In this manner, they develop their masculine and feminine identities. But because girls never acquire their "lost penis," Freud believed, they fail to develop an independent character like that of boys.

In many ways, such as in his commitment to science and his explorations of the unconscious, Freud seems the embodiment of twentieth-century thought. But over the past generation, his influence among American sex researchers has dwindled. Two of the most important reasons are his lack of empiricism and his inadequate description of female development.

Because of its limitations, Freud's work has become mostly of historical interest to mainstream sex researchers. It continues to exert influence in some fields of psychology but has been greatly modified by others. Even among contemporary psychoanalysts, Freud's work has been radically revised.

> The great question . . . which I have not been able to answer, despite my thirty years of research into the feminine soul, is "What does a woman want?"
>
> —*Sigmund Freud (1856–1939)*

Havelock Ellis (1859–1939)

Havelock Ellis, who became one of the most influential sexual thinkers and reformers in the twentieth century, was a child of the Victorian era. His youth in his native England was marked by the sexual repression and fears of that time. He set himself against those sexual inhibitions to free humanity from ignorance. He was among the first modern affirmers of sexuality. "Sex lies at the root of life," he wrote, "and we can never learn to reverence life until we know how to understand sex" (Ellis, 1900). He believed that the negators of sexuality used morality and religion to twist and deform sex until it became little more than sin and degradation.

Ellis was the earliest important modern sexual thinker. His *Studies in the Psychology of Sex* (the first six volumes of which were published between 1897 and 1910) consisted of case studies, autobiographies, and personal letters. One of his most important contributions was pointing out the relativity of sexual values. In the nineteenth century, Americans and Europeans alike believed that their society's dominant sexual beliefs were the only morally and naturally correct standards. But Ellis demonstrated not only that Western sexual standards were not the only moral standards but also that they were not necessarily rooted in nature. In doing so, he was among the first researchers to appeal to studies in animal behavior, anthropology, and history.

Ellis also challenged the view that masturbation was abnormal. He argued that masturbation was widespread and that there was no evidence linking it with any serious mental or physical problems. He recorded countless men and women who masturbated without ill effect. In fact, he argued, masturbation had a positive function: It relieved tension.

The nineteenth century viewed women as essentially "pure beings" who possessed reproductive rather than sexual desires. Men, by contrast, were driven by such strong sexual passions that their sexuality had to be severely controlled and repressed. In countless case studies, Ellis documented that women possessed sexual desires no less intense than those of men.

Ellis argued that a wide range of behaviors was normal, including much behavior that the Victorians considered abnormal. He argued that both masturbation and female sexuality were normal behaviors and that even the so-called abnormal elements of sexual behavior were simply exaggerations of the normal.

He also reevaluated homosexuality. The nineteenth century viewed homosexuality as the essence of sin and perversion. It was dangerous, lurid, and criminal. Ellis insisted that it was not a disease or a vice but a congenital condition: A person was born homosexual; one did not *become* homosexual. By insisting that homosexuality was congenital, Ellis denied that it could be considered a vice or a form of moral degeneracy because a person did not *choose* it. If homosexuality was both congenital and harmless, then, Ellis reasoned, it should not be considered immoral or criminal.

Alfred Kinsey (1894–1956)

Alfred Kinsey (1894–1956) shocked Americans by revealing how they actually behaved sexually. His scientific efforts led to the termination of his research funding because of political pressure.

Alfred A. Kinsey, a biologist at Indiana University and America's leading authority on gall wasps, destroyed forever the belief in American sexual innocence and virtue. He accomplished this through two books, *Sexual Behavior in the Human Male* (Kinsey et al., 1948) and *Sexual Behavior in the Human Female* (Kinsey et al., 1953). These two volumes statistically documented the actual sexual behavior of Americans. In massive detail, they demonstrated the great discrepancy between *public* standards of sexual behavior and *actual* sexual behavior. In the firestorm that accompanied the publication of Kinsey's books (popularly known as the *Kinsey Reports*), many Americans protested the destruction of their cherished ideals and illusions.

Sexual Diversity and Variation   What Kinsey discovered in his research was an extraordinary diversity in individual sexual behaviors. Among men, he found individuals who had orgasms daily and others who went months without orgasms. Among women, he found those who had never had orgasms and those who had them several times a day. He discovered one male who had ejaculated only once in 30 years and another who climaxed 30 times a week on average. "This is the order of variation," he commented dryly, "which may occur between two individuals who live in the same town and who are neighbors, meeting in the same place of business and coming together in common social activities" (Kinsey et al., 1948).

Reevaluation of Masturbation   Kinsey's work aimed at a reevaluation of the role of masturbation in a person's sexual adjustment. Kinsey made three points about masturbation: (1) It is harmless, (2) it is not a substitute for sexual intercourse but a distinct form of sexual behavior that provides sexual pleasure, and (3) it plays an important role in women's sexuality because it is a more reliable source of orgasm than heterosexual intercourse, and because its practice seems to facilitate women's ability to become orgasmic during intercourse. Indeed, Kinsey believed that masturbation is the best way to measure a woman's inherent sexual responsiveness because it does not rely on another person.

Same-Sex Behavior   Prior to Kinsey's work, an individual was identified as homosexual if he or she engaged in a single sexual act with a member of the same sex. Kinsey found, however, that many people had sexual experiences with members of both sexes. He reported that 50% of the men and 28% of the women in his studies had same-sex experiences; 38% of the men

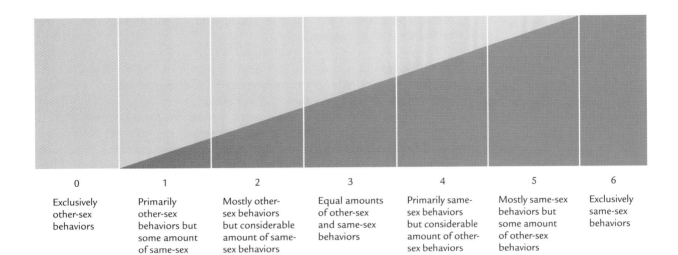

0	1	2	3	4	5	6
Exclusively other-sex behaviors	Primarily other-sex behaviors but some amount of same-sex behaviors	Mostly other-sex behaviors but considerable amount of same-sex behaviors	Equal amounts of other-sex and same-sex behaviors	Primarily same-sex behaviors but considerable amount of other-sex behaviors	Mostly same-sex behaviors but some amount of other-sex behaviors	Exclusively same-sex behaviors

FIGURE 2.1 The Kinsey scale focused on the degree to which a person engaged in other-sex and same-sex sexual behaviors.

and 13% of the women had orgasms during these experiences (Kinsey et al., 1948, 1953). Furthermore, he discovered that sexual preferences could change over the course of a person's lifetime. Kinsey's research led him to believe that it was erroneous to classify people as either heterosexual or homosexual. A person's sexuality was significantly more complex and fluid.

Kinsey wanted to eliminate the concept of heterosexual and homosexual *identities.* He did not believe that homosexuality, any more than heterosexuality, existed as a fixed psychological identity. Instead, he argued, there were only sexual acts, and acts alone did not make a person gay, lesbian, or heterosexual. It was more important to determine what proportion of behaviors were same-sex and other-sex than to label a person as gay, lesbian, or heterosexual.

He devised the Kinsey scale to represent the proportion of an individual's sexual behaviors with the same or other sex (Figure 2.1). This scale charted behaviors ranging from no behaviors with the same sex to behaviors exclusively with members of the same sex. These behaviors existed on a continuum. His scale radicalized the categorization of human sexual behavior (McWhirter, 1990).

Rejection of Normal/Abnormal Dichotomy   As a result of his research, Kinsey insisted that the distinction between normal and abnormal was meaningless. Like Ellis, he argued that sexual differences were a matter of degree, not kind. Almost any sexual behavior could be placed alongside another that differed from it only slightly. His observations led him to be a leading advocate of the toleration of sexual differences.

Although Kinsey's statistical methodology has been criticized, the two most important criticisms of his work are (1) his emphasis on the quantification of sexual behavior, and (2) his rejection of the psychological dimension.

Because Kinsey wanted to quantify behaviors, he studied only those behaviors that could be objectively measured. Thus, he defined sexual behaviors as those that lead to orgasm. By defining sexuality in this way, Kinsey reduced sexual behavior to genital activity. He excluded from his

I don't see much of Alfred anymore since he got so interested in sex.

—*Mrs. Kinsey*

research sexual activities, such as kissing and erotic fantasies, that do not ordinarily lead to orgasm.

He also neglected the psychological dimension of sexuality. Motivation and attitudes did not interest him because he did not believe they could be objectively measured. As a consequence, the role of emotions, such as love, did not enter into his discussion of sexuality.

Kinsey's lack of interest in the psychological dimension of human sexuality led him to reject homosexual/heterosexual *identities* as meaningless. Although a person's sexual behaviors may not correspond to his or her identity as homosexual or heterosexual, this identity is nevertheless a critical aspect of self-concept. By ignoring these elements, Kinsey seriously limited his understanding of human sexuality.

William Masters and Virginia Johnson

In the 1950s, William Masters, a St. Louis physician, became interested in treating sexual inadequacy—such problems as premature ejaculation and erection difficulties in men, and lack of orgasm in women. As a physician, he felt that a systematic study of human sexual response was necessary, but none existed. To fill this void, he decided to conduct his own research. Masters was joined several years later by Virginia Johnson. Later they married, and in 1992 they divorced.

William Masters and Virginia Johnson detailed the sexual response cycle in the 1960s and revolutionized sex therapy in the 1970s.

Masters and Johnson detailed the sexual response cycles of 382 men and 312 women during more than 10,000 acts of sexual behavior, including masturbation and sexual intercourse. The researchers combined observation with direct measurement of changes in male and female genitals using electronic devices.

Human Sexual Response (1966), their first book, became an immediate success among both researchers and the public at large. What made their work significant was not only their detailed descriptions of physiological responses, but the articulation of several key ideas. First, Masters and Johnson discovered that, physiologically, male and female sexual responses are very similar. Second, they demonstrated that women achieve orgasm primarily through clitoral stimulation. Penetration of the vagina is not needed for orgasm to occur. By demonstrating the primacy of the clitoris, Masters and Johnson destroyed once and for all the Freudian distinction between vaginal and clitoral orgasm. (Freud believed that the orgasm a woman experienced through masturbation was somehow physically and psychologically inferior to one experienced through sexual intercourse. He made no such distinction for men.) By destroying the myth of the vaginal orgasm, Masters and Johnson legitimized female masturbation.

In 1970, Masters and Johnson published *Human Sexual Inadequacy,* which revolutionized sex therapy by treating sexual problems simply as difficulties that could be easily treated using behavioral therapy. They argued that sexual problems were not the result of underlying neuroses or personality disorders. More often than not, problems resulted from a lack of information, poor communication between couples, or marital conflict. Their behavioral approach, which included "homework" exercises such as clitoral or penile stimulation, led to an astounding increase in the successful treatment of sexual problems. Their work made them pioneers in modern sex therapy.

National Health and Social Life Survey

In 1994, new figures were released showing us to be in a different place from when Kinsey did his research nearly 45 years ago. Researchers from the University of Chicago published, according to their own description, the "only comprehensive and methodologically sound survey of America's sexual practices and beliefs." Their findings, which were released under two titles—the popular trade book *Sex in America: A Definitive Survey* (Michael, Gagnon, Laumann, & Kolata, 1994) and a more detailed and scholarly version, *The Social Organization of Sexuality* (Laumann, Gagnon, Michael, & Michaels, 1994)—not only raised questions about research methodology in human sexuality but contradicted previous findings and beliefs about sex in America.

Researchers Robert T. Michael, John H. Gagnon, Stuart Michaels, and Edward O. Laumann.

The study was originally intended to be a federally funded one, but because of political opposition, it was completed with private funds. In it, the authors set out to do things right by randomly sampling 3,432 Americans, age 18 to 59, in 90-minute face-to-face interviews. Rigorous training of the interviewers, pretesting of the questionnaire, and built-in checkpoints to test the veracity of the responses were among the methods chosen to help ensure the accuracy and reliability of the test results. Nevertheless, a media storm accompanied the publication of the findings, charging the study with problems in such areas as age bias, sampling size, omission of certain subgroups, and interpretation of results.

Released as the first study to explore the social context of sexuality, the findings revealed:

- *Americans are largely monogamous.* The median number of sex partners since age 18 for men was six and for women, two.

- *On average, Americans have sex about once a week.* On frequency of sex, adults fell roughly into three groups: nearly 30% had sex with a partner only a few times a year or not at all, 35% had sex once or several times a month, and about 35% had sex at least two or more times a week.

- *Adultery is the exception, not the rule.* Among those who were married, 75% of men and 85% of women said they had been faithful to their spouse.

- *Most Americans are fairly traditional in the bedroom.* When respondents were asked to name their preferences from a long list of sexual practices, vaginal intercourse was considered "very appealing" by most of those interviewed. Ranking second, but far behind, was watching a partner undress. Oral sex ranked third.

- *Homosexuality is not as prevalent as originally believed.* Among men 2.8% and among women 1.4% described themselves as homosexual or bisexual.

- *Orgasms appear to be the rule for men, the exception for women.* Seventy-five percent of men claimed to have orgasms consistently with their partners, whereas only 29% of women did. Married women were most likely to report that they always or usually had orgasms.

- *Forced sex and the misperception of it remain critical problems.* Twenty-two percent of women said they had been forced to do sexual things they didn't want to do, usually by a loved one. Only 3% of men admitted to ever forcing themselves on women.

- *Three percent of adult Americans claim never to have had sex.*

Additional findings from this study are reported in subsequent chapters of this text.

EMERGING RESEARCH PERSPECTIVES

Although sex research continues to explore diverse aspects of human sexuality, some scholars feel their particular interests have been given insufficient attention. Feminists and gay and lesbian scholars have focused their research on issues that mainstream scholars have largely ignored. And ethnic research, only now beginning to be undertaken, points to lack of knowledge about the sexuality of African Americans, Latinos, Asian Americans, and other ethnic Americans. These emerging research perspectives enrich our knowledge of sexuality.

Feminist Scholarship

The initial feminist research generated an immense amount of groundbreaking work on women in almost every field of the social sciences and humanities. Feminists made gender and gender-related issues significant research questions in a multitude of academic disciplines. In the field of sexuality, feminism expanded the scope of research to include the subjective experience and meaning of sexuality for women; sexual pleasure; sex and power; pornography; and issues of female victimization, such as rape, the sexual abuse of children, and sexual harassment.

There is no single feminist perspective; instead, there are several. Neither is feminism a license for political rigidity, division, or intolerance of diversity (McCormick, 1996). Feminism centers on understanding female experience in cultural and historical context—that is, the social construction of gender and gender asymmetry (Pollis, 1988). **Social construction** is the development of social categories, such as masculinity, femininity, heterosexuality, and homosexuality, by society.

Feminists believe in these basic principles:

- *Gender is significant in all aspects of social life.* Like socioeconomic status and ethnicity, gender determines a person's position in society.

- *The female experience of sex has been devalued.* By emphasizing genital sex and such aspects of it as frequency of sexual intercourse and number of orgasms, both researchers and society ignore important aspects of female sexuality, such as kissing, caressing, love, commitment, and communication. Female sexuality in lesbian relationships is even more devalued. Until the 1980s, most research on homosexuality centered on men, making lesbians invisible.

- *Power is a critical element in male-female relationships.* Because women are subordinated to men as a result of our cultural beliefs about gender, women have less power than men. As a result, feminists believe men have defined female sexuality to benefit themselves. Not only do men decide when to initiate sex, but the man's orgasm takes precedence over the woman's orgasm. The most brutal form of the male expression of sexual power is rape.

- *Traditional empirical research needs to be combined with qualitative research and interpretive studies to provide a full understanding of human sexuality.* Because social science emphasizes objectivity and quantification, its methodology prevents us from fully exploring the complexity of what sex "means" and how it is personally experienced.

- *Ethnic diversity must be addressed.* Ethnic women, feminists point out, face a double stigma: being female *and* being from a minority group. Although very few studies exist on ethnicity and sexuality, feminists are committed to examining the role of ethnicity in female sexuality.

Despite its contributions, feminist research is often marginalized, and the feminist approach is considered subversive in many academic circles (McCormick 1996).

Gay and Lesbian Research

During the nineteenth century, sexuality became increasingly perceived as the domain of science, especially medicine. Physicians competed with ministers, priests, and rabbis in defining what was "correct" sexual behavior. But medicine's so-called scientific conclusions were not scientific; rather, they were morality disguised as science. "Scientific" definitions of healthy sex closely resembled religious definitions of moral sex. In studying sexual activities between men, medical researchers "invented" and popularized the distinction between heterosexuality and homosexuality (Gay, 1986; Weeks, 1986).

Early Researchers and Reformers   Although most physician-moralists condemned same-sex relationships as pathological as well as immoral, a few individuals stand out in their attempt to understand same-sex sexuality.

KARL HEINRICH ULRICHS (1825–1895)   Karl Ulrichs was a German poet and political activist who developed the first scientific theory about homosexuality in the 1860s (Kennedy, 1988). As a rationalist, he believed reason was superior to religious belief and therefore rejected religion as superstition. He argued from logic and inference and collected case studies from numerous men to reinforce his beliefs. Ulrichs maintained that men who were attracted to other men represented a third sex, whom he called "Urnings." Urnings were born as Urnings; their sexuality was not the result of immorality or pathology. Ulrichs believed that Urnings had a distinctive feminine quality about them that distinguished them from men who loved women. He fought for Urning rights and the liberalization of sex laws.

KARL MARIA KERTBENY (1824–1882)   Karl Kertbeny, a Hungarian physician, created the terms "heterosexuality" and "homosexuality" in his attempt to understand same-sex relationships (Feray & Herzer, 1990). Kertbeny believed that "homosexualists" were as "manly" as "heterosexualists." For this reason, he broke with Ulrichs's conceptualization of Urnings as

Magnus Hirschfeld (1868–1935) was a leading European sex reformer who championed homosexual rights. He founded the first institute for the study of sexuality, which was burned when the Nazis took power in Germany. Hirschfeld fled for his life.

inherently "feminine" (Herzer, 1985). Kertbeny argued that homosexuality was inborn and thus not immoral. He also maintained "the rights of man" (quoted in Herzer, 1985):

> The rights of man begin . . . with man himself. And that which is most immediate to man is his own body, with which he can undertake fully and freely, to his advantage or disadvantage, that which he pleases, insofar as in so doing he does not disturb the rights of others.

MAGNUS HIRSCHFELD (1868–1935)   In the first few decades of the twentieth century, there was a great ferment of reform in England and parts of Europe. While Ellis was the leading reformer in England, Magnus Hirschfeld was the leading crusader in Germany, especially for homosexual rights.

Hirschfeld was a homosexual and possibly a transvestite. He eloquently presented the case for the humanity of transvestites (Hirschfeld, 1991). And in defense of homosexual rights, he argued that homosexuality was not a perversion but the result of the hormonal development of inborn traits. His defense of homosexuality led to the popularization of the word "homosexual." Hirschfeld's importance, however, lies not so much in his theory of homosexuality as in his sexual reform efforts. In Berlin in 1897, he helped found the first organization for homosexual rights. He began the first journal devoted to the study of sexuality. In addition, he founded the first Institute of Sexual Science, where he gathered a library of more than 20,000 volumes.

When Hitler took power in Germany, the Nazis attacked the sex reform movement and destroyed Hirschfeld's institute. In fear for his life, Hirschfeld fled into exile and died several years later (Bullough, 1976; see Wolff, 1986, for Hirschfeld's biography).

EVELYN HOOKER   As a result of Kinsey's research, Americans learned that same-sex sexual relationships were widespread among both men and women. A few years later, psychologist Evelyn Hooker startled her colleagues by demonstrating that homosexuality in itself was not a psychological disorder. She found that ordinary gay men did not differ significantly in personality characteristics from similar heterosexual men (Hooker, 1957). The reverberations of her work continue to this day (McWhirter, 1990).

Earlier studies had erroneously found psychopathology among gay men and lesbians for two reasons. First, because most researchers were clinicians, their samples consisted mainly of gay men and lesbians who were seeking treatment. The researchers failed to compare their results against a control group of similar heterosexuals. (A **control group** is a group that is not being treated or experimented on; it controls for any variables that are introduced as a result of the treatment.) Second, researchers were predisposed to believing homosexuality was in itself a sickness, reflecting traditional beliefs about homosexuality. Consequently, emotional problems were automatically attributed to the client's homosexuality rather than to other sources.

Recent Contributions: Michel Foucault (1926–1984)   One of the most influential social theorists in the past quarter-century was the French thinker Michel Foucault. A cultural historian and philosopher, Foucault explored how society created social ideas and how these ideas operated to further the

established order. His most important work on sexuality was *The History of Sexuality, Volume I* (1980), a book that gave fresh impetus to scholars interested in the social construction of sex, especially those involved in gender and gay and lesbian studies.

A key idea in Foucault's work is the concept of discourse. *Discourse* refers to an organized body of knowledge (such as psychiatry) and its practitioners (psychiatrists) who create power over others (patients). Foucault uses the term to unify knowledge and power in a single concept. He is not interested in whether discourses reveal the "truth" about sexuality. Instead, he wants to discover who the "speakers" of the discourse are, their points of view, and the institutions that support them.

Foucault has challenged the belief that our sexuality is rooted in nature. Instead, he argues, it is rooted in society. Society "constructs" sexuality, including homosexuality and heterosexuality. Foucault's critics argue, however, that he underestimates the biological basis of sexual impulses and the role individuals have in creating their own sexuality.

Contemporary Gay and Lesbian Research In 1973, the American Psychiatric Association (APA) removed homosexuality from its list of psychological disorders in its *Diagnostic and Statistical Manual of Mental Disorders (DSM-II)*. The APA decision was reinforced by similar resolutions by the American Psychological Association and the American Sociological Association. More recently, in 1997 at its annual meeting, the American Psychological Association overwhelmingly passed a resolution stating that there is no sound scientific evidence on the efficacy of reparative therapies for gay men and lesbians. This statement reinforced the association's earlier stand that because there is nothing wrong with homosexuality, there is no reason to try to change sexual orientation through therapy.

As a result of the rejection of the psychopathological model, social and behavioral research on gay men and lesbians has moved in a new direction. Research no longer focuses primarily on the causes and cures of homosexuality. Most of the new research approaches homosexuality in a neutral manner. The only major exception to the shift in perspective is found in psychoanalytic literature.

Michel Foucault (1926–1984) of France was one of the most important thinkers who influenced our understanding of how society "constructs" human sexuality.

Directions for Future Research

In 1994, the National Institute of Child Health and Human Development initiated a 5-year study involving 19,000 teens and their sexual behavior. Researchers are conducting face-to-face interviews in the homes of teens, while at the same time assuring them confidentiality. The $21.4 million study has the potential to provide us with the broadest-based information about sexuality to date (Holden, 1994).

Historically, sex research has focused on preventive health, which "prioritizes sexuality as a social problem and behavioral risk" (di Mauro, 1995). In light of the HIV/AIDS pandemic and other social problems, this emphasis is important, but it fails to examine the full spectrum of individuals' behaviors or the social and cultural factors that drive those behaviors.

According to Diane di Mauro (1995), three priorities of applied and basic research in sexuality need to be recognized. They are (1) research that integrates an expanded definition of sexuality, one that provides a thorough knowledge of human sexuality; (2) relevant intervention research that is attuned to communication needs and incorporates appropriate evaluative processes; and (3) a more accepting and positive depiction of sexuality.

ETHNICITY AND SEXUALITY

Over the past several years, researchers have begun to recognize the significance of ethnicity in various aspects of American life, including sexuality. A recent review of ethnicity in 25 years of published sexuality research revealed a deficit in empirical investigation (Wiederman, Maynard, & Fretz, 1996). Though the results indicated modest increases in ethnic diversity of research samples, important questions must still be addressed. These include the differences that socioeconomic status plays in sexual behaviors, the way in which questions are posed in research studies, the research methods that are used, and the researcher's preconceived notions regarding ethnic differences. Although limited research is available, we attempt to provide some background to assist an understanding of sexuality and ethnicity.

African Americans

African Americans represent the largest ethnic group in America. Several factors must be considered when African American sexuality is studied: sexual stereotypes, socioeconomic status, Black subculture, and number of single adults.

Sexual stereotypes greatly distort our understanding of Black sexuality. One of the most common stereotypes is the depiction of African Americans as sexually driven (Murry, 1991). Although this is an age-old stereotype dating back to the fifteenth century, it continues to hold considerable strength among non-Blacks. Discussing African American men, Robert Staples (1991) writes: "Black men are saddled with a number of stereotypes that label them as irresponsible, criminalistic, hypersexual, and lacking in masculine traits."

Socioeconomic status is a person's ranking in society based on a combination of occupational, educational, and income levels. It is an important element in African American sexual values and behaviors (Staples & Johnson, 1993). Although stereotypes suggest that *all* Blacks have a low income, a well-educated and economically secure middle class has evolved (Giles, 1994). Middle-class Blacks share many sexual attitudes and values with middle-class Whites (Howard, 1988; Staples, 1988). For example, the overwhelming majority of births to single mothers are among low-income African Americans. But as income level increases among Blacks, births to single mothers decrease significantly (Staples, 1988).

Values and behaviors are shaped by culture and social class. The subculture of Blacks of low socioeconomic status is deeply influenced by poverty, discrimination, and structural subordination. In contrast to middle-class Whites and Blacks, low-income Blacks are more likely to engage in sexual intercourse at an earlier age and to have children outside of marriage. Because of the poverty, violence, and prejudice of inner-city life, low-income Black children do not experience a prolonged or "innocent" childhood. They are forced to become adults at an early age.

Premarital sexual activity is not considered immoral nor is it stigmatized, as it is in middle-class communities. Because sexual activity is regarded as natural, premarital sex is considered appropriate as relationships become more involved. Furthermore, as mere survival is not even guaranteed, adolescents may see no reason to wait for a future they may never have. In the inner-city subculture, boys tend to use sex exploitatively and competitively. For them, sex is not so much a means of achieving intimacy with partners as it is a way of achieving status among their male peers. For girls, sex is a means of demonstrating their maturity; it is a sign of their womanhood.

For inner-city Black adolescents, one becomes a woman by becoming a mother (Zinn & Eitzen, 1990). In 1995, 58% of Black households were headed by a single mother (U.S. Bureau of the Census, 1996). The Black community, which values children highly, generally does not stigmatize the unmarried mother. For Blacks of all classes, there is no such thing as an "illegitimate" or "illegally born" child. All children are considered valuable (Collins, 1991).

Sixty percent of African American women are single (U.S. Bureau of the Census, 1996). Among African Americans, there are approximately 1.5 million more women than there are "available" men. This gender imbalance is the result of high death rates, incarceration, and drug use among Black men, often attributable to the effects of discrimination. If they wish to have children, many African American women are likely to be unmarried single parents. Furthermore, the single lifestyle, whether White or Black, is associated with more sexual partners, a lack of contraceptive responsibility, and a greater likelihood of contracting STDs.

Although there has been a significant increase in African American research over the past decade, much still needs to be done (Taylor, Chatters, Tucker, & Lewis, 1991). For example, we need to (1) explore the sexual attitudes and behaviors of the general African American population, not merely adolescents; (2) examine Black sexuality from an African American cultural context; and (3) utilize a cultural equivalency perspective that rejects differences between Blacks and Whites as signs of inherent deviance. The **cultural equivalency perspective** is the view that the attitudes, values, and behaviors of one ethnic group are similar to those of another ethnic group.

Latinos

Latinos are the fastest-growing and second-largest ethnic group in the United States. Between 1980 and 1990, the Latino population increased by 35%, mostly as a result of immigration from Mexico. There is very little research, however, about Latino sexuality.

Two common stereotypes depict Latinos as sexually permissive and Latino males as pathologically *macho,* or hypermasculine. Like African Americans, Latino males are stereotyped as being promiscuous, engaging in excessive and indiscriminate sexual activities. No research, however, validates this stereotype. In fact, one study concludes that in contrast to the dominant stereotype, Latino males are significantly less experienced sexually than their Anglo peers (Padilla & O'Grady, 1987).

The macho stereotype paints Latino males as hypermasculine—swaggering and domineering. But the stereotype of machismo distorts its cultural meaning among Latinos. (The Spanish word was originally incorporated into English in the 1960s as a slang term to describe any male who was sexist.) Within its cultural context, however, **machismo** is a positive concept, characterized by a man's courage, strength, generosity, politeness, and respect for others. And in day-to-day functioning, relations between Latino men and women are significantly more egalitarian than the macho stereotype suggests. This is especially true among Latinos who are more acculturated (Sanchez, 1997). **Acculturation** is the process of adaptation of an ethnic group to the values, attitudes, and behaviors of the dominant culture.

Three important factors must be considered when Latino sexuality is studied: diversity of ethnic groups, significance of socioeconomic status, and degree of acculturation.

Latinos comprise numerous ethnic subgroups, the largest of which are Mexican American, Puerto Rican, and Cuban (Vega, 1991). Each group has its own unique background and set of cultural traditions that affect sexual attitudes and behaviors. For example, Latino adolescents differ in their contraceptive use according to their ethnic background (Durant, Pendergast, & Seymore, 1990). Fertility rates also differ between groups. The fertility rate of Mexican Americans, for example, is almost one-third higher than that of Anglos; by contrast, the fertility rate for Cuban Americans is lower than that of Anglos (Staples, 1988).

Socioeconomic status is important, as middle-class Latino values appear to differ from those of low-income Latinos. The birth rate for single women, for example, is significantly higher among low-income Latinas than among middle-class Latinas (Bean & Tienda, 1987). Furthermore, Latino ethnic groups rank differently on the socioeconomic scale. The middle class is largest among Cuban Americans, followed by Puerto Ricans, and then Mexican Americans.

Degree of acculturation may be the most important factor affecting sexual attitudes and behavior among Latinos. This can be viewed on a contin-

In studying Latino sexuality, it is important to remember that Latinos come from diverse ethnic groups, including Mexican American, Cuban American, and Puerto Rican, each with its own unique background and set of cultural values.

uum: traditional at one pole, bicultural in the middle, and acculturated at the other pole (Guerrero Pavich, 1986). (This same continuum may also be used with other ethnic groups, such as Europeans, Asian Americans, and Caribbean and Pacific Islanders.) *Traditional Latinos* were born and raised in Latin America; they adhere to the norms, customs, and values of their original homeland, speak mostly Spanish, and have strong religious ties. Foreign-born Latinos, who may number as many as 7 million, hold the most traditional values. *Bicultural Latinos* may have been born in either Latin America or the United States; they speak both Spanish and English, are able to function well in both Latino and Anglo cultures, and have moderate religious ties. *Acculturated Latinos* do not identify with their Latino heritage; they speak only English and have (at most) moderate religious ties.

Rebellion against the native culture may be expressed through sexual behavior (Sanchez, 1997). Traditional Latinos tend to place a high value on female virginity while encouraging males, beginning in adolescence, to be sexually active (Guerrero Pavich, 1986). Females are regarded according to a virgin/whore dichotomy—"good" girls are virgins, "bad" girls are sexual (Espín, 1984). Females are taught to put the needs of others, especially males, before their own. Among traditional Latinos, fears about American "sexual immorality" produce their own stereotypes of Anglos. Adolescent boys learn about masturbation from peers; girls rarely learn about it because of its tabooed nature. There is little acceptance of gay men and lesbians, whose relationships are often regarded as "unnatural" or sinful (Bonilla & Porter, 1990).

In traditional Latino culture, Catholicism plays an important role, especially in the realm of sexuality. The Church teaches premarital virginity and prohibits both contraception and abortion. For traditional Latinas, using contraception may lead to "considerable guilt and confusion on the part of the individual woman who feels she is alone in violating the cultural taboos against contraception" (Guerrero Pavich, 1986). Traditional Latinas are generally negative toward birth control; however, some evidence suggests that women are increasingly approving of and using available contraception (Baca-Zinn, 1994). Abortion is out of the question. Only the most acculturated Latinas view abortion as an option.

Among bicultural Latinos, there may be gender-role conflict (Salgado de Snyder, Cervantes, & Padilla, 1990). Emma Guerrero Pavich describes the conflicts some Latinas experience: "She observes the freedom and sexual expression 'Americanas' have. At first she may condemn them as 'bad women'; later she may envy their freedom. Still later she may begin to want those freedoms for herself" (Guerrero Pavich, 1986). For bicultural Latinos, sexual values and attitudes appear to lie at different points along the continuum, depending on the degree of acculturation.

There is significantly greater flux among Latinos as a result of continuing high rates of immigration and the acculturation process. Much current research on Latinos focuses on the acculturation of new immigrants. We know less, however, about bicultural Latinos and even less about acculturated Latinos.

Asian and Pacific Islander Americans

Asian and Pacific Islander Americans represent about 3.5% of the total population in the United States today. Among the oldest and largest groups are Japanese Americans and Chinese Americans. Other groups include Vietnamese, Laotians, Cambodians, Koreans, Filipinos, Asian Indians, Native Hawaiians, and other Pacific Islanders. Numbering more than 9 million people, they speak more than 30 different languages and represent a similar number of distinct cultures.

Significant differences in attitudes, values, and practices make it difficult to speak in general terms about these groups without stereotyping and oversimplifying. Given this caveat, it may be said that many Asian Americans are less individualistic and more relationship-oriented than members of other cultures. Individuals are seen as the products of their relationships to nature and other people (Shon & Ja, 1982). Asian Americans are less verbal and expressive in their interactions and often rely on indirection and nonverbal communication, such as silence and avoidance of eye contact as signs of respect (DelCarmen, 1990).

More than half of Chinese Americans are foreign-born. In traditional Chinese culture, in-laws of married women were responsible for safeguarding the wife's chastity and keeping her under the ultimate control of her husband. Where extended families worked and lived in close quarters for extended periods of time, many husbands and wives found it difficult to experience intimacy with one another. Though not much is known about mate selection of the foreign-born U.S. Chinese population, of those born in the United States, love and compatibility are the basis for marriage partners (Ishii-Kuntz, 1997a). As in other Asian American populations, the rate of cross-cultural marriage among younger Chinese Americans is higher than in their parents' and grandparents' generations. Still, Confucian principles,

Among Asian Americans (as with other ethnic groups), attitudes toward relationships, family, and sexuality are related to the degree of acculturation.

which teach women to be obedient to their husbands' wishes and needs and to be sexually loyal to their husbands, play a part in maintaining monogamy and holding down the divorce rate among traditional Chinese families (Ishii-Kuntz, 1997a). In contrast, men are expected to be sexually experienced, and their engaging in premarital sex is frequently accepted. Chinese American parents tend to teach their children to control their emotional expressions; thus affection is not often displayed openly (Uba, 1994).

For more than 100 years, Japanese Americans have maintained a significant presence in the United States, (Ishii-Kuntz, 1997b). Japanese cultural values of loyalty and harmony are strongly embedded in Confucianism and feudalism (loyalty to the ruler), yet Japanese lives are not strongly influenced by religion (Ishii-Kuntz, 1997b). Like Chinese Americans born in the United States, Japanese Americans born in the United States base partner selection more on love and individual compatibility than on family concerns (Nakano, 1990). Among the newest generation of Japanese Americans, the incidence of cross-cultural marriage has risen dramatically, to about 50–60% (Kitano, 1994).

Traditional Japanese values allowed sexual freedom for men but not for women. Traditionally, Japanese women were expected to remain pure; sexual permissiveness or infidelity on the part of women was considered socially disruptive and threatening (Ishii-Kuntz, 1997b). Over time, attitudes and conditions related to sexuality have changed, so that sexual activity is no longer considered solely procreational, and there is a greater use of contraceptives. Japanese Americans have one of the lowest divorce rates of any group in the United States. A desire not to bring shame on the family or on the community may partially account for this low rate.

Within most Asian cultures, self-disclosure is often viewed unfavorably. Quick self-disclosure of personal information may give the impression of emotional imbalance. Overall, educational achievement is highly valued, a strong sense of responsibility toward relatives exists, a failure to live up to the elders' expectations results in self-blame, and respect for elders is equated with respect for authority. As with other groups, the degree of acculturation may be the most important factor affecting sexual attitudes and behaviors. Compared with those who were raised in the United States, those who were born and raised in their original homeland tend to adhere more closely to their culture's norms, customs, and values.

> Men do not seek truth. It is the truth that pursues men who run away and will not look around.
>
> —*Lincoln Steffens (1866–1936)*

■   Popular culture surrounds us with sexual images disseminated through advertising, music, television, and film that form a backdrop to our daily living. Much of what is conveyed is simplified, stereotypical, shallow—and entertaining. But through sex research, we can gain tools for evaluating the mass of sex information disseminated through the media. Studying sex research enables us to understand how research is conducted and to be aware of its strengths and its limitations. Traditional sex research has been expanded in recent years by feminist and gay and lesbian research, which provides fresh insights and perspectives. Although the study of sexuality and ethnicity is only now beginning to emerge, it promises to enlarge our understanding of the diversity of attitudes, behaviors, and values in contemporary America.

SUMMARY

Sex, Advice Columnists, and Pop Psychology

- The *sex information/advice genre* transmits information to both entertain and inform; the information is generally oversimplified so that it does not interfere with the genre's primary entertainment purpose. Much of the information or advice conveys social norms. Although it uses the social science framework, it tends to overgeneralize and distort.

Thinking Critically About Sex

- *Objective statements* are based on observations of things as they exist in themselves. *Value judgments* are evaluations based on moral or ethical standards. *Opinions* are unsubstantiated beliefs based on an individual's personal thoughts. *Biases* are personal leanings or inclinations. *Stereotypes*, rigidly held beliefs about the personal characteristics of a group of people, are a type of *schema*, the organization of knowledge in our thought processes.

- *Attitudes* are predispositions to acting, thinking, or feeling certain ways toward things. *Behaviors* are the ways people act. Behaviors cannot necessarily be inferred from attitudes, or vice versa.

- *Fallacies* are errors in reasoning. The *egocentric fallacy* is the belief that others necessarily share one's own values, beliefs, and attitudes. The *ethnocentric fallacy* is the belief that one's own ethnic group, nation, or culture is inherently superior to any other.

Sex Research Methods

- Ethical issues are important concerns in sex research. The most important issues are *informed consent,* protection from harm, confidentiality, and the use of deception.

- In sex research, *sampling* is a particularly acute problem. To be meaningful, samples should be representative of the larger group from which they are drawn. But most samples are limited by volunteer bias, dependence on college students, underrepresentation of ethnic groups, and difficulties in sampling gay men and lesbians.

- The most important methods in sex research are clinical, survey, observational, and experimental. *Clinical research* relies on in-depth examinations of individuals or groups who come to the clinician seeking treatment for psychological or medical problems. *Survey research* uses questionnaires or interviews to gather information from a small representative sample of people. *Observational research* requires the researcher to observe interactions carefully in as unobtrusive a manner as possible. *Experimental research* presents subjects with various stimuli under controlled conditions in which their responses can be measured.

- Experiments are controlled through the use of *independent variables* (which can be changed by the experimenter) and *dependent variables* (which change in relation to changes in the independent variable). Clinical, survey, and observational research efforts, by contrast, are *correlational studies* that infer relationships between variables without manipulating them. In experimental research, physiological responses are often measured by *plethysmographs* or *strain gauges.*

The Sex Researchers

- Richard von Krafft-Ebing was one of the earliest sex researchers. His work emphasized the pathological aspects of sexuality.

- Sigmund Freud was one of the most influential thinkers in Western civilization. According to Freud's theory, personality consisted of three parts: *id, ego,* and *superego.* Freud believed there were five stages in psychosexual development: the *oral stage, anal stage, phallic stage, latency stage,* and *genital stage.*

- Havelock Ellis was the earliest modern sexual thinker. His ideas included the relativity of sexual values, the normality of masturbation, a belief in the sexual equality of men and women, the redefinition of "normal," and a reevaluation of homosexuality.

- Alfred Kinsey's work documented enormous diversity in sexual behavior, emphasized the role of masturbation in sexual development, and argued that the distinction between normal and abnormal behavior was meaningless. The Kinsey scale charts sexual activities along a continuum ranging from exclusive heterosexual behaviors to exclusive same-sex behaviors.

- William Masters and Virginia Johnson detailed the physiology of the human sexual response cycle. Their physiological studies demonstrated the similarity between male and female sexual responses; they demonstrated that women achieve orgasms through clitoral stimulation. Their work on sexual inadequacy revolutionized sex therapy through the use of behavioral techniques.

- The National Health and Social Life Survey is one of the largest and most comprehensive studies of sexual behavior published to date. Though controversy surrounds it, the study reveals new and interesting findings related to the social context of sexuality in America.

Emerging Research Perspectives

- There is no single feminist perspective in sex research.

- Most feminist research, however, focuses on gender issues, assumes that the female experience of sex has been devalued, believes power is a critical element in female-male relationships, argues that empirical research must be supplemented by qualitative research to capture the personal experience and meaning of sexuality, and explores ethnic diversity.

- Research on homosexuality has rejected the moralistic-pathological approach. Those who have conducted research in gay and lesbian studies include Karl Ulrichs, Karl Kertbeny, Magnus Hirschfeld, Evelyn Hooker, and Michel Foucault.

- Contemporary gay/lesbian research focuses on the psychological and social experience of being gay or lesbian.

Ethnicity and Sexuality

- The role of ethnicity in human sexuality has been largely overlooked until recently.

- *Socioeconomic status* is important in the study of African American sexuality. Other factors include stereotyping of Blacks as hypersexual and promiscuous, the importance of the African American subculture, and the large number of single women.

- Two common stereotypes about Latinos are that they are sexually permissive and that males are pathologically *macho.* Factors in studying Latino sexuality include the diversity of ethnic groups, such as Mexican American, Cuban American, and Puerto Rican; the role of socioeconomic status; and the degree of *acculturation*.

▪ Significant differences in attitudes, values, and practices make it difficult to speak in general terms about Asian and Pacific Islander Americans. Degree of acculturation may be the most important factor affecting sexual attitudes and behaviors. Religious and cultural values still play an important part in the lives of many Asian and Pacific Islander Americans.

SUGGESTED READING

Bullough, Vern L., & Bullough, Bonnie. (1995). *Sexual Attitudes Through the Ages*. New York: Prometheus Books. A history of sexual attitudes and a look at views about sex in a variety of cultures.

Geer, James, & O'Donohue, William (Eds.). (1987). *Theories of Human Sexuality*. New York: Plenum Press. A collection of essays briefly describing various theories of human sexuality.

Irvine, Janice. (1991). *Disorders of Desire: Sex and Gender in Modern American Sexology*. Philadelphia: Temple University Press. A critical examination, from a feminist perspective, of sexology, including the Kinsey studies, the work of Masters and Johnson, sex therapy, and gender research, especially gay/lesbian sexuality and transsexuality.

McKinney, Kathleen, & Sprecher, Susan (Eds.). (1989). *Human Sexuality: The Societal and Interpersonal Context*. New York: Ablex. Sociologically oriented essays on human sexuality.

Minton, Henry (Ed.). (1993). *Gay and Lesbian Studies: Emergence of a Discipline*. Binghamton, NY: Hawthorne Press. A collection of essays on the development of gay/lesbian studies.

Parker, Richard, & Gagnon, John (Eds.). (1995). *Conceiving Sexuality: Approaches to Sex Research in a Postmodern World*. New York: Routledge. A collection of essays exploring contemporary sex research.

3

Female Sexual Anatomy, Physiology, and Response

Although women and men are similar in many more ways than they are different, we tend to focus on the differences rather than the similarities. Various cultures hold diverse ideas about exactly what it means to be female or male, but just about the only differences that are consistent are actual physical differences, most of which relate to sexual structure and function. In this chapter and the following one, we discuss both the similarities and differences in the anatomy (body structures), physiology (body functions), and sexual response of males and females. This chapter introduces the sexual structures and functions of women's bodies, including the influence of hormones and the menstrual cycle. We also look at models of sexual arousal and response, the relationship of these to women's experiences of sex, and the role of orgasm. In Chapter 4, we discuss male anatomy and physiology, and in Chapter 5, we move beyond biology to look at gender and the meanings we ascribe to being male and female.

FEMALE SEX ORGANS: WHAT ARE THEY FOR?

Anatomically speaking, all embryos appear as females when their reproductive organs begin to develop (Figure 3.1). If it does not receive certain genetic and hormonal signals, the fetus will continue to develop as a female. In humans and most other mammals, the female, in addition to providing half the genetic instructions for the offspring, provides the environment in which it can develop until it becomes capable of surviving as a separate entity. She also nourishes the offspring, both during gestation (the period of carrying the young in the uterus) via the placenta and following birth via the breasts through lactation (milk production).

It is clear that the female sex organs serve a reproductive function. But they perform other functions as well. Some sexual parts serve to bring pleasure to their owners; they may also serve to attract potential sexual partners. Because of the mutual pleasure partners give each other, we can see that sexual structures also serve an important role in human relationships. People demonstrate their affection for one another by sharing sexual pleasure and generally form enduring partnerships at least partially on the basis of mutual sexual sharing. Let's look at the features of human female anatomy and physiology that provide pleasure to women and their partners and enable them to conceive and give birth.

External Structures (The Vulva)

The sexual and reproductive organs of both men and women are called **genitals,** or genitalia, from the Latin *genere,* to beget. The external female genitals are the mons pubis, the clitoris, the labia majora, and the labia minora, collectively known as the **vulva** (Figure 3.2). (People often use the word "vagina" when they are actually referring to the vulva. The vagina is an internal structure.)

The Mons Pubis The **mons pubis** (pubic mound), or **mons veneris** (mound of Venus), is a pad of fatty tissue that covers the area of the pubic

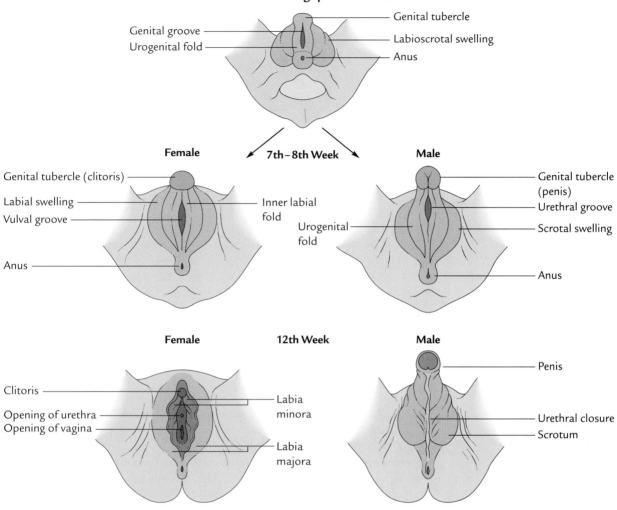

Undifferentiated stage prior to 6th week

Genital groove —
Urogenital fold —

— Genital tubercle
— Labioscrotal swelling
— Anus

Female   **7th–8th Week**   **Male**

Genital tubercle (clitoris) —
Labial swelling —
Vulval groove —

Anus —

— Inner labial fold

Urogenital fold —

— Genital tubercle (penis)
— Urethral groove
— Scrotal swelling

— Anus

Female   **12th Week**   **Male**

Clitoris —
Opening of urethra —
Opening of vagina —

— Labia minora

— Labia majora

— Penis

— Urethral closure
— Scrotum

FIGURE 3.1   Embryonic-Fetal Differentiation of the External Reproductive Organs. Female and male reproductive organs are formed from the same embryonic tissues. An embryo's external genitals are female in appearance until certain genetic and hormonal instructions signal the development of male organs. Without such instructions, the genitals continue to develop as female.

bone about 6 inches below the navel. Beginning in puberty, the mons is covered with pubic hair. In some women, this area is sensitive to sexual stimulation.

The Clitoris   The **clitoris** is the center of sexual arousal in the female. It contains a high concentration of nerve endings and is exquisitely sensitive to stimulation, especially at the tip of its shaft, the **glans clitoridis.** A fold of skin called the **clitoral hood** covers the glans when the clitoris is not engorged. Although the clitoris is structurally analogous to the penis (it is formed from the same embryonic tissue), its sole function is sexual arousal. (The penis serves the additional functions of urine excretion and semen ejaculation.) The shaft of the clitoris is both an external and an internal structure. The external portion is about 0.25–1.0 inch long. Internally, the shaft is divided into two branches called **crura** (singular *crus*), each of which is about 3 inches long. The crura contain two *corpora cavernosa*, hollow chambers that fill with blood and swell during arousal. When stimulated, the clitoris

Really that little dealybob is too far away from the hole. It should be built right in.

—*Loretta Lynn*

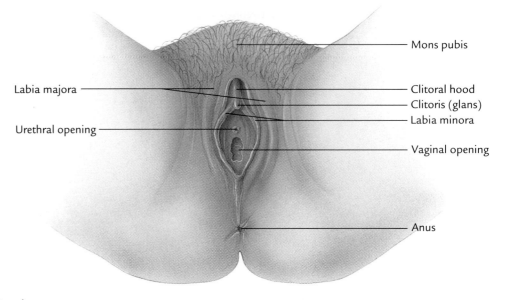

FIGURE 3.2   External Female
Sexual Structures (Vulva)

enlarges initially and then retracts beneath the hood just before and during orgasm. With repeated orgasms, it follows the same pattern of engorgement and retraction, although its swellings may not be as pronounced after the initial orgasm.

The Labia Majora and Labia Minora   The **labia majora** (major lips) are two folds of spongy flesh extending from the mons pubis and enclosing the labia minora, clitoris, urethral opening, and vaginal entrance. The **labia minora** (minor lips) are smaller folds within the labia majora that meet above the clitoris to form the clitoral hood. They are smooth and hairless and vary quite a bit in appearance from woman to woman. They are sensitive to the touch and swell during sexual arousal, doubling or tripling in size. The area enclosed by the labia minora is referred to as the **vestibule.** Within the vestibule, on either side of the vaginal opening, are two small ducts from the **Bartholin's glands** (or vestibular glands), which secrete a small amount of moisture during sexual arousal.

Internal Structures

The internal female sexual structures and reproductive organs include the vagina; the uterus and its lower opening, the cervix; the ovaries; and the fallopian tubes (Figure 3.3).

The Vagina   The **vagina,** from the Latin word for sheath, is a flexible, muscular structure that begins between the legs and extends diagonally toward the small of the back. The vagina serves two reproductive functions: It encompasses the penis during **coitus** (sexual intercourse) so that sperm will be deposited near the entrance of the uterus, and it is the **birth canal** through which an infant is born. Normally, the walls of the vagina are relaxed and

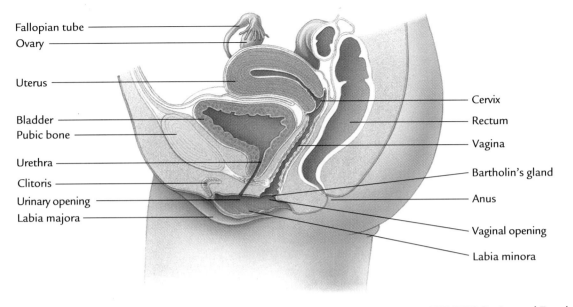

FIGURE 3.3 Internal Female Sexual Structures

collapsed together, but during sexual arousal, the inner two-thirds of the vagina expands. Mucous membranes line the vagina, providing lubrication during arousal. The opening of the vagina is known as the **introitus.** Prior to first intercourse or other intrusion, the introitus is partially covered by a thin membrane, the **hymen** (named for the Roman god of marriage). (Maintaining good vaginal health is discussed in Chapter 13.)

The hymen typically has one or several perforations, allowing menstrual blood and mucous secretions to flow out of the vagina (and generally allowing for tampon insertion). In many cultures, it is (or was) important for a woman's hymen to be intact on her wedding night. Blood on the nuptial sheets is taken as proof of her virginity. The stretching or tearing of the hymen may produce some pain or discomfort and possibly some bleeding. Usually there is little trouble inserting the penis through the hymen if the male is gentle and there is adequate lubrication. Prior to first intercourse, the hymen may be stretched somewhat by tampon insertion, by the woman's self-manipulation, or by a partner during noncoital sexual activity.

Fairly recently, controversial research has asserted that an erotically sensitive area, the **Grafenberg spot,** is located on the front wall of the vagina midway between the introitus and the cervix (on the vaginal side of the urethra). This area, also known as the **G-spot,** is described as being about the size of a small bean during its unaroused state and growing to the size of a dime during arousal (Ladas, Whipple, & Perry, 1982). Stimulation of the G-spot is said to lead to orgasm, and, in some women, the ejaculation of a clear fluid from the urethra. (It has been suggested that the Skene's glands, located inside the urethra and functioning in a way similar to that of the prostate in males, may be responsible for the liquid that is sometimes expelled during intense orgasms.) Masters and Johnson noted, however, in a study of 100 women, that fewer than 10% experienced any special sensitivity in that area (Masters, Johnson, & Kolodny, 1992). They suggest that additional research is necessary.

The Uterus and Cervix   The **uterus,** or womb, is a hollow, thick-walled, muscular organ held in the pelvic cavity by a number of flexible ligaments and supported by several muscles. It is pear-shaped, with the tapered end, the **cervix,** extending down and opening into the vagina. If a woman has not given birth, the uterus is about 3 inches long and 3 inches wide at the top; it is somewhat larger in women who have given birth. The uterus expands during pregnancy to the size of a volleyball or larger, to accommodate the developing fetus. The inner lining of the uterine walls, the **endometrium,** is filled with tiny blood vessels. During the menstrual cycle, this tissue is built up and then shed and expelled through the cervical **os** (opening), unless fertilization has occurred. In the event of pregnancy, the pre-embryo is embedded in the nourishing endometrium.

In addition to the more-or-less-monthly menstrual discharge, mucous secretions from the cervix also flow out through the vagina. These secretions tend to be somewhat white, thick, and sticky following menstruation, becoming thinner as ovulation approaches. At ovulation, the mucous flow tends to increase and to be clear, slippery, and stretchy, somewhat like egg white. (Birth control using cervical mucus to determine the time of ovulation is discussed in Chapter 11.)

The Ovaries   On each side of the uterus, held in place by several ligaments, is one of a pair of ovaries. The **ovary** is a **gonad,** an organ that produces **gametes,** the sex cells containing the genetic material necessary for reproduction. Female gametes are called **oocytes,** from the Greek words for egg and cell. (Oocytes are commonly referred to as eggs or **ova** [singular, **ovum**]. Technically, however, the cell does not become an egg until it completes its final stages of division following fertilization.) The ovaries are the size and shape of large almonds. In addition to producing oocytes, they serve the important function of hormone production. The basic female hormones, estrogen and progesterone, are discussed later in this chapter.

At birth the human female's ovaries contain 400,000–700,000 oocytes (Marieb, 1995; Masters, Johnson, & Kolodny, 1992). During childhood, many of these degenerate; then, beginning in puberty and ending after menopause, a total of about 400 oocytes mature and are released on a more-or-less-monthly basis. The release of an oocyte is called **ovulation.** The immature oocytes are embedded in saclike structures called **ovarian follicles.** The fully ripened follicle is called a *vesicular* or *Graffian follicle.* At maturation, the follicle ruptures, releasing the oocyte to begin its journey. After the oocyte emerges, the ruptured follicle becomes the **corpus luteum** (from Latin for yellow body), a producer of important hormones; it eventually degenerates.

The Fallopian Tubes   At the top of the uterus, one on each side, are two tubes known as **fallopian tubes,** uterine tubes, or oviducts. The tubes are about 4 inches long. They extend toward the ovaries but are not attached to them. Instead, the funnel-shaped end of each tube (the *infundibulum*) fans out into fingerlike *fimbriae,* which drape over the ovary but may not actually touch it. Tiny, hairlike *cilia* on the fimbriae become active during ovulation. Their waving motion conducts the oocyte that has been released from the ovary into the fallopian tube. Just within the infundibulum is the *ampulla,* the widened part of the tube in which fertilization normally occurs if sperm and oocyte are there at the same time. (The process of ovulation and the

THE MUCOUS MEMBRANES lining the walls of the vagina normally produce clear, white, or pale yellow secretions. These secretions pass from the cervix through the vagina and vary in color, consistency, odor, and quantity depending on the phase of the menstrual cycle, a woman's health, and her unique physical characteristics. It is important for you to observe your secretions periodically and note any changes, especially if symptoms accompany them. Call a health practitioner if you feel uncertain, suspicious, and/or have been exposed to a sexually transmitted disease.

Although the vaginal walls are generally moist, sexual excitement causes lubrication to increase substantially. This lubrication serves two biological purposes. First, it increases the possibility of conception by alkalinizing the normally acidic chemical balance in the vagina, thus making it more hospitable to sperm, which die faster in acid environments. Second, it makes coitus easier and more pleasurable for both you and your partner by reducing friction between the vaginal walls and penis.

Use the following chart to compare your personal observations with those of other women.

Vaginal Mucus and Secretions Chart

Color	Consistency	Odor	Other Symptoms	Possible Cause	What to Do
clear	slightly rubbery; stretchy	normal	——	ovulation; sexual stimulation	nothing
milky	creamy	normal	——	preovulation	nothing
white	sticky, curdlike	normal	——	postovulation; the pill	nothing
brownish	watery and sticky	normal or slightly different	——	last day of period; spotting	nothing
white	thin, watery, creamy	normal to foul or fishy	itching	*Gardnerella* bacteria or non-specific bacterial infection	see health practitioner
white	curdlike or flecks, slight amount of discharge	yeasty or foul	itching or intense itching	overgrowth of yeast cells, yeast infection	apply yogurt or vinegar solution, see health practitioner
yellow, yellow-green	smooth or frothy	usually foul	itchy; may have red dots on cervix	possible *Trichomonas* infection	see health practitioner
yellow, yellow-green	thick, mucous	none to foul	pelvic cramping or pelvic pain	possible infection of fallopian tubes	see health practitioner right away

Source: Strong, B., DeVault, C., & Sayad, B. (1998). *The Marriage and Family Experience* (7th ed.). Belmont, CA: Wadsworth.

Western culture tends to be ambivalent about breasts and nudity. Most people are probably comfortable with artistic portrayals of the nude female body, as in this photograph by Imogen Cunningham entitled Triangles.

events leading to fertilization are discussed later in this chapter; fertilization is covered in Chapter 12.)

Other Structures

There are several other important anatomical structures in the genital areas of both men and women. Although they may not serve reproductive functions, they may be involved in sexual activities. Some of these areas may also be affected by sexually transmitted diseases. In women, these structures include the urethra, anus, and perineum. The **urethra** is the tube through which urine passes; the **urethral opening** is located between the clitoris and the vaginal opening. Between the vagina and the **anus**—the opening of the rectum, through which excrement passes—is a diamond-shaped region called the **perineum.** This area of soft tissue covers the muscles and ligaments of the **pelvic floor,** the underside of the pelvic area extending from

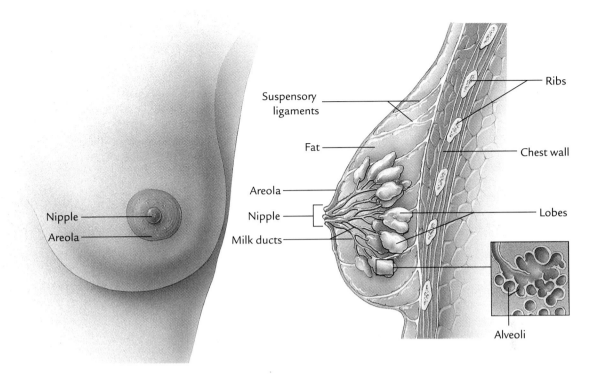

FIGURE 3.4   **The Female Breast**

the top of the pubic bone (above the clitoris) to the anus. (To learn more about this muscle and Kegel exercises, see Chapter 14.) The anus consists of two sphincters, circular muscles that open and close like valves. The tissue that rings the opening is tender and is erotically sensitive for some people.

In sex play or intercourse involving the anus or rectum, care must be taken not to rupture the delicate tissues. Anal sex, insertion of the penis into the rectum, is not considered safe, because abrasions of the tissue provide easy access for pathogens, such as HIV (the virus that causes AIDS), into the bloodstream (see Chapter 16). To practice safer sex, partners who engage in anal intercourse should use a well-lubricated condom.

The Breasts

Both women and men have breasts. At puberty, the female breasts begin to develop in response to hormonal stimuli (Figure 3.4). At maturity, the left breast is often slightly larger than the right (Rome, 1992).

The reproductive function of the breasts is to nourish the offspring through **lactation,** or milk production. A mature female breast, also known as a **mammary gland,** is composed of fatty tissue and 15–25 lobes that radiate around a central protruding nipple. Around the nipple is a ring of darkened skin called the **areola.** Tiny muscles at the base of the nipple cause it to become erect in response to touch, cold, or sexual arousal.

When a woman is pregnant, the structures within the breast undergo further development. Directly following childbirth, in response to hormonal signals, small glands within the lobes called **alveoli** begin producing milk. The milk passes into ducts, each of which has a dilated region for storage; the ducts open to the outside at the nipple. (Breast-feeding is discussed in detail in Chapter 12.) During lactation, a woman's breasts increase in size from enlarged glandular tissues and stored milk. In women who are not lactating, breast size depends mainly on fat content, often determined by hereditary factors.

In our culture, breasts also serve an erotic function. Many, but not all, women find breast stimulation intensely pleasurable, whether it occurs during breast-feeding or sexual contact. Men tend to be aroused by both the sight and the touch of women's breasts. Although there is no basis in reality, some believe that large breasts denote greater sexual responsiveness than small breasts.

> Uncorsetted, her friendly bust
> gives promise of pneumatic bliss.
>
> —*T. S. Eliot (1888–1965)*

FEMALE SEXUAL PHYSIOLOGY

The female reproductive cycle can be viewed as having two components (although, of course, multiple biological processes are involved): the ovarian cycle, in which eggs develop, and the menstrual, or uterine, cycle, in which the womb is prepared for pregnancy. These cycles repeat approximately every month for about 35 or 40 years. The task of directing these processes belongs to a class of chemicals called hormones.

Reproductive Hormones

Hormones are chemical substances that serve as messengers, traveling within the body through the bloodstream. Most hormones are composed of either amino acids (building blocks of proteins) or steroids (derived from cholesterol). They are produced by the ovaries and the endocrine glands—the adrenals, pituitary, and hypothalamus. Hormones assist in a variety of tasks, including development of the reproductive organs and secondary sex characteristics during puberty, regulation of the menstrual cycle, maintenance of pregnancy, initiation and regulation of childbirth, and initiation of lactation. Hormones that act directly on the gonads are known as **gonadotropins.** Among the most important of the female hormones are the **estrogens,** which affect the maturation of the reproductive organs, menstruation, and pregnancy, and **progesterone,** which helps to maintain the uterine lining. The principal hormones involved in a woman's reproductive and sexual life and their functions are described in Table 3.1.

The Ovarian Cycle

The development of female gametes is a complex process that begins even before a woman is born. In infancy and childhood, the cells that will develop into ova (eggs) undergo no further development. During puberty, hormones trigger the completion of the process of **oogenesis** (oh-uh-JEN-uh-sis), literally, "egg beginning" (Figure 3.5). This process, called the **ovarian cycle,** continues until a woman reaches menopause.

The ovarian cycle averages 28 days in length, although there is considerable variation among women, ranging from 21 to 40 days. In their own particular cycle length after puberty, however, most women experience little variation. Generally, ovulation occurs in only one ovary each month, alternating between the right and left sides with each successive cycle. If a sin-

TABLE 3.1 Female Reproductive Hormones		
Hormone	*Where Produced*	*Functions*
Estrogen (including estradiol, estrone, estriol)	Ovaries, adrenal glands, placenta (during pregnancy)	Promotes maturation of reproductive organs, development of secondary sex characteristics, and growth spurt at puberty; regulates menstrual cycle; sustains pregnancy
Progesterone	Ovaries, adrenal glands	Promotes breast development, maintains uterine lining, regulates menstrual cycle, sustains pregnancy
Gonadotropin-releasing hormone (GnRH)	Hypothalamus	Promotes maturation of gonads, regulates menstrual cycle
Follicle-stimulating hormone (FSH)	Pituitary	Regulates ovarian function and maturation of ovarian follicles
Luteinizing hormone (LH)	Pituitary	Assists in production of estrogen and progesterone, regulates maturation of ovarian follicles, triggers ovulation
Human chorionic gonadotropin (HCG)	Embryo and placenta	Helps sustain pregnancy
Testosterone	Adrenal glands and ovaries	Helps stimulate sexual interest
Oxytocin	Hypothalamus	Stimulates uterine contractions during childbirth
Prolactin	Pituitary	Stimulates milk production
Prostaglandins	All body cells	Mediate hormone response, stimulate muscle contractions

gle ovary is removed, the remaining one begins to ovulate every month. The ovarian cycle has three phases, called follicular, ovulatory, and luteal (Figure 3.6). As an ovary undergoes its changes, corresponding changes occur in the uterus. These changes, called the uterine, or menstrual, cycle, are discussed after the ovarian cycle.

Follicular Phase   On the first day of the cycle, **gonadotropin-releasing hormone (GnRH)** is released from the hypothalamus. GnRH begins to stimulate the pituitary to release **follicle-stimulating hormone (FSH)** and **luteinizing hormone (LH),** initiating the **follicular phase.** During the first ten days, 10 to 20 ovarian follicles begin to grow, stimulated by FSH and LH. In 98–99% of cases, just one of the follicles will mature completely during this period. (The maturation of more than one oocyte is one factor in multiple births.) All the developing follicles begin secreting estrogen. Under the influence of FSH and estrogen, the oocyte matures; it begins to bulge from the surface of the ovary.

Ovulatory Phase   The **ovulatory phase** begins at about day 11 and culminates with ovulation at about day 14. Stimulated by an increase of LH from the pituitary, the primary oocyte undergoes cell division and becomes ready for ovulation. The ballooning follicle wall thins and ruptures, and the oocyte enters the abdominal cavity near the beckoning fimbriae. Ovulation

FIGURE 3.5 **Oogenesis.** This diagram charts the development of an ovum, beginning with embryonic development of the oogonium and ending with fertilization of the secondary oocyte, which then becomes the diploid zygote. Primary oocytes are present in a female at birth; at puberty, hormones stimulate the oocyte to undergo meiosis.

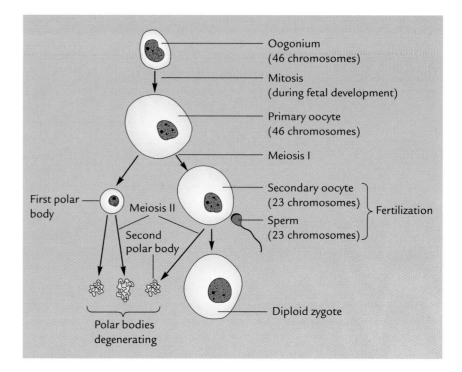

is now complete. Some women experience a sharp twinge on one side of the lower abdomen during ovulation. A very slight bloody discharge from the vagina may also occur.

Luteal Phase Following ovulation, estrogen levels drop rapidly, and the ruptured follicle, still under the influence of increased LH, becomes a corpus luteum, which secretes progesterone and small amounts of estrogen. Increasing levels of these hormones serve to inhibit pituitary release of FSH and LH. Unless fertilization has occurred, the corpus luteum deteriorates. In the event of pregnancy, the corpus luteum maintains its hormonal output, helping to sustain the pregnancy. The hormone human chorionic gonadotropin (HCG)—similar to LH—is secreted by the embryo and signals the corpus luteum to continue until the placenta has developed sufficiently to take over hormone production.

The **luteal phase** typically lasts from day 14 (immediately after ovulation) through day 28 of the ovarian cycle. Even when cycles are more or less than 28 days, the duration of the luteal phase remains the same; the time between ovulation and the end of the cycle is always 14 days. At this point, the ovarian hormone levels are at their lowest, GnRH is released, and FSH and LH levels begin to rise.

The Menstrual Cycle

As estrogen levels fall following the degeneration of the corpus luteum, the uterine lining (endometrium) is shed because it will not be needed to help sustain a fertilized ovum. The shedding of endometrial tissue and the bleeding that accompanies it are, collectively, a monthly event in the lives of

And if a woman shall have an issue, and her issue in her flesh be blood, she shall be separated seven days; and whatsoever touches her shall be unclean.

—*Leviticus 15:19*

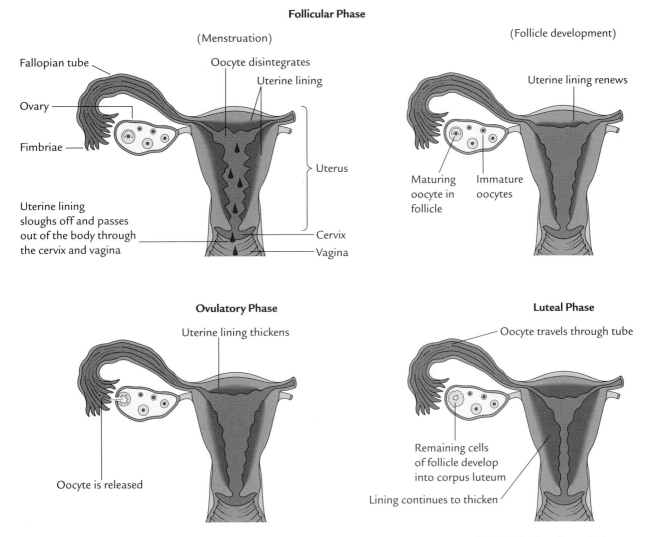

Follicular Phase

(Menstruation)

(Follicle development)

Fallopian tube

Oocyte disintegrates

Uterine lining

Uterine lining renews

Ovary

Fimbriae

Maturing oocyte in follicle

Immature oocytes

Uterine lining sloughs off and passes out of the body through the cervix and vagina

Uterus

Cervix

Vagina

Ovulatory Phase

Uterine lining thickens

Oocyte is released

Luteal Phase

Oocyte travels through tube

Remaining cells of follicle develop into corpus luteum

Lining continues to thicken

FIGURE 3.6 Ovarian and Menstrual Cycles. The ovarian cycle consists of the activities within the ovaries and the development of oocytes; it includes the follicular, ovulatory, and luteal phases. The menstrual cycle consists of events in the uterus. Hormones regulate these cycles.

women from puberty through menopause. Cultural and religious attitudes as well as personal experience influence our feelings about this phenomenon. (The physical and emotional effects of menstruation are discussed later in this section. The onset of menstruation and its effect on a woman's psychosexual development is discussed in Chapter 6. Menopause is discussed in Chapter 13.)

The **menstrual cycle** (or uterine cycle), like the ovarian cycle, is divided into three phases. What occurs within the uterus is inextricably related to what is happening in the ovaries, but only in their final phases do the two cycles actually coincide (Figure 3.7). The menstrual cycle consists of the menstrual, proliferative, and secretory phases.

Menstrual Phase   With hormone levels low because of the degeneration of the corpus luteum, the outer layer of the endometrium becomes detached from the uterine wall. The shedding of the endometrium marks the beginning of the **menstrual phase.** This endometrial tissue, along with mucus, other cervical and

FIGURE 3.7   The Menstrual Cycle, Ovarian Cycle, and Hormone Levels. This chart compares the activities of the ovaries and uterus and shows the relationship of hormone levels to these activities.

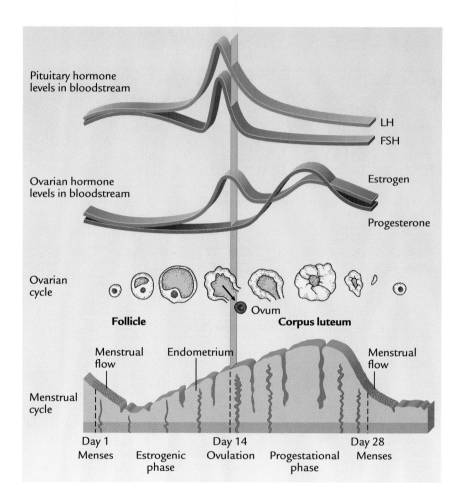

vaginal secretions, and a small amount of blood (2–5 oz per cycle), is expelled through the vagina. The menstrual flow, or **menses,** generally occurs over a period of 3–5 days. FSH and LH begin increasing around day 5, marking the end of this phase. A girl's first menstruation is known as **menarche.**

Proliferative Phase   The **proliferative phase** lasts about 9 days. During this time, the endometrium builds up in response to increased estrogen. The mucous membranes of the cervix secrete a clear, thin mucus with a crystalline structure that facilitates the passage of sperm. The proliferative phase ends with ovulation.

Secretory Phase   During the first part of the **secretory phase,** with the help of progesterone, the endometrium begins to prepare for the arrival of a fertilized ovum. Glands within the uterus enlarge and begin secreting glycogen, a cell nutrient. The cervical mucus thickens and starts forming a plug to seal off the uterus in the event of pregnancy. If fertilization does not occur, the corpus luteum begins to degenerate, as LH levels decline. Progesterone levels then fall, and the endometrial cells begin to die. The secretory phase lasts 14 days, corresponding with the luteal phase of the ovarian cycle. It ends with the shedding of the endometrium.

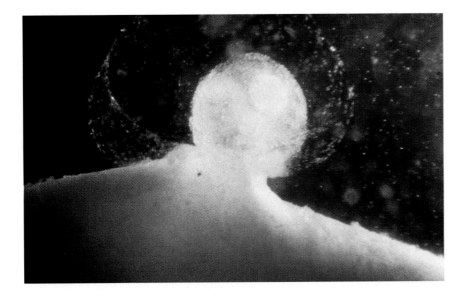

During ovulation, the ovarian follicle swells and ruptures, releasing the mature oocyte to begin its journey through the fallopian tube.

Menstrual Effects   For some women, menstruation is a problem. For others, it is simply a fact of life that creates little disruption. For individual women, the problems associated with their menstrual period may be physiological, emotional, or practical. About 70% of menstruating women notice at least one emotional, physical, or behavioral change in the week or so prior to menstruation. Most women describe the changes negatively: breast tenderness and swelling, abdominal bloating, irritability, cramping, depression, or fatigue. Some women also report positive changes, such as increased energy, heightened sexual arousal, or a general feeling of well-being. For most women, changes during the menstrual cycle are usually mild to moderate; they appear to have little impact on their lives. (Toxic shock syndrome, a blood infection associated with menstruation, is discussed in Chapter 13.) The most common problems associated with menstruation are discussed below.

PREMENSTRUAL SYNDROME   More severe menstrual problems have been attributed to what is commonly called **premenstrual syndrome (PMS),** a term used to describe the most commonly reported cluster of severe physical and emotional symptoms. Although up to 80% of women experience physical and behavioral changes premenstrually, 20–40% experience some difficulties, and some 2–10% report symptoms severe enough to impair work or relationships (Freeman, 1996). But because of the variety of symptoms and the difficulty involved in evaluating them, studies on PMS are contradictory and inconclusive. In 1994 the American Psychiatric Association included "premenstrual dysphoric disorder" (PMDD) in the fourth edition of its *Diagnostic and Statistical Manual of Mental Disorders (DSM-IV)*, which is used for psychiatric diagnosis. To be diagnosed with PMDD, a woman must have at least five of the eleven specific symptoms listed, which include depression, nervousness, irritability, and anxiety (grouped under dysphoria); bloating, swelling, and weight gain (grouped under fluid retention); breast tenderness; headache; fatigue; and food cravings (especially for salt, sugar, or chocolate).

Menstrual Period Slang
that time of the month
monthlies
the curse
female troubles
a visit from my friend
a visit from Aunt Sally
a visit from George
on the rag
on a losing streak
falling off the roof

IT IS A FACT THAT women have special needs and may face difficulties in the medical system. Whereas men are apt to receive medical care from one practitioner, women often receive either uncoordinated care from several physicians or care from a physician insensitive to, or untrained in finding, health problems peculiar to women. Gender bias is observed in the male-to-female ratio of physicians, the research decisions that are based on male subjects, and the observations by some that many male physicians are less focused on women's than men's medical needs. Recent studies have shown that, compared with women who see female practitioners, those who see male practitioners are less likely to have such diagnostic procedures as Pap smears and mammograms. They are also less likely to receive thorough diagnosis and treatment for coronary heart disease.

For these reasons, it is important for women to be aware and proactive in their medical care. That means selecting a male or female physician who is knowledgeable and sensitive to their needs and knowing what services to expect and making sure they get them. The basic

services unique to women are annual pelvic exams, Pap smears, and breast exams (including a mammogram every one to two years between ages 40 and 50, and annually thereafter).

To avoid duplication and to maximize observations and opinions, the best option—though not the cheapest—is for a woman to have both a gynecologist and a primary care physician and be sure they communicate with each other. Either kind of physician alone can fulfill a woman's health care needs; however, the combination is a better choice. Women should not be afraid to get a second (or third) opinion if they are confused, do not get a response to their symptoms, or are faced with differing diagnoses. It is important that women interview a new physician before seeking his or her care and be sure that the physician's attitude about women's health is similar to their own.

Source: Adapted from Lipman, M. (1994, May). "Office Visit: What Do Women Need?" *Consumer Reports on Health.*

For years, feminists have denied that menstruation makes any difference in behavior, pointing to the issue of biological sexism that keeps women out of positions of responsibility. Furthermore, they argue that PMS may be used against women in divorce and child custody cases.

The greatest difficulty in understanding PMS is knowing how to separate information that clearly indicates premenstrual symptoms from other aspects of a woman's physical and emotional health. Certain questions need to be answered before firm conclusions can be drawn. (For information on relieving premenstrual and menstrual symptoms, see pages R-11–R-12 in the Resource Center.)

DYSMENORRHEA   Some women experience pelvic cramping and pain during the menstrual cycle; this condition is called **dysmenorrhea.** There are two basic types. *Primary dysmenorrhea* is characterized by pain that begins with uterine shedding (or just before) and by the absence of pain at other times in the cycle. It can be very severe and may be accompanied by nausea, weakness, or other physical symptoms. In *secondary dysmenorrhea,* the symptoms may be the same, but there is an underlying condition or disease causing them; pain may not be limited to the menstrual phase alone. Secondary dysmenorrhea may be caused by pelvic inflammatory disease (PID), endometriosis, endometrial cancer, or other conditions (see Chapters 13 and 15).

The effects of dysmenorrhea can totally incapacitate a woman for several hours or even days. Once believed to be a psychological condition, primary dysmenorrhea is now known to be caused by high levels of **prostaglandins,** a type of hormone with a fatty-acid base that is found throughout the body. One type of prostaglandin is synthesized in the uterus and stimulates uterine contractions; excessive amounts cause tighter and longer contractions and keep oxygen from reaching the uterus and abdominal muscles (Rome, 1992). Taking drugs like ibuprofen (Motrin and Advil) relieves symptoms by inhibiting the production of prostaglandins. Some doctors may prescribe birth control pills.

AMENORRHEA   When women do not menstruate for reasons other than aging, the condition is called **amenorrhea.** A principal cause of amenorrhea is pregnancy. Lack of menstruation, if not a result of pregnancy, is categorized as either primary or secondary amenorrhea. Women who have passed the age of 16 and never menstruated are diagnosed as having *primary amenorrhea*. It may be that they have not yet reached their critical weight (when an increased ratio of body fat triggers menstrual cycle–inducing hormones) or that they are hereditarily late maturers. But it can also signal hormonal deficiencies, abnormal body structure, or hermaphroditism. Most primary amenorrhea can be treated with hormone therapy.

Secondary amenorrhea exists when a previously menstruating woman stops menstruating for several months. If it is not due to pregnancy, breast-feeding, or the use of hormonal contraceptives, the source of secondary amenorrhea may be found in stress, lowered body fat, heavy athletic training, or hormonal irregularities. Anorexia (discussed in Chapter 13) is a frequent cause of amenorrhea. If a woman is not pregnant, is not breast-feeding, and can rule out hormonal contraceptives as a cause, she should see her health practitioner if she has gone six months without menstruating.

Sexuality and the Menstrual Cycle

Although studies have tried to determine whether there is a biologically based cycle of sexual interest and activity in women that correlates with the menstrual cycle (such as higher interest around ovulation), the results have been conflicting. Researchers have found everything from no significant correlation (Bancroft, 1984; Meuwissen & Over, 1992) to significant correlations at different phases (Harvey, 1987; Matteo & Rissman, 1984). There is apparently a great deal of individual variation.

There is also variation in how people feel about sexual activity during different phases. If a woman believes she is ovulating, and if she and her partner do not want a pregnancy, they may feel negative or ambivalent about intercourse. If a woman is menstruating, she, her partner, or both of them may not wish to engage in intercourse or cunnilingus, for a number of reasons.

There is a general taboo in our culture, as in many others, against sexual intercourse during menstruation. This taboo may be based on religious beliefs. Among Orthodox Jews, for example, women are required to refrain from intercourse for seven days following the end of menstruation. They may then resume sexual activity after a ritual bath, the *mikvah*. Contact with blood may make some people squeamish. A man may view menstrual blood as "somehow dangerous, magical, and apparently not something he wants to get on his penis" (Delaney, Lupton, & Toth, 1988). Many women, especially at the beginning of their period, feel bloated or uncomfortable; they may experience breast tenderness or a general feeling of not wanting to be touched. Others may find that lovemaking helps relieve menstrual discomfort.

For come couples, just dealing with the logistics of bloodstains, bathing, and laundry may be enough to discourage them from intercourse at this time. For many people, however, menstrual blood holds no special connotation. It is important to note that although it is unusual, conception *can* occur during menstruation, especially if the woman has short or irregular cycles. Some women find that a diaphragm holds back the flow and facilitates lovemaking. Although it is not recommended that women engage in intercourse while a tampon is inserted because of possible injury to the cervix, cunnilingus is a possibility. And inventive lovers can, of course, find many ways to give each other pleasure that do not require putting the penis into the vagina.

Sexual intercourse during menstruation may carry health risks for women who have multiple sexual partners or whose partners may have been exposed to a sexually transmitted disease. Organisms, including HIV, have an easy pathway into a woman's bloodstream through the uterine walls exposed by endometrial shedding. Moreover, a woman with a pathogen in her blood, such as the hepatitis virus or HIV, can pass it to a partner in her menstrual blood. Therefore, during menstruation, as well as at other times, safer sex practices, including condom use, are strongly recommended. (See Chapter 15 for safer sex guidelines.)

FEMALE SEXUAL RESPONSE

Scientific research has contributed much to our understanding of sexual arousal and response. One way in which researchers investigate and describe phenomena is through the creation of models, hypothetical descriptions used to study or explain something. However, although models are useful as tools for general understanding or for assisting in the treatment of specific clinical problems (lack of arousal, for example), we should remember that they are only models.

Sexual Response Models

The **Masters and Johnson Four-Phase Model of Sexual Response** identifies the significant stages of response as excitement, plateau, orgasm, and resolution (Figure 3.8). Helen Singer Kaplan (1979) collapses the excitement and plateau phases into one, eliminates the resolution phase, and adds a phase to the beginning of the process. **Kaplan's Tri-Phasic Model of Sexual Response** includes the desire, excitement, and orgasm phases. These models are described and compared in Table 3.2.

Desire: Mind or Matter?

Desire is the psychological component of sexual arousal. Although we can experience desire without becoming aroused, and in some cases become aroused without feeling desire, some form of erotic thought or feeling is usually involved in our sexual behavior. The physical manifestations of sexual arousal involve a complex interaction of thoughts and feelings, sensory organs, neural responses, and hormonal reactions involving various parts of the body, including the cerebral cortex and limbic system of the brain, the

Those who restrain desire do so because theirs is weak enough to be restrained.

—*William Blake (1757–1827)*

Some desire is necessary to keep life in motion.

—*Samuel Johnson (1709–1784)*

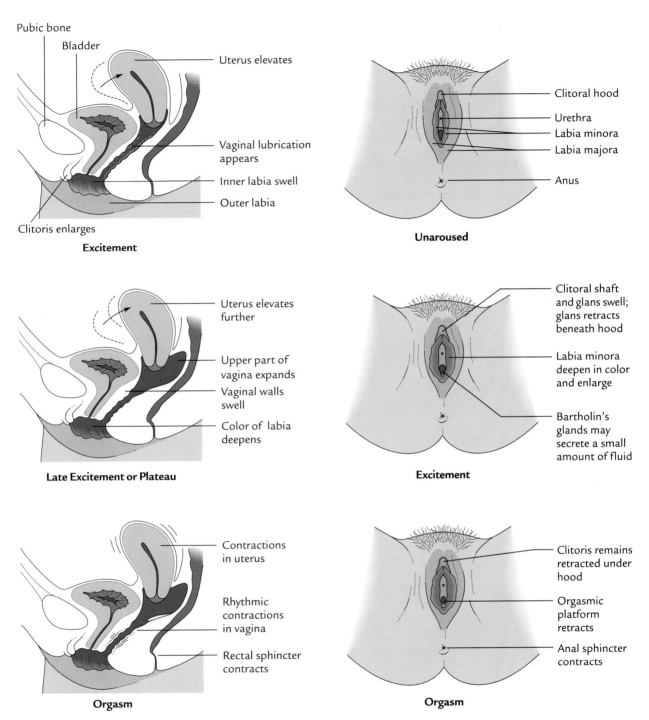

FIGURE 3.8 Stages of Female Sexual Response (internal, left; and external, right)

nervous system, the circulatory system, and the endocrine glands—as well as the genitals.

The Neural System and Sexual Stimuli   The brain is crucial to sexual response, yet relatively little is known about the manner in which the brain functions to create these responses. Through the neural system, the brain

TABLE 3.2 Sexual Response Models Compared: Masters/Johnson and Kaplan	
Psychological/Physiological Process	*Name of Phase*
Some form of thought, fantasy, or erotic feeling causes us to seek sexual gratification. (An inability to become sexually aroused may be due to a lack of desire, which can have a variety of causes.)	Desire (Kaplan)
Physical and/or psychological stimulation produces characteristic physical changes. In men, increased amounts of blood flow to the genitals produce erection of the penis; the scrotal skin begins to smooth out, and the testicles draw up toward the body. Later in this phase, the testes increase slightly in size. In women, vaginal lubrication begins, the upper vagina expands, the uterus is pulled upward, and the clitoris becomes engorged. In both women and men, the breasts enlarge slightly, and the nipples may become erect. Both men and women experience increasing muscular contractions.	Excitement (Masters/Johnson) — Excitement (Kaplan)
Sexual tension levels off. In men, the testes swell and continue to elevate. The diameter of the head of the penis swells slightly and may deepen in color. In women, the outer third of the vagina swells, lubrication may slow down, and the clitoris pulls back. Coloring and swelling of the labia increase. In both men and women, muscular tension, breathing, and heart rate increase.	Plateau (Masters/Johnson)
Increased tension peaks and discharges, affecting the whole body. Rhythmic muscular contractions affect the uterus and outer vagina in women. In men, there are contractions of the tubes that produce and carry semen, the prostate gland, and the urethral bulb, resulting in the expulsion of semen (ejaculation).	Orgasm (Masters/Johnson and Kaplan)
The body returns to its unaroused state. In women, this phase may not occur until after multiple orgasms.	Resolution (Masters/Johnson)

Passion, though a bad regulator, is a powerful spring.

—*Ralph Waldo Emerson (1803–1882)*

receives stimuli from the five senses plus one: sight, smell, touch, hearing, taste, *and* the imagination.

THE BRAIN   The brain, of course, plays a major role in all of our body's functions. Nowhere is its role more apparent than in our sexual functioning. The relationship between our thoughts and feelings and our actual behavior is not well understood (and what is known would require a course in neurophysiology to satisfactorily explain it). Cultural influences, as well as expectations, fantasies, hopes, and fears, combine with sensory inputs and hormonal messages to bring us to where we are ready, willing, and able to be sexual. Even then, potentially erotic messages may be short-circuited by the brain itself, which may inhibit as well as excite sexual responses. It is not known how the inhibitory mechanism works, but guilt, anxiety, fear, and negative conditioning will prevent the brain from sending messages to the genitals. In fact, the reason moderate amounts of alcohol and marijuana appear to enhance sexuality is that they reduce the control mechanisms of the brain that act as inhibitors.

Anatomically speaking, the areas of the brain that appear to be involved most in sexual behaviors of both men and women are the cerebral cortex and the limbic system. Interestingly, the sexual drive center, located in the nuclei of the hypothalamus, has been found to be twice as large in adult males as it is in adult females. Furthermore, there is a suggestion that the size of this area declines with advancing age (Levine, 1997). The cerebral cortex is the convoluted covering of most of the brain area. It is the area that is associated with conscious behavior such as perception, memory, communication, understanding, and voluntary movement. Beneath the cortex, the **limbic system,** which consists of several separate parts, is involved with emotions and feelings. There are extensive connections between the limbic system and the cerebral cortex, explaining perhaps why "emotions sometimes override logic and, conversely, why reason can stop us from expressing our emotions in inappropriate situations" (Marieb, 1995). Some parts of the limbic system have been dubbed "pleasure centers" (Olds, 1956) because their stimulation produces sexual arousal (Heath, 1972).

THE SENSES   An attractive person (sight), a body fragrance or odor (smell), a lick or kiss (taste), a loving caress (touch), and erotic whispers (hearing) are all capable of sending sexual signals to the brain. Many of the connections we experience between sensory data and emotional responses are probably products of the limbic system. Some sensory inputs may evoke sexual arousal without a lot of conscious thought or emotion. Certain areas of the skin, called **erogenous zones,** are highly sensitive to touch. These areas may include the genitals, breasts, mouth, ears, neck, inner thighs, and buttocks; erotic associations with these area vary from culture to culture and individual to individual. Our olfactory sense (smell) may bring us sexual messages below the level of our conscious awareness. Scientists have isolated chemical substances, called **pheromones,** that are secreted into the air by many kinds of animals including ants, moths, pigs, dogs, and monkeys. One function of pheromones, in animals at least, appears to be to arouse sexual interest (Kohl & Francoeur, 1995).

Fascinating work in this area, involving smell and the powerful influence it plays in partnership selection, has been done by Swiss zoologist Claus Wedekind (cited in Blum, 1997). In a study involving 44 college women and 49 college men, Wedekind gave each man a clean cotton T-shirt and asked him to sleep in it over a weekend. He also instructed the men to avoid colognes, deodorants, spicy foods, and cigarettes. The sweaty T-shirts were collected at the end of the weekend, and each was stored in a clean plastic box. At the time of each woman's ovulation (during which studies show that sense of smell becomes more acute), the woman was presented with a stack of plastic boxes containing both the sweaty T-shirts and some immaculately clean ones. The women were asked to rate every shirt for sexiness, pleasantness, and intensity of smell. The researchers found that the more different from her own was the man's MHC complex (genes that code for the body's own cells and send out an alert if unknown organisms are detected), the sexier the woman rated the shirt—and presumably, the man. This research correlated with previous results found with mice. Wedekind's study implies that biology disposes an individual toward a mate who would provide a healthy mixture of genes. Obviously, this is not the only cue we use in partnership selection, but it does suggest a subtle yet powerful link among MHC genes, smell, and sex. Definitive research on human pheromones, however, has yet to be developed.

Sensory inputs, such as the sight, touch, or smell of someone we love or the sound of his or her voice, may evoke desire and sexual arousal.

MANY OF US MEASURE both our sexuality and ourselves in terms of orgasm: Did we have one? Did our partner have one? Was it good? When we measure our sexuality by orgasm, however, we discount activities that do not necessarily lead to orgasm, such as touching, caressing, and kissing. We discount erotic pleasure as an end in itself. Our culture tends to identify sex with sexual intercourse, and the end of sexual intercourse is literally orgasm (especially male orgasm). As one female college student puts it: "The deification of intercourse belittles the other aspects of lovemaking that are equally valid and often more enjoyable" (Malcolm, 1984.)

An Anthropological Perspective

A fundamental, biological fact about orgasm is that the male orgasm and ejaculation are required for reproduction, whereas the female orgasm is not. The male orgasm is universal in both animal and human species, but sociobiologists and anthropologists have found immense variation in the experience of female orgasm. Anthropologists such as Margaret Mead (1975) found that some societies, such as the Mundugumor, emphasize the female orgasm, while it is virtually nonexistent in other societies, such as the Arapesh.

In our culture, women most consistently experience orgasm through clitoral stimulation; penile thrusting during intercourse is not always sufficient for orgasm. In cultures that cultivate female orgasm, according to sociobiologist Donald Symons (1979), there is, in addition to an absence of sexual repression, an emphasis placed on men's skill in arousing women. Among the Mangaians, for example, as boys enter adolescence, they are given expert advice on kissing and stimulating a woman's breasts, cunnilingus, and how to bring their partners to multiple orgasm before they themselves ejaculate (Marshall, 1971). In our own culture, among men who consider themselves (and are considered) good lovers, great emphasis is placed on their abilities to arouse and bring their partners to orgasm. These skills include not only penile penetration but, often more important, clitoral stimulation. The woman can, of course, also stimulate her own clitoris to experience orgasm.

The Tyranny of the Orgasm

Sociologist Philip Slater (1974) suggests that our preoccupation with orgasm is an extension of the Protestant work ethic, in which nothing is enjoyed for its own sake; everything is work, including sex. Thus, we "achieve" orgasm much as we achieve success. Those who achieve orgasm are the "successful workers" of sex; those who do not are the "failures."

As we look at our sexuality, we can see pressure to be successful lovers. Men talk of performance anxiety. We tend to evaluate a woman's sexual self-worth in terms of

Hormones   The sex drive, or libido, in both men and women is biologically influenced by the hormone testosterone. In men, testosterone is produced mainly in the testes. In women, it is produced in the adrenal glands and the ovaries. Although women produce much less testosterone than men, this does not mean they have less sexual interest; apparently, women are much more sensitive than men to testosterone's effects. The relationship between testosterone level and sexual interest is not well understood. Although a drop in testosterone often reduces sexual interest or functioning, this is not always the case.

Estrogen also plays a role in sexual functioning. In women, estrogens help maintain the vaginal lining; it is not clear how much of a role, if any, estrogen plays in maintaining the libido. Men also produce small amounts of estrogen, but its particular function is not known. Too much estrogen, however, can induce erection difficulties.

Experiencing Sexual Arousal

For both males and females, physiological changes during sexual excitement depend on two processes: vasocongestion and myotonia. **Vasocongestion** is the concentration of blood in body tissues. For example, blood fills the gen-

being orgasmic (able to have orgasms). For men, the significant question about women's sexuality has shifted from "Is she a virgin?" to "Is she orgasmic?"

Faking Orgasm

Although during sexual intercourse women are not as consistently orgasmic as men, there is considerable pressure on them to be so. In one study of almost 750 orgasmic women, 58% had faked orgasm at least once (Darling & Davidson, 1986). But the reason these women faked orgasm was not to protect their own feelings as much as to protect those of their partners. The most frequent reason given was the woman's desire to please her partner and to avoid hurting or disappointing him. Other reasons included fear of her own sexual inadequacy, to prevent her partner from seeking another partner, and to end boring or painful intercourse (Darling & Davidson, 1986).

"Was It Good for You?"

A question often asked following intercourse is, "Was it good for you?" or its variation, "Did you come?"

Such questions are usually asked by men rather than women, and women tend to resent them (Darling & Davidson, 1986). Part of the pressure to pretend having an orgasm is caused by these questions. What is really being asked? If the woman enjoyed intercourse? If she thinks the man is a good lover? Or is the question just a signal that the lovemaking is over?

If a partner cares about the other's enjoyment and wants to improve the couple's erotic pleasures, the appropriate time to inquire about lovemaking is not during or immediately following intercourse. Researchers Carol Darling and Kenneth Davidson (1986) advise that such discussion be initiated at a neutral time and place. Moreover, both women *and* men need to be free to inquire about their partner's satisfaction. The goal should be to increase a couple's fulfillment, rather than to complain about "performance" or soothe a ruffled ego. Even among lesbians, who undoubtedly are more acquainted with female anatomy than most men are, partners need to be aware of making assumptions about what is sexually arousing. One woman comments (cited in Boston Women's Health Book Collective, 1996): "The more women I sleep with, the more I realize you can't assume what you like is what she likes. There are tremendous differences. All kinds of stuff needs to be talked about and often isn't."

Malcolm writes:

> It is ironic and distressing that something so universal as sex is a conversational taboo. . . . Many of us don't talk openly with our partners. My friends and I have found that, in the long run, it is worth the struggle and awkwardness. Once you have worked out with your partner what each of you specifically can do to make the other feel best, you'll find real sexual pleasure.

ital regions of both males and females, causing the penis to become erect and the clitoris to swell. **Myotonia** is increased muscle tension accompanying the approach of orgasm; upon orgasm, the body undergoes involuntary muscle contractions and then relaxes. The sexual response pattern remains the same for all forms of sexual behavior, whether autoerotic or coital experiences, heterosexual or homosexual.

Sexual Excitement   For women, the first sign of sexual excitement is the moistening of the vaginal walls through a process called **sweating.** These secretions lubricate the vagina, enabling it to encompass the penis easily. The inner two-thirds of the vagina expands in a process called **tenting;** the vagina expands about an inch in length and doubles its width. Vasocongestion affects the labia differently depending on whether the woman has borne children. The minor lips begin to protrude outside the major lips during sexual excitement. Breathing and heart rate increase. These signs do not occur on a specific timetable; each woman has her own pattern of arousal, which may vary under different conditions, with different partners, and so on.

Contractions raise the uterus, but the clitoris remains virtually unchanged during this early phase. Although the clitoris responds more slowly than the penis to vasocongestion, it is, nevertheless, affected. The initial changes,

The reason so many women fake orgasms is that so many men fake foreplay.

—*Graffito*

however, are minor. Clitoral tumescence (swelling) occurs simultaneously with engorgement of the minor lips. During masturbation and oral sex, the clitoris is generally stimulated directly. During intercourse, clitoral stimulation is mostly indirect, caused by the clitoral hood being pulled over the clitoris or pressure in the general clitoral area. At the same time that these changes are occurring in the genitals, the breasts are also responding. The nipples become erect, and the breasts may enlarge somewhat because of the engorgement of blood vessels; the areolae may also enlarge. About 25% of women experience a **sex flush,** a rash that temporarily appears as a result of blood rushing to the skin's surface during sexual excitement.

As excitement increases, the clitoris retracts beneath the clitoral hood and virtually disappears. The minor lips become progressively larger until they double or triple in size. They deepen in color, becoming pink, bright red, or a deep wine-red color. This intense coloring is sometimes referred to as the "sex skin." When it appears, orgasm is imminent. Meanwhile, the vaginal opening and lower third of the vagina decrease in size as they become more congested with blood. This thickening of the walls, which occurs in the plateau stage of the sexual response cycle, is known as the **orgasmic platform.** The upper two-thirds of the vagina continues to expand, but lubrication decreases or may even stop. The uterus becomes fully elevated through muscular contractions.

Changes in the breasts continue. The areolae become larger, while, in contrast, the nipples decrease in relative size. If the woman has not breast-fed, her breasts may increase by up to 25% of their unaroused size; women who have breast-fed may have little change in size. An additional 75% of women experience a sex flush during this stage of response.

Orgasm   Continued stimulation brings **orgasm,** rhythmic contractions of the vagina, uterus, and pelvic muscles, accompanied by intensely pleasurable sensations. The inner two-thirds of the vagina does not contract; instead, it continues its tenting effect. The labia do not change during orgasm. The breasts also remain unchanged. Heart and respiratory rates along with blood pressure reach their peak during orgasm.

After orgasm, the orgasmic platform rapidly subsides. The clitoris re-emerges from beneath the clitoral hood. (If a woman does not have an orgasm once she is sexually aroused, the clitoris may remain engorged for several hours, possibly creating a feeling of frustration.) The labia slowly return to their unaroused state, and the sex flush gradually disappears. About 30–40% of women perspire as the body begins to cool.

Following orgasm, men experience a refractory period, in which they are unable to become aroused. By contrast, women are often physiologically able to be orgasmic immediately following the previous orgasm. As a result, women can have multiple orgasms if they continue to be stimulated. Though findings vary on the percentage of women who experience multiple orgasms (estimates range from 14% to 40%), what is clear is that wide variability exists among women and within any one woman from one time to another.

■   In the next chapter, we discuss the anatomical features and physiological functions that characterize men's sexuality and sexual response. The information in these two chapters should serve as a comprehensive basis for understanding the material that follows.

What is the earth? What are the body and soul without satisfaction?

—*Walt Whitman (1819–1892)*

SUMMARY

Female Sex Organs: What Are They For?

- All embryos appear as female at first. Genetic and hormonal signals trigger the development of male organs in those embryos destined to be male.

- Sex organs serve a reproductive purpose, but they perform other functions also: giving pleasure, attracting sex partners, and bonding in relationships.

- The external female *genitals* are known collectively as the *vulva*. The *mons pubis* is a pad of fatty tissue that covers the area of the pubic bone. The *clitoris* is the center of sexual arousal in the female. The *labia majora* are two folds of spongy flesh extending from the mons pubis and enclosing the other external genitals. The *labia minora* are smooth, hairless folds within the labia majora that meet above the clitoris.

- The internal female sexual structures and reproductive organs include the *vagina*, the *uterus*, the *cervix*, the *ovaries*, and the *fallopian tubes*. The vagina is a flexible muscular organ that encompasses the penis during sexual intercourse and is the *birth canal* through which an infant is born. The opening of the vagina, the *introitus*, is partially covered by a thin, perforated membrane, the *hymen*, prior to first intercourse or other intrusion.

- Controversial research has posited the existence of an erotically sensitive area, the *Grafenberg spot (G-spot)*, on the front wall of the vagina midway between the introitus and the cervix.

- The *uterus*, or womb, is a hollow, thick-walled, muscular organ; the tapered end, the *cervix*, extends downward and opens into the vagina. The lining of the uterine walls, the *endometrium*, is built up and then shed and expelled through the cervical *os* (opening) during menstruation. In the event of pregnancy, the pre-embryo is embedded in the nourishing endometrium. On each side of the uterus is one of a pair of ovaries, the female *gonads* (organs that produce *gametes*, sex cells containing the genetic material necessary for reproduction). At the top of the uterus are the *fallopian tubes*, or uterine tubes. They extend toward the ovaries but are not attached to them. The funnel-shaped end of each tube (the infundibulum) fans out into finger-like fimbriae, which drape over the ovary. Hairlike cilia on the fimbriae conduct the ovulated *oocyte* into the fallopian tube. The ampulla is the widened part of the tube in which fertilization normally occurs. Other important structures in the area of the genitals include the *urethra, anus,* and *perineum.*

- The reproductive function of the female breasts, or *mammary glands,* is to nourish the offspring through *lactation,* milk production. A breast is composed of fatty tissue and 15–25 lobes that radiate around a central protruding nipple. *Alveoli* within the lobes produce milk. Around the nipple is a ring of darkened skin called the *areola.*

Female Sexual Physiology

- *Hormones* are chemical substances that serve as messengers, traveling through the bloodstream. Important hormones that act directly on the gonads (*gonadotropins*) are *follicle-stimulating hormone (FSH)* and *luteinizing hormone (LH)*. Hormones produced in the ovaries are *estrogen*, which helps regulate the menstrual cycle, and *progesterone*, which helps maintain the uterine lining.

- At birth, the human female's ovaries contain 400,000–700,000 *oocytes*, female gametes. During childhood, many of these degenerate. In a woman's lifetime, about 400 oocytes will mature and be released, beginning in puberty when hormones trigger the completion of *oogenesis*, the production of oocytes, commonly called eggs or ova.

- The activities of the ovaries and the development of oocytes for ovulation, the expulsion of the oocyte, are described as the three-phase *ovarian cycle*, which is usually about 28 days long. The phases are *follicular* (maturation of the oocyte), *ovulatory* (expulsion of the oocyte), and *luteal* (hormone production by the corpus luteum).

- The *menstrual cycle* (or uterine cycle), like the ovarian cycle, is divided into three phases. The shedding of the endometrium marks the beginning of the *menstrual phase*. The menstrual flow, or *menses*, generally occurs over a period of 2–5 days. Endometrial tissue builds up during the *proliferative phase;* it produces nutrients to sustain an embryo in the *secretory phase.*

- The most severe menstrual problems have been attributed to *premenstrual syndrome (PMS),* a cluster of physical and emotional symptoms, which are not agreed upon because of contradictory studies. Some women experience pelvic cramping and pain during the menstrual cycle *(dysmenorrhea).* When women do not menstruate for reasons other than aging, the condition is called *amenorrhea.* A principal cause of amenorrhea is pregnancy.

Female Sexual Response

- The *Masters and Johnson Four-Phase Model of Sexual Response* identifies the significant stages of response as excitement, plateau, orgasm, and resolution. *Kaplan's Tri-Phasic Model of Sexual Response* consists of three phases: desire, excitement, and orgasm.

- The physical manifestations of sexual arousal involve a complex interaction of thoughts and feelings, sensory perceptions, neural responses, and hormonal reactions occurring in many parts of the body. For both males and females, physiological changes during sexual excitement depend on two processes: *vasocongestion,* the concentration of blood in body tissues, and *myotonia,* increased muscle tension with approaching orgasm.

- For women, the first sign of sexual excitement is the moistening of the vaginal walls, or *sweating.* The inner two-thirds of the vagina expands in a process called *tenting;* the labia may enlarge or flatten and separate; the clitoris swells. Breathing and heart rate increase. The nipples become erect, and the breasts may enlarge somewhat. The uterus elevates. As excitement increases, the clitoris retracts beneath the clitoral hood. The vaginal opening decreases by about one-third, and its outer third becomes more congested, forming the *orgasmic platform.*

- Continued stimulation brings *orgasm,* rhythmic contractions of the vagina, uterus, and pelvic muscles, accompanied by very pleasurable sensations. Women are often able to be orgasmic following a previous orgasm if they continue to be stimulated.

SUGGESTED READING

Borysenko, Joan. (1996). *A Woman's Book of Life: The Biology, Psychology and Spirituality of the Feminine Life Cycle.* New York: Riverhead Books. A scientific and provocative look at the feminine way of growth.

Boston Women's Health Book Collective. (1998). *Our Bodies, Ourselves: For the New Century.* New York: Simon and Shuster. A thorough, accurate, and proactive women's text covering a broad range of health issues.

Dan, Alice J., & Lewis, Linda L. (1992). *Menstrual Health in Women's Lives.* Urbana/Chicago: University of Illinois Press. A practical, positive self-help guide.

Lehrman, Karen. (1997). *The Lipstick Proviso: Women, Sex and Power in the Real World.* New York: Anchor/Doubleday. An inspiring and spirited celebration of autonomy, beauty, and the true diversity that exists among women.

McCormick, Naomi B. (1994). *Sexual Salvation: Affirming Women's Sexual Rights and Pleasures.* Westport, CT: Greenwood Publishing. A sex-positive perspective on the many aspects of women's sexual pleasure.

Sloan, Ethel. (1993). *The Biology of Women* (3rd ed.). New York: Delmar Publishers. The gynecological, sociological, and psychological factors that influence women's lives and health.

4

Male Sexual Anatomy, Physiology, and Response

*I*T'S CLEAR THAT MALE SEXUAL STRUCTURES and functions differ in many ways from those of females. What may not be as apparent, however, is that there are also a number of similarities in the functions of the sex organs and the sexual response patterns of both men and women. In the previous chapter, we learned that the sexual structures of both females and males derive from the same embryonic tissue. But when this tissue receives the signals to begin differentiation into a male, the embryonic reproductive organs begin to change their appearance dramatically.

MALE SEX ORGANS: WHAT ARE THEY FOR?

Like female sex organs, male sex organs serve several functions. In their reproductive role, a man's sex organs manufacture and store gametes and deliver them to a woman's reproductive tract. Some of the organs, especially the penis, provide a source of physical pleasure for both their owners and their owners' partners.

External Structures

The external male sexual structures are the penis and the scrotum.

The Penis   The **penis** (from the Latin word for tail) is the organ through which both sperm and urine pass. It is attached to the male perineum, the diamond-shaped region extending from the base of the scrotum to the anus.

The penis consists of three main sections: the root, the shaft, and the head (Figure 4.1). The **root** attaches the penis within the pelvic cavity; the body of the penis, the **shaft,** hangs free. At the end of the shaft is the enlarged head of the penis, the **glans penis,** and at its tip is the urethral opening. The rim at the base of the glans is known as the **corona.** On the underside of the penis is a triangular area of sensitive skin called the **frenulum,** which

FIGURE 4.1   External Male Sexual Structures

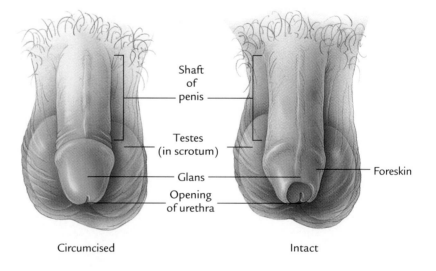

Shaft of penis

Testes (in scrotum)

Glans

Opening of urethra

Foreskin

Circumcised

Intact

attaches the glans to the foreskin. The glans penis is particularly important in sexual arousal because it contains a relatively high concentration of nerve endings, making it especially responsive to stimulation.

A loose skin covers the shaft of the penis and extends to cover the glans penis; the sleevelike covering of the glans is known as the **foreskin** or **prepuce.** It can be pulled back easily to expose the glans. In the United States, the foreskins of male infants are often surgically removed by a procedure called **circumcision.** As a result of this procedure, the glans penis is left exposed. The reasons for circumcision seem to be rooted more in tradition, hospital profits, and religious beliefs (it is an important ritual in Judaism and Islam) than in any firmly established health principles. Beneath the foreskin are several small glands that produce a cheesy substance called **smegma.** If smegma accumulates, it thickens and produces a foul odor. It is important for uncircumcised adult men to observe good hygiene by periodically retracting the skin and washing the glans to remove the smegma. Lack of proper hygiene may be associated with sexually transmitted diseases, urinary infections, and penile cancer (McAninch, 1989; Rotolo & Lynch, 1991). (For further discussion of circumcision, see Chapter 12.)

The shaft of the penis contains three parallel columns of erectile tissue. The two that extend along the front surface are known as the **corpora cavernosa** (cavernous bodies), and the third, which runs beneath them, is called the **corpus spongiosum** (spongy body), which also forms the glans (Figure 4.2). At the root of the penis, the corpora cavernosa form the **crura,** which are anchored by muscle to the pubic bone. The **urethra,** a tube that transports both urine and semen, runs from the bladder (where it expands to form the **urethral bulb**), through the spongy body, to the tip of the penis, where it opens to the outside. Inside the three chambers are a large number of blood vessels through which blood freely circulates when the penis is flaccid (relaxed). During sexual arousal, these vessels fill with blood and expand, causing the penis to become erect. (Sexual arousal, including erection, is discussed in greater detail later in the chapter.)

In an unaroused state, the *average* penis is slightly under 4 inches long, although there is a great deal of individual variation. When erect, penises become more uniform in size, as the percentage of volume increase is greater with smaller penises than with larger ones. But in an unaroused state, an individual's penis size may vary. Cold air, water, fear, or anxiety, for example, often causes the penis to be pulled closer to the body and to decrease in size. When the penis is erect, the urinary duct is temporarily blocked, allowing for the ejaculation of semen. But erection does not necessarily mean sexual excitement. A man may have erections at night during REM sleep, the phase of the sleep cycle when dreaming occurs (Chung & Choi, 1990), or when he is anxious, for example.

Myths and misconceptions about the penis abound, especially among men. Many people believe that the size of a man's penis is directly related to his masculinity, aggressiveness, sexual ability, or sexual attractiveness. Others believe there is a relationship between the size of a man's penis and the size of his hand, foot, thumb, or nose. In fact, the size of the penis is not specifically related to body size, weight, muscular structure, race or ethnicity, or sexual orientation; it is determined by individual heredity factors. Furthermore, there is no relationship between penis size and a man's ability to have sexual intercourse or to satisfy his partner (Masters & Johnson, 1966).

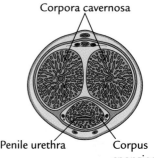

Corpora cavernosa

Penile urethra

Corpus spongiosum

FIGURE 4.2   Shaft of Penis (cross section)

It can safely be said that the adult male population suffers an almost universal anxiety in regard to penile size.

—*James F. Glenn, MD*

MAN'S PREOCCUPATION WITH HIS "GENERATIVE ORGAN" extends far back into history and appears in diverse cultures in every part of the world. The penis is an almost universal symbol of power and fertility. It may also be a source of considerable anxiety for the individual who happens to possess one.

Power to the Penis

Earthenware figurines from ancient Peru, ink drawings from medieval Japan, painted walls in the villas of Pompeii—in the art and artifacts from every corner of the world, we find a common theme: penises! And not just any old penises, but organs of such length, girth, and weight that they can barely be supported by their possessors. Whether as an object of worship or an object of jest, the giant penis has been (and continues to be) a symbol that holds deep cultural significance, especially in societies where men are dominant over women (Strage, 1980). Although it seems reasonable for the erect penis to be used as a symbol of love or at least lust, many of its associations appear to be as an instrument of aggression and power. In New Guinea, Kiwai hunters pressed their penises against the trees from which they would make their harpoons, thereby assuring the strength and straightness of their weapons. Maori warriors in New Zealand crawled under the legs of their chief so that the power of his penis would descend onto them (Strage, 1980).

In our society, many people would argue that men are deeply attached to symbolic images of their potency— cars, motorcycles, missiles, and especially guns. Lest they become confused as to which is the symbol and which the reality, young grunts in Marine bootcamp are instructed in the following drill (to be shouted with appropriate gestures):

> This is my rifle! This is my gun!
> This is for fighting! This is for fun!

To take away a man's gun is to threaten him with impotence. (The word "potent" is from the Latin *potens,* meaning ability or power; the word "impotent," in addition to meaning powerless, also implies the inability to get an erection.)

In many cultures, the penis has also represented fertility and prosperity. In India, large stone phalluses *(lingams),* associated with the Hindu god Siva, are adorned with flowers and propitiated with offerings. Ancient peoples as diverse as the Maya in Central America and the Egyptians in Africa believed that the blood from the penises of their rulers was especially powerful. Mayan kings ceremonially pierced their penises with sting-ray spines, and the pharaohs and high priests of Egypt underwent ritual circumcision. In other places, men have ritually offered their semen to assure a plentiful harvest.

It is a Freudian thesis, with which I am inclined to agree, that the pistol, whether in the hands of an amateur or a professional gunman, has significance for the owner as a symbol of virility, an extension of the male organ, and that excessive interest in guns is a form of fetishism.

—*Ian Fleming*
(creator of the James Bond character)

The Scrotum　Hanging loosely at the root of the penis is the **scrotum,** a pouch of skin that holds the two testicles. The skin of the scrotum is more heavily pigmented than the skin elsewhere on the body; it is sparsely covered with hair and divided in the middle by a ridge of skin. The skin of the scrotum varies in appearance under different conditions. When a man is sexually aroused, for example, or when he is cold, the testicles are pulled close to the body, causing the skin to wrinkle and become more compact. The changes in the surface of the scrotum help maintain a fairly constant temperature within the testicles (about 93°F). Two sets of muscles control these changes. The *dartos muscle,* a smooth muscle under the skin, contracts and causes the surface to wrinkle; the fibrous *cremaster muscle* within the scrotal sac causes the testes to elevate.

Internal Structures

Male internal reproductive organs and structures include the testes (testicles), seminiferous tubules, epididymis, vas deferens, ejaculatory ducts, seminal vesicles, prostate gland, and Cowper's (bulbourethral) glands (Figure 4.3).

"Phallic Phallacies"

It is interesting (but perhaps not surprising) that the responsibility of owning an instrument of great power can carry with it an equally great burden of anxiety. In some ways, the choice of the penis as a symbol of domination seems rather unwise. Any man (and a good many women) can tell you that a penis can be disturbingly unreliable and appear to have a mind of its own. For men who are already insecure about their abilities on the job or in the bedroom, the penis can take on meanings quite beyond those of procreation, elimination, or sensual pleasure. How can a man be expected to control his employees or his children when he can't control the behavior of his own penis?

As discussed in Chapter 2, Sigmund Freud believed that women are unconsciously jealous of men's penises (penis envy). In reality, those who appear to suffer the most from penis envy are men, who indeed possess a penis but often seem to long for a bigger one. The idea that "the larger the penis, the more effective the male in coital connection" is referred to by Masters and Johnson as a "phallic phallacy" (Masters & Johnson, 1966).

Another manifestation of penile anxiety, also named by Freud, is castration anxiety (see Chapter 2). Mark Strage points out that this term is misleading, for it does not describe what the actual fear is about. Castration is the removal of the testes, but castration anxiety is fear of losing the penis. In China and other parts of Asia and Africa, there have been documented epidemics of *koro* (a Japanese term), the conviction that one's penis is shrinking and is going to disappear. A doctor in Singapore in 1968 reported 4500 cases of *koro*, which appears to have no physiological basis but to grow in the psyches of anxiety-prone men (Yap, 1993).

Rising Anxiety

Strage (1980) makes the case that penile anxiety has resulted in men's efforts "to segregate women, to impute them with sinister intentions, and to persecute and punish them." Moreover, he goes on, "the level of this male anxiety rises as women, through no action or fault of their own, are perceived in a context of increased femaleness or sexuality." Finally, he states, men have devised ways "to resolve, or at least attenuate their anxiety—thereby inflicting harm on women, on the world, and, perhaps most grievously, on themselves."

For his own psyche's sake, as well as the sake of his partner and that of society, a man would do well to consider how his feelings about his penis and his masculinity affect his well-being. At this point, we can only speculate, but perhaps there will come a time when men will allow themselves to focus less on the size and performance of their equipment—both sexual and martial—and more on acceptance, communication, and the mutual sharing of pleasure.

The Testes   Inside the scrotum are the male reproductive glands or gonads, which are called **testicles** or **testes** (singular, *testis*). The testes have two major functions: sperm production and hormone production. Each olive-shaped testis is about 1.5 inches long and 1 inch in diameter and weighs about 1 ounce; as a male ages, the testis decreases in size and weight. The testicles are usually not symmetrical; the left testicle generally hangs slightly lower than the right one. Within the scrotal sac, each testicle is suspended by a **spermatic cord** containing nerves, blood vessels, and a vas deferens, the tube that carries sperm from the testicle (Figure 4.4). Within each testicle are around 1000 **seminiferous tubules,** tiny, tightly compressed tubes 1–3 feet long (they would extend several hundred yards if laid end to end). Within these tubes, the process of spermatogenesis, the production of sperm, takes place.

As a male fetus grows, the testes develop within the pelvic cavity; toward the end of the gestation period, the testes usually descend into the scrotum. In about 3–4% of cases, however, one or both of the testes fail to descend, a condition that usually corrects itself in a year or two (McClure, 1988).

The Epididymis and Vas Deferens   The epididymis and vas deferens (or ductus deferens) are the ducts that carry sperm from the testicles to the

> Nowhere does one read of a penis that quietly moseyed out for a look at what was going on before springing and crashing into action.
>
> —*Bernie Zilbergeld*

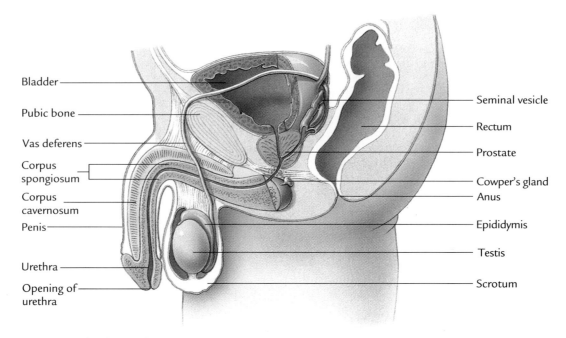

Bladder

Pubic bone

Vas deferens

Corpus spongiosum

Corpus cavernosum

Penis

Urethra

Opening of urethra

Seminal vesicle

Rectum

Prostate

Cowper's gland

Anus

Epididymis

Testis

Scrotum

FIGURE 4.3   Internal Male Sexual Structures

urethra for ejaculation. The seminiferous tubules merge to form the **epididymis,** a comma-shaped structure consisting of a coiled tube about 20 feet long, where the sperm finally mature. Each epididymis merges into a **vas deferens,** a tube about 18 inches long, extending into the abdominal cavity, over the bladder, and then downward, widening into the flask-shaped **ampulla.** The vas deferens joins the **ejaculatory duct** within the prostate gland. The vas deferens can be felt easily in the scrotal sac. Because it is easily accessible and is crucial for sperm transport, it is usually the point of ster-

FIGURE 4.4   Cross Section of a Testicle

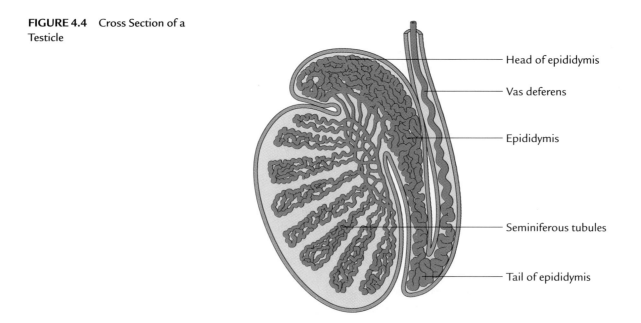

Head of epididymis

Vas deferens

Epididymis

Seminiferous tubules

Tail of epididymis

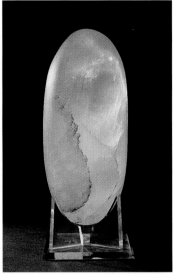

The penis is a prominent symbol in both ancient and modern art. Here we see a contemporary phallic sculpture in Frogner Park, Oslo, Norway, and a natural rock crystal lingam from India.

ilization for men. The operation is called a vasectomy (it is discussed fully in Chapter 11). A vasectomy does not affect the ability to ejaculate because only the sperm are transported through the vas deferens. Most of the semen that is ejaculated comes from the prostate gland and the seminal vesicles.

The Seminal Vesicles, Prostate Gland, and Cowper's Glands   At the back of the bladder lie two glands, each about the size and shape of a finger. These **seminal vesicles** secrete a fluid that makes up about 60% of the seminal fluid. Encircling the urethra just below the bladder is a small muscular gland about the size and shape of a chestnut. The **prostate gland** produces about 30–35% of the seminal fluid that makes up the ejaculated semen. These secretions flow into the urethra through a system of tiny ducts. Some men who enjoy receiving anal sex experience erotic sensations when the prostate is gently stroked; others find that contact with the prostate is uncomfortable. Men, especially if they are older, may be troubled by a variety of prostate problems, ranging from relatively benign conditions to more serious inflammations and prostate cancer. (Problems and diseases of the prostate are covered in Chapter 13.)

Below the prostate gland are two pea-sized glands connected to the urethra by tiny ducts. These are **Cowper's glands,** or **bulbourethral glands,** which secrete a thick, clear mucus prior to ejaculation. This fluid may appear at the tip of the erect penis; its alkaline content may help buffer the acidity within the urethra and provide a more hospitable environment for sperm. Fluid from the Cowper's glands may contain sperm that have remained in the urethra since a previous ejaculation or that have leaked in from the ampullae.

The Breasts and Other Structures

Male anatomical structures that do not serve a reproductive function but may be involved in or affected by sexual activities include the breasts, urethra, buttocks, rectum, and anus.

Male breasts, which are usually referred to euphemistically as "the chest," may or may not be considered erotic areas. Men are allowed to display their naked breasts in certain public settings. Whether the sight is sexually arousing depends on the viewer and the context.

Although the male breast contains the same basic structures as the female breast—nipple, areola, fat, and glandular tissue—the amounts of underlying fatty and glandular tissues are much smaller in men. Our culture appears to be ambivalent about the erotic function of a man's breasts. We usually do not even call them breasts, but refer to the general area as the chest. Some men find stimulation of their breasts to be sexually arousing, while others do not. **Gynecomastia,** the swelling or enlargement of the male breast, can occur during adolescence or adulthood. In puberty, gynecomastia is a normal response to hormonal changes, as we discuss in Chapter 6. In adulthood, its causes may include alcoholism, liver or thyroid disease, or cancer.

In men, the urethra serves as the passageway for both urine and semen. Because the urinary opening is at the tip of the penis, it is vulnerable to injury and infection. The sensitive mucous membranes around the opening may be subject to abrasion and can provide an entrance into the body for infectious organisms. Condoms, properly used, provide an effective barrier between this vulnerable area and potentially infectious secretions or other substances.

Men's buttocks may be a source of sexual attraction. For both women and men, the buttocks, anus, and rectum may be erotically sensitive. Both men and women may enjoy oral stimulation of the anus ("rimming"); the insertion of fingers, a hand ("fisting"), a dildo, or a penis into the rectum may bring erotic pleasure to both the receiver and the giver. (Anal sex is discussed more fully in Chapter 9; safer sex guidelines appear in Chapter 15.)

MALE SEXUAL PHYSIOLOGY

The reproductive processes of the male body include the production of hormones and the production and delivery of sperm, the male gametes. Although men do not have a monthly reproductive cycle comparable to that of women, they do experience regular fluctuations of hormone levels; there is also some evidence that men's moods follow a cyclical pattern.

Sex Hormones

Within the connective tissues of a man's testes are **Leydig cells** (also called interstitial cells), which secrete **androgens** (male hormones). The most important of these is testosterone, which triggers sperm production and regulates the sex drive. Other important hormones in male reproductive physiology are GnRH, FSH, and LH. In addition, men produce the protein hormone *inhibin* and small amounts of estrogen (Table 4.1). Figure 4.5 illustrates the involvement of these hormones in sperm production.

Testosterone   As discussed in Chapter 3, **testosterone** is a steroid hormone synthesized from cholesterol. In men, it is produced principally within the testes; small amounts are also secreted by the adrenal glands. During puberty, besides acting on the seminiferous tubules to produce sperm, testosterone targets other areas of the body. It causes the penis, testicles, and other reproductive organs to grow and is responsible for the development of **secondary sex characteristics,** such as pubic, facial, and underarm hair, and for the deepening of the voice. It also influences the growth of bones and increase of muscle mass and causes the skin to thicken and become oilier (leading to acne in many teenage boys). In addition to stimulating sexual interest, testosterone may also play a role in aggressiveness, according to some studies. Researcher Hilary Lips suggests, however, that these studies need to be carefully interpreted. Although there is some evidence that prenatal exposure to excess testosterone leads to increased rough-and-tumble play among children of both sexes (Hines, 1982; Reinisch, Ziemba-Davis, & Saunders, 1991), the connection between such play and actual aggressive behavior has not been adequately demonstrated (Lips, 1997). (For additional discussion on this issue, see "Think About It: Does Testosterone Cause Aggression?")

Male Cycles   Studies comparing men and women have found that both sexes are subject to changes in mood and behavior patterns (Lips, 1997).

TABLE 4.1 Male Reproductive Hormones		
Hormone	*Where Produced*	*Functions*
Testosterone	Testes, adrenal glands	Stimulates sperm production in testes, triggers development of secondary sex characteristics, regulates sex drive
GnRH	Hypothalamus	Stimulates pituitary during sperm production
FSH	Pituitary	Stimulates sperm production in testes
ICSH (LH)	Pituitary	Stimulates testosterone production in interstitial cells within testes
Inhibin	Testes	Regulates sperm production by inhibiting release of FSH
Relaxin	Prostate	Increases sperm motility

FIGURE 4.5 The Brain-Testicular Axis. The process of sperm production is regulated by this feedback system, which involves hormones produced by the hypothalamus, pituitary, and testes.

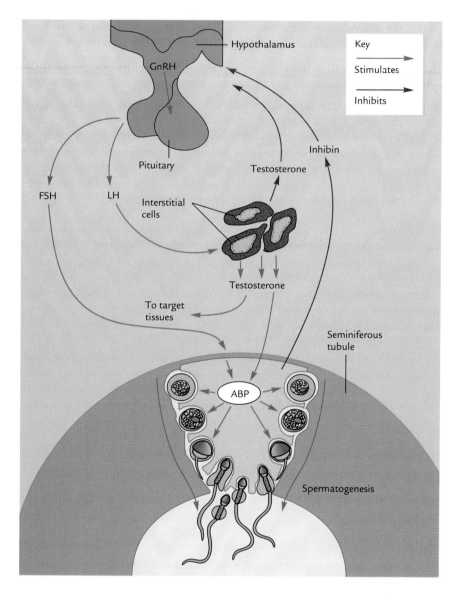

When people say women can't be trusted because they cycle every month, my response is that men cycle every day, so they should only be allowed to negotiate peace treaties in the evening.

—*June Reinisch*

Whereas such changes in women are often attributed (rightly or wrongly) to menstrual cycle fluctuations, it is not clear that male changes are related to levels of testosterone or other hormones, although there may well be a connection. Men do appear to undergo cyclic changes, although their testosterone levels do not fluctuate as dramatically as do women's estrogen and progesterone levels. On a daily basis, men's testosterone levels appear to be lowest around 8:00 P.M. and highest around 4:00 A.M. (Gorman, 1992). Moreover, their overall levels appear to be relatively lower in the spring and higher in the fall.

Spermatogenesis

Within the testes, from puberty on, **spermatogenesis,** the production of **sperm,** is an ongoing process. Every day, a healthy, fertile man produces sev-

Do HIGH TESTOSTERONE LEVELS cause a man to be violent? Is testosterone, according to some popular magazines, the "hormone from hell"? The distortions and the jokes that accompany this cholesterol derivative may lead us to believe so. Researchers, however, are far more cautious in their assessment of the hormone. Rather than endorsing a simple one-way cause-and-effect relationship, research now implicates testosterone as both a cause and effect of social behavior (Dabbs, 1992).

Testosterone is made by both sexes: Men make it mostly in the testes; women, primarily in the adrenal glands and the ovaries. Furthermore, the brain converts testosterone to estradiol (a female hormone). It is this flexibility of the hormone that makes the link between testosterone and behavior so precarious.

Many researchers do see a correlation between testosterone and personality. What complicates this equation, however, is the fact that testosterone levels are rarely stable; they appear to respond positively or negatively to almost every challenge, and not necessarily in a way we might predict.

An example of such a phenomenon is observed among athletes and soldiers (cited in Blum, 1997):

> [When wrestlers drive themselves to their physical limit] testosterone levels drop so hard they become comparable to the baseline of men who've been castrated—a bare trickle of hormone. Testosterone, in a sense, seems to take overexertion and stress to the point of exhaustion as a signal for retreat. The same phenomenon shows up in new soldiers in boot camp. . . . As testosterone levels drop (due to overexertion and muscle fatigue), so does the hormone's powerful influence on building up muscle. An overworked athlete starts losing muscle mass and strength. Once (however) the soldier marches off to battle, once the wrestler steps onto the competitive mat, testosterone rises again in response to challenge.

Thus it is that men's levels of testosterone can change in response to victory, defeat, or exhaustion.

Parallels can be seen in monkeys. If a male monkey sees an attractive and available female, his testosterone levels increase. They spike up even further if another monkey tries to compete for the same female. If a fight ensues, the winner's testosterone stays high or even climbs a little more, whereas the loser's levels fall by as much as 90% (Wallen, cited in Blum, 1997, p. 168). Though these studies are not directly related to aggression, they suggest the possibility of a link between testosterone and the experience of dominance.

Not all researchers might agree. Whereas some (Doering, Brodie, Kraemer, Becker, & Hamburg, 1974; Moyer, 1974) find little evidence of a correlation between circulating testosterone levels and aggression, others find testosterone to be associated with antisocial behaviors such as delinquency, alcohol and drug abuse, and military AWOL problems (Dabbs & Morris, 1990). Still others find that men producing high levels of testosterone are less likely to marry; however, if they do, they are more likely to divorce, have troubled relationships, have extramarital affairs, and become more violent with their spouse (Booth & Dabbs, 1993).

One logical place to search for a connection between testosterone and violence is among rapists. Robert Prentky (1985), a researcher who studies violent rape, found no such connection. What he did observe, however, was that high testosterone levels correlated with anger and with a desire to strike out. If testosterone indeed contributes to making a person more willing to strike out physically, that type of reaction could produce violent results. Examining this research, noted science writer Deborah Blum (1997) observes: "In an evolutionary context, the hormone might have become part of a competitive response, even an ingredient for success."

What must be considered in all studies related to hormones and behaviors is that even if a hormone triggers an emotional response or feeling, it doesn't inevitably lead to a specific behavior—in this case, violence. There are many ways to channel and express feelings. "Testosterone is only one of the many hormones in the human body, which may vary simultaneously and interact with one another in ways yet unknown" (Lips, 1997). Because the biology of violence in humans is extraordinarily complex and is judged by political, scientific, and human standards, it is impossible at this time to completely understand the relationship between testosterone and aggression.

eral hundred million sperm within the seminiferous tubules of his testicles (Figure 4.6). After they are formed in the seminiferous tubules, which takes 64–72 days, immature sperm are stored in the epididymis. It then takes about 20 days for the sperm to travel the length of the epididymis, during which time they become fertile and motile (able to move). Upon ejaculation,

FIGURE 4.6   Spermatogenesis. This diagram shows the development of spermatozoa, beginning with a single spermatogonium and ending with four complete sperm cells. Spermatogenesis is an ongoing process that begins in puberty. Several hundred million sperm are produced every day within the seminiferous tubules of a healthy man.

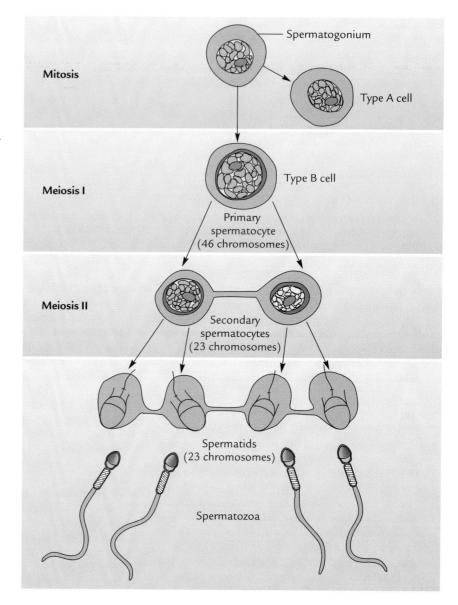

Mitosis — Spermatogonium — Type A cell

Meiosis I — Type B cell — Primary spermatocyte (46 chromosomes)

Meiosis II — Secondary spermatocytes (23 chromosomes)

Spermatids (23 chromosomes)

Spermatozoa

sperm in the tail section of the epididymis are expelled by muscular contractions of its walls into the vas deferens; similar contractions within the vas deferens propel the sperm into the urethra, where they are mixed with semen and then expelled from the urethral opening. Figure 4.7 shows a mature sperm cell.

The sex of the zygote produced by the union of egg and sperm is determined by the chromosomes of the sperm. The ovum always contributes a female sex chromosome (X), whereas the sperm may contribute either a female or a male sex chromosome (Y). The combination of two X chromosomes (XX) means that the zygote will develop as a female; with an X and a Y chromosome (XY), it will develop as a male. In some cases, combinations of sex chromosomes other than XX or XY occur, causing sexual development to proceed differently; these variations are discussed in Chapter 5.

In 1995, it was reported in the *New England Journal of Medicine* that sperm counts had declined significantly among men and that environmental toxins were possibly to blame (Auger, Kunstmann, Czyglik, & Jouannet, 1995). The researchers went on to claim that if the trend of the past few decades continued, there would be no human population in a couple of centuries.

Careful later research contradicts those findings. What other researchers have found is a variation in sperm count among men residing in different parts of the country. In these studies sperm counts for men ranged from a low of 48 million/cc for men residing in Iowa to a high of 134 million/cc for those in New York (Fisch, Ikeguchi, & Goluboff, 1996). What accounts for these regional differences is still unclear. Another team of researchers found no decline in semen quality in the past 21 years (Paulsen, Berman, & Wang, 1996). Finally, Dr. H. Fisch and his colleagues analyzed global variations in sperm. They argue that the previously reported decline probably resulted from previously unaccounted-for regional differences (Fisch, Goluboff, Olson, Feldshuh, Broder, & Barad, 1996). "We ought not to give up the vigilance that environmental toxicants might be affecting health [but] there is no substantial data set in this country, to say the least, to show that there are declining sperm counts," states Dr. Richard Sherins, director of male-infertility research at the Genetics and IVF Institute in Fairfax, Virginia (Kolata, 1996). Undoubtedly, this debate is likely to continue.

Semen Production

Semen, or **seminal fluid,** is the ejaculated liquid that contains sperm. The function of semen is to nourish sperm and provide them with a hospitable environment and means of transport when they are deposited within the vagina. Semen is mainly made up of secretions from the seminal vesicles and prostate gland, which mix together in the urethra during ejaculation. Immediately after ejaculation, the semen is somewhat thick and sticky from clotting factors in the fluid. This consistency keeps the sperm together initially; then the semen becomes liquefied, allowing the sperm to swim out. Semen ranges in color from opalescent or milky white to yellowish or grayish in tone upon ejaculation, but it becomes clearer as it liquefies. Normally, about 2–6 milliliters (about 1 teaspoonful) of semen are ejaculated at one time; this amount of semen generally contains between 100 million and 600 million sperm. Fewer than 100 sperm will reach the fallopian tubes.

MALE SEXUAL RESPONSE

At this point, it might be useful to review the material on sexual arousal and response in Chapter 3, including the models of Masters and Johnson and of Kaplan. Even though their sexual anatomy is quite different, women and men follow roughly the same pattern of excitement and orgasm, with two exceptions: (1) Generally (but certainly not always), men become fully aroused and ready for penetration in a shorter amount of time than women do; and (2) once men experience orgasm, they usually cannot have another one for some time, whereas women may experience multiple orgasms.

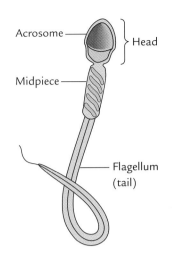

FIGURE 4.7 The Human Spermatozoon (Sperm Cell). The head contains the sperm's nucleus, including the chromosomes, and is encased in a helmetlike acrosome.

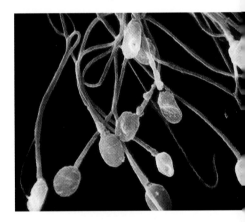

Between 100 million and 600 million sperm are present in the semen from a single ejaculation. Typically, following ejaculation during intercourse, fewer than 100 will get as far as a fallopian tube, where an ovulated oocyte may be present. Though many sperm assist in helping to dissolve the egg cell membrane, only one sperm ultimately achieves fertilization.

Male sexual response is far brisker and more automatic. It is triggered easily by things—like putting a quarter in a vending machine.

—Dr. Alex Comfort

Sexual arousal in men includes the processes of myotonia (increased muscle tension) and vasocongestion (engorgement of the tissues with blood). Vasocongestion in men is most apparent in the erection of the penis.

Erection

When a male becomes aroused, the blood circulation within the penis changes dramatically (Figure 4.8). During the process of **erection,** the blood vessels expand, increasing the volume of blood, especially within the corpora cavernosa. At the same time, expansion of the penis compresses the veins that normally carry blood out, so the penis becomes further engorged. (There are no muscles in the penis that make it erect, nor is there a bone in it.) Secretions from the Cowper's glands appear at the tip of the penis during erection.

Ejaculation and Orgasm

Increasing stimulation of the penis generally leads to **ejaculation,** the process by which semen is forcefully expelled from a man's body. When the impulses that cause erection reach a critical point, a spinal reflex sets off a massive discharge of nerve impulses to the ducts, glands, and muscles of the reproductive system. Ejaculation then occurs in two stages.

Emission   In the first stage, **emission,** contractions of the walls of the tail portion of the epididymis send sperm into the vas deferens. Rhythmic contractions also occur in the vas deferentia, ampullae, seminal vesicles, and ejaculatory ducts, which spill their contents into the urethra. The bladder's sphincter muscle closes to prevent urine from mixing with the semen and semen from entering the bladder, and another sphincter below the prostate also closes, trapping the semen in the expanded urethral bulb. At this point, the man feels a distinct sensation of **ejaculatory inevitability,** the point at which ejaculation *must* occur. These events are accompanied by increased heart rate and respiration, elevated blood pressure, and general muscular tension. About 25% of men experience a sex flush.

Expulsion   In the second stage of ejaculation, **expulsion,** there are rapid, rhythmic contractions of the urethra, the prostate, and the muscles at the base of the penis. The first few contractions are the most forceful, causing semen to spurt from the urethral opening. Gradually, the intensity of the contractions decreases and the interval between them lengthens. Breathing rate and heart rate may reach their peak at expulsion.

Some men experience **retrograde ejaculation,** the "backward" expulsion of semen into the bladder rather than out of the urethral opening. This malfunctioning of the urethral sphincters may be temporary (induced by tranquilizers, for example), but if it persists, the man should seek medical counsel to determine if there is an underlying problem. Retrograde ejaculation is not normally harmful; the semen is simply collected in the bladder and eliminated during urination.

Orgasm   The intensely pleasurable physical sensations and general release of tension that accompany ejaculation constitute the experience of *orgasm.*

Bring me my bow of burning gold.
Bring me my arrows of desire.

—*William Blake (1757–1827)*

An erection at will is the moral equivalent of a valid credit card.

—*Dr. Alex Comfort*

When the appetite arises in the liver, the heart generates a spirit which descends through the arteries, fills the hollow of the penis and makes it hard and stiff. The delightful movements of intercourse give warmth to all the members, and hence to the humor which is in the brain; this liquid is drawn through the veins which lead from behind the ears to the testicles and from them it is squirted by the penis into the vulva.

—*Constantinus Africanus (c. 1070)*

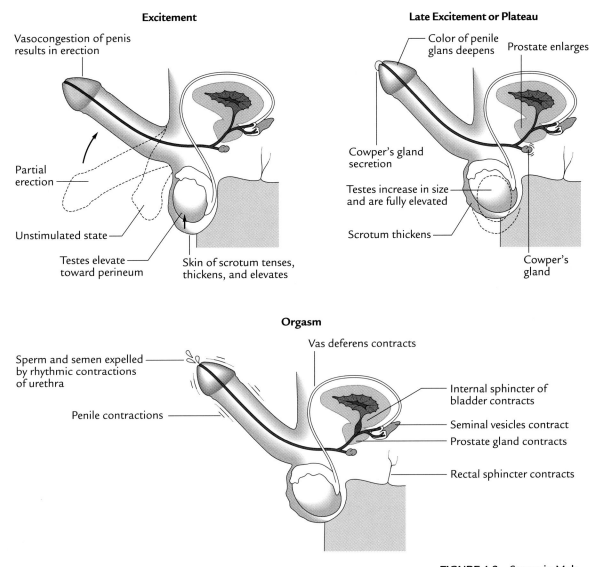

FIGURE 4.8 Stages in Male Sexual Response

Orgasm does not always occur with ejaculation, however. It is possible to ejaculate without having an orgasm and to experience orgasm without ejaculating. Following orgasm, men experience a **refractory period,** during which they are not capable of having an orgasm again. Refractory periods vary greatly in length, ranging from a few minutes to many hours (or even days, in some older men). Other changes occur immediately following orgasm. Erection diminishes as blood flow returns to normal, the sex flush (if there was one) disappears, and fairly heavy perspiration may occur. Men who experience intense sexual arousal without orgasm may feel some heaviness or discomfort in the testicles; this is generally not as painful as the common term "blue balls" implies. If discomfort persists, however, it may be relieved by a period of rest or by ejaculation through manual stimulation (by either the man or his partner). There is no harm to a man's health if he does not ejaculate frequently or at all. When the seminal vesicles are full,

THE ERECTION REFLEX CAN BE TRIGGERED by various sexual and nonsexual stimuli, including tactile stimulation (touching) of the penis or other erogenous areas; sights, smells, or sounds (usually words or sexual vocalizations); and emotions or thoughts. Even negative emotions, such as fear, can produce an erection. Conversely, emotions and thoughts can also inhibit erections, as can unpleasant or painful physical sensations. The erectile response is controlled by the parasympathetic nervous system, and as such, it cannot be consciously willed.

The length of time an erection lasts varies greatly from individual to individual and from situation to situation. With experience, most men are able to gauge the amount of stimulation that will either maintain the erection without causing orgasm or cause orgasm to occur too soon. Failure to attain an erection when one is desired is something most men experience at one time or another. (Erectile difficulties are discussed further in Chapter 14.)

There are, however, some things you can do to maximize your chances of producing viable erections. Because you need a steady flow of blood to your penis, you should get enough aerobic exercise to maintain your circulation. A diet low in fat and cholesterol and high in fiber and complex carbohydrates may also prevent hardening of the arteries, which restricts blood flow.

Some conditions, including diabetes, tension, and abnormalities in blood pressure, and some medications that treat the abnormalities may have an adverse effect on blood flow and erectile capacity. If any of these conditions are present, or if the failure to attain an erection is persistent, see your physician.

What can you do about unwanted erections at inappropriate times? Distract yourself or stop your thoughts or images. Remember, the brain is the most erotic (and unerotic) organ of the body.

feedback mechanisms diminish the quantity of sperm produced. Excess sperm die and are absorbed by the body.

■   In this chapter and the previous one, we have looked at the *physical* characteristics that designate us as female or male. But, as we will discover in the following chapter, there's more to gender than mere chromosomes or reproductive organs. How we feel about our male or female anatomy and how we act (our gender roles) also determine our identities as men or women.

SUMMARY

Male Sex Organs: What Are They For?

- In their reproductive role, a man's sex organs produce and store gametes and deliver them to a woman's reproductive tract. The *penis* is the organ through which both sperm and urine pass. The *shaft* of the penis contains two *corpora cavernosa* and a *corpus spongiosum*, which fill with blood during arousal, causing an erection. The head is called the *glans penis;* in uncircumcised men it is covered by the *foreskin*. Myths about the penis equate its size with masculinity and sexual prowess. The *scrotum* is a pouch of skin that hangs at the root of the penis. It holds the *testes*.

- The paired testes or testicles have two major functions: sperm production and hormone production. Within each testicle are about 1000 *seminiferous tubules*, where the production of sperm takes place. The seminiferous tubules merge to form the *epididymis*, a coiled tube where the sperm finally mature, and each epididymis merges into a *vas deferens,* which joins the *ejaculatory duct* within the *prostate gland.* The *seminal vesicles* and prostate gland produce semen, which nourishes and transports the sperm. Two tiny glands called *Cowper's* or *bulbourethral glands* secrete a thick, clear mucus prior to ejaculation.

- Male anatomical structures that do not serve a reproductive function but that may be involved in or affected by sexual activities include the breasts, *urethra,* buttocks, rectum, and anus.

Male Sexual Physiology

- The reproductive processes of the male body include the production of hormones and the production and delivery of sperm, the male gametes. Although men do not have a monthly reproductive cycle comparable to that of women, they do experience regular fluctuations of hormone levels; there is also some evidence that men's moods follow a cyclical pattern. The most important male hormone is *testosterone,* which triggers sperm production and regulates the sex drive. Other important hormones in male reproductive physiology are GnRH, FSH, LH, and inhibin.

- *Sperm* carry either an X chromosome, which will produce a female zygote, or Y chromosome, which will produce a male.

- *Semen,* or seminal fluid, is the ejaculated liquid that contains sperm. The function of the semen is to nourish sperm and provide them with a hospitable environment and means of transport when they are deposited within the vagina. It is mainly made up of secretions from the seminal vesicles and prostate gland. The semen from a single ejaculation generally contains between 100 million and 600 million sperm.

Male Sexual Response

- Male sexual response, like that of females, involves the processes of vasocongestion and myotonia. *Erection* of the penis occurs when sexual or tactile stimuli cause its chambers to become engorged with blood. Continuing stimulation leads to *ejaculation,* which occurs in two stages. In the first stage, *emission,* semen mixes with sperm in the urethral bulb. In the second stage, *expulsion,* semen is forcibly expelled from the penis, generally resulting in orgasm. Following orgasm is a **refactory period,** during which orgasm is not possible.

SUGGESTED READING

Bechtel, Stefan, & Roystains, Lawrence. (1997). *Sex: A Man's Guide.* Emmaus, PA: Rodale Press. Advice on more than 130 sex topics.

Castleman, Michael. (1989). *Sexual Solutions: A Guide for Men and Women Who Love Them.* New York: Touchstone Books. For heterosexual men (and women), the ins and outs of lovemaking; includes a reassuring section on penis size.

Eisler, Riane. (1995). *Sacred Pleasures: Sex, Myth, and the Politics of the Body.* New York: HarperCollins. A well-researched book that undermines the assumption of male aggression and domination, replacing it with a vision of partnership in society.

Yaffe, Maurice, & Fenwick, Elizabeth. (1989). *Sexual Happiness for Men: A Practical Approach.* New York: Holt. Illustrates and aims to enhance sexual responsiveness; also see the companion text for women.

Zilbergeld, Bernie. (1992). *The New Male Sexuality.* New York: Bantam Books. Explains both male and female anatomy and sexual response, plus communication, sexual problem solving, and much more. Authoritative, interesting, and readable; written for men (but recommended for women as well).

5

Gender and Gender Roles

*H*ow can you tell the difference between a man and a woman? Everyone knows that women and men are very basically distinguished by
their genitals. But accurate as this answer may be academically, it is not particularly useful in social situations. In most social situations—except in nud-
ist colonies and hot tubs, and while sunbathing *au naturel*—one's genitals
are usually not visible to the casual observer. One does not expose himself
or herself (or ask another to do so) for gender verification. We are more likely
to rely on secondary sex characteristics, such as breasts and body hair, or on
bone structure, musculature, and height. But even these characteristics are
not always reliable, given the great variety of shapes and sizes we come in
as human beings. And farther away than a few yards, we cannot always distinguish these characteristics. Instead of relying entirely on physical characteristics to identify males and females, we often look for other clues.

Culture provides us with an important clue for recognizing whether a
person is female or male in most situations: dress. In almost all cultures,
male and female clothing differs to varying degrees so that we can easily
identify a person's gender (Bullough, 1991). Some cultures, such as our own,
may accentuate secondary sex characteristics, especially for females. Traditional feminine clothing, for example, emphasizes a woman's gender: dress
or skirt, a form-fitting or low-cut top revealing the breasts (a secondary sex
characteristic), high heels, and so on. For adventuresome women, lacy
bustiers, garter belts, and brassieres, once considered undergarments, may
be worn as outerwear, emphasizing "femaleness." Most clothing, in fact, that
emphasizes or exaggerates secondary sex characteristics is female. Makeup
(red lipstick, rouge, eyeliner) and hairstyle also serve to mark or exaggerate
the differences between females and males. Even smells (perfume and after-
shave cologne) and colors (blue for boys, pink for girls) help distinguish
females and males.

Clothing and other aspects of appearance exaggerate the physical differences between women and men. And culture encourages us to accentuate
(or invent) psychological, emotional, mental, and behavioral differences. But
are men and women as different as we ordinarily think?

In this chapter, we examine some of the critical ways being male or female
affects us both as human beings and as sexual beings. We look at the connection between our genitals, our identity as female or male, and our feelings of being feminine or masculine. We also examine the relationship
between femininity, masculinity, and sexual orientation. Then we discuss
how masculine and feminine traits result from both biological and social
influences. We next focus on theories of socialization and how we learn to
act masculine and feminine in our culture. Then we look at traditional, contemporary, and androgynous gender roles. Finally, we examine intersexuality, transsexuality, and transgenderism, phenomena that raise complex issues
pertaining to gender and gender identity.

STUDYING GENDER AND GENDER ROLES

Let's start by defining some key terms, to establish a common terminology.
Keeping these definitions in mind will make the discussion clearer.

Lisa Lyon, 1981. Copyright © 1981 The Estate of Robert Mapplethorpe.

Whatever women do they must do twice as well as men to be thought half as good. Luckily, this is not difficult.

—Charlotte Whitton

Sex, Gender, and Gender Roles: What's the Difference?

The word **sex** refers to whether one is biologically female or male, based on genetic and anatomical sex. **Genetic sex** refers to one's chromosomal and hormonal sex characteristics, such as whether one's chromosomes are XY or XX, and whether estrogens or testosterone dominates the hormonal system. **Anatomical sex** refers to physical sex: gonads, uterus, vulva, vagina, penis, and so on.

Although "sex" and "gender" are often used interchangeably, gender is not the same as biological sex. **Gender** is femininity or masculinity, the social and cultural characteristics associated with biological sex. Whereas sex is rooted in biology, gender is rooted in culture. **Assigned gender** is the gender given by others, usually at birth. When a baby is born, someone looks at the genitals and exclaims, "It's a boy!" or "It's a girl!" With that single utterance, the baby is transformed from an "it" into a "male" or a "female." **Gender identity** is the gender a person believes him- or herself to be.

Gender role is the role a person is expected to perform as a result of being female or male in a particular culture. The term "gender role" is gradually replacing the traditional term "sex role" because "sex role" continues to suggest a connection between biological sex and behavior (Unger, 1991). Biological males are expected to act out masculine gender roles; biological females are expected to act out feminine gender roles. A **gender-role stereotype** is a rigidly held, oversimplified, and overgeneralized belief that all males and all females possess distinct psychological and behavioral traits. Stereotypes tend to be false or misleading, not only for the group as a whole ("women are more interested in relationships than sex") but for any individual in the group (Jane may be more interested in sex than relationships). Even if a generalization is statistically valid in describing a group average (males are generally taller than females), such generalizations do not necessarily predict whether Roberto will be taller than Tanya. **Gender-role attitude** refers to the beliefs a person has of him- or herself and others regard-

The moment we are born, we are identified as male or female and are socialized to fulfill masculine and feminine gender roles.

ing appropriate female and male personality traits and activities. **Gender-role behavior** refers to the actual activities or behaviors a person engages in as a female or a male.

Sex and Gender Identity

We develop our gender through the interaction of its biological and psychosocial components. The biological component includes genetic and anatomical sex; the psychosocial component includes assigned gender and gender identity.

Assigned Gender   When we are born, we are given an assigned gender based on anatomical appearance. Assigned gender is significant because it tells *others* how to respond to us. After all, one of the first questions an older child or adult asks upon seeing an infant is whether it's a girl or a boy. We have no sense of ourselves as females or males. We *learn* that we are a girl or a boy from the verbal responses of others. "What a pretty *girl*" or "What a good *boy*," our parents and others say. We are constantly given signals about our gender. Our birth certificate states our sex; our name, such as Paul or Paula, is most likely gender-coded. Our clothes, even in infancy, reveal our gender.

By the time we are 2 years old, we are probably able to identify ourself as a girl or a boy based on what we have internalized from what others have told us. But we don't really know *why* we are a girl or a boy. We don't associate our gender with our genitals. In fact, until the age of 3 or so, most children identify girls or boys by hairstyles, clothing, or other nonanatomical signs. At around age 3, we begin to learn that the genitals are what makes a person male or female. It still takes us a while to understand that we are *permanently* a boy or a girl. We often believe that we can become the other sex later.

Gender Identity   By about 24 months, we internalize and identify with our gender. We *think* we are a girl or a boy. This feeling of our femaleness or maleness is our gender identity. For most people, gender identity is permanent and is congruent with their sexual anatomy and assigned gender. Furthermore, it is virtually impossible to develop a personal identity without a gender identity as a female or a male (Money & Tucker, 1976). Our sense of femaleness or maleness is a core component of our identity.

Some cultures, however, put off instilling gender identity in males until later. They believe in a latent or dormant femaleness in males. As a consequence, such cultures institute rituals or ceremonies in childhood to ensure that males will identify themselves as males. In some East African societies, for example, male children are referred to as "woman-child"; there appear to be few social differences between boys and girls. Around age 7, the boy undergoes male initiation rites, such as circumcision, whose avowed purpose is to "make" the child into a man. Such ceremonies may be a kind of benign "brainwashing," helping the young male make the transition to a new gender identity with new role expectations. Other cultures allow older males to act out a latent female identity with such practices as the couvade, in which husbands mimic their wives giving birth. And in our own society, into the early years of this century, boys were dressed in gowns and wore their hair in long curls until age 2. At age 2 or 3, their dresses were replaced by pants and their hair cut. From then on, masculine socialization was stressed (Garber, 1991).

Masculinity and Femininity: Opposites or Similar?

Each culture determines the content of gender roles in its own way. Among the Arapesh of New Guinea, members of both sexes possess what we consider feminine traits. Both men and women tend to be passive, cooperative, peaceful, and nurturing. The father is said to "bear a child" as well as the mother; only the father's continual care can make a child grow healthily, both in the womb and in childhood. Eighty miles away, the Mundugumor live in remarkable contrast to the peaceful Arapesh. "Both men and women," Margaret Mead (1975) observed, "are expected to be violent, competitive, aggressively sexed, jealous, and ready to see and avenge insult, delighting in display, in action, in fighting." Biology creates males and females, but it is culture that creates our concepts of masculinity and femininity.

The traditional Western view of masculinity and femininity sees men and women as polar opposites. Our popular terminology, in fact, reflects this view. Women and men refer to each other as the "opposite sex." But this implies that women and men are opposites, that we have little in common with each other. Our gender stereotypes fit this pattern of polar differences: Men are aggressive, women are passive; men embody **instrumentality** and are task-oriented; women embody **expressiveness** and are emotion-oriented; men are rational, women are irrational; men want sex, women want love; and so on.

It is important to recognize that gender stereotypes, despite their depiction of men and women as opposites, are usually not all-or-nothing notions. Most of us do not think that only men are assertive or only women are nurturing. As individuals, along with our friends and family, we probably disapprove of this all-or-nothing notion. Stereotypes reflect *probabilities* that a woman or man will have a certain characteristic based on her or his gender.

One half the world cannot understand the pleasures of the other.

—Jane Austen (1775–1817)

The main difference between men and women is that men are lunatics and women are idiots.

—Rebecca West (1892–1983)

The perception of male/female psychological differences is far greater than they are in fact.

When we say that men are more independent than women, we mean there is a greater probability that a man will be more independent than a woman.

As technology becomes more advanced, we learn more about what contributes to making the sexes different. We are already beginning to get hints that our identities as men and women are a combination of nature and nurture. It is through new technology that researchers can catch brains in the act of cogitating, feeling, or remembering. Current research suggests that women engage more of their brains than men when they think sad thoughts, but possibly less when they solve SAT math problems (Begley, 1995). Other evidence has found that some differences between men and women may be due to differences in the part of the brain that controls emotional processing. In men, the part controlling action-oriented responses appears to be more active; in women, the part thought to control more symbolic emotional responses is more active (Gur, Mozley, Mozley et al., 1995). With continued interest in this subject, differences and similarities that we once attributed to learning or culture may be found to be biologically based. Add to this our choices, sense of identities, and life experiences, and we can begin to get a picture of what contributes to making each person unique.

Gender and Sexual Orientation

Gender, gender identity, and gender role are conceptually independent of sexual orientation (Lips, 1997). But, in many people's minds, these concepts are closely related to sexual orientation, discussed at greater length in Chapter 6. Our traditional notion of gender roles assumes that heterosexuality is a critical component of masculinity and femininity (Riseden & Hort, 1992). A "masculine" man is attracted to women and a "feminine" woman is attracted to men. From this assumption follow two beliefs about homosexuality: (1) If a man is gay, he cannot be masculine, and if a woman is lesbian, she cannot be feminine; and (2) if a man is gay, he must have some

Don't Judge a Man by His Lipstick or a Woman by Her Motorcycle Boots

A GROUP OF ADOLESCENT boys passed a lesbian with short hair, wearing a blue workshirt, a pair of old Levis, and motorcycle boots. One of the boys taunted her: "Are you a man or a woman?" She looked him straight in the eye: "I'm more man than you'll ever be and more woman than you'll ever be able to handle." The boy slunk away with his friends (Wolf, 1980).

Although the overwhelming majority of gay men and lesbians are as masculine or feminine as heterosexuals, some purposely act out effeminate or butch roles. (**Effeminacy** is the possession of femalelike qualities. Effeminate men or masculine-appearing women are not necessarily gay or lesbian; nor are they transvestites or cross-dressers.) In the gay/lesbian subculture, **butch** women are lesbians who dress and act in a stylized masculine manner; effeminate gay men are men who, without denying their maleness, mimic feminine characteristics in their dress and mannerisms. Many gay men and lesbians feel ambivalent about or hostile toward such men and women. They believe effeminate gay men and butch lesbians reinforce negative stereotypes about homosexuality.

Some elements of contemporary gay culture regard effeminate gay men as self-hating. The witty Quentin Crisp, who prided himself on his hennaed hair, makeup, red fingernails, and jewelry, however, viewed himself as both confrontational *and* self-protective. He did not want to pass as a woman, but to present himself as an "image of homosexuality that was outrageously effeminate" (Crisp, 1982). The effeminate gay man parodies masculinity and, like the cross-dresser, provokes confrontation because of his visibility. This arouses homophobia among some heterosexuals because they believe the men are flaunting their effeminacy. It arouses "transvestophobia" among some gay men because they believe effeminate dressing presents a distorted or stereotypical image of homosexuality as somehow "female" (Garber, 1991).

Since at least the 1890s, with the "invert" balls in New York, where lesbians dressed in tuxedoes and danced with others wearing gowns, butch-femme relationships have been an important element of the lesbian subculture in America and England (Faderman, 1991). (A **femme** is a feminine lesbian known by her butch partner choice; a butch is also referred to nonpejoratively in butch-femme culture as a **dyke** [Nestle, 1983].)

feminine characteristics, and if a woman is lesbian, she must have some masculine characteristics (Ross, 1983a). What these beliefs imply is that homosexuality is somehow associated with a failure to fulfill traditional gender roles (DeCecco & Elia, 1993). A "real" man is not gay; therefore, gay men are not "real" men. Similarly, a "real" woman is not a lesbian; therefore, lesbians are not "real" women.

Stereotypes of gay men often link them with "feminine" characteristics such as weakness, emotionality, and submissiveness. Such stereotypes can be traced back to the turn of the century, when both Havelock Ellis and Sigmund Freud (discussed in Chapter 2) believed that homosexuality was the result of "inversion," reversed gender roles. There are no conclusive findings on the relationship between sexual orientation and gender roles, however (Paul, 1993). Gay and lesbian roles may emphasize certain personality traits or behaviors during one time period and different ones at another time. These traits and behaviors are not necessarily inherent to being gay or lesbian. Like gender roles, gay and lesbian roles may reflect views on how people are expected to act.

Studies on attitudes toward gay men and lesbians indicate a relationship between negative attitudes and gender roles (Herek, 1984; Kite, 1984). A comparison between individuals who hold negative attitudes toward gay men and lesbians and those who hold neutral or positive attitudes found some evidence of differences. Those holding negative attitudes were more likely to adhere to traditional gender roles, stereotype men and women, and

Stereotypes fall in the face of humanity . . . this is how the world will change for gay men and lesbians.

—*Anna Quindlen*

During the 1950s, butch and femme were the dominant role models for young and working-class lesbians. (Middle-class and upper-class lesbians generally preferred to remain invisible during this time and lived their lives outside the lesbian subculture.) Butches assumed traditional masculine heterosexual roles, such as being the dominant partner and controlling their emotions, while femmes assumed feminine heterosexual roles, such as being submissive, supportive, and caring (Faderman, 1991). These "heterosexual" roles, however, did not translate erotically. Writer Joan Nestle (1983) notes: "Butch-femme relationships . . . were complex erotic and social statements, not phony heterosexual replicas. They were filled with a deeply lesbian language of stance, dress, gesture, love, courage, and autonomy."

Although the butch role may appear to be a male imitation, for women of the 1950s and earlier, it was empowering in contrast to the submissiveness of the traditional heterosexual female role. And unlike middle-class and wealthy lesbians, butches made themselves visible as lesbians. Femmes were not typical '50s females, either; they "were attracted to a rebel sexuality" and permitted themselves to be seen with butches whose outlaw status was clearly visible by their appearance (Faderman, 1991).

Beginning in the late 1960s, however, lesbian roles shifted in response to the challenges of women's liberation. Lesbian feminists rejected butch and femme as being heterosexual models. Instead, they sought a unique lesbian identity. Lesbians were to be strong women as women, not as lesbian imitations of men. The femme role was rejected as an imitation of a male-defined passive heterosexual female.

In the 1980s, butch-femme relationships reemerged in the lesbian subculture. But the new butch-femme relationship took on a distinctive sexual meaning that had been absent earlier: It was now mixed with erotic power, in which control and passivity became part of lesbian sex play. Seduction became an important element. "The goal was for women to use those roles for their own pleasurable ends," wrote historian Lillian Faderman (1991), "to demand freedom and sexual excitement as lesbians seldom dared before."

But just as many gay men feel uncomfortable with effeminacy, many lesbians also feel uncomfortable with butch and femme roles. They continue to view them as repressive relationships that mock the possibility of equality and strength in female-female relationships. What Faderman calls "the lesbian sex wars" continue today as lesbian-feminists and sexual radicals debate the "correctness" of butch-femme relationships.

support the sexual double standard, granting men greater sexual freedom than women. Males tended to be more negative than women toward gay men and lesbians. And heterosexual men tended to be more negative toward gay men than toward lesbians; heterosexual women were more negative toward lesbians than toward gay men.

Gender Theory

What is the relationship between our biological sex as male or female and our gender role as masculine or feminine? Do we act the way we act because our gender role is inbred in us or because of socialization? As we discussed in Chapter 1, biological explanations of gender differences focusing on genes and hormones have found increasing support in recent years. Research in the fields of sociobiology and evolutionary psychology has demonstrated that nature is an important determinant of gender development. Nature alone, however, doesn't account for the variety of gender-related characteristics seen across cultures or the ways in which gender roles are created. To really understand gender, we must look at social explanations as well as biological ones.

Traditionally, the social sciences have not paid much attention to *why* a culture develops its particular gender roles. They have been more interested in such topics as the process of socialization and male/female differences. In the 1980s, however, gender theory was developed to explore the role of gender in society. **Gender theory** argues that a society may be best understood by how it is organized according to gender. Gender is viewed as a basic element in social relationships, based on the socially perceived differences between the sexes that justify unequal power relationships (Scott, 1986). Imagine, for example, an infant crying in the night. In the mother/father parenting relationship, which parent gets up to take care of the baby? In most cases, the mother does because women are socially perceived to be nurturing, and it is the woman's "responsibility" as mother (even if she hasn't slept fully in four nights and is employed full-time). Yet the father could just as easily care for the crying infant. He doesn't, because caregiving is socially perceived as "natural" to women.

In psychology, gender theory focuses on (1) how gender is created and what its purposes are, and (2) how specific traits, behaviors, or roles are defined as male or female and how they create advantages for males and disadvantages for females. Gender theorists reject the idea that biology creates male/female differences. Gender differences are largely, if not entirely, created by society (Hare-Mustin & Marecek, 1990b; Lott, 1990).

The key to the creation of gender inequality lies in the belief that men and women are, indeed, "opposite" sexes; that they are opposite each other in personalities, abilities, skills, and traits. Furthermore, the differences between the sexes are unequally valued: Reason and aggressiveness (defined as male traits) are considered to be more valuable than emotion and passivity (defined as female traits). In reality, however, males and females are more like each other than they are different. Both are reasonable and emotional, aggressive and passive (Ferree, 1991).

> The war between the sexes is the only one in which both sides regularly sleep with the enemy.
>
> —*Quentin Crisp*

Gender is socially constructed (Lott, 1990). In other words, it is neither innate nor instinctive; it is the result of the exercise of cultural conditioning. Making the sexes appear to be opposite and of unequal value requires the suppression of natural similarities by the use of social power (Bem, 1995). The exercise of social power might take the form of greater societal value being placed on appearance over achievement for women, sexual harassment of women in the workplace or school, patronizing attitudes toward women, and so on.

There are several problems with gender theory, which derives many of its ideas and assumptions from social constructionism and conflict theory. Social constructionism discounts the role of biology rather than examining how biology and society may interact to create gender differences. Furthermore, it often overstates its case: Does the fact that a few cultures do not divide people into two genders *prove* that gender is entirely socially constructed? Perhaps ignoring the existence of gender is itself socially constructed. Conflict theory reduces interactions to issues of power and dominance, which, on the abstract level, may appear to be correct. But when applied to any specific male-female relationship, such a description may not be accurate. Furthermore, gender theory underestimates altruism, love as an antidote to power, and the actual amount of cooperation between men and women in day-to-day interactions. Finally, gender theory makes several erroneous assumptions about human beings: Women and men are passive recipients of gender roles, they are unable to form their own views and interpretations of society, and they are unable to change the roles and society in which they partake.

GENDER-ROLE LEARNING

As we have seen, gender roles are socially constructed and rooted in culture. How do individuals learn what their society expects of them as males or females?

Theories of Socialization

Although there are a number of ways of examining how we acquire our gender roles, two of the most prominent are cognitive social learning theory and cognitive development theory.

Cognitive social learning theory is derived from behaviorist psychology. In explaining our actions, behaviorists emphasize observable events and their consequences, rather than internal feelings and drives. According to behaviorists, we learn attitudes and behaviors as a result of social interactions with others (hence the term "social learning").

The cornerstone of cognitive social learning theory is the belief that consequences control behavior. Acts that are regularly followed by a reward are likely to occur again; acts that are regularly followed by a punishment are less likely to recur. Girls are rewarded for playing with dolls ("What a nice mommy!"), but boys are not ("What a sissy!").

This behaviorist approach has been modified recently to include **cognition**—mental processes that intervene between stimulus and response, such as evaluation and reflection. The cognitive processes involved in social learning include our ability to (1) use language, (2) anticipate consequences, and (3) make observations. By using language, we can tell our daughter that we like it when she does well in school and that we don't like it when she hits someone. A person's ability to anticipate consequences affects behavior. A boy doesn't need to wear lace stockings in public to know that such dressing will lead to negative consequences. Finally, children observe what others do. A girl may learn that she "shouldn't" play video games by seeing that the players in video arcades are mostly boys.

We also learn gender roles by imitation. Learning through imitation is called **modeling.** Most of us are not even aware of the many subtle behaviors that make up gender roles—the ways in which men and women use different mannerisms and gestures, speak differently, use different body language, and so on. We don't "teach" these behaviors by reinforcement. Children tend to model friendly, warm, and nurturing adults; they also tend to imitate adults who are powerful in their eyes—that is, adults who control access to food, toys, or privileges. Initially, the most powerful models that children have are their parents. As children grow older and their social world expands, so does the number of people who may act as their role models: siblings, friends, teachers, media figures. Children sift through the various demands and expectations associated with the different models to create their own unique selves.

In contrast to social learning theory, **cognitive development theory** focuses on the child's active interpretation of the messages he or she receives from the environment. Whereas social learning assumes that children and adults learn in fundamentally the same way, cognitive development theory stresses that we learn differently depending on our age. At age 2, children can correctly identify themselves and others as boys or girls, but they tend to base this identification on superficial features such as hair and clothing. Girls have long hair and wear dresses; boys have short hair and never wear dresses. Some children even believe they can change their gender by changing their clothes or hair length.

Cognitive development theory recognizes gender as a characteristic used to understand one's social environment and interact with it (Cross & Markus, 1993). Thus, a child compares him- or herself to others, including parents, and develops and attaches to masculine or feminine values. When children are 6 or 7, they begin to understand that gender is permanent; it is not something you can alter in the same way you can change your clothes. They acquire this understanding because they are capable of grasping the idea that basic characteristics do not change. A woman can be a woman even if she has short hair and wears pants. Although children can understand the permanence of gender, they tend to insist on rigid adherence to gender-role stereotypes.

According to cognitive social learning theory, boys and girls learn appropriate gender-role behavior through reinforcement and modeling. But, according to cognitive development theory, once children learn that gender is permanent, they independently strive to act like "proper" girls or boys. They do this on their own because of an internal need for congruence, the agreement between what they know and how they act. Also, children find performing the appropriate gender-role activities rewarding in itself. Models and reinforcement help show them how well they are doing, but the primary motivation is internal.

Gender-Role Learning in Childhood and Adolescence

It is difficult to analyze the relationship between biology and personality because learning begins at birth. Evidence shows, for example, that infant females are more sensitive than infant males to pain and to sudden changes of environment. Such responses may be encouraged by learning that begins immediately after birth.

In our culture, infant girls are usually held more gently and treated more tenderly than boys, who are ordinarily subjected to rougher forms of play. The first day after birth, parents characterize their daughters as soft, fine-featured, and small, and their sons as hard, large-featured, big, and attentive. Fathers tend to stereotype their sons more extremely than mothers do (Fagot & Leinbach, 1987). Although it is impossible for strangers to know the sex of a diapered baby, once they learn the baby's sex, they respond with gender stereotypes and expectations.

Parents as Socializing Agents   During infancy and early childhood, a child's most important source of learning is the primary caretaker, whether the mother, father, grandmother, or someone else. Many parents are not aware that their words and actions contribute to their children's gender-role socialization. Nor are they aware that they treat their daughters and sons differently because of their gender. Although parents may recognize that they respond differently to sons than to daughters, they usually have a ready explanation: the "natural" differences in the temperament and behavior of girls and boys. Parents may also believe they adjust their responses to each particular child's personality.

Children are socialized in gender roles through four very subtle processes: manipulation, channeling, verbal appellation, and activity exposure (Oakley, 1985).

- *Manipulation.* Parents manipulate their children from infancy onward. They treat a daughter gently, tell her she is pretty, and advise her that nice girls do not fight. They treat a son roughly, tell him he is strong, and advise him that big boys do not cry. Eventually, children incorporate their parents' views in such matters as integral parts of their personalities.

- *Channeling.* Children are channeled by directing their attention to specific objects. Toys, for example, are differentiated by sex. Dolls are considered appropriate for girls, cars for boys.

- *Verbal appellation.* Parents use different words with boys and girls to describe the same behavior. A boy who pushes others may be described as "active," whereas a girl who does the same is usually called "aggressive."

- *Activity exposure.* The activity exposure of girls and boys differs markedly. Although both are usually exposed to feminine activities early in life, boys are discouraged from imitating their mothers, whereas girls are encouraged to be "mother's little helper."

It is generally accepted that parents socialize their children differently according to gender (Block, 1983; Fagot & Leinbach, 1987). Fathers, more than mothers, pressure their children to behave in gender-appropriate ways. Fathers set higher standards of achievement for their sons than for their daughters; for their daughters, fathers emphasize the interpersonal aspect of their relationship. But mothers also reinforce the interpersonal aspect of the parent-daughter relationship. Both parents tend to be more restrictive of their daughters and to allow their sons more freedom and less intervention (Skolnick, 1992).

Various studies have indicated that ethnicity and class are important in influencing gender roles (Wilkinson, Zinn, & Chow, 1992; Zinn, 1990). Among Whites, working-class families tend to differentiate more sharply between boys and girls in terms of appropriate behavior than middle-class families do; they tend to place more restrictions on girls. African American families tend to socialize their children toward more egalitarian gender roles (Taylor, 1994). There is evidence that African American families socialize their daughters to be more independent than White families do. Indeed, among African Americans, the "traditional" female role model may never have existed. The African American female role model in which the woman is both wage-earner and homemaker is more typical and more accurately reflects African American experience (Basow, 1986).

As children grow older, their social world expands, and so do their sources of learning. Around the time children enter day care or kindergarten, teachers and peers become important influences.

Teachers as Socializing Agents

Day-care centers, nursery schools, and kindergartens are often the child's first experience in the wider world outside the family. Teachers become important role models for their students.

> What are little girls made of?
> Sugar and spice
> And everything nice.
> That's what little girls are made of.
> What are little boys made of?
> Snips and snails
> And puppy dogs' tails.
> That's what little boys are made of.
>
> —*Nursery rhyme*

Because most day-care, kindergarten, and elementary school teachers are women, children tend to think of child-adult interactions as primarily the province of women. In this sense, schools reinforce the idea that women are concerned with children and men are not (Koblinsky & Sugawara, 1984). Teachers also tend to be conventional in the gender-role messages they convey to children (Wynn & Fletcher, 1987). They may encourage different activities and abilities in boys and girls. There is research indicating that boys of all ages interrupt teachers in their activities much more than girls do, whereas teachers tend to interrupt girls more than they do boys (Henrick & Stange, 1991). Teachers often give children messages about appropriate activities, such as contact sports for boys and gymnastics or dance for girls. Academically, teachers tend to encourage boys more than girls in math and science and girls more than boys in language skills. Consequently, there is evidence of a downward spiral of test scores in math and science among girls, who earlier scored equal to or even higher than boys on nearly every standardized test (Sadker & Sadker, 1994). No such downward spiral is observed for boys.

Gender bias often follows students as they move into the college arena. Though little research is available on the effects of a college education on women, there is evidence that undergraduate women tend to report more discrimination and sexual bias in their academic departments than do male students (Fischer & Good, 1994). There is also inequality in athletics, based on opportunities for participation and availability of scholarship moneys.

Peers as Socializing Agents   **Peers,** a person's age-mates, become especially important when children enter school. By granting or withholding approval, friends and playmates influence what games children play, what they wear, what music they listen to, what television programs they watch, and even what cereal they eat. Peers provide standards for gender-role behavior in several ways (Absismaan, Crombie, & Freeman, 1993; Carter, 1987; Moller, Hymel, & Rubin, 1992):

▪ Peers provide information about gender-role norms through play activities and toys. Girls play with dolls that cry and wet or glamorous dolls with well-developed figures and expensive tastes. Boys play with dolls known as "action figures," such as *Star Wars* figures with guns, lasers, and bigger-than-life biceps.

▪ Peers influence the adoption of gender-role norms through verbal approval or disapproval. "That's for boys!" or "Only girls do that!" is a severe negative message when a girl plays with a football or a boy plays with dolls.

▪ Children's perceptions of their friends' gender-role attitudes, behaviors, and beliefs encourage them to adopt similar ones to be accepted. If a girl's friends play soccer, she is more likely to play soccer. If a boy's same-sex friends display feelings, he is more likely to display feelings.

Even though parents tend to fear the worst from peers, peers provide important positive influences. It is within their peer groups, for example, that adolescents learn to develop intimate relationships (Gecas & Seff, 1991). Adolescents in peer groups tend to be more egalitarian than parents, especially fathers (Thornton, 1989).

Media Influences   Much of television programming promotes or condones negative stereotypes about gender, ethnicity, age, and gay men and lesbians. Women are significantly underrepresented on television. Throughout the 1970s, men outnumbered women on prime-time TV 3 to 1; today it is about 2 to 1. (Even on "Sesame Street," 84% of the characters were male in 1992, compared with 76% 5 years earlier ["Muppet Gender Gap," 1993]). Men on television overwhelmingly gave directions to women, by a ratio of 7 to 3. Ninety percent of narrators in commercials are men, especially in commercials directed toward women in family roles: "For a clean toilet," the male voice intones, "buy . . . ." Magazine advertisements depicting women in traditional activities and roles have been increasing (Klassen, Jasper, & Schwartz, 1993). Blonde women are disproportionately represented; they are also more provocatively dressed ("Depiction of Women," 1993). Women in traditional roles as wives, mothers, and homemakers continue to dominate women's magazines. Over the past 30 years, however, career themes also have increased (Demarest & Gardner, 1992).

TV women are generally portrayed as emotional and needing emotional support; they are also sympathetic and nurturing. Not surprisingly, women are usually portrayed as wives, mothers, or sex objects (Vande Berg & Steckfuss, 1992). Earlier depictions of women as professionals characterized them as "tough broads" with aggressive attitudes; their portrayal has become more realistic. Women on television typically are under age 40, well-groomed, attractive, and excessively concerned with their appearance.

On television, male characters are shown as more aggressive and constructive than female characters. They solve problems and rescue others from danger. Only in recent years in prime-time series have males been shown in emotional, nurturing roles. Only 3% of the men are depicted performing household tasks, whereas 20% of the women are ("Depiction of Women," 1993).

Ethnic stereotypes continue to be standard fare in television: "the Native American in full headdress, the black man as villain, and Hispanics with lots of children" (Wardle, 1989). Gay men and lesbians are increasing in visibility in TV movies and in a few sitcoms, but the characters are coming under scrutiny by show sponsors and are often portrayed stereotypically—as sinister, comical, or the victims of AIDS—or solely in terms of their sexual orientation (Kalin, 1992; Tharp, 1991; Weir, 1992).

Gender Schema: Exaggerating Differences

Actual differences between females and males are minimal or nonexistent, except in levels of aggressiveness, verbal skills, and visual/spatial skills. Yet culture exaggerates these differences or creates differences where none otherwise exists (Carter, 1987). One way that culture does this is by creating a schema. Recall from Chapter 2 that a schema is a set of interrelated ideas that helps us process information by categorizing it in useful ways. We often categorize people by age, ethnicity, nationality, physical characteristics, and so on. Gender is one such way of categorizing.

Sandra Bem (1983) observes that although gender is not inherent in inanimate objects or in behaviors, we treat many objects and behaviors as if they were masculine or feminine. These gender divisions form a complex structure of associations that affects our perceptions of reality. Bem refers to this

When boys and girls participate in sports together, they develop comparable athletic skills. Segregation of boys and girls encourages the development of differences that otherwise might not occur.

cognitive organization of the world according to gender as **gender schema.** We use gender schemas in many dimensions of life, including activities (nurturing, fighting), emotions (compassion, anger), behavior (playing with dolls or action figures), clothing (dresses or pants), and even colors (pink or blue), considering some appropriate for one gender and some appropriate for the other.

Children are taught the significance of gender differences. They learn that "the dichotomy between male and female has intensive and extensive relevance to virtually every domain of human experience" (Bem, 1983). Thus, children learn very early that it is important whether someone is female or male. Children begin thinking in terms of gender schemas relatively early (Liben & Signorella, 1993). Knowledge about different aspects of gender is usually completed between ages 2 and 4.

Adults who have strong gender schemas quickly categorize people's behavior, personality characteristics, objects, and so on into masculine/feminine categories. They disregard information that does not fit their gender schema. Males with a high masculine schema tend to view women as stereotypically feminine, for example (Hudak, 1993).

Processing information by gender is important in cultures such as ours. First, gender-schema cultures make multiple associations between gender and other non–sex-linked qualities, such as affection and strength. Our culture regards affection as a feminine trait and strength as a masculine one. Second, such cultures make gender distinctions important, using them as a basis for norms, status, taboos, and privileges. Men are assigned leadership positions, for example, whereas women are placed in the rank and file (if not at home). Men are sexually assertive; women are sexually passive.

CONTEMPORARY GENDER ROLES

Within the past generation, there has been a significant shift from traditional toward more egalitarian gender roles. Although women's roles have changed more than men's, men's are also changing. These changes seem to affect all socioeconomic classes. Those from conservative religious groups, such as Mormons, Catholics, and fundamentalist and evangelical Protestants, adhere most strongly to traditional gender roles (Spence et al., 1985). Despite the ongoing disagreement, it is likely that the egalitarian trend will continue (Mason & Lu, 1988; Thornton, 1989).

Traditional Gender Roles

Most gender-role studies have focused on the White middle class. Very little research has been done on gender roles among African Americans, Latinos, Asian Americans, and other ethnic groups (Binion, 1990; Reid & Comas-Diaz, 1990). As a result, White middle-class students and researchers need to be careful not to project gender-role concepts or aspirations based on their values onto other groups. Too often such projections can lead to distortions or moral judgments. There is evidence, for example, that the feelings of low self-esteem and dependence often associated with traditional female roles do not apply to African American women. In contrast to middle-class Whites, African Americans have traditionally valued strong, independent women (Gump, 1980; E. Smith, 1982). And among Latinos, "machismo" has a positive meaning, denoting manliness, strength, and honor.

The Traditional Male Gender Role   What is it to be a "real" man in America? Bruce Feirstein (1982) parodied him in his book *Real Men Don't Eat Quiche*:

> *Question:* How many Real Men does it take to change a light bulb?
> *Answer:* None. Real Men aren't afraid of the dark.
>
> *Question:* Why did the Real Man cross the road?
> *Answer:* It's none of your damn business.

Central personality traits associated with the traditional male role—whether White, African American, Latino, or Asian American—include aggressiveness, emotional toughness, independence, feelings of superiority, and decisiveness. Males are generally regarded as being more power-oriented than females. Men demonstrate higher degrees of aggression, especially violent aggression (such as assault, homicide, and rape), dominance, and competitiveness. Although these tough, aggressive traits may be useful in the corporate world, politics, and the military (or in hunting sabre-toothed tigers), such characteristics are rarely helpful to a man in his intimate relationships, which require understanding, cooperation, communication, and nurturing.

Males from ethnic groups must move between dominant and ethnic cultures with different role requirements. They are expected to conform not only to the gender-role norms of the dominant group but to those of their own group as well. Black males, for example, must conform to dominant stereotype expectations (success, competition, and aggression) as well as to expectations of the African American community, most notably cooperation and the promotion of ethnic survival (Hunter & Davis, 1992). They must also confront negative stereotypes about Black masculinity, such as hypersexuality and violence.

Male Sexual Scripts   In sociology, a **script** refers to the acts, rules, and expectations associated with a particular role. It is like the script handed out to an actor. Unlike dramatic scripts, however, social scripts allow considerable improvisation within their general boundaries. We are given many scripts in life according to the various roles we play. Among them are sexual scripts that outline how we are to behave sexually when acting out our gender roles. Perceptions and patterns in sexual behavior are shaped by sexual scripts (Castillo & Leer, 1993). See Chapter 9 for further discussion on sexual scripts.

Bernie Zilbergeld (1992) suggests that the male sexual script includes the following:

■ *Men should not have (or at least should not express) certain feelings.* Men should not express doubts; they should be assertive, confident, and aggressive. Tenderness and compassion are not masculine feelings.

■ *Performance is the thing that counts.* Sex is something to be achieved, to win at. Feelings only get in the way of the job to be done. Sex is not for intimacy but for orgasm.

■ *The man is in charge.* As in other things, the man is the leader, the person who knows what is best. The man initiates sex and gives the woman her orgasm. A real man doesn't need a woman to tell him what women like; he already knows.

■ *A man always wants sex and is ready for it.* It doesn't matter what else is going on, a man wants sex; he is always able to become erect. He is a machine.

■ *All physical contact leads to sex.* Because men are basically sexual machines, any physical contact is a sign for sex. Touching is seen as the first step toward sexual intercourse, not an end in itself. There is no physical pleasure except sexual pleasure.

■ *Sex equals intercourse.* All erotic contact leads to sexual intercourse. Foreplay is just that: warming up, getting your partner excited for penetration. Kissing, hugging, erotic touching, and oral sex are only preliminaries to intercourse.

■ *Sexual intercourse leads to orgasm.* The orgasm is the proof of the pudding. The more orgasms, the better the sex. If a woman does not have an orgasm, she is not sexual. The male feels that he is a failure because he was not good enough to give her an orgasm. If she requires clitoral stimulation to have an orgasm, she has a problem.

Common to all these myths is a separation of sex from love and attachment. Sex is seen as performance.

The Traditional Female Gender Role   Although many of the features of the traditional male gender role, such as being in control, are the same across ethnic lines, there are striking ethnic differences in the female role.

Among Whites, the traditional female gender role centers around women as wives and mothers. When a woman leaves adolescence, she is expected to get married and have children. Although a traditional woman may work prior to marriage, she is not expected to defer marriage for work goals.

Husbands think we should know where everything is—like the uterus is a tracking device. He asks me, "Roseanne, do we have any Chee-Tos left?" Like he can't go over to the sofa cushion and lift it himself.

—*Roseanne*

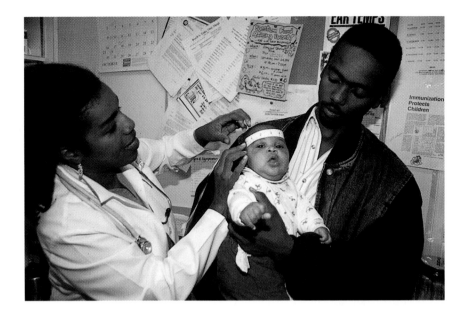

In recent years, the traditional role has been modified to include work and marriage. Work roles, however, are clearly subordinated to marital and family roles. Upon the birth of the first child, the woman is expected to remain home, if economically feasible, to become a full-time mother.

The traditional White female gender role does not extend to African American women. This may be attributed to a combination of the African heritage, slavery, which subjugated women to the same labor and hardships as men, and economic discrimination, which forced women into the labor force (Hatchett, 1991). African American men are generally more supportive than White or Latino men of more egalitarian gender roles for both women and men.

In traditional Latina gender roles, women subordinate themselves to men (Vasquez-Nuthall, Romero-Garcia, & DeLeon, 1987). But this subordination is based more on respect for the man's role as provider than on dominance (Becerra, 1988). Unlike in the Anglo culture, gender roles are strongly affected by age roles, in which the young subordinate themselves to the old. In this dual arrangement, notes Rosina Becerra (1988), "females are viewed as submissive, naive, and somewhat childlike. Elders are viewed as wise, knowledgeable, and deserving of respect." As a result of this intersection of gender and age roles, older women are treated with greater deference than younger women.

Female Sexual Scripts   Whereas the traditional male sexual script focuses on sex over feelings, the traditional female sexual script focuses on feelings over sex, on love over passion. The traditional female sexual script cited by Lonnie Barbach (1982) includes the following ideas:

> Women are made, not born.
> —*Simone de Beauvoir*

- *Sex is good and bad.* Women are taught that sex is both good and bad. What makes sex good? Sex in marriage or a committed relationship. What makes sex bad? Sex in a casual or uncommitted relationship. Sex is "so good" that you need to save it for your husband (or for someone with whom you are deeply in love). Sex is bad; if it is not sanctioned by love or marriage, you'll get a bad reputation.

▪ *Don't touch me "down there."* Girls are taught not to look at their genitals, not to touch them, especially not to explore them. As a result, women know very little about their genitals. They are often concerned about vaginal odors, making them uncomfortable about cunnilingus.

▪ *Sex is for men.* Men want sex, women want love. Women are sexually passive, waiting to be aroused. Sex is not a pleasurable activity as an end in itself; it is something performed by women *for* men.

▪ *Men should know what women want.* This script tells women that men know what they want, even if women don't tell them. Women are supposed to remain pure and sexually innocent. It is up to the man to arouse the woman, even if he doesn't know what a particular woman finds arousing. To keep her image of sexual innocence, she does not tell him what she wants.

▪ *Women shouldn't talk about sex.* Many women cannot talk about sex easily because they are not expected to have strong sexual feelings. Some women may know their partners well enough to have sex with them but not well enough to communicate their needs to them.

▪ *Women should look like models.* The media present ideally attractive women as beautiful models with slender hips, supple breasts, no fat; they are always young, with never a pimple, wrinkle, or gray hair in sight. As a result of these cultural images, many women are self-conscious about their physical appearance. They worry that they are too fat, too plain, too old. They often feel awkward without their clothes on to hide their imagined flaws.

▪ *Women are nurturers.* Women give, men receive. Women give themselves, their bodies, their pleasures to men. Everyone else's needs come first; his desire over hers, his orgasm over hers. If a woman always puts her partner's enjoyment first, she may be depriving herself of her own enjoyment. As Barbach (1982) points out, "If our attention is so totally riveted on another person, or on external events rather than on ourselves, it is impossible to experience the full pleasure and sensation of the sexual event."

▪ *There is only one right way to have an orgasm.* Women often "learn" that there is only one "right" way to have an orgasm: during sexual intercourse as a result of penile stimulation. But there are many ways to have an orgasm: through oral sex; manual stimulation before, during, or after intercourse; masturbation; and so on.

Changing Gender Roles

Contemporary gender roles are evolving from traditional hierarchical gender roles (in which one sex is subordinate to the other) to more egalitarian roles (in which both sexes are treated equally) and to androgynous roles (in which both sexes display the instrumental and expressive traits previously associated with one sex). Thus, contemporary gender roles often display traditional elements as well as egalitarian and androgynous ones.

The beautiful bird gets caged.
—*Chinese proverb*

Although attitudes toward motherhood are changing, especially among middle-class Whites, it continues to be highly valued in our culture.

Motherhood Reexamined   Changes in women's roles profoundly reinforce the contemporary trend to separate sex from reproduction. Record numbers of women are reexamining motherhood because of the conflicts child rearing creates with marriage and work. Parenthood may now be considered a choice because of the availability of birth control and the social acceptance of child-free lifestyles. Approximately 9.3% of American women between the ages of 18 and 34 do not plan to have children (U.S. Bureau of the Census, 1996).

Though there are differences in attitudes and customs in child rearing, mothers from all cultures share more similarities than they do differences. Hopes, aspirations, desire to survive, search for love, and need for family are very much the same for all mothers, regardless of ethnicity or socioeconomic status (DeGenova, 1997). For African American mothers, however, the scope and character of family life are greatly related to socioeconomic status. American families of African heritage that are impoverished and female-headed have vastly different patterns and expectations than do those from the working, middle, and upper classes (Wilkinson, 1997). For Latinas, lower socioeconomic status, lower level of education, strong affiliation with Catholicism, and strong belief in consanguineal relationships contribute to higher birth rates (Sanchez, 1997).

Involvement in the church is central to many families in supporting and supplementing family and community life. Regardless of a family's circumstances or finances, the health and economic needs of the children are of primary concern and are central to child raising. Child-centered homes, often nurtured and supported by an extended family, are the constant for which most mothers strive.

Many people are also reexamining fatherhood and the male role in the family. Many of those in the evolving men's movement share the beliefs of feminism: equal pay for equal work, more parental leave for mothers and fathers, and better child-care facilities (Wood, 1994). Others, such as those involved in Promise Keepers, embrace the expectations of traditional masculinity and seek the support of other men in defining themselves according to Biblical models.

> I don't know why people are afraid of new ideas. I am terrified of the old ones.
>
> —*John Cage (1912–1992)*

Contemporary Sexual Scripts   As gender roles change, so do sexual scripts. Traditional sexual scripts have been challenged by more liberal and egalitarian ones. Sexual attitudes and behaviors have become increasingly liberal for both White and African American males and females, although African American attitudes and behaviors continue to be somewhat more liberal (Gutherie, 1988; Peters & Wyatt, 1988; Weinberg & Wilson, 1988). Many college-age women have made an explicit break with the more traditional scripts, especially the good girl/bad girl dichotomy and the belief that "nice" girls don't enjoy sex (Moffatt, 1989). Older professional women who are single also appear to reject the old images (Davidson & Darling, 1988). We do not know how Latino sexuality and Asian American sexuality have changed, as there is almost no research on their sexual scripts, values, and behaviors.

Contemporary sexual scripts include the following elements for both sexes (Gagnon & Simon, 1987; Reed & Weinberg, 1984; Rubin, 1990; Seidman, 1989):

- Sexual expression is a positive good.
- Sexual activities are a mutual exchange of erotic pleasure.
- Sexuality is equally involving, and both partners are equally responsible.
- Legitimate sexual activities are not limited to sexual intercourse but also include masturbation and oral-genital sex.
- Sexual activities may be initiated by either partner.
- Both partners have a right to experience orgasm, whether through intercourse, oral-genital sex, or manual stimulation.
- Premarital sex is acceptable within a relationship context.

These contemporary scripts give increasing recognition to female sexuality. They are increasingly relationship-centered rather than male-centered. Women, however, are still not granted full sexual equality with males.

Androgyny

> Once made equal to man, woman becomes his superior.
>
> —*Socrates (c. 469–399 B.C.)*

Some scholars have challenged the traditional masculine/feminine gender-role dichotomy, arguing that such models are unhealthy and fail to reflect the real world. Instead of looking at gender roles in terms of polarized opposites, they suggest examining them in terms of androgyny (Roopnarine & Mounts, 1987). **Androgyny** refers to flexibility in gender roles and the unique combination of instrumental and expressive traits as influenced by individual differences, situations, and stages in the life cycle (Bem, 1975; Kaplan, 1979). (The term "androgyny" is derived from the Greek *andros,* man, and *gyne,* woman.) An androgynous person combines both the instrumental traits traditionally associated with masculinity and the expressive traits associated with traditional femininity. An androgynous lifestyle allows men and women to choose from the full range of emotions and behaviors, according to their temperament, situation, and common humanity, rather than their gender. Men are permitted to cry and display tenderness; they can touch, feel, and nurture without being considered effeminate. Women can be aggressive or career-oriented; they can seek leadership and can be mechanical or physical.

DID YOU EVER wonder what effect being androgynous might have on relationships, self-esteem, and even willingness to exercise? There is evidence that androgynous individuals and couples have a greater ability to form and sustain intimate relationships and adopt a wide range of behaviors and values (Ickes, 1993). Androgynous college students and other adults tend to have greater confidence in social situations than individuals who are **sex-typed,** following gender-role stereotypes. Masculine and androgynous people of both sexes are more independent and less likely to have their opinions influenced than are those who label themselves highly feminine. At the same time, feminine and androgynous people of both sexes appear to be more nurturing than those who describe themselves as typically masculine (Bem, Martyna, & Watson, 1976).

In addition, androgynous people have shown greater resilience to stress (Ross & Cohen, 1987). They are more aware of feelings of love and more expressive of them (Ganong & Coleman, 1987). Androgynous couples may have greater satisfaction in their relationships than sex-typed couples. Transcending traditional female and male behaviors and values, androgynous couples are more flexible in their responses to each other and to the environment. Androgyny even seems to affect health behaviors. Androgynous individuals, for example, are more likely to exercise and not to smoke (Shifren, Bauserman, & Carter, 1993).

Androgyny, however, does not necessarily equate to better. Some studies have indicated that androgyny may increase job-related stress and adversely affect emotional adjustment (Lee & Schurer, 1983; Rotherman & Weiner, 1983). As in many areas of human sexuality, more research needs to be conducted before we can make conclusive statements about the effects of androgyny on mental, marital, and physical health.

Flexibility and adaptability are important aspects of androgyny (Vonk & Ashmore, 1993). Individuals who are rigidly instrumental or expressive, despite the situation, are not considered androgynous. A woman who is always aggressive at work and passive at home, for example, would not be considered androgynous, as work may call for compassion and home life for assertion.

It is not clear what proportion of individuals may be identified as androgynous or traditional. Although it has been suggested that androgyny is a White middle-class concept, one study of African American women (Binion, 1990) indicated that 37% identified themselves as androgynous, 18% as feminine, and 24% as masculine. (The remaining women did not identify themselves.) That such a large percentage was androgynous or masculine, the study argues, is not surprising, given the demanding family responsibilities and cultural expectations that require instrumental and active traits.

Androgyny, like other personality theories, assumes that masculinity and femininity are basic aspects of an individual's personality. It assumes that when we are active, we are expressing our masculine side, and when we are sensitive, we are expressing the feminine side of our personality. Androgyny retains the concept of masculinity and femininity, and thus it retains some of the categories of bipolar gender-role thinking (Willemsen, 1993).

Living up to an androgynous gender role, however, may be just as stultifying to an individual as trying to be traditionally feminine or masculine. In advocating the expression of both feminine and masculine traits, perhaps we are imposing a new form of gender-role rigidity on ourselves. Bem, one of the leading proponents of androgyny, has become increasingly critical of the idea. She believes now that androgyny replaces "a prescription to be masculine or feminine with the doubly incarcerating prescription to be masculine *and* feminine. The individual now has not one but two potential sources of inadequacy to contend with" (Bem, 1983).

> Throughout history the more complex activities have been defined and redefined, now as male, now as female—sometimes as drawing equally on the gifts of both sexes. When an activity to which each sex could have contributed is limited to one sex, a rich, differentiated quality is lost from the activity itself.
>
> —*Margaret Mead (1901–1978)*

Androgyny allows greater flexibility in behavior.

WHEN GENDER IS AMBIGUOUS: INTERSEXUALITY, TRANSSEXUALITY, AND TRANSGENDERISM

For most of us, there is no question about our gender: We *know* we are female or male. We may question our femininity or masculinity, but rarely do we question being female or male. For hermaphrodites and transgendered individuals, however, "What sex am I?" is a real and painful question. Their dilemma, however, reinforces the fact that gender identity as male or female is not "natural" but learned.

Because our culture views sexual anatomy as a male/female dichotomy, it is difficult for many to accept the more recent view of anatomical sex differentiation as existing on a male/female continuum with several dimensions (Intersex Society of North America, 1995) (see Figure 5.1). Most people still think of genetic sex—XX or XY—as a person's "true sex." Yet approximately 0.2% of the population (1 in every 500 individuals) has a set of chromosomes other than these.

Intersexuality: Atypical Chromosomal and Hormonal Conditions

Researchers have long recognized the existence of individuals who are **intersexed,** that is, who display mixtures of male and female anatomical characteristics. Unusual genital or physical development can make a person's sex unclear. Usually such ambiguity is caused by chromosomal or hormonal errors during prenatal development. Sometimes a child is born with an underdeveloped penis or an enlarged clitoris, making it unclear whether the child is male or female. The most common chromosomal and hormonal errors in prenatal development are discussed below. They are summarized in Table 5.1.

Hermaphrodites   Many intersexed individuals are **hermaphrodites,** males or females possessing the sex characteristics of both sexes. A *true hermaphrodite* develops both male and female gonads: either one of each, two of each, or two ovotestes (gonads that have both ovarian and testicular tissue in the same gland). It is estimated that true hermaphrodism occurs in 0.015 per 1000 live births (Intersex Society of North America, 1995). The external appearance of a true hermaphrodite is ambiguous, with genital and other physical characteristics of both sexes. **Pseudohermaphrodites** have two testes or two ovaries but an ambiguous genital appearance. (Although rare among humans, hermaphroditism is fairly common in the animal world, where snails, for example, possess the reproductive organs of both sexes, changing "genders" for the purpose of copulation.)

Chromosomal Disorders   Chromosomal disorders are common. One study of 35,000 Danish newborns found that the incidence of sex chromosome disorders was 1 in 426 children, or 2.34 in 1000 (Nielsen & Wohlert, 1991). Chromosomal abnormalities occur when an individual has fewer or more X or Y chromosomes than normal. Two syndromes resulting from erroneous chromosomal patterns may result in gender confusion: Turner syndrome and Klinefelter syndrome. In both of these, the body develops with some marked physical characteristics of the other sex.

TABLE 5.1 Abnormalities in Prenatal Development						
	Chromosomal Sex*	*Gonads*	*Internal Reproductive Structures*	*External Reproductive Structures*	*Secondary Sex Characteristics*	*Gender Identity*
Chromosomal Abnormalities						
Turner syndrome	Female (45, XO)	Nonfunctioning or absent ovaries	Normal female except for ovaries	Underdeveloped genitals	No breast development or menstruation at puberty	Female
Klinefelter syndrome	Male (47, XXY)	Testes	Normal male	Small penis and testes	Female secondary sex characteristics develop at puberty	Male, but frequent gender confusion at puberty
Hormonal Abnormalities						
Androgen-insensitivity syndrome	Male (46, XY)	Testes, but body unable to utilize androgen (testosterone)	Shallow vagina, lacks normal male structures	Labia	Female secondary sex characteristics develop at puberty; no menstruation	Female
Congenital adrenal hyperplasia (pseudo-hermaphroditism)	Female (46, XX)	Ovaries	Normal female	Ambiguous tending toward male appearance; fused vagina and enlarged clitoris may be mistaken for empty scrotal sac and micropenis	Female secondary sex characteristics develop at puberty	Usually male unless condition discovered at birth and corrected by hormonal therapy
DHT deficiency	Male (46, XY)	Testes undescended until puberty	Partially formed internal structures but no prostate	Ambiguous; clitoral-appearing micropenis; penis enlarges and testes descend at puberty	Male secondary sex characteristics develop at puberty	Female identity until puberty; majority assume male identity later

*Chromosomal sex refers to 46, XX (female) or 46, XY (male). Sometimes a chromosome will be missing, as in 45, XO, or there will be an extra chromosome, as in 47, XXY. In these notations, the number refers to the number of chromosomes (46, in 23 pairs, is normal); the letters X and Y refer to chromosomes and O refers to a missing chromosome.

TURNER SYNDROME   Females with **Turner syndrome** are born lacking an X chromosome (notated as 45, XO). It is one of the most common chromosomal disorders among females, occurring about once in 2500 live births (Mullins, Lynch, Orten, & Youll et al., 1991). Infants and young girls with Turner syndrome appear normal externally, but they have no ovaries. At puberty, changes initiated by ovarian hormones cannot take place. The body does not gain a mature look or height, and menstruation cannot occur. The adolescent girl may question her femaleness because she does not menstruate or develop breasts or pubic hair like her peers. Girls with Turner syndrome may have academic problems and be involved in fewer social activities (Rovet & Ireland, 1994). Hormonal therapy, including estrogen therapy and human growth hormone (HGH) therapy, replaces the hormones necessary to produce normal adolescent changes, such as growth and menstruation (LaFranchi, 1992; Rongen-Westerlaken, Vanes, Wit, Otten, & Demuinkkeizer-Schrama, 1992; Rosenfeld, Frane, Attie, Brasel, Bursten, & Clara, 1992). Even with hormonal therapy, however, women with Turner syndrome will likely remain infertile, although they may successfully give birth through embryo transfer following in vitro fertilization with donated ova (Rogers, Murphy, Leeton, Hoise, & Beaton, 1992).

KLINEFELTER SYNDROME   Males with **Klinefelter syndrome** have one or more extra X chromosomes (47, XXY; 48, XXXY; or 49, XXXXY). Klinefelter syndrome is quite common, occurring in 1 in 500–1000 male births (Intersex Society of North America, 1995). The effects of Klinefelter are variable, and many men with Klinefelter are never diagnosed. The presence of the Y chromosome designates a person as male. It causes the formation of small, firm testes and ensures a masculine physical appearance. However, the presence of a double X chromosome pattern, which is a female trait, adds some female physical traits. At puberty, female secondary sex characteristics such as breasts and hips develop, and male characteristics tend to be weak: small penis and testes; scanty, soft body hair. The XXY male is often confused about his gender identity. He may be subject to teasing or ridicule by others. If the condition is identified early, many of the problems associated with it will respond to hormonal treatment (Mandoki, Sumner, Hoffman, & Riconda, 1991). Because of low testosterone levels, the vast majority of males with the syndrome are unable to experience erections; virtually all are sterile. So that they can develop male secondary sex characteristics like their peers, boys with Klinefelter are given testosterone. Men often continue the supplemental hormone throughout their lives to maintain a masculine appearance and libido.

Hormonal Disorders   Hormonal imbalances may cause males or females to develop physical characteristics associated with the other sex.

ANDROGEN-INSENSITIVITY SYNDROME   **Androgen-insensitivity syndrome**, or **testicular feminization**, is a genetic, inherited condition passed through X chromosomes (except for occasional spontaneous mutations) (Williams, Patterson, & Hughes, 1993; see Kaplan & Owett, 1993, for female androgen-deficiency syndrome). It occurs in 1 in 20,000 individuals (Intersex Society of North America, 1995). A genetic male (XY) is born with testes, but because of his body's inability to absorb testosterone, the estrogen influence prevails. From the earliest stages, therefore, his body tends toward a female appearance, failing to develop male internal and external reproductive structures. Externally the infant is female, with labia and vagina, but the internal female structures are not present. At puberty, the body develops breasts, hips, and other secondary female sex characteristics. The testes remain in the abdomen and are sterile. People with androgen insensitivity are usually assigned female gender status at birth (Gooren & Cohen-Kettenis, 1991; Shah, Wooley, & Costin, 1992).

Physically, individuals with androgen-insensitivity syndrome develop as typical females, except for their inability to menstruate. It is often not until puberty that the physical anomaly is discovered. Usually the person is comfortable about her female gender identity. She can enjoy sex and orgasm.

CONGENITAL ADRENAL HYPERPLASIA   In **congenital adrenal hyperplasia** (formerly known as adrenogenital syndrome), a genetic female (XX) with ovaries and a vagina develops externally as a male, the result of a malfunctioning adrenal gland. This condition is the most prevalent cause of intersexuality among females, with a frequency of about 1 in 20,000 births (Intersex Society of North America, 1995). It occurs when the adrenal gland produces androgen instead of androgen-inhibiting cortisone.

At birth, the child appears to be a male with a penis and an empty scrotum. The appearance, however, may be ambiguous. Some have only an enlarged clitoris, with or without a vaginal opening, some a micropenis, and some a complete penis and scrotum. When the situation is discovered at birth, the child is usually assigned female status, and treatment is given to promote female development. If the condition is discovered after the child establishes a male gender identity, a decision has traditionally been made to support the male gender identity or to initiate a sex change.

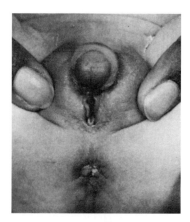

The genitals of a fetally androgenized female may resemble those of a male.

DHT DEFICIENCY   Because of a genetic disorder, some males are unable to convert testosterone to the hormone dihydrotestosterone (DHT). This disorder is known as **DHT deficiency.** DHT is required for the normal development of external male genitals. At birth, children with DHT deficiency have internal male organs but a clitorislike penis, undescended testes, a labialike scrotum, and a closed vaginal cavity. They are usually identified as girls. At puberty, however, their testes descend and their clitoris begins to resemble a penis.

A study of 18 children born with DHT deficiency in a small village in the Dominican Republic provides some evidence that hormones influence gender identity (Imperato-McGinley, 1974, 1979). Because of DHT deficiency, the children's penises were underdeveloped and resembled clitorides. The children led typical lives as girls, but when they reached adolescence, the DHT deficiency reversed and their bodies developed normal male characteristics. Their testes descended and their "clitorides" matured into penises.

If socialization were the most important factor in developing gender identity and gender roles, one would expect the children to remain psychologically female. Of the 18 children, however, only one chose to remain female. The others adopted male gender roles. The child who remained female married a man and became transgendered; another child who adopted the male gender identity and gender role cross-dressed.

The research was provocative because it suggests that gender identity is biologically determined rather than learned, and that gender identity can be changed without severe emotional trauma. The study has been criticized, however, on several counts. First, the children's genitals were ambiguous rather than completely female in appearance; it is unlikely that the children would have been treated as "normal" girls. Second, after the children developed penises, others may have encouraged them to act as males. Third,

EACH YEAR AN estimated 1000 babies are born in the U.S. with sex organs that cannot be classified as strictly male or strictly female. These sexually ambiguous infants are typically given a gender assignment (usually female) along with treatment to support the assignment, including surgery and, later, hormones and psychotherapy. Physicians have defended the practice of "correcting" ambiguous genitals, citing the success of current technology. Recently, however, this practice has undergone scrutiny by researchers and patients who point to the lack of evidence supporting its long-term success.

The protocol of surgical correction was established largely by Dr. John Money, a medical psychologist at Johns Hopkins Medical Center. Underlying Money's work are the beliefs that gender identity is determined not by biological traits but rather by the way a child is raised and that intersexed children are born psychosexually malleable. Since Money's research was first published, 15,000 sex reassignment procedures have been performed on infants. The American Academy of Pediatrics currently maintains that children born with ambiguous genitals "can be raised successfully as members of either sex" and recommends surgery within the first 15 months of life. The following beliefs are held strongly enough that they might be considered medical protocols: (1) individuals are psychosexually neutral at birth; (2) healthy psychosexual development is dependent on the appearance of one's genitals; (3) doubt about sex assignment should not be allowed; (4) sex should not be changed after 2 years of age.

The research of Dr. Milton Diamond, a noted endocrinologist and researcher now at the University of Hawaii, challenges the traditional pediatric postulates for sex assignment/reassignment. Diamond's research suggests that one's sexual identity is not fixed by the gender of rearing, that atypical as well as typical persons undergo psychosexual development, and that sexual orientation develops independent of rearing. As a result, Diamond recommends the adoption of a new set of postulates: (1) individuals are psychosexually biased at birth; (2) psychosexual development is related to but not dependent on the appearance of the genitals; (3) any doubt about gender, identity, or orientation should be discussed openly and fully; (4) change of sex should be supported whenever it is by informed choice (Diamond, 1997). His model urges physicians to show caution and conservatism in advising sex assignment/reassignment.

An emerging community of unhappy individuals willing to come out with their medical histories concurs with Diamond. They consider surgery to be a technology best delayed unless medically urgent (as when a genetic anomaly interferes with urination or creates a risk of infection) or requested by the individual. They believe that letting well enough alone is the better choice and that the erotic and reproductive needs of the adult should take precedence over the cosmetic needs of the child. Pointing to their own dissatisfaction as well as the lack of research supporting the long-term success of surgical treatment, they recommend that the professional community offer support and information to parents and the family and empower the intersexed individual to understand his or her status and choose (or reject) medical intervention (Intersex Society of North America, 1995).

No position has all the evidence in its favor, and resolution is not a simple matter. Nevertheless, many feel it is time that both professionals and families begin to question the research and listen to the stories of those whose lives have been affected by the practice known as "gender correction."

because DHT deficiency was relatively common for the village (the condition was known locally as *machihembra*—"male-female"), the transition from female to male may have been institutionalized. Finally, other studies conflict with the Dominican Republic studies. If there is a hormonal contribution to gender identity, it may be considerably weaker than the Dominican study suggests.

Transsexuality

Gender dysphoria is the state of dissatisfaction individuals experience when they feel they are trapped in a body of the "wrong" sex (Freund & Watson, 1993; Pauly, 1990). They feel they are not *really* the gender to which their genitals have "condemned" them. Gender-dysphoric people who wish to have, or have had, their genitals surgically altered to conform to their gender identity are known as **transsexuals.**

In transsexuality, a person's gender identity and sexual anatomy are at war. Transsexuals are convinced that by some strange quirk of fate they have been given a body of the wrong sex. They generally want to change their sex, not their personality. Many have little interest in sexual relationships. It is more important for them to acquire the anatomy of the desired gender than to have greater sexual satisfaction (Arndt, 1991; Braunthal, 1981).

Transsexuality revolves around issues of gender identity; it is a distinctly different phenomenon from homosexuality. Gay men and lesbians are not transsexuals. In contrast to transsexuals, lesbians and gay men feel confident of their female or male identity. Being lesbian or gay reflects sexual orientation rather than gender questioning. A study of female-to-male transsexuals and lesbians, for example, revealed that most members of both groups had sexual experiences with males, but the female-to-male transsexuals fantasized being males, whereas the lesbians completely identified with being female (McCauley & Ehrhardt, 1980). Furthermore, following surgery, transsexuals may or may not change their sexual orientation, whether it is toward members of the same, the other, or both sexes.

As mentioned, transsexuals often seek surgery to bring their genitals in line with their gender identity (Hausman, 1993). Male-to-female operations outnumber female-to-male by a ratio of 3 to 1. Some male-to-female transsexuals forgo the surgery but still identify themselves as women; they may choose to call themselves either transsexual or transgendered.

The prevalence of transsexuality is unknown, though it is estimated that there may be 1 transsexual per 50,000 people over age 15. There are also no known statistics on the number of postoperative transsexuals, but estimates range from 6000 to 11,000 in the United States (Selvin, 1993). Both of these numbers may be low, considering the cultural and religious biases, social stigmas, and financial constraints that many transsexual individuals experience. Some cultures, however, accept a gender identity that is not congruent with sexual anatomy and create an alternative third sex, as we saw in Chapter 1. "Men-women"—Native American two-spirits, Indian *hijas*, and Burmese *acaults*—are considered a third gender (Bullough, 1991; Coleman, Colgan, & Gooren, 1992; Roscoe, 1991). Members of this third gender are often believed to possess spiritual powers because of their "specialness."

There are no known definitive causes of transsexuality (Arndt, 1991; Bullough, 1991; Money, 1980). Among individuals known as *primary transsexuals*, transsexuality may begin in childhood; it is detectable sometimes in the first two years after birth. *Secondary transsexuals* experience gender dysphoria later, usually in adulthood. Parents of primary transsexuals often remark that their male children, who by age 4 or 5 identified themselves psychologically as girls, had acted as girls from the very beginning. Throughout childhood, these children engaged in girls' activities, play, and dress; they moved, walked, and ran as girls. Their playmates were girls. By the time the transsexual child reaches late adolescence, he may request an operation to change his genitals to those of a woman. The adolescent has usually learned the roles associated with femininity so well that he can easily pass as a woman in most situations.

Because primary transsexuals have lived much of their lives in their preferred gender (despite their genitals), they are often able to move into their

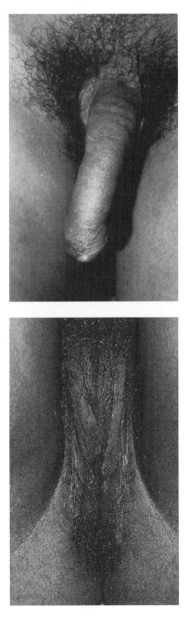

The genitals of a postoperative female-to-male transsexual, above, and the genitals of a postoperative male-to-female transsexual, below.

"new" gender with relative ease. Secondary transsexuals, however, who have lived most of their lives in their assigned gender, have more difficulty in making the transition to the behaviors associated with their preferred gender (Leavitt & Berger, 1990).

Until recently, transsexuality was considered a psychiatric disorder. However, the fourth edition of the American Psychiatric Association's *Diagnostic and Statistical Manual of Mental Disorders* no longer considers transsexuality per se an impairment. To be diagnosed with what is now called a **gender identity disorder,** one must show a strong and consistent cross-gender identity, demonstrate a persistent discomfort with one's sex or the gender role of one's sex, have a disturbance that is not concurrent with a physical intersex condition, and demonstrate a disturbance that causes clinically significant distress or impairment in social, occupational, or other areas of functioning. Given all of these conditions, assumptions of pathology or lack of psychological health among transgendered or transsexual individuals may no longer be warranted.

The Transgender Phenomenon

Within the past 10 years, there has been a major shift in the gender world. Upsetting old definitions and classification systems, a new **transgendered** community, one that embraces the possibility of numerous genders and multiple social identities, has emerged (Figure 5.1). This "complexity of gender offers serious challenges to scientific paradigms that conflate sex and gender" (Bolin, 1997).

Transgenderism is an inclusive category. The term "transgenderist" was first coined by Virginia Prince, the founding mother of the U.S. contemporary cross-dressing community, to describe someone who lives full-time in a gender role opposite to the gender role presumed by society to match the person's genetic sex (Richards, 1997). The key difference between a transsexual and a transgenderist is that the latter has no burning desire to alter his or her genitals to live in society in a role with which he or she feels comfortable. Thus, transgenderists do as little or as much as they wish to their bodies but stop short of genital surgery (Denny, 1997).

In past decades, those who were transgendered could escape from the traditional male and female categories only if they were "diagnosed" as transvestite or transsexual (Denny, 1997). This resulted in a larger number of "heterosexual" cross-dressers who were actually gay or bisexual or who had transsexual issues. It also involved diagnosis on the part of the psychiatric community and subsequent labeling and stigma. Over the past 5 years in North America, a paradigm shift has occurred that challenges the male/female polarization of gender, thereby making it more acceptable to live in a permanent preoperative state without the threat of "cure." This acceptance has "opened the door for political and scientific activism and the realization that being preoperative is not inevitably a way-station on the road to surgery" (Denny, 1997).

According to Dr. Walter O. Bockting, affiliated with the University of Minnesota School of Medicine's Human Sexuality Program, the paradigm shift in the transgendered experience includes changes in the following arenas (Bockting, 1997):

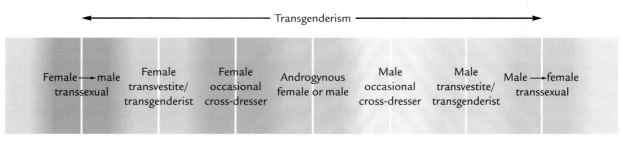

FIGURE 5.1 Nontraditional Gender Roles: The Gender Continuum. The concept of gender is viewed as a continuum, with a multitude of possible gender-variant behaviors.

■ *Sociocultural.* The prevailing gender schema of Western culture is challenged by transgendered identities that transcend two sexes. The number of transsexual men with vaginas, women with penises and breasts, and individuals who cross or transcend culturally defined gender lines is growing, and these people are becoming a more visible part of society.

■ *Interpersonal.* In coming out to their families, friends, and co-workers, transgenderists are now affirming their unique transgendered sexual identity. No longer conforming to a conventional heterosexual or homosexual pattern, they are creating unique gender roles and new sexual scripts in intimate relationships.

■ *Intrapersonal.* Self-affirmation of one's identity alleviates shame and is liberating. The pressure of trying to conform and the secrecy involved in hiding one's transgendered or transsexual status can be eliminated by coming out.

Transgenderist Sky Renfro describes his gender identity (cited in Feinberg, 1996):

My identity, like everything else in my life, is a journey. It is a process and an adventure that in some ways brings me back to myself, back into the grand circle of living. . . . My sense of who I am at any given time is somewhere on that wheel and the place that I occupy there can change depending on the season and life events as well as a number of other influences. Trying to envision masculine at one end of a line and feminine on the other, with the rest of us somewhere on that line, is a difficult concept for me to grasp. Male and female—they're so close to each other, they sit next to each other on that wheel. They are not at opposite ends as far as I can tell. In fact, they are so close that they're sometimes not distinguishable.

This paradigm shift in thinking regarding gender has implications for the clinical management of gender dysphoria. Treatment is no longer aimed at identifying the "true transsexual" but is open instead to the possibility of affirming a unique transgender identity and role (Bockting, 1997).

The fact that we are all human beings is infinitely more important than all the peculiarities that distinguish humans from one another.

—*Simone de Beauvoir (1908–1986)*

Treat people as if they were what they ought to be and you help them become what they are capable of being.

—*Johann Goethe (1749–1832)*

■ We ordinarily take our gender as female or male for granted. The making of gender, however, is a complex process involving both biological and psychological elements. Biologically, we are male or female in terms of genetic and anatomical makeup. Psychologically, we are male or female in terms of our assigned gender and our gender identity. Only in rare cases, as

MANY TRANSSEXUALS do not view their dilemma as a psychological problem but as a medical one. As a result, they tend to seek surgeons who may change their genitals rather than psychiatrists who can help them to examine and then to match their gender identity with their physical body. Sexual reassignment is not about sex but rather about matching one's gender identity to one's physiological status.

Gender-dysphoric individuals seeking **sex reassignment surgery (SRS),** the surgical process by which the reproductive organs are surgically altered from one sex to the other, go through a comprehensive treatment program prior to their operation. The goal of the surgery is to reduce the needless suffering and psychological adjustment problems that occur when the genitals do not conform to the brain's gender. In the early years of sex reassignment surgery, people who came to a professional saying they were transsexual were forced to prove it. More recently, client-centered programs have been designed in which people can obtain whatever therapeutic services they need. The following treatment modalities are often followed:

1. *Gender dysphoria therapy.* The client meets with a therapist or group of other gender-dysphoric individuals regularly for a period of 6 months. The client often demonstrates a persistent desire to be rid of his or her assigned gender and genitals, a feeling that has existed for at least 2 years prior to hormonal treatment (Chong, 1990). The therapist uses psychological tests and therapy to exclude mental disorders such as schizophrenia and to rule out individuals who may be confused about their sexual orientation or may simply wish to cross-dress. One study reported that 23% of those attending a gender-dysphoric clinic eventually were referred to sex reassignment surgery (Burns, Farrell, & Christie-Brown, 1990).

2. *Hormonal treatment.* Preoperative male-to-female transsexuals receive estrogen therapy, and preoperative female-to-male transsexuals receive testosterone therapy. These therapies induce the appropriate secondary sex characteristics, such as breasts for male-to-female transsexuals and facial and body hair and penises (enlarged clitorides) for female-to-male transsexuals. Dramatic changes are observable in the female-to-male therapies, such as male pattern baldness (if the gene is present), facial hair, and shifts of body weight.

3. *Living as a member of the preferred gender.* The client enters a real-life test lasting up to 2 years as a member of the preferred gender. This is not an easy task, for such subtle gender clues as mannerisms, voice inflections, and body movement, learned in childhood, must be altered.

4. *Sex reassignment surgery (SRS).* For male-to-female transsexuals, SRS involves a penile inversion technique in which doctors create a vaginal cavity with inverted penile skin. A clitoris is formed from penile corpus spongiosum, and inner and outer lips are crafted from scrotal tissue. Other cosmetic procedures, such as nose surgery, tracheal shave, and breast augmentation, may be performed to enhance femininity (Biber, 1997). By this time, electrolysis has probably been completed. Though there may be some decline in orgasmic capacity, most male-to-females report an enjoyment of sexual activities (Lief & Habschman, 1993). In female-to-male SRS, the ovaries, uterus, and breasts are removed. The clitoris, which has been enlarged by testosterone therapy, is refashioned into a penis, and the labia are formed into a scrotum. Several techniques may be used to simulate penile erection, ranging from the insertion of a semierect rod to the surgical implantation of an inflatable device. Most female-to-male transsexuals report an increase in orgasmic capacity (Lief & Habschman, 1993).

Between 6000 and 11,000 individuals have undergone surgery to correct nature's anatomical "mistake." Unfortunately, there have been few long-term studies of the impact of SRS on adjustment. Several factors appear to affect the satisfaction of postoperative transsexuals. First, the surgery must be skillfully done so that the transsexual will have a positive body image. Second, transsexual gay men and lesbians are generally more satisfied with their transsexual status than are heterosexuals (Blanchard et al., 1989). Third, female-to-male transsexuals appear to be more satisfied than male-to-female transsexuals in terms of sexual satisfaction and intimate relationships, both preoperatively and postoperatively (Kockott & Fahrner, 1988). Fourth, primary transsexuals have an easier adjustment than secondary transsexuals because of their greater amount of experience in their preferred gender (Leavitt & Berger, 1990).

Going public with the change involves significant risk for the transsexual, both personally and professionally. Because they are not specifically protected from discrimination in the workplace under the categories of "race, creed, color, ancestry, age, sex, sexual orientation, disability, or place of birth," transsexuals have good reason to be apprehensive. This situation is changing in a handful of cities where laws have been enacted to protect transsexuals. Legally, most states will issue new birth certificates, or amend existing ones, so they match the new status of the individual.

with chromosomal and hormonal disorders or gender dysphoria, is our gender identity problematic. For most of us, gender identity is rarely a source of concern. More often, what concerns us is related to our gender roles: Am I sufficiently masculine? Feminine? What it means to be feminine or masculine differs from culture to culture. Although femininity and masculinity are generally regarded as opposites in our culture, there are relatively few significant inherent differences between the sexes aside from males impregnating and females giving birth and lactating. The majority of social and psychological differences are exaggerated or culturally encouraged. All in all, women and men are more similar than different.

SUMMARY

Studying Gender and Gender Roles

- *Sex* is the biological aspect of being female or male. *Gender* is the social and cultural characteristics associated with biological sex. Normal gender development depends on both biological and psychological factors. Psychological factors include *assigned gender* and *gender identity. Gender roles* are the roles that tell us how we are to act as men and women in a particular culture.

- Although our culture encourages us to think that men and women are "opposite" sexes, they are more similar than dissimilar. Innate gender differences are generally minimal; differences are encouraged by socialization.

- Masculine and feminine stereotypes assume heterosexuality. If men or women do not fit the stereotypes, they are likely to be considered gay or lesbian. Gay men and lesbians, however, are as likely as heterosexuals to be masculine or feminine.

- *Gender theory* examines gender as a basic element in society and social arrangements. It focuses on how gender is created and how and why specific traits, behaviors, and roles benefit or cost women and men. In general, gender theorists believe gender differences are socially created to benefit men.

Gender-Role Learning

- *Cognitive social learning theory* emphasizes learning behaviors from others through *cognition* and *modeling. Cognitive development theory* asserts that once children learn gender is permanent, they independently strive to act like "proper" girls and boys because of an internal need for congruence.

- Children learn their gender roles from parents through manipulation, channeling, verbal appellation, and activity exposure. Parents, teachers, *peers*, and the media are the most important agents of socialization during childhood and adolescence.

- A *gender schema* is a set of interrelated ideas used to organize information about the world on the basis of gender. We use our gender schema to classify many non–gender-related objects, behaviors, and activities as male or female.

Contemporary Gender Roles

- The traditional male gender role is *instrumental*. It emphasizes aggression, independence, and sexual prowess. Traditional male sexual scripts include the denial of the expression of feelings, an emphasis on performance and being in charge, the belief that men always want sex and that all physical contact leads to sex, and assumptions that sex equals intercourse and that sexual intercourse always leads to orgasm.

- Traditional female roles are *expressive*. They emphasize passivity, compliance, physical attractiveness, and being a wife and mother. Female sexual *scripts* suggest that sex is good and bad (depending on the context); genitals should not be touched; sex is for men; men should know what women want; women shouldn't talk about sex; women should look like models; women are nurturers; and there is only one right way to experience an orgasm.

- Contemporary gender roles are more egalitarian than the traditional roles. Important changes affecting today's gender roles include increasing questioning, especially among White women, of motherhood as a core female identity; and the breakdown of the instrumental/expressive dichotomy.

- Contemporary sexual scripts are more egalitarian than traditional ones and include the belief that sex is a positive good, that it involves a mutual exchange, and that it may be initiated by either partner.

- *Androgyny* combines traditional female and male characteristics into a more flexible pattern of behavior, rather than seeing them as opposites. Evidence suggests that androgyny contributes to psychological and emotional health.

When Gender Is Ambiguous: Intersexuality, Transsexuality, and Transgenderism

- A number of hormonal and chromosomal disorders can affect gender development. Some of these can result in people who are known as *hermaphrodites* or *pseudohermaphrodites*. Chromosomal abnormalities include *Turner syndrome* and *Klinefelter syndrome*. Hormonal disorders include *androgen-insensitivity syndrome, congenital adrenal hyperplasia,* and *DHT deficiency.*

- *Gender dysphoria* is the state of dissatisfaction individuals may experience about their gender. People who have (or plan to have) surgery to construct the "appropriate" gender are known as *transsexuals.* This surgery is known as *sex reassignment surgery (SRS).* The causes of transsexuality are not known. Transsexuality per se is no longer considered a psychiatric disorder.

- A transgendered community, one that embraces the possibility of numerous genders and multiple social identities, has emerged. A *transgendered* individual is one who lives full-time in a gender role opposite to the gender role presumed by society to match that person's genetic sex.

SUGGESTED READING

Bonvillain, Nancy. (1998). *Women and Men: Cultural Constructs of Gender* (2nd ed.). Englewood Cliffs, New Jersey: Prentice-Hall. Highlights the importance of structural relationships and ideological constructs in supporting and legitimizing behaviors.

Bullough, Bonnie, Bullough, Vern L., & Elias, James (Eds.). (1997). *Gender Blending.* New York: Prometheus Books. A collection of scholarly and personal essays that point out the changes and the research being done around issues of gender.

Buss, David M. (1994). *The Evolution of Desire: Strategies of Human Mating.* New York: Basic Books. A sociobiological approach to human sexual behavior.

Fausto-Sterling, Anne. (1985). *Myths of Gender: Biological Theories About Women and Men.* New York: Basic Books. A well-written book by a developmental geneticist arguing that most biological explanations of gender differences are unscientific justifications for traditional gender roles that subordinate women to men.

Kimmel, Michael S., & Messner, Michael A. (1995). *Men's Lives* (2nd ed.). Englewood Cliffs, New Jersey: Prentice-Hall. A collection of essays on contemporary multiethnic masculinity.

Rhode, Deborah. (1997). *Speaking of Sex: The Denial of Gender Inequality.* Cambridge, MA: Harvard University Press. A book about sexual inequality and the law that combines empirical data, theoretical insight, and good sense.

Tavris, Carol. (1992). *The Mismeasure of Woman.* New York: Simon & Schuster. An examination of various misconceptions and biases that affect our understanding of women; includes critiques of sociobiology, the G-spot, premenstrual and postmenstrual syndromes, and the codependency and addiction movements.

Wainrib, Barbara Rubin (Ed.). (1992). *Gender Issues Across the Life Cycle.* New York: Springer. Clinically oriented essays on developmental issues facing men and women from adolescence through old age.

6

Sexuality Over the Life Span

*A*s we consider the human life cycle from birth to death, we cannot help but be struck by how profoundly sexuality weaves its way through our lives. From the moment we are born, we are rich in sexual and erotic potential, which begins to take shape in our sexual experimentations of childhood. As children, we are still unformed, but the world around us helps shape our sexuality. In adolescence, our education continues as a random mixture of learning and yearning. But as we enter adulthood, with greater experience and understanding, we develop a potentially mature sexuality. We establish our sexual orientation as heterosexual, gay, lesbian, or bisexual; we integrate love and sexuality; we forge intimate connections and make commitments; we make decisions regarding our fertility; we develop a coherent sexual philosophy. Then, in our middle years, we redefine sex in our intimate relationships, accept our aging, and reevaluate our sexual philosophy. Finally, as we become elderly, we reinterpret the meaning of sexuality in accordance with the erotic capabilities of our bodies. We come to terms with the possible loss of our partner and our own eventual decline. In all these stages, sexuality weaves its bright and dark threads through our lives.

In this chapter, we discuss both the innate and the learned aspects of sexuality, from infancy through late adulthood. We discuss both physical development and **psychosexual development,** which involves the psychological aspects of sexuality. We see how culture, the family, the media, and other factors affect children's feelings about their bodies and influence their sexual feelings and activities. We look at how the physical changes experienced by teenagers affect their sexual awareness and sexual identity as heterosexual, gay, or lesbian. We discuss adolescent sexual behaviors, sex education, teenage pregnancy, and teenage parenthood. Next, we turn to middle adulthood, where we look at developmental concerns, marital and extramarital sexuality, and divorce and sexuality. Finally, we look at sexuality in late adulthood, examining developmental issues, age, stereotypes, differences in aging between men and women, and the role of the partner in sustaining health.

SEXUALITY IN INFANCY AND CHILDHOOD

Our understanding of infant sexuality is based on observation and inference. It is obvious that babies derive sensual pleasure from stroking, cuddling, bathing, and other tactile stimulation. Ernest Borneman, a researcher of children's sexuality since the 1950s, suggests that the first phase of sexual development be called the cutaneous phase (from the Greek *kytos,* skin). During this period, an infant's skin can be considered a "single erogenous zone" (Borneman, 1983).

The young child's healthy psychosexual development lays the foundation for further stages of growth. Psychosexual maturity, including the ability to love, begins to develop in infancy, when babies are lovingly touched all over their appealing little bodies (which appear to be designed to attract the caresses of their elders).

Infants and very young children communicate by smiling, gesturing, crying, and so on. Before they understand our words, they learn to interpret our movements, facial expressions, body language, and tone of voice. Our

Conscience is the inner voice which warns us that someone may be looking.

—*H. L. Mencken (1880–1956)*

Kissing and cuddling are essential to an infant's healthy psychosexual development.

earliest lessons are conveyed in these ways. During infancy, we begin to learn how we "should" feel about our bodies. If a parent frowns, speaks sharply, or spanks an exploring hand, the infant quickly learns that a particular activity—touching the genitals, for example—is not right. The infant may or may not continue the activity, but if he or she does, it will be in secret, probably accompanied by the beginnings of guilt and shame (Renshaw, 1988).

Infants also learn about the gender role they are expected to fulfill. In our culture, baby girls are often handled more gently than baby boys. They are dressed up more and given soft toys and dolls to play with. Baby boys are expected to be "tough." Their dads may roughhouse with them and speak more loudly to them than to their sisters. They are given "boy toys"—blocks, cars, and tiny plastic "superheroes." This gender-role learning is reinforced as the child grows older (see Chapter 5).

Childhood Sexuality

Children become aware of sex and sexuality much earlier than many people realize. They generally learn to disguise their interest rather than risk the

Children are naturally curious about bodies. It is important that these kinds of explorations not be labeled "bad." Many sex educators advise parents to allow young children to observe each other naked in such settings as the bathroom or at the beach.

disapproval of their elders, but they continue as small scientists—collecting data, performing experiments, and attending conferences with their colleagues.

Curiosity and Sex Play   Starting as early as age 3, when they begin playful interaction with their peers, children begin to explore their bodies together. They may masturbate or play "mommy and daddy" and hug and kiss and lie on top of each other; they may play "doctor" so that they can look at each other's genitals (Berends & Caron, 1994). Letty Cottin Pogrebin (1983) suggests that we think of children as "students" rather than "voyeurs." It is important for them to know what others look like in order to feel comfortable about themselves.

Dr. Mary Calderone (1983b) stresses that children's sexual interest should never be labeled "bad," but that it may be called inappropriate for certain times, places, or persons. According to Calderone, "The attitude of the parents should be to socialize for privacy rather than to punish or forbid."

Children who participate in sex play generally do so with members of their own sex. Most go on to develop heterosexual orientations; some do not. But whatever a person's sexual orientation, it seems clear that childhood sex play does not create the orientation. The origins of homosexuality are not well understood; in some cases, there may indeed be a biological basis. Many gay men and lesbians say they first became aware of their attraction to members of the same sex during childhood, but many heterosexuals also report such feelings. Homosexual feelings and behaviors appear to be quite common and congruent with healthy psychological development in heterosexuals, lesbians, and gays (Van Wyk & Geist, 1984).

If children's natural curiosity about their sexuality is satisfied, they are likely to feel comfortable with their own bodies as adults (Renshaw, 1988). This is especially important for little girls, whose parents rarely discuss their daughters' genitals or teach the proper names for them (vulva, vagina, clitoris, urethra). Girls may learn to devalue their sexuality not because of the "mysterious and concealed nature" of their anatomy but because of the "mysterious and concealed nature of [their parents'] communication about it" (Pogrebin, 1983). By providing socially accepted guidelines for their children's behavior and accepting their children's sexual exploration as a positive and normal part of growth, parents can help facilitate the development of healthy sexuality in their children (Fishel, 1992; Harmon & Johnson, 1993).

Parents should be taught to bless, honor, dignify, conserve, and celebrate their children's sexuality.

—Committee report to SIECUS by an interfaith group of clergy

Masturbation and Permission to Feel Pleasure   It is a safe bet to say that most of us masturbate; it is also safe to say that most of us were raised to feel guilty about it. The message "If it feels good, it's bad" is often internalized at an early age, leading to psychological and sexual disorders in later life. Virtually all sex researchers and therapists advise that masturbation is not harmful. Some also suggest that there are physically harmful effects from "early sexual deprivation" (Money, 1980; Pogrebin, 1983). (Masturbation is discussed further in Chapter 9.)

Learning about sex in our society is learning about guilt.

—John Gagnon and William Simon

Children need to understand that pleasure from self-stimulation is normal and acceptable (Feitel, 1990). They also should know that self-stimulation is something we do in private, something that some people are uncomfortable with. It is important for young children to know the proper names of their genitals and what they are for (pleasure, elimination, future reproduction).

The Family Context

Family styles of physical expression and feelings about modesty and privacy vary considerably.

Family Nudity   Some families are comfortable with nudity in a variety of contexts: bathing, swimming, sunbathing, dressing, undressing. Others are comfortable with partial nudity from time to time: when sharing the bathroom, changing clothes, and so on. Still others are more modest and carefully guard their privacy. Most researchers and therapists would allow that all these styles can be compatible with the creation of sexually well-adjusted children, as long as some basic guidelines are observed:

- *Accept and respect a child's body (and nudity).* If 4-year-old Katie runs naked into her parents' dinner party, she should be greeted with friendliness, not horror or harsh words. If her parents are truly uncomfortable, they can help her get dressed matter-of-factly, without recrimination.

- *Do not punish or humiliate a child for seeing a parent naked, going to the bathroom, or making love.* If the parent screams or lunges for a towel, little Robbie will think he has witnessed something wicked or frightening. He can be gently reminded that mommy or daddy wants privacy at the moment.

▪ *Respect a child's need for privacy.* Many children, especially as they approach puberty, become quite modest. It is a violation of the child's developing sense of self not to respect his or her need for privacy. If 9-year-old Mark starts meticulously locking the bathroom door or 11-year-old Sarah covers her chest when a parent interrupts her while she is dressing, it is most likely a sign of normal development. Children whose privacy and modesty are respected will learn to respect those of others.

Expressing Affection   Families also vary in the amount and type of physical contact in which they participate. Some families hug and kiss, give back rubs, sit and lean on each other, and generally maintain a high degree of physical closeness. Some parents extend this closeness to their sleeping habits, allowing their infants and small children in their beds each night. (In many cultures, this is the rule rather than the exception.) Other families limit their contact to hugs and tickles. Variations of this kind are normal. Concerning children's needs for physical contact, we can make the following generalizations:

1. *All children (and adults) need freely given physical affection from those they love.* Although there is no prescription for the right amount or form of such expression, its quantity and quality both affect children's emotional well-being and the emotional and sexual health of the adults they will become (Hatfield, 1994; Kagan, 1976; Montauk & Clasen, 1989).

2. *Children should be told, in a nonthreatening way, what kind of touching by adults is "good" and what is "bad."* Children need to feel that they are in charge of their own bodies, that parts of their bodies are "private property," and that no adult has the right to touch them with sexual intent.

3. *It is not necessary to frighten a child by going into great detail about the kinds of things that might happen.* A better strategy is to instill a sense of self-worth and confidence in children, so they will not allow themselves to be victimized.

4. *We should listen to children and trust them.* Children need to know that if they are sexually abused, it is not their fault. They need to feel that they can tell about it and still be worthy of love.

SEXUALITY IN ADOLESCENCE

Puberty is the stage of human development when the body becomes capable of reproduction. For legal purposes (laws relating to child abuse, for example), puberty is considered to begin at age 12 for girls and age 14 for boys. **Adolescence** is the social and psychological state that occurs between the beginning of puberty and acceptance into full adulthood.

Psychosexual Development

Adolescents are sexually mature (or close to it) in a physical sense, but they are still learning their gender roles and social roles, and they still have much to learn about their sexual scripts (see Chapter 5). They may also be struggling to understand the meaning of their sexual feelings for others and their sexual orientation.

Physical Changes During Puberty   The physical changes of puberty are centered around the development of secondary sex characteristics (in both sexes) and the onset of menstruation (in girls) and ejaculation (in boys).

In girls, physical changes usually begin between ages 9 and 14. These include a rapid increase in height (called the growth spurt), the beginnings of breast development, the growth of pubic and underarm hair, and the onset of vaginal mucous secretions. Menarche, the onset of menstruation, follows within a year or two. The average age of menstruation is 12 or 13, although girls may begin menstruating as early as age 9 or as late as age 17. Although menstruation is a basic part of female maturation, a study by the manufacturers of Tampax tampons, conducted in the early 1980s, revealed that one-third of the girls and women polled did not know what was happening to them when they got their first menstrual period (Sarrel & Sarrel, 1984).

Breast development is a visible symbol of approaching womanhood. Some girls who develop early may feel awkward and embarrassed. Those who develop slowly may feel anxious and insecure.

In boys, physical changes include a growth spurt; hand and foot growth; muscle-mass growth; voice deepening; and hair growth on the face, the underarms, and the pubic area, and sometimes other parts of the body. The boy's penis and testicles also develop. Some boys reach puberty around the time they enter junior high school (about age 12); others, not until their later teens. Generally, however, they lag about 2 years behind girls in pubertal development.

At puberty, boys begin to ejaculate semen, which accompanies the experience of orgasm they may have been having for some time. Just as girls often do not know what is happening when they begin to menstruate, many boys are unnerved by the first appearance of semen as a result of masturbation, or by nocturnal emissions during sleep ("wet dreams"). Like menstruation for girls, the onset of ejaculation is a sexual milestone for boys. It is the beginning of their fertility. Kinsey called first ejaculation the most important psychosexual event in male adolescence (Kinsey et al., 1948).

Influences on Psychosexual Development   Besides biological forces, many other influences are involved in adolescent psychosexual development. Peer pressure, the perceived attitudes and opinions of their friends, is the single most powerful social influence on adolescents. One educator (De Armand, 1983) found that ninth-graders ranked "Friends/Peer Group" and "Everybody's Doing It" as their leading influences. Parents were ranked fifth or sixth by most. Other research has found the media, especially television, to be highly influential in shaping adolescent values, attitudes, and behavior (see Chapter 1).

PARENTAL INFLUENCE   Children learn a great deal about sexuality from their parents. For the most part, however, they don't learn because their parents set out to teach them but because they are avid observers of their parents' behavior. Much of what they learn concerns the hidden nature of sexuality.

As they enter adolescence, young people are especially concerned about their own sexuality, but they are often too embarrassed to ask their parents directly about these "secret" matters. And most parents are ambivalent about

Most mothers think that to keep young people from love making it is enough not to speak of it in their presence.

—*Marie Madeline de la Fayette (1678)*

their children's developing sexual nature. They are often fearful that their children (daughters especially) will become sexually active if they have "too much" information. They tend to indulge in wishful thinking: "I'm sure Jenny's not really interested in boys yet"; "I know Joey would never do anything like that." Parents may put off talking seriously with their children about sex, waiting for the "right time." Or they may bring up the subject once, make their points, breathe a sigh of relief, and never mention it again. Sociologist John Gagnon calls this the "inoculation" theory of sex education: "Once is enough" (Roberts, 1983). But children need frequent "boosters" where sexual knowledge is concerned. When a parent does undertake to educate a child about sex, it is usually the mother (Nolin & Petersen, 1992). Thus, most children grow up believing that sexuality is an issue that men don't deal with unless they have a specific problem.

Recent research indicates that parental concern and involvement with sons and daughters is a key factor in preventing risky behaviors, including early sexual intercourse (Resnick et al., 1997). Based on surveys from roughly 110,000 students from grades 7 through 12, the congressionally mandated and federally funded National Longitudinal Study of Adolescent Health found that young people who feel close to their parents, believe their parents and family members care about them, and are satisfied with their family relationships are the least likely to engage in risky behaviors. Among these behaviors are cigarette, alcohol, and marijuana use; violent behavior; suicide; and early sexual intercourse. The study also found that among those 1 in 5 adolescents who work 20 or more hours a week, there is increased emotional distress, smoking, substance abuse, and early sexual intercourse.

A strong bond with parents appears to lessen teenagers' dependence on the approval of their peers and their need for interpersonal bonding, which may lead to sexual relationships (DiBlasio & Benda, 1992; Miller & Fox, 1987). But parents also need to be aware of the importance of friends in their teenagers' lives. Families that stress familial loyalty and togetherness over interactions with others outside the family may set the stage for rebellion. Traditional Latino families, for example, may expect that daughters will spend most of their time at home, often caring for their siblings. This can lead to conflict because the "mainstream culture" expects teenagers of both sexes to be socially active (Guerrero Pavich, 1986).

Parents can also contribute to their children's feelings of self-worth by their ongoing demonstrations of acceptance and affection. Adolescents need to know that their sexuality is OK and that they are loved in spite of the changes they are going through (Gecas & Seff, 1991). Whereas low self-esteem increases vulnerability to peer pressure, high self-esteem increases adolescents' confidence and can enhance their sense of responsibility regarding their sexual behavior.

PEER INFLUENCE   Adolescents garner a wealth of misinformation from each other about sex. They also put pressure on each other to carry out traditional sex roles. Boys encourage other boys to be sexually active even if they are unprepared or uninterested. They must camouflage their inexperience with bravado, which increases misinformation; they cannot reveal sexual ignorance. Bill Cosby (1968) recalled the pressure to have sexual intercourse as an adolescent: "But how do you find out how to do it without blowin' the

fact that you don't know how to do it?" On his way to his first sexual encounter, he realized that he didn't have the faintest idea of how to proceed:

> So now I'm walkin', and I'm trying to figure out what to do. And when I get there, the most embarrassing thing is gonna be when I have to take my pants down. See, right away, then, I'm buck naked . . . buck naked in front of this girl. Now, what happens then? Do . . . do you just . . . I don't even know what to do . . . I'm gonna just stand there and she's gonna say, "You don't know how to do it." And I'm gonna say, "Yes, I do, but I forgot." I never thought of her showing me, because I'm a man and I don't want her to show me. I don't want nobody to show me, but I wish somebody would kinda slip me a note.

Even though many teenagers find their early sexual experiences less than satisfying, they still seem to feel a great deal of pressure to conform, which means continuing to be sexually active (DiBlasio & Benda, 1992). The following are typical statements from a group of teenagers in a study by Children's Home Society (De Armand, 1983): "I had to do it. I was the only virgin" (from a 15-year-old girl); "If you want a boyfriend, you have to put out" (from a 13-year-old girl); "You do what your friends do or you will be bugged about it" (from a 12-year-old boy). The students interviewed also said that "everyone" has to make the decision about having sexual intercourse by age 14. Researcher Charlotte De Armand comments that although, of course, "not 'everyone' is involved, certainly a large number of young people are making this decision at 14 or younger."

For boys, especially those with working-class backgrounds, adolescence is characterized by **homosociality,** relationships in which self-esteem and

In addition to biological factors, social forces strongly influence young teenagers. Peers are very important, especially for boys, whose self-esteem and social status may be linked to evaluations from their friends. Because certain types of violence and aggression are considered "manly" by our society, the boys in this photograph (left) take great pleasure in an arcade game featuring simulated warfare. For adolescent girls, the physical and hormonal changes of puberty often result in a great deal of interest (some would say obsession) with personal appearance. Cultural norms and media influences emphasizing female beauty reinforce this interest.

status are more closely linked to evaluations from people of the same sex than of the other sex. Homosociality has important consequences in terms of relationships with girls. To a boy in a relationship characterized as homosocial, a girlfriend's importance may lie in giving him status among other boys, his relationship with her being secondary. The generalized role expectations of males—that they must be competitive, aggressive, and achievement-oriented—carry over into sexual activities. They receive recognition for "scoring" with a girl, much as they would for scoring a touchdown or hitting a home run. Girls, by contrast, run the risk of being labeled as "sluts" by both male and female peers if they have sex in any context other than a steady relationship (Pipher, 1994).

Sexual encounters, as opposed to sexual relationships, function in large part to confer status among teenage boys. Those who have experienced rigidly homosocial activities during adolescence are often limited in the range of their later heterosexual relationships. In adolescence, they may learn to relate to women in terms of their own status needs, rather than as people. As a result, some men find it difficult to develop **heterosociality**, friendships with members of the other sex or relationships in which sexual activities involve respect or love for a woman. Heterosocial relationships bind boys and girls and men and women together, in striking contrast to homosocial relationships, in which girls or women are used to bind boys or men together. Some researchers have noted increasing levels of heterosocial relationships among adolescents (Borneman, 1983).

THE MEDIA   As discussed in Chapter 1, we know that erotic portrayals—nudity, sexually provocative language, and displays of sexual passion—are of great interest to the American viewing public. This public includes many curious and malleable children and adolescents. To the extent that these erotic images or actions outside a real-life context are mistaken for reality, they are potentially confusing at best and dangerously misleading at worst (Strasburger, 1995). A survey of 391 adolescents found a strong correlation between sexual activity and watching TV shows with high sexual content. It did not determine, however, if the viewing led to sexual activity, or whether the sexual activity led to increased interest in viewing such programs (Brown & Newcomer, 1991).

Although some would choose to protect young viewers by censoring what is shown on television or played on the radio, a more viable solution to sexual hype in the media is to balance it with information about real life. Parents can help their children understand that sexuality occurs in a context, that it is complex, and that it entails a great deal of personal responsibility. Themes from television can be used by parents to initiate discussions about sex, love, and desire (including the desire of advertisers to sell their products).

Most important of all, perhaps, parents can encourage their children to think for themselves. Because adolescents generally feel a strong need to conform to the ideals of their subculture, it can be especially hard for them to discriminate between what they think they should do and what they actually feel comfortable doing. Much of the process of becoming a mature adult involves the rejection of these images and the discovery and embracing of one's own unique identity.

Gay and Lesbian Adolescents During adolescence and early adulthood, sexual orientation becomes a very salient issue. In fact, few adolescents experience this to be a trouble- or anxiety-free time. Many young people experience sexual fantasies involving others of their own sex; some engage in same-sex play. For many, these feelings of sexual attraction are a normal stage of sexual development, but for 3–10% of the population the realization of a romantic attraction to members of their own sex will begin to grow (Laumann et al., 1994; Remafedi, Resnick, Blum, & Harris, 1992). Some gay men and lesbians report that they began to be aware of their "difference" in middle or late childhood. Some, but not all, gay men report "feminine" behaviors or occurrences, such as a preference for girls' games, playing with dolls, imagining themselves as a model or dancer, or being called a sissy. (A number of heterosexual men also report these childhood behaviors, however.) More predictive of adult gay orientation is a lack of "masculine" behaviors, such as a preference for boys' games, rough-and-tumble play, a desire to grow up like one's father, and imagining oneself to be a sports figure (Hockenberry & Billingham, 1987; Phillips & Over, 1992). Gay and lesbian adolescents usually have heterosexual dating experiences during their teens, but they report ambivalent feelings about them.

Society in general has difficulty dealing with the fact of adolescent sexuality. The fact of gay and lesbian (or bisexual) adolescent sexuality has been virtually impossible for society to deal with. The "assumed heterosexuality" of society, which includes social scientists, educators, health-care providers, and so on, has resulted in the virtual invisibility of gay, lesbian, and bisexual youth (Savin-Williams & Rodriguez, 1993).

For virtually all gay and lesbian teens, the process of coming to terms with their sexuality and with the expectations of their parents and peers is

Lesbian and gay teenagers often have an especially difficult time coming to terms with their sexuality because society generally disapproves of their orientation.

Nowadays the polite form of homophobia is expressed in safeguarding the family, as if homosexuals somehow came into existence independent of families and without family ties.

—*Dennis Altman*

WHAT CAUSES HOMOSEXUALITY? What causes heterosexuality? Many have asked the first question, but few have asked the second. Although researchers don't understand the origins of sexual orientation in general, they have nevertheless focused almost exclusively on homosexuality. Their explanations generally fall into either biological or psychological categories.

Biological Theories

The earliest researchers, including Krafft-Ebing, Hirschfeld, and Ellis, believed that homosexuality was something hereditary. The biological perspective, however, lost influence over the years; it was replaced by psychological theories, most notably psychoanalytic theories. Recently, there has been some renewed interest in the biological perspective. Today, many researchers, as well as many gay men and lesbians, believe that homosexuality is innate—people are "born" homosexual. Researchers point to possible genetic or hormonal factors.

In the first controlled genetic study of homosexuality in 40 years, researchers found a strong genetic link in male homosexuality (Bailey & Pillard, 1991). The researchers matched 157 identical and fraternal twin brothers and adopted brothers the same age to determine if there was a genetic component in homosexuality. (Identical twins are genetic clones, having developed from a single egg that split after fertilization. Fraternal twins develop simultaneously from two separate eggs.) The study found that if one identical twin was gay, there was a 52% chance that his brother was also gay, compared with a 22% likelihood among fraternal twins and an 11% likelihood among genetically unrelated (adopted) brothers. The researchers estimated that the genetic contribu-

tion to male homosexuality could range from 30% to 70%. Next they conducted a study of lesbian and heterosexual twins that came to similar conclusions. They found that if one identical twin was lesbian, there was about a 50% chance that her sister was also lesbian (Bailey, Pillard, Neale, & Agyei, 1993).

More recently, scientists studied genetic material from 40 pairs of gay brothers and discovered that 33 of the pairs had identical pieces of the end tip of the X chromosome (Hamer, Hu, Magnuson, Hu, & Pattatucci, 1993). Ordinarily, only half the pairs should have shared the same region. (The odds, in fact, of such an occurrence randomly happening were less than half of 1%.) This finding indicates that there may be one or more genes that play a role in predisposing some men to homosexuality. Researchers caution, however, that they have not identified a specific gene linked to homosexuality. Furthermore, because their findings have not been replicated, additional studies are necessary to validate their hypothesis. Finally, sexual orientation is an extremely complex biological and social phenomenon; a genetic link, if it exists, represents only part of the picture.

Other researchers have explored the possibility that homosexuality could have a hormonal basis. Because hormonal levels are sensitive to such factors as general health, diet, smoking, and stress, it is very difficult to control studies measuring sexual orientation. A review by researcher John Money (1988b) of controlled studies comparing hormone levels of adult gay men, lesbians, and heterosexuals found no difference in circulating hormones.

It has also been hypothesized that prenatal hormonal levels may affect fetal brain development. Animal experiments have found that prenatally manipulating hor-

confusing and painful. Although there is more understanding of homosexuality now than in decades past, and more counseling and support services are available in some areas, young gays and lesbians are still subject to ridicule and rejection. A recent survey found that teens who identified themselves as gay, lesbian, or bisexual were more likely than heterosexual teens to have attempted suicide in the past year ("Gay Teens," 1998). They were nearly 5 times more likely to have been absent from school because of fears about safety and more than 4 times as likely to have been threatened with a weapon at school. Very few gay and lesbian teens feel they can talk to their parents about their sexual orientation. Many (especially boys) leave home or are "kicked out" because their parents cannot accept their sexuality. It is sobering to think that a significant number of our children are forced into

mones can cause ewes (female sheep) to engage in the mounting behavior associated with rams (Money, 1988b). Because there is a critical prenatal period for brain development in human fetuses, it is possible that the fetus may be affected by changes in the mother's hormonal levels.

Because it is unethical to experiment with living fetuses, we cannot come to any meaningful conclusions about the effect of hormones on fetal brain development. There are some relevant studies, however. An analysis of maternal stress found no correlation among stress, hormonal fluctuation, and sexual orientation (Bailey, Willerman, & Parks, 1991). But it has been found that women who took the synthetic estrogen DES when pregnant were more likely to have daughters with bisexual or homosexual tendencies (Fagin, 1995). No such increase was found in males. The results suggest that although exposure to estrogenic chemicals in the womb is not a dominant cause of homosexuality, it may be one of many causes—some inborn and some learned.

In a study conducted by Simon LeVay (1991) on gay men and heterosexual men and women, LeVay found that the brain's anterior hypothalamus, which influences sexual behavior, was smaller among gay men than among those he assumed were heterosexuals. But because the study was conducted on the cadavers of gay men who had died from AIDS, the smaller hypothalamic size may have resulted from the disease. It may also have resulted from their behavior.

The present state of biological theories on sexual orientation "is one of inclusive complexity" (Bailey, 1995).

Social Constructionism and Psychological Theories

A different school of thought, known as social constructionism, regards sexual orientation as a malleable concept that varies from one culture to another. Daryl Bem, a social psychologist from Cornell University, advances this concept by theorizing that children who infrequently view members of the other sex (and in a minority of the cases, members of the same sex) see them as exotic. Exotic peers elicit physiological tingles and jolts that seem offensive at first but that fire up sexual desire later in life (Bower, 1996).

Psychoanalysis provided the earliest psychological theory accounting for the development of homosexuality. Freud believed that human beings were initially bisexual but gradually developed heterosexuality. But if children did not successfully resolve their Oedipus or Electra complex, their development would be arrested. In the 1960s, psychoanalyst Irving Bieber (1962), reflecting popular stereotypes, proposed that men became homosexual because they were afraid of women. In a study of 200 heterosexual and gay men, Bieber found that gay men tended to have overprotective, dominant mothers and passive or absent fathers in contrast to heterosexuals. A review of Bieber's and similar studies found that there was some evidence to support the view that males from such families are slightly more likely to be gay (Marmor, 1980c). But one women (Price, 1993) asks, tongue-in-cheek: "If having a dominant mother and a weak or absent father were truly a recipe for homosexuality, wouldn't most Americans be gay?"

Because research on the origins of sexual orientation examines homosexuality and not heterosexuality as well, there tends to be an underlying bias that homosexuality is not an acceptable or normal sexual variation. This bias has skewed research studies, especially psychoanalytic studies. As homosexuality has become increasingly accepted by researchers as a normal sexual variation, scholars have shifted their research from determining the "causes" of homosexuality to understanding the nature of gay and lesbian relationships.

secrecy and suffering because of society's reluctance to openly acknowledge the existence of homosexual orientations.

Nevertheless, evidence suggests a positive association between coming out to one's self and feelings of self-worth. Those who are out to self and have integrated a sexual identity with their overall personal identity are usually more psychologically well adjusted than individuals who have not moved through this process (Savin-Williams, 1995).

Developing a mature identity is more formidable for gay, lesbian, and bisexual individuals who also face issues of color. The racial or ethnic background of a youth may be both an impediment and an advantage in forming a sexual identity. Though racial, ethnic, and cultural communities can provide identification, support, and affirmation, all too often families and peer groups within the community present youth with biases and prejudices that undermine the process of self-acceptance as a lesbian or gay man. The young person may have to struggle with the question of whether sexual orientation or ethnic identification is more important; he or she may even have to choose one identity over the other.

Adolescent Sexual Behavior

Hormonal changes during puberty, which serve the human species by preparing each member for his or her reproductive function, bring about a dramatic increase in sexual interest.

Masturbation   If children have not begun masturbating before adolescence, the chances are good that they will begin once the hormonal and physical changes of puberty start. Masturbation is less common among African Americans and Latinos, however, than among Whites (Belcastro, 1985; Cortese, 1989). Although reliable statistics are not available, it is known that masturbation is more common among males than females. Data indicate that of those adolescents who do masturbate, boys do so about 3 times more frequently than girls (Leitenber, Detzer, & Srebnik, 1993). By the time adolescents enter college, about 5 out of 6 males and 7 or 8 out of 10 females masturbate (Sarrel & Sarrel, 1984). Rates of masturbation appear to be affected by a wide range of social factors, though it is not clear whether they are also affected by sexual interaction with a partner (Laumann et al., 1994). In addition to providing release from sexual tension, masturbation gives us the opportunity to learn about our own sexual functioning, knowledge that can later be shared with a sexual partner. Despite these positive aspects, adolescents, especially girls, often feel very concerned and guilty about their autoerotic activities.

First Base, Second Base: A Normative Sequence of Behaviors   Most heterosexual adolescent couples follow a normative pattern in the sequence of their sexual behaviors: hand-holding, embracing, kissing, fondling and petting, and (for some) intercourse (Miller, Christopherson, & King, 1993). A study in the United States showed that a normative behavior sequence for White adolescents progressed from necking, feeling breasts through clothing, feeling breasts directly, feeling female genitals, feeling penis directly, to intercourse (occurring least often) (Smith & Udry, 1985). The sequence was not predictable, however, for young Blacks. For example, more African American adolescents had experienced intercourse than had engaged in unclothed petting involving either the breasts or the genitals. For most teens, both White and Black, however, increasing commitment to the relationship brought an increased desire for sexual intimacy. Emotional involvement expands the range of sexual behavior that is normatively acceptable (Thornton, 1990). (It is interesting to note that the literature on adolescent sexual behavior rarely mentions the role of love in sexuality. "Commitment" and "emotional involvement" may be cited as reasons for sexual intimacy, but the word "love" is almost never used.)

Kissing is an important activity for teenage couples. An adolescent's first erotic kiss often proves to be an unforgettable experience, "a milestone, a rite of passage, the beginning of adult sexuality" (Alapack, 1991). It is largely

For most teens, increased commitment to the relationship is accompanied by increased sexual intimacy.

through kissing that we learn to be sexually intimate, to be comfortable with physical closeness, and to give and take sexual pleasure. Young couples may spend hours alternately kissing and gazing into each other's eyes.

Oral sex among teenagers, including heterosexuals, lesbians, and gays, has apparently become increasingly frequent in recent years, paralleling its growing acceptability in the culture at large (Wilson & Medora, 1990). In a study of junior high school students, cunnilingus was the most commonly reported form of oral sex. Among the girls surveyed, more had given or received oral sex than had engaged in intercourse; among the boys, more had engaged in intercourse than had given or received oral sex (Newcomer & Udry, 1985).

First Intercourse and Virginity   With the advent of the "sexual revolution" in the late 1960s, adolescent sexual behavior began to change. The average age for first intercourse dropped sharply, and almost as many girls as boys engaged in it. In the 1990s, however, a modification in this trend was observed. A survey of 10,487 people, titled "The 1995 National Survey of Family Growth," found that 50% of females age 15–19 had experienced sexual intercourse. This statistic, a drop from the 55% reported in 1990, is the first reported decline in more than two decades ("Teen Sex Down," 1997). A similar trend was reported for teenage males. The percentage of never-married males age 15–19 years who had ever had sexual intercourse declined from 60% in 1988 to 55% in 1995. When looking at the age of the female and her male partner, this same study found that of those women who had had their first voluntary intercourse before age 16, 66% reported that their partner was under 18, 21% said their partner was 18 or 19, 7% said their partner was between 20 and 22, and 6% said their partner was 23 or older. Approximately 16% of girls whose first intercourse was before age 16 reported that their first intercourse was not voluntary, compared with just 3% of women whose first intercourse was at age 20 or older.

The most significant predictors of sexual intercourse among teenagers are alcohol use, having a boyfriend or girlfriend, poor parental monitoring, and permissive parental sexual values (Small & Luster, 1994). In the past, peer pressure among girls was an important factor in limiting their sexual behavior. Today, girls' peers seem to exert the opposite effect. However, teenagers may feel compelled to act more sexually sophisticated than they actually are; they may lie to protect themselves from being thought of as immature. The context in which they "give up" their virginity is still important for many girls; most feel that they are doing it for love.

In spite of increased social pressure to engage in intercourse, there are "significant fractions of Americans who experience first coitus after marriage" (Thornton, 1990). Among older teens and young adults who have experienced intercourse, many say they wish they had postponed first intercourse until they were more emotionally mature. See Figure 6.1 for information showing ages and percentages of teenagers who have had and have not had intercourse.

Adolescents and Contraception   Many teenagers, especially younger ones, do not take measures to protect themselves against pregnancy or sexually transmitted diseases (STDs) when they begin having sexual intercourse. (Adolescents and STDs are discussed in Chapters 15 and 16.) Use of contraception is lowest among young teens, African Americans and Hispanics, and fundamentalist Protestants and highest among Jewish women and those whose mothers graduated from high school (Mosher & McNally, 1991). Among women of all ages, some 76% of all those who began having intercourse in the 1990s used contraception at first intercourse. Teenage males also showed an increase in use of contraceptives in the 1990s.

Condoms are the method of choice among sexually active teens. The increase in use, from 18% in the 1970s to 54% in the 1990s, was reported by those who had received information on sexually transmitted diseases, safer sex to prevent HIV, and how to say no to sex ("Teen Sex Down," 1997). Still, almost half said they did not use a condom the last time they had sex (CDC, 1995). Along with condoms, withdrawal (an unreliable method) is the method most frequently practiced by teenagers who use contraception, although it may be less common now than a decade ago.

Young women involved in serious relationships are more likely to use a reliable contraceptive method, such as the pill, than are those who are just beginning to have intercourse. Hormonal implants (Norplant) may prove to be a popular method for teenagers, although they are relatively new on the market and at present require the outlay of several hundred dollars for

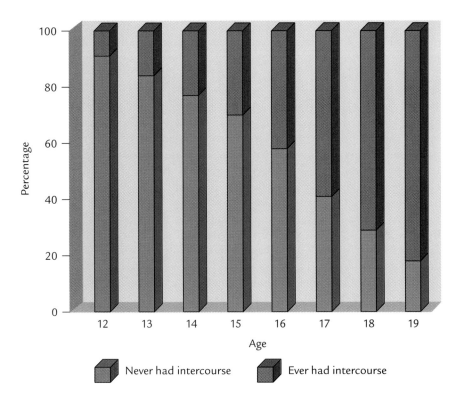

implantation. Implants do protect against pregnancy for 5 years, however. Among males, those who do poorly in school and lack long-term goals often have attitudes and practices that prevent them from using birth control. For reasons that are complex, these behaviors appear to be more common among teenagers of color, who may also view impregnating a woman as a sign of masculinity (Marsiglio & Shehan, 1993).

Adolescent Pregnancy

The Alan Guttmacher Institute, which researches family planning, indicates that about 22% of teenage girls between 15 and 19—more than a million American teenagers when girls under 15 are included—become pregnant every year in the United States. More than half of these pregnancies end in births (Figure 6.2). For nearly two-thirds of the births, the pregnancy was unintended ("Teen Sex Down," 1997).

In spite of the fact that nearly 4 in 10 teen pregnancies end in abortion (Alan Guttmacher Institute, 1996), teen pregnancies and births cost the United States more than $34 billion a year in medical, welfare, and related expenses (Center for Population Options, 1992). Since 1980, the rate of abortion has steadily declined, because fewer teenagers are becoming pregnant, and, in recent years, fewer pregnant teens have chosen to have an abortion.

Teen pregnancies trap most of the young mothers and fathers and their children in a downward spiral of lowered expectations and poverty. Because of poor nutrition and inadequate medical care during pregnancy, babies born to teenagers have twice the normal risk of low birth weight, which is responsible for numerous physical and developmental problems. Also, many of

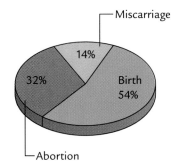

FIGURE 6.2.   Adolescent Pregnancy Outcomes. (*Source:* Alan Guttmacher Institute, 1996.)

these children will have disrupted family lives, absent fathers, and the attendant problems of poverty, such as poor diet, violent neighborhoods, limited health care, and limited access to education. They are also at higher risk of being abused than children born to older parents.

Why Teenagers Get Pregnant   Why do teenagers begin intercourse as early as they do, and why do they rarely use contraception? The forces of their hormones, combined with pressure from peers and the media, tend to propel teenagers into sexual activity before they are emotionally prepared for it. They often don't use contraception because they are afraid to acknowledge their sexuality; or they may have difficulties in obtaining it, be too embarrassed to ask for it, not know how to use it properly, or not have it readily available. They may underestimate the risks or not fully understand their implications. Results from a longitudinal study of youth reveal that race and ethnicity, poverty status, and family structure also play a role in adolescent and nonmarital childbearing (Trent & Crowder, 1997).

Not all teen pregnancies are accidental. About 20% of them are planned (Trent & Crowder, 1997). The pull of having someone to love them exclusively and unconditionally is strong for some girls. Some girls or couples see having a baby as a way to escape from an oppressive home environment. Both girls and boys may see parenthood as a way to enhance their status, to give them an aura of maturity, or to enhance their masculinity or femininity. Some believe a baby will cement a shaky relationship. (Many adult women and men choose to have babies for these same less-than-sensible reasons.) Unfortunately, for many expectant teens, parenthood may turn out to be as much a disaster as a blessing.

Teenage Mothers   Thirteen percent of all births in the United States are to teens. Most teenage mothers feel that they are "good" girls and that they became pregnant in a moment of unguarded passion. Apparently, most also say they would "do it again," although they would counsel other girls to use birth control in similar situations (Thompson, 1986). The reality of the *boy + girl = baby* equation often doesn't sink in until pregnancy is well advanced. This lack of realism makes it difficult (emotionally and physically) or impossible to have an abortion for those who might otherwise choose one. Teenage mothers are far more likely than other mothers to live below the poverty level and to receive welfare. In part because most teen mothers come from disadvantaged backgrounds, 28% of them remain poor in their 20s and early 30s, compared with 7% of mothers who first gave birth after adolescence (Alan Guttmacher Institute, 1996). Only about half of teen mothers finish high school, compared with 96% of girls who are not mothers (Wallis, 1985). They are significantly less likely to go on to college compared with women who delay childbearing. Planned Parenthood identifies teenage girls at greatest risk of becoming pregnant as those from single-parent homes, those whose mothers or sisters became pregnant in their teens, and those who do not do well in school (Beyette, 1986).

Not only are African American teens twice as likely to be sexually active as Whites, but their birth rates are also higher (Yawn & Yawn, 1997). This is partly explained by the way in which the forces of racism and poverty combine to limit the options of young people of color (Singh, 1986). (Poor Whites also have disproportionately high teenage birth rates.) But additional factors

COMPARED WITH OTHER Western countries, the United States has the highest rates of teen pregnancy, abortion, and childbirth (Carroll & Wolpe, 1996). The rates of teen pregnancy are 7 times higher than in the Netherlands and 17 times higher than in Japan (Society for Adolescent Medicine, 1991). The United States also leads Western countries in abortion rates by a wide margin. These countries have similar levels of sexual activity among teenagers. What is the reason for this huge birth rate discrepancy? In a word, contraception.

A multifaceted approach to reducing teen pregnancy is suggested by family planning experts, sociologists, demographers, and others who have studied these issues:

- The underlying issues of poverty and the racism that often reinforces it must be dealt with. There must be a more equitable distribution of income so that all children can have a true variety of educational, occupational, social, and personal options in their future.

- Contraception must be made available, along with practical information and a climate of openness about sexuality. This is one of the lessons to be learned from developed countries that have low teenage birth rates. Both sex education and tolerance of teenage sexual activity prevail in Western Europe.

The United States appears prudish and hypocritical by comparison.

- At the same time, schools, health-care agencies, and welfare agencies "have to be marching in the same direction, all at the same time" (Dryfoos, 1985). A concerted effort must be made to educate young people and to help them combat feelings of worthlessness and despair.

- Because parental attitudes play an important role in the sexual development of children, parents must also be educated so they become more knowledgeable and effective sex educators of their children. An emphasis on responsibility must prevail. At the same time, an appreciation of preexisting attitudes as well as a respect for cultural and ethnic differences must be built into any program that educates parents as well as their children.

- Reliable, specific information about sex and responsibility needs to be present on television and radio, in books, magazines, music, and advertisements. This requires a major overhaul in the way our society presents sex to its children and adolescents and may demand that adults reexamine their purchasing power.

contribute to pregnancy and childbirth among Black teens. For one thing, African American communities are far more accepting of births to unmarried women than their White counterparts; three-generation families are much more common, with the result that grandparents often have an active role in child rearing. (This is also true of Latino communities.) For another, there is often a great deal of pressure among young African American men (especially in communities with lower socioeconomic status) to prove their masculinity by engaging in sexual activity (Staples & Johnson, 1993; Yawn & Yawn, 1997). Another reason may be related to a lack of role models for African American girls (Wallis, 1985).

Teenage mothers have special needs. The most pressing that can be provided within the community are health care and education (Voydanoff & Donnelly, 1990). Regular prenatal (before the birth) care is essential to monitor fetal growth and the mother's health, including diet, possible sexually transmitted disease, and possible alcohol or drug use. Nevertheless, one-third of pregnant teens receive inadequate prenatal care. Babies born to young mothers are more likely to have childhood health problems and to be hospitalized than those born to older mothers (Alan Guttmacher Institute, 1996). After the birth, both mother and child need continuing care. The mother may need contraceptive counseling and services, and the child needs regular physical checkups and immunizations. Graduation from high school is an important goal of education programs for teenage mothers because it directly influences their employability and ability to support (or help support) themselves and their children. Many teenage mothers need financial assistance, at least until they complete their education. Programs such as TANF, food stamps, Medicaid, and WIC (Women, Infants, and Children, a program that provides coupons for essential foods) are often crucial to the survival of young mothers and their children. Such government programs are often underfunded and are periodically threatened with being cut off entirely. Even with programs such as these in place, most families need additional income to survive.

Coordination of health, educational, and social services is important because it reduces costs and provides the most comprehensive support (Voydanoff & Donnelly, 1990). School-based health clinics, which provide prenatal and postnatal care, contraception, and counseling, and teenage mother education programs, which provide general education, job skills, and life skills, are examples of coordinated care (Stevens-Simon & Beach, 1992). Such programs may be costly, but the costs of not providing these services are far greater.

Teenage Fathers   The incidence of teenage fatherhood is lower than that of teenage motherhood. The National Survey of Adolescent Males estimates the prevalence of teen fatherhood to be 2% for White males, 5% for African American males, and 2% for Hispanic males (Sonenstein, Pleck, & Ku, 1993). Teen fatherhood is not a function of any single risk factor (Thornberry, Smith, & Howard, 1997). Living in an inner city, having certain expectations and values about early childbearing, having poor school achievement, and engaging in delinquency behaviors seem to be pathways leading to adolescent fatherhood. Other risk factors include minority ethnic background and socioeconomic disadvantages.

Adolescent fathers typically remain physically or psychologically involved throughout the pregnancy and have "intimate feelings toward both mother and baby" (Robinson, 1988). Most continue to be involved with the mother during the pregnancy and for at least some period of time after the birth. About 10% of pregnant teenage couples marry, but the chances of the marriage working out are very slim (Robinson, 1988). It is usually difficult for teenage fathers to contribute much to the support of their children, although most express the intention of doing so during the pregnancy. Most have a lower income, less education, and more children than men who postpone having children until age 20 or more. They may feel overwhelmed at the responsibility and may doubt their ability to be good providers. Though many teenage fathers are the sons of absent fathers, most do want to learn to be fathers. Teen fathers are a seriously neglected group who face many hardships. Policy and intervention directed at reducing teen fatherhood will have to take into consideration the many factors that influence it and focus efforts throughout the life cycle (Thornberry, Smith, & Howard, 1997).

Sex Education

In the United States today, 70% of public school children receive some type of sex education before graduating from high school. As of 1993, 17 states required sex education, and 30 others recommended it (Carroll & Wolpe, 1996). Although many classes are far from comprehensive, a nationwide poll

Studies show that many teenage fathers continue to be involved with the mother during pregnancy and for at least some time following the birth. Most express interest in supporting their children, although in reality it often proves to be very difficult.

found that most Americans favor sex education, including AIDS education, endorse the use of condoms for prevention of disease and pregnancy, and favor integrating sex education into the elementary school curriculum (Kahn, 1990). Sex educators say that teenagers have pressing concerns about such subjects as contraception, abortion, masturbation, and homosexuality, yet these subjects are often considered taboo by schools. Why?

Different Values, Different Goals Among parents, teachers, and school administrators, there is substantial disagreement about what a "comprehensive"

IN TODAY'S WORLD, children and adolescents probably face more challenges relating to their sexuality than at any other time in history. In addition to the epidemic of AIDS and other STDs, factors contributing to the need for worldwide, culturally sensitive, and comprehensive sex education programs include the growing visibility of the media, changing attitudes toward sexuality, and increased mobility from family-centered communities to urban areas.

Europe

The Netherlands is a country hallmarked by its low rates of teenage pregnancy, abortion, and childbearing. Going against world opinion, the Netherlands initiated compulsory, comprehensive sex education programs and easily accessible birth control services for adolescents as early as the 1960s. Statistics bear out the success of these policies.

Its neighbor Belgium has a more complex social system. The division of church and government has resulted in two school systems. Because there is no standardized, government-endorsed sex education program, the provision of sex education depends largely on teacher motivation and local politics (Friedman, 1992). The relatively recent legalization of abortion has increased the number of family life and sexuality programs, though many programs still lack the comprehensive approach that seems to ensure success.

Like Denmark and Finland, Sweden enjoys a Nordic tradition of sexual openness. Swedes have long striven for an egalitarian lifestyle in which personal autonomy is respected, cohabitation is accepted, and gay and lesbian lifestyles are affirmed through policy. Reaching as far back as the 1920s, Sweden has also had an exceptionally long history of compulsory and standardized sex education programs. Acceptance of its curriculum and approach has been both community- and family-based.

Russia

A new government and new politics have led to some changes in policies and approaches to sex education in Russia. Abortion is clearly a major issue, with the average Russian woman having nearly seven pregnancies in her lifetime and anywhere from three to ten abortions (Shalin, 1990). Lack of information about sex, lack of contraceptives, high rates of prostitution, and essentially course in sex education should include. Some feel that only basic reproductive biology should be taught. Others see the prevention (or at least the reduction) of STDs as a legitimate goal of sex education. Still others would like the emphasis to be on the prevention of sexual activity among adolescents. Most sex educators seem to feel that *all* of these goals are worthy of pursuit. Many feel it's also important to address more controversial issues, such as the role of pleasure and desire, gay and lesbian sexual orientation, and the development of skills for making healthful, responsible decisions regarding sexual behavior. A common point of agreement is that the biology of sex must be taught within a larger context of building relationships based on dignity and respect (Gibbs, 1993).

Although the opposition to comprehensive sex education may be small, it is very vocal. The coalition, led by conservative parents, teachers, and religious groups, argues that to instruct children in the mechanics of birth control or abortion is to lead them down the path of self-destruction. In the absence of any national sex education consensus, the abstinence-only message has been quite successful in being adopted as the official curriculum in schools across the United States (Towle, 1993).

HIV/AIDS Education The alarming spread of sexually transmitted diseases, especially HIV infection and AIDS, has added to the controversy. Though condom use has increased since 1991, statistics show that almost half of high school students did not use condoms the last time they had sex (CDC, 1995a). In a survey of more than 4000 seventh- through twelfth-grade

nonexistent sex education in the schools are among the many issues faced by Russian society. Furthermore, both communism and the Russian Orthodox Church have opposed sexual and sensual images, seeing them as unimportant, distracting, and opposed to the goal of "social liberation" (Friedman, 1992). Thus a full language for sexual expression has been slow to develop. Sex education was not mandated for eighth-graders until the early 1980s and still falls short of what is needed. Advances in HIV/AIDS education and counseling have been left to the gay and lesbian community; however, it is still officially illegal in Russia to practice homosexuality. In short, Russian society appears to have much room for improvement in sex education.

Asia

In Japan, there is opposition to sex education. A sex education program in the schools was mandated in 1992 by the Japanese Ministry of Education, but response has been sluggish. Problems include lack of teacher support, lack of textbooks and teaching materials, an uncooperative Japanese school administration system, limited concepts of human sexuality in the culture, and an unbending educational philosophy that does not allow time for topics outside of the academic curriculum. According to a nationwide survey conducted in 1992, Japanese youth are more moderate in their sexual behavior than American youth; 22% of males and 16% of females had experienced sexual intercourse by the age of 18. The traditional value system, still held to by many Japanese youth, discourages premarital sexual activities and other unsanctioned sexual behaviors and may explain young people's moderate sexual behavior (Shimazaki, 1993–94). Sex education encourages individuals to make their own decisions and to take responsibility for their sexual choices; this tendency toward asserting one's individuality is also at odds with traditional Japanese values. Cultural values will probably have to change somewhat before sex education becomes firmly rooted in the schools and is viewed as a positive force in society.

In Hong Kong, formal sex education programs began appearing on television beginning in 1983. Conducted in a question-and-answer format and considered quite controversial, these programs first focused on women's sexuality and then on adolescent sexuality (Ng, 1993). Now that Hong Kong has been transferred to Chinese control, it will be interesting to watch how the new face of sex education evolves in that city.

teachers who taught subjects related to sex education, researchers found that most believed education regarding pregnancy, AIDS, and other STDs should be covered by grades seven and eight at the latest (Forrest & Silverman, 1989). The quality of HIV/AIDS education is also crucial because misinformation can cause unnecessary anxiety and fear.

Teaching About Homosexuality   Lessons about AIDS have brought the subject of homosexuality into the classroom. This is a highly controversial subject; some parents fear their children will "catch" it if they learn about it. Nevertheless, it is important for young people to understand that same-sex orientations are normal, for two principal reasons. One is that gay and lesbian teenagers need to have their identities validated; the other is that bias-related violence against gays and lesbians is largely perpetrated by teenage boys. Some school districts are taking steps to challenge prejudice against gays and lesbians. In 1992, the New York City Board of Education mandated that all curricula be revised to reflect diversity, including diversity in sexual orientation. (Parent opposition, however, forced cancellation of the curriculum.) In Los Angeles, a program called Project 10 offers counseling to gay and lesbian teens in the schools. In San Francisco, each school has a "gay-sensitive" staff member to work with gay and lesbian students (Humm, 1992; Uribe & Harbeck, 1991).

Too Little, Too Late   One reason sex education doesn't succeed better at reducing sexual activity, disease, and pregnancy may be that it is too little, too late. According to Leslie Kantor of the Sexuality Information and Education Council (1994), the most effective way to change behaviors is to provide opportunities for gaining knowledge, examining and modifying attitudes, and developing skills for implementing behaviors. This process can start as early as preschool with basic health information, lessons in self-esteem, and social skills development; over time, it can expand to include material relevant to student needs and concerns. By involving parents in the education process, a community can evolve that is educated and armed to face the complex issues of our times.

Abstinence-Only Programs   One kind of sex education curriculum that is increasing in popularity, often with the help of federal funds, stresses abstinence for teenagers as the only form of birth control. Such programs include Sex Respect, Facing Reality: Me & My World, My Future, and Teen Aid. There is little argument that children and adolescents should postpone sexual intercourse until they are mature. Not everyone, however, believes that schools should present sexuality in a negative light or attempt to scare young people into abstinence until they are married.

One argument for abstinence-only programs is that they reduce pregnancy rates. Evaluations of several programs claiming to have reduced pregnancy revealed that some of the data they reported were flawed (Kantor, 1994). For example, student attitudes and values were questioned, but not their behavior. And issues relating to anonymity and confidentiality were not clear.

Proponents of abstinence-only programs feel that information about sex damages a student's "natural modesty" and interferes with parent-child communication. Teachers and school administrators can maintain parental rights, however, by seeking and utilizing input from parents in developing curricula, by having parents included in curricular review committees, and by advocating "parental opt-out provisions," whereby parents can remove their child from any sex education program if they prefer to provide this type of education at home. The distinction between a parent rightfully interested in his or her own child's education and a parent who wants to restrict information from being taught to other people's children is an enormous one (Kantor, 1994).

The argument most often used against abstinence-only programs is that they are a thinly disguised effort to impose fundamentalist religious values on public school students, thus violating the constitutional separation of church and state (Towle, 1993). Furthermore, in court cases plaintiffs charge that abstinence-only programs are biased, sensationalist, and at times misleading. While state courts continue to rule on individual cases, sex educators and others wrestle with the real issue of combating misinformation. Such is the case with the Teen Aid program, which suggests that "the correct use of condoms does not prevent HIV infection but only delays it" and "the only way to avoid pregnancy is to abstain from genital contact." When accurate information is a matter of life and death, we cannot afford to be either modest or inaccurate.

Condoms in the Schools   Some school districts are attempting to address the problems of unintended pregnancies and sexually transmitted diseases among teenagers by making condoms available in the schools. Should schools be in the business of distributing condoms? This highly charged issue is creating controversy and causing moral and ideological debate among parents, clergy, politicians, and legislators.

For many, especially those in the public health community, the role of schools in distributing condoms is a health issue, that of preventing the spread of HIV infection, AIDS, and other STDs and reducing the number of unintended pregnancies. Many educators, however, view the issue with different priorities and restraints, the primary ones being staffing and liability.

Because the availability of condoms in schools is a relatively recent phenomenon, little is known about the most effective ways to make them available or about the impact of such availability on sexual behavior or condom use. A recent large-scale survey among high school students in New York City found that school-based condom availability can lower the risk of HIV and other STDs for urban teenagers (Guttmacher, Lieberman, Ward, Freudenberg, Radosh, & des Jarlais, 1997). The study also found that condom availability has a modest but significant effect on condom use and does not increase rates of sexual activity. Additional research has established that selling condoms through vending machines is not an effective method of distribution. Providing them free of charge through school staff, "condom bowls," or school-based health centers may, however, be very effective approaches (Kirby, 1993).

The way school officials approach the condom issue varies among communities, with a variety of factors influencing and affecting a community's interest, readiness, and ability to make condom availability a priority (Greene, 1993). The American Academy of Pediatrics (1995) has declared that, though sexual abstinence should be encouraged, youth should have access to condoms in the schools. Educators still have to face the problems of distribution logistics as well as possible liability concerns.

Additional well-designed research is needed to inform future action on this issue. (For further information, see *Condoms in the Schools* [Samuels & Smith, 1993], a publication from the Kaiser Family Foundation.)

Does Sex Education Lead to Sex?   "Learning and talking about sex do not have to mean giving permission," states Dr. Ruth Westheimer (1993), the well-known sex advisor. "On the contrary, I feel that a child knowing about his or her body will be able to deal with the pressure to have sex. This child can say no, I'll wait." Comprehensive sex education programs—those that integrate activities and personalize information, provide decision-making and assertiveness training, include information about avoiding undesirable consequences of sexual behavior, and promote the use of techniques to do so—tend to show that they can indeed reduce unprotected sexual activity (Kirby, 1992, 1993). In fact, sex education appears to discourage sexual interactions in some cases (Kirby, 1993).

Although much more research needs to be done on sex education and its impact on young people, most professionals agree that it is one of the most important preventive means we have. Young people, guided by their parents and armed with knowledge and self-confidence, can make informed decisions and direct their own sexual destinies.

SEXUALITY IN EARLY ADULTHOOD

Like other passages, the one from adolescence to early adulthood offers potential for growth if one is aware of and remains open to the opportunities this period brings.

Developmental Concerns

Several tasks challenge young adults as they develop their sexuality (Gagnon & Simon, 1973).

▪ *Establishing sexual orientation.* Children and adolescents may engage in sexual experimentation, such as playing doctor, kissing, and fondling, with members of both sexes. They do not necessarily associate these activities with sexual orientation. Instead, their orientation as heterosexual, gay, lesbian, or bisexual is in the process of emerging.

▪ *Integrating love and sex.* Traditional gender roles call for men to be sex-oriented and women to be love-oriented. In adulthood, the sex-versus-love opposition needs to be addressed. Instead of polarizing love and sex, people need to develop ways of uniting them.

▪ *Forging intimacy and making commitments.* Young adulthood is characterized by increasing sexual experience. Through dating, courtship, and cohabitation, individuals gain knowledge of themselves and others as potential partners. As relationships become more meaningful, the degree of intimacy and interdependence increases. Sexuality can be a means of enhancing intimacy and self-disclosure as well as a means of physical pleasure. As adults become more intimate, they need to develop their ability to make commitments.

▪ *Making fertility/childbearing decisions.* Childbearing is socially discouraged during adolescence, but it becomes increasingly legitimate in the twenties, especially if people are married. Fertility issues are often critical but unacknowledged, especially for single young adults.

▪ *Practicing safer sex to protect against sexually transmitted diseases.* An awareness of the various STDs and ways to best protect against them must be integrated into the communication, values, and behaviors of all young adults.

▪ *Evolving a sexual philosophy.* As individuals move from adolescence to adulthood, they reevaluate their moral standards, moving from moral decision making based on authority to standards based on their personal principles of right and wrong, caring, and responsibility. They become responsible for developing their own moral code, which includes sexual issues. In doing so, they need to evolve a personal philosophical perspective to give coherence to sexual attitudes, behaviors, beliefs, and values. They need to place sexuality within the larger framework of their lives and relationships. They need to integrate their personal, religious, spiritual, or humanistic values with their sexuality.

> It is the Man and Woman united that makes the complete Human Being. . . . A single man has not nearly the Value he would have in that State of Union. He is an incomplete Animal. He resembles the odd Half of a Pair of Scissors.
>
> —*Benjamin Franklin (1706–1790)*

Premarital Sexuality

Premarital sex refers to sexual activities, especially sexual intercourse, that take place prior to marriage. However, using "premarital sex" to describe sexual behavior among all unmarried adults is becoming increasingly questioned. We use **nonmarital sex** to refer to the sexual activities occurring primarily among unmarried adults over 30 and divorced or widowed men and women. Although this guideline is not absolute, it helps clarify the differences between these groups.

Premarital Sex: From Sin to Acceptance   A little more than a generation ago, virginity was the norm until marriage. Sex outside of marriage was considered sinful and immoral. In 1969, according to a Gallup survey, only 32% of the American population believed that premarital sex was acceptable (Lord, 1985). Today, however, values have shifted. Premarital sex among young adults (but not adolescents) in a relational context has become the norm (Sprecher & McKinney, 1993; Tranfer & Schoorl, 1992). Older Americans and groups with conservative religious backgrounds, such as Catholics and fundamentalist Protestants, continue to believe all nonmarital sex is morally wrong (Beck, Cole, & Hammond, 1991; Cochran & Beeghley, 1991). But religious conviction does not eliminate premarital sex. A survey of 1000 readers of the conservative *Christianity Today,* for example, found that 40% had engaged in premarital intercourse (Robinson, 1992).

The shift from sin to acceptance is the result of several factors. The advent of effective contraception, legal abortion, and changing gender roles legitimizing female sexuality have played major roles in this change. But one of the most significant factors may be traced to demography. Over the past 20 years, there has been a dramatic increase in unmarried men and women over age 18 (Cate & Lloyd, 1992). It is this group that has traditionally looked the most favorably on premarital intercourse. In 1995, the median age for first marriage for men was 26.7 years compared with 23.5 years in 1975. For women, the median age in 1995 was 24.5 years, compared with 21.1 years in 1975. On average, men and women have three additional years in which they may become sexually active prior to marriage.

Factors Leading to Premarital Sexual Involvement   What factors lead individual women and men to have premarital sexual intercourse? One study indicated that among women and men who had premarital sex, the most important factors were their love (or liking) for each other, physical arousal and willingness of both partners, and preplanning and arousal prior to the encounter (Christopher & Cate, 1984). Among nonvirgins, as with virgins, love or liking between the partners was extremely important (Christopher & Cate, 1984), but feelings of obligation or pressure were about as important as actual physical arousal.

Examining the sexual decision-making process more closely, researcher Susan Sprecher identifies individual, relationship, and environmental factors affecting the decision to have premarital intercourse (Sprecher, 1989; Sprecher & McKinney, 1993). Individual factors include previous sexual experience, sexual attitudes, personality characteristics, and gender. The

Among the most important factors associated with premarital sex for both men and women are their liking and loving each other, physical arousal and willingness, preplanning, and sexual arousal prior to their encounter.

more premarital sexual experience a man or woman has had in the past, the more likely he or she is to engage in sexual activities in the present.

Two of the most important factors determining sexual activity are the level of intimacy in the relationship and the length of time the couple have been together. Even those who are less permissive in their sexual attitudes accept sexual involvement if the relationship is emotionally intimate and long-standing. People who are less committed (or not committed) to a relationship are less likely to be sexually involved. Finally, people in relationships that share power equally are more likely to be sexually involved than those in inequitable ones.

Environmental factors may involve either the physical or the cultural environment. In the most basic sense, the physical environment affects the opportunity for sex. Because sex is a private activity, the opportunity for it may be precluded by the presence of parents, friends, roommates, or children (Tanfer & Cubbins, 1992). The cultural environment also affects premarital sex. The values of one's parents or peers may encourage or discourage sexual involvement. A person's ethnic group also affects premarital involvement: generally, African Americans are more permissive than Whites; Latinos are less permissive than Anglos (Baldwin, Whitely, & Baldwin, 1992). Furthermore, a person's subculture—such as the university or church environment, the singles world, the gay and lesbian community—exerts an important influence on sexual decision making.

Establishing Sexual Orientation

A critical task of adulthood is establishing one's sexual orientation as heterosexual, gay, lesbian, or bisexual. As mentioned earlier, in childhood and early adolescence, there is considerable sex play or sexual experimentation with members of the other sex and same sex. These exploratory experiences are tentative in terms of sexual orientation. But in late adolescence and young adulthood, men and women are confronted with the important developmental task of establishing intimacy. And part of the task of establishing intimate relationships is solidifying one's sexual orientation as heterosexual, gay, lesbian, or bisexual. A relatively small minority of individuals identify themselves as bisexual. **Bisexuality** refers to being sexually involved with or attracted to members of both sexes.

Most people develop a heterosexual identity by adolescence or young adulthood. Their task is simplified because their development as heterosexuals is approved by society (Wilkinson & Kitzinger, 1993). But for those who are lesbian, gay, bisexual, or unsure, development is filled with more doubt and anxiety. Because those who are attracted to members of the same sex are aware that they are violating deep societal taboos, it takes them longer to confirm their sexual orientation.

Statistics on Sexual Orientation   We do not know the numbers of men and women who are heterosexual, gay, lesbian, or bisexual. In large part, this is because homosexuality is stigmatized. Gay men and lesbians are often reluctant to reveal their identities in random surveys, and large-scale national surveys have been blocked until recently because of conservative opposition.

Some studies suggest that as many as 10% of Americans are lesbian or gay. Among women, about 13% have had orgasms with other women, but only 1–3% identify themselves as lesbian (Fay, Turner, Klassen, & Gagnon, 1989; Kinsey et al., 1948, 1953; Laumann et al., 1994; Marmor, 1980a). Among males, including adolescents, as many as 20–37% have had orgasms with other males, according to Kinsey's studies. Ten percent were predominantly gay for at least 3 years; 4% were exclusively gay throughout their entire lives (Kinsey et al., 1948). A review of studies on male same-sex behavior between 1970 and 1990 estimated that a minimum of 5–7% of adult men had had sexual contact with other men in adulthood. Based on their review, the researchers suggest that about 4.5% of men are exclusively gay (Rogers & Turner, 1991). A more recent large-scale study published by the University of Chicago of 3500 men and women reported that 2.8% of men and 1.4% of women describe themselves as homosexual or bisexual (Laumann et al., 1994).

What are we to make of these differences between studies? In part, the variances may be explained by different methodologies, interviewing techniques, sampling, or definitions of homosexuality. Furthermore, sexuality is more than simply sexual behaviors; it also includes attraction and desire. One can be a virgin or celibate and still be gay or heterosexual. Finally, because sexuality is varied and changes over time, its expression at any one time is not necessarily its expression at another time or for all time.

The Gay/Lesbian Identity Process   Identifying oneself as lesbian or gay takes considerable time and includes several phases, usually beginning in late childhood or early adolescence (Blumenfeld & Raymond, 1989; Troiden, 1988). **Homoeroticism,** feelings of sexual attraction to members of the same

"HETEROSEXUALITY" AND "HOMOSEXUALITY" arc terms used to categorize people according to the gender of their sexual partners. But, as noted in the discussion of Kinsey's work in Chapter 2, such categories do not always adequately reflect the complexity of sexual orientation or of human sexuality in general. Stephanie Sanders and her colleagues note that believing the labels "heterosexual" and "homosexual" reflect "actual sexual behavior patterns . . . leads to gross underestimates of the prevalence of behavioral bisexuality" (Sanders, Reinisch, & McWhirter, 1990).

Not everyone who has sexual experiences with members of both sexes identifies himself or herself as bisexual. Many more people who have had same-sex experiences identify themselves as heterosexuals than as bisexuals or homosexuals. The reason is simple: Most of these same-sex experiences took place during adolescent sexual experimentation and in situations where males and females are segregated according to sex. This behavior is much closer to childhood sex play than to adult sexuality because it lacks the commitment to a heterosexual, homosexual, or bisexual orientation. In addition, some people seek occasional same-sex contacts to supplement their heterosexual activity.

Those people who do define themselves as bisexual have partners of both sexes and reject both heterosexual and homosexual identities. Sometimes they have had only one or two same-sex experiences; nevertheless, they identify themselves as bisexual. They believe they can love and enjoy sex with both women and men. In other instances, those with predominantly homosexual experience and only limited heterosexual experience consider themselves bisexual. In most cases, bisexual people do not have sex with men one night and women the next. Their bisexuality is sequential. They are involved in heterosexual relationships for certain periods, ranging from a few weeks to years; later, they are involved in same-sex relations for another period of time.

Bisexual Identity Formation

In contrast to homosexuality, there is little research on bisexuality. (The exception is research on HIV/AIDS that examines bisexual behavior among men who identify themselves as heterosexual.) The process of bisexual identity formation appears to be complex, requiring the rejection of the two recognized categories of sexual orientation. Bisexuals often find themselves stigmatized by gay men and lesbians as well as by heterosexuals. Among heterosexuals, bisexuals are likely to be viewed as "really" homosexual. In the lesbian/gay community, they may be viewed as "fence-sitters," not willing to admit their supposed homosexuality, or as simply "playing" with their orientation (Weinberg, Williams, & Pryor, 1994).

The first model of bisexual identity formation was developed in 1994 by Martin Weinberg, Colin Williams, and D. W. Pryor (1994). According to this model, the process occurs in several stages. The first stage, often lasting years, is *initial confusion*. Many bisexuals are distressed to find they are sexually attracted to members of both sexes; others feel that their attraction to the same sex means an end to their heterosexuality; still others are disturbed by their inability to categorize their feelings as either heterosexual or homosexual. The second stage is *finding and applying the bisexual label*. For many, discover-

Bisexuality is not so much a cop-out as a fearful compromise.

—*Jill Johnston*

sex, almost always precedes lesbian or gay activity by several years (Bell, Weinberg, & Hammersmith, 1981).

The first phase is marked by fear and suspicion that somehow one's desires are different. At first, the person finds it difficult to label these emotional and physical desires for the same sex. His or her initial reactions often include fear, confusion, or denial (Herdt & Boxer, 1992).

In the second phase, the person actually labels these feelings of attraction, love, or desire as gay or lesbian feelings. The third phase includes the person's self-definition as gay. This may be difficult, for it entails accepting a label that society generally regards as deviant. Questions then arise about whether to tell parents or friends—whether to hide one's identity ("stay in the closet") or make it known ("come out of the closet").

Some or most gay men and lesbians may go through two additional phases. The next phase begins with a person's first gay or lesbian love affair (Troiden, 1988). This marks the commitment to unifying sexuality and affecing there is such a thing as bisexuality is a turning point; some find that their first heterosexual or same-sex experience permits them to view sex with *both* sexes as pleasurable; others learn of the term "bisexuality" from friends and are then able to apply it to themselves.

In the third stage, *settling into the identity*, the individual begins to feel at home with the label "bisexual." For many, self-acceptance is critical. A fourth stage is *continued uncertainty*. Bisexuals don't have a community or social environment that reaffirms their identity. Despite being settled in their sexual orientation, many feel persistent pressure from lesbians or gay men to relabel themselves as homosexual and to engage exclusively in same-sex activities.

Types of Bisexuals

Reserchers find that there is no single type of bisexual person (Weinberg et al., 1994). Instead, they have identified five types: pure, midrange, heterosexual leaning, homosexual leaning, and varied. The categories are based on the belief that sexual orientation consists of sexual feelings, sexual behaviors, and romantic feelings. Only 2% of the men and women studied were pure bisexuals, that is, were equally attracted to both genders in terms of sexual feelings, behaviors, and romantic inclination. About one-third of the men and women were midrange, that is, were mostly bisexual in their various feelings and behaviors. About 45% of the men and 20% of the women ranked themselves as heterosexual leaning. About 15% each of the men and women called themselves homosexual leaning. (Men were almost three times as likely to identify themselves as heterosexual leaning; women were divided more or less evenly between heterosexual leaning and homosexual leaning.) About 10% could be

identified as varied types. They were substantially more heterosexual on one dimension but much more homosexual on another dimension.

The Nature of Bisexual Relationships

For bisexuals, how do same-sex and other-sex relationships differ? In terms of sexual experiences, the most common difference reported by men and women was that when at least one partner was female, there was significantly more touching, hugging, and kissing and the quality of the interaction was slower, gentler, and softer. Male partners were viewed as less gentle, more urgent, and dominant. The researchers note: "Men seemed to get turned on by the sheer physicalness of the experience with other men. Women, however, often resented it." Both sexes noted physical differences, referring to the smoothness and softness of women and the muscularity and larger size of men. In describing the emotional aspects, both males and females said that sex with men was more impersonal and less sensitive, whereas sex with women was more caring and person-centered. But both sexes thought that their same-sex partner was more open and that they could understand her or him better; understanding the other sex was more difficult.

Bisexuals note that the nature of the relationship in terms of expressiveness, power, and bonding differs, depending on whether it is same-sex or other-sex. The most important difference is that it is more difficult for men to express their emotions. Another difference had to do with power. Women felt that their male partners were more controlling and that there was greater equality between women. Men were divided as to whether dominance issues were important in their same-sex relationships.

tion. Most lesbians and gay men have had such love affairs. The last phase a lesbian or gay man may enter is becoming involved in the gay subculture. A gay man or lesbian may begin acquiring exclusively gay friends, going to gay bars and clubs, or joining gay activist groups. In the gay/lesbian world, gay and lesbian identities incorporate a way of being in which sexual orientation is a major part of one's identity as a person.

For many, being lesbian or gay is associated with a total lifestyle and way of thinking. In making gay or lesbian orientation a lifestyle, **coming out,** publicly acknowledging one's homosexuality, has become especially important as an affirmation of one's sexual orientation. Coming out is a major decision because it may jeopardize many relationships, but it is also an important means of self-validation. By publicly acknowledging one's lesbian or gay orientation, a person begins to reject the stigma and condemnation associated with it. Generally, coming out to heterosexuals occurs in stages, first involving family members, especially the mother and siblings, and later the father.

Lesbians and gay men are often "out" to varying degrees. Some may be out to no one, not even themselves. Some are out only to their lovers, others to close friends and lovers but not to their families, employers, associates, or fellow students. Others may be out to everyone. Because of fear of reprisal, dismissal, or public reaction, gay and lesbian school teachers, police officers, members of the military, politicians, and members of other such professions are rarely out to their employers, co-workers, or the public.

Being Single

Over the past 25 years, there has been a staggering increase in the numbers of unmarried adults (never married, divorced, or widowed). Most of this increase has been the result of men and women, especially young adults, marrying later.

The New Social Context of Singlehood   Some of the results of this dramatic shift affecting unmarried young adults include:

▪ *Greater sexual experience.* Men and women who marry later are more likely to have more sexual experience and sexual partners than earlier generations. Premarital sex is becoming the norm among adults.

▪ *Widespread acceptance of cohabitation.* As young adults are deferring marriage longer, cohabitation has become an integral part of young adult life. Because gay men and lesbians are not legally permitted to marry, cohabitation has become for many of them a form of marriage.

▪ *Increased unintended pregnancies.* Because greater numbers of women are single and sexually active, more single women are likely to become unintentionally pregnant as a result of unprotected sexual intercourse or contraceptive failure.

▪ *Increased numbers of abortions and births to single women.* The increased number of unintended pregnancies has led to more abortions and births to single mothers. (About 20% of marriages take place with the woman being pregnant.) Birth to unmarried parents now rivals remarriage following divorce as a pathway by which children enter family structures (Acquilino, 1996). Fifty-eight percent of African American children, 42% of Hispanic children, and 25% of White children are born to an unmarried parent (Bryson & Casper, 1998). About a third of the unmarried parents are adolescents, and another third are between ages 20 and 24. They usually have become pregnant unintentionally.

▪ *Greater numbers of separated and divorced men and women.* Approximately 50% of all new marriages are likely to end in divorce (U.S. Bureau of the Census, 1997). Because of their previous marital experience, separated and divorced men and women tend to have different expectations about relationships than never-married young adults. Nearly half of all marriages are now remarriages for at least one partner.

▪ *Rise of single-parent families.* Today, 32% of all family groups with children are single-parent situations, the vast majority maintained by women. More than half of all children will be stepchildren by the year 2000 (U.S. Bureau of the Census, 1997). Single parenthood is most prevalent in African

The college social setting provides opportunities for students to meet and establish relationships.

American families, with 54% of the families headed by single parents, compared with 46% of Hispanic families and 24% of White families (Bryson & Casper, 1998).

The world that unmarried young adults enter is one in which greater opportunities than ever before exist for exploring intimate relationships.

The College Environment   The college environment is important not only for intellectual development but also for social development. The social aspects of the college setting—classes, dormitories, fraternities and sororities, parties, mixers, and sports events—provide opportunities for meeting others. For many, college is where people search for or find mates.

Dating in college is similar to high school dating in many ways. It may be formal or informal ("getting together"); it may be for recreation or to find a mate. Some of the features that distinguish college dating from high school dating, however, are the more independent setting (away from home, diminished parental influence, and so on), the increased maturity of each partner, more role flexibility, and the increased legitimacy of sexual interactions.

There appears to be a general expectation among students that they will engage in sexual intercourse at some point during their college career (Sprecher & McKinney, 1993) and that sexual involvement will occur within a loving relationship.

Sociologist Ira Reiss (1967) described four moral standards of premarital sexuality among college students. The first is the *abstinence standard,* which was the official sexual ideology in American culture until the 1950s and early 1960s. This belief holds that it is wrong for either men or women to engage in sexual intercourse before marriage regardless of the circumstances or their feelings for each other. The second is the *double standard,* widely practiced but rarely approved publicly, which permits men to engage in premarital intercourse. Women, however, are considered immoral if they do so. *Permissiveness with affection* represents a third standard. It describes sex between men and women who have an affectionate, stable, and loving relationship. This standard is widely held today (Sprecher, McKinney, Walsh, & Anderson, 1988; Sprecher & McKinney, 1993). *Permissiveness without affection* is the fourth standard. It holds that people may have sexual relationships with each other even if there is no affection or commitment.

Although acceptance of premarital sex is widespread among college students, there are limits. If a woman has sexual intercourse, most people believe it should take place in the context of a committed relationship. Women who "sleep around" are morally censured. Reflecting the continuing double standard, men are not usually condemned as harshly as women for having sex without commitment.

For gay men, lesbians, and bisexuals, the college environment is often liberating because many campuses are more accepting of sexual diversity than society at large is. College campuses often have lesbian, gay, and bisexual organizations that sponsor social events, dances, and get-togethers. There gays, lesbians, and bisexuals can freely meet others in open circumstances that permit meaningful relationships to develop and mature. Although prejudice against gay men, lesbians, and bisexuals continues to exist in colleges and universities, college life has been an important safe haven for many.

The Singles World   Men and women involved in the singles world tend to be older than college students; they range in age from 25 to 40. They have never been married, or, if they are divorced, they usually do not have primary responsibility for children. Single adults are generally working rather than attending school. The majority (nearly 22 million) of unmarried adults under 24 years of age live with someone else, usually their parents (Bryson & Casper, 1998).

Although dating in the singles world is somewhat different from dating in high school and college, there are similarities. Singles, like their counterparts in school, emphasize recreation and entertainment, sociability, and physical attractiveness.

The problem of meeting other single people is very often central. In college, students meet each other in classes or dormitories, at school events, or through friends. There are many meeting places and large numbers of eligibles. Because they are working, singles have less opportunity to meet available people. For single adults, friends, common interests, parties, work, and talking to a stranger are the most frequent means of meeting others.

To fill the demand for meeting other singles, the singles world has spawned a multibillion-dollar industry—bars, resorts, clubs, and housing. Singles increasingly rely on personal classified ads, where men advertise themselves as "success objects" and women advertise themselves as "sex objects" (Davis, 1990). These ads tend to reflect stereotypical gender roles. Men advertise for women who are attractive, de-emphasizing intellectual, professional, and financial considerations. Women advertise for men who hold jobs and who are financially secure, intelligent, emotionally expressive, and interested in commitment. Men are twice as likely as women to place ads. Additional forms of meeting others include video dating services, introduction services, computer bulletin boards, and 900 party-line phone services.

A recent study found that 10% of married couples met each other in bars, through ads, or on vacation. Twenty percent of those in short-term relationships met in a similar manner (Laumann et al., 1994).

Single men and women often rely on their church and church activities to meet other singles. About 8% of married couples meet in church (Laumann et al., 1994). Black churches are especially important for middle-class African Americans because they have less chance of meeting other African Americans in work and neighborhood settings. African Americans also attend Black-oriented concerts, plays, film festivals, and other social gatherings (Staples, 1991).

As a result of the growing acceptance of sexuality outside marriage, singles are presented with various sexual options. Some choose celibacy for religious or moral reasons. Others choose celibacy over casual sex; when they are involved in a committed nonmarital relationship, they may become sexually intimate. Some are temporarily celibate; they are taking "a vacation from sex." They utilize their celibacy to clarify the meaning of sexuality in their relationships.

Sexual experimentation is important for many. Although an individual may derive personal satisfaction from sexual experimentation, he or she must also manage the stress of conflicting commitments, loneliness, and a lack of connectedness. Although images of singles being especially sexual dominate our fantasies, their frequency of sexual intercourse is only about half that of married or cohabiting couples. In a recent study, 25% of nonpartnered singles had sex just a few times a year, compared with only 10% of married people (Laumann et al., 1994).

Many single women reject the idea of casual sex. Instead, they feel that sex must take place within the context of a relationship. In relationship sex, intercourse becomes a symbol of the degree of caring between two persons. Such relationships are expected to be "leading somewhere," such as to commitment, love, cohabitation, or marriage. As men and women get older, marriage becomes an increasingly important goal of a relationship.

Gay and Lesbian Singlehood   In the late nineteenth century, as a result of the stigmatization of homosexuality, groups of gay men and lesbians began congregating in their own secretive clubs and bars. There, in relative safety, they could find acceptance and support, meet others, and socialize. Today, some neighborhoods in large cities are identified with gay men and lesbians. These neighborhoods feature not only openly gay or lesbian bookstores,

THERE ARE NUMEROUS misconceptions about being gay or lesbian. These continue to circulate, adding to the fires of prejudice. The misconceptions include:

- *Misconception No. 1: Men and women are gay or lesbian because they can't get a heterosexual partner.* This belief is reflected in such remarks about lesbians as "All she needs is a good lay" (implying a man). Similar remarks about men include "He just needs to meet the right woman." Research indicates that lesbians and gay men have about as much heterosexual high school dating experience as their peers. Furthermore, the majority of lesbians have had sexual experiences with men; many of those experiences were pleasurable (Bell et al., 1981).

- *Misconception No. 2: Lesbians and gay men "recruit" heterosexuals to become gay.* People are not recruited or seduced into being gay any more than they are recruited into being heterosexual. Most gay men and lesbians have their first gay experience with a peer, either a friend or an acquaintance. They report having had homosexual feelings prior to their first experience (Bell et al., 1981).

- *Misconception No. 3: Gay men are child molesters.* This is a corollary to the recruitment misconception above. The overwhelming majority of child molesters are heterosexual males who molest girls; these men include fathers, stepfathers, uncles, and brothers. A large percentage of men who molest boys identify themselves as heterosexual (Arndt, 1991).

- *Misconception No. 4: Homosexuality can be caught.* Homosexuality is not the flu. Some parents express fear about having their children taught by homosexual teachers. They fear their children will model themselves after the teacher or be seduced by him or her. But a child's sexual orientation is often established by the time he or she enters school, and a teacher would not have an impact on that child's orientation (Marmor, 1980c).

- *Misconception No. 5: Gay men and lesbians could change if they wanted.* Most gay men and lesbians feel that they cannot change their sexual orientation. The belief that they should reflects assumptions that homosexuality is abnormal or sinful. Most psychotherapy with gay men and lesbians who are unhappy about their orientation aims at helping them adjust to it.

- *Misconception No. 6: Homosexuality is condemned in the Bible.* The Bible condemns same-sex sexual activities, not homosexuality. Some biblical scholars believe that the rejection of same-sex sexual activities is based on historical factors, including the lack of the concept of sexual orientation, the exploitative and abusive nature of much same-sex activity in ancient times, the belief that the purpose of sex was procreation, and purity or holiness concerns that such acts were impure (there were similar concerns about sexual intercourse with a menstruating woman). There is increasing debate among religious groups as to whether same-sex relationships are inherently sinful.

- *Misconception No. 7: All gays are effeminate; all lesbians are butches.* People often perceive the world selectively, paying attention to information that supports their stereotypes and ignoring information that contradicts them. Empirical research has demonstrated that perceptions of gay men as more theatrical, gentle, and liberated and of lesbians as more dominant, direct, forceful, strong, and nonconforming have been shaped more by cultural ideologies about homosexuality than by individuals' own unbiased observations (cited in Herek, 1995).

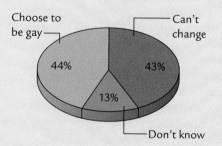

Percentage of Adults Who Believe Homosexuality Is Chosen or Can't Be Changed.

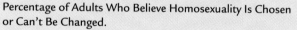

restaurants, coffeehouses, and bars but also churches, clothing stores, physicians, lawyers, and hair salons.

Gay and lesbian businesses, institutions, and neighborhoods are important for affirming positive identities; they enable gay men and lesbians to interact beyond a sexual context. They help make being lesbian or gay a complex social identity consisting of many parts—student, parent, worker, professional, churchgoer—rather than being simply a sexual role (Altman, 1982).

In these neighborhoods, men and women are free to express their affection as openly as heterosexuals. They experience little discrimination or intolerance and are involved in gay and lesbian social and political organizations. More recently, with increasing acceptance in some areas, many middle-class gay men and lesbians are moving to suburban areas. In the suburbs, however, they remain more discreet than they are in large cities (Lynch, 1992).

THE GAY MALE SUBCULTURE   The urban gay male subculture that emerged in the 1970s emphasized sexuality. Although relationships were important, sexual experiences and variety were even more important. Despite the emphasis on sex over relationships, however, two researchers found that most gay men in their study had at least one exclusive relationship (Weinberg & Williams, 1974). In fact, involvement in the gay subculture enhanced the likelihood of lasting relationships. The researchers speculated that closeted gay men were more likely than openly gay men to avoid attachments for fear of discovery.

With the rise of the HIV/AIDS epidemic in the 1980s and 1990s, the gay subculture has placed an increased emphasis on the relationship context of sex (Carl, 1986; Isensee, 1990). Relational sex has become the norm among large segments of the gay population (Levine, 1992). Most gay men have sex within dating or love relationships. (In fact, some AIDS organizations give classes on gay dating to encourage safer sex.)

African American gay men often experience a conflict between their Black and gay identities (Peterson, 1992). African Americans are less likely to disclose their gay identity because the Black community is less accepting of homosexuality than the White community. At the same time, African Americans may experience racial discrimination in the predominantly White gay community. Gay African Americans whose primary identity is racial tend to socialize in the Black community, where they are tolerated only as long as they are closeted. Few gay institutions are available to them. In most communities, they must rely on discreet friendship circles or clandestine bars to meet other gay Black men.

For gay Latinos in cities with large Latino populations, there is usually at least one gay bar. Such places usually specialize in dancing or female impersonation. The extent to which a gay Latino participates in the Anglo or Latino gay world depends on the individual's degree of acculturation (Carrier, 1992).

THE LESBIAN COMMUNITY   Beginning in the 1950s and 1960s, young and working-class lesbians developed their own institutions, especially women's softball teams and exclusively female gay bars as places to socialize. During the late 1960s and 1970s, lesbian separatists, lesbians who wanted to create a separate "womyn's" culture distinct from those of heterosexual women *and* gay men, rose to prominence. They developed their own music, literature, and erotica; they had their own clubs and bars. But by the middle of the 1980s, the lesbian community underwent a "shift to moderation" (Faderman, 1991). It became more diverse, welcoming Latinas, African American women, Asian American women, and older women. It also developed closer ties with the gay male community. Lesbians now view gay men as sharing much in common with them because of the prejudice directed against both groups.

Lesbians tend to value the emotional quality of relationships more than the sexual component. Lesbians usually form longer-lasting relationships than gay men (Tuller, 1988). Lesbians' emphasis on emotions over sex and the more enduring quality of their relationships reflect their socialization as women. Being female influences a lesbian more than being gay.

Cohabitation

In 1996 nearly 5.4 million unmarried heterosexual couples, or 5.3% of the unmarried adult population, were living together in the United States (U.S. Bureau of the Census, 1997). In contrast, only 400,000 heterosexual couples were cohabiting in 1960. Delaying marriage has increased the number of men and women cohabiting (Tanfer & Cubbins, 1992). For census purposes, heterosexuals who cohabit are called POSSLQs *(possel-kews)*, people of the other sex sharing living quarters.

A New Norm   Cohabitation is increasingly accepted at almost every level of society (Figure 6.3). By age 30, about 40–50% of all young adult women will have cohabited (Surra, 1991). Some scholars, in fact, believe that cohabitation is becoming institutionalized as part of the normal mate-selection process (Gwartney-Gibbs, 1986). The concept of **domestic partnership** has led to laws granting some of the protections of marriage to men and women, including gay men and lesbians, who cohabit in committed relationships.

Living together has become more widespread and accepted in recent years for several reasons. First, the general climate regarding sexuality is more liberal than it was a generation ago. Sexuality is more widely considered to be an important part of a person's life, whether or not he or she is married. The moral criterion for judging sexual intercourse has shifted; love rather than marriage is now widely regarded as making a sexual act moral. Second, the meaning of marriage is changing. Because of the dramatic increase in divorce rates over the past two decades, marriage is no longer thought of necessarily as a permanent commitment. Permanence is increasingly replaced by **serial monogamy,** a succession of marriages. Because the average marriage now lasts only 7 years, the distinction between marriage and living together is losing its clarity. Third, young adults are continuing to defer marriage. At the same time, they want the companionship found by living intimately with another person.

For young adults, there are a number of advantages to cohabitation. First, because their lives are often in transition—as they finish school, establish careers, or become more secure financially—cohabitation represents a "tentatively" committed relationship. Second, in cohabiting relationships, partners tend to be more egalitarian. They do not have to deal with the more structured roles of husband and wife. They are freer to develop their own individuality independent of marital roles. Third, the couple know they are together because they want to be, not because of the pressure of marital obligations.

Although there are a number of advantages to cohabitation, there may also be disadvantages. Parents may refuse to provide support for school to

MONOGAMY, n. A common misspelling. See "Monotony."

—*Robert Tefton*

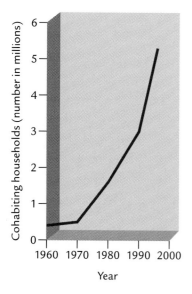

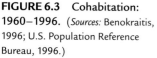

FIGURE 6.3   Cohabitation: 1960–1996. (*Sources:* Benokraitis, 1996; U.S. Population Reference Bureau, 1996.)

Many gay and lesbian couples choose to affirm their commitment in a marriage ceremony, although such unions are not legally recognized in most states.

a child who is living with someone; they may not welcome their child's partner into their home. Cohabiting couples also may find they cannot easily buy a house together because banks may not count their income as joint; they usually don't qualify for insurance benefits. If one partner has children, the other partner is usually not as involved as if the couple were married. Cohabiting couples who live together often find themselves socially stigmatized if they have a child. Finally, cohabiting relationships generally don't last more than 2 years; couples either break up or get married.

There is no consensus about whether cohabitation significantly increases or decreases later marital stability (DeMaris & Rao, 1992; Teachman & Polonko, 1990). Although couples who are living together often argue that cohabitation helps prepare them for marriage, such couples are statistically as likely to divorce as those who do not live together before marriage. People who live together before marriage tend to be more liberal, more sexually experienced, and more independent than people who do not live together before marriage. No conclusive research exists on the link between cohabitation and marital satisfaction.

Gay and Lesbian Cohabitation   In 1995, there were more than 1.5 million gay male or lesbian couples living together. The relationships of gay men and lesbians have been stereotyped as less committed than for heterosexual couples because (1) lesbians and gay men cannot legally marry, (2) they may not appear to emphasize sexual exclusiveness, and (3) heterosexuals misperceive love between lesbian and gay couples as being somehow less real than love between heterosexuals. Numerous similarities, however, exist between gay and heterosexual couples, according to Letitia Peplau (1981, 1988). Regardless of their sexual orientation, most people want a close, loving relationship with another person. For gay men, lesbians, and heterosexuals, intimate relationships provide love, romance, satisfaction, and security. There is one important difference, however. Heterosexual couples tend to adopt a traditional marriage model, whereas gay couples tend to have a "best-friend" model.

Few lesbian and gay relationships are divided into the traditional heterosexual provider/homemaker roles. Among heterosexuals, these divisions are gender-linked as male or female. In same-sex couples, however, tasks are often divided pragmatically, according to considerations such as who likes cooking more (or dislikes it less) and work schedules (Marecek, Finn, & Cardell, 1988). Most gay couples are dual-worker couples; neither partner supports or depends on the other economically. And because gay and lesbian couples are the same sex, the economic discrepancies based on greater male earning power are absent. Although gay couples emphasize egalitarianism, if there are differences in power, they are attributed to personality; if there is an age difference, the older partner is usually more powerful (Harry, 1988).

Because they confront societal hostility, lesbians and gay men fail to receive the general social support given heterosexuals in maintaining relationships. One rarely finds parents, for example, urging their gay male or lesbian children to make a commitment to a stable same-sex relationship or, if the relationship is rocky, to stick it out.

SEXUALITY IN MIDDLE ADULTHOOD

In the middle years, family and work become especially important. Personal time is spent increasingly on marital and family matters, especially if a couple has children. Sexual expression often decreases in frequency, intensity, and significance, replaced by family and work concerns. Sometimes the change reflects a higher value placed on family intimacy. At other times, it may reflect habit, boredom, or conflict.

Developmental Concerns

In the middle adult years, some of the psychosexual developmental tasks begun in young adulthood may be continuing. These tasks, such as intimacy issues or childbearing decisions, may have been deferred or only partly completed in young adulthood. Because of separation or divorce, people may find themselves facing the same intimacy and commitment tasks at age 40 they thought they had completed 15 years earlier (Cate & Lloyd, 1992). But life does not stand still; it moves steadily forward, ready or not. Other developmental issues appear, including the following ones:

▪ *Redefining sex in marital or other long-term relationships.* In new relationships, sex is often passionate, intense; it may be the central focus. But in

> Seldom, or perhaps never, does a marriage develop into an individual relationship smoothly and without crisis; there is no coming to consciousness without pain.
>
> —*Carl Jung (1875–1961)*

long-term marital or cohabiting relationships, habit, competing parental and work obligations, fatigue, and unresolved conflicts often erode the passionate intensity associated with sex. Sex may need to be redefined as a form of intimacy and caring. Individuals may also need to decide how to deal with the possibility, reality, and meaning of extramarital or extrarelational affairs.

- *Reevaluating one's sexuality.* Single women and men may need to weigh the costs and benefits of sex in casual or lightly committed relationships. In long-term relationships, sexuality often becomes less than central to relationship satisfaction. Nonsexual elements, such as communication, intimacy, and shared interests and activities, become increasingly important to relationships. Women who have deferred their childbearing begin to reappraise their decision: Should they remain child-free, race against their biological clock, or adopt a child? Some people may redefine their sexual orientation. One's sexual philosophy continues to evolve.

- *Accepting the biological aging process.* As people age, their skin wrinkles, their flesh sags, their hair turns gray (or falls out), their vision blurs—and they become, in the eyes of society, less attractive and less sexual. By their forties, their physiological responses have begun to slow noticeably. By their fifties, society begins to "neuter" them, especially women who have been through menopause. The challenge of aging is to come to terms with its biological mandate.

Marital Sexuality

When people marry, they may discover that their sexual lives are very different than they were before marriage. Sex is now morally and socially sanctioned. It is in marriage that the great majority of heterosexual interactions take place. Yet as a culture, we feel ambivalent about marital sex. On the one hand, marriage is the only relationship in which sexuality is legitimized. On the other hand, marital sex is an endless source of humor and ridicule.

Frequency of Sexual Interactions   Sexual intercourse tends to diminish in frequency the longer a couple is married. For newly married couples, the average rate of sexual intercourse is about three times a week. As couples get older, the frequency drops. In early middle age, married couples make love an average of one-and-a-half to two times a week. After age 50, the rate is about once a week or less. Decreased frequency, however, does not necessarily mean that sex is no longer important or that the marriage is unsatisfactory. It may be the result of biological aging and declining sexual drive (Call, Sprecher, & Schwartz, 1995). It often means simply that one or both partners are too tired. For dual-worker families and families with children, fatigue and lack of private time may be the most significant factors in the decline of frequency. Philip Blumstein and Pepper Schwartz (1982) found that most people attributed the decline in frequency of sexual intercourse to lack of time or physical energy or to "being accustomed" to each other. In addition, other activities and interests engage them besides sex.

Most married couples don't seem to feel that declining frequency is a major problem if their overall relationship is good (Cupach & Comstock, 1990; Sprecher & McKinney, 1993). Sexual intercourse is only one erotic bond

Marriage turns lovers into relatives.
—*John Rush*

Setting a good example for your children takes all the fun out of middle age.
—*William Feather*

The demands of parenting may diminish a couple's ability to be sexually spontaneous.

among many in marriage. There are also kissing, caressing, nibbling, stroking, massaging, candlelight dinners, walking hand-in-hand, looking into each other's eyes, and intimate words.

Sexual Satisfaction and Pleasure   In real life, higher levels of sexual satisfaction and pleasure seem to be found in marriage than in singlehood or extramarital relationships (Laumann et al., 1994). More than 50% of married men report that they are extremely satisfied physically and emotionally with their spouse. About 40% of married women report similar levels of satisfaction (Laumann et al., 1994). Almost 90% of married people report they enjoy great physical satisfaction in their marriage; 85% report great emotional satisfaction.

If a person has more than one sex partner, physical and emotional satisfaction begin to decline. Although most American marriages are monogamous, among those that are not, only 59% find sex with their spouse physically satisfying and only 55% are emotionally satisfied. It is impossible to say, however, whether lower levels of satisfaction cause people to seek out an extramarital partner or whether having another partner lowers levels of sexual satisfaction in marriage (Laumann et al., 1994; Michael et al., 1994).

About 75% of single, married, and cohabiting men always have orgasm with their partner, but those who are married report the highest rates of physical and emotional satisfaction with their partner. Among women, the rate of always having an orgasm varies. The highest—34%—is found among divorced women living alone, followed by married women, 30% of whom report always having an orgasm. Significantly, however, slightly more than 40% of the married women report being extremely sexually satisfied emotionally and physically with their partner. Only cohabiting women express higher rates of satisfaction (Laumann et al., 1994).

Laumann and his colleagues (1994) observe that sexual satisfaction in marriage is highest because partners tend to have greater emotional and social involvement in the relationship. Marital partners have the greatest commitment to pleasing each other, learning the other's likes, being sensitive to the other's needs. The longer the partnership is likely to last, the greater the commitment to making it work in various aspects—including the sexual aspect.

Lesbians, Gay Men, and Bisexuals in Heterosexual Marriages   Although there are no reliable studies, it is estimated that about 20% of gay men and 33% of lesbians have been married (Bell & Weinberg, 1978). Estimates run into the millions for married bisexual men and women (Gochoros, 1989; Hill, 1987). Relatively few men and women are consciously aware of their homosexuality or bisexuality at the time they marry. Those who are aware rarely disclose their feelings to their prospective partner (Gochoros, 1989). Like heterosexuals, lesbians and gay men marry because of pressure from family, friends, and girlfriend/boyfriend, genuine love for one's heterosexual partner, the wish for companionship, and the desire to have children (Bozett, 1987a).

When husbands or wives discover their partner's homosexuality or bisexuality, they initially experience shock, and then they feel deceived or stupid. Many feel shame (Hays & Samuels, 1989). "His coming out of the closet in some ways put the family in the closet," recalled one woman who felt ashamed to tell anyone of her situation (Hill, 1987). At the same time, homosexual or bisexual spouses often feel deeply saddened for hurting loved ones. If they have children, they fear losing them.

Extramarital Sexuality

A fundamental assumption in our culture is that marriages are monogamous. Each person remains the other's exclusive intimate partner, in terms of both emotional and sexual intimacy. Extramarital relationships violate that assumption.

A review of literature relating to the prevalence of extramarital sexuality found that between 15% and 25% of ever-married Americans report having had extramarital sex but that this behavior occurs infrequently during any year (1.5–4% during the preceding 12 months [Wiederman, 1997]). Also, it appears that men are at least somewhat more likely than women to report it. Very little is known about extramarital sex in relation to ethnicity; however, Black men and women reported higher rates during the preceding year

> What I have seen of the love affairs of other people has not led me to regret that deficiency in my experience.
>
> —*George Bernard Shaw (1856–1950)*

than White men and women. Similarly, Black women and Hispanic women reported higher rates than White women (Wiederman, 1997).

Although we tend to think of extramarital involvements as being sexual, they actually assume several forms (A. Thompson, 1983). They may be (1) sexual but not emotional, (2) sexual and emotional, or (3) emotional but not sexual (A. Thompson, 1984). Very little research has been done on extramarital relationships in which both people are emotionally but not sexually involved. Thompson's study, however, found that of 378 married and cohabiting people, the three types of extrarelational involvement were about equally represented.

Extrarelational Sex in Dating and Cohabiting Relationships   Both cohabiting couples and those in committed relationships usually have expectations of sexual exclusiveness. But, like some married men and women who take vows of fidelity, these couples do not always remain sexually exclusive. Blumstein and Schwartz (1983) found that those involved in cohabiting relationships had rates of extrarelational involvement similar to those of married couples, except that cohabiting males had somewhat fewer partners than husbands did. Gay men had more partners than cohabiting and married men. And lesbians had fewer partners than any other group.

Large numbers of both women and men have sexual involvements outside dating relationships that are considered exclusive. Of those who knew of their partner's affair, a large majority felt that it had hurt their own relationship. When both partners had engaged in affairs, each believed that their partner's affair had harmed the relationship more than their own had.

Extramarital Sex in Exclusive Marriages   In marriages that assume emotional and sexual exclusivity, mutuality and sharing are emphasized. Extramarital sexual relationships are assumed to be destructive of the relationship; nonsexual heterosexual relationships may also be judged threatening. The possibility of infecting one's husband or wife with an STD must also be considered.

As a result of marital assumptions, both sexual and nonsexual extramarital relationships take place without the knowledge or permission of the other partner. If the extramarital relationship is discovered, a marital crisis ensues. Many married people feel that the spouse who is unfaithful has broken a basic trust. Sexual accessibility implies emotional accessibility. When a person learns that his or her spouse is having an affair, the emotional commitment of that spouse is brought into question. How can you prove that you still have a commitment? You cannot—commitment is assumed; it can never be proved. Furthermore, the extramarital relationship may imply to the partner (rightly or wrongly) that he or she is sexually inadequate or uninteresting.

Extramarital Sex in Nonexclusive Marriages   There are several types of nonexclusive marriage (Weiss, 1983): (1) open marriage in which intimate but nonsexual friendships with others are encouraged, (2) open marriage in which outside sexual relationships are allowed, (3) swinging, and (4) group marriage/multiple relationships. The marriage relationship is considered the primary relationship in both nonsexual extramarital relationships and in open marriages and swinging relationships. Only the group marriage/mul-

There is one thing I would break up over, and that is if she caught me with another woman. I won't stand for that.

—*Steve Martin*

To be faithful to one is to be cruel to all the others.

—*Wolfgang Amadeus Mozart (1756–1791), Don Giovanni*

tiple relationships model rejects the primacy of the married relationship. Group marriage is the equal sharing of partners, as in polygamy; it may consist of one man and two women, one woman and two men, or two couples. The two most common types of consensual extramarital sex are sexually open marriages and swinging.

In **open marriage,** partners may mutually agree to allow sexual relationships with others. Little research has been done on open marriages. Blumstein and Schwartz (1983) found that 15–26% of the couples in their sample had "an understanding" that permitted extramarital relations in certain circumstances, such as the affair's occurring only out of town, never seeing the same person twice, never having sex with a mutual friend, and so on.

Two researchers found that successful sexually open marriages require (1) a commitment to the primacy of the marriage, (2) a high degree of affection and trust between the spouses, (3) good interpersonal skills to manage complex relationships, and (4) nonmarital partners who did not compete with the married partner (Knapp & Whitehurst, 1977).

Swinging (also called mate sharing or wife swapping) is a form of consensual extramarital sex in which couples engage in sexual activities with others in a social context clearly defined as recreational sex. These contexts may include swinging parties or commercial clubs. Married swingers swing together (Weiss, 1983). Forming an intimate relationship with an extramarital partner is prohibited. In terms of health, swinging may be an especially risky form of behavior.

Most sex research on consensual extramarital sex has been done on swinging (Weiss, 1983). It has been estimated that 2% of adult Americans have engaged in swinging. Although swingers are popularly perceived to be deviant, radical, or psychologically troubled, they tend not to differ significantly from most Americans. They tend to be White, overwhelmingly middle class, politically conservative, and quite "normal." They tend to be less religious than nonswingers (Jenks, 1985; Weiss, 1983).

Thou shalt not commit adultery . . .
unless in the mood.

—*W. C. Fields (1879–1946)*

Motivation for Extramarital Sex   People who engage in extramarital affairs have a number of different motivations, and affairs satisfy a number of different needs (Moultrup, 1990). John Gagnon (1977) describes the attraction extramarital affairs have for the people involved:

> Most people find their extramarital relationships highly exciting, especially in the early stages. This is a result of psychological compression: the couple gets together; they are both very aroused (desire, guilt, expectation); they have only three hours to be together. . . . Another source of attraction is that the other person is always seen when he or she looks good and is on best behavior, never when feeling tired or grubby, or when taking care of children, or when cooking dinner. . . . Each time, all the minutes that the couple has together are special because they have been stolen from all these other relationships. The resulting combination of guilt and excitement has a heightening effect, which tends to explain why people may claim that extramarital sex and orgasms are more intense.

Research by Ira Reiss (1980) suggests that extramarital affairs appear to be related to two variables: unhappiness of the marriage and/or extramarital sexual permissiveness. Generally speaking, in happy marriages, a partner is less likely to seek outside sexual relationships. If a person had premarital sex, he or she is more likely to have extramarital sex. Once the first prohibition is broken, the second holds less power.

Divorce and After

Divorce has become a major force in American life. A quick observation of demographics in this country points to a new and growing way of life: post-divorce singlehood. In 1997, 8.7% of men and 11% of women 18 and over were divorced (U.S. Bureau of the Census, 1997). A breakdown by ethnicity reveals that 9.1% of Whites, 10.7% of African Americans, and 7.9% of Latinos were divorced in 1995 (U.S. Bureau of the Census, 1996).

Scholars suggest that divorce does not represent a devaluation of marriage but, oddly enough, an idealization of it. We would not divorce if we did not have such high expectations for marriage's ability to fulfill various needs (Furstenberg & Cherlin, 1991; Furstenberg & Spanier, 1987). Our high divorce rate further tells us that we may no longer believe in the permanence of marriage. Instead, we remain married only as long as we are in love, or until a potentially better partner comes along (Glenn, 1991).

Dating Again   A first date after years of marriage and subsequent months of singlehood evokes some of the same emotions felt by inexperienced adolescents. Separated or divorced men and women who are beginning to date again may be excited and nervous; worry about how they look; and wonder whether it's OK to hold hands, kiss, or make love. They may feel that dating is incongruous with their former selves, or they may be annoyed with themselves for feeling excited and awkward. Furthermore, they have little idea of the norms of postmarital dating (Spanier & Thompson, 1987).

Dating serves several important purposes for separated and divorced people. Primarily, it is a statement to both the former spouse and the world at large that the person is available to become someone else's partner (Vaughan, 1986). Also, dating is an opportunity to enhance one's self-esteem (Spanier & Thompson, 1987). Free from the stress of an unhappy marriage, people may discover, for example, that they are more interesting and charming than either they or (especially) their former spouses had imagined. And dating initiates people into the singles subculture, where they can experiment with the freedom about which they may have fantasized when they were married.

Several features of dating following marital separation and divorce differ from premarital dating. For one thing, dating does not seem to be a leisurely matter. Divorced people usually feel too pressed for time to waste it on a first date that might not go well. And dating may be less spontaneous if the divorced woman or man has primary responsibility for children. The parent must make arrangements about child care; he or she may wish not to involve the children in the dates. In addition, finances may be strained; divorced mothers may have income only from low-paying or part-time jobs or from welfare benefits, while having many child-care expenses. In some cases, a father's finances may be strained by paying alimony or child support. Finally, separated and divorced men and women often have a changed sexual ethic based on the simple fact that there are few (if any) divorced virgins (Spanier & Thompson, 1987).

Sexual activity is an important component in the lives of separated and divorced men and women. Engaging in sexual relations for the first time following separation helps people accept their newly acquired single status. Because sexual fidelity is usually an important element in marriage, becoming sexually active with someone other than one's spouse is a dramatic symbol that the old marriage vows are no longer valid (Spanier & Thompson, 1987). Men initially tend to enjoy their sexual freedom following divorce, but women generally do not find it as meaningful. For men, sexual experience following separation is linked with their sense of well-being; it seems to reassure them and bolster their self-confidence. In contrast, sexual activity is not as strongly connected to a woman's sense of well-being (Spanier & Thompson, 1987). After a while, sex becomes a secondary consideration in dating, as people look for a deeper, more intimate relationship.

Little is known about the sexual behavior of divorced men and women. Using national data on 340 divorced people, one study found that the level of sexual activity for the divorced was much lower than earlier studies and popular mythology suggest (Stack & Gundlach, 1992). Over a year's time, the study found that 74% had either a single partner or none; 16% of the men and 34% of the women had no partner.

Single Parenting   Nearly one-third of all families consist of single parents. Today, 10 million children under age 18 live with one parent (Bryson & Casper, 1998). Ethnicity is an important demographic factor related to single parenthood: In 1997, among White children, 25% lived in single-parent families; among African American children, 58% lived in such families; among Hispanics, 42% lived in single-parent families (Bryson & Casper, 1998). White single mothers were more likely to be divorced than their African American or Latina counterparts, who were more likely to be unmarried at the time of birth or widowed.

Single parents are not often a part of the singles world, which involves more than simply not being married. It requires leisure and money, both of which single parents generally lack because of their parenting responsibilities. Because of stereotypes of single women being sexually "loose," single mothers are often cautious about developing new relationships (Kissman & Allen, 1993).

The presence of children affects a divorced woman's sexual activity. Single divorced parents are less likely than divorced women without children to be sexually active (Stack & Gundlach, 1992). Children enormously complicate a single parent's sexual decision making. A single mother must decide, for example, whether to permit a man to spend the night with her when her children are present. This is often an important symbolic act for a woman, for several reasons. First, it involves her children in her romantic relationships. Women are often hesitant to again expose their children to the distress associated with the memory of the initial parental separation and divorce, often painfully seared into everyone's mind. Second, it reveals to her children that their mother is sexual, which may make her feel uncomfortable. Third, it opens her up to receiving moral judgments from her children regarding her sexuality. Single parents are often fearful that their children will lose respect for them, which may happen sometimes when children

Because of their child-rearing responsibilities, single parents are usually not part of the singles world.

reach middle childhood. And finally, having someone sleep over may trigger the resentment and anger the children feel toward their parents for splitting up. They may feel deeply threatened and act out.

SEXUALITY IN LATE ADULTHOOD

Sexuality is one of the least understood aspects of life in old age. Many older people continue to adhere to the standards of activity or physical attraction they held when they were young (Creti & Libman, 1989). They need to overcome the taboos and stereotypes about aging they held when they were younger so that they can enjoy their sexuality in their later years (Kellett, 1991).

Developmental Concerns

Many of the psychosexual tasks older Americans must undertake are directly related to the aging process.

▪ *Changing sexuality.* As older men's and women's physical abilities change with age, their sexual responses change as well. A 70-year-old, though still sexual, is not sexual in the same manner as an 18-year-old. As men and women continue to age, their sexuality tends to be more diffuse, less genital, and less insistent. Chronic illness and increasing frailty understandably result in diminished sexual activity. These considerations contribute to the ongoing evolution of the individual's sexual philosophy.

▪ *Loss of a partner.* One of the most critical life events is the loss of a partner. After age 60, there is a significant increase in spousal deaths. Because having a partner is the single most important factor determining an older person's sexual interactions, the death of the partner signals a dramatic change in the survivor's sexual interactions.

One of the most famous twentieth-century sculptures is Auguste Rodin's The Kiss, *which depicts young lovers embracing. Here, the aging model Antoni Nordone sits before the statue that immortalized his youth.*

Older adults accomplish these tasks within the context of continuing aging. Resolving these tasks as we age helps us to accept the eventuality of our death.

Stereotypes of Aging

Our society stereotypes aging as a lonely and depressing time, but most studies of older adults find that they express relatively high levels of satisfaction and well-being. It is poverty and poor health that make old age difficult. But even so, the aged have lower levels of poverty than most Americans, including young adults, women, and children. More important, until their mid-seventies, most older people report few if any restrictions on their activities because of health.

The sexuality of older Americans tends to be invisible. Society tends to discount their sexuality (Libman, 1989). In fact, one review of the literature on aging concludes that the decline in sexual activity among aging men and women is more cultural than biological in origin (Kellett, 1991). Several factors account for this in our culture (Barrow & Smith, 1992). First, we associate sexuality with the young, assuming that sexual attraction exists only between those with youthful bodies. Interest in sex is considered normal and virile in 25-year-old men, but in 75-year-old men, it is considered lecherous. Second, we associate the idea of romance and love with the young; many of us find it difficult to believe that the aged can fall in love or love intensely. Third, we continue to associate sex with procreation, measuring a woman's femininity by her childbearing and maternal role and a man's masculinity by the children he sires. Finally, the aged do not have as strong sexual desires as the young, and they do not express them as openly. Intimacy is especially valued and important for an older person's well-being (Mancini & Blieszner, 1992).

Aging gay men and lesbians face a double stereotype: They are old *and* gay. But like other stereotypes of aging Americans, this one reflects myths rather than realities. Most gay men and lesbians are satisfied with their sexual orientation; about half are worried about aging (Berger, 1982; Kehoe, 1988).

Stereotypes and myths about aging are not the only factors that affect the sexuality of the aged. The narrow definition of sexuality contributes to the problem. Sexual behavior is defined by researchers and the general population in terms of masturbation, sexual intercourse, and orgasm. But sexuality has emotional, sensual, and relationship aspects that are enjoyed by all people, regardless of age.

Sexuality, Partner Availability, and Health

As age increases, so often does the number of health problems. Hypertension, cardiovascular disease, cancer, diabetes, and arthritis may occur, causing a debilitation of overall health and sexual well-being. Therapies to control or treat these maladies may also cause adverse reactions or changed body image and may require education, support, reevaluation of the therapies, or an alteration in the sexual habits of those affected. Often, older adults indicate that they continue to feel sexual desires; they simply lack the ability to express them because of their health.

The greatest determinants of an older person's sexual activity are the availability of a partner and health. A major study of older people found that only 7% of those who were single or widowed were sexually active, in contrast to 54% of those living with a partner (Verwoerdt et al., 1969). Frequency of sexual intercourse of the latter group, with an average age of 70, ranged from three times a week to once every two months. Those who described their sexual feelings as having been weak or moderate in their youth stated that they were without sexual feelings. More recently, researchers studying 800 married couples over age 60 found that more than half of the sample (and 24% of those older than 76) had had sexual intercourse within the previous month (Marsiglio & Donnelly, 1991). Masturbation continued to be a pleasurable activity for those with and without partners (Pratt & Schmall, 1989).

After age 75, a significant decrease in sexual activity often takes place. In spite of the fact that 17% of men and women expressed a desire for sexual activity (C. White, 1982), most families, nursing homes, and society in general make no provisions for the sexuality of older people. Instead, they actively discourage sexual expression—not only sexual intercourse but also masturbation—or try to sublimate erotic interests into crafts or television or

The greatest determinants of an aged person's sexual activity are the availability of a partner and health.

to deaden them with medication. Such manipulations do little to satisfy erotic needs.

It is not the loss of sexuality alone that older people must face, of course. Many older widows do not miss the sexual aspect of their married lives as much as the social aspects. It is the companionship, the activity, the pleasure found in their partners that many older people miss most acutely (Malatesta, Chambless, Pollack, & Cantor, 1989).

Male and Female Differences

Older women and men face different problems sexually. Physiologically, men are less responsive. The decreasing frequency of intercourse and the increasing time required to attain an erection produce anxieties in many older men about erectile dysfunction (impotence)—anxieties that may very well lead to such dysfunction. When the natural slowing down of sexual responses is interpreted as the beginning of erectile dysfunction, this self-diagnosis triggers a vicious spiral of fears and even greater difficulty in having or maintaining an erection.

Among older adults, fantasies become more diffuse, turning from those that are obviously sexual to those centering more on pleasurable experiences in general (Barclay, 1980). As some men get older, their erotic performance becomes more dependent on fantasies; they are less responsive to simple tactile stimulation of the genitals.

Women, who are sexually capable throughout their lives, have different concerns. They face greater social constraints than men. Women are confronted with an unfavorable sex ratio (27 unmarried men per 100 unmarried women over age 65), a greater likelihood of widowhood, and norms against marrying younger men. Grieving over the death of a partner, isolation, and depression also affect their sexuality. Finally, there is a double standard of aging. In our culture, as men age, they become distinguished; as women age,

You can take no credit for beauty at sixteen. But if you are beautiful at sixty, it will be your soul's own doing.

—*Marie Stopes (1880–1958)*

ENVISION YOURSELF NOW. How do you look? How do you feel about your sexuality? Move the clock ahead 45 years from now (or adjust it accordingly so that you are 70 years old). How do you feel about the way you look? Are you in a relationship? Are you sexual? If the image of you as a sexual person is dimmed by a different body image, lack of a partner, or poor health, you are not alone. Most of us (including physicians and other health professionals) have been indoctrinated by restrictive attitudes or an absence of images about older adults and their sexuality. A few facts about sex and aging are in order:

▪ *People remain sexual throughout their lives.* Though individuals may not be sexually active, they still have sexual histories, knowledge, and values that must not be denied. Though sexual activity declines over the decades and many older people choose abstinence as a lifestyle, physicians and health-care workers need to recognize that sexual feelings are healthy throughout life. With this understanding, they will be better able to alleviate feelings of guilt and remorse among older people about their sexuality.

▪ *Many older people have a need for a good sexual relationship.* Loss of health, friends, partner, children, and career may cause depression and a profound sense of loneliness. An excellent antidote to the loss is a loving, intimate, secure sexual relationship.

▪ *Sexual physiology changes with age.* Being aware of potential changes often helps older people accept and deal with them. Males may often have less turgid erections, less forceful ejaculations, and a longer refractory period. A longer refractory period may simply mean there may be sexual relations without ejaculation. Men and their partners can learn that there can be gratifying sex without an erect penis. The slowing down of the sexual response cycle means that foreplay can be prolonged and intimacy and gratification increased.

Although some women celebrate the arrival of menopause, finding it liberating from the concerns of pregnancy and menstruation, others find it disturbing, embarrassing, or painful. Vaginal dryness, the most common symptom and one that can make sexual intercourse quite painful, can be alleviated by an over-the-counter water-soluble lubricant or by saliva. Hormone replacement therapy or an estrogen cream can also remedy this problem. Hot flashes and bone loss leading to osteoporosis are additional problems that women must contend with and should discuss with their physician.

▪ *Changes in body image may have a profound impact on sexuality.* This is particularly true in our society, where image and youth are valued over age and wisdom. Older people must try to reverse the influence of years of conditioning and consciously reevaluate their images of sex and aging.

▪ *Use it or lose it.* This is not an empty phrase. Sexual activity is a physiological function that tends to deteriorate if not exercised; it is particularly fragile in the elderly. Sexual activity appears to keep the vagina more elastic, flexible, and lubricated. According to Masters, Johnson, and Kolodny (1992), intercourse and/or masturbation at least once a week over a period of years helps to keep the mucous secretions active, maintains muscle tone, and helps preserve the shape and size of the vagina.

▪ *Older people are better lovers.* Think about what experience and time bring to an individual. In the case of sexuality, experience brings awareness of self and (we hope) sensitivity to others. Given the quantity of leisure time and the slower-paced lifestyle of many older adults, relationships can often be nurtured and enjoyed. A more accepting attitude about self, others, and life in general can help to make people better sexual partners later in life.

Source: Adapted from Cross, R. (1993, June–July). "What Doctors and Others Need to Know; Sex Facts on Human Sexuality and Aging." *SIECUS Report,* 7–9.

they simply get older. Femininity is connected with youth and beauty; as women age, they tend to be regarded as more masculine. A young woman, for example, is "beautiful," but an older woman is "handsome," a term ordinarily used for men of any age.

▪ As this chapter has shown, psychosexual development occurs on a continuum rather than as a series of discrete stages. Each person develops in his or her own way, according to personal and social circumstances and the dictates of biology. As adolescents grow toward sexual maturity, the gap between their physiological development and their psychological development begins to narrow; their emotional and intellectual capabilities begin to "grow into" their bodies. Nearing adulthood, young people become less dependent on their elders and more capable of developing intimacy on a new level. In young adulthood, tasks that define adult sexuality include establishing sexual orientation, making commitments, entering long-term intimate relationships, and making childbearing decisions. None of these tasks is accomplished overnight. Nor does a task necessarily end as a person moves into a new stage of life.

In middle adulthood, individuals face new tasks involving the nature of their long-term relationships. Often these tasks involve reevaluating these relationships. As people enter late adulthood, they need to adjust to the aging process—to changed sexual responses and needs, declining physical health, the loss of a partner, and their own eventual death. Each stage is filled with its own unique meaning, which gives shape and significance to life and to sexuality.

SUMMARY

Sexuality in Infancy and Childhood

- *Psychosexual development* begins in infancy, when we begin to learn how we "should" feel about our bodies and our gender roles. Infants need stroking and cuddling to ensure healthy psychosexual development.

- Children learn about bodies through various forms of sex play. Their sexual interest should not be labeled "bad" but may be called inappropriate for certain times, places, or persons. Children need expressions of physical affection and to be told nonthreateningly about "good" and "bad" touching by adults.

Sexuality in Adolescence

- *Puberty* is the biological stage when reproduction becomes possible. The psychological state of puberty is *adolescence,* a time of growth and often confusion as the body matures faster than the emotional and intellectual abilities. The traits of adolescence are culturally determined.

- Pubertal changes in girls begin between ages 9 and 14. They include a growth spurt, breast development, pubic and underarm hair, vaginal secretions, and menarche (first menstruation). Pubertal changes in boys generally begin about 2 years later than in girls. They include a growth spurt, voice deepening, hair growth, development of external genitals, and the ejaculation of semen.

- Children and adolescents often learn from their parents that sex is secretive, and "bad." A strong bond between parent and child reduces the risk of early sexual involvement and pregnancy.

- Peers are the strongest influence on the values, attitudes, and behavior of adolescents. They are also a source of much misinformation regarding sex.

- The media present highly charged images of sexuality that are often out of context. Parents can counteract media distortions by discussing the context of sexuality with their children and controlling access to television.

- Young gays and lesbians are largely invisible because of society's assumption of heterosexuality. Gays and lesbians may begin to come to terms with their homosexuality during their teenage years. Because of society's reluctance to acknowledge homosexuality openly, most gay, lesbian, and bisexual teens suffer a great deal of emotional pain.

- Most adolescents engage in masturbation. White adolescent heterosexual couples generally follow a normative sequence of adolescent behaviors, from hand-holding to intercourse. African American teens do not necessarily follow such a sequence. For most teenagers, increased emotional involvement leads to increased sexual activity.

▪ Most teenagers have pressing concerns about sexuality, and most parents favor sex education for their children. Yet the subject remains controversial in many school districts. This is mainly the result of opposition from a vocal minority. Areas of controversy include homosexuality, contraception (versus abstinence), and condom availability.

▪ The United States leads the world's developed nations in teen pregnancies, births, and abortions. Adolescents get pregnant mainly because they do not use contraception or use it improperly; some get pregnant intentionally.

▪ Black communities are more accepting of births outside of marriage than are White communities. Teenage mothers' principal needs are for health care, including prenatal care, and education, including parenting and life skills and job training. Many teenage fathers are eager to help support the families they've created.

▪ Part of the solution to reducing teenage pregnancy is to work toward eliminating the poverty and racism that limit the options and lower the self-esteem of many adolescents.

Sexuality in Early Adulthood

▪ Developmental tasks in young adulthood include establishing sexual orientation, integrating love and sex, forging intimacy and making commitments, making fertility/childbearing decisions, and evolving a sexual philosophy.

▪ *Premarital sex* among young adults (but not adolescents) in a relational context has become the norm. An important factor in this shift is the surge in numbers of unmarried men and women.

▪ Factors leading to premarital sexual involvement include individual factors, relationship factors, and environmental factors. Ethnicity also affects premarital involvement.

▪ A critical task of adulthood is establishing one's sexual identity as heterosexual, gay, lesbian, or bisexual. Between 3% and 10% of Americans have had a significant amount of same-sex sexual contact. Identifying oneself as a lesbian, a gay male, or

a bisexual, however, is complex and includes several phases. *Coming out* is publicly acknowledging one's homosexuality or bisexuality. Though relatively few people identify themselves as *bisexual*, the existence of the term points to the fact that human sexual behavior cannot be easily categorized.

▪ The large increase in the number of unmarried adults has dramatically altered the nature of singlehood in our society.

▪ The two most widely held standards regarding premarital sexual intercourse are permissiveness with affection and the double standard. For gay men and lesbians, the college environment is often liberating because of greater acceptance.

▪ Among single men and women not or no longer attending college, meeting others can be a problem. Singles often meet at work, clubs, resorts, housing complexes, and churches.

▪ With the rise of the HIV/AIDS epidemic, the gay subculture has placed an increased emphasis on the relationship context of sex.

▪ The contemporary lesbian community is currently more moderate and diverse than in prior years. Lesbians' emphasis on emotions over sex and the more enduring quality of their relationships reflect their socialization as women.

▪ Cohabitation has become more widespread and accepted in recent years. More than 1.5 million gay or lesbian couples and 3.6 million heterosexual couples cohabit. *Domestic partnerships* provide some legal protection for cohabiting couples in committed relationships.

Sexuality in Middle Adulthood

▪ Developmental issues of sexuality in middle adulthood include redefining sex in long-term relationships, reevaluating one's sexuality, and accepting the biological aging process.

▪ In marriage, sex tends to diminish in frequency the longer a couple are married. Most married couples don't feel that declining frequency is a major problem if their overall relationship is good.

▪ Extrarelational sexual involvement exists in dating, cohabiting, and marital relationships. In monogamous marriages, extramarital sexual relationships are assumed to be destructive of the relationship and are kept secret. Nonexclusive marriages permit extramarital sex. Successful sexually *open marriages* require commitment to the primacy of the marriage, a high degree of affection and trust, good interpersonal skills, and extramarital partners who do not compete with the marital partner.

- Extramarital affairs appear to be related to two variables: unhappiness of the marriage and/or premarital sexual permissiveness.

- Approximately 50% of all first marriages will probably end in divorce. Sexual experiences following divorce are linked to well-being, especially for men. Single parents are usually not a part of the singles world because the presence of children constrains their freedom.

Sexuality in Late Adulthood

- Many of the psychosexual tasks older Americans must undertake are directly related to the aging process, including changing sexuality and the loss of a partner. Most studies of older adults find that they express relatively high levels of satisfaction and well-being. Older adults' sexuality tends to be invisible because we associate sexuality and romance with youth and procreation.

- Sexual behavior in late adulthood often becomes more intimacy-based, involving touching and holding rather than genital activity. Physiologically, men are less responsive. Women's concerns are more social than physical; they have an unfavorable sex ratio, a greater likelihood of widowhood, and the double standard of aging.

- The greatest determinants of an older person's sexual activity are the availability of a partner and health. After age 75, a significant decrease in sexual activity takes place because of health problems.

SUGGESTED READING

The following journals contain articles on adolescent psychosexual development, sex education, and other issues concerning teenagers: *SIECUS Reports; Family Planning Perspectives,* published by the Alan Guttmacher Institute; and *Journal of Adolescence.*

Blumstein, Philip, & Schwartz, Pepper. (1983). *American Couples: Money, Work, Sex.* New York: William Morrow. A classic work examining power as expressed in money, work, and sex in cohabiting, married, gay, and lesbian relationships.

Calderone, Mary S., & Johnson, Eric W. (1989). *The Family Book About Sexuality* (Rev. ed.). New York: Harper & Row. An excellent guide for parents who want to transmit humanistic values about sexuality to their children.

D'Augelli, Anthony R., & Patterson, Charlotte (Eds.). (1995). *Lesbian, Gay, and Bisexual Identities Over the Lifespan: Psychological Perspectives.* New York: Oxford University Press. An overview of psychological research and theory on lesbian, gay, and bisexual identities by leading scholars.

Gullotta, Thomas P., Adams, Gerald R., & Montemayor, Raymond (Eds.). (1993). *Adolescent Sexuality.* Newbury Park, CA: Sage. Research in many areas of adolescent sexuality, including sexual behavior, gay and lesbian teenagers, teenage pregnancy, and promoting sexual responsibility.

Irvine, Janice M. (1995). *Sexuality Education Across Cultures.* San Francisco, CA: Jossey-Bass. A discussion of sexual attitudes and behaviors and how we communicate about sexuality in light of cultural differences.

Klein, Marty. (1992). *Ask Me Anything.* New York: Simon & Schuster. A book for adults (teachers, parents, therapists) who want to be prepared to give straightforward, knowledgeable answers to any question a child may ask about sex.

Pipher, Mary. (1994). *Reviving Ophelia: Saving the Selves of Adolescent Girls.* New York: Ballantine Books. Insight into the lives of teenage girls and the pressures that our culture inflicts on them.

Rubin, Lillian. (1991). *Erotic Wars: What Happened to the Sexual Revolution?* New York: Harper & Row. An examination of changing sexual mores among young adults and married couples.

Sprecher, Susan, & McKinney, Kathleen. (1993). *Sexuality.* Newbury Park, CA: Sage. A comprehensive examination of sexuality within the context of close relationships, such as dating, cohabitation, and marriage.

Strasburger, Victor C. (1995). *Adolescents and the Media: Medical and Psychological Impact.* Thousand Oaks, CA: Sage. A state-of-the-art review of research findings demonstrating the role of the media in the behavior and development of adolescents.

Weinberg, Martin, Williams, Colin, & Pryor, Douglas. (1994). *Dual Attraction: Understanding Bisexuality.* New York: Oxford University Press. The first major scientific study on the nature of bisexuality.

7

Love, Intimacy, and Sexuality

*L*OVE IS ONE of the most profound human emotions, and it manifests itself in various forms across all cultures. In our culture, love binds us together as partners, parents, children, and friends. It is a powerful force in the intimate relationships of almost all individuals, regardless of sexual orientation; it crosses all ethnic boundaries. We make major life decisions, such as whom we marry, based on love. We make sacrifices for it, sometimes sacrificing even our lives for those we love.

Love is both a feeling and an activity. A person feels love for someone and acts in a loving manner. But we can also be angry with the person we love, or feel frustrated, bored, or indifferent. This is the paradox of love: It encompasses opposites. A loving relationship includes affection and anger, excitement and boredom, stability and change, bonds and freedom. Its paradoxical quality makes some ask whether they are really in love when they are not feeling "perfectly" in love or when their relationship is not going smoothly. Love does not give us perfection, however; it gives us meaning. In fact, as sociologist Ira Reiss (1980) suggests, a more important question to ask is not if one is feeling love, but, "Is the love I feel the kind of love on which I can build a lasting relationship or marriage?"

In this chapter, we examine the relationship between sex and love. We look at the always perplexing question of the nature of love. Then we examine the ways that social scientists study love to gain new insights into it. We then turn to the darker side of love—jealousy—to understand its dynamics. Finally, we see how love transforms itself from passion to intimacy, providing the basis for long-lasting relationships.

Love doesn't make the world go round. Love is what makes the ride worthwhile.

—*Franklin P. Jones*

LOVE AND SEXUALITY

Love and sexuality are intimately intertwined (Aron & Aron, 1991). Although marriage was once the only acceptable context for sexual intercourse, for most people today, love legitimizes sex outside of marriage. With the "sex with affection" standard of sexual relations, we use individualistic rather than social norms to legitimize sexual relations. Our sexual standards have become personal rather than institutional. This shift to personal responsibility makes love even more important in sexual relationships.

We can even see this connection between love and sex in our everyday use of words. Think of the words we use to describe sexual interactions. When we say that we "make love," are "lovers," or are "intimate" with someone, we generally mean that we are sexually involved. But this sexual involvement carries overtones of relationship, caring, or love. Such potential meanings are absent in such technically correct words as "sexual intercourse," "fellatio," and "cunnilingus," as well as in such obscene words as "fuck" and "screw."

Men, Sex, and Love

Men and women who are not in an established relationship have different expectations. Men are more likely than women to separate sex from affection. Studies consistently demonstrate that for the majority of men, sex and

At the start of a relationship, it is often impossible to tell whether one's feelings are infatuation or the beginning of love.

love can be easily separated (Blumstein & Schwartz, 1983; Carroll, Volk, & Hyde, 1985; Laumann et al., 1994).

Although men are more likely than women to separate sex and love, Linda Levine and Lonnie Barbach (1983) found in their interviews that men indicated that their most erotic sexual experiences took place in a relational context. Most men in the study responded that it was primarily the emotional quality of the relationship that made their sexual experiences special.

Researchers suggest that heterosexual men are not as different from gay men in terms of their acceptance of casual sex as might be thought. Heterosexual men, they maintain, would be as likely as gay men to engage in casual sex if women were equally interested. Women, however, are not as interested in casual sex; as a result, heterosexual men do not have as many willing partners as gay men do (Blum, 1997; Foa, Anderson, Converse, & Urbansky, 1987).

Women, Sex, and Love

Women generally view sex from a relational perspective. In the decision to have sexual intercourse, the quality and degree of intimacy of a relationship were more important for women than men (Christopher & Cate, 1984). Women were more likely to report feelings of love if they were sexually involved with their partners than if they were not sexually involved (Peplau, Rubin, & Hill, 1977). For women, love is also more closely related to feelings of self-esteem.

Women generally seek emotional relationships; some men initially seek physical relationships. This difference in intentions can place women in a bind. Carole Cassell (1984) suggests that women face a "damned if you do, damned if you don't" dilemma in their sexual relationships. If a woman has sexual intercourse with a man, he says good-bye; if she doesn't, he says he respects her and still says good-bye.

Traditionally, women were labeled "good" or "bad" based on their sexual experience and values. "Good" women were virgins, sexually naive, or passive, whereas "bad" women were sexually experienced, independent, and passionate. According to Lillian Rubin (1990), this attitude has not entirely changed. Rather, we are ambivalent about sexually experienced women. One exasperated woman leaped out of her chair and began to pace the floor, exclaiming to Rubin, "I sometimes think what men really want is a sexually experienced virgin. They want you to know the tricks, but they don't like to think you did those things with anyone else."

Gay Men, Lesbians, and Love

Love is equally important for heterosexuals, gay men, lesbians, and bisexuals (Aron & Aron, 1991; Keller & Rosen, 1988; Kurdek, 1988; Peplau & Cochran, 1988). Many heterosexuals, however, perceive lesbian and gay love relationships as less satisfying and less loving than heterosexual ones. It is well documented that love is important for gay men and lesbians; their relationships have multiple emotional dimensions and are not based solely on sex, as others might believe (Adler, Hendrick, & Hendrick, 1989).

Men in general are more likely to separate love and sex than women; gay men are especially likely to make this separation. Although gay men value love, they also value sex as an end in itself. Furthermore, they place less emphasis on sexual exclusiveness in their relationships. Many gay men appear to successfully negotiate sexually open relationships. Keeping the sexual agreements they make appears to matter most for these men. Data from 560 self-selected gay couples indicate that the pursuit of outside sex should not be taken as evidence that sex between the partners is lacking (Demian, 1994).

Although lesbians share sex less often than gay male or heterosexual couples, they tend to be more satisfied with their sexual lives and report a greater sense of intimacy with their partner (Schureurs, 1993). For many, caressing, nongenital stimulation, and affectionate foreplay are the preferred expressions of sexuality and love.

For lesbians, gay men, and bisexuals, love has special significance in the formation and acceptance of their identities. Although significant numbers of men and women have had sexual experiences with members of the same sex or both sexes, relatively few identify themselves as gay or lesbian. As we saw in Chapter 6, same-sex sexual interactions are not in themselves sufficient to acquiring a gay or lesbian identity. An important element in solidifying such an identity is loving someone of the same sex. Love signifies a commitment to being lesbian or gay by unifying the emotional and physical dimensions of a person's sexuality (Troiden, 1988). For the gay man or lesbian, it marks the beginning of sexual wholeness and acceptance. In fact, some researchers believe that the ability to love someone of the same sex, rather than having sex with him or her, is the critical element that distinguishes being gay or lesbian from being heterosexual (Money, 1980).

For lesbians, gay men, and bisexuals, love is an important component in the formation and acceptance of their sexual orientation. The public declaration of love and commitment is a milestone in the lives of many couples.

The only queer people are those who don't love anybody.

—*Rita Mae Brown*

Sex Without Love

Is love necessary for sex? We may assume that it is, but that assumption is based on motives and values. The question cannot be answered by reference to empirical or statistical data. It becomes a more fundamental one: Is sexual activity legitimate in itself, or does it require justification? To believe that sex does not require love as a justification, argues researcher John Crosby (1985), does not deny the significance of love and affection in sexual relations. In fact, love and affection are important and desirable for enduring relationships. They are simply not necessary, Crosby believes, for affairs in which erotic pleasure is the central feature.

Ironically, although sex without love violates our overt beliefs about sexuality, it is the least threatening form of extrarelational sex. Even those who accept their partner's having sex outside the relationship find it especially difficult to accept their partner's having a meaningful affair. "They believe that two intense romantic relationships cannot co-exist and that one would have to go" (Blumstein & Schwartz, 1983).

Love Without Sex: Celibacy as a Choice

In a society that often seems obsessed with sexuality, it may be surprising to find individuals who counter the culture by choosing celibacy as a lifestyle. **Celibacy,** not engaging in any kind of sexual activity, is not necessarily a symptom of a problem or disorder. It may be a choice for some, such as those who have taken religious vows or are in relationships where deep affection and respect provide adequate fulfillment. For others, it is a result of life circumstances, such as the absence of a partner or imprisonment. Still others report very low interest in sex or express concern over the spread of HIV or other sexually transmitted diseases. The National Social Life Survey found that 4% of men and 14% of women rarely or never think about sex (Laumann et al., 1994).

Individuals who choose celibacy may report a better appreciation of the nature of friendship and an increased respect for the bonds and boundaries of marriage (Norris, 1996). In giving up their sexual pursuits, celibate individuals may seek to learn to relate to others as human beings and to listen without possessiveness and without imposing themselves. Although these traits may also be developed within a sexual relationship, those who choose celibacy as a lifestyle may feel that it frees up energy for personal growth or other kinds of relationships in a way that would not otherwise be possible for them.

HOW DO I LOVE THEE? APPROACHES AND ATTITUDES RELATED TO LOVE

For most people, love and sex are closely linked in an ideal intimate relationship. Love reflects the positive factors—such as caring—that draw people together and sustain them in a relationship. Sex reflects both emotional and physical elements in a relationship, such as closeness and sexual excitement, that differentiate romantic love from other forms of love, such as

> Love and you shall be loved. All love is mathematically just, as much as two sides of an algebraic equation.
>
> —*Ralph Waldo Emerson (1803–1882)*

parental love or the love between friends. Although the two are related, they are not necessarily connected. One can exist without the other. It is possible to love someone without being sexually involved, and it is possible to be sexually involved without love.

Attitudes and Behaviors Associated with Love

A review of the research finds a number of attitudes, feelings, and behaviors associated with love (Kelley, 1983). Notice how some of these are also associated with sex.

Positive attitudes and feelings toward the other bring people together. Zick Rubin (1973) found that four feelings identify love. These feelings are:

- *Caring for the other,* wanting to help him or her.
- *Needing the other,* having a strong desire to be in the other's presence and to have the other care for you.
- *Trusting the other,* mutually exchanging confidences.
- *Tolerating the other,* including his or her faults.

Of these, caring appears to be the most important, followed by needing, trusting, and tolerating (Steck, Levitan, McLane, & Kelley, 1982). J. R. Davitz (1969) identified similar feelings associated with love but noted, in addition, that respondents reported feeling an inner glow, optimism, and cheerfulness. They felt harmony and unity with the person they loved. They were intensely aware of the other person, feeling that they were fully concentrated on him or her.

Love is also expressed in certain behaviors. One study found that romantic love is expressed in several ways (Swensen, 1972). Notice that the expression of love often overlaps thoughts of love:

- *Verbally expressing affection,* such as saying, "I love you."
- *Self-disclosing,* such as revealing intimate facts about oneself.
- *Giving nonmaterial evidence,* such as emotional and moral support in times of need, and respecting the other's opinion.
- *Expressing nonverbal feelings,* such as feeling happier, more content, more secure when the other is present.
- *Giving material evidence,* such as gifts, flowers, small favors, or doing more than your share of something.
- *Physically expressing love,* such as hugging, kissing, making love.
- *Tolerating the other,* such as accepting his or her idiosyncrasies, peculiar routines, or forgetfulness about putting the cap on the toothpaste.

Research supports the belief that people "walk on air" when they are in love. Researchers have found that those in love view the world more positively than those who are not in love (Hendrick & Hendrick, 1988).

Styles of Love

Sociologist John Lee describes six basic styles of love (Borrello & Thompson, 1990; Lee, 1973, 1988). These styles of love, he cautions, describe relationship

> LOVE, A temporary insanity, curable by marriage.
>
> —*Ambrose Bierce (1842–1914)*

> It is only with the heart that one can see rightly; what is essential is invisible to the eye.
>
> —*Antoine de Saint-Exupéry (1900–1944)*

styles, not individual styles. The style of love may change as the relationship changes or when individuals enter different relationships.

Eros was the ancient Greek god of love, the son of Aphrodite. (The Romans called him Cupid.) As a style of love, **eros** is the love of beauty. Erotic lovers delight in the tactile, the sensual, the immediate; they are attracted to beauty (though beauty is in the eye of the beholder). They love the lines of the body, its feel and touch. They are fascinated by every detail of their beloved. Their love burns brightly but soon flickers and dies.

The word "mania" comes from the Greek word for madness, and as a style of love, **mania** is obsessive and possessive. For manic lovers, nights are marked by sleeplessness and days by pain and anxiety. The slightest sign of affection brings ecstasy for a short while, only to disappear. Satisfactions last but a moment before they must be renewed. Manic love is roller-coaster love.

Ludus is the Latin word for play, and **ludus** represents playful love. For ludic lovers, love is a game, something to play at rather than to become deeply involved in. Love is ultimately *ludic*rous. Love is for fun; encounters are casual, carefree, and often careless. "Nothing serious" is the motto of ludic lovers.

Storge (STOR-gay), companionate love, from the Greek word for natural affection, is the love between companions. It is, wrote Lee, "love without fever, tumult, or folly, a peaceful and enchanting affection." It begins usually as friendship and then gradually deepens into love. If the love ends, that also occurs gradually, and the couple often become friends once again. Of such love Theophile Gautier wrote, "To love is to admire with the heart; to admire is to love with the mind."

Agape (AH-ga-pay), altruistic love, from the Greek word for brotherly love, is the traditional Christian love that is chaste, patient, and undemanding; it does not expect to be reciprocated. It is the love of saints and martyrs. Agape is more abstract and ideal than concrete and real. It is easier to love all of humankind than an individual in this way.

Pragma, from the Greek word for business, is practical love. Pragmatic lovers are, first and foremost, businesslike in their approach to looking for someone who meets their needs. They use logic in their search for a partner, seeking background, education, personality, religion, and interests that are compatible with their own. If they meet a person who satisfies their criteria, erotic, manic, or other feelings may develop. But, as Samuel Butler warned, "Logic is like the sword—those who appeal to it shall perish by it."

In addition to these pure forms, there are mixtures of the basic types: storgic-eros, ludic-eros, and storgic-ludus.

Lee believes that to have a mutually satisfying relationship, a person has to find a partner who shares the same style and definition of love. The more different two people are in their styles of love, the less likely it is they will understand each other's love. (To find your style of love, see the box on pages 210–211.)

Recent research reports the absence of significant gender differences in love attitudes across adulthood (Montgomery & Sorell, 1997). Individuals throughout the life stages of marriage report love attitudes involving passion, romance, friendship, and self-giving love. The information contradicts the notion that romantic, passionate love is the privilege of youth and young relationships.

According to sociologist John Lee, there are six styles of love: eros, mania, ludus, storge, agape, and pragma. What style do you believe this couple illustrates? Why?

The Triangular Theory of Love

The **triangular theory of love,** developed by Robert Sternberg (1986), emphasizes the dynamic quality of love relationships. This theory sees love as composed of three elements, as in the points of a triangle. These elements are intimacy, passion, and decision/commitment (Figure 7.1). Each can be enlarged or diminished in the course of a love relationship, which will affect the quality of the relationship. They can also be combined in different ways. Each combination produces a different type of love, such as romantic love, infatuation, empty love, liking, and so on. Partners may combine the components differently at different times in the same love relationship.

The Components of Love Intimacy refers to the warm, close, bonding feelings we get when we love someone. According to Sternberg and Grajek (1984), there are ten signs of intimacy:

1. Wanting to promote your partner's welfare.
2. Feeling happiness with your partner.
3. Holding your partner in high regard.
4. Being able to count on your partner in time of need.
5. Being able to understand each other.
6. Sharing yourself and your possessions with your partner.
7. Receiving emotional support from your partner.
8. Giving emotional support to your partner.
9. Being able to communicate with your partner about intimate things.
10. Valuing your partner's presence in your life.

FIGURE 7.1 According to Robert Sternberg's triangular theory of love, the three triangle points are intimacy, passion, and decision/commitment.

If love does not know how to give and take without restrictions, it is not love, but a transaction that never fails to lay stress on a plus and a minus.

—*Emma Goldman (1869–1940)*

JOHN LEE, WHO DEVELOPED the idea of styles of love, also developed a questionnaire that allows men and women to identify their style of love. Complete the questionnaire to identify your style of love. Then ask yourself to which style of love you find yourself drawn in others. Is it the same as your own or different?

Consider each characteristic as it applies to a current relationship that you define as love, or to a previous one if that is more applicable. For each, note whether the trait is *almost always* true (AA), *usually* true (U), *rarely* true (R), or *almost never* true (AN).

	Eros	Ludus	Storge	Mania	Ludic-Eros	Storgic-Eros	Storgic-Ludus	Pragma
1. You consider your childhood less happy than the average of peers.	R		AN	U				
2. You were discontented with life (work, etc.) at the time your encounter began.	R		AN	U	R			
3. You have never been in love before this relationship.					U	R	AN	R
4. You want to be in love or have love as security.	R	AN		AA		AN	AN	U
5. You have a clearly defined ideal image of your desired partner.	AA	AN	AN	AN	U	AN	R	AA
6. You felt a strong gut attraction to your beloved on the first encounter.	AA	R	AN	R		AN		
7. You are preoccupied with thoughts about the beloved.	AA	AN	AN	AA			R	
8. You believe your partner's interest is at least as great as yours.		U	R	AN			R	U
9. You are eager to see your beloved almost every day; this was true from the beginning.	AA	AN	R	AA		R	AN	R
10. You soon believed this could become a permanent relationship.	AA	AN	R	AN	R	AA	AN	U
11. You see "warning signs" of trouble but ignore them.	R	R		AA		AN	R	R
12. You deliberately restrain frequency of contact with partner.	AN	AA	R	R	R	R	U	
13. You restrict discussion of your feelings with beloved.	R	AA	U	U	R		U	U
14. You restrict display of your feelings with beloved.	R	AA	R	U	R		U	U
15. You discuss future plans with beloved.	AA	R	R				AN	AA
16. You discuss wide range of topics, experiences with partner.	AA	R				U	R	AA
17. You try to control relationship, but feel you've lost control.	AN	AN	AN	AA	AN	AN		
18. You lose ability to terminate relationship first.	AN	AN		AA	R	U	R	R

	Eros	Ludus	Storge	Mania	Ludic-Eros	Storgic-Eros	Storgic-Ludus	Pragma
19. You try to force beloved to show more feeling, commitment.	AN	AN		AA		AN	R	
20. You analyze the relationship, weigh it in your mind.			AN	U		R	R	AA
21. You believe in the sincerity of your partner.	AA			U	R	U	AA	
22. You blame partner for difficulties of your relationship.	R	U	R	U	R	AN		
23. You are jealous and possessive but not to the point of angry conflict.	U	AN	R		R	AN		
24. You are jealous to the point of conflict, scenes, threats, etc.	AN	AN	AN	AA	R	AN	AN	AN
25. Tactile, sensual contact is very important to you.	AA		AN		U	AN		R
26. Sexual intimacy was achieved early, rapidly in the relationship.	AA		AN	AN	U	R	U	
27. You take the quality of sexual rapport as a test of love.	AA	U	AN		U	AN	U	R
28. You are willing to work out sex problems, improve technique.	U	R		R	U		R	U
29. You have a continued high rate of sex, tactile contact throughout the relationship.	U		R	R	U	R		R
30. You declare your love first, well ahead of partner.		AN	R	AA		AA		
31. You consider love life your most important activity, even essential.	AA	AN	R	AA		AA	R	R
32. You are prepared to "give all" for love once under way.	U	AN	U	AA	R	AA	R	R
33. You are willing to suffer abuse, even ridicule from partner.		AN	R	AA			R	AN
34. Your relationship is marked by frequent differences of opinion, anxiety.	R	AA	R	AA	R	R		R
35. The relationship ends with lasting bitterness, trauma for you.	AN	R	R	AA	R	AN	R	R

To diagnose your style of love, look for patterns across characteristics. If you consider your childhood less happy than that of your friends, were discontent with life when you fell in love, and very much want to be in love, you have "symptoms" that are rarely typical of eros and almost never true of storge, but that do suggest mania. Where a trait does not especially apply to a style of love, the space in that column is blank. Storge, for instance, is not the *presence* of many symptoms of love, but precisely their absence: it is cool, abiding affection.

Source: J. A. Lee. "The Styles of Love." Reprinted with permission from *Psychology Today Magazine*, ©1974 (Sussex Publishers, Inc.).

The passion component refers to the elements of romance, attraction, and sexuality in your relationship. These may be fueled by desires to increase self-esteem, to be sexually active or fulfilled, to affiliate with others, to dominate, or to subordinate.

The decision/commitment component consists of two separate parts, a short-term part and a long-term part. The short-term part refers to your decision that you love someone. You may or may not make the decision consciously. But it usually occurs before you decide to make a commitment to that person. The commitment represents the long-term part; it is the maintenance of love. But a decision to love someone does not necessarily entail a commitment to maintaining that love.

> Don't threaten me with love, baby.
> —*Billie Holiday (1915–1959)*

Kinds of Love   The intimacy, passion, and decision/commitment components can be combined in eight basic ways, according to Sternberg. These combinations form the basis for classifying love:

1. Liking (intimacy only)
2. Infatuation (passion only)
3. Romantic love (intimacy and passion)
4. Companionate love (intimacy and commitment)
5. Fatuous love (passion and commitment)
6. Consummate love (intimacy, passion, and commitment)
7. Empty love (decision/commitment only)
8. Nonlove (absence of intimacy, passion, and commitment)

These types represent extremes that probably few of us experience. Not many of us, for example, experience infatuation in its purest form, in which there is absolutely *no* intimacy. And empty love, in fact, is not really love at all. These categories are nevertheless useful for examining the nature of love.

LIKING: INTIMACY ONLY   Liking represents the intimacy component alone. It forms the basis for close friendships but is neither passionate nor committed. As such, liking is often an enduring kind of love. Boyfriends and girlfriends may come and go, but good friends remain.

INFATUATION: PASSION ONLY   Infatuation is "love at first sight." It is the kind of love that idealizes its object; it rarely sees the other as a "real" person who sometimes has bad breath (but is worthy of being loved nonetheless). Infatuation is marked by sudden passion and a high degree of physical and emotional arousal. It tends to be obsessive and all-consuming; one has no time, energy, or desire for anything or anyone but the beloved (or thoughts of him or her). To the dismay of the infatuated individual, infatuations are usually asymmetrical: One's passion (or obsession) is rarely returned equally. And the greater the asymmetry, the greater the distress in the relationship.

ROMANTIC LOVE: INTIMACY AND PASSION   Romantic love combines intimacy and passion. It is similar to liking except it is more intense as a result of physical or emotional attraction. It may begin with an immediate union of the two components, with friendship that intensifies with passion, or with passion that also develops intimacy. Although commitment is not an essential element of romantic love, it may develop.

COMPANIONATE LOVE: INTIMACY AND COMMITMENT   Companionate love is essential to a committed friendship. It often begins as romantic love, but as the passion diminishes and the intimacy increases, it is transformed into companionate love. Some couples are satisfied with such love; others are not. Those who are dissatisfied in companionate love relationships may seek extrarelational affairs to maintain passion in their lives. They may also end the relationship to seek a new romantic relationship that they hope will remain romantic.

FATUOUS LOVE: PASSION AND COMMITMENT   Fatuous or deceptive love is whirlwind love; it begins the day a couple meet, quickly results in cohabitation or engagement, then marriage. It goes so fast one hardly knows what happened. Often enough, nothing much really did happen that will permit the relationship to endure. As Sternberg (1988) observes, "It is fatuous in the sense that a commitment is made on the basis of passion without the stabilizing element of intimate involvement—which takes time to develop." Passion fades soon enough, and all that remains is commitment. But commitment that has had relatively little time to deepen is a poor foundation on which to build an enduring relationship. With neither passion nor intimacy, the commitment wanes.

CONSUMMATE LOVE: INTIMACY, PASSION, AND COMMITMENT   Consummate love is born when intimacy, passion, and commitment combine to form their unique constellation. It is the kind of love we dream about but do not expect in all our love relationships. Many of us can achieve it, but it is difficult to sustain over time. To sustain it, we must nourish its different components, for each is subject to the stress of time.

EMPTY LOVE: DECISION/COMMITMENT ONLY   Empty love involves staying together solely for appearance' sake or for the sake of the children.

NONLOVE: ABSENCE OF INTIMACY, PASSION, AND COMMITMENT   Nonlove can take many forms, such as attachment for financial reasons, fear, or the fulfillment of neurotic needs.

The Geometry of Love   The shape of the love triangle depends on the intensity of the love and the balance of the parts. Intense love relationships create triangles with greater area; such triangles occupy more of one's life. Just as love relationships can be balanced or unbalanced, so can love triangles. The balance determines the shape of the triangle (Figure 7.2). A relationship in which the intimacy, passion, and commitment components are equal forms an equilateral triangle. But if the components are not equal, unbalanced triangles form. The size and shape of a person's triangle give a good pictorial sense of how that person feels about another. The greater the match between the triangles of the two partners in a relationship, the more each is likely to experience satisfaction in the relationship.

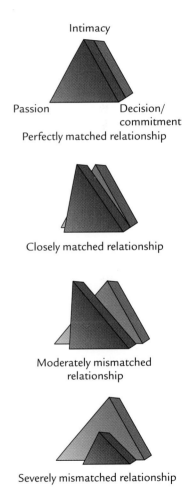

FIGURE 7.2 According to the triangular theory of love, the shape and size of each person's triangle indicates how well each is matched to the other.

Love as Attachment

Human beings need to bond with other people. At the same time, many people fear bonding. Where do these contradictory impulses and emotions come from? Can they ever be resolved?

Attachment theory, the most prominent approach to the study of love, helps us understand adult relationships, what goes wrong in them, and what to do when things do go wrong. In this theory, love is seen as a form of **attachment,** a close, enduring emotional bond that finds its roots in infancy (Hazan & Shaver, 1987; Shaver, 1984; Shaver, Hazan, & Bradshaw, 1988). Research suggests that romantic love and infant/caregiver attachment have similar emotional dynamics. These include the following:

Attachment

- Attachment bond's formation and quality depend on attachment object's (AO) responsiveness and sensitivity.
- When AO is present, infant is happier.
- Infant shares toys, discoveries, objects with AO.
- Infant coos, talks baby talk, "sings."
- Feelings of oneness with AO.

Romantic Love

- Feelings of love are related to lover's interest and reciprocation.
- When lover is present, person feels happier.
- Lovers share experience and goods; give gifts.
- Lovers coo, sing, and talk baby talk.
- Feelings of oneness with lover.

The implications of attachment theory are far-reaching. Attachment affects the way we process information, interact with others, and view the world. Quite basically, it influences our ability to love and see ourselves as lovable. One study showed that we can carry an attachment style with us for life; this style predisposes us to behave in certain ways in love relationships (Shaver et al., 1988). In a later study, researchers found a significant association between attachment styles and relationship satisfaction (Brennan & Shaver, 1995).

The core elements of love appear to be the same for children as they are for adults: the need to feel emotionally safe and secure. When a partner responds to a need, for instance, adults sense the world as home, a safe place. In this respect, we don't differ greatly from children.

The most basic concept of attachment theory is that to be whole adults, we do not need to deny the fact that we are also vulnerable children. In a secure, intimate adult relationship, it is neither demeaning or diminishing nor pathologic to share honest emotions. It is the capacity to be vulnerable and open and accepting of others' giving that makes us lovable and human.

Based on observations made by Mary Ainsworth and colleagues (1978, cited in Shaver et al., 1988), Shaver and colleagues (1988) hypothesized that the styles of attachment developed in childhood—secure, anxious/ambivalent, and avoidant—continue through adulthood. Their surveys revealed similar styles in adult relationships.

According to attachment theory, the holding and cuddling behaviors between parents and babies resemble those of adult lovers.

Adults with **secure attachments,** for example, found it relatively easy to get close to others. They felt comfortable depending on others and having others depend on them. They didn't frequently worry about being abandoned or having someone get too close to them. More than anxious/ambivalent and avoidant adults, they felt that others generally liked them; they believed that people were generally well-intentioned and good-hearted. Their love experiences tended to be happy, friendly, and trusting. They accepted and supported their partners. On average, their relationships lasted 10 years. About 56% of the adults in the study were secure. A recent study reported that secure adults find greater satisfaction and commitment in their relationships than those with other attachment styles (Pistole, Clark, & Tubbs, 1995).

Adults with **anxious/ambivalent attachments** felt that others did not get as close as they themselves wanted. They worried that their partners didn't really love them or would leave them. They also wanted to merge completely with another, which sometimes scared others away. More than others, they felt that it is easy to fall in love. Their experiences in love were often obsessive and marked by desire for union, high degrees of sexual attraction, and jealousy. Their love relationships lasted an average of 5 years. Between 19% and 20% of the adults were identified as anxious/ambivalent.

Adults with secure attachments find it easy to get close to others.

Adults with **avoidant attachments** felt discomfort in being close to others; they were distrustful and fearful of being dependent. More than others, they believed that romance seldom lasts, but that at times it can be as intense as it was at the beginning. Their partners wanted more closeness than they did. Avoidant lovers feared intimacy and experienced emotional highs and lows and jealousy. Their relationships lasted an average of 6 years. Twenty-three to 25% of the adults in the study were avoidant.

In adulthood, the attachment style developed in infancy combines with sexual desire and caring behaviors to give rise to romantic love. It is this combination that lays the groundwork for a relationship with another.

Friendship and Love

Friendship and love breathe life into humanity. They bind us together, provide emotional sustenance, buffer us against stress, and help to preserve our physical and mental well-being.

What distinguishes love from friendship? Two researchers (Todd & Davis, 1985) set out to distinguish the differences between the characteristics of love and friendship. In their study of 250 college students and community members, they found that although love and friendship were alike in many ways, some crucial differences make love relationships both more rewarding and more vulnerable. Best-friend relationships were similar to spouse/lover relationships in several ways: level of acceptance, trust, and respect and levels of confiding, understanding, spontaneity, and mutual acceptance. Levels of satisfaction and happiness with the relationship were also found to be similar for both groups. What separated friends from lovers was that lovers had much more fascination and a greater sense of exclusiveness with their partners than did friends. Though love had a greater potential for distress, conflict, and mutual criticism, it ran deeper and stronger than friendship.

Friendship appears to be the foundation for a strong love relationship. Shared interests and values, acceptance, trust, understanding, and enjoyment are at the root of friendship and a basis for love. Adding the dimensions of passion and emotional intimacy alters the nature of the friendship and creates new expectations and possibilities.

Although some believe that marriage should satisfy all their needs, it is important to remember that when people marry, they do not cease to be separate individuals. Friendships and patterns of social behavior continue, so the mix of friendship and love must be understood as it affects marital satisfaction.

With men and women marrying later than ever before and women being an integral part of the workforce, close friendships, including with other-sex friends, are more likely to be a part of the tapestry of relationships in people's lives. Partners need to communicate and seek understanding regarding the nature of activities and degree of emotional closeness they find acceptable in their partner's friendships. Boundaries should be clarified and opinions shared. Many couples find cross-sex friendships acceptable and even desirable. Like other significant issues involving partnerships, success in balancing a love relationship and other friendships depends on the ability to communicate concerns and on the maturity of the people involved.

UNREQUITED LOVE

As most of us know from painful experience, love is not always returned. Several researchers (Baumeister, Wotman, & Stillwell, 1993) accurately captured some of the feelings associated with **unrequited love** (love that is not returned) in the title of their research article: "Unrequited Love: On Heartbreak, Anger, Guilt, Scriptlessness, and Humiliation." They found that unrequited love is distressing for both the would-be lover and the rejecting partner. Would-be lovers felt both positive and intensely negative feelings about their unlucky attempt at a relationship. The rejectors, however, felt uniformly negative about the experience. Unlike the rejectors, the would-be lovers felt that the attraction was mutual, that they had been led on, and that the rejection had never been clearly communicated. Rejectors, by contrast, felt that they had not led the other person on; moreover, they felt guilty about hurting him or her. Nevertheless, many found the other person's persistence intrusive and annoying; they wished the other would have simply gotten the hint and gone away. Rejectors saw would-be lovers as self-deceptive and unreasonable; would-be lovers saw their rejectors as inconsistent and mysterious.

> 'Tis better to have loved and lost
> Than never to have loved at all.
>
> —*Alfred, Lord Tennyson (1809–1892)*

Styles of Unrequited Lovers

Unrequited love presents a paradox: If the goal of loving someone is an intimate relationship, why should we continue to love a person with whom we cannot have such a relationship? Arthur Aron and his colleagues addressed this question in a study of almost 500 college students (Aron et al., 1989). The researchers found three different styles underlying the experience of unrequited love:

▪ *The Cyrano style*—the desire to have a romantic relationship with a specific person regardless of how hopeless the love is. In this style, the benefits of loving someone are so great that it does not matter how likely it is that the love will be returned. Being in the same room with the beloved—because he or she is so wonderful—may be sufficient. This style is named after Cyrano de Bergerac, a seventeenth-century musketeer, whose love for Roxanne was so great that it was irrelevant that she loved someone else.

▪ *The Giselle style*—the misperception that a relationship is more likely to develop than it actually is. This might occur if one misreads the other's cues, such as in mistakenly believing that friendliness is a sign of love. This style is named after Giselle, the tragic ballet heroine who was misled by Count Albrecht to believe that her love was reciprocated.

▪ *The Don Quixote style*—the general desire to be in love, regardless of whom one loves. In this style, the benefits of being in love—such as being viewed as a romantic or the excitement of extreme emotions—are more important than actually being in a relationship. This style is named after Cervantes's Don Quixote, whose love for the common Dulcinea was motivated by his need to dedicate knightly deeds to a lady love. "It is as right and proper for a knight errant to be in love as for the sky to have stars," Don Quixote explained.

Attachment Theory and Unrequited Love

Using attachment theory, the researchers found that some people were predisposed to be Cyranos, others Giselles, and still others Don Quixotes. Anxious/ambivalent adults tended to be Cyranos, avoidant adults often were Don Quixotes, and secure adults were likely to be Giselles. Those who were anxious/ambivalent were most likely to experience unrequited love; those who were secure were least likely to experience such love. Avoidant adults experienced the greatest desire to be in love in general; yet they had the least probability of being in a specific relationship. Anxious/ambivalent adults showed the greatest desire for a specific relationship; they also had the least desire to be in love in general.

JEALOUSY

Beware, my lord, of jealousy. It is the green-eyed monster that mocks the meat it feeds on.

—*William Shakespeare (1564–1616)*

Many of us think that the existence of jealousy proves the existence of love. We may try to test someone's interest or affection by attempting to make him or her jealous by flirting with another person. If our date or partner becomes jealous, the jealousy is taken as a sign of love (Salovey & Rodin, 1991; G. White, 1980a). But provoking jealousy proves nothing except that the other person can be made jealous. Making jealousy a litmus test of love is dangerous, for jealousy and love are not necessarily companions. Jealousy may be a more accurate yardstick for measuring insecurity or immaturity than love (Pistole, 1995).

It's important to understand jealousy for several reasons. First, jealousy is a painful emotion filled with anger and hurt. This churning emotion can turn us inside out, making us feel out of control. If we can understand jealousy, especially when it is irrational, then we can eliminate some of its pain. Second, jealousy can help cement or destroy a relationship. Jealousy helps maintain a relationship by guarding its exclusiveness. But in its irrational or extreme forms, it can destroy a relationship by its insistent demands and attempts at control. We need to understand when and how jealousy is functional and when it is not. Third, jealousy is often linked to violence (Follingstad, Rutledge, Berg, & Hause, 1990; Laner, 1990; Riggs, 1993). It is a factor in precipitating violence in dating relationships among both high school and college students (Burcky, Reuterman, & Kopsky, 1988; Stets & Pirog-Good, 1987). Marital violence and rape are often provoked by jealousy (Russell, 1990). Rather than being directed at a rival, jealous aggression is often used against the partner (Paul & Galloway, 1994).

What Is Jealousy?

Jealousy is an aversive response that occurs because of a partner's real, imagined, or likely involvement with a third person (Bringle & Buunk, 1985; Sharpsteen, 1993). Jealousy sets boundaries for the behaviors that are acceptable in relationships; the boundaries cannot be crossed without evoking jealousy (Reiss, 1986). Though a certain amount of jealousy can be expected in any loving relationship, it is important that partners communicate openly about their fears and boundaries. Jealousy doesn't necessarily signal difficulty between partners, nor does it have to threaten the relationship (Wiederman & Allgeier, 1993).

The Psychological Dimension   As most of us know, jealousy is a painful emotion. It is an agonizing compound of hurt, anger, depression, fear, and doubt. When we are jealous, we may feel less attractive and acceptable to our partner. Jealous responses are most intense in committed or marital relationships because both assume "specialness." This specialness occurs because one's intimate partner is different from everyone else. With him or her, we are most confiding, revealing, vulnerable, caring, and trusting. There is a sense of exclusiveness. To be intimate outside the relationship violates that sense of exclusiveness because intimacy (especially sexual intimacy) symbolizes specialness. Words such as "disloyalty," "cheating," and "infidelity" reflect the sense that an unspoken pledge has been broken. This unspoken pledge is the normative expectation that serious relationships, whether dating or marital, will be sexually exclusive.

As our lives become more and more intertwined, we become less and less independent. For some, this loss of independence increases the fear of losing the partner. But it takes more than simple dependency to make a person jealous. To be jealous, we also need to lack self-esteem and have a feeling of insecurity, either about ourselves or about our relationships (McIntosh, 1989; Pistole, 1995). Insecure people tend to feel jealous in their relationships. This is true for both Whites and African Americans (McIntosh, 1989).

Types of Jealousy   Social psychologists suggest that there are two types of jealousy: suspicious and reactive (Bringle & Buunk, 1991). **Suspicious jealousy** occurs when there is no reason to be suspicious, or when only ambiguous evidence exists for suspecting that a partner is involved with a third

> Love is like quicksilver in the hand. Leave the fingers open and it stays. Clutch it, and it darts away.
>
> —*Dorothy Parker (1893–1967)*

ASSUMING THE FOLLOWING statements were true for you, which would you reveal to a partner or spouse?

- In order to become aroused and maintain arousal, you need to fantasize about another person or situation.

- You have had an extrarelational affair.

- You no longer find your partner physically attractive.

- (For women only) You rarely experience orgasm during intercourse.

If you would not reveal this information to your partner, are you being deceptive? Or are these just private issues? How does deception differ from privacy?

Deception involves betrayal and delusion; it often takes the form of lies, omissions, fabrications, or secrets. Counselors and psychologists agree that though deception is extremely common in intimate relationships, it has the power to destroy closeness and intimacy and ultimately to shatter trust. Whether or not a deception is revealed, it creates distance and disorientation in the relationship. It erodes bonds and blocks authentic communication and trust. Deception strips away spontaneity and often leaves a couple operating on a higher level of anxiety, states psychologist Harriet Lerner, author of *The Dance of Deception* (1993).

There are differences, some cultural and some personal, in what people consider acceptable and proper to reveal. Many people, for instance, do not reveal their sexual fantasies to their partners, considering it neither necessary nor valuable to do so. They consider this a matter of privacy rather than one of deceptiveness. Deception typically originates with betrayal or involves lies and secrets that drive couples apart.

Are you deceptive in your primary relationship? If so, in the process of identifying and confronting deception, it is valuable to understand your motivations. Are they the result of unfounded criticism by a partner? Anger toward one's partner about an extrarelational relationship? Boredom in the bedroom? Dissatisfaction with the quality of communication? Or stonewalling an idea or project? Perhaps you don't understand why your behavior exists. The reasons and motivations are often complex, with their expression rooted in our early life experiences and the ways we have learned to behave. For some, therapy is a way to help unravel, understand, and communicate what often seems beyond comprehension.

If one believes that truth and intimacy are connected, then truth is usually the preferred choice. Given the high cost of deception, it is worthwhile to try to understand the reason for the deceit, confront it with honesty, and communicate openly about it. This approach, though difficult and painful, will ultimately strengthen the relationship, whereas continued deception will only erode it further.

Source: Adapted from Adler, E. (1994, August 24). "How the Tangled Web of Deception Hurts Relationships." *San Francisco Chronicle.*

---

person. **Reactive jealousy** occurs when a partner is involved in a current, past, or anticipated relationship with another person.

Suspicious jealousy tends to occur most often when a relationship is in its early stages. The relationship is not firmly established, and the couple is unsure about its future. The smallest distraction, imagined slight, or inattention can be taken as evidence of interest in another person. Even without *any* evidence, a jealous partner may worry ("Is he or she seeing someone else but not telling me?"). The partner may engage in vigilance, watching his or her partner's every move ("I'd like to audit your human sexuality class"). He or she may snoop, unexpectedly appearing in the middle of the night to see if someone else is there ("I was just passing by and thought I'd say hello"). The partner may try to control the other's behavior ("If you go to your friend's party without me, we're through").

Sometimes, however, suspicions are valid. Suspicious jealousy, in fact, may be a reasonable response to circumstantial evidence. Robert Bringle and Bram Buunk believe that a certain amount of suspicious jealousy may be functional. They observe that "emotional reactions to these [circumstantial] events may forewarn the partner of what will happen if there are serious transgressions and thereby serve the role of *preventing* extradyadic involvements" (Bringle and Buunk, 1991).

Reactive jealousy occurs when one learns of a partner's present, past, or anticipated sexual involvement with another person. This usually provokes the most intense jealousy. If the affair occurred during the current relationship, the discovering partner may feel that the entire relationship has been based on a lie. Trust is questioned. Every word and event must be reevaluated: "If you slept with each other when you said you were going to the library, did you also sleep with him/her when you said you were going to the laundromat?" Or, "How could you say you loved me when you were seeing him/her?" The damage can be irreparable.

Boundary Markers As we noted earlier, jealousy represents a boundary marker. It points out what the boundaries are in a particular relationship. It determines how, to what extent, and in what manner others can interact with members of the relationship. It also shows the limits to which the members of the relationship can interact with those outside the relationship. Culture prescribes the general boundaries of what evokes jealousy, but individuals adjust them to the dynamics of their own relationship.

Boundaries may vary depending on the type of relationship, gender, sexual orientation, and ethnicity. Although the majority of people believe sexual exclusiveness to be important in serious dating relationships and cohabitation, it is virtually mandatory in marriage (Blumstein & Schwartz, 1983; Buunk & van Driel, 1989). Fewer than 2% of adults believe that having sex with someone other than a spouse is "not wrong at all" (Laumann et al., 1994). Men are generally more restrictive than women; heterosexuals are more restrictive than gay men and lesbians. Although we know very little about jealousy and ethnicity, traditional Latinos and new Latino and Asian immigrants tend to be more restrictive than Anglos or African Americans (Mindel, Habenstein, & Wright, 1988). Despite variations in where the boundary lines are drawn, jealousy functions to guard those lines.

Managing Jealousy

Jealousy can be unreasonable, based on fears and fantasies, or realistic, a reaction to genuine threats or events. Unreasonable jealousy can become a problem when it interferes with an individual's well-being or that of the relationship. Dealing with irrational suspicions can often be very difficult, for such feelings touch deep recesses in ourselves. As we noted earlier, jealousy is often related to personal feelings of insecurity and inadequacy. The source of such jealousy lies within ourselves, not within the relationship.

If we can work on the underlying causes of our insecurity, then we can deal effectively with our irrational jealousy. Excessively jealous people may need considerable reassurance, but at some point they must also confront their own irrationality and insecurity. If they do not, they emotionally imprison their partner. Their jealousy may destroy the very relationship they have been desperately trying to preserve.

But jealousy is not always irrational. Sometimes there are real reasons, such as the relationship boundaries being violated. In this case, the cause lies not within ourselves but within the relationship. If the jealousy is well

Jealousy is not a barometer by which the depth of love can be read. It merely records the depth of the lover's insecurity.

—*Margaret Mead (1901–1978)*

founded, the partner may need to modify or end the relationship with the third party whose presence initiated the jealousy. Modifying the third-party relationship reduces the jealous response and, more important, symbolizes the partner's commitment to the primary relationship. If the partner is unwilling to do this, because of a lack of commitment, unsatisfied personal needs, or problems in the primary relationship, the relationship is likely to reach a crisis. In such cases, jealousy may be the agent for profound change.

There are no set rules for dealing with jealousy. Each person must deal with it using his or her own understanding and insights. As with many of life's puzzling problems, jealousy has no simple answers.

THE TRANSFORMATION OF LOVE: FROM PASSION TO INTIMACY

Ultimately, passionate or romantic love may be transformed or replaced by a quieter, more lasting love. Otherwise, the relationship will likely break up, and each person will search for another who will once again ignite his or her passion.

Although love is one of the most important elements of our humanity, it seems to come and go. The kind of love that stays is what we might call **intimate love.** In intimate love, each person knows he or she can count on the other. The excitement comes from the achievement of other goals—from creativity, from work, from child rearing, from friendships—as well as from the relationship. The key to making love stay does not seem to be in love's passionate intensity but in transforming it into intimate love. Intimate love is based on commitment, caring, and self-disclosure.

Commitment is an important component of intimate love. It is a determination to continue a relationship or marriage in the face of bad times as well as good (Reiss, 1986). It is based on conscious choice rather than on feelings, which, by their very nature, are transitory. Commitment is a promise of a shared future, a promise to be together, come what may.

Commitment has become an important concept in recent years. We seem to be as much in search of commitment as we are in search of love or marriage. We speak of "making a commitment" to someone or to a relationship. A "committed" relationship has become almost a stage of courtship, somewhere between dating and being engaged or living together.

Caring is the making of another's needs as important as your own. It requires what the philosopher Martin Buber called an "I-Thou" relationship. Buber described two fundamental ways of relating to people: I-Thou and I-It. In an I-Thou relationship, each person is treated as a Thou—that is, as a person whose life is valued as an end in itself. In an I-It relationship, each person is treated as an It; the person has worth only as someone who can be used. When a person is treated as a Thou, his or her humanity and uniqueness are paramount.

Self-disclosure is the revelation of personal information that others would not ordinarily know because of its riskiness. When we self-disclose, we reveal ourselves—our hopes, our fears, our everyday thoughts—to others. Self-disclosure deepens others' understanding of us. It also deepens our own understanding, for we discover unknown aspects as we open ourselves to others.

ALTHOUGH WE GENERALLY make commitments because we love someone, love alone is not sufficient to make a commitment last. Our commitments seem to be affected by several factors that can strengthen or weaken the relationship. Ira Reiss (1980) believes that there are three important factors: the balance of costs to benefits, normative inputs, and structural constraints.

The Balance of Costs to Benefits

Whether we like it or not, human beings have a tendency to look at romantic, marital, and sexual relationships from a cost-benefit perspective. Most of the time, when we are satisfied, we are unaware that we may judge our relationships in this manner. But when there is stress or conflict, we often ask ourselves, "What am I getting out of this relationship?" Then we add up the pluses and minuses. If the result is on the plus side, we are encouraged to continue the relationship; if the result is negative, we are more likely to discontinue it, especially if the negativity continues over a long period of time. By this system, sexual interactions can have a positive or negative value. But although sex is important, it is generally not the only factor; it is not even necessarily the most important factor.

Normative Inputs

Normative inputs for relationships are the values that you, your partner, and society hold about love, relationships, marriage, and family. These values can either sustain or detract from a commitment. How do you feel about a love commitment? If you are heterosexual, a marital commitment? Do you believe that marriage is for life? If you are gay, lesbian, or bisexual, what are the values you and your partner bring to your relationship in terms of commitment? How do you create your own positive norms in the face of negative societal norms?

Structural Constraints

The structure of a relationship will add to or detract from commitment. Depending on the type of relationship—whether it is dating, living together, or marriage—there are different structural roles and expectations. In marital relationships, there are partner roles (husband/wife) and economic roles (employed worker/homemaker). There may also be parental roles (mother/father). There is usually the expectation of monogamy. In gay and lesbian relationships, the marital relationship model is replaced by the best-friends model, in which sexual exclusiveness is generally negotiable.

These different factors interact to increase or decrease commitment in a relationship. Commitments are more likely to endure in marriage than in cohabiting or dating relationships, which tend to be relatively short-lived. They are more likely to last in heterosexual relationships than in gay or lesbian relationships (Testa, Kinder, & Ironson, 1987). The reason commitments tend to endure in marriage may or may not have anything to do with a couple's being happy. Marital commitments tend to last because of norms, and structural constraints may compensate for the lack of personal satisfaction.

For most people, love seems to include commitment and commitment includes love. Though the two seem to overlap considerably, we can mistakenly assume that if someone loves us, he or she is also committed to us. It is not uncommon for one partner to believe there is more commitment in a relationship than there actually is. Even if a person is committed, it is not always clear what the commitment means: Is it a commitment to the partner or to the relationship? For a short time or for a long time? Is it for better and for worse?

Without self-disclosure, we remain opaque and hidden. If others love us, such love leaves us with anxiety: Are we loved for ourselves, or for the image we present to the world?

Together, these elements help transform love. But in the final analysis, perhaps the most important means of sustaining love are our words and actions; caring words and deeds provide the setting for maintaining and expanding love (Byrne & Murnen, 1988).

■ The study of love is only beginning, but it is already helping us to understand the various components that make up this complex emotion. Although there is something to be said for the mystery of love, understanding how it works in the day-to-day world may help us keep our love vital and growing.

> Everyone has experienced that truth: that love, like a running brook, is disregarded, taken for granted; but when the brook freezes over, then people begin to remember how it was when it ran, and they want it to run again.
>
> —*Khalil Gibran (1833–1931)*

SUMMARY

Love and Sexuality

- Sexuality and love are intimately related in our culture. Sex is most highly valued in loving relationships. Sex with affection rivals marriage as an acceptable moral standard for intercourse. Love is valued by heterosexual men and women, gay men, lesbians, and bisexuals.

- Men are more likely than women to separate sex from love; women tend to view sex within a relational context. Gay men are more likely than heterosexual men to be involved in purely sexual relationships.

- For a variety of reasons, some choose *celibacy* as a lifestyle. These individuals may find a better appreciation of the nature of friendship and an increased respect for the bonds of long-term partnerships.

How Do I Love Thee? Approaches and Attitudes Related to Love

- Attitudes and feelings associated with love include caring, needing, trusting, and tolerating. Behaviors associated with love include verbal, nonverbal, and physical expression of affection, self-disclosure, giving of nonmaterial and material evidence, and tolerance.

- According to John Lee, there are six basic styles of love: *eros, mania, ludus, storge, agape,* and *pragma.*

- The *triangular theory of love* views love as consisting of three components: intimacy, passion, and decision/commitment.

- The *attachment* theory of love views love as being similar in nature to the attachments we form as infants. The attachment (or love) styles of both infants and adults are *secure, anxious/ambivalent,* and *avoidant.*

- Friendship is often the foundation for a strong love relationship. What separates friends from lovers is that lovers have more fascination and a greater sense of exclusiveness with their partners.

Unrequited Love

- *Unrequited love*—love that is not returned—is distressing for both the would-be lover and the rejecting partner. A person's style of attachment affects the way in which he or she experiences unrequited love.

Jealousy

- *Jealousy* is an aversive response to a partner's real, imagined, or likely involvement with a third person. Jealous responses are most likely in committed or marital relationships because of the presumed "specialness" of the relationship, symbolized by sexual exclusiveness.

- As individuals become more interdependent, there is a greater fear of loss. Fear of loss, coupled with insecurity about self or the relationship, increases the likelihood of jealousy.

- There are two types of jealousy: suspicious and reactive. *Suspicious jealousy* occurs when there is no reason to be suspicious or only ambiguous evidence. *Reactive jealousy* occurs when a partner reveals a current, past, or anticipated relationship with another.

- Jealousy acts as a boundary marker for relationships. Boundaries vary according to type of relationship, gender, sexual orientation, and ethnicity.

The Transformation of Love: From Passion to Intimacy

- Time affects romantic relationships. *Intimate love* is based on *commitment, caring,* and *self-disclosure,* the revelation of information not normally known by others.

- Love alone is not sufficient to make a commitment last. Three factors that can strengthen or weaken a relationship are the costs versus benefits, normative inputs, and structural constraints.

SUGGESTED READING

Ackerman, Diane. (1994). *A Natural History of Love.* New York: Random House. A historical and cultural perspective on love.

Feeney, Judith, & Noller, Patricia. (1996). *Adult Attachment.* Thousand Oaks, CA: Sage. A coherent account of diverse strands of attachment research.

Hendrick, Susan, & Hendrick, Clyde. (1991). *Romantic Love.* Newbury Park, CA: Sage. A concise review of social science research on romantic love.

Peck, M. Scott. (1978). *The Road Less Traveled: A New Psychology of Love, Traditional Values, and Spiritual Growth.* New York: Simon & Schuster. A psychological/spiritual approach to love that sees love's goal as spiritual growth.

Sternberg, Robert, & Barnes, Michael (Eds.). (1988). *The Psychology of Love.* New Haven: Yale University Press. An excellent collection of essays by some of the leading researchers in the area of love.

Weber, Ann L., & Harvey, John (Eds.). (1994). *Perspectives on Close Relationships.* Boston: Allyn & Bacon. A collection of scholarly essays on various aspects of intimate relationships.

White, Greg, & Mullen, Paul. (1989). *Jealousy: A Clinical and Multidisciplinary Approach.* New York: Guilford. A comprehensive examination of what we know about jealousy (and its treatment).

8

Communicating About Sex

*C*OMMUNICATION IS THE THREAD that connects sexuality and intimacy. The quality of the communication affects the quality of the relationship, and the quality of the relationship affects the quality of the sex (Cupach & Metts, 1991). Good relationships tend to have good sex; bad relationships often have bad sex. Sex, in fact, frequently serves as a barometer for the quality of the relationship. The ability to communicate about sex is important in developing and maintaining both sexual and relationship satisfaction. (Cupach & Comstock, 1990; Metts & Cupach, 1989). People who are satisfied with their sexual communication also tend to be satisfied with their relationship as a whole (Noller & Fitzpatrick, 1991).

Most of the time, we don't think about our ability to communicate. Only when problems arise do we consciously think about it. Then we become aware of our limitations in communicating, or more often, what we believe are the limitations of others: "You just don't get it, do you?" "You're not listening to me." And as we know, communication failures are marked by frustration.

There are generally two types of communication problems in relationships. The first problem is the failure to self-disclose. The second is poor communication skills. Although much of what we discuss here refers to interpersonal communication in general, such knowledge will enrich your ability to communicate about sexual issues as well.

It's important to realize, however, that not all of a relationship's problems are communication problems. Often we understand each other very clearly; the problem is that we are unable or unwilling to change or compromise. Good communication will not salvage a bad relationship or the "wrong" relationship. But good communication will allow us to see our differences. It will allow us to see the consequence of our actions or inactions, and it will provide us with the ability to make informed decisions.

In this chapter, we examine the characteristics of communication and how different contexts affect it. We discuss forms of nonverbal communication, such as touch, which are especially important in sexual relationships. Then we examine the different ways we communicate about sex in intimate relationships. We explore ways we can develop our communication skills in order to enhance our relationships. Finally, we look at the different types of conflicts in intimate relationships and how to resolve them.

> Words are given to man to enable him to conceal his true feelings.
>
> —*Voltaire (1694–1778)*

THE NATURE OF COMMUNICATION

Communication is a transactional process by which we convey symbols, such as words, gestures, and movements, to establish human contact, exchange information, and reinforce or change our attitudes and behaviors and those of others. Communication takes place simultaneously within cultural, social, and psychological contexts. These contexts affect our ability to communicate clearly by prescribing rules (usually unwritten or unconscious) for communicating about various subjects, including sexuality.

The Cultural Context

The cultural context of communication refers to the language, values, beliefs, and customs in which communication takes place. On the whole, reflecting our Judeo-Christian heritage, our culture has viewed sexuality negatively. Sexual topics are often tabooed. Children and adolescents are discouraged from obtaining sexual knowledge; they learn they are not supposed to talk about sex. Censorship abounds in the media, with the ever-present "beep" on television or the "f—k" in newspapers and magazines to indicate a "forbidden" sexual word. Our language has few words for describing "the sex act" except scientific or impersonal ones ("sexual intercourse," "coitus," or "copulation"), moralistic ones ("fornication"), euphemistic ones ("doing it," "being intimate," or "sleeping with"), and tabooed ones ("fucking"). A few terms place sexual interactions in a relational category, such as "making love." But love is not always involved—as in, for example, a single encounter between strangers—and the term does not capture the erotic quality of sex. Furthermore, the gay and lesbian subculture has developed its own sexual argot, or slang, because society prohibits the open discussion or expression of homosexuality.

Different ethnic groups within our culture also have different language patterns that affect the way they communicate about sexuality. African American culture creates distinct communication patterns (Hecht, Collier, & Ribeau, 1993). Among African Americans, for example, language and expressive patterns are characterized by, among other things, emotional vitality, realness, and valuing direct experience (White & Parham, 1990). Emotional vitality is expressed in the animated, expressive use of words. Realness refers to "telling it like it is," using concrete, nonabstract words. Direct experience is valued because "there is no substitute in the Black ethos for actual experience gained in the course of living" (White & Parham, 1990). In sexual (and other) matters, "mother wit," practical or experiential knowledge, may be valued over knowledge gained from books or lectures.

Among Latinos, especially traditional Latinos, there is the assumption that sexual matters will not be discussed openly (Guerrero Pavich, 1986). Confrontations are to be avoided; negative feelings are not to be expressed. As a consequence, nonverbal communication is especially important. Women are expected to read men's behavior for clues to their feelings and to discover what is acceptable. Because confrontations are unacceptable and sex cannot be openly discussed, secrets are important. They are shared between friends but not between partners. Sometimes secrets are hinted at; at times of crisis, they may be revealed through anger.

Asian Americans tend to be less individualistic than other Americans in general. Whereas mainstream American culture views the individual as self-reliant and self-sufficient, Asian American subcultures are more relationally oriented. Asian Americans are less verbal and expressive in their interactions than White Americans. They rely to a great degree on indirection and nonverbal communication, such as silence and the avoidance of eye contact as signs of respect (Del Carmen, 1990).

Because harmonious relationships are highly valued, Asian Americans have a greater tendency to avoid direct confrontation if possible. Japanese Americans, for example, "value implicit, nonverbal, intuitive communication over explicit, verbal, the rational exchange of information" (Del Carmen, 1990). In order to avoid conflict, verbal communication is often indirect or ambiguous; it skirts around issues rather than confronting them. As a consequence, Asian Americans rely on each other to interpret the meaning of a conversation or nonverbal clues.

The Social Context

The social context of communication refers to the roles we play in society. These roles are derived from being members of different groups. As men and women, we play out masculine and feminine roles. As members of marital units, we act out roles of husband and wife. As members of cohabiting units, we perform heterosexual, gay, or lesbian cohabiting roles.

Roles exist in relationship to other people. Without a female role, there would be no male role; without a wife role, there would be no husband role. Because roles exist in relationship to others, **status,** a person's position or ranking in a group, is important. In traditional gender roles, men are accorded higher status than women; in traditional marital roles, husbands are superior in status to wives. And in terms of orientation, society awards higher status to heterosexuals than to gay men, lesbians, and bisexuals. Because of this male/female disparity, heterosexual relationships tend to have a greater power imbalance than gay and lesbian couples (Lips, 1997).

The Psychological Context

Although the cultural and social contexts are important factors in communication, they do not *determine* how people communicate. The psychological context of communication does that. We are not prisoners of culture and society, but unique individuals. We may accept some cultural or social aspects, such as language taboos, but reject, ignore, or modify others, such as traditional gender roles. Because we have distinct personalities, we express our uniqueness by the way we communicate: We may be assertive or submissive, rigid or flexible, sensitive or insensitive; we may exhibit high self-esteem or low self-esteem.

Our personality characteristics affect our ability to communicate, change, or manage conflict. Rigid people, for example, are less likely to change than flexible ones, regardless of the quality of communication. People with high self-esteem may be more open to change because they do not necessarily take conflict as an attack on themselves. Personality characteristics such as having negative or positive feelings about sex affect our sexual communication more directly.

Nonverbal Communication

There is no such thing as not communicating. Even when you are not talking, you are communicating by your silence (an awkward silence, a hostile silence, a tender silence). You are communicating by the way you position your body and tilt your head, through your facial expressions, your physical distance from another person, and so on. Look around you. How are the people in your presence communicating nonverbally?

Much of our communication of feeling is nonverbal. We radiate our moods: A happy mood invites companionship; a solemn mood pushes people away. Joy infects; depression distances—all without a word being said. Nonverbal expressions of love are particularly effective—a gentle touch, a loving glance, or the gift of a flower.

One of the problems with nonverbal communication, however, is the imprecision of its messages. Is a person frowning or squinting? Does the

> The cruelest lies are often told in silence.
>
> —*Robert Louis Stevenson (1850–1894)*

Proximity, eye contact, and touching are important components of nonverbal communication. What do you think this man and woman are "saying" to each other?

smile indicate friendliness or nervousness? A person may be in reflective silence, but we may interpret the silence as disapproval or distance.

The ability to correctly interpret nonverbal communication appears to be an important ingredient in successful relationships. "I can tell when something is bothering him/her" reveals the ability to read nonverbal clues, such as body language. This ability is especially important in ethnic groups and cultures that rely on nonverbal expression of feelings, such as Latino and Asian cultures. Although the value placed on nonverbal expression may vary among groups and across cultures, the ability to communicate and understand nonverbally remains important in all cultures.

Three of the most important forms of nonverbal communication are proximity, eye contact, and touching.

Proximity   Nearness in physical space and time is called **proximity.** Where we sit or stand in relation to another person signifies a level of intimacy or relationship. Many of our words that convey emotion relate to proximity, such as feeling "distant" or "close" or being "moved" by someone. We also "make the first move," "move in" on someone else's partner, or "move in together."

In a social gathering, the face-to-face distances between people when they start a conversation are clues to how the individuals wish to define the relationship. All cultures have an intermediate distance in face-to-face interactions that is neutral. In most cultures, decreasing the distance signifies an invitation to greater intimacy or a threat. Moving away denotes the desire to terminate the interaction. When you stand at an intermediate distance from someone at a party, you send the message, "Intimacy is not encouraged." If you want to move closer, however, you risk the chance of rejection.

Because of cultural differences, there can be misunderstandings. The neutral intermediate distance for Latinos, for example, is much closer than for Anglos, who may misinterpret the same distance as "too close for comfort." In social settings, this can lead to problems. As Carlos Sluzki (1982) points out, "A person raised in a non-Latino culture will define as seductive behavior the same behavior that a person raised in a Latin culture defines as socially neutral." An Anglo may interpret the behavior as an invitation for intimacy, while the Latino may interpret it as neutral. Because of the miscue, the Anglo may withdraw or flirt, depending on his or her feelings. If the Anglo flirts, the Latino may respond to what he or she believes is the other's initiation. Additionally, among people whose culture features greater intermediate distances and less overt touching, such as Asian Americans, neutral responses may be misinterpreted negatively by those outside the culture.

Eye Contact   Much can be discovered about a relationship by watching how people look at each other. Making eye contact with another person, if only for a split second longer than usual, is a signal of interest. Brief and extended glances, in fact, play a significant role in women's expression of initial interest (Moore, 1985). When you can't take your eyes off another person, you probably have a strong attraction to him or her. In addition to eye contact, dilated pupils may be an indication of sexual interest.

Research suggests that the amount of eye contact between a couple in conversation can distinguish between those who have high levels of conflict and those who don't. Those with the greatest degree of agreement have the greatest eye contact with each other (Beier & Sternberg, 1977). Those in conflict tend to avoid eye contact (unless it is a daggerlike stare). As with proximity, however, the level of eye contact may differ by culture.

Touching   It is difficult to overestimate the significance of touch. A review of the research on touch finds it to be extremely important in human development, health, and sexuality (Hatfield, 1994). Touch is the most basic of all senses. Skin contains receptors for pleasure and pain, heat and cold, roughness and smoothness. "Touch is the mother sense and out of it, all the other senses have been derived," writes anthropologist Ashley Montagu (1986). Touch is a life-giving force for infants. If babies are not touched, they may fail to thrive and may even die. We hold hands and cuddle with small children and those we love.

"HOW CAN I BECOME more openly affectionate when expressing affection was discouraged by my family when I was growing up?"

"My partner likes to touch and be touched, but I am uncomfortable with both. How can we overcome these differences?"

These are questions students ask over and over in human sexuality classes. These questioners are aware of the deep need and value of human touch. So profound is this need that infants have been observed wasting and becoming ill, in spite of good physical care, as a result of lack of touch and cuddling. Among adults, professionals see a correlation between marital happiness and physical affection: The happiest couples often tend to be the most demonstrative couples. The response to touch is indeed physical: Biochemical reactions produced by touch can cause an increase in heart rate, a drop in blood pressure, and an easing of pain.

A variety of factors appear to contribute to each individual's need for and ability to touch. Among these, culture is a strong determinant. Studies show that Americans tend to touch less than people from many Latin American countries, the Middle East, and Russia. Families also have a key role in influencing how comfortable people are with touch. Both quantity and quality of touch among adults and between adults and children are observed by children and then translated into behavior that often repeats itself in later adulthood. Inborn differences, gender, and individual preferences also influence touching.

Regardless of where the patterns and preferences originate, problems can occur in relationships if distinct discrepancies exist between partners in sending or receiving touch. Misunderstandings, discomfort, and a widening gap in the ability of each person to emotionally connect with the other often result.

The most obvious and possibly the most difficult solution to this problem is honest communication. Communication can replace assumptions (about why someone is not being touched), ignorance (about what does and does not feel good), misplaced anger and resentment (about the importance of touch), and misinterpretation (about the meaning of touch). Communication in a nonthreatening and relaxed environment can begin to help unravel and expose in a new way existing patterns and behaviors.

Discussing what touch means to each person is a beginning. For some, touch means intimacy; for others, it represents safety; and for still others, it signals a readiness for sex. Often, the absence of touch is merely a response to previous learning. But the absence of touch can elicit feelings in another ranging from abandonment to rage. Sharing the meaning of touch may expand its definition and allow it to find a place in one's patterns of expression.

If touching is an issue in your relationship, experiment with nonsexual touching. Learn to enjoy giving and receiving touch. Give and accept feedback nondefensively. Give feedback, especially verbal cues, about what does and does not feel good. Initiate touch when it is appropriate, even though it may be awkward at first. Don't be afraid to be adventurous in learning and utilizing methods that are pleasing to both you and your partner.

At the same time, be prepared to accept individual differences. In spite of forthright and ongoing communication, people still have unique comfort levels. Again, honest feedback will help you and your partner find a mutually acceptable level. If you are both able to understand and enjoy the rich and powerful messages that touch sends, then your relationship as a whole can be enriched by yet another dimension.

But touch can also be a violation. Strangers or acquaintances may touch as if they were more familiar than they are. Your date or partner may touch you in a manner you don't like or want. And sexual harassment includes unwelcomed touching (see Chapter 17).

As with eye contact, touching is a form of communication. The amount of contact, from almost imperceptible touches to "hanging all over each other," helps differentiate lovers from strangers. How and where a person is touched can suggest friendship, intimacy, love, or sexual interest.

Levels of touching differ among cultures and ethnic groups. Studies show that Americans touch much less, at least in public, than do Russians, Greeks, and people in many Latin American countries (Brenton, 1990). Although the value placed on nonverbal expression may vary among groups and cultures, the ability to communicate and understand nonverbally remains important in all cultures.

What about gender differences in touching? Despite stereotypes of women touching and men avoiding touch, studies suggest that there are no consistent differences between the sexes in the amount of overall touching (Andersen, Lustig, & Andersen, 1987). Men do not seem to initiate touch with women any more than women do with men. Women are markedly unenthusiastic, however, about receiving touches from strangers and express greater concern in general about being touched. For women, there is greater touch avoidance unless there is a relational context with the man. However, in situations with sexual overtones, men initiate more touching than women (Blumstein & Schwartz, 1983).

Touch often signals intimacy, immediacy, and emotional closeness. In fact, touch may very well be the *closest* form of nonverbal communication. One researcher writes: "If intimacy is proximity, then nothing comes closer than touch, the most intimate knowledge of another" (Thayer, 1986). And touching seems to go hand-in-hand with self-disclosure. Those who touch appear to self-disclose more; in fact, touch seems to be an important factor in prompting others to talk more about themselves (Heslin & Alper, 1983; Norton, 1983).

Sexual behavior relies above all else on touch: the touching of self and others; the touching of hands, faces, chests, arms, necks, legs, and genitals. (Sex is a contact sport, some say, with more truth than they realize.) In sexual interactions, touch takes precedence over sight: We often close our eyes to caress, kiss, and make love. In fact, we close our eyes to better focus on the sensations aroused by touch; we shut out visual distractions to intensify the tactile experience of sexuality. When touching leads to sexual arousal, the sensual aspects are all too often hurried along in order to initiate sexual activity (Love & Robinson, 1994).

> Married couples who love each other tell each other a thousand things without talking.
>
> —*Chinese proverb*

SEXUAL COMMUNICATION

Communication is important in understanding, developing, and maintaining sexual relationships. In childhood and adolescence, communication is critical for transmitting sexual knowledge and values and in forming our sexual identities. As we establish our relationships, communication enables us to signal sexual interest and initiate sexual interactions. In developed relationships, communication allows us to explore and maintain our sexuality as a couple.

Sexual Communication in Beginning Relationships

Our interpersonal sexual scripts provide us with "instructions" on how to behave sexually, including the initiation of potentially sexual relationships. Because as a culture we share our interpersonal sexual scripts, we know how we are supposed to act at the beginning of a relationship. The very process of acting out interpersonal scripts, in fact, communicates sexual meanings (Simon & Gagnon, 1987). But how do we begin relationships? What is it that attracts us to someone?

The Halo Effect   Imagine yourself unattached at a party. You notice some-one standing next to you as you reach for some chips. In a split second, you decide whether you are interested in him or her. On what basis do you make that decision? Is it looks, personality, style, sensitivity, intelligence, or what?

If you're like most people, you base this decision, consciously or unconsciously, on appearance. Physical attractiveness is particularly important during the initial meeting and early stages of a relationship. If you don't know anything else about a person, you tend to judge on appearance.

Most people would deny that they are attracted to others just because of their looks. We like to think we are deeper than that. But looks are important unconsciously. We tend to infer qualities based on looks. This inference is based on what is known as the **halo effect,** the assumption that attractive or charismatic people possess more desirable social characteristics than others. In one well-known experiment, students were shown pictures of attractive people and asked to describe what they thought these people were like (Dion, Berscheid, & Walster, 1972). Attractive men and women were assumed to be more sensitive, kind, warm, sexually responsive, strong, poised, and outgoing than others; they were assumed to be more exciting and to have better characters than "ordinary" people. Research indicates that, overall, the differences in perceptions between very attractive and average people are minimal (Cowley, 1996).

Interest and Opening Lines   After we have sized someone up based on his or her appearance, what happens next in interactions between men and women? (Gay and lesbian beginning relationships are discussed later.) Does the man initiate the encounter? On the surface yes, but in reality, the woman often "covertly initiates . . . by sending nonverbal signals of availability and interest" (Metts & Cupach, 1989). The woman will "glance" at the man once or twice and "catch" his eye; she may smile or flip her hair. If the man moves into her physical space, the woman then relies on nodding, leaning close, smiling, or laughing.

If the man believes the woman is interested, he then initiates a conversation using an "opening line." The opening line tests the woman's interest and availability. There is an array of opening lines that men use. According to women, the most effective are innocuous, such as "I feel a little embarrassed, but I'd like to meet you" or "Are you a student here?" The least effective are sexually blunt, such as "You really turn me on."

The First Move and Beyond   After we first meet someone, we weigh each other's attitudes, values, and philosophy to see if we are compatible. We evaluate the other person's sense of humor, intelligence, "partner" potential, ability to function in a relationship, sex appeal, and so on. Based on our overall judgment, we may continue the relationship. If the relationship continues in a romantic vein, we may decide to move into one that includes some kind of physical intimacy. To signal this transition from nonphysical to physical intimacy, one of us must "make the first move." Making the first move marks the transition from a potentially sexual relationship to one that is actually sexual.

If the relationship develops along traditional gender-role patterns, one of the partners, usually the male, will make the first move to initiate sexual intimacy, whether it is kissing, petting, or engaging in sexual intercourse (Benokraitis, 1993; O'Sullivan & Byers, 1992). The point at which this occurs

Whereas a lot of men used to ask for conversation when they really wanted sex, nowadays they often feel obliged to ask for sex even when they really want conversation.

—*Katherine Whitehorn*

When women and men are interested in meeting each other, the woman will often covertly initiate by sending non-verbal messages of interest. If the man believes the woman is interested, he will then initiate the conversation with an "opening line."

generally depends on two factors: the level of intimacy and the length of the relationship (Sprecher, 1989). The more emotionally involved the couple, the more likely they will be sexually involved as well. The duration of the relationship also affects the likelihood of sexual involvement.

Initial sexual involvement can occur as early as the first meeting or later, as part of a well-established relationship. Although some people become sexually involved immediately ("lust at first sight"), the majority begin their sexual involvements in the context of an ongoing relationship.

In new or developing relationships, communication is generally indirect and ambiguous about sexuality. There is considerable flirtation (Abrahams, 1994). As one communication scholar notes about developing relationships, "The typical relationship process is not dominated by open, direct communication, but rather involves the construction of a web of ambiguity by which parties signal their relationship indirectly" (Baxter, 1987). Direct strategies are sometimes used to initiate sexual involvement, but these usually occur when the person is confident in the other's interest or is not concerned about being rejected.

In new relationships, we communicate *indirectly* about sex because, although we want to become sexually involved with the other person, we also want to avoid rejection. By using indirect strategies, such as turning down the lights, moving closer, touching the other's face or hair, we may test the other's interest in sexual involvement. If the other person responds positively to our cues, we can initiate a sexual encounter.

WE MAY CATCH the flu in a crowded bus or subway, but we won't be intimate enough (presumably) to give or get a sexually transmitted disease. Acquiring an STD requires that we get intimately close to another person. Just as getting STDs requires intimacy, so does preventing them. Avoiding an STD may even require more intimacy than getting one, because very often it means we have to talk. Learning to communicate isn't always easy. It can be embarrassing, especially if we are unaccustomed to sharing personal and sexual feelings. But it gets easier with practice. And when you come right down to it, embarrassment is not as bad as herpes, gonorrhea, or AIDS.

Important elements in communicating about STDs include initiating the discussion, mutual disclosure of relevant information, and joint decision making.

Initiating the Discussion

In some situations, we may be able to use nonverbal communication regarding STD prevention. Although it may lack the depth and intimacy that words can produce, nonverbal communication is certainly preferable to no communication at all. For example, if you think you are going to have sex with someone, you can be sure to have a condom with you, and, if you are a man, you can simply put it on at the appropriate time. If you are a woman, you can offer a condom to your partner when the moment is right. If your partner agrees, all will be well with this very minimal amount of communicating. But if your partner recoils in horror and says, "Yuck,

I never use those," it's likely that you will need to begin verbal communication if you are serious about protection.

It is preferable to initiate a discussion of safer sex before you are entangled in a passionate embrace. In the "heat of the moment," we are all susceptible to suspending our ability to think clearly and rationally. "Oh well, just this once won't matter," we may think. But it may matter very much indeed. When sexual intimacy appears on the horizon of a relationship, we need to be prepared with strategies for introducing the topics of contraception and STD prevention. Some people are able to state their concerns simply and directly: "Do you have condoms, or shall I get some?" Others may need to broach the subject more indirectly: "What do you think about safer sex?" or "It's not easy for me to talk about this, but I think we should decide about protection." Once the ice has been broken, the other person will usually be receptive and responsive to a discussion. There's a good chance he or she has been trying to find the courage to say the same thing.

Mutual Disclosure

When we embark on a relationship that includes sexual activity, it is important to have some information about our partner's sexual health. It would be nice if our partner simply volunteered the relevant information, but that is probably not going to occur. We are most likely going to have to ask some very personal questions. One of the best ways to get someone to disclose personal informa-

Because so much of our sexual communication is indirect, ambiguous, or nonverbal, there is a high risk of misinterpretation between women and men. Both men and women may say "no" to sex while actually desiring it (Sprecher, Hatfield, Cortese, Potapova, & Levitskaya, 1994). There are four basic reasons that misunderstandings occur (Cupach & Metts, 1991).

First, men and women tend to disagree about *when* sexual activities should take place in a relationship. Men more than women tend to want sexual involvement earlier and with a lower level of intimacy.

Second, men may be skeptical about women's refusals. Men often misinterpret women's cues, such as misinterpreting a woman's friendly touch as a sexual cue. Men also believe that women often say "no" when they actually mean "coax me." Men believe that women say "no" as token resistance.

Third, because sexual communication is indirect, women may be unclear in signaling their disinterest. A woman may turn her face aside, move a man's hand back to its proper place, say that it's getting late, or try to change the subject. Research indicates that women are most effective when they make strong, direct verbal refusals; men become more compliant if women

tion is to reveal important personal information about ourselves. There is always some risk involved in self-disclosure. For example, you may say, "Before we go any further, you should know that I had an outbreak of herpes two years ago. It hasn't recurred so there's very little chance that I'm contagious at this time, but I wanted you to know." If your partner does not know the facts about herpes, he or she may react negatively to your disclosure. But it is more likely that your honesty will be appreciated. (Besides, there's a 1 in 6 chance your partner has herpes, too!)

The information that potential sex partners should disclose to each other includes:

- Having an STD or symptoms that might indicate an STD.
- A possible recent exposure to an STD.
- A past history of STDs.
- Current lifestyles, including multiple sex partners and injection drug use.
- A past history of many sex partners, gay or bisexual male partners, or partners with a history of injection drug use.
- HIV status (positive or negative, as determined by an HIV blood test). This is especially important for gay or bisexual men, injection drug users, and their sex partners.

If both partners are sincerely concerned about the other's well-being, they will probably be able to overcome any feelings of embarrassment, guilt, or shame and share this important information. For this reason, rela-tionships that develop over time and are founded on mutual caring and trust are likely to be safer sexually than one-night stands. Unfortunately, a person with no emotional investment in a relationship may not always be motivated to tell the truth. Taking some time to get to know your partner is a good way to help ensure your own sexual good health.

Joint Decision Making

If partners use a condom during intercourse, they probably are doing so by mutual consent. Either they have both agreed it is important to use a condom or one of them has proposed condom use and the other has tacitly agreed by going along with it. What may not be clear is that if two people have sex without using a condom, they have mutually agreed that protection is unimportant or unnecessary. Perhaps they have not discussed their decision with each other, but it is a decision nonetheless. Perhaps one (or even both) of the partners would rather be using a condom but hasn't said anything because of embarrassment or fear of rejection. In choosing not to discuss the subject, the person has made the decision to risk getting an STD. In order to have safer sex, both partners need to agree on what practices they will engage in and under what circumstances they will or will not use condoms. Otherwise, "one partner who is not motivated to practice safer sex may not cooperate with the other partner, may undercut the other partner's resolve, or may refuse to use condoms properly" (Darrow & Siegel, 1990).

are persistent in such refusals (Christopher & Frandsen, 1990; Murnen, Perot, & Byrne, 1989).

Fourth, men are more likely than women to interpret nonsexual behavior or cues as sexual. As William Cupach and Sandra Metts (1991) write, "Men may wear sex-colored glasses." Although both men and women flirt for fun, men are more likely to flirt with a sexual purpose. Reflecting their own tendencies, men are more likely to interpret a woman's flirtation as sexual.

Directing Sexual Activity   As we begin a sexual involvement, we have several tasks to accomplish. First and foremost, we must practice safer sex (see Chapter 15). We should gather information about our partner's sexual history, determine whether he or she knows how to practice safer sex, and use condoms. Unlike much of our sexual communication, which is nonverbal or ambiguous, practicing safer sex requires direct verbal discussion. Second, we must discuss birth control (unless both partners have agreed to try for pregnancy). Contraceptive responsibility, like safer sex, requires verbal communication (see Chapter 11).

In addition to communicating about safer sex and contraception, we also need to communicate about what we like and what we need sexually. What kind of foreplay do we like? Afterplay? Do we like to be orally or manually stimulated during intercourse? If so, how? What does each partner need to be orgasmic? Many of our needs and desires can be communicated nonverbally by movements or by giving our partner physical cues. But if our partner does not pick up our nonverbal signals or cues, we need to discuss them directly and clearly to avoid ambiguity.

Gay and Lesbian Relationships   Gay men and lesbians, like heterosexuals, rely on both nonverbal and verbal communication in expressing sexual interest in others. Unlike heterosexuals, however, they cannot necessarily assume that the person in whom they are interested is of the same sexual orientation. Instead, they must rely on specific identifying factors, such as meeting at a gay or lesbian bar, wearing a gay/lesbian pride button, participating in gay/lesbian events, or being introduced by friends to others identified as lesbian or gay. In situations where sexual orientation is not clear, gay men and lesbians use "gaydar," gay radar, in which they look for clues as to orientation. They give ambiguous cues as to their own orientation while looking for cues from the other. These cues can include mannerisms, speech patterns, slang usage, or lingering glances. They may also include the mention of specific places for entertainment or recreation that are frequented mainly by lesbians or gay men, songs that can be interpreted to have "gay" meanings, such as "Strangers in the Night" or "Secret Love," or movies with gay or lesbian themes, such as *Torch Song Trilogy* or *Boys on the Side*.

Like heterosexuals, gay men and lesbians prefer innocuous opening lines. To prevent awkwardness, the opening line usually does not make an overt reference to orientation unless the other person is clearly lesbian or gay.

Once a like orientation is established, lesbians and gay men use nonverbal communication to express interest. There are mutual glances, smiles, subtle body movements. Someone initiates a conversation with an opening line. In these beginning interactions, physical appearance is important, especially for gay males.

Because of their socialization as males, gay men are more likely than lesbians to initiate sexual activity earlier in the relationship. In large part, this is because both partners are free to initiate and because men are not expected to refuse sex as women are. But this same sexual socialization makes it difficult for some gay men to refuse sexual activity. Lesbians do not initiate sex as often as do gay or heterosexual men. In contrast to men, they often feel uncomfortable because women have not been socialized to sexually initiate. Philip Blumstein and Pepper Schwartz (1983) write that "many lesbians are not comfortable in the role of sexual aggressor and it is a major reason why they have sex less often than other kinds of couples."

Sexual Communication in Established Relationships

As a relationship develops and becomes established, the partners begin modifying their individual sexual scripts as they interact with each other. The scripts become less rigid and conventional as each adapts to the uniqueness of his or her partner. The couple develop a shared sexual script. Through their sexual interactions, they learn what each other likes, dislikes, wants, or needs. Much of this learning takes place nonverbally: Partners in

Partners in established relationships tend to develop a shared sexual script. Touching and sharing feelings (by smiling or laughing, for example) are two forms of nonverbal communication that help people learn about each other.

established relationships, like those in emerging relationships, tend to be indirect and ambiguous in their sexual communication. The reason that partners are indirect in established relationships is the same as for those in new relationships: They want to avoid rejection. Indirection allows them to express sexual interest while at the same time protecting themselves from loss of face.

Initiating Sexual Activity　Within established relationships, men continue to overtly initiate sexual encounters more frequently than women. But women continue to signal their willingness. They pace the frequency of intercourse by showing their interest with nonverbal cues, such as giving a "certain look" or lighting candles by the bed. They may also overtly suggest "doing the wild thing." Their partners pick up on the cues and "initiate" sexual interactions. In marital relationships, many women feel more comfortable with overtly initiating sex. In part, this may be related to the decreasing significance of the double standard as relationships continue. In a new relationship, the woman initiating intercourse may be viewed negatively, as a sign of promiscuity. But in an established relationship, the woman's initiation may be viewed positively, as an expression of love. The increase may also be the result of couples becoming more egalitarian in their gender-role attitudes. Not surprisingly, sexual initiations are more often successful in marital relationships than in new or dating relationships.

Some people act as if talking about sex will reduce the possibility of its happening. Thus, there may be little communication between the transition from thinking about sexual activity to actually experiencing it (Wight, 1992). The claim "it just happened" is a reflection of this type of occurrence.

Unlike in new relationships, sexual disinterest is communicated verbally in established relationships (Byers & Heinlein, 1989). In established relationships, a direct refusal is not considered as much of a threat to the relationship as it is in new relationships. In an established relationship, refusals are usually accompanied by a face-saving explanation, "I'd like to but I'm too tired." "You are pretty sexy, but I have to finish studying for my exam." "Let's wait until after the kids go over to their friend's." Such direct refusals are also more effective than indirect ones.

Lesbian and Gay Interactions   In both lesbian and gay relationships, the more emotionally expressive partner is likely to initiate sexual interaction (Blumstein & Schwartz, 1983). The gay or lesbian partner who talks more about feelings, who spontaneously gives his or her partner hugs or kisses, is the one who most often begins sexual activity.

One of the key differences between heterosexuals and gay males and lesbians, however, is how they handle extrarelational sex. In marriage and committed heterosexual relationships, both partners are expected to be sexually exclusive; when heterosexual men and women engage in affairs, they ordinarily keep such matters secret. In gay and lesbian culture, by contrast, sexual exclusivity is often negotiable. Sexual exclusiveness is not necessarily equated with commitment or fidelity. It is acceptable, sometimes expected, to be open with one's partner about extrarelational sex.

As a result of these differing norms, lesbians and gay men must decide early in the relationship whether they will be sexually exclusive (Isensee, 1990). If they choose to have a nonexclusive relationship, they need to discuss how outside sexual interests will be handled. They must decide whether to tell each other, whether to have affairs with friends; they should discuss what degree of emotional involvement is acceptable, and how to deal with jealousy. They need to deal with STD and HIV risks resulting from a third person's being in the relationship.

Gender Differences in Marital Communication   For some time, researchers have been aware of gender differences in general communication patterns. More recently, they have discovered specific gender differences in marital communication (Klinetob & Smith, 1996; Noller & Fitzpatrick, 1991; Thompson & Walker, 1989).

▪ *Wives send clearer messages to their husbands than their husbands send to them.* Wives tend to be more sensitive and responsive to their husbands' messages, both during conversation and during conflict. They are more likely to reply to either positive messages or negative messages than are their husbands, who may not reply at all to such statements.

▪ *Husbands more than wives tend to give neutral messages or to withdraw.* An example would be, "It doesn't matter to me." Wives give more positive or negative messages. Because women tend to smile or laugh when they send messages, however, they send fewer clearly neutral messages. The neutral responses of husbands make it more difficult for wives to decode what their partners are really trying to say. Imagine a wife responding to her husband's

Men and women use the same words but speak a different language.

—*Deborah Tannen*

sexual overture by saying, "Let's do it later, when I'm not so tired." Her husband gives a neutral response: "Whatever." But the response is unclear: Does the husband really not care, or is he pretending he doesn't to avoid possible conflict?

- *Wives tend to set the emotional tone of an argument.* Although communication differences in arguments between husbands and wives are usually small, wives escalate conflict with negative verbal and nonverbal messages ("Don't give me that!") or de-escalate arguments by setting an atmosphere of agreement ("I would feel hurt/upset too if that happened to me"). Husbands' inputs are less important in setting the climate for resolving or escalating conflicts. Wives tend to use emotional appeals and threats more than husbands, who tend to reason, seek conciliation, and try to postpone or end an argument. A wife is more likely to ask, "Don't you love me?" whereas a husband is more likely to say, "Be rational."

DEVELOPING COMMUNICATION SKILLS

Studies suggest that poor communication skills precede the outset of marital problems (Markman, 1981; Markman, Duncan, Storaasli, & Howes, 1987). The material that follows will help you understand and develop your skills in communicating about sexual matters.

Developing Self-Awareness

Before we can communicate with others, we must first know how we feel ourselves. Yet we often place obstacles in the way:

- We suppress "unacceptable" feelings, especially anger, hurt, frustration, and jealousy. After a while, we don't even consciously experience them.
- We deny our feelings. If we are feeling hurt and our partner looks at our pained expression and asks us what we're feeling, we may reply, "Nothing." We may feel nothing because we have anesthetized our feelings.
- We displace or project our feelings. Instead of recognizing that we are jealous, we may accuse our partner of being jealous; instead of feeling hurt, we may say our partner is hurt.

Becoming aware of ourselves requires us to become aware of our feelings. Perhaps the first step toward this self-awareness is realizing that feelings are simply emotional states—they are neither good nor bad in themselves. As feelings, however, they need to be felt, whether they are warm or cold, pleasurable or painful. They do not necessarily need to be acted out or expressed. We do not need to censor our feelings or deny them. It is the acting out that holds the potential for problems or hurt.

Feelings are valuable guides for action. If we feel irritated at our partner, the irritation is a signal that something is wrong, and we can work toward change. But if we suppress or deny our feelings, perhaps because we are fearful of conflict, we do not have the impetus for change. The cause remains, and the irritation increases until it is blown out of proportion; a minor annoyance becomes a major source of anger.

> To say what we think to our superiors would be inexpedient; to say what we think to our equals would be ill-mannered; to say what we think to our inferiors is unkind. Good manners occupy the terrain between fear and pity.
>
> —*Quentin Crisp*

RESEARCHERS STUDYING marital satisfaction have found a number of communication patterns that offer clues to enhancing our intimate relationships (Hendrick, 1981; Noller & Fitzpatrick, 1991; Schaap, Buunk, & Kerkstra, 1988). They found that men and women in satisfied relationships tend to have the following common characteristics regarding communication:

- *The ability to disclose or reveal private thoughts and feelings, especially positive ones, to each other.* Dissatisfied spouses tend to disclose mostly negative thoughts to their partners. Satisfied couples say such things as "I love you," "You're sexy," or "I feel vulnerable; please hold me." Unhappy couples may also say they love each other, but more often they say things like "Don't touch me; I can't stand you," "You turn me off," or "This relationship makes me miserable and frustrated."

- *The expression by both partners of more-or-less equal levels of affective disclosures.* Both partners in satisfied couples are likely to say such words as "You make me feel happy," "I love you more than I can ever say," or "I love the way you touch me."

- *More time spent talking, discussing personal topics, and expressing feelings in positive ways.* Satisfied couples talk about their sexual feelings, the fun they have in bed together.

- *A willingness to accept conflict but to engage in conflict in nondestructive ways.* Satisfied couples view conflict as a natural part of intimate relationships. When they have sexual disagreements, they do not accuse or blame; instead, they seek common ground and are willing to compromise.

- *Less frequent conflict and less time spent in conflict.* Both satisfied and unsatisfied couples, however, experience conflicts about the same topics, especially about communication, sex, and personality characteristics.

- *The ability to accurately encode (send) verbal and nonverbal messages and accurately decode (understand) such messages from their spouses.* This ability to send and understand nonverbal messages is especially important for men. In satisfied couples, for example, if a man wants his partner to initiate sex more often, he can say, "I'd like you to initiate sex more often," and his partner will understand the message correctly. In dissatisfied couples, the man may stop initiating sex, hoping his partner will be forced to initiate more often in order to have sex. Or he may ask his partner to initiate sex more often, but his partner may mistakenly interpret the request as a personal attack.

Many of these communication patterns appear to hold true for gay and lesbian relationships as well.

The other night I said to my wife, Ruth: "Do you feel that the sex and excitement has gone out of our marriage?" Ruth said: "I'll discuss it with you during the next commercial."

—*Milton Berle*

If you don't risk anything, you risk even more.

—*Erica Jong*

Talking About Sex

Good communication is central to a healthy intimate relationship. Unfortunately, it is not always easy to establish or maintain.

Obstacles to Sexual Discussions The process of articulating our feelings about sex can be very difficult. There are several reasons for this. First, we rarely have models for talking about sex. As children and adolescents, we probably never spoke with our parents about sex. If we talked about sex in their presence, they probably discouraged it or felt uncomfortable. We learned that sex is not an appropriate subject of conversation in "polite" company.

Second, talking about sexual matters defines us as being interested in sex, and interest in sex is often identified with being sexually obsessive, immoral, prurient, or "bad." If the sexual topic is tabooed, we risk further danger of being labeled "bad."

Third, we may feel that talking about sex will threaten our relationship. We don't talk about tabooed sexual feelings, fantasies, or desires because we fear our partner may be repelled or disgusted. We also are reluctant to talk about sexual difficulties or problems because of their inherent riskiness.

Sexual vocabulary can also be a problem. We shift our sexual vocabulary depending on the context or to whom we are talking. Some words are uncomfortable or inappropriate in different contexts. To describe sexuality, we have medical terms that objectify and de-eroticize it: "penis," "vulva," "vagina," "sexual intercourse." These are the words we use in formal situations, as in medical or academic settings or when talking with our parents or our children; they are the acceptable terms for the printed page and for talk shows.

Slang words retain their sexual connotations: "cock," "cunt," "screw." There are the "dirty" words of our language. They are most often used in informal settings, among friends or peers. Gay men and lesbians have developed their own colloquial or slang terms.

Colloquial and slang words have powerful connotations. To modify their power, we have euphemisms, terms such as "making love" and "sleeping together," whose emotional impact stands somewhere between medical and slang terms. And, finally, we have our own private vocabulary of "pet names" for sexual body parts, such as "Miss Muff" or "Wilbur," that may develop within a relationship and be shared only with our partner (Cornog, 1986).

Because men and women tend to use a different sexual vocabulary, it can be difficult for them to communicate with each other about sexual matters. A woman may be offended by the vocabulary her boyfriend uses among his friends; the man may think his girlfriend is unduly reticent because she uses euphemisms to describe sexuality. A couple must often negotiate the language they will use in order not to offend each other. Sometimes this problem will be resolved into open, acceptable communication; at other times, it may result in silence.

Keys to Good Communication   Being aware of communication skills and actually using them are two separate matters. Furthermore, even though we may be comfortable sharing our feelings with another, it may be more difficult to discuss our sexual preferences and needs. Self-disclosure, trust, and feedback are three keys to good communication.

SELF-DISCLOSURE   Self-disclosure creates the environment for mutual understanding (Derlega, Metts, Petronio, & Margulis, 1993). Most people know us only through the conventional roles we play as female/male, wife/husband, parent/child. These roles, however, do not necessarily reflect our deepest selves. If we act as if we are nothing more than our roles, we may reach a point at which we no longer know who we are.

Through the process of self-disclosure we not only reveal ourselves to others, we also discover who we are. We discover the depths of feeling we have hidden, repressed, or ignored. We nurture forgotten aspects of ourselves by bringing them to the surface. Moreover, self-disclosure is reciprocal. In the process of our sharing, others share themselves with us. Men are less likely than women, however, to disclose intimate aspects of themselves (Lips, 1997). Because they have been taught to be strong, they are more reluctant to express tenderness or feelings of vulnerability. Women find it easier to disclose their feelings because they have been taught from childhood to

A little sincerity is a dangerous thing, and a great deal of it is absolutely fatal.

—*Oscar Wilde (1854–1900)*

IF YOU WANT to avoid intimacy, here are ten rules that have proved effective in nationwide testing with lovers, husbands and wives, parents, and children. Follow these guidelines, and we guarantee you'll never have an intimate relationship.

1. *Don't talk.* This is the basic rule for avoiding intimacy. If you follow this one rule, you will never have to worry about being intimate again. Sometimes, however, you may be forced to talk. But don't talk about anything meaningful. Talk about the weather, baseball, class, the stock market—anything but feelings.

2. *Never show your feelings.* Showing your feelings is almost as bad as talking, because feelings are ways of communicating. If you cry or show anger, sadness, or joy, you are giving yourself away. You might as well talk, and if you talk you could become intimate. So the best thing to do is remain expressionless (which, we admit, is a form of communication, but at least it's sending the message that you don't want to be intimate).

3. *Always be pleasant.* Always smile, always be friendly, especially if something's bothering you. You'll be surprised at how effective hiding negative feelings from your partner is in preventing intimacy. It may even fool your partner into believing that everything's OK in your relationship.

4. *Always win.* If you can't be pleasant, try this one. Never compromise, never admit that your partner's point of view may be as good as yours. If you start compromising, it's an admission that you care about your partner's feelings, which is a dangerous step toward intimacy.

5. *Always keep busy.* Keeping busy at school or work will take you away from your partner, and you won't have to be intimate. Your partner may never figure out that you're using work to avoid intimacy. Because our culture values hard work, he or she will feel unjustified in complaining. Devoting yourself to your work will give your partner the message that he or she is not as important as your work. You can make your partner feel unimportant in your life without even talking!

6. *Always be right.* There is nothing worse than being wrong, because it is an indication that you are human. If you admit you're wrong, you might have to

---

express themselves (Tannen, 1990). These differences can drive wedges between men and women. Even when people live together or are married, they feel lonely because there is no contact. And the worst kind of loneliness is feeling alone when we are with someone with whom we want to feel close.

> Ninety-nine lies may save you, but the hundredth will give you away
>
> —*West African proverb*

TRUST   When we talk about intimate relationships, the two words that most frequently pop up are "love" and "trust." Trust is the primary characteristic we associate with love. But what, exactly, is trust? **Trust** can be defined as a belief in the reliability and integrity of a person. When a person says, "Trust me," he or she is asking for something that does not easily occur. For trust to develop, three conditions must exist:

1. *The relationship must have a strong likelihood of continuing.* We generally do not trust strangers or people we have just met with information that makes us vulnerable, such as our sexual anxieties. We trust people with whom we have a significant relationship.

2. *Behavior must be predictable.* If we are married or in a committed relationship, we trust that our partner will not do something that will hurt us, such as have an affair. In fact, if we discover that our partner is involved in an affair, we often speak of our trust being violated or destroyed. If trust is destroyed, it is because the predictability of sexual exclusiveness is no longer there.

admit your partner's right, and that will make him or her as good as you. If he or she is as good as you, then you might have to consider your partner, and before you know it, you will be intimate!

7. *Never argue.* If you can't always be right, don't argue at all. If you argue, you might discover that you and your partner are different. If you're different, you may have to talk about the differences in order to make adjustments. And if you begin making adjustments, you may have to tell your partner who you really are, what you really feel. Naturally, these revelations may lead to intimacy.

8. *Make your partner guess what you want.* Never tell your partner what you want. That way, when your partner tries to guess and is wrong (as he or she often will be), you can tell your partner that he or she doesn't really understand or love you. If your partner did love you, he or she would know what you want without asking. Not only will this prevent intimacy, but it will drive your partner crazy as well.

9. *Always look out for number one.* Remember, you are number one. All relationships exist to fulfill your needs, no one else's. Whatever you feel like doing is just fine. You're OK; your partner's not OK. If your partner can't satisfy your needs, he or she is narcis-

sistic; after all, you are the one making all the sacrifices in the relationship.

10. *Keep the television on.* Keep the television turned on at all times: during dinner, while you're reading, when you're in bed, and while you're talking (especially if you're talking about something important). This rule may seem petty compared with the others, but it is good preventive action. Watching television keeps you and your partner from talking to each other. Best of all, it will keep you both from even noticing that you don't communicate. If you're cornered and have to talk, you can both be distracted by a commercial, a seduction scene, or the sound of gunfire. And when you actually think about it, wouldn't you rather be watching "Seinfeld" reruns anyway?

This list is not complete. Everyone knows additional ways for avoiding intimacy. These may be your own inventions or techniques you have learned from your boyfriend or girlfriend, husband or wife, friends, or parents. To round out this compilation, list additional rules for avoiding intimacy on a separate sheet of paper. The person with the best list wins—and never has to be intimate again.

3. *Each person must have options.* If we were marooned on a desert island alone with our partner, he or she would have no choice but to be sexually monogamous. But if a third person, sexually attractive to our partner, swam ashore a year later, our partner would have an alternative. Our partner would then have a choice of being sexually exclusive or nonexclusive; his or her behavior would then be evidence of trustworthiness—or its absence.

Trust is critical in close relationships for two reasons. First, self-disclosure requires trust because it makes you vulnerable. A person will not self-disclose if he or she believes the information may be misused, by mocking or revealing a secret, for example. Second, the degree to which you trust a person influences the way you are likely to interpret ambiguous or unexpected messages from him or her. If your partner says he or she wants to study alone tonight, you are likely to take the statement at face value if you have a high level of trust. But if you have a low level of trust, you may believe he or she is going to be meeting someone else.

Self-disclosure is reciprocal. If we self-disclose, we expect our partner to self-disclose as well. As we self-disclose, we build trust; as we withhold self-disclosure, we erode trust. To withhold ourselves is to imply that we don't trust the other person, and if we don't, he or she will not trust us.

FEEDBACK   A third critical element in communication is **feedback,** the ongoing process in which participants and their messages create a given result and are subsequently modified by that result. If my partner

> When in doubt, tell the truth.
> —*Mark Twain (1835–1910)*

> A half-truth is a whole lie.
> —*Yiddish proverb*

FIGURE 8.1 Communication Loop. In successful communication, feedback between the sender and receiver ensures that both understand (or are trying to understand) what is being communicated. For communication to be clear, the message and the intent behind the message must be congruent. Nonverbal and verbal components must also support the intended message. Verbal aspects of communication include not just language and word choice but characteristics such as tone, volume, pitch, rate, and periods of silence.

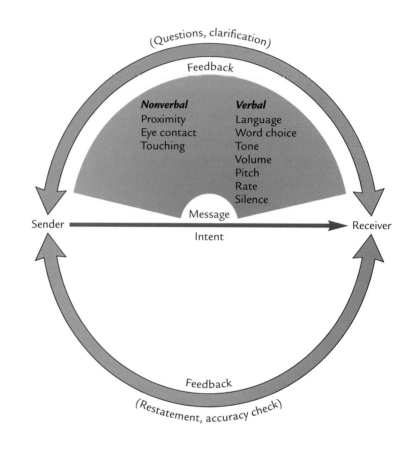

self-discloses to me, my response to that self-disclosure is my feedback. My partner's response is feedback to my feedback. It is a continuous process (Figure 8.1). The most important form of feedback for improving relationships is *constructive* feedback. Constructive feedback focuses on self-disclosing information that will help your partner understand the consequences of his or her actions on you and on the relationship. For example, if your partner discloses his or her doubts about the relationship, you can respond in a number of ways. Among these are remaining silent, venting anger, expressing indifference, or giving constructive feedback. Of these responses, constructive feedback is the most likely to encourage positive change.

CONFLICT AND INTIMACY

Conflict is the communication process in which people perceive incompatible goals and interference from others in achieving their goals. Conflict is a special type of communication.

We expect love to unify us, but sometimes it doesn't. Two people do not become one when they love each other, although at first they may have this feeling. Their love may not be an illusion, but their sense of ultimate oneness is. In reality, we retain our individual identities, needs, wants, and pasts—even while loving one another. It is a paradox that the more intimate two people become, the more likely they may be to experience conflict. In

Conflict is natural in intimate relationships because each person has her or his own unique identity, values, needs, and history.

fact, it is a lack of arguing that can signal trouble in a relationship because it may mean that issues are not being resolved (Kipnis & Herron, 1993). Conflict itself is not dangerous to intimate relationships; it is the manner in which the conflict is handled. The presence of conflict does not necessarily indicate that love is going or has gone. It may mean that love is *growing.*

Conflict in relationships is expressed differently by different ethnic groups. Non-Latino Whites tend to seek either dominance, which is confrontational and controlling, or integration, which is solution-oriented. They seem to believe that conflict is more natural and expected in a relationship, perhaps because of the high value placed on individualism. Both African Americans and Mexican Americans view conflict less positively; they believe that conflict has both short-term and long-term negative effects. A comparison between Whites and African Americans found that Whites tend to be more solution-oriented than Blacks, who tend to be more controlling. In interpersonal relationships, both groups tend to identify conflict in terms of issues and goals. By contrast, Mexican Americans view conflict more in relationship terms; conflict occurs when a relationship is out of balance or harmony (Collier, 1991).

These differing views of conflict and conflict resolution affect each group's willingness to deal with sexual conflicts. Understanding these differences will help in resolving sexual problems and issues.

GIVING CONSTRUCTIVE, effective feedback is an important skill in any intimate relationship. The following guidelines (developed by David Johnston for the Minnesota Peer Program) will help you engage in constructive dialogue and feedback with your partner:

- *Focus on "I" statements.* An "I" statement is a statement about *your* feelings: "I feel unloved." By contrast, "You" statements tell another person how *he* or *she* is, feels, or thinks: "You don't love me." "You" statements are often blaming or accusatory. Because "I" messages don't carry blame, the recipient is less likely to be defensive or resentful.

- *Focus on behavior rather than on the person.* If you focus on a person's behavior rather than on the person, you are more likely to secure change, because a person can change behaviors, but not himself or herself. If you want your partner to stimulate your clitoris during intercourse, say, "I'd like you to touch my clitoris while we're making love because it would help me have an orgasm." This statement focuses on behavior that can be changed. If you say, "You're not a particularly hot lover," you are attacking the person, and he is likely to respond defensively: "Talk about crummy lovers—how come you need my help to have an orgasm? What's wrong with you?"

- *Focus feedback on observations rather than on inferences or judgments.* Focus your feedback on what you actually observe rather than what you think the behavior means. "I don't receive enough stimulation during intercourse to have an orgasm" is an observation. "You don't really care about how I feel because you never try to help me have an orgasm" is an inference that the partner's sexual interactions indicate a lack of regard. The inference moves the discussion from sexual stimulation to the partner's caring.

- *Focus feedback on observations based on a more-or-less continuum.* Behaviors fall on a continuum. Your partner doesn't *always* do or not do a particular thing. When you say your partner does something sometimes, or even most of the time, you are *measuring* behavior. "The last three times you wanted to make love I didn't want to because of the way you smelled" is a measuring statement; its accuracy can be tested. But if you say your partner *always* (or *never*) does something, you are probably distorting reality. "You *always* smell when you come to bed" or "You *never* take a shower before sex" is probably an exaggeration that may provoke a hostile response. "What do you mean? I showered last month. You got some kind of hang-up?"

Sexual Conflicts

Common mistakes such as using sex as a scapegoat for nonsexual problems and using fights as a cover-up for other problems frequently lead to additional arguments and misunderstandings. Clinging to these patterns can interfere with problem solving and inhibit conflict resolution.

Fighting About Sex   Fighting and sex can be intertwined in several different ways. A couple may have a disagreement about sex that leads to a fight. For example, if one person wants to have sexual intercourse and the other does not, they may fight.

Sex can also be used as a scapegoat for nonsexual problems. If a man is angry because his wife has called him a lousy provider, he may take it out on her sexually by calling her a lousy lover. They fight about their lovemaking rather than about the real issue, his provider role.

Finally, a fight can be a cover-up. If a man feels sexually inadequate and does not want to have sex as often as his partner, he may pick a fight and make his partner so angry that the last thing she would want to do is to be sexual with him.

It's hard to tell during a fight if there are deeper causes than the one about which a couple are currently fighting. If you repeatedly fight about sexual

- *Focus feedback on sharing ideas or offering alternatives rather than giving advice.* No one likes being told what to do. Unsolicited advice often produces anger or resentment, because advice implies that you know more about what a person needs to do than he or she does. Advice implies a lack of respect. But by sharing ideas and offering alternatives, you give the other person the freedom to decide based on his or her own perceptions and goals. "What you need to do is pay attention to some of my needs" is advice. "I wish I could be more orgasmic in intercourse. Let's try some other things. If I had more clitoral stimulation, like your rubbing my clitoris when we are making love . . . something like that would be great. . . . Or I could stimulate myself. What do you think?" Such responses offer alternatives.

- *Focus feedback according to its value for the recipient.* If your partner says something that upsets you, your initial response may be to lash back. A cathartic response may make you feel better for the time being, but it may not be useful for your partner. For example, your partner says that he or she has been faking orgasms. You can respond with anger or accusations, or you can express concern and try to find out why he or she felt it was necessary.

- *Focus feedback on the amount the recipient can process.* Don't overload your partner with your response.

Your partner's disclosure may touch deep, pent-up feelings in you, but he or she may not be able to comprehend all that you say. If you respond to your partner's revelation of doubts about your relationship with a listing of all the doubts you have *ever* experienced about it, you may overwhelm your partner.

- *Focus feedback at the appropriate time and place.* When you discuss anything of importance, choose an appropriate time and place so that nothing will distract you. Choose a time when you are not likely to be interrupted. Turn the television off, and put the answering machine on. Also, choose a time that is relatively stress-free. Talking about something of great personal importance just before an exam or a business meeting is likely to sabotage any attempt at communication. Finally, choose a place that will provide privacy; don't start an important conversation if you are worried about people overhearing or interrupting you. A crowded dormitory lounge during "South Park," a kitchen filled with kids, a football stadium during a big game, and a car full of people on the way to the beach are inappropriate places.

Building these behaviors into your communication patterns will help you nurture your relationships in both the short and the long term.

issues without getting anywhere, the ostensible cause may not be the real one. If fighting does not clear the air and make intimacy possible again, you should look for other reasons for the fights. It may be useful to talk with your partner about why the fights do not seem to accomplish anything. Step back and look at the circumstances of the fight, what patterns occur, and how each of you feels before, during, and after a fight.

Sexuality and Power Conflicts   In power struggles, sexuality can be used as a weapon, but this is generally a destructive tactic (Szinovacz, 1987). A classic strategy for the weaker person in a relationship is to withhold something that the more powerful one wants. In male-female struggles, this is often sex. By withholding sex, a woman gains a certain degree of power (Kaplan, 1979). Men also use sex in its most violent form: They use rape (including date rape and marital rape) to overpower and subordinate women (see Chapter 17).

In long-term gay male relationships, refusing sex can take on symbolic meaning. Refusing sex is sometimes associated with power struggles occurring as a result of having two sexual initiators (Blumstein & Schwartz, 1983). Because initiating sex is associated with power and dominance, two men being sexually assertive can become a form of competition. The man who feels himself less powerful can try to reassert his power by refusing his partner's sexual advances. In many lesbian relationships, power issues are often disguised because of the commitment of both partners to equality. In these cases, power struggles are often indirect and obscure (Burch, 1987). Sexual rejection or lack of interest may hide issues of power.

Genuine intimacy appears to require equality in power relationships. Decision making in the happiest marriages seems to be based not on coercion or "tit for tat" but on caring, mutuality, and respect for the other person. Women who feel vulnerable to their mates may withhold feelings or pretend to feel what they do not. Unequal power in marriage may encourage power politics, as each partner struggles to keep or gain power.

It is not easy to change unequal power relationships after they become embedded in the overall structure of a relationship, yet they can be changed. Talking, trying to understand, and negotiating are the best approaches. Still, in attempting changes, a person may risk estrangement or the breakup of a relationship. He or she must weigh the possible gains against the possible losses in deciding whether change is worth the risk.

Conflict Resolution

The way in which a couple deal with conflict resolution reflects and perhaps contributes to their marital happiness (Boland & Follingstad, 1987).

For a marriage to be peaceful, the husband should be deaf and the wife blind.

—*Spanish proverb*

Strategies for Resolving Conflicts   There are several ways to end conflicts. You can give in, but unless you believe that the conflict ended fairly, you are likely to feel resentful. You can try to impose your will through the use of power, force, or the threat of force. But using power to end conflict leaves your partner with the bitter taste of injustice. Or you can end the conflict through negotiation. In negotiations, both partners sit down and work out their differences until they can come to a mutually acceptable agreement.

Sometimes, even if we sincerely commit ourselves to working out our problems, it is difficult to see our own role in sustaining a pattern of interaction. If a couple are unable to resolve their conflicts, they should consider entering relationship counseling. A therapist or other professional can often help identify underlying problems, as well as help a couple develop negotiating skills.

Conflict Resolution and Relationship Satisfaction   Happy couples tend to act in positive ways to resolve conflicts, such as changing behaviors (putting the cap on the toothpaste rather than denying responsibility) and presenting reasonable alternatives (purchasing toothpaste in a pump dispenser). Unhappy or distressed couples, in contrast, use more negative strategies in attempting to resolve conflicts ("If the cap off the toothpaste bothers you, then you put it on"). A study of happily and unhappily married couples found distinctive communication traits as these couples tried to resolve their conflicts (Ting-Toomey, 1983). The communication behaviors of happily married couples displayed the following traits:

▪ *Summarizing.* Each person summarized what the other said. "Let me see if I can repeat the different points you were making."

- *Paraphrasing.* Each put what the other said into his or her own words. "What you are saying is that you feel bad when I don't acknowledge your feelings."

- *Validation.* Each affirmed the other's feelings. "I can understand how you feel."

- *Clarification.* Each asked for further information to make sure that he or she understood what the other was saying. "Can you explain what you mean a little bit more to make sure that I understand you?"

In contrast, unhappily married couples displayed the following reciprocal patterns:

- *Confrontation.* Each member of the couple confronted. "You're frigid!" "Not me, buddy. It's you who can't get it up."

- *Confrontation and defensiveness.* One confronted, while the other defended himself or herself. "You're a lousy lover!" "I did what you told me you wanted and you still can't come."

- *Complaining and defensiveness.* One complained, while the other was defensive. "I try to please you but it still does no good!" "I am too tired and distracted."

Negotiating Conflicts

Conflicts can be solved through negotiation in three major ways: agreement as a gift, bargaining, and coexistence.

AGREEMENT AS A GIFT   If you and your partner disagree on an issue, you can freely agree with your partner as a gift. If a woman wants her partner to stimulate her clitoris, and he doesn't want to because he feels it reflects badly on him, he can agree to try it because he cares about his partner. Similarly, a woman who does not want to try oral sex can try as a gift of caring. (Neither the man nor the woman, however, needs to continue if the activity continues to be objectionable.)

Agreement as a gift is different from giving in. When you give in, you do something you don't want to do. But when you agree without coercion or threats, the agreement is a gift of love. As in all exchanges of gifts, there will be reciprocation. Your partner will be more likely to give you a gift of agreement in return.

BARGAINING   Bargaining means making compromises. But bargaining in relationships is different from bargaining in the marketplace or in politics. In relationships, you don't want to get the best deal for yourself, but the most equitable deal for both you *and* your partner. At all points during the bargaining process, you need to keep in mind what is best for the relationship, as well as for yourself, and trust your partner to do the same. In a relationship, both partners need to win. The purpose of conflict resolution in a relationship is to solidify the relationship, not to make one partner the winner and the other the loser. Achieving your end by exercising coercive power or withholding love, affection, or sex is a destructive form of bargaining. If you get what you want, how will that affect your partner and the relationship? Will your partner feel you're being unfair and become resentful? A solution has to be fair to both of you, or it won't enhance the relationship.

> Hatred does not cease by hatred at any time. Hatred ceases by love. This is an unalterable law.
>
> —*Siddhartha Gautama, the Buddha* (c. 563–483 B.C.)

COEXISTENCE   Sometimes differences can't be resolved, but they can be lived with. If a relationship is sound, differences can be absorbed without undermining the basic ties. All too often we regard differences as threatening rather than as the unique expression of two personalities. If one person likes to masturbate, the partner can accept it as an expression of his or her unique sexuality.

■   If you can't talk about what you like and what you want, there is a good chance you won't get either one. Communication is the basis for good sex and good relationships. Communication and intimacy are reciprocal: Communication creates intimacy, and intimacy, in turn, creates good communication.

If we fail to communicate, we are likely to turn our relationships into empty facades. Each person acts according to a role rather than revealing his or her deepest self. But communication is learned behavior. If we have learned *not* to communicate, we can learn *how* to communicate. Communication allows us to expand ourselves and to maintain our relationships.

SUMMARY

The Nature of Communication

- The ability to communicate is important in developing and maintaining ongoing relationships. Couples satisfied with their sexual communication tend to be satisfied about their relationships as a whole.

- *Communication* is a transactional process by which we convey symbols, such as words, gestures, and movements, to establish human contact, exchange information, and reinforce or change the attitudes and behaviors of ourselves and others.

- Communication takes place within cultural, social, and psychological contexts. The cultural context refers to the language, values, beliefs, and customs in which communication takes place. Ethnic groups communicate about sex differently, depending on their language patterns and values. The social context refers to the roles we play in society that influence our communication. The most important roles affecting sexuality are those relating to gender and sexual orientation. The psychological context refers to our personality characteristics, such as having positive or negative feelings about sex.

- Communication includes both verbal and nonverbal communication. The ability to correctly interpret nonverbal messages is important in successful relationships. *Proximity*, eye contact, and touching are especially important forms of nonverbal communication.

Sexual Communication

- In initial encounters, physical appearance is especially important. Because of the *halo effect*, we infer positive qualities about people based on their appearance. Women typically send nonverbal cues to men indicating interest; men then begin a conversation with an "opening line."

- The "first move" marks the transition to physical intimacy; the male generally initiates. In initiating the first sexual interaction, communication is generally nonverbal, ambiguous, and indirect. Sexual disinterest is usually communicated nonverbally. With sexual involvement, the couple must communicate verbally about contraception, STD prevention, and sexual likes and dislikes.

- Unless there are definite clues as to orientation, gay men and lesbians try to determine through nonverbal cues whether others are appropriate partners. Because of male gender roles, gay men initiate sex earlier than heterosexuals; for parallel reasons, lesbians initiate sex later.

- In established relationships, many women feel more comfortable in initiating sexual interactions. Sexual initiations are more likely to be accepted in established relationships; sexual disinterest is communicated verbally. Women do not restrict sexual activities any more than men.

- Research indicates that happily married couples disclose private thoughts and feelings to partners, express equal levels of affective disclosure, spend more time together talking or expressing feelings in positive ways, are willing to engage in conflict in nondestructive ways, have less frequent conflict and spend less time in conflict, and accurately encode and decode messages.

- There are gender differences in marital communication. Wives send clearer messages; husbands tend to give neutral messages, whereas wives tend to give more positive or negative messages; and wives tend to set the emotional tone and escalate arguments more than husbands.

Developing Communication Skills

- Achieving self-awareness is an important first step in developing communication skills. Obstacles to talking about sex include a lack of role models, fear of being identified as "bad," cultural and personal taboos on unacceptable sexual subjects, and a lack of adequate vocabulary. Sexual vocabulary shifts according to context.

- The keys to effective communication are self-disclosure, trust, and feedback. *Self-disclosure* is the revelation of intimate information about ourselves. *Trust* is the belief in the reliability and integrity of another person. *Feedback* is a constructive response to another's self-disclosure.

Conflict and Intimacy

- *Conflict* is natural in intimate relationships. Conflicts about sex can be specific disagreements about sex, arguments that are ostensibly about sex but that are really about nonsexual issues, or disagreements about the wrong sexual issue.

- In resolving conflicts, happily married couples communicate by summarizing, paraphrasing, validating, and clarifying. Unhappily married couples use confrontation, confrontation and defensiveness, and complaining and defensiveness. Conflict resolution may be achieved through negotiation in three ways: agreement as a freely given gift, bargaining, and coexistence.

SUGGESTED READING

Cupach, W. R., & Spitzberg, B. H. (Eds.). (1994). *The Darkside of Interpersonal Communication*. Hillsdale, NJ: Lawrence Erlbaum. A conversation about conversational dilemmas, distressed relationships, and other issues that stress families.

Derlega, Valerian, Metts, Sandra, Petronio, Sandra, & Margulis, Steven. (1993). *Self-Disclosure*. Newbury Park, CA: Sage. How self-disclosure affects intimate relationships in terms of closeness, privacy, feelings of vulnerability, and love.

Hecht, Michelle, Collier, Mary Jane, & Ribeau, Sidney. (1993). *African American Communication*. Newbury Park, CA: Sage. A synthesis of research on African American communication and culture, including effective and ineffective communication patterns.

Satir, Virginia. (1988). *The New Peoplemaking* (Rev. ed.). Palo Alto, CA: Science and Behavior Books. One of the most influential (and easy to read) books of the past 25 years on communication and family relationships.

Scarf, Maggie. (1995). *Intimate World: Life Inside the Family*. New York: Random House. An exploration by a counseling psychologist of issues such as conflict, power, and intimacy.

Tannen, Deborah. (1990). *You Just Don't Understand: Women and Men in Conversation*. New York: William Morrow. A best-selling, intelligent, and lively discussion of how women use communication to achieve intimacy and men use communication to achieve independence.

Ting-Toomey, Stella, & Korzenny, Felipe (Eds.). (1991). *Cross-Cultural Interpersonal Communication*. Newbury Park, CA: Sage. A ground-breaking collection of scholarly essays on communication and relationships among different ethnic and cultural groups, including African American, Latino, Korean, and Chinese ethnic groups and cultures.

9

Sexual
Expression

SEXUAL EXPRESSION is a complex process through which we reveal our sexual selves. Sexual expression involves more than simply sexual behaviors. It involves our feelings as well. "Behavior can never be unemotional," one scholar observes (Blechman, 1990). As human beings, we do not separate feelings from behavior, including sexual behavior. Our sexual behaviors are rich with emotions, ranging from love to anxiety, from desire to antipathy.

To fully understand our sexuality, we need to examine our sexual behaviors *and* the emotions we experience along with them. If we studied sexual activities apart from our emotions, we would distort the human meaning of sexuality. It would make our sexual behaviors appear mechanistic, nothing more than genitals rubbing against each other.

In this chapter, we first discuss sexual attractiveness. Next, we turn to sexual scripts that give form to our sexual drives. Then we examine the most common sexual behaviors, both autoerotic behaviors, such as fantasies and masturbation, and interpersonal behaviors, such as oral-genital sex, sexual intercourse, and anal eroticism.

> Sex is one of the nine reasons for reincarnation. . . . The other eight are unimportant.
>
> —*Henry Miller (1891–1980)*

SEXUAL ATTRACTIVENESS

Sexual attractiveness is an important component in sexual expression. As we shall see, there are few universals in what people from different cultures consider attractive.

A Cross-Cultural Analysis

In a landmark cross-cultural survey by Clelland Ford and Frank Beach (1951), the researchers discovered that there appear to be only two characteristics that women and men universally consider important in terms of sexual attractiveness: youth and good health. All other aspects may vary significantly from culture to culture. Why should only youth and health be universals? Why not also small feet or curly hair?

Although we may never find an answer, sociobiologists offer a possible but untestable explanation. They theorize, as we saw in Chapter 1, that all animals instinctively want to reproduce their own genes. Consequently, both humans and other animals adopt certain reproductive strategies. One of these strategies is choosing a mate capable of reproducing one's offspring. Human males prefer females who are young because young women are the most likely to be fertile. Good health is also related to reproductive potential. Healthy women are more likely to be fertile and capable of rearing their children. Evolutionary psychologist David Buss (1994) notes that our ancestors looked for certain physical characteristics that indicated a woman's health and youth. Buss found certain physical features that are cross-culturally associated with beauty: good muscle tone; full lips; clear, smooth skin; lustrous hair; clear eyes. Our ancestors also looked for behavioral cues, such as animated facial expression; a bouncy, youthful gait; and a high energy level. These observable physical cues to youth and health (and hence to reproductive capacity) constitute the standards of beauty in many cultures.

Vitality and health are important to human females. Women prefer men who are slightly older than they are, because an older man is likely to be more stable and mature and have greater resources to invest in children. Similarly, in the animal kingdom, females choose mates who provide resources, such as food and protection. Among American women, Buss points out, countless studies indicate that economic security and employment are much more important for women than for men (Buss, 1994). If you look in the personal ads in any newspaper, you'll find this gender difference readily confirmed. A woman's ad typically reads: "Lively, intelligent woman seeks professional, responsible gentleman for committed relationship." A man's ad typically reads: "Looking for sexy woman interested in having a good time. Send photo."

Women prefer men who are in good health. They want someone who will be physically fit to be a good provider. If a woman chooses someone with hereditary health problems, she risks passing on his poor genes to her children. An unhealthy partner is also more likely to die sooner, cutting the woman and her children off from resources. Ford and Beach (1951) found that signs of ill health (including open sores, lesions, and excessive pallor) are universally considered unattractive.

Aside from youth and good health, however, Ford and Beach found no universal standards of physical sexual attractiveness. In fact, the study found that there is considerable variation from culture to culture in what parts of the body are considered erotic. In some cultures, the eyes are the key to sexual attractiveness; in others, height and weight; and in still others, the size and shape of the genitals. In our culture, female breasts are considered erotic; in others, they are not.

Cultures that agree on which body parts are erotic may still disagree on what constitutes attractiveness. In terms of female beauty, American culture considers a slim body attractive. But worldwide, Americans are in the minority, for the type of female body most desired cross-culturally is plump. Similarly, we prefer slim hips, but the majority of cultures in Ford and Beach's study found wide hips most attractive. In our culture, large breasts are ideal, but others prefer small breasts, and still others, long and pendulous breasts. In the past decade, well-defined pectoral and arm muscles have become part of the ideal male body.

The Halo Effect Revisited

A pair of powerful spectacles has sometimes sufficed to cure a person in love.

—*Friedrich Nietzsche*

As discussed in Chapter 8, attractive people are surrounded by a halo effect. The halo effect extends to assumptions about sexuality. A study of men from two universities found that among the various traits attributed to attractive women, the trait most affected by their appearance was their sexual behavior (Tanke, 1982). Attractive women were viewed as more sexually warm, exciting, and permissive than unattractive ones.

Although most studies on sexuality and attractiveness relate to beliefs about attractive people, an intriguing study of 100 college women found some evidence indicating a relationship between attractiveness and actual sexual behavior (Stelzer, Desmond, & Price, 1987). Attractive women were significantly more likely to engage in sexual intercourse and oral sex than the other women. This finding suggests that the halo effect may create a self-

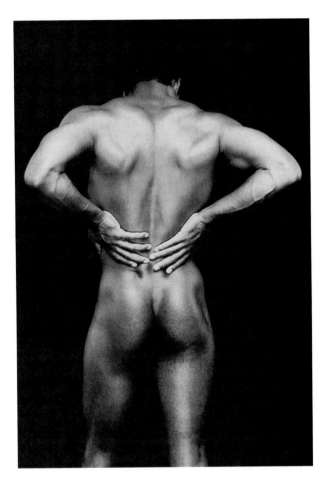

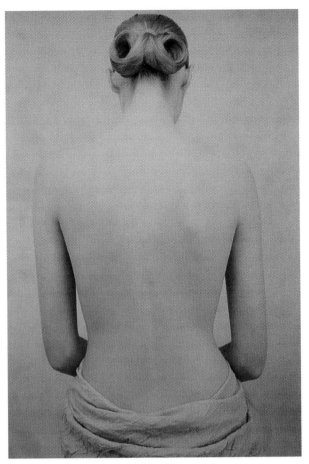

Cultures that agree on which body parts are erotic may still disagree on what constitutes attractiveness.

fulfilling expectation about sexual behavior. Because attractive women are *expected* to be more sexually active, they *become* more sexually active.

Another study found that attractive women are more likely to be on top during sexual intercourse and to engage in cunnilingus and fellatio (Blumstein & Schwartz, 1983). The researchers speculate that attractiveness bestows sexual power on women. Being attractive increases women's self-esteem and permits them to express themselves more freely.

Although attractiveness is important, it's good to remember that looks aren't everything. Looks are most important to certain types or groups of people and in certain situations or locations, such as classes, parties, and bars, where people do not interact extensively with each other daily. Looks are less important to those in ongoing relationships and to adults over 30 or so (Hatfield & Sprecher, 1986). Attractiveness remains important, however, in established relationships as well. Blumstein and Schwartz (1983) found that the happiest people in cohabiting and married relationships thought of their partners as attractive. People who found their partners attractive had the best sex lives. Another study found that women whose partners' faces and other body parts were most symmetrical enjoyed a significantly higher frequency of orgasms during sexual intercourse than did those with less symmetrical mates (Furlow & Thornhill, 1996).

How MUCH SEXUAL DESIRE is "normal," and what can couples do when one partner has more—or less—desire than the other?

Although there is a great deal of variability in sexual desire, it is generally held that "healthy" individuals experience desire regularly and take advantage of appropriate opportunities for sexual expression when they arise. Individuals who are persistently uninterested in sexual expression and do not report sexual fantasies are said to be experiencing hypoactive sexual desire disorder (American Psychiatric Association, 1994). For such individuals, therapy may be recommended.

Of course, terms like "regularly," "appropriate," and "persistent" are very subjective. The *DSM-IV* uses these terms to avoid defining low desire in terms of frequency of sexual activity, because some people have sex out of feelings of obligation or coercion rather than interest or desire (Wincze & Carey, 1991). Instead, the manual defines desire in terms of the individual's feelings and encourages clinical evaluation when a problem is experienced. (Note that sexual abstinence—deliberately refraining from sexual expression—is not considered a disorder and should not be labeled as such.)

Regardless of measurements and clinical judgments, it is apparent to couples when one individual is more interested in sex than the other. Sometimes differences stem from such issues as timing, cleanliness, and appro-

priate stimulation techniques; issues like these can often be resolved through honest discussion, feedback, and practice. Elements contributing to a successful outcome in any discussion of sex include awareness, taking enough time to talk about it, using positive communication, and having a sense of humor.

Often, problems arise because individuals' expectations are based on fantasy, media influences, or lack of information. A woman may, for instance, ask herself why she is unable to reach orgasm during intercourse, or a man may wonder why his erection fails even though he wants to have intercourse. In the case of the woman, is she aware of the effects of clitoral stimulation? Has she practiced stimulation techniques on herself and effectively demonstrated them to her partner? Does she position herself during intercourse in such a way as to maximize the opportunities for stimulation? If she knows that most women require prolonged and effective amounts of stimulation up to and through orgasm, she may be able to enjoy intercourse more fully and may then feel more desire.

In the case of the man, does he know that lack of desire is a fairly common and often temporary problem? Does he know what kinds and amounts of stimulation are most effective for him? Does he feel comfortable using fantasy? Has he told his partner what he likes? Has he tried to discover noncoital means of pleasure with his

Sexual Desire

Desire can exist separately from overtly physical sexual expression. As discussed in Chapter 3, desire is the psychobiological component that motivates sexual behavior. But almost no scientific research exists on sexual desire. One of the most important reasons researchers have avoided studying it is that desire is difficult to define and quantify.

Sexual desire is affected by erotophilia and erotophobia. **Erotophilia** is a positive emotional response to sexuality, and **erotophobia** is a negative emotional response to sexuality. In recent years, researchers have hypothesized that the place where someone falls on the erotophilic/erotophobic continuum strongly influences his or her overt sexual behavior (Fisher, 1986). In contrast to erotophobic individuals, for example, erotophilic men and women accept and enjoy their sexuality, seek out sexual situations, engage in more autoerotic and interpersonal sexual activities, enjoy talking about sex, and are more likely to obtain and use contraception. Furthermore, erotophilic people are more likely to have positive sexual attitudes, to engage in more involved sexual fantasies, and to have seen more erotica than erotophobic people.

A person's emotional response to sex is also linked to how he or she eval-

> The degree and kind of a person's sexuality reaches up into the ultimate pinnacle of his spirit.
>
> —*Friedrich Nietzsche (1844–1900)*

partner? Once again, open and honest communication is the key to successful sexual interactions.

When the situation is partner-specific—that is, each person masturbates successfully and/or desires or fantasizes about others but does not desire or respond to a given partner—the problem is obviously more complex and difficult to solve. The couple may be bored with each other or with the way they make love, or they may fear pregnancy or STDs. Other factors that interfere with desire and arousal are anger, depression, an imbalance of power between the partners, and an inability to associate love with sexual desire. Some men (and perhaps women) experience what is referred to as the "madonna-whore syndrome." They report low sexual desire with their regular partners (usually their wives) but are aroused and can function with women they consider "slutty." Trying a few of the techniques listed below may help with this problem. Some prescription drugs have been shown to reduce sexual desire and inhibit orgasm. When this is the case, individuals and couples may require the help of a physician or therapist to overcome their differences.

If you and your partner are experiencing problems stemming from differences in desire, there are some simple techniques you can use to increase interest and provide novelty in the bedroom. To set the stage, find a place where you are assured of no interruptions or distractions. Allow enough time to discover each other again. Approach lovemaking with an open mind and a sense of humor and fun. And try some of these techniques:

- Find a different location to make love—the bathroom or shower, on the floor or in the pool, or in a hotel room.
- Undress each other slowly, taking time to touch and enjoy the removal of each article of clothing.
- Use erotic films that appeal to each of you. If you don't have the same taste, alternate videos from time to time.
- Prolong pleasuring and foreplay by using body oils and lotions; give each other erotic massages.
- Bathe together, taking the time to wash and enjoy each other.
- If you are comfortable doing so, use "sex toys," such as vibrators or feathers.
- Share sexual fantasies, using graphic language if you are comfortable with it.
- Tell each other what feels good.

Because fluctuations in desire are a normal part of life, as are differences in desire between partners, individuals may choose masturbation as an acceptable and pleasurable outlet for sexual desire. Like all areas of sexual functioning, the important thing to remember, when sexual appetites differ, is that open and honest communication paves the way to fulfillment.

uates other aspects of sex. Erotophilic individuals, for example, tend to evaluate sexually explicit material more positively. In fact, one study found that erotophilics identified explicit movies as erotic, whereas erotophobics described the same films as pornographic (Byrne, Fisher, Lambreth, & Mitchell, 1974).

Researchers have found intriguing evidence of a relationship between erotophilia/erotophobia and personality traits. Erotophobic individuals tend to be more authoritarian, believing in rules and order. They experience higher levels of guilt about sexual matters, feeling guilty about masturbation and premarital sex. They are more rigid in their gender roles, believing that men and women are basically different, especially about sexual matters, and they are less likely to use contraceptives (Byrne & Schulte, 1990; Fisher, Byrne, White, & Kelley, 1988).

But erotophilic and erotophobic traits are not fixed. Positive experiences can alter erotophobic responses over time. In fact, some therapy programs work on the assumption that consistent positive feelings, such as love, affirmation, caring, touching, and communication, can do much to diminish the fear of sex. Positive sexual experiences can help dissolve much of the anxiety that underlies erotophobia.

SEXUAL SCRIPTS

As you recall from Chapter 5, gender roles have an immense impact on how we behave sexually, for sexual behavior and feelings depend more on learning than on biological drives. Our sexual drives can be molded into almost any form. What is "natural" is what society calls natural; there is very little spontaneous, unlearned behavior. Sexual behavior, like all other forms of social behavior (such as courtship, classroom behavior, and sports), relies on scripts.

Scripts are like plans that organize and give direction to our behavior. The sexual scripts we receive strongly influence our sexual activities as men and women in our culture. As William Gagnon (1977) writes:

> A script is simpler than the activity we perform. . . . It is like a blueprint or roadmap or recipe, giving directions but not specifying everything that must be done. Regardless of its sketchiness, the script is often more important than the concrete acts. It is our script that we carry from action to action, modified by our concrete acts, but not replaced by them. Scripts do change, as new elements are added and old elements are reworked, but very few people have the desire, energy, or persistence to create highly innovative or novel scripts.

Our sexual scripts have three main components: cultural, intrapersonal, and interpersonal.

▪ *Cultural component.* The cultural component provides the general pattern that sexual behaviors are expected to take. Our general cultural script, for example, emphasizes heterosexuality, gives primacy to sexual intercourse, discourages masturbation, and so on.

▪ *Intrapersonal component.* The intrapersonal component deals with the internal and physiological states that lead to, accompany, or identify sexual arousal, such as a pounding heart, erection or vaginal lubrication, and so on.

▪ *Interpersonal component.* The interpersonal component deals with the shared conventions and signals that enable two people to engage in sexual behaviors, such as body language, words, and erotic touching.

Cultural Scripting

Many are saved from sin by being inept at it.

—*Mignon McLaughlin*

Our culture sets the general contours of our sexual scripts. It tells us which behaviors are acceptable ("moral" or "normal") and which are unacceptable ("immoral" or "abnormal"). Among middle-class White Americans, the norm is a sequence of sexual events consisting of kissing, genital caressing, and sexual intercourse. If large numbers of people did not share these conventions, there would be sexual chaos. Imagine a scenario in which two people from different cultures try to initiate a sexual encounter. The one from our culture follows our culture's sexual sequence, and the other from a different culture follows a sequence beginning with sexual intercourse, moving to genital caressing, and ending with passionate kissing. At least initially, such a couple might experience endless frustration and confusion as one tried to initiate the sexual encounter with kissing and the other with sexual intercourse.

Yet this kind of confusion occurs fairly often because there is not necessarily a direct correlation between what our culture calls erotic and what any particular individual calls erotic. Culture sets the general pattern, but there is too much diversity in terms of individual personality, socioeconomic status, and ethnicity for everybody to have exactly the same erotic script. Thus, sexual scripts can be highly ambiguous.

We may believe that everyone shares our own particular script, projecting our experiences onto others and assuming that they share our erotic definitions of objects, gestures, and situations. But often, they initially do not. Our partner may have come from a different socioeconomic group or religious background and may have had far different learning experiences. Each has to learn the other's sexual script and be able to complement and adjust to it. If our scripts are to be integrated, we must make our needs known through words, gestures, or movements. This is the reason many people view their first intercourse as somewhat of a comedy or tragedy—or perhaps a little bit of both.

Intrapersonal Scripting

On the intrapersonal level, sexual scripts enable people to give meaning to their physiological responses. The meaning depends largely on the situation. An erection, for example, does not always mean sexual excitement. Young boys sometimes have erections when they are frightened, anxious, or worried. In the morning, men may experience erections that are unaccompanied by arousal. Adolescent girls sometimes experience sexual arousal without knowing what their sensations mean. They report them as funny, weird kinds of feelings; or as anxiety, fear, or an upset stomach. The sensations are not linked to a sexual script until the girl becomes older and physiological states acquire a definite erotic meaning.

The intrapersonal, internal script also determines what physiological events our minds will become aware of. During masturbation or intercourse, for example, an enormous number of physiological events occur simultaneously, but we are aware of only a few of them. These are the events we associate with sexual arousal, such as increasing heartbeat and tensing muscles. Others, such as curling toes, may not filter through to our consciousness.

Finally, internal scripts provide a sequence of body movements by acting as mechanisms that activate biological events and release tension. We learn, for example, that we may create an orgasm by manipulating the penis or clitoris during masturbation.

Interpersonal Scripting

The interpersonal level is the area of shared conventions, which make sexual activities possible. Very little of our public life is sexual. Yet there are signs and gestures—verbal and nonverbal—that define encounters as sexual. We make our sexual motives clear by the way we look at each other, the tone of our voices, the movements of our bodies, and other culturally shared phenomena. A bedroom or a motel room, for example, is a potentially erotic location; a classroom, office, or factory is not. The movements we use in arousing ourselves or others are erotic activators. Within a culture, there are normative scripts leading to sexual intercourse.

In our society, passionate kissing is part of the cultural script for sexual interactions.

People with little sexual experience, especially young adolescents, are often unfamiliar with sexual scripts. What do they do after kissing? Do they embrace? Caress above the waist? Below? Eventually, they learn a comfortable sequence based on cultural inputs and personal and partner preferences. For gay men and lesbians, learning the sexual script is more difficult because it is socially stigmatized. The sexual script is also related to age. Older children and young adolescents often limit their scripts to kissing, holding hands, and embracing, and they feel completely satisfied. Kissing for them may be as exciting as intercourse for more experienced people. When the range of their scripts increases, the earlier stages lose some of their sexual intensity.

AUTOEROTICISM

Autoeroticism consists of sexual activities that involve only the self. Autoeroticism is an *intrapersonal* activity rather than an *interpersonal* one. It includes sexual fantasies, erotic dreams, and masturbation. A universal phenomenon in one form or another (Ford & Beach, 1951), autoeroticism is one of our earliest expressions of sexual stirrings. It is also one that traditionally has been condemned in our society. By condemning it, however, our culture sets the stage for the development of deeply negative and inhibitory attitudes toward sexuality.

Sexual Fantasies and Dreams

Men and women, but especially men, think about sex often. According to a national representative sample, 54% of American men and 19% of American women think about sex at least once a day. Forty-three percent of the men and 67% of the women think about sex a few times per week or per month (Laumann et al., 1994).

"A fantasy is a map of desire, mastery, escape, and obscuration," wrote Nancy Friday (1980), "the navigational path we invent to steer ourselves between the reefs and shoals of anxiety, guilt, and inhibition." Erotic fantasy is probably the most universal of all sexual behaviors. Nearly everyone has experienced such fantasies, but because they touch on feelings or desires considered personally or socially unacceptable, they are not widely discussed.

Occurring spontaneously or as a result of outside stimuli, fantasies are part of the body's regular healthy functioning. Research indicates that sexual fantasies are related to sexual drives: The higher the sexual drive, the higher the frequency of sexual fantasies and level of satisfaction in one's sexual life (Leitenberg & Henning, 1995). Fantasies help create an equilibrium between our environment and our inner selves, seeking a balance between the two (Wilson, 1978). They usually accompany our masturbatory experiences to enhance them, as well as oral-genital sex, sexual intercourse, and other interpersonal experiences. According to Dr. Ethel Person, professor of psychiatry at Columbia University, fantasies can also affect our lives by influencing the work we do, the people we love, the places we call home, and our ideas of who we are and who we are destined to become (Person, 1995).

Our erotic fantasies develop with our experiences, although there are distinct gender differences. Sexual fantasies usually develop between the ages of 11 and 13, with boys experiencing them earlier (Leitenberg & Henning, 1995) and feeling more positive about them than girls (Gold & Gold, 1991). Overall, men fantasize more often than do women (Hsu et al., 1994), and their fantasies tend to be more visual, impersonal, and active than women's, which are generally more passive and romantic (Barbach, 1995; Leitenberg & Henning, 1995).

The Function of Sexual Fantasies Sexual fantasies have a number of important functions. First, fantasies help direct and define our erotic goals. They take our generalized sexual drives and give them concrete images and specific content. We fantasize about certain types of men or women and reinforce our attraction through fantasy involvement. Unfortunately, our fantasy model may be unreasonable or unattainable, which is one of the pitfalls of fantasy; we can imagine perfection, but we can rarely find it in the real world.

Second, sexual fantasies allow us to plan or anticipate situations that may arise. Fantasies provide a form of rehearsal, allowing us to practice in our minds how to act in various situations. Our fantasies of what *might* take place on a date, after a party, or in bed with our partner give us a certain amount of preparation.

Third, erotic fantasies provide escape from a dull or oppressive environment. Routine or repetitive labor often gives rise to fantasies as a way of coping with boredom. Fourth, even if our sexual lives are satisfactory, we may indulge in sexual fantasies to bring novelty and excitement into the relationship. Many people fantasize about things they would not actually do in

The only way to get rid of temptation is to yield to it.

—*Oscar Wilde (1854–1900)*

real life. Fantasy offers a safe outlet for sexual curiosity. One researcher (Wilson, 1978) notes:

> We all have a need for adventure, but set limits on how far we permit curiosity to determine our actual behavior. This limit varies according to our personality and stage of development. Imagining an experience is less radical than doing it, so our criterion of what is socially and personally acceptable often falls between the two. The nice thing about fantasy is that it allows us to explore, yet at the same time retain our physical safety and avoid hurting other people

One study found that some women are capable of experiencing orgasm solely through fantasy (Whipple, Ogden, & Komisaruk, 1992).

Fifth, sexual fantasies have an expressive function in somewhat the same manner that dreams do. Our sexual fantasies may offer a clue to our current interests, pleasures, anxieties, fears, or problems. Because fantasies use only a few details from the stream of reality, what we select is significant, expressing feelings that often lie beneath the surface of our consciousness (Sue, 1979). Fantasies of extramarital relationships, for example, may signify deep dissatisfaction with a marriage, whereas fantasies centering around impotence may represent fears about sexuality or a particular relationship.

> When two people make love, there are at least four people present—the two who are actually there and the two they are thinking about.
>
> —*Sigmund Freud (1856–1939)*

Fantasies During Intercourse A sizable number of people fantasize during sex. The fantasies are usually a continuation of daydreams or masturbation fantasies, transforming one's partner into a Brad Pitt or Tyra Banks. Various studies report that 60–90% of the respondents fantasize during sex, depending on gender and ethnicity (Cado & Leitenberg, 1990; Knafo & Jaffe, 1984; Price & Miller, 1984). Women who fantasize about being forced into sexual activity or about being victimized do not necessarily want this to actually occur (Leitenberg & Henning, 1995). Rather, it has been found that these women tend to be more interested in a variety of sexual activities and to be more sexually experienced (Gold, Balzano, & Stamey, 1991).

Erotic Dreams Almost all of the men and two-thirds of the women in Kinsey's studies reported having had overtly sexual dreams (Kinsey et al., 1948, 1953). Sexual images in dreams are frequently very intense. Although people tend to feel responsible for fantasies, which occur when awake, they are usually less troubled by sexual dreams.

Overtly sexual dreams are not necessarily exciting, although dreams that are apparently nonsexual may cause arousal. It is not unusual for individuals to awaken in the middle of the night to find their bodies moving as if they were making love. They may also experience nocturnal orgasm. About 2–3% of a woman's orgasms may be nocturnal, whereas for men the number may be around 8% of their total orgasms (Kinsey et al., 1948, 1953). About 50% of the men interviewed by Kinsey had more than five nocturnal orgasms a year, but less than 10% of the women experienced them that frequently.

Dreams almost always accompany **nocturnal orgasm** (or **emission**). The dreamer may awaken, and men usually ejaculate. Although the dream content may not be overtly sexual, it is always accompanied by sensual sensations. Erotic dreams run the gamut of sexual possibilities: heterosexual, homosexual, or autoerotic; incestuous, dominance and submission, bestial, fetishistic. Women seem to feel less guilt or fear about nocturnal orgasms than men do, accepting them more easily as pleasurable experiences.

Masturbation

People **masturbate** by rubbing, caressing, or otherwise stimulating their genitals to give themselves sexual pleasure or to release sexual tension (Figures 9.1 and 9.2). They may masturbate during particular periods or throughout their entire lives. Kinsey and his colleagues (1953) reported that 92% of the men and 58% of the women they interviewed said they had masturbated. Today, there appears to be a slight increase in both incidence and frequency. Nevertheless, gender differences continue to be significant (Atwood & Gagnon, 1987; Leitenberg, Detzer, & Srebnik, 1993).

Attitudes toward masturbation and masturbatory behaviors vary along ethnic lines. Whites are quite accepting of masturbation, for example, whereas African Americans are less so. The differences can be explained culturally. Because Whites tend to begin coital activities later than Blacks, Whites regard masturbation as an acceptable alternative to sexual intercourse. Black culture, by contrast, accepts sexual activity at an earlier age. In this context, Blacks may view masturbation as a sign of personal and sexual inadequacy. As a result, many Blacks tend to view sexual intercourse as normal and masturbation as deviant (Cortese, 1989; Kinsey et al., 1948; Wilson, 1986). Masturbation is becoming more accepted within the African American community as a legitimate sexual activity (Figure 9.3).

Latinos, like African Americans, are more conservative than Anglos in their attitudes about masturbation (Cortese, 1989; Padilla & O'Grady, 1987). For many, masturbation is not considered an acceptable sexual option for either men or women (Guerrero Pavich, 1986). In part, this is because of the cultural emphasis on sexual intercourse and the influence of Catholicism,

> MASTURBATION, n. An extremely disgusting act performed on a regular basis by everyone *else*.
>
> —*Robert Tefton*

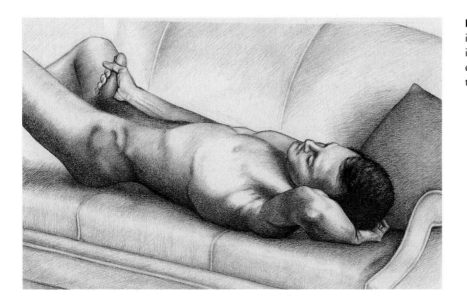

FIGURE 9.1 Masturbation is an important form of sexual behavior in which individuals explore their erotic capacities and bring pleasure to themselves.

FIGURE 9.2   Many people "discover" their sexual potential through masturbation. Sometimes women learn to be orgasmic through masturbation, then carry this knowledge over into their relationships.

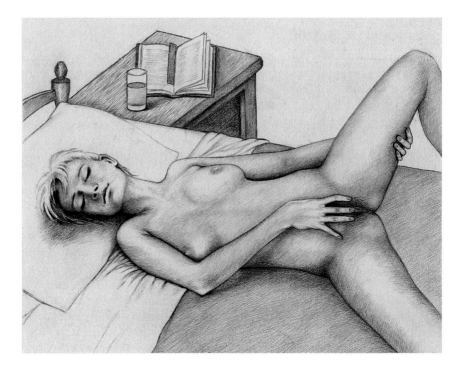

which regards masturbation as sinful. As with other forms of sexual behavior, however, acceptance becomes more likely as Latinos become more assimilated.

Masturbatory behavior is influenced by education, ethnicity, and religion; however, education is particularly dramatic in influencing rates of masturbation (Billy, Tanfer, Grady, & Klepinger, 1993; Laumann et al., 1994). Eighty percent of men who have graduate degrees report having masturbated in the past year, with the rate declining with less education to 45% of those who have not completed high school. A similar pattern was found to occur among women, with 60% of those who have attended graduate school having masturbated in the past year, declining to 25% among women who have not finished high school. The better educated also report masturbating more frequently.

Age is also significantly related to the frequency of masturbation (Laumann et al., 1994). Interestingly, young adults, often believed to have the highest levels of autoerotic activity, are less likely to have masturbated in the past year than those who are slightly older (24–35). The distribution rates seem to follow a U-shaped curve for both men and women, with the proportion not masturbating decreasing in the next two age groups and then stabilizing at about one-third of the men and one-half of the women until age 50. For people over 50, one-half of the men and 70% of the women report no masturbation. These figures may represent negative social attitudes, personal guilt, or unwillingness to admit to masturbating. Nevertheless, by the time married men and women reach their eighties, the most common overt genital activity is masturbation (Weizman & Hart, 1987).

Fewer women than men report orgasm usually or always, even with similar rates of masturbation. Researchers point out that their results suggest

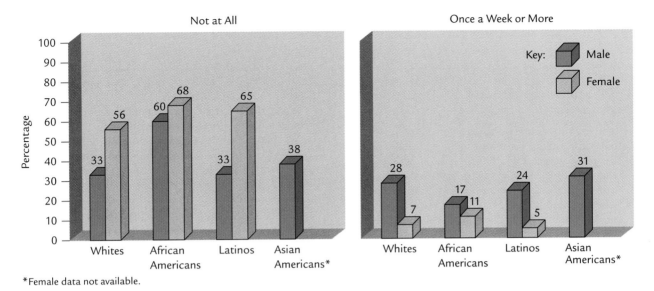

*Female data not available.

FIGURE 9.3 Frequency of Masturbation by Ethnicity in One Year. (*Source:* Adapted from Laumann et al., 1994, p. 82.)

that "young women in our society simply do not find masturbation as pleasurable or acceptable as do young men." They point out that women, more than men, have been socialized to associate sex with romance, relationships, and emotional intimacy. Their results, they note, suggest that "the recent effort to encourage women to take more responsibility for their own sexuality and the explicit suggestion to masturbate more has not altered this socialization process" (Leitenbeg, Detzer, & Srebnik, 1993).

Masturbation is an important means of learning about our bodies (Atwood & Gagnon, 1987). Through masturbation, children and adolescents learn what is sexually pleasing, how to move their bodies, and what their natural rhythms are. The activity has no harmful physical effects. Although masturbation often decreases significantly when individuals make love regularly, it is not necessarily a temporary substitute for sexual intercourse but a legitimate form of sexual activity in its own right. Sex therapists may encourage clients to masturbate as a means of overcoming specific sexual problems and discovering their personal sexual potential. Masturbation, whether practiced alone or mutually with a partner, is also a form of safer sex, because ordinarily there is no exchange of semen, vaginal secretions, or blood, which could transmit HIV or other organisms that cause STDs (see Chapters 15 and 16). Regarding masturbation, former U.S. Surgeon General M. Joycelyn Elders, M.D., states (Elders & Kilgore, 1997):

> Masturbation, practiced consciously or unconsciously, cultivates in us a humble elegance—an awareness that we are part of a larger natural system, the passions and rhythms of which live on in us. Sexuality is part of creation, part of our common inheritance, and it reminds us that we are neither inherently better nor worse than our sisters and brothers. Far from evil, masturbation just may render heavenly contentment in those who dare.

We are capable of experiencing genital pleasure from birth through old age. Male infants have been observed with erect penises a few hours after birth. A baby boy may laugh in his crib while playing with his erect penis (although he does not ejaculate). Baby girls sometimes move their bodies

> Masturbation is an intrinsically and seriously disordered act.
>
> —*Vatican Declaration on Sexual Ethics*

> Masturbation is the primary sexual activity of mankind. In the nineteenth century it was a disease: in the twentieth, it's a cure.
>
> —*Thomas Szasz*

MASTURBATION HAS A long history of being associated with sin or psychopathology. Our traditional aversion to it can be traced to antiquity. The Judeo-Christian grounding for the prohibition against masturbation is found in the story of Onan (Genesis 38:7–19):

> And Er, Judah's first born, was wicked in the sight of the Lord; and the Lord slew him. And Judah said unto Onan, Go in unto thy brother's wife, and marry her, and raise up the seed to thy brother. And Onan knew that the seed should not be his; and it came to pass, when he went in unto his brother's wife, that he spilled it on the ground, lest that he should give seed to his brother. And the thing which he did displeased the Lord; whereupon he slew him also.

Although God struck Onan down, it is not clear why he was slain: Was it because of withdrawal (coitus interruptus) or because he had disobeyed God's command? (The general consensus among biblical scholars is that he was slain for the sin of disobedience [Bullough, 1976].) But despite the message's reference to withdrawal, the "sin of Onan" has traditionally been interpreted as masturbation. "Onanism," in fact, has been used interchangeably with "masturbation." And because Onan was slain, masturbation has been viewed as a particularly heinous sexual offense in the eyes of God. In the Talmudic tradition, masturbation was made a capital offense. Christianity identified it as a form of sodomy, so-called unnatural sexual acts, which, at different times, was punishable by burning.

In the Judeo-Christian tradition, masturbation was treated as a sin with a high price: damnation. The nineteenth century, however, exacted a new tribute from the sinner: physical debilitation, insanity, or death. Under the leadership of physicians, the consequences of masturbation shifted from moral to physical. They believed that semen contained precious nutrients that were absorbed by the body to sustain life and growth. The Swiss physician Tissot had first warned of the physical dangers of masturbation in 1758, asserting that weakness was caused by the loss of semen and the draining of "nervous energy" from the brain. By the middle of the nineteenth century, physicians warned of a masturbatory plague that was enveloping the civilized world (Gay, 1986).

For nineteenth-century Americans, masturbation was *the* sexual evil against which individuals had to struggle. Children were especially susceptible to the practice. Victorians believed that children were not *naturally* sexual but learned to be sexual through exposure to vice and bad examples. By refusing to recognize spontaneous childhood sexuality, Victorians were able to sustain the myth of childhood innocence.

---

rhythmically, almost violently, appearing to experience orgasm. And men as old as 102 have reported masturbating. In fact, for older adults, because of the loss of partners, masturbation regains much of the primacy it lost after adolescence as a means of sexual pleasure.

Childhood   Children often accidentally discover that playing with their genitals is pleasurable and continue this activity until reprimanded by an adult (see Chapter 6). By the time they are 4 or 5, children have usually been taught that adults consider this form of behavior "nasty." Parents generally react negatively to masturbation, regardless of the age and gender of the child. Later, this negative attitude becomes generalized to include the sexual pleasure that accompanies the behavior. Children thus learn to conceal their masturbatory play.

Adolescence   When boys and girls reach adolescence, they no longer regard masturbation as ambiguous play; they know that it is sexual. As discussed in Chapter 6, this is a period of intense change emotionally and biologically. Complex emotions are often involved in adolescent masturbation. Teenagers may feel guilt and shame for engaging in a practice that their parents and other adults indicate is wrong or bad, and they may be fearful of discovery. A girl who feels vaginal lubrication or finds stains on her underpants for the

Because children learned about masturbation by associating with "vile" playmates or being exposed to suggestive books, songs, or pictures, it became the parents' duty to closely supervise their children's friends and activities. These fears virtually compelled parents to interfere with their children's developing sexuality (Foucault, 1980). Because masturbation was a "secret vice," parents were to be suspicious of everything. Responsible parents, despite their reticence about sex, warned their children against the dangers of "self-abuse." There were patented devices to be attached to the child's penis so that if he touched it, an alarm sounded in his parents' bedroom, alerting them to the danger. Parents and masturbators alike purchased penile rings embedded with sharp prongs, which promised freedom from self-abuse.

Dr. Homer Bostwick (1860) received patients who were suffering from the "damnable effects of masturbation," recording a case history that describes the treatment:

> I advised him to have 25 leeches applied to the perinaeum [base of the penis] immediately, and sit over a bucket of hot water as soon as they should drop off, so that the steam and warm bathing would keep up further bleeding. I ordered the leeches to be followed by a blister, and hot poultices, hot mustard, hip baths, etc., etc. I had his bowels opened with a dose of castor oil, and confined him to a light gruel, vegetable, and fruit diet, advising him to scrupulously avoid everything stimulating, to drink nothing but cold water and mucilaginous fluids.

The treatments continued for five weeks, until the man was pronounced "cured" and returned home. ("He was, of course, somewhat weakened and debilitated," Bostwick concluded.)

The almost hysterical fear of masturbation helped sustain the severe sexual restrictions that characterized the nineteenth century. Masturbatory hysteria instilled sexual fears and anxieties in the children of the nineteenth century. As these children grew into adults, they were vulnerable to believing the myths of sexual danger that would regulate their adult lives.

Fears about masturbation continued in diminished form throughout the first half of the twentieth century. Masturbation was no longer associated with death and insanity, however, but with arrested psychological development in children and neuroses in adults. Today, it continues to be viewed as immoral and a sign of emotional immaturity by many conservative religious denominations, especially by the Roman Catholic Church, which declared masturbation "an intrinsically and seriously disturbed act" (Patton, 1986). Until the late 1970s, *The Boy Scout Handbook* warned against the moral and psychological dangers of masturbation (Rowan, 1989).

first time may be frightened, as may a boy who sees the semen of first ejaculation. Although open discussion could alleviate fears, frank talk is not always possible in a setting that involves shame.

According to one survey of those adolescents who do masturbate, boys do so approximately 3 times more often than girls (Leitenberg, Detzer, & Srebnik, 1993). By the end of adolescence, virtually all males and about three-quarters of females have masturbated to orgasm. These gender differences may be the result of social conditioning and communication. Most boys discuss masturbatory experiences openly, relating different methods and recalling "near misses" when they were almost caught by their parents. Among boys, masturbation is a subject for camaraderie. In contrast, girls usually learn to masturbate through self-discovery. Because "nice girls" are not supposed to be sexual, they seldom talk about their own sexuality but hide it, repress it, or try to forget it. Although White males are most likely to have their first ejaculation during masturbation, African American males more often experience their first ejaculation during sexual intercourse (Staples & Johnson, 1993). Comparable information is not available for female Black adolescents and young adults.

Adulthood Masturbation continues after adolescence, although the frequency often declines among men and increases among women.

WOMEN AND MASTURBATION   One way in which women become familiar with their own sexual responsiveness is through masturbation. Women who masturbate appear to hold more positive sexual attitudes and are more likely to be orgasmic than women who don't masturbate (Kelly, Strassberg, & Kircher, 1990). Among women who experience multiple orgasms, 26% experience them through masturbation (Darling, Davidson, & Jennings, 1991). Although the majority of women feel that orgasms experienced through masturbation differ from those experienced in sexual intercourse, they feel the same levels of sexual satisfaction (Davidson & Darling, 1986).

Though no two women masturbate in exactly the same manner, a number of common methods are used to achieve orgasm. Most involve some type of manual clitoral stimulation, by using the fingers, rubbing against an object, or using a vibrator.

Since the glans clitoridis is often too sensitive for prolonged direct stimulation, women tend to stroke gently on the shaft of the clitoris. Another common method, which exerts less direct pressure on the clitoris, is to stroke the mons areas or the minor lips. Individual preferences play a key role in what method is chosen, how rigorous the stimulation is, how often masturbation occurs, and whether it is accompanied by erotic aids, such as a vibrator, sensual oils, or other types of stimuli. A number of women, for instance, may find that running a stream of warm water over the vulva or sitting near the jet stream in a hot tub is sexually arousing. Stimulation of the breasts and nipples is also very common, as is stroking the anal region. Some women enjoy inserting a finger or other object into their vagina. Using common sense in relation to cleanliness, such as not inserting an object or finger from the anus into the vagina and keeping vibrators and other objects used for insertion clean, helps to prevent infection.

MEN AND MASTURBATION   Like women, men have individual preferences and patterns of masturbating. Nearly all methods involve some type of direct stimulation of the penis with the hand. Typically, the penis is grasped and stroked at the shaft, with up-and-down or circular movements of the hand, so that the edge of the corona around the glans and the frenulum on the underside are stimulated. The amount of pressure, how rapid the strokes are, the number of fingers used, and how far up and down the hands move vary from one man to another. Whether the breasts, testicles, anus, or other parts of the body are stimulated is also individual, but it appears to be the up-and-down movement or rubbing of the penis that triggers orgasm. Just before orgasm, the stroking tends to increase, and then to slow or stop during ejaculation.

To add variety or stimulation, some men may elect to use erotic materials, artificial vaginas, inflatable dolls, or rubber pouches in which to insert their penis. Regardless of the aid or technique, it is important to pay attention to cleanliness to prevent bacterial infections.

MASTURBATION AND MARRIAGE   Most people continue to masturbate after they marry, although the rate is significantly lower. Hunt reported that among married men in their late twenties or early thirties, about 72% masturbated, with a median frequency of 24 times a year (Hunt, 1974). Sixty-eight percent of the married women of this age group masturbated according to the median frequency. A *Redbook* survey of 100,000 women indicated that almost 75% masturbated during marriage—20% occasionally and 20% often (Tavris & Sadd, 1977). The frequency was significantly higher among women who rated their marriages as unsatisfactory, suggesting that they masturbated because their personal and sexual relationships were unfulfilling.

There are many reasons for continuing the activity during marriage: Masturbation is a pleasurable form of sexual excitement, a spouse is away or unwilling, sexual intercourse is not satisfying, the partner(s) fear(s) sexual inadequacy, the individual acts out fantasies, or he or she seeks to release tension. During times of marital conflict, masturbation may act as a distancing device, with the masturbating spouse choosing masturbation over sexual intercourse as a means of emotional protection (Betchen, 1991).

INTERPERSONAL SEXUALITY

We often think that sex is sexual intercourse and that sexual interactions end with orgasm (usually the male's). But sex is not limited to sexual intercourse. Heterosexuals engage in a wide variety of sexual activities, which may include erotic touching, kissing, and oral and anal sex. Except for sexual intercourse, gay and lesbian couples engage in basically the same sexual activities as do heterosexuals.

Touching

Where does sex begin for you? Whether it begins with the heart or the genitals, touch is the fire that melds the two into one. Touching is both a sign of caring and a signal for arousal.

Touching does not need to be directed toward genitals or erogenous zones. The entire body is responsive to a touch or a caress. Although women appear to be especially responsive to touch, traditional male sex roles give little significance to touching. Some men regard touching as simply a prelude to intercourse. When this occurs, touch is transformed into a demand for intercourse rather than an expression of intimacy or erotic play. The man's partner may become inhibited from touching or showing affection for fear her gestures will be misinterpreted as a sexual invitation.

Masters and Johnson suggest a form of touching they call "pleasuring." **Pleasuring** is nongenital touching and caressing. Neither partner tries to sexually stimulate the other; they simply explore, discovering how their bodies respond to touching. The man guides the woman's hand over his body, telling her what feels good; she then takes his hand and moves it over her body, telling him what she likes.

Such sharing gives each a sense of his or her own responses; it also allows each to discover what the other likes and dislikes. We can't assume we know what a particular person likes, for there is too much variation between people. Pleasuring opens the door to communication; couples discover that the entire body, not just the genitals, is erogenous.

Nude or clothed massages, back rubs, foot rubs, scalp massages—all are soothing and loving forms of touch. The sensuousness of touching may be enhanced by the use of lubricating oils. Such erotic touching is a form of safer sex.

Pleasuring is the giving and receiving of erotic pleasure for its own sake.

Other forms of touching are more directly sexual, such as caressing, fondling, or rubbing our own or our partner's genitals or breasts. Sucking or licking earlobes, the neck, toes, or the insides of thighs, palms, or arms can be highly stimulating. Oral stimulation of a woman's or man's breasts or nipples is often exciting. Moving one's genitals or breasts over a partner's face, chest, breasts, or genitals is very erotic for some people.

Stimulating your partner's clitoris or penis with your hand or fingers can increase excitement or lead to orgasm. Inserting a finger or fingers into your partner's wet vagina and rhythmically moving it at the pace your partner likes may be pleasing. Some women like to have their clitoris licked or stimulated with one hand while their vagina is being penetrated with the other. Men like having their penises lubricated so that their partner's hand glides smoothly over the shaft and glans penis. (Be sure to use a water-based lubricant if you plan to use a condom later, because oil-based lubricants may cause the condom to deteriorate.) Masturbating while your partner is holding you can be highly erotic for both people. Mutual masturbation can also be intensely sexual. Some people use sex toys, such as dildos, vibrators, or ben-wah balls to enhance sexual touching. (These are discussed in Chapter 14.)

As we enter old age, touching becomes increasingly significant as a primary form of erotic expression. Touching in all its myriad forms, ranging from holding hands to caressing, massaging to hugging, walking with arms around each other to fondling, becomes the touchstone of eroticism for the elderly.

Kissing

Kissing is usually our earliest interpersonal sexual experience, and its primal intensity may be traced back to our suckling as infants. The kiss is magic: Fairy tales keep alive the ancient belief that a kiss can undo spells and bring a prince or princess back to life. Parental kisses show love and often remedy the small hurts and injuries of childhood.

Kissing is probably the most acceptable of all premarital sexual activities (Jurich & Polson, 1985). The tender lover's kiss symbolizes love, and the erotic lover's kiss, of course, simultaneously represents and *is* passion. Both men and women regard kissing as a romantic act, a symbol of affection as well as desire (Tucker, 1992; Tucker, Marvin, & Vivian, 1991).

The lips and mouth are highly sensitive to touch and are exquisitely erotic parts of our bodies. Kisses discover, explore, and excite the body. They also involve the senses of taste and smell, which are especially important because they activate unconscious memories and associations. Often we are aroused by familiar smells associated with particular sexual memories: a person's body scent, a perfume associated with an erotic experience. In some languages—among the Borneans, for example— the word "kiss" literally translates as smell. In fact, among the Eskimos and Maoris, there is no mouth kissing, only the touching of noses to facilitate smelling.

Although kissing may appear innocent, it is in many ways the height of intimacy. The adolescent's first kiss is often regarded as a milestone, a rite of passage, the beginning of adult sexuality (Alapack, 1991). It is an important developmental step, marking the beginning of a young person's sexuality. Blumstein and Schwartz (1983) report that many of their respondents cannot imagine engaging in sexual intercourse without kissing. In fact, they found that those who have a minimal (or nonexistent) amount of kissing feel distant from their partners but may have intercourse anyway as a physical release. (Interestingly, both female and male prostitutes are more willing to engage in oral sex, sexual intercourse, or other sexual activities than to kiss their clients, specifically *because* kissing symbolizes intimacy.)

The amount of kissing differs according to sexual orientation. Lesbian couples tend to engage in kissing more than heterosexual couples, whereas gay male couples kiss less than heterosexual couples (Blumstein & Schwartz, 1983).

Ordinary kissing is considered safer sex. French kissing is probably safe, unless the kiss is hard and draws blood or either partner has sores or cuts in or around the mouth. (See Chapter 16 for further discussion of kissing and HIV.)

Oral-Genital Sex

In recent years, oral sex has become a part of our sexual scripts. The two types of oral-genital sex are cunnilingus and fellatio, which may be performed singly or simultaneously. **Cunnilingus** is the erotic stimulation of a woman's vulva by her partner's mouth and tongue. The word is derived

> The kiss originated when the first male reptile licked the first female reptile, implying in a subtle, complimentary way that she was as succulent as the small reptile he had for dinner the night before.
>
> —*F. Scott Fitzgerald (1896–1940)*

> I wasn't kissing her, I was whispering in her mouth.
>
> —*Chico Marx*

> I'd love to kiss you, but I just washed my hair.
>
> —*Bette Davis*

Chimps Do It, Humans Do It: Cross-Species Sexual Behavior

IMMORAL! PROMISCUOUS! Sex addicts! Those are some of the terms moralistic observers might apply to the bonobo chimpanzees if they discovered a troop of them in the wild. Bonobos are constantly engaging in sex. It appears to be one of their favorite pastimes. Members of a troop seem to engage in sex with every other member of their group, including the young. Some females exchange sex for food offerings by males. "Prostitution! Call the police," the moralists would exclaim. But those who study primates would point to the various uses of sex among bonobos. These chimpanzees use sex for pleasure, to relieve tension, to control aggression, to gain access to food, to assert dominance—and, of course, to reproduce (de Waal, 1995; Pavelka, 1995).

All animals engage in sexual behavior. Humans share many behaviors in common with nonhuman animals. Our sexuality, however, is distinct from that of other mammals in many ways. For example, rules imposed by society govern our sexual behavior. And much, if not all, of our sexual behavior is learned. Because different societies and groups have different attitudes, values, and ideas concerning sexuality, there is immense variation in human sexuality across cultures. Sexual behavior among animals, however, is biologically controlled and similar within a given species.

To understand sexual behavior across species, we must understand the role of the brain's cortex. The larger the cortex, the outer layer of the brain, the higher the species. In lower animals (those with a small brain cortex), sexual behavior is controlled by lower brain centers and hormonal changes that activate spinal reflexes. Higher species with a larger brain cortex have more control over their sexual responses. Having a large cortex, humans have few, if any, built-in sexual restraints or directions. Because we don't have innate biological wiring that directs our sexual activity, our sexuality depends on learning. Although reproduction seems to be the primary aim for most animals, sex serves purposes other than reproduction for human beings, including giving and receiving pleasure. For humans, sex may be used to cement the pair-bond between heterosexual and same-sex couples.

Masturbation

Human beings masturbate. So do other mammals, especially primates such as monkeys, chimpanzees, and apes. Some of us have been startled at the zoo by a male gibbon ape greeting us by masturbating with his hands or feet, or a female gibbon inserting objects into her vagina (Mootnick & Baker, 1994). In zoos, masturbation among gibbons typically accompanies the excitement related to food, interrupted copulation, or the presence of humans. Raised as captive animals, they use masturbation as a way to greet and identify with humans. It was once believed that apes engaged in this "unnatural" activity because they were captive, but researchers have discovered that apes also engage in masturbation in the wild.

Other animals find ingenious ways of masturbating. Male red deer rub their antlers against shrubs; this sensuous exercise produces an erection and ejaculation. Female porcupines may take a stick in their front paws and walk around straddling it. The vibration against the genitals appears to give them great pleasure. And many of us have been embarrassed by a dog mounting our leg, using our body as a masturbatory device.

Some female macaque monkeys have also been observed to have orgasm during masturbation. They display the same physiological characteristics as human females, such as increased heart rate and uterine contraction (Wallen, 1995).

Copulation and Oral-Genital Contact

Unlike humans and other primates, most animals engage in sexual behavior only periodically, when the female is in heat and capable of reproduction. For lower mam-

> As for the topsy turvy tangle known as *soixante-neuf,* personally I have always felt it to be madly confusing, like trying to pat your head and rub your stomach at the same time.
>
> —*Helen Lawrenson*

from the Latin *cunnus,* vulva, and *lingere,* to lick. **Fellatio** is the oral stimulation of a man's penis by his partner's sucking and licking. It is from the Latin *fellare,* to suck. When two people orally stimulate each other simultaneously, their activity is sometimes called "sixty-nine." The term comes from the configuration "69," which visually suggests the activity.

For people of every orientation (especially among high school and college students), oral sex is an increasingly important and healthy aspect of their sexual selves (Wilson & Medora, 1990). Psychologist Lilian Rubin reports that young women today express pleasure about oral sex, in contrast to 20 years ago; a minority of middle-aged women, who earlier believed oral

mals, male-female sex is strictly for reproduction, so female sexual interest and responsiveness are directly tied to when she is most fertile. To indicate to males that she is in heat, a female may emit chemical substances known as pheromones or display genital swelling, both of which attract males to her for the purpose of mating.

Among primates, sexual behavior is less controlled by the female estrus (heat) cycle. Among bonobos, as we have noted, males and females may copulate when the female is not in heat (de Waal, 1995).

Animals also engage in oral-genital stimulation, especially when the female is in estrus. The male licks the female's genitals in response to the pheromones she gives off while in heat. Although females will also orally stimulate the male's genitals, it occurs less frequently.

Sex among animals may also be used for nonsexual purposes, such as when a male baboon signals defeat by "presenting," raising his rump in the female sexual posture. Dominant male monkeys use mounting, the male sexual posture, to demonstrate subordination of other males. Some squirrels use phallic aggression against competing males by forcefully displaying their erect penis (Wickler, 1973).

Same-Sex Sexual Behavior

Although most research on animal sexual behavior has focused on male-female pairs, many species besides our own display same-sex sexual behavior. Homosexuality is not unique to humans; it may be a part of our mammalian heritage. In many species, males mount other males in sexual displays. In species that form lasting pairs, such as ducks, some males appear to form long-term bonds with other males (Lorenz, 1966). In their classic study of animal and human behavior, Clelland Ford and Frank Beach (1951) suggest that mammals are basically bisexual.

Human Differences

Despite similarities, however, humans and animals differ significantly in their sexual behavior. Human sexuality has a number of important features, including the following:

- Psychological and emotional elements as well as physiological ones.
- The ability and willingness of females to engage in sexual behavior at any time during their hormonal cycle.
- The ability to exercise conscious control rather than being subject to biological control.
- The learning of sexual beliefs, attitudes, and behaviors.
- A lower significance for the role of reproduction.
- A higher significance for the role of erotic pleasure.
- Nonsexual purposes, such as cementing relationships and communicating.
- Greater variability due to cultural differences.

sex was "dirty" or immoral, continue to feel some ambivalence (Rubin, 1990). Of the men and women in various studies, 70–90% report that they have engaged in oral sex (Billy, Tanfer, Grady, & Klepinger, 1993; Janus & Janus, 1993; Laumann et al., 1994). Blumstein and Schwartz (1983) found that 50% of gay couples, 39% of lesbian couples, and 30% of heterosexual couples usually or always had oral sex as part of their lovemaking routine.

Although oral-genital sex is increasingly accepted by White middle-class Americans, it remains less permissible among some ethnic groups. As shown in Figure 9.4, African Americans, for example, have lower rates of oral-genital sex than Whites because many Blacks consider it immoral (Laumann

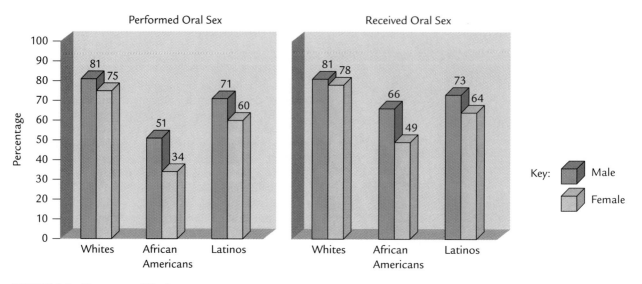

FIGURE 9.4 Frequency of Oral-Genital Sex by Ethnicity in One Year. (*Source:* Adapted from Laumann et al., 1994, p. 141.)

et al., 1994; Wilson, 1986). A large-scale national study found that 81% of White men had performed oral sex, compared with 51% of African American men and 71% of Latino men. Eighty-one percent of White men had received oral sex, compared with 66% of African American men, and 73% of Latinos. Oral sex is increasingly accepted, however, among Black women (Wyatt, Peters, & Gutherie, 1988). This is especially true if they have a good relationship and communicate well with their partners (Wyatt & Lyons-Rowe, 1990). Among married Latinos, oral sex is relatively uncommon. When oral sex occurs, it is usually at the male's instigation, as women are not expected to be interested in erotic variety (Guerrero Pavich, 1986). Although little is known about older Asian Americans and Asian immigrants, college-age Asian Americans appear to accept oral-genital sex to the same degree as middle-class Whites (Cochran, Mays, & Leung, 1991).

A study of university students of both sexes found that a person's attitudes toward his or her genitals may be an important facet of sexual interaction (Reinholtz & Muehlenhard, 1995). Someone who believes his or her genitals are attractive and sexy may be more comfortable during sexual interaction than someone who feels self-conscious about them. Furthermore, this same study found that the vast majority of participants who had engaged in oral sex had both performed and received it. For college students, oral sex is more acceptable after the early stages of a relationship; students are more likely to approve of it for people in general than for their close friends, brothers, or sisters (Sprecher et al., 1989).

Cunnilingus   In cunnilingus, a woman's genitals are stimulated by her partner's tongue and mouth, which gently and rhythmically caress and lick her clitoris and the surrounding area (Figure 9.5). During arousal, the mouth and lips can nibble, lick, and kiss the inner thighs, the stomach, the mons pubis, and then move to the sensitive labia minora. Orgasm may be brought on by rhythmically stimulating the clitoris. During cunnilingus, some women also enjoy insertion of a finger into the vagina or anus for extra stimulation.

FIGURE 9.5 Cunnilingus

Many women find cunnilingus one of the most arousing sexual activities. According to a major study, 33% of the women found cunnilingus very appealing, 35% found it somewhat appealing, and 32% did not find it appealing. Seventy-seven percent of the men, however, reported enjoying performing cunnilingus (Laumann et al., 1994).

Among lesbians, cunnilingus is a common activity for experiencing orgasm. In contrast to heterosexual couples, lesbian couples may be more inventive, less restrained, and more involved (Califia, 1979). This may be partly because, as women, each partner can identify with what the other may enjoy. But as many as 25% of the lesbians in Blumstein and Schwartz's study (1983) engaged in cunnilingus rarely or never. Instead, they relied on holding, kissing, manual stimulation, and pressing themselves erotically against each other. Nevertheless, the more often lesbians in the study had oral sex, the more likely they were to be satisfied with their sex lives and partners.

Some women, however, have concerns regarding cunnilingus. The most common worries revolve around whether the other person is enjoying it and, especially, whether the vulva has an unpleasant odor (Hite, 1976; Reinholtz & Muehlenhard, 1995). Concerns about vaginal odors may be eased by washing. Undeodorized white soap will wash away unpleasant smells without disturbing the vagina's natural erotic scent. If an unpleasant odor arises from the genitals, it may be because the woman has a vaginal infection.

A woman may also worry that her partner is not enjoying the experience because the partner is giving pleasure rather than receiving it. What she may not recognize is that such sexual excitement is often mutual. Because our mouths and tongues are erotically sensitive, the giver finds erotic excitement in arousing his or her partner.

Because of concerns about the spread of HIV through oral sex, experts have recommended the use of rubber dams over the vulva during cunnilingus. These devices may be the kind used in dental work, or they may be

FIGURE 9.6   Fellatio

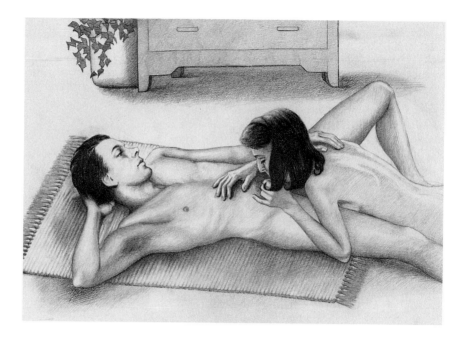

made by cutting a square sheet from a nonlubricated latex condom or rubber surgical glove. Though the risk of contracting HIV during oral-genital sex has not yet been established, experts suggest that any barrier that prevents the mixing of body fluids reduces the risks. These types of barriers, however, will not prevent all sexually transmitted diseases, such as transmission of organisms that cause urethral or vaginal infections from the mouth or transmission of throat infections from the genitals.

Fellatio   In fellatio, a man's penis is taken into his partner's mouth. The partner licks the glans penis and gently stimulates the shaft (Figure 9.6). If the penis is not erect, it usually will become erect within a few minutes. The partner sucks more vigorously as excitement increases, down toward the base of the penis and then back up, in a rhythmical motion, being careful not to bite hard or scrape the penis with the teeth. While the man is being stimulated by mouth, his partner can also stroke the shaft of the penis by hand. Gently playing with the testicles is also arousing as long as they are not held too tightly. As in cunnilingus, the couple should experiment to discover what is most stimulating and exciting. The man should be careful not to thrust his penis too deeply into his partner's throat, for that may cause a gagging reflex. He should let his partner control how deeply the penis goes into the mouth. The gag reflex can also be reconditioned by slowly inserting the penis into the mouth at increasing depth over a number of times. Some women feel that fellatio is more intimate than sexual intercourse, whereas others feel that it is less intimate. It is the most common form of sexual activity performed on men by prostitutes (Freund, Lee, & Leonard, 1991).

A national representative sample indicated that 83% of the men found fellatio appealing. Only 17% found it unappealing. By contrast, only 57% of the women reported that performing fellatio was appealing (Laumann et al.,

1994). Although men are generally enthusiastic about fellatio, women have mixed feelings about it (Blumstein & Schwartz, 1983). Some find it highly arousing; others feel it is a form of submissiveness, especially if they sense that their partner demands it. If the woman's partner is too demanding or directing, she may feel he is being controlling or selfish. If she accedes to his wishes, she may feel psychologically coerced. This sense of coercion may block the pleasure she might otherwise have enjoyed by engaging in fellatio.

For gay men, fellatio is an important component of their sexuality. As with sexual intercourse for heterosexual men, however, fellatio is only one activity in their sexual repertoire. Generally speaking, the more often gay couples engage in giving and receiving oral sex, the more satisfied they are (Blumstein & Schwartz, 1983). Because oral sex often involves power symbolism, reciprocity is important. If one partner always performs oral sex, he may feel he is subordinate to the other. The most satisfied gay couples alternate between giving and receiving oral sex.

A common concern about fellatio centers around ejaculation. Should a man ejaculate into his partner's mouth? Some people find the taste of semen slightly bitter, but others like it. Some find it exciting to suck even harder on the penis during or following ejaculation; others do not like the idea of semen in the mouth. For many, a key issue is whether to swallow the semen. Some swallow it, others spit it out; many rinse their mouth afterward. It is simply a matter of personal preference, and the man who is receiving fellatio should accept his partner's feelings about it and avoid equating a dislike for swallowing semen with a personal rejection.

Some partners worry, as they should, about the transmission of HIV through fellatio (see Chapter 16). It is possible to contract HIV orally if there are sores or openings within the mouth. Excessive toothbrushing, flossing, biting on the side of the mouth, and/or abrasions (from orthodontia or dental work) can cause small cuts in the mouth that allow the HIV virus, if present, to enter the bloodstream. A condom worn during fellatio will ensure safer sex.

Sexual Intercourse

Throughout the world, there are more than 100 million acts of sexual intercourse daily. As a result, there are 910,000 conceptions and 350,000 transmissions of STDs each day (World Health Organization, 1992). But pregnancy and disease are only the most overt consequences. Sexual intercourse has intense personal meaning (Cate, Long, Angera, & Draper, 1993; Schwartz, 1993). It is a source of pleasure, communication, and love. If forced, however, it becomes an instrument of aggression and pain. Its meaning changes depending on the context in which we engage in it (Sprecher & McKinney, 1993). How we feel about sex may depend as much (or more) on the feelings and motives we bring to it as on the techniques we use or the orgasms we experience.

Significance Although sexual intercourse is important for most sexually involved couples, the significance of it differs between men and women (Blumstein & Schwartz, 1983; Sprecher & McKinney, 1993). For men, sexual intercourse is only one of several sexual activities that they enjoy. For many

> The sexual act is in time what the tiger is in space.
>
> —*Georges Bataille*

FIGURE 9.7   Face-to-Face, Man Above

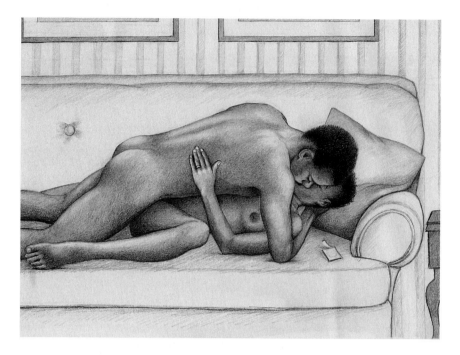

heterosexual women, however, intercourse is central to their sexual satisfaction. More than any other heterosexual sexual activity, sexual intercourse involves equal participation by both partners. Both partners equally and simultaneously give and receive. As a result, women feel a greater shared intimacy than they do in other sexual activities.

Positions   There are two basic positions in sexual intercourse—face-to-face and rear-entry—although the playfulness of the couple, their movement from one bodily configuration to another, and their ingenuity can provide an infinite variety. The same positions played out in different settings can cause an intensity that transforms the ordinary into the extraordinary.

The most common position is face-to-face with the man above (Figure 9.7). Many people prefer this position, for several reasons. First, it is the traditional, correct, or "official" position in our culture, which many people find reassuring and validating of their sexuality. (The man-above position is commonly known as the missionary position because it was the position missionaries encouraged people to use.) Second, it can allow the man maximum activity, movement, and control of coitus, validating the traditional gender roles, in which the man controls and the woman responds. Third, it allows the woman freedom to stimulate her clitoris to assist in her orgasm. The primary disadvantages are that it limits the woman's movement and that she may feel too much weight on her if her partner does not raise himself with his arms or elbows.

Another common position is face-to-face with the woman above (Figure 9.8). The woman either lies above her partner or sits astride him. This position allows the woman maximum activity, movement, and control. She can control the depth to which the penis penetrates. Additionally, when the woman sits astride her partner, either of them can caress or stimulate her vulva and clitoris. A disadvantage is that some men or women may feel

FIGURE 9.8   Face-to-Face, Woman Above

uneasy about the woman assuming a position that signifies an active role in coitus.

Intercourse can also be performed with the man positioned behind the woman. There are several variations on the rear-entry position. The woman may kneel supported on her arms and receive the penis in her vagina from behind. The couple may lie on their sides, with the woman's back to her partner (Figure 9.9). This position offers variety and may be particularly suitable during pregnancy. This position facilitates clitoral stimulation by the woman. Generally, it is also possible for the man to stimulate her during intercourse. Some people object to the rear-entry position as being "animal-like." Or they may feel it inhibits intimacy or resembles anal intercourse.

In the face-to-face side position, both partners lie on their sides facing each other (Figure 9.10). Each partner has greater freedom to caress and stimulate the other. The major drawback is that some may find it difficult to keep the penis inside the vagina.

The agents that cause sexually transmitted diseases, including HIV, can be passed on through heterosexual intercourse. Unless you are in a mutually monogamous relationship and have both tested HIV-negative, it is important to use a condom every time you have sex.

Anal Eroticism

Anal eroticism refers to sexual activities involving the anus, whose delicate membranes (as well as tabooed nature) make it erotically sensitive for many people. These activities include **analingus,** the licking of the anal region (colloquially known as "rimming" or "tossing salad"). Anal-manual contact consists of stimulating the anal region with the fingers; sometimes an entire fist may be inserted (known as "fisting" among gay White males and "finger-

FIGURE 9.9   Rear-Entry

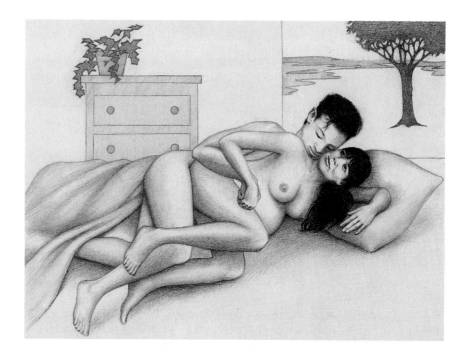

FIGURE 9.10   Face-to-Face on Side

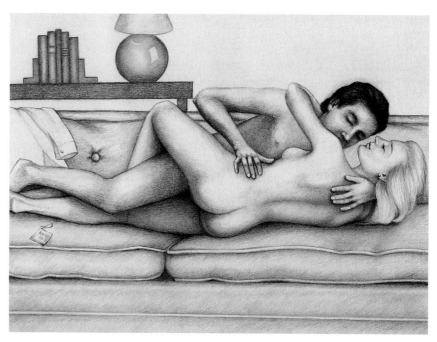

ing" by gay African Americans). Many couples engage in this activity along with fellatio or sexual intercourse.

Anal intercourse refers to the male's inserting his erect penis into his partner's anus. Both heterosexuals and gay men participate in anal intercourse. In a recent study, 10% of sexually active heterosexual couples reported engaging in anal intercourse during one year, but it is not a common practice after it has been experienced once. For heterosexuals, it is more of an

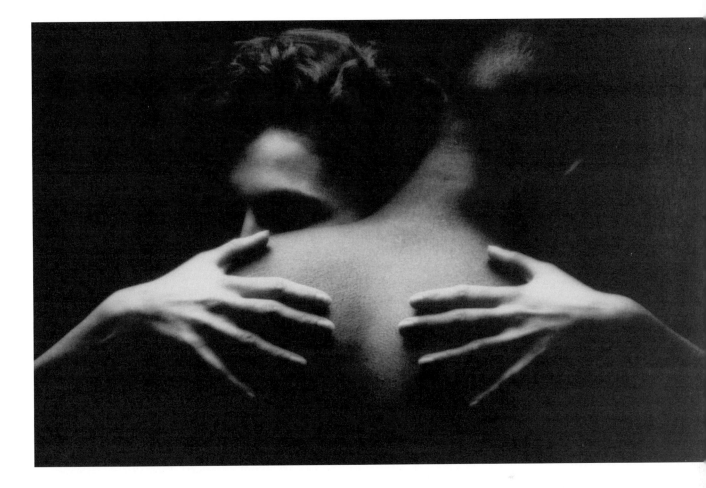

experimental activity (Laumann et al., 1994). About 25% of heterosexual adults have engaged in anal sex (Seidman & Rieder, 1994).

Anal intercourse is a major mode of sexual interaction for gay men. In fact, there are more colloquial terms for anal eroticism among gay men than for any other form of sexual activity (Mays, Cochran, Bellinger, & Smith, 1992; Mays, Cochran, Smith, & Daniels, 1993). A national study of anal sex practices by American men (orientation not stated) found considerable variation by ethnicity (Billy et al., 1993). Among men age 20–39, about 21% of Whites, 13.6% of African Americans, and 24% of Latinos have experienced anal intercourse.

Among gay men, anal intercourse is less common than oral sex, but it is, nevertheless, an important ingredient to the sexual satisfaction of many gays (Berger, 1991; Blumstein & Schwartz, 1983). Although heterosexual imagery portrays the person who penetrates as "masculine" and the penetrated person as "feminine," this imagery does not generally reflect gay reality. For both partners, anal intercourse is regarded as masculine.

Although anal sex may heighten eroticism for those who engage in it, from a health perspective it is riskier than most other forms of sexual interaction. The rectum is particularly susceptible to sexually transmitted diseases (Agnew, 1986). Because of HIV, anal intercourse is potentially the most dangerous form of sexual interaction. Anal intercourse is the most prevalent mode of transmitting HIV sexually, among both gay men and heterosexuals (Voeller, 1991). The delicate rectal tissues are easily lacerated, allowing the AIDS virus (carried within semen) to enter the bloodstream. If a couple practice anal intercourse, they should engage in it *only* if both are certain that they are free from HIV *and* if they use a condom. When there is oral stimulation to the anal region, a rubber dam can be placed over the area to protect against transmission of HIV, other STDs, and bacteria. As a result of safer-sex campaigns and powerful new drugs, the AIDS death rate has been dramatically lowered (Peyser, 1997). Nevertheless, AIDS is still a devastating fatal disease.

If the penis or a foreign object is inserted in the anus, it must be washed before insertion into the vagina because it may cause a bacterial infection. Other health hazards associated with anal erotic practices include rupturing the rectum with foreign objects, and laceration of the anus or rectal wall through the use of enemas. Licking the anus puts individuals at risk of acquiring HIV, hepatitis, or other sexually transmitted diseases (see Chapters 15 and 16).

■   As we have seen, sexual behaviors cannot be separated from attraction and desire. Our autoerotic activities are as important to our sexuality as are our interpersonal ones. Although the sexual behaviors we have examined in this chapter are the most common ones in our society, many engage in other, less typical activities. We discuss these atypical behaviors in Chapter 10.

SUMMARY

Sexual Attractiveness

- The characteristics that constitute sexual attractiveness vary across cultures. Youth and good health appear to be the only universals. Our culture prefers slender women with large breasts and men with well-defined arm and pectoral muscles. Both men and women are attracted to the buttocks of the other sex.

- Because of the halo effect, attractive people are assumed to be more sexual and permissive than unattractive people. Attractive college women may be more likely to have engaged in sexual intercourse and oral sex than unattractive women.

- Sexual desire is affected by *erotophilia*, a positive emotional response to sex, and by *erotophobia*, a negative response to sex.

Sexual Scripts

- Sexual scripts organize our sexual impulses. They have three major components: cultural, intraper-

sonal, and interpersonal. The cultural script provides the general patterns sexual behaviors are expected to take in a particular society. The intrapersonal script interprets our physiological responses as sexual or not. The interpersonal script is the shared conventions and signals that make sexual activities between two people possible.

Autoeroticism

- *Autoeroticism* refers to sexual activities that involve only the self. These activities include sexual fantasies, erotic dreams and *nocturnal orgasm*, and *masturbation*, or stimulation of the genitals for pleasure.

- Sexual fantasies and dreams are probably the most universal of all sexual behaviors; they are normal aspects of our sexuality. Erotic fantasies have several functions: they take our generalized sexual drives and help define and direct them, they allow us to plan or anticipate erotic situations, they provide pleasurable escape from routine, they introduce novelty, and they offer clues to our unconscious.

- Most men and women masturbate. Masturbation may begin as early as infancy and continue throughout old age. Attitudes toward masturbation vary across ethnic groups.

Interpersonal Sexuality

- The erotic potential of touching has been undervalued because our culture tends to be orgasm-oriented, especially among males. *Pleasuring* is a means by which couples get to know each other erotically through touching and caressing.

- Erotic kissing is usually our earliest interpersonal sexual experience and is regarded as a rite of passage into adult sexuality.

- Oral-genital sex is becoming increasingly accepted, especially among young adults. *Cunnilingus* is the stimulation of the vulva with the tongue; it is engaged in by both heterosexuals and lesbians. *Fellatio* is the stimulation of the penis with the mouth; it is engaged in by both heterosexuals and gay men.

- Sexual intercourse is a complex interaction between two people. It is both a means of reproduction and a form of communication.

- Anal eroticism refers to sexual activities involving the anus. It is engaged in by heterosexuals, gay men, and lesbians.

SUGGESTED READING

Arbramson, Paul R., & Pinkerton, Steven D. (Eds.). (1995). *Sexual Nature, Sexual Culture.* Chicago: University of Chicago Press. A collection of scholarly essays examining the contributions of nature and nurture to the development of human sexuality. Includes a number of essays reporting the latest research on cross-species sexual behavior.

Barbach, Lonnie. (1984). *For Each Other: Sharing Sexual Intimacy.* New York: Bantam. A best-selling book describing women's sexual activities, attitudes, and feelings.

Comfort, Alex. (1991). *The New Joy of Sex* (Rev. ed.). New York: Crown. An updated version of the contemporary classic on sex and sexuality.

Dodson, Betty. (1987). *Sex for One.* New York: Harmony Publications. Self-discovery techniques through masturbation for women and men; includes sensitive illustrations.

Kroll, Ken, & Klein, Erica Levy. (1992). *Enabling Romance: A Guide to Love, Sex, and Relationships for the Disabled.* New York: Harmony Books. A discussion by hundreds of men and women with disabilities of stereotypes, different ways of being sexual, the use of sex toys, and strengthening relationships.

Loulan, JoAnn. (1984). *Lesbian Sex.* San Francisco: Spinsters Books. One of the most popular books on lesbian sexuality and sexual enhancement.

Michael, Robert T., Gagnon, John, Laumann, Edward, & Kolata, Gina. (1994). *Sex in America: A Definitive Survey.* Boston: Little, Brown. A lay version of *The Social Organization of Sexuality* by Edward Laumann and his colleagues, cited throughout this textbook; emphasizes the social context of sexuality and is based on interviews with almost 3500 respondents in a national representative survey.

Silverstein, Charles, & Picano, Felice. (1992). *The New Joy of Gay Sex.* New York: HarperCollins. An illustrated guide to gay male sexuality.

Zilbergeld, Bernie. (1992). *The New Male Sexuality Book.* Boston: Little, Brown. An updated version of the classic work on male sexuality, describing sexual myths, communication, and sexual expression.

10

Atypical and Paraphilic Sexual Behavior

I N A PARTICULARLY VICIOUS election campaign, the late Florida senator Claude Pepper was accused of being a "shameless extrovert," whose sister was known to be a New York "thespian." His opponent claimed that the senator "practiced celibacy" prior to marriage and later engaged in "nepotism" with his sister-in-law (Catchpole, 1992). These "accusations," which Pepper's opponent hoped would imply some kind of unnatural or perverted activity, refer simply to the senator's being outgoing (an extrovert), having an actress sister (a thespian), being sexually abstinent prior to marriage (celibacy), and giving his sister-in-law preferential treatment because of their relationship (nepotism). But the use of clinical- or moral-sounding terms points to the power of labeling. Sometimes, labels help us understand behavior; at other times, they interfere. This is especially true as we examine unusual or atypical sexual activities.

In this chapter, we examine atypical sexual behaviors, such as cross-dressing and domination and submission, which are not within the range of sexual behaviors in which people typically engage. Then we turn to sexual behaviors that are classified by the American Psychiatric Association as paraphilias. The noncoercive paraphilias include fetishism and transvestism. And finally we examine the coercive paraphilias, which include zoophilia, pedophilia, sexual sadism, sexual masochism, and necrophilia.

ATYPICAL VERSUS PARAPHILIC BEHAVIOR

The range of human sexual behavior is almost infinite. Yet most of our activities and fantasies, such as coitus, oral-genital sex, masturbation, and our orientation as heterosexual, gay, lesbian, or bisexual, cluster within a general range of behaviors and desires. Those behaviors and fantasies that do not fall in this general range are considered atypical. In this chapter, we use the term **atypical sexual behavior** to refer to those consensual behaviors that are not *statistically* typical of American sexual behaviors. It is important to remember, however, that atypical does not necessarily mean abnormal; it simply means that the majority of people do not engage in that particular behavior. Sexual behaviors that are classified as mental disorders are known as paraphilias. Atypical sexual behaviors tend to differ from paraphilic ones in that paraphilic behaviors tend to be compulsive, long-standing, and distressing to the individual.

According to the American Psychiatric Association's *Diagnostic and Statistical Manual of Mental Disorders,* 4th ed. *(DSM-IV)* (1994), a **paraphilia** is a mental disorder characterized by recurrent intense sexual urges, sexually arousing fantasies, or behaviors lasting at least 6 months and involving (1) nonhuman objects, (2) the suffering or humiliation of oneself or one's partner, or (3) children or other nonconsenting people. In addition, "the person has acted upon these urges or is markedly distressed by them" (American Psychiatric Association, 1994). A person with a paraphilia is known as a **paraphiliac.**

The distinction between atypical and paraphilic behavior is sometimes more a difference of degree than kind. For example, many men find that certain objects, such as black lingerie, intensify their sexual arousal; for others, these objects are necessary for arousal. In the first case, there is nothing

ARE YOU A SEX ADDICT? As you read descriptions of sexual addiction, you may begin to think that you are. But don't believe everything you read. Consider the following description.

"The moment comes for every addict," writes psychologist Patrick Carnes (1983, 1991), who developed and marketed the idea of sexual addiction, "when the consequences are so great or the pain so bad that the addict admits life is out of control because of his or her sexual behavior." Money is spent on pornography, affairs threaten a marriage, masturbation replaces jogging, fantasies interrupt studying. . . . Sex, sex, sex is on the addict's mind. And he or she has no choice but to engage in these activities.

Sex addicts' lives are filled with guilt or remorse, according to Carnes. They cannot make a commitment; instead, they move from one affair to another. They make promises to themselves, to their partners, and to God to stop, but they cannot. Like all addicts, they are powerless before their addiction (Butts, 1992; Carnes, 1983, 1991). Their addiction is rooted in deep-seated feelings of worthlessness, despair, anxiety, and loneliness. These feelings are temporarily allayed by the "high" obtained from sexual arousal and orgasm. Sex addicts, writes Carnes, go through a four-step cycle:

1. *Preoccupation with sex, an obsessive search for sexual stimulation.* Everything passes through a sexual filter. Sex becomes an intoxication, a high.

2. *Ritualization, or special routines that lead to sex.* The ritual may include body oils and massage, cruising, watching others, candles next to the bed, champagne.

3. *Compulsive sexual behavior.* This includes masturbation, bondage, extramarital affairs, exhibitionism, or incest.

4. *Despair: the realization that the person is incapable of changing.* Guilt, feelings of isolation, or suicidal tendencies may be present.

Carnes identifies several levels of sexual addiction, categorized according to behavior. The first level of behavior includes excessive masturbation, numerous heterosexual relationships, interest in pornography, relations with prostitutes, and homosexuality. The second level includes exhibitionism, voyeurism, and obscene phone calls. The third level includes child molestation, incest, and rape. The addict moves from one level of behavior to the next in search of excitement and satisfaction.

Sexual addiction is viewed in the same light as alcoholism and drug addiction; it is an activity over which the addict has no control. And as for alcoholism, a 12-step treatment program for sex addiction has been established by the National Council on Sexual Addiction/Compulsivity (Corley, 1994). The first step is for the addict to admit that he or she is helpless to end the addiction. Subsequent steps include turning to a Higher Power for assistance, listing all moral shortcomings, asking forgiveness from those who have been harmed and making amends to them, and finding a spiritual path to wholeness.

After reading this description of sexual addiction, do you feel a little uneasy? Do some of the signs of sexual addiction seem to apply directly to you? Are you wondering, "Am I a sex addict?" Don't worry; you're probably not. The reason you might think you're suffering

particularly unusual. In fact, a study of almost 200 students found that 16% of the women and 7% of the men had recently worn erotic garments (Person, Terestman, Myers, & Goldberg, 1989). But if a man were unable to become excited without the lingerie and the purpose of sex was to bring him in contact with the panties, the behavior would be considered paraphilic.

It is also important to recognize that seemingly scientific or clinical terms may not be scientific at all. Instead, they may be pseudoscientific terms hiding moral judgments, as in the case of the terms "nymphomania" and "satyriasis." **Nymphomania** is a pejorative term, usually referring to "abnormal or excessive" sexual desire in a woman. It is usually applied to sexually active single women. What is "abnormal" or "excessive" is often defined moralistically rather than scientifically. Nymphomania is not recognized as a clinical condition by the *DSM-IV* (American Psychiatric Association, 1994). Although the term "nymphomania" dates back to the seventeenth century, it was popularized in the nineteenth century by Krafft-Ebing and others.

from sexual addiction is that its definition taps into many of the underlying anxieties and uncertainties we feel about sexuality in our culture. The problem lies not in you but in the concept of sexual addiction.

Although the sexual addiction model has found some adherents among clinical psychologists, they are clearly a minority. There are some people, it is true, who are compulsive in their sexual behaviors, but compulsion is not addiction. The influence of the sexual addiction model is not the result of its impact on therapy, psychology, and social work. Its influence is due mainly to its popularity with the media, where talk-show hosts interview so-called sex addicts and advice columnists caution their readers about the signs of sexual addiction. The popularity of an idea is no guarantee of its validity, however.

The sexual addiction model has been rejected by a number of sex researchers as nothing more than pop psychology. These researchers suggest that the idea of sexual addiction is really repressive morality in a new guise. It is a conservative reaction to sexual diversity, eroticism, and sex outside of monogamous relationships. It makes masturbation a sign of addiction, just as in earlier times masturbation was viewed as a sign of moral degeneracy. According to the sexual addiction model, sex is healthy if it takes place within a relationship; outside a relationship, it is pathological (Levine & Troiden, 1988).

Critiques of the sexual addiction model by sex researchers have undermined its credibility (Kavich-Sharon, 1994; Satel, 1993). First, the researchers point out, addiction requires physiological dependence on a chemical substance arising from habitual use. Sex is not a substance. Nor is there physiological distress, such as diarrhea, convulsions, or delirium, from withdrawal. Second, research fails to convincingly document sexual addiction as a clinical condition. There is virtually no empirical evidence to support the sexual addiction model. What little evidence there is comes from small clinical samples in which there are no comparable control groups. Indeed, the case studies Carnes describes in his book are not even real. "The stories used in this book," Carnes (1983, 1991) writes, "are fictionalized composites." As a result, one study calls the sexual addiction movement dangerously oversimplified (Klein, 1991).

Third, there is no sexual hierarchy. Suggesting that masturbation leads to pornography, pornography to exhibitionism, and exhibitionism to rape borders on the irresponsible. Fourth, the sexual addiction model is highly moralistic. The committed, monogamous, heterosexual relationship is the model against which all other behaviors are measured. Nonprocreative sex such as masturbation is viewed as symptomatic. Gay and lesbian sex is also considered symptomatic. Fifth, the characteristics of the addictive process—"preoccupation, ritualization, compulsive sexual behavior"—are subjective and value-laden. Sociologists Martin Levine and Richard Troiden (1988) note: "Each of these characteristics could just as well describe the intense passion of courtship or the sexual routines of conventional couples." Nor is there evidence to support the notion that a person goes through three levels of behavior in search of greater excitement. "Carnes' notion of levels of addiction is a classic instance of moral judgment parading as scientific fact" (Levine & Troiden, 1988).

If your sexual fantasies and activities are distressing to you, or your behaviors are emotionally or physically harmful to yourself or others, you should consult a therapist. The chances are, however, that your sexuality and your unique expression of it are as normal as anyone else's.

Physicians and psychiatrists used the term to pathologize women's sexual behavior if it deviated from nineteenth-century moral standards. Even today, "nymphomania," "nymphomaniac," and "nympho" retain pathological connotations.

Satyriasis, referring to "abnormal" or "uncontrollable" sexual desire in men, is less commonly used than "nymphomania" because men are expected to be more sexual than women. For this reason, definitions of satyriasis infrequently include the adjective "excessive." Instead, reflecting ideas of male sexuality as a powerful drive, "uncontrollable" becomes the significant adjective. Satyriasis is not recognized by the American Psychiatric Association (1994).

As you continue this chapter, remember to distinguish clearly between the use of the various terms clinically, judgmentally, or casually. It can be tempting to define a behavior you don't like or approve of as paraphilic. But unless you are clinically trained, you cannot diagnose someone (including yourself) as having a mental disorder.

Through me forbidden voices.
Voices of sexes and lusts . . .
Voices veiled, and I remove the veil,
Voices indecent by me clarified and
    transfigured.

—*Walt Whitman (1819–1892)*

ATYPICAL SEXUAL BEHAVIORS

Atypical sexual behaviors are not rare. Although the majority of people do not engage in these activities, they are not necessarily uncommon. In this section we discuss the incidence of these behaviors and one of the more controversial and widespread forms—domination and submission.

Incidence of Atypical Sexual Behaviors

A study of recent sexual behaviors and fantasies among 193 college and graduate students found that 23% of the women and 38% of the men had recently watched their partner masturbate (Person et al., 1989). Fourteen percent of the women and 6% of the men had used sex toys. Eleven percent of the women and 18% of the men had performed sexual acts in front of mirrors. And 5% of the women and 4% of the men had watched others engage in sexual intercourse. In terms of fantasies, 10% of the men and the women had imagined themselves members of the other gender. Ten percent of the women and 5% of the men had fantasized themselves as prostitutes. One film critic suggests that the popularity of vampire movies and novels may reflect our fascination with forbidden impulses or obsessions about which we may fantasize but that we will never act out (James, 1992).

Domination and Submission

Domination and submission (D/S) refers to sexual arousal derived from the *consensual* acting out of sexual scenes in which one person dominates and the other submits. The term **sadomasochism (S&M)** is also used by the general public to describe domination and submission, but it is no longer used as a clinical term in psychiatry and psychology to describe consensual domination and submission (Breslow, 1989).

Ah beautiful, passionate body,
That never has ached with a heart!
On the mouth though the kisses are
    bloody,
Though they sting till it shudder and
    smart
More kind than the love we adore is
They hurt not the heart nor the brain
Oh bitter and tender Dolores
Our Lady of Pain.

—*Algernon Swinburne (1837–1909)*

Domination and submission are forms of fantasy sex. The critical element is not pain, but power. The dominant partner is all-powerful and the submissive partner is all-powerless. Significantly, the amount or degree of "pain," which is usually feigned or slight, is controlled by the submissive partner. As such, fantasy plays a central role, especially for the submissive person (Arndt, 1991).

A large-scale study of a nonclinical population found that the majority involved in domination and submission did so as "a form of sexual enhancement which they voluntarily and mutually choose to explore" (Weinberg, Williams, & Moser, 1984). As such, domination and submission is not paraphilic. To be considered paraphilic, such behavior requires the suffering or humiliation of oneself or one's partner to be real, not merely simulated (American Psychiatric Association, 1994). (Sexual sadism and sexual masochism, which are considered paraphilias, are discussed later in the chapter.)

Domination and submission take many forms. The participants generally assume both dominant and submissive roles at different times; few are interested only in being "top" or "bottom" (Moser, 1988). Probably the most widely known form is bondage and discipline. **Bondage and discipline (B&D)** refers to activities in which a person is bound with scarves, leather straps, underwear, handcuffs, chains, or other such devices while another

Bondage and discipline, or B&D, often involves leather, handcuffs, and other restraints as part of its scripting.

simulates or engages in light to moderate discipline activities, such as spanking, whipping, and so on. The bound person may be blindfolded or gagged. A woman specializing in disciplining a person is known as a **dominatrix,** and her submissive partner is called a slave.

Bondage and discipline may take place in specialized settings called "dungeons" furnished with restraints, body-suspension devices, racks, whips, and chains (Stoller, 1991). Eleven percent of both men and women have had experience with bondage, according to one study (Janus & Janus, 1993).

Another common form of domination and submission is *humiliation,* in which the person is debased or degraded (Arndt, 1991). Five percent of the men and 7% of the women in the Janus study had engaged in verbal humiliation (Janus & Janus, 1993). One-third of the submission respondents in another study received enemas ("water treatment"), were urinated on ("golden showers"), or defecated on ("scat") (Breslow, Evans, & Langley, 1985). In the Janus study, 6% of the men and 4% of the women had participated in golden showers (Janus & Janus, 1993). Humiliation activities may include servilism, babyism, kennelism, and tongue lashing. In *servilism,* the person desires to be treated as a servant or slave. In *babyism,* the person acts in an infantile manner—using baby talk; wearing diapers; being pampered, scolded, or spanked by his or her "mommy" or "daddy." *Kennelism* refers to being treated like a dog (wearing a studded dog collar and being tied to a

IT'S NEARLY IMPOSSIBLE to watch MTV, televised sports, or fashion events these days without seeing someone with a small tattoo or ring discreetly (or not so discreetly) displayed on his or her body. As the latest expression of individuality, piercing and tattooing have attracted a diverse set of enthusiasts and have moved into mainstream culture.

Every culture and time has had its own standards of beauty and sexual attractiveness, and piercing and tattooing have been used to enhance both. A pierced navel was considered a sign of royalty among the ancient Egyptians, and the Crusaders of the Middle Ages were tattooed with crucifixes to ensure a Christian burial.

Tattooing in our culture has become widespread and nearly routine, with tattoo "studios" presenting their services as art. The tattooing procedure involves injecting dye into the skin, resulting in a permanent marking. Potential problems associated with the painful procedure include the risk of infection, including infection with hepatitis or HIV. Between 12 and 20 million Americans have tattoos; studies indicate that nearly half these people want them removed, most often because of psychological discomfort and/or job discrimination (Marin, Hannah, Colin, Annin, & Gegax, 1995). Although the removal procedure is also painful, new technology and lower costs have allowed many individuals to have their tattoos removed. Using the flickering beam of a laser, physicians can explode the indelible ink into minute particles, which are absorbed and discarded by the body.

"The last taboo is the body," states Fakir Musafar, considered by many to be the father of the "modern primitive movement" (Ryan, 1997). Musafar believes that the popularity of body modification is the final stage of evolution that began in the 1960s, when young people challenged religion, family, and government. Like tattooing, body piercing has become increasingly popular as a dra-

leash) or ridden like a horse, while the dominant partner applies whips or spurs. *Tongue lashing* is verbal abuse by a dominant partner who uses language that humiliates and degrades the other.

People engage in D/S in private or as part of an organized subculture complete with clubs and businesses catering to the acting out of D/S fantasies (Stoller, 1991). This subculture is sometimes known as "the velvet underground." There are scores of noncommercial D/S clubs throughout the

Betty Page, who has become a cult figure among those interested in domination and submission, was one of the most photographed women in the 1950s.

matic way to help define oneself. What keeps piercing exotic is not only the look but the pain factor that accompanies it. "Pain is relative," says Musafar (cited in Ryan, 1997). "People in other cultures can transmit the strong physical sensation of pain into ecstasy, healing and many other states. It's a way of using the body to explore inner space and spiritual dimensions." For some, the pain is viewed as a drug, a way of releasing anxiety, and/or a means of erotic stimulation. Psychologists report that cutting and other self-injury provide relief by releasing endorphins, which can actually boost one's mood (Ryan, 1997).

Piercing capitalizes on a fascination with the look of deviance, with its sadomasochistic undertones. If placed strategically, rings and studs provide both physical stimulation and psychological titillation. The most common site for piercing, besides the earlobe, is the nipple, followed by the navel. Other sites include the tongue, lips, labia, frenulum, and scrotum. Each type of piercing involves a specific method of puncturing and a prescribed course of healing. Some plastic surgeons report a doubling of business involving stitching together body parts damaged by piercing.

A third practice is branding. Used as a hazing rite of passage in some Black fraternities, it is now becoming more common in the mainstream, with some clubs offering branding as a stage show. Hot-iron branding leaves a scar that may be treated with steroid injections but that can never be totally removed.

Because all these markings are considered permanent and potentially dangerous, the procedures should be performed only by professionals. Keys to safety and satisfaction include basic aftercare, which involves keeping the site clean and avoiding contact with dirty hands, saliva, or other body fluids; an awareness of anatomy and knowledge of proper healing procedures on the part of the person providing the services; proper placement of the marks or piercings; and the use of sterile tools ("Piercing Exquisite, " 1998).

United States (Arndt, 1991). The clubs are often specialized: lesbian S&M, dominant men/submissive women, submissive men/dominant women, gay men's S&M, and transvestite S&M. Leather sex bars are meeting places for gay men who are interested in D/S. The D/S subculture includes D/S videos, Web sites, books, and magazines.

The world of D/S is secretive, but the degree of secrecy depends on the different groups involved and the types of activities they undertake. The world of heterosexual D/S is more hidden; their contacts are limited to private, small networks (Weinberg & Kamel, 1983).

> Don't do unto others as you would they should do unto you. Their taste may be different.
>
> —*George Bernard Shaw (1856–1950)*

NONCOERCIVE PARAPHILIAS

Incidence of Paraphilias

We have no reliable estimates of the number of individuals who are paraphiliacs. But research suggests that many of the activities of convicted sex offenders, such as exhibitionism, voyeurism, and pedophilia, may also be present in the general population (Finkelhor, Hotaling, Lewis, & Smith, 1990; Koss, 1988; Templeman & Stinnett, 1991). A study of 60 college men attempted to find out what percentage of the young male nonoffender, nonclinical population engaged in coercive atypical sexual behaviors (Templeman & Stinnett, 1991). By collecting life histories of the men, the researchers found that 65% had engaged in some form of sexual misconduct, such as voyeurism, obscene phone calling, or sexually rubbing themselves against a woman. The study concluded that young men were easily aroused to diverse stimuli, blurring the distinction between typical and atypical behavior.

The overwhelming majority of paraphilias occur among men. Paraphilias occur among heterosexuals, gay men, male bisexuals, and transsexuals. It is important to realize that sexual orientation is not related to paraphilia. A gay exhibitionist, for example, is considered paraphilic not because of his attraction to other men but because he exposes his genitals (Levine, Risen, & Althof, 1990).

Males are most likely to engage in paraphilic activities between ages 15 and 25. Paraphiliacs generally lack control over their behavior. It is not uncommon for them to participate in a variety of paraphilic activities (Fedora, Reddon, Morrison, & Fedora, 1992) and to be unable to maintain a conventional sexual relationship (Golwyn & Selvie, 1992).

An important aspect of paraphilias is whether they involve coercion. Noncoercive paraphilias are regarded as relatively benign or harmless because they are victimless. Noncoercive paraphilias include fetishism and transvestism.

Fetishism

We attribute special or magical powers to many things: a lucky number, a saint's relic, an heirloom, a lock of hair, or an automobile. These objects possess a kind of symbolic magic (Belk, 1991). We will carry our boyfriend's or girlfriend's photograph (and sometimes talk to it or kiss it), ask for a keepsake if we part, become nostalgic for an old love when we hear a particular song. All these are normal, but they point to the symbolic power of objects, or fetishes.

Fetishism is sexual attraction to objects, which become for the fetishist sexual symbols. Instead of relating to another person, a fetishist gains sexual gratification from kissing a shoe, caressing a glove, drawing a lock of hair against his or her cheek, or masturbating with a piece of underwear. But a fetishist's focus is not necessarily an inanimate object; he may be attracted to a woman's feet, ears, breasts, legs, or elbows or to any other part of her body (Cautela, 1986). (According to the *DSM-IV*, exclusive attraction to body parts is known as **partialism**.) Some researchers consider *Playboy's* centerfold to be fetishistic in its focus on female breasts and genitals (Rosegrant, 1986). Reports of types of fetishes even include arousal from sneezes (King, 1990). According to the Janus study, 11% of the men and 6% of the women had engaged in fetishistic behaviors (Janus & Janus, 1993).

Fetishistic behavior may be viewed as existing on a continuum, or existing in degrees, moving from a slight preference for an object, to a strong preference for it, to the necessity of the object for arousal, and finally to the object as a substitute for a sexual partner (McConaghy, 1993). Most people have slight fetishistic traits: Men describe themselves as leg men or breast men; they prefer dark-haired or light-haired partners. Some women are attracted to muscular men, others to hairy chests, and still others to shapely buttocks. It is only when a person develops a strong preference for an object that his or her attachment moves outside the range of statistical normality.

Transvestism

Transvestism is the wearing of clothing of the other sex, usually for sexual arousal. The term is derived from the Latin *trans,* cross, and *vestire,* to dress.

Of all the sexual aberrations, the most peculiar is chastity.

—*Remy de Gourmont (1858–1915)*

Girls will be boys and boys will be girls
It's a mixed up, muddled up, shook up world . . .

—*The Kinks,*"Lola"

Inanimate objects or parts of the body, such as the foot, may be sexualized by some people.

One study found that 6% of men and 3% of women reported cross-dressing (Janus & Janus, 1993). Although the literature indicates that cross-dressing occurs almost exclusively in males, there are studies of women who have erotic attachment to men's garments (Bullough & Bullough, 1993; Stoller, 1982).

Transvestism covers a broad range of behaviors. Some transvestites prefer to wear only one article of clothing (usually a brassiere or panties) of the other sex in the privacy of their home; others choose to don an entire outfit in public. The distinction between fetishism and transvestism involves the wearing of the garment versus the viewing or fondling of it. The frequency of cross-dressing ranges from a momentary activity that produces sexual excitement, usually through masturbation, to more frequent and long-lasting behavior, depending on the individual, available opportunities, and mood or stressors.

Cross-dressing is not necessarily a paraphilia. It may be a source of humor and parody, as the traditional boundaries of gender are explored and challenged.

Those hot pants of hers were so damned tight, I could hardly breathe.

—Benny Hill

Some who cross-dress are considered psychologically disordered, as in **fetishistic transvestism.** According to the American Psychiatric Association (1994), people with this disorder are heterosexual men who, over a period of at least 6 months, act upon intense, usually distressful, sexual urges and fantasies involving the wearing of women's clothes. Because many transvestites contend they are not abnormal but merely revealing a legitimate source of sexual expression and arousal, they resist and shun this diagnosis.

Transvestites are usually quite conventional in their masculine dress and attitudes. Dressed as women or wearing only one women's garment, they may become sexually aroused and masturbate or have sex with a woman.

EACH YEAR VAST NUMBERS of ordinary men dress as women during Halloween, Mardi Gras, and Carnival. **Cross-dressing** is a staple of television shows, such as "Martin," "Saturday Night Live," and "In Living Color." It has been the focus of many movies, including *The Birdcage* and *Mrs. Doubtfire*. Rock culture includes cross-dressed performances by Little Richard, Alice Cooper, Mick Jagger, David Bowie, and Madonna. In the gay subculture, cross-dressing (or **drag**) is a source of humor and parody. In all these cases, cross-dressing represents a loosening of traditional boundaries. Behind masks and costumes, men and women play out fantasies that are forbidden to them in their daily lives.

As can readily be seen, people cross-dress for a wide variety of reasons. Some people cross-dress to relieve the pressure associated with traditional gender roles. Others are satirizing or parodying social conventions. Still others want to challenge what they see as narrow views of gender and sexuality.

Given the humor, playfulness, and sense of relaxation apparent in many cases of cross-dressing, how do we distinguish this phenomenon from fetishistic transvestism, which is considered a paraphilia? If those who cross-dress are labeled paraphiliacs, what effect does it have on them? Does such labeling create mental distress in an otherwise relatively well-adjusted person?

Questions like these lead us to consider the effect of labeling in general and to ask, "What's in a name?" Although clinical labels and definitions help professionals to diagnose illnesses and create treatment plans, labeling can also cause problems. Consider the difference between a 7-year-old boy who is called "active" and one who is labeled "hyperactive." Or between a person described as "compassionate" and one labeled "co-dependent." Or between someone said to have a lot of libido and someone labeled a "sex addict." In each case, the label adds a clinical dimension to the person's behavior. Labeling can have a profound effect both on an individual's self-concept and on the perceptions and behaviors of those involved with the person.

Among those who cross-dress, being labeled a paraphiliac can contribute to maladaptation by fostering unnecessary shame and guilt. It can even become a self-fulfilling prophecy if the person begins to experience significant distress and impairment as a result of being labeled. Although cross-dressing is atypical, the majority of cross-dressers are not maladapted or mentally disordered, nor is their behavior pathological. To label all those who cross-dress as paraphiliacs is inaccurate and potentially harmful.

As time passes, however, the erotic element of the female garment may decrease and their comfort level increase. The majority of transvestites have no desire to undertake a sex-change operation. If they do, there may be an accompanying diagnosis of gender dysphoria. Transvestites are rarely attracted to other men (G. R. Brown, 1995; Wise & Meyer, 1980). They believe they have both masculine and feminine personalities within them. Their feminine personality appears when they cross-dress; sometimes they give their feminine personality a name (Brierly, 1979). Transvestites may even walk around town as women and not be recognized.

Over two-thirds of transvestites are or have been married. In fact, a number of them marry in hopes of "curing" their desire to cross-dress. Of those who marry, about two-thirds have children. Some voluntarily reveal their cross-dressing after marriage, but the majority have it discovered. Invariably, the transvestites' partners are distressed and blame themselves for somehow "emasculating" their partners. Some transvestites and their wives and families are able to adjust to the cross-dressing. Data suggest, however, that wives merely tolerate rather than support their husbands' cross-dressing (Brown & Collier, 1989; Bullough & Weinberg, 1988). But often the stress is too great, and separation follows soon after the transvestism is discovered.

As transvestism is neither dangerous nor reversible (Wise & Meyer, 1980), the preferred clinical treatment is to help the transvestite and those close to

> I don't think painting my fingernails is a big deal. It's not like I'm sitting home by myself trying on lingerie. . . . When I cross-dress now, it's just another way I can show all the sides of Dennis Rodman.
>
> —*Dennis Rodman*

> I don't mind drag—women have been female impersonators for some time.
>
> —*Gloria Steinem*

Ru-Paul is a well-known cross-dresser. Cross-dressing has been an important part of popular culture, especially comedy, since Shakespeare's time.

Nine out of ten men who prefer Camels end up with women.

—*Anonymous*

him accept his cross-dressing. Though most individuals who engage in transvestism do not seek professional help (G. R. Brown, 1995), those who do often must deal with their feelings of guilt and shame (Peo, 1988).

Why does our culture seem disproportionately preoccupied with cross-dressing? Our interest, writes Marjorie Garber (1992), reflects a "crisis in categories." She asserts that the categories of male/female and heterosexual/homosexual are inadequate for describing the full range of human experience. Just as bisexuality challenges the heterosexuality/homosexuality dichotomy, cross-dressing challenges the traditional masculine/feminine dichotomy. Can a man wearing a dress really be a man? Can a heterosexual male wearing a dress really be heterosexual? Cross-dressing destroys our usual either/or ways of categorizing people (Garber, 1992).

COERCIVE PARAPHILIAS

Few noncoercive paraphilias are brought to public attention because of their private, victimless nature. But coercive paraphilias, which involve victimization, are the subject of concern by society because of the harm they cause others.

All of these paraphilias involve some kind of coercive or nonconsensual relationship with another person or with an animal. A study of more than 400 outpatient sex offenders found that they attempted over 239,000 sex crimes, of which the majority were exhibitionism, voyeurism, obscene phone calls, and frotteurism (sexually rubbing against another person). These disorders also appear to be linked to child sexual abuse and rape. As many as 80% of rapists begin their assaultive behavior with "hands-off" sexual behavior, such as exhibitionism, voyeurism, obscene phone calls, and so on. Of exhibitionists, 29.7% were involved in child sexual abuse, and 29.2% were involved in rape. Of voyeurs, 13.8% were involved in child sexual abuse and 20.2% in rape (Knopp, 1984).

Zoophilia

Zoophilia, sometimes referred to as "bestiality," involves deriving sexual excitement from animals (American Psychiatric Association, 1994). Kinsey reported that about 8% of the men and 3% of the women he surveyed had experienced at least one sexual contact with animals. Seventeen percent of the men who had been reared on farms had had such contact, but these activities accounted for less than 1% of their total sexual outlet (Kinsey et al., 1948, 1953). Sexual contact with animals usually takes place among adolescents and is a transitory phenomenon. Among adults, such contact usually occurs when human partners are not available (Money, 1981).

Voyeurism

Viewing sexual activities is a commonplace activity. As we saw earlier, relatively large percentages of individuals have used mirrors to view themselves in sex acts, watched their partners masturbate, or watched others having intercourse (Person et al., 1989). Americans' interest in viewing sexual activities has spawned a multibillion-dollar sex industry devoted to fulfilling visual desires. Erotic magazines, books, X-rated videos, and pornographic Web sites are widely available. Topless bars, strip and peep shows, and erotic dancing attest to the attraction of visual erotica.

As Arndt (1991) notes, "Since looking at erotic scenes is so pervasive among males, it is difficult to determine when these acts are pathological." It is generally agreed, however, that the critical difference between casual, consensual viewing and voyeurism is consent.

Voyeurism involves recurring, intense sexual urges and fantasies to secretly observe another person who is nude, disrobing, or engaging in sexual activity (American Psychiatric Association, 1994). To be considered paraphilic behavior, voyeurism must be preferred over sexual relations with another or be indulged in with some risk. The sexual arousal often occurs when the risk of being discovered is high. In order to become aroused, the voyeur must hide and remain unseen, and the person or couple being watched must be unaware of the voyeur's presence. The excitement is intensified by the possibility of being discovered. Sometimes the voyeur will masturbate while peering through a window or keyhole.

Very little study has been done of voyeurs, the majority of whom are young men (Davidson & Neale, 1993). Voyeurs do not seek random females to watch undress or engage in sexual activities; instead, they seek out females they find sexually attractive. What voyeurs consider arousing differs from one voyeur to another. Some require viewing nude bodies, breasts, or vulvas; others desire watching sexual intercourse or lesbian sex. Voyeurism appears to appeal primarily to heterosexual men (Arndt, 1991), most of whom are content to keep their distance from their victim.

Exhibitionism

Also known as "indecent exposure," **exhibitionism** is the recurring, intense urge or fantasy to display one's genitals to an unsuspecting stranger (American Psychiatric Association, 1994). The individual has acted on these urges or is greatly disturbed by them. Although exhibitionists derive sexual gratification from the exposure of their genitals, the exposure is not a prelude or invitation to intercourse. Instead, it is an escape from intercourse, for the man never exposes himself to a willing woman—only to strangers or near-strangers. Typically, the exhibitionist obtains sexual gratification after exposing himself as he fantasizes about the shock and horror he caused his victim (Blair & Lanyon, 1981). Others experience orgasm as they expose themselves; still others may masturbate during the act of exhibitionism (American Psychiatric Association, 1994). Exhibitionists generally expose themselves to children, adolescents, and young women; they rarely expose themselves to older women. In those few instances in which a woman shows interest, the exhibitionist immediately flees (Stoller, 1977). Usually, there is no physical contact.

Exhibitionism is a fairly common paraphilia; more than one-third of all males arrested for sexual offenses are arrested for exhibitionism. Many of the men arrested for exhibitionism have also engaged in voyeurism, frotteurism, obscene phone calling, and attempted rape (Lang, Checkley, & Pugh, 1987). Seven percent of college men in one study expressed interest in exhibiting themselves; 2% actually had (Templeman & Stinnett, 1991). Another study found that exhibitionistic offenders became slightly more

Some people like to exhibit their bodies within public settings that are "legitimized," such as Mardi Gras. Such displays may be exhibitionistic, but they are not considered exhibitionism in the clinical sense.

aroused by descriptions of exposure than nonoffending men (Marshall, Eccles, & Barabee, 1991). Because of the widespread incidence of exhibitionism, at least half of adult women may have witnessed indecent exposure at least once in their lives (Arndt, 1991).

The stereotype of the exhibitionist as a dirty old man, lurking in parks or building entryways, dressed only in a raincoat and sneakers, is erroneous. (Fewer than 10% of exhibitionists are more than 50 years old, although a few may be as old as in their eighties when they first begin [Arndt, 1991; Kenyon, 1989].)

Exhibitionists appear to find fully clothed women more erotic than nude or partially nude women. For some reason, they misinterpret neutral or noneretic signals from women as erotic (Fedora, Reddon, & Yeudall, 1986). Most reportedly hope that the women will enjoy the experience (Lang, Checkley, & Pugh, 1987).

Exhibitionists are generally introverted, insecure, or sexually inadequate men (Arndt, 1991; Marshall et al., 1991). They feel impotent as men, and their sexual relations with their wives are usually poor. This sense of impotence gives rise to anger and hostility, which they direct toward other women by exhibiting themselves.

Telephone Scatologia

Telephone scatologia, the making of obscene phone calls, is considered a paraphilia because the acts are compulsive and repetitive or because the associated fantasies cause distress to the individual.

Those who engage in this behavior typically get sexually aroused when their victim reacts in a shocked or horrified manner. Obscene phone calls are generally made randomly, by chance dialing or phone book listings.

The overwhelming majority of callers are male, but there are some female obscene callers as well (Saunders & Awad, 1991). Male callers frequently

AN OBSCENE PHONE CALL can be shocking or even traumatizing. A person who receives such a call may feel attacked, singled out, or victimized. If you have had this experience, it may be helpful to know that the obscene phone caller very often picks the victim randomly from a phone book or just by dialing and is merely trying to elicit a response. Obscene phone callers rarely follow up their verbal intrusions with physical attacks on their victims. Horror, anger, and shock are the reactions the caller anticipates and finds arousing; thus, your initial response is critical.

If you receive an obscene phone call, the best thing to do is to quietly hang up the telephone. Banging down the receiver or trying to retaliate by screaming or scolding gives the caller the desired response. The telephone company claims that tactics such as pretending to be hard of hearing, blowing a whistle into the telephone, pretending to go to another phone, and letting the phone remain off the hook simply are not necessary. If the phone immediately rings again, don't answer it. If obscene calls are repeated, the telephone company suggests changing your number (many companies will do this at no charge) or, in more serious cases, working with law enforcement departments to trace the calls. A relatively new service available through many telephone companies is "call trace." When the recipient of a call enters a designated code, the telephone company can trace the call. Following a certain number of traces to the same telephone number, the offender will receive a warning that the unlawful behavior must stop. Abuse of this warning results in police or civil legal intervention.

make their female victims annoyed, frightened, anxious, upset, or angry, while the callers themselves often suffer from feelings of inadequacy and insecurity (Matek, 1988). The victims of male callers often feel violated. But female callers have a different effect on male recipients, who generally do not feel violated or who may enjoy the call as titillation (Matek, 1988).

Frotteurism

Frotteurism (also known as "frottage") involves recurrent, intense urges or fantasies—lasting over a period of at least 6 months—to touch or rub against a nonconsenting person for the purpose of sexual arousal and gratification (American Psychiatric Association, 1994). It is not known how many people practice frotteurism, but one study of normal college males found that 21% had engaged in at least one frotteuristic act (Templeman & Stinnett, 1991).

The frotteur usually carries out his touching or rubbing in crowded subways or buses or at large sporting events or rock concerts. When he enters a crowd, his initial rubbing can be disguised by the crush of people. He usually rubs against his victim's buttocks or thighs with his erect penis inside his pants. At other times, he may use his hands to rub a woman's buttocks, pubic region, thighs, or breasts. Generally, he rubs against the woman for 60–90 seconds. If he ejaculates, he stops. If he doesn't, he usually moves on to find another victim (Abel, 1989).

Frotteurism often occurs with other paraphilias, especially exhibitionism, voyeurism, pedophilia, and sadism, the sexually arousing infliction of pain. It is also associated with rape.

Necrophilia

Necrophilia is sexual activity with a corpse. It is regarded as nonconsensual because a corpse is obviously unable to give consent. There are relatively few instances of necrophilia, yet it retains a fascination in horror literature,

> The dead person who loves will love forever and will never be weary of giving and receiving caresses.
>
> —*Ernest Jones*

especially vampire stories and legends, and in gothic novels. It is also associated with ritual cannibalism in other cultures. Within our own culture, *Sleeping Beauty* features a necrophilic theme, as does the crypt scene in Shakespeare's *Romeo and Juliet.* Some heavy metal music deals with necrophilia (Rosman & Resnick, 1989).

A review of 122 cases of supposed necrophilia or necrophilic fantasies found only 54 instances of true necrophilia (Rosman & Resnick, 1989). The study found that neither sadism, psychosis, nor mental impairment was inherent in necrophilia. Instead, the most common motive for necrophilia was the possession of a partner who neither resisted nor rejected. In order to find such "partners," necrophiliacs often choose occupations giving them access to corpses, such as mortician or morgue attendant. Yet even some who have access to bodies nevertheless commit murder as part of their necrophilic behavior.

Pedophilia

Pedophilia refers to "recurrent intense sexual urges and sexually arousing fantasies involving sexual activity with a prepubescent child or children" that the individual, referred to as a **pedophile,** has acted upon or finds distressing (American Psychiatric Association, 1994). The children are age 13 or younger. A pedophile must be at least 16 and at least 5 years older than the child. (A late adolescent is not considered pedophilic if he or she is involved in an ongoing sexual relationship with a 12-year-old or older child.) A large number of arrested pedophiles currently are or previously have been involved in exhibitionism, voyeurism, or rape. In this section, we discuss only pedophilia. Nonpedophilic child sexual abuse and incest, their impact on the victim, and prevention of child sexual abuse are discussed in Chapter 17. Child sexual abuse is illegal in every state.

Sexual attraction to children is fairly widespread in the nonoffending population. A study of child-focused thoughts and fantasies among 193 male college students found that 21% reported sexual attraction to children, 9% had sexual fantasies of children, and 5% had masturbated to such fantasies (Briere & Runtz, 1989). These individuals tended to have had negative early sexual experiences; they reported dominance attitudes toward women, as well as a likelihood of raping them.

The actual incidence of child abuse in this country and abroad is staggering. National surveys indicate the percentage of girls victimized ranges from 20% to 33% and of boys, from 10% to 16% (Finkelhor, 1993, 1994; Guidry, 1995; Williams, 1994). Because of the stigmatization of the victim of abuse, especially when the victim is male, it is estimated that rates of sexual abuse of boys are actually much higher than those reported (Hack, Osachuk, & DeLuca, 1994). Although these rates are only estimates, they suggest that 1 out of 4 people in the United States has been a victim of childhood sexual abuse. Similar rates have been found worldwide (Finkelhor, 1994).

For most adult men and women, whether they are heterosexual, gay, or lesbian, the gender of their partner is important. But heterosexual/homosexual orientation is less important to pedophiles. For pedophiles, it is more important that the child *is* a child (Freund & Watson, 1993; Freund, Watson,

Dickey, & Rienzo, 1991). As a consequence, many heterosexually identified men may molest boys or boys and girls. Homosexually identified men may molest both boys and girls, although they are less likely to molest girls (Arndt, 1991; Freund et al., 1991). Men who molest boys are almost 7 times as likely to be imprisoned as those who molest girls (Walsh, 1994).

Cross-Sex Pedophilia　Some male pedophiles seek to sexually molest female children, the majority of whom are between ages 8 and 9. Adolescent pedophiles, averaging 15 years of age, sexually misuse girls around age 7 (Arndt, 1991). About half the pedophiles report stressful events, such as marital or work conflict, personal loss, or rejection, preceding the act of molestation. Many are fearful that their sexual abilities are decreasing or that they are impotent. Alcohol consumption, resulting in disinhibition, is involved in 30–50% of the offenses. One-third claim that viewing explicit child pornography led, at least occasionally, to their committing the offense (Marshall, 1988).

Seduction and enticement are often used to manipulate children. In these instances, the pedophile is known to the girl. The pedophile befriends the girl, talking to her, giving her candy, taking her to the store, going for walks with her, letting her watch TV at his house. Gradually, he initiates tactile contact with her, such as having her sit on his lap, rough-housing with her, or giving her a back rub. Eventually, he will attempt to fondle her (Lang & Frenzel, 1988). If she resists, he will stop and try later. He will try added inducements or pressure but will rarely use force (Groth, Hobson, & Gary, 1982). The image of a man in a trenchcoat using candy or other bribes to lure young children into the backseat of a car represents only a small percentage of actual perpetrators. As Table 10.1 demonstrates, the molester is more likely to be a relative or someone else the victim knows. Even though

TABLE 10.1	Relationship Between the Child Victim and the Perpetrator of Sexual Abuse	
	Female Victims (%)	*Male Victims (%)*
Stranger	7	4
Teacher	3	4
Family friend	29	40
Mother's boyfriend	2	1
Older friend of victim	1	4
Older relative	29	13
Older brother	9	4
Stepfather	7	1
Father	7	1
Other	19	17
Number of cases	289	166

Source: Laumann et al., 1994.

Note: The columns add to more than 100% because some respondents were abused by more than one adult.

these latter cases are far more common, they are much less likely to be reported because of the pressures and consequences the molester uses to threaten the child.

Pedophilic acts rarely involve sexual intercourse. The pedophile usually seeks to fondle or touch the child, usually on her genitals, legs, and buttocks. Sometimes the pedophile exposes himself and has the child touch his penis. Occasionally, oral or anal stimulation is involved (Arndt, 1991; Laumann et al., 1994).

Although a pedophile may have sexual relationships with women, they are not necessarily his preferred partners. About half of pedophiles are or have been married. Most married pedophiles claim their marriages are happy, although they describe their wives as controlling and sexually distant. Their frequency of marital intercourse does not differ from that of nonoffenders, but many report a low sex drive and erectile difficulties. Few have serious mental disorders, such as psychosis (Arndt, 1991).

Same-Sex Pedophilia   Same-sex pedophilia is a complicated phenomenon. It does not appear to be as closely linked to homosexuality as cross-sex pedophilia is to heterosexuality. A different kind of psychosexual dynamic seems to be at work for a large number of same-sex pedophiles. Although most same-sex pedophiles have little interest in heterosexual relationships, a significant number do not identify themselves as gay. One study of imprisoned offenders, for example, found that more than half identified themselves as heterosexual or bisexual. Many reject a gay identity or are homophobic. Although some people believe that pedophilia is the means by which the gay community "recruits" boys into homosexuality, pedophiles are soundly rejected by the gay subculture (Peters, 1992).

The mean age of the molested boy is between 10 and 12. A large number of pedophiles describe feelings of love, friendship, or caring for the boy. Others blatantly entice or exploit their victims. Force is rarely used. Voluntary interviews with 27 same-sex pedophiles reveal four themes to explain their involvement with children: (1) Their pedophilic desire feels "natural" to them, (2) children are appealing because they are gentle and truthful, (3) adult-child sexual involvement can be positive for the child, and (4) the relationship is characterized by romantic love, not casual sex (Li, 1990). Such views are generally regarded as cognitive distortions or rationalizations. Adult-child sexual relationships are by definition exploitive. The majority of children report feelings of victimization (Finkelhor, 1990).

The most common activities are fondling and masturbation, usually the man masturbating the boy. Other acts include oral-genital sex, with the adult fellating the boy, and anal sex, with the adult assuming the active role.

Female Pedophilia   Although there are relatively few reports of female pedophiles, there appears to be a small percentage (Arndt, 1991; Rowan, 1988). Female pedophilia appears to be underreported for two reasons (Rowan, 1988). First, male/female stereotypes disguise female sexual contact with children. Men are viewed as aggressive and sexual; women are viewed as maternal and nurturing. Because of these stereotypes, women are given greater freedom than men in touching children and expressing feelings for them. As a consequence, when a pedophilic female embraces, kisses, or pets a child, her behavior may be viewed as nurturing rather than sexual. But when a nonpedophilic male does the same thing, his behavior may be misinterpreted as sexual. Second, the majority of male children who have sexual contact with adult women generally view the experience positively rather than negatively. As a consequence, they do not report the contact (Condy, Templer, Brown, & Veaco, 1987).

Adult female sexual contact with young boys is fairly common. A study of almost 1600 male and female college students and prison inmates found that 16% of male college students and 46% of male prison inmates had sexual contacts with women when they were 12 years old or younger and the women were in their early twenties (Condy et al., 1987). More than half of the men in the study reported having sexual intercourse with the women. The majority of the women were friends, neighbors, babysitters, or strangers. Among the women in the study reporting sexual contact with boys, 0.5% were college students, and 7.5% were prisoners.

More than half the college males and two-thirds of the prisoners in the study reported that, at the time, they felt their childhood experiences with adult females were positive. Twenty-five percent of the college males and 6% of the male prisoners regarded it as negative. And 12% of the college males and 25% of the prisoners regarded the experience as mixed. The critical factor affecting how they evaluated the experience was whether force was used. Those forced into sex generally regarded the experience as negative.

Female sexual abuse of male children differs from male sexual abuse of female children in several significant ways (Condy et al., 1987; Cooper, Swaminath, Baxter, & Poulin, 1990; Fritz, Stoll, & Wagner, 1981; Okami, 1991). First, half the female sexual abusers have sexual intercourse with the male children, whereas relatively few male abusers have sexual intercourse with the female children. Second, female abusers force male children to engage in sexual activities significantly less frequently than male abusers force female children. Third, male children tend not to be as traumatized by female abusers as female children are by male abusers.

Sexual Sadism and Sexual Masochism

Although we tend to think of sadism and masochism as different aspects of a single phenomenon, sadomasochism, sadists are not necessarily masochists, nor are masochists necessarily sadists. Sadism and masochism are separate but sometimes related phenomena. In order to make this distinction clear, the American Psychiatric Association (1994) has created separate categories: sexual sadism and sexual masochism.

There is no clear dividing line between sexual sadism and sexual masochism, and domination and submission. In the case of sadism, coercion separates sexual sadism from domination. But in consensual behaviors, there is no clear distinction. A rule of thumb separating consensual sexual sadism and masochism from domination and submission may be that the activities are extreme, compulsive, and dangerous. Sadomasochistic sex partners often make specific agreements ahead of time concerning the amount of pain and punishment that will occur during sexual activity. Nevertheless, the acting out of fantasies involves risk, such as physical injury (for example, a deep cut through the skin); thus, it is important that individuals communicate their preferences and limits before they engage in any new activity.

> I had to give up masochism—I was enjoying it too much.
>
> —*Mel Calman*

Sexual Sadism   According to the *DSM-IV,* a person may be diagnosed with **sexual sadism** if, over a period of at least 6 months, he or she experiences intense, recurring sexual urges or fantasies involving real (not simulated) acts in which physical or psychological harm (including humiliation) is inflicted upon a victim for purposes of sexual arousal. The individual has acted on these urges or finds them extremely distressful (American Psychiatric Association, 1994). Characteristic symptoms include obsessive, compelling sexual thoughts and fantasies involving acts centering on a victim's physical suffering. The victim may be a consenting masochist or someone abducted by a sadist. The victim may be tortured, raped, mutilated, or killed; often the victim is physically restrained and blindfolded or gagged (Money, 1990).

Most rapes are not committed by sexual sadists, but sadistic rapes do account for about 5% of all stranger rapes (Groth, 1979). Sadistic rapes are the most brutal. The rapist finds "intentional maltreatment gratifying and takes pleasure in torment, anguish, distress, helplessness, and suffering" (Groth, 1979). There is often bondage and a ritualistic quality to such rapes.

Sexual Masochism   For a diagnosis of **sexual masochism** to be made, a person must experience for a period of at least 6 months intense, recurring sexual urges or fantasies involving real (not simulated) acts of being "humiliated, beaten, bound, or otherwise made to suffer." The individual has acted on these urges or is highly distressed by them (American Psychiatric Association, 1994). The degree of pain one must experience to achieve sexual arousal varies from symbolic gestures to severe mutilations.

Autoerotic Asphyxia   **Autoerotic asphyxia,** a form of sexual masochism linking strangulation with masturbation, causes up to 1000 deaths annually. Those who participate in this activity seek to heighten their masturbatory arousal and orgasm by cutting off the oxygen supply to the brain. A person may engage in this practice either alone or with a partner (American Psychiatric Association, 1994). If death occurs, it is usually accidental.

Because of the secrecy and shame that accompany this and other masturbatory activities, it is difficult to estimate the number of individuals who find this practice arousing. Reports by survivors are extremely rare. Although the majority of those who die accidentally are adolescent heterosexual males, men in their twenties and thirties have also been victims of this practice (Hazelwood, Burgess, & Dietz, 1983).

The practice involves a variety of techniques, all of which cut off oxygen to the brain and can cause death. It is suggested that the interference with the blood supply to the brain causes cerebral anoxia (lack of oxygen), which is experienced as giddiness, light-headedness, and exhilaration, thereby heightening and reinforcing the masturbatory sensation (Resnick, 1972).

Individuals often use ropes, cords, or chains along with padding around the neck to prevent telltale signs. Others may place bags or blankets over their heads. Still others inhale asphyxiating gases such as aerosol sprays or amyl nitrate ("poppers"), a drug used to treat heart pain. The corpses are usually found either naked or partially clothed, often in women's clothing. Various forms of bondage have also been observed (Blanchard & Hucker, 1991).

The characteristic features that rule out the possibility of suicide are the presence of pornographic materials, the use of a mirror or video camera, evidence of penile engorgement and/or ejaculation, and the absence of a suicide note (Sheehan & Garfinkel, 1988).

The origins of the syndrome are obscure but are believed to date back to the seventeenth century (Rosenblum & Faber, 1979). During that time period, some people in England experimented with self-hanging as a possible cure for impotence (Resnik, 1972). Anthropologists have reported observing similar practices among Eskimo children, some Indian tribes in North and South America, and a few Asian societies (Rosenblum & Faber, 1979).

Although researchers have some understanding of why people participate, it is more important that medical personnel, parents, and other adults be aware of this practice so they can recognize signs of it and respond with strategies commensurate with its seriousness. Those who engage in such sexual practices rarely realize the potential consequences of their behavior; therefore, parents and others must be alert to physical and other telltale signs. An unusual neck bruise; bloodshot eyes; disoriented behavior, especially after the person has been alone for a while; and unexplained possession of or fascination with ropes or chains are the key signs (Saunders, 1989). Until we as a society can educate about, recognize, and respond to autoerotic asphyxia assertively and with compassion, we can expect to see more deaths as a result of this practice.

■ Studying atypical and paraphilic sexual behaviors reveals the variety and complexity of sexual behavior. It also underlines the limits of tolerance. Some unconventional sexual behaviors, undertaken in private between consenting adults as the source of erotic pleasure, are of concern only to the people involved. As long as physical or psychological harm is not done to the self or others, it is no one's place to judge. Coercive paraphilic behavior, however, may be injurious and should be treated.

SUMMARY

Atypical Versus Paraphilic Behavior

- *Atypical sexual behavior* is consensual behavior in which less than the majority of individuals engage. Atypical sexual behavior is not abnormal behavior, the definition of which varies from culture to culture and from one historical period to another.

- Recurring, intense, sexually arousing fantasies, urges, or behaviors involving nonhuman objects, suffering or humiliation, or children or other nonconsenting persons or animals are known as *paraphilias*. Paraphilias tend to be injurious, compulsive, and long-standing. They may be noncoercive or coercive.

Atypical Sexual Behaviors

- *Domination and submission (D/S)*, also known as *sadomasochism (S&M)*, is a form of fantasy sex with power as the central element.

Noncoercive Paraphilias

- Although there are no reliable statistics on the number of individuals involved, paraphilic activities are widespread in the nonoffender population.

- *Fetishism* is sexual attraction to objects.

- *Transvestism* is the wearing of clothes of a member of the other sex, usually for sexual arousal.

Coercive Paraphilias

- *Zoophilia* involves deriving sexual excitement from animals.

- *Voyeurism* is the nonconsensual and secret observation of others for the purpose of sexual arousal.

- *Exhibitionism* is the exposure of the genitals to a nonconsenting stranger.

- *Telephone scatologia* is the nonconsensual telephoning of strangers and use of obscene language.

- *Frotteurism* involves touching or rubbing against a nonconsenting person for the purpose of sexual arousal.

- *Necrophilia* is sexual activity with a corpse.

- *Pedophilia* refers to sexual arousal and contact with children age 13 or younger by adults, or with children age 11 or younger by adolescents older than age 16. Child sexual abuse is illegal in every state. For most *pedophiles,* the fact that a child is a child is more important than gender. Heterosexuals and gay men may both be pedophilically attracted to boys; gay pedophiles are less attracted to girls.

- The majority of pedophiles know their victim. About half of pedophiles have been married. The most common activities are fondling and masturbation.

- There are relatively few reported cases of female pedophilia, but it may be underreported for two reasons. Because of stereotypes of female nurturance, pedophilic activities may not be recognized; and the majority of male children apparently view the event positively or neutrally.

- *Sexual sadism* refers to sexual urges or fantasies of intentionally inflicting real physical or psychological pain or suffering on a partner. About 5% of all rapes are sadistic.

- *Sexual masochism* is the recurring sexual urge or fantasy of being humiliated or caused to suffer through real acts, not simulated ones.

- *Autoerotic asphyxia* is a form of sexual masochism linking strangulation with masturbatory activities.

SUGGESTED READING

Arndt, William B., Jr. (1991). *Gender Disorders and the Paraphilias.* Madison, CT: International Universities Press. A comprehensive look at transvestism, transsexuality, and the paraphilias.

Dailey, Dennis (Ed.). (1988). *The Sexually Unusual: A Guide to Understanding and Helping.* New York: Harrington Park Press. A thoughtful and often compassionate examination of what are usually considered paraphilias.

Favazza, A. R. (1996). *Bodies Under Siege: Self-Mutilation and Body Modification in Culture and Psychiatry* (2nd ed.). Baltimore: Johns Hopkins University Press. A report on the self-mutilation that some individuals go through for a variety of personal and cultural reasons.

Garber, Marjorie. (1992). *Vested Interests: Cross-Dressing and Cultural Anxiety.* New York: Routledge. A provocative study of the role of cross-dressing in contemporary culture. Cross-dressers, the author argues, call attention to cultural inconsistencies about being male and female in our society.

Maletsky, Barry M. (1991). *Treating the Sexual Offender.* Newbury Park, CA: Sage. An extensive and detailed examination of sex offenders, most of whom were offenders against children.

Stoller, Robert J. (1991). *Pain and Passion: A Psychoanalyst Explores the World of S&M.* New York: Plenum. Theories and research about sadomasochism, as well as insights into the S&M subculture.

11

Contraception and Birth Control

*T*ODAY, MORE THAN EVER BEFORE, we are aware of the impact of fertility on our own lives as well as on the world. Reproduction, once considered strictly a personal matter, is now a subject of open debate and political action. Yet regardless of our public views, we must each confront fertility on a personal level. In taking charge of our reproductive destinies, we must be informed about the available methods of birth control. But information is only part of the picture. We also need to understand our own personal needs, values, and habits so that we can choose methods we will use consistently, thereby minimizing our risks.

In this chapter, we begin by examining the psychology of risk taking and the role of individual responsibility in contraception. We then describe in detail the numerous contraceptive devices and techniques (including abstinence) that are used today: methods of use, effectiveness rates, advantages, and possible problems. Finally, we look at the process of abortion and its effect on individuals and society.

The command "be fruitful and multiply" was promulgated according to our authorities, when the population of the world consisted of two people.

—*Dean Inge (1860–1954)*

RISK AND RESPONSIBILITY

In the United States, nearly 60% of pregnancies are unintended (CDC, 1997b). Although on average a woman has only about a 2–4% chance of becoming pregnant during intercourse without contraception, timing affects the odds:

- If intercourse occurs the day before ovulation, the chance of pregnancy is about 30%.

- If intercourse occurs on the day of ovulation, the chance of pregnancy is about 15%.

- Over a period of a year, couples who do not use contraception have a 90% chance of pregnancy.

Because the potential for getting pregnant is so high for a sexually active couple, it would seem reasonable that sexually active couples would use contraception to avoid unintended pregnancy. Unfortunately, all too often this is not the case. One major study found that during their first intercourse, only about 59% of couples used contraception (Abma, Chandra, Mosher, Peterson, Piccinino, 1997). However, as men and women age, they become more consistent contraceptive users. About 64% of all women who could become pregnant do use some form of contraception (U.S. Dept. of Health and Human Services, 1997).

Numerous studies have indicated that the most consistent users of contraception are men and women who explicitly communicate about the subject. Those at greatest risk are those in casual dating relationships and those who infrequently discuss contraception with their partners or others. A review of the literature on the interpersonal factors in contraceptive use concludes: "Individuals in stable, serious relationships of long duration who had frequent, predictable patterns of sexual activity were most likely to use contraception" (Milan & Kilmann, 1987).

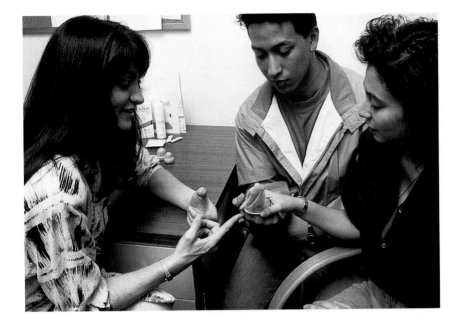

Planning contraception requires us to acknowledge our sexuality. One way a responsible couple can reduce the risk of pregnancy is by visiting a family planning clinic—together.

Women, Men, and Birth Control: Who Is Responsible?

Because women bear children and have most of the responsibility for raising them, they may have a greater interest than their partners in controlling their fertility. Also, it has generally been easier to keep one egg from being fertilized once a month than to stop millions of sperm during each act of intercourse. For these and other reasons, responsibility for birth control has traditionally been seen as the woman's job, but attitudes are changing. A recent large-scale survey (Billy, Grady, Lincoln-Hanson, & Tanfer, 1996) has revealed that we as a society no longer view the responsibility for birth control to lie with women. Rather, the majority of men (as well as women) perceive that there is gender equality in sexual decision making and equal responsibility for decisions about contraception. Eighty-eight percent of the men surveyed agreed that a man has the same responsibilities as a woman for the children they have together. This attitude shift is taking hold in such countries as Italy and Japan, where male methods of contraception (such as withdrawal or condoms) are used more than female methods. Although withdrawal is not considered a reliable method of birth control, the condom is quite effective when used properly, especially in combination with a spermicide.

In addition to using a condom, a man can help take contraceptive responsibility by (1) exploring ways of making love without intercourse; (2) helping to pay doctor or clinic bills and sharing the cost of pills, implants, or other birth control supplies; (3) checking on supplies, helping to keep track of the woman's menstrual cycle, and helping his partner with her part in the birth control routine; and (4) in a long-term relationship, if no (or no more) children are wanted, having a vasectomy.

MOST PEOPLE KNOW they are taking a chance when they don't use contraception. But, as demonstrated in Kristin Luker's classic study (1975) of contraceptive risk taking, the more frequently a person takes chances with unprotected intercourse without resultant pregnancy, the more likely he or she is to take chances again. A subtle psychology develops: Somehow, apparently by willpower, "good vibes," or the gods' kindly intervention, the woman does not get pregnant. Eventually, the woman or couple will feel almost magically invulnerable to pregnancy. Each time they are lucky, their risk taking is reinforced.

The consequences of an unintended pregnancy—economic hardships, adoption, or abortion—may be overwhelming. So why do people take chances in the first place? Part of the reason is faulty knowledge. People often underestimate how easy it is to get pregnant. Or, they may not know how to use a contraceptive method correctly.

Let's examine some of the perceived costs of contraceptive planning versus the anticipated benefits of pregnancy.

Perceived Costs of Contraceptive Planning

One reason people avoid taking steps to prevent pregnancy is that they don't want to acknowledge their own sexuality. On the surface, it may seem fairly simple to acknowledge that we are sexual beings, especially if we have conscious sexual desires and engage in sexual intercourse. Yet acknowledging our sexuality is not necessarily easy, for it may be accompanied by feelings of guilt, conflict, and shame. The younger or less experienced we are, the more difficult it is to acknowledge our sexuality.

Planning contraception requires us to admit not only that we are sexual but also that we plan to be sexually active. Without such planning, men and women can pretend that their sexual intercourse "just happens"—in a moment of passion, when they have been drinking, or when the moon is full—even though it may happen frequently.

Another reason people don't use contraception is difficulty in obtaining it. It is often embarrassing for sexually inexperienced people to be seen in contexts that identify them as sexual beings. The person who sits behind you in your chemistry class may be sitting next to you in the waiting room of the family planning clinic. If you go to the drugstore to buy condoms, who knows if your mother, teacher, or minister might be down the aisle buying toothpaste (or contraceptives, for that matter) and might see you? The cost of contraceptives is also a problem for some. Although free or low-cost contraceptives may be obtained through family planning clinics or other agencies, people may have transportation or work considerations that keep them away.

Many people also have trouble planning and continuing contraception. Contraceptive developments in the past few decades (especially the pill) shifted responsibility from the man to the woman. Required to more consciously define themselves as sexual, women have had to abandon traditional, passive sexual roles. Some women, however, are reluctant to plan contraceptive use because they fear they will be regarded as sexually aggressive or promiscuous.

Because it is women who get pregnant, men tend to be unaware of their responsibility or to downplay their role in conception and pregnancy, although with the reemerging popularity of the condom, responsibility may become more balanced (especially if women insist on it). Nevertheless, males, especially adolescents, often lack the awareness that supports contraceptive planning. Yet males are more fertile than females. The average male is fertile 24 hours a day for 50 years or more. Females, in contrast, are fertile only a day or two out of the month for 35 or so years.

Preventing Sexually Transmitted Diseases

Most sexually transmitted diseases (STDs), if treated in their early stages, are not particularly dangerous. AIDS is the notable exception; it is a terminal illness. Because of AIDS, people are much more aware of their vulnerability to STDs. (STDs are discussed in Chapter 15; HIV and AIDS are discussed in Chapter 16.)

Fortunately, there are contraceptive methods that do excellent double duty as prophylactics (disease-preventers). Latex rubber as well as polyurethane condoms provide a barrier against the herpes virus, chlamydia, gonococcus, and HIV (the AIDS virus). They work both ways, protecting

Many people, especially women using the pill, practice birth control consistently and effectively within a steady relationship but give up their contraceptive practices if the relationship breaks up. They define themselves as sexual only within the context of a relationship. When men or women begin a new relationship, they may not use contraception because the relationship has not yet become established. They do not expect to have sexual intercourse or to have it often, so they are willing to take chances.

Using contraceptive devices such as a condom or diaphragm may destroy the feeling of "spontaneity" in sex. For those who justify their sexual behavior by romantic impulsiveness, using these devices seems cold and mechanical. Others do not use them because they feel doing so would interrupt the passion of the moment. A survey of 5331 heterosexual Americans found that 41% believed that condoms reduce sexual pleasure, 37% worried that suggesting condom use would cause their partner to distrust them, and 35% were embarrassed about buying condoms (Choi, Rickman, & Catania, 1994). Males, Blacks, Latinos, and less-educated people were more likely than others to dislike condoms. The researchers concluded that condom use should be portrayed as "a caring and responsible behavior for men."

Anticipated Benefits of Pregnancy

Many men and women fantasize that even an "accidental" pregnancy might be beneficial. Ambivalence about pregnancy is a powerful incentive *not* to use contraception (Demb, 1991). What are some of the perceived benefits of pregnancy?

First, for many, being pregnant proves that a woman is indeed feminine on the most fundamental biological level. Getting a woman pregnant provides similar proof of masculinity for a man. Being a mother is one of the most basic definitions of traditional womanhood. In an era in which there is considerable confusion about women's roles, pregnancy helps, even forces, a woman to define herself in a traditional manner. Young men may also find the idea of fatherhood compelling. They may feel that fathering a child will give them a sense of accomplishment and an aura of maturity.

Pregnancy also proves beyond any doubt that a person is fertile. Many men and women have lingering doubts about whether they can have children. This is especially true for couples who have used contraception for a long time, but it is also true for those who constantly take chances. If they have taken chances many times without pregnancy resulting, they may begin to have doubts about their fertility.

Another anticipated benefit of pregnancy is that it requires a couple to define their relationship and commitment to each other. It is a form of testing, albeit often an unconscious one. It raises many questions that must be answered. How will the partner react? Will it lead to marriage or a breakup? Will it solidify a marriage or a relationship? Will the partner be loving and understanding, or will he or she be angry and rejecting? What is the real nature of the commitment? Many men and women unconsciously expect their partners to be pleased, but this is not always the reaction they get.

Finally, pregnancy involves not only the couple but their parents as well (especially the woman's). Pregnancy forces a young person's parents to pay attention and deal with him or her as an adult. Being pregnant puts a female on the very verge of adulthood, for in most cultures, marriage and motherhood are major rites of passage. Similarly, fatherhood is an adult status for a male, transforming him from a boy into a man. Pregnancy may mean many things in regard to the parent-child relationship. It may be a sign of rebellion, a form of punishment for a parental lack of caring, a plea for help and understanding, or an insistence on autonomy, independence, or adulthood.

the wearer of the condom from a disease carried by his partner, and vice versa. (Animal membrane condoms, however, do *not* protect against all disease-carrying organisms—notably the viruses, which include HIV—and should only be used for contraception by couples in mutually monogamous relationships who know they are free of STDs.)

It is vital to note that condoms (or any other methods) do *not* guarantee absolute protection from STDs, just as they do not guarantee absolute protection from pregnancy. They have been known to leak, break, or slip off. Furthermore, disease may be spread by hands, mouth, and genital areas other than the penis and vagina (if there are herpes lesions on the scrotum or vulva, for example).

What is the message of these posters? What myths or stereotypes do they challenge?

Spermicides, chemicals that kill sperm, offer protection against some STDs. For this reason, condoms pretreated with spermicide or used with spermicidal foam or film can provide extra protection, although there is no way to be sure that *all* the disease organisms will be killed.

Barrier methods for women—the diaphragm, cervical cap, and female condom—help protect against diseases of the cervix and uterus. The prophylactic function of these barriers is increased when they are used with spermicide.

There is no absolute guarantee against contracting an STD (or becoming pregnant) except total abstinence from sexual intercourse. Therefore, the value of caution and sound judgment for sexually active people cannot be overstated.

METHODS OF CONTRACEPTION AND BIRTH CONTROL

The methods we use to prevent pregnancy or to keep it from progressing vary widely according to our personal beliefs, tastes, health, and other life circumstances. For many people, especially women, the search for an "ideal" method of birth control is one of ongoing frustration. Some methods pose health risks to certain women, others run counter to religious or moral beliefs, and others are inconvenient or aesthetically displeasing. There are several methods and techniques to choose from, however, and scientific research is slowly increasing our options for safe and effective contraception. Most individuals and couples can find a method that they can use with comfort and, most important, with regularity.

Birth Control and Contraception: What's the Difference?

Although the terms "birth control" and "contraception" are often used interchangeably, there is actually a subtle difference in meaning. **Birth control** is any means of preventing a birth from taking place. Thus, methods that prevent a fertilized egg from implanting in the uterine wall (such as the IUD in some instances) and methods that remove the **conceptus**—the fertilized egg, embryo, or fetus—from the uterus (such as "morning-after" pills and surgical abortions) are forms of birth control. These are not, however, true contraceptive methods. **Contraception,** the prevention of conception altogether, is the category of birth control in which the sperm and egg are prevented from uniting. This is done in a variety of ways, including barrier methods, such as condoms and diaphragms, which place a physical barrier between sperm and egg; spermicides, which kill the sperm before they can get to the egg; and hormonal methods, such as the pill and implants, which inhibit the release of the oocyte from the ovary.

Choosing a Method

To be fully responsible in using birth control, a person must know what options he or she has available, how reliable these methods are, and the advantages and disadvantages (including possible side effects) of each method. Thus, it is important to be aware of your own personal health issues, as well as the specifics of the methods themselves.

> The best contraceptive is a glass of cold water: not before or after, but instead.
>
> —*Pakistani delegate to the International Planned Parenthood Conference*

Choosing the best form of birth control for yourself and your partner, especially if you have not been practicing contraception, is not easy. But knowing the facts about the methods gives you a solid basis from which to make decisions, and more security once a decision is reached. If you need to choose a birth control method for yourself, remember that *the best method is the one you will use consistently.* (For help in choosing which method of birth control might be the most comfortable, see "Guidelines for Choosing a Contraceptive Method.") When you are having intercourse, a condom left in a purse or wallet, a diaphragm in the bedside drawer, or a forgotten pill in its packet on the other side of town is *not* an effective means of birth control.

In the following discussions of method effectiveness, "theoretical effectiveness" implies perfectly consistent and correct use; "user effectiveness" refers to *actual* use (and misuse) based on studies by health-care organizations, medical practitioners, academic researchers, and pharmaceutical companies. User effectiveness is sometimes significantly lower than theoretical effectiveness because of factors that keep people from using a method properly or consistently These factors may be inherent in the method or may be the result of a variety of influences on the user.

Sexual Abstinence and Outercourse

Before we begin our discussion of devices and techniques for preventing conception, we must acknowledge the oldest and most reliable birth control method of all. **Abstinence**—refraining from sexual intercourse—is a legitimate personal choice. Those who choose not to express their sensuality or sexuality through genital contact, however, are sometimes stigmatized as uptight, frigid, or weird. The term "celibacy" is sometimes used interchangeably with "abstinence." We use the word "abstinence" because "celibacy" often implies the avoidance of *all* forms of sexual activity and, often, the religious commitment to not marry or to maintain a nonsexual lifestyle.

IT IS IMPORTANT to choose a method of birth control that works. All the methods offered at a family planning clinic will work well—if you use them properly.

It is also important to choose a method you will like! To make an informed decision, ask yourself these questions: What type of birth control are you thinking about? Have you ever used it before? If yes, how long did you use it?

Circle Your Answers

Are you afraid of using this method?	Yes	No	Don't know
Would you rather not use this method?	Yes	No	Don't know
Will you have trouble remembering to use this method?	Yes	No	Don't know
Have you ever become pregnant while using this method?	Yes	No	Don't know
Will you have trouble using this method carefully?	Yes	No	Don't know
Do you have unanswered questions about this method?	Yes	No	Don't know
Does this method make menstrual periods longer or more painful?	Yes	No	Don't know
Does this method cost more than you can afford?	Yes	No	Don't know
Does this method ever cause serious health problems?	Yes	No	Don't know
Do you object to this method because of religious beliefs?	Yes	No	Don't know
Have you already had problems using this method?	Yes	No	Don't know
Is your partner opposed to this method?	Yes	No	Don't know
Are you using this method without your partner's knowledge?	Yes	No	Don't know
Will using this method embarrass you?	Yes	No	Don't know
Will using this method embarrass your partner?	Yes	No	Don't know
Will you enjoy intercourse less because of this method?	Yes	No	Don't know
Will this method interrupt lovemaking?	Yes	No	Don't know
Has a nurse or doctor ever told you not to use this method?	Yes	No	Don't know

Do you have any "Don't know" answers? If you do, ask your clinic counselor, college's health staff, or physician to help you with more information.

Do you have any "Yes" answers? "Yes" answers mean you may not like this method. Ask a medical person to talk this over with you. You may need to think about another method.

Source: Adapted from Hatcher et al., 1994.

Individuals who choose not to have intercourse are still free to express affection (and give and receive sexual satisfaction if they so desire) in a variety of ways. Ways to show love without making babies include talking, hugging, massaging, kissing, petting, and manual and oral stimulation of the genitals. Those who choose sexual abstinence as their method of birth control need to communicate this clearly to their dates or partners. They should also be informed about other forms of contraception. And, in the event that either partner experiences a change of mind, it can't hurt to have a condom handy. An advantage of abstinence is that refraining from sexual activity allows a couple to get to know and trust each other gradually before facing the emotions and stresses brought about by high degrees of intimacy.

Another method of preventing pregnancy, often overlooked, is **outercourse**—the choice to be sexual without engaging in penile-vaginal intercourse. Considered by some to be a viable method of birth control, outer-

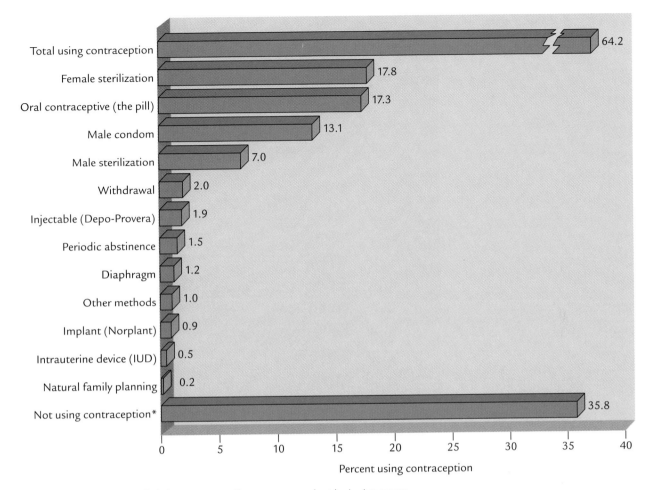

FIGURE 11.1 Types of Contraceptives Used by Men and Women Age 15–44 in the United States, 1995. (*Source:* U.S. Department of Health and Human Services, 1997.)

*Includes being surgically sterile, being pregnant, seeking pregnancy, and not having intercourse.

course includes a variety of sexual behaviors, among them, kissing, massage, petting, manual masturbation, and oral and anal sex. As a method of birth control, outercourse is simple to use, inexpensive, pleasurable, highly effective if the man keeps his penis away from the woman's vagina, and relatively free of side effects. In addition to preventing pregnancy, it may also be chosen as a primary or temporary activity during an outbreak of a sexually transmitted disease or immediately following childbirth or abortion.

Hormonal Methods: The Pill and Implants

In addition to the tried-and-true birth control pill, other forms of hormonal contraception are also available. These include capsules that are implanted under a woman's skin and injectable hormones for both women and men.

The Pill   **Oral contraceptives,** popularly called "the pill," are the most popular form of reversible contraception in the United States (Figure 11.1). The pill is actually a series of pills (20, 21, or 28 to a package) containing

Oral Contraceptives

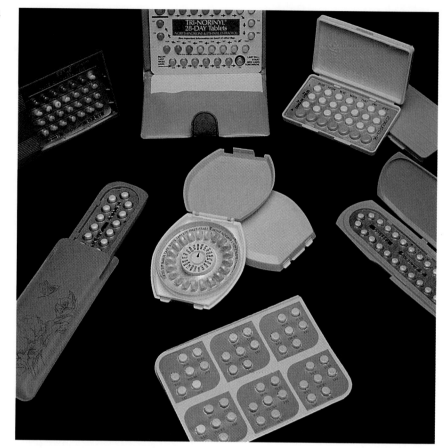

synthetic estrogen and/or progesterone that regulates egg production and the menstrual cycle. When taken for birth control, oral contraceptives accomplish some or all of the following:

- Inhibit ovulation.
- Thicken cervical mucus (preventing sperm entry).
- Change the lining of the uterus to inhibit implantation of the fertilized ovum.
- Alter the rate of ovum transport.

The pill produces basically the same chemical conditions that would exist in a woman's body if she were pregnant.

Oral contraceptives must be prescribed by a physician or family planning clinic. Approximately 32 combinations are available, containing various amounts of hormones. Most commonly prescribed are the combination pills, which contain a fairly standard amount of estrogen (usually about 35 micrograms) and different doses of progestin according to the pill type. In the triphasic pill, the amount of progestin is altered during the cycle, purportedly to approximate the normal hormonal pattern. (The various manufacturers of the triphasic pills seem to disagree with one another, however, as to what constitutes a normal hormonal pattern [Hatcher et al., 1994].) There is also a "minipill" containing progestin only, but it is generally prescribed only for women who should not take estrogen. It is considered slightly less effective than the combined pill, and it must be taken with precise, unfailing regularity to be effective.

With the 20- and 21-day pills, one pill is taken each day until they are all used; 2–5 days later, the menstrual flow will begin, which typically is quite light. (If the flow does not begin, the woman should start the next series of pills 7 days after the end of the last series. If she repeatedly has no flow, she should talk to her health-care practitioner.) On the fifth day of her menstrual flow, the woman starts the next series of pills.

The 28-day pills are taken continuously. Seven of the pills have no hormones. They are there simply to avoid breaks in the routine; some women prefer them because they find them easier to remember.

The pill is considered the most effective birth control method available (except for sterilization) when used correctly. The pill is not effective when used carelessly. It must be taken every day, as close as possible to the same time each day. If one is missed, it should be taken as soon as the woman remembers, and the next one taken on schedule. If two are missed, the method cannot be relied on, and an additional form of contraception should be used for the rest of the cycle. A year's supply of birth control pills costs between $100 and $300.

Birth control pills in no way protect against sexually transmitted diseases. Women on the pill should consider the additional use of a condom to reduce the risk of STDs.

EFFECTIVENESS   The combined pill is more than 99.5% effective theoretically. User effectiveness (the rate shown by actual studies) is between 95% and 98%. Progestin-only pills are somewhat less effective and may contribute to irregular bleeding. However, they have fewer side effects and health risks than the combined pill.

ADVANTAGES   Pills are easy to take. They are dependable. No applications or interruptions are necessary before or during intercourse. Some women experience side effects that please them, such as more regular or reduced menstrual flow, fewer menstrual cramps, enlarged breasts, or less acne. There may also be an increase in bone mass among women in their twenties.

POSSIBLE PROBLEMS   There are many possible side effects, which may or may not bother the user, from taking the pill. Those most often reported are

- Change (usually a decrease) in menstrual flow
- Breast tenderness
- Nausea or vomiting
- Weight gain or loss

Some of the other side effects are

- Spotty darkening of the skin
- Nervousness, dizziness
- Loss of scalp hair
- Change in appetite
- Change (most commonly, a decrease) in sex drive

TABLE 11.1	ACHES: Symptoms of Possible Problems Associated with the Birth Control Pill	
Initial	*Symptom*	*Possible Problem*
A	Abdominal pain (severe)	Gallbladder disease, liver tumor, or blood clot
C	Chest pain (severe) or shortness of breath	Blood clot in lungs or heart attack
H	Headaches (severe)	Stroke, high blood pressure, or migraine headache
E	Eye problems: blurred vision, flashing lights, or blindness	Stroke, high blood pressure, or temporary vascular problems at many possible sites
S	Severe leg pain (calf or thigh)	Blood clot in legs

Source: Adaped from Hatcher et al., 1994.

- Mood changes
- Increase in body hair
- Increase in vaginal discharges and yeast infections

These side effects can sometimes be eliminated by changing the prescription, but not always. Certain women react unfavorably to the pill because of existing health factors or extra sensitivity to female hormones. Women with heart or kidney diseases, asthma, high blood pressure, diabetes, epilepsy, gall bladder disease, or sickle-cell anemia and those prone to migraine headaches or depression are usually considered poor candidates for the pill. Certain medications may react differently or unfavorably with the pill, either diminishing in their therapeutic effect or interfering with oral contraceptive effectiveness. Thus, it is important to check with your doctor before starting any new prescriptions if you are taking the pill.

The pill also creates certain health risks, but to what extent is a matter of controversy. (For a summary of symptoms of possible problems associated with the birth control pill, see Table 11.1.) Women taking the pill stand a greater chance of problems with circulatory diseases, blood clotting, heart attack, and certain kinds of liver tumors. There is also an increased risk of contracting chlamydia, an STD. The health risks are low for the young (about half the number of risks encountered at childbirth), but they increase with age. The risk for smokers, women over 35, and those with certain other health disorders is about four times as great as childbirth. For women over 40, the risks are considered high. Current literature on the pill especially emphasizes the risks for women who smoke. Definite risks of cardiovascular complications and various forms of cancer exist because of the synergistic action of the ingredients in cigarettes and oral contraceptives.

A number of studies have linked pill use with certain types of cancer, but they are not conclusive. The risk of some types of cancer, such as ovarian and endometrial, appears to be significantly *reduced* by pill use (Hankinson, Colditz, Hunter, Spencer, Rosner, & Stampflau, 1992). On the other hand, a link between cervical cancer and long-term pill use has been suggested by several studies (Vessey et al., 1983; World Health Organization, 1992). Reg-

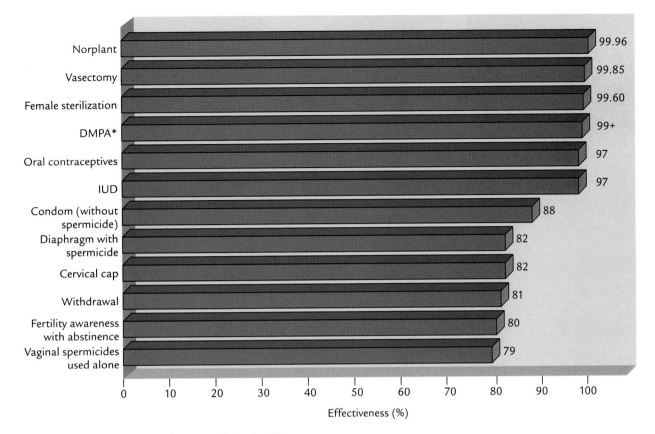

*Failure rates for Depo-Provera vary but are usually less than 1%.

FIGURE 11.2 Effectiveness Rates of Various Contraceptive Methods During the First Year of Use. (*Source:* Adapted from Hatcher et al., 1990, p. 134.)

ular Pap smears (see Chapter 13) are recommended as an excellent defense against cervical cancer for pill users and nonusers alike.

Findings regarding the pill and breast cancer have been conflicting. Recently, however, a worldwide epidemiological study analyzing more than 53,000 women with breast cancer and another 100,000 without the disease found that women who are currently using combined oral contraceptives or have used them in the past 10 years are at a slightly increased risk of having breast cancer diagnosed (Collaborative Group on Hormonal Factors in Breast Cancer, 1996). This same study also reported no evidence of an increased risk 10 or more years after use was stopped. Furthermore, the cancers that were diagnosed in women who had used oral contraceptives were less advanced clinically than the cancers that were diagnosed in those who had never used them.

Certain other factors may need to be taken into account in determining if oral contraceptives are appropriate. Young girls who have not matured physically may have their development slowed by early pill use. Nursing mothers cannot use pills containing estrogen because the hormone inhibits milk production. Some lactating women use the minipill successfully (Hatcher et al., 1994).

Millions of women use the pill with moderate to high degrees of satisfaction. For many women, if personal health or family history does not contraindicate it, the pill is both effective (Figure 11.2) and safe.

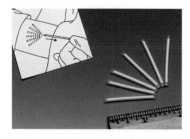

Contraceptive implants are inserted under the skin of a woman's arm in a 10-minute office procedure. One set of implants prevents pregnancy for 5 years.

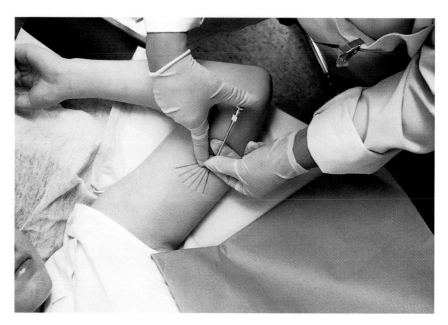

Implants   In December 1990, the FDA approved the contraceptive **implant,** a set of thin, matchstick-sized capsules containing levonorgestrel (a progestin) that is implanted under a woman's skin. Over a period of up to 5 years, the hormone is slowly released. When the implants are removed, which may be done at any time, fertility is restored. A set of soft tubes is surgically implanted under the skin of the upper arm in a simple office procedure with a local anesthetic. Once implanted, the capsules are not visible (or are barely visible) but may be felt under the skin. The implants, under the trade name **Norplant,** are currently on the market in more than 14 countries. The cost of the implant, including insertion and removal, ranges from $375 to $700, depending on where it is obtained. The cost may seem high, but it is probably less expensive than a 5-year supply of birth control pills; however, the up-front costs may be too high for some women (Westfall & Main, 1995).

More than 1 million American women received Norplant implants during the first 3 years after it came on the market, but sales dropped sharply beginning in 1992. Although surveys have shown a high satisfaction rate among Norplant users, negative publicity associated with lawsuits against the manufacturer caused sales to plummet from 800 units a day to about 60 (Kolata, 1995). Many of the law firms involved in these lawsuits are the same ones involved in earlier devastating suits against the manufacturers of silicone breast implants. (One such manufacturer, Dow Corning Corporation, filed for bankruptcy in 1995 as a result.) Norplant has been found to be safe in a number of controlled studies, but whether American women will continue to have the implant as a contraceptive option remains to be seen.

EFFECTIVENESS   Although Norplant has not been observed or tested to the degree that other contraceptives have, initial reports indicate an effectiveness rate of 99.01% in the first year, decreasing slowly with each additional year of use. The effectiveness rate at the end of 5 years of use is about 96.3%. Effectiveness rates are slightly lower for women who weigh more than 155 lb. The implants should be removed after 5 years, as their effectiveness drops sharply in the sixth year. New implants may be inserted at that time. Removable progestin implants such as Norplant may be the most effective reversible contraceptive now available.

ADVANTAGES   Convenience is clearly a big advantage of the implant. Once the implant is in, there's nothing to remember, buy, do, or take care of. Because implants contain no estrogen, users generally experience fewer side effects than with the pill. Many users report light to nonexistent menstrual flow and a reduction in menstrual cramps and pain. The risk of endometrial cancer may be reduced (Hatcher et al., 1994). The thickened cervical mucus resulting from Norplant use has a protective effect against pelvic inflammatory disease. (PID is discussed further in Chapter 15.) In addition, fertility is not compromised; a woman's ability to become pregnant returns within 24 hours after removal of the implant (Darney, 1994).

POSSIBLE PROBLEMS   Side effects of contraceptive implants may be similar to those of oral contraceptives. The chief negative side effect, experienced by about half of implant users, is a change in the pattern of menstrual bleeding, such as lengthened periods, spotting between periods, or having no bleeding at all. The menstrual cycle usually becomes more regular after 1 year of use (Cullins, 1994). Nevertheless, more than 1 in 10 women have the implant removed within 1 year because of side effects (Frank, Poindexter, Cornin, Cox, & Bateman, 1993). Progestin implants should not be used by women with acute liver disease, breast cancer, blood clots, or unexplained vaginal bleeding, nor should they be used by women who are breast-feeding or those who may possibly be pregnant. Implant users are advised not to smoke. Difficult and painful removal of the device has also been reported (Roberts, 1994). Possible long-term negative effects are not known at this time.

Depo-Provera (DMPA)   The injectable contraceptive medroxyprogesterone acetate, **Depo-Provera,** or **DMPA,** which provides protection from pregnancy for 3–6 months, is used in more than 80 countries throughout the world and has recently been approved for use in the United States. Generally speaking, DMPA has been considered to be remarkably free of serious side effects and complications. In approximately half the women taking DMPA, menstruation stops completely after a year of use (Stehlin, 1997). Menstrual spotting, weight gain, headaches, breast tenderness, dizziness, and mood changes have also been reported, though less frequently (Earl & David, 1994). DMPA may also contribute to delayed fertility (up to a year in some cases) until its effects wear off. However, because the drug does not accumulate in the body, the return to fertility is independent of the number of injections received, though it may be affected by a woman's height and weight (Stehlin, 1997). The effectiveness rate is 99%, on par with Norplant. A woman should get her first injection of DMPA within 5 days of the start of her menstrual period. The drug is effective immediately. A year's protection with DMPA (given in four injections at 3-month intervals) costs about $150.

HUMANS ARE A very inventive species. In the area of birth control, however, some of our inventions do not deserve to be patented. "Traditional" birth control techniques such as withdrawal and lactation have some merit in that they work some of the time for some people. Other methods, such as Coca Cola douches or plastic bag condoms, are worse than useless; they may be harmful.

Coitus Interruptus (Withdrawal)

The oldest contraceptive technique known is **coitus interruptus** (also known as *withdrawal*, or "pulling out"), which involves removing the penis from the vagina before ejaculation. This method is widely used throughout the world and can be considered somewhat successful for *some* people. Success may depend on technique, on combination with calendar methods, or on the physical characteristics of the partners (such as the tendency toward infertility in one or both partners).

A problem with this method is its riskiness. Secretions from the man's Cowper's glands, urethra, or prostate, which sometimes seep into the vagina before ejaculation, can carry thousands of healthy sperm. Also, the first few drops of ejaculate carry most of the sperm. If the man is slow to withdraw or allows any ejaculate to spill into (or near the opening of) the vagina, the woman may get pregnant. A man using this method should wipe off any fluid at the tip of the penis before insertion into the vagina. If he has difficulty determining when he is about to ejaculate, he should *not* rely on withdrawal for contraception. The theoretical effectiveness rate of using coitus interruptus is 84%. The actual user effectiveness rate is 81%. Although it is generally considered an unreliable method of birth control, coitus interruptus is certainly better than nothing.

Douching

Douching involves flushing the vagina with water or a medicated liquid. As a contraceptive method it is faulty because after ejaculation, douching is already too late. By the time a woman can douche, the sperm may already be swimming through the cervix into the uterus. The douche liquid may even push the sperm into the cervix. Douching with any liquid, especially if done often, tends to upset the normal chemical balance in the vagina and may cause irritation or infection.

Lactation

When a woman breast-feeds her child after giving birth, she may not begin to ovulate as long as she continues to nourish her child exclusively by breast-feeding. When used as a method of birth control, nursing should be done at least every 4 hours, and little or no other foods or liquids should be given to the baby. Although some women do not ovulate while lactating, others do. Cycles may begin immediately after delivery or in a few months. The woman never knows when she will begin to be fertile. Lactation is considered a contraceptive method in some countries, but the success rate is low, especially if used longer than 6 months.

Mythical Methods

There are many myths among young and old about contraception. Widely known methods that are *totally* useless include:

- Standing up during or after intercourse (sperm have no problem swimming "upstream").
- Taking a friend's pill the day of, or the day after, intercourse (doesn't work, and may even be dangerous).
- Only having intercourse occasionally (it is when, not how often, that makes a difference; once is enough, if the woman is fertile at that time).
- Using plastic wrap or plastic bags as condoms (too loose, undependable, and unsanitary).

Barrier Methods: The Condom, Female Condom, Diaphragm, and Cervical Cap

Barrier methods are designed to keep sperm and egg from uniting. The barrier device worn by men is the condom. Barrier methods available to women are the diaphragm, the cervical cap, and the female condom. The effectiveness of all barrier methods is increased by use with spermicides, which are discussed later in this chapter.

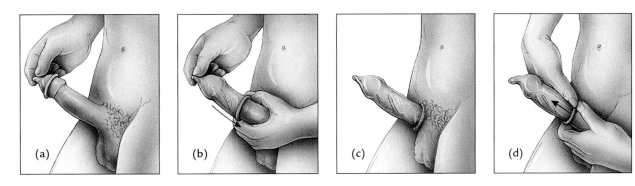

FIGURE 11.3   Using a Condom. (a) Place the rolled condom on the erect penis, leaving about a half-inch of space at the tip (first, squeeze any air out of the condom tip). (b) Roll the condom down, smoothing out any air bubbles. (c) Roll the condom to the base of the penis. (d) After ejaculation, hold the condom base while withdrawing the penis.

The Condom   A **condom** (or **male condom**) is a thin, soft, flexible sheath of latex rubber, polyurethane, or processed animal tissue that fits over the erect penis to prevent semen from being transmitted (Figure 11.3). Condoms are available in a variety of sizes, shapes, and colors. Some are lubricated, and some are treated with spermicides. They are easily obtainable from drugstores and family planning clinics, and most kinds are relatively inexpensive. Condoms are the third most widely used form of birth control in the United States (after sterilization and the pill). Their use has increased significantly since the late 1980s, due in large part to their effectiveness in helping prevent the spread of STDs. A condom costs anywhere from about 50¢ (for "plain") to $1.50 (for "fancy"). They are often available free from college health services, family planning clinics, and AIDS education programs.

Condoms provide effective contraception when properly used. One recent study found that when used in experienced, motivated populations, their efficacy in preventing pregnancy may equal that of the most reliable forms of contraception (Rosenberg & Waugh, 1997). *Latex* and *polyurethane* condoms (but not those made of animal tissue) also help guard against the transmission of a number of sexually transmitted diseases such as chlamydia, gonorrhea, genital herpes, and HIV/AIDS. Due to increased publicity regarding the transmissibility of HIV, both heterosexuals and gay men are increasingly using condoms as prophylactic devices. Condom use does not guarantee *total* safety from STDs, however, because sexual partners may also transmit certain diseases by hand, mouth, and genital areas other than the penis or vagina. Condoms may also occasionally tear or leak. As mentioned above, animal tissue (or "lambskin") condoms can be permeated by viruses such as HIV. Therefore, they should be used only for contraceptive purposes by monogamous couples who understand that such condoms do not protect against STDs.

A condom made of polyurethane (Avanti) is now available. Polyurethane has been demonstrated to be at least as effective as latex as a barrier against sperm- and virus-sized particles. It is thinner than latex, allowing for excellent transmission of heat and receptivity to feeling, and it is 40% stronger than latex. This condom may be used with oil-based lubricants and presents a welcome alternative for those allergic to latex. The cost is about $10.50 for a package of six.

Another nonlatex condom is made of a material called Tactylon. Like latex and polyurethane, the material does not permit the passage of sperm, viruses, or bacteria and thus should provide good protection against disease

"Hear me, and hear me good, kid. Unroll the condom all the way to the base of the erect penis, taking care to expel the air from the reservoir at the tip by squeezing between the forefinger and thumb . . ." Reproduced by Special Permission of PLAYBOY Magazine. Copyright © 1989 by PLAYBOY.

Male Condoms

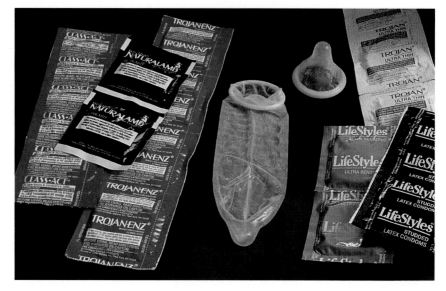

and pregnancy (Winikoff & Wymelenberg, 1997). This condom is very thin, strong, and extremely stretchy. Like polyurethane, it is not damaged by oils. Tactylon condoms should be available soon.

WOMEN AND CONDOM USE   Today, nearly half of male condoms are purchased by women, and condom advertising and packaging increasingly reflect this trend (Winikoff & Wymelenberg, 1997). Four key points are relevant to the issue of women and condom use (Hatcher et al., 1994).

- Women have more to lose than men when it comes to sexually transmitted diseases; they can suffer permanent infertility, for example.
- Men infected with STDs infect 2 out of 3 of their female partners, whereas women with STDs transmit the illness to 1 out of 3 male partners.
- Condoms help protect women against unplanned pregnancy, ectopic pregnancy, bacterial infections such as vaginitis and PID, viral infections such as herpes and HIV, cervical cancer, and infections that may harm a fetus or an infant during delivery.
- A woman has the right to insist on condom use. Even if a woman regularly uses another form of birth control, such as the pill or an IUD, she may want to have the added protection provided by a condom, especially if it has been treated with spermicide (which provides further protection against disease organisms). Contraceptive aerosol foam and contraceptive film (a thin, translucent square of tissue that dissolves into a gel) are the most convenient spermicidal preparations to use with condoms.

It is now vitally important that we find a way of making the condom a cult object of youth.

—*Germaine Greer*

EFFECTIVENESS   Condoms are 98–99% effective theoretically. User effectiveness is about 88%. Failures sometimes occur from mishandling the condom, but they are usually the result of not putting it on until after some semen has leaked into the vagina, or simply not putting it on at all. When

CONDOMS CAN BE very effective contraceptive devices when used properly. They also can protect against STDs. Here are some tips for their use.

- Use condoms every time you have sexual intercourse; this is the key to successful contraception and disease prevention.

- Use a spermicide with the condom. Foam and film are both easy to apply.

- Always put the condom on before the penis touches the vagina.

- Leave about a half-inch of space at the condom tip, and roll the condom all the way down to the base of the penis.

- Withdraw the penis soon after ejaculation. Make sure someone holds the base of the condom firmly against the penis as it is withdrawn.

- After use, check the condom for possible tears. If you did not use a spermicide and you find a tear or hole, immediately insert spermicidal foam or jelly into the vagina. This may reduce the chance of pregnancy. If torn condoms are a persistent problem, use a water-based lubricant, such as K-Y jelly, or a spermicide to reduce friction.

- Do not reuse a condom.

- Keep condoms in a cool, dry, and convenient place.

- To help protect against HIV and other organisms, always use a latex rubber or polyurethane condom, *not* one made of animal tissue.

If you or your partner is uncomfortable with condom use, consider the following:

- *Stand your ground.* (This is important for women because it is generally men who object to condoms.) Unless you want to be pregnant and are sure your partner is free of STDs, you need protection during sex. If he says no to condoms, you can say no to him. If he cares about you, he will work with you to find birth control and safer sex methods that suit you both.

- *Communication is crucial.* It may seem "unromantic," but planning your contraception strategy before you are sexually entangled is essential. Consider visiting a family planning clinic for counseling—together. The issue of protection must be dealt with by both of you.

- *Keep your sense of humor and playfulness.* Condoms can provide lots of laughs, and laughter and sex go well together.

---

used in anal sex, a male condom is more likely to break and slip than when used for vaginal sex, although these problems still occur infrequently (Winikoff & Wymelenberg, 1997).

ADVANTAGES   Condoms are easy to obtain. They are easy to carry in a wallet or purse. Latex rubber and polyurethane condoms help protect against STDs, including herpes and AIDS. They are inexpensive or can be free.

POSSIBLE PROBLEMS   The chief drawback of a condom is that it must be put on after the man has become aroused but before penetration. This interruption is the major reason for users to neglect or "forget" to put them on. Some men complain that sensation is dulled, and (very rarely) cases of allergy to rubber are reported. Men who experience significant loss of feeling with a condom are advised to try other kinds. Many of the newer condoms are very thin (but also strong); they conduct heat well and allow quite a bit of sensation to be experienced. Latex condoms that are flavored, glow in the dark, or are brightly colored may not be as protective as plain condoms. The condom user (or his partner) must take care to hold the sheath at the base of his penis when he withdraws, in order to avoid leakage. Latex condoms should be used with water-based lubricants only because oil-based lubricants such as Vaseline can weaken the rubber. Vaginally applied

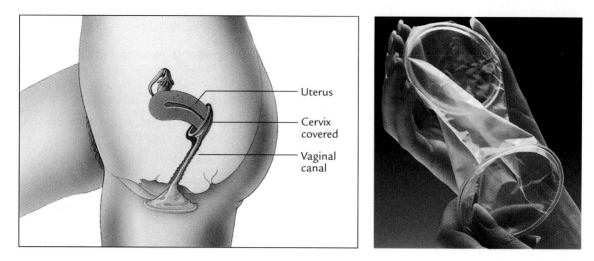

FIGURE 11.4   The Female Condom in Position. The female condom, a sheath of soft polyurethane, is anchored around the cervix with a flexible ring (much like a diaphragm). A larger ring secures the sheath outside the vagina and also helps protect the vulva.

medications such as Monistat (for yeast infections) and Premarin (an estrogen cream) may also cause condom breakage. If a condom breaks, slips, or leaks, there are some things a person can do (see the section titled "Emergency Contraception" on pages 342–343).

The Female Condom   Currently, there is one **female condom** available for women. Called Reality, it is a disposable, soft, loose-fitting polyurethane sheath with a diaphragmlike ring at each end. It measures 3 in. in diameter and 6 to 7 in. long and is designed to line the inner walls of the vagina and protect women against sperm, bacteria, and viruses. One ring, which is sealed shut, is inside the sheath and is used to insert and anchor the condom against the cervix. The larger outer ring remains outside the vagina and acts as a barrier, protecting the vulva and the base of the penis (Figure 11.4). The pouch is lubricated both inside and out and is meant for one-time use. It can be inserted up to 8 hours before intercourse and can be used without additional spermicide. The cost of female condoms ranges from $7 to $9 for a package of three.

EFFECTIVENESS   The effectiveness rates for female condoms are similar to those for other barrier methods in protecting against pregnancy, ranging from 86.7% to 98.4%. In laboratory tests, this condom was not permeated by HIV, indicating that is has promise both for contraception and for the control of STDs.

ADVANTAGES   One advantage of the female condom over the male condom is that it not only protects the vagina and cervix from sperm and microbes, but it is sized so that the open end also covers a woman's external genitals and the base of her partner's penis, thus offering both people excellent protection against disease (Winikoff & Wymelenberg, 1997). Because polyurethane is stronger than latex, the device is less likely than the male latex condom to break. Female condoms may prove advantageous for women whose partners are reluctant to use a male condom, in part because they do not constrict the penis as do male latex condoms ("Female Condom," 1996). They also give women an additional way to control their fertility.

POSSIBLE PROBLEMS   The female condom is relatively problem-free. The major complaint is aesthetic: Some women dislike the complete coverage of the female genitals provided by the condom (one of its chief health advantages) and don't want to use it for this reason ("Female Condom," 1996).

The Diaphragm   A **diaphragm** is a rubber cup with a flexible rim that is placed deep inside the vagina, blocking the cervix, to prevent sperm from entering the uterus and fallopian tubes. Different women require different sizes, and a woman's size may change, especially after a pregnancy; the size must be determined by an experienced practitioner. Diaphragms are available by prescription from doctors and family planning clinics. Somewhat effective by itself, the diaphragm is highly effective when used with a spermicidal cream or jelly. (Creams and jellies are considered more effective than foam for use with a diaphragm.) Diaphragm users should be sure to use an adequate amount of spermicide and to follow their practitioner's instructions with care. Diaphragms are relatively inexpensive—about $25, plus the cost of spermicide and the initial exam and fitting.

Diaphragm

The diaphragm can be put in place up to 2 hours before intercourse. It should be left in place 6 to 8 hours afterward. A woman should not dislodge it or douche before it is time to remove it. If intercourse is repeated within 6 hours, the diaphragm should be left in place but more spermicide should be inserted with an applicator. However, a diaphragm should not be left in place for more than 24 hours. To remove a diaphragm, the woman inserts a finger into the vagina and under the front of the diaphragm rim and then gently pulls it out. The diaphragm should be washed in mild soap and water and patted dry before being put away in its storage case.

A diaphragm should be replaced about once a year; the rubber may deteriorate and lose elasticity, thus increasing the chance of splitting. Any change in the way the diaphragm feels calls for a visit to a doctor or clinic to check the fit. A woman who gains or loses a lot of weight should also have the fit of her diaphragm checked.

EFFECTIVENESS   Numerous studies of diaphragm effectiveness have yielded varying results. Typical user effectiveness (actual statistical effectiveness) is in the 81–83% range. Consistent, correct use is essential to achieve maximum effectiveness. For this reason, the risk of diaphragm failure is approximately double for women who are under 25 (and therefore more fertile than older women) or who have intercourse four times weekly or more (Hatcher et al., 1994).

ADVANTAGES   The diaphragm can be put in place up to 2 hours before the time of intercourse. For most women, there are few health problems associated with its use. It helps protect against diseases of the cervix (see Chapter 13) and PID (see Chapter 15). Cancer of the cervix has been found to be much less common in women who consistently use a diaphragm during intercourse for at least 5 years (Winikoff & Wymelenberg, 1997).

POSSIBLE PROBLEMS   Some women dislike handling or placing diaphragms, or the mess or smell of the chemical contraceptives used with them. Some men complain of rubbing or other discomfort caused by the diaphragm. Occasionally, a woman will be allergic to rubber. Some women have a

Cervical Cap

slightly increased risk of repeated urinary tract infections (see Chapter 15). Because there is a small risk of toxic shock syndrome (TSS) associated with its use, a woman should not leave a diaphragm in the vagina for more than 24 hours (Hatcher et al., 1994).

The Cervical Cap   The **cervical cap** is a small rubber barrier device that fits snugly over the cervix; it is held in place by suction and can be filled with spermicidal cream or jelly. Following intercourse, it must remain in place for at least 6 hours. Cervical caps come in different sizes and shapes, though only four styles are available in the United States. Proper fit is extremely important, and not everyone can be fitted. Fitting must be done by a physician or a health-care practitioner.

EFFECTIVENESS   There is a limited amount of research data in this country regarding the cervical cap's effectiveness. Reported user effectiveness ranges from 79% to 92%.

ADVANTAGES   The cervical cap may be more comfortable and convenient than the diaphragm for some women. Much less spermicide is used than with the diaphragm; spermicide need not be reapplied if intercourse is repeated. The cap can be inserted many hours before intercourse and can be worn for as long as 48 hours. It does not interfere with the body physically or hormonally. It may also protect against some STDs, but not AIDS.

POSSIBLE PROBLEMS   Some users are bothered by an odor that develops from the interaction of the cap's rubber with either vaginal secretions or the spermicide. There is some concern that the cap may contribute to erosion of the cervix. If a partner's penis touches the rim of the cap, it can become displaced during intercourse. Theoretically, the same risk of TSS exists for the cervical cap as for the diaphragm.

Spermicides

A **spermicide** is a substance that is toxic to sperm. The most commonly used spermicide in products sold in the United States is the chemical **nonoxynol-9.** Spermicidal preparations are available in a variety of forms: bioadhesive gel, foam, film, cream, jelly, and suppository. Some condoms are also treated with spermicides. Spermicidal preparations are considered most effective when used in combination with a barrier method of contraception. Spermicidal preparations are sold in tubes, packets, or other containers that hold about 12–20 applications. The cost per use is about 50¢ to $2.50.

Another benefit of spermicides is that they may provide significant protection against microorganisms, such as those that cause gonorrhea and chlamydia. The risk of cervical cancer and hepatitis B may also be reduced (Hatcher et al., 1994). Some evidence suggests that nonoxynol-9 provides women with some protection against HIV infection, but there is also evidence that it causes mucosal inflammation and sores when used frequently (several times a day for many days) or in high doses (Elias & Heise, 1993; Winikoff & Wymelenberg, 1997). Such sores could actually increase the possibility of HIV infection if exposure occurred. Because of conflicting study results, nonoxynol-9 should not be relied on as a regular method of HIV (or any STD) prevention ("Spermicide Fails," 1998). It can also encourage the presence of *Candida albicans,* the organism that causes yeast infections. Furthermore, there is no way to ensure that any spermicide will kill *all* the viruses or other organisms that may be present. (For further information on STD prevention, see Chapter 15.)

Bioadhesive Gel   Newly available under the trade name Advantage 24, **bioadhesive gel** is a gel combined with a small amount of nonoxynol-9 that clings to the cervix and walls of the vagina for up to 24 hours. The product is not washed away by a man's ejaculate or a woman's secretions or menstrual blood. Once the gel is applied, intercourse can take place at any time within 24 hours; however, a new application of gel should be made with each act of intercourse.

The product is sold in prefilled applicators for one-time use. Before insertion, the applicator should be shaken and then used to deposit the gel close to the cervix. The cost is $8 for three applications, less if purchased in a larger quantity or at a family planning center.

Contraceptive Foam   **Contraceptive foam** is a chemical spermicide sold in aerosol containers. It is a practical form of spermicide for use with a condom. Methods of application vary with each brand, but foam is usually released deep in the vagina either directly from the container or with an applicator. The foam forms a physical barrier to the uterus, and its chemicals inactivate sperm in the vagina. It is most effective if inserted no more than half an hour before intercourse. Shaking the container before applying the foam increases its foaminess so that it spreads further. The foam begins to go flat after about half an hour. It must be reapplied when intercourse is repeated.

EFFECTIVENESS   Foam has a theoretical effectiveness rate of 98.5%. User failure brings its effectiveness down to as low as 71%. Failure tends to

Since if the parts be smooth conception is prevented, some anoint that part of the womb on which the seed falls with oil of cedar, or with ointment of lead or with frankincense, commingled with olive oil.

—*Aristotle (384–322 B.C.)*

result from not applying the foam every single time the couple has intercourse, from relying on foam inserted hours before intercourse, from relying on foam placed hurriedly or not placed deep enough in the vagina, or from foam whose expiration date has passed. If used properly and consistently, however, foam is quite reliable. Used with a condom, foam is highly effective.

ADVANTAGES   Almost no medical problems are associated with the use of foam. Foam may help provide protection against STDs.

POSSIBLE PROBLEMS   Some women dislike applying foam. Some complain of messiness, leakage, odor, or stinging sensations. Occasionally, a woman or man may have an allergic reaction to the foam. Because it is impossible to know how much remains in a container of foam, it is wise to keep a backup can available at all times.

Contraceptive Film   **Contraceptive film** (also called vaginal contraceptive film, or VCF) is a relatively new spermicidal preparation. It is sold in packets of small (2-in.-square), translucent tissues. This paper-thin tissue contains nonoxynol-9, which dissolves into a sticky gel when inserted into the vagina. It is placed directly over the cervix, not less than 15 minutes or more than 1 hour before intercourse. It remains effective for 2 hours after insertion. Contraceptive film works effectively in conjunction with the male condom.

EFFECTIVENESS   Extensive research has not been done on the effectiveness of film because of its relative newness on the market. The highest effectiveness rates reported are 82–90%. Proper and consistent use with a condom will greatly increase effectiveness.

ADVANTAGES   Many women find film easy to use. It is easily obtained from a drugstore and is easy to carry in a purse, wallet, or pocket.

POSSIBLE PROBLEMS   Some women may not like inserting the film into the vagina. Some women may be allergic to it. Increased vaginal discharge and temporary pain while urinating after using contraceptive film have been reported.

Creams and Jellies   Spermicidal creams and jellies come in tubes and are inserted with applicators or placed inside diaphragms or cervical caps. These chemical spermicides can be bought without prescription at most drugstores. They work in a manner similar to foams but are considered less effective when used alone. Like foam, jellies and creams may provide some protection against STDs. This factor makes their use with a diaphragm even more attractive.

Vaginal Suppositories   These chemical spermicides are inserted into the vagina before intercourse. Body heat and fluids dissolve the ingredients, which will inactivate sperm in the vagina after ejaculation. They must be inserted early enough to dissolve completely before intercourse.

Contraceptive Film

EFFECTIVENESS OF CREAMS, JELLIES, AND VAGINAL SUPPOSITORIES   Reports on these methods vary widely. It is suspected that the variations are connected with each user's technique of application. Directions for use that come with these contraceptives are not always clear. Jellies, creams, and vaginal suppositories should be used in conjunction with a barrier method for maximum effectiveness.

ADVANTAGES   Spermicidal creams, jellies, and suppositories are simple to use and easy to obtain, with virtually no medical problems. They may help protect against certain common STDs and may reduce the danger of acquiring pelvic inflammatory disease. The use of spermicides does not affect any pregnancy that may follow (Winikoff & Wymelenberg, 1997).

POSSIBLE PROBLEMS   Some people have allergic reactions to spermicides. Some women dislike the messiness, odor, or necessity of touching their own genitals. Others experience irritation or inflammation, especially if they use any of the methods frequently. A few women lack the vaginal lubrication to dissolve the suppositories in a reasonable amount of time. And a few women complain of having anxiety about the effectiveness of these methods during intercourse.

The IUD (Intrauterine Device)

The **intrauterine device,** or **IUD,** is a tiny plastic or copper device that is inserted into the uterus through the cervical os (opening) to prevent conception (Figure 11.5). The type of device inserted determines how long it may be left in place; the range is 1 year to indefinitely.

FIGURE 11.5 An IUD (Progestasert) in Position

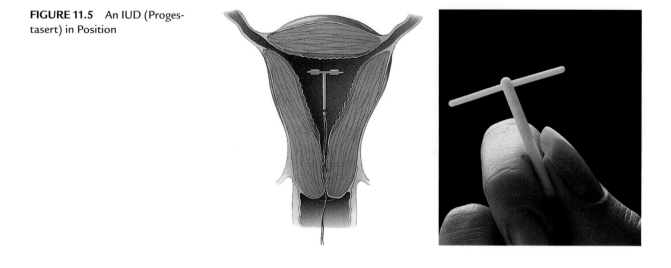

Although most IUDs have been withdrawn from the U.S. market because of the proliferation of lawsuits against their manufacturers in recent years, they are still considered a major birth control method. The two IUDs currently available in the United States are the Copper T-380A, marketed as the ParaGard, and the progesterone T device, marketed as the Progestasert IUD. The Copper T-380A is made of polyethylene; the stem of the T is wrapped with fine copper wire. It can be left in place for 10 years. More than 8 million Copper T-380As have been distributed worldwide. The Progestasert is also in the form of a T. It is made of a polymer plastic with a hollow stem containing progesterone, which is continually released. The Progestasert is effective for 1 year. At the time an IUD is removed, a new one may be inserted. The cost of an IUD, including insertion, ranges from $300 to $700. IUDs must be inserted and removed by a trained practitioner.

IUDs apparently work in a number of ways, some of which are not yet clearly understood. Both IUD types produce a reaction on the uterus that causes production of white blood cells and prostaglandins. Their presence in the uterus and fallopian tubes interferes with the movement of sperm and egg. If the IUD also contains copper, the effect on sperm and eggs is enhanced by the copper's ability to kill the sperm or diminish their ability to fertilize the egg. In addition, IUDs change the movement of the egg as it passes though the fallopian tube, thereby altering the sensitive timing normally required for impregnation.

EFFECTIVENESS   IUDs are 97–99% effective theoretically. User effectiveness is 90–96%. The Copper T-380A has the lowest failure rate of any IUD developed to date.

ADVANTAGES   Once inserted, IUDs require little care. They don't interfere with spontaneity during intercourse. If used over a period of years, they are also relatively inexpensive.

POSSIBLE PROBLEMS   Insertion may be painful. Heavy cramping usually follows and sometimes persists. Menstrual flow usually increases, often significantly. An estimated 2–8% of IUD users, especially women who have never been pregnant, expel the device within the first year. This usually happens during the first 3 months after insertion. The IUD can be reinserted, however, and many women retain it the second time.

The IUD has been associated with increased risk of pelvic inflammatory disease (see Chapter 15). Recent studies suggest, however, that most cases of pelvic infection that occur with an IUD in place are attributable to sexually transmitted diseases and that women at low risk for STDs are also at low risk for pelvic infection while they are using an IUD (Rosenfield, Peterson, & Tyler, 1997). However, because of the risk of sterility induced by PID, many physicians recommend that women planning to have children use alternative methods. Women who have had PID or who have multiple sex partners should be aware that an IUD will place them at significantly greater risk of PID, STDs, and other infections.

The IUD cannot be inserted in some women because of unusual uterine shape or position. Until recently, it was considered difficult to insert and less effective for teenage girls, but newer, smaller IUDs have been found to provide good protection even for young teenagers. Occasionally, the device perforates the cervix. This usually happens at the time of insertion, if it happens at all. Removal sometimes requires a minor surgical procedure.

Sometimes pregnancy or ectopic pregnancy (implantation within the fallopian tube) occurs and is complicated by the presence of the IUD. If the IUD is not removed, there is about a 50% chance of a miscarriage (Hatcher et al., 1994). Because there is increased blood flow in the uterus during pregnancy, an infection (if one is present) can travel rapidly through the woman's bloodstream and may cause death. Still, the overall rate of IUD-related mortality appears to be low compared with the mortality rates associated with pregnancy and other forms of contraception (CDC, 1997b).

Fertility Awareness Methods

Fertility awareness methods of contraception require substantial education, training, and diligence. They are based on a woman's knowledge of her body's reproductive cycle. Requiring a high degree of motivation and self-control, these methods are not for everyone. Fertility awareness is also referred to as "natural family planning." Some people make the following distinction between the two. With fertility awareness, the couple may use an alternative method (such as a diaphragm with jelly or a male condom with foam) during the fertile part of the woman's cycle. Natural family planning does not include the use of any contraceptive device and is thus considered to be more natural; it is approved by the Catholic church.

Fertility awareness methods include the calendar (rhythm) method, the basal body temperature (BBT) method, the cervical mucus method, and the symptothermal method, which combines the latter two. These methods are not recommended for women who have irregular menstrual cycles, including postpartum and lactating mothers.

All women can benefit from learning to recognize their fertility signs. It is useful to know when the time of greatest likelihood of pregnancy occurs, both for women who wish to avoid pregnancy and for those who want to become pregnant.

It is now quite lawful for a Catholic woman to avoid pregnancy by resort to mathematics, though she is still forbidden to resort to physics and chemistry.

—*H. L. Mencken (1880–1956)*

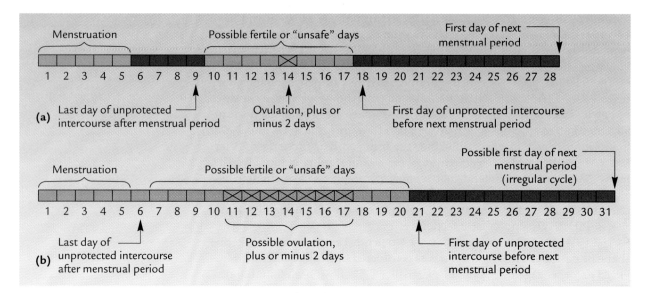

FIGURE 11.6 Fertility Awareness Calendar. To use the calendar method or other fertility awareness methods, a woman must keep track of her menstrual cycles. (a) The top chart shows probable safe and unsafe days for a woman with a regular 28-day cycle. (b) The bottom chart shows safe and unsafe days for a woman whose cycles range from 25 to 31 days. Note that the woman with an irregular cycle has significantly more unsafe days. The calendar method is most effective when combined with the basal body temperature (BBT) and cervical mucus methods.

Women who miscalculate are called mothers.

—*Abigail Van Buren*

The Calendar (Rhythm) Method The **calendar (rhythm) method** is based on calculating "safe" days, which depends on the range of a woman's longest and shortest menstrual cycles. It may not be practical or safe for women with irregular cycles. For women with regular cycles, the calendar method is reasonably effective because the period of time when an oocyte is receptive to fertilization is only about 24 hours. Because sperm generally live 2–4 days, the maximum period of time in which fertilization could be expected to occur may be calculated with the assistance of a calendar.

Ovulation generally occurs 14 (plus or minus 2) days before a woman's menstrual period. (However, ovulation *can* occur anytime during the cycle, including during the menstrual period.) Taking this into account, and charting her menstrual cycles for a minimum of 8 months to determine the longest and shortest cycles, a woman can determine her expected fertile period. Figure 11.6 shows the interval of fertility calculated in this way. During the fertile period, a woman must abstain from sexual intercourse or use an alternative method of contraception. A woman using this method must be meticulous in her calculations, keep her calendar up to date, and be able to maintain an awareness of what day it is. Statistically, only about one-third of all women have cycles regular enough to use this method satisfactorily.

The Basal Body Temperature (BBT) Method A woman's temperature tends to be slightly lower during menstruation and for about a week afterward. Just before ovulation, it dips a few fractions of a degree; it then rises sharply (one-half to nearly one whole degree) following ovulation. It stays high until just before the next menstrual period.

A woman practicing the **basal body temperature (BBT) method** must record her temperature every morning upon waking for 6–12 months to have an accurate idea of her temperature pattern. This change can best be noted using a basal body temperature thermometer and taking the temperature in the morning, before getting out of bed. When she is quite sure she recognizes the rise in temperature and can predict about when in her cycle it will happen, she can begin using the method. She will abstain from intercourse or use an alternative contraceptive method for 3–4 days before the expected rise, and for 4 days after it has taken place. If she limits intercourse to only the "safe" time after her temperature has risen, the method is more effective. The method requires high motivation and control. For greater accuracy, it may be combined with the cervical mucus method described next.

The Cervical Mucus Method   Women who use the **cervical mucus method** determine their point in the menstrual cycle by examining the mucous secretions of the cervix. In many women, there is a noticeable change in the appearance and character of cervical mucus prior to ovulation. After menstruation, most women experience a moderate discharge of cloudy, yellowish, or white mucus. Then, for a day or two, a clear, slippery mucus is secreted. Ovulation occurs immediately after the clear, slippery mucous secretions appear. The preovulatory mucus is elastic in consistency, rather like raw egg white, and a drop can be stretched between two fingers into a thin strand. Following ovulation, the amount of discharge decreases markedly. The 4 days before and the 4 days after these secretions are considered the unsafe days. An alternative contraception method may be used during this time. The method requires training and a high degree of motivation to be successful. This method may be combined with the BBT method for greater effectiveness.

The Symptothermal Method   When the BBT and cervical mucus methods are used together, the approach is called the **symptothermal method.** Additional signs that may be useful in determining ovulation are midcycle pain in the lower abdomen on either side (*Mittelschmerz*) a very slight discharge of blood from the cervix ("spotting"), breast tenderness, feelings of heaviness, and/or abdominal swelling.

EFFECTIVENESS OF FERTILITY AWARENESS METHODS   It is problematic to calculate the effectiveness of fertility awareness methods. With this type of contraception, in a sense, the user *is* the method: The method's success or failure rests largely on her diligence. Women who wish to rely on fertility awareness methods of contraception should enroll in a class at a clinic. Learning to read one's own unique fertility signs is a complex process requiring one-on-one counseling and close monitoring. For those who have used fertility awareness with unfailing dedication, these methods have been demonstrated to have effectiveness as high as 99%. Many studies, however, show fairly high failure rates with these methods. Some researchers believe this is due to risk taking during the fertile phase. In addition, there is always some difficulty in predicting ovulation with pinpoint accuracy; thus, there is a greater chance of pregnancy as a result of intercourse before ovulation than as a result of intercourse following it. Furthermore, there is evidence that sperm may survive as long as 5 days inside a woman's body, suggesting that a reliably "safe" period of time may be very short indeed and consequently hard to predict. All fertility awareness methods increase in effectiveness if intercourse is unprotected only during the safe period following ovulation.

ADVANTAGES   Fertility awareness (or natural family planning) methods are acceptable to most religious groups. They are free and pose no health risks. If a woman wishes to become pregnant, awareness of her own fertility cycles is very useful.

POSSIBLE PROBLEMS   These methods are not suitable for women with irregular menstrual cycles or couples who are not highly motivated to use them. Some couples who practice abstinence during fertile periods may begin to take risks out of frustration. These couples may benefit by exploring other forms of sexual expression, and counseling can help.

Sterilization

Among married couples in the United States, sterilization (of one or both partners) is the most popular form of birth control. **Sterilization** involves surgical intervention that makes the reproductive organs incapable of producing or delivering viable gametes (sperm and eggs). Annually, about 1 million Americans choose this method of family planning, which is also known as **voluntary surgical contraception** (Hatcher et al., 1994). Before 1975, most sterilizations in this country were performed on men, but currently, women choose to be sterilized at twice the rate of men.

Sterilization for Women   Female sterilization is now a relatively safe, simple, and common procedure for many women, most of whom are over 30. Most female sterilizations are **tubal ligations,** familiarly known as "tying the tubes" (Figure 11.7). The two most common operations are laparoscopy and minilaparotomy. Less commonly performed types of sterilization for women are culpotomy, culdoscopy, and hysterectomy. Generally, this surgery is not reversible; only women who are completely certain that they want no (or no more) children should choose this method.

Sterilization for women is quite expensive. Surgeon, anesthesiologist, and hospital fees are substantial. Costs may range from $1200 to $3000, although a high cost does not necessarily guarantee a better quality procedure. Most health insurance policies will cover all or part of the cost of sterilization for both men and women. In some states, Medicaid pays for certain patients.

LAPAROSCOPY AND MINILAPAROTOMY   Sterilization by **laparoscopy** is the most frequently used method and usually requires a day or less in the hospital or clinic. General anesthesia is usually recommended. The woman's abdomen is inflated with gas to make the organs more visible. The surgeon inserts a rodlike instrument with a viewing lens (the laparoscope) through a small incision at the edge of the navel and locates the fallopian tubes. Through this incision or a second one, the surgeon inserts another instrument that closes the tubes, usually by electrocauterization (burning). Special small forceps that carry an electric current clamp the tubes and cauterize

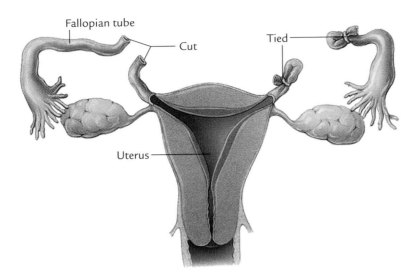

FIGURE 11.7   Tubal Ligation

them. The tubes may also be closed off or blocked with tiny rings, clips, or plugs. There is a recovery period of several days to a week. During this time, the woman will experience some tenderness and some vaginal bleeding. Rest is important. Local or general anesthesia is used with **minilaparotomy.** A small incision is made in the lower abdomen, through which the fallopian tubes are brought into view. They are then tied off or sealed with electric current, clips, or rings. Recovery is the same as with laparoscopy.

CULPOTOMY AND CULDOSCOPY   In these operations, an incision is made at the back of the vagina. In **culpotomy,** the tubes are viewed through the incision and then tied or otherwise blocked, then cut. **Culdoscopy** is the same procedure but uses a viewing instrument called a culdoscope. The advantage of these procedures is that they leave no visible scars. They require more expertise on the part of the surgeon, however, and have higher complication rates than laparoscopy and minilaparotomy.

HYSTERECTOMY   Hysterectomy (surgical removal of the uterus) is not performed for sterilization except under special circumstances. Because it involves the removal of the entire uterus, it is both riskier and more costly than other methods. It involves greater recovery time and, for some women, is potentially more difficult psychologically. It may be appropriate for women who have a uterine disease or other problem that is likely to require a future hysterectomy anyway. (Hysterectomy is discussed at greater length in Chapter 13.)

EFFECTIVENESS OF STERILIZATION FOR WOMEN   Surgical contraception is one of the most effective contraceptive methods available. However, a recent study of more than 10,500 women who underwent tubal sterilization found that the risk of sterilization failure is higher than previously reported, an average of 2–5%, depending on the method performed and the patient's age (Peterson, 1996). In extremely rare instances (less than one-quarter of 1%),

BECAUSE STERILIZATION IS PERMANENT, the decision to have this procedure done is a serious one. If you are considering sterilization, ask yourself these questions:

- *Are there any circumstances in which I might later want children?* Should a child die or a new relationship develop, would a child enhance or enrich your life? If, however, you have a health problem that can make pregnancy unsafe, if you do not wish to pass on a hereditary disease or disability, or if you have all the children you want, sterilization may be a good choice.

- *What are the circumstances in which sterilization makes sense?* Sterilization may be a good choice if you and your partner cannot or do not want to use the reversible contraceptive methods currently available.

- *Which partner should get sterilized?* Medically speaking, a vasectomy is simpler, safer, and less expensive than a female sterilization. However, a number of other issues are often tied to this decision, making it less clear-cut.

- *How does my partner feel about the decision?* Although the permission of a spouse is not legally required for sterilization, the decision should certainly be discussed beforehand.

- *Am I eligible for sterilization?* Individuals who wish to be sterilized must be legally competent to make this decision, which usually means being over age 21 and mentally competent. If the sterilization is being paid for with federal funds, the person must sign a consent form for voluntary surgical contraception and then wait 30 days before having the surgery. Federally funded sterilizations include those paid for by Medicaid or performed in U.S. public health, military, or Indian Health Service facilities.

- *How might I feel as a result of this procedure?* If your sense of masculinity or femininity is tied to your fertility, this procedure may not be best for you. Also, if you are young, if you are not sure about having children, or if you are considering sterilization because of pressure from a partner or the hope that it will solve conflict within the relationship, then this is probably not a good decision for you.

Source: Adapted from Winikoff & Wymelenberg, 1997.

probably because of improperly performed surgery, a tube may reopen or grow back together, allowing an egg to pass through.

Once sterilization has been done, no other method of birth control will ever be necessary. (A woman who risks exposure to STDs, however, may wish to protect herself with a condom.)

ADVANTAGES   Sterilization does not reduce or change a woman's feminine characteristics. It is not the same as menopause and does not hasten the approach of menopause, as some people believe. A woman still has her menstrual periods until whatever age menopause naturally occurs for her. The regularity of menstrual cycles is also not affected. In fact, many women become regular after being sterilized ("Does Female Sterilization," 1996). Her ovaries, uterus (except in the case of hysterectomy), and hormonal system have not been changed. The only difference is that sperm cannot now reach her eggs. (The eggs, which are released every month as before, are reabsorbed by the body.) Sexual enjoyment is not diminished. In fact, a high percentage of women report that they feel more relaxed during intercourse because anxiety about pregnancy has been eliminated. There seem to be no harmful side effects associated with female sterilization.

Sterilization should be considered irreversible. Only 15–25% percent of women who attempt to have their tubal ligations reversed succeed in conceiving.

FIGURE 11.8   Vasectomy

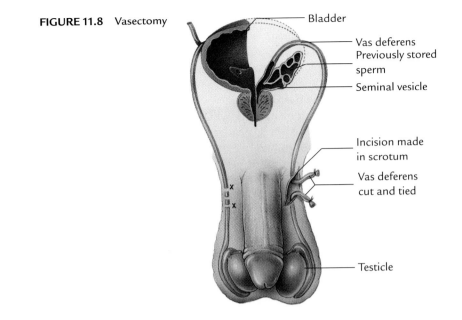

- Bladder
- Vas deferens Previously stored sperm
- Seminal vesicle
- Incision made in scrotum
- Vas deferens cut and tied
- Testicle

POSSIBLE PROBLEMS   The tubal ligation itself is a relatively safe procedure. With electrocauterization, there is a chance that other tissues in the abdomen may be damaged or that infection will occur, especially if the surgeon is not highly skilled. There may also be complications from anesthesia.

Sterilization for Men   A **vasectomy** is a minor surgical procedure that can be performed in a doctor's office under a local anesthetic. It takes approximately half an hour. In this procedure, the physician makes a small incision (or two incisions) in the skin of the scrotum. Through the incision, each vas deferens (sperm-carrying tube) is lifted, cut, tied, and often cauterized with electricity (Figure 11.8). After a brief rest, the man is able to walk out of the office; complete recuperation takes only a few days. Some 500,000 vasectomies are performed each year in the United States.

A man may retain some viable sperm in his system for days or weeks following a vasectomy. He should use other birth control until his semen has been checked, about 8 weeks following the operation.

EFFECTIVENESS   Vasectomies are 99.85% effective. In very rare cases, the ends of a vas deferens may rejoin. But this is virtually impossible if the operation is correctly performed.

ADVANTAGES   No birth control method will ever be needed again. But the man may still wish to use a condom to prevent getting or spreading an STD. Sexual enjoyment will not be diminished; the man will still have erections and orgasms and ejaculate semen. Vasectomy is relatively inexpensive compared with female sterilization. Depending on where the surgery is performed, it costs between $350 and $1000 (Winikoff & Wymelenberg, 1997).

POSSIBLE PROBLEMS   Compared with other birth control methods, the complication rates for vasectomy are very low. Most problems occur when proper antiseptic measures are not taken during the operation, or when the man exercises too strenuously in the few days after it. Hematomas (bleeding under the skin) and granulomas (clumps of sperm) can be treated with ice packs and rest. Epididymitis (inflammation of the tiny tubes that connect the testicle and vas deferens) can be treated with heat and scrotal support.

A few men, those who equate fertility with virility and potency, may experience psychological problems following vasectomy. However, most men experience no adverse psychological reactions if they understand what to expect and have the opportunity to express their concerns and ask questions.

Among men who attempt to have their vasectomies reversed, about 50% of the surgeries are successful. The cost is high, and it is not covered by insurance in many cases. Vasectomy should be considered permanent.

Emergency Contraception

No birth control device is 100% effective: Condoms may tear, spermicides expire, or a device may not be used correctly. Intercourse sometimes occurs unexpectedly, or rape may occur. **Emergency contraception** (also referred to as postcoital or morning-after birth control) following unprotected intercourse can prevent conception from occurring or expel a newly formed blastocyst. Measures to accomplish this are now safe, easily available, and legal. There is also an Emergency Contraception Hotline you can call for help: 1 888 NOT-2-LATE.

Emergency Contraceptive Pill (ECP)   The principal form of emergency contraception is the **emergency contraceptive pill (ECP),** also known as the morning-after pill. It is generally a combined estrogen-progestin birth control pill, given in a larger-than-normal dose under medical supervision, within 72 hours after unprotected intercourse. This initial dose is followed with a second dose taken 12 hours later; the treatment is often referred to as the Yuzpe Regimen (Trussell & Stewart, 1996). ECPs are both cost-effective (ranging from $25 to $100) and relatively safe compared with the alternatives of abortion or childbirth (Reuters Health Information Services, 1997). This method can reduce the chance of pregnancy by about 75% (Winikoff & Wymelenberg, 1997). Information regarding the use of regular birth control pills as ECPs is available at many family planning clinics. The ECP has recently been approved by the Food and Drug Administration specifically for emergency birth control and is available by prescription for about $20.

Minipill   The minipill is the second most common type of emergency birth control. It contains progestin but no estrogen. Prescribed for women who can't take estrogen—those who are breast-feeding, who smoke, or who are allergic to estrogen—minipills can be taken up to 2 days after unprotected sex. (A second dose is taken 12 hours after the first one.) Like the ECP, the minipill reduces the chance of pregnancy by 75%. Fees for the minipill (like the ECP) can range from $25 to $100, depending on the services needed ("Emergency Birth Control," 1997).

Copper IUD   Another form of postcoital birth control is the insertion of a copper IUD within 7 days after unprotected intercourse. This method is not recommended for women who have not had children, have multiple sex partners, or have a history of pelvic inflammatory disease. An IUD should also not be inserted if the woman is at risk for a sexually transmitted disease because insertion while an infection is present can lead to PID. This method should be chosen only if a woman wishes to continue to use the IUD as a contraceptive. Copper IUDs can be 99% effective when used in this manner (Winikoff & Wymelenberg, 1997). If a woman becomes pregnant with an IUD already in place, there is about a 50% chance of a miscarriage occurring (Hatcher et al., 1994). Still, as mentioned earlier, the overall rate of IUD-related mortality appears to be low compared with the mortality rates associated with pregnancy and other forms of contraception (CDC, 1997b).

ABORTION

When most people hear the word "abortion," they think of a medical procedure. But **abortion,** or expulsion of the conceptus, can happen naturally or can be made to happen in one of several ways. Many abortions happen spontaneously—because a woman suffers a physical trauma, because the conceptus is not properly developed, or, more commonly, because physical conditions within the uterus break down and end the development of the conceptus. Approximately one-third of all abortions reported in a year in the United States are **spontaneous abortions;** these are commonly referred to as miscarriages (see Chapter 12). In this section, however, we examine *induced abortions,* intentionally terminated pregnancies, of which there are about 1.2 million reported in a year in the United States. Unless otherwise noted, when we refer to abortion, we mean induced abortion.

Under safe, clean, and legal conditions, abortion is a very safe medical procedure. Self-administered or under illegal, clandestine conditions, abortion can be very dangerous. The continued availability of legal abortion is considered by most physicians, psychologists, and public health professionals to be critical to the public's physical and mental well-being (Stephenson, Wagner, Badea, & Serbanescu, 1992; Susser, 1992).

Abortions cannot be examined as if they are all the same. Distinctions must be made, for example, among wanted, unintended, and unwanted pregnancies. It is also important to know at what stage of pregnancy an abortion occurs. Abortions occurring during the first trimester, for example, use simpler procedures, involve an embryo or less-developed fetus, and are psychologically more positive than abortions occurring later (Adler, David, Major, Roth, Russo, & Wyatt, 1990). Finally, it is important to know the woman's age and motivation because these vary considerably and are associated with different emotional responses.

Methods of Abortion

An abortion can be induced in several ways. Surgical methods are most common in this country, but the use of medications is also possible, as is suction. Methods for early abortions (those performed in the first 3 months of pregnancy) differ from those for late abortions (those performed after the third month).

Mifepristone with Misoprostol   The most commonly used drug combination for terminating early pregnancy worldwide is **mifepristone with misoprostol** (formerly known as **RU-486**). Mifepristone prevents the cells of the uterine lining from getting the progesterone they need to support a blastocyst (fertilized ovum); the embryo therefore dies and is expelled by the uterus. This method is most effective when used during the early weeks of pregnancy.

When used alone, mifepristone is 65–80% effective in terminating an early pregnancy. When combined with misoprostol (a prostaglandin), the success rate for early first-trimester abortion exceeds 95% (Winikoff & Wymelenberg, 1997). Vacuum aspiration may be required in approximately 5% of cases.

In 11 years of use in Europe, there have been few serious medical problems associated with this method. Some of the side effects include cramping, abdominal pain, and bleeding, like that of a heavy period. There may also be nausea, vomiting, and diarrhea. Because a small, single dose is used and most of the drug is eliminated from the body in a few days, the risk of long-term health effects is low.

In spite of the controversy that has surrounded it and other methods of abortion, the Food and Drug Administration is expected to release this drug on the American market sometime within the next few years.

Suction Method   Blurring the lines between contraception and abortion is a new technique that offers abortions to women as early as 8–10 days after conception and before they have missed a period (Lewin, 1997). A hand-held syringe is used to remove the contents of the womb. A combination of better ultrasound imaging that shows the gestational sac in its earliest stages and very sensitive pregnancy tests that can detect pregnancy as soon as the blastocyst is implanted in the womb have made this new technique possible. Technically, very early abortions are the same as what was previously called menstrual extraction. What makes the suction method different from the earlier procedure is the smaller size of the instrument and the presence of a positive pregnancy test. The procedure is now available at most family planning clinics.

Surgical Methods   Surgical methods include vacuum aspiration, dilation and evacuation (D & E), hysterotomy, and several other methods. To facilitate the dilation of the cervix prior to abortion, the health-care practitioner may use a metal or other type of dilator or insert a **laminaria,** a small stick of sterilized, compressed seaweed, into the cervical opening. The laminaria expands gradually, dilating the cervix gently in the process. It must be placed at least 6 hours prior to the abortion.

VACUUM ASPIRATION (FIRST-TRIMESTER METHOD)   **Vacuum aspiration** is performed under local anesthesia. The cervix is dilated with a series of graduated rods (a laminaria may have been used to begin dilation). Then, a small tube attached to a vacuum is inserted through the cervix. The uterus is gently vacuumed, removing the conceptus, placenta, and endometrial tissue (Figure 11.9). If the pregnancy is less than 9 weeks, a large syringe may be used. The entire process takes 10–15 minutes.

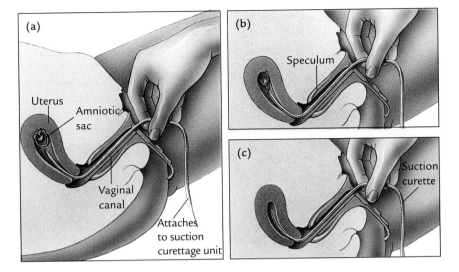

(a)

Uterus

Amniotic sac

Vaginal canal

Attaches to suction curettage unit

(b)

Speculum

(c)

Suction curette

FIGURE 11.9 Vacuum Aspiration. (a) The vagina is opened with a speculum, and a thin vacuum tube is inserted through the cervix into the uterus. (b) The uterus is gently vacuumed. (c) The curette end of the vacuum tube may be used to gently scrape the uterine wall; the conceptus and other contents of the uterus are suctioned out.

Curettage (scraping with a curette, a small spoon-shaped instrument) may follow. The patient returns home the same day. She will experience cramping, bleeding, and, possibly, emotional reactions over the following days. Serious complications are unusual for a legal, properly performed abortion. If a pregnancy progresses past 12 weeks, vacuum aspiration is not used because the uterine walls have become thinner, making perforation and bleeding more likely.

DILATION AND EVACUATION (D & E) (SECOND-TRIMESTER METHOD) **Dilation and evacuation (D & E)** is usually performed between the 13th and 26th weeks of pregnancy. Only about 10% of abortions in the United States are carried out in the second trimester, and most of them are done in the first few weeks of the trimester. Local or general anesthesia is used. The cervix is slowly dilated, and the fetus is removed by alternating curettage and solution. The patient is given an intravenous solution of the hormone oxytocin to encourage contractions and limit blood loss. Because it is a second-trimester procedure, a D & E is somewhat riskier and often more traumatic than a first-trimester abortion.

HYSTEROTOMY (SECOND-TRIMESTER METHOD) In **hysterotomy,** the fetus is removed through an incision made in the woman's abdomen. This is essentially a cesarean section—major surgery requiring several days in the hospital. This type of procedure is extremely rare and is limited to cases in which a woman's uterus is so malformed that a D & E would be dangerous (Winikoff & Wymelenberg, 1997).

Other Methods of Abortion Abortion can also be induced medically with injections or suppositories. These abortions are performed during the second trimester and generally require hospitalization. Prostaglandins, saline solutions, and urea are used in this way, alone or in various combinations. For the most part, however, these methods have been replaced by the safer and much speedier D & E.

As discussed in Chapter 3, many cells of the body contain prostaglandins, fatty-acid-based hormones that are active in many body processes, including reproduction. Prostaglandins are injected into the amniotic sac (which contains the fetus within the uterus) or administered as vaginal suppositories to stimulate uterine contractions and induce abortion. Some of the side effects associated with their use are gastrointestinal symptoms, cervical lacerations, and temperature elevation. Saline solutions and solutions of urea are toxic to the fetus and can be injected amniotically. These solutions are relatively inexpensive; they are generally considered more effective when used in combination with prostaglandins.

A Decline in the Prevalence of Abortion

The number of abortions performed in the United States has declined over the past 20 years (CDC, 1997a). The number performed in 1995—1,211,000—represented a decrease of 4.5% from 1994. Women who obtained legal abortions in 1995 were predominantly White and unmarried. As in the previous year, one-fifth of the women who obtained legal abortions were adolescents, and 33% were aged 20–24. More than half of all legal abortions were performed during the first 8 weeks of gestation; approximately 88% were performed during the first 12 weeks of pregnancy. Researchers offer several possible reasons for the declining abortion rate:

- Emphasis on prevention of unintended pregnancy, particularly among teenagers.
- Reduced access to the procedure, especially in rural areas. Currently, 84% of U.S. counties have no doctor or facility providing abortions.
- The aging of the baby boomers.
- Greater use of condoms because of fear of AIDS.
- An increase in single women keeping their babies.
- The influence of anti-abortion activists, along with pressure on hospitals to perform fewer abortions.
- Changing attitudes toward abortion or toward childbirth.

Women and Abortion

A key research issue concerns the psychological effects of legal abortion on women who obtain them. A report released by the American Psychological Association reviewing the scientific literature on the psychological effects of legal abortion concluded that most women feel the most distress immediately *preceding* an abortion and feel relief following it (Adler, David, Major, Roth, Russo, & Wyatt, 1990). Only a small minority of women report adverse psychological effects (Major & Cozzarelli, 1992).

There are many stereotypes about women who have an abortion: They are selfish, promiscuous, single, unwilling to accept family responsibilities, childless, nonmaternal, depressed, sinful, and immoral (Gordon, 1990; Petchesky, 1990). Furthermore, national public opinion surveys depict a "simplistic image" of women's reasons for abortion (Adler, David, Major, Roth, Russo, & Wyatt, 1992). Because few women openly discuss their abortion experiences, stereotypical views of abortion continue unchallenged.

Women generally have multiple reasons for wanting an abortion (Adler et al., 1992; Torres & Forrest, 1988). An important study by Aida Torres and Jacqueline Forrest (1988) came to the following conclusions:

1. *The abortion decision is complex, with several factors at play.* It is not undertaken lightly. The multiple reasons most commonly cited by women include concern about how a child would change her life, not being able to afford a child, problems in the relationship, or not wanting to be a single parent.

2. *The woman's developmental life stage is important.* Eleven percent of the women stated they were "too immature" or "too young" to have a child; 21% said they were "unready for responsibility."

3. *Many reasons have to do with women's relationships with other people or educational or economic circumstances.* Decisions do not reflect just the woman's personal concerns and circumstances. Twenty-three percent said their husband or partner didn't want a child. More than two-thirds said they couldn't afford a child. These reasons point to women's ongoing sense of responsibility to others or outside circumstances.

These researchers found that being White, African American, or Latina had little influence in abortion decision making. Latinas were only slightly less likely than non-Latinas to say they did not want additional children.

Making an abortion decision, regardless of the ultimate outcome, raises many emotional issues for women. There is no painless way of dealing with an unwanted pregnancy. For many, such a decision requires a reevaluation of their relationships, an examination of their childbearing plans, a search to understand the role of sexuality in their lives, and an attempt to clarify their life goals.

Men and Abortion

In the abortion decision-making process, the man is often forgotten. Attention is usually focused on the woman, who is making an agonizing decision. If the man is thought of, it is often with hostility and blame. And yet the man, like the woman, may be undergoing his own private travail, experiencing guilt and anxiety, feeling ambiguous about the possibility of parenthood.

A common feeling men experience is powerlessness. They may try to remain cool and rational, believing that if they reveal their confused feelings, they will be unable to give their partners emotional support. Because the drama is within the woman and her body, a man may feel he must not influence her decision.

There is the lure of fatherhood, all the same. A pregnancy forces a man to confront his own feelings about parenting. Parenthood for males, as for females, is a profound passage into adulthood. For young men, there is a mixture of pride and fear about the potential for being a father and an adult.

After an abortion, many men feel residual guilt, sadness, and remorse. It is not uncommon for some men to temporarily experience erectile or ejaculatory difficulties. It is fairly common for couples to split up after an abortion; the stress, conflict, and guilt can be overwhelming. Many abortion clinics now provide counseling for men, as well as women, involved in an abortion.

The Abortion Debate

On a national level, acceptance of abortion has risen somewhat in recent years. Data collected in 1994 by the National Opinion Research Center at the University of Chicago showed that 91% of U.S. men and women thought that abortion should be legal in cases where maternal health or life was at stake, 82% if there is a strong chance of fetal defect, and 84% if the pregnancy is a result of rape. Forty-six percent felt that abortion should be available for any reason, up from 36% in 1988 ("How the Public Views Abortion," 1994).

In the abortion debate, those who believe abortion should be prohibited generally identify themselves as "pro-life." Those who support a woman's right to choose for herself whether to have an abortion generally identify themselves as "pro-choice."

The Pro-Life Argument   For those who oppose abortion, there is a basic principle from which their arguments follow: The moment an egg is fertilized, it becomes a human being, with the full rights and dignity afforded other humans. An embryo is no less human than a fetus, and a fetus is no less human than a baby. Morally, aborting an embryo is the equivalent of killing a person.

Even though the majority of those opposing abortion would consider rape and incest (and sometimes a defective embryo or fetus) to be exceptions, the pro-life leadership generally opposes any justification for an abortion, except to save the life of the pregnant woman. To abort the embryo of a rape or incest survivor, they reason, is still taking an innocent human life.

In addition, pro-life advocates argue that abortion is the first step toward a society that eliminates undesirable human beings. If we allow the elimination of embryos, they argue, what is to stop the killing of the disabled, the elderly, or the merely inconvenient? Finally, pro-life advocates argue that there are thousands of couples who want to adopt children but are unable to do so because so many pregnant women choose to abort rather than give birth.

The Pro-Choice Argument   Those who believe that abortion should continue to be legal present a number of arguments. First, for pro-choice men and women, the fundamental issue is who decides whether a woman will bear children: the woman or the government. Because women continue to bear the primary responsibility for rearing children, pro-choice advocates believe that women should not be forced to give birth to unwanted children. Becoming a mother alters a woman's role more profoundly than almost any other event in her life. When women have the *choice* of becoming mothers, they are able to decide the timing and direction of their lives.

Second, although pro-choice advocates support sex education and contraception to eliminate much of the need for abortion, they believe that abortion should continue to be available as birth control backup. Because no contraceptive method is 100% effective, unintended pregnancies occur even among the most conscientious contraceptive users.

Third, if abortion is made illegal, large numbers of women nevertheless will have illegal abortions, substantially increasing the likelihood of dangerous complications, infections, and death. Those who are unable to have

> I have noticed that all the people who favor abortion have already been born.
>
> —*Ronald Reagan*

> There are few absolutes left in the age after Einstein, and the case of abortion like almost everything else is a case of relative goods and ills to be evaluated one against the other.
>
> —*Germaine Greer*

an abortion may be forced to give birth to and raise a child they did not want.

Abortion and Religion   Although the morality of abortion is often hotly debated among Christians and Jews, there are no direct statements in the Old or New Testaments regarding abortion. Neither Moses, Jesus, nor Paul addressed the question. Any scriptural basis for or against abortion is inferred or based on interpretation.

A key element in both pro-choice and pro-life arguments turns on when *human* life begins. Both pro-life and pro-choice supporters believe that the conceptus *is* life. They disagree as to whether it is *human* life in the same sense as the life of those of us who have been born. The debate, however, is theological rather than scientific. The answer to the question of *when* embryonic or fetal life becomes *human* life depends on one's moral or religious beliefs rather than on scientific evidence. And even among religious groups, there is no unanimity. During the Middle Ages, for example, it was believed that the soul entered a male conceptus 40 days after conception but waited 80 days before entering a female. Because the conceptus did not become human until it was ensouled, aborting an "unensouled" conceptus was not considered grounds for excommunication. It was not until 1869 that Pope Pius IX promulgated the doctrine that the soul entered the ovum at the time of fertilization. From this doctrine follows the belief that to abort an embryo or fetus is to kill a human being. Many Protestants accept similar beliefs about the soul and conception. As a result of such beliefs, Catholics and Christian fundamentalists are the most likely to oppose abortion as immoral (Wills, 1990).

Other religious groups, such as Methodists, Unitarians, and other mainstream Protestants, tend to support abortion choice (Wenz, 1992). Although they generally believe that an embryo or a fetus is life, they also believe that other human issues must be considered. The Methodist church, for example, asserts that the "sanctity of unborn human life makes us reluctant to approve abortion" but adds that "we recognize tragic conflicts of life with life that may justify abortion" (Granberg, 1991; Kellstedt & Smidt, 1991). And some Catholics support abortion rights based on the primacy of conscience, which asserts that every Catholic has the right to follow his or her conscience in matters of morals.

Constitutional Issues   In 1969 in Texas, 21-year-old Norma McCorvey, a single mother, discovered she was pregnant. In the hope of obtaining a legal abortion, she lied to her doctor, saying that she had been raped. Her physician informed her, however, that Texas prohibited all abortions except those to save the life of the mother. He suggested she travel to California, where she could obtain a legal abortion. But she had no money. Two lawyers heard of her situation and took her case in order to challenge abortion restrictions as an unconstitutional invasion of the individual's right to privacy. For the case, McCorvey was given "Roe" as a pseudonym. In 1970, a court in Texas declared the law unconstitutional, but the state appealed the decision. Meanwhile, McCorvey had the baby and gave her child up for adoption. Ultimately, the case reached the Supreme Court, where the court issued its famous *Roe v. Wade* decision in 1973 (*Roe v. Wade* 410 U.S. 113 [1973]).

> If men could get pregnant, abortion would be a sacrament.
>
> —*Florynce Kennedy (attributed)*

Under the 1973 *Roe* decision, a woman's right to abortion was guaranteed as a fundamental right, part of the constitutional right to privacy (Tribe, 1992). In delivering the Court's opinion in *Roe*, Justice William Brennan stated (*Roe v. Wade* 410 U.S. 113 [1973]):

> The right to privacy . . . is broad enough to encompass a woman's decision whether or not to terminate a pregnancy. The detriment that the State would impose upon the pregnant woman by denying this choice altogether is apparent. Specific and direct harm medically diagnosable even in early pregnancy may be involved. Maternity, or additional offspring, may force upon the woman a distressful life and future. Psychological harm may also be imminent. Mental and physical health may be taxed by childcare. There is also the distress, for all concerned, associated with the unwanted child, and there is the problem of bringing a child into a family already unable, psychologically or otherwise, to care for it. In other cases, as in this one, the . . . stigma of unwed motherhood may be involved. All these are factors the woman and her responsible physician necessarily will consider in consultation.

At the time, only four states permitted abortion at the woman's discretion.

The *Roe* decision created a firestorm of opposition among political and religious conservatives and fueled a conservative political resurgence (Wills, 1990). But because abortion was determined a fundamental right by the *Roe* decision, efforts by the states to curtail it failed.

The 1989 *Webster v. Reproductive Rights* case (109 S.CT.3040) was a turning point. For the first time, the Court rejected the definition of abortion as a fundamental right. Instead, abortion became a "limited constitutional right." Under the new standard, the Court gave states the right to limit abortion access provided the limitations did not place an "undue burden" on the pregnant woman. States were allowed to impose extensive restrictions, as long as they did not actually prohibit abortion.

In 1992, the landmark decision of *Planned Parenthood v. Casey* (112 S.CT.279) replaced *Webster* as the reigning constitutional doctrine on abortion and government regulation. Under the *Casey* ruling, a law regulating abortion is unconstitutional "if its purpose or effect is to place a substantial obstacle in the path of a woman seeking an abortion before the fetus attains viability."

RESEARCH ISSUES

Most users of contraception find some drawback to whatever method they choose. Hormonal methods may be costly or have undesirable side effects. Putting on a condom or inserting a diaphragm may seem to interrupt lovemaking too much. The inconveniences, the side effects, and the lack of 100% effectiveness—all these point to the need for more effective and more diverse forms of contraception than we have now.

High development costs, government regulations, and marketing priorities all play a part in restricting contraceptive research. The biggest barrier to developing new contraceptive techniques, however, is the fear of lawsuits, according to a 1990 report by two federal agencies, the National Research Council and the Institute of Medicine. Pharmaceutical manufacturers will not easily forget that the IUD market was virtually destroyed in the 1970s and 1980s by numerous costly lawsuits. Although a number of the suits, especially those against A. H. Robbins, the manufacturer of the Dalkon Shield, may have been justified, the result (in addition to the bankruptcy of Robbins) was the removal of almost all IUDs from the American market. Safety was not an issue in most cases. Indeed, due to the apparent eagerness of the American public to sue for huge amounts of money and the subsequent publicity, many people, both in this country and abroad, have acquired "rather inaccurate views about contraceptive methods, believing the risks to be much greater and the benefits to be much smaller than they actually are" (Forrest, 1986).

Another reason for limited contraceptive research is extensive government regulation, which requires extensive product testing. Although no one wants to be poisoned by medicines, perhaps it wouldn't hurt to take a closer look at the process by which new drugs become available to the public. Approval from the Food and Drug Administration takes an average of 7.5 years. Drug patents are in effect for only 17 years, so the pharmaceutical companies have less than 10 years to recover their developmental costs once a medication is approved for sale. Furthermore, pharmaceutical corporations are not willing to expend millions in research only to have the FDA refuse to approve the marketing of new discoveries. According to Carl Djerrasi (1979), the "father" of the birth control pill, safety is a relative, not an absolute, concept. We may need to reexamine the question "How safe is safe?" and weigh potential benefits along with possible problems.

> A lily pond, so the French riddle goes, contains a single leaf. Each day the number of leaves doubles—two leaves the second day, four the third, eight the fourth, and so on. Question: If the pond is completely full on the thirtieth day, when is it half full? Answer: On the twenty-ninth day. The global lily pond in which four billion of us live may already be half full.
>
> —*Lester Brown*

■ Control over our fertility helps us control our lives. It also allows the human race to survive and, at least in parts of the world, to prosper. The topic of birth control provokes much emotional controversy. Individuals and institutions alike are inclined to believe in the moral rightness of their particular stance on the subject, whatever that stance may be. As each of us tries to find his or her own path through the quagmire of controversy, we can be guided by what we learn. We need to arm ourselves with knowledge—not only about the methods and mechanics of contraception and birth control but also about our own motivations, needs, weaknesses, and strengths.

SUMMARY

Risk and Responsibility

- Over the period of 1 year, couples who do not use contraception have a 90% chance of pregnancy. Most couples do not use contraception during their first intercourse. As people become older, they tend to become more consistent users of contraceptive methods.

- Many people knowingly risk pregnancy by having unprotected intercourse. The more "successful" they are at risk taking, the more likely they are to take chances again. People also take risks because of faulty knowledge, denial of their sexuality, or a subconscious desire for a child.

- Because women are the ones who get pregnant, they may have greater interest than men in controlling their fertility. More men are now sharing the responsibility.

Methods of Contraception and Birth Control

- *Birth control* is any means of preventing a birth from taking place. *Contraception* is birth control that works specifically by preventing the union of sperm and egg.

- The most reliable method of birth control is *abstinence*—refraining from sexual intercourse. Another method of birth control is *outercourse*—using any avenue of sexual intimacy except penile-vaginal intercourse.

- *Oral contraceptives* are the most widely used form of reversible birth control in the United States. Birth control pills contain synthetic hormones: progestin and (usually) estrogen. The pill is highly effective if taken regularly. There are side effects and possible problems that affect some users. The greatest risks are to smokers, women over 35, and women with certain health disorders, such as cardiovascular problems.

- Thin capsules containing progestin that are implanted under the skin of a woman's arm protect against pregnancy for 5 years. When they are removed, fertility is restored. These *implants* (marketed as *Norplant*) may be the most effective reversible contraceptive ever marketed. The injectable hormone *Depo-provera (DMPA)* is now available in the United States. It is administered at 3-month intervals.

- A *condom* (or *male condom*) is a thin sheath of latex, rubber, polyurethane, or processed animal tissue that fits over the erect penis and prevents semen from being transmitted. It is the third most widely used birth control method in the United States. Condoms are very effective for contraception when used correctly, especially in combination with spermicidal foam or film. Latex and polyurethane condoms also help provide protection against STDs.

- The *female condom, diaphragm,* and *cervical cap* are barrier methods used by women. The diaphragm and cervical cap cover the cervical opening. They are used with spermicidal jelly or cream. The diaphragm and cervical cap are effective if used properly. Female condoms, in addition to lining the vagina, cover much of the vulva, providing more protection against disease organisms.

- *Spermicides* are chemicals that are toxic to sperm. *Nonoxynol-9* is the most common ingredient. *Contraceptive foam* provides fairly good protection when used alone, but other preparations are more effective if combined with a barrier method. Other spermicidal products are *bioadhesive gel, film,* cream, jelly, and vaginal suppositories.

- An *intrauterine device (IUD)* is a tiny plastic or metal device that is inserted through the cervical os into the uterus. It disrupts the fertilization and implantation processes.

- *Fertility awareness methods* (or natural family planning) involve a woman's awareness of her body's reproductive cycles. These include the *calendar (rhythm), basal body temperature (BBT), cervical mucus,* and *symptothermal methods.* These methods are suitable only for women with regular menstrual cycles and high motivation.

- Surgical *sterilization* (or *voluntary surgical contraception*) is the most popular form of birth control among married couples and women in this country. The most common form for women is *tubal ligation,* closing off the fallopian tubes. The surgical procedure that sterilizes men is a *vasectomy,* in which each vas deferens (sperm-carrying tube) is closed off. These methods of birth control are very effective.

- *Emergency contraception* (postcoital or "morning-after" birth control) following unprotected intercourse can prevent conception or expel a blastocyst. The "morning-after" pill, minipill, and copper IUD are the most common methods currently used.

Abortion

- *Abortion,* the expulsion of the conceptus from the uterus, can be *spontaneous* or induced. *Mifepristone with misoprostol* (formerly known as *RU-486*) is available worldwide to terminate early pregnancy. It is expected to be available in this country soon. Surgical methods of abortion are *vacuum aspiration, dilation and evacuation (D & E),* and *hysterotomy.* Nonsurgical methods utilize injections of prostaglandins, saline solution, or urea solution. Abortion is generally safe if done in the first trimester. Second-trimester abortions are significantly riskier.

- In the United States, there are about 1.2 million abortions annually. The abortion rate has declined slightly in recent years, possibly due to reduced access, an aging population, and greater use of condoms.

- For women, the abortion decision is complex; their developmental/life stage is important, and their reasons for choosing abortion have to do with relationships or educational or economic circumstances. Men often feel powerless and ambivalent; many men feel residual guilt and sadness following an abortion.

- In the abortion controversy, pro-life advocates argue that life begins at conception, that abortion leads to euthanasia, and that many who want to adopt are unable to because fewer babies are born as a result of abortion. Pro-choice advocates argue that women have the right to decide whether to continue a pregnancy, that abortion is needed as a birth control alternative because contraceptives are not 100% effective, and that if abortion is not legal, women will have unsafe illegal abortions. A key issue in the debate is when the embryo or fetus becomes human life.

- The current reigning constitutional doctrine on abortion was established by *Planned Parenthood v. Casey* in 1992, which states that a law regulating abortion is unconstitutional if it represents a substantial obstacle to a woman seeking an abortion.

Research Issues

- High development costs, government regulations, and marketing priorities all play a part in restricting contraceptive research. The biggest barrier, however, is the fear of lawsuits.

SUGGESTED READING

Chesler, Ellen. (1992). *A Woman of Valor: Margaret Sanger and the Birth Control Movement in America.* New York: Simon & Schuster. The biography of Margaret Sanger, who, in the early decades of this century, fought for women's contraceptive rights, an idea as divisive then as abortion rights are today.

Greer, Germaine. (1984). *Sex and Destiny.* New York: Harper & Row. A critique of the politics of fertility that is brilliant, controversial, opinionated, passionate, and refreshing; covers a wide range of topics, including contraception, abortion, infanticide, eugenics, and population control.

Hatcher, Robert, Stewart, F., Trussel, J., Kowal, D., Guest, F., Stewart, G., & Cates, W. (1994). *Contraceptive Technology* (16th ed.). New York: Irvington. A comprehensive and technically reliable book on developments in contraceptive technology; updated regularly.

Luker, Kristin. (1975). *Taking Chances.* Berkeley, CA: University of California Press. A major work on contraceptive risk taking; one of the most influential books in the field.

Tribe, Laurence. (1992). *Abortion: The Clash of Absolutes.* New York: Norton. An incisive, balanced book on the social, medical, political, legal, religious, and moral aspects of the abortion debate.

Winikoff, Beverly, & Wymelenberg, Suzanne. (1997). *The Whole Truth About Contraception.* Washington, DC: National Academy of Sciences. A user-friendly and scientifically accurate guide to the methods of birth control.

12

Conception, Pregnancy, and Childbirth

*T*HE BIRTH OF A WANTED CHILD is considered by many parents to be the happiest event of their lives. Today, however, pain and controversy surround many aspects of this completely natural process. As we struggle to balance the rights of the mother, the father, the fetus, and society itself in these matters, we find ourselves considering the quality of life as well as life's mere existence.

For most American women, pregnancy will be relatively comfortable and the outcome predictably joyful. Yet for increasing numbers of others, especially among the poor, the prospect of having children raises the specters of drugs, disease, malnutrition, and familial chaos. And there are those couples who have dreamed of and planned for families for years, only to find that they are unable to conceive.

In this chapter, we view pregnancy and childbirth from biological, social, and psychological perspectives. We consider pregnancy loss, infertility, and reproductive techniques. And we look at the challenges of the transition to parenthood.

FERTILIZATION AND FETAL DEVELOPMENT

As you will recall from Chapter 3, once the secondary oocyte has been released from the ovary, it drifts into the fallopian tube, where it may be fertilized if live sperm are present (Figure 12.1). If the pregnancy proceeds without interruption, the birth will occur in approximately 266 days. (Traditionally, physicians count the first day of the pregnancy as the day on which the woman began her last menstrual period; they calculate the due date to be 280 days, which is also 10 lunar months, from that day.)

The Fertilization Process

The oocyte remains viable for 12–24 hours after ovulation; most sperm are viable in the female reproductive tract for 12–48 hours, although some "super sperm" may be viable for up to 72 hours (Marieb, 1992). Therefore, for fertilization to occur, intercourse must take place within a period of 3 days before and 1 day after ovulation.

Of the millions of sperm ejaculated into the vagina, only a few thousand (or even just a few hundred) actually reach the fallopian tubes. The others leak from the vagina or are destroyed within its acidic environment. Those that make it into the cervix (which is easier during ovulation, when the cervical mucus becomes more fluid) may still be destroyed by white blood cells within the uterus. Furthermore, the sperm that actually reach the oocyte within a few minutes of ejaculation are not yet capable of getting through its outer layers. They must first undergo **capacitation,** the process by which their membranes become fragile enough to release the enzymes from their acrosomes (the helmetlike coverings of the sperm's nuclei). It takes 6–8 hours for this acrosomal reaction to occur. Enzymes from hundreds of sperm must be released in order for the oocyte's outer layers (the corona radiata and the zona pellucida) to soften sufficiently to allow a sperm to be absorbed.

If your parents didn't have any children, there's a good chance that you won't have any.

—*Clarence Day (1874–1935)*

Expectant parents who want a boy will get a girl, and vice versa; those who practice birth control will get twins.

—*John Rush*

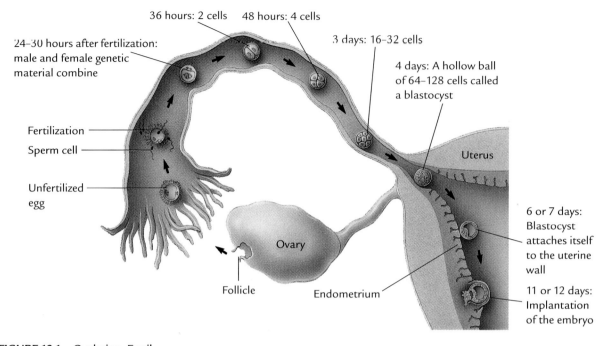

FIGURE 12.1 Ovulation, Fertilization, and Development of the Blastocyst. This drawing charts the progress of the ovulated oocyte (unfertilized egg) through fertilization and pre-embryonic development.

Once a single sperm is inside the oocyte cytoplasm, an electrical reaction occurs that prevents any other sperm from entering the oocyte. Immediately, the oocyte begins to swell, detaching the sperm that still cling to its outer layer. Then it completes the final stage of cell division and becomes a mature ovum by forming the ovum nucleus. The nuclei of sperm and ovum then release their chromosomes, which combine to form the diploid zygote, containing 23 pairs of chromosomes. (Each parent contributes one chromosome to each of the pairs.) Fertilization is now complete, and preembryonic development begins. Within 9 months, this single cell, the zygote, may become the 6000 billion cells that constitute a human being.

Development of the Conceptus

Following fertilization, the zygote undergoes a series of divisions, during which the cells replicate themselves. After 4 or 5 days, there are about 100 cells, now called a **blastocyst.** On about the fifth day, the blastocyst arrives in the uterine cavity, where it floats for a day or two before implanting in the soft, blood-rich uterine lining (endometrium), which has spent the past 3 weeks preparing for its arrival. The process of **implantation** takes about 1 week. Human chorionic gonadotropin (HCG) secreted by the blastocyst maintains the uterine environment in an "embryo-friendly" condition and prevents the shedding of the endometrium, which would normally occur during menstruation.

The blastocyst, or pre-embryo, rapidly grows into an **embryo,** which will, in turn, be referred to as a **fetus** after the eighth week of **gestation** (pregnancy). During the first 2 or 3 weeks of development, the **embryonic membranes** are formed. These include the **amnion** (amniotic sac), a membranous sac that will contain the embryo and **amniotic fluid;** the **yolk sac,** producer

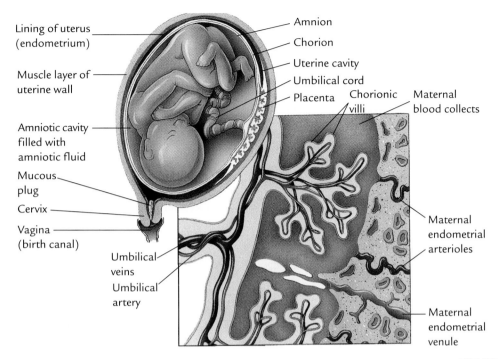

Lining of uterus (endometrium)

Muscle layer of uterine wall

Amniotic cavity filled with amniotic fluid

Mucous plug

Cervix

Vagina (birth canal)

Umbilical veins

Umbilical artery

Amnion

Chorion

Uterine cavity

Umbilical cord

Placenta

Chorionic villi

Maternal blood collects

Maternal endometrial arterioles

Maternal endometrial venule

FIGURE 12.2 **The Fetus in the Uterus and a Cross Section of the Placenta.** The placenta is the organ of exchange between mother and fetus. Nutrients and oxygen pass from the mother to the fetus, and waste products pass from the fetus to the mother via blood vessels within the umbilical cord.

of the embryo's first blood cells and the germ cells that will develop into gonads; and the **chorion,** the embryo's outermost membrane (Figure 12.2).

During the 3rd week, extensive cell migration occurs, and the stage is set for the development of the organs. The first body segments and the brain begin to form. The digestive and circulatory systems begin to develop in the 4th week, and the heart begins to pump blood. By the end of the first month, the spinal cord and nervous system have also begun to develop. The 5th week sees the formation of arms and legs. In the 6th week, the eyes and ears form. At 7 weeks, the reproductive organs begin to differentiate in males; female reproductive organs continue to develop. At 8 weeks, the fetus is about the size of a thumb, although the head is nearly as large as the body. The brain begins to function to coordinate the development of the internal organs. Facial features begin to form, and bones begin to develop. Arms, hands, fingers, legs, feet, toes, and eyes are almost fully developed at 12 weeks. At 15 weeks, the fetus has a strong heartbeat, some digestion, and active muscles. Most bones are developed by then, and the eyebrows appear. At this stage, the fetus is covered with a fine, downy hair called **lanugo.**

Throughout its development, the fetus is nourished through the **placenta.** The placenta begins to develop from part of the blastocyst following implantation. It grows larger as the fetus does, passing nutrients from the mother's bloodstream to the fetus, to which it is attached by the **umbilical cord.** The placenta serves as a biochemical barrier; it allows dissolved substances to pass to the fetus but blocks blood cells and large molecules.

By 5 months, the fetus is 10–12 inches long and weighs between ½ and 1 lb. The internal organs are well developed, although the lungs cannot function well outside the uterus. At 6 months, the fetus is 11–14 inches long and weighs more than 1 lb. At 7 months, it is 13–17 inches long and weighs about 3 lb. At this point, most healthy fetuses are viable—that is, capable of

> What was your original face before you were born?
>
> *—Zen koan (riddle)*

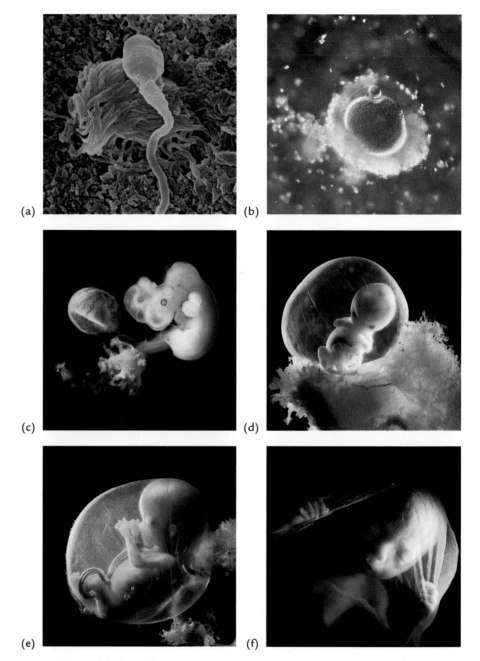

(a) After ejaculation, several million sperm move through the cervical mucus toward the fallopian tubes; an ovum has moved into one of the tubes. On their way to the ovum, millions of sperm are destroyed in the vagina, uterus, or fallopian tubes. Some go the wrong direction in the vagina, and others swim into the wrong tube. (b) The mother's and father's chromosomes have united, and the fertilized ovum has divided for the first time. After about 1 week, the blastocyst will implant itself in the uterine lining. (c) The embryo is 5 weeks old and is ⅖ of an inch long. It floats in the embryonic sac. The major divisions of the brain can be seen, as well as an eye, hands, arms, and a long tail. (d) The embryo is now 7 weeks old and is almost 1 inch long. Its external and internal organs are developing. It has eyes, nose, mouth, lips, and tongue. (e) At 12 weeks, the fetus is over 3 inches long and weighs almost 1 ounce. (f) At 16 weeks, the fetus is more than 6 inches long and weighs about 7 ounces. All its organs have been formed. The time that follows is now one of simple growth.

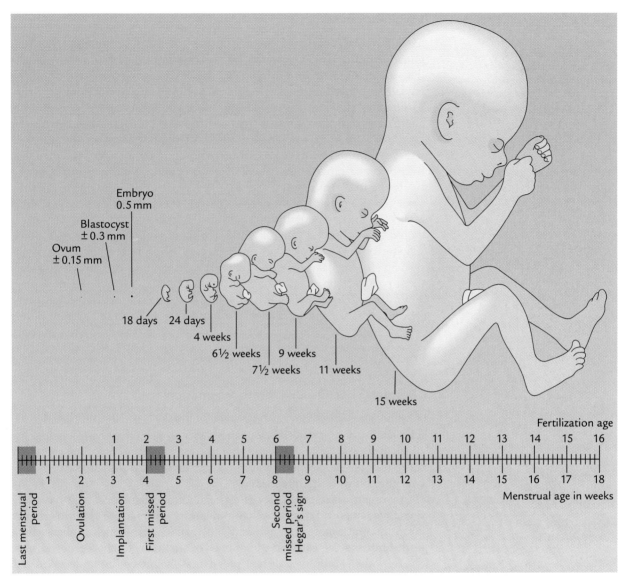

Embryo
0.5 mm

Blastocyst
± 0.3 mm

Ovum
± 0.15 mm

18 days   24 days

4 weeks

6½ weeks   9 weeks

7½ weeks   11 weeks

15 weeks

Fertilization age

Menstrual age in weeks

Last menstrual period

Ovulation

Implantation

First missed period

Second missed period
Hegar's sign

FIGURE 12.3   Growth of the Embryo and Fetus. In this drawing, the actual sizes of the developing embryo and fetus are shown, from conception through the first 15 weeks.

surviving outside the womb. (Although some fetuses are viable at 5 or 6 months, they require specialized care to survive.) The fetus spends the final 2 months of gestation growing rapidly. At term (9 months), it will be about 20 inches long and will weigh about 7 lb (Figure 12.3).

BEING PREGNANT

Pregnancy is an important life event for both women and their partners. From the moment it is discovered, a pregnancy affects people's feelings about themselves, their relationships with their partners, and the interrelationships of other family members as well.

Everyone wants to know when his or her baby's going to be born. It is fairly simple to figure out the date: Add 7 days to the first day of the last menstrual period. Then subtract 3 months and add 1 year. For example, if a woman's last menstrual period began on July 17, 1999, add 7 days (July 24). Next, subtract 3 months (April 24). Then add 1 year. This gives the expected date of birth as April 24, 2000. Few births actually occur on the date predicted, but 60% of babies are born within 5 days of the predicted time.

Pregnancy Tests

Chemical tests designed to detect the presence of **human chorionic gonadotropin (HCG),** secreted by the developing placenta, can usually determine pregnancy approximately 2 weeks following a missed (or spotty) menstrual period. Pregnancy testing may be done in a doctor's office or family planning clinic, or home pregnancy tests may be purchased in most drugstores. The directions must be followed closely. Blood analysis can also be used to determine if a pregnancy exists. Although such tests diagnose pregnancy with better than 95% accuracy, no absolute certainty exists until a fetal heartbeat and movements can be detected or ultrasound is performed.

The first reliable physical sign of pregnancy can be distinguished about 4 weeks after a woman misses her period. By this time, changes in her cervix and pelvis are apparent during a pelvic examination. At this time the woman would be considered to be 8 weeks pregnant, according to medical terminology; physicians calculate pregnancy as beginning at the time of the woman's last menstrual period rather than at the time of actual fertilization (because that date is often difficult to determine). Another signal of pregnancy, called **Hegar's sign,** is a softening of the uterus just above the cervix, which can be felt during a vaginal examination. In addition, a slight purple hue colors the labia minora; the vagina and cervix also take on a purplish color rather than the usual pink.

Changes That Occur During Pregnancy

A woman's feelings during pregnancy will vary dramatically according to who she is, how she feels about pregnancy and motherhood, whether the pregnancy was planned, whether she has a secure home situation, and many other factors. Her feelings may be ambivalent; they will probably change over the course of the pregnancy.

A woman's first pregnancy is especially important because it has traditionally symbolized her transition to maturity. Even as social norms change and it becomes more common and "acceptable" for women to defer childbirth until they've established a career or for them to choose not to have children, the significance of first pregnancy should not be underestimated. It is a major developmental milestone in the lives of mothers—and of fathers as well (Marsiglio & Donnelley, 1991).

A couple's relationship is likely to undergo changes during pregnancy. It can be a stressful time, especially if the pregnancy was unanticipated. Communication is especially important during this period, because each partner may have preconceived ideas about what the other is feeling. Both partners may have fears about the baby's well-being, the approaching birth, their ability to parent, and the ways in which the baby will interfere with their own relationship. All of these concerns are normal. Sharing them, perhaps in the setting of a prenatal group, can deepen and strengthen the relationship. If the pregnant woman's partner is not supportive or if she does not have a partner, it is important that she find other sources of support—family, friends, women's groups—and that she not be reluctant to ask for help.

A pregnant woman's relationship with her own mother may also undergo changes. In a certain sense, becoming a mother makes a woman the equal of her own mother. She can now lay claim to being treated as an adult.

Couples who defer parenthood until other components of their lives, such as careers, are solidified express increased satisfaction with their lives and their marital relationships.

Women who have depended on their mothers tend to become more independent and assertive as their pregnancy progresses. Women who have been distant, hostile, or alienated from their own mothers may begin to identify with their mothers' experience of pregnancy. Even women who have delayed childbearing until their thirties may be surprised to find their relationships with their mothers changing and becoming more "adult." Working through these changing relationships is a kind of "psychological gestation" that accompanies the physiological gestation of the fetus.

The first trimester (3 months) of pregnancy may be difficult physically for the expectant mother. She may experience nausea, fatigue, and painful swelling of the breasts. She may also have fears that she may miscarry or that the child will not be normal. Her sexuality may undergo changes, resulting in unfamiliar needs (for more, less, or differently expressed sexual love), which may in turn cause anxiety. (Sexuality during pregnancy is discussed further in the box that accompanies this section.) Education about the birth process and her own body's functioning and support from partner, friends, relatives, and health-care professionals are the best antidotes to fear.

During the second trimester, most of the nausea and fatigue disappear, and the pregnant woman can feel the fetus move within her. Worries about miscarriage will probably begin to diminish, too, for the riskiest part of fetal development has passed. The pregnant woman may look and feel radiantly happy. She will very likely feel proud of her accomplishment and be delighted as her pregnancy begins to show. She may feel in harmony with life's natural rhythms. Some women, however, may be concerned about their increasing size. They may fear that they are becoming unattractive. A partner's attention and reassurance will ease these fears.

The third trimester may be the time of the greatest difficulties in daily living. The uterus, originally about the size of the woman's fist, has now

IT IS NOT UNUSUAL for a woman's sexual feelings and actions to change during pregnancy, although there is great variation among women in these expressions of sexuality. Some women feel beautiful, energetic, sensual, and interested in sex, whereas others feel awkward and decidedly unsexy. Some studies indicate a lessening of women's sexual interest during pregnancy and a corresponding decline in coital frequency; others show a shift in the type of activities preferred (Hart, Cohen, Gingold, & Homburg, 1991). It is also quite possible for a woman's sexual feelings to fluctuate during this time. Men may also feel confusion or conflicts about sexual activity. They, like many women, may have been conditioned to find the pregnant body unerotic. Or they may feel deep sexual attraction to their pregnant partners, yet fear their feelings are "strange" or unusual. They may also worry about hurting their partner or the baby.

Although there are no "rules" governing sexual behavior during pregnancy, a few basic precautions should be observed:

- If the woman has had a prior miscarriage, she should check with her health practitioner before having intercourse, masturbating, or engaging in other activities that might lead to orgasm. Powerful uterine contractions could induce a spontaneous abortion in some women, especially during the first trimester.

- If there is bleeding from the vagina, the woman should refrain from sexual activity and consult her physician or midwife at once.

- If the insertion of the penis into the vagina causes pain that is not easily remedied by a change of position, the couple should refrain from intercourse.

- Pressure on the woman's abdomen should be avoided, especially during the final months of pregnancy.

- Late in pregnancy, an orgasm is likely to induce uterine contractions. Generally, this is not considered harmful, but the pregnant woman may want to discuss it with her practitioner. (Occasionally, labor begins when the waters break as the result of orgasmic contractions.)

A couple, especially if it is their first pregnancy, may be uncertain as to how to express their sexual feelings. The following guidelines may be helpful:

- Even during a normal pregnancy, sexual intercourse may be uncomfortable. The couple may want to try such positions as side-by-side or rear-entry, to avoid pressure on the woman's abdomen and to facilitate more shallow penetration. (See illustrations of different sexual positions in Chapter 9.)

- Even if intercourse is not comfortable for the woman, orgasm may still be intensely pleasurable. She may wish to consider the possibilities of masturbation (alone or with her partner) or of cunnilingus. It is important to note that air should *not* be blown into the vagina during cunnilingus.

- Both partners should remember that there are no "rules" about sexuality during pregnancy. This is a time for relaxing, enjoying the woman's changing body, talking a lot, touching each other, and experimenting with new ways—both sexual and nonsexual—of expressing affection.

enlarged to fill the pelvic cavity and pushes up into the abdominal cavity, exerting increasing pressure on the other internal organs (Figure 12.4). Water retention (edema) is a fairly common problem during late pregnancy. Edema may cause swelling in the face, hands, ankles, and feet, but it can often be controlled by cutting down on salt and carbohydrates. If dietary changes do not help this condition, a pregnant woman should consult her physician. Her physical abilities are limited by her size. She may need to cut back or stop her work. A family dependent on the pregnant woman's income may suffer a severe financial crunch.

The woman and her partner may become increasingly concerned about the upcoming birth. Some women experience periods of depression in the month preceding their delivery; they may feel physically awkward and sexually unattractive. Many feel an exhilarating sense of excitement and anticipation marked by energetic bursts of industriousness. They feel that the

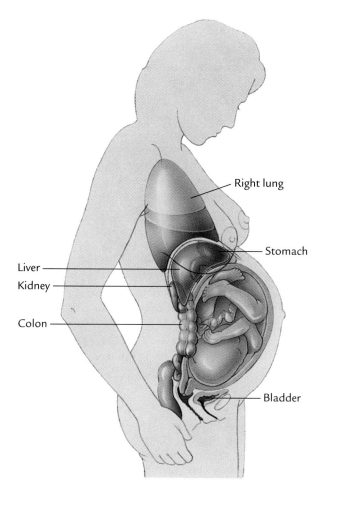

FIGURE 12.4 Mother and Fetus in Third Trimester of Pregnancy. The expanding uterus affects the mother's internal organs, causing feelings of pressure and possible discomfort.

Right lung

Stomach

Liver

Kidney

Colon

Bladder

fetus is a member of the family. Both parents may begin talking to the fetus and "playing" with it by patting and rubbing the mother's belly.

The principal developmental tasks for the expectant mother and father can be summarized as follows:

Tasks of an Expectant Mother

- Development of an emotional attachment to the fetus
- Differentiation of the self from the fetus
- Acceptance and resolution of the relationship with the woman's own mother
- Resolution of dependency issues (generally involving parents or husband/partner)
- Evaluation of practical and financial responsibilities

Tasks of an Expectant Father

- Acceptance of the pregnancy and attachment to the fetus
- Acceptance and resolution of the relationship with the man's own father
- Resolution of dependency issues (involving wife/partner)
- Evaluation of practical and financial responsibilities

Complications of Pregnancy and Dangers to the Fetus

Usually, pregnancy proceeds without major complications. Good nutrition is one of the most important factors in having a complication-free pregnancy. However, some women experience minor to serious complications.

Effects of Teratogens   Substances other than nutrients may reach the developing embryo or fetus through the placenta. Although few extensive studies have been done on the subject, toxic substances in the environment can also affect the health of the fetus. Whatever a woman breathes, eats, or drinks is eventually received by the conceptus in some proportion. A fetus's blood-alcohol level, for example, is equal to that of the mother (Rosenthal, 1990). **Teratogens,** substances that cause defects (such as brain damage or physical deformities) in developing embryos or fetuses, are directly traceable in only about 2–3% of cases of birth defects. (See the box "Pregnancy and Drugs Don't Mix.") They are thought to be linked to 25–30% of such cases; the causes of the remaining cases remain unknown (Healy, 1988).

Chemicals and environmental pollutants are also potentially threatening. Continuous exposure to lead, most commonly in paint products or water from lead pipes, has been implicated in a variety of learning disorders. Mercury, from fish contaminated by industrial wastes, is a known cause of physical deformities. Solvents, pesticides, and certain chemical fertilizers should be avoided or used with extreme caution both at home and in the workplace.

Infectious Diseases   Infectious diseases can also damage the fetus. If a woman contracts German measles (rubella) during the first 3 months of pregnancy, her child may be born with physical or mental disabilities. Immunization against rubella is available, but it must be done before the woman is pregnant; otherwise, the injection will be as harmful to the fetus as the disease itself. Group B streptococcus, a bacterium carried by 15–40% of pregnant women, is harmless to adults but can be fatal to newborns. Each year, about 12,000 infants are infected; 1600–2000 of them die. The American Academy of Pediatrics recommends that all pregnant women be screened for strep B. Antibiotics administered to the newborn during labor can greatly reduce the danger.

Sexually Transmitted Diseases   Sexually transmitted diseases may also damage the fetus. The Centers for Disease Control and Prevention (CDC) recommends that all pregnant women be screened for hepatitis B, a virus that can be passed to the infant at birth. If the mother tests positive, her child can be immunized immediately following birth. A woman with gonorrhea may expose her child to blindness from contact with the infected vagina; the baby will need immediate antibiotic treatment. A woman with HIV or AIDS has a 25–40% chance of passing the virus to the fetus via the placenta (Cowley, 1991; Fischl, Dickinson, Segal, Flannagan, & Rodriguez, 1987). The number of infants with HIV or AIDS is increasing as more women become infected with the virus either before or during pregnancy (see Chapter 16). However, if the drug AZT is administered to the pregnant woman, it can significantly reduce the possibility of HIV transmission ("Routine AZT Use," 1996).

AMONG THE LESSONS most of us learn from our parents is to be good to our children. This lesson is crucial during pregnancy, when the unborn child is most vulnerable to substances generated by the mother. But many of us do not put this lesson into action: Between 1979 and 1990, there was a 456% increase in the number of drug-affected newborns discharged from hospitals (Dicker & Leighton, 1994).

Because the placenta does not block all substances from entering the fetus's bloodstream, it is prudent to assume that there is no safe drug. With the exception of a handful of prescription and over-the-counter medications, all drugs—including alcohol, tobacco, street drugs, and many legal drugs—may have the potential to cause physical damage, malformation, or miscarriage. The most devastating outcomes occur for pregnant women who lack information about drugs and whose judgment is impaired because they are under the influence of uncontrolled street drugs or alcohol.

The following is a partial list of drugs and their effects on the fetus. Not well understood or studied are the effects of the father's drug use on the health of the fetus. Regardless, it is prudent for both partners to assume healthy lifestyles before considering pregnancy.

Alcohol

Studies have linked chronic ingestion of alcohol during pregnancy to fetal alcohol syndrome (FAS), which can include unusual facial characteristics, small head and body size, congenital heart defects, defective joints, poor mental capabilities, and abnormal behavior patterns in the newborn. Lesser amounts of alcohol may result in fetal alcohol effect (FAE), the most common problem of which is growth retardation (Waterson & Murray-Lyon, 1990). FAS and FAE are often difficult to diagnose right away, but the incidence of fetal alcohol syndrome is probably in the range of 4000–12,000 cases per year. There are thousands more cases of FAE (SAMHSA, 1993). The CDC reports that FAS is 6 times more common in African Americans than in Whites and 30 times more common in Native Americans (Rosenthal, 1990a). The rate is higher among those with low socioeconomic status (Abel, 1995). Most experts counsel pregnant women to abstain entirely from alcohol because there is no safe quantity known at this time.

continued

The increasingly widespread incidence of genital herpes may present some hazards for newborns. About 1000 cases of neonatal herpes are reported yearly. The herpes simplex virus may cause brain damage and is potentially life-threatening for these infants (Gelven, 1996). Careful monitoring by a physician can determine whether a vaginal delivery should take place. Although the harmful potential of neonatal herpes should not be underestimated, if the appropriate procedures are followed by the infected mother and her physician or midwife, the chance of infection from genital lesions is minimal. Testing for genital herpes may be recommended for both expectant parents. A simple blood test, the Western Blot, can now be used to detect the presence of the virus. Once the baby is born, a mother who is experiencing an outbreak of either oral or genital herpes should wash her hands often and carefully and not permit contact between her hands, contaminated objects, and the baby's mucous membranes (inside of eyes, mouth, nose, penis, vagina, vulva, and rectum). If the father is infected, he should do likewise until the lesions have subsided.

In the early 1980s, syphilis was rarely seen in infants. In the early 1990s, however, the incidence greatly increased, peaking at about 4400 cases before beginning to decline. In 1995 more than 1500 cases of congenital syphilis were reported (CDC, 1996b). The principal reason for this resurgence is lack of prenatal care, which normally includes testing for syphilis. Most infants with syphilis have no obvious symptoms and suffer no long-term effects if they are treated promptly with antibiotics.

Opiates and Cocaine

Mothers who regularly use opiates (heroin, morphine, codeine, and opium) are likely to have infants who are addicted at birth. A study in New York of drug-exposed infants revealed that the opiate-exposed babies showed more neurological damage than the cocaine-exposed babies, and that those infants exposed to polydrug abuse (both opiates and cocaine) were worse off than those exposed to any single drug in terms of gestational age at birth, birth weight, and length of hospital stay (Kaye, Elkind, Goldberg, & Tytun, 1989). It should be noted that many drug-exposed infants have been exposed to alcohol as well.

Tobacco

Cigarette smoking affects the unborn child (Ellard et al., 1996). Babies born to women who smoke during pregnancy are an average of one-quarter to one-half pound lighter at birth than babies born to nonsmokers. Second-hand smoke breathed by the mother is also considered dangerous to the developing fetus (Healy, 1988; Martinez et al., 1994). Smoking has been implicated in sudden infant death syndrome (SIDS), respiratory disorders in children, and various adverse pregnancy outcomes. Maternal smoking during pregnancy may also create a serious risk for smoking dependence in female offspring (Kandel, Wu, & Davies, 1994).

Prescription and Over-the-Counter Drugs

Prescription drugs should be used only under careful medical supervision because some may cause serious harm to the fetus. The most dramatic illustration of the teratogenic effects of a prescription drug occurred in the 1950s, when the drug thalidomide, given to alleviate morning sickness, caused severe birth defects in more than 10,000 babies. Thalidomide has been off the market for more than 40 years, but it is scheduled to reappear soon because it has proven beneficial in treating leprosy, some cancers, and autoimmune diseases such as lupus (Cowley, 1997). It is also being investigated as a treatment for AIDS. Isotretinoin (Acutane), a popular anti-acne drug, has been implicated in more than 1000 cases of severe birth defects. Vitamins, aspirin, and other over-the-counter drugs, as well as large quantities of caffeine-containing food and drink (coffee, tea, cola, chocolate) should be avoided or used only under medical supervision. Vitamin A in large doses can cause serious birth defects.

Ectopic Pregnancy   In **ectopic pregnancy** (tubal pregnancy), the incidence of which has more than quadrupled in the past 20 years, the fertilized egg implants itself in the fallopian tube. Generally, this occurs because the tube is obstructed, most often as a result of pelvic inflammatory disease (Hilts, 1991). The pregnancy will never come to term. The embryo may spontaneously abort, or the embryo and placenta will continue to expand until they rupture the fallopian tube. Salpingectomy (removal of the tube) and abortion of the conceptus may be necessary to save the mother's life.

Toxemia and Preeclampsia   **Toxemia,** which may appear in the 20th to 24th week of pregnancy, is characterized by high blood pressure and edema. It can generally be treated through nutritional means. If untreated, toxemia can develop into preeclampsia after the 24th week.

    Preeclampsia is characterized by increasingly high blood pressure. Toxemia and preeclampsia are also known as gestational edema-proteinuria-hypertension complex. If untreated, they can lead to eclampsia, maternal convulsions that pose a serious threat to mother and child. Eclampsia is not common; it is prevented by keeping the blood pressure down through diet, rest, and sometimes medication. It is important for a pregnant woman to have her blood pressure checked regularly.

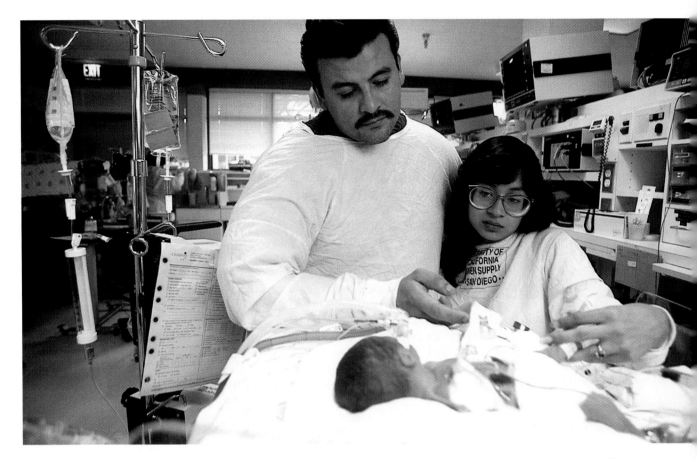

Low birth weight (prematurity) affects about 7% of newborns in the United States. Adequate prenatal care significantly reduces the risk of low birth weight.

Low Birth Weight Prematurity, or **low birth weight (LBW),** is a major complication in the third trimester of pregnancy, affecting about 7% of newborns yearly (about 289,700 in 1996) in the United States (National Center for Health Statistics, 1998). The fundamental problem of prematurity is that many of the infant's vital organs are insufficiently developed. An LBW baby usually weighs less than 5.5 lb at birth. Most premature infants will grow normally, but many will experience disabilities. LBW infants are subject to various respiratory problems as well as infections. Feeding, too, is a problem because the infants may be too small to suck a breast or bottle, and their swallowing mechanisms may be too underdeveloped to permit them to drink. As premature infants get older, problems such as low intelligence, learning difficulties, poor hearing and vision, and physical awkwardness may become apparent.

Premature delivery is one of the greatest problems confronting obstetrics today. About half the cases are related to teenage pregnancy, smoking, poor nutrition, and poor health in the mother (Pear, 1992; Schneck, Sideras, Fox, & Dupuis, 1990); the causes of the other half are unknown.

Prenatal care is extremely important as a means of preventing prematurity. One-third of all LBW births could be averted with adequate prenatal care (Scott, 1990a). We need to understand that if children's needs are not met today, we will all face the consequences of their deprivation tomorrow. The social and economic costs are bound to be very high.

Diagnosing Abnormalities of the Fetus

Both the desire to bear children and the desire to ensure that those children are healthy have encouraged the development of new diagnostic technologies. In cases where serious problems are suspected, these technologies may be quite helpful, but sometimes it seems that they are used "simply because they're there."

Ultrasound examinations use high-frequency sound waves to create a picture of the fetus in the uterus. The sound waves are transmitted through a quartz crystal; when they detect a change in the density, the sound waves bounce back to the crystal. The results are interpreted on a televisionlike screen; the picture is called a **sonogram.** Sonograms are used to determine fetal age and the location of the placenta; when used with amniocentesis (see below), they help determine the fetus's position so that the needle may be inserted safely. Often, it is possible to determine the fetus's sex during ultrasound. More extensive ultrasound techniques can be used to gain further information if there is the possibility of a problem with fetal development.

In **amniocentesis,** amniotic fluid is withdrawn from the uterus with a long, thin needle inserted through the abdominal wall (the position of the fetus is determined by ultrasound) (Figure 12.5). The fluid is then examined for evidence of possible birth defects such as Down syndrome, cystic fibrosis, Tay-Sachs disease, spina bifida, and conditions that are caused by chromosomal abnormalities. The sex of the fetus can also be determined. About 80–90% of amniocentesis tests are performed in cases of "advanced" maternal age, usually when the mother is over 35. The test is generally performed at about 16 weeks of pregnancy, although recently some physicians have begun performing "early amniocentesis" at 10–12 weeks. Amniocentesis carries a slight risk (a 0.5–2% chance of fetal death, depending on how early in pregnancy the test is performed) (Brandenburg, Jahoda, Pijpers, Reuss, Kleyer, & Wladmiroff, 1990; Hanson, Happ, Tennant, Hune, & Peterson, 1990; Stranc, 1997).

An alternative to amniocentesis more recently introduced in the United States is **chorionic villus sampling (CVS)** (see Figure 12.5). This procedure involves removal through the abdomen (by needle) or through the cervix (by catheter) of tiny pieces of the membrane that encases the embryo; it can be performed between 9 and 11 weeks of pregnancy. There may be a somewhat greater-than-normal chance of miscarriage with CVS due to the possible introduction of infectious microorganisms at the time of the procedure (Baumann, Jovanovic, Gellert, & Rauskolb, 1991). There have been reports of limb deformities in infants whose mothers underwent CVS; however, at this time these cases are not well understood and assignment of a cause is considered controversial (Stranc, 1997).

Alpha-fetoprotein (AFP) screening is a test (or series of tests) performed on the mother's blood after 16 weeks of pregnancy. It reveals defects of the spine, spinal cord, skull, and brain, such as anencephaly and spina bifida. It is much simpler than amniocentesis but sometimes yields false positive results (Samuels & Samuels, 1996). If the results are positive, other tests, such as amniocentesis and ultrasound, will be performed to confirm or negate the AFP screening findings.

For approximately 95% of women who undergo prenatal testing, the results are negative. The results of amniocentesis and AFP screening can't be

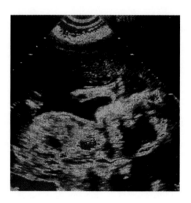

The pictures produced by ultrasound are called sonograms. They are used to determine fetal age, position of the fetus and placenta, and possible developmental problems.

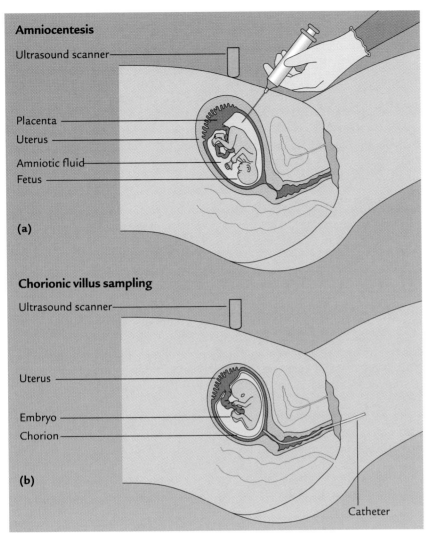

FIGURE 12.5 (a) Amniocentesis and (b) Chorionic Villus Sampling.

determined, however, until approximately 20 weeks of pregnancy; consequently, if the pregnancy is terminated through abortion at this stage, the process is likely to be physically and emotionally difficult. If a fetus is found to be defective, it may be carried to term, aborted, or, in rare but increasing instances, surgically treated while still in the womb (Kolata, 1990).

Pregnancy Loss

The loss of a child through **miscarriage** (spontaneous loss of a fetus before it can survive on its own), stillbirth, or death during early infancy is often a devastating experience that has been largely ignored in our society. The statement, "You can always have another one," may be meant as consolation, but it is particularly chilling to the ears of a grieving mother. In the past few years, however, the medical community has begun to respond to the emotional needs of parents who have lost a pregnancy or an infant.

Spontaneous Abortion   Spontaneous abortion, or miscarriage, is a powerful natural selective force toward bringing healthy babies into the world. About 1 out of 4 women is aware she has miscarried at least once (Beck, 1988). Studies indicate that at least 60% of all miscarriages are due to chromosomal abnormalities in the fetus. The first sign that a pregnant woman may miscarry is vaginal bleeding (spotting). If a woman's symptoms of pregnancy disappear and she develops pelvic cramps, she may be miscarrying; the fetus is usually expelled by uterine contractions. Most miscarriages occur between the 6th and 8th weeks of pregnancy. Evidence is increasing that certain occupations involving exposure to chemicals increase the likelihood of spontaneous abortions.

Infant Mortality   The U.S. infant mortality rate, although at its lowest point ever, remains far higher than that of most of the developed world. The U.S. Public Health Service reported 6.68 deaths for every 1000 live births in 1995 (U.S. Bureau of the Census, 1996). Among developed nations, our country ranks 20th for low infant mortality, meaning that 19 countries have *lower* infant mortality rates than the United States. Of the more than 35,000 American babies less than 1 year old who die each year, most are victims of the poverty that often results from racial or ethnic discrimination. The infant mortality rate for African Americans is more than twice that for Whites. Native Americans are also at high risk; for example, about 1 out of every 67 Navajo infants dies each year (Wilkerson, 1987). Up to one-third of infant deaths could be prevented if mothers were given adequate health care (Scott, 1990b).

Recent studies of prenatal care and birth outcomes have found that recipients of food and nutritional counseling through the federal program known as WIC (Special Supplemental Food Program for Women, Infants, and Children) have a much better chance of having healthy babies than do women of comparable ethnicity and socioeconomic status who are not in the WIC program (Frisbie, Biegler, de Turk, Forbes, & Pullum, 1997). One study estimated that one year of WIC expenditures could save society as much as $800 million in federal and state Medicaid expenditures (Avruch & Cackley, 1995).

Although many infants die of poverty-related conditions, others die from congenital problems (conditions appearing at birth) or from infectious diseases, accidents, or other causes. Sometimes the causes of death are not apparent; more than 3000 infant deaths per year are attributed to **sudden infant death syndrome (SIDS),** a perplexing phenomenon wherein an apparently healthy infant dies suddenly while sleeping. Sleeping position may be one variable contributing to SIDS in vulnerable infants. The American Academy of Pediatrics recommends that infants be placed on their backs for sleeping. Maternal smoking during pregnancy and exposure of the baby to secondhand smoke are also implicated in some SIDS deaths (Klonoff-Cohen et al., 1995; Seachrist, 1995). No one knows what all the factors are that contribute to this unpredictable event (Brazelton, 1995). Recently, closer investigation of a number of alleged SIDS deaths has led to the appalling discovery that some of them, perhaps 5–10%, were actually cases of infanticide in which the infants were smothered (Firstman & Talan, 1997; Southall, 1997). Physicians are now urged to consider all factors and to report any suspicions when presented with SIDS cases or repeated "near-SIDS" cases, especially if there has already been a SIDS death in the family (Begley, 1997b).

Coping with Loss   The depth of shock and grief felt by many who lose an infant before or during birth can be difficult for those who have not had a similar experience to understand. What they may not realize is that most women form a deep attachment to their children even before birth. At first, the attachment may be to a fantasy image of the unborn child. During the course of the pregnancy, the mother forms an acquaintance with her infant through the physical sensations she feels within her. Thus, the death of the fetus can also represent the death of a dream and of a hope for the future. This loss must be acknowledged and felt before psychological healing can take place (Vredeveldt, 1994).

The healing process takes time—months, a year, perhaps more for some. Support groups or counseling is often helpful, especially if healing does not seem to be progressing—if, for example, depression and physical symptoms don't appear to be diminishing (DeSpelder & Strickland, 1999).

> Dear Auntie will come with presents and will ask, "Where is our baby, sister?" And, Mother, you will tell her softly, "He is in the pupils of my eyes. He is in my bones and in my soul."
>
> —*Rabindranath Tagore (1864–1941)*

INFERTILITY

Some couples experience the pain of loss when they plan to have a child and then discover that they cannot get pregnant. **Infertility** is broadly defined as the inability to conceive a child after trying for a year or more. The problem of infertility has attracted a growing amount of public attention in recent years. In 1995, for example, about 7.1% of married couples (2.1 million), many of whom had deferred pregnancy because of career plans or later marriages, discovered they were infertile. About 1 million were childless and infertile (CDC, American Society for Reproductive Medicine, & RESOLVE, 1997). The greatest increase in infertility is found among women in the 35- to 44-year-old age bracket. Infertility among young African American couples is almost twice that of White couples.

Female Infertility

Most cases of infertility among women are due to physical factors. Hormones, stress, immunological factors, and environmental factors may also be involved.

Physical Causes   The leading cause of female infertility is blocked fallopian tubes, generally the result of **pelvic inflammatory disease (PID),** an infection of the fallopian tubes or uterus that is usually the result of a sexually transmitted disease (see Chapter 15). It can be caused by *gonococcus, Chlamydia,* or several other organisms. About 1 million cases of PID are treated each year; doctors estimate that about half of the cases go untreated because PID is often symptomless, especially in the early stages (Hilts, 1991; Mueller, Luz-Jimenez, Daling, Moore, McKnight, & Weiss, 1992). Treated early, PID can now be cured with a course of the new oral antibiotic oxflaxacin (trade name, Floxin) (Griffin & Mason, 1997; "New PID Treatment," 1997). Generally, only the woman with PID seeks treatment, and the man from whom she contracted the STD that caused it may continue to pass it on. Surgery, including laser surgery, may restore fertility if the damage has not progressed too far.

The second leading cause of infertility in women is **endometriosis;** it is most prevalent in women age 30 and over, many of whom have postponed childbirth. In this disease, uterine tissue grows outside the uterus, often appearing on the ovaries, in the fallopian tubes (where it may also block the tubes), and in the abdominal cavity. In its most severe form it may cause painful menstruation and intercourse, but most women with endometriosis are unaware that they have it. Hormone therapy and sometimes surgery are used for treatment.

A below-normal percentage of body fat, due to excessive dieting or exercise, may inhibit ovulation and delay pregnancy. In addition, benign growths such as fibroids and polyps on the uterus, ovaries, or fallopian tubes may also affect a woman's fertility. Surgery may restore fertility in many of these cases.

Hormonal and Psychological Causes   In addition to physical causes, there may be hormonal reasons for infertility. The pituitary gland may fail to produce sufficient hormones (follicle-stimulating hormone, or FSH, and luteinizing hormone, or LH) to stimulate ovulation, or it may release them at the wrong time. Stress, which may be increased by the anxiety of trying to become pregnant, may also contribute to lowered fertility. Occasionally, immunological causes may be present, the most important of which is the production of sperm antibodies by the woman. For an unknown reason, a woman may be allergic to her partner's sperm, and her immune system will produce antibodies to destroy them.

Environmental Factors   Toxic chemicals, such as those found in paint, solvents, and insecticides, or exposure to radiation therapy can threaten a woman's reproductive capacity. Smoking appears to reduce fertility in women (Laurent, Thompson, Addy, Garrison, & Moore, 1992). High caffeine intake (three cups of coffee or eight sodas a day) may also reduce women's odds of conceiving by as much as 26% ("Caffeine Intake," 1997; "Effects of Caffeine," 1996; "Women, Coffee and Fertility," 1995). Evidence indicates that the daughters of mothers who took diethylstibestrol (DES), a drug once thought to increase fertility and reduce the risk of miscarriage, have a significantly higher infertility rate.

Nature also plays a part. Beginning around age 30, a woman's fertility naturally begins to decline. By age 35, about one-quarter of women are infertile (Carroll, 1990).

Male Infertility

The primary causes of male infertility are low sperm count, lack of sperm motility, and blocked passageways. Some studies show that there is a variation in sperm counts among men residing in different parts of the country (Fisch, Ikeguchi, & Goluboff, 1996). What accounts for these regional differences is still unclear.

As with women, environmental factors may contribute to men's infertility. Increasing evidence suggests that toxic substances, such as lead or chemicals found in some solvents and herbicides, are responsible for decreased sperm counts. Smoking may produce reduced sperm counts or abnormal sperm. Prescription drugs such as cimetidine (Tagamet, for ulcers), prednisone (a corticosteroid that reduces tissue inflammation), or some medications for urinary tract infections have also been shown to affect the number of sperm that a man produces.

Large doses of marijuana cause decreased sperm counts and suppression of certain reproductive hormones. These effects are apparently reversed when marijuana smoking stops. Men are more at risk than women from environmental factors because they are constantly producing new sperm cells; for the same reason, men may also recover faster once the affecting factor has been removed.

Sons of mothers who took DES may have increased sperm abnormalities and fertility problems. Too much heat may temporarily reduce a man's sperm count (the male half of a couple trying to conceive may want to stay out of the hot tub for a while). A fairly common problem is the presence of a varicose vein called a **varicocele** above the testicle. Because it impairs circulation to the testicle, the varicocele causes an elevated scrotal temperature and thus interferes with sperm development. The varicocele may be surgically removed, but unless the man has a fairly good sperm count to begin with, his fertility may not improve.

Emotional Responses to Infertility

By the time a couple seek medical advice about their fertility problems, they may have already experienced a crisis in confronting the possibility of not being able to become biological parents. Many such couples feel they have lost control over a major area of their lives (Golombok, 1992; Olshansky, 1992). A number of studies suggest that women generally are more intensely affected than men (Andrews, Abbey, & Halman, 1991; Brand, 1989; McEwan, Costello, & Taylor, 1987; Wright, Duchesne, Sabourin, Bissonnette, Benoit, & Girard, 1991).

Infertility Treatment

Almost without exception, fertility problems are physical, not emotional, despite myths to the contrary (Figure 12.6). The two most popular myths are that anxiety over becoming pregnant leads to infertility and that if an infertile couple adopt a child, the couple will then be able to conceive on their own. Neither has any basis in medical fact, although it is true that some presumably infertile couples have conceived following an adoption. (This does not mean, however, that one should adopt a child to remedy infertility.) About 10–14% of infertility cases are unexplained. In some of these cases, fertility is restored for no discernible reason; in others, the infertility remains a mystery.

The techniques and technologies developed to achieve conception include fertility drugs, intrauterine insemination, sperm and egg banks, surrogate motherhood, and a number of procedures collectively known as **assisted reproductive technology (ART)**. ART includes in vitro fertilization and techniques known as GIFT, ZIFT, and ICSI (discussed in the sections that follow).

Some of these techniques raise ethical questions not faced before by society. For example, it is theoretically possible that within a few years you could go down to your local fertility center and order up a baby that would be an

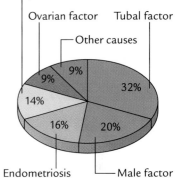

FIGURE 12.6 Primary Diagnoses for Assisted Reproductive Technology Procedures, 1995. *Tubal factor,* accounting for one-third of all diagnoses, means the woman's fallopian tubes are damaged or blocked; *male factor* means there is a problem with sperm count or motility; *endometriosis* means there is uterine tissue in abnormal locations, which can affect both fertilization and implantation; *ovarian factor* means the ovaries are not producing eggs normally; *other causes* include problems with the uterus, such as unusual shape or fibroid tumors, and exposure to DES as a fetus; *unexplained cause* means that no cause of infertility can be found, despite testing. (*Source:* CDC, ASRM, & RESOLVE, 1997.)

THE DESIRE TO HAVE healthy, happy, beautiful children is understandable, basic, and human. But in the face of today's reproductive technology, many of us may have to search our souls for the answers to a number of ethical questions. When faced with infertility, the possibility of birth defects, or the likelihood of a difficult labor, we need to weigh the possible benefits of a given technique against the costs and risks involved. What are your feelings about the following reproductive issues?

- *Fetal diagnosis.* If you (or your partner) were pregnant, would you choose to have ultrasound? Should ultrasound be used routinely in all pregnancies or only in selected cases, such as when the mother is over 35 or there is a suspected problem? When would you consider amniocentesis appropriate? Should all fetuses be electronically monitored during birth (entailing the attachment of electrodes to the infant's scalp in the uterus), or should this technique be reserved for problem births? Would you want your child to be routinely monitored in this way?

- *Cesarean section.* How would you determine that C-section was necessary for yourself or your partner? Should vaginal delivery be attempted first?

What if it was a breech birth? What if you (or your partner) had had a previous C-section?

- *Intrauterine insemination and in vitro fertilization (IVF).* Should these techniques be available to anyone who wants them? Under what circumstances, if any, would you use these techniques? What are the rights of all the parties involved: parents, donors, physicians, child? What are the embryo's or fetus's rights? For example, does a frozen embryo have the "right to life" if its parents die before it is implanted in a surrogate? Can you envision a situation in which you would want to donate ova or sperm? What if your partner wanted to?

- *Older motherhood.* Modern reproductive technology has made it possible for women who have gone through menopause to give birth following IVF. What issues does this raise for these older mothers? For fathers? For the children? Are these decisions solely up to the mother? Both parents? Or should society be involved?

- *Surrogate motherhood.* Should a woman be allowed to "carry" a pregnancy for a couple using father-donated sperm? Does it matter if profit is involved? Should a contract involving surrogate motherhood

---

> Rarely is moral queasiness a match for the onslaught of science.
>
> —*Sharon Begley*

exact replica of you (Begley, 1997a; Sternberg, 1998). For further discussion of reproductive ethics, see the box "The Ethics of Reproductive Technology."

Medical Intervention   In cases where infertility is a result of impaired ovulatory function in women, it may be remedied with medication. Treatment may include hormones that stimulate the ovarian follicles or regulate the menstrual cycle (Toback, 1992). Hormone therapy may be used alone or in combination with the techniques discussed below. About 10–20% of the pregnancies achieved with the help of "fertility drugs" result in multiple births as the result of more than one egg being released by the ovary (Rosenthal, 1992). This possibility was dramatically made clear in 1997 with the birth of septuplets to a young mother who took Metrodin after she and her husband failed to conceive a second child after 16 months of trying (Leo, 1997). That all seven babies survived is unusual, because multiple births pose higher risks to both mothers and infants (Belluck, 1998; Perlman, 1997). Twins are about 10 times more likely than babies born alone to have very low birth weights (3.3 lb or less); triplets are more than 30 times more likely to have very low birth weights and 3 times more likely to have severe disabilities than infants born alone (Dr. Barbara Luke, cited in Rosenthal, 1992).

Current medical research is focusing increasingly on "male factor infertility." Approaches for treating men include new methods of sperm evalua-

be legally binding? Whose rights should take precedence, those of the surrogate (who is the biological mother) or of the couple (which includes the biological father)? What are the child's rights? Who decides? Can you think of a circumstance when you might wish to have the services of a surrogate mother? Could you be a surrogate or accept your partner's being one?

For all the preceding techniques, consider the following questions: Who is profiting (scientists, physicians, businesspeople, donors, parents, children)? Who is bearing the greatest risks? How great are the costs—monetary and psychological—and who is paying them? What are the long-range goals of this technology? Are we "playing God"? How might this technology be abused? Are there certain techniques you think should be outlawed?

- *Abortion.* When do you think human life begins? Do we ever have the right to take human life? Under what conditions, if any, should abortion be permitted? Whenever the pregnant woman requests it? If there is a serious birth defect? If there is a minor birth defect (such as a shortened limb)? If the fetus is the "wrong" sex? If rape or incest led to the pregnancy? Under what conditions, if any, would you have an abortion or want your partner to have one?

If you had an unmarried pregnant teenage daughter, would you encourage her to have one?

- *Tissue donation.* Is it appropriate to use the tissues or organs of human corpses for medical purposes? Is it appropriate to use aborted fetuses for tissue donation? For research?

- *Life and death.* Is prolonging the life of an infant always the most humane choice? What if prolonging life also prolongs suffering? Should life be prolonged whenever possible, at all costs? Who decides?

- *Human cloning.* Scientists expect that cloning—manipulating a cell from an organism so that it develops into an exact duplicate of the original organism—will be technologically possible for human replication within 10 years. Should the cloning of humans be allowed? Can you think of any circumstances in which human cloning might be acceptable? Should the use of human embryos or human cells in cloning research be allowed?

- *Fertility and fulfillment.* Do you think your reproductive values and feelings about your own fertility (or lack of it) are congruent with reality, given the world's population problems? For you, are there viable alternatives to conceiving or bearing a child? What are they? Would adoption be one alternative? Why?

tion and processing, and the use of medication to improve sperm velocity (Go, 1992; Meacham & Lipshultz, 1991; Ohninger & Alexander, 1991).

Intrauterine Insemination   When childlessness is the result of male infertility (or low fertility) or a genetically transmitted disorder carried by the male, couples may try **intrauterine insemination (IUI),** also known as **artificial insemination (AI).** Single women who want children but who have not found an appropriate partner or who wish to avoid emotional entanglements have used this technique, as have lesbian couples. The American Society for Reproductive Medicine estimates that there are about 50,000 births a year from donor intrauterine insemination (CDC, ASRM, & RESOLVE, 1997).

During ovulation, semen is deposited by syringe near the cervical opening. The semen may come from the partner; if he has a low sperm count, several collections of semen may be taken and frozen and then collectively deposited in the woman's vagina, improving the odds of conception. If the partner had a vasectomy earlier, he may have had his semen frozen and stored in a sperm bank. If the man is sterile or has a genetically transferable disorder, **therapeutic donor insemination (TDI),** also known as artificial insemination by donor (AID), may be used. Anonymous donors—often medical students—are paid nominal amounts for their deposits of semen.

Intrauterine insemination tends to produce males rather than females; in the general population, about 51% of the children born are male, but this figure reaches about 60% when conception is achieved artificially. Intrauterine insemination has a success rate of about 60% for infertile couples.

Some lesbians, especially those in committed relationships, are choosing to create families through artificial insemination. To date, there are no reliable data on the number of such births, but anecdotal information indicates that it is in the thousands. There are many questions raised when a lesbian couple contemplate having a baby in this way: Who will be the birth mother? What will the relationship of the other mother be? Will the donor be known or unknown? If known, will the child have a relationship with him? Will the child have a relationship with the donor's parents? Which, if any, of the child's grandparents will have a relationship with him or her? Will there be a legal contract between the parenting parties? There are few precedents to learn from or role models to follow in these cases. Another issue that such couples have to face is that the nonbiological parent may have no legal tie to the child (in some states the nonbiological parent may adopt the child as a "second parent"). Furthermore, society may not recognize a nonbiological parent as a "real" parent, because children are expected to have only one real mother and one real father.

In Vitro Fertilization   **In vitro fertilization (IVF)** entails combining sperm and oocyte in a laboratory dish and subsequently implanting the blastocyst, or pre-embryo, into the uterus of the mother or a surrogate. To help increase the chances of pregnancy, several oocytes are generally collected, fertilized, and implanted. The mother takes hormones to regulate her menstrual cycle so that the uterus will be prepared for the fertilized ovum. Sometimes the eggs or the embryos are frozen and stored, to be used at a later date. The egg can come from the mother or from a donor. If a donor oocyte is used, the donor may be artificially inseminated with the father's sperm and the embryo removed from the donor and transplanted in the mother-to-be's uterus. More commonly, oocytes are "harvested" from the mother's or donor's ovary, which has been hormonally stimulated to produce 12–18 eggs instead of the usual one. This procedure is done by inserting a 16-inch needle into the ovary by way of the vagina and drawing out the egg cells, which are then mixed with the father's sperm. In two days, between two and seven blastocysts are implanted in the mother's uterus. Usually, not all the embryos develop successfully, but sometimes all or most of them do. Therefore, the American Society for Reproductive Medicine discourages the transfer of a large number of embryos (more than three or four) because of the increased likelihood of multiple births (CDC, ASRM, & RESOLVE, 1997) (Figure 12.7).

These procedures are all quite costly (a single attempt, or "cycle," typically costs $8000) and must usually be repeated a number of times before a viable pregnancy results. The average cost of an in vitro delivery is $72,000. In 1995, the success rate for IVF was 22.3% (CDC, ASRM, & RESOLVE, 1997). About 70% of all ART procedures involve in vitro fertilization. IVF, along with the techniques discussed below, resulted in 11,315 live deliveries (and 16,520 babies) in 1995 (CDC, ASRM, & RESOLVE, 1997).

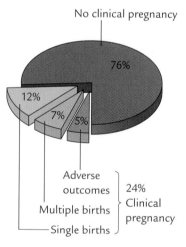

No clinical pregnancy

76%

12%

7%

5%

Adverse outcomes

Multiple births

Single births

24% Clinical pregnancy

FIGURE 12.7 Results of Assisted Reproductive Technology Cycles, 1995. Most ART cycles (76%) performed in 1995 did not produce a pregnancy. However, 12% produced a single birth and 7% produced a multiple birth, for a combined "take-home baby" rate of 19%. (*Source:* CDC, ASRM, & RESOLVE, 1997.)

When in vitro procedures are used to combat infertility, there is about a 1 in 3 chance of a multiple birth.

GIFT and ZIFT   Another fertilization technique, **gamete intrafallopian transfer (GIFT),** may be recommended for couples who have no known reason for their infertility. In this process, sperm and eggs are collected from the parents and deposited together in the fallopian tube following laparoscopic surgery. In 1995, about 6% of ART procedures used GIFT (Figure 12.8).

In **zygote intrafallopian transfer (ZIFT),** eggs and sperm are united in a petri dish and then transferred immediately to the fallopian tube to begin cell division. In 1995, about 2% of ART procedures involved ZIFT. GIFT and ZIFT have higher success rates than IVF but are more invasive, and many women are not suitable candidates for these procedures. As with IVF, both GIFT and ZIFT carry an increased risk of multiple pregnancy (Bollen, Camus, Staessen, Tournaye, Devroey, & Van Steirteghem, 1991).

ICSI   A revolutionary new method of fertilization, **intercytoplasmic sperm injection (ICSI),** developed by a Belgian physician, involves the direct injection of a single sperm into an oocyte in a laboratory dish (Kolata, 1993). As in IVF, the blastocyst is then transferred to the mother. Before its developer proved otherwise, it was believed that such a technique would not work because it bypasses both the capacitation of the sperm and the softening of the oocyte's outer layers (which requires the presence of several hundred sperm). ICSI holds great promise for many men who have low sperm counts or large numbers of abnormal sperm. In 1995, about 11% of ART procedures used ICSI.

Surrogate Motherhood

The idea of **surrogate motherhood,** in which one woman bears a child for another, is not new. In the Old Testament (Genesis 16:1–15), Abraham's wife,

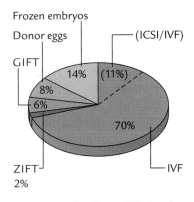

Frozen embryos
Donor eggs
GIFT
ZIFT
2%
(ICSI/IVF)
14%
(11%)
8%
6%
70%
IVF

FIGURE 12.8   Types of Assisted Reproductive Technology Procedures, United States, 1995. In 1995, 59,142 ART cycles were carried out. Most of these cycles (78%) used fresh embryos developed from the couple's own egg and sperm; 14% used frozen embryos from nondonated eggs; and 8% used donated eggs. The most common procedure by far was IVF (70%), including ICSI (11%), followed by GIFT (6%) and ZIFT (2%). (*Source:* CDC, ASRM, & RESOLVE, 1997.)

Sarah, finding herself unable to conceive, arranged for her husband to impregnate the servant Hagar. These days, the procedures are considerably more complex, and the issues are definitely cloudier.

Some people question the motives of surrogate mothers. Women have had babies for their friends and even for their relatives. In 1991, a South Dakota woman became the first American "surrogate granny" when she was implanted with the fertilized ova of her daughter, who had been born without a uterus (Plummer & Nelson, 1991). Some women simply extend this kind of altruism to women they don't know. Women's motivations for becoming surrogates are varied. The major ones given are money (they are usually paid $10,000–$25,000 or more), enjoying being pregnant, and unreconciled birth traumas, such as abortion or relinquishing a child for adoption.

In the United States, there are thought to be several hundred births to surrogate mothers each year. A number of privately run agencies have been created to match surrogates and couples, highlighting the commercial potential of surrogate motherhood. Although new technologies to assist human reproduction have brought hope and joy to many couples, they have also raised new ethical issues. The commercial aspect of surrogate motherhood is just one of these difficult issues.

GIVING BIRTH

Throughout pregnancy, numerous physiological changes occur to prepare the woman's body for childbirth. Hormones secreted by the placenta regulate the growth of the fetus, stimulate maturation of the breasts for lactation, and ready the uterus and other parts of the body for labor. During the later months of pregnancy, the placenta produces the hormone **relaxin,** which increases flexibility in the ligaments and joints of the pelvic area. In the last trimester, most women occasionally feel uterine contractions that are strong but generally not painful. These are called **Braxton Hicks contractions.** They exercise the uterus, preparing it for labor.

Labor and Delivery

During labor, contractions begin the **effacement** (thinning) and **dilation** (opening up) of the cervix. It is difficult to say exactly when labor starts, which helps explain the great differences reported in lengths of labor for different women. When the uterine contractions become regular, true labor begins. During these contractions, the lengthwise muscles of the uterus involuntarily pull open the circular muscles around the cervix. This process generally takes 2–36 hours. Its duration depends on the size of the baby, the baby's position in the uterus, the size of the mother's pelvis, and the condition of the uterus. The length of labor tends to shorten after the first birth experience.

Labor can generally be divided into three stages. The first stage is usually the longest, lasting 4–16 hours. An early sign of first-stage labor is the expulsion of a plug of slightly bloody mucus that has blocked the opening of the cervix during pregnancy. At the same time or later on, there is a second fluid discharge from the vagina. This discharge, often referred to as the "breaking of the waters," is the amniotic fluid, which comes from the

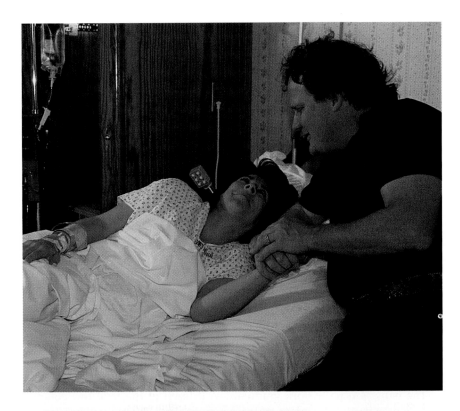

During labor, uterine contractions cause the opening and thinning of the cervix. The length of labor varies from woman to woman and birth to birth; it is usually between 4 and 16 hours. During transition, the end of first-stage labor, contractions are the most intense. Encouragement from her partner can help the mother relax (top). The second stage of labor is the delivery of the infant. In this photograph, the mother is coached to push as the baby's head begins to crown (bottom right). The baby may be ready to nurse following delivery. Medical staff can give advice for getting started (bottom left).

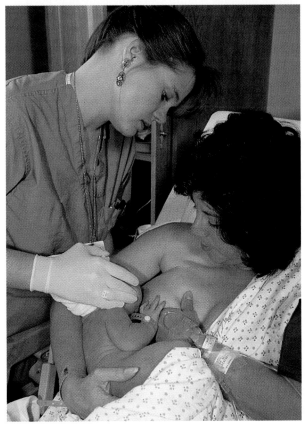

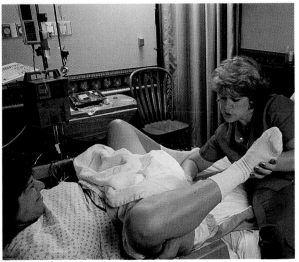

> If men had to have babies, they would only ever have one each.
>
> —*Diana, Princess of Wales*
> *(1961–1997)*

ruptured amnion. (Because the baby is subject to infection after the protective membrane breaks, the woman should receive medical attention soon thereafter, if she has not already.)

The hormone **oxytocin** produced by the fetus, along with prostaglandins from the placenta, stimulates strong uterine contractions. At the end of the first stage of labor, which is called **transition,** the contractions come more quickly and are much more intense than at the beginning of labor. Many women report transition as the most difficult part of labor. During the last part of first-stage labor, the baby's head enters the birth canal. This marks the shift from dilation of the cervix to expulsion of the infant. The cervical opening is now almost fully dilated (about 10 cm [4 in.] in diameter), but the baby is not yet completely in position to be pushed out. Some women feel despair, isolation, and anger at this point. Many appear to lose faith in those assisting in the birth. A woman may find that management of the contractions seems beyond her control; she may be afraid that something is wrong. At this time, she needs the full support and understanding of her helpers. Transition is usually, though not always, brief (half an hour to 1 hour).

Second-stage labor begins when the baby's head moves into the birth canal and ends when the baby is born. During this time, many women experience a great force in their bodies. Some women find this the most difficult part of labor. Others find that the contractions and bearing down bring a sense of euphoria.

The baby is usually born gradually. With each of the final few contractions, a new part of the infant emerges (Figure 12.9). The baby may even cry before he or she is completely born, especially if the mother did not have medication.

The baby will still be attached to the umbilical cord connected to the mother, which is not cut until it stops pulsating. He or she will appear wet, often covered by a waxy substance called **vernix.** The head may look oddly shaped at first, from the molding of the soft plates of bone during birth. This shape is temporary; the baby's head usually achieves a normal appearance within 24 hours.

After the baby has been delivered, the uterus continues to contract, expelling the placenta, also called the afterbirth, and completing the third and final stage of labor. The doctor or midwife will examine the placenta to make sure it is whole. If the practitioner has any doubt that the entire placenta has been expelled, he or she may examine the uterus to make sure no parts of the placenta remain to cause adhesions or hemorrhage. Immediately following birth, the attendants assess the physical condition of the **neonate,** or newborn. Heart rate, respiration, color, reflexes, and muscle tone are individually rated with a score of 0 to 2. The total, called an **Apgar score,** will be at least 8 if the child is healthy. For a few days following labor (especially if it is a second or subsequent birth), the mother will probably feel strong contractions as the uterus begins to return to its prebirth size and shape. This process takes about 6 weeks. She will also have a bloody discharge called **lochia,** which continues for several weeks.

Following birth, if the baby has not been drugged by anesthetics administered to the mother, he or she will probably be alert and ready to nurse. Breast-feeding (discussed later) provides benefits for both mother and child.

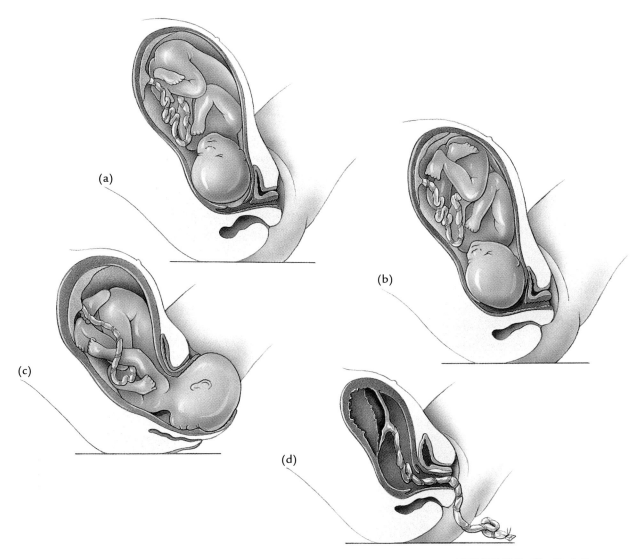

(a)

(b)

(c)

(d)

FIGURE 12.9 The Birth Process: Labor and Delivery. (a) First stage: cervix beginning to dilate. (b) Transition: cervix dilated. (c) Second stage: delivery of the infant. (d) Third stage: delivery of the placenta.

If the infant is a boy, the parents will need to decide about circumcision, the surgical removal of the foreskin of the penis (see the box "The Question of Circumcision").

Choices in Childbirth

Women and couples planning the birth of a child have decisions to make in a variety of areas: place of birth, birth attendant(s), medications, preparedness classes, circumcision, breast-feeding—to name just a few. The "childbirth market" is beginning to respond to consumer concerns, so it's important for prospective consumers to fully understand their options.

Hospital Birth   Because of impersonal, routine care at some facilities, some hospitals are responding to the need for a family-centered childbirth. Fathers

And you shall circumcise the flesh of your foreskin: and it shall be a token of the covenant between Me and you.

—*Genesis 17:9–14*

IN 1975, WHEN about 93% of newborn boys were circumcised, the American Academy of Pediatrics and the American College of Obstetricians and Gynecologists issued a statement declaring that there is "no absolute medical indication" for routine **circumcision.** This procedure, which involves slicing and removing the sleeve of skin (foreskin) that covers the glans penis, has been performed routinely on newborn boys in the United States since the 1930s. Although it is obviously painful, circumcision is often done without anesthesia. Parents should discuss with their pediatrician the use of an anesthetic cream or medication. Circumcision carries medical risks, including excessive bleeding, infection, and faulty surgery.

In 1989, the American Academy of Pediatrics modified its stance on circumcision, stating that "newborn circumcision has potential medical benefits and advantages as well as disadvantages and risks." The Academy recommended that "the benefits and risks should be explained to the parents and informed consent obtained." This change was at least partially in response to several studies indicating a *possible* connection between lack of circumcision and urinary tract infections, penile cancer, and sexually transmitted diseases (Wiswell, 1990). Those studies have been contradicted by others, however (Altschul, 1989; Canadian Paediatric Society, 1996). Circumcision clearly does not guarantee protection from STDs or infections. Physician George Denniston (1992) puts the issue in perspective:

> Performing 100 . . . surgeries to possibly prevent one treatable urinary tract infection is not valid preventive medicine. . . . Penile cancer occurs in older men at the rate of approximately 1 per 100,000. The idea of per-

---

Wash, don't amputate.

—*Alex Comfort, MD*

Minor surgery is one that is performed on someone else.

—*Eugene Robin, MD*

and other relatives or close friends often participate today. Some hospitals permit rooming-in, in which the baby stays with the mother rather than in the nursery, or a modified form of rooming-in. Regulations vary as to when the father and other family members and friends are allowed to visit.

Some form of anesthetic is administered during most hospital deliveries, as well as various hormones (to intensify the contractions and to shrink the uterus after delivery). The most common form of anesthetic administration is the **epidural,** in which a pain-killing drug is continuously administered through a tiny catheter placed in the woman's lower back. When administered properly, an epidural eliminates the sensations of labor and numbs the body from the lower belly to the knees. The mother isn't the only recipient of the drug, however; it goes directly through the placenta to the baby, in whom it may reduce heart and respiration rates. Epidural anesthesia may be accompanied by artificial rupture of the amniotic membranes, fetal monitoring, and the placement of a urinary catheter. It entails a higher risk of vacuum or forceps delivery and cesarean section than does a drug-free birth.

During delivery, the mother will probably be given an **episiotomy,** a surgical procedure that enlarges the vaginal opening by cutting through the perineum toward the anus. Although an episiotomy may be helpful if the infant is in distress, it is usually performed routinely in order to prevent possible tearing of the perineum. Episiotomies are performed in about 80% of first vaginal births in hospitals; yet one midwife who has assisted at more than 1200 births reports a rate of less than 1% (Armstrong & Feldman, 1990). A Canadian study of 703 uncomplicated births found no advantage to routine episiotomies; the disadvantages were pain and bleeding (Klein et al., 1992). The authors recommended that "liberal or routine use of episiotomy be abandoned."

forming 100,000 . . . procedures on newborns to possibly prevent cancer in one elderly man is absurd.

There is a clear need for long-range comparative studies of circumcised and intact males (Maden et al., 1993; Poland, 1990). The effects of circumcision on sexual functioning also need to be assessed because the removal of the foreskin destroys numerous nerve endings (Taylor, Lockwood, & Taylor, 1996). Additionally, factors such as hygiene and number of sexual partners must be taken into consideration. Education can help prevent problems by teaching boys to clean under their foreskin and, if they become sexually active, to use a condom.

Almost 60% of newborn boys were circumcised in 1990, according to the National Center for Health Statistics. Although this represents a substantial drop from 93% in 1975, it still places the United States far ahead of other Western countries, which circumcise less than 1% of their newborn boys. The exception is Israel. In Judaism, the ritual circumcising, the *brit milah* or *bris*, is an important religious event. Within the Jewish community, some parents are developing alternative *brit milah* ceremonies (Rothenberg, 1991). Circumcision has religious significance for Muslims as well.

Aside from religious reasons, the other reasons given by parents for circumcising their infants are "cleanliness" and "so he'll look like his dad." A circumcised penis is not necessarily any cleaner than an uncircumcised one. Infants do not require cleaning under their foreskins; adults do. If reasonable cleanliness is observed, an intact penis poses no more threat of disease to a man's sexual partner than a circumcised one would. As for "looking like dad," there is no evidence to suggest that little boys are seriously traumatized if dad's penis doesn't look exactly like theirs.

A growing movement of parents and medical practitioners is seeking to educate prospective parents so that they can make informed choices about circumcising their infant sons.

The baby is usually delivered on a table. If such factors as medication or exhaustion slow labor, he or she may be pulled from the womb with a vacuum extractor (which has a small suction cup that fits onto the baby's head) or forceps. (In some cases of acute fetal distress, these instruments may be crucial in order to save the infant's life, but they are sometimes used by physicians as a substitute for patience and skill.)

Cesarean Section   **Cesarean section,** or **C-section,** is the removal of the fetus by an incision in the mother's abdominal and uterine walls. In 1970, 5.5% of American births were done by cesarean section. Today, cesarean births account for about 22.8% of all births (CDC, 1995b).

Although there is a decreased mortality rate for infants born by C-section, the mothers' mortality rate is higher. As with all major surgeries, there are possible complications, and recovery can be slow and difficult.

Hoping to reduce the number of C-sections, the National Institutes of Health (NIH) have issued the following guidelines:

1. Because a woman has had a previous cesarean delivery does not mean that subsequent deliveries must be C-sections; whenever possible, women should be given the option of a vaginal birth.

2. Abnormal labor does not mean that a C-section is necessary. Sleep or medication may resolve the problems. Only after other measures have been tried should a physician perform a cesarean, unless the infant is clearly in danger.

3. Breech babies—those who enter the birth canal buttocks-first or feet-first—do not necessarily require C-sections. A physician's experience using his or her hands to deliver the baby vaginally is crucial.

The Huichol people of Mexico traditionally practiced couvade. The father squatted in the rafters above the laboring mother. When the mother experienced a contraction, she would pull the ropes that had been attached to his scrotum, so that he could "share" the experience of childbirth.

PROSPECTIVE PARENTS must make many important decisions. The more informed they are, however, the better able they will be to decide what is right for them. If you were planning a birth, how would you answer the following questions?

- Who will be the birth attendant—a physician, a nurse-midwife? Do you already have someone in mind? If not, what criteria are important to you in choosing a birth attendant? Have you considered hiring a labor assistant, or *doula*, a professional childbirth companion employed to guide the mother during labor?

- Who will be present at the birth—the husband or partner? Other relatives or friends? Children? How will these people participate? Will they provide emotional support and encouragement? Will they provide practical help, such as "coaching" the mother, giving massages, fetching supplies, taking photographs or videos? Can these people be sensitive to the needs of the mother?

- Where will the birth take place—in a hospital, in a birth center, at home? If in a hospital, is there a choice of rooms?

- What kind of environment will you create in terms of lighting, room furnishings, and sounds? Is there special music you would like to hear?

- What kinds of medication, if any, do you feel comfortable with? Do you know what the options are for pain-reducing medications? What about hormones to speed up or slow down labor? How do you feel about having an IV inserted as a precaution, even if medication is not planned? If you should change your mind about medication part of the way through labor, how will you communicate this to your attendants?

If a woman does not want a C-section unless it is absolutely necessary, she should learn about her physician's attitude about and record on performing cesareans. It is noteworthy that the greatest number of cesareans are performed in the socioeconomic group of women with the lowest medical risk. In a study of 245,854 births, the C-section rate for middle- and upper-income women was 22.9%, whereas for lower-income women it was 3.2% (Gould, Davey, & Stafford, 1989). Therefore, it is assumed that cesareans are often performed for reasons other than medical risk. The U.S. Public Health Service has set a goal for reducing the overall C-section rate to no more than 15% and the repeat rate to 65% by the year 2000 (National Center for Health Statistics, 1994). To achieve these goals, it recommends:

1. Addressing the issue of physician malpractice in certain instances
2. Eliminating physicians' financial incentives for cesareans, which are currently more lucrative than vaginal deliveries
3. Publishing C-section rates of physicians and hospitals
4. Increasing physician training in options for normal labor and delivery

Prepared Childbirth   Increasingly, Americans are choosing among such childbirth alternatives as prepared childbirth, rooming-in birthing centers, home birth, and midwives.

Prepared childbirth (or natural childbirth) was popularized by Grantly Dick-Read (1972), who observed that fear causes muscles to tense, which in turn increases pain and stress during childbirth. He taught both partners about childbirth and gave them physical exercises to ease muscle tension. Encouraged by Dick-Read's ideas, women began to reject anesthetics during

- What about fetal monitoring? Will there be machines attached to you or the baby? What types and degree of monitoring do you feel comfortable with?

- What is your attendant's policy regarding food and drink during labor? What kinds of foods or drinks, such as ice cream, fruit, juices, or ice chips, do you think you (or your partner) might want to have?

- What about freedom of movement during labor? Will you (or your partner) want the option of walking around during labor? Will there be a shower or bath available? Will the baby be delivered with the mother lying on her back with her feet in stirrups, or will she be free to choose her position, such as squatting or lying on her side?

- Do you want a routine episiotomy? Under what conditions would it be acceptable?

- What do you wish the role of instruments or other interventions, such as forceps or vacuum extraction, to be? Who will determine if and when they are necessary?

- Under what conditions is a cesarean section acceptable? Who will decide?

- Who will "catch" the baby as she or he is born? Who is going to cut the umbilical cord, and at what point will it be cut?

- What will be done with the baby immediately after birth? Will he or she be with the mother or the father? Who will bathe and dress the baby? What kinds of tests will be done on the baby, and when? What other kinds of procedures, such as shots and medicated eyedrops, will be given, and when?

- Will the baby stay in the nursery, or is there rooming-in? Is there a visiting schedule?

- How will the baby be fed—by breast or bottle? Will feeding be on a schedule or "on demand"? Is there someone with breast-feeding experience available to answer questions if necessary? Will the baby have a pacifier between feedings?

- If the baby is a boy, will he be circumcised? When?

labor and delivery and were consequently able to take a more active role in childbirth, as well as be more aware of the whole process.

In the 1950s, Fernand Lamaze (1956, 1970) developed a method of prepared childbirth based on knowledge of conditioned reflexes. Women learn to mentally separate the physical stimulus of uterine contractions from the conditioned response of pain. With the help of a partner, women use breathing and other exercises throughout labor and delivery. Although Lamaze did much to advance the cause of prepared childbirth, he has been criticized by other childbirth educators as too controlling or even "repressive," according to Armstrong and Feldman (1990). A woman does not give birth, they write, "by direction, as if it were a flight plan."

Prepared childbirth, then, is not so much a matter of controlling the birth process as of understanding it and having confidence in nature's plan. Clinical studies consistently show better birth outcomes for mothers who have had prepared childbirth classes. Prepared mothers (who usually attend classes with the father or other partner) handle pain more successfully, use less medication and anesthesia, express greater satisfaction with the childbirth process, and experience less postpartum depression than women who undergo routine hospital births (Hetherington, 1990).

Birthing Rooms and Centers Birth (or maternity) centers, institutions of long standing in England and other European countries, have now been developed in the United States. Although they vary in size, organization, and orientation, birth centers share the view that childbirth is a normal, healthy process that can be assisted by skilled practitioners (midwives or physicians) in a homelike setting. The mother (or couple) has considerable autonomy in deciding the conditions of birth: lighting, sounds, visitors,

Childbirth classes enable both partners to understand and share the birth process.

delivery position, and so on. Some of these centers can provide some kinds of emergency care; all have procedures for transfer to a hospital if necessary.

An extensive survey of 11,814 births in birth centers concluded that "birth centers offer a safe and acceptable alternative to hospital confinement for selected pregnant women, particularly those who have previously had children, and that such care leads to relatively few cesarean sections" (Rooks, Weatherby, Ernst, Stapleton, Rosen, & Rosenfield, 1989).

Home Birth   Home births have increased during the past two decades, although they still constitute a small fraction of total births, amounting to not quite 2%, according to available data. Careful medical screening and planning that eliminate all but the lowest-risk pregnancies can make this a viable alternative for some couples. A couple can create their own birth environment at home, and home births cost considerably less, usually at least one-third less, than hospital delivery. With the supervision of an experienced practitioner, parents have little to worry about. But if a woman is at risk, she is wiser to give birth in a hospital where medical equipment is readily available.

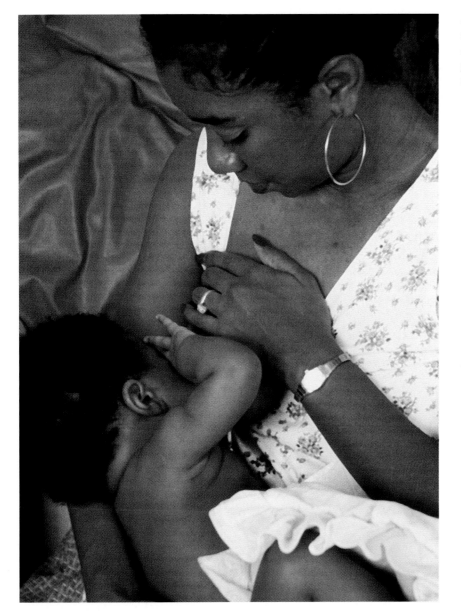

Breast-feeding provides the best nutrition for infants. It also helps protect against many infectious diseases and gives both mother and child a sense of well-being.

All is beautiful
All is beautiful
All is beautiful, yes!
Now Mother Earth
And Father Sky
Join one another and meet
forever helpmates
All is beautiful
All is beautiful
All is beautiful, yes!
Now the night of darkness
And the dawn of light
Join one another and meet
forever helpmates
All is beautiful
All is beautiful
All is beautiful, yes!
Now the white corn
And the yellow corn
Join one another and meet
forever helpmates
All is beautiful
All is beautiful
All is beautiful, yes!
Life that never ends
Happiness of all things
Join one another and meet
forever helpmates
All is beautiful
All is beautiful
All is beautiful, yes!

—*Navajo Night Chant*

Midwifery   The United States has an increasing number of certified nurse-midwives who are registered nurses trained in obstetrical techniques. They are qualified for routine deliveries and minor medical emergencies. They also often operate as part of a total medical team that includes a backup physician. Their fees are generally considerably less than a doctor's. Nurse-midwives usually participate in both hospital and home births, although this may vary according to hospital policy, state law, and the midwife's preference.

If a woman decides she wants to give birth with the aid of a midwife outside a hospital setting, she should have a thorough medical screening to make sure she or her infant will not be at risk during delivery. She should

IF YOU ARE A WOMAN who plans to have children, you will have to decide whether to breast- or bottle-feed your child. Perhaps you already have an idea that breast-feeding is healthier for the baby but are not sure why.

The following list of benefits and advantages should help you understand why breast-feeding is recommended (assuming that the mother is healthy and has a good diet). The American Academy of Pediatrics now recommends breast-feeding for an infant's first year (Gartner, 1997).

Physical Benefits of Breast-Feeding

- Breast milk contains antibodies that protect the baby from many infectious diseases for at least 6 months.
- It forms softer curds in the infant's stomach, making digestion and elimination easier.
- It puts less stress on the infant's immature liver and kidneys because its total protein is lower than that of other mammalian milk.
- It is high in cholesterol, which is needed for proper development of the nervous tissue.
- It causes fewer allergic reactions because of its concentration and type of protein.
- It is a better source of nutrition for low birth weight babies because nature adapts the content of the mother's milk to meet the infant's needs.
- Babies who have been breast-fed have fewer problems with tooth decay.
- Breast-feeding is thought to encourage the development of the dental arch, helping prevent the need for orthodontia later on.
- For mothers, hormonal changes stimulated by breast-feeding cause the uterus to contract and return to its normal size.
- Breast-feeding mothers reduce their risk of ovarian cancer, early breast cancer, and postmenopausal hip fractures due to osteoporosis.

Psychological Benefits of Breast-Feeding

- The close physical contact of breast-feeding provides a sense of emotional well-being for mother and baby.
- Sustaining the life of another through her milk may affirm a woman's sense of self and ability to give.
- Breast-feeding is natural and pleasurable.

Health and Logistical Advantages of Breast-Feeding

- It requires no buying, mixing, or preparation of formulas.
- Is not subject to incorrect mixing or spoilage.
- Breast milk is clean and is not easily contaminated.
- Breast-feeding provides some protection against pregnancy (if the woman is breast-feeding exclusively).
- The breast is always available.

Bottle-Feeding

For those women whose work schedules, health problems, or other demands prohibit them from breast-feeding, holding and cuddling the baby while bottle-feeding can contribute to the sense of emotional well-being that comes from a close parent-baby relationship. Bottle-feeding affords a greater opportunity for fathers to become involved in the feeding of the baby. Working women and mothers whose lifestyles or choices do not include breast-feeding often find bottles more convenient.

Regardless of the choices that parents make regarding their infants' feeding, it may well be the care and love with which it is done that are most important to the growth and development of a healthy child.

---

learn about the midwife's training and experience, what type of backup services the midwife has in the event of complications or emergencies, and how the midwife will handle a transfer to a hospital if necessary.

Breast-Feeding

About three days after childbirth, **lactation**—the production of milk—begins. Before lactation, sometimes as early as the second trimester, a yellowish liquid called **colostrum** is secreted by the nipples. It is what nourishes the newborn infant before the mother's milk comes in. Colostrum is high in protein and contains antibodies that help protect the baby from infectious diseases. Hormonal changes during labor begin the changeover from colostrum to milk, but unless a mother nurses her child, her breasts will soon stop producing milk. If she chooses not to breast-feed, she is usually given an injection of estrogen soon after delivery to stop lactation. It is not certain, however, whether estrogen is actually effective; furthermore, it may cause an increased risk of blood clotting.

Currently about 60% of new mothers breast-feed. Only about 20% continue to do so after 6 months, however ("Mothers Urged to Breast-Feed," 1997).

BECOMING A PARENT

Men and women who become parents enter a new phase of their lives. Even more than marriage, parenthood signifies adulthood—the final, irreversible end of youthful roles. A person can become an ex-spouse but never an ex-parent. The irrevocable nature of parenthood may make the first-time parent doubtful and apprehensive, especially during the pregnancy. Yet, for the most part, parenthood has to be learned experientially, although ideas can modify practices. A person may receive assistance from more experienced parents, but, ultimately, each new parent has to learn on his or her own.

Many of the stresses felt by new parents closely reflect gender roles. Overall, mothers seem to experience greater stress than fathers. When we speak of "mothering" a child, everyone knows what we mean: nurturing, caring for, diapering, soothing, loving. Mothers generally "mother" their children almost every day of the year for at least 18 consecutive years. The meaning of "fathering" is quite different. Nurturant behavior by a father toward his child has not typically been referred to as "fathering." Because the lines between roles are becoming increasingly blurred as fathers take a more active role in the raising of their children, however, the verb "to parent" has been used to describe the child-tending behaviors of both mothers and fathers.

The time immediately following birth is a critical period for family adjustment. No amount of reading, classes, and expert advice can prepare expectant parents for the real thing. The 3 months or so following childbirth (the "fourth trimester") constitute the **postpartum period.** This time is one of physical stabilization and emotional adjustment. The abrupt transition from being a nonparent to being a parent may create considerable stress. Parents take on parental roles literally overnight, and the job goes on without relief around the clock. Many parents express concern about their ability to meet all the responsibilities of child rearing.

New mothers, who may well have lost most of their interest in sexual activity during the last weeks of pregnancy, will probably find themselves returning to prepregnancy levels of desire and coital frequency. Some women, however, may have difficulty reestablishing their sexual lives because of fatigue, physiological problems such as continued vaginal bleeding, and worries about the infant.

Before I got married, I had six theories about bringing up children. Now I have six children and no theories.

—*John Wilmot, Earl of Rochester (1647–1680)*

We learn from experience. A man never wakes up his second baby just to see it smile.

—*Grace Williams*

A loud noise at one end and no sense of responsibility at the other.

—*Father Ronald Knox (1888–1957)*

ALTHOUGH STATISTICS are difficult to obtain, researchers believe that there are between 6 million and 14 million children in the United States with at least one gay parent (Kantrowitz, 1996). Most of these parents are or have been married; consequently, many children of lesbians and gay men begin their lives in "traditional" families, even though separation or divorce may occur later on. Adoption, insemination, surrogacy, and foster parenting are also options being used increasingly by both singles and couples who are lesbian or gay (Goldman, 1992; Ricketts & Achtenberg, 1989). Because of the nontraditional nature of these families, it is difficult to determine the number of gays and lesbians who choose these alternatives.

Studies of gay fathers indicate that "being gay is compatible with effective parenting" (Bozett, 1987b; Goldman, 1992; Harris & Turner, 1985). Furthermore, it appears that gays who disclose their orientation to their children and who have a stable gay relationship tend to provide better-quality parenting than those who remain married and keep their sexual orientation hidden (Barret & Robinson, 1990).

Heterosexual fears about gays and lesbians as parents center around concerns about parenting abilities, fears of sexual abuse, and worries that the children will "catch" the homosexual orientation. All of these fears are unwarranted. A review of the literature on children of gay men and lesbians found virtually no documented cases of sexual abuse by gay parents or their lovers; such exploitation appears to be disproportionately committed by heterosexuals (Barret & Robinson, 1990; Cramer, 1986).

Fears that gay and lesbian parents may reject children of the other sex also appear unfounded. Such fears reflect two common misconceptions: that being gay or lesbian is a rejection of members of the other sex, and that people are able to choose their sexual orientation. A number of studies of children of lesbians and gays found the parents' orientation to have no impact on the children's sexual orientation or their feelings about their gender (Flaks, Ficher, Masterpasqua, & Joseph, 1995; Patterson, 1992). According to Dr. Michael Lamb, chief of the Section on Social and Emotional Development at the National Institute of Child Health and Human Development, "What evidence there is suggests there are no particular developmental or emotional deficits for children raised by gay or lesbian parents. . . . These kids look OK" (quoted in Goldman, 1992).

Despite the abundance of research and millions of case scenarios to support the above conclusion, gays and lesbians still fight for the legal rights and protections they deserve. Because they cannot legally marry and because of pervasive anti-gay prejudices, such issues as custody, visitation, and adoption remain legal dilemmas or obstacles for many contemplating or trying to become parents.

A number of services and programs have been established to assist prospective gay and lesbian parents in sorting through the myriad questions and issues they face. In the end, it is the welfare of the child that society aims to support. This can best be achieved with loving, caring, responsible parents, regardless of sexual orientation.

Cleaning and scrubbing can wait till tomorrow.
For babies grow up we've learned to our sorrow.
So quiet down cobwebs, dust go to sleep.
I'm rocking my baby and babies don't keep.

—*Anonymous*

The postpartum period also may be a time of significant emotional upheaval. Even women who had easy and uneventful deliveries may experience a period of "postpartum blues," characterized by alternating periods of crying, unpredictable mood changes, fatigue, irritability, and occasionally mild confusion or lapses of memory. New mothers often have irregular sleep patterns because of the needs of their newborn, the discomfort of childbirth, or the strangeness of the hospital environment. Some mothers may feel lonely, isolated from their familiar world.

Biological, psychological, and social factors are all involved in postpartum depression. Biologically, during the first several days following delivery, there is an abrupt fall in certain hormone levels. The physiological stress accompanying labor, as well as dehydration, blood loss, and other physical factors, contributes to lowering the woman's stamina. Psychologically, conflicts about her ability to mother and communication problems with the infant or partner may contribute to the new mother's feelings of depression and helplessness. Finally, the social setting into which the child is born is important, especially if the infant represents a financial or emotional burden for the family. Postpartum counseling prior to discharge from the hospital can help new parents gain perspective on their situation so that they know what to expect and can evaluate their resources. Although the postpartum blues are felt by many mothers (and even some fathers), they usually don't last more than a couple of weeks.

■ For many, the arrival of a child is one of life's most important events. It signifies adulthood and conveys social status to those who are now parents. It creates the lifelong bonds of family. And it can fill the new parents with a deep sense of accomplishment and well-being.

SUMMARY

Fertilization and Fetal Development

- Fertilization of the oocyte by a sperm usually takes place in the fallopian tube. The chromosomes of the ovum combine with those of the sperm to form the diploid zygote; it divides many times to form a *blastocyst*, which *implants* itself in the uterine wall.

- The blastocyst becomes an *embryo* and then a *fetus*, which is nourished through the *placenta*, via the *umbilical cord*.

Being Pregnant

- The first reliable chemical pregnancy test can be made 2 to 4 weeks after a woman misses her menstrual period. *Hegar's sign* can be detected by a trained examiner. Pregnancy is confirmed by the detection of the fetal heartbeat and movements, or examination by *ultrasound*.

- A woman's feelings vary greatly during pregnancy. It is important for her to share her fears and to have support from her partner, friends, relatives, and health-care workers. Her feelings about sexuality are likely to change during pregnancy. Men may also have conflicting feelings. Sexual activity is generally safe unless there is pain, bleeding, or history of miscarriage.

- Harmful substances may be passed to the embryo or fetus through the placenta. Substances that cause birth defects are called *teratogens;* these in-clude alcohol, tobacco, certain drugs, and environmental pollutants. Infectious diseases, such as rubella, may damage the fetus. Sexually transmitted diseases may be passed to the infant through the placenta or the birth canal during childbirth.

- *Ectopic pregnancy, toxemia, preeclampsia,* and *low birth weight (prematurity)* are the most common complications of pregnancy.

- Abnormalities of the fetus may be diagnosed using ultrasound, *amniocentesis, chorionic villus sampling (CVS),* or *alpha-fetoprotein (AFP) screening.*

- Some pregnancies end in *spontaneous abortion (miscarriage);* about 1 in 4 women is aware she has miscarried at least once. Infant mortality rates in the United States are extremely high compared with those in other industrialized nations. Loss of a pregnancy or death of a young infant is recognized as a serious life event.

Infertility

- *Infertility* is the inability to conceive a child after trying for a year or more. The primary causes of female infertility are blocked fallopian tubes (often the result of pelvic inflammatory disease), endometriosis, and hormonal abnormalities. The primary causes of male infertility are low sperm count, blocked passageways, and lack of sperm motility. Couples with fertility problems often feel they have lost control over an important area of their lives.

- Techniques for combating infertility include hormonal treatments, *intrauterine insemination, in vitro fertilization, GIFT, ZIFT,* and *ICSI. Surrogate motherhood* is also an option for childless couples, but it raises many legal and ethical issues.

Giving Birth

- In the last trimester of pregnancy, a woman feels *Braxton Hicks contractions.* These contractions also begin the *effacement* and *dilation* of the cervix to permit delivery.

- Labor can be divided into three stages. First-stage labor begins when uterine contractions become regular. When the cervix has dilated approximately 10 cm, the baby's head enters the birth canal; this is called *transition.* In second-stage labor, the baby emerges from the birth canal. In third-stage labor, the *placenta (afterbirth)* is expelled.

- *Cesarean section* is the removal of the fetus by an incision through the mother's abdomen into her uterus. A dramatic increase in C-sections has led to criticism that the procedure is used more often than necessary.

- *Prepared childbirth* encompasses a variety of methods that stress the importance of understanding the birth process and of relaxation and emotional support of the mother during childbirth.

- Birth centers and birthing rooms in hospitals are providing attractive alternatives to hospital birth settings for normal births. Instead of medical doctors, many women now choose trained nurse-midwives.

- *Circumcision* has been performed routinely in this country for many years. Debate in the medical community still exists regarding its usefulness. Circumcision holds religious meaning for Jews and Muslims.

- About 60% of American women breast-feed their babies today. Mother's milk is more nutritious than formula or cow's milk and provides immunity to many diseases. Nursing offers emotional rewards to mother and infant.

Becoming a Parent

- Because the roles involving "mothering" and "fathering" are becoming blurred, the term "to parent" has been used to describe child-tending behaviors.

- A critical adjustment period—the *postpartum period*—follows the birth of a child. The mother may experience feelings of depression (sometimes called "postpartum blues") that are a result of biological, psychological, and social factors.

- Lesbian and gay parents often face additional challenges because society tends to view them with suspicion. Gay and lesbian parenting, however, appears to differ very little from heterosexual parenting.

SUGGESTED READING

For the most current research findings in obstetrics, see *Obstetrics and Gynecology, The New England Journal of Medicine,* and *JAMA: Journal of the American Medical Association.*

Eisenberg, Arlene, Hathaway, Sandy, & Merkoff, Heidi E. (1991). *What to Expect While You're Expecting* (Rev. ed.). New York: Workman. A thorough and thoroughly readable "encyclopedia" for expectant and new parents.

Harper, Barbara. (1994). *Gentle Birth Choices.* Rochester, VT: Healing Arts Press. A thoughtful exploration of birth alternatives, with photographs.

Iovine, Vicki. (1995). *The Girlfriends' Guide to Pregnancy.* New York: Pocket Books. Subtitled "Everything Your Doctor Won't Tell You," this book takes a humorous yet practical and down-to-earth look at pregnancy and birth.

Kitzinger, Sheila. (1997). *The Complete Book of Pregnancy and Childbirth* (Rev. ed.). New York: Knopf. A thorough guide, newly revised, by the "mother" of modern midwifery, with beautiful photographs.

Leach, Penelope. (1997). *Your Baby and Child: From Birth to Age Five* (Rev. ed.). New York: Knopf. Complete, concise, sympathetic advice for parents and parents-to-be.

Marrs, Richard, Bloch, Lisa Friedman, & Silverman, Kathy Kirtland. (1998). *Dr. Richard Marrs' Fertility Book.* New York: Knopf. An up-to-date guide to the myriad choices faced by infertile couples.

Nilsson, Lennart, and Hamberger, Lars. (1990). *A Child Is Born.* New York: Delacourt/Seymour Lawrence. The story of birth, beginning with fertilization, told in stunning photographs with text.

Pryor, Karen, & Pryor, Gayle. (1991). *Nursing Your Baby.* New York: Pocket Books. A comprehensive and compassionate guide to breast-feeding.

Shapiro, Jerrold Lee. (1993). *The Measure of a Man: Becoming the Father You Wish Your Father Had Been.* New York: Delacorte. Practical, empathetic advice from one dad to others, with lots of examples.

Vaughn, Christopher. (1996). *How Life Begins: The Science of Life in the Womb.* New York: Dell. A fascinating look at the first 9 months of human life.

Vredeveldt, P. (1994). *Empty Arms: Emotional Support for Those Who Have Suffered Miscarriage or Stillbirth.* Sisters, OR: Questar. A sensitive guide to dealing with grief following pregnancy loss.

13

The Sexual Body in Health and Illness

*T*HE INTERRELATEDNESS OF OUR PHYSICAL HEALTH, our psychological well-being, and our sexuality is complex. It's not something that most of us even think about, especially as long as we remain in good health. But as we age, we are more and more likely to encounter physical problems and limitations, many of which may profoundly influence our sexual lives. Our bodies may appear to betray us in a variety of ways: They grow too much or not enough or in the wrong places, they develop aches and pains and strange symptoms, and they are subject to devastating injuries and diseases. We need to inform ourselves about these problems so that we can deal with them effectively.

In this chapter, we examine our attitudes and feelings about our bodies, in addition to looking at specific health issues. We begin with a discussion of body image and eating disorders. We then look at the effects of alcohol and other drugs on our sexuality. We next discuss aging and its effects on the sexual lives of both women and men. Then we turn to issues of sexuality and disability. We discuss the physical and emotional effects of specific diseases such as diabetes, heart disease, arthritis, and cancer as they influence our sexual functioning. Finally, other issues specific to women or men are addressed.

As we grow emotionally as well as physically, we may also develop new perceptions of what it means to be healthy. We may discover new dimensions in ourselves to lead us to a more fulfilled and healthier sexual life.

LIVING IN OUR BODIES: THE QUEST FOR PHYSICAL PERFECTION

Health is more than the absence of disease, and sexual health is more than healthy sex organs. According to the World Health Organization (1992), "sexual health is the integration of the physical, emotional, intellectual, and social aspects of sexual being, in ways that are positively enriching and that enhance personality, communication, and love." Sexual health has to do with how we function biologically, but it is also a function of our behavior and our awareness and acceptance of our bodies. In terms of sexuality, health requires us to know and understand our bodies, to feel comfortable with them. It requires a woman to feel at ease with the sight, feeling, and smell of her vulva; to be comfortably aware of her breasts—their shape, size, and contours. Sexual health requires a man to accept his body, including his genitals, and to be aware of physical sensations such as lower back pain or a feeling of congestion in his bladder. A sexually healthy man abandons the idea that masculinity means he should ignore his body's pains, endure stress, and suffer in silence.

Our general health affects our sexual functioning. Fatigue, stress, and minor ailments all affect our sexual interactions. If we ignore these aspects of our health, we are likely to experience a decline in our sexual drive, as well as suffer physical and psychological distress. A person who always feels tired or is constantly ill or debilitated is likely to feel less sexual than a healthy, rested person. Health and sexuality are gifts we must care for and respect.

Contrary to popular stereotypes, people of all shapes and sizes can lead healthy and happy lives.

We have to have faith in ourselves. I have never met a woman who, deep down in her core, really believes she has great legs. And if she suspects she might have great legs, then she's convinced that she has a shrill voice and no neck.

—*Cynthia Heimel*

When I go to the beauty parlor, I always use the emergency entrance. Sometimes I just go for an estimate.

—*Phyllis Diller*

Muscles I don't care about—my husband likes me to be squishy when he hugs me.

—*Dixie Carter*

Eating Disorders

Many of us are willing to pay high costs—physically, emotionally, and financially—to meet the expectations of our culture and to feel worthy, lovable, and sexually attractive. Although having these desires is clearly a normal human characteristic, the means by which we try to fulfill them can be extreme and even self-destructive. Many American women and some men try to control their weight by dieting at some time in their lives, but some people's fear and loathing of fat (often combined with fear or disgust regarding sexual functions) impels them to extreme forms of eating behavior. Compulsive overeating (also called binge eating) and compulsive overdieting (purging)—and combinations thereof—are the behaviors classified as eating disorders. The eating disorders we will discuss are known as anorexia nervosa, bulimia, and binge eating disorder. A recent study of college female athletes found that 15% of swimmers, 62% of gymnasts, and 32% of all varsity athletes exhibited disordered eating patterns (Wardlow, 1997).

Although most studies of eating disorders have singled out White middle-class and upper-class women, these problems transcend ethnic and socioeconomic boundaries. A study of teenagers in New Mexico found the highest prevalence of "disturbed eating" among Native Americans (Smith & Krejci, 1991). Other research suggests that ethnic minority women, poor women, and lesbians have generally been excluded from such research, and that women in these groups may develop eating disorders in response to traumas arising from racism, poverty, and sexism as well as sexual abuse (B. W. Thompson, 1992).

Michael P. Levine (1987; 1993) defines **eating disorders** as eating and weight management practices that have the following characteristics:

1. They reduce a person's health and vigor and threaten his or her life.
2. They are carried out in secrecy, reducing the person's ability to fulfill obligations to self and others.

3. The person suffers from obsessions, anxiety, irritability, depression, and guilt.

4. The person becomes increasingly self-absorbed as well as emotionally unstable.

5. The person is out of control.

Anorexia Nervosa   "Anorexia" is the medical term for loss of appetite. The term "anorexia nervosa" is a misnomer for the condition it purports to describe. Those with anorexia are, in fact, obsessively preoccupied with food; they live in a perpetual struggle with the pangs of hunger. Dr. Hilde Bruch (1978), a pioneer in the study of eating disorders, defined **anorexia nervosa** as the "relentless pursuit of excessive thinness." It affects women more often than men by a ratio of 20 to 1 (American Psychiatric Assn., 1994). Anorexia usually develops between the ages of 10 and 30; the average age of onset is 17. An estimated 0.5–1% of young women in their late teens and early twenties develop anorexia (Hales, 1997).

Most anorexics share a number of characteristics. They are ruled by a desire for thinness, the conviction that their bodies are too large (even in the face of evidence to the contrary), and the "grim determination" to sustain weight loss (Levine, 1987). Typically, a person with anorexia has a body weight at least 15% below normal. Quite often the illness begins with a significant amount of weight loss; later the person becomes debilitated and ill as a result, but she refuses help and so continues in a potentially life-threatening downward spiral. Like other eating disorders, anorexia is often the "tip of the iceberg," a symptom of an underlying psychological disturbance or set of disturbances (Zerbe, 1992).

Physiologically, anorexics suffer from **amenorrhea,** delay of menarche or cessation of menstrual periods for at least three menstrual cycles; they may also suffer from hypothermia, the body's inability to maintain heat. In men, testosterone levels decline. Adolescents with this disorder may not achieve the secondary sex characteristics that are normal for this time, such as breast development and a growth spurt. Other symptoms include the growth of lanugo (fine body hair), insomnia, constipation, dry skin and hair, problems with teeth and gums, and weakening and thinning of the bones.

Behaviorally, anorexics often exhibit hyperactivity, social withdrawal, binge eating, and purging with self-induced vomiting, laxatives, or diuretics. The accumulated physical and psychological effects of anorexia are profound. The mortality rate is believed to be about 4%.

Bulimia   The word "bulimia" is derived from Greek roots meaning "ox hunger." **Bulimia** is characterized by episodes of uncontrolled overeating (binge eating), which the person then tries to counteract by purging—vomiting, exercising, or dieting excessively, or using laxatives or diuretics.

Many people with bulimia viewed themselves with extreme disdain during childhood, grappled with obesity at a young age, and have a history of conflict with their parents ("Community Study," 1997). Other traits that may distinguish the individual with bulimia from others include childhood physical and sexual abuse, severe physical health problems, perfectionism, and parents who have suffered from depression. Bulimia has also been shown to

The body that is idealized by ultra-thin fashion models is impossible for most women to obtain without imperiling their health.

develop more frequently in women who had begun to menstruate by age 12 than in those who began later. Early changes in body shape associated with puberty may be seen as another incentive to diet. Other characteristics associated with bulimia are dramatic weight fluctuation, emotional instability, and a high need for approval. Bulimia is more prevalent than anorexia; 1–3% of adolescent and young women develop it (American Psychological Assn., 1994).

Binge Eating Disorder   A recently recognized eating disorder, **binge eating disorder,** more commonly known as compulsive overeating, is similar to bulimia except that there is no purging behavior. Loss of control may be accompanied by a variety of symptoms, including rapid eating, eating to the point of discomfort or beyond, continual eating throughout the day, and eating large amounts when not hungry. Obsessive thinking, embarrassment, and feelings of guilt and disgust often accompany the overeating (American Psychological Assn., 1994). Those with binge eating disorder are often overweight; many are dieters. Evidence indicates that between 25% and 45% of obese dieters, most of whom are women, may have binge eating disorder.

Retreating from Sexuality

Clinicians who work with eating-disordered patients often find that they have histories of abuse, including incest or other sexual abuse (Simpson &

Ramberg, 1992). They may also have been raised to be fearful of sex and to view the body as dirty or sinful. Sexual dysfunctions and inhibitions are common among those with severe eating disorders (Rothschild, Fagan, Woodall, & Andersen, 1991; Zerbe, 1992).

Eating disorders, especially anorexia, often develop during adolescence. It is not unusual for adolescents to experience fear and feelings of power-lessness as their bodies and roles change. For some women, eating is a strat-egy used to cope with a variety of abusive situations. Control over the size of their bodies is one of the few forms of control that women have been allowed to exercise (Boston Women's Health Book Collective, 1992). The refusal of food, in spite of the intense demands of hunger, may be equated with strength.

Many people with eating disorders are ambivalent toward their bodies and their sexual natures in general. An adolescent girl may feel (possibly on a subconscious level) that accepting a "curvy" woman's body means accept-ing a traditional gender role. Becoming asexual by becoming excessively fat or thin can be seen as a rebellion against models of feminine subservience and ineffectiveness. Acquiring an asexual body is also a means of retreating from the powerful forces of sexuality. For adolescents especially, sexuality appears dangerous and evil on the one hand, desirable and beautiful on the other. The conflict generated by these opposing views can result in sexual-ity's becoming "curiously disembodied from the person" (Orbach, 1982).

Sexual abuse may also be involved in rejection of the body (Young, 1992). Through self-starvation, a young woman may demonstrate her wish to sim-ply disappear. Others may express their rejection of sexuality by insulating themselves in a protective layer of fat.

ALCOHOL, DRUGS, AND SEXUALITY

Alcohol and other drugs can significantly affect our sexual health and well-being. In the minds of many Americans, sex and alcohol (or sex and "recre-ational" drugs) go together like a hamburger and fries. Although experience shows us that sexual performance and enjoyment generally decrease as alco-hol or drug levels increase, many people persist in believing the age-old myths. One study of 125 women age 15–31 found that 65% had combined alcohol use with sex in the preceding month, and that 43% had used alco-hol at the time of their first sexual experience (Flanigan, 1990). In a survey of 243 single college students, only 19% of those over 21 had never had sex as a result of intoxication (Butcher, Manning, & O'Neal, 1991).

Alcohol Use and Sexuality

The belief that alcohol and sex go together, although not new, is certainly reinforced by popular culture. Alcohol advertising often features beautiful women, barely clothed. Beer drinkers are portrayed as young, healthy, and fun-loving. Wine drinkers are romantics, surrounded by candlelight and roses. Those who choose Scotch are the epitome of sophistication. These images reinforce long-held cultural myths associating alcohol with social prestige and sexual enhancement (Leigh, 1990; Roenrich & Kinder, 1991; Whitbeck & Hoyt, 1991).

Because of the ambivalence we often have about sex ("It's good but it's bad"), many people feel more comfortable about initiating or participating in sexual activities if they have had a drink or two. This phenomenon of activating behaviors that would normally be suppressed is known as **disinhibition** (Woods & Mansfield, 1981). Although a small amount of alcohol may have a small disinhibiting, or relaxing, effect, greater quantities can result in aggression, loss of judgment, poor coordination, and loss of consciousness. Studies have shown that there may be an indirect relationship between substance abuse and behavioral disinhibition ("Risky Sex," 1998). This means that some people who are under the influence of alcohol are less able to process the negative consequences of an action (e.g., not using a condom) or the cues that normally inhibit them (e.g., having sex with someone they might not otherwise choose to have sex with). Alcohol is also generally detrimental to sexual performance and enjoyment. Furthermore, ingestion of large amounts of alcohol by both men and women can contribute to infertility and birth defects.

Alcohol affects the ability of both men and women to become sexually aroused. Men may have difficulty achieving or maintaining an erection, and women may not experience vaginal lubrication. Physical sensations are likely to be dulled. Chronic users of alcohol typically experience desire and arousal difficulties (O'Farrell, Choquette, & Birchler, 1991; Schiavi, Schreiner-Engle, Mandeli, Schanzer, & Cohen, 1990). This may be due in part to poor general health and also to lowered production of reproductive hormones. Alcohol has been demonstrated to affect RNA in male rats, suppressing its function in testosterone and sperm production (Emanuele, Tentler, Emanuele, & Kelley, 1991). Researchers have determined that drinking a six-pack of beer in less than 2 hours can halt a man's RNA activity for up to 12 hours. (This does not mean, however, that no sperm are present; production is slowed, but most men will remain fertile.)

Alcohol use also puts people at high risk for numerous unwanted or dangerous consequences. These include unwanted intercourse, sexual violence, pregnancy, and sexually transmitted diseases. The disinhibiting effect of alcohol allows some men to justify acts of sexual violence they would not otherwise commit (Abbey, 1991; Roenrich & Kinder, 1991). Men may expect that alcohol will make them sexually aggressive and act accordingly; they may believe that if a woman drinks, she is consenting to have sex. Additionally, a woman who has been drinking may have difficulty in sending and receiving cues about expected behavior and in resisting assault (Abbey, 1991). Alcohol use is often a significant factor in sexual violence of all types. The American College Health Association estimates that drinking contributes to approximately two-thirds of all violence on campus and one-third of all emotional and academic problems. Furthermore, it may play a role in 90% of rapes and sexual assaults (Rivinus & Larimer, 1993).

Drug Use and Sexuality

Human beings have always been interested in the effects of drugs and other concoctions on sexual interest and performance. Substances that supposedly increase sexual desire or improve sexual performance are called **aphrodisiacs.** Painstaking research, both personal and professional, inevitably leads to the same conclusion: one's inner fantasy life, coupled with an interested and

Among college students, the use of alcohol is associated with increased risk of unwanted intercourse, sexual violence, pregnancy, and sexually transmitted diseases.

responsive partner, is the most powerful and effective aphrodisiac available. Nevertheless, the search continues for the magic potion.

Most recreational drugs, although perceived as increasing sexual enjoyment, actually have the opposite effect. (Many prescribed medications have negative effects on sexual desire and functioning as well.) Marijuana and alcohol continue to be the most widely used and abused drugs among people anxious to increase libido and performance. Although drugs may reduce inhibitions and appear to enhance the sexual experience, many also have the capacity to interfere with sexual functioning and even cause impotence and infertility.

The effects of marijuana are in large part determined by the expectations of its users ("Marijuana and Sex," 1996); therefore, no definitive statement can be made about how marijuana affects sexual encounters. Specific answers about its effects in a relationship can be found by looking at the role it plays in a couple's life. In some cases marijuana (or any drug) can become a crutch to help people deal with situations or behaviors they find uncomfortable.

Some evidence suggests that marijuana stimulates the body to convert testosterone to estrogen, resulting in delayed puberty for young teenage boys ("Effects of Marijuana," 1995). Long-term marijuana use can also cause or contribute to low motivation to achieve and low sex drive.

The substance amyl nitrate is reputed to intensify orgasmic pleasure. It is a fast-acting smooth muscle relaxant and coronary vasodilator, meaning it expands blood vessels around the heart. Medically, it is used to relieve attacks of angina. Some people attempt to intensify their orgasms by "popping" an amyl nitrate vial and inhaling the vapor. The drug causes engorgement of the blood vessels in the penis. It also causes a drop in blood pressure, which may result in feelings of dizziness and giddiness. The most common side effects are severe headaches, fainting, and, because it is flammable, risk of burns.

Another drug widely considered to be an aphrodisiac is cantharides, or "Spanish fly." Derived from a specific beetle, this substance is produced by

WHAT WOULD YOU BE WILLING to do to obtain the "perfect body"? Exercise 3 hours a day at the gym? Spend hundreds of dollars each month on exercise equipment and gym fees? Take anabolic steroids? For many, this last alternative offers the quickest and most dramatic route to a toned and muscular body. Unfortunately for the many thousands who choose this alternative, it is also the most dangerous.

Anabolic steroids are synthetic derivatives of testosterone, the male hormone that helps the body to build muscle and synthesize protein. Beyond this function, the mechanism of action of steroids is unclear. Though anabolic steroids are legitimately prescribed to combat some diseases, both male and female athletes may often take 10 times the recommended dosage to increase muscle mass, improve strength, and promote tissue growth. Abuse can have serious and long-lasting negative effects on the health of the user.

In men, acne, baldness, and changes in sexual desire are the most common side effects of anabolic steroids. In addition, steroids can cause a decrease in sperm production as well as infertility if used over a prolonged period. The size of the testicles may decrease, and men may have a difficult time achieving and maintaining an erection. In women, steroids usually have a masculinizing effect; they may cause the growth of facial hair, a deepening of the voice, shrinkage of the breasts, menstrual irregularities, an enlargement of the clitoris, and, if the woman is genetically predisposed, male pattern baldness. These side effects are permanent.

When they first begin to use steroids, before any negative effects appear, users often report an increase in libido, a heightened sense of sexuality, and euphoria. But these feelings are offset by the depression that occurs if the athlete goes off the drug. As use continues, larger doses must be taken to achieve the highs that were experienced early on. Psychological and physical dependence follows, accompanied by dramatic emotional highs and lows. The user may experience personality changes, becoming hostile, paranoid, or violent.

Steroid abuse may also have significant effects on the cardiovascular system, leading to atherosclerosis. Increased water retention combined with atherosclerosis causes high blood pressure, another problem experienced by abusers. Liver structure and function are disrupted, but this process stops when steroid use is discontinued. Because steroids are often injected, users are at risk for HIV infection from sharing unclean needles.

Anabolic steroids sold on the "black market" include a wide range of drugs, many approved only for animals. Because there is little or no quality control, users are at extreme risk. Although we know many of the dangers associated with these drugs, it may be years before their full effects on athletes using them now begin to surface.

Source: Adapted from *Health Tips,* a publication of the California Medical Education and Research Foundation, February 1992.

drying and heating the insects' bodies until they disintegrate into a powder. There have not yet been controlled studies to confirm its aphrodisiac effect ("Aphrodisiacs," 1996). Taken internally, the substance causes acute irritation and inflammation of the genitourinary tract, including the kidneys, bladder, and urethra. It can result in permanent tissue damage and death. This substance is banned in the United States.

LSD and other psychedelic drugs (including mescaline and psilocybin) have no positive effects on sexual ability. They may actually cause constant and painful erections, a condition called **priapism**.

Cocaine, a central nervous system stimulant, reduces inhibitions and enhances feelings of well-being. But regular use nearly always leads to sexual dysfunction in both men and women, as well as an inability to achieve erection or orgasm. Cocaine also lowers sperm count. The same levels of sexual impairment occur among those who sniff the drug and those who smoke it as "freebase." Those who inject cocaine experience the greatest dysfunction.

Ecstasy (MDMA) is a hallucinogenic amphetamine that produces heightened arousal, a mellowing effect, and an enhanced sense of self ("Ecstasy

Effects," 1996). The drug is illegal and has no legitimate use. It has been associated with dehydration due to physical exertion without breaks for water; heavy use has been linked to paranoia, liver damage, and heart attacks.

Derived from the bark of the yohimbe tree of West Africa, yohimbine has been used for centuries as an aphrodisiac. The scientifically manufactured form of the drug, yohimbine hydrochloride, has been approved by the FDA for treating erectile problems as well as low blood pressure ("Aphrodisiacs," 1996). Effectiveness ranges from 40% to 80%, depending on the study. This is good news for those whose sexual problems are caused by antidepressants or other medications.

Aside from the adverse physical effects of drugs themselves, a major negative consequence of substance abuse is that it puts many people at significant risk of acquiring sexually transmitted diseases, including HIV infection. Addiction to cocaine, especially in the smokable form known as "crack," has led to the widespread practice of bartering sex for cocaine. This practice, as well as the practice of injecting cocaine or heroin, combined with the low rate of condom use, has led to epidemics of STDs, including AIDS, in many urban areas. For additional information on drugs and violence, see Chapter 17.

SEXUALITY AND AGING

Men and women tend to view aging differently. As men approach their fifties, they generally fear the loss of their sexual capacity but not their attractiveness; in contrast, women generally fear the loss of their attractiveness but not their sexuality.

Most older studies on aging and sexuality indicated a decline in sexual desire or interest as people age. More recent studies seem to indicate, however, that although physiological functions such as lubrication and erection may be slowed, sexual interest, enjoyment, and satisfaction often remain strong (Greeley, 1992; Mulligan & Moss, 1991; Schiavi et al., 1990). Expressions of sexuality among older adults seem to depend on the cultural attitudes of the society (Greer, Herkov, & Hill, 1994). In a longitudinal study, almost 700 middle-aged women were interviewed twice, at a 6-year interval (Hällstrom & Samuelsson, 1990). Almost two-thirds of the women studied experienced no significant change in their levels of desire after 6 years. Although 27% experienced a decline, 10% actually experienced an increase. What is most notable about this study is that it shows the impact of marital satisfaction and mental health on sexual desire. Not surprisingly, many of the women whose desire decreased over 6 years felt that their marriages lacked intimacy, had spouses who were alcoholic, and were themselves depressed. Such an unhappy combination is a sure antidote to desire. Those whose desire increased had initially experienced weaker desire, had troubled marriages, and had been depressed. Six years later, as their marriages improved and their mental health improved, their desire increased, moving them closer to the average.

Among older lesbian and gay couples, as well as heterosexual pairs, the happiest are those with a strong commitment to the relationship. The need for intimacy, companionship, and purpose transcends issues of sexual orientation (Lipman, 1986).

> You only possess what will not be lost in a shipwreck.
>
> —*El-Ghazaki*

Marital satisfaction and emotional health foster the desire for sexual intimacy in lasting relationships.

Because our society tends to desexualize the old, aging people may interpret their slower responses as signaling the end of their sexuality. Education programs for older people, in which they learn about anatomy, physiology, and sexual response, have been shown to be helpful in dispelling myths, building confidence, and giving permission to be sexual (Goldman & Carroll, 1990; Kellett, 1991).

Women's Issues

Beginning sometime in their forties, most women begin to experience a decline in fertility. The ovaries produce less and less estrogen, and ovulation becomes less regular. This period of gradual change and adjustment is referred to as **perimenopause.** Over a few years' time, menstrual periods become irregular and eventually stop, usually between the ages of 45 and 55. This period of time is referred to as the **climacteric.** The average age of **menopause,** the complete cessation of menstruation, is 52, although about 10% of women complete it before age 40 (Beck, 1992). Most women experience some physiological or psychological symptoms during menopause, but for only about 5–15% of women are the effects severe enough to cause them to seek medical assistance (Brody, 1992).

Physical Effects of Menopause   The most common physical effects of menopause are hot flashes and vaginal symptoms, such as dryness, thinning of the vaginal walls, and pain or bleeding during intercourse. These effects may begin while a woman is still menstruating and may continue after menstruation has ceased. As many as 75% of women experience some degree of hot flashes, which usually diminish within 2 years following the end of menopause. A **hot flash** is a period of intense warmth, flushing, and (often) perspiration, typically lasting for a minute or two (but ranging anywhere from 15 seconds to 1 hour in length). Some women perspire so heavily that they soak through their clothing or bedclothes. A hot flash occurs when falling estrogen levels cause the body's "thermostat" in the brain to trigger dilation (expansion) of blood vessels near the skin's surface, producing a sensation of heat. Some women who are going through menopause experience insomnia (which can be related to hot flashes), mood changes, changes in sexual interest (more commonly a decrease), urinary incontinence, weakening of pelvic floor muscles, headaches, or weight gain.

Long-term effects related to lowered estrogen levels may be experienced by some women. **Osteoporosis,** the loss of bone mass, leads to problems such as wrist and hip fractures in about 25% of mainly postmenopausal White and Asian women and Latinas; African American women are less susceptible to osteoporosis (Greenwood, 1992). Women who are fair-skinned or thin or who smoke are at increased risk for osteoporosis. Lowered estrogen can also contribute to diseases of the heart and arteries related to rising levels of LDL ("bad" cholesterol) and falling levels of HDL ("good" cholesterol). Hereditary factors also play a part in cardiovascular disease.

Many women do not consider menopause a medical condition and therefore do not feel it requires any special treatment. Others may be bothered enough by attendant symptoms to seek medical advice or assistance. Some women may be concerned about the possibility of future problems, such as osteoporosis. Others may be concerned about changes in their sexual feelings or patterns, or about the implications of fertility loss, aging, and changing standards of attractiveness. Because physicians may have a tendency to treat menopause as a medical "problem," women may find themselves subjected to treatments they don't understand or would not choose if they were better informed. It's important that women seek out practitioners who will work with them to meet their needs in the ways that are most appropriate for each individual.

Diagnosis of osteoporosis can be made through bone densitometry, a quick, painless procedure that can reveal signs of osteoporosis long before symptoms appear. The cost to patients is $100–$200. Premenopausal women should consider testing if they have a bone-threatening medical condition such as type I diabetes, rheumatoid arthritis, or hyperthyroidism. Thin-boned men over 65 might also consider having the test.

Newly developed treatments can control osteoporosis indefinitely. Because the disease stems mainly from the loss of estrogen at menopause, replacing estrogen, along with progesterone, is currently the most common treatment. The cost is $25 per month. In 1995, the FDA approved an oral medication (trade name Fosamax) and a nasal spray (sold as Miacalcin), both of which have been found to significantly lower the risk of fractures (Cowley & Underwood, 1996). Inconvenience and/or costs play a role in the use of either one of these drugs. For women who don't like these options, a slow-release formulation of sodium fluoride (the same ingredient that protects teeth) is being considered by the FDA for approval and should soon be available. Other approaches include exercise and calcium supplements to reduce bone loss.

Other changes that may reduce the physical effects of menopause include low-cholesterol diets, exercise and nutritional supplements to lower cholesterol, topical lubricants to counteract vaginal dryness, and Kegel exercises to strengthen pelvic floor muscles. Frequent sexual stimulation (by self or partner) may help maintain vaginal moistness. For women who smoke, quitting smoking provides benefits in many areas, including reducing the risk of osteoporosis, less intense hot flashes, and an improved sense of well-being (Greenwood, 1992).

Hormone Replacement Therapy   The administration of estrogen—often combined with progestin—in the form of pills, vaginal cream, or a small adhesive patch is known as **hormone replacement therapy (HRT).** The pills are usually taken daily; progestin pills may be added for part or all of the cycle. The woman will often take pills for part of a month and then stop taking them, to allow the uterine lining to be shed. Some women prefer to apply estrogen directly to the vagina in the form of a cream; this may be done either daily or less frequently. The estrogen patch, worn on the back or abdomen, must be changed every few days. Additional progestin may also be prescribed.

HRT has both benefits and risks. A woman should investigate before beginning treatment. The principal benefits of HRT are that it greatly reduces the risks of osteoporosis, heart attack, and stroke; it virtually eliminates hot flashes; and it allows the vaginal walls to remain supple and moist. This last effect can have a positive impact on the sexual interactions of those women who would otherwise experience pain or bleeding with intercourse (Walling, Andersen, & Johnson, 1990). The possible risks of HRT include an increased chance of cancer of the uterine lining and a 5% increase in the risk of breast cancer (Huang et al., 1997); there is also the possibility of PMS-like symptoms. Adding progestin to part of the cycle is thought to prevent endometrial cancer, but it may have unpleasant side effects for some women.

The risk of breast cancer may be higher in women with a family history of the disease. Weight gain and increased body mass are also associated with postmenopausal breast cancer, increasing the risk by 16%. By comparison, HRT increases the risk by 5%. The combination of these two factors (weight gain and HRT) accounts for almost one-third of postmenopausal breast cancers (Huang et al., 1997). Women who take HRT for less than 5 years do not appear to be at increased risk of breast cancer. Although long-term use of estrogen dramatically reduces an older woman's risk of dying from a heart attack, it gradually increases her risk of breast cancer. After a decade of use, the increase in risk of cancer begins to cancel out the lowered risk of heart attack (Grodstein et al., 1997).

The effects of HRT on postmenopausal memory loss and Alzheimer's disease have only recently begun to be explored. Though several studies have found beneficial effects, a group of Yale University researchers reviewing 19 studies of the effects of HRT on memory found inadequate evidence to support the conclusion that HRT improves cognitive function in postmenopausal women or women with Alzheimer's dementia (Haskell, Richardson, & Horwitz, 1997).

Psychological Aspects of Menopause   Many women find they feel relieved when they no longer have to worry about getting pregnant. Not having to worry about birth control may be very liberating. Most women are pleased when they no longer have to deal with a monthly menstrual flow. Some women may be bothered by the physical effects of menopause, whereas for others, the positive psychological effects are greater. Even though most women close to their fifties no longer wish to bear children, the knowledge that she is no longer capable of reproduction may be painful for a woman. In addition to grieving for the loss of her fertility, she may also feel that she is losing her sexual attractiveness. Because women in our society are often judged on the basis of their appearance and youthfulness, those who have "used their glamour and sexiness to attract men and enhance their self-esteem" may find aging particularly painful (Greenwood, 1992).

Men's Issues

Changes in male sexual responsiveness begin to become apparent when men are in their forties and fifties, a period of change sometimes referred to as the **male climacteric.** Some 15% of U.S. men are completely impotent by 70 (up from 5% at 40) and one-third experience at least occasional erectile difficulties (Cowley, 1996). For about 5% of men, these physical changes of aging are accompanied by experiences such as fatigue, an inability to concentrate, depression, loss of appetite, and a decreased interest in sex (Kolodny, Masters, & Johnson, 1979). As a man ages, his frequency of sexual activity declines; achieving erection requires more stimulation and time, and the erection may not be as firm (Mulligan & Moss, 1991). Ejaculation takes longer and may not occur every time the penis is stimulated; the force of the ejaculation is less than before, as is the amount of ejaculate (Zilbergeld, 1992). The refractory period is extended (up to 24 hours or longer in older men). Sexual interest and enjoyment generally do not decrease (Schiavi et al., 1990). Although some of the changes are related directly to age and a normal decrease in testosterone production, others may be the result of diseases associated with aging (Mulligan, Retchin, Chinchilli, & Bettinger, 1988; Whitbourne, 1990). Poor general health, diabetes, atherosclerosis, urinary incontinence, and some medications can contribute to sexual dysfunction.

It is important for older men to understand that slower responses are a normal function of aging and are unrelated to the ability to give or receive sexual pleasure. "The senior penis," writes Bernie Zilbergeld (1992), "can still give and take pleasure, even though it's not the same as it was decades ago."

About half of men over age 50 are affected to some degree by **benign prostatic hypertrophy,** an enlargement of the prostate gland. The enlarged prostate may put pressure on the urethra, resulting in the frequent and urgent need to urinate. It does not affect sexual functioning. If the blockage of the urethra is too severe, surgery can correct the problem. The surgery may lead to **retrograde ejaculation,** in which the ejaculate is released into the bladder instead of the urethra upon orgasm. Retrograde ejaculation is not dangerous, and the sensations of orgasm are generally unchanged (Thompson, 1990).

Male anxiety about aging has led to a heavy demand for remedies and treatments. Though largely untested, some antidotes are available. Testosterone is currently the most widely known and prescribed drug among these. Used to maintain muscle mass and reduce cholesterol, it also increases energy and libido. Side effects include an increased risk of prostate tumors, lower rates of HDL ("good" cholesterol), and blocked sperm ducts. Other drugs used include DHEA (dehydroepiandrosterone, a naturally occurring hormone produced in the adrenal glands and now used by those who believe that it can improve mood, memory, energy, and libido), melatonin, and human growth hormone. As with testosterone, the long-term risks and rewards remain uncertain (Cowley, 1996).

Making medical history as the most successful prescription drug ever is Viagra, a medication that helps men achieve and sustain erections. Used for men suffering from impotence caused by peripheral vascular disease (hardening of the arteries of the penis), the pill is taken an hour before intercourse. The drug acts by enhancing the smooth muscle relaxant effects of nitric oxide, a substance that is normally released locally in response to sexual stimulation. This smooth muscle relaxation allows blood to enter and pool in the penis, leading to an erection (U.S. Food & Drug Administration, 1998). Viagra typically costs about $10 a pill. It has a success rate of 70% (Adler, 1998).

As with any drug product, there are side effects in some people. The most common ones include headache, flushing, stomach ache, and mild and temporary visual changes. Men who are currently using medicines that contain nitrates, such as nitroglycerin, should not use Viagra because taken together the two medications can lower blood pressure (USFDA, 1998). Physicians are concerned about patients who order Viagra from the Internet or obtain it without having a full medical history taken and an examination performed to determine the cause of their impotence. Men who have medical conditions that may cause sustained erection (such as sickle-cell disease or leukemia) or an abnormally shaped penis may not be able to take the drug.

With Viagra on the market, the line between medical necessity and emotional well-being has become blurred. Insurance companies and government agencies are questioning the limits of their responsibility for coverage of the drug. As of the printing of this book, a few groups have taken action for or against payment.

Although Viagra has been approved by the Food & Drug Administration for men only, doctors are free to prescribe it in any way they see fit as long as they believe there is a medical reason. Consequently, women are beginning to seek treatment with Viagra to restore lost sex lives caused by hysterectomies, high cholesterol, and age. Researchers believe that Viagra boosts blood flow to the vagina, increasing a woman's lubrication and sensitivity to stimulation ("Viagra Might Help," 1998).

The key to Viagra's instant marketing success may be that there are no appealing alternative treatments for erectile dysfunction available. Vacuum pumps, hypodermic injections, or inserts may improve performance but often take away desire. If Viagra lives up to the hopes and expectations of the millions suffering from impotence or anorgasmia, there may be a significant improvement in the quality of life for many.

SEXUALITY AND DISABILITY

A wide range of disabilities and physically limiting conditions affect human sexuality, yet the sexual needs and desires of those with disabilities have been generally overlooked and ignored. In 1987, Ellen Stohl, a young woman who uses a wheelchair, created controversy by posing seminude for an eight-page layout in *Playboy*. Some people (including some editors at *Playboy*) felt the feature could be construed as exploitive of disabled people. Others, Stohl among them, felt that it would help normalize society's perception of people with disabilities. She said, "I realized I was still a woman. But the world didn't accept me as that. Here I am a senior in college [with] a 3.5 average, and people treat me like I'm a 3-year-old" (quoted in Cummings, 1987).

A study of lesbians and gay men with disabilities found that they were dealing with several issues affecting their sexuality (Lew-Starowicz, 1994). Their main problems were difficulty finding a partner and lack of acceptance of their sexual orientation.

Physical Limitations

Many people are subject to sexually limiting conditions for some or all of their lives. These conditions may be congenital, appearing at birth, such as cerebral palsy (a neuromuscular disorder) and Down syndrome (a developmentally disabling condition). They may be caused by a disease such as diabetes, arthritis, or cancer or be the result of an accident, as in the case of spinal cord injuries.

Changing Expectations   Educating people with physical limitations about their sexual potential and providing a holistic approach that includes counseling to build self-esteem and combat negative stereotypes are increasingly being recognized as crucial issues by the medical community (Burling, Tarvydas, & Maki, 1994; Rieve, 1989).

To establish sexual health, people with disabilities must overcome previous sexual performance expectations and realign them with their actual sexual capacities. In cases where the spinal cord is completely severed, for example, there is no feeling in the genitals, but that does not eliminate sexual desires or put a stop to other possible sexual behaviors. Many men with spinal cord damage are able to have erections or partial erections; some may ejaculate, although the orgasmic feelings accompanying ejaculation are generally absent. Those who are not capable of ejaculation may be able to father a child through electroejaculation sperm retrieval and intrauterine insemination of the man's partner. In this procedure, the prostate gland is electrically stimulated through the rectum, causing erection and ejaculation.

Women with spinal cord injuries generally do not experience orgasm, although they are able to experience sensuous feelings in other parts of their bodies. People with spinal cord injuries (and anyone else, for that matter) may engage in oral or manual sex—anything, in fact, they and their partners find pleasurable and acceptable. They may discover new erogenous areas of their bodies, such as their thighs, necks, ears, or underarms. A study by the Kinsey Institute and Indiana University of 186 people (140 men and 46 women) with spinal cord injuries found that the injury affected masturbation, coitus, noncoital sex, sexual response during sleep, and fertility (Donohue & Gebhard, 1995). Within 3 years of the injury, however, 95% of the women (excluding three who were virgins) and 90% of the men had resumed coitus.

Spinal cord injuries do not usually affect fertility. Many women with such injuries are able to have painless childbirth, although forceps delivery, vacuum extraction, or cesarean section may be necessary.

Overcoming Guilt   A major problem for many of those with disabilities is overcoming the guilt they feel because their bodies don't meet the cultural "ideal." They often live in dread of rejection, which may or may not be realistic, depending on whom they seek as partners. Many people with disabilities have rich fantasy lives. This is fortuitous, because imagination is a key ingredient to developing a full sexual life. Robert Lenz, a consultant in the field of sexuality and disability, received a quadriplegic (paralyzed from the neck down) spinal cord injury when he was 16 (Lenz & Chaves, 1981). In the film *Active Partners,* he says:

> One thing I do know is that I'm a much better lover now than I ever was before. There are a lot of reasons for that, but one of the biggest is that I'm more relaxed. I don't have a list of do's and don'ts, a timetable or a proper sequence of moves to follow, or the need to "give" my partner an orgasm every time we make love. Sex isn't just orgasm for me; it's pleasuring, playing, laughing, and sharing.

Major functions of therapists working with people with disabilities are to give their clients "permission" to engage in sexual activities that are appropriate to their capacities and to suggest new activities or techniques (Kolodny, Masters, & Johnson, 1979). Clients should also be advised about the use of vibrators, artificial penises and vaginas, and other aids to sexual excitement.

Vision and Hearing Impairment

Loss of sight or hearing, especially if it is total and has existed from infancy, presents many difficulties in both the theoretical and the practical understanding of sexuality. A young person who has been blind from birth is unlikely to know what a person of the other sex actually "looks" (or feels) like. Children who are deaf often do not have parents who communicate well in sign language; as a result, they may not receive much instruction about sex at home, nor are they likely to understand abstract concepts such as "intimacy." Older individuals who experience significant losses of sight or hearing may become depressed, develop low self-esteem, and withdraw from contact with others. Because they don't receive the visual or auditory cues that most of us take for granted, the hearing-impaired or sight-impaired may have communication difficulties within their sexual relationships. These difficulties can often be overcome with education or counseling, depending on the circumstances. Schools and programs for visually and hearing-impaired children offer specially designed curricula for teaching about sexuality.

Chronic Illness

Diabetes, cardiovascular disease, and arthritis are three of the most prevalent diseases in America. Although these conditions are not always described as disabilities, they may require considerable adjustments in a person's sexuality because they (or the medications or treatments given to control them) may affect libido, sexual capability or responsiveness, and body image. Many older couples find themselves dealing with issues of disease and disability in addition to aging (Power-Smith, 1991).

There may be other disabling conditions, too numerous to discuss here, that also affect our lives or those of people we know. Some of the information presented here may be applicable to conditions not specifically dealt

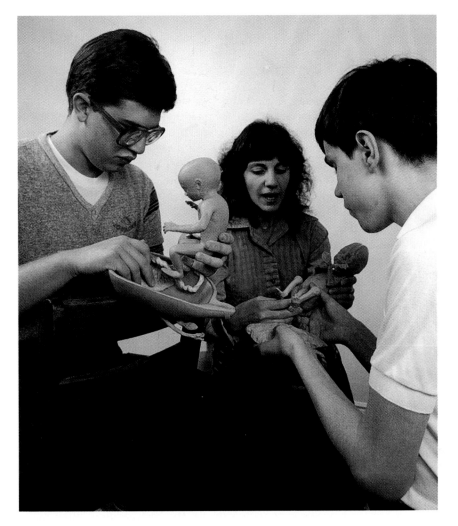

Children with physical or developmental disabilities may have special needs when it comes to sexuality education. Here, students with visual impairments take a hands-on approach to learning about pregnancy and childbirth with the help of lifelike models.

with, such as multiple sclerosis or postpolio syndrome. We encourage readers with specific questions regarding sexuality and chronic diseases to seek out networks, organizations, and self-help groups that specialize in those issues.

Diabetes **Diabetes mellitus,** commonly referred to simply as diabetes, is a chronic disease characterized by an excess of sugar in the blood and urine, due to a deficiency of insulin, a protein hormone. Nerve damage or circulatory problems caused by diabetes can cause sexual problems (Bemelmans, Meuleman, Doesburg, Notermans, & Debruyne, 1994). Men with diabetes are more affected sexually by their disease than are women. Almost half of men with diabetes experience erectile dysfunctions, although there is apparently little or no relationship between the severity of the diabetes and the dysfunction. Heavy alcohol use and poor blood sugar control also increase the risk of erectile problems.

Women who have diabetes generally experience little or no decline in libido and are able to lubricate during sexual activity. There is conflicting opinion, however, about the effects of diabetes on women's orgasmic response (Ellenberg, 1980; Kolodny, 1971). One study has found there to be less physiological arousal to sexual stimulation in women with diabetes (Wincze, Albert, & Bansal, 1993).

Cardiovascular Disease   A heart attack or stroke is a major event in a person's life, affecting important aspects of daily living. Following an attack, a person often enters a period of depression in which the appetite declines, sleep habits change, and there is fatigue and a loss of libido. There is often an overwhelming fear of sex based on the belief that sexual activity might provoke another heart attack or stroke (Renshaw, 1995). The wives of male heart attack patients also express great concern about sexuality. They are fearful of the risks, concerned over their husbands' sexual difficulties, and apprehensive during intercourse about possible symptoms of another attack. Usually, sexual activity is safe 2 to 3 weeks after the heart attack patient returns home from the hospital, but it depends on the individual's physical and psychological well-being. He or she should consult with a physician.

Arthritis   Whereas more men suffer from cardiovascular disease, the majority of people with arthritis are women. About 20 million people have symptoms of arthritis, most of them older women, but the disease may afflict and disable children and adolescents as well. Arthritis is a painful inflammation and swelling of the joints, usually of the knees, hips, and lower back, which may lead to deformity of the limbs. Sometimes the joints can be moved only with great difficulty and pain; sometimes they cannot be moved at all. The cause of arthritis is not known.

Sexual intercourse may be painful or impossible for arthritic women because they are not able to rotate their hip joints or spread their legs sufficiently for their partners to enter in the male-above position (Renshaw, 1995). Simply the pressure of their partners' bodies can cause excruciating pain. A woman with this type of arthritis may experiment to find a position that is comfortable for her. For men with arthritis, the best position is the male-above position. Oral sex, general pleasuring of the body, and creative sexual positioning have definite advantages for those with arthritis.

Developmental Disabilities

About 6 million Americans have varying degrees of developmental disabilities (sometimes referred to as "mental retardation"). The sexuality of those who are developmentally disabled has only recently been widely acknowledged by those who work with them. Their sexual rights are just beginning to be recognized, although there is a great deal of debate about these issues. The capabilities of the developmentally disabled vary widely. Mildly or moderately disabled people may be able to learn to behave appropriately, protect themselves from abuse, and understand the basics of reproduction. Some may manage to marry, work, and raise families with little assistance (Monat-Haller, 1982; Pincus, 1988).

Sex education is of great importance for adolescents who have developmental disabilities. Some parents may fear that this will "put ideas into their heads," but it is more likely, given the combination of explicit media presentations and the effects of increased hormonal output, that the ideas are

Lament of a Coronary

My doctor has made a prognosis
That intercourse fosters thrombosis,
But I'd rather expire fulfilling desire
Than abstain, and suffer neurosis.

—*Anonymous*

already there. It may be difficult or impossible to teach more severely affected people how to engage in safe sexual behaviors. There is ongoing debate about the ethics of mandatory birth control devices—such as IUDs or implants—or sterilization for those who are developmentally disabled. These issues are especially salient in cases where there is the chance of passing the disability genetically to a child.

The Sexual Rights of People with Disabilities

Although many of the concerns of people with disabilities are becoming more visible through the courageous efforts of certain groups and individuals, much of their lives still remains hidden. There is a marked tendency on the part of the rest of humanity to put its collective head in the sand, believing that what it doesn't see does not exist. But none of us is immune to accidents or to numerous debilitating diseases and conditions. By refusing to recognize the existence and concerns of those with physical and developmental limitations, the rest of us do a profound disservice to our fellow human beings—and, ultimately, to ourselves.

The sexual rights of those with disabilities include:

1. The right to sexual expression
2. The right to privacy
3. The right to be informed and to have access to needed services, such as contraceptive counseling, medical care, genetic counseling, and sex counseling
4. The right to choose one's marital status
5. The right to have or not have children
6. The right to make one's own decisions and develop to one's fullest potential

SEXUALITY AND CANCER

In ancient Greece, physicians examining the invasive tissues extending from malignant breast tumors thought these tissues looked like the jutting claws of a crab. From the Greek word for crab, *karkinos,* we have derived our word "cancer." Cancer, however, is not a single disease; it is more than 300 distinct illnesses that can affect any organ of the body. These various cancers grow at different speeds and have different treatment success and failure rates. Most cancers, but not all (leukemia, for example), form solid tumors.

All cancers have one thing in common: They are the result of the aberrant behavior of cells. Cancer-causing agents (carcinogens) are believed to jumble up the DNA's messages, causing the cell to abandon its normal functions. Tumors are either benign or malignant. **Benign tumors** usually are slow growing and remain localized. **Malignant tumors,** however, are cancerous. Instead of remaining localized, they invade nearby tissues and disrupt the normal functioning of vital organs. The process by which the disease spreads from one part of the body to another unrelated part is called **metastasis.** This metastatic process, not the original tumor, accounts for 80% of cancer deaths.

Women and Cancer

Because of their fear of breast cancer and cancer of the reproductive organs, some women avoid having regular breast examinations or Pap tests. If a woman feels a breast lump or her doctor tells her she has a growth in her uterus, she may plunge into despair or panic. These reactions are understandable, but they are also counterproductive. Most lumps and bumps are benign conditions, such as uterine fibroids, ovarian cysts, and fibroadenomas of the breast.

Breast Cancer   The most common cancer among women is breast cancer, causing almost as many deaths among American women as lung cancer. In 1997, an estimated 182,000 women were diagnosed with breast cancer and nearly 46,000 died. Approximately 80% of women diagnosed with the disease survive at least 5 years; the majority achieve a complete cure.

Because of increasing success in the treatment of breast cancer, more emphasis is being placed on the quality of the patient's life after diagnosis. The aftermath of treatment (which often includes disfigurement) and the possibility of recurrence are ongoing issues and raise new physical and psychological concerns. The concept of "survivorship" requires a major shift in public attitudes. We should begin to think of cancer, not as a death sentence, but as a chronic disease we can live with.

"Breast cancer" is a catch-all term for at least 15 different types of tumors. Each type has a different rate of growth and tendency to metastasize in different organs. By the time a breast tumor is large enough to be felt, it is usually at least 2 years old. A slow-growing tumor can take as long as 9 years to develop to the size of a pea. During this time, in approximately half the cases, there has already been some micrometastasis—miscroscopic spreading of malignant cells—to other organs. Some cancerous cells are destroyed by the body's own immune system; others continue to grow slowly.

Because the incidence is high in industrialized countries, breast cancer has often been referred to as a disease of modern Western civilization. Whether this connection has to do with the high-fat, low-fiber diet of most Americans, their sedentary lifestyle, or high levels of obesity is uncertain. It has recently been found that avoiding adult weight gain may be a significant objective in preventing breast cancer (Huang et al., 1997). Other principal risk factors include a family history of breast cancer, a previous cancer (breast or other), being childless or bearing children later in life (starting after age 30), early menstruation, late menopause, and a history of fibrocystic disease. Alcohol consumption and smoking have also been implicated in the development of breast cancer. The connection for many of these risk factors may be levels of estrogen in the bloodstream. Estrogen promotes the growth of cells in a variety of sites. Alcohol can increase estrogen levels, as can fat cells. Estrogen-responsive cells, which include those in the breast and uterus, seem to be the most susceptible. In spite of the number of risk factors that have been identified, the majority of all new cases of breast cancer are diagnosed in women who have no known risk factors for the disease.

LESBIANS AND BREAST CANCER   In 1993, an epidemiologist with the National Cancer Institute reported that lesbians have a hypothetical risk of developing breast cancer that is 2 to 3 times higher than that of heterosexual women ("Lesbians' Cancer Risk," 1993). Cancer researcher Suzanne Haynes estimated that lesbians have a 1-in-3 lifetime chance of breast cancer based on known risk factors and information from a 1987 survey of lesbian health. Smoking, alcohol use, lack of childbearing, and poor access to health care are all factors that contribute to breast cancer risk; these are all apparently more common among lesbians (due in part to psychological and social pressures resulting from discrimination) than among heterosexual women.

DETECTION   The American Cancer Society recommends the following program for early detection of breast cancer:

1. Monthly breast self-examination (BSE) for all women over age 20 (see the Resource Center).
2. A clinical breast exam by a physician every 3 years.
3. **Mammograms** (low-dose X-ray screening) every year for most women over age 40. (Individual risk factors should be considered in determining the frequency of mammograms; the value of mammograms for women in their forties is still an area of debate.)

No one denies that mammograms, which can detect a lump only one-eighth of an inch in diameter, can find tumors sooner than manual exams. Depending on how rapidly a tumor grows, mammography can detect a tumor 2 years before a manual exam. The accuracy of a mammogram depends, to some extent, on when it is done. Mammograms are twice as likely to miss cancer in women if performed during the two weeks before their period begins (Sepah, 1998). Women 50 and older who have annual mammograms have a mortality rate 30% lower than women of the same age who do not. In the past few years, however, researchers have observed that early detection doesn't benefit younger women as much as it does women over the age of 50 (Begley, 1997). According to the National Cancer Institute, mammograms miss as many as 25% of invasive cancers in women age 40–49, compared with 10% in older women. In addition, some tumors detected early are not necessarily curable. Several factors should be considered before electing to have a mammogram, including risks, limitations, and costs. Regardless of the decision a woman makes, the significance of breast self-exam should not be underestimated.

It is important to recognize that most breast lumps—75–80%—are *not* cancerous. Many disappear on their own. Of lumps that are surgically removed for diagnostic purposes (biopsied), 80% prove to be benign. Most are related to **fibrocystic disease** (a common and generally harmless breast condition, not really a disease at all), or they are fibroadenomas (round, movable growths, also harmless, that occur in young women).

TREATMENT   Surgical removal of the breast is called **mastectomy.** The leading treatments for breast cancer are modified radical mastectomy and simple (or total) mastectomy. In modified radical mastectomy, the entire breast is removed, along with the lining of the underlying chest muscles and some or all of the nearby lymph nodes. Less drastic is simple mastectomy, which involves the removal of only the breast and a few lymph nodes if necessary. Another approach, increasingly popular, is known as **lumpectomy.** It involves removal of only the tumor and lymph nodes, thus sparing the breast and underlying muscle. Lumpectomy is generally followed by radiation treatments to halt the further spread of cancerous cells.

About 65%, or 117,000, of the 180,000 breast cancers diagnosed among American women each year are classified as early stage (1 and 2). Of these, three-quarters are eligible for breast-conserving therapy (lumpectomy) (Altman, 1998). National guidelines published in 1992 state that doctors should not use age, prognosis, or tumor type as criteria in choosing mastectomy over breast conservation therapy. Nevertheless, in a recent large-scale study of 18,000 women treated for early stage breast cancer in 1994, scientists found that more than half of those eligible for a lumpectomy underwent mastectomy instead (Altman, 1998). The most important message from this study is that if you are told you need a mastectomy, be sure to ask why.

Other treatments for cancer are radiation and chemotherapy (treatment with powerful drugs or hormones). When combined with conventional chemotherapy, radiation has recently been found to dramatically reduce the risk of death among young women who have undergone a mastectomy ("Breast Cancer Studies," 1997).

Some who have considered surgically removing a healthy breast to avoid future breast cancer can now contemplate taking a daily pill to prevent the disease. One such drug, tamoxifen, works by keeping estrogen from stimulating the cancer cells. A large-scale, 4-year study found women at high risk for breast cancer reduced their chances of getting the disease 45% by taking tamoxifen (Mishra, 1998). The drug also brings with it increased risk of uterine cancer and blood clot of the lungs. Despite the difficult choices associated with its use, tamoxifen marks a significant step in the fight against breast cancer.

A woman who undergoes a mastectomy is confronted with the loss of one or several visible parts of her body. First, she has lost her breast. Second (in the case of radical surgery), the removal of chest muscles and auxiliary lymph tissues not only leaves visible scars but also may restrict the movement and strength of her arm. Psychologically, the loss of her breast may symbolize for her the loss of sexuality; she may feel scarred and be fearful of rejection, because breasts in American culture are such primary sexual symbols (Kaplan, 1992). She also may experience a definite decrease in her sexual excitability. Because the breasts play an important role in sexual arousal and foreplay for many woman, their loss may prevent some women from becoming fully aroused sexually.

Much of the emotional adjustment after a mastectomy depends on how the woman's partner reacts. She is often fearful that her partner will reject her; the two may find themselves unable to discuss their sexuality. Some men are initially shocked and feel repulsion and confusion. Other men may be fearful of resuming intercourse lest they hurt their partners. If the relationship prior to the mastectomy was good and the couple was sexually happy, the postmastectomy adjustment will be less difficult. It has recently been found that regular aerobic exercise can alleviate anxiety and depression and facilitate recovery in breast cancer survivors ("Breast Cancer Survivors," 1997).

BREAST RECONSTRUCTION   Because most breast cancer is treated by surgical removal of the breast, the subject of breast reconstruction—literally,

Surviving cancer can deepen one's appreciation of life. Notice the tattoo along this woman's mastectomy scar.

building a new breast—is one of paramount interest to many women (and those who care about them).

In 1978, the total number of American women who had undergone breast reconstruction was 15,000. Today, due to sophisticated plastic surgery and the fact that most insurance companies are willing to provide coverage for it, breast reconstruction is undertaken by more than 100,000 women annually. An estimated 2 million American women have had silicone implants.

Women who wanted to have their breasts restored were once thought of by the medical community and society at large as vain or neurotically insecure, but current thinking is becoming more compassionate and humane. Although many women do not feel the need to restore a missing breast or at least do not feel it strongly enough to go through additional surgery, many others welcome the opportunity to restore their feelings of physical integrity and balance. For these women, reconstruction is an important step in recovering from breast cancer.

Depending on a woman's age, general health, type of tumor, and individual preference, breast reconstruction may be performed at the same time as mastectomy or several months (or longer) afterward. The reconstructive surgery itself varies according to the extent of the mastectomy and how much muscle, skin, and underlying tissue remain with which to work. For women who have undergone modified radical or total mastectomy, the operation involves inserting a breast-shaped implant under the remaining chest muscle. In cases of radical mastectomy, extra muscle and skin must be taken from another part of the body to cover the implant. This may be done by rotating a flap of the latissimus dorsi muscle and a covering piece of skin from the back to the chest. Or it may involve using skin and fatty tissue from the abdominal area, a procedure known as a "transflap."

The implants are usually pouches filled with saline solution or silicone gel; polyurethane foam forms are also used. Although the safety of silicone implants has been challenged and the manufacturer (Dow Corning) has agreed to a 3.2-billion-dollar settlement, they are still used in some cases. During reconstructive surgery or in a subsequent operation, the surgeon may also attach a nipple fashioned out of skin from the labia, inner thigh, inside of the mouth, or other tissue. If there are no cancerous cells in it, the woman's own nipple sometimes can be saved ("banked") by temporarily attaching it to another part of the body, such as the inner thigh, and moving it to the new breast after reconstruction. Common problems involve scarring, impaired arm movement, and swelling of the upper arm. Physical therapy can help restore mobility in the arm and upper body. Implants occasionally "migrate" or leak, especially with age. One study showed 63.6% of breast implants that had been in place for between 1 and 25 years had ruptured or were leaking (Brown, Silverman, & Berg, 1997). Pain or swelling in conjunction with silicone implants should be reported to the physician at once. Additional surgeries may be required to make adjustments and repairs.

Deciding about breast reconstruction involves many issues. It is not a decision contemplated lightly by women who have already undergone the pain and trauma of cancer and surgery. But it provides a significant option to many by filling an important need.

Cervical Cancer and Cervical Dysplasia   **Cervical dysplasia,** also called **cervical intraepithelial neoplasia (CIN),** is a condition of the cervical epithelium (covering membrane) that *may* lead to cancer if it is not treated. It is more common than cancer of the breast or uterus. Because cervical dysplasia is confined to the cervix, it can be treated easily. Approximately 15% of sexually active teenage girls show evidence of CIN (Biro, Rosenthal, Wildley, & Hillard, 1991).

The more advanced and dangerous malignancy is invasive cancer of the cervix (ICC). More than 80% of the tumors that appear on the cervix stem from infection by the sexually transmitted human papillomavirus. Additional risk factors include multiple sex partners and being a daughter of a mother who was given diethylstibestrol (DES) during pregnancy, sexual intercourse before age 18, cigarette smoking, and low socioeconomic status. When detected in its early stages, the disease is both preventable and curable ("Cervical Cancer," 1997). Women between the ages of 35 and 60 account for 60% of all cases.

DETECTION: THE PAP TEST   The most reliable means of making an early detection of cervical cancer is the **Pap test** (or Pap smear). This is a simple procedure that can not only detect cancer but also reveal changes in cells that make them precancerous. A Pap test can warn against cancer even before it begins.

The Pap test is usually done during a pelvic exam and takes about a minute or so. Cell samples are gently and usually painlessly scraped from the cervix and examined under a microscope. If any are suspicious, the physician will make further exams. Women should have a Pap test yearly unless their physician recommends differently. Unfortunately, the test is not as effective in detecting cancer in the body of the uterus, which occurs in women most frequently during or after menopause.

TREATMENT   Cervical dysplasia is very responsive to treatment in its early stages. With an irregular Pap smear, a **biopsy**—surgical removal of tissue for diagnosis—may be performed. Some abnormalities clear up on their own, so the physician may wait several months and do a follow-up smear. There may be some risk in delaying treatment, however. If the cervix shows visible signs of abnormality, a biopsy should be performed at once. Cervical biopsies are done with the aid of a colposcope, an instrument that contains a magnifying lens. Sometimes conization, the removal of a cone of tissue from the center of the cervix, is performed. This procedure is time-consuming and requires hospitalization. Depending on the extent and severity of the dysplasia and whether it has progressed to cancer, other treatment options range from electric cauterization (or cryosurgery) to laser surgery, radiotherapy, or hysterectomy.

Ovarian Cancer   Cancers of the ovaries are relatively rare. They make up only about 4% of all female cancers, yet they are among the most deadly. New evidence links pregnancy, breast-feeding, or taking oral contraceptives with a lower risk of ovarian cancer, perhaps because each gives the woman a rest from ovulation and eases wear and tear on the ovaries ("Ovulation Cycles," 1997). Ovarian cancer is hard to diagnose because there are no symptoms in the early stages; it is not usually detectable by a Pap smear. Diagnosis is done by pelvic examination and needle aspiration (removal of fluid) or biopsy. Treatment involves surgical removal of the tumor and ovary, often followed by radiation or chemotherapy. Follow-up care is especially important. New data suggest that acetaminophen significantly reduces the risk of ovarian cancer (Cramer, Harlow, Titus-Ernstoff, Bohlke, Welch, & Greenberg, 1998).

Uterine Cancer   More than 99% of cancers of the uterus involve the endometrium, the lining of the uterus. Certain women appear more at risk of developing endometrial cancer than others. White women contract endometrial cancer at almost twice the rate of African American women. Other risk factors include extreme obesity, childlessness, late menopause, diabetes, hypertension, certain ovarian disorders, breast and ovarian cancer, radiation exposure, menstrual irregularity, and inherited characteristics. Estrogen is associated with endometrial cancer. The safety of hormone replacement therapy continues to be controversial; HRT may increase the risk of endometrial cancer at least 4 to 7 times, although the administration of progestin with the estrogen appears to reduce the risk substantially (Greenwood, 1992).

Hysterectomy   The surgical removal of the uterus is known as a **hysterectomy.** A simple hysterectomy removes the uterus and a portion of the vagina, and a radical hysterectomy involves the additional removal of ovaries, fallopian tubes, cervix, and adjacent tissues. Certain conditions make a hysterectomy necessary: (1) when a cancerous or precancerous growth cannot be treated otherwise; (2) when noncancerous growths on the uterus become so large that they interfere with other organs (such as when they hinder bladder or bowel functions) or cause pain or pressure; (3) when bleeding is so heavy that it cannot be controlled or when it leads to anemia; (4) when severe infection cannot be controlled in any other way. If a woman's physician recommends a hysterectomy, she should have the opinion confirmed by a second physician.

A hysterectomy is performed by removing the uterus surgically through the vagina or through an abdominal incision. At the same time, there may be an **oophorectomy,** removal of one or both ovaries, because of endometriosis, cysts, or tumors. If both ovaries are removed from a premenopausal woman, she may begin hormone therapy to control the symptoms caused by the lack of estrogen. But because estrogen therapy may be linked to increased breast cancer risk, such therapy should be undertaken with caution.

For many couples, a hysterectomy may cause a major crisis. For others, it brings well-founded fears. The absence of the cervix and uterus deprives a woman of certain sensations that may have been important for both arousal and orgasm. Removal of the ovaries can result in lowered libido because testosterone (the sex-drive hormone) is mainly produced there. Furthermore, the absence of ovarian estrogen can cause menopausal symptoms such as vaginal dryness and thinning of the vaginal walls. Therapy and self-help groups for posthysterectomy patients can be very useful for women who wish to increase sexual desire and pleasure. **Androgen replacement therapy**—testosterone administered orally, by injection, or by a slow-release pellet placed under the skin—may be helpful to some women.

Most women recover well from hysterectomy, although fatigue and depression are not unusual during the first few weeks. It's important for a woman who has had a hysterectomy to us common sense, follow her doctor's instructions, and not try to become too active too soon. It's also important for her to have the support and attention of friends and family members.

A recently approved alternative to a hysterectomy, called ThermaChoice, involves using a heated balloon that in just 8 minutes destroys the cause of excessive menstrual bleeding that is not the result of fibroids or uterine cancer ("An Alternative," 1997).

Men and Cancer

Generally speaking, men are less likely than women to get regular checkups and to seek help at the onset of symptoms. This tendency can have unfortunate consequences where reproductive cancers are concerned, because early detection can often mean the difference between life and death. Prostate and testicular cancer both appear to be increasing dramatically, so it is of paramount importance that men pay attention to what goes on in their genital and urinary organs. Just as women should regularly examine their breasts, men should regularly examine their testicles. Men over 40 should have an annual rectal examination of the prostate gland.

HEADLINES LINKING VASECTOMY to prostate cancer or birth control pills to breast cancer send waves of fear through the population. Each time word of a new medical risk reaches us, we are thrown into confusion and possibly even despair. What do we do if we've just had a type of surgery that supposedly had no negative side effects, and now we read that it does? Or if we've been taking a medication that is suddenly purported to cause a life-threatening disease? Health writer Jane Brody advises: Don't panic (Brody, 1993).

In assessing newly discovered medical "risks," we need to proceed calmly and carefully. Brody offers five questions for consideration:

1. *What is the source of the report?* The most reliable studies appear in professional journals and on Web sites that are subject to peer review, such as *The New England Journal of Medicine, Journal of the American Medical Association, Lancet,* and *Med Pulse.* Unpublished reports from conferences and studies done at private, non-government-funded institutions are probably not as reliable. Also potentially less reliable are the many Web sites that do not publish the credentials of an author or source of publication or that are not supported by a governmental or reputable agency.

2. *Are there other studies on the same subject?* Even in scientific studies, results can occur by chance alone. It is therefore important that findings be replicated by independent researchers before they are used as the basis for making radical changes.

3. *What is the degree of risk compared with the benefits?* Even when doubled or tripled, a risk that was initially small does not become great (a 2% risk increases to a 4–6% risk, for example). A 50% risk that increases by half (to 75%), however, is much more alarming. Also, a procedure or medication may increase some risks but greatly reduce others, so it is important not to generalize but to consider risks versus benefits case by case.

4. *Are there comparable but safer alternatives?* It may take some investigation, but there may be alternatives or variations to a procedure that are less risky. Taking progestin along with estrogen, for example, greatly reduces the risk of uterine cancer for women choosing HRT.

5. *Is the research biologically explainable or supported by animal studies?* If the study results are only theoretical and not based on actual biological findings, Brody suggests that researchers should be sent "scurrying to the laboratory." A risk that may be serious should be scientifically demonstrated as soon as possible.

Prostate Cancer   Prostate cancer is the most common form of cancer among men; after lung and colon cancer, it is the cause of most cancer deaths. Prostate cancer strikes 1 out of every 9 men; 80% of cases are diagnosed in men over age 65. According to the American Cancer Society, approximately 184,500 new cases are diagnosed in this country each year, and almost 42,000 men die of the disease annually. As a man gets older, his chances of developing prostate cancer increase. One study reports a genetic link between brothers (Narod, 1995). Prostate cancer is about 30% more common in African American men than in White men, and African Americans are 2–3 times more likely to die as a result of it. Although scientists cannot explain the racial disparity, theories range from genetics to lack of health care access and distrust of the mostly White medical establishment ("Prostate Cancer Kills Blacks," 1998). A high intake of dietary fat has also been implicated.

DETECTION   Various signs may point to prostate cancer, a slow-growing disease. Although these signs are more likely to indicate prostatic enlargement or benign tumors than cancer, they should never be ignored. They include:

- Weak or interrupted flow of urine
- Inability to urinate or difficulty in beginning to urinate

- Frequent need to urinate, especially at night; bed-wetting
- Urine flow that is not easily stopped
- Painful or burning urination
- Continuing pain in lower back, pelvis, or upper thighs

The first step in diagnosing prostate cancer is to have a physician conduct a digital exam. By inserting a finger into the rectum, the physician can usually feel an irregular or unusually firm area on the prostate that may indicate a tumor. If the physician discovers a suspicious area, he or she will then make a battery of tests including X rays, urine and blood analyses, and biopsy.

A blood test, called the **prostate-specific antigen (PSA) test,** can be used to help diagnose prostate cancer with 90% accuracy. Although controversial, the test is most useful when repeated over time to chart the rate of change. The American Cancer Society recommends offering this test to men over 50 as long as they are first told about the uncertainties of the treatment for prostate cancer and that the PSA results can be misleading. Ultrasound is often used as a follow-up to the PSA test to detect lumps too small to be felt. A needle biopsy of suspicious lumps can be performed to determine if the cells are benign or malignant. A large new study concludes that routine use of the PSA test could prevent 27,000 (or 69%) of the 39,000 prostate cancer deaths in the United States each year (Haney, 1998). The researchers predicted that if men started testing at age 50, when their risk of advanced prostate cancer is still small, testing could practically eliminate its deadly spreading stages.

TREATMENT   If detected early, prostate cancer has a high cure rate. Depending on the stage of the cancer, treatment may include surgery, hormone treatment, radiation therapy, or chemotherapy. If the cancer has not spread beyond the prostate gland, all or part of the gland is removed by surgery. Radical surgery has a high cure rate, but it often results in incontinence and erectile dysfunction. A less invasive and equally effective treatment involves radiation (via radioactive seeds) surgically implanted in the prostate. Although the 5-year survival rate for this procedure is 87%, it can also cause erectile dysfunction, rectal problems, or damage to the urinary tract.

Some men choose to have penile implants following prostate surgery so that intercourse will again be possible. In any event, sensitive sex counseling should be an integral part of treatment. Some men who retain the ability to become erect experience retrograde ejaculation and are infertile because semen does not pass out of the urethra.

Testicular Cancer   Although cancer of the testes accounts for only 1% of cancer in men, it is the most common form found in men between the ages of 29 and 35. For reasons that are still unclear, the highest incidence is found in White males. Because one factor that puts a man at risk is undescended testicles, this condition should be corrected in early childhood. Malignancies that start in the testes can spread to the lymph nodes or lungs and then are reported at those sites. If testicular cancer is caught early, it is curable; if it is found later, it is often deadly. Except for the rarest form of testicular cancer, the cure rate is about 95%.

DETECTION The first sign of testicular cancer is usually a painless lump or slight enlargement and a change in the consistency of the testicle; the right testicle is more often involved than the left. Although the tumors that grow on the testes are generally painless, there is often a dull ache in the lower abdomen and groin, accompanied by a sensation of dragging and heaviness. If the tumor is growing rapidly, there may be severe pain in the testicles.

Because of the lack of symptoms and pain in the early stage, men often do not go to a doctor for several months after discovering a slightly enlarged testicle. This delay accounts for the fact that in 88% of patients with testicular cancer, it has already metastasized by the time it is diagnosed.

A self-examination is the best line of defense against metastasis of testicular cancer. It only takes a couple of minutes and should be performed once a month (see the Resource Center). Suspicious findings should be reported to a physician at once.

TREATMENT After the affected testicle is removed, an artificial one may be inserted in the scrotal sac. Radiation treatment or chemotherapy may follow. Although the cure rate for all testicular cancer is over 95% (provided the disease has not widely metastasized), the aftermath of treatment is problematic for some men. Sperm-banking and support groups may be helpful resources for some men and their partners.

OTHER SEXUAL HEALTH ISSUES

In this section we discuss two disorders of the female reproductive system, toxic shock syndrome and endometriosis, as well as some other sexual health issues. Sexually transmitted diseases and related problems are discussed in Chapter 15.

Toxic Shock Syndrome

Toxic shock syndrome (TSS) is caused by the *Staphylococcus aureus* bacterium, a common agent of infection. This organism is normally present in the body and usually does not pose a threat. Tampons, especially the superabsorbent type, or other devices that block the vagina or cervix during menstruation apparently lead to the creation of an ideal culture medium for the overgrowth of staph bacteria.

The risk of developing TSS is quite low; about 3 out of 100,000 women develop it. The FDA advises all women who use tampons to reduce the already low risk by using sanitary napkins during part of their menstrual periods (at night, for example). Tampons should be changed frequently. It is also advisable not to leave a diaphragm or cervical cap in place for more than 24 hours.

TSS can be treated effectively with antibiotics if it is detected. The warning signs are fever (101°F or higher), diarrhea, vomiting, muscle aches, and/or a sunburnlike rash. Early detection is critical; otherwise, TSS can do significant damage.

IN MORE THAN 20 AFRICAN COUNTRIES, some parts of Asia, and immigrant communities elsewhere, female infants, girls, or young women may undergo **clitoridectomy,** or **female circumcision:** having their clitoris slit or cut out entirely and all or part of their labia sliced off. The sides of their vulvas or their vaginal openings may be stitched together—a process called **infibulation**—leaving only a tiny opening for the passage of urine and menstrual blood. These surgeries are generally performed with a knife, razor, or even a tin can lid or piece of broken glass, without anesthesia; conditions are often unsanitary. The effects of these devastatingly painful operations include bleeding, infections, infertility, scarring, the inability to enjoy sex, and, not uncommonly, death. Upon marriage, a young woman may undergo considerable pain and bleeding as the entry to the vagina is reopened by tearing her flesh. In childbirth, the old wounds must be reopened surgically, or tearing will result. In spite of these dreadful consequences, as many as

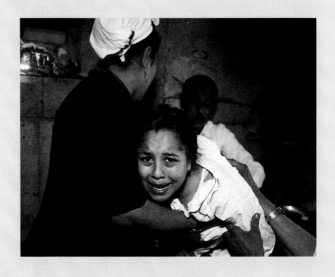

Endometriosis

Sometimes called the "career woman's disease," **endometriosis** may affect as many as 10 million American women. Its nickname derives from its apparent prevalence among women who have delayed childbearing. It occurs in roughly 10–15% of premenopausal women. Endometriosis involves the growth of endometrial tissue (uterine lining) outward into the organs surrounding the uterus. It is a major cause of infertility.

Symptoms of endometriosis include pain (usually pelvic pain, which can be very intense) and abnormal menstrual bleeding. It is usually diagnosed by palpation (feeling) and laparoscopic examination.

Treatment is a complex issue. The woman's age, her childbearing plans, and the extent of the disease are all significant factors. Hormone therapies designed to interfere with ovulation can help. Sometimes birth control pills are prescribed. A synthetic male hormone, danazol, stops ovulation and thus causes shrinkage of endometrial tissues. It does have masculinizing side effects, however, and it is very expensive. A synthetic hormone, nafarelin, similar to gonadotropin-releasing hormone (GRH), also shows promise. Pregnancy can help if it is feasible for a woman to arrange her childbearing plans accordingly. Surgery is also a possibility, and it may be the only choice if the endometriosis is severe.

Prompt treatment is crucial if endometriosis is suspected. It is also important for the woman who has endometriosis to inform herself about the disease and thoroughly investigate the options, because treatment for this condition is very much an individual matter.

70–100 million female infants, girls, and women alive today are estimated to have undergone this operation (Perlez, 1990; Simons, 1993; A. Walker, 1992). It has recently been reported that 97% of nearly 15,000 Egyptian women polled had been circumcised. At the end of 1997, however, the Egyptian courts finally banned the practice ("Ban on Female Circumcision," 1997).

This ancient custom, practiced mainly by Muslims, but also by Christians and animists, is difficult for outsiders to understand. Why would a loving mother allow this to be done to her defenseless daughter, and even hold her down during the procedure? As with many other practices (including male circumcision in our own culture), the answer is "tradition." Although the surgery undoubtedly began as a way of controlling women's sexuality (it virtually eliminates the possibility of sexual pleasure), many Muslims believe (erroneously) that it is required by the Koran, the Islamic holy book (Simons, 1993). Clitoridectomy was practiced by physicians in the nineteenth century in both England and the United States, mainly as a cure for masturbation, which was thought to awaken women's insatiable sexual appetites (Barker-Benfield, 1976). It continued in this country until at least 1937. "Female castration" (oophorectomy) and hysterectomy were practiced as cures for a variety of psychological disorders, especially between 1880 and 1900 but continuing well into this century.

In Africa, female circumcision is opposed by many national leaders and is illegal in a number of countries. African medical workers stress the health dangers and feel that education has helped curb the practice to some degree. But there is still strong social pressure for it, and the operations are often carried out in secret. Raakiya Omaar, the Somali head of Africa Watch, a human rights organization, told an interviewer (Perlez, 1990):

> The older women still feel young girls are never going to get married unless they are circumcised. . . . It's such a long, embedded social tradition that if Western people say, "this is barbaric," it backfires. Emphasis must be put on the medical aspects, not the sexual issues.

Lesbian Health Issues

In addition to many of the medical concerns shared by all women, lesbians face additional difficulties. Several studies have found that lesbians encounter prejudice and discrimination when seeking health care (Robertson, 1992; Stevens, 1992). First, it may be assumed that they are heterosexual, leading to the inclusion of inappropriate questions, comments, or procedures and the exclusion of appropriate measures. Second, if they do disclose their orientation, they are likely to be treated with hostility. As a result of these experiences, lesbians are less likely than heterosexuals to seek health care. Thus, they may put themselves at higher risk for diseases that could be detected early on. Older lesbians are especially vulnerable because they are not generally as willing to disclose their sexual orientation; they often feel "invisible." Surveys of lesbians regarding health-care choices have found preferences for female practitioners, holistic approaches, preventive care and education, and woman-managed clinics (Lucas, 1992; Trippet & Bain, 1992).

Prostatitis

Many of men's sexual health problems are related to sexually transmitted diseases. One condition affecting men that is not sexually transmitted is **prostatitis,** the inflammation of the prostate gland. It affects as many as 30–40% of American men between 20 and 40 years of age. There are two types: infectious prostatitis and congestive prostatitis. Infectious prostatitis is generally caused by *E. coli* bacteria. Congestive prostatitis usually results from abstention from ejaculation or infrequent ejaculation. It is sometimes called the "priest's disease."

The prostate secretes most of the fluid portion of a man's ejaculate (semen). If a man does not ejaculate, this fluid begins to decompose, and the prostate becomes congested, causing congestive prostatitis. Congestive prostatitis can also be caused by dramatic changes in a man's sexual behavior patterns. The prostate develops its own production pattern based on the man's sexual activity; therefore, if a highly active man cuts back his sexual routine, his prostate will continue its high production and become congested with too much fluid over a period of time. Similarly, if the man goes from no orgasms a day to several, he may develop congestive prostatitis.

Symptoms of prostatitis include swelling in the genital area, a feeling of heat, and pain. Frequently, there is pain in the lower back. When there is infection, there may be a thin mucous discharge from the penis that may be visible in the morning before urination. Acute prostatitis often results in a loss of libido and painful ejaculations; chronic prostatitis is often associated with sexual dysfunctions.

Infectious prostatitis is treated with antibiotics. But treatment may be problematic, because antibiotics are unable to pass into the prostatic fluid, which acts as a reservoir for the infection. Congestive prostatitis may be treated with warm baths and prostatic massage, which is done by inserting a finger in the anus and gently massaging the prostate. If the prostatitis is especially painful, any form of sexual excitement should be avoided.

DES Daughters and Sons

Between 1941 and 1971, an estimated 6 million women used **diethylstilbestrol,** or **DES,** a synthetic estrogen, to prevent miscarriages, particularly if they had a previous history of miscarriage or bleeding during pregnancy or were diabetic. About 3 million women whose mothers took DES were born during these years. They range in age now from early adulthood to middle age. Some grown children of women who were given DES while pregnant have developed genital tract abnormalities, including cancer. DES sons and daughters need to be aware of their special health needs and to seek treatment accordingly.

▪ In this chapter we've explored issues of self-image and body image as they interact with our society's ideas about beauty and sexuality. We've considered the effects of alcohol and certain drugs on our sexuality. We've looked at aging, physical limitations and disabilities, and cancer and other health issues. Our intent is to give you information to assist you in personal health issues and to stimulate thinking about how society deals with certain aspects of sexual health. We encourage you to learn more about your own body and your own sexual functioning. If things don't seem to work right, if you don't feel well, or if you have questions, see your physician or other health-care practitioner. If you're not satisfied, get a second opinion. Read about health issues that apply to you and the people you're close to. Because we live in our bodies, we need to appreciate and respect them. By taking care of ourselves physically, we can maximize our pleasures in sexuality and in life.

SUMMARY

Living in Our Bodies: The Quest for Physical Perfection

- Our society is preoccupied with bodily perfection. As a result, *eating disorders* have become common, especially among young women. Eating disorders reduce a person's health and vigor; are carried out in secrecy; are accompanied by obsessions, depression, anxiety, and guilt; lead to self-absorption and emotional instability; and are characterized by a lack of control. Those with eating disorders may have a history of psychological or sexual abuse in childhood.

- *Anorexia nervosa* is characterized by an all-controlling desire for thinness. Those with anorexia, usually female teenagers, are convinced that their bodies are too large, no matter how thin they actually are. Sexual dysfunction often accompanies anorexia. Those with anorexia diet (and often exercise) obsessively. Anorexia is potentially fatal.

- *Bulimia* is characterized by episodes of uncontrolled overeating (binge eating), counteracted by purging—vomiting, dieting, exercising excessively, or taking laxatives or diuretics.

- *Binge eating disorder* is similar to bulimia except that the purging does not occur.

Alcohol, Drugs, and Sexuality

- Drugs and alcohol are commonly perceived as enhancers of sexuality, although in reality this is rarely the case. These substances have the effect of *disinhibition,* activating behaviors that would otherwise be suppressed.

- Some people use alcohol to give themselves permission to be sexual. Some men may use alcohol to justify sexual violence. People under the influence of alcohol or drugs tend to place themselves in risky sexual situations, such as exposing themselves to sexually transmitted diseases.

Sexuality and Aging

- Although some physical functions may be slowed by aging, sexual interest, enjoyment, and satisfaction remain high for many older people. Women tend to be more concerned about the loss of attractiveness, whereas men tend to worry about their sexual capacity.

- In their forties, women's fertility begins to decline. Generally, between ages 45 and 55, *menopause,* the cessation of menstrual periods, occurs. Other physical changes occur, which may or may not present problems. The most common are hot flashes, changes in the vagina, and a gradual loss of bone mass. *Hormone replacement therapy (HRT)* is sometimes used to treat these symptoms. Women need to weigh the risks and benefits of HRT.

- Men need to understand that slower sexual responses are a normal part of aging and are not related to the ability to give or receive sexual pleasure. About half of men experience some degree of prostate enlargement after age 50. If it is severe, surgery can be performed.

Sexuality and Disability

- A wide range of disabilities and physical limitations can affect sexuality. People with these limitations need support and education so they may enjoy their full sexual potential. Society as a whole needs to be aware of the concerns of the disabled and to allow them the same sexual rights as others.

- Chronic illnesses, such as diabetes, cardiovascular disease, and arthritis, pose special problems for a sexual life. People with these diseases (and their partners) can learn what to expect of themselves sexually and how to best cope with their particular conditions.

Sexuality and Cancer

- Cancer (in its many forms) occurs when cells begin to grow aberrantly. Most cancers form tumors. *Benign tumors* grow slowly and remain localized. *Malignant tumors* can spread throughout the body. When malignant cells are released into the blood or lymph system, they begin to grow away from the original tumor; this process is called *metastasis.*

- Breast cancer is the most common cancer among women. Although the survival rate is improving, those who survive it may still suffer psychologically. Breast self-examination and *mammograms* (low-dose X-ray screenings) are the principal methods of detection. Surgical removal of the breast is called *mastectomy;* surgery that removes only the tumor and surrounding lymph nodes is called *lumpectomy.* Radiation and chemotherapy are also used to fight breast cancer. The decision to undertake breast reconstruction involves many issues.

▪ *Cervical dysplasia,* or *cervical intraepithelial neoplasia (CIN),* the appearance of certain abnormal cells on the cervix, can be diagnosed by a *Pap test.* It may then be treated by *biopsy,* cauterization, cryosurgery, or other surgery. If untreated, it may lead to cervical cancer.

▪ The most common gynecological cancer that poses a serious threat is uterine cancer; more than 99% of these cancers affect the endometrium, the uterine lining. Uterine cancer is treated with surgery (hysterectomy), radiation, or both.

▪ *Hysterectomy* is the surgical removal of the uterus. Conditions requiring hysterectomy are (1) when cancerous or precancerous growth cannot be treated otherwise, (2) when noncancerous growths interfere with other organs, (3) when heavy bleeding cannot be otherwise controlled, and (4) when severe infection cannot be otherwise controlled. Other problems may sometimes require hysterectomy. The removal of the ovaries *(oophorectomy)* will precipitate menopausal symptoms because the estrogen supply stops.

▪ Prostate cancer is the most common form of cancer among men. If detected early, it has a high cure rate. One possible test is the *prostate-specific antigen (PSA) test.* Surgery, radiation, hormone therapy, and chemotherapy are possible treatments. If the entire prostate is removed, sterility results, and erectile difficulties may occur.

▪ Testicular cancer primarily affects young men between the ages of 29 and 35. If caught early, it is curable; if not, it may be deadly. Self-examination is the key to detection; even slight symptoms should be reported at once.

Other Sexual Health Issues

▪ *Toxic shock syndrome (TSS)* is a potentially fatal disease caused by *Staphylococcus aureus* bacteria. Using superabsorbent tampons or a diaphragm or

cervical cap for more than 24 hours can increase a woman's risk of getting TSS. The disease is easily cured with antibiotics if caught early.

▪ In some parts of the world, female infants, girls, or young women may undergo *clitoridectomy,* or *female circumcision*—the surgical removal of the clitoris and all or part of the labia. *Infibulation* refers to the stitching together of the sides of the vulva or vaginal opening.

▪ *Endometriosis* is the growth of endometrial tissue outside the uterus. It is a major cause of infertility. Symptoms include intense pelvic pain and abnormal menstrual bleeding. Treatment depends on a number of factors. Various hormone treatments and types of surgery are employed.

▪ Lesbians tend to have poorer health care than heterosexual women, partly because they face hostility from health-care practitioners. Fear of discrimination may keep them from getting early diagnosis of serious diseases, such as breast cancer.

▪ *Prostatitis* is the inflammation of the prostate gland. Congestive prostatitis is usually the result of abstention from ejaculation or infrequent ejaculation. Infectious prostatitis is difficult to treat, although antibiotics are prescribed for it; chronic prostatitis is painful and can lead to sexual dysfunctions.

▪ *DES (diethylstilbestrol)* is a synthetic estrogen that was widely prescribed between 1941 and 1971 to prevent miscarriages. Women who took DES, and their children, are subject to genital tract abnormalities, including cancer. DES sons and daughters need to be aware of their special health risks and seek treatment accordingly.

SUGGESTED READING

Journals with articles relevant to sexual health include: *JAMA: Journal of the American Medical Association, The New England Journal of Medicine, Women and Health,* and the British journal *Lancet.*

Greenwood, Sadja. (1992). *Menopause, Naturally: Preparing for the Second Half of Life.* Volcano, CA: Volcano Press. A compassionate and comprehensive guide through menopause by a female physician.

Hepburn, Cuca, & Gutierrez, Bonnie. (1988). *Alive and Well: A Lesbian Health Guide.* Freedom, CA: Crossing

Press. A comprehensive guide addressing the health needs of lesbians, who are often excluded from sensitive medical care.

Love, Susan. (1995). *Dr. Susan Love's Breast Book* (2nd ed.). Reading, MA: Addison-Wesley. Breast care and information on breast cancer from a leading authority.

Love, Susan. (1997). *Dr. Susan Love's Hormone Book.* New York: Random House. A book about menopause and hormone replacement therapy by a leading authority in the field.

Peterson, K. Jean. (1996). *Health Care for Lesbians and Gay Men.* New York: Haworth Press. Highlights the special needs of gay and lesbian individuals and discusses how homophobia and heterosexism affect them.

Schover, Leslie. (1997). *Sexuality and Fertility After Cancer.* New York: Wiley. Examines the broad range of issues that affect those with cancer and ways to address them.

West, James W., & Ford, Betty. (1997). *The Betty Ford Center Book of Answers: Help for Those Struggling with Substance Abuse and for the People Who Love Them.* New York: Pocket Books. Practical and insightful advice for people dealing with alcohol and drug abuse.

White, Evelyn C. (Ed.). (1990). *The Black Women's Health Book: Speaking for Ourselves.* Seattle, WA: Seal Press. Addresses issues typically faced by African American women in seeking competent and compassionate health care.

14

Sexual Enhancement and Therapy

*T*HE QUALITY OF OUR SEXUALITY is intimately connected to the quality of our lives and relationships. Because our sexuality is an integral part of ourselves, it reflects our excitement and boredom, intimacy and distance, emotional well-being and distress, health and illness. As a consequence, our sexual desires and activities ebb and flow. Sometimes they are highly erotic; at other times, they may be boring. Furthermore, many of us who are sexually active may sometimes experience sexual difficulties or problems. A review of 23 studies on sexual problems found that nearly half the men and women reported occasional or frequent lack of desire, problems in arousal or orgasm, and painful intercourse (Spector & Carey, 1990). The widespread variability in our sexual functioning suggests how "normal" at least occasional sexual difficulties are. Bernie Zilbergeld (1992) writes:

> Sex problems are normal and typical. I know, I know, all of your buddies are functioning perfectly and never have a problem. If you really believe that, I have a nice piece of oceanfront property in Kansas I'd like to talk to you about.

In this chapter, we examine some ways to enhance your sexuality to bring you greater pleasure and intimacy. Then we look at several common sexual problems and their causes. Finally, we see how those problems are treated.

SEXUAL ENHANCEMENT

Improving the quality of one's sexual relationship is referred to as **sexual enhancement.** There are several sexual-enhancement programs for people who function well sexually but who nevertheless feel they can improve the quality of their sexual interactions and relationships. The programs generally aim at providing accurate information about sexuality, developing communication skills, fostering positive attitudes, and increasing self-awareness (Cooper, 1985). In some ways, your study of human sexuality examines many of the same cognitive, attitudinal, and communication themes explored in sexual-enrichment programs.

Zilbergeld (1992) suggests that there are six requirements for what he calls "great sex." They form the basis of many sexual-enhancement programs:

1. Accurate information about sexuality, especially your own and your partner's

2. An orientation toward sex based on pleasure, such as arousal, fun, love, and lust, rather than performance and orgasm

3. Being involved in a relationship that allows each person's sexuality to flourish

4. An ability to communicate verbally and nonverbally about sex, feelings, and relationships

5. Being equally assertive and sensitive about your own sexual needs and those of your partner

6. Accepting, understanding, and appreciating differences between partners

Self-Awareness

Being aware of your own sexual needs is often critical to enhancing your sexuality. Because of gender-role stereotypes and negative learning about sexuality, we often lose sight of our own sexual needs.

What Is Good Sex?   Sexual stereotypes present us with images of how we are supposed to behave sexually. Images of the "sexually in charge" man and the "sexual, but not too sexual" woman may interfere with our ability to express our own individual sexual feelings, needs, and desires. We follow the scripts and stereotypes we have been socialized to accept, rather than our own unique responses. Following these cultural images may impede our ability to have what therapist Carol Ellison calls "good sex." In an essay about intimacy-based sex therapy, Ellison (1985) writes that you will know you are having good sex if you feel good about yourself, your partner, your relationship, and what you're doing. It's good sex if, after a while, you still feel good about yourself, your partner, your relationship, and what you did. Good sex does not necessarily include orgasm or intercourse. It can be kissing, holding, masturbating, oral sex, anal sex, and so on. It can be heterosexual, gay, lesbian, or bisexual.

Zilbergeld (1992) suggests that to fully enjoy our sexuality, we need to explore our "conditions for good sex." There is nothing unusual about requiring conditions for any activity. For a good night's sleep, for example, each of us has certain conditions. We may need absolute quiet, no light, a feather pillow, an open window. Others, however, can sleep during a loud dormitory party, curled up in the corner of a stuffy room. Of conditions for good sex, Zilbergeld writes:

> In a sexual situation, a condition is anything that makes you more relaxed, more comfortable, more confident, more excited, more open to your experience. Put differently, a condition is something that clears your nervous system of unnecessary clutter, leaving it open to receive and transmit sexual messages in ways that will result in a good time for you.

Discovering Your Conditions for Good Sex   Different individuals report different conditions for good sex. Some common conditions, according to Zilbergeld (1992), include:

▪ *Feeling intimate with your partner.* Intimacy is often important for both men and women, despite stereotypes of men wanting only sex. Partners who are feeling distant from each other may need to talk about their feelings before becoming sexual. Emotional distance can take the heart out of sex.

▪ *Feeling sexually capable.* Generally, feeling capable relates to an absence of anxieties about sexual performance. For men, these include anxiety about becoming erect or ejaculating too soon. For women, anxieties include worry about painful intercourse or lack of orgasm. For both men and women, they include worry about whether one is a good lover.

▪ *Feeling trust.* Both men and women may need to know they are emotionally safe with their partner. They need to feel confident that they will not be judged, ridiculed, or talked about.

Good sex involves the ability to communicate nonverbally—through laughter and good times—as well as verbally.

■ *Feeling aroused.* A person does not need to be sexual unless he or she is sexually aroused or excited. Simply because your partner wants to be sexual does not mean that you have to be.

■ *Feeling physically and mentally alert.* This condition requires a person not to feel particularly tired, ill, stressed, or preoccupied. It requires that one not be excessively under the influence of alcohol or drugs.

■ *Feeling positive about the environment and situation.* A person may need privacy, to be in a place where he or she feels protected from intrusion. Each needs to feel that the other is sexually interested and wants to be sexually involved.

Each individual has his or her own unique conditions for good sex. If you are or have been sexually active, to discover your conditions for good sex, think about the last few times you were sexual and were highly aroused. Compare those times to other times when you were much less aroused (Zilbergeld, 1992). Make a list of the factors that were different between the two. Consider the following areas: your feelings about your partner at the time (intimate, distant, indifferent, or angry, for example); how interested you were in being sexual; anxieties about sexual performance; the surroundings; preoccupation, worry, or stress about nonsexual matters; your health; whether you were using alcohol or other drugs.

Put the list away for a few days, and then see if there is anything you want to add or change. Reword the list so that each of the conditions is specific. For example, if you wrote "Felt pressured to have sex," rewrite as "Need to feel unpressured." When you rewrite these conditions, you can get a clearer sense of what your conditions for good sex are. Communicate your needs to your partner.

Homework Exercises   We are often unaware of our body and our erotic responses. Sexual-enhancement programs often specify exercises to undertake in private. Such "homework" exercises require individuals to make a time commitment to themselves or their partner. Typical assignments include the exercises below. If you feel comfortable with any of the assignments, you might want to try one or more. (For additional exercises for men, see Zilbergeld, 1992; for exercises for women, see Barbach, 1982.)

▪ *Mirror examination.* Use a full-length mirror to examine your nude body. Use a hand mirror to view your genitals. Look at all your features in an uncritical manner; view yourself with acceptance.

▪ *Body relaxation and exploration.* Take 30 minutes to an hour to fully relax. Begin with a leisurely shower or bath; then, remaining nude, find a comfortable place to touch and explore your body and genitals.

▪ *Masturbation.* In a relaxed situation, with body oils or lotions to enhance your sensations, explore ways of touching your body and genitals that bring you pleasure. Do this exercise for several sessions without having an orgasm; experience erotic pleasure without orgasm as its goal. If you are about to have an orgasm, decrease stimulation. After several sessions without having an orgasm, continue pleasuring yourself until you have an orgasm.

▪ *Erotic aids.* Devices designed to enhance erotic responsiveness, such as vibrators, dildos, oils, and lotions, are referred to as **erotic aids.** Erotic devices are also called **sex toys,** emphasizing their playfulness. A major study found that 2.9% of men and 3.3% of women bought sex toys during the previous year (Laumann et al., 1994). You may wish to try using a sex toy or shower massage as you masturbate, with your partner or by yourself. You may also want to view videos at home or read erotic poetry or stories to yourself or your partner. Many of these exercises can also be done with a partner; each takes turns erotically exploring the other.

Intensifying Erotic Pleasure

One of the most significant elements in enhancing one's physical experience of sex is intensifying arousal. Intensifying arousal centers sexual experience on erotic pleasure rather than on sexual performance. This can be done in many ways, some of which are described below.

Sexual Arousal   Sexual arousal refers to the physiological responses, fantasies, and desires associated with sexual anticipation and sexual activity. We

have different levels of arousal, and they are not necessarily associated with particular types of sexual activities. Sometimes we feel more sexually aroused when we kiss than when we have sexual intercourse or oral sex. Masturbation may sometimes be more exciting that oral sex or coitus.

The first element in increasing sexual arousal is having your conditions for good sex met. If you need privacy, find a place to be alone; if you need a romantic setting, go for a walk on the beach by moonlight, or listen to music with candlelight; if you want limits on your sexual activities, tell your partner; if you need a certain kind of physical stimulation, show or tell your partner what you like.

A second element in increasing arousal is focusing on the sensations you are experiencing. Once you begin an erotic activity, such as massaging or kissing, do not let yourself be distracted. When you're kissing, don't think about what you're going to do next or about an upcoming test. Instead, focus on the sensual experience of your lips and heart. Zilbergeld (1992) writes:

> Focusing on sensations means exactly that. You put your attention in your body where the action is. When you're kissing, keep your mind on your lips. This is *not* the same as thinking about your lips or the kiss; just put your attention in your lips. As you focus on your sensations, you may want to convey your pleasure to your partner. Let him or her know through your sounds and movements that you are excited.

Alternatives to Intercourse   Waiting, delays, and obstacles may intensify arousal. This is one of the pleasures of sexual abstinence that may get lost soon after one begins coitus. Lonnie Barbach (1982) suggests that sexually active people may intensify arousal by placing a ban on sexual intercourse for a period of time. If you are gay or lesbian, you may place a comparable ban on your preferred activity. During this time, instead explore other ways of being erotic or sexual. Barbach (1982), JoAnn Loulan (1984), and Zilbergeld (1992) suggest the following activities, among others:

License my roving hands, and let
    them go,
Behind, before, above, between,
    below.

—*John Donne (1572–1631)*

▪ Sit or lie down close to each other. Gaze into each other's eyes to establish an intimate connection. Gently caress each other's face and hair as you continue gazing. Tell each other what fantasies you have about the other.

▪ Bathe or shower with your partner, soaping his or her body slowly and sensually but not touching the genitals. At another time, you may want to include genital stimulation.

▪ Give and receive a sensual, erotic massage. Do not touch the genitals, but massage around them teasingly. Use body oils and lotions to increase tactile sensitivity. Later, you may want to include genital stimulation.

▪ Use your lips, tongue, and mouth to explore your partner's body, especially the neck, ears, nipples, inner thighs, palms, fingers, feet, and toes. Take your time.

▪ "Dirty dance" together, feeling the curves and textures of your partner's body; put your hands under your partner's clothes, and caress him or her. Kiss and caress each other as you slowly remove each other's clothing. Then hold each other close, kiss and massage each other, explore each other's body with your mouth, tongue, and lips.

SEXUAL DISORDERS AND DYSFUNCTIONS

Sexual disorders and dysfunctions refer to difficulties individuals experience in their sexual functioning. Heterosexuals, gay men, and lesbians experience similar kinds of sexual problems (Margolies, Becher, & Jackson-Brewer, 1988). Determining the origins of sexual problems, however, is often complex and difficult (Davis-Joseph, Tiefer, & Melman, 1995).

Sexual dysfunctions are generally defined as impaired physiological responses that prevent individuals from functioning sexually, such as erectile difficulties or absence of orgasm. Common sexual dysfunctions among men include erectile dysfunction, the inability to have or maintain erection; premature ejaculation, the inability to delay ejaculation; inhibited ejaculation, the inability to ejaculate; and delayed ejaculation, prolonged delay in ejaculating. Common dysfunctions among women include anorgasmia, the absence of orgasm; vaginismus, the tightening of the vaginal muscles, prohibiting penetration; and dyspareunia, painful intercourse.

Recently, researchers and therapists have become interested in defining and treating sexual disorders as well as dysfunctions. **Sexual disorders** include such problems as hypoactive sexual desire, low or absent sexual desire, and sexual aversion, a consistently phobic response to sexual activities or the idea of such activities. Disorders are similar to sexual dysfunctions insofar as they limit an individual's ability to be sexual. But properly speaking, disorders affect the brain's arousal capabilities rather than physiological responses. Individuals with sexual disorders retain their ability to respond physically; the problem is that they have no desire to be sexual. They have shut down their brains' erotic centers. Figure 14.1 shows the percentage of heterosexual adults in the general U.S. population who reported experiencing sexual problems during the previous year (Laumann et al., 1994).

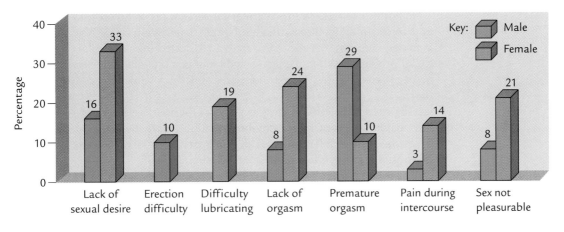

FIGURE 14.1 Heterosexual Sexual Dysfunctions in a Nonclinical Sample. (*Source:* Adapted from Laumann et al., 1994, pp. 370–371.)

Sexual Disorders

Hypoactive sexual desire and sexual aversion may be deeply rooted psychological problems; they are difficult to treat (Hawton, Catalan, & Fagg, 1991).

Hypoactive Sexual Desire   Low or absent sexual desire, or **hypoactive sexual desire (HSD),** is a widespread problem. Kaplan (1979) described the characteristics of a person experiencing hypoactive sexual desire, also known as **inhibited sexual desire:**

> [He] behaves as though his sexual circuits have been "shut down." He loses interest in sexual matters, will not pursue sexual gratification, and if a sexual situation presents itself, is not moved to avail himself of the opportunity.

HSD is fairly common in both men and women (Apt, Hurlbert, & Powell, 1993). As Figure 14.1 shows, it is more common among women. Lifelong HSD, however, is quite rare.

Hypoactive sexual desire is related to other sexual dysfunctions insofar as it is rooted in anxieties. Usually, however, it stems from deeper, more intense sexual anxieties, greater hostility toward the partner, and more pervasive defenses than are found in people with erectile and orgasmic difficulties (Hawton et al., 1991; H. S. Kaplan, 1987). Sometimes HSD is a means of coping with other sexual dysfunctions that precede it. Kolodny, Masters, and Johnson (1979) observe: "By developing a low interest in sexual activity, the person avoids the unpleasant consequences of sexual failure such as embarrassment, loss of self-esteem, and frustration."

There appear to be a number of causes of HSD (Hawton et al., 1991; H. S. Kaplan, 1979). Depression is one significant cause. HSD also commonly reflects unsolved relationship problems (Trudel, Boulos, & Matte, 1994). Over a period of time, if anger is not resolved, it may develop into resentment or hatred that colors every aspect of the relationship. Most people cannot experience sexual desire for someone with whom they are angry or whom they deeply resent.

In addition, stress, traumatic marital separation or divorce, loss of work, and forced retirement are frequently associated with HSD. When a person is under stress, energies and resources are directed toward dealing with emotional problems. When the stress ends, the person usually reexperiences his or her sexual desires. Drugs, hormone deficiency, and illness also decrease desire.

Gay men and lesbians may experience hypoactive sexual desire if they are unable to accept their sexual orientation (Margolies et al., 1988; Reece, 1988). Because of HIV and AIDS, some gay men have become especially depressed and have lost their sexual desire.

The treatment for most sexual dysfunctions involves some form of behavior modification. The treatment for HSD is often more complicated, however, and usually involves multifaceted and intensive interventions. Many times therapy is directed at helping couples resolve their interpersonal problems (Hawton et al., 1992). Sometimes, as in the case of menopausal women, 35% of whom experience a gradual or sudden loss of sexual interest, testosterone supplements in conjunction with estrogen replacement therapy have made a dramatic difference in restoring libido ("Rx for Lost Libido," 1996).

Sexual Aversion   A consistently phobic response to sexual activities or the idea of such activities is known as **sexual aversion** (H. S. Kaplan, 1987). It is often confused with hypoactive desire because avoidance often manifests itself as a lack of interest in sexual matters. Closer examination, however, may show that the lack of desire is a defense against anxiety-causing situations, such as intimacy or touch (Ponticas, 1992). More women than men experience sexual aversion.

In cases of sexual aversion, the frequency of intercourse typically falls to once or twice a year (or less). Although it is not uncommon for some people to be uninterested in or to dislike various forms of noncoital sexual activity, they nevertheless enjoy (or tolerate) sexual intercourse. A person experiencing sexual aversion, however, feels overwhelming anxieties about *any* kind of sexual contact. A mere kiss, touch, or caress may cause a phobic response out of fear that it might lead to something sexual. Sometimes these responses are internalized, but at other times, they can lead to physical responses such as sweating, nausea, vomiting, or diarrhea. Anticipating sex often provokes greater anxiety than the sexual activity itself.

Sexual aversion often results from severely negative parental attitudes during childhood; sexual trauma, such as rape or sexual abuse; consistent sexual pressure from a long-term partner; and gender identity confusion (Masters, Johnson, & Kolodny, 1992). Many cases of sexual aversion appear to be linked to adolescent difficulty with body image or self-esteem. Adolescent boys with gynecomastia (transitory breast enlargement), girls with excessive body or facial hair, and adolescents of both sexes with acne or obesity problems often avoid the sexual experimentation and activity typical for their age.

As with heterosexuals, gay men and lesbians may enjoy certain activities, such as kissing or mutual masturbation, but feel aversive to other activities. For gay men, sexual aversion often focuses on issues of anal eroticism (Reece, 1988). For lesbians, aversion frequently focuses on cunnilingus (Nichols, 1987), which is often the preferred activity among lesbians for reaching orgasm.

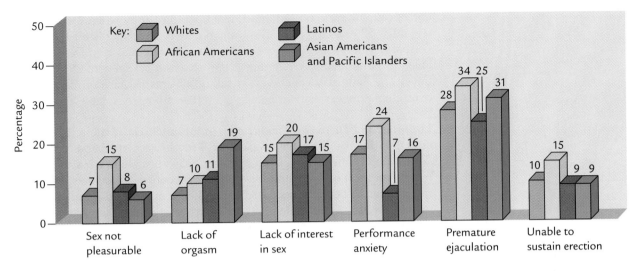

FIGURE 14.2 Male Sexual Dysfunctions by Ethnicity. (*Source:* Adapted from Laumann et al., 1994, p. 370.)

Male Sexual Dysfunctions

Both males and females may experience desire disorders. They may also experience dyspareunia, painful intercourse, but it is relatively uncommon among men. Most specifically, male sexual problems focus on the excitement stages of the response cycle: the ability to have or maintain an erection, and premature or delayed ejaculation. Figure 14.2 shows the percentage of males, by ethnicity, in the general U.S. population who reported experiencing various sexual problems during the previous year (Laumann et al., 1994).

Erectile Dysfunctions The inability to have or maintain an erection during intercourse is known as **erectile dysfunction.** (Erectile dysfunctions were previously called "impotence.") Such dysfunctions are common; between 10 and 20 million American men suffer erectile dysfunctions at some point in their lives ("New Pills," 1997). Roughly 50% of all new cases occur among men over the age of 40 (Feldman, Goldstein, Hatzichristou, Krane, & McKinlay, 1994). Erectile dysfunctions are divided into primary and secondary dysfunctions. Those men with primary erectile dysfunction have never had an erection; those with secondary erectile dysfunction have had erections in the past. Secondary erectile dysfunctions are more common than primary dysfunctions and are easier to treat, because they are often situational in origin.

Erectile difficulties may occur because of fatigue, too much alcohol, certain medical conditions, depression, conflict, or a host of other transitory reasons. Approximately 80% of erectile difficulties involve some organic (as opposed to psychological) impairment ("New Pills," 1997). Despite their common and usually temporary occurrence, erectile difficulties deeply affect a man's masculine self-concept.

Premature Ejaculation In **premature ejaculation,** a man, with minimal stimulation, is unable to control or delay his ejaculation as long as he wishes, resulting in personal or interpersonal distress. Approximately 29% of men experience premature ejaculation (Laumann et al., 1994). Although it is one of the most common sexual dysfunctions of heterosexual men in sex therapy, women more than men complain about it (Masters & Johnson, 1970).

> Thou treacherous, base deserter of
> my flame,
> False to my passion, fatal to my
> fame,
> Through what mistaken magic dost
> thou prove
> So true to lewdness, so untrue to
> love?
>
> —*John Wilmot, Earl of Rochester*
> *(1647–1680)*

Often, couples are confused, bewildered, and unhappy when the man consistently ejaculates too early. The woman may be sexually dissatisfied, while her partner may feel that she is too demanding. He may also feel considerable guilt and anxiety. They may begin to avoid sexual contact with each other. The man may experience erectile problems because of his anxieties over premature ejaculation; he may withdraw from sex completely.

Inhibited and Delayed Ejaculation   In **inhibited ejaculation,** the penis is erect, but the man is unable to ejaculate. Because ejaculation and orgasm are separate phenomena, the man may nevertheless be able to have an orgasm. In mild forms, it occurs with some frequency. About 4–9% of men have experienced this difficulty (Spector & Carey, 1990). In **delayed ejaculation,** the man is not able to ejaculate easily in intercourse; it may take 40 minutes of concentrated thrusting before ejaculation occurs.

Anxiety-provoking situations can interfere with a man's ejaculatory reflex. He may not be able to have an orgasm in certain situations in which he feels guilt or conflict. He may experience orgasm only from masturbation. Often this inhibition is overcome when the situation or partner changes or when the man engages in a fantasy, receives additional stimulation, or is distracted.

Female Sexual Dysfunctions

Most female sexual difficulties center on the orgasmic phase, although occasionally women experience vaginismus or dyspareunia during the excitement phase. Figure 14.3 shows the percentage of females, by ethnicity, in the general U.S. population who reported experiencing sexual problems during the previous year (Laumann et al., 1994).

Vaginismus   In **vaginismus,** the muscles around the vaginal entrance go into involuntary spasmodic contractions, preventing the insertion of the penis. During the nineteenth century, vaginismus was one of the most common complaints among women, who were taught to dread intercourse or to perform it perfunctorily. Today, about 2% of women are estimated to experience vaginismus (Renshaw, 1988). Vaginismus is essentially a conditioned response that reflects fear, anxiety, or pain. It may result from negative attitudes about sexuality, harsh early sexual experiences, sexual abuse or rape, or painful pelvic examinations (Vandeweil, Jaspers, Schultz, & Gal, 1990).

Dyspareunia   Painful intercourse, or **dyspareunia,** often occurs because a woman is not entirely aroused before her partner attempts intercourse (Lazarus, 1989). About 15% of women have reported dyspareunia (Laumann et al., 1994). Men may attempt intercourse too early, either because they are in a rush or because they mistake lubrication alone as a sign that their partner is ready for intercourse. Sexual inhibitions, a poor relationship with her partner, or hormonal imbalances may contribute to a woman's dyspareunia. Women past menopause have decreased vaginal lubrication and lose much of the elasticity of the vagina from a decrease in estrogen production. The use of lubricating jelly or estrogen therapy may help. Vaginitis, endometriosis, or pelvic inflammatory disease may make intercourse painful. If longer stimulation or the use of lubricants does not relieve the dyspareunia, a

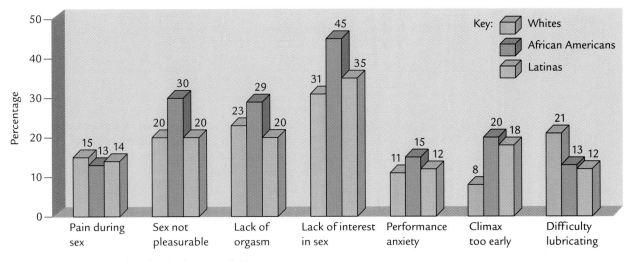

Data on Asian Americans and Pacific Islanders not available.

FIGURE 14.3 **Female Sexual Dysfunctions by Ethnicity.** (*Source:* Adapted from Laumann et al., 1994, p. 371.)

woman should consult her physician or health-care practitioner to determine the cause.

Anorgasmia The condition of not being orgasmic is called **anorgasmia.** (Anorgasmia is also known as orgasmic dysfunction, inorgasmia, and preorgasmia.) It is the most common female dysfunction seen by sex therapists; 18–76% of women in therapy are anorgasmic (Spector & Carey, 1990). (Previously, anorgasmia was known as "frigidity," a pejorative term connoting emotional coldness.) There are several types of anorgasmia.

In *primary anorgasmia,* a woman has never experienced an orgasm. Various studies suggest that approximately 5–10% of American women have never experienced orgasm (Spector & Carey, 1990). In *secondary anorgasmia,* a woman has previously experienced orgasm in sexual intercourse but no longer does so. In *situational anorgasmia,* a woman has had orgasms in certain situations, such as when masturbating, but not when being sexually stimulated by her partner.

Absence of orgasm may occur for any number of reasons, such as lack of effective penile stimulation during intercourse, insufficient manual stimulation of the clitoris by the woman or her partner, or insufficient duration of intercourse. Not being orgasmic, however, does not mean a woman is not sexual; many anorgasmic women rate their sexual experiences positively (Raboch & Raboch, 1992).

PHYSICAL CAUSES OF SEXUAL DYSFUNCTIONS

Until recently, researchers believed that most sexual dysfunction was psychological in origin. Current research challenges this view as more is learned about the intricacies of sexual physiology, such as the subtle influences of hormones. Our vascular, neurological, and endocrine systems are sensitive to changes and disruptions. As a result, various illnesses may have an adverse effect on our sexuality. Some prescription drugs, such as medication for hypertension or for depression, may affect sexual responsiveness. Chemotherapy and radiation treatment for cancer affect sexual desire and responsiveness.

Physical Causes in Men

Diabetes and alcoholism are the two leading causes of erectile dysfunctions; together they account for several million cases. Alcoholism, smoking, and drug use are widely associated with sexual dysfunctions (Vine, Margolin, Morrison, & Hulka, 1994). Diabetes, which causes erectile dysfunction in as many as 1 million men, damages blood vessels and nerves, including those within the penis. Other causes of sexual difficulties include lumbar-disc disease and multiple sclerosis, which interfere with the nerve impulses regulating erection (J. Weiss, 1992). Atherosclerosis is another major physical problem causing blockage of the arteries, including the blood flow necessary for erection. Spinal cord injuries may affect erectile abilities (Stein, Chamberlin, Lerner, & Gladshteyn, 1993). Smoking may also contribute to sexual difficulties. One study found that men who are heavy smokers are 50% more likely to experience erectile dysfunction that nonsmokers (National Center for Environmental Health, 1995). Bicycle-induced sexual difficulties can occur as a result of flattening of the main penile artery, thereby temporarily blocking the blood flow required for erections ("A Very Sore Spot," 1997).

A condition in which calcium deposits and tough fibrous tissue develop in the corpora cavernosa within the penis is known as **Peyronie's disease.** This problem occurs primarily in older males and can be quite painful. The disease results in a curvature of the penis that, in severe cases, interferes with erection and intercourse (Wilson & Delk, 1994). Medical treatments can alleviate the source of discomfort.

Prolonged and painful erection, occurring when blood is unable to drain from the penis, is called **priapism.** Lasting from several hours up to a few days, this problem is not associated with sexual thoughts or activities. Rather, it results from certain medications, including some antidepressants and excessive doses of penile injections. Certain medical conditions, such as sickle-cell disease and leukemia, may also cause priapism ("What Is Priapism?" 1997).

Although sexual dysfunctions often reflect conflict and discord within a relationship or disrupt a relationship, if the dysfunction is due to cancer, paraplegia, or diabetes, there may be less relationship strain. If the relationship was stable before the onset of the illness, a couple may have a satisfactory relationship without sexual intercourse. Other forms of sexual interaction may also provide sexual intimacy and pleasure. "When the bond between the mates is love and intimacy," observes Peter Martin (1981), "the loss of sex due to physical illness does not make the marriage an unhappy one."

Physical Causes in Women

Organic causes of anorgasmia in women include medical conditions such as diabetes and heart disease, hormone deficiencies, and neurological disorders, as well as drug use and alcoholism. Spinal cord injuries may affect sexual responsiveness (Stein et al., 1993). Multiple sclerosis can decrease vaginal lubrication and sexual response (J. Weiss, 1992).

Dyspareunia may result from an obstructed or thick hymen, clitoral adhesions, a constrictive clitoral hood, or a weak **pubococcygeus,** the pelvic floor muscle surrounding the urethra and, in women, the vagina. Antihistamines used to treat colds and allergies, as well as marijuana, may reduce vaginal lubrication. Endometriosis and ovarian and uterine tumors and cysts may affect a woman's sexual response.

The skin covering the clitoris can become infected. Women who masturbate too vigorously can irritate their clitoris, making intercourse painful. Men can stimulate their partners too roughly, causing soreness in the vagina, urethra, or clitoral area. Dirty hands may cause a vaginal or urinary tract infection.

Treatment of Physical Problems

Sexual dysfunctions are often a combination of physical and psychological problems (LoPiccolo, 1991). Even people whose disorders are physical may develop psychological or relationship problems as they try to cope with their difficulties. Thus, treatment for organically based dysfunctions may need to include psychological counseling.

Coital pain caused by inadequate lubrication and thinning vaginal walls often occurs as a result of decreased estrogen associated with menopause. Lubricants or hormone replacement therapy, discussed in Chapter 13, often resolves the difficulties. There are no other widely used medical treatments for organic female sexual difficulties.

Most medical and surgical treatment for men centers on erectile dysfunctions. Often these problems are due to illnesses or injuries that impair the vascular system, affecting penile vasocongestion. Microsurgery may correct the blood-flow problem, but it is not always successful (Mohr & Beutler, 1990; Puech-Leao, 1992; Weidner, Weiske, Rudnick, Becker, Schroeder-Printzen, & Brahler, 1992).

Suction devices may be used to induce and maintain an erection. A vacuum chamber is placed over the flaccid penis and the air suctioned out, causing blood to be drawn into the penis. When the penis is erect, an elastic ring is placed around the base of the penis to prevent the blood from exiting. The chamber is removed, and the penis stays erect as long as the band is intact.

Erections may also be assisted by implanting a penile prosthesis in the penis and testicles. There are two types of penile implants. One type consists of a pair of semirigid rods embedded in the cavernous bodies of the penis. They are relatively easy to implant, but the penis remains permanently semierect. The second type is an inflatable implant that permits the penis to be either erect or flaccid. A pair of inflatable tubes is implanted in the penis's cavernous bodies, a fluid-filled reservoir is inserted near the bladder, and a pump is placed in the scrotum. To get an erection, the man or his partner squeezes the scrotal pump, and fluid fills the empty tubes, causing an erection. A release valve is triggered to empty the fluid from the tubes back into the reservoir. Figure 14.4 illustrates several treatments available for erectile dysfunctions.

Suppositories, injections, and more recently, oral medications have become the treatment of choice for many men with erectile dysfunction. Unlike vacuum devices or surgery, which can be quite painful or clumsy, these remedies are easy to use and produce instant erections when injected

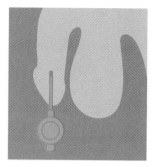
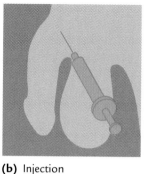
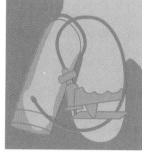

(a) Suppository   **(b)** Injection   **(c)** Vacuum pump   **(d)** Implant

FIGURE 14.4   Treatments Available for Erectile Dysfunctions. (a) Use of a suppository involves the delivery of alprostadil in gel form through an applicator inserted into the tip of the penis. The suppository is inserted 5 to 10 minutes before sex. The erection can last an hour. (b) Injection therapy involves the injection of a chemical 10 minutes to 2 hours before sex. The erection can last an hour or more. (c) The vacuum pump removes air from around the sheathed penis, pulling blood into it. It is used just before sex. The erection lasts until the elastic ring at the base of the penis is taken off. (d) Surgical implants involve the use of a malleable or inflatable pump and a reservoir of saline solution which is bent or pumped into position. The erection lasts until the pump is unbent or drained. Oral medication to enhance the possibility of erection has recently become available and is helpful in some cases. (*Source:* Leland, 1997.)

or inserted into the penis. Pills are the next frontier. Recently, the Food and Drug Administration has approved the oral medication Viagra (see Chapter 13) and is reviewing several others, each of which has shown success in treating mild or partial erectile dysfunction (Leland, 1997).

Treatment for erectile impairment provides both promise and potential for unforeseen social consequences. Opening questions of culture as well as pharmacology, these remedies "reduce complex human endeavors to biology, then monkey with the biology" (Leland, 1997). Author Bernard Absell (1995) has raised questions about the meaning of chemically enhanced erections and the consequences of a market-driven quest for the perfect penis. However, for those individuals and couples who have suffered because of lack of intimacy, remedies for erectile dysfunction open the doors to the possibility of improved psychological and interpersonal well-being.

PSYCHOLOGICAL CAUSES OF SEXUAL DYSFUNCTIONS

Sexual dysfunctions may have their origin in any number of psychological causes. Some dysfunctions originate from immediate causes, others from conflict within the self, and still others from a particular sexual relationship. Gay men and lesbians often have unique issues affecting their sexual functioning.

Immediate Causes

The immediate causes of sexual dysfunctions lie in the current situation, including fatigue, stress, ineffective sexual behavior, and sexual anxieties.

Fatigue and Stress Many dysfunctions have fairly simple causes. Men and women may find themselves physically exhausted from the demands of work or child rearing. They may bring their fatigue into the bedroom in the form of sexual apathy or disinterest. "I'm too tired to make love tonight" may be a truthful description of a person's feelings. What these couples may need is not therapy or counseling but a vacation, relief from their daily routines.

Long-term stress can also contribute to lowered sexual drive and less responsiveness. A man or woman preoccupied with making ends meet, with an unruly child, or with prolonged illness can temporarily lose his or her sexual desire.

Ineffective Sexual Behavior Helen Singer Kaplan (1974) found that a surprising amount of ignorance and misinformation prevents couples from being effectively sexual with each other. Ineffective sexual behavior appears to be especially relevant in explaining why many women do not experience orgasm in sexual interactions. The couple may not be aware of the significance of the clitoris or the necessity for direct stimulation.

Some gay men and lesbians have not learned effective sexual behaviors because they are inexperienced. They have grown up without easily accessible sexual information or positive role models (Reece, 1988).

Sexual Anxieties   A number of anxieties, such as performance anxiety, can lead to sexual problems. If a man fails to experience an erection or a woman is not orgasmic, he or she may feel anxious and fearful. The anxiety may block the very response the man or woman desires.

Performance anxieties may give rise to **spectatoring,** the process in which a person becomes a spectator of his or her sexual performance (Masters & Johnson, 1970). When people become spectators of their sexual activities, they critically evaluate and judge whether they are "performing" well or whether they are doing everything "right" for having orgasms. Helen Kaplan (1983) believes spectatoring is involved in most orgasmic dysfunctions.

Performance anxiety may be even more widespread among gay men. Rex Reece (1988) writes: "Many gay men move in a social, sexual milieu where sexual arousal is expected immediately or soon after meeting someone. If response is not rapidly forthcoming, rejection is very likely."

Excessive Need to Please a Partner   Another source of anxiety is an excessive need to please a partner (H. S. Kaplan, 1974). A man who experiences this anxiety may want a speedy erection to please (or impress) his partner. He may feel he must always delay his orgasm until after his partner's. A woman who experiences this anxiety may want to have an orgasm quickly to please her partner. She may worry that she is not sufficiently attractive to her partner.

One result of the need to please is that men and women may pretend to have orgasms. (The great cinematic faked orgasm took place when Meg Ryan demonstrated faking an orgasm in a deli in the film "When Harry Met Sally.") One study found that two-thirds of the women and one-third of the men reported faking orgasm (Darling & Davidson, 1986). Women fake orgasm most often to avoid disappointing their partner or hurting his feelings. Both also fake orgasm to present a false image of their sexual performance. Unfortunately, faking orgasm miscommunicates to the partner that each is equally satisfied. Because the orgasmic problem is not addressed, resentment and anger may simmer.

Conflict Within the Self

Our religious traditions tend to view sex as inherently dangerous, as lust and fornication. Sexual intercourse within marriage is the only sexual behavior and context endorsed by *all* Christian and Jewish denominations. Premarital intercourse, oral sex, cohabitation, and gay and lesbian relationships are condemned to various degrees. As a consequence, religious background may contribute to sexual problems (Simpson & Ramberg, 1992). Masters, Johnson, and Kolodny (1992) note that rigid religious upbringing is associated with vaginismus, primary anorgasmia, and erectile dysfunction. Ideas of the inherent sinfulness of sexuality are not as culturally pervasive as they

CHILDHOOD SEXUAL ABUSE and adult sexual assault or rape are widespread and often have a severe impact on sexual functioning. As a result of abuse or assault, issues of trust, safety, and intimacy may interfere with a person's sexual responsiveness. Sexuality becomes associated with exploitation, pain, and even terror. A common response is for a person to experience sexual dysfunctions.

Survivors of childhood sexual abuse may find it difficult to relax and enjoy sexual activities; they may avoid sex, experience a lack of desire, or be unable to experience orgasm (Beitchman, Zucker, Hood, daCosta, Akman, & Cassavia, 1992). A recent study reports that survivors of multiple incidents of familial sexual abuse are significantly more likely to experience a lack of desire and an inability to experience orgasm (Kinzl, Traweger, & Biebel, 1995). Those who suffered only a single abuse incident experienced no more problems than nonvictims. Another study found that survivors may develop aversive responses to what was done to them during the assault (McNew & Abell, 1995). If they were fondled, for example, erotic touching may produce fear and disgust.

Psychotherapy is often useful for couples in which a partner experienced childhood abuse (J. Brown, 1995).

Therapists can help survivors understand that their current dysfunction or aversion is related to their childhood exploitation rather than caused by their partner. They can help the survivor establish trust and enable the partner to understand the underlying dynamics.

Sexual assault or rape in adulthood also affects a woman's sexuality (Nadelson, 1990). Some begin avoiding sexual interactions, because sex reminds them of the rape. Those who are less depressed, however, have fewer sexual difficulties (Mackey, Sereika, Weissfeld, Hacker, Zender, & Heard, 1992). The two most common sexual problems are fear of sex and a lack of sexual desire (Howard, 1980). Both White and African American women report similar sexual problems (Wyatt, 1992).

In a 3-year study of 100 rape victims, women who did not develop sexual problems as a result of the rape had explained their rape to their partners, who were warm, empathetic, and responsive to them (Howard, 1980). Recovery from the rape trauma was accelerated by letting the woman determine when sex with her partner would take place. A number of women who did not develop sexual problems had refrained from sexual activities with their partners for a period of time.

once were, but they are still powerful forces that form notions of sexuality as we mature.

Negative attitudes toward sex held by parents are frequently associated with sexual problems later (McCabe, 1994). Much of the process of growing up is a casting off of the sexual guilt and negativity instilled from childhood. And among gay men and lesbians, internalized homophobia, self-hatred because of one's homosexuality, is a major source of conflict traced to a conservative religious upbringing (Nichols, 1988; Reece, 1988).

Severely damaging sources of sexual dysfunction are childhood sexual abuse, adult sexual assault, and rape. Guilt and conflict do not usually eliminate a person's sex drive; rather, they inhibit the drive and alienate a person from his or her sexuality. A person may come to see sexuality as something bad or "dirty," rather than something to happily affirm. Sexual expression is forced "to assume an infinite variety of distorted, inhibited, diverted, sublimated, alienated and variable forms to accommodate the conflict" (H. S. Kaplan, 1974).

Relationship Causes

Sexual problems do not exist in a vacuum, but usually within the context of a relationship (Crowe, 1995). Most frequently, married couples go into therapy because they have a greater investment in the relationship than couples who are dating or living together. Sexual difficulties in a dating or cohabiting relationship often do not rise to the surface. It is often easier for unmarried couples to break up than to change the patterns that contribute to their sexual problems.

If left unresolved, rage, anger, disappointment, and hostility often become a permanent part of couple interaction. Desire discrepancies become sources of conflict rather than of acceptance. Underlying fears of rejection or abandonment may help form the relationship structure. But these factors vastly influence the nature and quality of the relationship between partners.

TREATING SEXUAL PROBLEMS

There are several approaches to sex therapy, the most important ones being behavior modification and psychosexual therapy. William Masters and Virginia Johnson were the pioneers in the cognitive-behavioral approach, whereas the most influential psychosexual therapist is Helen Singer Kaplan. The cognitive-behavioral approach works well with sexual dysfunctions, such as erectile and orgasmic problems. Psychosexual therapy is more effective in treating sexual disorders, such as hypoactive desire and sexual aversion (Atwood & Dershowitz, 1992).

Masters and Johnson: A Cognitive-Behavioral Approach

In this section, we examine the program developed by Masters and Johnson in the treatment of sexual dysfunctions. Their work has been the starting point for contemporary sex therapy. Not only did they reject the Freudian model of tracing sexual problems to childhood; they relabeled sexual problems as sexual dysfunctions rather than aspects of neuroses. Masters and Johnson (1970) argued that the majority of sexual dysfunctions are the result of sexual ignorance, faulty techniques, or relationship problems. They treated dysfunctions using a combination of cognitive and behavioral techniques, and they treated couples rather than individuals. In cases where a partner was unavailable, Masters and Johnson used, as part of their therapeutic team, **sex surrogates,** whose role it was to have sexual interactions with a client.

Dysfunctional Couples Cognitive-behavioral therapists approach the problems of erectile and orgasmic difficulties by dealing with the couple rather than the individual. They regard sexuality as an interpersonal phenomenon rather than an individual one. In fact, they tell their clients that there are no dysfunctional individuals, only dysfunctional couples, and that faulty sexual interaction is at the root of sexual problems. Neither individual is to blame; rather, it is their mutual interaction that sustains a dysfunction.

Therapists using this approach attempt to take into therapy only those couples who are genuinely committed to their relationship. Treatment lasts 12 days on the average. During this time, couples are seen daily by the therapists. They are told not to attempt sexual intercourse until they are given permission by their therapist team, a man and a woman. In this way, each partner is immediately relieved of any pressure to perform, thus easing anxieties and allowing the development of a more relaxed attitude toward sex.

Case Histories   The first morning, each individual is interviewed separately by the therapist of the same sex; in the afternoon, the interview is repeated by the therapist of the other sex. The therapists are careful not to assign blame to either partner, for it is the couple, rather than the individual, who are being treated.

After the interviews and the case histories have been taken, the couple meet with both therapists to discuss what has been learned so far. The therapists explain what they have learned about the couple's personal and sexual interaction, encouraging the man and woman to expand or correct what they are saying. Then the therapists discuss the sexual myths and fallacies that the couple hold that may interfere with their sexual interaction.

Sensate Focus   At the end of the third day, the therapists introduce **sensate focus,** focusing on touch and the giving and receiving of pleasure. The other senses—smell, sight, hearing, and taste—are worked on indirectly as a means of reinforcing the touch experience. To increase their sensate focus, the couple are given "homework" assignments. In the privacy of their own room, they are to take off their clothes so that nothing will restrict their sensations. One partner must give pleasure and the other receive it. The giver touches, caresses, massages, and strokes his or her partner's body everywhere except the genitals and the breasts. The purpose is not sexual arousal but simply sense awareness.

Through the fourth day, therapy is basically the same for any type of sexual dysfunction. Thereafter, the therapists begin to focus on the particular dysfunction affecting the couple.

Treating Male Dysfunctions   The therapists use different techniques for treating the specific dysfunction.

ERECTILE DYSFUNCTIONS   When the problem is erectile difficulties, the couple are taught that fears and anxieties are largely responsible and that the removal of these fears is the first step in therapy. Once the fear is removed, the man is less likely to be an observer of his sexuality; he can become an actor rather than a spectator or judge.

After the sensate focus exercises have been integrated into the couple's behavior, they are told to play with each other's genitals, but not to attempt an erection. Often, erections may occur because there is no demand on the man; but he is encouraged to let his penis become soft again, then erect, then soft, as reassurance that he can successfully have erections. This builds his confidence and his partner's by letting her know that she can excite him.

During this time, the couple is counseled on other aspects of their relationship that contribute to their sexual difficulties. Then, about the tenth day, the couple attempt their first intercourse, if the man has had erections with some success. Eventually, in the final session, the man will have an orgasm.

PREMATURE EJACULATION   Cognitive-behavioral therapists treat premature ejaculation by using initially the same pattern they use in treating erectile dysfunctions. They concentrate especially on reducing fears and anxieties and increasing sensate focus and communication. Then they use a simple exercise called the **squeeze technique** (Figure 14.5). (This technique was developed in the 1950s and remains the most effective treatment to date [St.

> Full nakedness! All joys are due to thee,
> As souls unbodied, bodies unclothed must be,
> To taste whole joys.
>
> —*John Donne*

FIGURE 14.5 The Squeeze Technique. This exercise is effective in treating premature ejaculation.

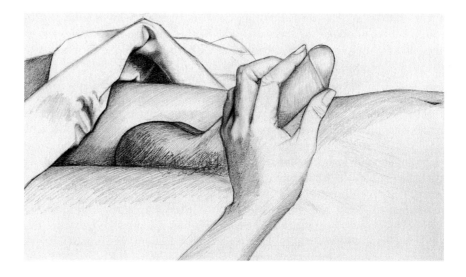

Lawrence & Madakasira, 1992].) The man is brought manually to a full erection. Just before he is about to ejaculate, his partner squeezes his penis with thumb and forefinger just below the corona. After 30 seconds of inactivity, the partner arouses him again and, just before he ejaculates, squeezes again. Using this technique, the couple can continue for 15–20 minutes before the man ejaculates.

INHIBITED EJACULATION   Inhibited ejaculation is treated by having the man's partner manipulate his penis. The partner asks for verbal and physical direction to bring him the most pleasure possible. It may take a few sessions before the man reaches his first orgasm. The idea is to identify his partner with sexual pleasure and desire. He is encouraged to feel stimulated, not only by his partner, but also by her erotic responses to him. After the man has reached orgasm through manual stimulation, he then proceeds to vaginal intercourse. With further instruction and feedback, the man is able to function sexually without fear of ejaculatory inhibition.

Treating Female Dysfunctions   Each female dysfunction is treated differently in behavior modification therapy.

ANORGASMIA   After the sensate focus sessions, the woman's partner begins to touch and caress her vulva; she guides his hand to show him what she likes. The man is told, however, not to stimulate the clitoris directly because it may be extremely sensitive and stimulation may cause pain instead of pleasure. Instead, he caresses and stimulates the area around the clitoris, the labia, and the upper thighs. During this time, the couple are told not to attempt orgasm because it would place undue performance pressure on the woman. They are simply to explore the woman's erotic potential and discover what brings her the greatest pleasure.

VAGINISMUS   Vaginismus is one of the easiest sexual dysfunctions to eliminate, using vaginal dilators, plastic penile-shaped rods. The woman uses a set of dilators graduated in diameter. She inserts one before going to bed at night, taking it out in the morning. As soon as the woman is able to receive a dilator of one size without having vaginal spasms, a larger one is used. In most cases, the vaginismus disappears.

Helen Singer Kaplan: Psychosexual Therapy

Helen Singer Kaplan (1974, 1979, 1983) modified Masters and Johnson's behavioral treatment program to include psychosexual therapy. The cognitive-behavioral approach works well for excitement and orgasmic dysfunctions resulting from mild to mid-level sexual anxieties. But if the individual experiences severe anxieties resulting from intense relationship or psychic conflicts or from childhood sexual abuse or rape, a behavioral approach alone frequently does not work. Such severe anxieties usually manifest themselves in sexual aversion or hypoactive sexual desire.

The role of the therapist in such instances is to provide clients with insight into the origins of the dysfunction. Individuals with desire disorders, for example, often resist behavioral exercises such as sensate focus and pleasuring. They may respond to these exercises with boredom, anxiety, or discomfort; they resist experiencing pleasure. The therapist can intervene by pointing out that they are actively (consciously or unconsciously) creating inhibitions by focusing on negative feelings ("She makes strange sounds"; "His arms are too hairy"), by distracting themselves with thoughts of work or household matters, or by calling up performance fears ("I won't be able to come").

The therapist creates a crisis by confronting individuals with their resistances, then pointing out that they are in control of their resistances and that they can change if they want to. Some individuals will improve as a result of the crisis. Others, however, feel powerless to change. They require additional psychosexual therapy to gain insight into their disorders. They need to discover and resolve the unconscious roots of their disorders to permit themselves to experience desire once again for their partners.

Other Therapeutic Approaches

Both cognitive-behavioral and psychosexual therapy are expensive and take a considerable amount of time. In response to these limitations, brief sex therapy, self-help, and group therapy have developed.

PLISSIT Model of Therapy   One of the most widespread models used by sex therapists is the **PLISSIT model** (Annon, 1974, 1976). PLISSIT is an acronym for the four progressive levels of sex therapy: **p**ermission, **l**imited **i**nformation, **s**pecific **s**uggestions, and **i**ntensive **t**herapy.

The first level in the PLISSIT model is *permission giving*. At one time or another, most sexual behaviors were prohibited by important figures in our lives. Because desires and activities such as fantasies or masturbation were not validated, we often question their "normality" or "morality." We shroud them in secrecy or cover them with shame. Without permission to be sexual, we may experience sexual disorders and dysfunctions.

Sex therapists act as "permission givers" for us to be sexual. They become authority figures who validate our sexuality by helping us accept our sexual feelings and behaviors. They reassure us and help us clarify our sexual

SEX THERAPY ASSUMES a Western middle-class model of sexuality. Although this model may be effective in explaining and treating sexual difficulties among White middle-class Americans, it may be ineffective in treating members of other cultures and ethnic groups. As Yoav Lavee (1991) notes, the dominant Western model makes four assumptions about sexuality:

- Sex is primarily a means of exchanging pleasure.
- Both partners are equally involved.
- People need and want information about sex.
- Communication is important for good sexual relationships.

These assumptions about sexuality, however, are not universal. In the United States, there is considerable variation among the many non-Western cultural and ethnic groups, such as Native American, Asian, Middle Eastern, and East Indian (Lavee, 1991; McGoldrick, Pearce, & Giordano, 1982).

Among some non-Western clients, the issues focus on men's obtaining sexual pleasure; there is little concern about women's pleasure. In treating Arab, North African, and Asian Jews in Israel, Lavee (1991) found that his clients were primarily men who complained about erectile difficulties. Premature ejaculation was problematical only when it interfered with the man's pleasure. When both husband and wife were invited to attend therapy, usually only the man attended. Finally, individuals and couples alike resisted suggestions of sensate focus exercises. Even if they did agree to do them, most did not follow through; many dropped out of therapy.

Although White middle-class Americans tend to use the services of medical and mental health-care professionals, including sex and family therapists, members of various ethnic groups consult such professionals considerably less often. Two reasons may explain this. First, because ethnic minorities tend to be poorer than Whites, they do not have the financial resources. Second, physical and mental health have often been defined in terms of White middle-class standards of physical and psychological functioning and behavior. Therefore, members of ethnic minorities have been stereotypically misdiagnosed. For decades, for example, it was asserted that African American men had weak masculine identities because of the absence of fathers in families; the presence of strong, independent women was thought to be emasculating. African American males allegedly overcompensated by being obsessed with sex and "promiscuous." Such misdiagnosis has a long history. During slavery times, for example, some Blacks were diagnosed as suffering from "drapetomania," a disease that caused them to run away (Wilkinson & Spurlock, 1986).

For Latinos, the myth of the supermasculine "macho" male dominated the mental health profession and continues to have influence (Guerrero Pavich, 1988). Because of the prevalence of stereotypes masquerading as diag-

values. They also validate our ability to say no to activities in which we are uncomfortable.

The second level is giving *limited information.* This information is limited to the specific area of difficulties. If a woman is anorgasmic in intercourse, for example, the therapist might explain that not all women are orgasmic in coitus without additional manual stimulation before, during, or after penetration. The therapist might discuss the effects of drugs such as alcohol, marijuana, and cocaine on sexual responsiveness.

The third level is *specific suggestions.* If permission giving and limited information are not sufficient, the therapist next suggests specific "homework" exercises. If a man experiences premature ejaculation, the therapist may suggest that he and his partner try the squeeze technique. An anorgasmic woman might be instructed to masturbate with or without her partner to discover the best way for her partner to assist her in experiencing orgasm.

The fourth level is *intensive therapy.* If the individual still continues to experience a sexual problem, he or she will need to enter intensive therapy, such as psychosexual therapy.

noses, many members of ethnic groups are suspicious of the mental health-care professions (Wilkinson, 1986; P. Wilson, 1986).

Many issues must be considered when treating members of diverse cultural and ethnic groups. One is the differing cultural definitions of what is a problem. If the purpose of sex is male pleasure or reproduction, then most female "problems" disappear as long as they do not interfere with sexual intercourse. Low sexual desire and lack of orgasm in women are deemed irrelevant. Vaginismus and painful intercourse are perceived as problems only if they prevent sexual intercourse. These beliefs are consistent with cultural beliefs that women are not supposed to seek or experience sexual pleasure. Female sexual problems in male-centered cultures are usually viewed as reproductive ones, especially infertility.

We do not know whether women's perceptions necessarily support some or all of these cultural views. In male-centered societies, it is difficult for women to speak out. Furthermore, tradition and socialization, as well as the fear of being labeled immoral, lead many women to accept and embrace beliefs that appear highly alien to us.

The second issue to consider is that there are different "explanations" of what causes sexual problems. In many of the world's rural areas, erectile and infertility problems are blamed on sorcery or supernatural causes, and most cultures have folk remedies to deal with them. Although treatments vary from culture to culture, many have stood the test of time and may be quite effective among those for whom they were formulated.

The third issue is that there are cultural differences concerning *whom* to consult for problems. If the problem is thought to be caused by supernatural forces, *curanderos*, curers, are called in Latin America to furnish the victim with charms or medicines to ward off the evil. Sometimes priests are called in to pray for deliverance (Lavee, 1991).

In American society there is also considerable variation about whom to call for treatment. Among individualistic, White, working-class and middle-class American men, no one is called. The man is supposed to solve the problem by himself; talking to others is a sign of weakness (Rubin, 1976). African Americans tend to use the extended family network, although women are more willing than men to initiate therapy (Hines & Boyd-Franklin, 1982). Among Asian Americans, sexual problems are expected to be worked out within the family, especially between the spouses. Traditional Irish Americans and Latinos are more likely to turn to priests (Espín, 1984; McGoldrick, 1982).

Because there is considerable cultural and ethnic variation, Lavee (1991) writes:

> If the client's sexual values are different, we ought to remember that a well-integrated life philosophy, that has proven effective for many generations, stands behind them. It may therefore be easier and wiser to fit the treatment to the client's values than to attempt to "teach" them what healthy sex is.

Self-Help and Group Therapy The PLISSIT model provides a sound basis for understanding how partners, friends, books, self-help exercises, and group therapy may be useful in helping us deal with the first three levels of therapy: permission, limited information, and specific suggestions. Partners, friends, books, and group therapy sessions under a therapist's guidance, for example, may provide permission for us to engage in sexual exploration and discovery. From these sources, we may learn that many of our sexual fantasies and behaviors are very common. Such methods are most effective when dysfunctions arise from a lack of knowledge or mild sexual anxieties. They also are considerably less expensive than most other types of sex therapy.

The first step in dealing with a sexual problem can be to turn to your own immediate resources. Begin by discussing the problem with your partner; find out what he or she thinks. Discuss specific strategies that might be useful. Sometimes simply communicating your feelings and thoughts will resolve the difficulty. Seek out friends with whom you can share your feelings and anxieties. Find out what they think. Ask them whether they have

KEGEL EXERCISES were originally developed by Dr. Arnold Kegel (KAY-gul) to help women with problems controlling urination. They were designed to strengthen and give you voluntary control of a muscle called the pubococcygeus (pew-bo-kawk-SEE-gee-us), or P.C. for short. The P.C. muscle is part of the sling of muscle stretching from your pubic bone in front to your tailbone in back. Because the muscle encircles not only the urinary opening but also the outside of the vagina, some of Dr. Kegel's patients discovered a pleasant side effect—increased sexual awareness. (Men may also benefit from doing Kegels!)

Why Do Kegel Exercises?

Learning Kegel exercises:

- Can help you be more aware of feelings in your genital area
- Can increase circulation in the genital area
- May help increase sexual arousal started by other kinds of stimulation
- Can be useful during childbirth to help control the strength and duration of pushing
- Can be helpful after childbirth to restore muscle tone in the vagina

Identifying Your P.C. Muscle

Sit on the toilet. Spread your legs apart. See if you can stop and start the flow of urine without moving your legs. That's your P.C. muscle, the one that turns the flow on and off. If you don't find it the first time, don't give up; try again the next time you have to urinate.

How to Do the Exercises

- *Slow Kegels.* Tighten the P.C. muscle as you did to stop the urine. Hold it for a slow count of three. Relax it.
- *Quick Kegels.* Tighten and relax the P.C. muscle as rapidly as you can.
- *Pull in—Push out.* Pull up the entire pelvic floor as though trying to suck water into your vagina. Then push or bear down as if trying to push the imaginary water out. (This exercise will use a number of "stomach" or "abdominal" muscles as well as the P.C. muscle.)

At first, do ten of each of these three exercises (one "set") five times every day. Each week, increase the number of times you do each exercise by five (15, 20, 25, etc.). Keep doing five "sets" each day.

Exercise Guidelines

- You can do these exercises any time during daily activities that don't require a lot of moving around. Some examples include while driving your car, watching television, doing dishes, sitting in school or at your desk, or lying in bed.
- When you start, you will probably notice that the muscle doesn't want to stay "contracted" during "Slow Kegels" and that you can't do "Quick Kegels" very fast or evenly. Keep at it. In a week or two you will probably notice that you can control the muscle quite well.
- Sometimes the muscle will start to feel a little tired. Not surprising. You probably haven't used it very much before. Take a few seconds' rest and start again.
- A good way to check on how you are doing is to insert one or two lubricated fingers into your vagina.
- Remember to keep breathing naturally and evenly while doing your Kegels!

had similar experiences and how they handled them. Try to keep your perspective—and your sense of humor.

Group therapy may be particularly valuable for providing us with an open, safe forum in which we can discuss our sexual feelings. It is an opportunity to experience and discover that many of our sexual behaviors, fantasies, and problems are very common. The presence of a therapist in these sessions can provide valuable insight and direction. Another benefit of group therapy is that it is often less expensive than most other types of therapy.

Gay, Lesbian, and Bisexual Sex Therapy

Until recently, sex therapy treated sexual dysfunctions and disorders as implicitly heterosexual. The model for sexual functioning, in fact, was generally orgasmic heterosexual intercourse. There was virtually no mention of gay, lesbian, or bisexual sexual concerns.

For gay men, lesbians, and bisexuals, sexual issues differ from those of heterosexuals in several ways. First, although gay men and lesbians may have desire, erectile, or orgasmic difficulties, the context in which they occur may differ significantly from that of heterosexuals. Problems among heterosexuals most often focus on sexual intercourse, whereas gay, bisexual, and lesbian sexual difficulties focus on other behaviors. Gay men in sex therapy, for example, most often experience aversion toward anal eroticism (Reece, 1988). Lesbians in sex therapy frequently complain about aversive feelings toward cunnilingus. Anorgasmia, however, is not frequently viewed as a problem (Margolies et al., 1988). Heterosexual women, by contrast, frequently complain about lack of orgasm.

Second, lesbians, gay men, and bisexuals must deal with both societal homophobia and internalized homophobia (Friedman, 1991; Margolies et al., 1988). Fear of violence makes it difficult for gay men, bisexuals, and lesbians to openly express their affection in the same manner as heterosexuals. As a consequence, lesbians, bisexuals, and gay men learn to repress their expressions of feelings in public; this repression may carry over into private as well. Internalized homophobia may result in diminished sexual desire, creating sexual aversion and fostering guilt and negative feelings about sexual activity.

Third, gay men must deal with the association between sex and HIV infection that has cut a deadly swath through the gay community. Grieving over the death of friends, lovers, and partners has left many depressed. In turn, this affects sexual desire and creates high levels of sexual anxiety. Many are fearful of contracting HIV even if they practice safer sex. And HIV-positive men, even if they are practicing safer sex, are often afraid of transmitting the infection to their loved ones (Friedman, 1991; Rudolph, 1989b; Shannon & Woods, 1991).

These unique lesbian, bisexual, and gay concerns require that sex therapists expand their understanding and treatment of sexual problems. If the therapist is not gay or lesbian, he or she needs to have a thorough knowledge of homosexuality and the gay and lesbian world. Therapists further need to be aware of their own assumptions and feelings about homosexuality. Some therapists continue to believe that homosexuality is morally wrong and convey their beliefs to their clients under the guise of therapy (Coleman, Rosser, & Strapko, 1992). Therapists working with gay, bisexual, or lesbian clients need to develop inclusive models of sexual treatment that are "gay-positive."

Seeking Professional Assistance

Because something is not "functioning" according to a therapist's model does not necessarily mean that something is wrong. You need to evaluate your sexuality in terms of your own and your partner's satisfaction and the meanings you give to your sexuality. If, after doing this, you are unable to resolve your sexual difficulties yourself, seek professional assistance. It is important to realize that seeking such assistance is not a sign of personal weakness or failure. Rather, it is a sign of strength, for it demonstrates an ability to reach out and a willingness to change. It is a sign that you care for your partner, your relationship, and yourself. As you think about therapy, consider the following points:

- What are your goals in therapy? Are you willing to make changes in your relationship to achieve your goals?

- Do you want individual, couple, or group therapy? If you are in a relationship, is your partner willing to attend therapy?

- What characteristics are important for you in a therapist? Do you prefer a female or a male therapist? Is the therapist's age, religion, or ethnic background important to you?

- What are the therapist's professional qualifications? There are few certified sex therapy programs; most therapists who treat sexual difficulties come from various professional backgrounds, such as psychiatry, clinical psychology, psychoanalysis, marriage and family counseling, and social work. Because there is no licensing in the field of sex therapy, it is important to seek out those trained therapists who have licenses in their generalized field. This way, the patient has recourse if questionable practices arise. It is worth noting that professionals view sexual contact between themselves and the client as unethical and unlawful.

- What is the therapist's approach? Is it behavioral, psychosexual, psychoanalytic, religious, spiritual, feminist, or something else? What is the therapist's attitude toward gender roles? Do you feel comfortable with the approach?

- If necessary, does the therapist offer a sliding-scale fee, based on your level of income?

- If you are lesbian, gay, or bisexual, does the therapist affirm your sexual orientation? Does the therapist understand the special problems gays, bisexuals, and lesbians face?

- After a session or two with the therapist, do you have confidence in him or her? If not, discuss your feelings with the therapist. If you believe your dissatisfaction is not a defense mechanism, change therapists.

Just how successful is sex therapy? Nobody really knows. Though Masters and Johnson have reported higher success rates than other therapists, some of their methods of evaluating patients have come under attack. What constitutes success or failure is subjective and open to interpretation. Much of therapy's success depends on a person's willingness to confront painful feelings and to change. This entails time, effort, and often considerable amounts of money. But, ultimately, the difficult work may reward you with greater satisfaction and a deeper relationship.

■ As we consider our sexuality, it is important to realize that sexual difficulties and problems are commonplace. But sex is more than orgasms or certain kinds of activities. Even if we have difficulties in some areas, there are other areas in which we may be fully sexual. If we have erectile or orgasmic problems, we can use our imagination to expand our repertoire of erotic activities. We can touch each other sensually, masturbate alone or with our partner, caress, kiss, eroticize and explore our bodies with fingers and tongues. We can enhance our sexuality if we look at sex as the mutual giving and receiving of erotic pleasure, rather than a command performance. By paying attention to our conditions for good sex, maintaining intimacy, and focusing on our erotic sensations and those of our partner, we can transform our sexual relationships.

> Impulse arrested spills over, and the flood is feeling, the flood is passion, the flood is even madness: It depends on the force of the current, the height and strength of the barrier. . . . Feeling lurks in that interval of time between desire and its consummation.
>
> —*Aldous Huxley (1894–1963)*

SUMMARY

Sexual Enhancement

- Many people experience sexual difficulties or problems at one time or another. Nearly half of the men and women in various surveys report occasional or frequent lack of desire, problems in arousal or orgasm, and painful intercourse. The widespread variability of sexual functioning suggests the "normality" of at least occasional sexual difficulties.

- *Sexual enhancement* refers to improving the quality of one's sexual relationship. Sexual-enhancement programs generally aim at providing accurate information about sexuality, developing commu-nication skills, fostering positive attitudes, and increasing self-awareness. Awareness of your own sexual needs is often critical to enhancing your sexuality. Enhancing sex includes the intensification of arousal.

Sexual Disorders and Dysfunctions

- *Sexual dysfunctions* are impaired physiological responses. *Sexual disorders* are problems affecting the brain's arousal capabilities.

- *Hypoactive sexual desire (HSD)* is low sexual desire. Depression is probably the most common cause. Anger toward the partner, stress, traumatic marital separation or divorce, loss of work, anxiety, and guilt are frequently associated with HSD. *Sexual aversion* is a consistently phobic response to sexual activities or the idea of such activities.

▪ Male sexual problems focus on the excitement stage. *Erectile dysfunction* is the inability to have or maintain an erection during intercourse. Erectile difficulties may occur because of fatigue, too much alcohol, smoking, depression, conflict, certain medical conditions, or a host of other transitory reasons.

▪ *Premature ejaculation* is the inability to control or delay ejaculation as long as desired, causing personal or interpersonal distress. In *inhibited ejaculation,* the penis is erect but the man is unable to ejaculate. In *delayed ejaculation,* the man is not able to ejaculate easily in intercourse.

▪ In *vaginismus,* the muscles around the vaginal entrance go into spasmodic contractions. Vaginismus is essentially a conditioned response that reflects fear, anxiety, or pain. *Dyspareunia,* painful intercourse, often occurs because a woman is not entirely aroused before her partner attempts intercourse. Sexual inhibitions, a poor relationship with her partner, or hormonal imbalances may contribute to dyspareunia.

▪ *Anorgasmia* refers to the condition of not being orgasmic. Absence of orgasm may occur from a lack of effective penile stimulation during intercourse, insufficient manual stimulation of the clitoris by the woman or her partner, or insufficient duration of intercourse. Not being orgasmic, however, does not mean a woman is not sexual; many anorgasmic women rate their sexual experiences positively.

Physical Causes of Sexual Dysfunctions

▪ Diabetes and alcoholism are the two leading causes of erectile dysfunctions. Some prescription drugs affect sexual responsiveness.

▪ Coital pain caused by inadequate lubrication and thinning vaginal walls often occurs as a result of decreased estrogen associated with menopause. Lubricants or hormone replacement therapy often resolves the difficulties.

▪ Illnesses or injuries may impair the vascular system, affecting penile vasocongestion. Microsurgery may correct the blood-flow problem, but it is not always successful. Medications may be injected into the penis to dilate the blood vessels. Oral medication may be used to stimulate an erection. Suction devices may be used to induce and maintain an erection. Erections may also be assisted by implanting a penile prosthesis.

Psychological Causes of Sexual Dysfunctions

▪ Sexual dysfunctions may have their origin in any number of psychological causes. The immediate causes of sexual dysfunctions lie in the current situation, including fatigue and stress, ineffective sexual behavior, sexual anxieties, and an excessive need to please one's partner. Conflict within the self, caused by religious teachings, guilt, negative learning, and internalized homophobia, can contribute to dysfunctions, as can relationship conflicts.

Treating Sexual Problems

▪ Masters and Johnson developed a cognitive-behavioral approach to sexual difficulties. They relabeled sexual problems as dysfunctions rather than neuroses or diseases, used direct behavior-modification practices, and treated couples rather than individuals. Treatment includes *sensate focus* exercises without intercourse, different "homework" exercises, and finally, "permission" to engage in sexual intercourse. Kaplan's psychosexual therapy program combines behavioral exercises with insight therapy.

▪ The *PLISSIT model* of sex therapy refers to four progressive levels: permission, limited information, specific suggestions, and intensive therapy. Individuals and couples can often resolve their difficulties by talking over their problems with their partners or friends, reading self-help books, and attending sex therapy groups. If they are unable to resolve their difficulties in these ways, they should consider intensive sex therapy.

▪ There are three significant concerns for gay men, bisexuals, and lesbians in sex therapy: (1) The context in which problems occur may differ significantly from that of heterosexuals; there may be issues revolving around anal eroticism and cunnilingus. (2) They must deal with both societal homophobia and internalized homophobia. (3) Gay men must deal with the association between sex and HIV/AIDS.

- In seeking professional assistance for a sexual problem, it is important to realize that seeking help is not a sign of personal weakness or failure, but rather a sign of strength.

SUGGESTED READING

Barbach, Lonnie. (1982). *For Each Other: Sharing Sexual Intimacy*. New York: Doubleday. A thoughtful book that explores women's sexuality; includes exercises.

Heiman, Julia, & LoPiccolo, Joseph. (1988). *Becoming Orgasmic: A Sexual Growth Program for Women*. Englewood Cliffs, NJ: Prentice-Hall. Suggestions on how to develop one's orgasmic responsiveness.

Leiblum, Sandra, & Rosen, Raymond (Eds.). (1990). *Principles and Practice of Sex Therapy: Update for the 1990s*. New York: Guilford Press. A collection of essays designed for professionals on various aspects of sex therapy.

Ogden, Gina. (1994). *Women Who Love Sex*. New York: Pocket Books. Profiles of women who take great pleasure in, and discover important meaning in, their sexuality.

Schnarch, David. (1997). *Passionate Marriage: Sex, Love, and Intimacy in Emotionally Committed Relationships*. New York: Norton. An honest, straightforward book that seeks to enhance the sex lives of individuals within committed relationships.

Torgovnick, Marianna. (1996). *Primitive Passions: Men, Women, and the Quest for Ecstasy*. New York: Random House. Insights into our ideas about spirituality and gender and the hidden but vital part of ourselves; encompasses religion, art, psychology, literature, and other aspects of our culture.

Zilbergeld, Bernie. (1992). *The New Male Sexuality*. New York: Bantam Books. The book most widely recommended by therapists for men on enhancing sexual relationships. Women can profit equally from it, not only for themselves but also in understanding male sexuality.

15

Sexually Transmitted Diseases

*T*HE CONSEQUENCES OF SEXUALLY TRANSMITTED DISEASES (STDs) are felt on both personal and societal levels. Personal costs range from inconvenience and discomfort to severe pain, serious illness, infertility, and even death. Society as a whole pays for the damage caused by STDs.

In this chapter and the next one, we discuss the factors that contribute to the "STD epidemic" in this country, and we explore the particular issues affecting women. This chapter contains an overview of the incidence, symptoms, and treatment of the principal STDs that affect Americans, with the exception of HIV/AIDS, which is the subject of Chapter 16. Much of this chapter is devoted to the prevention of STDs, including positive health behaviors, safer sex practices, and communication skills.

> O rose, thou art sick!
> The invisible worm
> That flies in the night,
> In the howling storm,
> Has found thy bed
> Of crimson joy,
> And his dark secret love
> Does thy life destroy.
>
> —*William Blake (1757–1827)*

X-RATED DISEASES: THE PSYCHOLOGICAL IMPACT OF STDS

Our culture extols the attractions of uninhibited sexual activity (during which no one ever uses a condom or contracts a disease) in movies, music, television programs, and advertising. But people who follow this lead and end up with a sexually transmitted disease may feel ashamed and guilty. What is going on here?

The deep ambivalence our society feels about sexuality is clearly brought to light by the way in which we deal with sexually transmitted diseases. If we think we have strep throat, we waste no time getting ourselves to a health center or doctor to obtain the appropriate medication. We probably take precautions not to spread the germs to those around us, and we have no hesitation about calling a friend or our boss and croaking, "Guess what? I've got strep throat!"

But let's say we're experiencing some discomfort when we urinate, and there's an unusual discharge. We will likely try to ignore the symptoms at first. We hope they'll go away if we just don't think about them. But they don't. Pretty soon, we're feeling some actual pain, and we know something is definitely not right. With fear and trepidation, we slink into the clinic or doctor's office, hoping we don't see anyone we know so we won't have to explain why we're there. The doctor or clinician examines our "private parts," which makes us very uncomfortable, and he or she asks us a lot of embarrassing questions. When we pick up our prescription, we can't look the pharmacist in the eye. And then there's the whole problem of telling our partner—or, worse yet, partners—about our predicament. Sound familiar? We hope not! But for millions of Americans, especially among those under age 25, at least part of this scenario will ring true.

Why all this emotion over an STD but not over strep throat? Where does all the fear, hesitation, denial, embarrassment, guilt, shame, and humiliation come from? Why are STDs the only class of illnesses we categorize by their *mode of transmission* rather than by the type of organism that causes them? All these questions stem from a common source: Americans are confused about sex! And because we, as a society, are so ambivalent and anxious, we don't deal with STDs rationally. We pretend we won't get them and ignore them when we do. We lie to ourselves and our partners. And even if we feel *we* wouldn't put someone down or think badly of him or her for having an

STD, if we get one ourselves, we feel embarrassed, ashamed, and guilty. We may even feel (or others may tell us) we are being punished by God or fate for being sinful or bad.

THE STD EPIDEMIC

The **incidence,** or number of new cases, of STDs occurring each year in this country is estimated to be more than 12 million (Figure 15.1). Three million of these cases, roughly one-quarter of all new cases, occur among teenagers (CDC, 1997f). Two-thirds of STD cases occur in people under age 25. Young women under age 24 may be more at risk for STDs than older women because the cells lining the cervix are immature and more easily infected and because younger women may have less immunity to infection (National Women's Health Resource Center [NWHRC], 1998). Based on reports from publicly funded clinics and private practitioners, public-health officials can only estimate the number of STD cases. Reporting regulations vary. For example, reports of syphilis are thought to be the most accurate because of the strict laws regarding both screening (testing) and reporting. Gonorrhea reporting, however, is less complete. Although public clinics are required to report gonorrhea cases, private physicians are not, and many, in fact, do not. Therefore, officials must calculate the numbers as best they can. The same is

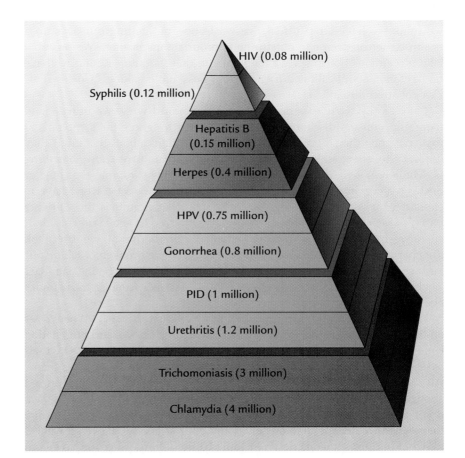

FIGURE 15.1   Annual STD Incidence.   It is estimated that each year more than 12 million Americans will get an STD. (*Source:* ASHA, 1998b.)

HIV (0.08 million)

Syphilis (0.12 million)

Hepatitis B (0.15 million)

Herpes (0.4 million)

HPV (0.75 million)

Gonorrhea (0.8 million)

PID (1 million)

Urethritis (1.2 million)

Trichomoniasis (3 million)

Chlamydia (4 million)

THIS SCALE WAS developed by William Yarber, Moham-mad Torabi, and C. Harold Veenker to measure the atti-tudes of young adults to determine whether they are at high or low risk for contracting a sexually transmitted disease. Follow the directions, and mark your responses to the statements below. Then calculate your risk as indi-cated.

Read each statement carefully. Indicate your first reaction by writing the letter that corresponds to your answer.

Key
SA = Strongly Agree
A = Agree
U = Undecided
D = Disagree
SD = Strongly Disagree

1. How one uses his/her sexuality has nothing to do with STDs.

2. It is easy to use the prevention methods that reduce one's chances of getting an STD.

3. Responsible sex is one of the best ways of reducing the risk of STDs.

4. Getting early medical care is the main key to pre-venting the harmful effects of STDs.

5. Choosing the right sex partner is important in reduc-ing the risk of getting an STD.

6. A high frequency of STDs should be a concern for all people.

7. People with an STD have a duty to get their sex part-ners to seek medical treatment.

8. The best way to get a sex partner to STD treatment is to take him/her to the doctor with you.

9. Changing one's sex habits is necessary once the pres-ence of an STD is known.

10. I would dislike having to follow the medical steps for treating an STD.

11. If I were sexually active, I would feel uneasy doing things before and after sex to prevent getting an STD.

12. If I were sexually active, it would be insulting if a sex partner suggested we use a condom to avoid getting an STD.

13. I dislike talking about STDs with my peers.

14. I would be uncertain about going to the doctor un-less I was sure I really had an STD.

continued

true for other STDs. Furthermore, a large number of STD cases may go entirely undiagnosed because they produce no symptoms or the symptoms are ignored and go untreated, especially among people with limited access to health care. It is quite likely that the **prevalence,** or total number of cases, of STDs is greater, not smaller, than the current estimates. This can be seen when the incidence of new cases is added to those that have already been diagnosed but cannot be cured, as is the case with viral STDs, such as herpes.

In addition to the ambivalence about being sexual that leads to risk tak-ing, there are several other reasons for the increase of STD cases. These fac-tors include changes in society, the particular biological characteristics of the disease organisms, and the way in which diseases are spread within groups of people.

A recent analysis of STD statistics has revealed wide discrepancies between racial and ethnic groups (CDC, 1997f). For example, gonorrhea rates in Black adolescents (15–19 years of age) are almost 25 times greater than those in White adolescents. The rate of primary and secondary syphilis in African Americans is nearly 50 times that in Whites, and among Hispanics, it is about 3 times that of Whites. Congenital syphilis (babies born with the disease) has decreased nationally in recent years, but births to Black and His-panic mothers accounted for 90% of the 1160 cases reported in 1996, although only 23% of the total female population is Black or Hispanic. These differ-ences in STD occurrence by race and ethnicity in the United States serve as

15. I would feel that I should take my sex partner with me to a clinic if I thought I had an STD.

16. It would be embarrassing to discuss STDs with one's partner if one were sexually active.

17. If I were to have sex, the chance of getting an STD makes me uneasy about having sex with more than one partner.

18. I like the idea of sexual abstinence (not having sex) as the best way of avoiding STDs.

19. If I had an STD, I would cooperate with public-health people to find the source of my infection.

20. If I had an STD, I would avoid exposing others while I was being treated.

21. I would have regular STD checkups if I were having sex with more than one partner.

22. I intend to look for STD signs before deciding to have sex with anyone.

23. I will limit my sexual activity to just one partner because of the chances of getting an STD.

24. I will avoid sexual contact any time I think there is even a slight chance of getting an STD.

25. The chance of getting an STD would not stop me from having sex.

26. If I had a chance, I would support community efforts toward controlling STDs.

27. I would be willing to work with others to make people aware of STD problems in my town.

Scoring

Calculate points as follows: Items 1, 10–14, 16, and 25: Strongly Agree = 5, Agree = 4, Undecided = 3, Disagree = 2, Strongly Disagree = 1. Items 2–9, 15, 17–24, 26, and 27: Strongly Agree = 1, Agree = 2, Undecided = 3, Disagree = 4, Strongly Disagree = 5.

The higher the score, the stronger the attitude that predisposes a person toward risky sexual behaviors. You may also calculate your points within three subscales: items 1–9 represent the "belief subscale," items 10–18 the "feeling subscale," and items 19–27 the "intention to act" subscale.

Source: Adapted from Yarber, Torabi, & Veenker, 1989.

reminders of the inequities in health status, socioeconomic status, and access to high-quality medical care that exist in this country. Reporting biases also undoubtedly play a role in race differentials.

Social Factors

Social and cultural factors contributing to the spread of STDs are listed below.

■ *Changes in acceptable sexual behavior.* Changing patterns have led to the widespread acceptance of sexual activity outside of marriage, for both women and men.

■ *Inconsistent condom use.* Beginning in the 1960s with the advent of the pill and the IUD, condom use declined dramatically, removing a very effective method of **prophylaxis,** or protection, from mainstream use. Condom use has begun to increase, however, in recent years because of the serious nature of AIDS. Still, it is obvious from the prevalence of STDs today that a large portion of the population remains unconvinced about the efficacy of condoms in STD prevention (Cates & Stone, 1992).

■ *Disagreements about sex education.* Educational efforts regarding STDs (and sexuality in general) are often hampered by vocal minorities who feel that knowledge about sex is what causes people to engage in it.

Social factors contributing to the spread of STDs include acceptance of sexual activity outside of marriage and the excessive consumption of alcohol.

■ *Confusion about moral and medical issues.* This confusion discourages funding for research and treatment of illnesses that are seen as somehow "deserved." For example, significant funding for AIDS research did not begin until it was clear that heterosexuals as well as gay men were threatened (Altman, 1985; Shilts, 1987).

■ *Inability of the health-care system to meet society's needs.* STDs are rampant in low-income urban areas where health services are limited and health-care workers may not be responsive to the community's needs. Racism, or at least an insensitivity to ethnic issues, may be partly responsible. Funds for public-health programs—to provide education, diagnosis, treatment, partner tracing, and follow-up—are limited, to say the least. Health-care agencies often find themselves vying with one another for funding.

■ *Alcohol and drug abuse.* These abuses contribute indirectly to the spread of STDs by impairing people's ability to make rational decisions about sexual conduct. The exchange of sex for drugs may contribute to the spread of STDs such as syphilis.

Biological Factors

The characteristics of certain organisms and the diseases they produce also contribute to STD transmission (Alexander, 1992).

▪ *Absence of symptoms.* Many STDs are **asymptomatic**—that is, they produce no symptoms, especially in the first stages. A person may have an STD and infect others without knowing that he or she is affected.

▪ *Resistance to treatment.* Because resistant strains of viruses, bacteria, and other pathogens are continuously developing, antibiotics that have worked in the past may no longer be effective. Infected people may continue to transmit the disease, either because they believe they have been cured or because they never have any symptoms. The clinician or the patient may underrate the value of a follow-up examination to ensure that the initial treatment has worked or to try an alternative medication if necessary.

▪ *Lack of a cure.* Some STDs, such as herpes, genital warts, and HIV, cannot be cured. A person who carries any of these viruses is always theoretically able to transmit them to others.

PRINCIPAL STDS

In this section we discuss the principal STDs by their mode of transmission and infection, starting with chlamydia and progressing through the bacterial STDs (gonorrhea, urinary tract infections, and syphilis) and then the viral STDs (genital warts, genital herpes, and hepatitis). Table 15.1 (pages 468–469) summarizes information about the principal sexually transmitted diseases.

Chlamydia

The most common STD in the United States, affecting more than 4 million people each year, is caused by an organism called *Chlamydia trachomatis,* commonly known as **chlamydia,** which has properties of both a bacterium and a virus. It affects the urinary tract and reproductive organs of both women and men. Chlamydia is responsible for as many as 80% of all cases of tubal infertility (NWHRC, 1998). Furthermore, women who develop the infection 3 or more times have as great as a 75% chance of becoming infertile. Untreated chlamydia can be quite painful and can lead to conditions requiring hospitalization, including acute arthritis. Infants of mothers infected with chlamydia may develop dangerous eye, ear, and lung infections.

Although *C. trachomatis* has undoubtedly been around for centuries, it is only within the past 15 years that large-scale screening has been possible. Chlamydial infection appears to occur throughout the general population, although the rates are highest in the 15- to 19-year-old and 20- to 24-year-old populations (CDC, 1997f).

About 80% of women with chlamydia show no symptoms until serious complications have arisen (Ault & Faro, 1993; Keim, Woodard, & Anderson, 1992). When early symptoms do occur, they are likely to include:

▪ Unusual vaginal discharge

▪ Burning sensation when urinating and frequent urination

- Unexplained vaginal bleeding between menstrual periods (Krettek, Arkin, Chaisilwattana, & Monif, 1993)

Later symptoms, occurring up to several months after exposure, are:

- Low abdominal pain
- Bleeding between menstrual periods
- Low-grade fever

One-third to one-half of men are asymptomatic when first infected. Men's symptoms may include:

- Unusual discharge from the penis
- Burning sensation when urinating
- Itching and burning around the urethral opening (urethritis)
- Pain and swelling of the testicles
- Low-grade fever

The last two symptoms may indicate the presence of chlamydia-related **epididymitis,** inflammation of the epididymis. Untreated epididymitis can lead to infertility. For both women and men, early symptoms appear 7–21 days after exposure, if they appear at all. Chlamydia responds well to antibiotic therapy, generally with doxycycline.

In many instances, chlamydia is not detected unless the affected person is tested for it in the process of being treated for something else, or unless he or she has been named as a partner, or "contact," of someone diagnosed with chlamydial infection (CDC, 1997f). Because so many people with chlamydial infections are asymptomatic, it is a sound health practice for those who are sexually active—especially if they have numerous partners—to be checked for it regularly (every 3–6 months). Several tests can be used to detect chlamydia. One kind tests a urine sample; another tests fluid from a man's penis or a woman's cervix. A Pap smear does not test for chlamydia (American Social Health Association [ASHA], 1998a).

Gonorrhea

Gonorrhea, the second most prevalent STD, affects an estimated 800,000 Americans yearly (ASHA, 1998b). Popularly referred to as "the clap" or "drip," gonorrhea is caused by the *Neisseria gonorrhoeae* bacterium. The organism thrives in the warm, moist environment provided by the mucous membranes lining the mouth, throat, vagina, cervix, urethra, and rectum. Symptoms of gonorrhea, if they occur, appear within 2–21 days of exposure. Men tend to experience the symptoms of gonorrhea more readily than women, notably as a watery discharge ("drip") from the penis, the first sign of urethritis. ("Gonorrhea" is from the Greek, meaning "flow of seed.") Other symptoms in men may include:

- Itching or burning at the urethral opening
- Pain when urinating

If untreated, the disease soon produces these other symptoms:

- Thick yellow or greenish discharge
- Increasing discomfort or pain with urination

I had the honor
To receive, worse luck!
From a certain empress
A boiling hot piss.

—*Frederick the Great of Prussia*
(1712–1786)

TABLE 15.1   Principal Sexually Transmitted Diseases

STD and Infecting Organism	Symptoms	Time from Exposure to Occurrence	Medical Treatment	Comments
Chlamydia (Chlamydia trachomatis)	Women: 80% asymptomatic; others may have vaginal discharge or pain with urination. Men: 30–50% asymptomatic; others may have discharge from penis, burning urination, pain and swelling in testicles, or persistent low fever.	7–21 days	Antibiotics	If untreated, may lead to pelvic inflammatory disease (PID) and subsequent infertility in women.
Genital herpes (herpes simplex virus)	Small sore or itchy bumps on genitals, becoming blisters that may rupture, forming painful sores; possibly swollen lymph nodes; flulike symptoms with first outbreak.	3–20 days	No cure, although acyclovir and related medications may relieve symptoms. Nonmedical treatments may also help relieve symptoms.	Virus remains in the body, and outbreaks of contagious sores may recur. Many people have no symptoms after the first outbreak.
Genital warts (human papillomavirus)	Variously appearing bumps (smooth, flat, round, clustered, fingerlike, white, pink, brown, etc.) on genitals: usually penis, anus, vulva, vagina, or cervix.	1–6 months (usually within 3 months)	Surgical removal by freezing or laser therapy if warts are large or cause problems. (About 80% of warts eventually reappear.)	Virus remains in the body after warts are removed.
Gonorrhea (Neisseria gonorrhoeae)	Women: 50–80% asymptomatic; others may have symptoms similar to chlamydia. Men: itching, burning or pain with urination, discharge from penis ("drip").	2–21 days	Antibiotics	If untreated, may lead to pelvic inflammatory disease (PID) and subsequent infertility in women.
Hepatitis (hepatitis A or B virus)	Fatigue, diarrhea, nausea, abdominal pain, jaundice, darkened urine due to impaired liver function.	1–4 months	No medical treatment available; rest and fluids are prescribed until the disease runs its course.	Hepatitis B more commonly spread through sexual contact. Both A and B can be prevented by vaccinations.

TABLE 15.1   continued

STD and Infecting Organism	Symptoms	Time from Exposure to Occurrence	Medical Treatment	Comments
HIV infection and AIDS (human immunodeficiency virus)	Possible flulike symptoms but often no symptoms during early phase. Variety of later symptoms, including weight loss, persistent fever, night sweats, diarrhea, swollen lymph nodes, bruiselike rash, persistent cough.	Several months to several years (most commonly within 6 months)	No cure available, although antiviral drug combinations may suppress viral activity, and many symptoms and opportunistic infections can be treated with medications. Good general health practices can delay or reduce the severity of symptoms.	Cannot be self-diagnosed; a blood test must be performed to determine the presence of the virus.
Pelvic inflammatory disease (PID) (women only)	Low abdominal pain, bleeding between menstrual periods, persistent low fever.	Several weeks or months after exposure to chlamydia or gonorrhea (if untreated)	Penicillin or other antibiotics; surgery	Caused by untreated chlamydia or gonorrhea; may lead to chronic problems such as arthritis and infertility.
Syphilis (*Treponema pallidum*)	*Stage 1:* Red, painless sore (chancre) at bacteria's point of entry. *Stage 2:* Skin rash over body, including palms of hands and soles of feet.	*Stage 1:* 1–12 weeks *Stage 2:* 6 weeks to 6 months after chancre appears	Penicillin or other antibiotics	Easily cured, but untreated syphilis can lead to ulcers of internal organs and eyes, heart disease, neurological disorders, and insanity.
Urethritis (various organisms)	Painful and/or frequent urination; discharge from penis; women may be asymptomatic.	1–3 weeks	Antibiotics	Laboratory testing is important to determine appropriate treatment.
Vaginitis (*Gardnerella vaginalis*, *Trichomonas vaginalis*, or *Candida albicans*)	Intense itching of vagina and/or vulva, unusual discharge with foul or fishy odor, painful intercourse. Men who carry organisms may be asymptomatic.	2–21 days	Depends on organism; oral medications include metronidazole and clindamycin. Vaginal medications include clotrimazole and miconazole.	Not always acquired sexually. Other causes include contact with a contaminated toilet seat, stress, oral contraceptives, pregnancy, tight pants or underwear, antibiotics, douching, and dietary

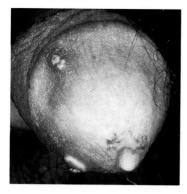

Gonorrhea infection in men is often characterized by a discharge from the penis.

Although most men seek treatment by this stage, some do not. Even if the symptoms diminish, the bacteria are still present. Those who do not get treatment can still infect their partners and may develop serious complications, such as abscesses of the prostate gland and epididymitis.

Up to 80% of women with gonorrhea show no symptoms or very mild symptoms, which many tend to ignore. Because untreated gonorrhea, like untreated chlamydia, can lead to pelvic inflammatory disease (PID), it is important for women to be on guard for symptoms and to be treated if they think they may have been exposed to gonorrhea (if they have had multiple sex partners, for example). Symptoms a woman may experience include:

- Thick yellow or white vaginal discharge
- Burning sensation when urinating
- Unusual pain during menstruation
- Severe lower abdominal pain

Gonorrhea may be passed to an infant during childbirth, causing conjunctivitis (an eye infection) and even blindness if not treated. (Most states require that all newborn infants have their eyes treated with antibiotics in the event that they may have been exposed to gonorrhea in the birth canal.) Penicillin and related antibiotics are effective against most strains of gonorrhea; tetracycline may be used in the case of allergy or resistance to penicillin. In 1996, however, 29% of the gonorrhea diagnosed was resistant to penicillin, tetracycline, or both (CDC, 1997f). Because *N. gonorrhoeae* can evolve rapidly into penicillin-resistant strains, a variety of antibiotics may need to be tried before the infection is eliminated (Hook, Sondheimer, & Zenilman, 1995). There is strong evidence that gonococcal infections facilitate HIV transmission; however, the specific mechanism through which this occurs is unclear (CDC, 1997f).

Urinary Tract Infections (NGU/NSU)

Both women and men are subject to sexually transmitted infections of the urinary tract. Among the several organisms that cause these infections, the most common and most serious is *Chlamydia* (ASHA 1998b). *Urinary tract infections* are sometimes referred to as **nongonococcal urethritis (NGU)** or **nonspecific urethritis (NSU).** In men **urethritis,** inflammation of the urethra, may produce:

- Burning sensation when urinating
- Burning or itching around the opening of the penis
- White or yellowish discharge from the penis

Women are likely to be asymptomatic. They may not realize they are infected until a male partner is diagnosed. If a woman does have symptoms, they are likely to include:

- Itching or burning while urinating
- Unusual vaginal discharge

It is important to have a laboratory test for an unusual discharge from the penis or vagina so that the appropriate antibiotic can be prescribed. Tetracycline and erythromycin are usually effective against NGU. Untreated

NGU may result in permanent damage to the reproductive organs of both men and women, resulting in infertility; problems in pregnancy, resulting in premature delivery or low birth weight; and/or eye, ear, and lung infections in newborns. The most common urinary tract infection among women, cystitis, is discussed later in this chapter.

Syphilis

When **syphilis** first appeared in Europe in the late 1490s, its early manifestations were considerably more horrible than they appear today. Whether syphilis was introduced to Europe from the New World by Spanish explorers or from Africa by those who plied the slave trade is debated by historians. Its legacy of suffering, however, is debated by no one.

In the 1940s, it was found that penicillin very effectively killed *Treponema pallidum,* the bacterium that causes syphilis. At last the disease that had caused widespread pain, anguish, and death for centuries began to fade from view in most parts of the developed world. In the United States, strict control measures were instituted, requiring the testing of many citizens for syphilis, including those in the armed services and couples seeking marriage licenses. Health departments and medical laboratories were (and are) required to report all cases of syphilis to the government. Despite these efforts, however, beginning in the 1980s, the number of cases in the United States began increasing dramatically, especially within inner cities. In 1990, the syphilis rate was the highest it had been since the 1940s and more than 10 times as high as rates in other developed countries (Kilmarx et al., 1997). Since then, the rate has declined to an estimated 120,000 cases annually (ASHA, 1998b). The current epidemic appears to be concentrated mainly in urban areas and among young, heterosexual minority populations. In some instances it appears to be correlated with crack cocaine use, possibly related to the practice of exchanging sex (principally fellatio) for the drug (Kilmarx et al., 1997).

T. pallidum is a spiral-shaped bacterium (a **spirochete**) that requires a warm, moist environment, such as the genitals or the mucous membranes inside the mouth, to survive. It is spread through vaginal, anal, and oral sexual contact. A mother infected with syphilis can pass it to the fetus through the placenta. Because neonatal syphilis can lead to brain damage and death, it is imperative for pregnant women to be screened for it within the first trimester. If they are treated during this period, the newborn will not be affected. Untreated syphilis in adults may lead to brain damage, heart disease, blindness, or death. As it appears today, syphilis progresses through four discrete stages, although it is most often treated during the first two:

1. *Primary syphilis.* The first symptom of syphilis appears 1–12 weeks after contact with an infected partner. It is a small, red, pea-sized bump that soon develops into a round, painless sore called a **chancre** (SHANK-er). The chancre may be covered by a crusty scab; it may be hard around the edges and ringed by a pink border. It appears at the site where the bacterium initially entered the body, usually within the vagina or on the cervix in women or on the glans of the penis in men. The chancre may also appear on the labia, the shaft of the penis, the testicles, or the rectum, within the mouth, or on the lips. Unless it is in a visible area, it may not be noticed. Without treatment, it will disappear in 1–5 weeks,

And he died in the year fourteen-twenty.
Of the syphilis, which he had a-plenty.

—*François Rabelais (1490–1553)*

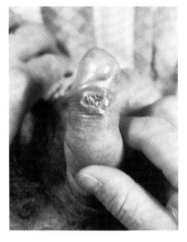

The first symptom of syphilis is a red, pea-sized bump called a chancre at the site where the bacterium originally entered the body.

The Tuskegee Syphilis Study: "A Tragedy of Race and Medicine"

IN 1932 IN MACON COUNTY, Alabama, the U.S. Public Health Service, with the assistance of the Tuskegee Institute, a prestigious Black college, recruited 600 African American men to participate in an experiment involving the effects of untreated syphilis on Blacks. Of this group, 399 men had been diagnosed with syphilis, and 201 were controls. The study was originally meant to last 6–9 months, but "the drive to satisfy scientific curiosity resulted in a 40-year experiment that followed the men to 'end point' (autopsy)" (Thomas & Quinn, 1991). The history of this experiment—the racial biases that created it, the cynicism that fueled it, and the callousness that allowed it to continue—is chillingly chronicled by James Jones (1993) in *Bad Blood: The Tuskegee Experiment—A Tragedy of Race and Medicine.*

The purpose of the study was to determine if there were racial differences in the developmental course of syphilis. There was speculation in the (White) medical world that tertiary syphilis affected the cardiovascular systems of Blacks, whereas it affected Whites neurologically. The racial prejudice behind this motivation may seem hard to fathom today, yet, as we shall see, the repercussions still reverberate strongly through African American communities.

Much of the original funding for the study came from the Julius Rosenwald Foundation (a philanthropic organization dedicated to improving conditions within African American communities), with the understanding that treatment was to be a part of the study. Although Alabama law required prompt treatment of diagnosed venereal diseases, the Public Health Service managed to ensure that treatment was withheld from the participants. In the 1940s, the Public Health Service kept draft boards from ordering treatment for 250 A-1 registrants who were part of the experiment. It involved health departments across the country in a conspiracy to withhold treatment from subjects who had moved from Macon County. Even after 1951, when penicillin became the standard treatment for syphilis, the Public Health Service

refused to treat the Tuskegee "subjects" on the grounds that the experiment was a "never-again-to-be-repeated opportunity" (Jones, 1993).

The Tuskegee participants were never informed that they had syphilis. The Public Health Service, assuming they would not understand medical terminology, referred to it as "bad blood," a term used to describe a variety of ailments in the rural South. The participants were not told their disease was sexually transmitted, nor were they told it could be passed from mother to fetus. We can only speculate on the extent to which this wanton disregard for human life allowed the disease to spread and wreak its misery and death in the Black South and beyond.

It was not until 1966 that anyone within the public-health system expressed any moral concern over the study. Peter Buxtun, an investigator for the Public Health Service, wrote a concerned letter to the director of the Division of Venereal Diseases, William Brown. Nothing changed. In 1968, Buxtun wrote a second letter, questioning the study's ramifications in light of the current climate of racial unrest in the nation. Dr. Brown showed the letter to the Centers for Disease Control (CDC), which convened a panel to discuss the issue. Having reviewed the study, the panel decided to allow it to continue until "end point." In 1972, Peter Buxtun told his story to Edith Lederer, a friend who was an international reporter for the Associated Press. Ultimately the story was assigned to Jean Heller, who broke it in the *Washington Post* on July 25, 1972, whereupon it became front-page news across the country. A congressional subcommittee headed by Senator Edward Kennedy began hearings in 1973. The results included the rewriting of the Department of Health, Education, and Welfare's regulations on the use of human subjects in scientific experiments. A $1.8 billion class-action suit was filed on behalf of the Tuskegee participants and their heirs. A settlement for $10 million was made out of court.

Since the original disclosure and outcry, there has

but the bacterium remains in the body, and the person is still highly contagious.

2. *Secondary syphilis.* Untreated primary syphilis develops into secondary syphilis about 6 weeks after the chancre has disappeared. The principal symptom at this stage is a skin rash that neither itches nor hurts. The rash is likely to occur on the palms of the hands and the soles of the feet, as well as on other areas of the body. The individual may also

been little discussion of the Tuskegee experiment within the public-health system or in the public media. (David Feldman's powerful 1989 play, *Miss Evers' Boys,* and an hour-long 1992 PBS documentary are the exceptions.) Stephen Thomas and Sandra Crouse Quinn (1991) of the Minority Health Research Laboratory at the University of Maryland's Department of Health cite the "failure of public health professionals to comprehensively discuss the Tuskegee experiment" as an ongoing "source of misinformation [that] helps to maintain a barrier between the Black community and health care service providers." Current public-health efforts to control the spread of HIV infection, AIDS, and other STDs raise the specter of genocide among many members of the African American community. For example, in 1990, as part of an HIV education program conducted by the Southern Christian Leadership Conference with CDC funding, a survey of 1056 Black church members found that 35% of them believed AIDS to be a form of genocide and another 30% were unsure. Thirty-four percent thought the virus was manmade, and an additional 44% were unsure.

A tremendous gap exists in this country between the health-care needs of minority-status families and the beliefs within those communities. In order to begin to close the gap, we must, as stated by Thomas and Quinn (1991), "recognize that Blacks' belief in AIDS as a form of genocide is a legitimate attitudinal barrier rooted in the history of the Tuskegee Syphilis study." On both physiological and psychological levels, there is much healing to be done.

(For reflections on the legacy of the Tuskegee study, see Caplan, 1992; King, 1992; and J. H. Jones, 1992.)

'NOW can we give him penicillin?'

Editorial cartoon by Tony Auth, *Philadelphia Inquirer,* July 1972. (Courtesy Tony Auth)

experience flulike symptoms. The rash or other symptoms may be very mild or may pass unnoticed. The person is still contagious.

3. *Latency.* If secondary syphilis is not treated, the symptoms disappear within 2–6 weeks, beginning the latent stage. The infected person may feel no further symptoms for years, or perhaps will never experience any. Or he or she may have symptoms that are vague or difficult to diagnose without a blood test to screen for *T. pallidum.* After about a

year, the bacterium can no longer be spread to sex partners, although a pregnant women can still transmit the disease to her fetus.

4. *Tertiary syphilis.* In the United States, syphilis is rarely seen in its tertiary stage because treatment usually prevents the disease from progressing that far. The symptoms of tertiary syphilis may appear years after the initial infection. Possible effects include the following:

  ▪ Gummas (large ulcers) within the muscles, liver, lungs, eyes, or endocrine glands
  ▪ Heart disease
  ▪ Neurosyphilis (leading to "general paralysis" or "paresis,") involving the brain and spinal cord, and leading to muscular paralysis, psychosis, and death

In the primary, secondary, and early latent stages, syphilis can be successfully treated with penicillin (Goldmeier & Hay, 1993). Later stages may require additional injections. Other antibiotics can be used if the infected person is allergic to penicillin.

Genital Warts

About 500,000 to 1 million Americans develop **genital warts** every year (CDC 1997f). The virus responsible for these warts, **human papillomavirus (HPV),** exists in numerous different strains; one of the most prevalent types is *condyloma acuminatum.* An estimated two-thirds of the partners of people with HPV contract the infection (Cowley, 1991). The virus is transmitted through direct contact with the warts, which are highly contagious. Many cases may be passed along by people who are asymptomatic or haven't noticed the warts. Studies of people with genital warts show that HPV is correlated with earlier onset of sexual activity, more sexual partners, and less condom use than among controls (Shah, 1997). Some types of HPV are being studied as risk factors for cervical cancer. Additional factors such as first intercourse at an early age, smoking, and the presence of other STDs combined with HPV may increase one's risk of developing cervical cancer (ASHA, 1997b). Therefore, any woman with a history of genital warts should have an annual Pap smear. The virus has also been found in cancers of other organs, including the penis and anus.

Genital warts may appear within several weeks after sexual relations with an infected person, may take months to appear, or may never appear (ASHA, 1997b). When they do appear, they generally range in size from a pencil point to a quarter of an inch in diameter. They may be flat, bumpy, round, or smooth; white, gray, pink, or brown. Some look like miniature cauliflowers; others, like tiny fingers. In men, genital warts usually develop on the shaft or glans of the penis or around the anus. In women, they are found on the cervix, vaginal wall, vulva, or anus. Warts inside the cervix, vagina, or rectum are difficult to detect without examination. The virus can be transmitted from an infected pregnant mother to her baby during vaginal delivery if warts are present on the cervix or in the vagina. For reasons that are not yet understood, genital warts proliferate during pregnancy and regress after delivery. If the warts cause discomfort or problems (such as interfering with urination), they may be removed by cryosurgery (freezing) or laser surgery. Removal of the warts does not eliminate HPV from the person's sys-

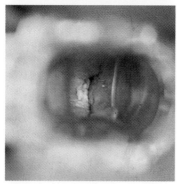

Genital warts appear in a variety of forms. In women, genital warts may appear on the vaginal wall.

tem. Because the virus can lie dormant in the cells, in some cases warts can return months or even years after treatment (ASHA, 1997b). The extent to which a person can still transmit HPV after the visible warts have been removed is unknown. A condom may help to prevent transmission.

Genital Herpes

Genital herpes, caused by the **herpes simplex virus (HSV),** is carried by an estimated 45 million Americans, or roughly 1 in 5 people over age 12 (Doheny, 1998). Since the 1970s, diagnoses of genital herpes have increased 30%. The greatest increase in the incidence of genital herpes is in White teens and young adults. The incidence is increasing by approximately 200,000–500,000 each year (CDC, 1997f). HSV exists in two strains: HSV type 1, which is usually responsible for cold sores and fever blisters around the mouth; and HSV type 2, which is usually associated with genital lesions. (An estimated 4 out of 5 Americans carry the HSV type 1 virus [ASHA, 1997a].) Both types of HSV, however, can and do develop equally well on the mouth or genitals. Serious complications from HSV are rare in adults but may result if the individual's general health is not good or the immune system is depressed. Having genital herpes can put people at greater risk for HIV because the presence of the herpes lesions can facilitate its transmission (Doheny, 1998). Although the spread of herpes to newborns is rare, and most mothers with a history of herpes have normal vaginal deliveries, newborns can contract HSV if they come into contact with active lesions during birth. This may result in infections of the eyes, skin, or mucous membranes; infections of the central nervous system; or even death.

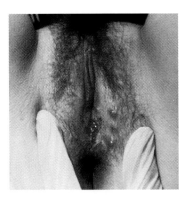

Women may develop herpes lesions on the vulva, perineum, or anus or within the vagina.

For many people with HSV, the initial infection is the most severe. Sometimes it is the only outbreak a person experiences. Within 3–20 days after exposure, small bumps called vesicles or papules appear on the genitals: penis, anus, perineum, vulva, or vagina. The papules may itch at first; they then form blisters or pustules that rupture, forming small, often painful, ulcers. These sores may be further irritated by tight clothing, moisture, or urine. In addition, an affected person may experience:

- Swollen lymph nodes in the groin
- Flulike symptoms

The first outbreak lasts an average of 12 days, and subsequent outbreaks may last 5 days each. Individuals with HSV experience an average of 4–5 subsequent outbreaks. They may begin with feelings of itchiness or tingling at the site where the lesions will appear. Just prior to the outbreak is a period of a few days known as the **prodrome.** During this time, and while there are actual lesions, the virus is active; live viruses are shed from the affected areas and are spread upon contact. Some people with HSV may shed the virus without experiencing symptoms (ASHA, 1996c). Although the mechanism of recurrence is poorly understood and highly individual, people who experience recurrent herpes outbreaks note they are often preceded by excessive friction in the genital area. Outbreaks have also been reported following surgical trauma.

Herpes Hysteria   Although most people with HSV experience little or no discomfort from it after the initial outbreak, they may experience intense psychological pain and distress from the knowledge that they are carrying an incurable STD. Even though most Americans carry one or both types of HSV, society as a whole still tends to regard people with STDs as deviant, immoral, or otherwise suspect. This attitude, so indicative of our national ambivalence about sexuality, does little to help us deal realistically with STDs, especially those that cannot be cured.

Most people who experience symptoms of HSV find them manageable, if sometimes uncomfortable. Drug therapy may be helpful for those with persistent symptoms. With reasonable caution (abstinence during outbreaks, condoms if one is unsure) and candor (disclosure of risks to one's partner), the likelihood of spreading HSV is significantly reduced. Care should also be taken not to spread oral herpes to the genitals via oral sex. Fear of stigmatization is one of the principal factors responsible for the spread of herpes because it keeps people from dealing rationally with the issue.

Managing HSV   There is no treatment that can cure herpes, but there are medications that can help to keep the virus in check (ASHA, 1996c). The antiviral drug acyclovir (trade name Zovirax) is often helpful in reducing or suppressing HSV symptoms. It can be administered either orally (as a pill) or topically (as an ointment). Valacyclovir (trade name Valtrex) uses acyclovir as its active ingredient, but it is better absorbed by the body and can be taken less often. Famcyclovir (trade name Famvir) works in a similar way to acyclovir, but it is also better absorbed and can be taken less often. All three drugs, which appear to be equally effective, work by disrupting the virus's ability to reproduce. All are safe and have virtually no side effects. Genital herpes appears to respond better to the oral than to the topical medications. Patients can choose either episodic therapy, which involves taking medication during an outbreak to speed healing, or suppressive therapy, which means taking antiviral medication every day to hold HSV in check.

Other methods reported to be useful in preventing, shortening the duration of, or lessening the severity of recurrent outbreaks are:

- *Plenty of rest.* For the immune system to work at its highest capacity, the body needs rest.

- *A balanced diet.* Healthy eating also fosters a healthy immune system. Avoiding foods that appear to trigger outbreaks may be helpful.

- *L-lysine.* The amino acid L-lysine, taken orally, is reportedly helpful to a number of people.

- *No tight clothes.* Tight jeans, tight or nylon underwear, and nylon pantyhose create an ideal warm, moist environment for HSV. Loose-fitting cotton clothing is recommended.

- *Keeping the area cool and dry.* If lesions do appear, an icepack may provide temporary relief. Baby powder or cornstarch may be used to absorb moisture.

- *Aspirin or other pain relievers.* Medications may be helpful in relieving the discomfort that is associated with an outbreak.

Reasonable Precautions   HSV can be spread by hand to another person or even to a different location on one's own body. Anyone experiencing an outbreak should wash his or her hands frequently with soap. Caution should also be taken not to touch one's eyes (or another's) if one has touched a lesion. Serious eye infection can result. Individuals should tell their partners and together decide about what precautions are right for them. Because having sex during a recognized outbreak puts an uninfected partner at risk, one should abstain from sex when signs and symptoms of either oral or genital herpes are present. Use of a condom reduces the chance of infection. Spermicides should be used along with condoms, not in place of them. Pregnant women or their partners who have HSV should be sure to discuss precautionary procedures with their medical practitioners.

Hepatitis

Hepatitis is a viral disease affecting the liver. The most common types of the virus that can be sexually transmitted are hepatitis A and hepatitis B. A third type, hepatitis C, is a common virus passed primarily through contact with infected blood; risk of transmittal from sexual partners or from mothers to newborns during birth is low (CDC, 1997c). Hepatitis A is most often contracted as a result of unsanitary conditions, in contaminated food or water. It is believed to be transmitted sexually mainly via infected fecal matter—for example, during oral-anal sex ("rimming") or anal intercourse. A highly effective vaccine can prevent hepatitis A, and immune serum globulin injections provide some immunity. Although the symptoms of hepatitis A are similar to those of hepatitis B, the disease is not considered as dangerous. Affected individuals usually recover within 6 weeks and develop immunity against reinfection.

Hepatitis B is 100 times more infectious than HIV (ASHA, 1996a). It is commonly spread through sexual contact, in blood, semen, saliva, vaginal secretions, and urine. It can also be contracted by using contaminated needles and syringes, including those used in ear piercing, acupuncture, and tattooing, or by sharing the toothbrush or razor of an infected person. It affects an estimated 300,000 Americans annually, most of whom are adolescents and young adults (ASHA, 1996a). Although most are unaware of its presence, an estimated 1.5 million people in the United States are chronic carriers of the virus. The incidence of hepatitis B is declining among gay men (probably due to safer sex practices) and increasing among heterosexuals. Anyone can get hepatitis B, but those in their teens and twenties are at greater risk. Because hepatitis B spreads "silently," that is, without easily noticeable symptoms, many people are not aware it is in their communities.

Hepatitis B can be prevented by a simple, widely available vaccination. The Centers for Disease Control and Prevention recommend routine vaccination for those most at risk, including people with more than one sexual partner, teenagers, gay men, IV drug users, and health-care workers who come into contact with blood. Screening for hepatitis B is also recommended for pregnant women so that their newborns can be immediately vaccinated if necessary. The vaccine is safe and effective and provides lasting protection.

Hepatitis C, once referred to as "non-A, non-B hepatitis," now infects 30,000 Americans annually, 85% of whom develop chronic infections. Currently, 4 million people nationwide (four times the number of those infected with HIV) carry this blood-borne virus (Hall, 1998). Risk of infection from sexual activity is low unless it involves blood contact; having multiple sex partners increases the risk. Most cases of hepatitis C can be traced to blood transfusions before 1992, the sharing of needles during injection drug use, and accidental needle-sticks. Known as "the silent epidemic," the disease damages the liver over the course of many years, even decades, before symptoms appear. To date, there is no vaccine.

The symptoms of hepatitis include:

- Fatigue

- Diarrhea

- Nausea

- Abdominal pain

- Jaundice (caused by accumulating blood pigments not destroyed by the liver)

- Darkened urine

- Enlarged liver, which can lead to cirrhosis or liver cancer (Your chances of getting liver cancer are 200 times higher if you are a hepatitis B carrier.)

There is no medical treatment for hepatitis. Rest and fluids are recommended until the disease runs its course, generally in a few weeks. Occasionally, serious liver damage or death results.

Vaginal Infections

Vaginal infections, or **vaginitis,** affect 3 out of 4 women at least once in their lives. These infections are often, although not always, sexually transmitted. They may also be induced by an upset in the normal balance of vaginal organisms by such things as stress, birth control pills, antibiotics, nylon underwear, and douching. The three principal types of vaginitis are bacterial vaginosis, candidiasis, and trichomonal infection.

Bacterial Vaginosis   Bacterial vaginal infections, referred to as **bacterial vaginosis,** may be caused by a number of different organisms, most commonly *Gardnerella vaginalis,* often a normal inhabitant of the healthy vagina. An overabundance of *Gardnerella,* however, produces:

- Vaginal itching

- Whitish discharge, with a fishy odor that is more pronounced when the discharge is combined with semen

Most men who carry *Gardnerella* are asymptomatic; some may experience inflammation of the urethra or glans. Bacterial vaginosis in women is commonly treated with metronidazole (Flagyl), unless the woman is pregnant or breast-feeding; then clindamycin may be prescribed. Some people experience unpleasant side effects, such as nausea, with metronidazole. There is disagreement about the usefulness of treating men unless they actually have symptoms (Bowie, Hammerschlag, & Martin, 1994; Braverman & Strasburger, 1994). However, if a man has symptoms, then treating him is necessary to prevent infection or reinfection of his partner.

Candidiasis   The fungus *Candida albicans* is normally present in the healthy vagina of many women. Various conditions may cause *C. albicans* to multiply rapidly, producing the condition known as **candidiasis** (can-di-DYE-a sis), moniliasis, or, more commonly, yeast infection. Symptoms include:

- Intense itching of the vagina and vulva
- A lumpy, cottage-cheese-like discharge

   C. albicans may be transmitted sexually, although this does not necessarily lead to symptoms. Conditions that may induce candidiasis include dietary imbalances (eating large amounts of dairy products, sugars, and artificial sweeteners), taking antibiotics or birth control pills, and pregnancy. The yeast organism, if not already present in the woman's vagina, can be transmitted from the anus via wiping back-to-front or on the surface of a menstrual pad; it can also be transmitted through sexual contact, because the foreskin of an uncircumcised male partner can harbor the organism. Clotrimazole (Gyne-Lotrimin) and miconazole (Monostat) are available over the counter as vaginal creams or suppositories for the treatment of yeast infections. A woman who is uncertain about the symptoms should be medically diagnosed.

Trichomoniasis   *Trichomonas vaginalis* is a single-celled protozoan responsible for about 25% of all cases of vaginitis. **Trichomoniasis,** commonly referred to simply as "trich" (pronounced TRICK), is a hardy parasite that may survive for several hours on damp items such as towels and toilet seats. Its principal mode of transmission, however, is sexual intercourse. Even though they are often asymptomatic, men may carry *Trichomonas.* If men do exhibit symptoms, they tend to be those associated with urethritis (Krieger et al., 1993). The symptoms of trichomoniasis can be very unpleasant for women. They include:

- Intense itching of the vagina and vulva
- A frothy, unpleasant-smelling vaginal discharge
- Painful intercourse

   Metronidazole (Flagyl) is effective in treating trichomoniasis. To prevent reinfection, both partners must be treated, even if the man is asymptomatic (Braverman & Strasburger, 1994).

Other STDs

A number of other sexually transmitted diseases appear in the United States but with less frequency than they do in some developing countries.

- *Chancroid* is a painful sore or group of sores on the penis, caused by the bacterium *Hemophilus ducreyi.* Women may carry the bacterium but are generally asymptomatic for chancroid.

- *Cytomegalovirus (CMV)* is a virus of the herpes group that affects people with depressed immune systems. A fetus may be infected with CMV in the uterus.

- *Enteric infections* are intestinal infections caused by bacteria, viruses, protozoans, or other organisms that are normally carried in the intestinal

> Sex is a pleasurable exercise in plumbing, but be careful or you'll get yeast in your drainpipe.
>
> —*Rita Mae Brown*

tract. Amebiasis, giardiasis, and shigellosis are typical enteric infections. They often result from anal sex or oral-anal contact.

▪ *Granuloma inguinale* appears as single or multiple nodules, usually on the genitals, that become lumpy but painless ulcers that bleed on contact.

▪ *Lymphogranuloma venereum (LGV)* begins as a small, painless lesion at the site of infection and then develops into a painful abscess, accompanied by pain and swelling in the groin.

▪ *Molluscum contagiosum,* caused by a relatively large virus, is characterized by smooth, rounded, shiny lesions that appear on the trunk, on the genitals, or around the anus.

Parasites

Although they are not diseases per se, parasites such as scabies and pubic lice can be spread by sexual contact.

Scabies   The red, intensely itchy rash caused by the barely visible mite *Sarcoptes scabiei* is called **scabies.** It usually appears on the genitals, buttocks, feet, wrists, knuckles, abdomen, armpits, or scalp as a result of the mites' tunneling beneath the skin to lay their eggs and the baby mites' making their way back to the surface. It is highly contagious and spreads quickly among people who have close contact, both sexual and nonsexual. The mites can also be transferred on clothes, towels, and bedding. Scabies is usually treated with a prescribed lotion containing lindane, applied at bedtime and washed off in the morning. Young children and pregnant or nursing women should obtain an alternate prescription to lindane, because it can be toxic to infants and young children. Clothing, towels, and bedding of people who have scabies should be disinfected by washing in hot water and drying in high heat, or by dry cleaning.

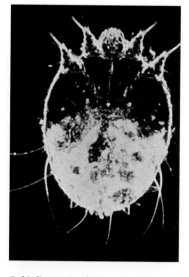

Pubic lice, or "crabs," are easily spread during intimate contact; they may also be transmitted on bedclothes, towels, or underwear.

Pubic Lice   The tiny *Phthirus pubis,* commonly known as a "crab," moves easily from the pubic hair of one person to that of another (probably along with several of its relatives). When **pubic lice** mate, the male and female grasp adjacent hairs; the female soon begins producing eggs (nits), which she attaches to the hairs at the rate of about three eggs a day for 7–10 days. The nits hatch within 7–9 days and begin reproducing in about 2 weeks, creating a very ticklish (or itchy) situation. Pubic lice can be transmitted nonsexually. They may fall into underwear, sheets, or towels, where they can survive up to a day *and* lay eggs that hatch in about a week. Thus, it is possible to get crabs simply by sleeping in someone else's bed, wearing his or her clothes, or sharing a towel.

A person can usually tell when he or she has pubic lice. There is intense itching, and upon inspection, one discovers a tiny, pale, crablike louse or its minuscule, pearly nits attached near the base of a pubic hair. There are both prescription and over-the-counter treatments for pubic lice. A gamma-benzene solution sold as Kwell may be prescribed. Other preparations such as Nix (permethrin) and RID (A-200 pyrinate) do not require a prescription. In addition to killing all the lice and nits on the body, the person must wash all infected linen and clothing in hot water and dry it on high heat, or the crabs may still be around, waiting and hungry.

STDS AND WOMEN

STDs affect men and women similarly in some ways and differently in others. Overall, the consequences for women appear to be more serious than those for men. Generally speaking, heterosexual women contract STDs more readily than men and risk greater damage to their health and reproductive functioning. As a group, lesbians are at the lowest risk for STDs; they are not immune, however, and can still benefit by observing safer sex guidelines and basic hygiene to avoid transmitting organisms such as HSV by hand.

Biological Sexism

Where STDs are concerned, there is a kind of "biological sexism" working to the disadvantage of women. According to Robert Hatcher and colleagues (1994), this is partly a result of the "fluid dynamics of intercourse," wherein "women are apparently more likely than men to acquire a sexually transmitted infection from any single sexual encounter." For example, the risk of acquiring gonorrhea from a single "coital event" when one partner is infectious is approximately 25% for men and 50% for women. Long-term effects of STDs for women include pelvic inflammatory disease, ectopic pregnancy, infertility, and cervical cancer.

A woman's anatomy may increase her susceptibility to STDs. The warm, moist interiors of the vagina and uterus are ideal environments for many organisms. The thin, sensitive skin inside the labia and the mucous membranes lining the vagina may also be more permeable to infecting organisms than the skin covering a man's genitals. Additionally, menstruation may cause a woman to be more vulnerable. As the endometrium sloughs off the uterine walls, tiny blood vessels rupture, causing bleeding and incidentally providing a pathway for infecting organisms directly into the woman's bloodstream. (If a woman has a bloodborne disease, such as hepatitis or HIV/AIDS, it may also be passed to her partner in menstrual blood.)

Women who use barrier methods of contraception, such as the diaphragm or female condom, tend to better protected against STDs than women who rely on men to use a condom (Rosenberg, Davidson, Chen, Judson, & Douglas, 1992).

Pelvic Inflammatory Disease (PID)

Pelvic inflammatory disease (PID), also known as **salpingitis,** is one of the leading causes of female infertility. Approximately 1 million cases of PID occur annually, resulting in about 165,000 hospitalizations of women age 15–44 (ASHA, 1998b). PID begins with an initial infection of the fallopian tube (or tubes) by an organism such as *C. trachomatis* or *N. gonorrhoeae,* which makes it possible for bacteria to invade and develop (Ault & Faro, 1993). As the infection spreads, the tubes swell and fester, often causing acute pain. Scar tissue begins to form within the tubes; it may block the passage of eggs en route to the uterus or cause a fertilized egg to implant within the tube itself—an ectopic pregnancy. PID occurs more commonly in women who have had a number of sex partners, women with a previous history of PID, and very young women. A woman may be more susceptible to PID during the first few days of her period, or if she uses an IUD.

Symptoms of PID include:

- Lower abdominal pain
- Cervical discharge
- Cervical tenderness
- Fever

Because definitive diagnosis of PID usually requires laparoscopy (an expensive examination involving minor surgery to insert the viewing instrument), physicians may go ahead and prescribe antibiotics once such conditions as appendicitis and ectopic pregnancy have been ruled out. Untreated PID can lead to life-threatening conditions such as pelvic abscesses and ectopic pregnancy. Once the infection is under control, further examination and treatment may be necessary to prevent infertility, ectopic pregnancy, or chronic abdominal pain, all of which may result from scar tissue buildup. To prevent reinfection, women with PID should be sure their partners are examined and treated for STDs.

Cystitis

A bladder infection that affects mainly women, **cystitis** is often related to sexual activity, although it is not transmitted from one partner to another. Cystitis is characterized by:

- Painful, burning urination
- A nearly constant need to urinate

Cystitis occurs when a bacterium such as *Escherichia coli*, normally present in the lower intestine and in fecal material, is introduced into the urinary tract. This can occur when continuous friction (from intercourse or manual stimulation) in the area of the urethra traumatizes the tissue and allows nearby bacteria to enter the urinary tract. It often occurs at the beginning of a sexual relationship, when sexual activity is high (hence the nickname "honeymoon cystitis"). If cystitis is not treated promptly, more serious symptoms will occur:

- Lower abdominal pain
- Fever
- Kidney pain

Damage to the kidneys may occur.

PREVENTING STDS

It seems that STDs should be easy to prevent, at least in theory. But in reality, STD prevention involves a subtle interplay of knowledge, psychological factors, and behaviors. In other words, STD prevention *is* easy, *if* you know the facts, *if* you believe in prevention, and *if* you act in accordance with your

An important part of controlling the spread of STDs is having free access to condoms and relevant information. Here, peer educator Kevin Turner, also known as Mr. Condom, distributes condoms and STD facts in Seattle.

knowledge and belief. In the earlier part of this chapter, you read the facts. Now let's think about the psychological and behavioral components of preventing STDs. (For measures to prevent cystitis or steps to treat it if it does occur, see the Resource Center.)

Risk Taking

The psychology of risk taking where STDs are concerned is similar in many ways to the psychology of contraceptive risk taking. Our ambivalence about sexuality may cause us to deny that we are sexual creatures at the same time that we are engaging in sexual behaviors that put us at risk. Thus, we may not use a condom because our partner "doesn't look like the type to have an STD," or we may be monogamous "except for once in a while." Denying our sexuality in this way is not just psychologically unhealthy—it is physically dangerous.

ALTHOUGH WE ARE aware of STDs and their consequences, many of us do not take steps to prevent them unless we perceive the disease as a specific threat to ourselves. The **health belief model** helps explain the psychology behind our sexual health behaviors (Darlow & Siegel, 1990; Rosenstock, 1974). According to this model, four factors must be present for an individual to take action to avoid a disease:

1. The person must believe that he or she is personally susceptible to it.
2. The individual must believe that the disease would have at least a moderately severe effect on his or her life.
3. He or she must believe that taking a particular action will reduce susceptibility to or severity of the disease.
4. He or she must believe that the costs of prevention (or treatment) are worth the benefits.

Let's take a closer look at each of these factors.

Susceptibility

People tend to underestimate their risk of getting STDs. They may not understand that the risk of STD infection goes up exponentially with each new sex partner. This is because when we have sex with someone, we are potentially in contact with all the sexually transmitted organisms of every person our partner has ever had sex with, which include (potentially) all the organisms of those with whom each of our partner's former partners have had sex, and so on. Furthermore, people persist in believing that they can distinguish a person who has an STD simply by looking at her or him (Balshem, Oxman, Van Rooven, & Girod, 1992).

Severity

In the "Age of AIDS," we can hardly afford to be blasé about the consequences of getting an STD. Moreover, the consequences (especially for women) of STDs such as chlamydia, gonorrhea, and genital warts may be painful, expensive, and heartbreaking, even if they are not usually life-threatening.

Appropriate Action

Knowledge about ways to prevent, recognize, and treat STDs enables us to act in ways that benefit our health. For example, we are more likely to use a condom if we believe it will help us avoid getting an STD. If we don't understand how condoms work or if we are unaware of their proven effectiveness, we may not use them or may use them only grudgingly at our partner's insistence.

Benefits Versus Costs

People may not act to prevent STDs because they perceive the costs as being too high. The costs could include the embarrassment of talking to a partner about STDs, the monetary expense of treatment, the inconvenience of buying or putting on a condom, or the change of lifestyle from many partners to a single, monogamous relationship. A person has to determine if these kinds of costs are worth the benefits of preventive action or treatment, such as feeling healthy, being pain-free, not having to worry about getting infected, and not passing an STD to a partner.

Abstinence

The most absolutely foolproof method of STD prevention is abstaining from intimate sexual contact, specifically penile-vaginal intercourse, anal intercourse, and oral sex. Hugging, massaging, kissing, petting, and mutual masturbation are all ways of sharing intimacy that are extremely unlikely to transmit STDs. (But watch out for colds!)

Abstinence is the only reliable course of action for a person who has an STD or whose partner has an STD (or a suspected STD). Freely chosen abstinence is a legitimate personal choice regarding sexuality. People who wish to be abstinent need to communicate their preferences clearly and unambiguously to their dates or partners. They also need to learn to avoid

SAFER SEX PRACTICES are an integral part of good health practices. (Many people prefer the term "safer sex" to "safe sex" because all sexual contact carries at least a slight risk—a condom slipping off, perhaps—no matter how careful we try to be.)

Safer Practices

- Hugging
- Kissing (but possibly not deep, French kissing)
- Massaging
- Petting
- Masturbation (solo or mutual, unless there are sores or abrasions on the genitals or hands)
- Erotic videos, books, etc.

Possibly Safe Practices

- Deep, French kissing, unless there are sores in the mouth
- Vaginal intercourse with a latex or polyurethane condom and spermicide
- Fellatio with a latex or polyurethane condom

- Cunnilingus, if the woman is not menstruating or does not have a vaginal infection (a latex dental dam provides extra protection)
- Anal intercourse with a latex or polyurethane condom and spermicide (experts disagree about whether this should be considered "possibly safe" even with a condom because it is the riskiest sexual behavior without one)

Unsafe Practices

- Vaginal or anal intercourse without a latex or polyurethane condom
- Fellatio without a latex or polyurethane condom
- Cunnilingus, if the woman is menstruating or has a vaginal infection and a dental dam is not used
- Oral-anal contact
- Contact with blood, including menstrual blood
- Semen in the mouth
- Sharing vibrators, dildos, etc., without washing them between uses

---

high-pressure sexual situations and to stay away from alcohol and drugs, which can impair their judgment.

Good Health, Safer Sex

When we value ourselves, our bodies, and our lives, we are likely to practice good health behaviors, such as eating well, exercising, getting enough rest, and seeking medical care when we need it. When we become sexual, we need to develop particular habits and patterns to promote our continuing good health. Specific health behaviors that help protect us from STDs include:

- Good genital hygiene (simply washing with mild soap and warm water, especially under the foreskin for uncircumcised males, before and after sex)
- Consistent use of a latex or polyurethane condom
- Practicing safer sex
- Knowing the signs and symptoms of STDs
- Talking to a partner about past and current exposure, or possible exposure, to an STD
- Examining self and partner for genital sores or unusual discharge

- Seeking medical care at the onset of symptoms and/or getting tested regularly if you have multiple sex partners
- Following treatment instructions

People who are sexually active with more than one partner should have a medical examination to screen for STDs every 3–6 months. This is especially important for women because they are often asymptomatic.

Acquiring an STD requires that we get intimately close to another person. Avoiding an STD demands even more intimacy because very often it means having to talk. Putting aside embarrassment or learning to communicate isn't always easy—but it's a lot simpler than dealing with herpes, gonorrhea, or AIDS.

> We kill our selves, to propagate our kinde.
>
> —John Donne (1572–1631)

■ As individuals, we have the knowledge and means to protect ourselves from STDs. As a society, we should have a larger goal. In the words of King Holmes and the other editors of *Sexually Transmitted Diseases* (1990), "We must acknowledge and correct the failure of society and of politicians to support the basic needs for public health in general and for STD control in particular."

SUMMARY

X-Rated Diseases: The Psychological Impact of STDs

- Although the media and popular culture encourage us to express ourselves sexually, Americans continue to experience a great deal of embarrassment, guilt, and shame over their sexuality. This deep ambivalence discourages us from dealing realistically with sexually transmitted diseases (STDs).

The STD Epidemic

- The *incidence* of STDs occurring in the United States each year is estimated to be more than 12 million cases. Social factors include changes in sexual mores, decreased condom use due to the advent of the pill and IUD, obstruction of educational efforts and research by vocal minorities who confuse medical issues with moral ones, inadequate health-care facilities, and the misuse of alcohol and drugs. Biological factors include the fact that many STDs are *asymptomatic,* as well as the evolution of strains of viruses and bacteria that are resistant to prescribed antibiotics.

Principal STDs

- The principal STDs affecting Americans are *chlamydia, gonorrhea, urinary tract infections, syphilis, genital warts, genital herpes, hepatitis, vaginitis,* and *HIV/AIDS.* Parasites that may be sexually transmitted include *scabies* and *pubic lice.*

STDs and Women

- There is a kind of "biological sexism" where STDs are concerned. Women tend to be more susceptible to STDs than men and to experience graver consequences, such as *pelvic inflammatory disease (PID),* an infection of the fallopian tubes that can lead to infertility, and ectopic pregnancy. Intense stimulation of the vulva can irritate the urethra, leading to *cystitis* (bladder infection).

Preventing STDs

- STD prevention involves the interaction of knowledge, psychological factors, and behaviors to avoid taking risks. Abstinence is a legitimate personal strategy for avoiding STDs. Good health behaviors, including safer sex, are very effective in protecting against STDs. Consistent condom use is an important component of safer sex.

- The *health belief model* is used to help explain the psychology behind our sexual health behaviors. In order to take action to avoid a disease, according to this model, a person must believe that he or she is personally susceptible to it, the disease would have at least a moderately severe effect on his or her life, taking a particular action would reduce the susceptibility to or severity of the disease, and the costs are worth the benefits.

SUGGESTED READING

Brandt, Allan M. (1987). *No Magic Bullet: A Social History of Venereal Disease in the United States Since 1880.* New York: Oxford University Press. An informative and very readable history of the social and political aspects of STDs.

Hatcher, Robert. (1995). *Safely Sexual.* New York: Irvington. A practical and sensitive guide to safer sex and pregnancy prevention.

Holmes, King K., Sparling, P. F., Mardh, R. A., Stanley, M., Stammo, W. E., Piot, P., & Wasserheit, J. (Eds.). (1998). *Sexually Transmitted Diseases* (3rd ed.). New York: McGraw-Hill. The definitive collection of recent research by leading authorities on STDs in the United States and Europe.

Jones, James. (1993). *Bad Blood: The Tuskegee Syphilis Experiment—A Tragedy of Race and Medicine* (Rev. ed.). New York: Free Press. A fascinating—and chilling—account of a 40-year experiment by the Public Health Service, using African Americans in the rural South as human guinea pigs. Discusses the experiment's impact on current HIV/AIDS prevention efforts in the Black community.

Quétel, Claude. (1992). *The History of Syphilis.* Baltimore: Johns Hopkins University Press. A fascinating social and scientific journey across 500 years with *T. pallidum.*

16

HIV and AIDS

OVER THE PAST 20 YEARS, no single phenomenon has changed the face of sexuality as much as the appearance of the microscopic virus known as **HIV,** or **human immunodeficiency virus.** In the early 1980s, physicians in San Francisco, New York, and Los Angeles began noticing repeated occurrences of formerly rare diseases among young and relatively healthy men. Kaposi's sarcoma, a cancer of the blood vessels, and pneumocystis carinii pneumonia, a lung infection that is usually not dangerous, had become killer diseases because of the breakdown of the immune system of the men in whom these diseases were being seen (Centers for Disease Control, 1982). Even before the virus responsible for the immune-system breakdown was discovered, the disease was given a name: acquired immune deficiency syndrome, or AIDS. At first, AIDS within the United States seemed to be confined principally to three groups: gay men, Haitians, and people with hemophilia. Soon, however, it became apparent that no particular group could afford to be complacent: the disease spread into communities with high rates of intravenous drug use and into the general population, including heterosexual men and women (and their children) at all socioeconomic levels. The far-reaching consequences of the AIDS epidemic, in addition to the pain and loss directly caused by the illness, have included widespread fear, superstition, and hatred. Ignorance of its modes of transmission has fueled the flames of homophobia among some people. Among other people, it has kindled a general fear of sexual expression. In many communities, however, it has engendered compassion and solidarity as people have come together to care for those who are living with HIV or AIDS and to educate themselves and others. Although the crisis is not over, the availability of new drugs has allowed many individuals with HIV or AIDS to live longer, healthier, and more productive lives.

Although researchers know a great deal about the virus and the way it works, among the general public, misinformation abounds. By now most of us know how HIV is spread. And yet, for a variety of reasons, people continue engaging in behaviors that put them at risk. Our goal in this chapter is to present a solid grounding in the biological aspects of the disease and in its psychological and sociological aspects as well. Because it is not likely that a cure for AIDS will be found in the near future, we must develop the attitudes and behaviors that will stop its deadly progression. AIDS *is* preventable. We hope that the material in this chapter will help you make healthy, informed choices for yourself and become a force for education and positive change in the community. Because of the tremendous amount of AIDS research being conducted, some of the information presented here will be outdated by the time the book appears in print. We anxiously await and welcome these new findings. For updates on HIV/AIDS research findings and news, contact one of the agencies or Web sites listed in the Resource Center at the back of the book.

We begin the chapter by exploding some common myths about AIDS and then go on to describe the disease, the virus itself, and the workings of the immune system. We next discuss modes of transmission, the effects of HIV and AIDS on certain groups of people, means of prevention, HIV testing, and current treatments. Then we deal with the demographic aspects of the epidemic—its effect on various communities and groups: the gay community, women, children, teenagers and college students, older adults, ethnic minorities, and the poor. The final section of the chapter is about living with

> Ring around the rosy,
> Pocket full of posies.
> Ashes! Ashes!
> We all fall down.
>
> *—Nursery rhyme*

HIV or AIDS. We offer practical advice for those who have the virus or whose friends or loved ones do. For a directory of organizations to contact for information or counseling regarding HIV and AIDS, refer to the Resource Center following Chapter 18.

WHAT IS AIDS?

AIDS is an acronym for **acquired immune deficiency syndrome.** This condition is so named for the following reasons:

A   Acquired, because it is not inherited

I   Immune, because it affects the immune system, which protects the body against foreign organisms

D   Deficiency, because the body lacks immunity

S   Syndrome, because the symptoms occur as a group

To receive an AIDS diagnosis under the Centers for Disease Control (CDC) classification system (and thus be eligible for treatments, programs, and insurance funds that would not otherwise be available), a person must, in most cases, have a positive blood test indicating the presence of HIV antibodies and a T-cell count (discussed later) below 200 (CDC, 1994b). If the T-cell count is higher, the person must have one or more of the diseases or conditions associated with AIDS (discussed shortly). If a person has HIV antibodies, as measured by a blood test, but does not meet the other criteria, he or she is said to "have HIV," "be HIV-positive," or "be living with HIV." Infection with HIV produces a spectrum of diseases that progress from a latent or asymptomatic state to AIDS as a late manifestation. The rate of this progression varies (CDC, 1998b).

At the beginning of 1993, T-cell count, along with cervical cancer/CIN (cervical intraepithelial neoplasia), pulmonary tuberculosis, and recurrent bacterial pneumonia, was added to the CDC definition of AIDS. These additions led to a dramatic increase in the number of people who "officially" have AIDS.

AIDS Myths and Facts

Myths and rumors about HIV and AIDS abound. Many are kept alive by the media, especially the tabloid newspapers, read by millions, and certain talk-show hosts and newspaper columnists. Some politicians and religious leaders, especially those with "anti-sex" agendas, are also responsible for the spread of misinformation. We briefly discuss some common myths below. As you read the chapter, you will understand more about the issues that are raised.

▪ *Myth:* If you're not in a high-risk group, you don't have to worry about AIDS.

Fact: Equating *low* risk with *no* risk is one of the deadliest myths about AIDS. Statistics won't seem very relevant if you happen to be the "1 out of 100" (or whatever the number). The only way to stop AIDS is for everyone to take responsibility for his or her behavior.

- *Myth:* Scientists have not actually seen HIV.

Fact: Researchers have seen HIV innumerable times (through a microscope, of course) and understand a great deal about it. Because the presence of the virus is determined by testing for the antibodies that the immune system develops to fight HIV, people may erroneously assume that the virus itself cannot be found. It can be, but the tests would be prohibitively expensive and involve unnecessary pain and risk.

- *Myth:* HIV was developed in the laboratory as germ warfare against gays or Blacks, or it was spread through contaminated vaccines, such as the polio vaccine.

Fact: There are many theories about the origin of HIV. Some are grounded in science, but others have sprung solely from fear or paranoia. The pattern of HIV's spread does not ultimately support any of these theories. There is not a shred of evidence that the virus was made in a laboratory, nor have any traces of it been found in samples of frozen early vaccines. The most promising work in the search for HIV's origin is based on the obvious—but not yet well-understood—relationship of HIV (especially HIV-2) to SIV (simian immunodeficiency virus) (Essex & Kanki, 1988). SIV is widely prevalent among African green monkeys, but it is not deadly to them. Scientists hope that by studying SIV they will discover mechanisms by which HIV can be weakened or disabled.

- *Myth:* The AIDS virus is easy to "catch."

Fact: The virus is easy to catch only in intimate situations when infected blood, semen, vaginal secretions, or breast milk have a direct pathway into the bloodstream of an uninfected person. The virus is delicate and dies quickly when exposed to spermicide, bleach, and a variety of other disinfectants. It can't survive in the open air. It is not spread by handshakes, hugs, or kisses when blood is not present.

- *Myth:* Latex condoms have naturally occurring holes that are 50 times bigger than the human immunodeficiency virus, so condoms do not really provide protection.

Fact: Good-quality latex and polyurethane condoms do not have such holes. Laboratory tests have shown that virus-sized particles do not normally leak from highly rated brands (see the Resource Center for information) (Voeller, 1991). Although lambskin and lower-rated brands have been shown to leak minute amounts of virus-sized particles in laboratory studies, researchers nevertheless conclude that "worst-case condom barrier effectiveness" is "at least 10,000 times better than not using a condom at all" (Carey, Herman, Retta, Rinaldi, Herman, & Athey, 1992). Numerous studies of couples in which one person is HIV-positive and one is not have shown extremely low rates of transmission when latex condoms are consistently used (CDC, 1993a; de Vincenzi, 1994).

- *Myth:* HIV doesn't cause AIDS.

Fact: Most AIDS researchers are appalled at well-publicized claims (by other researchers) that the connection between HIV and AIDS is coincidental rather than causative. It is dangerous to publicize this sort of conclusion, because it may encourage people infected with HIV, or those who are involved with them, to engage in unsafe practices (Osborn, 1996). Although the exact way (or ways) in which HIV destroys the immune system is still

Many people who are HIV-positive continue to feel healthy and lead active lives, as attested to by Magic Johnson. Here, the renowned basketball player attends an AIDS fundraising event with Elizabeth Taylor and k. d. lang.

under investigation, there is no reason to doubt that it is the cause of AIDS (Ascher, Sheppard, Winkelstein, & Vittinghoff, 1993; Maddox, 1993).

▪ *Myth:* If you are HIV-positive, it means you have AIDS.

Fact: Although it currently appears that nearly all those who test positive for HIV will develop AIDS eventually, having the virus is not the same as having AIDS. Many people who are HIV-positive feel perfectly normal and healthy. If they maintain a healthful lifestyle, their immune system may continue to function well for a number of years. It is important to remember, though, that anyone who is HIV-positive can transmit the virus regardless how healthy he or she may look or feel.

Conditions Associated with AIDS

The CDC currently lists 27 clinical conditions to be used in diagnosing AIDS along with HIV-positive status (CDC, 1996c). These conditions fall into several categories: opportunistic infections, cancers, conditions associated specifically with AIDS, and conditions that *may* be diagnostic for AIDS under certain circumstances. The most commonly occurring diseases and conditions within these categories are listed here.

Opportunistic Infections   Diseases that take advantage of a weakened immune system are known as **opportunistic infections (OIs).** Normally, these infections do not develop in healthy people or are not life-threatening. Common OIs associated with HIV are:

- **Pneumocystis carinii pneumonia (PCP).** The most common opportunistic infection of people with AIDS; a lung disease caused by a common organism (probably a protozoan or fungus) that is not usually harmful. The organisms multiply, resulting in the accumulation of fluid in the lungs (pneumonia).

- *Mycobacterium avium intracellulare (MAI).* An atypical tuberculosis, usually affecting the lungs; may also affect the liver, spleen, lymphatic system, bone marrow, gastrointestinal tract, skin, or brain. MAI is the most common form of TB among people with AIDS. It is resistant to most antibiotics.

- *Mycobacterium tuberculosis (TB).* An infection that generally occurs in the lungs and may appear at other sites, such as the lymph nodes. This "old-fashioned" form of TB is infectious but treatable with common antibiotics.

- *Bacterial pneumonia.* Accumulation of fluid in the lungs due to the presence of any of several common bacteria. Multiple episodes of bacterial pneumonia may occur in people with AIDS.

- *Toxoplasmosis.* A disease of the brain and central nervous system caused by a parasite frequently present in cat feces.

Cancers   Certain types of cancer are commonly associated with AIDS, including the following:

- **Kaposi's sarcoma.** A cancer of the blood vessels, causing red or purple blotches to appear under the skin; rare in healthy people, except in older men of central African or Mediterranean descent. Among people with AIDS, it is more common in gay or bisexual men than in women or heterosexual men.

- *Lymphomas.* Cancers of the lymphatic system. Lymphomas may also affect the brain.

- *Invasive cervical cancer.* Cancer or dysplasia (CIN) of the cervix that can lead to cancer. Cervical cancer and CIN are more common in women who are HIV-positive than in other women. Cervical cancer can lead to uterine cancer if untreated.

Clinical Conditions   Conditions that are specifically linked to AIDS include:

- **Wasting syndrome.** Severe weight loss, usually accompanied by weakness and persistent diarrhea.

- *HIV encephalopathy (AIDS dementia).* Impairment of mental functioning, changes in mood or behavior, or impaired movement caused by direct infection of the brain with HIV.

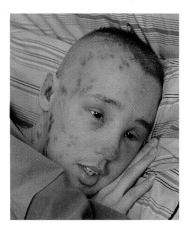

Kaposi's sarcoma is a cancer of the blood vessels commonly associated with AIDS. It causes red or purple blotches to appear under the skin's surface.

Other Infinctions . Infections listed by the CDC that may lead to an AIDS diagnosis under certain circumstances include:

- *Candidiasis (thrush).* A fungal (yeast) infection affecting the mouth, throat, esophagus, trachea, lungs, or vagina. Recurring candidiasis is especially common in women with AIDS.

- *Herpes simplex.* A common viral STD. Persistent lesions (lasting a month or more) or lesions on the lungs or esophagus may be diagnostic for AIDS.

- *Cytomegalovirus (CMV).* A virus of the herpes family, often sexually transmitted. In people with AIDS, it can lead to encephalitis (a brain infection), retinitis (infection of the retina that can lead to blindness), pneumonia, or hepatitis.

Because the immune systems of people with HIV may not be functioning well (and those of people with advanced AIDS certainly are not), they may be subject to numerous other infections that would not normally be much of a problem, such as colds, flus, and intestinal infections. Health precautions for people living with HIV are discussed later in the chapter.

Symptoms of HIV Infection and AIDS

A person with HIV may feel fine, or he or she may experience one or more of the symptoms that follow. A person who has received an AIDS diagnosis is more likely to experience at least some of these symptoms. It is important to remember, however, that all of these are also common symptoms of conditions that are not related to HIV or AIDS. *AIDS cannot be self-diagnosed.* A person who is experiencing persistent discomfort or illness should be checked out by a medical practitioner. Symptoms that may be associated with HIV or AIDS include:

- Unexplained persistent fatigue
- Unexplained fever, chills, or night sweats for a period of several weeks or more
- Unexplained weight loss greater than 10 lb or 10% of body weight in less than 2 months
- Swollen lymph nodes in the neck, armpits, or groin that are unexplained and last more than 2 months. This condition is called *lymphadenopathy.*
- Pink, purple, or brown blotches on or under the skin or inside the mouth, nose, eyelids, or rectum that do not disappear
- Persistent fuzzy white spots or other sores in the mouth (indicative of either *hairy leukoplakia* or candidiasis)
- Persistent dry cough and shortness of breath
- Persistent diarrhea

In addition, women may experience the following:

- Abnormal Pap smears
- Persistent vaginal candidiasis
- Abdominal cramping (due to PID)

Understanding AIDS: The Immune System

The principal components of blood are plasma (the fluid base), red blood cells, white blood cells, and platelets.

Leukocytes   Two to three pounds of body weight are accounted for by the body's approximately 1 trillion white blood cells, or **leukocytes.** Twenty to fifty million white cells circulate in the blood, and billions more are distributed throughout the body in the lymph nodes (located mainly in the neck, face, armpits, and groin), spleen, and other lymphatic tissues (within connective tissue, throughout the small intestine, in the tonsils). There are several kinds of leukocytes, all of which play major roles in defending the body against invading organisms or mutant (cancerous) cells. Because HIV invades and eventually kills some kinds of leukocytes, it impairs the body's ability to ward off infections and other harmful conditions that ordinarily would not be threatening. The principal type of leukocyte we discuss is the lymphocyte.

Macrophages, Antigens, and Antibodies   White blood cells called **macrophages,** literally "big eaters," are formed within the bone marrow. Although some circulate in the blood, most migrate to lymph nodes or lymphatic tissues, where they wait for foreign particles to be brought to them. The macrophage engulfs the foreign particle and displays the invader's antigen (*anti*body *gene*rator) like a signal flag on its own surface. **Antigens** are large molecules that are capable of stimulating the immune system and then reacting with the antibodies that are released to fight them. **Antibodies** bind to antigens, inactivate them, and mark them for destruction by killer cells. If the body has been previously exposed to the organism (by fighting it off or being vaccinated), the response is much quicker because memory cells are already biochemically programmed to respond.

B Cells and T Cells   The **lymphocytes** (a type of leukocyte) crucial to the immune system's functioning are **B cells** and several types of **T cells.** Like macrophages, **helper T cells** are programmed to "read" the antigens and then begin directing the immune system's response. They send chemical signals to B cells, which begin making antibodies specific to the presented antigen. Helper T cells also stimulate the proliferation of B cells and T cells (which are genetically programmed to replicate, or make copies of themselves) and activate both macrophages and **killer T cells,** transforming them into agents of destruction whose only purpose is to attack and obliterate the enemy. **Suppressor T cells** are activated when an antigen has been successfully destroyed. They slow and finally stop the immune response. T cells are also identified by the type of protein receptor (called CD4 or CD8) they display on their surface. Helper T cells display CD4; killer T cells and suppressor T cells display CD8. The number of helper T cells in an individual's body is an important indicator of how well the immune system is functioning, as we discuss later.

The Virus

A **virus** is a protein-coated package of genes that invades a cell and alters the way in which the cell reproduces itself. In some ways, viruses are really

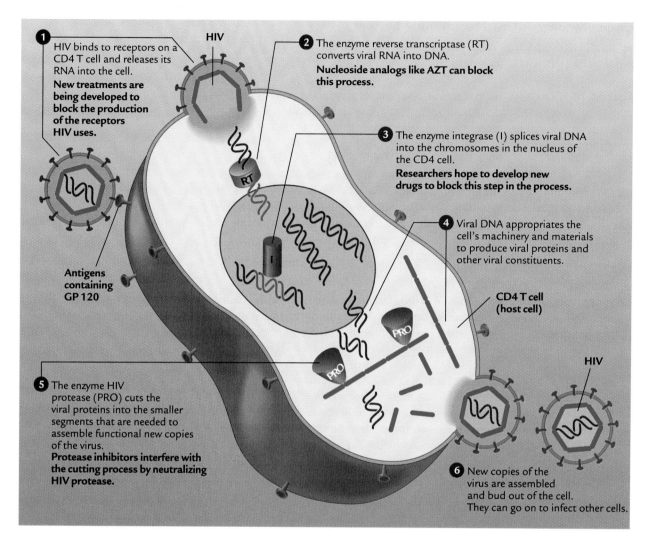

1 HIV binds to receptors on a CD4 T cell and releases its RNA into the cell.
New treatments are being developed to block the production of the receptors HIV uses.

HIV

2 The enzyme reverse transcriptase (RT) converts viral RNA into DNA.
Nucleoside analogs like AZT can block this process.

3 The enzyme integrase (I) splices viral DNA into the chromosomes in the nucleus of the CD4 cell.
Researchers hope to develop new drugs to block this step in the process.

4 Viral DNA appropriates the cell's machinery and materials to produce viral proteins and other viral constituents.

Antigens containing GP 120

CD4 T cell (host cell)

HIV

5 The enzyme HIV protease (PRO) cuts the viral proteins into the smaller segments that are needed to assemble functional new copies of the virus.
Protease inhibitors interfere with the cutting process by neutralizing HIV protease.

6 New copies of the virus are assembled and bud out of the cell. They can go on to infect other cells.

FIGURE 16.1 The Infection of a CD4 T Cell by HIV. Different classes of drugs block the replication of HIV at different points in the virus's life cycle.

very primitive entities. They have no life on their own. They can't propel themselves independently, and they can't reproduce unless they are inside a host cell. It would take 16,000 human immunodeficiency viruses to cover the head of a pin in a single layer. Under strong magnification, HIV resembles a spherical pincushion, bristling with tiny pinheadlike knobs (Figure 16.1). These knobs are the antigens, which contain a protein called GP 120; the CD4 receptors on a helper T cell are attracted (fatally, as it turns out) to GP 120. Within the virus's protein core is the genetic material (RNA) that carries the information the virus needs to replicate itself. Also in the core is an enzyme called **reverse transcriptase,** which enables the virus to "write" its RNA (the genetic software or program) into a cell's DNA. Viruses with the ability to reverse the normal genetic writing process are known as **retroviruses.** There are numerous variant strains of HIV as a result of mutations (Chermann, cited in Challice, 1992). The virus begins undergoing genetic variation as soon as it has infected a person, even before antibodies develop

A T cell infected with HIV begins to replicate the virus, which buds from the cell wall, eventually killing the host cell.

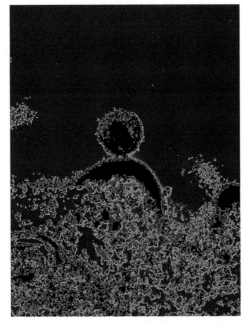

(Pang, Shlesinger, Daar, Moudgil, Ho, & Chen, 1992). This tendency to mutate is one factor that makes HIV difficult to destroy.

Effect on T Cells   When HIV enters the bloodstream, helper T cells rush to the invading viruses, as if they were specifically designed for them. Normally at this stage, a T cell reads the antigen, stimulating antibody production in the B cells and beginning the process of eliminating the invading organism. In the case of HIV, however, although antibody production does begin, the immune process starts to break down almost at once. HIV injects its contents into the host T cell and copies its own genetic code into the cell's genetic material (DNA). As a result, when the immune system is activated, the T cell begins producing HIV instead of replicating itself. The T cell is killed in the process. HIV also targets other types of cells, including macrophages, *dendritic cells* (leukocytes found in the skin, lymph nodes, and intestinal mucous membranes), and brain cells.

HIV-1 and HIV-2   Almost all cases of HIV in the United States involve the type of the virus known as HIV-1. Ten subtypes of HIV-1 have been identified worldwide (Kreiger, 1996). Subtype B is by far the most common in North America. Scientists note that different strains may differ in their effects on the body—which cells they prefer to attack, for example—indicating the need for further research. Another type, HIV-2, as been found to exist mainly in West Africa. HIV-2 has only a 60–90% chance of being detected by the standard HIV test, although more extensive testing will reveal its presence. Most people in the United States are not likely to have HIV-2—unless they are from West Africa or have had intimate contact with a West African. There were 9 confirmed cases of HIV-2 in this country in 1995 (CDC, 1996c). Overall, it appears that HIV-2 takes longer then HIV-1 to damage the immune system; it may not always develop into AIDS (Essex & Kanki, 1988).

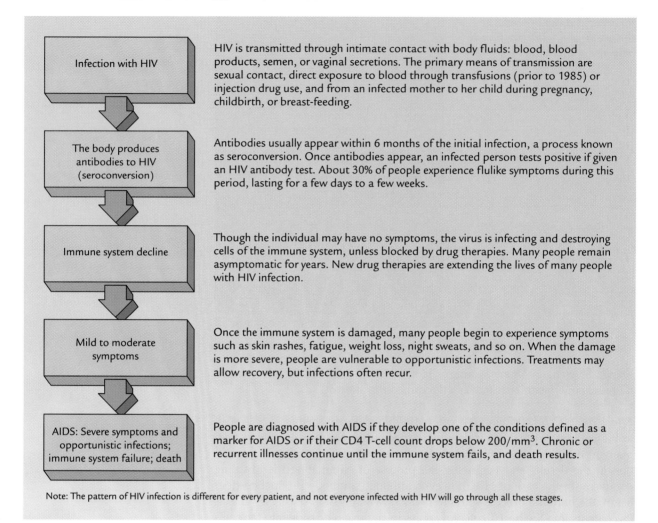

Infection with HIV	HIV is transmitted through intimate contact with body fluids: blood, blood products, semen, or vaginal secretions. The primary means of transmission are sexual contact, direct exposure to blood through transfusions (prior to 1985) or injection drug use, and from an infected mother to her child during pregnancy, childbirth, or breast-feeding.
The body produces antibodies to HIV (seroconversion)	Antibodies usually appear within 6 months of the initial infection, a process known as seroconversion. Once antibodies appear, an infected person tests positive if given an HIV antibody test. About 30% of people experience flulike symptoms during this period, lasting for a few days to a few weeks.
Immune system decline	Though the individual may have no symptoms, the virus is infecting and destroying cells of the immune system, unless blocked by drug therapies. Many people remain asymptomatic for years. New drug therapies are extending the lives of many people with HIV infection.
Mild to moderate symptoms	Once the immune system is damaged, many people begin to experience symptoms such as skin rashes, fatigue, weight loss, night sweats, and so on. When the damage is more severe, people are vulnerable to opportunistic infections. Treatments may allow recovery, but infections often recur.
AIDS: Severe symptoms and opportunistic infections; immune system failure; death	People are diagnosed with AIDS if they develop one of the conditions defined as a marker for AIDS or if their CD4 T-cell count drops below 200/mm^3. Chronic or recurrent illnesses continue until the immune system fails, and death results.

Note: The pattern of HIV infection is different for every patient, and not everyone infected with HIV will go through all these stages.

FIGURE 16.2 The General Pattern of HIV Infection

AIDS Pathogenesis: How the Disease Progresses

As discussed earlier, when viruses are introduced into the body, they are immediately snatched up by helper T cells and whisked off to the lymph nodes. Although HIV begins replication right away within the host cells, the virus itself may not be detectable in the blood for some time. HIV antibodies, however, are generally detectable in the blood within 2–6 months (the testing process is discussed later). The process in which a person develops antibodies is called **seroconversion**. A person's **serostatus** is HIV-negative if antibodies to HIV are not detected and HIV-positive if antibodies are detected.

T-Cell (CD4) Count T-cell count—also called CD4 count—refers to the number of helper T cells that are present in a cubic milliliter of blood. A healthy person's T-cell count averages about 1000, but it can range from 500 to 1600, depending on a person's general health and whether he or she is fighting off an illness.

Phases of Infection   The pace of disease progression is variable, with the time between infection with HIV and development of AIDS ranging from a few months to as long as 17 years (the average is 10 years) (CDC, 1998a). When a person is first infected with HIV, he or she may experience severe flulike symptoms as the immune system goes into high gear to fight off the invader. The person's T-cell count may temporarily plunge as the virus begins rapid replication. During this period, the virus is dispersed throughout the lymph nodes, where it replicates, a process called "seeding" (Kolata, 1992). HIV may also be trapped within dendritic cells (Langhoff & Hasteline, 1992). The virus may stay localized in these areas for years, but it continues to replicate and destroy T cells. Most researchers agree that it does not have an actual "dormant" period, as previously believed (Kolata, 1992). Detecting infection early and beginning treatment can reduce viral load and possibly an individual's infectiousness (Cates, Chesney, & Cohen, 1997).

As time goes by, the T cells gradually diminish in number, destroyed by newly created HIV. During this phase, as the number of infected cells goes up, the number of T cells goes down, generally to between 200 and 500 per milliliter of blood.

When AIDS is in the advanced phase, the lymph nodes appear "burned out" (Israelski, 1992). The T cells and other fighter cells of the immune system are no longer able to trap foreign invaders. Infected cells continue to increase, and the T-cell count drops to under 200. The virus is detectable in the blood. At this point, the person is fairly ill to very ill. The T-cell count may continue to plummet to zero. The general progression of HIV infection is shown in Figure 16.2.

EPIDEMIOLOGY AND TRANSMISSION OF HIV

Epidemiology is the study of the incidence, process, distribution, and control of a disease. An *epidemic* is the wide and rapid spread of a contagious disease. In this country over the past 15–20 years, the number of people diagnosed with AIDS has grown from a few dozen to more than 641,000 (approximately 1 in 300) (CDC, 1997e; Kreiger, 1996). Worldwide, more than 30 million people may be infected with HIV or AIDS (Figure 16.3). Rates of infection are rising in the Caribbean, Latin America, Africa, the Middle East, eastern Europe, and central Asia. The steepest rises are occurring in southern and Southeast Asia (Pan American Health Organization [PAHO], 1997). It is estimated that 10 million Asians will die of AIDS-related causes before the year 2015 (Shenon, 1996). In 1997, new infections occurred among 5.8 million adults and children worldwide, and approximately 2.3 million died from the disease. Thus far, it is estimated that nearly 12 million individuals have died from HIV/AIDS (AHO, 1997). These numbers suggest that it is not unreasonable to refer to HIV/AIDS as an epidemic.

A great deal has been discovered about AIDS since it first perplexed physicians and scientists in 1981. Much of what we now know regarding HIV transmission is due to the work of epidemiologists who track the progress of the disease in the United States and throughout the world.

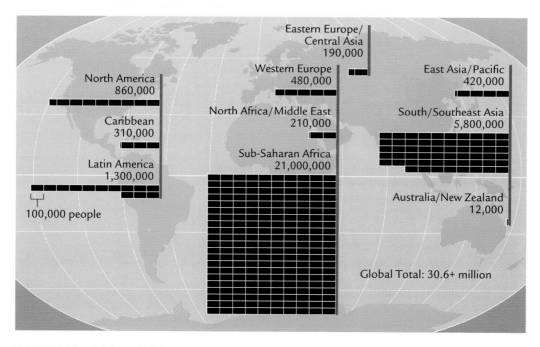

FIGURE 16.3 Adults and Children Estimated Worldwide to Be Living with HIV/AIDS, 1997. (*Source:* UNAIDS/WHO Report, June 1998.)

Epidemiology of HIV/AIDS

At this book's publication, the latest figures from the CDC indicated that, since 1981, 641,086 people have been diagnosed with AIDS in the United States (CDC, 1997e). Of these, 78% were men, 21% were women, and 1% were children under 13 years of age. An additional 88,586 were diagnosed with HIV, excluding those who were tested anonymously (CDC, 1997e). For the first time since the beginning of the AIDS epidemic, the annual estimated number of Americans newly diagnosed with AIDS declined in 1997, from an estimated 68,137 in 1996 to 60,161. Also for the first time, in 1996 the estimated deaths among persons with AIDS declined, to 37,500 from 50,000 in 1995. Between 800,000 and 1 million people in the United States were estimated to be infected with HIV. About 50% of the total reported U.S. AIDS cases involved gay or bisexual men. Women, Blacks, Latinos, and those with heterosexually acquired HIV infections account for the greatest growth in the epidemic. Injection drug use and sex with at-risk partners, especially among heterosexuals and young homosexual/bisexual men, also continue to challenge HIV prevention programs (CDC, 1994b).

Currently, the face of HIV/AIDS is changing (Figure 16.4). Gay men have tended to modify their sexual behaviors; heterosexuals have not, and heterosexual transmission is becoming more common, with the increase expected to continue. The role of IV and injection drug use in the spread of HIV is also increasing as HIV-infected drug users pass the virus to each other in blood and to female partners during sexual activity. Pregnant women may also infect the fetus in utero. The importance of education in changing behaviors has been demonstrated in some populations, notably the gay community, where the rate of new infection has slowed markedly.

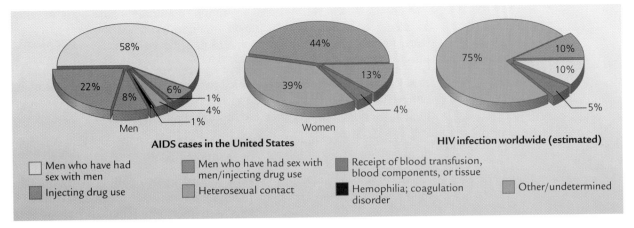

AIDS cases in the United States

Men — 58%, 22%, 8%, 6%, 1%, 4%, 1%

Women — 44%, 13%, 39%, 4%

HIV infection worldwide (estimated) — 75%, 10%, 10%, 5%

- ☐ Men who have had sex with men
- ☐ Injecting drug use
- ☐ Men who have had sex with men/injecting drug use
- ☐ Heterosexual contact
- ☐ Receipt of blood transfusion, blood components, or tissue
- ■ Hemophilia; coagulation disorder
- ☐ Other/undetermined

FIGURE 16.4 Current HIV Transmission Patterns for Adults and Adolescents. (*Source:* Data from CDC, 1997e; Purvis, 1996–97.)

Myths and Modes of Transmission

Before we discuss further the ways in which HIV has been shown to be transmitted, we should mention some of the ways in which it is *not* transmitted. You *cannot* get HIV from:

- *Casual contact.* Normal household or social contact does not transmit HIV. Shaking hands, hugging, kissing, playing, and providing personal care such as bathing, feeding, and dressing are extremely unlikely to transmit HIV. Extensive studies of households with an HIV-infected member have shown no evidence of transmission through casual contact.

- *Inanimate objects.* HIV cannot live outside the body fluids in which it is normally found. It cannot survive on countertops, toilet seats, drinking fountains, telephones, eating utensils, and so on. If a surface or object is contaminated by infected blood or semen, it can be disinfected with bleach, alcohol, hydrogen peroxide, Lysol, or other household cleaners.

- *Blood donation.* In the United States, it is not possible to get HIV from donating blood. Sterilized needles are used to draw the blood and they are disposed of afterward; they are never reused.

- *Animals.* Household pets and farm animals can neither get HIV nor pass it on. Laboratory chimpanzees may be intentionally infected with HIV, but there are no known cases of transmission from chimps to humans.

- *Insect bites.* Extensive research has shown that HIV is not transmitted by biting insects such as mosquitoes. The virus has been demonstrated not to replicate in flies, ticks, or mosquitoes.

- *Saliva.* About 1% of people with HIV have detectable virus in their saliva. The amounts are very small, and enzymes in the saliva are hostile to the virus. There are no known cases of transmission from saliva, although theoretically there could be a slight risk if the saliva from a person with advanced AIDS were to enter another's bloodstream or if a person with HIV had blood in the mouth.

■ *Tears or sweat.* HIV exists in minute quantities in the tears of some infected people, but researchers have found no evidence of transmission via tears. Researchers have been unable to find the virus in the sweat of HIV-infected people.

■ *Vaccines.* The processes by which vaccines are manufactured effectively remove or inactivate HIV. In the United States, sterile, fresh needles are used to give vaccinations, and they are destroyed after use.

■ *Water.* HIV cannot live or replicate in water. It is not transmitted in drinking water, nor in hot tubs or swimming pools.

For HIV to replicate in the body, it must have a path of entry into the bloodstream. The most common modes of transmission involve HIV-infected semen, blood, or vaginal secretions. Activities or situations that may promote transmission include:

- Vaginal or anal intercourse without a latex or polyurethane condom, fellatio without a latex or polyurethane condom, cunnilingus without a latex or other barrier.

- Sharing needles contaminated with HIV-infected blood during injection drug use, tattooing, home injections of medications, or self-administered steroid injections.

- Passage of the virus from mother to fetus in the uterus (20–50% chance) or in blood during delivery.

- Breast-feeding, if the mother is HIV-positive

- Sharing sex toys, such as dildos or vibrators, without disinfecting them

- Accidental contamination when infected blood enters the body through the mucous membranes of the eyes or mouth or through cuts, abrasions, or punctures in the skin

- Before April 1, 1985, from contaminated blood (transfusions) or organs (transplants)

The first three modes of transmission are the most common. We discuss each of these in greater detail in the following sections.

Sexual Transmission

Semen and vaginal secretions of people with HIV may contain infected cells, especially in the later phases of AIDS. Latex barriers, condoms, dental dams, and surgical gloves can provide good protection against the transmission of HIV if used properly.

Anal Intercourse   The riskiest form of sexual interaction for both men and women is receiving anal sex. The membrane lining the rectum is delicate and ruptures easily, exposing tiny blood vessels to infection from virus-carrying semen. Infected blood from the rectum may also enter the penis through the mucous membrane at the urethral opening. Heterosexual anal intercourse is more common than many people realize; studies show that 9% of heterosexual couples practice it (Laumann et al., 1994). Unprotected anal intercourse is reported to be 5 times riskier than vaginal intercourse as a mode of HIV transmission in women (Seidman & Rieder, 1994).

Vaginal Intercourse   Vaginal sex is also quite risky as an HIV transmission route, especially for women. A number of explanations are associated with this reality. First is the fact that semen contains a higher concentration of HIV than any other bodily fluid (Forrest, 1991). Second, the large area of exposed mucosal tissue in the vagina puts women at an additional disadvantage to men in terms of exposure (Seidman & Rieder, 1994). Third, a large number of couples regularly engage in unprotected vaginal intercourse (Seidman & Rieder, 1994). Finally, adolescent females are biologically more susceptible to HIV than older women because their immature cervixes may be more easily infected (Braverman & Strasburger, 1994). Men contract HIV from women during intercourse at a small fraction of the rate that women contract it from men (Billy, Tanfer, Grady, & Klepinger, 1993). Menstrual blood containing HIV can facilitate transmission of the virus to a sex partner (de Vincenzi et al., 1992), as can infected vaginal secretions containing many leukocytes.

Oral Sex   HIV may be transmitted through oral sex between heterosexuals, gay men, or lesbians (Lifson et al., 1990; UCSF, 1991). Infection can occur when semen or vaginal secretions from a person with HIV get into an uninfected person's body via sores or cuts in or around the person's mouth, such as cold sores (herpes) or lesions from gum disease. A recent case appears to have been transmitted via mucous membrane exposure in blood-contaminated saliva during "deep kissing" (CDC, 1997h).

Sex Toys   HIV can be transmitted in vaginal secretions on such objects as dildos and vibrators; therefore, it is very important that these objects not be shared or that they be washed thoroughly before use.

Drug Use

Sharing needles or other paraphernalia (including cotton pieces) used to inject drugs provides an ideal pathway for HIV (CDC, 1996a). Infection via the bloodstream is called **parenteral transmission.** An intravenous drug user (IVDU) or injection drug user (IDU) may have an immune system that has already been weakened by poor health, poor nutrition, or an STD. (Because it is more inclusive, the term "injection drug use" is now preferred to "intravenous drug use.") Injection drug users who become infected often pass the virus sexually to their partners (Ross, Wodak, Gold, & Miller, 1992).

Sobering statistics from the CDC indicate that nearly 50% of new HIV infections are occurring among drug addicts. These cases involve both injection drug users and users of crack cocaine (CDC, 1997e). Both men and women addicted to crack may go on binges and have sex with multiple partners, often for crack or the money to buy it (Kolata, 1995).

When we think of injection drug use, we usually think in terms of psychotropic (mind-affecting) drugs such as heroin or cocaine. We may conjure up images of run-down tenement rooms or "shooting galleries," where needles are passed around. But these are not the only settings for sharing drugs. HIV transmission in connection with the recreational use of injection drugs also occurs among people who are of middle or upper socioeconomic status. Moreover, injection drug use exists among athletes who may share

Sharing needles and other injection drug paraphernalia is a common mode of HIV transmission via infected blood. Groups such as the AIDS Brigade provide clean needles for injection drug users.

needles for steroids to increase muscle mass. HIV can be transmitted just as easily in a brightly lit locker room or upscale living room as in a dark alley.

Mother-to-Child Transmission

The passing of a disease from mother to child in the womb is known as **perinatal transmission.** Infants whose mothers are HIV-positive will have HIV antibodies at birth. This does not necessarily mean they will become infected with the virus, however. Treatment during pregnancy can help an HIV-infected woman protect her baby from becoming infected. Since 1994, there has been a two-thirds reduction in the risk for perinatal HIV transmission with ZDV (AZT) therapy. (Drugs used in HIV treatment are discussed later in the chapter.) Recent evidence shows that the rate of mother-to-infant transmission plummeted to 2%, and in some cases lower than 1% when C-section is used with AZT therapy (Irvine, 1998). Without such treatment, 15–25% of all infants born to HIV-infected mothers will have the virus and will eventually develop symptoms (CDC, 1998b).

It is not known exactly how HIV is passed from mother to fetus, although it is generally accepted that HIV manages to cross the placental barrier. It has been found that the likelihood of the offspring's becoming infected rises with the amount of the virus in a pregnant woman's blood ("AIDS Test," 1995). The CDC (1998b) now recommends that all pregnant women be tested for HIV as early in the pregnancy as possible and, if infected, be given the drug ZDV (AZT) at 14–34 weeks' gestation and during labor. The drug should also be given to infants of infected mothers for the first 6 weeks of life. Furthermore, HIV-infected women should be advised not to breast-feed their infants (CDC, 1998b).

Uncommon Modes of Transmission

Although the great majority of HIV infections are acquired in the ways just discussed, many people still worry about getting the virus through casual (nonsexual) contact or accidents. There is also concern about transmission through blood transfusions, although this mode is very unlikely today in countries that routinely test donated blood for HIV.

Nonsexual Contact   As mentioned earlier in this chapter, nonsexual, casual contact that typically occurs with health-care workers, with family members, and in school and day-care settings is highly unlikely to transmit HIV under ordinary circumstances. For example, a study of 89 household members caring for HIV-positive children showed no seroconversion to HIV-positive status. Close personal contact—bathing, cleaning up blood and body fluids, sharing dishes and utensils, and hugging and kissing—was common. After 4 months or longer, no indication of HIV was found in other family members (Rogers et al., 1990).

Much media attention has focused on the possibility of transmission in health-care situations, either from infected providers (doctors, dentists, nurses, and so on) to their patients or from infected patients to their care providers. All studies of these situations show that the risk of transmission is very low, especially if standard infection control precautions and common sense are observed (CDC, 1998a).

Accidents   People sometimes express concern about the possibility of accidental blood exchange—during children's play or contact sports, for example. Although it is theoretically possible for blood to be passed in this way, it is highly unlikely that the blood of one person could spill into another person's open wound and from there enter the bloodstream. (It was this kind of fear, expressed by professional basketball players, that led HIV-positive basketball superstar Magic Johnson to retire once and for all.)

Medical and dental accidents are also feared, although the chance of transmission in these situations is slight. Greater awareness among both patients and health-care providers of the risk factors associated with HIV transmission has led to increased testing for HIV and early diagnosis of the infection (CDC, 1998a).

Blood Transfusions and Organ Donations   Theoretically, donated blood, plasma, body organs, and semen are all capable of sustaining HIV. Because of this, today medical procedures involving these materials include either screening for HIV or destroying it. Since April 1, 1985, blood has been screened for HIV. Plasma is treated to inactivate any virus that may be present. The chance of being infected with HIV via blood transfusion is estimated at 1 per 2 million units. Donated organs are screened for HIV, and there are guidelines regarding semen donation for artificial insemination (discussed in Chapter 12).

Factors Contributing to Infection

Although most researchers agree that HIV is responsible for AIDS, many believe there may be additional factors that need to come into play before the immune system is seriously impaired. There are certain actions or conditions that appear to put some people at higher risk than others for infection with HIV. And other conditions may make a person with HIV more prone to developing AIDS.

Researchers have found that certain physiological or behavioral factors increase the risk of contracting HIV. For people of both sexes, these include behaviors already discussed, such as anal intercourse, multiple sex partners, and injection drug use. Other factors are having an STD, especially if genital lesions are present (Chirgwin, DeHovitz, Dillon, & McCormack, 1991; Hook et al., 1992; Martin, Gresenguet, Massanga, Georges, & Testa, 1992). Herpes lesions and syphilitic chancres, for example, provide a pathway for HIV into the body. Throat inflammation due to gonorrhea, syphilis, or herpes may also increase susceptibility during oral sex (UCSF, 1991). Multiple exposure to HIV also increases the risk of contracting it, although it can be transmitted in a single encounter. Moreover, a person in the early phase of AIDS is likely to pass on greater quantities of the virus (Cates, Chesney, & Cohen, 1997). Noninjection "recreational" drug use is also considered a risk factor for HIV. In part this is because drug use is associated with risk taking in general (Doll et al., 1991). As previously mentioned, there is a connection between crack cocaine use and STDs, including HIV (Carlson & Siegal, 1991; Chirgwin et al., 1991). The exchange of sex (especially fellatio) for crack is commonplace.

Factors that may tend to place women at higher risk include cervical ectopy (displacement or abnormal position), which may be associated with adolescence, pregnancy, use of oral contraceptives (Moss et al., 1991), IUD use, or being over age 45. For men, contact with HIV-infected menstrual blood may be a risk factor (de Vincenzi et al., 1992).

Cofactors, conditions that *may* make a person who is HIV-positive more likely to develop AIDS, include a history of STDs, drug use, alcohol use, poor nutrition, stress, smoking, pregnancy, and repeated exposure to HIV. Individual genetic conditions that predispose some people to developing AIDS may exist, as well as genetic elements that provide resistance to HIV or the development of AIDS (Johnson, 1993). There is a need for more research concerning possible cofactors for AIDS development.

AIDS DEMOGRAPHICS

The statistical characteristics of populations are called **demographics.** Public-health researchers often look at groups of people in terms of age, socioeconomic status, living area, ethnicity, or sex in order to understand the dynamics of disease transmission and prevention. In instances where sexually transmitted diseases are involved, they also look at sexual behaviors. This may entail studying groups based on sexual orientation as well as other characteristics that may be considered risk markers. No one is exempt from HIV exposure by virtue of belonging or not belonging to a specific group. Certain groups, however, appear *as a whole* to be at greater risk than others, or to face special difficulties where HIV is concerned. Many individuals within these groups may not be at risk, however, because they do not engage in risky behaviors.

The Gay Community

"AIDS has given a human face to an invisible minority," says Robert Bray of the National Gay and Lesbian Task Force. As of 1997, 309,247 gay and

The poor homosexuals—they have declared war upon nature and now nature is exacting an awful retribution.

—*Pat Buchanan*

Members of Act Up focus public attention on issues affecting people with HIV and AIDS.

bisexual men had been diagnosed with AIDS (CDC, 1997e). Nearly 185,000 have died. Another several hundred thousand are estimated to be infected with HIV. Although epidemiologists do not know for certain how HIV first arrived in the gay community, they do know that it spread like wildfire mainly because anal sex is such an efficient mode of transmission. Furthermore, initial research, education, and prevention efforts were severely hampered by a lack of government and public interest in what was perceived to be a "gay disease" (Shilts, 1987). Now, nearly 20 years after the virus first appeared, the gay community continues to reel under the repeated blows dealt by AIDS. Overall, sexual practices have become much safer, and the rate of new infection has fallen dramatically. But men who were infected years ago continue to grow sick and die.

Many members of the gay community have lost dozens of their friends. They may be coping with multiple-loss syndrome, a psychological condition that may be characterized by depression, hypochondria, feelings of guilt, sexual dysfunction, or self-destructive behavior.

In spite of the initial lack of public support for the fight against AIDS, or perhaps at least partly because of it, the gay and lesbian communities rallied together in a variety of ways to support each other, educate themselves and the public, and influence government policies. Grass-roots projects such as clinics, self-help groups, and information clearinghouses were created by people from both the gay and the straight communities whose lives were affected by HIV. The role of volunteers remains a crucial component of many AIDS organizations. Many people have devoted themselves to supporting the HIV/AIDS community or educating the public.

It appears that in recent years, some gay men have abandoned safer sexual practices. It is speculated that despair within the gay community may have led some men to intentionally put themselves at risk (Peyser, 1997). Feelings of invulnerability among younger men may also be at work (Lemp et al., 1994; Osmond et al., 1994; Ramafedi, 1994). Such may be the case with

Fear = Silence
Silence = Death
Knowledge = Power

—*AIDS Coalition to Unleash Power (ACT UP)*

I think God did send AIDS for a reason. It was to show how mean and sinful a healthy man can be toward a sick man.

—*Joe Bob Briggs*

a new generation of gay men who have begun practicing unsafe sex again in what is referred to as *bareback sex*. A recent study found that 25% of the young men who had sex with other men surveyed had engaged in higher-risk sex because they are less concerned about AIDS ("Lesbian, Gay, and Bisexual Youth," 1997). Cyberspace seems to be the most visible source for discussion of barebacking. This practice appears to have become more common in part because of what has come to be called the "morning-after" pill. This still-experimental treatment, which requires taking a potent combination of AIDS drugs for 28 days, may prevent HIV from taking root if it is begun within a few days of exposure to the virus ("Health & Safety," 1998). The CDC is considering recommending the drugs for gay men, rape victims, and injection drug users.

Members of the gay community not only empower themselves to face the AIDS epidemic, they inspire and empower many outside the community to lend their voices and support to the cause of AIDS prevention. Nonetheless, the perception of AIDS as a gay disease rather than a viral disease lingers, and some who have moral objections to homosexual behavior still blame AIDS on gays.

Women and HIV

More than 98,000 women are currently diagnosed with AIDS in this country; several hundred thousand are estimated to be infected with HIV (CDC, 1997e). AIDS among women represented 22% of all cases reported in 1997. Most were infected through injection drug use (32%) or heterosexual contact with an infected partner (38%). Although women as a group are not at special risk for HIV, the activities that put them at risk include injection drug use, being a sex partner of an injection drug user or a gay or bisexual man, or having multiple sex partners.

Women are often diagnosed at a later stage than men. They are also one-third more likely to die without an AIDS-defining condition than are HIV-infected men. There are two principal reasons for this. First, women are not generally perceived to be at risk for HIV, so neither they nor their physicians are alert to signs of HIV infection they may exhibit. Second, women generally serve in caretaking roles for their children, partners, and other relatives. They may also be breadwinners. Consequently, they may not seek care for themselves until they are quite ill.

Among the most pressing needs of women with HIV is inclusion in clinical trials for HIV and AIDS treatments. Women have generally been excluded from such trials, partly because AIDS has not been perceived to affect women. But because women's physiology is different from men's, especially in regard to hormones, it is imperative that they have access to new and experimental therapies, so that what works for them—and what does not—can be discovered (Minkoff & Dehovitz, 1991).

Issues of poverty, racism, and sexism also need to be addressed if all women are to receive the care they need. Not only are HIV-positive women of color largely excluded from quality medical care; lesbians with HIV are practically invisible. Although as a group they are not at high risk for HIV, lesbians can and do contract the virus in the same ways as heterosexuals. (Health-care issues of lesbians were discussed in Chapter 13.)

Pregnancy is a particularly painful dilemma for a woman with HIV. Issues that must be considered include the chance of the child's being HIV-infected, the desire of the woman to have a child, the probability that the child will be orphaned, the effect of HIV on the pregnancy, and the effect of pregnancy on the course of HIV infection (Smeltzer & Whipple, 1991).

Children and HIV

As of December 1997, 8,086 children had been diagnosed with AIDS and thousands more with HIV (CDC, 1997e). Most of these cases were acquired perinatally. The impact of HIV is greatest among 1- to 4-year-olds, particularly African American and Latino children. Of children in this age group in New York State, AIDS is the leading cause of death among Latino children and the second leading cause of death among African American children. As the number of infected women rises, so does the burden on families and society, which must care for hundreds (or possibly thousands) of orphans, many of whom have HIV or AIDS (Chu, Buehler, Oxtoby, & Kolbourne, 1991).

The incidence of AIDS among children has been affected by recommendations by the CDC, which suggests routine counseling and voluntary prenatal HIV testing for women and the use of ZDV to prevent perinatal transmission (CDC, 1998b).

Teens and College Students

HIV cases are increasing rapidly among young people (CDC, 1997e; Rosenberg, Biggar, & Goedert, 1994). The CDC and the American College Health Association estimate that 1 in 500 college students is infected with HIV (CDC, 1997d). (We should bear in mind that most of those in their twenties were probably infected in their teens.) Young gays, Blacks, Latinos, and runaways are among those most affected, but others are also at increasing risk, including Whites, heterosexuals, and rural teens.

Adolescence and risk taking often seem to go together like peanut butter and jelly. Because teenagers often have a sense of invulnerability, they may put themselves at great risk without really understanding what it means. Public-health officials support education about condoms for sexually active teenagers (Roper, Petersen, & Curran, 1993).

> I have never shared needles. And obviously I'm not a gay man. The only thing I did was something every single one of you has already done or will do.
>
> —*Krista Blake, infected with HIV as a teenager*

Older Adults

Between 1991 and 1997, the number of new AIDS cases rose twice as fast among older people (age 50 and over) as they did among young adults. In 1997, 11% of AIDS cases were diagnosed among people 50 and older (CDC, 1997e). Compared with the early days of the epidemic, when most cases among older adults were contracted through a blood transfusion, more cases are now the result of unprotected sex and injection drug use. Contributing to the higher rates among both men and women are the similarity of diseases that signal AIDS to the illnesses associated with aging, a lack of awareness on the part of physicians, and a sense among older people that they are not vulnerable to AIDS ("Number of AIDS Cases," 1998). When older

People of color are disproportionately represented in HIV/AIDS statistics. For African American and Latino men, the average survival time following diagnosis is 2 years or less.

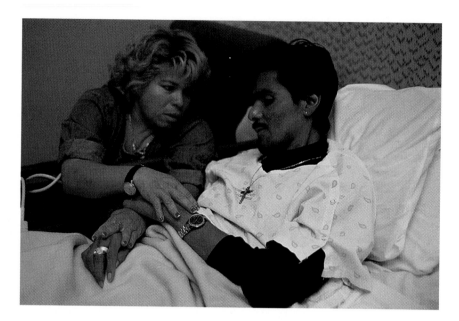

people are diagnosed with AIDS, it is more often in the later stages. In 1996, 13% of people 50 and older died within a month of their AIDS diagnosis, compared with 6% of those between 13 and 49. Given what we know about the virus that causes AIDS, it is quite apparent that it does not discriminate.

Poverty, Ethnicity, and HIV

HIV and AIDS, like many of society's ills, are often linked with poverty that is enforced by racism and discrimination. The disease is a significant presence among the homeless. Despair often fosters unsafe behaviors, and poverty and prejudice limit access to health care. Poor people in ethnic communities plagued with crime and violence may find themselves trapped in a vicious downward spiral. Until there is social and economic justice, even education and health care may not be sufficient to stem the rising tide of HIV. In 1993, AIDS became the leading cause of death among all Americans aged 25–44 (Altman, 1995). In 1996, it dropped to second place, following unintentional injuries (CDC, 1998a). Although the death toll for AIDS in the United States declined in 1996, the decrease was far more striking among White people than it was among people of color and women. African Americans and Latinos are disproportionately represented in HIV/AIDS statistics. White AIDS patients live an average of 3 years after diagnosis, yet African American and Latino men survive 2 years or less. Following diagnosis, African American women's average survival time is 18 months to 2 years; that of Latinas is a mere 3 months.

Ethnic communities are often suspicious of outsiders, whom they may perceive as interfering or threatening. In Chapter 15, we discussed the infamous Tuskegee syphilis study and its effects on African Americans' perceptions of the health-care establishment. In 1988, the CDC began to respond to the need for ethnically sensitive programs by establishing grants for 32 ongoing HIV prevention programs targeting specific ethnic groups, including

African Americans, Latinos, Native Americans, and Alaskan natives. One group targeted Asian Americans and Pacific Islanders (Holman, Jenkins, Gayle, Duncan, & Lindsey, 1991). Until the health issues of ethnic communities are consistently approached with sensitivity, it will be difficult to ascertain the best means of providing optimum assistance and care (Doll et al., 1991; Mays & Jackson, 1991; Wyatt, 1991).

PREVENTION AND TREATMENT

As a whole, our society remains in denial about the realities of HIV risk. Many assume their partners are not HIV infected because they look healthy, "clean," and/or attractive. In addition, the federal response to AIDS has failed to lay out a coherent strategic plan of action (Presidential Advisory Council on HIV/AIDS, 1997). With tens of thousands of Americans—as many as half of them teenagers or young adults—becoming infected with HIV each year, hope is fragile, and apathy is an enemy in the fight against this disease. To assess your own attitudes toward HIV prevention, see "Practically Speaking: HIV-Prevention Attitude Scale."

Protecting Ourselves

To protect ourselves and those we care about from HIV, there are some things we should know in addition to the basic facts about transmission and prevention.

What We Need to Know   First, we should be aware that the use of alcohol and drugs significantly increases risky behaviors. If we are serious about protecting ourselves, we need to assess our risks when we are clearheaded and act to protect ourselves. Second, we need to develop our communication skills so that we can discuss risks and prevention with our partner or potential partner. If we want our partner to disclose information about past high-risk behavior, we have to be willing to do the same. Third, we may need to have information on HIV testing. If we have engaged in high-risk behavior, we may want to be tested for our own peace of mind and that of our partner. If we test positive for HIV, we need to make important decisions regarding our health, sexual behavior, and lifestyle. Fourth, if we are sexually active with more than one long-term, monogamous partner, we need to become very familiar with condoms.

Condoms   Although America has responded to the threat of AIDS by increased purchasing of condoms, condom use remains low among many segments of the population. Following Surgeon General Koop's 1987 report endorsing condoms for safer sex, there was a 50% increase in condom sales (*U.S. News and World Report,* 1994). Although increased sales imply increased use, it is clear that many people remain unconvinced regarding either their own vulnerability to HIV or the usefulness of condoms in preventing its spread.

Although any sexual activity involving semen, vaginal fluid, or blood carries some degree of risk, condoms have repeatedly been demonstrated to effectively reduce risk. As we have stressed before, condoms do not

READ EACH STATEMENT carefully. Record your immediate reaction to each statement by writing the letter that corresponds to your answer. There is no right or wrong answer for each statement, so mark your own response.

Key
A = Strongly agree
B = Agree
C = Undecided
D = Disagree
E = Strongly disagree

1. I am certain that I could be supportive of a friend with HIV.
2. I feel that people with HIV got what they deserve.
3. I am comfortable with the idea of using condoms for sex.
4. I would dislike the idea of limiting sex to just one partner to avoid HIV infection.
5. It would be embarrassing to get the HIV antibody test.
6. It is meant for some people to get HIV.
7. Using condoms to avoid HIV is too much trouble.
8. I believe that AIDS is a preventable disease.
9. The chance of getting HIV makes using IV drugs stupid.

10. People can influence their friends to practice safe behavior.
11. I would shake hands with a person having HIV.
12. I will avoid sex if there is a slight chance that the partner might have HIV.
13. If I were to have sex, I would insist that a condom be used.
14. If I used IV drugs, I would not share the needles.
15. I intend to share HIV facts with my friends.

Scoring
Calculate the total points for each statement using the following point values. Items 1, 3, 8–15: Strongly agree = 5, Agree = 4, Undecided = 3, Disagree = 2, Strongly disagree = 1. For the remaining items: Strongly agree = 1, Agree = 2, Undecided = 3, Disagree = 4, Strongly disagree = 5.

The higher the score, the more positive the prevention attitude.

Source: William L. Yarber, Professor of Health Education, Indiana University, Bloomington; Mohammad Torabi, Professor of Health Education, Indiana University, Bloomington; L. Harold Veenker, Professor Emeritus of Health Education, Purdue University, Lafayette, IN.

guarantee 100% safety from HIV. Abstinence is safer. But if we choose to have sex, using a condom significantly reduces the risk (just as putting on a seat belt improves your safety when riding in a car).

Getting the Word Out

Education is the key to AIDS prevention. Yet, despite widespread public educational efforts on the part of public-health officials and AIDS organizations, many people remain uninformed about and unsympathetic to people with AIDS and HIV—at least until it strikes someone they care about.

AIDS has changed us forever. It has brought out the best in us, and the worst.

—*Michael Gottlieb, MD*

Obstacles to Education: Blame and Denial HIV/AIDS is still seen by many people as a disease of "marginalized" groups, those who are outside the mainstream of American life as it is portrayed on reruns of "Leave It to Beaver" and "The Brady Bunch." (Robert Reed, the actor who played the role of the Brady dad, died of AIDS-related causes in 1992.) People who are not White, not middle class, and not heterosexual are often viewed with suspicion by people who are. People who are gay or lesbian are often ignored or reviled even within their own ethnic communities. People who use drugs are written off as useless, worthless, and criminal. Prostitutes are frequently blamed for spreading STDs, even though they undoubtedly contract the disease from their clients, who more than likely have or will spread it to their partner or partners.

Some of this intolerance stems from conservative religious beliefs that sexuality in general and homosexuality in particular are sinful. People with these views often tend to blame those with HIV for their own illness. But it isn't just religious conservatives who have these kinds of attitudes. A study of college students' attitudes toward people with HIV found they blamed gay men more than heterosexuals for getting AIDS when sexual contact was the mode of transmission. They also believed that a person who got HIV through a blood transfusion was less responsible for getting it than one who got it sexually or through injection drugs. Men were more apt than women to blame the person for getting AIDS (Dowell, LoPresto, & Sherman, 1991).

Such blaming has consequences that are both ugly and dangerous. Although one effect of AIDS has been to make gay men more visible and less suspect, another has been to attract hate-motivated violence against them. Men who have been victims of vicious incidents of gay bashing report that their attackers accuse them of causing AIDS (Webb, 1992). Projecting the blame for AIDS onto certain groups not only stigmatizes people in those groups; it also keeps the blamer from looking into his or her own behavior. This denial is one of the biggest obstacles AIDS educators face. And it affects not only adults, but their children, too.

Teaching About HIV and AIDS It is difficult to determine the effect, if any, of public education on the spread of AIDS. Experts at the 12th International AIDS Conference in Geneva report that although prevention campaigns are succeeding in a few countries, those successes are spotty, even in so-called advanced nations like the United States (Perlman, 1998). Some elementary and secondary schools teach sex education and STD prevention, but such teaching remains controversial. "Teens are at the mercy of adults," writes Barbara Kantrowitz (1992), "—parents, teachers, politicians—who often won't give young people the information they desperately need to make the right choices about their sexual behavior." Fear abounds among adults: fear that sex education will lead to sex, that teaching about homosexuality will lead to people becoming gay, that discussion of sexuality is immoral. Some conservative groups feel that sex education should be done by parents, but often these same parents are the least informed.

Most parents want AIDS education for their children, especially those of high school age. However, there is good evidence that younger adolescents are becoming sexually active, and they are notoriously the least informed and least likely to use protection (Sonenstein et al., 1991). Current sex educators believe that the focus should be on self-esteem, communication, critical thinking, and building refusal skills. They believe abstinence should be stressed as a positive, healthy, mature, and socially acceptable choice. For those who are sexually active, which seems inevitable for most older teens, the facts about risks and prevention, including the effectiveness of properly used condoms, should be taught and reinforced (Mangasarian, 1993; Roper et al., 1993).

Outreach Programs Outreach programs for groups who are at particularly high risk for HIV can be very effective if they are sensitive to the unique

Educating students and other groups with trained speakers who are HIV-positive is an effective way to provide information and sensitize audiences to issues surrounding HIV. Here, speakers from Project First Hand share their stories of living with HIV with a university class.

cultural, ethnic, and social issues that apply to these groups. Education about risk, prevention, and testing is often most effective when given by peers from the community in question (Kantrowitz, 1992). Here are some examples of programs that are used to reach specific groups of people:

- Trained teen peer-counselors who talk to teenagers in clinics or classrooms; young people who are living with HIV can be especially effective by simply telling their stories (Mota, 1991). Peer-group support and reinforcement have been shown to reduce risky behaviors among adolescents (Jemmott, Jemmott, & Fong, 1992).

- Gay men who distribute condoms and safer sex information in "public sex environments," such as parks, roadside rest stops, and public restrooms (Beckstein, 1990).

- Young African American or Latino men who distribute clean needles, bleach kits, and condoms in ethnic neighborhoods where there is high drug use. Such programs have effectively demonstrated that they can reduce the spread of HIV (CDC, 1995c).

- Latina women who counsel other women in their neighborhoods about risks, safer sex, health care, and communication.

- Former prostitutes or other sex workers and injection drug users who can talk about their own lives to members of these risk groups; if they are HIV-positive, their comments can be especially effective.

Community-based clinics, staffed by community members, can provide a variety of services, including examinations and treatment for STDs, HIV testing, and counseling. Drug education and treatment programs are increasingly needed in communities where injection drug and crack use are rampant (Kolata, 1995). But many communities simply do not have the funds for such programs.

Needle-exchange programs, especially those that include information about risks and HIV prevention, also play an important role. However, these programs are controversial because some people believe they endorse or encourage drug use. Others feel that because the drug use already exists, saving lives should be the first priority. Although needle-exchange programs are illegal in some areas, they are often allowed to continue as long as the workers keep a low profile. Needle-exchange activists believe that high priority should be given to legalizing and expanding these programs, which are cost-effective and have the potential of saving thousands of lives (Day, 1995).

HIV Testing

Free or low-cost and anonymous or confidential HIV testing is available in many areas, although in some places, people are turned away from testing sites because of a lack of funding.

Types of Tests Almost everyone who has the HIV virus develops antibodies within 2–6 months after exposure. The most common tests look for these antibodies. Occasionally, a person with HIV will not have discernible antibodies when tested; if there is reason to suspect HIV, other tests can be performed that will be definitive (Pan, Sheppard, Winkelstein, & Levy, 1991).

The most common test for HIV is called the **ELISA,** an acronym for enzyme-linked immunosorbent assay. This simple blood test screens for the antibodies to HIV that are usually present 2 months after infection with the virus. A negative test result—meaning no antibodies are found—is considered highly (99.7%) accurate if received 6 months after the date of last possible exposure. In the event of a positive or inconclusive test result, a person should be retested; in ELISA tests on the general population, only about 20–30% of seropositive results are true positives indicating HIV infection. The test used to recheck positive ELISA results is called the **Western blot.** In the Western blot procedure, the antibodies are tested to determine whether they are specific to HIV. Usually, Western blot results are clearly either positive or negative; if there is an inconclusive result, the person should be tested again in 6 months; a few people who are HIV-negative repeatedly get inconclusive results. If necessary, more complex tests can be performed, including HIV-antigen (polymerase chain reaction, or PCR, tests), recombinant DNA-HIV tests, and CD4 receptor T-cell counts.

For those who choose not to get their test results at a clinic or doctor's office, the Food and Drug Administration approved, in 1996, two home-use HIV kits. Currently, only one, the Home Access HIV-1 Test System, remains on the market. Included in the kit is information about how HIV is transmitted and prevented. The kit is more than 99% sensitive for detecting HIV infection ("Home-Use HIV Test Kits," 1998) and costs about $30.

Unlike many common home tests, the Home Access system does not provide users with a result at home. Instead, the user collects a blood sample, mails it anonymously with the kit's code number, and calls 3–7 days later for the test results. Those who test negative get their results via a recorded message; those who test positive speak to a counselor. Inadequate counseling, a false sense of security if the test turns out negative, and insufficient information about the increased risk for other STDs are issues that concern many health-care providers (Kisabeth, Pontius, Statland, & Galper, 1997). Those using the Internet to locate and purchase tests are warned to be cautious about the many kits that are marketed yet not approved for sale ("Home Access Health," 1997). In spite of the number of concerns and caveats, home testing is a viable option for those who might otherwise not get tested.

Getting Tested   Most people who go for an HIV test are anxious. Even though the vast majority of test results are negative, there is still the understandable fear that one has drawn the short straw. For many people, there are probably also feelings of ambivalence or guilt about the risky behaviors that led them to this situation. Because of these kinds of responses, which are normal, counseling is an important part of the testing process. It is important for people being tested to understand what their risks for HIV actually are and to know what the results mean. It is also important for everyone, no matter what the results of their tests are, to understand the facts of transmission and prevention. For the majority who test negative, practicing abstinence or safer sex, remaining monogamous, avoiding injection drug use, and other preventive measures can eliminate much of the anxiety associated with HIV. (These measures reduce the risk of other diseases as well.)

Counseling is vitally important for those who are HIV-positive. Early treatment and positive health behaviors are essential to retaining good health and prolonging life. Pregnancy counseling should be made available for women. It is also essential for a person to know that he or she can pass the virus to others.

Partner Notification   Theoretically, both current and past partners should be notified so that they can be tested and receive counseling. There is considerable controversy surrounding the issues of disclosure of HIV serostatus and partner notification. The rights of the individual to privacy may be in direct conflict with the public's right to know. From a public-health standpoint, mandatory contact tracing would be a helpful way to slow down the spread of HIV. But from a civil rights standpoint, it would be a gross violation. Moreover, in some instances it would be impossible to track down all contacts, such as in cases involving prostitution or anonymous sexual encounters. AIDS counselors and health-care practitioners currently encourage those with HIV to make all possible efforts to contact past and current partners. In some cases, counselors try to make such contacts, with their clients' permission.

Treatments

The issues surrounding treatments for HIV infection and AIDS are multifaceted. Many kinds of questions, some of which have no easy answers, are brought to light. The issues often involve an interplay of medicine, ethics, economics, and law. Ultimately, it is government policy that determines the direction of most AIDS research, treatment, and services.

The major issues that will influence the future direction of government policy regarding HIV and AIDS include (1) how provisions for health care for the uninsured and underinsured will be made on state and national levels, (2) the effectiveness of policies designed to change risky sexual behaviors, (3) the effectiveness of programs to change behaviors of injection drug users, and (4) the development of the disease itself (Fox, 1991).

Guidelines state that viral load tests and T-cell counts should be used together to help make decisions about starting or changing a treatment. **Viral load tests** measure the amount of HIV in the bloodstream and serve as an indicator for determining the risk of progressing to AIDS.

Today, there are 11 major AIDS drugs approved by the Food and Drug Administration. They fall into three categories. One type consists of therapies to treat symptoms and infections; these include antibiotics, pain medications, and so on. Among the most common drugs used to treat the opportunistic infections associated with AIDS are preventive antibiotics such as Septra and Bactrim, dapsone, and aerosolized pentamidine, all of which can be very effective against pneumocystis. Because deadly reservoirs of the AIDS virus can lurk silently inside the immune system cells, treatments should continue indefinitely (Perlman, 1997).

The second type of treatment consists of drugs that affect the virus in some way. This category includes the antiretroviral drugs that act directly on the virus to change or delay the way in which it progresses. The newest drugs in this category are the *protease inhibitors,* which block an enzyme called protease that helps assemble the virus at a later stage in its life cycle. Another group of antiviral drugs is the nucleoside analogs (examples are AZT [azidothymidine] and ZVD [zidovudine]), which work by blocking reverse transcriptase, the enzyme used by HIV to copy its genetic material into a host cell's DNA (see Figure 16.1, page 496).

The third type of treatment includes therapies designed to bolster the immune system's natural responses. Most physicians agree that early detection of HIV is essential for deriving optimum benefits from medical care and healthy lifestyle choices.

The most effective treatment for HIV to date is early and aggressive treatment with a combination of two nucleoside analogs (such as AZT and ddI) and one protease inhibitor (such as saquinavir, indinavir, or nelfinavir), sometimes referred to as a "cocktail" ("Positive News," 1997). Using three drugs rather than two helps ensure that the treatment will continue to be effective against the virus, which mutates rapidly and can become resistant to drugs ("Stanford AIDS Study," 1998). The new drug combinations have cut the death rates by 70% and have curbed the rate of opportunistic infections by 73% (Palella, Delaney, Moorman, Loveless, Fuher, Satten, & Aschman et al., 1998). Patients practicing this regimen must maintain close communication with their physicians, because dangerous side effects can develop.

As new drug combinations change the course of HIV infection, questions arise about how best to use the drugs, who will pay for them, how to address the discarding of the most powerful drugs because of their unbearable side effects, and how the delay of symptoms and death will affect patients. Because antiretroviral drugs are very expensive, they are not an option for everyone. The annual cost of a regimen of the "cocktail," for example, is approximately $20,000. Further, physicians may judge that some patients will be less able or likely to follow the complicated drug regimen accurately. Another issue is that many people diagnosed with HIV infection have already faced their own mortality; now they must adopt a new attitude. For some, this may mean learning to live with a manageable chronic disease rather than a death sentence—a course that will require a different kind of courage and perseverance.

The search for a cure for AIDS continues. Learning more about the genetics of the small number of HIV-infected individuals who remain healthy may lead to new therapies that can help others. Gene therapy, in which the immune system is reconstructed with genetically altered resistant cells, is one potentially promising approach. Researchers are working on microbicides, agents that kill pathogens, as well as a vaccine that can be used to prevent HIV. Even if their success proves transient, the new approaches should improve patients' prospects by creating more obstacles to the virus.

LIVING WITH HIV OR AIDS

People with AIDS, sometimes referred to as PWAs, and people with HIV, PWHs, have the same needs as everyone else—and a few more. If you are HIV-positive, in addition to dealing with the special issues of loss and grief, you will need to pay special attention to maintaining good health. If you are caring for someone with HIV or AIDS, you also have special needs.

If You Are HIV-Positive

A positive antibody test is scary to just about anyone. Many people view it as a death sentence, while others try to pretend it just isn't true. Whatever else it may be, a positive test result is valuable news. It is news that may make it possible to actually save your life. If you hadn't learned about your status in this way, you would probably not have known until a serious opportunistic infection announced the presence of HIV. At that point, many of your best medical options would have been lost and you might have spread the virus to others who would not have been otherwise exposed ("After You've Tested," 1990).

Taking Care of Your Health   It is important to find a physician who has experience working with HIV and AIDS, and—even more important, perhaps—who is sensitive to the issues confronted by PWHs and PWAs. In addition to appropriate medical treatment, factors that can help promote your continuing good health include good nutrition, plenty of rest, appropriate exercise, limited (or no) alcohol use, and stress reduction. People with HIV or AIDS should stop smoking tobacco because it increases susceptibility to PCP. Also, you need to reduce your chances of exposure to infectious organisms. This doesn't mean shutting yourself up in a room and never coming out. It simply means you need to take more than ordinary care not to expose yourself to infectious organisms—for example, in spoiled or improperly cooked foods, or unwashed glasses or utensils used by sick household members, or from certain kinds of pets. Your doctor or nearest HIV/AIDS resource group should have more information on these measures.

In addition, if you decide to have sexual relations, it means practicing safer sex, even if your partner is also HIV-positive. Researchers caution that one can become reinfected with different HIV strains (Chermann, cited in Challice, 1992). Moreover, STDs of all kinds can be much worse for people with an impaired immune system. HIV doesn't mean an end to being sex-

The Names Project has created a giant quilt, each square of which has been lovingly created by friends and families of people who have died of AIDS. The quilt now contains more than 41,000 panels.

ual, but it does suggest that different ways of expressing love and lust may need to be explored.

It is recommended that women who are HIV-positive have Pap tests every 6–12 months. Cervical biopsies may also be necessary to determine whether CIN or cancer is present.

Other Needs   Besides taking care of one's physical health, a person who is living with HIV needs to take care of psychological and emotional needs. The stigma and fear surrounding HIV and AIDS often make it difficult to just get on with the business of living. Suicide is the leading cause of non-HIV-related death among people who are HIV-positive (Israelski, 1992). Among gay and bisexual men, social support is generally better for Whites than for Blacks; in Black communities, there tends to be less affirmation from primary social support networks and less openness about sexual orientation (Ostrow et al., 1991). Women, who usually concern themselves with caring for others, may not be inclined to seek out support groups and networks (Kline, Kline, & Oken, 1992). But people who live with HIV and AIDS say that it's important not to feel isolated. If you are HIV-positive, we encourage you to seek support from AIDS organizations in your area. (See the Resource Center for referrals to groups in your area, or check your local telephone directory.)

If You Are Caring for Someone with HIV or AIDS

When someone you know is diagnosed with HIV or AIDS, you, as a support person, should be aware of the uncharted territory ahead in terms of discrimination, experimental drug treatments, the unpredictable course of the disease, new and strong emotions, and the hope that always accompanies each treatment. Added to all this are a changing sense of time and increasing feelings of urgency, which intensify all of the above.

Caring for someone with HIV or AIDS also means dealing with your own profound emotions. This includes confronting your fears about death and dying, accepting your changing relationship with your friend or partner, and addressing your anger, depression, loneliness, guilt, and/or sense of abandonment.

To help your friend or partner, you may need to actively seek information and support from legal, medical, and psychological resources. National, state, and city hotlines, referral agencies, texts, professionals with experience and compassion, and support groups can be found by searching through telephone directories and/or libraries in your region. Reaching out and sharing empower you to meet the challenges you face today and will undoubtedly continue to face in the future.

What we learn in times of pestilence [is] that there are more things to admire in men than to despise.

—*Albert Camus (1913–1960)*

■   "Education is going to be the vaccine for AIDS," says June Osborn, dean of the University of Michigan's School of Public Health and former chair of the National Commission on AIDS. As we have seen, there are many public misperceptions concerning HIV and AIDS, and the denial of risk appears to be epidemic in many areas. But AIDS can be prevented. We hope that this chapter has provided you with information that will serve as your vaccine.

SUMMARY

What Is AIDS?

- *AIDS* is an acronym for *acquired immune deficiency syndrome.* In order for a person to receive an AIDS diagnosis, he or she must have a positive blood test indicating the presence of *HIV (human immunodeficiency virus)* antibodies and have a T-cell count below 200; if the T-cell count is higher, the person must have 1 or more of the 27 diseases or conditions associated with AIDS. These include *opportunistic infections,* such as *Pneumocystis carinii pneumonia* and tuberculosis; cancers, such as *Ka-posi's sarcoma,* lymphomas, and cervical cancer or CIN; and conditions associated with AIDS, such as *wasting syndrome* and AIDS dementia. Other conditions may lead to an AIDS diagnosis, including persistent candidiasis and outbreaks of herpes.

- A host of symptoms are associated with HIV/ AIDS. Because these symptoms may be indicative of many other diseases and conditions, HIV and AIDS cannot be self-diagnosed; testing by a clinician or physician is necessary.

- *Leukocytes,* or white blood cells, play major roles in defending the body against invading organisms and cancerous cells. One type, the *macrophage,* engulfs foreign particles and displays the invader's *antigen* on its own surface. *Antibodies* bind to antigens, inactivate them, and mark them for destruction by *killer T cells.* Other white blood cells called *lymphocytes* include *helper T cells,* which are programmed to "read" the antigens and then begin directing the immune system's response. The number of helper T cells in an individual's body is an important indicator of how well the immune system is functioning.

- *Viruses* are primitive entities; they can't propel themselves independently, and they can't reproduce unless they are inside a host cell. Within the human immunodeficiency virus's protein core is the genetic material (RNA) that carries the information the virus needs to replicate itself. A *retrovirus* can "write" its RNA (the genetic program) into a host cell's DNA.

- Although HIV begins replication right away within the host cells, it is not detectable in the blood for some time—often years. HIV antibodies, however, are generally detectable in the blood within 2–6 months. A person's *serostatus* is HIV-negative if antibodies are not present and HIV-positive if antibodies are detected. "T-cell count" or "CD4 count" refers to the number of helper T cells that are present in a cubic milliliter of blood. A healthy person has a T-cell count in the range of 500–1600.

- When a person is first infected with HIV, he or she may experience severe flulike symptoms. During this period, the virus is dispersed throughout the lymph nodes and other tissues. The virus may stay localized in these areas for years, but it continues to replicate and to destroy T cells. As the number of infected cells goes up, the number of T cells goes down. In advanced AIDS, the T-cell count drops to under 200, and the virus itself is detectable in the blood.

Epidemiology and Transmission of HIV

- More than 641,000 people are currently diagnosed with AIDS in the United States; between 800,000 and 1 million are estimated to be infected with HIV. Worldwide, more than 30 million people are infected with HIV or have developed AIDS. Heterosexual transmission is becoming more common and is expected to continue to increase. The role of injection drug use in the spread of HIV is increas-

ing as HIV-infected drug users pass the virus to each other in blood and to women partners during sexual activity. Crack cocaine use is also implicated in the heterosexual transmission of HIV. Women may infect their children in utero or through breast-feeding.

- HIV is not transmitted by casual contact.

- Activities or situations that may promote transmission include sexual transmission through vaginal or anal intercourse without a condom; fellatio without a condom; cunnilingus without a latex or other barrier; sharing needles contaminated with infected blood; in utero infection from mother to fetus, from blood during delivery, or in breast milk; sharing sex toys without disinfecting them; accidental contamination when infected blood enters the body through mucous membranes (eyes or mouth) or cuts, abrasions, or punctures in the skin (relatively rare); or blood transfusions administered before April 1, 1985.

- Certain physiological or behavioral factors increase the risk of contracting HIV. In addition to anal intercourse, multiple sex partners, and injection drug use, these factors include having an STD (especially if genital lesions are present), multiple exposure to HIV, and drug and alcohol use.

AIDS Demographics

- Studying *demographics,* such as age, socioeconomic status, living area, ethnicity, or sex, can help researchers understand the dynamics of disease transmission and prevention. In instances where sexually transmitted diseases are involved, they also examine sexual behaviors. Certain groups appear as a whole to be at greater risk than others or to face special difficulties where HIV is concerned, including gay men, women, teenagers, and young inner-city African Americans.

- The gay and lesbian communities, along with other concerned individuals, have rallied together in a variety of ways to support people with HIV and AIDS, to educate themselves and the public, and to influence government policies.

- Women face unique issues where HIV is concerned. As the number of infected women rises, the number of infected children is also expected to rise. Because teenagers often have a sense of invulnerability, they may put themselves at great risk without really understanding the consequences that may result.

▪ HIV/AIDS is often linked with poverty enforced by racism and discrimination. As of December 1997, HIV/AIDS was the second leading cause of death among all Americans age 25–44.

Prevention and Treatment

▪ To protect ourselves and those we care about from HIV, we need to be aware that alcohol and drug use significantly increases risky behaviors, develop communication skills so that we can talk with our partner, and get information on HIV testing. If we are sexually active with more than one long-term, monogamous partner, we need to use condoms consistently.

▪ Free or low-cost anonymous or confidential HIV testing is available in many areas, although in some places people are turned away from testing sites because of a lack of funding. The most common test, *ELISA,* looks for antibodies to the virus.

▪ There are three basic types of medical treatments for HIV and AIDS: therapies to treat the symptoms and infections, such as antibiotics and pain medications; drugs that affect the virus in some way; and therapies that boost the immune system.

Living with HIV or AIDS

▪ An HIV or AIDS diagnosis may be a cause for sadness and grieving, but it also can be a time for reevaluation and growth. Those whose friends or family members are living with HIV, or who are themselves HIV-positive, need information, practical support, and emotional support.

▪ Early detection of HIV can greatly enhance both the quality and quantity of life. Appropriate med-

ical treatment and a healthy lifestyle are important. People with HIV or AIDS also need to practice safer sex and consider seeking support from AIDS organizations. AIDS caregivers need support, too.

SUGGESTED READING

Ahmed, P. I. (1992). *Living and Dying with AIDS.* New York: Plenum Press. A collection of papers that offer personal and practical perspectives on HIV and AIDS.

Arno, Peter S., & Feiden, Karyn L. (1992). *Against the Odds: The Story of AIDS Drug Development, Politics and Profits.* New York: HarperCollins. A fascinating and frustrating story of what can occur when human medical needs conflict with those of business and government.

DiClemente, Ralph J. (1992). *Adolescents and AIDS.* Newbury Park, CA: Sage. A well-researched and sobering report on the risks teenagers face (and take).

Luna, G. Cajetan. (1997). *Youths Living with HIV.* Binghamton, NY: Haworth Press. Explores the struggles and adaptations of HIV-infected young Americans.

Senechek, David. (1998). *Placing AIDS and HIV in Remission: A Guide to Aggressive Medical Therapy for People with HIV Infection.* San Francisco: Senyczak Publications. An explanation by a physician in lay terms of the nature of the virus that causes AIDS and the remarkable new drugs that bring it to a standstill.

Shilts, Randy. (1987). *And the Band Played On: People, Politics and the AIDS Epidemic.* New York: St. Martin's Press. The fascinating story behind the "discovery" of AIDS, complete with real heroes and, unfortunately, real villains.

Stine, Gerald J. (1993). *Acquired Immune Deficiency Syndrome: Biological, Medical, Social, and Legal Issues.* Englewood Cliffs, NJ: Prentice-Hall. A factual study of the AIDS epidemic.

Valdiserri, R. O. (1994). *Gardening in Clay: Reflections on AIDS.* Ithaca, NY: Cornell University Press. A moving and informative series of essays by a person whose brother died from complications of AIDS.

17

Sexual Coercion: Harassment, Aggression, and Abuse

*A*LTHOUGH SEXUALITY PERMITS US to form and sustain deep bonds and intimate relationships, it may also have a darker side. For some people, sex is linked with coercion, degradation, aggression, and abuse. In these cases, sex becomes a weapon. Sex can be a means to exploit, humiliate, or harm others. In this chapter, we first examine the various aspects of sexual harassment, including the distinction between flirting and harassment and sexual harassment in schools, colleges, and the workplace. Next we look at harassment, prejudice, and discrimination directed against gay men and lesbians. Then we examine sexual aggression, including date rape and stranger rape, the motivations for rape, and the consequences of rape. Finally, we discuss child sexual abuse, examining the factors contributing to abuse, the types of sexual abuse and their consequences, and programs for preventing child sexual abuse.

SEXUAL HARASSMENT

Sexual harassment refers to two distinct types of behavior: the abuse of power for sexual ends and the creation of a hostile environment. In abuse of power, sexual harassment consists of unwelcomed sexual advances, requests for sexual favors, or other verbal or physical conduct of a sexual nature as a condition of instruction or employment (Frazier, Cochran, & Olson, 1995). Refusal to comply may result in reprisals (Charney & Russell, 1994). Only a person with power over another can commit the first kind of harassment (Pierce, 1994). In a **hostile environment,** someone acts in sexual ways that interfere with a person's performance at school or in the workplace. Such harassment is illegal. Sexual harassment may be regarded as a form of gender discrimination that contributes to a hostile and intimidating work environment (Murrell, Olson, & Frieze, 1995). In 1996, 15,889 sexual harassment charges were filed, up from 6,883 in 1991 (Goldberg, 1997).

Sexual harassment is a mixture of sex and power; power may often be the dominant element. In school and in the workplace, men devalue women by calling attention to their sexuality. Sexual harassment may be a way to keep women "in their place" and make them feel vulnerable.

There are other forms of behavior that, although not illegal, are considered by many to be sexual harassment. These include unwelcomed whistles, taunts, and obscenities directed from a man or group of men to a woman walking past them. They also include a man "talking to" a woman's breasts or body during conversation, or persistently giving her "the once over" as she walks past him, sits down, or enters or leaves a room. Such incidents may make women feel uncomfortable and vulnerable. (They have been described, in fact, as "little rapes.") The cumulative effect of these behaviors is to lead women to limit their activities, to avoid walking past groups of men, and to stay away from beaches, concerts, parties, and sports events unless they are accompanied by others (Bowman, 1993).

Flirtation Versus Harassment

There is nothing wrong with flirtation per se. A certain smile, look, or compliment can give zest and pleasure to both people. But persistent and unwelcomed flirtation can be sexual harassment if the flirtatious person holds power over the other, or if the flirtation creates a hostile school or work environment. Whether flirtation is sexual harassment depends on three factors. These apply to male-female, male-male, and female-female interactions.

1. *Whether you have equal power.* A person's having power over you limits your ability to refuse, for fear of reprisal. For example, if a professor or teaching assistant in your class asks you for a date, you are placed in an awkward position. If you say no, will your grade suffer? Will you be ignored in class? What other consequences might occur? If your boss at work asks for dates, you may be similarly concerned about losing your job, being demoted, or having your work environment become hostile. Ninety percent of the harassment claims filed in 1995 were by women (Wolfe, 1996). Because sexual harassment is typically perpetrated by people who have power over their victims, this statistic is not surprising.

2. *Whether you are approached appropriately.* "Hi babe, nice tits, wanna screw?" and "Hey stud, love your buns, wanna do it?" are patently offensive. But approaches that are complimentary ("You look really nice today"), indirect ("What do you think of the course?"), or direct ("Would you like to have some coffee?") are acceptable because they do not pressure you. You have the opportunity to let the overture pass, respond positively, or politely decline.

3. *Whether you wish to continue contact.* If you find the other person appealing, you may want to continue the flirtation. You can express interest or flirt back. But if you don't, you may want to stop the interaction by not responding or by responding in a neutral or discouraging manner.

The issue is complicated by several factors related to culture and gender. Differing cultural expectations may lead to misinterpretation. For example, when a Latino, whose culture encourages mutual flirting, says *"muy guapa"* (good looking) to a Latina walking by, the words may be meant *and* received as a compliment. But when a Latino says the same to a non-Latina, he may be dismayed to find the woman insulted. He perceives her as uptight, and she perceives him as rude, but each is misinterpreting the other because of cultural differences.

Three significant gender differences may contribute to sexual harassment. First, men are generally less likely to perceive activities as harassing than are women (Jones & Remland, 1992; Popovich, Gehlauf, Jolton, & Somers, 1992). Second, men tend to misperceive women's friendliness as sexual interest (Johnson, Stockdale, & Saal, 1991; Stockdale, 1993). Third, men are more likely than women to perceive male-female relationships as adversarial (Reilly, Lott, Caldwell, & DeLuca, 1992).

Power differences also affect perception. Personal questions asked by an instructor or supervisor, for example, are more likely to be perceived as sexual harassment than they would be if a student or co-worker asked them. What needs to be clear is the basis of the relationship: is it educational, business, or professional, or is it romantic or sexual? Flirtatious or sexual ways of relating are inappropriate in the first three contexts.

Harassment in School and College

Sexual harassment in various forms is widespread. It does not necessarily begin in adulthood; it may begin as early as middle childhood.

Harassment in Elementary and High School   It's a "time-honored" practice for boys to "tease" girls: flipping up their skirts, calling them names, touching their breasts, spreading sexual gossip, and so on. If such behavior is defined as teasing, its impact is discounted; it is just "fun." But if the behavior is thought of as sexual harassment, then the acts may be evaluated in a new light. Such behavior, researcher Carrie Herbert (1989) found, leads girls to "become more subordinated, less autonomous, and less capable of resisting. This behavior controls the girls through intimidation, embarrassment, or humiliation."

Among students, sexual harassment occurs most often when boys are in groups. Their motives may often be homosocial—heightening their group status by denigrating girls—rather than based on any specific animosity toward a particular girl (Carr, 1992). Harassment is usually either ignored by adults or regarded as normal or typical behavior among boys—"Boys will be boys." Girls are frequently blamed for the harassment because they did not "stand up for themselves" or they took the incidents "too seriously" (Herbert, 1989).

Harassment in College   Sexual harassment on college and university campuses has become a major concern in recent years. Various studies suggest that 20–50% of female college students have experienced some form of harassment from other students, faculty members, or administrators (Bursik, 1992; Paludi, 1990; Sundt, 1994). Many men have also been victimized, with estimates varying from 9% to 20% (Mazel & Percival, 1989; Sundt, 1994).

Two major problems in dealing with issues of sexual harassment are gender differences in levels of tolerance and attribution of blame. Women are often blamed for not taking a "compliment" and for provoking unwanted sexual attention by what they wear or how they look. These attitudes also seem to be widely held in college settings, especially among men.

Because of sexual harassment, students may find it difficult to study; others worry about their grades. If the harasser is an instructor controlling grades, students fear reporting the harassment. They may use strategies such as avoiding courses taught by the harasser. In extreme cases, the emotional consequences may sometimes be as severe as for those who are raped (Paludi, 1990). However, many students view the dating of students by professors as unethical behavior rather than harassment (Quatrella & Wentworth, 1995).

Most universities and colleges have developed sexual harassment policies. Although such policies help make students aware of harassment issues, their effectiveness depends on educating students about what constitutes harassment (Gressman et al., 1992; Williams, Lam, & Shively, 1992). Younger female students, in particular, are often unable to define clearly harassing situations as harassment, despite feelings of discomfort (Bremer, Moore, &

Sexual harassment, particularly in the workplace, creates a stressful and hostile environment for the victim.

Bildersee, 1991; Jaschick & Fretz, 1991). With the exception of coercive or highly intrusive behaviors, many students are uncertain about what behaviors constitute sexual harassment (Fitzgerald & Ormerod, 1991).

If a student finds herself or himself sexually harassed, the first step is to request the harasser to stop. The person may not be aware of the impact of his or her behavior. If he or she does not stop, the student should consult an advisor, resident assistant, counselor, or dean.

Harassment in the Workplace

Issues of sexual harassment are complicated in the workplace because work, like college, is one of the most important places where adults meet potential partners. As a consequence, sexual undercurrents or interactions often take place. Flirtations, romances, and affairs are common in the work environment. Drawing the line between flirtation and harassment can be filled with ambiguity—especially for men. Many women do not realize they were being harassed until much later. When they identify the behavior, they report feeling naive or gullible as well as guilty and ashamed. As they learn more about sexual harassment, they are able to identify their experiences for what they were—harassment (Kidder, Lafleur, & Wells, 1995).

Furthermore, sexuality and power issues can become intertwined. Power can manifest itself in sexual coercion or harassment (Bargh & Raymond, 1995). Sexual harassment tends to be most pervasive in formerly all-male occupations. In these occupations, sexual harassment is a means of exerting control over women and asserting male dominance. Such male bastions as the building trades, the trucking industry, law enforcement, and the military have been especially resistant to women entering (Niebuhr & Boyles, 1991; Schmitt, 1990). Female African American firefighters report high levels of harassment (Yoder & Aniakudo, 1995). Sexual harassment can be perpetrated by fellow employees as well as by supervisors. Recognizing this, the U.S.

Supreme Court recently ruled that employers are liable for their supervisors' behavior even if companies were unaware of their actions (Sward, 1998).

Sexual harassment can have a variety of consequences for the victim, including depression, anxiety, shame, humiliation, and anger (Charney & Russell, 1994; Paludi, 1990). To help protect themselves from the rising costs of sexual harassment, more employers are opting to purchase insurance policies for sexual harassment, discrimination, or wrongful discrimination. Fifty percent of the Fortune 500 companies have bought such coverage, presumably because suing has gotten easier and more lucrative ("An Insurance Policy," 1998).

ANTI-GAY/LESBIAN HARASSMENT, PREJUDICE, AND DISCRIMINATION

Many Americans feel profoundly ambivalent about gay men and lesbians. A large-scale survey conducted by the *New York Times* in 1993 found that 55% believed sexual behavior between adult gay men or lesbians is morally wrong (Schmalz, 1993). At the same time, 78% believed gay men and lesbians should have equal job opportunities. Yet 42% believed laws should not be passed to guarantee equal rights for gay men and lesbians.

Researchers have identified two forms of discrimination or bias against gay men and lesbians: heterosexual bias and anti-gay prejudice. We explain the distinctions between the two in the following sections.

Heterosexual Bias

Heterosexual bias, also known as **heterosexism,** is the tendency to see the world in heterosexual terms and to ignore or devalue homosexuality (Herek, Kimmel, Amaro, & Melton, 1991; Rich, 1983). Heterosexual bias may take numerous forms. Examples of this type of bias are:

▪ *Ignoring the existence of lesbians and gay men.* Discussions of various aspects of human sexuality may ignore gay men and lesbians, assuming that such individuals do not exist, are not significant, or are not worthy of inclusion. Without such inclusion, discussions of human sexuality are really discussions of *heterosexual* sexuality.

▪ *Segregating lesbians and gay men from heterosexuals.* Where sexual orientation is irrelevant, separating gay men and lesbians from others is a form of segregation, as in proposals to separate HIV-positive gay men (but not other HIV-positive individuals) from the general population.

▪ *Subsuming gay men and lesbians into a larger category.* Sometimes it is appropriate to make sexual orientation a category in data analysis, as in studies of adolescent suicide rates. If orientation is not included, findings may be distorted (Herek et al., 1991).

Prejudice, Discrimination, and Violence

Anti-gay prejudice is a strong dislike, fear, or hatred of gay men and lesbians because of their homosexuality. **Homophobia** is an irrational or phobic fear of gay men and lesbians. Not all anti-gay feelings are phobic in the clinical sense of being excessive and irrational, but they may be unreasonable or biased. (The feelings may, however, be within the norms of a biased culture.) Because prejudice may not be clinically phobic, "homophobia" is being increasingly replaced by the nonclinical phrase "anti-gay prejudice" (Haaga, 1991).

As a belief system, anti-gay prejudice justifies discrimination based on sexual orientation. In his classic work on prejudice, Gordon Allport (1958) states that social prejudice is acted out in three stages: offensive language, discrimination, and violence. Gay men and lesbians experience all three stages. They are called "faggot," "dyke," "queer," and "homo." They are discriminated against in terms of housing, employment opportunities, adoption, parental rights, family acceptance, and so on. And they are the victims of violence, known as **gay-bashing** or **queer-bashing.** Among college students, anti-gay prejudice often extends to those heterosexuals who voluntarily room with a lesbian or gay man. They are assumed to have "homosexual tendencies" and to have many of the negative stereotyped traits of gay men and lesbians, such as poor mental health.

Effects on Heterosexuals   Anti-gay prejudice adversely affects heterosexuals as well as gay men and lesbians. First, it creates fear and hatred, negative emotions that cause distress and anxiety. Second, it alienates heterosexuals from their gay family members, friends, neighbors, and co-workers. Third, it limits their range of behaviors and feelings, such as hugging or being emotionally intimate with same-sex friends, for fear that such intimacy may be "homosexual." Fourth, among men, it may lead to exaggerated displays of masculinity to prove that one is not gay, that is, effeminate.

Discrimination and Antidiscrimination Laws   As mentioned, gay men, lesbians, and bisexuals are discriminated against in many areas and experience high levels of stress as a result (Meyer, 1995). They face imprisonment in some states for engaging in oral and anal sex, for which heterosexuals are seldom prosecuted. Medical and public-health efforts against HIV/AIDS were inhibited initially because AIDS was perceived as "the gay plague" and was considered by some to be "punishment" against gay men for their "unnatural" sexual practices (Altman, 1985). The fear of HIV/AIDS has contributed to increased anti-gay prejudice among some heterosexuals (Lewes, 1992). Anti-gay prejudice influences parental reactions to their gay and lesbian children, often leading to estrangement (Holtzen & Agresti, 1990). And in some cases, a gay man's advances toward a homophobic male have led to manslaughter. Such sexual advances have been used as grounds for acquittal. (The bias in such a defense can be seen if one imagines a woman being allowed to kill a man for making a sexual advance.)

Gay men and lesbians have been seeking legislation to protect themselves from discrimination based on sexual orientation. Just recently, a federal law was passed protecting employees from being sexually harassed in the workplace by people of the same sex ("Same-Sex Harassment," 1998). Such legislation guarantees lesbians and gay men equal protection under the law. Public opinion supports equal employment opportunities for gay men and lesbians.

Violence Against Gay Men and Lesbians Violence against gay men and
lesbians has a long history. At times, such violence has been sanctioned by
religion. During the Middle Ages, the Inquisition burned "sodomites." In the
sixteenth century, England's King Henry VIII made sodomy punishable by
death. In our own times, homosexuals were among the first victims of the
Nazis, who killed 50,000 in concentration camps. Because of worldwide violence and persecution against lesbians and gay men, the Netherlands, Germany, and Canada in 1992 granted asylum to men and women based on

During the Middle Ages, gay men (called sodomites) were burned at the stake as heretics (previous page). In Germany in 1933, the Nazis burned Magnus Hirschfeld's library and forced him to flee the country (above). Gay men and lesbians were among the first Germans the Nazis forced into concentration camps, where over 50,000 of them were killed. Today, violence against gay men and lesbians, known as gay-bashing, continues (right). The pink triangle recalls the symbol the Nazis required lesbians and gay men to wear, just as they required Jews to wear the Star of David.

their homosexuality (Farnsworth, 1992). Today, gay men and lesbians continue to be the targets of violence. Anti-gay and lesbian incidents increased 2% from 1993 to 1994. Nearly half of the incidents involved physical assault, with 62% of the victims sustaining injury (New York City Gay and Lesbian Anti-Violence Project, 1995).

Personal Sources of Anti-Gay Prejudice Anti-gay prejudice in people may come from several sources (Marmor, 1980a): (1) a deeply rooted insecurity concerning a person's own sexuality and gender identity, (2) a strong fundamentalist religious orientation, and (3) simple ignorance concerning homosexuality. The literature also indicates fairly consistent gender differences in attitudes toward lesbians and gay men (Herek, 1984). Heterosexuals tend to have more negative attitudes toward gays of their own sex than of the other sex. Heterosexual men tend to be less tolerant than heterosexual women (Whitley & Kite, 1995).

Much anti-gay prejudice is conveyed through some of our social institutions, especially conservative religious groups and the military, as well as by the film industry (Herek & Berrill, 1992). Christianity and Judaism have been particularly important in reinforcing negative views of homosexuality. The spectrum of religious opinion runs from full equality for lesbians and gay men among Quakers and other groups that value tolerance to total rejection in Catholic and many fundamentalist teachings.

An important task in religion is separating religious beliefs from prejudice. Prejudice can masquerade as belief. During the nineteenth century, for example, the Bible was quoted extensively to justify slavery (F. G. Wood, 1990), and today it is quoted to justify intolerance of homosexuality. John Boswell (1980) points out that the Bible consistently condemns hypocrisy, the pursuit of wealth, adultery, and prostitution, but Western culture does not consider hypocrites, greedy people, adulterers, or prostitutes unnatural, nor does it persecute them. He writes, "Biblical strictures have been employed with great selectivity by all Christian states, and in a historical context *what* determines the selection is clearly the crucial issue."

Despite hostility, many religious lesbians and gay men have formed their own churches and synagogues, such as the Metropolitan Community Church. Denominational caucuses, including the Catholic group Dignity, Lutherans Concerned, and Presbyterians for Lesbian and Gay Concerns, have emerged to advocate tolerance within the churches.

Ending Anti-Gay Prejudice

Although legislation to prohibit discrimination is important for ending prejudice, education and positive social interactions are also important vehicles for change. Negative attitudes about homosexuality may be reduced by arranging positive interactions between heterosexuals and gay men, lesbians, and bisexuals. These interactions should be in settings of equal status, common goals, cooperation, and a moderate degree of intimacy. Such interactions may occur when family members or close friends come out. Other interactions should emphasize common group membership (such as religious, social, ethnic, or political) on a one-to-one basis. Religious volunteers working with people with HIV or AIDS often find their prejudice decreasing as they give care and comfort (Kayal, 1992).

SEXUAL AGGRESSION

In recent years, we have increasingly expanded our knowledge about sexually aggressive acts and their consequences. We have expanded our focus beyond stranger rape and examined the consequences of sexually aggressive acts on survivors. Earlier, researchers had focused primarily on **rape,** usually defined as penile-vaginal penetration performed against a *woman's* will through the use or threat of force. They assumed rape was committed by strangers for the purpose of sexual gratification. In their work, researchers generally examined the sexual psychopathology of male offenders and the characteristics of women that "precipitated" rapes, such as acting docile, living alone, and dressing in a certain way (White & Farmer, 1992).

In the 1970s, feminists challenged the belief that rape is an act of sexual deviance. Instead, they argued that rape is an act of violence and aggression against women. The principal motive is power, not sex (Brownmiller, 1975). As a result of feminist influence, the focus of research shifted.

Contemporary research now views rape as a category of sexual aggression. **Sexual aggression** refers to sexual activity, including petting, oral-genital sex, anal intercourse, and sexual intercourse, performed against a person's will through the use of force, argument, pressure, alcohol or drugs, or authority (Cate & Lloyd, 1992; Muehlenhard, Ponch, Phelps, & Giusti, 1992). Unlike rape, which by definition excludes men as victims, sexual aggression includes both women *and* men as victims. It also includes gay men and lesbians, who have been excluded from such research because of rape's heterosexual definition (Muehlenhard et al., 1992). **Sexual coercion** is a broader term than "rape" or "sexual aggression." It includes arguing, pleading, and cajoling, as well as force and the threat of force.

The Nature and Incidence of Rape

In rape, sex is a means of achieving power or releasing anger and hatred. Rape *forces* its victim into an intimate physical relationship with the rapist against her or his will. The victim does not experience pleasure; she or he experiences terror. In most cases, the victim is a woman; sometimes the victim is a man. In almost every case, however, the assailant is a man. The weapon in rape is the penis (which may be supplemented by a knife or a gun); the penis is used to attack, subordinate, and humiliate the victim.

Rape is not only an act but also a threat. As small girls, women are warned against taking candy from strangers, walking alone down dark streets, and leaving doors and windows unlocked. Men may fear assault, but women fear assault *and* rape. As a result, many women live with the possibility of being raped as a part of their consciousness. Rape and the fear of rape are facts of life for women; this is not true for men.

As many as 683,000 adult women were raped in 1990, according to a report sponsored by the Department of Health and Human Services (National Victim Center, 1992). The Department of Justice stated in 1994 that half of the rapes reported to the police involved girls who were under the age of 18. (See Figures 17.1 and 17.2 for types of rape and ages of rape victims.)

A large-scale survey reported that 1.3% of the men surveyed and nearly 22% of the women had been forced to have sex by a man. On the other hand, only 2.8% of the men in the survey reported forcing a woman to have sex (Laumann et al., 1994). A study of first sexual intercourse found that 6% of the undergraduate women had sex against their will (Bajracharya, Sarvela, & Isberner, 1995). A look at first sexual intercourse among younger women (grades 8–12) found sexual assault to occur up to 26% of the time, though it is seldom reported (Rhynard, Krebs, & Glover, 1997).

> Undismayed, he plucks the rose
> In the hedgerow blooming.
> Vainly she laments her woes,
> Vainly doth her thorns oppose,
> Gone her sweet perfuming.
>
> —*German art song*

> The fear of sexual assault is a special fear: its intensity in women can best be likened to the male fear of castration.
>
> —*Germaine Greer*

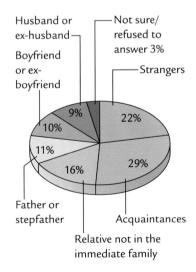

FIGURE 17.1   Types of Rape. (*Source:* Data from National Victim Center, 1992.)

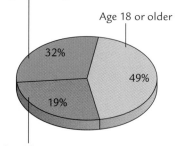

FIGURE 17.2   Ages of Rape Victims. (*Source:* Data from National Victim Center, 1992.)

Although earlier estimates of rape suggested that African American women were more likely to be sexually assaulted than White women, newer estimates do not find significant ethnic differences (Wyatt, 1992). A community study comparing Latino and Anglo rape rates found a significantly lower incidence among Latinos. The researchers speculate that the lower rate may be attributed to *machismo,* which requires men to be protective of women (Sorenson & Siegel, 1992). The lower rate, however, may also be attributed to Latinas' greater reluctance to report rape because of the strong emphasis on female virginity and purity in Latino culture.

Myths About Rape

Our society has a number of myths about rape, which serve to encourage rather than discourage it. Such myths blame women for their own rapes as if they somehow "deserved" them or were responsible for them. In fact, in a large national sample, two-thirds of the women who were raped worried they might be blamed for their assaults (National Victim Center, 1992).

Belief in rape myths is part of a larger belief structure that includes gender-role stereotypes, sexual conservatism, acceptance of interpersonal violence, and the belief that men are extremely different from women. Men are more likely than women to believe rape myths (Brady, Chrisler, Hosdale, & Osowiecki, 1991; Kalof & Wade, 1995; Quackenbush, 1991; Reilly et al., 1992). Sandra Byers and Raymond Eno (1991) found that acceptance of rape-supportive myths among college men was associated with the use of physical force, verbal coercion, and belief in "uncontrollable physical arousal." It is unclear what impact, if any, exposure to sexually explicit material has on the acceptance of rape myths. Results from studies are contradictory (Allen, Emmers, Gebhardt, & Giery, 1995; Davies, 1997).

Ethnicity and gender appear to influence the acceptance of rape myths. Both White and African American women are less likely than men of either group to accept rape myths, interpersonal violence, gender-role stereotyping, and adversarial relationships. Furthermore, African American women's attitudes toward these behaviors and beliefs are significantly less traditional than those of White women (Kalof & Wade, 1995).

Myth #1: Women Want to Be Raped   It is popularly believed that women have an unconscious wish to be raped. The fact that many women have rape fantasies is cited as proof. This myth supports the misconception that a woman enjoys being raped because she sexually "surrenders." The myth perpetuates the belief that rape is a sexual act rather than a violent one.

Myth #2: Women Ask for It   Many people believe that women "ask for it" by their behavior. According to one study, 25% of male students believe this myth (Holcomb, Holcomb, Sondag, & Williams, 1991). Another study found that provocative dress on the part of the victim of a date rape resulted in a greater perception that the victim was responsible and the rape was justified (Cassidy & Hurrell, 1995). Despite some attempts to reform rape laws, women continue to bear the brunt in proving their accusations (Goldberg-Ambrose, 1992).

Myth #3: Women Are Raped Only by Strangers   Women are warned to avoid or distrust strangers as a way to avoid rape; such advice, however, isolates them from normal social interactions. Furthermore, studies indicate that approximately three-quarters of all rapes are committed by nonstrangers such as acquaintances, friends, dates, husbands, or relatives (National Victim Center, 1992).

Myth #4: Women Could Avoid Rape If They Really Wanted To   This myth reinforces the stereotype that women "really" want to be raped or that they should curtail their activities. In one study, 25% of male students believed this myth (Holcomb et al., 1991). Women are often warned not to be out after dark alone. Approximately two-thirds of rapes/sexual assaults occur between 6 P.M. and 6 A.M., but nearly 6 out of 10 occur at the victim's home or the home of a friend, relative, or neighbor (Greenfeld, 1997). Women are also approached at work, on their way to or from work, or at church, or they are kidnapped from shopping centers or parking lots at midday. Restricting women's activities does not seem to have an appreciable impact on rape.

Myth #5: Women Cry Rape for Revenge   This myth suggests that women who are left by men accuse them of rape as a means of revenge. About 25% of the men in one study believed this (Holcomb et al., 1991). FBI crime statistics show that only about 2% of rape reports are false; this rate is lower than the rate for most other crimes. False reporting is unlikely because of the many obstacles that women face before an assailant is brought to trial and convicted.

Myth #6: Rapists Are Crazy or Psychotic   Very few men who rape are clinically psychotic. The vast majority are psychologically indistinguishable from other men, except that rapists appear to have more difficulty handling hostile feelings. Studies on date rape find that rapists differ from nonrapists primarily in such ways as greater hostility toward women, acceptance of traditional gender roles, and greater willingness to use force (Cate & Lloyd, 1992).

Myth #7: Most Rapists Are Black Men   Most rapists and their victims are members of the same race or ethnic group. The Black rapist myth reinforces racism by calling up the sexual stereotype of the "oversexed" Black man. It conjures images of African American men preying on White women. There is no evidence to suggest that Black rapists prefer White women. Rapists appear to attack women on the basis of opportunity, not ethnicity (South & Felson, 1990).

Forms of Rape

Rapists may be acquaintances, dates, husbands, fathers, or other family members, as well as strangers.

Date Rape   The most common form of rape is sexual intercourse with a dating partner that occurs against the victim's will, with force or the threat of force. It is known as **date rape** or **acquaintance rape.** One study found that women are more likely than men to define date rape as a crime. Men are less likely than women to agree that the assailant should have stopped when the woman asked him to. Disturbingly, respondents considered date rape less serious when the woman was African American (Foley, Evancic, Karnik, & King, 1995).

Date rapes are usually not planned. Two researchers (Bechhofer & Parrot, 1991) describe a typical date rape:

> He plans the evening with the intent of sex, but if the date does not progress as planned and his date does not comply, he becomes angry and takes what he feels is his right—sex. Afterward, the victim feels raped while the assailant believes that he has done nothing wrong. He may even ask the woman out on another date.

Alcohol and/or drugs are often involved in date rapes. One study found that 70% of women who had been date-raped had been drinking or taking drugs prior to the rape. Seventy-one percent said their assailant had been drinking or taking drugs (Copenhaver & Gauerholz, 1991). Male and female drunkenness is believed by students to be an important cause of date rape (Gillen & Muncher, 1995). There are often high levels of alcohol and drug use among middle school and high school students who have unwanted sex. When both people are drinking, they are viewed as more sexual. Men who believe in rape myths are more likely to see drinking as a sign that females are sexually available (Abbey & Harnish, 1995).

INCIDENCE   Lifetime experience of date rape ranges from 15% to 28% for women, according to various studies. If the definition is expanded to include attempted intercourse as a result of verbal pressure or the misuse of authority, then women's lifetime incidence increases significantly. When all types of unwanted sexual activity are included, ranging from kissing to sexual intercourse, 25–50% of college women report sexual aggression in dating (Cate & Lloyd, 1992). Among college students, the most likely victimizer is a peer (Bridgeland, Duane, & Stewart, 1995). There is also considerable sexual coercion in gay male relationships and in lesbian relationships, although less among lesbians than among gay males and heterosexuals (Waterman, Dawson, & Bologna, 1989).

NO MEANS NO   There is confusion about what constitutes consent. As we saw in Chapter 8, much sexual communication is nonverbal and ambiguous. The fact that we don't usually give verbal consent for sex indicates the significance of nonverbal clues. Nonverbal communication is imprecise, however. It can be misinterpreted easily if not reinforced verbally. For example, men frequently mistake a woman's friendliness for sexual interest (Johnson et al., 1991; Stockdale, 1993). They often misinterpret a woman's cuddling, kissing, and fondling as interest in engaging in sexual intercourse (Gillen & Muncher, 1995; Muehlenhard, 1988). A woman must make her boundaries clear verbally, and men need to avoid misinterpreting clues.

Our sexual scripts often assume "yes" unless a "no" is directly stated (Muehlenhard et al., 1992). This makes individuals "fair game" unless they explicitly say "no." The assumption of consent puts women at a disadvantage. Because men traditionally initiate sex, a man can initiate sex whenever

Sexual assault peer educators at Brown University dramatize date rape to make students aware of its dynamics.

he desires without the woman explicitly consenting. A woman's withdrawal can be considered "insincere" because consent is always assumed. Such thinking reinforces a common sexual script in which men initiate and women refuse so as not to appear "promiscuous." In this script, the man continues believing that the woman's refusal is "token." Some common reasons for offering "token" refusals include not wanting to appear "loose," unsureness of how the partner feels, inappropriate surroundings, and game playing (Muehlenhard & McCoy, 1991). Token resistance often occurs after the tenth date, whereas resistant behavior generally occurs earlier (Shotland & Hunter, 1995). Because some women sometimes say "no" when they mean "coax me," male-female communication may be especially unclear regarding consent. Furthermore, men are more likely than women to think of male-female relationships as a "battle of the sexes" (Reilly et al., 1992). Because relationships are conflictual, they believe, refusals are to be expected as part of the battle. A man may feel he "should" persist since his role is to conquer, even if he's not interested in sex (Muehlenhard & Schrag, 1991; Muehlenhard & McCoy, 1991).

PROFILE   A review of research (Cate & Lloyd, 1992) found that sexually coercive men, in contrast to noncoercive ones, tend to:

- Hold traditional beliefs about women and women's roles.
- Display hostility toward women.
- Believe in rape-supportive myths.
- Accept general physical violence.
- Express anger and dominance sexually.
- Report high levels of sexual activity.
- Use exploitative techniques.

Women involved in sexually coercive dating relationships do not differ significantly from those in noncoercive relationships (Cate & Lloyd, 1992). They have more or less the same levels of self-esteem, assertiveness, feminist ideology, and belief in rape-supportive myths.

Stranger Rape   The majority of rapes *reported* to the police are stranger rapes. A typical stranger rape scenario does not necessarily involve an unknown assailant hiding in the bushes or a stairwell on a dark night. Rather, it is likely to involve a chance meeting with a man who seems friendly and congenial. The woman relaxes her guard because the man seems nice, even protective. He casually maneuvers her to an isolated place—an alley, park, apartment, or house—where the rape occurs.

A study of women age 57–82 who were raped found that they were more likely to have been raped by strangers and to have been raped in their homes than younger rape victims (Muram, Miller, & Cutler, 1992). Stranger rapes are more likely to involve guns or knives than date rapes. Almost one-third of stranger rapes involve weapons (Harlow, 1991). A stranger rape is more likely to be taken seriously by the police because it reflects the rape stereotype better than date or marital rape (Russell, 1990).

Marital Rape   Throughout the United States, a husband can be prosecuted for raping his wife, although 26 states limit the conditions, such as requiring extraordinary violence. Only 17 states offer full legal protection to wives (Muehlenhard et al., 1992). Laws against marital rape, however, have not been widely enforced. In the few cases in which husbands have been convicted of marital rape, they were separated and living apart from their wives.

Many people discount rape in marriage as a "marital tiff" that has little to with "real" rape (Finkelhor & Yllo, 1985). Women are more likely than men to believe that a husband would use force to have sexual intercourse with his wife. White women are more likely than African American women to identify sexual coercion in marriage as rape (Cahoon, Edmonds, Spaulding, & Dickens, 1995). When college students were asked to describe marital rape, they created "sanitized" images: "He wants to and she doesn't, so he does anyway." "They are separated but he really loves her, so when he comes back to visit, he forces her because he misses her." The realities are very different.

In Diana Russell's 1982 study on marital rape, 930 randomly selected women in San Francisco were interviewed. Eighty-seven out of the 644 women who had ever been married (about 13%) had been raped by their husbands. Russell found that force was used in 84% of the rapes and the threat of force in 9%. (The remaining victims were asleep, intoxicated, or surprised and not able to resist.) Of the wives who were raped, 31% reported their rapes as isolated events that occurred only once. But another 31% reported that they had been raped more than 20 times. Other studies of wives who had been raped by their husbands reported that 59–87% were raped multiple times (cited in Russell, 1990).

Marital rape victims experience betrayal, anger, humiliation, and guilt. Following their rape, many wives feel intense anger toward their husbands. A minority feel guilt and blame themselves for not being better wives. Others develop negative self-images and view their lack of sexual desire as a reflection of their own inadequacies rather than as a consequence of abuse.

Gang Rape   Gang rape may be perpetrated by strangers or acquaintances. It may be motivated not only by power but also by male-bonding factors (Sanday, 1990). It is a common form of adolescent rape, most often occurring with strangers (Holmes, 1991). Among adults, gang rape disproportionately occurs in tightly knit groups, such as fraternities, athletic teams, street gangs, or military units. When gang rape takes place on campus, the attackers may know the woman, who may have been invited to a party or apartment. Alcohol is often involved (O'Sullivan, 1991). The assailants demonstrate their masculinity and "share" a sexual experience with their friends.

A study compared 44 college women who experienced gang sexual assault to 44 who were individually assaulted (Gidyez & Koss, 1990). In general, gang sexual assaults were more violent. The victims of gang assaults offered greater resistance and were more likely to report the attack to the police. Gang assault victims were also more traumatized. As a result, they were more likely to contemplate suicide and seek psychotherapy.

People who would not rape alone may rape in groups for several reasons (O'Sullivan, 1991). Responsibility is diffused in a group; no single individual is to blame. A person may lose his sense of individuality and merge with the group's standards. He might model his behavior on the sexual aggressiveness of the others.

Statutory Rape   Consensual sexual intercourse with a girl beneath a state's **age of consent,** the age at which a person is legally deemed capable of giving informed consent, is termed **statutory rape.** It may not matter whether the male is the same age as, older than, or younger than the girl. If a female is younger than a certain age—varying from age 14 in Hawaii to 18 in 16 states—the court ignores her consent. The enforcement of statutory rape laws, however, is generally sporadic, accidental, or arbitrary.

Male Rape   Sexual assaults against males may be perpetrated by other men or by women. Most rapes of men are by other men. (In some states, the word "rape" is used only to define a forced act of vaginal sexual intercourse, whereas an act of forced anal intercourse is termed "sodomy." More recently, states have started using gender-neutral terms, such as "sexual assault" or "criminal sexual conduct," regardless of whether the victim is a man or a woman. To be specific, we have chosen the term "male rape.")

The Bureau of Justice Statistics (1997) reports that in 1994 there were approximately 4,890 rapes of males age 12 and over in the United States. Experts, however, believe that male rape statistics vastly underrepresent the actual number of males who are raped (National Victim Center, 1997b). Though society is becoming increasingly aware of male rape, the lack of tracking of sexual crimes against men and the lack of research about their effects on victims are indicative of the attitude held by society at large—that although male rape occurs, it is not an acceptable topic for discussion.

There are also many reasons why male victims do not come forward and report being raped. Perhaps the main reason is the fear of many that they will be perceived as homosexual. Male sexual assault has nothing to do with the sexual orientation of the attacker or the victim, just as a sexual assault does not make the victim gay, bisexual, or heterosexual. Male rape is a violent crime that affects heterosexual men as often as gay men (National Victim Center, 1997b). Furthermore, the sex of the victim does not appear to be of significance to half of the offenders (Groth & Burgess, 1980).

Although many people believe that the majority of male rape incidents occur in prison, research suggests that the conditions for male rape are not unique to prison. Rather, all men, regardless of who or where they are, should be regarded as potential victims (Lipscomb et al., 1992).

In the aftermath of an assault, many men blame themselves, believing that they in some way gave permission to the rapist (Brochman, 1991). Male rape victims suffer from fears similar to those felt by female rape victims, including the belief that they actually enjoyed or somehow contributed to the rape. Some men may suffer additional guilt because they became sexually aroused or ejaculated during the rape. These are normal, involuntary physiological reactions and do not imply consent or enjoyment. Another concern for male rape victims is society's belief that men should be able to protect themselves and that the rape was somehow their own fault.

Research indicates differences in how gay men and heterosexual men react in the aftermath of rape. Although gay men may have difficulties in their sexual and emotional relationships with other men and think that the assault occurred because they are gay, heterosexual men often begin to question their sexual identity and are more disturbed by the sexual aspect of the assault than by the violence involved (Brochman, 1991).

Although they are uncommon, there are some instances of women sexually assaulting men. Despite being threatened with knives and guns, the men were able to have erections (Sarrell & Masters, 1982). After the assaults, the men suffered rape trauma syndrome similar to that experienced by women (discussed later). They experienced sexual difficulties, depression, and anxiety. Most felt abnormal because they did respond sexually during the assault. Because they were sexually assaulted by women, they doubted their masculinity.

Motivations for Rape

Most stranger rapes and some acquaintance or marital rapes can be characterized as *anger rapes, power rapes,* or *sadistic rapes* (Groth, Burgess, & Holmstrom, 1977). This typology has been very influential, but it is based on interviews with incarcerated stranger rapists. As a result, it may not reflect the

A CHEAP AND POWERFUL SEDATIVE called Rohypnol is finding its way into the hands of sexual predators and street gangs across the country. Sometimes referred to as "roofie," "rope," "Roche," or "R-2," the white, dime-sized drug can be slipped into alcoholic or other beverages to cause severe mental incapacitation and amnesia in its victims. Those committing sexual assault rely on the drug's effects to make it difficult, if not impossible, for the rape victim to recall the circumstances surrounding the sexual assault (Woodworth, 1996).

The effects of Rohypnol are similar to alcohol intoxication. Taken alone and in low doses, Rohypnol can produce drowsiness, dizziness, motor incoordination, memory loss, dry mouth, and visual disturbances. Higher doses can cause coma and death. More commonly, the drug is combined with alcohol, marijuana, or amphetamines. Heroin addicts use Rohypnol to enhance the effects of heroin; cocaine addicts use it to modulate the effect of cocaine binges. Within 10–20 minutes after the drug is taken, the victim will feel dizzy, disoriented, and either hot or cold; she or he will sometimes have trouble speaking or moving. Most victims pass out and have no memory of what happened to them while they were under the drug's influence. The effects may persist for 8 hours or more (Monroe, 1997).

Rohypnol ranks as the most widely prescribed sedative/sleeping pill in Europe, but it is not approved for sale in the United States. Most Rohypnol that is obtained in this country is smuggled from Mexico and South America, where it is sold legally. In 1996, President Clinton signed into law the "Drug-Induced Rape Prevention and Punishment Act of 1996," which makes it a felony to distribute Rohypnol or similar substances to someone without that person's knowledge and with the intent to commit violence, including rape, against that person. In response to the threat the drug poses to communities and individuals, the Drug Enforcement Administration has taken specific and numerous actions to eliminate Rohypnol abuse and trafficking (Woodworth, 1996).

To protect yourself from drugs like Rohypnol, it is essential to know of its existence and to watch what you drink at parties or on dates. Do not take any drinks (soda, coffee, or alcohol) from someone you do not know well and trust. Refuse open-container beverages. If you think you've been drugged, call 911 or get to an emergency room. If possible, try to keep a sample of the beverage (Monroe, 1997).

In response to concerns, the manufacturer of Rohypnol recently reformulated the drug to make it easier for people to identify it in drinks. The new drug will turn light-colored beverages blue and will also form small, chunky pieces in the mouth. However, it may take a while for this new Rohypnol to hit the streets ("Rohypnol," 1997). In the meantime, in unfamiliar dating or party situations, stay alert and aware!

---

motivations of the majority of rapists, who are acquaintances, boyfriends, and husbands.

Anger Rape   Anger rapists are physically brutal; as a consequence of their extreme violence, their victims often require hospitalization. These rapes account for approximately 40% of stranger rapes (Groth & Birnbaum, 1978). Nicholas Groth (1979) described anger rapes in this way:

> The assault is characterized by physical brutality. Far more actual force is used . . . than would be necessary if the intent were simply to overpower the victim and achieve sexual penetration. . . . His aim is to hurt and debase his victim, and he expresses contempt for her through abusive and profane language. . . .

Power Rape   Representing about 55% of stranger rapes in Groth and Jean Birnbaum's (1978) study, power rapes are acts of dominance. Typically, the rapist does not want to hurt the woman but to dominate her sexually. The rape may be triggered by what the rapist regards as a slight to his masculinity. He attempts to restore his sense of power, control, and identity by raping. He uses sex to compensate for his sense of inadequacy. He uses only as much force as necessary to rape his victim.

Sadistic Rape   A violent fusion of sex and aggression, sadistic rapes are by far the most brutal. A sadistic rapist finds "intentional maltreatment of his victim intensely gratifying and takes pleasure in her torment, anguish, distress, helplessness and suffering" (Groth & Birnbaum, 1978). Bondage is often involved, and the rape may have a ritualistic quality. The victim is often severely injured and may not survive the attack. Although sadistic rapes are overwhelmingly the most brutal, they are also the least frequent. About 5% of the stranger rapes in Groth and Birnbaum's study were sadistic.

The Aftermath of Rape

According to the National Victim Center (1992), more than two-thirds of the women who were raped in 1990 were not physically injured. Twenty-four percent received minor injuries, and 4% sustained serious injuries (Figure 17.3).

It is important that rape victims gain a sense of control over their lives to counteract the helplessness they experienced during their rape (Robertson, 1990). They need to cope with the depression and other symptoms resulting from their trauma.

Although White and African American women experience rape in more or less the same proportion, the African American woman's experience may be somewhat different. As Gail Wyatt (1992) writes, "In American culture, rape and sexual vulnerability have a unique history because of the sexual exploitation of slaves for over 250 years." Historically, there were no penalties for the rape of Black women by Whites. Because Whites believed African American women were promiscuous by nature, they believed Black women could not actually be raped. Contemporary White stereotypes continue to view Black women as promiscuous. There are three important consequences of this stereotype. First, African American women who are raped assume that they are less likely to be believed than White women, especially if the rapist is White. Second, African American women are less likely to report the rape to the police, whom they view as unsympathetic to Blacks in general and to raped Black women in particular. Third, African American women are less likely to seek treatment and support to help the healing process.

Rape victims may soon be offered anti-HIV drugs for protection in case they have been exposed to AIDS. Although the risk of contracting HIV from a sexual assault is small—about 5 in 1000—victims should be given the option so that they can make an informed choice ("Victims May Be Offered," 1997).

Rape Trauma Syndrome   Rape is a traumatic event, to which a woman may have a number of responses. The emotional changes she undergoes as a result of rape are collectively known as **rape trauma syndrome.** Rape survivors are likely to experience depression, anxiety, restlessness, and guilt. These responses are consistent with **posttraumatic stress disorder (PTSD),** a group of characteristic symptoms that follow an intensely distressing event outside a person's normal life experience (Bownes, O'Gorman, & Sayers,

> If a man seizes a betrothed virgin in the city and lies with her, then you shall bring them both out to the gate of the city, and you shall stone them to death, the young woman because she did not cry for help, though others could have heard her, and the man because he violated his neighbor's wife.
>
> —Deuteronomy 22:23–24

> If a man seizes a virgin who is not betrothed and lies with her and they are discovered, then the man shall give the young woman's father 50 silver shekels and he shall have her as his wife because he has violated her.
>
> —Deuteronomy 22:28–29

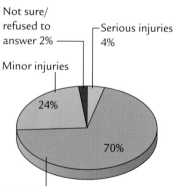

Not sure/
refused to
answer 2%
Serious injuries
4%

Minor injuries

24%

70%

No injuries

FIGURE 17.3   Injuries from Rape.
(*Source:* Data from National Victim Center, 1992.)

1991a, 1991b; Foa & Riggs, 1995). Both Whites and African Americans experience similar symptoms (Wyatt, 1992). A large-scale study found that nearly 31% of all those who had been a victim of forcible rape had developed PTSD (National Victim Center, 1992).

Rape trauma syndrome consists of two phases: an acute phase and a long-term reorganization phase. The acute phase begins immediately following the rape. It may last for several weeks or more. In the first few hours after a rape, the woman's responses are characterized by feelings of self-blame and fear. She may believe that she was somehow responsible for the rape: She was wearing something provocative, she should have kept her doors locked, she should have been suspicious of her attacker. Self-blame, however, leads to higher rates of depression (Frazier, 1991).

The woman is shaken by fears: that the attacker will return, that she may be killed, that others will react negatively. She may act out these feelings through expressive, controlled, or combined reactions. An expressive response leaves the woman crying, expressing signs and feelings of fear, anger, rage, anxiety, and tension. If she controls her responses, she hides her feelings and tries to appear calm. Nevertheless, there are often signs of tension: headaches, irritability, sleeplessness, restlessness, and jumpiness. Women may also feel humiliated, angry, embarrassed, vengeful, and fearful. Women are more likely than men to express these varied symptoms following rape (Sorenson & Siegel, 1992).

Following the acute phase, the rape survivor enters the long-term reorganization phase. The rape is a crisis in a woman's life and relationships (Nadelson, 1990). If the rape took place at home, the woman may move, fearing that the rapist will return. Some women develop fears of being indoors if the rape occurred indoors, while those raped outside sometimes fear being outdoors. About 3 months after their rapes, 60% of the women in one study reported depression. Forty percent rated their depression as severe (Mackey et al., 1992).

Long-term stress reactions are often exacerbated by the very systems designed to assist people. These systems and individuals have sometimes

Singer Tori Amos (herself a rape survivor) founded the Rape, Abuse, and Incest National Network (RAINN), an organization that operates a national toll-free hotline for victims of sexual assault (see the Resource Center).

proven to be more psychologically damaging to survivors than the rape itself (National Organization for Victim Assistance, 1992), a phenomenon referred to as *secondary victimization*. Examples of these support systems and individuals include the criminal justice system; the media; emergency and hospital room personnel; social workers; and family, friends, employers, and clergy. Nevertheless, the most important thing you can do to help someone you care about who suffers from symptoms of PTSD is to help her or him get professional help (National Victim Center, 1995).

Effects on Sexuality   Typically, women find that their sexuality is severely affected for a short time or longer after a rape (Nadelson, 1990). Some begin avoiding sexual interactions, because sex reminds them of the rape. Those who are less depressed, however, have fewer sexual difficulties (Mackey et al., 1992). Two common sexual problems are fear of sex and a lack of sexual desire. Both White and African American women report similar sexual problems (Wyatt, 1992).

CHILD SEXUAL ABUSE

Child sexual abuse, by both relatives and non-relatives, occurs widely. **Child sexual abuse** is *any* sexual interaction (including fondling, sexual kissing, and oral sex, as well as vaginal or anal penetration) between an adult and a prepubertal child. It does not matter whether the child is perceived by the adult to be engaging in the sexual activity voluntarily. Because of the child's age, he or she cannot give informed consent; the activity can only be considered as self-serving to the adult.

In 1996, approximately 3,126,000 children were reported to Child Protective Services as alleged victims of child mistreatment. Of these cases, 9%, or roughly 281,000, involved sexual abuse (National Victim Center, 1995). According to the congressionally mandated *Third National Incidence Study of Child Abuse and Neglect* (Sedlak & Broadhurst, 1996), girls are sexually abused 3 times more often than boys; however, boys are more likely to die from or be seriously injured by their abuse. The risk of being sexually abused does not vary among races, but children from lower-income groups and from single-parent families are more frequently victims. From age 3 on, children are at a constant rate of risk. Every incident of child sexual abuse costs the victim and society $99,000 (Miller, Cohen, & Wiersema, 1996), not to mention the loss of trust, relationship, and sense of self that often accompanies sexual abuse.

Child sexual abuse is generally categorized in terms of kin relationship. **Extrafamilial abuse** is sexual abuse by unrelated people. **Intrafamilial abuse** is sexual abuse by biologically related people and step relatives. The abuse may be pedophilic or nonpedophilic. (As explained in Chapter 10, pedophilia refers to an adult's sexual attraction to children.) **Nonpedophilic sexual abuse** refers to an adult's sexual interaction with a child that is not sexually motivated; the most important nonsexual motives are power and affection.

The victimization may include force or the threat of force, pressure, or taking advantage of trust or innocence. The most serious or harmful forms of child sexual abuse include actual or attempted penile-vaginal penetration, fellatio, cunnilingus, and analingus, with or without the use of force. Other serious forms range from forced digital penetration of the vagina to fondling of the breasts (unclothed) or simulated intercourse without force. The least serious forms of sexual abuse range from kissing to intentional sexual touching of the clothed genitals or breasts or other body parts, with or without the use of force (Russell, 1984).

Most victimized children are between 8 and 12 years of age. Although boys and girls are equally likely to be abused (Kilpatrick, Edmunds, & Seymour, 1992), we have only recently recognized the sexual abuse of boys. This neglect has been part of the more general neglect of all sexual victimization of males. The most likely offenders of girls are stepfathers; boys are most often abused by unrelated males (Levesque, 1994). Research shows that regardless of whether the perpetrators were intrafamilial or extrafamilial, child sexual abuse victims are equally traumatized (Whitcomb, 1994).

General Preconditions for Child Sexual Abuse

Researchers have found that intrafamilial and extrafamilial sexual abuse share many common elements. Because there are so many variables—such as the age and sex of the victims and perpetrators, their relationship, the type of acts involved, and whether there was force—one cannot automatically say that abuse within the family is more harmful than extrafamilial abuse.

David Finkelhor (1984) believes there are four preconditions that need to be met by the offender for sexual abuse to occur. These preconditions apply to pedophilic, nonpedophilic, incestuous, and nonincestuous abuse.

1. *Motivation to sexually abuse a child.* This consists of three components: (a) emotional congruence, in which relating sexually to a child fulfills some important emotional need; (b) sexual arousal toward the child; and (c) blockage, in which alternative sources of sexual gratification are not available or are less satisfying.

2. *Overcoming internal inhibitions against acting on motivation.* Inhibitions may be overcome by the use of alcohol or poor impulse control.

3. *Overcoming external obstacles to committing sexual abuse.* The most important obstacle appears to be the supervision and protection a child receives from others, such as family members, neighbors, and the child's peers. The mother is especially significant in protecting children. Growing evidence suggests that children are more vulnerable to abuse when the mother is absent, neglectful, or incapacitated in some way through illness, marital abuse, or emotional problems.

4. *Undermining or overcoming a child's potential resistance to the abuse.* The abuser may use outright force or select psychologically vulnerable targets. Certain children may be more vulnerable because they feel insecure, needy, or unsupported and will respond to the abuser's offers of attention, affection, or bribes. Children's ability to resist may be undercut because they are young or naive or have a special relationship to the abuser as friend, neighbor, or family member.

According to Finkelhor (1984), *all* four factors must come into play for sexual abuse to occur. Each factor acts as a filter for the previous one. Some people have strong motivation to sexually abuse a child. Of these, however, only some are able to overcome their internal inhibitions, fewer can overcome the external obstacles, and still fewer can overcome the child's resistance.

Forms of Intrafamilial Sexual Abuse

The incest taboo is nearly universal in human societies. **Incest** is generally defined as sexual intercourse between people too closely related to legally marry (usually interpreted to mean father-daughter, mother-son, or brother-sister). (The few documented exceptions to the incest taboo involve brother-sister marriages in the royal families of ancient Egypt, China, Peru, and Hawaii.) Sexual abuse in families can involve blood relatives, most commonly uncles and grandfathers, and step relatives, most often stepfathers and step-brothers. In grandfather-granddaughter abuse, the grandfathers frequently have sexually abused their children as well.

It is not clear what type of familial sexual abuse is the most frequent (Peters et al., 1986; Russell, 1986). Some researchers believe that father-daughter (including stepfather-daughter) abuse is the most common; others think that brother-sister abuse is most common. Still other researchers believe that incest committed by uncles is the most common (Russell, 1986). Mother-son sexual relations are considered to be rare (or are underreported).

Father-Daughter Sexual Abuse   There is general agreement that the most traumatic form of sexual victimization is father-daughter abuse, including that committed by stepfathers. One study indicated that 54% of the girls sexually abused by their fathers were extremely upset (Russell, 1986). In contrast, 25% who were abused by other family members reported the same degree of emotional upset. Over twice as many abused daughters reported serious long-term consequences. Some factors contributing to the severity of father-daughter sexual relations include the following:

- Fathers were more likely to have engaged in penile-vaginal penetration than other relatives (18% versus 6%).
- Fathers sexually abused their daughters more frequently than other perpetrators abused their victims (38% of the fathers sexually abused their daughters 11 or more times, compared with a 12% abuse rate for other abusing relatives).
- Fathers were more likely to use force or violence than others (although the numbers for both fathers and others were extremely low).

In the past, many have discounted the seriousness of sexual abuse by a stepfather because there is no *biological* relationship. The emotional consequences are just as serious, however. Sexual abuse by a stepfather still represents a violation of the basic parent-child relationship.

Brother-Sister Sexual Abuse   There are contrasting views concerning the consequences of brother-sister incest. Researchers generally have expressed little interest in it. Most have tended to view it as harmless sex play or sexual exploration between mutually involved siblings. The research, however, has generally failed to distinguish between exploitative and nonexploitative brother-sister sexual activity. One study found that brother-sister incest can be a devastating invasion of individual boundaries (Canavan, Myers, & Higgs, 1992). Sibling incest needs to be taken seriously (Adler & Schultz, 1995). Russell (1986) suggests that the idea that brother-sister incest is usually harmless and mutual may be a myth. In her study, the average age difference between the brother (age 17.9 years) and sister (10.7 years) is so great that the siblings can hardly be considered peers. The age difference represents a significant power difference. Furthermore, not all brother-sister sexual activity is "consenting"; considerable physical force may be involved.

Uncle-Niece Sexual Abuse   Alfred Kinsey (Kinsey et al., 1953) and Diane Russell (1986) found the most common form of intrafamilial sexual abuse to involve uncles and nieces. Russell reported that almost 5% of the women in her study had been molested by their uncles, slightly more than the percentage abused by their fathers. The level of severity of the abuse was generally less in terms of the type of sexual act and the use of force. Although such abuse does not take place within the nuclear family, many victims found it quite upsetting. One-quarter of the respondents indicated long-term emotional effects (Russell, 1986).

Children at Risk

Incest does not discriminate. It occurs in families that are financially privileged as well as those of low socioeconomic status. All racial and ethnic groups are vulnerable, as are members of all religious traditions. Boys and girls, infants and adolescents are victims of incest. Incest occurs between fathers and daughters, fathers and sons, mothers and daughters, and mothers and sons. Perpetrators can be family members or people without a direct blood or legal relationship to the victim, such as a parent's lover or a live-in nanny (National Victim Center, 1997a).

Nevertheless, not all children are equally at risk for sexual abuse. Although any child can be sexually abused, some groups of children are more likely to be victimized than others. A review (Finkelhor & Baron, 1986) of the literature indicates that those children at higher risk for sexual abuse are in the following groups:

- Female children
- Preadolescent children (particularly between the ages of 10 and 12)
- Children with absent or unavailable parents
- Children whose relationships with their parents are poor
- Children whose parents are in conflict
- Children who live with a stepfather

Effects of Child Sexual Abuse

Until recently, much of the literature on child sexual abuse has been anecdotal, case studies, or small-scale surveys of nonrepresentative groups. Nevertheless, numerous well-documented consequences of child sexual abuse hold true for both intrafamilial and extrafamilial abuse. These include both initial and long-term consequences. Many child sexual abuse survivors experience symptoms of posttraumatic stress disorder (McLeer, Deblinger, Henry, & Ovraschel, 1992).

UNTIL THE LATE 1960s, child sexual abuse was believed to be virtually nonexistent. Before the rise of the feminist movement in the 1970s, women's reports of such abuse were generally downplayed or dismissed as neurotic fantasies.

Over the past two decades, we have become painfully aware of the extent of child sexual abuse. Most recently, some women and men have stated that they had been sexually abused during childhood but had repressed their memories of it. They say they had forgotten their abuse and later recovered the memory of it, often through the help of therapists. When these recovered memories surface, those accused of the abuse often profess shock and deny that the abuse ever took place. Instead, they insist that these memories are figments of the imagination. Who is to be believed—the person making the accusation or the accused?

The question of whom to believe has given rise to a vitriolic memory war: recovered memories versus false memories. Each side has its proponents; emotions run high, and debates often deteriorate into shouting matches. A **repressed memory** is a memory of a powerfully traumatic event that is buried in the unconscious and produces symptoms, such as anxiety or nervousness. The individual is unaware of the existence of her or his repressed memories. According to Freud, who developed the concept of repression, the content of the memory could be an actual event or a fantasized one. More recently, research suggests that some victims of incest may suffer from biochemically induced amnesia. Triggered by a severe trauma, the amnesia occurs as a result

of a number of complex endocrine and neurological changes. Any immediate and/or latent memory of the incident is repressed (Matsakis, 1991). A **recovered memory** is a repressed memory brought to consciousness so that the individual is aware of it. It is assumed that the recovered memory describes an actual event that has been repressed. A **false memory** is a fictitious memory of an event that never occurred (Bass & Davis, 1988; Terr, 1994; Yapko, 1994).

According to advocates of recovered memory, repressed memories are brought to consciousness through the use of various therapeutic techniques. Clients are encouraged to reimagine their childhood. Their recovered memories may be very vivid, detailed, and concise (Terr, 1994). If a person has certain symptoms, including anxiety, low sexual desire, or an inability to maintain relationships, some therapists may infer that these are symptoms of repressed memories and that their client was sexually abused. Ellen Bass and Laura Davis wrote in *The Courage to Heal* (1988): "If you are unable to remember any specific instances . . . but still have a feeling that something abusive happened, it probably did." The researchers noted that they had not encountered a single woman who "suspected she might have been abused, explored it, and determined that she was not." If the client does not remember the abuse, the therapist may use various techniques, such as hypnosis, dream interpretation, relaxation or free association, to help in the recovery of memories. One study of women who were sexually abused as children suggests that abuse memories might be forgotten (Williams, 1994). Researchers report inter-

In recent years, some adults have claimed that they repressed their childhood memories of abuse and only later, as adults, recalled them. These accusations have given rise to a fierce controversy about the nature of memories of abuse, as described in the box "The Memory Wars."

Initial Effects   The initial consequences of sexual abuse occur within the first 2 years. The proportion of victimized children who experience these disturbances ranges from one-quarter to almost two-thirds, depending on the study. Some of the typical effects are:

- *Emotional disturbances,* including fear, anger, hostility, guilt, and shame.
- *Physical consequences,* including difficulty in sleeping, changes in eating patterns, and pregnancy. Childhood STDs are frequently a consequence of sexual abuse (Anderson, 1995).
- *Sexual disturbances,* including significantly higher rates of open masturbation, sexual preoccupation, and exposure of the genitals (Hibbard & Hartman, 1992).

viewing 129 adult women in the 1990s who, according to documentation from the 1970s, were confirmed as sexually abused children. Seventeen years later, the researchers found that 38% of them did not remember the abuse that had been confirmed earlier. The study did not indicate whether these women suffered symptoms consistent with repression of abuse.

In the past several years, there has been a response to the recovered memory movement by parents who assert they have been falsely accused. One group of accused parents began the False Memory Foundation (Yapko, 1994). They developed the term **false memory syndrome**, which they define as a collection of fictitious memories elicited by a therapist and believed by the client to be authentic and accurate. ("False memory syndrome" is not recognized by any scientific or psychiatric organization.)

Critics of recovered memories make several points:

- *The absence of evidence of memory repression.* There are no controlled laboratory experiments supporting the theory that people repress memories of traumatic events. Studies indicate that concentration camp and crime victims over age 6, for example, have not repressed their traumatic experiences (Crews, 1995).

- *The unreliability and impermanence of memories.* Events are forgotten, reconstructed, combined with other events, and remembered. We use our memories to create a narrative or story about our self; they help explain who we are, to form and validate our self-image. Sometimes we combine and confuse memories or even invent them to validate ourselves. Early

memories, for example, are often distorted with a normal "retrospective bias" (Boakes, 1995; Loftus & Ketcham, 1994).

- *The ability to "create" false memories.* Laboratory experiments demonstrate that false memories can be created by repeatedly questioning subjects until they "remember" events that never actually happened. Some young children were tricked, for example, into falsely believing that they were once hospitalized (Ceci, Loftus, Leichtman, & Bruck, 1994).

- *Therapeutic suggestion.* Some therapists may unwittingly plant the suggestion in the mind of their clients that they were abused (Yapko, 1994).

What are we to make of the recovered versus false memory debate? A review of the research by the American Psychological Association (1994) came to four conclusions:

1. Most people who were sexually abused as children at least partially remember the abuse.

2. Memories of sexual abuse that have been forgotten may later be remembered.

3. False memories of events that never happened may occur.

4. The process by which accurate or inaccurate recollections of childhood abuse are made is not well understood.

Because firm scientific conclusions cannot be made at this time, the debate is likely to continue to rage.

- *Social disturbances,* including difficulties at school, truancy, running away from home, and early marriages by abused adolescents. (A large proportion of homeless youth are fleeing parental sexual abuse [Athey, 1991].)

Ethnicity appears to influence how a child responds to sexual abuse. A recent study compared sexually abused Asian American children with a random sample of abused White, African American, and Latino children (Rao, Diclemente, & Poulton, 1992). The researchers found that Asian American children suffered less sexually invasive forms of abuse. They tended to be more suicidal and to receive less support from their parents than non-Asians. They were also less likely to express anger or to act out sexually. These different responses point to the importance of understanding cultural context when treating ethnic victims.

Long-Term Effects   Although there can be some healing of the initial effects, child sexual abuse may leave lasting scars on the adult survivor

A therapist helps a child deal with his sexual abuse.

(Beitchman et al., 1992; Jumper, 1995). These adults often have significantly higher incidences of psychological, physical, and sexual problems than the general population. Abuse may predispose some women to sexually abusive dating relationships (Cate & Lloyd, 1992).

Long-term effects include the following (Beitchman et al., 1992; Browne & Finkelhor, 1986; Elliott & Briere, 1992; Wyatt, Guthrie, & Notgass, 1992):

- *Depression,* the symptom most frequently reported by adults sexually abused as children.

- *Self-destructive tendencies,* including suicide attempts and thoughts of suicide (Jeffrey & Jeffrey, 1991; "Risk of Suicide," 1996).

- *Somatic disturbances and dissociation,* including anxiety and nervousness, eating disorders (anorexia and bulimia), feelings of "spaciness," out-of-body experiences, and feelings that things are "unreal" (DeGroot, Kennedy, Rodin, & McVey, 1992; Walker, Katon, Hansom, & Harrop-Griffiths, 1992; Young, 1992).

- *Negative self-concept,* including feelings of low self-esteem, isolation, and alienation.

- *Interpersonal relationship difficulties,* including difficulties in relating to both sexes, parental conflict, problems in responding to their own children, and difficulty in trusting others.

- *Revictimization,* in which women abused as children are more vulnerable to rape and marital violence.

- *Sexual problems,* in which survivors find it difficult to relax and enjoy sexual activities, or in which they avoid sex and experience hypoactive (inhibited) sexual desire and lack of orgasm.

One study of revictimization found that among rape survivors, about 66% had a history of child sexual abuse (Urquiza & Goodlin-Jones, 1994). Another study found that women most likely to be harassed at work and in social settings had also been sexually abused as children (Wyatt & Riederle, 1994). There is serious concern that a woman's continued revictimization could lead to a decline in her sense of well-being and make her more vulnerable sexually.

Gay men and lesbians who were sexually abused as children or adolescents may have additional issues to deal with. This is especially true if they were in the process of becoming aware of their sexual orientation. They may have avoided telling anyone about the abuse because of their orientation and out of fear of being blamed if their homosexuality were suspected by a family member or caseworker. The community may be unsupportive. The survivor's age and stage in the coming-out process are particularly significant (Arey, 1995; Burke, 1995). The abuse may create or intensify self-directed homophobia.

Sexual Abuse Trauma   The consequences of child sexual abuse may create a traumatic dynamic that affects the child's ability to deal with the world. Angela Browne and David Finkelhor (1986) suggest a model of **sexual abuse trauma** that contains four components: traumatic sexualization, betrayal, powerlessness, and stigmatization. When these factors converge as a result of sexual abuse, they affect the child's cognitive and emotional orientation to the world. They create trauma by distorting a child's self-concept, world view, and emotional development. These consequences affect abuse survivors not only as children but also as adults.

TRAUMATIC SEXUALIZATION   Traumatic sexualization refers to the process in which the sexually abused child's sexuality develops inappropriately and becomes interpersonally dysfunctional. Sexually traumatized children learn inappropriate sexual behaviors (such as manipulating an adult's genitals for affection), are confused about their sexuality, and inappropriately associate certain emotions—such as loving and caring—with sexual activities. Childhood sexual abuse may be associated with the reasons some women later become prostitutes (Simons & Whitbeck, 1991).

Sexual issues may become especially important when abused children become adults. Survivors may suffer flashbacks, sexual dysfunctions, and negative feelings about their bodies. They may also be confused about sexual norms and standards. A fairly common confusion is the belief that sex may be traded for affection. Some women label themselves as "promiscuous," but this label may be more a result of their negative self-image than their actual behavior.

BETRAYAL   Children feel betrayed when they discover that someone on whom they have been dependent has manipulated, used, or harmed them. Children may also feel betrayed by other family members, especially mothers, for not protecting them from abuse.

As adults, survivors may experience depression as a manifestation, in part, of extended grief over the loss of trusted figures. Some may find it difficult to trust others. Other survivors may feel a deep need to regain a sense of trust and become extremely dependent. Distrust may manifest itself in hostility and anger. In adolescents, antisocial or delinquent behavior may be a means of protecting themselves from further betrayal. Anger may express a need for revenge or retaliation. At other times, distrust may manifest itself in social isolation and avoidance of intimate relationships.

POWERLESSNESS   Children experience a basic kind of powerlessness when their bodies and personal space are invaded against their will. A child's powerlessness is reinforced as the abuse is repeated.

In adulthood, powerlessness may be experienced as fear or anxiety; the person feels unable to control events. Adult survivors often believe that they have impaired coping abilities. This feeling of ineffectiveness may be related to the high incidence of depression and despair among survivors. Powerlessness may also be related to increased vulnerability or revictimization by rape or marital violence; survivors feel unable to prevent subsequent victimization. Other survivors may attempt to cope with their earlier powerlessness by an excessive need to control or dominate others.

STIGMATIZATION   Stigmatization, the guilt and shame about sexual abuse that are transmitted to abused children and then internalized by them, is communicated in numerous ways. The abuser blames the child or, through his secrecy, communicates a sense of shame. If the abuser pressures the child for secrecy, the child may also internalize feelings of shame and guilt. Children's prior knowledge that their family or community considers such activities deviant may contribute to their feelings of stigmatization.

As adults, survivors may feel extreme guilt or shame about having been sexually abused. They may have low self-esteem because they feel that the abuse made them "damaged merchandise." They also feel different from others, because they mistakenly believe that they alone have been abused.

Treatment Programs

There is a growing trend to deal with child sexual abuse, especially father-daughter sexual abuse, through therapy programs working in conjunction with the judicial system, rather than by breaking up the family by removing the child or the offender (Nadelson & Sauzier, 1986). Because the offender is often also the breadwinner, incarcerating him may greatly increase the family's emotional distress. The district attorney's office may work with clinicians in evaluating the existing threat to the child and deciding whether to prosecute or refer the offender for therapy (or both). The goal is not simply to punish the offender, but to try to help the victim and the family come to terms with the abuse.

Many of these clinical programs work on several levels at once: They treat the individual, the father-daughter relationship, the mother-daughter relationship, and the family as a whole. They work on developing self-esteem and improving the family and marital relationships. If appropriate, they refer individuals to alcohol- or drug-abuse treatment programs.

A crucial component of many treatment programs is individual and family attendance at self-help group meetings. Self-help groups are composed of incest survivors, offenders, mothers, and other family members. Groups such as Parents United and Daughters and Sons United help offenders acknowledge their responsibility and understand the impact of the abuse on all those involved.

Preventing Sexual Abuse

The idea of preventing sexual abuse is relatively new (Berrick & Barth, 1992). Prevention programs began about a decade ago, a few years after programs were started to identify and help child and adult survivors of sexual abuse. Such prevention programs have been hindered, however, by three factors (Finkelhor, 1986a, 1986b):

- Sexual abuse is complicated by differing concepts of what constitutes appropriate sexual behaviors and partners, which are not easily understood by children.

- Sexual abuse, especially incest, is a difficult topic for adults to discuss with children. Children who are frightened by their parents, however, may be less able to resist abuse than those who are given strategies of resistance.

- Sex education is controversial. Even where it is taught, instruction often does not go beyond physiology and reproduction. The topic of incest is especially opposed.

In confronting these problems, child abuse prevention (CAP) programs have been very creative. These programs typically aim at three audiences: children, parents, and professionals, especially teachers. CAP programs aimed at children include plays, puppet shows, filmstrips, videotapes, books, and comic books to teach children that they have rights. Children have the right to control their own bodies (including their genitals) and to feel "safe," and they have the right not to be touched in ways that feel confusing or wrong. The CAP programs stress that the child is not at fault when such abuse does occur. These programs generally teach three strategies (Gelles & Conte, 1991). First, children are taught to say "no." Second, they are told to get away from the assailant or situation. Third, they are instructed to tell a trusted adult about what happened (and to keep telling until they are believed). It is not known how well these strategies work, because assessment studies cannot ethically duplicate the various situations.

Other programs focus on educating parents, who, it is hoped, will in turn educate their children. These programs aim at helping parents discover abuse or abusers by identifying warning signs. Such programs, however, need to be culturally sensitive, as Latinos and Asians may be reluctant to discuss these matters with their children (Ahn & Gilbert, 1992). Parents seem reluctant in general to deal with sexual abuse issues with their children, according to David Finkelhor (1986a). Many do not feel that their children are at risk, are fearful of unnecessarily frightening their children, and may also feel uncomfortable about talking with their children about sex in general, much less about such tabooed subjects as incest. In addition, parents may not believe their own children or may feel uncomfortable confronting a suspected abuser, who may be a partner, an uncle, a friend, or a neighbor.

CAP programs also seek to educate professionals, especially teachers, physicians, mental-health professionals, and police officers. Because of their

One objective of child-abuse prevention programs is to teach children the difference between "good" touching and "bad" touching.

close contact with children and their role in teaching children about the world, teachers are especially important. Professionals are encouraged to be watchful for signs of sexual abuse and to investigate children's reports of such abuse.

In 1997 the Supreme Court ruled in favor of what is now referred to as Megan's Law. Enacted in 1995, the law calls for schools, day-care centers, and youth groups to be notified about moderate-risk sex offenders in the community. For high-risk offenders, the law requires that the police go door-to-door notifying neighborhood residents. It also requires sex offenders who have been paroled or recently released from prison to register with local authorities when moving to a community. The law is named for Megan Kanka, a 7-year-old who was raped and murdered by a twice-convicted sex offender who lived across the street from her. Although parts of the law have been challenged, the Supreme Court has rejected objections (Carelli, 1998). Most communities see the law as a welcome victory for their children.

■ Sexual harassment, anti-gay harassment and discrimination, sexual aggression, and sexual abuse of children represent the darker side of human sexuality. Their common thread is the humiliation, subordination, or victimization of others. But we need not be victims. We can educate ourselves and others about these activities; we can work toward changing attitudes and institutions that support these destructive and dehumanizing behaviors.

SUMMARY

Sexual Harassment

- *Sexual harassment* includes two distinct types of illegal harassment: the abuse of power for sexual ends and the creation of a *hostile environment*. Sexual harassment may begin as early as middle childhood. In college, 20–50% of female students and 9–20% of male students have experienced some form of sexual harassment from other students, faculty members, or administrators.

- In the workplace, fellow employees as well as supervisors may engage in sexual harassment. In many instances, harassment may not represent sexual attraction as much as an exercise of power.

Anti-Gay/Lesbian Harassment, Prejudice, and Discrimination

- Researchers have identified two forms of discrimination or bias against gay men and lesbians: heterosexual bias and anti-gay prejudice. *Heterosexual*

bias includes ignoring, segregating, and submerging gay men and lesbians into larger categories that make them invisible.

- *Anti-gay prejudice* is a strong dislike, fear, or hatred of gay men and lesbians. It is acted out through offensive language, discrimination, and violence. Anti-gay prejudice is derived from a deeply rooted insecurity concerning a person's own sexuality and gender identity, a strong fundamentalist religious orientation, or simple ignorance.

- Much anti-gay prejudice is supported by conservative religious institutions. In considering homosexuality from a religious perspective, individuals need to separate religious beliefs from prejudice.

Sexual Aggression

- *Rape* is penile-vaginal penetration performed against a woman's will. *Sexual aggression* refers to any sexual activity against a person's will through the use of force, argument, pressure, alcohol/drugs, or authority. *Sexual coercion,* a broader term than "rape" or "sexual aggression," includes arguing, pleading, and cajoling as well as force or the threat of force.

- Myths about rape encourage rape by blaming women. Men are more likely than women to believe rape myths.

- *Date rape* is the most common form of rape. Date rapes are usually not planned. Alcohol or drugs are often involved. There is also considerable sexual coercion in gay male relationships; there is less coercion in lesbian relationships. There is considerable confusion and argument about consent, especially because much sexual communication is nonverbal and ambiguous.

- The majority of reported rapes are by strangers. Stranger rapes are more likely to involve guns or knives than date rapes.

- In most states, a husband can be prosecuted for raping his wife. Marital rape victims experience feelings of betrayal, anger, humiliation, and guilt.

- Gang rape may be perpetrated by strangers or acquaintances. It may be motivated by power and by male-bonding factors.

- Most male rape victims have been raped by other men. Because the motive in sexual assaults is power and domination, sexual orientation is often irrelevant.

- Most stranger rapes (and some acquaintance or marital rapes) can be characterized as anger rapes, power rapes, or sadistic rapes. This typology, however, may not reflect the motivations of the majority of rapists, who are acquaintances, boyfriends, and husbands.

- The emotional changes women undergo as a result of rape are collectively known as *rape trauma syndrome*. Women develop depression, anxiety, restlessness, and guilt. The symptoms following rape are consistent with *posttraumatic stress disorder (PTSD)*. Rape trauma syndrome consists of an acute phase and a long-term reorganization phase. A *secondary victimization* may accompany both. Women find their sexuality severely affected for a short time or for longer after rape.

Child Sexual Abuse

- *Child sexual abuse* is any sexual interaction between an adult and a prepubertal child. *Incest* is sexual intercourse between individuals too closely related to legally marry.

- The preconditions for sexual abuse include motivation to sexually abuse a child, overcoming internal inhibitions against acting on the motivation, overcoming external obstacles, and undermining or overcoming the child's potential resistance.

- The initial effects of abuse include physical consequences and emotional, social, and sexual disturbances. Child sexual abuse may leave lasting scars on the adult survivor.

- *Sexual abuse trauma* includes traumatic sexualization, betrayal, powerlessness, and stigmatization. Treatment programs simultaneously treat the individual, the father-child relationship, the mother-child relationship, and the family as a whole.

- Child abuse prevention (CAP) programs have been hindered by different concepts of appropriate sexual behavior, adult fear of discussion, and controversy over sex education. Prevention programs generally teach children to say "no," to get away from the assailant or situation, and to tell a trusted adult about what happened.

SUGGESTED READING

Bergen, Raquel Kennedy. (1996). *Wife Rape: Understanding the Response of Survivors and Service Providers.* Thousand Oaks, CA: Sage. Addresses the deep pain and humiliation suffered by married women as a result of sexual assault by their husbands.

Draucker, Claire Burke. (1992). *Counseling Survivors of Childhood Sexual Abuse.* Newbury Park, CA: Sage. A comprehensive examination of treating adult survivors of childhood sexual abuse, using case studies.

Fontes, Lisa Aronson (Ed.). (1995). *Sexual Abuse in Nine North American Cultures: Treatment and Prevention.* Thousand Oaks, CA: Sage. Examines the impact of culture on child sexual abuse, including ways in which cultural norms can be used to protect children and help them recover from abuse; includes chapters on African Americans, Puerto Ricans, Asian Americans, Jews, gay men, and lesbians.

Hasbany, Richard (Ed.). (1990). *Homosexuality and Religion.* New York: Haworth Press. A survey of recent Christian and Jewish positions on homosexuality; current biblical and theological scholarship; gay and lesbian ministers, priests, and rabbis; and pastoral counseling for gay men and lesbians.

Herek, Gregory, and Benl, Kevin (Eds.). (1991). *Hate Crimes: Confronting Violence Against Lesbians and Gay Men.* Newbury Park, CA: Sage. An overview of violence against gay men and lesbians: the context, the perpetrators, and responses.

Parrot, Andrea, and Bechhofer, Laurie (Eds.). (1991). *Acquaintance Rape: The Hidden Crime.* New York: John Wiley. A collection of scholarly essays on date rape.

Wiehe, Vernon R. (1997). *Sibling Abuse: Hidden Physical, Emotional, and Sexual Trauma.* Thousand Oaks, CA: Sage. Defines terminology, describes various forms of abuse, cites incidence, and offers firsthand accounts to help us better understand sibling violence.

Wright, Lawrence. (1994). *Remembering Satan.* New York: Knopf. A stunning, balanced account of a family in which the father is alleged to have committed satanic abuse with his daughters; explores issues of recovered and false memories and the social/religious context in which charges of satanic abuse occur.

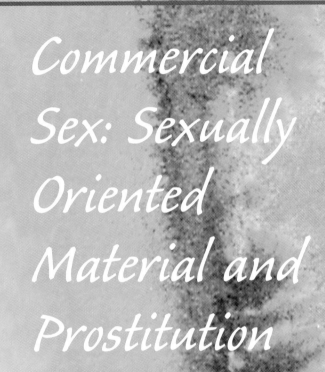

18

Commercial Sex: Sexually Oriented Material and Prostitution

Money and sex are bound together in the production and sale of sexually oriented material and in prostitution. Money is exchanged for sexual images or descriptions portrayed by videos, films, electronic media, magazines, books, music, and photographs that depict people in explicit or suggestive sexual activities. Money is also exchanged for sexual services provided by streetwalkers, call girls, massage parlor workers, and other sex workers. The sex industry is a multibillion-dollar industry with countless millions of consumers and customers. As a nation, however, we feel profoundly ambivalent about sexually oriented material and prostitution. Many condemn it as immoral and exploitative and wish to censor or eliminate it. Others find it harmless, an erotic diversion, or an aspect of society that cannot (or should not) be regulated; they believe censorship and police action do greater harm than good.

In this chapter, we examine sexually oriented material, including depictions of sex in popular culture, the role of technology in developing new forms of sexually oriented material, the effects of sexually oriented material, and censorship issues. Then we examine prostitution, focusing on females and males working in prostitution, the legal issues involved, and the impact of HIV/AIDS.

SEXUALLY ORIENTED MATERIAL IN CONTEMPORARY AMERICA

Studying sexually oriented material objectively is difficult because it touches deep and often conflicting feelings we have about sexuality. Some enjoy it, others feel it is degrading, and still others believe it may lead to violence or moral chaos.

Is It Pornography or Erotica? Is It Obscene?

Much of the discussion about sexually oriented material concerns the question of whether such material is erotic or pornographic. Unfortunately, there is a lack of agreement about what constitutes erotica or pornography. Part of the problem is that erotica and pornography are subjective terms. **Erotica** describes sexually oriented material that can be evaluated positively. (The word "erotica" is derived from the Greek *erotikos,* meaning a love poem.) It often involves mutuality, respect, affection, and a balance of power (Stock, 1985). **Pornography** represents sexually oriented material that is generally evaluated negatively. ("Pornography" is a nineteenth-century word derived from the Greek *porne,* meaning prostitute, and *graphos,* meaning depicting.) Although the U.S. judicial system has not been able to agree on a consistent definition of "pornography," such material might include anything that depicts sexuality and causes sexual arousal to the viewer. Pornography is legal in the United States; however, materials that are considered to be obscene are not. Although the legal definition for **obscenity** varies, the term generally implies a personal or societal judgment that something is offensive. Often material involving the use of violence and aggression or degrading and dehumanizing situations is deemed to be obscene. Because such a determination involves a judgment, critics often point to the subjective

Perversity is the muse of modern literature.

—*Susan Sontag*

How can you accuse me of liking pornography when I don't even have a pornograph?

—*Groucho Marx (1895–1977)*

nature of this definition. (For a further discussion of obscenity, and the law, see pages 565–568).

The same sexually oriented material may evoke a variety of responses in different people. Some people may enjoy the material, others may be repulsed, and still others may simultaneously feel aroused and guilty. "What I like is erotica, but what you like is pornography," may be a facetious statement, but one that's not entirely untrue. It has been found that people view others as more adversely affected by sexually explicit material than themselves (Gunther, 1995). Judgments about sexually explicit material tend to be relative.

Because of the tendency to use "erotica" as a positive term and "pornography" as a negative term, we will use the neutral term "sexually oriented material" whenever possible. **Sexually oriented material** is material such as photographs, videos, films, magazines, or books whose primary themes, topics, or depictions involve sexuality or cause sexual arousal. **Sexually explicit material** is material that intimately depicts sexual activities, the vulva, the erect penis, or the anus. This material is also considered **hardcore.** Other sexually oriented material may be considered **softcore** if it is not explicit, such as the depiction of nudes in *Playboy*. Sometimes however, the context of studies we are citing may require us to use either "erotica" or "pornography," rather than "sexually oriented material." This is especially true if the studies use those terms or are clearly making a positive or negative evaluation.

Sexually Oriented Material and Popular Culture

In the nineteenth century, technology transformed the production of sexually oriented material. Cheap paper and large-scale printing, combined with mass literacy, created an enormous market for books and drawings, including sexually explicit material. Today, technology is once again extending the forms in which this material is conveyed.

Over the past few decades, sexually oriented material, especially softcore, has become an integral part of popular culture. *Playboy* and *Penthouse* are among the most widely circulated magazines in America. The depiction of sexual activities is not restricted to books and magazines, however. Various establishments offer live adult entertainment. Bars, for example, feature topless dancers. Some clubs or adult entertainment establishments employ erotic dancers who expose themselves and simulate sexual acts before their audience. The video and VCR revolution has been so great that bedrooms have supplanted adult theaters, or "porno" movie houses, for the viewing of sexually oriented videos, which account for 15–25% of all videocassettes sold. Mainstream X-rated videos generally depict stereotypical gender roles, but sexual aggression is not typical (Davis & Bauserman, 1993). When it does occur, the victim is rarely depicted as enjoying it.

Videocassettes have had a profound effect on *who* views erotic films. Adult movie houses were the domain of men; relatively few women entered them. But with erotic videos available in the privacy of the bedroom, women also have become consumers of sexually oriented films and videos. The inclusion of women in the audience has led to **femme porn,** sexually oriented material catering to women and heterosexual couples. Femme porn avoids violence, is less male-centered, and is more sensitive to women's

> Obscenity is whatever happens to shock some elderly and ignorant magistrate.
>
> —*Bertrand Russell (1872–1970)*

The video and VCR revolution drove "porno" movie houses out of business as individuals became able to view X-rated videos in the privacy of their own homes. More than 200 million X-rated videos are rented annually.

erotic fantasies. (For more about other types of sexually oriented forms of mass media, see Chapter 1.)

A Blurring of Boundaries   As sexual themes, ideas, images, and music continue to expand in art, literature, and popular culture, the boundaries increasingly blur between what is socially acceptable and what is considered obscene. Thus, we are confronted with such questions as: Is Michael Jackson's crotch-grabbing obscene or expressive? Are the explicit talk shows of Ricki Lake and Howard Stern prurient or informative?

Looking at beauty pageants, we can see how essentially sexual portrayals of women may be defined as either legitimate or illegitimate. Women walking down a runway in bathing suits while their beauty and grace are judged is an all-American tradition. To some people, however, such pageants exploit women as sex objects. Consider the ironies involved in pop singer and actress Vanessa Williams's becoming Miss America. In 1985, Williams was forced to give up her crown when nude photographs of her were made public in *Penthouse* magazine. When Williams appeared in *Penthouse,* she crossed the boundary that separates legitimate from illegitimate portrayals of sex. Miss America, according to Ellen Goodman (1985), is "a virginal sex object" who projects feelings of availability and innocence, allure but inexperience. *Penthouse* projects images of sexuality and experience; there are no "virgins" in *Penthouse.* Both Miss America and *Penthouse,* however, sell fantasy sex. Goodman writes:

> Pageants and penthouses are both in the flesh biz. A beauty contest displays a woman solely as a body; a pornographer subdivides that body into parts. Both make their subject into an object, both offer her up for the pleasure of the devouring public.

The Miss America pageant and *Penthouse* illustrate some of the problems involved in labeling material obscene. Both the pageant and the magazine

The performances of rock artists are often highly sexual; Madonna uses sexuality as an integral theme in her videos and concerts.

essentially transform women into sex objects, yet one is accepted by society and the other is not.

Content and Themes Many of the themes found in sexually oriented and explicit material are also found in the mainstream media. Many music videos, TV shows, and movies, for example, contain sexual scenes and innuendoes, the subordination of women, and violence. They differ primarily in their explicitness. When researchers analyzed the contents of sexually explicit media, they found the following characteristics (Zillmann, 1994).

1. Sexual encounters take place between individuals who have just met. The participants are strangers and make no attempt to gain knowledge about each other. They usually express no interest in seeing each other again to develop a relationship. Their encounter remains solely sexual.

2. A few individuals are featured and have sex consecutively with different partners. Sex is fundamentally impersonal; people are bodies, not human beings.

The older one grows, the more one likes indecency.

—*Virginia Woolf (1882–1941)*

3. No matter what sexual activities are being portrayed, they give euphoric pleasure to all participants.

Another study examined the dynamics between the individuals. An analysis of 443 sexually explicit scenes in 45 X-rated videos found four themes (Greenberg, 1994). The most common theme (37%) was reciprocity, accompanied by mutual consent and satisfaction. Domination was represented in 28% of the scenes, in which one person, usually the male, controlled the sex act. Exploitation, in which one person used coercion or higher status to get his or her way, accounted for 26% of the scenes. Autoeroticism accounted for 9% of the scenes.

There is some evidence, however, that sexually explicit videos are moving away from impersonal sex to more romantic views of sexual encounters (Quackenbush, Strassberg, & Turner, 1995). This trend may be the result of women's becoming an increasingly large segment of the market. Women traditionally place sexual relationships within a romantic or relationship context. One experimental study found that women who viewed videos targeted at a female audience were more aroused, absorbed, and positive about such videos than they were toward impersonal videos (Mosher & MacIan, 1994).

With few exceptions, most studies are of material featuring White heterosexuals. As a result, we know very little about sexually explicit material directed toward ethnic groups, such as African Americans and Latinos, or toward gay men and lesbians. Such research is virtually nonexistent.

There have been some studies of interracial sex in sexually explicit videos. One study found that African American actors were of lower status and were stereotyped (Cowan & Campbell, 1994). African American women were more often the targets of sexual aggression than White women. And Black men showed fewer intimate behaviors, such as touching or expressing positive emotions, than White men. Interracial sexual interactions showed more aggression than same-race interactions. A study of racial prejudice in sexually explicit media, such as magazines, books, and videos, found that depictions of ethnic women reinforced ethnic stereotypes (Mayall & Russell, 1993). African American women were represented as sexually dangerous and contemptible, Latinas were portrayed as sexually voracious yet submissive, and Asian women were depicted as pliant dolls.

Gay male sex is rarely shown in heterosexual videos, presumably because it would make heterosexual men uncomfortable. But heterosexual videos may sometimes portray lesbian sex because many heterosexual men find such depictions sexually arousing.

The Effects of Sexually Oriented Material

There are a number of concerns about the effects of sexually oriented material. Does it cause people to engage in deviant acts? Is it a form of sex discrimination against women? And, finally, does it cause violence against women?

Sexual Expression   People who read or view sexually explicit material usually recognize it as fantasy; they use it as a release from their everyday world. Exposure to sexually oriented material temporarily encourages sexual expression and may activate a person's *typical* sexual behavior pattern.

> Western man, especially the Western critic, still finds it very hard to go into print and say: "I recommend you go and see this because it gave me an erection."
>
> —*Kenneth Tynan*

Sexually oriented materials deal with fantasy sex, not sex as we know it in the context of human relationships. Sexually explicit sex usually takes place in a world in which people and situations are defined in exclusively sexual terms. People are stripped of their nonsexual connections.

People are interested in sexually oriented material for a number of reasons. First, people enjoy the sexual sensations erotica arouses. It can be a source of pleasure. Masturbation or other sexual activities, pleasurable in themselves, may accompany the use of sexually oriented material or follow it. Second, since the nineteenth century, sexually oriented material has been a source of sexual information and knowledge. Eroticism generally is hidden from view and discussion. When sexuality is discussed in the family, in schools, or in public, it is discussed moralistically, rationally, or objectively. Most discussions are limited to sexual intercourse; other activities are avoided. Because the erotic aspects of sex are rarely talked about, sexually oriented material fills the void. In fact, several studies of college students have found that sexually oriented material is an important source of sex information, especially concerning oral sex (Duncan & Donnelly, 1991; Duncan & Nicholson, 1991). Third, sexually oriented material, like fantasy, may provide an opportunity for people to rehearse sexual activities. Fourth, reading or viewing sexually oriented material for pleasure or to enhance one's fantasies or masturbatory experiences may be regarded as safer sex.

Sexually oriented material may perform an additional function for gay men by allowing safer sex and reaffirmation. Being HIV-positive or a person with AIDS creates anxieties about HIV transmissions to others. But gay sexually oriented material permits those with HIV or AIDS to explore their own sexuality with masturbatory images and scenes while refraining from sexual encounters with a partner.

> The worst that can be said about pornography is that it leads not to anti-social acts but to the reading of more pornography.
>
> —*Gore Vidal*

Variation in Personal Response   Men tend to react more positively to sexually explicit material than women (Thompson, Chaffe, & Oshagan, 1990). Men more than women believe sexually explicit material has positive effects, such as sexual release and a lowering of inhibitions. Both believe, however, that sexually explicit material may have negative effects, such as dehumanizing women and causing a loss of respect between men and women.

Why does one person evaluate sexually explicit material negatively and another positively? The answer seems to lie in the person's emotional response to the material. A person's erotophobic/erotophilic attitudes affect his or her response to sexually oriented material (see Chapter 9). Erotophilic people tend to respond positively to such material; erotophobic people do not. Ira Reiss (1990) writes:

> Our reactions to sexually arousing films or books provide insight into our personal sexual attitudes. What we really are reacting to is not the objective material but rather a projection of our own innermost feelings concerning the type of sexuality presented. We may feel that sexuality being portrayed is too revealing, too embarrassing, too suggestive, or too private.

Sexual Aggression   In 1970, the President's Commission on Pornography and Obscenity concluded that pornography did not cause harm or violence. It recommended that all legislation restricting adult access to it be repealed as inconsistent with the First Amendment.

Pornography is the theory and rape is the practice.

—Robin Morgan

In the 1980s, President Ronald Reagan established a new pornography commission under Attorney General Edwin Meese. In 1986, the Attorney General's Commission on Pornography stated that "the most prevalent forms of pornography" were violent; it offered no evidence, however, to substantiate its assertion (U.S. Attorney General's Commission on Pornography [AGCOP], 1986). There is no evidence, in fact, to indicate that the majority of sexually explicit material is violent.

In the 1970s, feminists and others who worked to increase rape awareness began to call attention to the violence against women portrayed in the media. They found rape themes in sexually explicit material especially disturbing, believing those images reinforced rape myths. There is no evidence, however, that nonviolent sexually oriented material is associated with actual sexual aggression against women. Even the conservative Commission on Pornography agreed that nonviolent sexually oriented material had no such effect (AGCOP, 1986). But it did assert that "some forms of sexually explicit materials bear a causal relationship . . . to sexual violence." It presented no scientific evidence as proof, however.

The relationship between violent sexually oriented material and sexual aggression against women remains an issue of contention (Davies, 1997). The most important studies suggesting a link between sexually oriented material and sexual violence have been experimental ones.

Even though experimental studies are more likely than correlational studies to suggest a negative impact of exposure to pornography, even experimental studies may not find such an impact (Allen, D'Alessio, Emmers, & Gebhart, 1996; Davies, 1997; Fisher & Grenier, 1994). Recent experiments have found no effect from exposure to violent pornography (Bauserman, 1996; Fisher & Grenier, 1994). Prior to viewing material of a woman enjoying being raped, some research subjects were provoked by a female researcher; others were not. After viewing the material, both groups could talk with the researcher over an intercom or send her an electrical shock. Exposure to violent material—even among those provoked—produced no antifemale aggression, fantasies, or attitudes.

Sex Discrimination   Since the 1980s, feminists have been divided about sexually explicit material. One segment of the feminist movement, which identifies itself as antipornography, views sexually explicit material as inherently degrading and dehumanizing to women. Many in this group believe that sexually explicit material provides the social basis for women's subordination by turning them into sex objects. They argue that sexually explicit material inhibits women's equal rights by encouraging the exploitation and subordination of women.

Feminist and other critics of this approach point out that it has an antisexual bias that associates sex with exploitation. Sexually explicit images, rather than specifically sexist images, are singled out. Further, discrimination and the subordination of women in Western culture have existed since ancient times, long before the rise of sexually oriented material. The roots of subordination lie far deeper. One researcher even suggests that differences in response to sexually explicit mass media are the result of inherited differences (Malamuth, 1996). The elimination of sexual depictions of women would not alter discrimination against women significantly, if at all. Finally, some feminists believe that the approach represents a double standard. One recent study suggests that exposure to pornography and its effects are related to broad and fundamental ways of understanding men, women, and gender relations (Frable, Johnson, & Kellman, 1997).

Child Pornography   Child pornography is a form of child sexual exploitation. Children involved in pornography, who are usually between ages 8 and 16, are motivated by friendship, interest in sexuality, offers of money, or threats. Younger children may be unaware that their photographs are being used sexually. Many of these children are related to the photographer. Many children who have been exploited in this way exhibit distress and poor adjustment; they may suffer from depression, anxiety, and guilt. Many engage in destructive and antisocial behavior.

Although the courts have generally continued to oppose censoring sexually explicit material and to affirm the individual's right to possess such material, a major exception is child pornography. In 1990, the Supreme Court affirmed the right to prosecute individuals for the possession of child pornography (*Osborne v. Ohio*, No. 88-5986).

Censorship, Sexually Oriented Material, and the Law

To censor means to examine in order to suppress or delete anything considered objectionable. **Censorship** occurs when the government, private groups, or individuals impose their moral or political values on others by suppressing words, ideas, or images they deem offensive. *Obscenity* is the state of being contrary to generally accepted standards of decency or morality. During the first half of this century, under American obscenity laws, James Joyce's *Ulysses* and the works of D. H. Lawrence were prohibited, Havelock Ellis's *Studies in the Psychology of Sex* was banned, nude paintings were ripped from gallery and museum walls, and everything but tender kisses was banned from the movies for years.

U.S. Supreme Court decisions in the 1950s and 1960s eliminated much of the legal framework supporting literary censorship on the national level. But censorship continues to flourish on the state and local levels, especially among schools and libraries. The women's health book *The New Our Bodies, Ourselves* has been a frequent object of attack because of its feminist perspective and descriptions of lesbian sexuality. More recently, two children's books have been added to the list of most censored books: Leslea Newman's *Heather Has Two Mommies* and Michael Willhoite's *Daddy's Roommate*. Both books have come under attack because they describe children in healthy lesbian and gay families. Judy Blume's books for teenagers, J. D. Salinger's *The Catcher in the Rye*, and the *Sports Illustrated* swimsuit issue are regular items on banned-book lists. Exhibits of the photographs taken by the late Robert Mapplethorpe have been strenuously attacked for "promoting" homoeroticism.

Obscenity Laws   It is difficult to arrive at a legal definition of obscenity for determining whether a specific illustration, photograph, novel, or movie is obscene. Traditionally, American courts considered material obscene if it tended to corrupt or deprave its user. Over the years, the law has been debated in a number of court cases. This process has resulted in a set of guidelines for determining what is obscene:

Congress shall make no law respecting an establishment of religion, or prohibiting the free exercise thereof; or abridging the freedom of speech, or of the press, or the right of the people peaceably to assemble, and to petition the Government for a redress of grievances.

—*First Amendment to the Constitution of the United States*

If a man is pictured chopping off a woman's breast, it only gets an "R" rating; but if, God forbid, a man is pictured kissing a woman's breast, it gets an "X" rating. Why is violence more acceptable than tenderness?

—*Sally Struthers*

Two of the most heavily censored books in America are Leslea Newman's Heather Has Two Mommies, *about a lesbian family, and Michael Will- hoite's* Daddy's Roommate *(shown here), about a child who visits his gay father and his roommate. These books are opposed because they depict loving gay and lesbian families.*

1. The dominant theme of the work must appeal to prurient sexual inter- ests and portray sexual conduct in a patently offensive way.

2. Taken as a whole, the work must be without serious literary, artistic, political, or scientific value.

3. A "reasonable" person must find the work, when taken as a whole, to possess no social value.

The problem with these criteria, as well as the earlier standards, is that they are highly subjective. Who is a reasonable person? There are also many instances in which reasonable people disagree about whether material has social value. Most of us, however, would probably find that a reasonable person has opinions regarding obscenity that closely resemble our own. (Otherwise, we would think that he or she was unreasonable.)

As we saw earlier, our evaluation of sexually explicit material is closely related to how we feel about such material. Our judgments are not based on reason but on emotion. Justice Potter Stewart's exasperation in *Jacobelis v. Ohio* (1965) reveals a reasonable person's frustration in trying to define pornography: "But I know it when I see it."

If America persists in the way it's go- ing, and the Lord doesn't strike us down, He ought to apologize to Sodom and Gomorrah.

—*Jesse Helms*

The Issue of Child Protection   In 1988, the United States passed the Child Protection and Obscenity Enforcement Act, which supports stiff penalties for those who involve children in the making and distribution of pornography. Since then, the development and distribution of child pornography of all types have been targeted by the Attorney General's Office (Dickerson, 1994), resulting in an increase in both new legislation and prosecutions (Servi, 1995). Most recently, the Communications and Decency Act of 1996 tried to address the problem of sexual exploitation of children and teens over the Internet. However, in July 1997, the United States Supreme Court ruled that the statute was not constitutional because it violated the First Amendment's guarantee of free speech. One side of this argument is represented by those

Rock, Rap, and Righteousness: Censorship and Popular Music

FROM ITS BEGINNING, rock and roll music, with its overt sexual themes, has attracted censors. In the 1950s, sociology writer Vance Packard testified before the U.S. Senate that rock and roll stirred "the animal instinct in modern teenagers" by its "raw savage tone." When Elvis ("The Pelvis") Presley appeared on "The Ed Sullivan Show," he was filmed only from the waist up. When the Rolling Stones appeared on the show several years later, words from the song "Satisfaction" were bleeped out; Mick Jagger had to change the words of "Let's Spend the Night Together" to "let's spend some time together" (Heins, 1993).

The current cycle of music censorship began in 1985 when Tipper Gore (wife of Vice President Al Gore) heard Prince's "Darling Nikki," a song about masturbation. She organized Parents' Music Resource Center (PMRC) to focus public attention on the explicitness of rock music. Senate hearings were called to pressure record companies to label offensive music. Frank Zappa, one of America's foremost rock innovators and composers, defended rockers' artistic freedom. "Masturbation is not illegal. If it is not illegal, why should it be illegal to sing about?" (Chapple & Talbot, 1990).

Because the hearings intimidated the record companies, they began labeling potentially offensive music. In 1990, the major record companies adopted a "sexually explicit lyrics" label (Heins, 1993). Although the label was not meant to suggest that record stores should refuse to sell labeled recordings to minors, police in some areas warned music stores that such records were considered obscene. Major retailers, such as Sears and J.C. Penney, announced that they would not carry labeled recordings.

Since the late 1980s, local officials have attempted to shut down shows by the Beastie Boys, Run-DMC, and LL Cool J. LL Cool J was arrested for making lewd movements on stage. In 1990, Washington became the first state to ban the sale of music with explicit sexual lyrics to minors.

Marjorie Heins (1993) writes:

Creative works are constitutionally protected in large part because of the critical role they play in a society that values individual autonomy, dignity, and growth;

it also expresses, defines, and nourishes the human personality. Art speaks to our emotions, our intellects, our spiritual lives, and also our physical and sexual lives. Artists celebrate joy and abandon, but they also confront death, depression, and despair. For some of us, rock 'n' roll or rap artists may play these roles and provide these connections; for others, classical composers, sculptors, or playwrights may elicit the most powerful responses.

By the early 1990s, it became common practice to "censor by suggestion." Police departments or district attorneys warned retailers to remove certain music, especially rap or rock, because, they suggested, it might be obscene. Since obscenity could only be tested in court, many stores withdrew the material because they could not bear the expense of a costly court trial. Although the police denied this was censorship, it short-circuited the legal process. As Justice William Brennan observed, "People do not lightly disregard public officers' thinly veiled threats to institute criminal proceedings against them if they do not come around" (quoted in Heins, 1993).

Many critics complain about the themes of sex, violence, suicide, incest, and sexism found in contemporary music. Although these themes may be objectionable, they are not unique to rock and rap. Wolfgang Amadeus Mozart's opera *Don Giovanni* begins with a famous aria enumerating the hundreds of women Don Juan has seduced. The Greek tragedy *Oedipus Rex* is about incest. Some of the works of such great artists as Brueghel, Rembrandt, Goya, and Picasso (to name but a few) deal with seduction, incest, bestiality, rape, and sadism.

There is no doubt that some popular music is repugnant, tasteless, vulgar, puerile, degrading, racist, sexist, homophobic, offensive, lewd, and stupid. But Supreme Court decisions have long demonstrated our inability to create objective criteria for determining what is obscene. When we consider popular music, it is important to remember that the purpose of the Constitution's First Amendment is not to judge art but to protect our freedom of expression. As the Supreme Court stated in *Cohen v. California* (1971): "One man's lyric may be another's vulgarity."

who agree with Deputy Solicitor General Waxman's warning that "the Internet threatens to give every child with access to a connected computer a free pass into the equivalent of every adult bookstore and video store in the country" (cited in Levy, 1997). The other side is represented by those who feel their rights to free speech, including information about sexually transmitted diseases, gay rights, and free speech debates, may be blocked as a

To slurp or not to slurp at the fountain of filth is a decision to which each of us is entitled.

—*Stephen Kessler*

result of censorship. Nonetheless, sending and keeping child pornography remains a crime that law enforcement officers vigorously pursue (Kowalski, 1997).

Our inability to find criteria for objectively defining obscenity makes it potentially dangerous to censor such material. We may end up using our own personal standards for restricting freedom of speech guaranteed by the First Amendment. By enforcing our own biases, we endanger the freedom of others.

> I may disagree with what you say but I will defend to the death your right to say it.
>
> —*Voltaire (1694–1778)*

PROSTITUTION

The exchange of sexual acts, such as sexual intercourse, fellatio, anal intercourse, discipline and bondage, and obscene insults, for money and/or goods is called **prostitution**. Both men and women, including transvestites and transsexuals, work as prostitutes.

Females Working in Prostitution

> Prostitution gives her an opportunity to meet people. It provides fresh air and wholesome exercise, and keeps her out of trouble.
>
> —*Joseph Heller,* Catch 22

During the 1980s, an estimated 80,000 women worked in prostitution (Potterat, Woodhouse, Muth, & Muth, 1990). This estimate may be considerably smaller than the actual number because many women engage in prostitution occasionally or drift in and out. There is little agreement on anything but the more blatant forms of solicitation and definitions of prostitution. Many women who accept money or drugs for sexual activities do not consider themselves prostitutes. According to Janus and Janus (1993), 5% of the women in their representative study reported exchanging sex for money, and 20% of the men, money for sex. Laumann et al. (1994) reported that 16% of the men surveyed ever paid for sex.

Sex as Work   Prostitutes often identify themselves as "working girls" or "sex workers," probably an accurate description of how they perceive themselves in relationship to sex. They are usually not prostitutes because they like anonymous sex and multiple partners per se, but because they perceive it as good-paying work. They generally do not expect to enjoy sex with their customers. They separate sex as a physical act for which they are paid from sex as an expression of intimacy and pleasure. One prostitute (quoted in Zausner, 1986) describes her feelings about sex:

> I don't think about sex when I'm working. You have to be a good actress to make men think that you like it when you don't. I only enjoy sex if I'm with someone I care about.

Although prostitutes may be willing to perform various sexual acts, many will not kiss; they regard kissing as a particular form of intimacy which they reserve for men they care about.

Entrance into Prostitution   One study found that the majority of prostitutes began working as prostitutes at an average age of 21.8 (Albert, Warner, Hatcher, Trussell, & Bennett, 1995). But many young prostitutes are under age 16 when they begin (Weisberg, 1985).

Childhood sexual abuse is often a factor in both adolescent girls' and boys' entrance into prostitution, for two reasons (Simons & Whitbeck, 1991; Widom & Kuhns, 1996). First, sexual abuse increases the likelihood that a preadolescent or adolescent will become involved in deviant street culture and activities. Physically and sexually abused youths are more likely to be rejected by their conventional peers and become involved in delinquent activities. Second, one of the primary reasons young people flee home is parental abuse—generally sexual abuse for girls, physical abuse for boys.

Girls are generally introduced into prostitution by pimps, men upon whom prostitutes are emotionally and financially dependent. Prostitutes give their pimps the money they earn. In turn, pimps provide housing, buy them clothes and jewelry, and offer them protection on the streets. Although girls meet their pimps in various ways, pimps most frequently initiate the contact. They use both psychological and physical coercion. Many girls and young women are "sweet-talked" into prostitution by promises of money, protection, and companionship. Adolescent prostitutes are more likely than adults to have pimps.

Once involved with pimps, women are frequently abused by them. The women also run the risk of abuse and violence from their customers. Street-walkers are especially vulnerable.

Personal Background and Motivation   Adult prostitutes are often women who were targets of early male sexual aggression, had extensive sexual experience in adolescence, were rejected by peers because of sexual activities, and were not given adequate emotional support by their parents. There are high rates of physical and sexual abuse (including intrafamilial abuse) and neglect in their childhoods (Widom & Kuhns, 1996; Zausner, 1986). Their parents failed to provide them with a model of affectionate interaction. As a result, as the girls grew up, they tended to be anxious, to feel lonely and isolated, and to be unsure of their own identity. Another common thread running through the lives of most prostitutes is an economically disadvantaged background (Goode, 1994).

Adolescent prostitutes describe their general psychological state of mind as very negative, depressed, unhappy, or insecure at the time they first entered prostitution. There were high levels of drug use, including alcohol, marijuana, cocaine, and/or heroin, and many of those who became drug addicts later turned to prostitution in order to survive and maintain their drug habit (Graham & Wisch, 1994; Miller, 1995). Their emotional state made them particularly vulnerable to pimps.

No single motive seems to explain why a person becomes a prostitute. It is probably a combination of environmental, social, financial, and personal factors that leads a woman to this profession. When women describe the most attractive things about life in the prostitution subculture, they describe them in monetary and material terms. One prostitute notes, "I said to myself how can I do these horrible things and I said money, money, money" (Weisberg, 1990). Compared with a minimum-wage job, which may be the only alternative, prostitution appears to be an economically rational decision. But prostitutes also are aware of the psychological and physical costs. They fear the dangers of physical and sexual abuse, AIDS and other sexually transmitted diseases, harassment, jail, and legal expenses. They are also aware of the damage done to their self-esteem from stigmatization and rejection by family and society, negative feelings toward men and sex, bad working conditions, lack of a future, and control by pimps (Weisberg, 1985).

In many countries of the world, the availability of prostitutes has become part of the tourist economy, with the money paid to prostitutes an important part of the national income ("Asia," 1996; Baker, 1995). In developing countries such as Thailand and the Philippines, where social and economic conditions combine with a dominant male hierarchy and acceptance of a double standard, prostitution is seen by many as a necessary and accepted occupation.

Prostitutes exhibit a range of feelings toward their customers. Some may project onto others their feelings of being deviant. If customers regard prostitutes as bad, the women feel that the so-called respectable people who come to them are worse—hypocrites, freaks, weirdos, and perverts who ask them to perform sexual acts that the women often consider degrading. Prostitutes encounter such people frequently and may generalize from these experiences. Other prostitutes, however, are accepting and nonjudgmental of their customers. "My customers are people like everyone else," reports one prostitute (Zausner, 1986). "If they're nice to me and don't try to fuck with me, then I like them."

Forms of Female Prostitution   Female prostitutes work as streetwalkers, in brothels, in massage parlors, and as call girls.

STREETWALKERS   By far the greatest number of prostitutes are streetwalkers. Streetwalking is usually the first type of prostitution in which adolescents become involved; it is also the type they prefer. Women working as streetwalkers are often high school dropouts or runaways who fled abusive homes. Because streetwalkers make their contacts through public solicitation, they are more visible and more likely to be arrested. Without the ability to easily screen her customers, the streetwalker is more likely to be victimized, beaten, robbed, or raped. One study found that more than 90% of street prostitutes had been sexually assaulted (Miller & Schwartz, 1995). The study also found that people often consider prostitutes to be "unrapable" or even deserving of being raped.

Streetwalkers in one study worked an average of 5 days a week and had 4 or 5 clients a day, half of whom were repeats (Freund, Leonard, & Lee, 1989). Fellatio was their most common activity; less than one-quarter of their contacts involved sexual intercourse.

BROTHELS   Brothels can be found in most large cities. They are legal in some counties in Nevada, where there are approximately 32 legal brothels employing about 300 licensed prostitutes (Albert et al., 1995). One study found that the average number of clients over a 1-month period was 111 (Albert et al., 1995). A major attraction of brothels is their comfortable and personable atmosphere. In brothels, men can sit and have a cup of coffee or a drink, watch television, or casually converse with the women. Many customers are regulars. Sometimes they go to the brothel simply to talk or relax rather than to engage in sex.

Because of their inability to screen clients, streetwalkers are the most likely of prostitutes to be victimized.

Some brothels, such as B&D dungeons, which cater to bondage and discipline customers, specialize in different types of sex. These "dungeons" are equipped with whips, racks, leg irons; they replicate a gothic atmosphere. Women in such brothels adopt pseudonyms such as "Madam Lash" or add the prefix "Mistress" to their first names. They dress in black, studded leather and make themselves up as forbidding dominatrices (plural of "dominatrix," a woman who dominates).

MASSEUSES   There are relatively few brothels any longer; most have been replaced by massage parlors. The major difference between brothels and massage parlors is that brothels present themselves as places of prostitution, whereas massage parlors try to disguise their intent. Some massage parlors offer customers any type of sexual service they wish for a fee, which is negotiated with the masseuses. But most are "massage and masturbation only" parlors. These so-called M-and-M parlors are probably the most widespread; their primary service is the "local" or "relief" massage in which there is only masturbation. By limiting sex to masturbation, these parlors are able to avoid legal difficulties, because most criminal sex statutes require genital penetration, oral sex, discussion of fees, and explicit solicitation for criminal prosecution. Women who work M-and-M parlors are frequently referred to as "hand whores"; these women, however, often do not consider themselves prostitutes, although they may drift into prostitution later. Many masseuses run newspaper ads for their services and work on an out-call basis, meeting customers at their hotel rooms or homes.

Prostitution is legal and subject to government regulation in some parts of Nevada.

CALL GIRLS   Call girls have the highest status among prostitutes. They are usually better educated than other prostitutes, often come from a middle-class background, dress fashionably, and live on "the right side of the tracks." A call girl is expensive; her fees may be $100–$250 an hour or $500–$2500 a night. She operates through contacts and referrals; instead of the street, she takes to the telephone and arranges to meet her customers. Call girls often work for escort services that advertise through newspapers.

Males Working in Prostitution

Although there is extensive research about prostitution, most of it concerns female prostitution. Most research on male prostitution focuses on street hustlers, the male equivalent of streetwalkers. There are other kinds of male prostitutes, such as call boys, masseurs, and prostitutes who work out of gay bars, who have not been extensively investigated. Men tend to enter into the life of prostitution early, usually by the age of 16 (Cates and Markley, 1992). Few males who work as prostitutes are gigolos, heterosexual men providing sexual services for women in exchange for money. Gigolos are probably more the products of male fantasies—being paid for "having fun"—than reality. The overwhelming majority of male prostitutes sell their sexual services to other males. The most common types of sexual behaviors male prostitutes engage in are fellatio, either alone or with other activities (99%); anal sex (80%); and oral stimulation of the anus, also called rimming (63%) (Morse, Simon, Balson, & Osofsky, 1992).

Male prostitution is shaped by three subcultures: the peer delinquent subculture, the gay subculture, and the transvestite subculture. Young male prostitutes are called "chickens," and the customers who are attracted to them are known as "chickenhawks."

In female adolescent prostitution, the pimp plays a major role: He takes a girl's money and maintains her in the life. By contrast, there is usually no pimp role in male prostitution. Most males are introduced to prostitution

The movie My Own Private Idaho, *starring Keanu Reeves and the late River Phoenix, depicted the lives of young street hustlers.*

through the influence of their peers. A typical male begins when a friend suggests he can make "easy money" on the streets. Hustlers usually live alone or with roommates, whereas female streetwalkers usually live with their pimps. Many of the psychological symptoms associated with hustling are as attributable to the delinquent environment as to the hustler's innate psychological condition (Simon et al., 1992).

The **peer delinquent subculture,** an antisocial youth subculture, is part of delinquent street life characterized by male and female prostitution, drug dealing, panhandling, theft, and violence. Young people in this culture sell sex like they sell drugs or stolen goods—as a means of making money. Teenage hustlers may not consider themselves gay because they are selling sex rather than seeking erotic gratification. Instead, they may identify themselves as bisexual or heterosexual. They may find their customers in urban "sex zones"—adult bookstores, topless bars, and X-rated movie houses—which cater to the sexual interests of people of all sexual orientations. They are more likely to work the street than bars.

In contrast to male delinquent prostitutes, gay male prostitutes engage in prostitution as a means of expressing their sexuality *and* making money (Weisberg, 1990). They identify themselves as gay and work primarily in gay neighborhoods or gay bars. Many are "pushed-away" children who fled their homes when their parents and peers rejected them because of their sexual orientation (Kruks, 1991). The three most important reasons they give for engaging in prostitution are money, sex, and fun/adventure.

Very little is known about male transvestite prostitutes (Boles & Elifson, 1994). They are a diverse group and are distinct from other male and female prostitutes (Elifson, Boles, Posey, & Sweat, 1993). Their clients are both heterosexual and gay males. Many of their heterosexual clients believe the transvestites are women, but others are aware that the prostitutes are transvestites. Transvestite prostitutes can be found in most major cities.

Another type of male prostitute is the **she-male,** a male who has undergone breast augmentation. The she-male's client may mistakenly believe that the he is a she. Often the client is another she-male or a male who knows that the prostitute is genitally a male (Blanchard, 1993).

Prostitution and the Law

Arrests for prostitution and calls for cleanups seem to be a communal ritual practiced by influential segments of the population to reassert their moral, political, and economic dominance. The arrests are symbolic of community disapproval. They are not effective in ending prostitution.

Female prostitution is the only sexual offense for which women are extensively prosecuted; the male patron is seldom arrested. Prostitutes are subject to arrest for various activities, including vagrancy and loitering, but the most common charge is for solicitation. **Solicitation,** a word, gesture, or action that implies an offer of sex for sale, is defined vaguely enough that women who are not prostitutes occasionally are arrested on the charge because they act "suspiciously." It is usually difficult to witness a direct transaction in which money passes hands, and such arrests are also complicated by involving the patron. Laws may also include actions not ordinarily associated with prostitution; for example, some states define prostitution as offering oneself for promiscuous and indiscriminate intercourse without payment.

There are periodic attempts to repeal laws criminalizing prostitution because it is perceived as a victimless crime: Both the woman and her customer engage in it voluntarily. Others, especially feminists, want to repeal such laws because they view prostitutes as being victimized by their pimps, their customers, and the police and legal system (Barry, 1995; Bullough & Bullough, 1996). Studies of prostitutes and their clients, as well as psychological and sociological studies, provide significant support for decriminalization (Rio, 1991).

Reformers propose that prostitution be either legalized or decriminalized. Those who support legalizing prostitution want to subject it to licensing and registration by police and health departments, as in Nevada and parts of Europe. Those who propose decriminalization want to remove criminal penalties for engaging in prostitution; prostitutes would be neither licensed nor registered. Some prostitutes have organized for decriminalization and support in a group called COYOTE (Call Off Your Old Tired Ethics). COYOTE also advocates the unionization of prostitutes and recognition of their work as satisfying a widespread public demand for their services.

Whatever one's opinion about decriminalizing adult prostitution, treating adolescent prostitution as a crime needs to be reevaluated. Treating juvenile prostitutes as delinquents overlooks the fact that, in many ways, adolescent prostitutes are more victims than criminals. As researchers examine such social problems as the sexual and physical abuse of children, running away, and adolescent prostitution, they are discovering a disturbing interrelationship. The law, nevertheless, does not view adolescent prostitution as a response to victimization and an attempt to survive on the streets. Instead, it deals with it as a criminal behavior and applies legal sanctions. A more appropriate response might be to offer counseling, halfway houses, alternative schooling, or job training as options.

I regret to say that we of the FBI are powerless to act in case of oral-genital intimacy, unless it has in some way obstructed interstate commerce.

—*J. Edgar Hoover (1895–1972)*

The Impact of HIV/AIDS

Prostitution has received increased attention as a result of the HIV/AIDS epidemic. There are several reasons that female and male prostitutes are at higher risk than the general population. First, many prostitutes are injection drug users, and injection drug use is one of the primary ways of transmitting HIV infection (CDC, 1997e; Morse, Simon, Osofsky, Balson, & Gaumer, 1991). Women exchanging sex for crack in crack houses are also at high risk for HIV (Inciardi, 1995). Second, prostitutes are at higher HIV risk because they have multiple partners. Third, prostitutes do not always require their customers to use condoms. The male prostitutes are at even greater risk than female prostitutes because of their high-risk sexual practices, especially anal intercourse, and their high-risk gay/bisexual clientele. One study reported that in some urban areas the rate of HIV infection among male prostitutes is 50% or higher (Boles & Elifson, 1994).

The question of who acts as the bridge population in the spread of AIDS generates controversy. Although some point to the male clients of prostitutes (Dingman, 1996), others claim that the prostitutes themselves, both male and female, are responsible for much of the heterosexual transmission of HIV. Many male prostitutes reported having girlfriends or wives, some of whom were also prostitutes. The male prostitutes indicated that they believed the majority of their clients were heterosexual or bisexual.

Fear of contracting AIDS from women is prompting some men to turn to children for sex ("AIDS Fear," 1996). "The AIDS epidemic has become both a cause and a consequence of the trade in children for sex," states Peter Piot, executive director of the United Nations global AIDS agency. Although statistics showing the rate of HIV infection among child prostitutes are unavailable, small samples indicate that as many as 50% of underage sex workers could have the virus.

Supporters of continued criminalization of prostitution point to the prevalence of HIV/AIDS as an additional reason for arresting prostitutes. Prostitutes, they argue, are likely to contribute to the AIDS epidemic. Some suggest additional penalties for prostitutes who have AIDS or test positive for the virus. Those who wish to decriminalize prostitution point out that the current laws have not diminished prostitution. Further, they argue, if prostitution were regulated and prostitutes were made subject to routine STD/HIV testing, there would be a greater likelihood of preventing HIV transmission. In Nevada, for example, where brothel prostitution is legal, health officials require monthly mandatory HIV tests and the use of condoms. According to one study involving more than 20,000 HIV tests to women employed in Nevada brothels, none tested positive for HIV (Albert et al., 1995).

What can we learn from all of the above? That clients of prostitutes are putting themselves *as well as their partners* at high risk for HIV if they do not use condoms.

■   The world of commercial sex is one our society approaches with confusion. Society simultaneously condemns sexually explicit material and prostitution, while it also provides their customers. Because of conflicting attitudes and behaviors, our society rarely approaches the issues surrounding sexually explicit material and prostitution with disinterested logic.

SUMMARY

Sexually Oriented Material in Contemporary America

- There is a lack of agreement about what constitutes *erotica, pornography,* and *obscenity* because they are subjective terms. The same *sexually oriented material* (or *sexually explicit material*) may evoke a variety of responses in different people.

- X-rated videos have increased the consumption of sexually oriented films by women. The inclusion of women in the audience has led to *femme porn.*

- People who read or view sexually explicit material usually recognize it as fantasy. They use it as a release from their everyday world. Pornography temporarily encourages sexual expression, activating a person's typical sexual behavior pattern. People are interested in sexually oriented material because they enjoy sexual sensations, it is a source of sexual information and knowledge, it enables people to rehearse sexual activities, and it is safer sex. For gay men, sexually oriented material offers safer sex and reaffirmation.

- In 1970, the President's Commission on Pornography and Obscenity concluded that pornography does not cause harm or violence. Over the years, there have been controversy and debate over the effects of pornography. There is no evidence, however, that nonviolent sexually oriented material is associated with sexual aggression against women, nor is there evidence that sexually violent material produces lasting changes in attitudes or behaviors.

- Some feminists believe that sexually oriented material represents a form of sex discrimination against women because it places them in what they believe to be a degrading and dehumanizing context. Others believe that opponents of sexually oriented material have an antisex bias.

- Child pornography is a form of sexual exploitation. Child pornography is not widespread; it appeals to a very limited audience. Courts have prohibited its production, sale, and possession.

- The legal guidelines for determining whether a work is obscene are: (1) the dominant theme of the work must appeal to prurient sexual interests and portray sexual conduct in a patently offensive way;

(2) taken as a whole, the work must be without serious literary, artistic, political, or scientific value; and (3) a reasonable person must find the work, when taken as a whole, to possess no social value. The inability to find criteria for objectively defining obscenity makes it potentially dangerous to censor such material.

Prostitution

- Prostitution is the exchange of sexual acts for money and/or goods. Both men and women work as prostitutes. Women are generally introduced into prostitution by pimps. Adolescent prostitutes describe their psychological state as negative when they first entered prostitution. Streetwalkers run the risk of abuse and violence from their customers. Prostitutes report various motives for entering prostitution, including earning quick and easy money, the prostitution subculture, and the excitement of "the life."

- Streetwalkers are the most numerous prostitutes. Others work in brothels, but massage parlors are more widespread. Some masseuses have intercourse with clients, but most provide only masturbation. Call girls have the highest status among prostitutes.

- Most research on male prostitution focuses on street hustlers. Male prostitution is shaped by the peer delinquent, gay, and transvestite subcultures. The three most important reasons given for engaging in prostitution are money, sex, and fun/adventure.

- Arrests for prostitution are symbols of community disapproval; they are not effective in ending prostitution. Female prostitution is the only sexual offense for which women are extensively prosecuted; the male patron is seldom arrested. Decriminalization of prostitution is often urged because it is a victimless crime, or because prostitutes are victimized by their pimps, customers, police, and the legal system. Some people advocate regulation by police and health departments.

- Prostitutes are at higher risk for HIV/AIDS than the general population because many are injection drug users, have multiple partners, and do not always require their customers to use condoms. Female and male prostitutes and their customers may provide a pathway for HIV into the general heterosexual community.

SUGGESTED READING

Barry, K. (1995). *The Prostitution of Sexuality: The Global Exploitation of Women.* New York: New York University Press. Brings attention to the lack of choice facing many women who are prostitutes and argues that only under decriminalization can prostitutes leave the life without stigma.

Delacoste, Frédérique, & Alexander, Priscilla (Eds.). (1991). *Sex Work: Writing by Women in the Sex Industry.* Pittsburgh, PA: Cleis Press. A collection of short, personal stories by women who work as prostitutes, masseuses, topless dancers, models, and actresses, many of whom regard themselves as feminists.

Donnerstein, Edward, Penrod, Steven, & Linz, Daniel (Eds.). (1987). *The Question of Pornography: Research Findings and Policy Implications.* New York: Free Press. A review of the scientific research on sexually oriented material, its effects, and the legal issues involved.

Heins, Marjorie. (1993). *Sex, Sin, and Blasphemy: A Guide to America's Censorship Wars.* New York: New Press. Recent censorship battles—and what's at stake—in art, music, dance, and the mass media by a leader of the American Civil Liberties Union's Art Censorship Project.

Steward, Samuel M. (1992). *Understanding the Male Hustler.* New York: Haworth Press. A look at the world of male prostitution from the hustler's point of view.

Tisdale, Sallie. (1994). *Talk Dirty to Me: An Intimate Philosophy of Sex.* New York: Doubleday. A positive perspective on a woman's personal exploration of erotica and sexuality.

Weisberg, Kelly D. (1990). *Children of the Night.* New York: Free Press. An outstanding scholarly work on the world of adolescent prostitution.

Resource Center

ALCOHOL AND DRUGS

Al-Anon Family Groups
1600 Corporate Landing Parkway
Virginia Beach, VA 23454
(800) 344-2666 or 757-563-1600
http://www.al-anon.alateen.org

A worldwide fellowship for relatives and friends of alcoholics who "share their experience, strength, and hope in order to solve their common problems and help others do the same."

Alcohol Treatment Referral Hotline
(800) ALCOHOL (252-6465)

Provides referrals to local intervention and treatment providers.

Alcoholics Anonymous (AA)
P.O. Box 459, Grand Central Station
New York, NY 10163
(212) 870-3400

A voluntary worldwide fellowship of people who meet together to attain and maintain sobriety. Check your telephone directory for local chapters.

Narcotics Anonymous World Services Office
P.O. Box 9999
Van Nuys, CA 91409
(818) 773-9999
http://www.wsoinc.com

Similar to Alcoholics Anonymous; sponsors 12-step meetings and provides other support services for drug abusers.

National Clearinghouse for Alcohol and Drug Information (NCADI)
P.O. Box 2345
Rockville, MD 20847
(800) 729-6686; (301) 468-2600
http://www.health.org

Provides a referral service, answering inquiries on alcohol- and drug-related subjects by telephone or mail.

Rational Recovery
P.O. Box 800
Lotus, CA 95651
(916) 621-2667

An alternative to Alcoholics Anonymous.

Web of Addictions
http://www.well.com/user/woa

Provides a wealth of information about substance abuse and dependence.

BREAST-FEEDING (SEE INFANT CARE)

CANCER

**American Cancer Society (ACS) and
Reach for Recovery**
1599 Clifton Road NE
Atlanta, GA 30329
(800) ACS-2345 (227-2345)
http://www.cancer.org

ACS provides information and support for people with cancer. Local chapters can be found by checking your telephone directory. Reach for Recovery is a group for breast cancer survivors.

Breast Cancer Action
55 New Montgomery Street, Ste. 323
San Francisco, CA 94105
(415) 243-9301
bcaction@hooked.net

Provides information and suggests political action for women with breast cancer.

Encore

Contact your local YWCA for information on Encore, a support organization for women with breast cancer.

National Cancer Institute
Office of Cancer Communication
31 Center Drive, MSC 2580, Bldg. 31, Rm. 10A16
Bethesda, MD 20892-2580
(800) 4-CANCER (422-6237)
http://www.nci.nih.gov
http://wwwicic.nci.nih.gov

Provides information on treatment options, screening, clinical trials, and newly approved anti-cancer drugs.

New York Online Access to Health (NOAH): Cancer
http://www.noah.cuny.edu/cancer/cancer.html

Provides information about cancer and links to related sites.

Oncolink / The University of Pennsylvania Cancer Center Resource
http://www.oncolink.upenn.edu

Contains information on different kinds of cancer and answers to frequently asked questions.

CHILDREN AND ADOLESCENTS

CDC Infants' and Children's Health Page
http://www.cdc.gov/diseases/infant.html

Provides information on prenatal care, birth defects, breast-feeding, and other topics.

Family Education Network
http://www.families.com

Provides information about education, safety, health, and other family-related issues.

The Fatherhood Project / Families and Work Institute
330 Seventh Avenue
New York, NY 10001
(212) 465-2044

A national research project that provides information and promotes "wider options for male involvement in child rearing."

Go Ask Alice
http://www.columbia.edu/cu/healthwise/alice.html

Sponsored by the Columbia University Health Service; professional and peer educators provide answers to many topics relating to interpersonal relationships and communication.

Search Institute
700 South 3rd Street, Ste. 210
Minneapolis, MN 55415
(612) 870-9511; (800) 888-7828

Researches and evaluates mentor programs throughout the country.

CHRONIC ILLNESS

American Diabetes Association
1660 Duke Street
Alexandria, VA 22314
(800) 342-2383
http://www.diabetes.org

Provides information and referrals relating to diabetes.

American Heart Association
7272 Greenville Avenue
Dallas, TX 75231
(800) 242-8721; (214) 373-6300
http://www.americanheart.org

Provides information and referrals relating to heart disease prevention and treatment.

Arthritis Foundation
1330 West Peachtree Street
Atlanta, GA 30309
(800) 283-7800
http://www.arthritis.org

Provides information and referrals relating to arthritis and other rheumatic diseases.

DRUG ABUSE (SEE ALCOHOL AND DRUGS)

EATING DISORDERS

The American Anorexia-Bulimia Association
165 West 46th Street, Ste. 1108
New York, NY 10036
(212) 575-6200

Information and referrals for people with eating disorders and their families.

Ask the Dietitian / Overweight
http://www.dietitian.com/overweig.htm

Provides questions and answers on many topics related to weight control.

Eating Disorders Shared Awareness (EDSA)
http://www.something-fishy.com/ed.html

Provides information about eating disorders, including prevention, signs, symptoms, treatment, and tips for helping a friend, as well as links to resources and support groups.

Go Ask Alice
http://www.columbia.edu/cu/healthwise/alice.html

Sponsored by Columbia University Health Service, provides answers to a wide variety of questions about weight management, diet, and exercise.

National Association of Anorexia Nervosa and Associated Disorders
P.O. Box 7
Highland Park, IL 60035
(847) 831-3438

Provides written materials, referrals, and counseling.

Overeaters Recovery Group
http://www.hiwaay.net/recovery

Contains many links to online support for overeaters and information on the 12-step program sponsored by Overeaters Anonymous.

FAMILY PLANNING (ALSO SEE PREGNANCY, INFANT CARE)

Advocates for Youth
1025 Vermont Avenue NW, Ste. 210
Washington, DC 20005
(202) 347-5700

Seeks to improve adolescent decision-making through life planning and other sexuality education programs.

Alan Guttmacher Institute
120 Wall Street
New York, NY 10005
(212) 248-1111
http://www.agi-usa.org

A nonprofit organization that provides research findings and policy analysis in the areas of family planning and reproductive rights.

Office of Population Affairs / Department of Health and Human Services
4350 East West Highway
Bethesda, MD 20814
(301) 594-4000
http://www.dhhs.gov/progorg/opa

Provides materials on contraception, STDs, adoption, and general reproductive health care.

Planned Parenthood Federation of America
810 Seventh Avenue
New York, NY 10019
(202) 785-3351 (to order publications)
(800) 230-PLAN (230-7526) (for a list of clinics)
http://www.plannedparenthood.org

Provides information, counseling, and medical services related to reproduction and sexual health to anyone who wants them, regardless of age, social group, or ability to pay. Most cities have a Planned Parenthood organization listed in the telephone directory.

Public Health Departments

Counties throughout the United States have county health clinics that provide low-cost family planning services. Some cities also have public health clinics. Look in your telephone directory under headings such as these:
   Department of Health
   Family Planning
   Family Services
   Health
   Public Health Department
   (City or County's Name) Health (or Medical) Clinic

Zero Population Growth (ZPG)
1400 16th Street NW, Ste. 320
Washington, DC 20036
(800) 767-1956
http://www.zpg.org.zpg

A nonprofit membership organization that works to achieve a sustainable balance between the earth's population and its environment and resources.

GAY, LESBIAN, BISEXUAL, AND TRANSGENDER RESOURCES

Indiana University's Gay, Lesbian, Bisexual, and Transsexual Home Page
http://www.Indiana.edu/~glbtserv

Access to global information on GLBT issues.

Intersex Society of North America
P.O. Box 31791
San Francisco, CA 94131
http://www.isna.org

A peer support and advocacy group operated by and for intersexuals.

National Federation of Parents and Friends of Lesbians and Gays (PFLAG)
1101 14th Street NW, Ste. 1030
Washington, DC 20005
(202) 638-4200
http://www.pflag.org

Provides information and support for those who care about gay and lesbian individuals. Write or call for the number of a parent contact in your area, or check your telephone directory for regional offices. Publications are available.

National Gay and Lesbian Task Force
2320 17th Street NW
Washington, DC 20009-2702
(202) 332-6483
(202) 332-6219 (TTY)
http://www.ngltf.org/main.html

Provides information and referrals on gay and lesbian issues and rights.

Yahoo / Lesbians, Gays, and Bisexuals
http://www.yahoo.com/society_and_culture/
lesbian_gay_and_bisexual

A Web site and search engine that contains many links to information and support for lesbians, gays, and bisexuals.

GENERAL HEALTH INFORMATION

American College Health Association
P.O. Box 28937
Baltimore, MD 21240-8937
(410) 859-1500

A professional association that focuses on health promotion to the college community.

American Medical Association
http://www.ama-assn.org/JAMA

Provides information for the general public seeking to learn about medical conditions and physicians.

Centers for Disease Control and Prevention (CDC)
1600 Clifton Road NE
Atlanta, GA 30333
(404) 332-4555 (CDC Infoline)
(404) 639-3311
http://www.cdc.gov

Inquiries from the public on topics such as preventive medicine, health education, and STDs (including AIDS) can be directed to the Public Inquiries Office at the CDC. The office also answers questions on family planning and public health problems. Inquiries are answered directly or referred to an appropriate resource.
   Many other government Web sites provide access to sexuality and health-related materials:
   National Library of Medicine: http://www.nlm.
      nih.gov
   National Institutes of Health: http://www.nih.gov
   World Health Organization: http://www.who.ch

Food and Drug Administration
Circulation Dept., HF1-43
5600 Fishers Lane
Rockville, MD 20857
(301) 443-3220

Publishes a monthly bulletin that reviews new drugs and medical devices (including condoms) and evaluates drug treatments and effects.

Healthfinder
http://www.healthfinder.gov

Launched by the U.S. government in 1997, this site is a gateway to online publications, Web sites, support, and self-help groups that produce reliable information.

Medicine Net
http://www.medicinenet.com

Provides health information and news, and an ask-the-doctor feature.

Medscape, Inc.
http://www.medscape.com

Provides a wide range of articles, interactive communication, and links to other resources.

National Health Information Center (NHIC)
P.O. Box 1133
Washington, DC 20013-1133
(800) 336-4797 (referral database)
http://nhic-nt.health.org

A central clearinghouse designed to refer consumers to health information resources; offers a variety of publications.

University of Wisconsin, Stevens Point Wellness Links
http://wellness.uwsp.edu/college_health

Includes links to the top 100 wellness sites; organized by topic.

HIV/AIDS

Basic Statistics on HIV and AIDS
http://www.cdc.gov/nchstp/hiv_aids/stats/
hasrlink.htm

The Centers for Disease Control and Prevention posts tables containing statistics on the number of AIDS cases in the United States, by a broad range of categories, at this Web site.

CDC National AIDS Clearinghouse
P.O. Box 6003
Rockville, MD 20849
(800) 458-5231
http://www.cdcnac.org

Provides information on services and educational resources. Also provides copies of Public Health Service publications.

CDC National HIV and AIDS Hotline
(800) 342-AIDS (342-2437)
(800) 344-SIDA (344-7432) (Spanish)
(800) 243-7889 (TTY, deaf access)

Provides information and referrals relating to HIV and AIDS.

HIV InSite: Gateway to AIDS Knowledge
http://hivinsite.ucsf.edu

Provides information about prevention, education, treatment, clinical trials, and new developments.

Journal of the American Medical Association HIV/AIDS Information Center
http://www.ama-assn.org/special/hiv

Provides a daily news summary, expert advice, general information, and an extensive glossary.

The NAMES Project Foundation AIDS Memorial Quilt
http://www.aidsquilt.org

Includes the story behind the quilt, images of quilt panels, and information and links relating to HIV infection.

INFANT CARE

La Leche League International
1400 N. Meacham Road
Schaumberg, IL 60173-4840
(800) LA-LECHE (525-3243)
(708) 519-7730 (Counseling Hotline)
http://www.lalecheleague.org

Provides advice and support for nursing mothers. Write for a brochure or catalog of its numerous publications. For local groups, check your local telephone directory or call the league's Counseling Hotline.

INFERTILITY

Center for Surrogate Parenting, Inc.
8383 Wilshire Boulevard, Ste. 750
Beverly Hills, CA 90211
(213) 655-1974 (collect calls accepted)
(800) 696-4664

A private organization that matches prospective parents and surrogates for a fee. Extensive screening is involved. Write or call for further information.

Infertility Resources
http://www.ihr.com/infertility/index.html

Designed for people experiencing infertility difficulties, this site provides information for individuals and professionals.

International Council on Infertility Information Dissemination
http://www.inciid.org

A Web site that provides information on current research and treatment for infertility.

Resolve
1310 Broadway
Somerville, MA 02144-1779
(617) 623-0744
(617) 623-0252 (fax)

A national nonprofit organization focusing on infertility; refers callers to chapters across the nation, provides fact sheets on male and female infertility, and publishes a newsletter and a directory of infertility resources. Phone counseling is also offered. There is a small charge for publications.

MEN'S HEALTH AND ISSUES

At-Home Dad: Home Page
http://www.parentsplace.com/readroom/athomedad/index.html

Provides information, referrals, and support relating to the many issues facing at-home dads.

Men's Issues Page
http://info-sys.home.vix.com/pub/men/
http://www.vix.com/pub/men

Discussions on a wide variety of issues.

The Fatherhood Project
Families and Work Institute
330 7th Ave., 14th Floor
New York, NY 10001
(212) 465-2044

A national research demonstration and dissemination project designed to encourage wider options for male involvement in child rearing. Pamphlets are available on various subjects related to families and work.

PREGNANCY (ALSO SEE FAMILY PLANNING, INFANT CARE)

American College of Nurse-Midwives
818 Connecticut Avenue NW, Ste. 900
Washington, DC 20006
(202) 728-9860

Write or call for a directory of certified nurse-midwives in your area or to get information on accredited university-affiliated nurse-midwifery education programs.

California Teratogen Information Service
University of California at San Diego Medical Center
(800) 532-3749

The latest information about the effects of drugs and medications on unborn babies, free of charge. Pregnant women who have been exposed to suspected teratogens (substances harmful to the fetus) can also participate in a free follow-up program after birth. Confidentiality is maintained.

National Abortion Rights Action League (NARAL)
1156 15th Street NW, Ste. 700
Washington, DC 20005
(202) 828-9300
http://www.naral.org

A political organization concerned with family planning issues and dedicated to making abortion "safe, legal, and accessible" for all women. It is affiliated with many state and local organizations. A newsletter and brochures are available.

National Right to Life Committee
419 Seventh Street NW, Ste. 500
Washington, DC 20004
(202) 626-8800
http://www.nrlc.org

Provides information on alternatives to abortion and the politics of the pro-life movement.

Olen Interactive Pregnancy Calendar
http://www.olen.com/baby

Provides a calendar describing the development of a baby from conception to birth.

Online Birth Center
http://www.efn.org/~djz/birth/birthindex.html

Information on a wide range of pregnancy- and birth-related topics, including high-risk situations and alternative health resources.

PREGNANCY LOSS AND INFANT DEATH

National SHARE Office
St. Joseph's Health Center
300 First Capitol Drive
St. Charles, MO 63301
(314) 947-6164

With its affiliate groups, offers support for parents who have experienced miscarriage, stillbirth, or the death of a baby. Check your local telephone directory for groups, which may also be listed under "Sharing Parents," "Hoping and Sharing," "HAND," or a similar heading.

Sudden Infant Death Syndrome (SIDS) Alliance
1314 Bedford Avenue, Ste. 210
Baltimore, MD 21208
(800) 221-SIDS (221-7437)

Provides information, counseling, and referrals to families who have lost a child to SIDS; local chapters and free literature.

RAPE AND SEXUAL ABUSE

Family Violence Prevention Fund
383 Rhode Island Street, Ste. 304
San Francisco, CA 94103
(800) END-ABUSE (799-7233)
http://www.fvpf.org/fund

Provides information and referrals for individuals concerned about domestic violence.

National Clearinghouse on Marital and Date Rape
2325 Oak Street
Berkeley, CA 94708
(510) 524-1582
24 hours (message tape)

Provides information, referrals, seminars, and speakers covering numerous aspects of marital and date rape. There is a nominal charge for publications and consultation services. Calls are returned, collect.

National Committee to Prevent Child Abuse (NCPCA)
332 S. Michigan Avenue, Ste. 1600
Chicago, IL 60604
(312) 663-3520
http://www.childabuse.org

Provides statistics, information, and publications relating to child abuse.

National Victim Center
http://www.nvc.org

An advocacy group for crime victims; Web site provides statistics, news, and links to related sites.

National Violence Hotlines
(800) 422-4453 (child abuse)
(800) 799-SAFE (domestic violence)
(800) 222-2000 (family violence)

Provides information, referral services, and crisis intervention.

Parents United
232 E. Gish Road
San Jose, CA 95112
(408) 453-7616

With related groups Daughters and Sons United and Adults Molested as Children United, a self-help group for family members affected by incest and child sexual abuse; provides referrals to treatment programs and self-help groups throughout the country; offers a number of informative publications, including a bimonthly newsletter.

Rape, Abuse, and Incest National Network (RAINN)
(800) 656-HOPE (656-4673)

A national hotline that provides information, counseling, and referrals for victims of sexual assault.

Rape Crisis Centers
Check your telephone directory under Rape Crisis Center or a similar listing to find the local crisis center nearest you; the service is available in almost all cities.

SEX EDUCATION AND THERAPY

American Association of Sex Educators, Counselors, and Therapists (AASECT)
P.O. Box 238
Mt. Vernon, IA 52314-0238
(319) 895-8407

An interdisciplinary professional organization devoted to the promotion of sexual health through the development and advancement of the fields of sex therapy, sex counseling, and sex education; provides professional education and certification for sex educators, counselors, and therapists; publishes a newsletter and the *Journal of Sex Education and Therapy*.

Healthy Sexuality
http://beWell.com/healthy/sexuality

Provides information related to sexual behaviors, sex therapy, midlife sex, and more.

Institute for the Advanced Study of Human Sexuality
http://home.netinc.ca/~sexorg/index.htm

A Web site containing a large collection of information and answers to frequently asked questions about sexuality.

Kinsey Institute for Research in Sex, Gender, and Reproduction
313 Morrison Hall
Indiana University
Bloomington, IN 47405
(812) 855-7686
http://www.indiana.edu/~kinsey

One of the oldest and most respected institutions doing research on sexuality.

New York University Sexual Disorders Screening
http://www.med.nyu.edu/Psych/screens/sdsm.html (men)
http://www.med.nyu.edu/Psych/screens/sdsf.html (women)

Provides interactive online screening tests for common sexual disorders.

Sex Information and Education Council of the United States (SIECUS)
130 W. 42nd Street, Ste. 350
New York, NY 10036
(212) 819-9770
http://www.siecus.org

A nonprofit educational organization that promotes "healthy sexuality as an integral part of human life," SIECUS provides information or referrals to anyone who requests them. It maintains an extensive library and computer database. Publications include sex education guides for parents (in English and Spanish) and a comprehensive bimonthly journal, *SIECUS Report*. Memberships are available.

SEXUALLY TRANSMITTED DISEASES (ALSO SEE HIV/AIDS, GENERAL HEALTH INFORMATION)

American Social Health Association
P.O. Box 13827
RTP, NC 27709
(800) 653-HEALTH (653-4325); (919) 361-8400
http://sunsite.unc.edu/ASHA

Provides information on all aspects of STDs. Confidentiality is maintained.

CDC National Center for Infectious Diseases
1600 Clifton Road
Atlanta, GA 30333
(404) 639-3311
http://www.cdc.gov/ncidod/ncid.htm

Provides numerous publications on many diseases, including a journal devoted to infectious diseases.

Herpes Resource Center
P.O. Box 13827
Research Triangle Park, NC 27709-9940
(919) 361-8488

Provides referrals for people who are infected with the herpes virus or who think they may be. Services are confidential.

SINGLE PARENTS

Parents Without Partners (PWP)
401 N. Michigan Avenue
Chicago, IL 60611
(312) 644-6610
(800) 637-7974

A mutual support group for single parents and their children; has numerous local groups with more than 85,000 members. PWP offers educational programs and literature, including *The Single Parent* magazine. It also offers scholarships for PWP children.

Single Mothers by Choice (SMC)
P.O. Box 1642
Gracie Station
New York, NY 10028
(212) 988-0993

A national group that supports single women over 30 who are considering or have chosen motherhood; offers workshops, support groups, a newsletter, and related information about donor insemination and adoption. SMC has chapters throughout the United States.

Single Parent Resource Center
http://rampages.onramp.net/~beuhamil/singleparentresourcece_478.html

Information and referrals for single parents.

TERMINAL ILLNESS

National Hospice Organization (NHO)
1901 N. Moore Street, Ste. 901
Arlington, VA 22209
(703) 516-4928
http://www.nho.org

Hospices provide support and care for people in the final phase of terminal disease. The hospice "team" provides personalized care to minister to the physical, spiritual, and emotional needs of the patient and family. Call or write for literature and referral information.

WOMEN'S HEALTH AND ISSUES

American Medical Association—Women's Health Information Center

http://www.ama-assn.org/special/womenh/newsline

Provides a newsline, journal scan, contraceptive information, STD information, and referrals to Web sites focusing on women's health issues.

The Endometriosis Association
8585 N. 76th Place
Milwaukee, WI 53223
(800) 992-3636

Provides information and referrals for women with endometriosis.

National Organization for Women (NOW)
1000 16th Street NW, Ste. 700
Washington, DC 20036
(202) 331-0066
http://now.org/now

An organization of women and men who support "full equality for women in truly equal partnerships with men." NOW promotes social change through research, litigation, and political pressure. A newspaper and other publications are available. Many cities have local chapters. Membership dues vary.

PMS Access / Women's Health America Group
429 Gammon Place
P.O. Box 259641
Madison, WI 53725
(800) 222-4767
http://www.womenshealth.com

Provides information about PMS, as well as links to other sites dealing with PMS and women's health issues.

A Woman's Guide to Sexuality
http://www.plannedparenthood.org

Provided by Planned Parenthood (see Family Planning), this guide explores sexuality and relationships. Although there is no separate URL for the women's guide, it can be accessed at this site.

Women's Net @igc (Women's Issues Online)
http://www.igc.apc.org/womensnet

A wide variety of topics and referrals is made available through this Web site.

Women's Health

RELIEVING MENSTRUAL SYMPTOMS

To date, the causes of premenstrual syndrome (PMS) are unknown, there is no laboratory test that identifies it, and there are no universally effective ways to relieve its symptoms. For women, recognizing their menstrual patterns, learning about their bodies, and recognizing and dealing with existing difficulties can be useful in heading off or easing potential problems. Different remedies work for different women. We suggest you try varying combinations of them and keep a record of your response to each. Following are suggestions for relieving the more common premenstrual and menstrual symptoms; both self-help and medical treatments are included.

For Premenstrual Symptoms

- *Diet.* Moderate amounts of protein and substantial amounts of carbohydrates (such as fresh fruits and vegetables, whole-grain breads and cereals, beans, rice, and pasta) are recommended. Reduce or avoid salt, sugar, and caffeine products such as coffee and colas. Keep in mind that although you may crave chocolate, it may have a negative effect on you; try fruit or popcorn instead, and see how you feel. Frequent small meals may be better than two or three large meals. Some women find relief by taking a maximum 300-mg-per-day dose of vitamin B_6 during their menstrual period. Excessive doses of this vitamin over prolonged periods, however, can cause neurological problems.
- *Alcohol and tobacco.* Avoid them.
- *Exercise.* Moderate exercise is suggested, but be sure to include a daily regimen of at least 30–45 minutes of movement (U.S. Surgeon General, 1996). Aerobic exercise brings oxygen to body tissues and stimulates the production of endorphins, chemical substances that help promote feelings of well-being. Yoga may also be helpful, especially the "cobra" position.
- *Medical treatments.* There is much controversy within the medical profession about treatment for PMS. Progesterone therapy, once advocated as a treatment, is now considered ineffective in treating PMS (Freeman, Rickels, Sondheimer, & Polansky, 1990; Robinson & Garfinkel, 1990). Selective serotonin-

reuptake inhibitors, such as Prozac and Zoloft, have been found to be effective in treating PMS in some women. These drugs block the reuptake of serotonin in the brain and substantially reduce tension and irritability in some women with severe symptoms (Freeman, 1996; Squires, 1997; Steiner et al., 1995). They are generally used throughout the month. Drawbacks of the drugs include their cost ($300–$500 per month) and the fact that they place women in a kind of temporary menopause, complete with hot flashes (Squires, 1997). In addition, women may experience nausea, insomnia, fatigue, dizziness, decreased libido, and/or delayed orgasm (Freeman, 1996). No medication for PMS has yet received FDA approval. Current research suggests that the most effective treatment for most women involves stress management; a reduction in caffeine, nicotine, and salt; a well-balanced diet; and exercise (Meyer & Deitsch, 1996; Robinson & Garfinkel, 1990). When symptoms are severe enough to impair work and relationships, a woman should seek medical attention.

- *Support groups.* Therapy or support groups may help some women deal with the ways PMS affects their lives. They may also help women deal with issues that may be exacerbated by the stress of coping with PMS.

For Cramps

- *Relaxation.* Rest, sleep, and relaxation exercises can help reduce pain from uterine and abdominal cramping, especially in combination with one or more of the remedies listed below.
- *Heat.* A heating pad or hot-water bottle (or, in a pinch, a cat) applied to the abdominal area may help relieve cramps; a warm bath may also help.
- *Massage.* Lower back massage or other forms of massage, such as acupressure, Shiatsu, or polarity therapy, are quite helpful for many women. See *The New Our Bodies, Ourselves* (Boston Women's Health Book Collective, 1998) for guidelines for menstrual massage.
- *Herbal remedies.* Herbal teas, especially raspberry leaf, are helpful for some women. Health food stores carry a variety of teas, tablets, and other preparations. Use them as directed, and stop using them if you experience additional discomfort or problems.
- *Prostaglandin inhibitors.* Antiprostaglandins reduce cramping of the uterine and abdominal muscles. Aspirin is a mild prostaglandin inhibitor. Ibuprofen, a highly effective prostaglandin inhibitor, was often prescribed for menstrual cramps (as Motrin) before it became available over the counter. Aspirin increases menstrual flow slightly, whereas ibuprofen reduces it.

Stronger antiprostaglandins may be prescribed. Taking medication at the first sign of cramping—as opposed to waiting until the pain is severe—increases its effectiveness greatly.

- *Orgasm.* Some women report relief of menstrual congestion and cramping at orgasm (with or without a partner).

If pain cannot be controlled with these methods, further medical evaluation is needed. The symptoms may indicate an underlying problem, such as endometriosis or pelvic inflammatory disease (PID).

GYNECOLOGICAL SELF-EXAMINATION

In a space that is comfortable for you, take time to look at your outer genitals, using a mirror and a good light. The name given to female outer genitals is the vulva. The large, soft folds of skin with hair on them are the outer lips, or labia majora. The color, texture, and pattern of this hair vary widely among women. Inside the outer lips are the inner lips, or labia minora. These have no hair and vary in size from small to large and protruding. They extend from below the vagina up toward the pubic bone, where they form a hood over the clitoris. If you pull back the hood you will be able to see your clitoris. The size and shape of the clitoris, as well as the hood, vary widely among women. These variations have nothing to do with a woman's ability to respond sexually. You may also find some cheesy white matter under the hood. This is called smegma and is normal.

Below the clitoris is a smooth area and then a small hole. This is the urinary opening, or meatus. Below the urinary opening is the vaginal opening, which is surrounded by rings of tissue. One of these, which you may or may not be able to see, is the hymen. Just inside the vagina, on both sides, are the Bartholin's glands. They may secrete a small amount of mucus during sexual excitement but little else of their function is known; if they are infected, they will be swollen, but otherwise you won't notice them. The smooth area between your vagina and anus is called the perineum.

Once you're familiar with the normal appearance of your outer genitals, you can check for unusual rashes, soreness, warts, or parasites, such as crabs.

You can also examine your inner genitals, using a speculum, flashlight, and mirror. A speculum is an instrument used to hold the vaginal walls apart, allowing a clear view of the vagina and cervix. You should be able to obtain a speculum and information about doing an internal exam from a clinic that specializes in women's health or family planning.

It is a good idea to observe and become aware of what the normal vaginal discharges look and feel like (refer back to Chapter 3 for more information). Colors vary from white to gray, and secretions change in consistency from thick to thin and clear (similar to egg white that is stretched between the fingers) over the course of the menstrual cycle. Distinct changes or odors, along with burning, bleeding between menstrual cycles, pain in the pelvic region, itching, or rashes, should be reported to a physician.

In doing a vaginal self-exam, you may initially experience some fear or uneasiness about touching your body. In the long run, however, your patience and persistence will pay off in increased body awareness and a heightened sense of personal health.

MAINTAINING VAGINAL HEALTH

Here are some simple guidelines that may help a woman avoid getting vaginitis:

- Do not use vaginal deodorants, especially deodorant suppositories or tampons. They upset the natural chemical balance of the vagina. Despite what pharmaceutical companies may advertise, a healthy vagina does not have a bad odor. If the vagina does have an unpleasant smell, then something is wrong, and you should check with your doctor or clinic.
- For the same reason, do not use douches, except medicated douches that have been recommended by a clinician or vinegar solutions for yeast infections.
- Maintain good genital hygiene by washing regularly (about once a day is fine) with mild soap. Bubble baths and strongly perfumed soaps may cause irritation to the vulva.
- After a bowel movement, wipe the anus from front to back, away from the vagina, to prevent contamination with fecal bacteria.
- Wear cotton underpants and pantyhose with a cotton crotch. Nylon does not "breathe," and it allows heat and moisture to build up, creating an ideal environment for infectious organisms to reproduce.
- If you use a vaginal lubricant, be sure it is water-soluble. Oil-based lubricants such as Vaseline encourage bacterial growth.
- If you have candidiasis (yeast infection), try douching every 2 or 3 days with a mild vinegar solution (2 tablespoons of vinegar to 1 quart of warm water). You can also try applying plain yogurt twice a day to the vulva and vagina. (It must be plain yogurt that contains live lactobacillus culture.) Adding yogurt to your diet and avoiding foods with a high sugar content may also help.
- If you are diagnosed with a vaginal infection, particularly trichomoniasis, be sure to have your partner treated also, to avoid being reinfected.

PREVENTING AND TREATING CYSTITIS

The following precautions may help a woman avoid cystitis:

- Urinate frequently, to avoid the buildup of highly acidic urine.
- Urinate before sexual activity and immediately afterward, to flush bacteria from the urethra.
- Drink plenty of fluids (water is best), especially just before and just after intercourse.
- Eat a well-balanced diet and get plenty of rest, especially if your resistance is low.
- If you use a diaphragm and are troubled by cystitis, have it checked for proper fit. You may need a smaller size, or you may need to consider another form of contraception.

If you have cystitis:

- Drink copious amounts of water (at least 16 glasses a day). It won't hurt you, as long as you urinate frequently. A pinch of baking soda in a glass of water may help neutralize the urine's acidity. Some women find that drinking cranberry juice provides relief. Coffee, tea, colas, and alcohol are not advisable because they may irritate the urinary tract.
- Pain and itching may be relieved by spraying or sponging water on the urethral opening. If urination is very painful, try urinating while sitting in a few inches of warm water (in the bathtub or a large pan).
- If symptoms persist or in the case of a fever, see your doctor or clinic. Sulfa drugs or other antibiotics will usually clear up the symptoms within a few days. (A caution about sulfa drugs: 10–14% of African Americans have an inherited deficiency of a blood enzyme called glucose-6-phosphate-dehydrogenase [G6PD]; sulfa drugs may cause a serious anemic reaction in individuals with this deficiency.)

BREAST SELF-EXAMINATION

All women age 20 and older should perform a monthly breast self-exam to help in the early detection of breast cancer. When performed regularly, breast self-exam helps you get to know how your breasts normally feel. You will then quickly be able to feel any changes.

The best time to do a breast self-exam is right after your period, when your breasts are not tender or swollen. If you do not have regular periods or sometimes skip a month, do breast self-exam on the same day every month. If you discover a lump or detect any changes, seek medical attention. Most breast lumps and changes are not cancerous, but it's best to be sure.

1. Lie down and put a pillow under your right shoulder. Place your right arm behind your head.

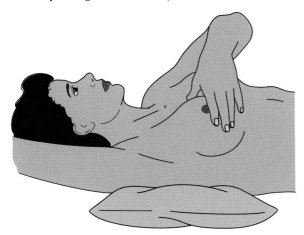

2. Use the finger pads of the three middle fingers on your left hand to feel your right breast for lumps or thickening. Your finger pads are the top third of each finger.

3. Press firmly enough to know how your breast feels. If you're not sure how hard to press, ask your health-care provider. Alternatively, try to copy the way your health-care provider uses the finger pads during a breast exam. Learn what your breast feels like most of the time. A firm ridge in the lower curve of each breast is normal.

4. Move around the breast in a set way. You can choose (a) the circle pattern, (b) the up-and-down pattern, or (c) the wedge pattern. Use the same pattern every time you examine your breasts to help make sure that you've gone over the entire breast area and to remember how your breast feels.

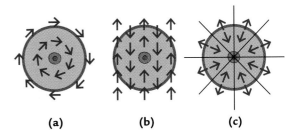

(a)   (b)   (c)

5. Using the same technique, examine your left breast with the finger pads of your right hand.

6. If you find any changes, see your health-care provider right away.

For added safety, you should also check your breasts while standing in front of a mirror right after you do your breast self-exam each month. See if there are any changes in the way your breasts look, such as dimpling of the skin, changes in the nipple, or redness or swelling.

You might also want to do a breast self-exam while you're in the shower. Your soapy hands will glide over wet skin, making it easy to check how your breasts feel.

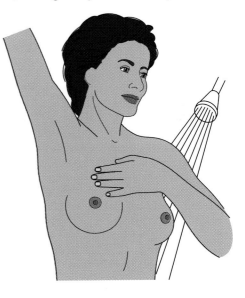

Source: How to Do Breast Self-Examination. © 1997, American Cancer Society, Inc. Used with permission.

Pregnancy and Childbirth _____

MAKING A BIRTH PLAN

Prospective parents must make many important decisions. The more informed they are, the better able they will be to decide what is right for them. If you were planning a birth, how would you answer the following questions?

1. Who will be the birth attendant—a physician, a nurse-midwife? Do you already have someone in mind? If not, what criteria are important to you in choosing a birth attendant? Have you considered hiring a labor assistant (sometimes called a *doula,* a professional childbirth companion employed to guide the mother during labor)?
2. Who will be present at the birth—your spouse or partner? Other relatives or friends? Children? How will these people participate? Will they provide emotional support and encouragement? Will they provide practical help, such as "coaching" the mother, giving massages, fetching supplies, taking photographs or videos? Can these people be sensitive to the needs of the mother?
3. Where will the birth take place—in a hospital, in a birth center, at home? If in a hospital, is there a choice of rooms?
4. What kind of environment will you create in terms of lighting, room furnishings, and sounds? Is there special music you would like to hear?
5. What kinds of medication, if any, do you feel comfortable with? Do you know what the options are for pain-reducing medications? What about hormones to speed up or slow down labor? How do you feel about having an IV inserted as a precaution, even if medication is not planned? If you should change your mind about medication partway through labor, how will you communicate this to your attendants?
6. What about fetal monitoring? Will there be machines attached to the mother or the baby? What types and degree of monitoring do you feel comfortable with?
7. What is your attendant's policy regarding food and drink during labor? What kinds of foods or drinks, such as ice cream, fruit, juices, or ice chips, do you think you (or your partner) might want to have?
8. What about freedom of movement during labor? Will you (or your partner) want the option of walking around during labor? Will there be a shower or bath available? Will the baby be delivered with the mother lying on her back with her feet in stirrups, or will she be free to choose her position, such as squatting or lying on her side?
9. Do you want a routine episiotomy? Under what conditions would it be acceptable?
10. What do you wish the role of instruments or other interventions, such as forceps or vacuum extraction, to be? Who will determine if and when they are necessary?
11. Under what conditions is a cesarean section acceptable? Who will decide?
12. Who will "catch" the baby as she or he is born? Who will cut the umbilical cord, and at what point will it be cut?
13. What will be done with the baby immediately after birth? Will he or she be with the mother or the father? Who will bathe and dress the baby? What kinds of tests will be done on the baby, and when? What other kinds of procedures, such as shots and medicated eyedrops, will be given, and when?
14. Will the baby stay in the nursery, or is rooming-in available? Is there a visiting schedule?
15. How will the baby be fed—by breast or bottle? Will feeding be on a schedule or "on demand"? Is there someone with breast-feeding experience available to answer questions if necessary? Will the baby have a pacifier between feedings?
16. If the baby is a boy, will he be circumcised? When?

PRACTICAL TIPS ABOUT BREAST-FEEDING

Some women start breast-feeding with perfect ease and hardly any discomfort. For others, it can be frustrating and sometimes painful, but it need not be. Midwife Raven Lang (1992) tells us that the following method will lead to successful breast-feeding.

- When you first put the baby to your breast, limit her to 1 minute per breast. Try not to nurse again for a half hour to an hour. If the baby fusses, give her the end of your little finger (or a pacifier) to suck.
- The second hour, let her nurse 2 minutes at each breast; the third hour, 3 minutes; the fourth hour, 4 minutes; and so on.
- Your baby will not want to nurse every hour of the day and night (although it may seem like it). The basic rule to follow is: Increase your nursing time by only 1 minute per breast with each subsequent feeding, until you are nursing comfortably for as long a session as you and the baby both enjoy.
- Remember that for the first three days, the baby is getting colostrum only. By the time your true milk comes in on the third day, things should be going smoothly. Also, even a slow-nursing infant gets about four-fifths of her nourishment during the first 5 minutes.

Lang says that although mothers are generally most effective when they care for their babies "by feel" rather than "by the book" (or in this case, "by the clock"), the process of establishing breast-feeding is an exception to this "rule."

Most women find that a good nursing bra, one that provides good uplift and that opens easily for nursing, makes breast-feeding easier and more comfortable. Many wear such a bra day and night during the months they are nursing.

Rest and relax as much as possible during the months that you are breast-feeding, especially at the beginning. Your body is doing a tremendous amount of work and needs extra care.

While nursing, find a position that is comfortable for you and your baby: A footstool, a pillow, and a chair with arms are often helpful.

Touch the baby's cheek with the nipple to start. She will turn her head to grasp the nipple. (If you try to push her to the nipple with a finger touching her other cheek or chin, she will turn away from the nipple toward the finger.)

Allow her to grasp the entire dark-colored part of the breast in her mouth. She gets the milk by squeezing it from the nipple, not by actually sucking. Her grasp on your nipple may hurt for the first few seconds, but the pain should disappear once she is nursing in a good rhythm. When you want to remove her mouth from your breast, first break the suction by inserting your finger in the corner of her mouth. This will prevent sore nipples.

A small amount of milk may come out of your nipples between feedings. A small nursing pad or piece of sanitary napkin inserted in the bra over the nipple will absorb this milk, keeping the bra clean and preventing irritation of the nipple.

If your entire breast becomes sore, you may be able to relieve the pain simply by lifting and supporting the breast with one hand during nursing. Hot compresses between nursing sessions may further relieve soreness.

If you notice a spot of tenderness or redness on your breast or nipple that persists for more than two feedings, be sure to seek advice from your breast-feeding support group or physician promptly.

If you have difficulty beginning to breast-feed, don't give up! Ask friends, women's centers, clinics, or the local La Leche League chapter for help. Don't worry about not having enough milk; the more your baby nurses, the more you'll produce.

Men's Health

TESTICULAR SELF-EXAMINATION

Just as women practice breast self-examination each month, men should practice preventive medicine by doing testicular self-examination regularly.

The best time to discover any small lumps is right after a hot shower or bath, when the skin of the scrotum is most relaxed. Each testicle should be gently rolled between the thumb and fingers of both hands, slowly and carefully. Learn what the collecting structure at the back of the testicle (the epididymis) feels like so that you won't mistake it for an abnormality. The testicles should feel smooth except for the epididymis. If you find any lump or growth, it most often will be on the front side of the testicle.

Any hard lumps, enlargements, or contour changes should be promptly reported to your urologist or another health-care practitioner.

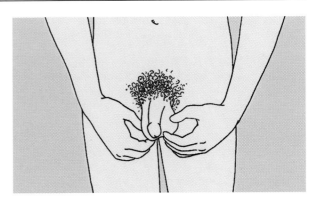

Preventing and Treating Sexually Transmitted Diseases ____

A VISIT TO AN STD CLINIC

Let's say you think you may have an STD. Perhaps you've noticed a peculiar discharge from your vagina or penis, and it hurts when you urinate. Or maybe you noticed some unusual little bumps on your partner's genitals— *after* you'd made love. So you decide that a visit to your local STD clinic or your college health clinic is in order. You call first to see if you need an appointment. (Check the yellow pages of your telephone directory under Clinics, Family Planning, or Health Services if you don't know the number.)

After an uncomfortable, semisleepless night, you find yourself at the clinic at 10:00 the next morning. Here's a version of what might happen next:

- The receptionist gives you a clipboard with a bunch of papers to fill out. The most important of these is a medical/sexual history. Take your time filling it out, and include any information you think might be helpful to the clinician who will see you and recommend treatment. You return the papers to the receptionist.
- You wait. Most clinics are working within a limited budget. They may have a small staff and a large clientele. Bring your patience (and a book).
- Your name or number is called. You go into another room and sit down to talk with a counselor or social worker. (This may instead happen after your medical exam, or be combined with it.) She or he is there to give you information and to answer your questions, in addition to getting more specific details about the reason for your visit. The more honest and straightforward you are about your sexual activities, the more help you will be able to receive. Health-care workers are not interested in passing judgment on you; they are there to help you get well. Your records will be kept confidential.
- Depending on your symptoms, you may next be asked for a urine sample or a blood sample. The health-care worker should explain the reasons for any test or procedure.
- Next, you go to an examination room. If you are a woman, you will probably be instructed to remove your clothes from the waist down and cover yourself with a paper gown or drape. You will probably lie down on an examining table with your feet in stirrups so that the clinician can have a clear view of your genital area and give you a vaginal examination. If you are a man, you will probably be asked to remove your pants or simply to lower them. The clinician who examines you may be a physician, intern, public-health nurse, nurse practitioner, or other medically

trained person. Depending on your symptoms, the clinician may use a cotton swab to take a small sample of the affected tissue or discharge for microscopic evaluation or culturing. For men, this may involve squeezing the glans to produce the discharge. For women, it may involve the insertion of a speculum to open the vagina and then a gentle swabbing of the cervix. (A note for women: If you are examined by a man, the law requires that a female assistant be present.) Be sure to tell the clinician about any discomfort or pain you experience during the exam. After the examination, you dress and go back to the waiting room or to a conference room.

- The clinician, counselor, or another health-care worker discusses your diagnosis with you. In some cases, treatment will be started right away. In others, you may have to wait several days for lab results. In any event, it is imperative to follow the clinic's instructions exactly. If you have questions, be sure to ask.
- You get your medication from the clinic or pharmacy and begin taking it.
- You inform you partner (or partners) of your diagnosis and insist that he or she (or they) seek immediate treatment. This is critically important for halting the spread of an STD and preventing your own possible reinfection.
- You refrain from sexual activity until the clinician tells you it is safe. You return for a follow-up visit if required.
- You decide that next time, you'll use a condom.

LEARNING TO LOVE LATEX

"It's like taking a shower in a raincoat!" goes the old (male) complaint about wearing a condom. Many of the complainers, however, have not actually tried using condoms or have tried only one or two kinds. Becoming a virtuoso of safer sex requires becoming experienced with different varieties of condoms and other latex products. Although the idea of using a piece of rubber as part of normal sexual activity may appear clinical to the uninitiated, experienced safer-sex practitioners have found ways to turn latex protective devices into sexual enhancers.

Latex Care

Latex products that are used in safer sex include condoms, dental dams, gloves, and finger covers. Proper care of these products helps ensure their effectiveness as barriers to disease-causing organisms. Here are some guidelines for latex care:

- Check the expiration date on the package of your latex product. Latex deteriorates with age; its shelf life averages 2½–5 years.
- Keep your latex away from the heat. For example, don't leave condom packets in the sun or in your glove compartment. It's all right to carry condoms in your wallet, but don't leave them there for more than 2 weeks or so.
- Handle latex with care. Be especially careful not to tear your latex product when you open the package. Be careful with long fingernails.
- Keep all oil-based products away from your latex. These include oil-based lubricants (such as Vaseline), massage oils, cocoa butter, and vaginal medications such as estrogen preparations and antifungal creams. To see what oil does to latex, try this experiment: Rub a little massage oil, cooking oil, or Vaseline into a condom. Wait a minute or so and then stretch the latex and see what happens.

Dental Dams

Because HIV and other STDs can be transmitted in vaginal fluids (including menstrual blood), it's important to know how to practice cunnilingus safely. Organisms from genital sores or lesions, such as herpes, also can be spread during oral or manual sexual contact. There are several products that can provide barrier protection during these activities.

Dental dams are squares of latex used by dentists to isolate a particular tooth during dental procedures. They can usually be obtained at family planning clinics, women's clinics, or AIDS organizations. During sex, dams can be used over the vulva or anus while it is being orally or manually stimulated.

Some people have found an alternative to dental dams that is more comfortable for them—plastic wrap! Although no tests have been performed on the efficacy of plastic wrap as a barrier against disease organisms, it is thought to provide protection equivalent to that of latex dams when used according to similar guidelines. You can cut it to any size (the more area it covers, the better). Don't expose it to heat (including hot water), however, and don't reuse it. An additional caveat is to be aware of the risk of inhalation during use.

Another alternative for cunnilingus is a condom that has been cut open and flattened. You can snip the condom on one side before unrolling it. Use sharp scissors, and cut from the rolled edge to the center of the tip and then simply unroll it. You'll find the thin latex to be an excellent transmitter of heat and touch. A condom can also be slipped over the fingers for clitoral, vaginal, or anal stimulation. Latex gloves and finger covers (cots) also provide protection during manual sexual activities where there are sores, cuts, or abrasions.

Condom Sense

Basic guidelines for condom use are given in Chapter 11. Here are a few additional suggestions to help you use condoms safely and pleasurably.

- Some brands are more highly rated for safety than others. A *Consumer Reports* study found the most effective condoms to be Sheik (Excita/Extra Ribbed and Classic), Ramses (Extra Ribbed, Extra, and Sensitol), Lifestyles (regular, Vibra-Ribbed, and spermicide), Trojan-Enz, Touch, Saxon, Rough Rider, Gold Circle, Class Act, and Kimono ("How Reliable Are Condoms?" 1995). The best-selling brand, Trojan, was generally rated low, as was Lifestyles Ultra Sensitive. Many Japanese condoms are considered to be of high quality because they are individually tested, rather than randomly tested, as American condoms are. For up-to-date studies, check your library, family planning clinic, or AIDS resource center.
- To maximize your pleasure, try different kinds of condoms. Some brands and styles may fit more comfortably than others. Some, including the Japanese brands, are quite thin and allow a lot of sensitivity. Some brands of thinner condoms may be more prone to tearing than others. In cases of tears or slippage, apply spermicide or lubricant with nonoxynol-9 to reduce the chance of infection. If one brand consistently tears, try a different one.
- If breakage is a problem no matter what kind of condom you use (some people are just friskier than others), consider "double bagging"—using two condoms! Some folks swear by this.

There is no product or practice (except abstinence) that can guarantee 100% safety from HIV and other STDs, but with a little latex and common sense, we can provide a lot of protection for ourselves and those we care about.

Preventing Sexual Assault

There are no guaranteed ways to prevent sexual assault or coercion. Each situation, assailant, and targeted woman or man is different (Fischhoff, 1992). But rape education courses may be effective in reducing the rape myths that provide support for sexual aggression (Fonow, Richardson, & Wemmerus, 1992).

To reduce the risk of date rape, consider these guidelines:

- When dating someone for the first time, go to a public place, such as a restaurant, movie, or sports event.
- Share expenses. A common scenario is a date expecting you to exchange sex for his or her paying for dinner, the movie, drinks, and so on.
- Avoid using drugs or alcohol if you do not want to be sexual with your date. Such use is associated with date rape (Abbey, 1991).
- Avoid ambiguous verbal or nonverbal behavior. Make sure your verbal and nonverbal messages are identical. If you only want to cuddle or kiss, for example, tell your partner that those are your limits. Tell him or her that if you say no, you mean no. If necessary, reinforce your statement emphatically, both verbally and physically (pushing him or her away).

To reduce the risk of stranger rape, consider the guidelines below. But try to avoid becoming overly vigilant; use reasonable judgment. Do not let fear control your life.

- Do not identify yourself as a person living alone, especially if you are a woman. Use initials on the mailbox and in the telephone directory.

- Don't open your door to strangers; keep your house and car doors locked. Have your keys ready when you approach your car or house. Look in the back seat before getting into your car.
- Avoid dark and isolated areas. Carry a whistle or airhorn. Let people know where you are going.
- If someone approaches you threateningly, turn and run. If you can't run, resist. Studies indicate that resisting an attack by shouting, causing a scene, or fighting back can deter the assailant. Fighting and screaming may reduce the level of the abuse without increasing the level of physical injury. Most women who are injured during a rape appear to have been injured *before* resisting (Ullman & Knight, 1991). Trust your intuitions, whatever approach you take.
- Take self-defense training. It will raise your level of confidence and your fighting abilities. You may be able to scare off the assailant, or you may gain the opportunity to escape. Many women take self-defense training following an incidence of sexual aggression to reaffirm their sense of control.

If you are sexually assaulted (or the victim of an attempted assault), report the assault as soon as possible. You are probably not the assailant's first victim. As much as you might want to, do not change clothes or shower. Semen and hair or other materials on your body or clothing may be very important in arresting and convicting a rapist. You may also want to contact a rape crisis center; its staff members are knowledgeable about dealing with the police and the traumatic aftermath of rape. But most important, remember that you are not at fault. The rapist is the only one to blame.

Glossary

abortion The expulsion of the conceptus, either spontaneously or by induction.

abstinence Refraining from sexual intercourse.

acculturation The process of adaptation by an ethnic group to the attitudes, behaviors, and values of the dominant culture.

acquired immune deficiency syndrome (AIDS) A chronic disease caused by the human immunodeficiency virus (HIV), in which the immune system is weakened and unable to fight opportunistic infections, such as pneumocystitis carinii pneumonia (PCP) and Kaposi's sarcoma.

adolescence The social and psychological state that occurs between the beginning of puberty and acceptance into full adulthood.

agape In John Lee's typology of love, altruistic love.

age of consent The age at which a person is legally deemed capable of giving consent.

alpha-fetoprotein (AFP) screening A blood test of a pregnant woman's blood to determine the existence of neural tube defects.

alveoli (singular, *alveolus*) Small glands within the female breast that begin producing milk following childbirth.

amenorrhea The absence of menstruation, unrelated to aging.

amniocentesis A process in which amniotic fluid is withdrawn by needle from the uterus and then examined for evidence of possible birth defects.

amnion An embryonic membranous sac containing the embryo and amniotic fluid.

amniotic fluid The fluid within the amniotic sac that surrounds the embryo or fetus.

ampulla The widened part of the fallopian tube or the vas deferens.

anal intercourse The insertion of the erect penis into the partner's anus.

anal stage In Freudian theory, the period from age 1 to 3, during which the child's erotic activities center on the anus.

analingus The licking of the anal region.

anatomical sex Identification as male or female based on physical sex characteristics, such as gonads, uterus, vulva, vagina, penis, and so on.

androgen Any of the male hormones, including testosterone.

androgen-insensitivity syndrome or **testicular feminization** A genetic, hereditary condition passed through X chromosomes in which a genetic male is born with testes but is unable to absorb testosterone; as a result, the estrogen influence prevails, and his body tends toward a female appearance, failing to develop male internal and external sex organs.

androgen replacement therapy The administration of testosterone to increase sex drive, especially after oophorectomy.

androgyny The unique and flexible combination of instrumental and expressive traits in accordance with individual differences, situations, and stages in the life cycle.

anorexia nervosa An eating disorder characterized by the pursuit of excessive thinness.

anorgasmia A sexual dysfunction characterized by the absence of orgasm.

antibody A cell that binds to the antigen of an invading cell, inactivating it and marking it for destruction by killer cells.

anti-gay prejudice A strong dislike, fear, or hatred of gay men and lesbians because of their homosexuality.

antigen A molecular structure on the wall of a cell capable of stimulating the immune system and then reacting with the antibodies that are released to fight it.

anus The opening of the rectum, consisting of two sphincters, circular muscles that open and close like valves.

anxious/ambivalent attachment A style of infant attachment characterized by separation anxiety and insecurity in relation to the primary caregiver.

Apgar score The cumulative rating of the newborn's heart rate, respiration, color, reflexes, and muscle tone.

aphrodisiac A substance that supposedly increases sexual desire or improves sexual performance.

areola A ring of darkened skin around the nipple of the breast.

assigned gender The gender ascribed by others, usually at birth.

assisted reproductive technology (ART) A group of procedures developed to achieve conception in cases of infertility; includes in vitro fertilization, GIFT, ZIFT, and ICSI.

asymptomatic   Without symptoms.

attachment   The emotional tie between an infant and his or her primary caregiver.

attitude   The predisposition to act, think, or feel in certain ways toward particular things.

atypical sexual behavior   Consensual sexual activity that is not statistically typical of American sexual behavior.

autoerotic asphyxia   A form of sexual masochism linking strangulation with masturbation.

autoeroticism   Sexual self-stimulation or behavior involving only the self; includes masturbation, sexual fantasies, and erotic dreams.

avoidant attachment   A style of infant attachment characterized by avoidance of the primary caregiver as a defense against rejection.

B cell   A type of lymphocyte involved in antibody production.

bacterial vaginosis   A vaginal infection commonly caused by the bacterium *Gardnerella vaginalis*.

Bartholin's gland   One of two small ducts on either side of the vaginal opening that secretes a small amount of moisture during sexual arousal. Also known as vestibular gland.

basal body temperature (BBT) method   A contraceptive method based on a woman's temperature in the morning upon waking; when the temperature rises, the woman is fertile.

behavior   The way a person acts.

benign prostatic hypertrophy   Enlargement of the prostate gland, affecting more than half of men over age 50.

benign tumor   A nonmalignant (noncancerous) tumor that is slow growing and remains localized.

bias   A personal leaning or inclination.

biased sample   A nonrepresentative sample.

binge eating disorder   An eating disorder characterized by rapid eating, eating to the point of discomfort or beyond, continual eating, and eating when not hungry. Also called compulsive overeating.

bioadhesive gel   A spermicide that clings to the cervix and walls of the vagina for up to 24 hours.

biopsy   The surgical removal of tissue for diagnosis.

birth canal   The passageway through which an infant is born; the vagina.

birth control   Any means of preventing a birth from taking place, including contraception and abortion.

bisexuality   A sexual orientation in which one is attracted to members of both sexes.

blastocyst   A collection of about 100 human cells that develops from the zygote.

bondage and discipline (B&D)   Sexual activities in which one person is bound while another simulates or engages in light or moderate "discipline" activities, such as spanking and whipping.

Braxton Hicks contractions   Uterine contractions during the last trimester of pregnancy that exercise the uterus, preparing it for labor.

bulimia   An eating disorder characterized by episodes of uncontrolled overeating followed by purging (vomiting).

butch   A lesbian who dresses and acts in a stylized masculine manner. *See also* femme.

calendar (rhythm) method   A contraceptive method based on calculating "safe" days depending on the range of a woman's longest and shortest menstrual cycles.

candidiasis   A yeast infection caused by the fungus *Candida albicans*. Also known as moniliasis.

capacitation   The process by which a sperm's membranes become fragile enough to release the enzymes from its acrosomes.

caring   Making another's needs as important as one's own.

castration anxiety   In Freudian theory, the belief that the father will cut off the child's penis because of rivalry for the mother/wife.

celibacy   Not engaging in any kind of sexual activity.

censorship   The suppression of words, ideas, or images by a government, private groups, or individuals based on their political or moral values.

cervical cap   A small rubber contraceptive barrier device that fits snugly over the cervix.

cervical dysplasia or **cervical intraepithelial neoplasia (CIN)**   A condition of the cervical epithelium (covering membrane) that may lead to cancer if not treated.

cervical mucus method   A contraceptive method using a woman's cervical mucus to determine ovulation.

cervix   The end of the uterus, opening toward the vagina.

cesarean section (C-section)   Removal of the fetus by an incision in the mother's abdominal and uterine walls.

chancre   A round, pea-sized, painless sore symptomatic of the first stage of syphilis.

child sexual abuse   Any sexual interaction (including fondling, erotic kissing, oral sex, and genital penetration) between an adult and a prepubertal child.

chlamydia   An STD caused by the *Chlamydia trachomatis* organism. Also known as chlamydial infection.

chorion   The embryo's outermost membrane.

chorionic villus sampling (CVS)   A procedure in which tiny pieces of the membrane that encases the embryo are removed and examined for evidence of possible birth defects.

CIN   *See* cervical dysplasia.

circumcision   The surgical removal of the foreskin, which covers the glans penis.

climacteric   The time during which a woman's menstrual periods become increasingly irregular prior to menopause. Also refers to the normal diminishing sexual activity that occurs among men as they age.

clinical research The in-depth examination of an individual or group by a clinician who assists with psychological or medical problems.

clitoral hood A fold of skin covering the glans of the clitoris.

clitoridectomy The surgical removal of the clitoris and all or part of the labia. Also known as female circumcision.

clitoris (plural, *clitorides*) An external sexual structure that is the center of arousal in the female; located above the vagina at the meeting of the labia minora.

cofactor A condition that may make a person who is HIV-positive more likely to develop AIDS.

cognition Mental processes that intervene between stimulus and response, such as evaluation and reflection.

cognitive development theory A child development theory that views growth as the mastery of specific ways of perceiving, thinking, and doing that occurs at discrete stages.

cognitive social learning theory A child development theory that emphasizes the learning of behavior from others, based on the belief that consequences control behavior.

coitus Sexual intercourse.

coitus interruptus The removal of the penis from the vagina prior to ejaculation. Also called withdrawal.

colostrum A yellowish substance containing nutrients and antibodies that is secreted by the breast 2 or 3 days prior to actual milk production.

coming out The public acknowledgment of one's gay, lesbian, or bisexual orientation.

commitment A determination, based on conscious choice, to continue a relationship or a marriage.

communication A transactional process in which symbols, such as words, gestures, and movements, are used to establish human contact, exchange information, and reinforce or change attitudes and behaviors.

conceptus In medical terminology, the developing human offspring from fertilization through birth.

condom or **male condom** A thin, soft, flexible sheath of latex rubber or polyurethane (or processed animal tissue) that fits over the erect penis to prevent semen from being transmitted and to help protect against sexually transmitted diseases. *See also* female condom.

conflict A communication process in which people perceive incompatible goals and interference from others in achieving their goals.

congenital adrenal hyperplasia A condition in which a genetic female with ovaries and a vagina develops externally as a male as a result of a malfunctioning adrenal gland. Previously known as adrenogenital syndrome.

contraception The prevention of conception.

contraceptive film A small, translucent tissue that contains spermicide and dissolves into a sticky gel when inserted into the vagina.

contraceptive foam A chemical spermicide dispensed in an aerosol container.

control group A group that is not being treated in an experiment.

corona The rim of tissue between the glans and the penile shaft.

corpora cavernosa The hollow chambers in the shaft of the clitoris or penis that fill with blood and swell during arousal.

corpus luteum The tissue formed from a ruptured ovarian follicle that produces important hormones after the oocyte emerges.

corpus spongiosum A column of erectile tissue within the penis enclosing the urethra.

correlational study The measurement of two or more naturally occurring variables to determine their relationship to each other.

Cowper's gland or **bulbourethral gland** One of two small structures below the prostate gland that secrete a clear mucus into the urethra prior to ejaculation.

cross-dressing Wearing the clothing of a member of the other sex.

crura (singular, *crus*) The internal branches of the clitoral or penile shaft.

culdoscopy A form of tubal ligation in which an incision is made at the back of the vagina and the tubes are viewed with a culdoscope.

culpotomy A form of tubal ligation in which a small incision is made at the back of the vagina.

cultural equivalency perspective The view that attitudes, behaviors, and values of diverse ethnic groups are basically similar, with differences resulting from adaptation to historical and social forces, such as slavery, discrimination, or poverty.

cultural relativity The perspective that any custom must be evaluated in terms of how it fits within the culture as a whole.

cunnilingus Oral stimulation of the female genitals.

curettage Scraping of the inside of the uterus with a small spoon-shaped instrument called a curette.

cystitis A bladder infection affecting mainly women that is often related to sexual activity, although it is not transmitted from one partner to another.

date rape or **acquaintance rape** Sexual intercourse with a dating partner that occurs against the victim's will, with force or the threat of force.

deception Actions aimed at betraying, misleading, or deluding another person, including lies, omissions, fabrications, and secrets.

delayed ejaculation A sexual dysfunction characterized by the male's inability to ejaculate easily during intercourse.

demographics The statistical characteristics of human populations.

dependent variable　In an experiment, a factor that is likely to be affected by changes in the independent variable.

Depo-Provera (DMPA)　An injectable contraceptive containing medroxyprogesterone acetate (DMPA).

deviant sexual behavior　Sexual behavior that diverges from the norm.

DHT deficiency　A genetic disorder in which some males are unable to convert testosterone to the hormone dihydrotestosterone (DHT), required for the normal development of external male genitals. Usually identified as girls at birth, the children begin to develop male genitals at adolescence.

diabetes mellitus　A chronic disease characterized by excess sugar in the blood and urine due to a deficiency of insulin.

diaphragm　A rubber cup with a flexible rim that is placed deep inside the vagina, blocking the cervix, to prevent sperm from entering the uterus.

diethylstilbestrol (DES)　A synthetic estrogen once used to prevent miscarriages; associated with a possible increased cancer risk among the women who took it and their children.

dilation　Opening up of the cervix during labor.

dilation and evacuation (D & E)　A second-trimester abortion method in which the cervix is slowly dilated and the fetus removed by alternating solution and curettage.

disinhibition　The phenomenon of activating behaviors that would normally be suppressed.

domestic partnership　A legal category granting some rights ordinarily reserved to married couples to committed, cohabiting heterosexual, gay, and lesbian couples.

domination and submission (D/S)　Sexual activities involving the consensual acting out of fantasy scenes in which one person dominates and the other submits.

dominatrix　In bondage and discipline, a woman who specializes in "disciplining" a submissive partner.

drag　Cross-dressing, often with comic intent.

dyke　In the butch-femme subculture, a nonpejorative term referring to a lesbian who dresses and acts in a stylized masculine manner. Outside the butch-femme subculture, a pejorative term for a "nonfeminine" woman, whether lesbian or heterosexual.

dysmenorrhea　Pelvic cramping and pain experienced by some women during menstruation.

dyspareunia　A female sexual dysfunction characterized by painful intercourse.

eating disorder　Eating and weight-management practices that endanger a person's physical and emotional health.

ectopic pregnancy　A pregnancy in which the fertilized egg implants in a fallopian tube instead of in the uterus. Also known as tubal pregnancy.

effacement　Thinning of the cervix during labor.

effeminacy　Having feminine qualities.

ego　In Freudian theory, the self.

egocentric fallacy　An erroneous belief that one's own personal experience and values are held by others in general.

ejaculation　The process by which semen is forcefully expelled from the penis.

ejaculatory duct　One of two structures within the prostate gland connecting with the vasa deferentia.

ejaculatory inevitability　The point at which ejaculation *must* occur.

Electra complex　In Freudian theory, the female child's erotic desire for the father and simultaneous fear of the mother.

ELISA　A simple blood test that screens for HIV antibodies; the most common test for HIV.

embryo　The early form of life in the uterus between the stages of blastocyst and fetus.

embryonic membrane　One of the embryo's membranes, including the amnion, yolk sac, chorion, and allantois.

emergency contraception　A form of birth control involving the early expulsion of an ovum that may have been fertilized. Also known as postcoital birth control or morning-after birth control.

emergency contraceptive pill (ECP)　A two-dose estrogen-progestin pill taken within 72 hours of unprotected intercourse to prevent conception or expel a just-fertilized ovum. Also called the Yuzpe Regimen.

emission　The first stage of ejaculation, in which sperm and semen are propelled into the urethral bulb.

endometriosis　A disease caused by endometrial tissue (uterine lining) spreading and growing in other parts of the body; a major cause of infertility.

endometrium　The inner lining of the uterine walls.

epididymis　The coiled tube, formed by the merging of the seminiferous tubules, where sperm mature.

epididymitis　Inflammation of the epididymis.

epidural　A method of anesthetic delivery during childbirth in which a pain-killing drug is continuously administered through a catheter in the woman's lower back.

episiotomy　A surgical procedure during childbirth that enlarges the vaginal opening by cutting through the perineum toward the anus.

erectile dysfunction　A sexual dysfunction characterized by the inability to have or maintain an erection during intercourse. Previously referred to as impotence.

erection　The process of the penis becoming rigid through vasocongestion; an erect penis.

erection reflex　The response to arousal in which the penis becomes erect; may be triggered by a variety of stimuli.

erogenous zone   Any area of the body that is highly sensitive to touch and associated with sexual arousal.

eros   In John Lee's typology of love, the love of beauty.

erotic aid or **sex toy**   A device, such as a vibrator or dildo, or a product, such as oils or lotions, designed to enhance erotic responsiveness.

erotica   Sexually oriented material that can be evaluated positively.

erotophilia   A positive emotional response to sexuality.

erotophobia   A negative emotional response to sexuality.

estrogen   The principal female hormone, regulating reproductive functions and the development of secondary sex characteristics.

ethnic group   A group of people distinct from other groups because of cultural characteristics transmitted from one generation to the next.

ethnicity   Ethnic affiliation or identity.

ethnocentric fallacy or **ethnocentrism**   The belief that one's own ethnic group, nation, or culture is innately superior to others.

exhibitionism   A paraphilia involving recurrent, intense urges to expose the genitals to another, nonconsenting person.

experimental research   The systematic manipulation of an individual or the environment to learn the effect of such manipulation on behavior.

expressiveness   Revealing or demonstrating one's emotions.

expulsion   The second stage of ejaculation, characterized by rapid, rhythmic contraction of the urethra, prostate, and muscles at the base of the penis, causing semen to spurt from the urethral opening.

extrafamilial abuse   Child sexual abuse by someone unrelated to the child.

fallacy   An error in reasoning that affects our understanding of a subject.

fallopian tube   One of two uterine tubes extending toward an ovary.

false memory   A fictitious memory of an event that never occurred.

false memory syndrome   A collection of fictitious memories elicited by a therapist and believed by the individual to be authentic and accurate; whether such a syndrome exists is a matter of debate.

feedback   The ongoing process in which participants and their messages create a given result and are subsequently modified by that result.

fellatio   Oral stimulation of the penis.

female circumcision   The surgical removal of the clitoris and all or part of the labia. Also known as clitoridectomy.

female condom   A soft, loose-fitting, disposable polyurethane sheath with a diaphragm-like ring at each end that covers the cervix, vaginal walls, and part of the external genitals to prevent conception and to help protect against sexually transmitted diseases.

femme   A feminine lesbian with a butch partner. *See also* butch.

femme porn   Sexually oriented material catering to women and heterosexual couples.

fertility awareness method   One of several contraceptive methods based on a woman's knowledge of her body's reproductive cycle, including calendar (rhythm), basal body temperature (BBT), cervical mucus, and symptothermal methods.

fetishism   A paraphilia in which a person is sexually attracted to certain objects.

fetishistic transvestite   A heterosexual male who cross-dresses for sexual arousal.

fetus   The stage of life from 8 weeks of gestation to birth.

fibrocystic disease   A common and generally harmless breast condition in which fibrous tissue and benign cysts develop in the breast.

follicle-stimulating hormone (FSH)   A hormone that regulates ovulation.

follicular phase   The phase of the ovarian cycle during which a follicle matures.

foreskin or **prepuce**   The portion of the sleevelike skin covering the shaft of the penis that extends over the glans penis.

frenulum   The triangular area of sensitive skin on the underside of the penis, attaching the glans to the foreskin.

frotteurism   A paraphilia involving recurrent, intense urges to touch or rub against a nonconsenting person for the purpose of sexual arousal.

gamete   A sex cell containing the genetic material necessary for reproduction; an oocyte (ovum) or sperm.

gamete intrafallopian transfer (GIFT)   An ART technique in which oocyte and sperm are collected and then deposited together in the fallopian tube.

gay-bashing or **queer-bashing**   Violence directed against gay men or lesbians because of their sexual orientation.

gender   The social and cultural characteristics associated with being male or female.

gender dysphoria   Dissatisfaction with one's gender.

gender identity   The gender one feels himself or herself to be.

gender identity disorder   A psychiatric diagnosis in which one's gender identity is inconsistent with one's anatomical gender, causing significant distress or impairment.

gender role   The role a person is expected to perform as a result of being male or female in a particular culture. Preferred over the term *sex role*.

gender schema   A set of interrelated ideas used to organize information about the world on the basis of gender.

gender theory   A theory that a society is best understood by how it is organized according to gender.

gender-role attitude   Beliefs about appropriate male and female personality traits and activities.

gender-role behavior   The activities in which individuals engage in accordance with their gender.

gender-role stereotype   A rigidly held, oversimplified, and overgeneralized belief that all males and all females possess distinct psychological and behavioral traits.

genetic sex   Identification as male or female based on chromosomal and hormonal sex characteristics.

genital herpes   An STD caused by the herpes simplex virus (HSV).

genital stage   In Freudian theory, the period in which adolescents become interested in genital sexual activities, especially sexual intercourse.

genital warts   An STD caused by the human papilloma virus (HPV).

genitals   The reproductive and sexual organs of males and females. Also known as genitalia.

gestation   Pregnancy.

glans clitoridis   The erotically sensitive tip of the clitoris.

glans penis   The head of the penile shaft.

gonad   An organ (ovary or testis) that produces gametes.

gonadotropin   A hormone that acts directly on the gonads.

gonadotropin-releasing hormone (GnRH)   A hormone that stimulates the pituitary gland to release follicle-stimulating hormone (FSH) and luteinizing hormone (LH), initiating the follicular phase of the ovarian cycle.

gonorrhea   An STD caused by the *Neisseria gonorrhoeae* bacterium.

Grafenberg spot   According to some researchers, an erotically sensitive area on the front wall of the vagina midway between the introitus and the cervix. Also known as G-spot.

gynecomastia   Swelling or enlargement of the male breast.

halo effect   The assumption that attractive or charismatic people possess more desirable social characteristics than others.

health belief model   A health behavior model arguing that four factors must be present for an individual to take action to avoid a disease: belief in personal susceptibility, belief that the disease would have at least a moderately severe effect on one's life, belief that taking a particular action will reduce susceptibility to or the severity of the disease, and belief that the costs of prevention or treatment are worth the benefits.

Hegar's sign   The softening of the uterus above the cervix, indicating pregnancy.

helper T cell   A lymphocyte that "reads" antigens and directs the immune system's response.

hepatitis   A viral disease affecting the liver; several types of the virus can be sexually transmitted.

hermaphrodite   A person with both male and female gonads: either one of each, two of each, or two ovotestes (gonads that have both ovarian and testicular tissue in the same gland). Also known as true hermaphrodite.

herpes simplex virus (HSV)   The virus that causes genital herpes.

heterosexual bias or **heterosexism**   The tendency to see the world in heterosexual terms and to ignore or devalue homosexuality.

heterosexuality   Sexual orientation in which emotional and sexual attraction are directed toward members of the other sex.

heterosociality   Relationships with the other sex that are based on respect and friendship.

homoeroticism   Sexual attraction, desire, or impulses directed toward members of the same sex; homosexuality.

homophobia   An irrational or phobic fear of gay men and lesbians. *See also* anti-gay prejudice; heterosexual bias.

homosexuality   Sexual orientation in which emotional and sexual attraction are directed toward members of the same sex.

homosociality   Relationships in which self-esteem and status are more closely linked to evaluations from people of the same sex than of the other sex.

hormone   A chemical substance that acts as a messenger within the body, regulating various functions.

hormone replacement therapy (HRT)   The administration of estrogen, often with progestin, in the form of pills, vaginal cream, or a small adhesive patch.

hostile environment   As related to sexuality, a work or educational atmosphere that interferes with a person's performance because of sexual harassment.

hot flash   An effect of menopause consisting of a period of intense warmth, flushing, and perspiration, typically lasting 1–2 minutes.

human chorionic gonadotropin (HCG)   A hormone secreted by the developing placenta and needed to support a pregnancy.

human immunodeficiency virus (HIV)   The virus that causes AIDS.

human papilloma virus (HPV)   The virus that causes genital warts.

hymen   A thin membrane partially covering the introitus prior to first intercourse or other breakage.

hypoactive sexual desire (HSD) or **inhibited sexual desire**   A sexual disorder characterized by low or absent sexual desire.

hysterectomy   The surgical removal of the uterus.

hysterotomy   A second-trimester abortion method in which the fetus is removed through an incision made in the woman's abdomen; an extremely rare procedure.

id In Freudian theory, the instincts.

implant A contraceptive method that involves insertion of thin, matchstick-sized capsules containing a progestin under the skin of a woman's arm.

implantation The process by which a blastocyst becomes embedded in the uterine wall.

in vitro fertilization (IVF) An ART procedure that combines sperm and oocyte in a laboratory dish and transfers the blastocyst to the mother's uterus.

incest Sexual intercourse between individuals too closely related to legally marry, usually interpreted to mean father-daughter, mother-son, or brother-sister.

incidence Number of new cases of a disease within a specified time, usually 1 year.

independent variable In an experiment, a factor that can be manipulated or changed.

induction A type of reasoning in which arguments are formed from a premise to provide support for its conclusion.

infertility The inability to conceive a child after trying for a year or more.

infibulation The stitching together of the sides of the vulva or vaginal opening; part of the process of female circumcision.

informed consent Assent given by a mentally competent individual at least 18 years old with full knowledge of the purpose and potential risks and benefits of participation.

inhibited ejaculation A sexual dysfunction characterized by the male's inability to ejaculate despite an erection and stimulation.

instrumentality Being oriented toward tasks and problem solving.

intercytoplasmic sperm injection (ICSI) An ART procedure in which a single sperm is injected into an oocyte in a laboratory dish and the resultant blastocyst is transferred to the mother's uterus.

intersexuality A combination of male and female anatomical structures.

intimate love Love based on commitment, caring, and self-disclosure.

intrafamilial abuse Child sexual abuse by biologically and step-related individuals.

intrauterine device (IUD) A T-shaped device inserted into the uterus through the cervical os to prevent conception or implantation of the fertilized egg.

intrauterine insemination (IUI) or **artificial insemination (AI)** A means of achieving pregnancy by depositing semen by syringe near the cervical opening during ovulation.

introitus The opening of the vagina.

jealousy An aversive response that occurs because of a partner's real, imagined, or likely involvement with a third person.

Kaplan's Tri-Phasic Model of Sexual Response A model that divides sexual response into three phases: desire, excitement, and orgasm.

Kaposi's sarcoma A rare cancer of the blood vessels that is common among people with AIDS.

Kegel exercises A set of exercises designed to strengthen and give voluntary control over the pubococcygeus and to increase sexual pleasure and awareness.

killer T cell A lymphocyte that attacks foreign cells.

Klinefelter syndrome A condition in which a male has one or more extra X chromosomes, causing the development of female secondary sex characteristics.

labia majora (singular, *labium majus*) Two folds of spongy flesh extending from the mons pubis and enclosing the labia minora, clitoris, urethral opening, and vaginal entrance. Also known as major lips.

labia minora (singular, *labium minus*) Two small folds of skin within the labia majora that meet above the clitoris to form the clitoral hood. Also known as minor lips.

lactation The production of milk in the breasts (mammary glands).

laminaria A small stick of seaweed placed into the cervical opening about 6 hours prior to an abortion to dilate the cervix.

lanugo The fine, downy hair covering the fetus.

laparoscopy A form of tubal ligation using a viewing lens (the laparoscope) to locate the fallopian tubes and another instrument to cut or block and close them.

latency stage In Freudian theory, the period from age 6 to puberty in which sexual impulses are no longer active.

leukocyte White blood cell.

Leydig cell Cell within the testes that secretes androgens. Also known as an interstitial cell.

libido The sex drive.

limbic system A group of structures in the brain associated with emotions and feelings; involved with producing sexual arousal.

lochia A bloody vaginal discharge following childbirth.

low birth weight (LBW) Prematurity; a condition in which the newborn weighs less than 5.5 lb; a major complication in the third trimester of pregnancy.

ludus In John Lee's typology of love, playful love.

lumpectomy Breast surgery that removes only the malignant tumor and surrounding lymph nodes.

luteal phase The phase of the ovarian cycle during which a follicle becomes a corpus luteum and then degenerates.

luteinizing hormone (LH) A hormone involved in ovulation.

lymphocyte A type of leukocyte active in the immune response.

machismo In Latino culture, highly prized masculine traits.

macrophage   A type of white blood cell that destroys foreign cells.

male condom   *See* condom.

malignant tumor   A cancerous tumor that invades nearby tissues and disrupts the normal functioning of vital organs.

mammary gland   A mature female breast.

mammogram   A low-dose X ray of the breast.

mania   In John Lee's typology of love, obsessive love.

mastectomy   The surgical removal of the breast.

Masters and Johnson Four-Phase Model of Sexual Response   A model that divides sexual response into four phases: excitement, plateau, orgasm, and resolution.

masturbation   Stimulation of the genitals for pleasure.

menarche   The onset of menstruation.

menopause   The complete cessation of menstruation.

menses   The menstrual flow, in which the endometrium is discharged.

menstrual cycle   The more-or-less monthly process during which the uterus is readied for implantation of a fertilized ovum. Also known as uterine cycle.

menstrual phase   The shedding of the endometrium during the menstrual cycle.

metastasis   The process by which cancer spreads from one part of the body to another unrelated part via the bloodstream or lymphatic system.

mifepristone with misoprostol   A drug combination used to terminate early pregnancies. Formerly known as RU-486.

minilaparotomy   A form of tubal ligation in which a small incision is made in the lower abdomen.

miscarriage   The spontaneous expulsion of the fetus from the uterus; also called spontaneous abortion.

modeling   The process of learning through imitation of others.

mons pubis   In the female, the mound of fatty tissue covering the pubic bone; the pubic mound. Also known as mons veneris.

mons veneris   The pubic mound; literally, mountain of Venus. Also known as mons pubis.

moral principle   In Freudian theory, the principle by which the individual conscience is guided by morals and values.

mucus method   *See* cervical mucus method.

myotonia   Increased muscle tension.

necrophilia   A paraphilia involving recurrent, intense urges to engage in sexual activities with a corpse.

neonate   A newborn.

neurosis   A psychological disorder characterized by anxiety or tension.

nocturnal orgasm or **emission**   Male orgasm and ejaculation while sleeping; usually accompanied by erotic dreams. Also known as wet dream.

nongonococcal urethritis (NGU)   Urethral inflammation caused by something other than the gonococcus bacterium.

nonmarital sex   Sexual activities occurring primarily among single adults over 30 and widowed men and women.

nonoxynol-9   The sperm-killing chemical in spermicide.

nonpedophilic sexual abuse   An adult's sexual interaction with a child that is motivated not by sexual desire but rather by nonsexual motives, such as power or affection.

nonspecific urethritis (NSU)   Inflammation of the urethra with an unspecified, nongonococcal cause.

norm   A cultural rule or standard of behavior.

normal sexual behavior   Behavior that conforms to a group's average or median patterns of behavior.

Norplant   The trade name of a contraceptive implant that is inserted under the skin of a woman's arm.

nymphomania   A pseudoscientific term referring to "abnormal" or "excessive" sexual desire in a woman.

objectivity   The observation of things as they exist in reality as opposed to our feelings or beliefs about them.

obscenity   That which is deemed offensive to "accepted" standards of decency or morality.

observational research   A method of gathering information in which a researcher systematically and unobtrusively observes behavior.

Oedipal complex   In Freudian theory, the male child's erotic desire for his mother and simultaneous fear of his father.

oocyte   The female gamete, referred to as an egg or ovum.

oogenesis   The production of oocytes; the ovarian cycle.

oophorectomy   The removal of one or both ovaries.

open marriage   A marriage in which both partners agree to allow each other to have openly acknowledged and independent relationships with others, including sexual ones.

opinion   An unsubstantiated belief or conclusion about what seems to be true according to an individual's personal thoughts.

opportunistic infection (OI)   An infection that normally does not occur or is not life threatening, but that takes advantage of a weakened immune system.

oral contraceptive   A series of pills containing synthetic estrogen and/or progesterone that regulates egg production and the menstrual cycle. Commonly known as "the pill."

oral stage   In Freudian theory, the period lasting from birth to age 1 in which infant eroticism is focused on the mouth.

orgasm   The climax of sexual excitement, including rhythmic contractions of muscles in the genital area and intensely pleasurable sensations; usually accompanied by ejaculation in males beginning in puberty.

orgasmic platform   A portion of the vagina that undergoes vasocongestion during sexual arousal.

os   The cervical opening.

osteoporosis   The loss of bone mass.

outercourse   A method of birth control using all avenues of sexual intimacy except penile-vaginal intercourse.

ovarian cycle   The more-or-less monthly process during which oocytes are produced.

ovarian follicle   A saclike structure in which an oocyte develops.

ovary   One of a pair of organs that produces oocytes.

ovulation   The release of an oocyte from the ovary during the ovarian cycle.

ovulatory phase   The phase of the ovarian cycle during which ovulation occurs.

ovum (plural, *ova*)   An egg; an oocyte; the female gamete.

oxytocin   A hormone produced by the fetus that stimulates strong uterine contractions.

Pap test   A method of testing for cervical cancer by scraping cell samples from the cervix and examining them under a microscope.

paraphilia   A mental disorder characterized by recurrent, intense, sexually arousing fantasies, sexual urges, or behaviors generally lasting at least 6 months and involving nonhuman objects, the suffering or humiliation of oneself or one's partner, or children or other nonconsenting persons.

paraphiliac   A person who has a paraphilia.

parenteral transmission   Infection via the bloodstream.

partialism   A paraphilia in which a person is sexually attracted to a specific body part.

participant observation   A method of observational research in which the researcher participates in the behaviors being studied.

pathological behavior   Behavior deemed unhealthy or diseased by current medical standards.

pedophile   A person who is sexually attracted to children.

pedophilia   A paraphilia characterized by recurrent, intense urges to engage in sexual activities with a prepubescent child.

peer   An age-mate.

peer delinquent subculture   An antisocial youth subculture.

pelvic floor   The underside of the pelvic area, extending from the top of the pubic bone to the anus.

pelvic inflammatory disease (PID)   An infection of the fallopian tube (or tubes) caused by an organism, such as *C. trachomatis* or *N. gonorroehae*, in which scar tissue may form within the tubes and block the passage of eggs or cause an ectopic pregnancy; a leading cause of female infertility. Also called salpingitis.

penis   The male organ through which semen and urine pass.

penis envy   In Freudian theory, female desire to have a penis.

perimenopause   A period of gradual changes and adjustments a woman's body goes through prior to menopause, before menstruation stops completely.

perinatal transmission   The passing of a disease from mother to fetus.

perineum   An area of soft tissue between the genitals and the anus that covers the muscles and ligaments of the pelvic floor.

Peyronie's disease   A painful male sexual dysfunction, resulting in curvature of the penis, that is caused by fibrous tissue and calcium deposits developing in the corpora cavernosa of the penis.

phallic stage   In Freudian theory, the period from age 3 through 5, during which both male and female children exhibit interest in the genitals.

pheromone   A sexually arousing chemical substance secreted into the air by many kinds of animals.

placenta   The organ of exchange between the mother and the fetus.

pleasure principle   In Freudian theory, the principle that organisms (including people) seek pleasure and avoid pain.

pleasuring   Erotic, nongenital touching.

plethysmograph   A device attached to the genitals to measure physiological response.

PLISSIT model   A model for sex therapy consisting of four progressive levels: **P**ermission, **L**imited Information, **S**pecific **S**uggestions, and **I**ntensive **T**herapy.

pneumocystis carinii pneumonia (PCP)   An opportunistic lung infection caused by a common, usually harmless organism; the most common opportunistic infection among people with AIDS.

pornography   Sexually oriented material that is generally evaluated negatively.

postpartum period   The period (about 3 months) following childbirth, characterized by physical stabilization and emotional adjustment.

post-traumatic stress disorder (PTSD)   A group of characteristic symptoms, such as depression, that follows an intensely distressing event outside a person's normal life experience.

pragma   In John Lee's typology of love, practical love.

preeclampsia   A condition in pregnancy characterized by increasingly high blood pressure.

premarital sex   Sexual activities, especially sexual intercourse, taking place prior to marriage or among adolescents or young adults.

premature ejaculation   A sexual dysfunction characterized by the inability to control or delay ejaculation as long as desired, causing distress.

premenstrual syndrome (PMS)   A set of severe symptoms associated with menstruation.

prepared childbirth   An approach to childbirth that encourages the mother's understanding of the process and teaches exercises to reduce tension; also known as natural childbirth.

prevalence Overall occurrence; the total number of cases of a disease.

priapism Prolonged and painful erection due to the inability of blood to drain from the penis.

prodrome A period prior to a viral outbreak when live viruses are shed from the affected areas.

progesterone A female hormone that helps regulate the menstrual cycle and sustain pregnancy.

proliferative phase The building up of the endometrium in response to increased estrogen during the menstrual cycle.

prophylaxis Protection from disease.

prostaglandins A type of hormone with a fatty-acid base that stimulates muscle contractions.

prostate gland A muscular gland encircling the urethra that produces about one-third of the seminal fluid.

prostate-specific antigen (PSA) test A blood test used to help diagnose prostate cancer.

prostatitis Inflammation of the prostate gland.

prostitution The exchange of sex for money and/or goods.

proximity Nearness in physical space and time.

pseudohermaphrodite A person with two testes or two ovaries but an ambiguous genital appearance.

psychoanalysis A psychological system developed by Sigmund Freud that traces behavior to unconscious motivations.

psychosexual development Development of the psychological components of sexuality.

puberty The stage of human development when the body becomes capable of reproduction.

pubic lice *Phthirus pubis,* colloquially known as crabs; tiny lice that infest the pubic hair.

pubococcygeus A part of the muscular sling stretching from the pubic bone in front to the tailbone in back.

random sample A portion of a larger group collected in an unbiased way.

rape Penile-vaginal penetration against a woman's will through the use or threat of force.

rape trauma syndrome The emotional changes an individual undergoes as a result of rape.

reactive jealousy A type of jealousy that occurs because of a partner's current, past, or anticipated relationship with another person.

reality principle In Freudian theory, the principle by which the external world exerts influence on the organism.

recovered memory A repressed memory brought to consciousness so that the individual is aware of it.

refractory period For men, a period following orgasm during which they are not capable of having an orgasm again.

relaxin A hormone produced by the placenta in the later months of pregnancy that increases flexibility in the ligaments and joints of the pelvic area. In men, relaxin is contained in semen, where it assists in sperm motility.

representative sample A small group representing a larger group in terms of age, sex, ethnicity, socioeconomic status, orientation, and so on.

repressed memory A memory of a powerfully traumatic event that is buried in the unconscious and produces symptoms, such as anxiety or nervousness.

repression A psychological mechanism that keeps people from becoming aware of hidden memories and motives because they arouse guilt or pain.

retrograde ejaculation The backward expulsion of semen into the bladder rather than out of the urethral opening.

retrovirus A virus capable of reversing the normal genetic writing process, causing the host cell to replicate the virus instead of itself.

reverse transcriptase An enzyme in the core of a retrovirus enabling it to write its own genetic program into a host cell's DNA.

root The portion of the penis attached to the pelvic cavity.

RU-486 *See* mifepristone with misoprostol.

sadomasochism (S&M) A popular, nonclinical term for domination and submission.

salpingitis *See* pelvic inflammatory disease.

satyriasis A pseudoscientific term referring to "abnormal" or "uncontrollable" sexual desire in a man.

scabies A red, intensely itchy rash appearing on the genitals, buttocks, feet, wrists, knuckles, abdomen, armpits, or scalp, caused by the barely visible mite *Sarcoptes scabiei.*

schema A set of interrelated ideas that helps us process information by organizing it in useful ways.

scientific method A systematic approach to acquiring knowledge by collecting data, forming a hypothesis, testing it empirically, and observing the results.

script In sociology, the acts, rules, and expectations associated with a particular role.

scrotum A pouch of skin that holds the two testicles.

secondary sex characteristics The physical changes that occur as a result of increased amounts of hormones targeting other areas of the body.

secretory phase The phase of the menstrual cycle during which the endometrium begins to prepare for the arrival of a fertilized ovum; without fertilization, the corpus luteum begins to degenerate.

secure attachment A style of infant attachment characterized by feelings of security and confidence in relation to the primary caregiver.

self-disclosure The revelation of personal information that others would not ordinarily know because of its riskiness.

semen The ejaculated fluid containing sperm. Also known as seminal fluid.

seminal vesicle   One of two glands at the back of the bladder that secrete about 60% of the seminal fluid.

seminiferous tubule   Tiny, tightly compressed tubes in which spermatogenesis takes place.

sensate focus   The focusing on touch and the giving and receiving of pleasure as part of the treatment of sexual difficulties.

serial monogamy   A succession of monogamous marriages.

seroconversion   The process by which a person develops antibodies.

serostatus   The absence or presence of antibodies for a particular antigen.

sex   Identification as male or female based on genetic and anatomical sex characteristics.

sex flush   A rash that temporarily appears as a result of blood rushing to the skin's surface during sexual excitation.

sex information/advice genre   A media genre that transmits information and norms about sexuality to a mass audience.

sex reassignment surgery (SRS)   The surgical process by which the reproductive organs are surgically altered from one sex to the other.

sex surrogates   Sex partners who assist sexually dysfunctional clients without spouses or other partners in sex therapy.

sex-typed   Following gender-role stereotypes.

sexual abuse trauma   A dynamic marked by traumatic sexualization and feelings of betrayal, powerlessness, and stigmatization exhibited by children and adults who have been sexually abused.

sexual aggression   Any kind of sexual activity performed against a person's will through the use of force, argument, pressure, alcohol or drugs, or authority.

sexual aversion   A sexual disorder characterized by a consistently phobic response to sexual activities or the idea of such activities.

sexual coercion   A broad term referring to any kind of sexual activity initiated with another person through the use of argument, pressure, pleading, or cajoling, as well as force, pressure, alcohol or drugs, or authority.

sexual disorder   An impairment of an individual's sexual responsiveness caused by interference with the brain's arousal capacity.

sexual dysfunction   An impaired physiological response that prevents an individual from functioning sexually, such as erectile difficulties or absence of orgasm.

sexual enhancement   Improvement in the quality of one's sexual relationship.

sexual harassment   The abuse of power for sexual ends; the creation of a hostile work or educational environment because of unwelcomed conduct or conditions of a sexual nature.

sexual impulse   An inclination to act sexually.

sexual masochism   A paraphilia characterized by recurrent, intense urges to engage in real (not fantasy) sexual acts in which the person is humiliated, harmed, or otherwise made to suffer.

sexual orientation   The pattern of sexual and emotional attraction based on the gender of one's partner.

sexual sadism   A paraphilia characterized by recurrent, intense urges to engage in real (not fantasy) sexual acts in which the person inflicts physical or psychological harm on a victim.

sexual variation   Sexual variety and diversity in terms of sexual orientation, attitudes, behaviors, desires, fantasies, and so on.

sexually explicit material or **hardcore**   Material that intimately depicts sexual activities, the vulva, the erect penis, or the anus.

sexually oriented material   Material such as photographs, videos, films, magazines, or books whose primary themes, topics, or depictions involve sexuality or cause sexual arousal.

shaft   The body of the penis.

she-male   A male who has undergone breast augmentation.

smegma   A cheesy substance produced by several small glands beneath the foreskin of the penis and hood of the clitoris.

social construction   The development of social categories, such as masculinity, femininity, heterosexuality, and homosexuality, by society.

socioeconomic status   Ranking in society based on a combination of occupational, educational, and income levels.

softcore   Nonexplicit sexually oriented material.

solicitation   In terms of prostitution, a word, gesture, or action that implies an offer of sex for sale.

sonogram   A visual image created by ultrasound.

spectatoring   The process in which a person becomes a spectator of his or her sexual activities, thereby causing sexual dysfunctions or disorders.

sperm   The male gamete. Also known as a spermatozoon.

spermatic cord   A tube suspending the testicle within the scrotal sac, containing nerves, blood vessels, and a vas deferens.

spermatogenesis   The process by which a sperm develops from a spermatid.

spermicide   A substance that is toxic to sperm.

spirochete   A spiral-shaped bacterium.

spontaneous abortion   The natural expulsion of the conceptus, commonly referred to as miscarriage.

squeeze technique   A technique for the treatment of premature ejaculation in which the partner squeezes the man's erect penis below the glans immediately prior to ejaculation.

status   An individual's position or ranking in a group.

statutory rape   Consensual sexual intercourse with a female under the age of consent.

stereotype   A set of simplistic, rigidly held, overgeneralized beliefs about a person or group of people.

sterilization or **voluntary surgical contraception**   A surgical procedure that makes the reproductive organs incapable of producing or "delivering" viable gametes (sperm and eggs).

storge   In John Lee's typology of love, companionate love.

strain gauge   A device resembling a rubber band that is placed over the penis to measure physiological response.

sudden infant death syndrome (SIDS)   A phenomenon in which an apparently healthy infant dies suddenly while sleeping.

superego   In Freudian theory, the conscience.

suppressor T cell   A type of lymphocyte that is activated when an antigen has been successfully destroyed; slows and then stops the immune response.

surrogate motherhood   An approach to infertility in which one woman bears a child for another.

survey research   A method of gathering information from a small group to make inferences about a larger group.

suspicious jealousy   A type of jealousy that is groundless or that arises from ambiguous evidence.

sweating   The moistening of the vagina by secretions from its walls.

swinging   A form of consensual extramarital sex in which couples engage in sexual activities with others in a social context clearly defined as recreational sex. Also called mate sharing; wife swapping.

sympto-thermal method   A fertility awareness method combining the basal body temperature and cervical mucus methods.

syphilis   An STD caused by the *Treponema pallidum* bacterium.

T cell   Any of several types of lymphocytes involved in the immune response.

telephone scatologia   A paraphilia involving recurrent, intense urges to make obscene telephone calls.

tenting   The expansion of the inner two-thirds of the vagina during sexual arousal.

teratogen   A toxic substance that causes birth defects.

testicle or **testis** (plural, *testes*)   One of the paired male gonads inside the scrotum.

testosterone   A steroid hormone associated with sperm production, the development of secondary sex characteristics in males, and the sex drive in both males and females.

therapeutic donor insemination (TDI)   Intrauterine insemination in which the semen is from a donor rather than from the woman's husband.

toxemia   High blood pressure and edema that may occur between the 20th and 24th weeks of pregnancy.

toxic shock syndrome (TSS)   A potentially life-threatening condition caused by the *Staphylococcus aureus* bacterium and linked to the use of superabsorbent tampons.

transgender   An inclusive gender category; a transgenderist is someone who lives full-time in a gender role opposite to the gender role presumed by society to match the person's genetic sex.

transition   The end of the first stage of labor, when the infant's head enters the birth canal.

transsexual   A person whose genitals and gender identity as male or female are discordant. Postsurgical transsexuals have surgically altered their genitals to fit their gender identity.

transvestism   A clinical term referring to the wearing of clothing of the other sex, usually for sexual arousal.

triangular theory of love   A theory developed by Robert Sternberg emphasizing the dynamic quality of love as expressed by the interrelationship of three elements: intimacy, passion, and decision/commitment.

trichomoniasis   A vaginal infection caused by *Trichomonas vaginalis*. Also known as trich.

trust   Belief in the reliability and integrity of another person, process, thing, or institution.

tubal ligation   The cutting and tying off (or other method of closure) of the fallopian tubes so that ova cannot be fertilized.

Turner syndrome   A chromosomal disorder affecting females born lacking an X chromosome, resulting in the failure to develop ovaries.

two-spirit   In many cultures, a male who assumes female dress, gender role, and status.

ultrasound   The use of high-frequency sound waves to create a visual image of the fetus in the uterus.

umbilical cord   The cord connecting the placenta and fetus, through which nutrients pass.

unrequited love   Love that is not returned.

urethra   The tube through which urine (and in men, semen) passes.

urethral bulb   The expanded portion of the urethra at the bladder.

urethral opening   The opening in the urethra through which urine is expelled.

urethritis   Inflammation of the urethra.

uterus   A hollow, thick-walled, muscular organ held in the pelvic cavity by flexible ligaments and supported by several muscles. Also known as womb.

vacuum aspiration   A first-trimester form of abortion using vacuum suction to remove the conceptus and other tissue from the uterus.

vagina   In females, a flexible, muscular organ that begins between the legs and extends diagonally toward the small of the back. It encompasses the penis during sexual intercourse and is the pathway (birth canal) through which an infant is born.

vaginismus   A sexual dysfunction characterized by muscle spasms around the vaginal entrance, preventing the insertion of a penis.

vaginitis   Any of several kinds of vaginal infection.

value judgment   An evaluation as "good" or "bad" based on moral or ethical standards rather than objective ones.

variable   An aspect or factor that can be manipulated in an experiment.

varicocele   A varicose vein above the testicle that may cause lowered fertility in men.

vas deferens (plural, *vasa deferentia*)   One of two tubes that transport sperm from the epididymis to the ejaculatory duct within the prostate gland.

vasectomy   A form of surgical sterilization in which each vas deferens is severed, thereby preventing sperm from entering the seminal fluid.

vasocongestion   Blood engorgement of body tissues.

vernix   The waxy substance that sometimes covers an infant at birth.

vestibule   The area enclosed by the labia minora.

viral load test   A blood test that measures the amount of HIV in the bloodstream and serves as an indicator for determining the risk of progressing to AIDS.

virus   A protein-coated package of genes that invades a cell and alters the way in which the cell reproduces itself.

voyeurism   A paraphilia involving recurrent, intense urges to view nonconsenting others while they are engaged in sexual activities.

vulva   The collective term for the external female genitals.

wasting syndrome   Severe weight loss, usually accompanied by weakness and persistent diarrhea; a condition linked to AIDS.

Western blot   A test to determine whether antibodies are specific to HIV.

yolk sac   The producer of the embryo's first blood cells and the germ cells that will develop into gonads.

zoophilia   A paraphilia involving recurrent, intense urges to engage in sexual activities with animals.

zygote intrafallopian transfer (ZIFT)   An ART technique in which oocyte and sperm are combined in a laboratory dish and immediately transferred to the fallopian tube.

Bibliography

Abbey, A. (1991). "Acquaintance Rape and Alcohol Consumption on College Campuses: How Are They Linked?" *Journal of the American College Health, 39*(4), 165–169.

Abbey, A., Halman, L. J., & Andrews, F. M. (1992). "Psychosocial, Treatment, and Demographic Predictors of the Stress Associated with Infertility." *Fertility and Sterility, 57*(1), 122–128.

Abbey, A., & Harnish, R. J. (1995, March). "Perception of Sexual Intent: The Role of Gender, Alcohol Consumption, and Rape Supportive Attitudes." *Sex Roles, 32*(5–6), 297–313.

Abel, E. P. (1995). "An Update on Incidence of Fetal Alcohol Syndrome." *Neurotoxicology and Teratology, 17*(4), 437.

Abel, G. (1989). "Paraphilias." In H. I. Kaplan & B. Sadock (Eds.), *Comprehensive Textbook of Psychiatry, Vol. I* (5th ed.), Baltimore, MD: Williams & Wilkins.

Abma, J. C., Chandra, A., Mosher, W. D., Peterson, L., & Piccinino, L. (1997). "Fertility, Family Planning & Women's Health: New Data from the 1995 National Survey of Family Growth." National Center for Health Statistics. *Vital Health Statistics, 23*(19).

Aboukler, J. P., & Swart, A. M. (1993). "Preliminary Analysis of the Concorde Trial." *Lancet, 341*(8849), 889–890.

Abrahams, M. F. (1994). "Perceiving Flirtations Communication." *Journal of Sex Research, 31*(4), 283–292.

Absell, B. (1995). *The Pill: A Biography of the Drug That Changed the World.* New York: Random House.

Absi-Semaan, N., Crombie, G., & Freeman, C. (1993). "Masculinity and Femininity in Middle Childhood: Developmental and Factor Analyses." *Sex Roles: A Journal of Research, 28*(3–4), 187–202.

Ackerman, D. (1990). *A Natural History of the Senses.* New York: Random House.

Adelman, M. B. (1992). "Sustaining Passion: Eroticism and Safe-Sex Talk." *Archives of Sexual Behavior, 21*, 481–494.

Adler, J. (1992, October 19). "Must Boys Always Be Boys?" *Newsweek*, p. 7.

Adler, J. (1998, May 4). "Take a Pill and Call Me Tonight." *Newsweek*, p. 48.

Adler, N. A., & Schutz, J. (1995, July). "Sibling Incest Offenders." *Child Abuse & Neglect, 19*(7), 811–819.

Adler, N. E. (1992). "Unwanted Pregnancy and Abortion: Definitional and Research Issues." *Journal of Social Issues, 48*(3), 19–35.

Adler, N. E., David, H. P., Major, B. N., Roth, S. H., Russo, N. F., & Wyatt, G. E. (1990). "Psychological Responses After Abortion." *Science, 246*, 41–44.

Adler, N. E., David, H. P., Major, B. N., Roth, S. H., Russo, N. F., & Wyatt, G. E. (1992). "Psychological Factors in Abortion: A Review." *American Psychologist, 47*(10), 1194–2204.

Adler, N., Hendrick, S., & Hendrick, C. (1989). "Male Sexual Preference and Attitudes Toward Love and Sexuality." *Journal of Sex Education and Therapy, 12*(2), 27–30.

"Advance Report of Final Natality Statistics, 1991." (1993, September 9). *Monthly Vital Statistics Report* (Centers for Disease Control and Prevention) *42*,3 (Suppl.), 1–6.

AGCOP. *See* U.S. Attorney General's Commission on Pornography.

Ageton, S. (1983). *Sexual Assault Among Adolescents.* Lexington, MA: Lexington Books.

Agnew, J. (1986). "Problems Associated with Anal Erotic Activity." *Archives of Sexual Behavior, 15*(4), 307–314.

Ahn, H. N., & Gilbert, N. (1992). "Cultural Diversity and Sexual Abuse Prevention." *Social Service Review, 66*(3), 410–428.

Ahrons, C., & Rogers, R. (1987). *Divorced Families.* New York: W. W. Norton.

"AIDS and Children: A Family Disease." (1989, November). *World AIDS Magazine*, pp. 12–14.

"AIDS Fear Fuels Demand for Sex with Children." (1996). *AIDS Weekly Plus*, pp. 23–25.

"AIDS Test for Pregnant Women." (1995, February 23). *San Francisco Chronicle.*

"AIDS Transmission from Mother to Baby; Risk Tied to Amount of Virus in Woman." (1994). *San Francisco Chronicle.*

Ainsworth, M., et al. (1978). *Patterns of Attachment: A Psychological Study of the Strange Situation.* Hillsdale, NJ: Erlbaum.

Alan Guttmacher Institute (1986). *Teenage Pregnancy in Developed Countries.* New Haven, CT: Yale University Press.

Alan Guttmacher Institute. (1994). *Sex and American Teenagers.* New York: Author.

Alan Guttmacher Institute. (1996). *Teen Sex and Pregnancy.* New York: Author.

Alapack, R. (1991). "The Adolescent First Kiss." *Humanistic Psychologist, 19*(1), 48–67.

Albert, A. E., Warner, D. L., Hatcher, R. A., Trussell, J., & Bennett, C. (1995, March 21). "Condom Use Among Female Commercial Sex Workers in Nevada's Legal Brothels." Paper available from Family Planning Program, Emory University School of Medicine, Atlanta, GA.

Alcott, W. (1868). *The Physiology of Marriage.* Boston: J. P. Jewett.

Alexander, L. L. (1992). "Sexually Transmitted Diseases: Perspectives on This Growing Epidemic." *Nurse Practitioner, 17*(10), 31ff.

Alexander, W., & Judd, B. (1986). "Differences in Attitudes Toward Nudity in Advertising." *Psychology: A Quarterly Journal of Human Behavior, 23*(1), 26–29.

Allen, A., D'Alessio, D., Emmers, T. M., & Gebhardt, L. (1996). "The Role of Educational Briefings in Mitigating Effects of Experimental Exposure to Violent Sexually Explicit Material: A Meta-Analysis." *Journal of Sex Research, 33*(2), 135–141.

Allen, M., Emmers, T., Gebhardt, L., & Giery, M. A. (1995, December). "Exposure to Pornography and Acceptance of Rape Myths." *Journal of Communication, 45*(1), 5–26.

Allgeier, A. R. (1982). "Sexuality and Gender Roles in Middle-Aged and Elderly Persons." In E. Allgeier & N. McCormick (Eds.), *Gender Roles and Sexual Behavior.* Mountain View, CA: Mayfield.

Allport, G. (1958). *The Nature of Prejudice.* Garden City, NY: Doubleday.

Aloni, R., Heller, L., Keren, O., Mendelson, E., & Davidoff, G. (1992). "Noninvasive Treatment for Erectile Dysfunction in the Neurologically Disabled Population." *Journal of Sex & Marital Therapy, 18*(3), 243–249.

Althof, S. E., Turner, L. A., Levine, S. B., Bodner, J., Kursh, E. D., & Resnick, M. I. (1992). "Through the Eyes of Women: The Sexual and Psychological Responses of Women to Their Partner's Treatment with Self-Injection or External Vacuum Therapy." *Journal of Urology, 147*(4), 1024–1027.

"An Alternative to Hysterectomies." (1997, December 13). *Monterey Herald,* p. A-1.

Altman, D. (1982). *The Homosexualization of America, the Americanization of the Homosexual.* New York: St. Martin's Press.

Altman, D. (1985). *AIDS in the Mind of America.* Garden City, NY: Doubleday.

Altman, L. K. (1995, January 31). "AIDS Is Leading Killer of Those 25–44 in U.S." *San Jose Mercury News,* p. A7.

Altman, L. K. (1996, January 30). "Study: Drug Combo Potent Against AIDS." *San Francisco Chronicle,* p. A-10.

Altman, L. K. (1998, May 19). "Thousands of Mastectomies Needless." *Monterey County Herald,* p. A-7.

Altschul, M. S. (1989, July). "Cultural Bias and the Urinary Tract Infection (UTI) Controversy." *Truth Seeker,* pp. 43–45.

Alvarez, F., et al. (1988). "New Insights on the Mode of Action of Intrauterine Devices in Women." *Fertility and Sterility, 49,* 768–773.

American Academy of Pediatrics. (1995). *Condom Availability for Youth.* Elkgrove, IL: Author.

American Psychiatric Association. (1994). *Diagnostic and Statistical Manual of Mental Disorders* (4th ed.). Washington, DC: Author.

American Psychological Association. (1994). *Interim Report of the APA Working Group on Investigation of Memories of Childhood Abuse.* Washington, DC: Author.

American Social Health Association (ASHA). (1996a). Hepatitis B. Available: http://sunsite.unc.edu/ASHA/std/hepb.html#why (Last visited 2/14/98).

American Social Health Association (ASHA). (1996b). NGU (Nongonococcal Urethritis). Available: http://sunsite.unc.edu/ASHA/std/ngu.html#whatis (Last visited 2/14/98).

American Social Health Association (ASHA). (1996c). Questions and Answers About Herpes. Available: http://sunsite.unc.edu/ASHA/std/herqa.html#whatis (Last visited 2/14/98).

American Social Health Association (ASHA). (1997a). *Herpes Simplex and Pregnancy* (Pamphlet).

American Social Health Association (ASHA). (1997b). HPV Questions and Answers. Available: http://sunsite.unc.edu/ASHA/hpv/hpvqa.html#what (Last visited 2/14/98).

American Social Health Association (ASHA). (1998a). Chlamydia: What You Should Know. Available: http://sunsite.unc.edu/ASHA/std/chlam.html#intro (Last visited 2/14/98).

American Social Health Association (ASHA). (1998b). STD Statistics. Available: http://www.ashastd.org/std/stats/html

Ames, M. A., & Houston, D. (1990). "Legal, Social, and Biological Definitions of Pedophilia." *Archives of Sexual Behavior, 19*(4), 333–342.

Andersen, D. A., Lustig, M. W., & Andersen, J. F. (1987). "Regional Patterns of Communication in the United States: A Theoretical Perspective." *Communication Monographs, 54,* 128–144.

Anderson, C. (1995, February). "Childhood Sexually Transmitted Diseases: One Consequence of Sexual Abuse." *Public Health Nursing, 12*(1), 41–46.

Anderson, J. R. (1989). "Gynecologic Manifestations of AIDS and HIV Disease." *The Female Patient, 14,* 57ff.

Andersson, M. (1994). *Sexual Selection.* Princeton, NJ: Princeton University Press.

Andrews, F. M., Abbey, A., & Halman, L. J. (1991). "Stress from Infertility, Marriage, Factors, and Subjective Well-Being of Wives and Husbands." *Journal of Health and Social Behavior, 32*(3), 238–253.

Andrews, S. (1992, November 2). "The Naked Truth." *San Jose Mercury News,* pp. 1, 4.

Aneshensel, C., Fielder, E., & Becerra, R. (1989). "Fertility and Fertility-Related Behavior Among Mexican-American and Non-Hispanic White Females." *Journal of Health and Social Behavior, 30*(1), 56–78.

Annon, J. (1974). *The Behavioral Treatment of Sexual Problems.* Honolulu, HI: Enabling Systems.

Annon, J. (1976). *Behavioral Treatment of Sexual Problems: Brief Therapy.* New York: Harper & Row.

"Aphrodisiacs: Do They Ever Work?" (1996, December). *Sex Over Forty, 15*(7), 1–5.

Applebome, P. (1993, January 28). "Military People Split Over Ban on Homosexuals." *The New York Times,* p. A10.

Applebome, P. (1993, February 1). "Homosexual Issues Galvanizes Conservative Foes of Clinton." *The New York Times,* pp. A1, A8.

Apt, C., Hurlbert, D., & Powell, D. (1993). "Men with Hypoactive Sexual Desire Disorder: The Role of Interpersonal Dependency and Assertiveness." *Journal of Sex Education and Therapy, 19*(2), 108–116.

Aral, S., & Holmes, K. K. (1990). "Epidemiology of Sexual Behavior and Sexually Transmitted Diseases." In K. K. Holmes et al. (Eds.), *Sexually Transmitted Diseases* (2nd ed.). New York: McGraw-Hill.

Arey, D. (1995). "Gay Males and Sexual Child Abuse." In L. A. Fontes (Ed.), *Sexual Abuse in Nine North American Cultures: Treatment and Prevention.* Thousand Oaks, CA: Sage Publications.

Armstrong, P., & Feldman, S. (1990). *A Wise Birth.* New York: William Morrow.

Armsworth, M. W. (1991). "Psychological Responses to Abortion." *Journal of Counseling and Development, 69,* 377–379.

Arndt, W. B., Jr. (1991). *Gender Disorders and the Paraphilias.* Madison, CT: International Universities Press.

Arno, P. S., & Feiden, K. L. (1992). *Against the Odds: The Story of AIDS Drug Development.* New York: HarperCollins.

Aron, A., & Aron, E. (1991). "Love and Sexuality." In K. McKinney & S. Sprecher (Eds.), *Sexuality in Close Relationships.* Hillsdale, NJ: Erlbaum.

Aron, A., Dutton, D. G., & Aron, E. N. (1989b). "Experiences of Falling in Love." *Journal of Social and Personal Relationships 6,* 243–257.

Aron, A., & Strong, B. (1999). "Prototypes of Love and Sexuality."

Ascher, M. S., Sheppard, H. W., Winkelstein, W., & Vittinghoff, E. (1993, March 11). "Does Drug Use Cause AIDS?" *Nature, 362*(6416), 103–104.

Ash, M. (1980). "The Misnamed Female Sex Organ." In M. Kirkpatrick (Ed.), *Women's Sexual Development*. New York: Plenum Press.

ASHA. *See* American Social Health Association.

"Asia: Child Prostitution in Cambodia." (1996). *The Economist, 7955,* 338.

Athey, J. L. (1991). "HIV Infection and Homeless Adolescents." *Child Welfare, 70*(5), 517–528.

Atwood, J. D., & Dershowitz, S. (1992). "Constructing a Sex and Marital Therapy Frame: Ways to Help Couples Deconstruct Sexual Problems." *Journal of Sex and Marital Therapy, 18*(3), 196–218.

Atwood, J. D., & Gagnon, J. (1987). "Masturbatory Behavior in College Youth." *Journal of Sex Education and Therapy, 13,* 35–42.

Auger, J., Kuntsmann, J. M., Czyglik, F., & Jouannet, P. (1995). "Decline in Semen Quality Among Fertile Men in Paris During the Past 20 Years." *New England Journal of Medicine, 332*(5), 281–285.

Ault, K. A., & Faro, S. (1993). "Pelvic Inflammatory Disease: Current Diagnostic Criteria and Treatment Guidelines." *Postgraduate Medicine, 93*(2), 85–86, 89–91.

Avruch, S., & Cackley, A. P. (1995). "Savings Achieved by Giving WIC Benefits to Women Prenatally." *Public Health Reports, 110,* 27–34.

Baca-Zinn, M. (1994). "Feminist Rethinking from Racial-Ethnic Families." In M. Baca-Zinn & B. Thorton-Dill (Eds.), *Women of Color in U.S. Society.* Philadelphia: Temple University Press.

Bachrach, C. (1984). "Contraceptive Practice Among American Women, 1973–1982." *Family Planning Perspectives, 16*(6), 253–258.

Bailey, J. M. (1995). "Biological Perspectives on Sexual Orientation." In A. R. D'Augelli & C. J. Patterson (Eds.), *Lesbian, Gay, and Bisexual Identities Over the Lifespan: Psychological Perspectives.* New York: Oxford University Press.

Bailey, J. M., & Pillard, R. C. (1991). "A Genetic Study of Male Sexual Orientation." *Archives of General Psychiatry, 48*(12), 1089–1096.

Bailey, J. M., Pillard, R. C., Neale, M. C., & Agyei, Y. (1993). "Heritable Factors Influence Sexual Orientation in Women." *Archives of General Psychiatry, 50*(3), 217–223.

Bailey, J. M., Willerman, L., & Parks, C. (1991). "A Test of the Maternal Stress Theory of Human Male Homosexuality." *Archives of Sexual Behavior, 20,* 277–293.

Bajracharya, S., Sarvela, P., & Isberner, F. R. (1995, January). "A Retrospective Study of First Sex Intercourse Experiences Among Undergraduates." *Journal of American College Health, 43*(4), 169–177.

Baker, B. (1993). "The Female Condom." *Ms., 3*(5), 80–81.

Baker, C. P. (1995). "Child Chattel: Future Tourists for Sex." *Insight on the News, 11,* p. 11.

Baldwin, J. D., Whitely, S., & Baldwin, J. I. (1993). "The Effect of Ethnic Group on Sexual Activities Related to Contraception and STDs." *Journal of Sex Research, 29*(2), 189–206.

Balshem, N., Oxman, G., Van Rooven, D., & Girod, K. (1992). "Syphilis, Sex and Crack Cocaine: Images of Risk and Morality." *Social Science and Medicine, 35*(2), 147–160.

Bancroft, J. (1984). "Hormones and Human Sexual Behavior." *Journal of Sex and Marital Therapy, 10,* 3–21.

Ban on Female Circumcision Reinstated in Egypt. (1997). Available: http://www.ama-assn.org/special/womh/newsline/reuters/12301825.htm (Last visited 1/27/98).

Barbach, L. (1982). *For Each Other: Sharing Sexual Intimacy.* Garden City, NY: Doubleday.

Barbach, L. G. (1995). Cited in Goleman, D. (1995, June 14). "Sex Fantasy Research Said to Neglect Women." *The New York Times,* p. C-14.

Barclay, A. (1980). "Changes in Sexual Fantasy with Age." *Medical Aspects of Human Sexuality,* 15ff.

Bargh, J. A., & Raymond, P. (1995, March). "The Naive Misuse of Power: Nonconscious Sources of Sexual Harassment." *Journal of Social Issues, 51*(1), 85–96.

Barkan, S., & Bracken, M. (1987). "Delayed Childbearing: No Evidence for Increased Low Risk of Low Birth Weight and Preterm Delivery." *American Journal of Epidemiology, 125*(1), 101–109.

Barker-Benfield, G. J. (1976). *The Horrors of the Half-Known Life: Male Attitudes Toward Women and Sexuality in Nineteenth-Century America.* New York: Harper & Row.

Barnes-Kedar, I., Amiel, A., Maor, O., & Fejgin, M. (1993). "Elevated Human Chorionic Gonadotropin Levels in Pregnancies with Sex Chromosome Abnormalities." *American Journal of Medical Genetics, 45*(3), 356–357.

Barnett, W., Freudenberg, N., & Wille, R. (1992). "Partnership After Induced Abortion—A Prospective Controlled Study." *Archives of Sexual Behavior, 21*(5), 443–455.

Baron, L. (1983). "Sex Differences in Attitudes and Experiences of Romantic Love." *Dissertation Abstracts International, 43,* 372A.

Barret, R. L., & Robinson, B. E. (1990). *Gay Fathers.* Lexington, MA: Lexington Books.

Barrow, G., & Smith (1992). *Aging, Ageism, and Society.* St. Paul, MI: West.

Barrows, S. (1986). *Mayflower Madam.* New York: Arbor House.

Barry, K. (1995). *The Prostitution of Sexuality: The Global Exploitation of Women.* New York: University Press.

Bartell, G. D. (1970). "Group Sex Among the Mid-Americans." *Journal of Sex Research, 6,* 113–130.

Basow, S. A. (1986). *Gender Stereotypes: Traditions and Alternatives* (2nd ed.). Pacific Grove, CA: Brooks/Cole.

Basow, S. A. (1992). *Gender: Stereotyping and Roles.* Pacific Grove, CA: Brooks/Cole.

Bass, E., & Davis, L. (1988). *The Courage to Heal.* New York: Harper Perennial.

Baumann, P., Jovanovic, V., Gellert, G., & Rauskolb, R. (1991). "Risk of Miscarriage After Transcervical and Transabdominal CVS in Relation to Bacterial Colonization of the Cervix." *Prenatal Diagnosis, 11*(8), 551–557.

Baumeister, R. F. (1988a). "Gender Differences in Masochistic Scripts." *Journal of Sex Research, 25,* 478–499.

Baumeister, R. F. (1988b). "Masochism as an Escape from Self." *Journal of Sex Research, 25*(1), 28–59.

Baumeister, R., Wotman, S. R., & Stillwell, A. M. (1993). "Unrequited Love: On Heartbreak, Anger, Guilt, Scriptlessness, and Humiliation."

Bauserman, R. (1990). "Objectivity and Ideology: Criticism of Theo Sandfort's Research on Man-Boy Sexual Relations." *Journal of Homosexuality, 20*(1–2), 297–312.

Bauserman, R. (1996, December). "Sexual Aggression and Pornography: A Review of Correlational Research." *Basic & Applied Social Psychology, 18*(4), 405–427.

Baxter, L. A. (1987). "Cognition and Communication in Relationship Process." In R. Burnett, P. McGhee, & D. Clarke (Eds.), *Accounting for Relationships: Explanation, Representation, and Knowledge.* London: Methuen.

Bayer, R. (1981). *Homosexuality and American Psychiatry: The Politics of Diagnosis.* New York: Basic Books.

Bean, F., & Tienda, M. (1987). *The Hispanic Population of the United States.* New York: Russell Sage Foundation.

Becerra, R. (1988). "The Mexican American Family." In C. Mindel et al. (Eds.), *Ethnic Families in America: Patterns and Variations* (3rd ed.). New York: Elsevier North Holland.

Bechhofer, L., & Parrot, L. (1991). "What Is Acquaintance Rape?" In A. Parrot & L. Bechhofer (Eds.), *Acquaintance Rape: The Hidden Crime.* New York: John Wiley.

Beck, M. (1988, August 15). "Miscarriages." *Newsweek,* pp. 46–49.

Beck, M. (1992, May 25). "Menopause." *Newsweek,* pp. 71–79.

Beck, S. H., Cole, B. S., & Hammond, J. A. (1991). "Religious Heritage and Premarital Sex: Evidence from a National Sample of Young Adults." *Journal for the Scientific Study of Religion, 30*(2), 173–180.

Beckman, K. A., & Burns, G. L. (1990). "Relation of Sexual Abuse and Bulimia in College Women." *International Journal of Eating Disorders, 9,* 487–492.

Begley, S. (1995, March 27). "Gray Matters." *Newsweek,* pp. 48–54.

Begley, S. (1997a, March 10). "Little Lamb, Who Made Thee?" *Newsweek,* pp. 53–59.

Begley, S. (1997b, February 24). "The Mammogram War." *Newsweek,* pp. 55–60.

Begley, S. (1997c, September 22). "The Nursery's Littlest Victims." *Newsweek,* pp. 72–73.

Behar, R. (1989). "Sexual Witchcraft, Colonialism, and Women's Powers: Views from the Spanish Inquisition." In A. Lavrin (Ed.), *Sexuality and Marriage in Colonial Latin America.* Lincoln, NE: University of Nebraska Press.

Beier, E., & Sternberg, D. (1977). "Marital Communication." *Journal of Communication, 27*(3), 92–97.

Beitchman, J. H., Zucker, K. J., Hood, J. E., daCosta, G. A., Akman, D., & Cassavia, E. (1992). "A Review of the Long-Term Effects of Child Sexual Abuse." *Child Abuse and Neglect, 16*(1), 101–128.

Belcastro, P. (1985). "Sexual Behavior Differences Between Black and White Students." *Journal of Sex Research, 21*(1), 56–67.

Belk, R. (1991). "The Ineluctable Mysteries of Possessions." *Journal of Social Behavior and Personality, 6*(6), 17–55.

Belknap, J. (1989). "The Sexual Victimization of Unmarried Women by Non-Relative Acquaintances." In M. Pirog-Good & J. Stets (Eds.), *Violence in Dating Relationships.* New York: Praeger.

Bell, A., & Weinberg, M. (1978). *Homosexualities: A Study of Diversities Among Men.* New York: Simon & Schuster.

Bell, A., Weinberg, M., & Hammersmith, S. (1981). *Sexual Preference: Its Development in Men and Women.* Bloomington, IN: Indiana University Press.

Bello, D., Pitts, R., & Etzel, M. (1983). "The Communication Effects of Controversial Sexual Content in Television Programs and Commercials." *Journal of Advertising, 12*(3), 32–43.

Belluck, P. (1998, January 3). "Heartache Frequently Visits Parents with Multiple Births." *The New York Times,* p. A1.

Belsky, J. (1986, September). "Transition to Parenthood." *Medical Aspects of Human Sexuality, 20,* 56–59.

Belsky, J., et al. (1984). *The Child in the Family.* Reading, MA: Addison-Wesley.

Bem, S. L. (1974). "The Measurement of Psychological Androgyny." *Journal of Consulting and Clinical Psychology, 42,* 151–162.

Bem, S. L. (1975). "Androgyny vs. the Tight Little Lives of Fluffy Women and Chesty Men." *Psychology Today, 9*(4), 58–59ff.

Bem, S. L. (1981). "Gender Schema Theory: A Cognitive Account of Sex Typing." *Psychological Review, 88,* 354–364.

Bem, S. L. (1983). "Gender Schema Theory and Its Implications for Child Development: Raising Gender-Aschematic Children in a Gender Schematic Society." *Signs, 8*(4), 598–616.

Bem, S. L. (1989). "Genital Knowledge and Gender Constancy in Preschool Children." *Child Development, 60*(3), 649–662.

Bem, S. L. (1995). "Dismantling Gender Polarization and Compulsory Heterosexuality: Should We Turn the Volume Up or Down?" *Journal of Sex Research 32*(4), 329–332.

Bem, S. L., & Lewis, S. A. (1975). "Sex Role Adaptability: One Consequence of Psychological Androgyny." *Journal of Personality and Social Psychology, 31*(4), 634–643.

Bem, S. L., Martyna, W., & Watson, C. (1976). "Sex Typing and Androgyny: Further Explorations of the Expressive Domain." *Journal of Personality and Social Psychology, 34,* 1016–1023.

Bemelmans, B., Meuleman, E., Doesburhg, W., Notermans, S., & Debruyne, F. (1994). "Erectile Dysfunction in Diabetic Men: The Neurological Factor Revisited." *Journal of Urology, 151,* 884–889.

Bennett, W. (1982). *The Dieter's Dilemma: Eating Less and Weighing More.* New York: Basic Books.

Benokraitis, N. V. (1993). *Marriages and Families: Changes, Choices, and Constraints.* Englewood Cliffs, NJ: Prentice-Hall.

Benokraitis, N. V. (1996). *Marriages and Families.* Englewood Cliffs, NJ: Prentice-Hall.

Benshoof, J. (1993). "Planned Parenthood v. Cases: The Impact of the Undue Burden Standard on Reproductive Health Care." *JAMA: Journal of the American Medical Association, 269*(17), 2249–2257.

Benson, D., & Thompson, G. (1982). "Sexual Harassment on a University Campus: The Confluence of Authority Relations, Sexual Interest, and Gender Stratification." *Social Problems, 29,* 236–251.

Bera, W., et al. (1991). *Male Adolescent Sexual Abuse.* Newbury Park, CA: Sage Publications.

Berends, M. M., & Caron, S. L. (1994). "Children's Understanding and Knowledge of Conception and Birth: A Developmental Approach." *Journal of Sex Education and Therapy, 20*(1), 18–29.

Bergen, D. J., & Williams, J. E. (1991). "Sex Stereotypes in the United States Revisited: 1972–1988." *Sex Roles, 24*(7/8), 413–423.

Berger, A. A. (1991). "Of Mice and Men: An Introduction to Mouseology; or Anal Eroticism and Disney." *Journal of Homosexuality, 21*(1–2), 155–165.

Berger, R. M. (1982). "The Unseen Minority: Older Gays and Lesbians." *Social Work, 27,* 236–242.

Bernard, J. (1982). *The Future of Marriage* (2nd ed.). New York: Columbia University Press.

Bernstein, H. (1991, February 5). "Ruling May Curb Harassment." *Los Angeles Times,* p. 3.

Berrick, J. D., & Barth, R. P. (1992). "Child Sexual Abuse Prevention—Research Review and Recommendations." *Social Work Research and Abstracts, 28,* 6–15.

Berscheid, E. (1983). "Emotion." In H. H. Kelley et al. (Eds.), *Close Relationships.* New York: W. H. Freeman.

Berscheid, E., & Walster, E. H. (1974). "A Little Bit About Love." In T. L. Huston (Ed.), *Foundations of Interpersonal Attraction.* New York: Academic Press.

Bérubé, A. (1988, September). "Caught in the Storm: AIDS and the Meaning of Natural Disaster." *Out/Look,* 8–19.

Betchen, S. (1991). "Male Masturbation as a Vehicle for the Pursuer/Distancer Relationship in Marriage." *Journal of Sex and Marital Therapy, 17*(4), 269–278.

Betts, K. (1994, April). "Body Language." *Vogue,* 345–347.

Beyette, B. (1986, October 17). "Teen Sex-Education Campaign Launched." *Los Angeles Times,* pp. 20, 22.

Biber, S. H. (1997). "Current State of Transsexual Surgery: A Brief Overview." In B. Bullough, V. L. Bullough, & J. Elias (Eds.), *Gender Blending,* New York: Prometheus Books.

Bieber, I. (1962). *Homosexuality: A Psychoanalytic Study.* New York: Basic Books.

Bills, S. A., & Duncan, D. F. (1991). "Drugs and Sex: A Survey of College Students' Beliefs." *Perceptual and Motor Skills, 72,* 1293–1294.

Billy, J., Grady, W. R., Lincoln-Hansen, J., & Tanfer, K. (1996). "Men's Perceptions of Their Roles and Responsibilities Regarding Sex, Contraception and Childrearing." *Family Planning Perspectives, 28*(5), 221–227.

Billy, J. O., Tanfer, K., Grady, W. R., & Klepinger, D. H. (1993). "The Sexual Behavior of Men in the United States." *Family Planning Perspectives, 25*(2), 52–60.

Billy, J. O., & Udry, J. R. (1985). "The Influence of Male and Female Best Friends on Adolescent Sexual Behavior." *Adolescence, 20*(77), 21–32.

Binion, V. (1990). "Psychological Androgyny: A Black Female Perspective." *Sex Roles, 22*(7–8), 487–507.

Binsacca, B. D., et al. (1987). "Factors Associated with Low Birth Weight in an Inner-City Population." *American Journal of Public Health, 77*(4), 505–506.

Biro, F. M., Rosenthal, S. L., Wildley, L. S., & Hillard, P. A. (1991). "The Sexual Behavior of Men in the United States." *Family Planning Perspectives, 25*(2), 52–60.

Black, R. D. (1991). "Women's Voices After Pregnancy Loss: Couples' Patterns." *Social Work in Health Care, 16*(2), 19–36.

Blackwood, E. (1984). "Sexuality and Gender in Certain Native American Tribes: The Case of Cross-Gender Females." *Signs, 10,* 27–42.

Blair, C., & Lanyon, R. (1981). "Exhibitionism: Etiology and Treatment." *Psychological Bulletin, 89,* 439–463.

Blakeslee, S. (1991, October 30). "Simplifying the Surgical Removal of Precancerous Cervical Lesions." *The New York Times,* p. B9.

Blanchard, R. (1993, March). "The She-Male Phenomena and the Concept of Partial Autogynephilia." *Journal of Sex and Marital Therapy, 19*(1), 69–76.

Blanchard, R., Clemmensen, L., & Steiner, B. (1986). "Phallometric Detection of Fetishistic Arousal in Heterosexual Male Cross-Dressers." *Journal of Sex Research, 22*(4), 452–462.

Blanchard, R., & Hucker, S. (1991). "Age, Transvestism, Bondage, and Concurrent Paraphilic Activities in 117 Fatal Cases of Autoerotic Asphyxia." *British Journal of Psychiatry, 159,* 371–377.

Blanchard, R., Steiner, B. W., Clemmensen, L. H., & Dickey, R. (1989). "Prediction of Regrets in Postoperative Transsexuals." *Canadian Journal of Psychiatry, 34*(1), 43–45.

Blatch, H. (Ed.). (1922). *Elizabeth Cady Stanton.* New York: Harper & Row.

Blechman, E. A. (1990). *Emotions and the Family: For Better or for Worse.* Hillsdale, NJ: Erlbaum.

Block, J. (1983). "Differential Premises Arising from Differential Socialization of the Sexes: Some Conjectures." *Child Development, 54,* 1335–1354.

Blum, D. (1997). *Sex on the Brain.* New York: Viking.

Blum, R., et al. (1992). "American Indian–Alaska Native Youth Health." *Journal of the American Medical Association, 267,* 1637.

Blumberg, M. L., & Lester, D. (1991). "High School and College Students' Attitude Toward Rape." *Adolescence, 26*(103), 727–729.

Blumenfeld, W., & Raymond, D. (1989). *Looking at Gay and Lesbian Life.* Boston: Beacon Press.

Blumstein, P., & Schwartz, P. (1983). *American Couples.* New York: McGraw-Hill.

Boakes, J. (1995). "False Memory Syndrome" [Commentary]. *The Lancet, 346*(8982), 1048–1050.

Boland, J., & Follingstad, D. (1987). "The Relationship Between Communication and Marital Satisfaction: A Review." *Journal of Sex and Marital Therapy, 13*(4), 286–313.

Boland, R. (1992). "Selected Legal Developments in Reproductive Health in 1991." *Family Planning Perspectives, 24*(4), 178–185.

Boles, A. J., & Curtis-Boles, H. (1986). "Black Couples and the Transition to Parenthood." *The American Journal of Social Psychiatry, 6*(1), 27–31.

Boles, J., & Elifson, E. W. (1994, July). "The Social Organization of Transvestite Prostitution and AIDS." *Social Science and Medicine, 39*(2), 85–93.

Bolin, A. (1997). "Transforming Transvestism and Transsexualism: Polarity, Politics, and Gender." In B. Bullough, V. L. Bullough, & J. Elias (Eds.), *Gender Blending.* New York: Prometheus Books.

Bollen, N., Camus, M., Staessen, C., Tournaye, H., Devroey, P., & VanSteirteghem, A. C. (1991). "The Incidence of Multiple Pregnancy After In Vitro Fertilization and Embryo Transfer, Gamete, or Zygote Intrafallopian Transfer." *Fertility and Sterility, 55*(2), 314–318.

Bonilla, L., & Porter, J. (1990). "A Comparison of Latino, Black, and Non-Hispanic White Attitudes Toward Homosexuality." *Hispanic Journal of Behavioral Sciences, 12,* 437–452.

Booth, A., & Dabbs, J. M., Jr. (1993, December). "Testosterone and Men's Marriages." *Social Forces, 72*(2), 463–477.

Borhek, M. (1988). "Helping Gay and Lesbian Adolescents and Their Families: A Mother's Perspective." *Journal of Adolescent Health Care, 9*(2), 123–128.

Borneman, E. (1983). "Progress in Empirical Research on Children's Sexuality." *SIECUS Report,* 1–5.

Borrello, G., & Thompson, B. (1990). "A Note Regarding the Validity of Lee's Typology of Love." *Journal of Psychology, 124*(6), 639–644.

Boston Women's Health Book Collective. (1996). *The New Our Bodies, Ourselves.* New York: Simon and Schuster.

Bostwick, H. (1860). *A Treatise on the Nature and Treatment of Seminal Disease, Impotency, and Other Kindred Afflictions.* (12th ed.). New York: Burgess, Stringer.

Boswell, J. (1980). *Christianity, Social Tolerance, and Homosexuality.* Chicago: University of Chicago Press.

Botcking, W. O. (1997). "Transgender Coming Out: Implications for the Clinical Management of Gender Dysphoria." In B. Bullough, V. L. Bullough, & J. Elias (Eds.), *Gender Blending.* New York: Prometheus Books.

Boulton, M., Hart, G., & Fitzpatrick, R. (1992). "The Sexual Behavior of Bisexual Men in Relation to HIV Transmission." *AIDS Care, 4*(2), 165–175.

Bouman, P. G. (1988). "Sex Reassignment Surgery in Male-to-Female Transsexuals." *Annals of Plastic Surgery, 21*(6), 526–531.

Bower, B. (1996, August 10). "From Exotic to Erotic: Roots of Sexual Orientation Found in Personality, Childhood Friendships." *Science News, 150,* 88–89.

Bowie, W., Hammerschlag, M., & Martin, D. (1994). "STDs in '94: The New CDC Guidelines." *Patient Care,* pp. 29–50.

Bowlby, J. (1969, 1973, 1980). *Attachment and Loss, Vols. I–III.* New York: Basic Books.

Bowman, C. G. (1993). "Street Harassment and the Informal Ghettoization of Women." *Harvard Law Review, 106*(3), 517–580.

Bownes, I. T., O'Gorman, E. C., & Sayers, A. (1991a). "Assault Characteristics and Post-Traumatic Stress Disorder in Rape Victims." *Acta Psychiatrica Scandinavica, 83,* 27–30.

Bownes, I. T., O'Gorman, E. C., & Sayers, A. (1991b). "Psychiatric Symptoms, Behavioral Responses and Post-Traumatic Stress Disorder in Rape Victims." Division of Criminological and Legal Psychology First Annual Conference. *Issues in Criminological and Legal Psychology, 1,* 25–33.

Bowser, B. P., Fullilove, M. T., & Fullilove, R. E. (1990). "African-American Youth and AIDS High-Risk Behavior: The Social Context and Barriers to Prevention." *Youth and Society, 22*(1), 54–66.

Bozett, F. W. (1987a). "Children of Gay Fathers." In F. W. Bozett (Ed.), *Gay and Lesbian Parents.* New York: Praeger.

Bozett, F. W. (Ed.). (1987b). *Gay and Lesbian Parents.* New York: Praeger.

Brady, E. C., Chrisler, J. C., Hosdale, D. C., & Osowiecki, D. M. (1991). "Date Rape: Expectations, Avoidance, Strategies, and Attitudes Toward Victims." *Journal of Social Psychology, 131*(3), 427–429.

Brand, H. J. (1989). "The Influence of Sex Differences on the Acceptance of Infertility." *Journal of Reproductive and Infant Psychology, 7*(2), 129–131.

Brandenburg, H., Jahoda, M. G., Pijpers, L., Reuss, A., Kleyer, W. J., & Wladmiroff, J. W. (1990). "Fetal Loss Rate After Chorionic Villus Sampling and Subsequent Amniocentesis." *American Journal of Medical Genetics, 35*(2), 178–180.

Braunthal, H. (1981). "Working with Transsexuals." *International Journal of Social Psychology, 27*(1), 3–12.

Braverman, P., & Strasburger, V. (1993). "Contraception." *Clinical Pediatrics, 32,* 725–735.

Braverman, P., & Strasburger, V. (1994, January). "Sexually Transmitted Diseases." *Clinical Pediatrics, 26*–37.

Brazelton, T. B. (1995, February 27). "Confusion Over Sleep Positions, SIDS." *San Francisco Chronicle.*

"Breast Cancer Studies Find Radiation Helps." (1997, October 2). *San Francisco Chronicle,* p. A-4.

Breast Cancer Survivors: Exercise Speeds Psychosocial Recovery. (1997). Reuters Health Information Services, Inc. Available from JAMA Women's Health Information Center: http://www.ama-assn.org/special/womh/newsllne/reuters/01222012.htm (Last visited 1/27/98).

Bremer, B. A., Moore, C. T., & Bildersee, E. F. (1991). "Do You Have to Call It 'Sexual Harassment' to Feel Harassed?" *College Student Journal, 25*(3), 258–268.

Brennan, K., & Shaver, P. R. (1995, March). "Dimensions of Adult Attachment, Affect Regulation, and Romantic Relationship Functioning." *Personality and Social Psychology Bulletin, 21*(3), 267–283.

Brenton, M. (1990, July/August). "The Importance of Touch." *Bridal Guide,* pp. 134, 136.

Breslow, N. (1989). "Sources of Confusion in the Study and Treatment of Sadomasochism." *Journal of Social Behavior and Personality, 4*(3), 263–274.

Breslow, N., Evans, L., & Langley, J. (1985). "On the Prevalence and Roles of Females in the Sadomasochistic Subculture: Report on an Empirical Investigation." *Archives of Sexual Behavior, 14,* 303–317.

Bridgeland, W. M., Duane, E. A., & Stewart, C. S. (1995, March). "Sexual Victimization Among Undergraduates." *College Student Journal 29*(1), 16–25.

Briere, J. (1992). "Methodological Issues in the Study of Sexual Abuse Effects." *Journal of Consulting and Clinical Psychology, 60*(2), 196–204.

Briere, J., & Runtz, M. (1989). "University Male's Sexual Interest in Children: Predicting Potential Indices of 'Pedophilia' in a Nonforensic Sample." *Child Abuse and Neglect, 13*(1), 65–75.

Brierly, H. (1979). *Transvestism.* New York: Pergamon Press.

Bringle, R., & Buunk, B. (1985). "Jealousy and Social Behavior: A Review of Personal, Relationship, and Situational Determinants." In P. Shaver (Ed.), *Review of Personality and Social Psychology, Vol. 6: Self, Situation, and Social Behavior.* Newbury Park, CA: Sage Publications.

Bringle, R., & Buunk, B. (1991). "Extradyadic Relationships and Sexual Jealousy." In K. McKinney & Susan Sprecher (Eds.), *Sexuality in Close Relationships.* Hillsdale, NJ: Erlbaum.

Brinton, L. A., et al. (1986). "Long-Term Use of Oral Contraceptives and Risk of Invasive Cervical Cancer." *International Journal of Cancer, 38,* 339ff.

Brochman, S. (1991, July 30). "Silent Victims: Bringing Male Rape Out of the Closet." *The Advocate, 582,* 38–43.

Brody, J. E. (1992). "Estrogen Is Found to Improve Mood, Not Just Menopause Symptoms." *The New York Times,* p. 141.

Brody, J. E. (1993, February 24). "Don't Panic. Before Worrying About All the Medical Studies, Take a Close Look at the Evidence." *The New York Times,* p. B7.

Brotman, B. (1992, July 19). "Why Abortion Rights Is a White Fight." *San Jose Mercury News,* p. A4.

Brown, G. R. (1995). "Cross-Dressing Men Often Lead Double Lives." *Menninger Letter,* pp. 4–5.

Brown, G. R., & Collier, Z. (1989). "Transvestites' Women Revisited: A Nonpatient Sample." *Archives of Sexual Behavior, 18,* 73–83.

Brown, J. (1995). "Treating Sexual Dysfunctions in Survivors of Sexual Abuse and Assault." In M. Hunter (Ed.), *Adult Survivors in Sexual Abuse: Treatment Innovations.* Thousand Oaks, CA: Sage Publications.

Brown, J. D., & Newcomer, S. F. (1991). "Television Viewing and Adolescents' Sexual Behavior." *Journal of Homosexuality, 21*(1–2), 77–91.

Brown, J. D., & Schulze, L. (1990). "The Effects of Race, Gender, and Fandom on Audience Interpretations of Madonna's Music Videos." *Journal of Communication, 40,* 88–102.

Brown, P. L. (1990, October 4). "Where to Put the TV Set?" *The New York Times,* p. 4.

Brown, S. L., Silverman, B. G., & Berg, W. A. (1997, November 22). "Rupture of Silicon-Gel Breast Implants: Causes, Sequelae, and Diagnosis." *Lancet, 350*(9090), 1531.

Browne, A., & Finkelhor, D. (1986). "Initial and Long-Term Effects: A Review of the Research." In D. Finkelhor (Ed.), *Sourcebook on Child Sexual Abuse.* Beverly Hills, CA: Sage Publications.

Brownmiller, S. (1975). *Against Our Will: Men, Women, and Rape.* New York: Simon & Schuster.

Brozan, N. (1986, June 21). "Early Detection Is Key in Breast Cancer." *The New York Times,* pp. 19, 20.

Bruce, K. E., Shrum, J. C., Trefethen, C., & Slovik, L. F. (1990). "Students' Attitudes About AIDS, Homosexuality, and Condoms." *AIDS Education and Prevention, 2*(3), 220–234.

Bruch, H. (1978). *The Golden Cage: The Enigma of Anorexia Nervosa.* Cambridge, MA: Harvard University Press.

Bryant, C. (1982). *Social Deviancy and Social Proscription.* New York: Human Sciences Press.

Bryant, Z. L., & Coleman, M. (1988). "The Black Family as Portrayed in Introductory Marriage and Family Textbooks." *Family Relations, 37*(3), 255–259.

Bryson, K., & Casper, L. M. "Household and Family Characteristics, March 1977." *Current Population Reports,* Series P-20–509.

Buchanan, P. (1993, February 15). "Is the GOP Falling into Humpty Dumpty Country?" *San Jose Mercury News,* p. A12.

Buchholz, E., & Gol, B. (1986). "More Than Playing House: A Developmental Perspective on the Strengths in Teenage Motherhood." *American Journal of Orthopsychology, 56*(3), 347–359.

Budiansky, S. (1988, April 18). "The New Rules of Reproduction." *U.S. News and World Report,* pp. 66–69.

Bullough, B., & Bullough, V. (1996). "Female Prostitution: Current Research and Changing Interpretations." *Annual Review of Sex Research, 7,* 158–180.

Bullough, B., Bullough, V. L., & Elias, J. (Eds.). (1997). *Gender Blending.* New York: Prometheus Books.

Bullough, V. (1976). *Sexual Variance in Society and History.* New York: John Wiley.

Bullough, V. (Ed.) (1979). *The Frontiers of Sex Research.* Buffalo, NY: Prometheus.

Bullough, V. (1991). "Transvestism: A Reexamination." *Journal of Psychology and Human Sexuality, 4*(2), 53–67.

Bullough, V. L., & Bullough, B. (1993). *Cross Dressing, Sex and Gender.* Philadelphia: University of Pennsylvania Press.

Bullough, V., & Weinberg, J. S. (1988). "Women Married to Transvestites: Problems and Adjustments." *Journal of Psychology and Human Sexuality, 1,* 83–104.

Burch, B. (1987). "Barriers to Intimacy: Conflicts Over Power, Dependency, and Nurturing in Lesbian Relationships." In Boston Lesbian Psychologies Collective (Ed.), *Lesbian Psychology: Explorations and Challenges.* Urbana, IL: University of Chicago Press.

Burcky, W., Reuterman, N., & Kopsky, S. (1988). "Dating Violence Among High School Students." *School Counselor, 35*(5), 353–358.

Bureau of Justice Statistics. (1997). *Criminal Victimization in the United States, 1994.* Washington, DC: U.S. Department of Justice.

Burke, M. (1995). "Lesbians and Sexual Child Abuse." In L. A. Fontes (Ed.), *Sexual Abuse in Nine North American Cultures: Treatment and Prevention.* Thousand Oaks, CA: Sage Publications.

Burling, K., Tarvydas, V. M., & Maki, D. R. (1994). "Human Sexuality and Disability: A Holistic Interpretation of Rehabilitation Counseling." *Journal of Applied Rehabilitation Counseling, 25*(1), 10–16.

Burnett, R., McGhee, P., & Clarke, D. (Eds.). *Accounting for Relationships: Explanation, Representation and Knowledge.* London: Methuen.

Burnham, M. (1992). "The Supreme Court Appointment Process and the Politics of Sex and Gender." In T. Morrison (Ed.), *Raceing Justice, En-Gendering Power.* New York: Pantheon.

Burns, A., Farrell, M., & Christie-Brown, J. (1990). "Clinical Features of Patients Attending a Gender-Identity Clinic." *British Journal of Psychiatry, 157,* 265–268.

Bursik, K. (1992). "Perceptions of Sexual Harassment in an Academic Context." *Sex Roles, 27*(7–8), 401–412.

Burt, M. (1980). "Cultural Myths and Supports for Rape." *Journal of Personality and Social Psychology, 38,* 217–230.

Buss, D. M. (1994). "The Strategies of Human Mating." *American Scientist, 82*(3), 238–249.

Butcher, A. H., Manning, D. T., & O'Neal, E. C. (1991). "HIV-Related Sexual Behaviors of College Students." *Journal of American College Health, 40*(3), 115–118.

Butter, I. H., & Kay, B. J. (1990). "Self-Certification in Law Midwives Organizations—A Vehicle for Professional Autonomy." *Social Science and Medicine, 30*(12), 1329–1339.

Butts, J. D. (1981). "Adolescent Sexuality and Teenage Pregnancy from a Black Perspective." In T. Ooms (Ed.), *Teenage Pregnancy in a Family Context.* Philadelphia: Temple University Press.

Butts, J. D. (1992). "The Relationship Between Sexual Addiction and Sexual Dysfunction." *Journal of Health Care for the Poor and Underserved, 3*(1), 128–135.

Buunk, B., & Hupka, R. (1987). "Cross-Cultural Differences in the Elicitation of Sexual Jealousy." *Journal of Sex Research, 23*(1), 12–22.

Buunk, B., & van Driel, B. (1989). *Variant Lifestyles and Relationships.* Newbury Park, CA: Sage Publications.

Buxton, R. (1991). "Dr. Ruth Westheimer: Upsetting the Normalcy of the Late-Night Talk Show." *Journal of Homosexuality, 21*(1–2), 139–153.

Byers, E. S., & Eno, R. J. (1991). "Predicting Men's Sexual Coercion and Aggression from Attitudes, Dating History, and Sexual Response." *Journal of Psychology and Human Sexuality, 4*(3), 55–70.

Byers, E. S., & Heinlein, L. (1989). "Predicting Initiations and Refusals of Sexual Activities in Married and Cohabiting Heterosexual Couples." *Journal of Sex Research, 26,* 210–231.

Bygdeman, M., Swahn, M. L., Gemzell-Danielsson, K., & Svalander, P. (1993). "Mode of Action of RU 486." *Annals of Medicine, 25*(1), 61–64.

Byrd, W., et al. (1990). "A Prospective Randomized Study of Pregnancy Rates Following Intrauterine and Intracervical Insemination Using Frozen Donor Sperm." *Fertility and Sterility, 53*(3), 521–527.

Byrne, D., Fisher, W. A., Lambreth, J., & Mitchell, H. E. (1974). "Evaluations of Erotica: Facts or Feelings?" *Journal of Personality and Social Psychology, 29,* 111–116.

Byrne, D., & Murnen, K. (1988). "Maintaining Love Relationships." In R. Sternberg & M. Barnes (Eds.), *The Psychology of Love.* New Haven, CT: Yale University Press.

Byrne, D., & Schulte, L. (1990). "Personality Dispositions as Mediators of Sexual Responses." *Annual Review of Sex Research, 1,* 93–117.

Byrne, D., et al. (1977). "Negative Sexual Attitudes and Contraception." In D. Byrne & L. A. Byrne (Eds.), *Exploring Human Sexuality.* New York: Harper & Row.

Cado, S., & Leitenberg, H. (1990). "Guilt Reactions to Sexual Fantasies During Intercourse." *Archives of Sexual Behavior, 19*(1), 49–63.

"Caffeine Intake and Delayed Conception." (1997). *Nutrition Research Newsletter, 16*(5), 58.

Cahoon, D., Edmonds, E. M., Spaulding, R. M., & Dickens, J. C. (1995, March). "A Comparison of the Opinions of Black and White Males and Females Concerning the Occurrence of Rape." *Journal of Social Behavior & Personality, 10*(1), 91–100.

Calderone, M. (1983a). "Fetal Erection and Its Message to Us." *SIECUS Report, 11*(5–6), 9–10.

Calderone, M. S. (1983b). "Childhood Sexuality: Approaching the Prevention of Sexual Disease." In G. Albee et al. (Eds.), *Promoting Sexual Responsibility and Preventing Sexual Problems.* Hanover, NH: University Press of New England.

Califia, P. (1979). "Lesbian Sexuality." *Journal of Homosexuality, 4,* 255–266.

California Medical Education and Research Foundation. (1992, February). "Health Tips; Anabolic Steroids and Steroid Alternatives." San Francisco: California Medical Association Newsletter.

Call, V., Sprecher, S., & Schwartz, P. (1995, August). "The Incidence and Frequency of Marital Sex in a National Sample." Journal of Marriage and the Family, 57(3), 639–652.

Callan, V. (1985). "Perceptions of Parents, the Voluntarily and Involuntarily Childless: A Multidimensional Scaling Analysis." Journal of Marriage and the Family, 47(4), 1045–1050.

Callendar, C., & Kochems, L. (1985). "Men and Not-Men: Male Gender-Mixing Statuses and Homosexuality." Special issue: Anthropology and Homosexual Behavior. Journal of Homosexuality, 11, 165–178.

Callendar, C., et al. (1983). "The North American Berdache." Current Anthropology, 24(4), 443–456.

Canadian Paediatric Society, Fetus and Newborn Committee. (1996). "Neonatal Circumcision Revisited." Canadian Medical Association Journal, 154(6), 769–780.

Canavan, M. M., Myers, W. J., & Higgs, D. C. (1992). "The Female Experience of Sibling Incest." Journal of Marital and Family Therapy, 18, 129–142.

Cantor, M. (1987). "Popular Culture and the Portrayal of Women: Content and Control." In M. Beth & M. M. Ferree (Eds.), Analyzing Gender. Newbury Park, CA: Sage Publications.

Cantor, M. (1991). "The American Family on Television: From Molly Goldberg to Bill Cosby." Journal of Comparative Family Studies, 22(2), 205–216.

Caplan, A. L. (1992). "Twenty Years After: The Legacy of the Tuskegee Syphilis Study. When Evil Intrudes." Hastings Center Report, 22(6), 29–32.

Carelli, R. (1998, February 24). "High Court Turns Down Megan's Law Challenges." San Francisco Chronicle, p. A-1.

Carey, R. F., Herman, W. A., Retta, S. M., Rinaldi, J. E., Herman, B. A., & Athey, T. W. (1992). "Effectiveness of Latex Condoms as a Barrier to Human Immunodeficiency Virus-Sized Particles Under Conditions of Simulated Use." Sexually Transmitted Diseases, 19(4), 230–234.

Carl, D. (1986). "Acquired Immune Deficiency Syndrome: A Preliminary Examination of the Effects on Gay Couples and Coupling." Journal of Marital and Family Therapy, 12(3), 241–247.

Carlson, R. G., & Siegal, H. A. (1991). "The Crack Life: An Ethnographic Overview of Crack Use and Sexual Behavior Among African-Americans in a Midwest Metropolitan City." Journal of Psychoactive Drugs, 23(1), 11–20.

Carmen, A., & Moody, H. (1985). Working Women: The Subterranean World of Street Prostitution. New York: Harper & Row.

Carnes, P. (1983). Out of Shadows. Minneapolis, MN: CompCare Publications.

Carnes, P. (1991). "Progress in Sex Addiction: An Addiction Perspective." In R. T. Francoeur (Ed.), Taking Sides: Clashing Views on Controversial Issues in Human Sexuality (3rd ed.). Guilford, CT: Dushkin.

Carr, P. (1992, February 16). "Sexual Harassment Pushes Its Way into the Schoolyard." San Jose Mercury News, pp. 1L, 8L.

Carrera, M. (1980). "Sexual Learning in the Elementary School." In E. Roberts (Ed.), Childhood Sexual Learning: The Unwritten Curriculum. Cambridge, MA: Ballinger.

Carrera, M. (1981). Sex: The Facts, the Acts, and Your Feelings. New York: Crown.

Carrier, J. (1992). "Miguel: Sexual Life History of a Gay Mexican American." In G. Herdt (Ed.), Gay Culture in America: Essays from the Field. Boston: Beacon Press.

Carrier, J., Joseph, C., Nguyen, B., & Su, S. (1992). "Vietnamese American Sexual Behaviors and the HIV Infection." Journal of Sex Research, 29(4), 547–560.

Carroll, J. (1990, March 5). "Tracing the Causes of Infertility." San Francisco Chronicle, pp. 3ff.

Carroll, J., Volk, K. D., & Hyde, J. J. (1985). "Differences in Males and Females in Motives for Engaging in Sexual Intercourse." Archives of Sexual Behavior, 14, 131–139.

Carroll, J. L., & Wolpe, P. R. (1996). Sexuality and Gender in Society. New York: HarperCollins

Carter, B., & McGoldrick, M. (Eds.). (1989). The Changing Family Life Cycle (2nd ed.). Boston: Allyn & Bacon.

Carter, D. B. (Ed.). (1987). Current Conceptions of Sex Roles and Sex Typing. New York: Praeger.

Cary, A. (1992, April 18). "Big Fans on Campus." TV Guide, pp. 26–31.

Cass, V. C. (1983). "Homosexual Identity: A Concept in Need of Definition." Journal of Homosexuality, 9(2–3), 105–126.

Cassell, C. (1984). Swept Away. New York: Simon & Schuster.

Cassidy, L., & Hurrell, R. M. (1995). "The Influence of Victim's Attire on Adolescents' Judgments of Date Rape." Adolescence, 30(118), 319–404.

Castillo, C. O., & Leer, J. H. (1993). "Ambiguous Stimuli: Sex in the Eye of the Beholder." Archives of Sexual Behavior, 22, 131–143.

Catchpole, T. (1992, November). "A Short History of Political Tricks." Playboy, pp. 86–87, 169.

Cate, R. M., & Lloyd, S. A. (1992). Courtship. Newbury Park, CA: Sage Publications.

Cates, J. A., & Markley, J. (1992). "Demographic, Clinical, and Personality Variables Associated with Male Prostitution by Choice." Adolescence, 27, 695–706.

Cates, W., Chesney, M. A., & Cohen, M. S. (1997, December). "Primary HIV Infection—A Public Health Opportunity." American Journal of Public Health, 87(12), 1928–1930.

Cates, W. J., & Stone, K. M. (1992). "Family Planning, Sexually Transmitted Diseases and Contraceptive Choices: A Literature Update. Part I." Family Planning Perspectives, 24(2), 75–84.

Cautela, J. E. (1986). "Behavioral Analysis of a Fetish: First Interview." Journal of Behavior Therapy and Experimental Psychiatry, 17(3), 161–165.

CDC. See Centers for Disease Control or Centers for Disease Control and Prevention.

Ceci, S., Loftus, E., Leichtman, M., & Bruck, M. (1994). "The Role of Source Misattributions in the Creation of False Beliefs in Preschoolers." International Journal of Clinical and Experimental Hypnosis, 42, 304–320.

Center for Population Options. (1992). Teenage Pregnancy and Too-Early Childbearing: Public Costs, Personal Consequences.

Centers for Disease Control. (1982). "Update on Acquired Immune Deficiency Syndrome (AIDS)—United States." Morbidity and Mortality Weekly Report, 31(37).

Centers for Disease Control and Prevention. (1993). "Update: Barrier Protection Against HIV Infection and Other Sexually Transmitted Diseases." Morbidity and Mortality Weekly Report, 42(30), 589–596.

Centers for Disease Control and Prevention. (1995a). National Youth Risk Behavior Survey. Washington, DC.

Centers for Disease Control and Prevention. (1995b). "Rates of Cesarean Delivery—United States, 1993." Morbidity and Mortality Weekly Report, 44, 303–307.

Centers for Disease Control and Prevention, Division of STD/HIV Prevention. (1995c). *Sexually Transmitted Disease Surveillance Report, 1994.*

Centers for Disease Control and Prevention. (1996a). "AIDS Associated with Injection Drug Use: United States, 1995." *Morbidity and Mortality Weekly Report, 45,* 392–398.

Centers for Disease Control and Prevention. (1996b). Sexually Transmitted Disease Surveillance Report, 1995. Available: http://wonder.cdc.gov/wonder/STD/Title3600.html

Centers for Disease Control and Prevention. (1996c). "Surveillance Report: U.S. AIDS Cases Reported Through December 1995." *HIV/AIDS Surveillance Report, 7*(2), 1–10.

Centers for Disease Control and Prevention. (1997a, December 5). "Abortion Surveillance: Preliminary Analysis, United States, 1995." *Morbidity and Mortality Weekly Report, 46*(48).

Centers for Disease Control and Prevention. (1997b, October 17). "Current Trends—IUD Safety: Report of a Nationwide Physician Survey." *Morbidity and Mortality Weekly Report, 46*(41).

Centers for Disease Control and Prevention. (1997c). Facts About Hepatitis A and C. Available: http://www.cdc.gov/od/oc/media/fact/hepac.htm (Last visited 2/19/98).

Centers for Disease Control and Prevention. (1997d). HIV/AIDS and College Students. Available: gopher://cdc.org:72/00/11pathfinders/collpath.txt (Last visited 2/28/98).

Centers for Disease Control and Prevention. (1997e). *HIV/AIDS Surveillance Report, 1997, 9*(2), 1–44.

Centers for Disease Control and Prevention, Division of STD Prevention. (1997f, September). Sexually Transmitted Disease Surveillance Report, 1996. Available: http://wonder.cdc.gov/wonder/STD/STDD007.PCW.html (Last visited 2/19/98).

Centers for Disease Control and Prevention. (1997g). "Surveillance Report: U.S. AIDS Cases Reported Through Mid-June, 1997." *HIV/AIDS Surveillance Report, 9*(1), 1–10.

Centers for Disease Control and Prevention. (1997h). "Transmission of HIV Possibly Associated with Exposure of Mucous Membrane to Contaminated Blood." *Morbidity and Mortality Weekly Report, 46*(27), 620–624.

Centers for Disease Control and Prevention. (1997i). "Update: Perinatally Acquired HIV/AIDS, United States, 1997." *Morbidity and Mortality Weekly Report, 46*(46), 1086–1093.

Centers for Disease Control and Prevention. (1997j, May). *Vital and Health Statistics: Fertility, Family Planning, and Women's Health: New Data from the 1995 National Survey of Family Growth.* Series 23, No. 19. Hyattsville, MD: U.S. Department of Health and Human Services.

Centers for Disease Control and Prevention. (1998a). CDC AIDS Information. Available: http://www.cdc.gov/nchstp/hiv_aids/hivinfo/vfax/ (Last visited 4/11/98).

Centers for Disease Control and Prevention. (1998b). "1998 Guidelines for Treatment of STDs." *Morbidity and Mortality Weekly Report, 47* (No. RR-1).

Centers for Disease Control and Prevention, American Society for Reproductive Medicine (ASRM), & RESOLVE. (1997, December). *1995 Assisted Reproductive Success Rates.* Hyattsville, MD: U.S. Department of Health and Human Services.

Cervical Cancer Kills 25,000 Latin American Women Each Year. (1997, April 18). Available: http://www.medscape.com/other/PAHO/1997/apr/CervicalCancerKillsWomen.html (Last visited 9/21/97).

Challice, J. (1992, May). "AIDS Research." *PAACNotes,* 121–124.

Chapman, A. (1988). "Male-Female Relations: How the Past Affects the Present." In H. McAdoo (Ed.), *Black Families* (2nd ed.). Beverly Hills, CA: Sage Publications.

Chappel, S., & Talbot, D. (1990). *Burning Desires: Sex in America.* New York: Signet.

Charney, D., & Russell, R. (1994). "An Overview of Sexual Harassment." *American Journal of Psychiatry, 151,* 10–17.

Chiasson, M. A., Stoneburner, R. L., & Joseph, S. C. (1990). "Human Immunodeficiency Virus Transmission Through Artificial Insemination." *Journal of Acquired Immune Deficiency Syndromes, 3*(1), 69–72.

Chirgwin, K., DeHovitz, J. A., Dillon, D. S., & McCormack, W. M. (1991). "HIV Infection, Genital Ulcer Disease, and Crack Cocaine Use Among Patients Attending a Clinic for Sexually Transmitted Diseases." *American Journal of Public Health, 81*(12), 1576–1579.

Choi, K. H., Rickman, R., & Catania, J. A. (1994). "What Heterosexuals Believe About Condoms." *New England Journal of Medicine, 331,* 406–497.

Chong, J. M. (1990). "Social Assessment of Transsexuals Who Apply for Sex Reassignment Therapy." *Social Work in Health Care, 14*(3), 87–105.

Chrisman, R., & Allen, R. (Eds.). (1992). *Court of Appeal: The Black Community Speaks Out on the Racial and Sexual Politics of Clarence Thomas vs. Anita Hill.* New York: Ballantine.

Christian-Smith, L. K. (1990). *Becoming a Woman Through Romance.* New York: Routledge.

Christopher, F., & Cate, R. (1984). "Factors Involved in Premarital Decision-Making." *Journal of Sex Research, 20,* 363–376.

Christopher, F. S., & Frandsen, M. M. (1990). "Strategies of Influence in Sex and Dating." *Journal of Social and Personal Relationships, 7,* 89–105.

Chu, S. Y., Buehler, J. W., Oxtoby, M. J., & Kilbourne, B. W. (1991). "Impact of the Human Immunodeficiency Virus Epidemic on Mortality in Children, United States." *Pediatrics, 87*(6), 806–810.

Chu, S. Y., Peterman, T. A., Doll, L. S., Buehler, J. W., & Curran, J. W. (1992). "AIDS in Bisexual Men in the United States: Epidemiology and Transmission to Women." *American Journal of Public Health, 82*(2), 220–224.

Chung, W., & Choi, H. (1990). "Erotic Erection Versus Nocturnal Erection." *The Journal of Urology, 143,* 294–297.

Clanton, G., & Smith, L. (1977). *Jealousy.* Englewood Cliffs, NJ: Prentice-Hall.

Clapper, R. L., & Lipsitt, L. P. (1991). "A Retrospective Study of Risk-Taking and Alcohol-Mediated Unprotected Intercourse." *Journal of Substance Abuse, 3*(1), 91–96.

Clark, D. (1992). "Cagney & Lacey: Feminist Strategies of Detection." In M. E. Brown (Ed.), *Television and Women's Culture: The Politics of the Popular.* Newbury Park, CA: Sage Publications.

Clift, E. (1990, July 2). "The Right Wing's Cultural Warrior." *Newsweek,* p. 51.

Cochran, J. K., & Beeghley, L. (1991). "The Influence of Religion on Attitudes Toward Nonmarital Sexuality: A Preliminary Assessment of Reference Group Theory." *Journal of the Scientific Study of Religion, 30*(1), 45–63.

Cochran, S. D., Mays, V. M., & Leung, L. (1991). "Sexual Practices of Heterosexual Asian-American Young Adults: Implications for Risk of HIV Infection." *Archives of Sexual Behavior, 20*(4), 381–394.

Cogen, R., & Steinman, W. (1990). "Sexual Function and Practice in Elderly Men of Lower Socioeconomic Status." *Journal of Family Practice, 31*(2), 162–166.

Cohen, B. (1992, September 14). "Discrimination: The Limits of the Law." *Newsweek*, pp. 35–40.

Cohen, J. (1993). "Early AZT Takes a Pounding in French-British 'Concorde' Trial." *Science, 260*(5105), 157.

Colapinto, J. (1997, December 11). "The True Story of John/Joan." *Rolling Stone, 775*, 54–72, 92–97.

Colditz, G. A., et al. (1993). "Family History, Age, and Risk of Breast Cancer—Prospective Data from the Nurses Health Study." *Journal of the American Medical Association, 270*(3), 338–343.

Cole, E., & Rothblum, E. (1990). "Commentary on 'Sexuality and the Midlife Woman.'" Special Issue: Women at Midlife and Beyond. *Psychology of Women Quarterly, 14*(4), 509–512.

Cole, W. (1992). "Incest Perpetrators: Their Assessment and Treatment." *Psychiatric Clinics of North America, 15*(3), 689–701.

Coleman, E., Colgan, P., & Gooren, L. (1992). "Male Cross-Gender Behavior in Myanmar (Burma): A Description of the Acault." *Archives of Sexual Behavior, 21*(3), 313–321.

Coleman, E., Rosser, B. R., & Strapko, N. (1992). "Sexual and Intimacy Dysfunction Among Homosexual Men and Women." *Psychiatric Medicine, 10*(2), 257–271.

Coleman, M., & Ganong, L. (1991). "Remarriage and Stepfamily Research in the 1980s: Increased Interest in an Old Form." In A. Booth (Ed.), *Contemporary Families: Looking Forward, Looking Back.* Minneapolis, MN: National Council on Family Relations.

Collaborative Group on Hormonal Factors in Breast Cancer. (1996, June 22). "Breast Cancer and Hormonal Contraceptives: Collaborative Reanalysis of Individual Data on 53,297 Women With Breast Cancer and 100,239 Women Without Breast Cancer from 54 Epidemiological Studies." *Lancet, 347*, 1713–1727.

Collier, M. J. (1991). "Conflict Competence Within African, Mexican, and Anglo American Friendships." In S. Ting-Toomey & Felipe Korzenny (Eds.), *Cross-Cultural Interpersonal Communication.* Newbury Park, CA: Sage Publications.

Collins, P. H. (1991). "The Meaning of Motherhood in Black Culture." In R. Staples (Ed.), *The Black Family* (4th ed.). Belmont, CA: Wadsworth.

"Community Study Traces Bulimia's Origins." (1997, July 5). *Science News, 152*, 7.

Conant, J., & Wingert, P. (1987, August 24). "You'd Better Sit Down, Kids." *Newsweek*, p. 58.

Condry, J., & Condry, S. (1976). "The Development of Sex Differences: A Study of the Eye of the Beholder." *Child Development, 47*(4), 812–819.

Condy, S., Templer, D. E., Brown, R., & Veaco, L. (1987). Parameters of Sexual Contact of Boys with Women." *Archives of Sexual Behavior, 16*(5), 379–394.

Connor, S. (1994, August 28). "Downward Spiral in Quality of Sperm." *San Francisco Chronicle.*

"Contraceptive Couldn't Pass FDS Inspection." (1995, January 21). *San Jose Mercury News.*

Cook, A., et al. (1982). "Changes in Attitudes Toward Parenting Among College Women: 1972 and 1979 Samples." *Family Relations, 31*, 109–113.

Cooper, A. (1985). "Sexual Enhancement Programs: An Examination of Their Current Status and Directions for Future Research." *Archives of Sexual Behavior, 21*(4), 387–404.

Cooper, A., & Stoltenberg, C. D. (1987). "Comparison of a Sexual Enhancement and a Communication Training Program on Sexual and Marital Satisfaction." *Journal of Counseling Psychology, 34*, 309–314.

Cooper, A. J., Swaminath, S., Baxter, D., & Poulin, C. (1990). "A Female Sex Offender with Multiple Paraphilias." *Canadian Journal of Psychiatry, 35*(4), 334–337.

Copenhaver, S., & Gauerholz, E. (1991). "Sexual Victimization Among Sorority Women: Exploring the Link Between Sexual Violence and Institutional Practices." *Sex Roles, 24*, 31–41.

Corby, N. H., Wolitski, R. J., Thornton-Johnson, S., & Tanner, W. M. (1991). "AIDS Knowledge, Perception of Risk, and Behaviors Among Female Sex Partners of Injection Drug Users." *AIDS Education and Prevention, 3*(4), 353–366.

Corea, G. (1985). *The Mother Machine: Reproductive Technology from Artificial Insemination to Artificial Wombs.* New York: Harper & Row.

Corley, M. D. (1994). "The Question of Research into Sexual Addiction." *Contemporary Sexuality, 28*(8), 8.

Cornett, C., & Hudson, R. (1985). "Psychoanalytic Theory and Affirmation of the Gay Lifestyle: Are They Necessarily Antithetical?" *Journal of Homosexuality, 12*(1), 97–108.

Cornog, M. (1986). "Naming Sexual Body Parts: Preliminary Patterns and Implications." *Journal of Sex Research, 22*(3), 399–408.

Cortese, A. (1989). "Subcultural Differences in Human Sexuality: Race, Ethnicity, and Social Class." In K. McKinney & S. Sprecher (Eds.), *Human Sexuality: The Societal and Interpersonal Context.* Norwood, NJ: Ablex.

Cosby, B. (1968, December). "The Regular Way." *Playboy*, pp. 288–289.

Cosgray, R. E., Hanna, V., Fawley, R., & Money, M. (1991). "Death from Auto-Erotic Asphyxiation in Long-Term Psychiatric Setting." *Perspectives in Psychiatric Care, 27*(1), 21–24.

Courtright, J., & Baran, S. (1980). "The Acquisition of Sexual Information by Young People." *Journalism Quarterly, 57*(1), 107–114.

Couzinet, B., et al. (1986, December 18). "Termination of Early Pregnancy by the Progesterone Antagonist RU 486 (Mifepristone)." *New England Journal of Medicine, 315*(25), 1565–1670.

Cowan, G., & Campbell, R. R. (1994, September). "Racism and Sexism in Interracial Pornography: A Content Analysis." *Psychology of Women Quarterly, 18*(3), 323–328.

Cowley, G. (1991, December 9). "Sleeping with the Enemy." *Newsweek*, pp. 58–59.

Cowley, G. (1996, September 16). "Attention Aging Men." *Newsweek*, pp. 68–75.

Cowley, G. (1996, June 3). "The Biology of Beauty." *Newsweek*, pp. 61–64.

Cowley, G. (1997, May 19). "Gender Limbo." *Newsweek*, pp. 64–66.

Cowley, G. (1997, October 6). "Bitter Pill." *Newsweek*, p. 57.

Cowley, G., & Underwood, A. (1996, December 9). "Scanning the Skeleton." *Newsweek*, p. 70.

Cramer, D. (1986). "Gay Parents and Their Children: A Review of Research and Practical Implications." *Journal of Counseling and Development, 64*, 504–507.

Cramer, D., & Roach, A. (1987). "Coming Out to Mom and Dad: A Study of Gay Males and Their Relationships with Their Parents." *Journal of Homosexuality, 14*(1–2), 77–88.

Cramer, D. W., Harlow, B. L., Titus-Ernstoff, L., Bohlke, R., Welch, W. R., & Greenberg, E. R. (1998, January 10). "Over-the-Counter Analgesics and Risk of Ovarian Cancer." *Lancet, 351*(9096), 104.

Cramer, R. E., Dragna, M., Cupp, R. G., & Stewart, P. (1991). "Contrast Effects in the Evaluation of the Male Sex Role." *Sex Roles, 24*(3–4), 181–193.

Creti, L., & Libman, E. (1989). "Cognition and Sexual Expression in the Aging." *Journal of Sex and Marital Therapy, 15*(2), 83–101.

Crews, F. (1994, November 17). "Revenge of the Repressed." *The New York Review of Books,* pp. 54–60.

Crisp, Q. (1982). *The Naked Civil Servant.* New York: New American Library.

Cross, S. E., & Markus, H. R. (1993). "Gender in Thought, Belief, and Action: A Cognitive Approach." In A. E. Beall & R. J. Sternberg (Eds.), *The Psychology of Gender.* New York: Guilford Press.

Crowe, M. (1995, June). "Couple Therapy and Sexual Dysfunction." *Interpersonal View of Psychiatry, 7*(2), 195–204.

Cruikshank, M. (1992). *The Gay and Lesbian Liberation Movement.* New York: Routledge.

Crum, C. P., et al. (1984). "Human Papillomavirus Type 16 and Early Cervical Neoplasm." *New England Journal of Medicine, 310,* 880–883.

Cuber, J. (1969). "Adultery: Reality vs. Stereotype." In G. Newbeck (Ed.), *Extramarital Relations.* Englewood Cliffs, NJ: Prentice-Hall.

Cullins, V. E. (1994). "Comparison of Adolescent and Adult Experiences with Norplant Levonorgestrel Contraceptive Implants." *Obstetrics and Gynecology, 83,* 1026–1032.

Cummings, J. (1987, June 8). "Disabled Model Defies Sexual Stereotypes." *The New York Times,* p. 17.

Cupach, W. R., & Comstock, J. (1990). "Satisfaction with Sexual Communication in Marriage." *Journal of Social and Personal Relationships, 7,* 179–186.

Cupach, W. R., & Metts, S. (1991). "Sexuality and Communication in Close Relationships." In K. McKinney & S. Sprecher (Eds.), *Sexuality in Close Relationships.* Hillsdale, NJ: Erlbaum.

Curie-Cohen, M., et al. (1979). "Current Practice of Artificial Insemination by Donor in the United States." *New England Journal of Medicine, 300*(11), 585–590.

Curtis, T. (1993, April). "The Female Condom." *Self,* 138–141; 176–179.

Cushner, I. M. (1986). "Reproductive Technologies: New Choices, New Hopes, New Dilemmas." *Family Planning Perspectives, 18*(3), 129–132.

Dabbs, J. M., Jr. (1992). "Testosterone Measurement in Social and Clinical Psychology." *Journal of Social and Clinical Psychology, 11*(3), 209–211.

Dabbs, J. M., Jr., & Morris, R. (1990). "Testosterone, Social Class, and Antisocial Behavior in a Sample of 4,462 Men." *Psychological Science 1*(3), 209–211.

Dailey, D. (Ed.). (1988). *The Sexually Unusual.* New York: Harrington Press.

Dancey, C. (1992). "The Relationship of Instrumentality and Expressivity to Sexual Orientation in Women." *Journal of Homosexuality, 23*(4), 73–82.

Darling, C. A., & Davidson, J. K. (1986). "Enhancing Relationships: Understanding the Feminine Mystique of Pretending Orgasm." *Journal of Sex and Marital Therapy, 12,* 182–196.

Darling, C. A., Davidson, J. K., & Conway-Welch, C. (1990). "Female Ejaculation: Perceived Origins, the Grafenberg Spot/Area, and Sexual Responsiveness." *Archives of Sexual Behavior, 19,* 29–47.

Darling, C. A., Davidson, J. K., & Cox, R. P. (1991). "Female Sexual Response and the Timing of Partner Orgasm." *Journal of Sex and Marital Therapy, 17*(1), 3–21.

Darling, C. A., Davidson, J. K., & Jennings, D. A. (1991). "The Female Sexual Response Revisited: Understanding the Multiorgasmic Experience in Women." *Archives of Sexual Behavior, 20,* 527–540.

Darling-Fisher, C., & Tiedje, L. (1990). "The Impact of Maternal Employment Characteristics on Fathers' Participation in Child Care." *Family Relations, 39*(1), 20–26.

Darney, P. (1994). "Hormonal Implants: Contraception for a New Century." *American Journal of Obstetrics and Gynecology, 170,* 1536–1543.

Darrow, W. W., & Siegel, K. (1990). "Preventive Health Behavior and STDs." In K. K. Holmes et al. (Eds.), *Sexually Transmitted Diseases* (2nd ed.). New York: McGraw-Hill.

Davenport, W. (1987). "An Anthropological Approach." In J. Geer & W. O'Donohue (Eds.), *Theories of Human Sexuality.* New York: Plenum Press.

Davey, R. T., Goldschmidt, R. H., & Sande, M. A. (1996). "Anti-HIV Therapy in 1996." *Patient Care 30*(9).

Davidson, J. K., & Darling, C. A. (1986). "The Impact of College-Level Sex Education on Sexual Knowledge, Attitudes, and Practices: The Knowledge/Sexual Experimentation Myth Revisited." *Deviant Behavior, 7,* 13–30.

Davidson, J. K., Darling, C. A., & Conway-Welch, C. (1989). "The Role of the Grafenberg Spot and Female Ejaculation in the Female Orgasmic Response: An Empirical Analysis." *Journal of Sex and Marital Therapy, 15*(2), 102–120.

Davies, K. A. (1997, June). "Voluntary Exposure to Pornography and Men's Attitudes Towards Feminism and Rape." *Journal of Sex Research, 34*(2), 131–138.

Davis, C. M., & Bauserman, R. (1993). "Exposure to Sexually Explicit Materials: An Attitude Change Perspective." *Annual Review of Sex Research, 4,* 121–129.

Davis, R. C., et al. (1991). "Supportive and Unsupportive Responses of Others to Rape Victims: Effects on Concurrent Victim Adjustment." *American Journal of Community Psychology, 19*(3), 443–451.

Davis, S. (1990). "Men as Success Objects and Women as Sex Objects: A Study of Personal Advertisements." *Sex Roles, 23,* 43–50.

Davis, S. M., & Harris, M. B. (1982). "Sexual Knowledge, Sexual Interest, and Sources of Sexual Information of Rural and Urban Adolescents from Three Cultures." *Adolescence, 17*(66), 471–492.

Davis-Joseph, B., Tiefer, L., & Melman, A. (1995). "Accuracy of the Initial History and Physical Examination to Establish the Etiology of Erectile Dysfunction." *Urology, 45*(3), 498–502.

Davison, G., & Neale, J. (1993). *Abnormal Psychology* (6th ed.). New York: John Wiley.

Davitz, J. R. (1969). *The Language of Emotion.* New York: Academic Press.

Dawson, D. (1986). "The Effects of Sex Education on Adolescent Behavior." *Family Planning Perspectives, 18*(4), 162ff.

Day, D. (1995). *The Needle Exchange Activist's Handy Guide to 1995 National AIDS Data.* Princeton, NJ: Dogwood Center.

De Armand, C. (1983). "Let's Listen to What the Kids are Saying." *SIECUS Report,* 3–4.

"Death Rates for Minority Infants Were Underestimated, Study Says." (1992, January 8). *The New York Times,* p. A10.

Deaux, K., & Lewis, L. L. (1983). "Components of Gender Role Stereotypes." *Psychological Documents, 13* (Ms. No. 2583), 25.

De Cecco, J. P. (Ed.). (1988). *Gay Relationships.* New York: Haworth Press.

De Cecco, J. P., & Elia, J. P. (1993). "A Critique and Synthesis of Biological Essentialism and Social Constructionist Views of Sexuality and Gender. Introduction." *Journal of Homosexuality, 24*(3–4), 1–26.

De Cecco, J. P., & Elia, J. P. (1993). "If You Seduce a Straight Person, Can You Make Them Gay—Issues in Biological Essentialism Versus Social Constructionism in Gay and Lesbian Identities. Preface." *Journal of Homosexuality, 24*(3–4), R23–R24.

De Cecco, J. P., & Shively, M. (1983). "From Sexual Identity to Sexual Relationships: A Conceptual Shift." *Journal of Homosexuality, 9*(2–3), 1–26.

DeGenova, M. K. (1997). *Families in Cultural Context: Strengths and Challenges in Diversity.* Mountain View, CA: Mayfield.

Degler, C. (1980). *At Odds.* New York: Oxford University Press.

De Groot, J. M., Kennedy, S. H., Rodin, G., & McVey, S. (1992). "Correlates of Sexual Abuse in Women with Anorexia Nervosa and Bulimia Nervosa." *Canadian Journal of Psychiatry, 37*(7), 516–581.

De La Chappelle, A. (1983). "Sex Chromosome Abnormalities." In A. F. Emery & D. L. Rimarin (Eds.), *Principles and Practices of Medical Genetics.* New York: Churchill Livingstone.

Delaney, J., Lupton, M. J., & Toth, E. (1988). *The Curse: A Cultural History of Menstruation.* New York: Dutton.

Del Carmen, R. (1990). "Assessment of Asian-Americans for Family Therapy." In F. Serafica, A. Schwebel, R. Russell, P. Isaac, & L. Myers (Eds.), *Mental Health of Ethnic Minorities.* New York: Praeger.

Demarest J., & Gardner, J. (1992). "The Representation of Women's Roles in Women's Magazines Over the Past 30 Years." *Journal of Psychology, 126*(4), 357–369.

DeMaris, A., & Rao, K. V. (1992, February). "Premarital Cohabitation and Subsequent Marital Stability in the United States: A Reassessment." *Journal of Marriage and the Family, 54*(1), 178–190.

de Mauro, D. (1990). "Sexuality Education 1990." *SIECUS Report, 18*(2), 1–9.

Demb, J. M. (1991). "Abortion in Inner-City Adolescents: What the Girls Say." *Family Systems Medicine, 9,* 93–102.

Demb, J. M. (1992). "Are Gay Men Artistic? A Review of the Literature." *Journal of Homosexuality, 23*(4), 83–92.

Demian, A. S. B. (1994). "Relationship Characteristics of American Gay and Lesbian Couples: Findings from a National Survey." *Journal of Gay and Lesbian Social Services, 1*(2), 101–117.

D'Emilio, J., & Freedman, E. (1988). *Intimate Matters: A History of Sexuality in America.* New York: Harper & Row.

Denniston, G. C. (1992, July). "Unnecessary Circumcision." *Female Patient, 17,* 13–14.

Denny, D. (1997). "Transgender: Some Historical, Cross-Cultural, and Contemporary Models and Methods of Coping and Treatment." In B. Bullough, V. L. Bullough, & J. Elias (Eds.), *Gender Blending.* New York: Prometheus Books.

Derlega, V. J., Metts, S., Petronio, S., & Margulis, S. (1993). *Self-Disclosure.* Newbury Park, CA: Sage Publications.

DES Action. (1980). *You May Be a DES Daughter.* San Francisco: DES Action/California.

DeSpelder, L. A., & Strickland, A. (1999). *The Last Dance: Encountering Death and Dying* (6th ed.). Mountain View, CA: Mayfield.

"Detailed U.S. AIDS Report Offers Hints, Warnings." (1993, June 11). *Baltimore Sun,* p. 3A.

de Vincenzi, I. (1994). "A Longitudinal Study of Human Immuno-Deficiency Virus Transmission by Heterosexual Partners." *New England Journal of Medicine, 331*(6), 341.

de Vincenzi, I., et al. (1992). "Comparison of Female to Male and Male to Female Transmission of HIV in 563 Stable Couples." *British Medical Journal, 304*(6830), 809–813.

Dewaraja, R., & Money, J. (1986). "Transcultural Sexology: Formicophilia, a Newly Named Paraphilia in a Young Buddhist Male." *Journal of Sex and Marital Therapy, 12*(2), 139–145.

De Young, M. (1988). "The Indignant Page: Techniques of Neutralization in the Publications of Pedophile Organizations." *Child Abuse and Neglect, 12*(4), 583–591.

De Young, M. (1989). "The World According to NAMBLA." *Journal of Sociology and Social Welfare, 16*(1), 111–126.

Diamond, M. (1997). "Sexual Identity and Sexual Orientation in Children with Traumatized or Ambiguous Genitalia." *Journal of Sex Research, 32*(2), 199–212.

Diaz, E. (1990). "Public Policy, Women, and HIV Disease." *SIECUS Report, 19,* 4–5.

Di Blasio, F. A., & Benda, B. B. (1992). "Gender Differences in Theories of Adolescent Sexual Activity." *Sex Roles, 27*(5–6), 221–236.

Dicker, & Leighton. (1994).

Dickerson, J. (1994, November 21). "Censoring Cyberspace." *Time,* pp. 102–104.

Dick-Read, G. (1972). *Childbirth Without Fear* (4th ed.). New York: Harper & Row.

Di Mauro, Diane. (1995). "Executive Summary. Sexuality Research in the United States: An Assessment of the Social and Behavioral Sciences." New York: Social Science Research Council. Available: http://www.indiana.edu/~kinsey/SSRC/sexreas2.html

Dimen, M. (1984). "Politically Correct? Politically Incorrect?" In C. S. Vance (Ed.), *Pleasure and Danger: Exploring Female Sexuality.* New York: Routledge & Kegan Paul.

Dingman, D. J. (1996). "Clients, Not Prostitutes, Seen as Central to AIDS Spread." *AIDS Weekly Plus,* pp. 5–7.

Dion, K. K., Berscheid, E., & Walster, E. (1972). "What Is Beautiful Is Good." *Journal of Personality and Social Psychology, 24,* 285–290.

Diop, C. A. (1987). *Precolonial Black Africa.* Trenton, NJ: Africa World.

"Disrupting the Assembly Line." (1996, December 2). *Newsweek.*

Dittmar, H., & Bates, B. (1987). "Humanistic Approaches to the Understanding and Treatment of Anorexia Nervosa." *Journal of Adolescence, 10,* 57–69.

Djerrasi, C. (1979). *The Politics of Contraception.* New York: Norton.

Dodd, R. Y. (1992). "The Risk of Transfusion-Transmitted Infection." *New England Journal of Medicine, 327*(6), 419–421.

Doering, C. H., Brodie, H. K. H., Kraemer, H. C., Becker, H. B., & Hamburg, D. A. (1974). "Plasma Testosterone Levels and Psychological Measurements in Men Over a 2-Month Period." In R. C. Friedman, R. M. Richart, & R. L. Vande Wiele (Eds.), *Sex Differences in Behavior.* New York: John Wiley.

Does Female Sterilization Affect Menstrual Patterns? (1996, June). *Family Health International.* Available: http://www.ama-assn.org/special/contra/support/educate/fpfaq71.htm (Last visited 1/20/98).

Doheny, K. (1998, January 19). "Genital Herpes Epidemic Grows." *Los Angeles Times,* pp. S-1, S-6.

Doll, L. S., et al. (1991). "Homosexual Men Who Engage in High-Risk Sexual Behavior. A Multicenter Comparison." *Sexually Transmitted Diseases, 18*(3), 170–175.

Donat, P. L., & D'Emilio, J. (1992). "A Feminist Redefinition of Rape and Sexual Assault: Historical Foundations and Change." *Journal of Social Issues, 48*(1), 9–22.

Donohue, J., & Gebhard, P. (1995, March). "The Kinsey Institute/Indiana University Report of Sexuality and Spinal Cord Injury." *Sexuality and Disability, 13*(1), 7–85.

Donovan, P. (1986). "New Reproductive Technologies: Some Legal Dilemmas." *Family Planning Perspectives, 18,* 57ff.

Dowell, K. A., LoPresto, C. T., & Sherman, M. F. (1991). "When Are AIDS Patients to Blame for Their Disease? Effects of Patients' Sexual Orientation and Mode of Transmission." *Psychological Reports, 69*(1), 211–219.

Downey, J., Elkin, E. J., Erhard, A. A., Meyer, B. H. F., Bell, J. J., & Morishima, K. J. (1991). "Cognitive Ability and Everyday Functioning in Women with Turner Syndrome." *Journal of Learning Disabilities, 24*(1), 32–39.

Drugger, K. (1988). "Social Location and Gender-Role Attitudes: A Comparison of Black and White Women." *Gender and Society, 2*(4), 425–448.

Dryfoos, J. (1985). "What the United States Can Learn About Prevention of Teenage Pregnancy from Other Developed Countries." *SIECUS Report, 14*(2), 1–7.

Duncan, D. F. (1991). "Who Does Have a Test for AIDS?" *Psychological Reports, 68*(1), 138.

Duncan, D. F., & Donnelly, J. W. (1991). "Pornography as a Source of Sex Information for Students at a Private Northeastern University." *Psychological Reports, 68*(3, Pt. 1), 781–782.

Duncan, D. F., & Nicholson, T. (1991). "Pornography as a Source of Sex Information for Students at a Southeastern State University." *Psychological Reports, 68*(3, Pt. 1), 802.

Dunkle, J. H., & Francis, P. L. (1990). "The Role of Facial Masculinity/Femininity in the Attribution of Homosexuality." *Sex Roles, 23*(3–4), 157–167.

Durant, R., Pendergast, R., & Seymore, C. (1990). "Contraceptive Behavior Among Sexually Active Hispanic Adolescents." *Journal of Adolescent Health, 11*(6), 490–496.

Dwyer, S. M., & Myers, S. (1990). "Sex Offender Treatment: A Six-Month to Ten-Year Follow-Up Study." *Annals of Sex Research, 3*(3), 305–318.

Eagly, A. H. (1987). *Sex Differences in Social Behavior: A Social-Role Interpretation.* Hillsdale, NJ: Erlbaum.

Eakins, P. S. (1989). "Free-Standing Birth Centers in California." *Journal of Reproductive Medicine, 34*(12), 960–970.

Earl, D., & David, D. (1994). "Depo-Provera: An Injectable Contraceptive." *American Family Physician, 49*(4), 891--894.

Earls, C. M., & David, H. (1990). "Early Family and Sexual Experiences of Male and Female Prostitutes." *Canada's Mental Health, 38,* 7–11.

Eber, M., & Wetli, C. (1985). "A Case of Autoerotic Asphyxia." *Psychotherapy, 22*(3), 662–668.

Ecstasy Effects. (1996, May 31). Available: http://www.columbia.edu/cu/healthwise/0925.html (Last visited 1/29/98).

Edelman, R. (1986). "Adaptive Training for Existing Male Transsexual Gender Role: A Case History." *Journal of Sex Research, 22*(4), 514–519.

"Effects of Caffeine Consumption on Delayed Conception." (1996). *Journal of American Dietetic Association, 96*(6), 619.

Effects of Marijuana on Libido and Fertility. (1995, October 5). Available: http://www.columbia.edu/cu/healthwise/0682.html (Last visited 1/29/98).

Eichler, M. (1989). "Reflections on Motherhood, Apple Pie, the New Reproductive Technologies and the Role of Sociologists in Society." *Society-Société, 13*(1), 1–5.

Elders, M. J., & Kilgore, B. (1997). The Dreaded 'M' Word. Available: http://www.nervemag.com/Elders/mword/mword.shtml (Last visited 10/4/97).

Eldh, J. (1993). "Construction of a Neovagina with Preservation of the Glans Penis as a Clitoris in Male Transsexuals." *Plastic and Reconstructive Surgery, 91*(5), 895–903.

Elias, C., & Heise, L. (1993). "The Development of Microbicides: A New Method of HIV Prevention for Women." New York: The Population Council.

Elifson, K. W., Boles, J., Posey, E., & Sweat, M. (1993). "Male Transvestite Prostitutes and HIV Risk." *American Journal of Public Health, 83*(2), 260–262.

Ellard, G. A., et al. (1996). "Smoking During Pregnancy: The Dose Dependence of Birthweight Deficits." *British Journal of Obstetrics and Gynaecology, 103*(8), 806–813.

Ellenberg, M. (1980). "Vaginal Lubrication in Diabetic Women." *Medical Aspects of Human Sexuality, 14,* 66

Elliott, D. M., & Briere, J. (1992). "Sexual Abuse Trauma Among Professional Women: Validating the Trauma Symptom Checklist (TSC-40)." *Child Abuse and Neglect, 16*(3), 391ff.

Ellis, H. (1900). *Studies in the Psychology of Sex.* Philadelphia: F. A. Davis.

Ellis, H. (1938). *Psychology of Sex: A Manual for Students.* New York: Harcourt Brace Jovanovich.

Ellison, C. (1985). "Intimacy-Based Sex Therapy." In W. Eicher & G. Kockott (Eds.), *Sexology.* New York: Springer-Verlag.

Emanuele, M. A., Tentler, J., Emanuele, N. V., & Kelley, M. R. (1991). "In Vivo Effects of Acute ETOH on Rat Alpha-Luteinizing and Beta-Luteinizing Hormone Gene Expression." *Alcohol, 8*(5), 345–348.

Emergency Birth Control. (1997). Santa Cruz, CA: ETR Associates.

Emery, A. F., & Rimarin, D. L. (Eds.). (1983). *Principles and Practices of Medical Genetics.* New York: Churchill Livingstone.

Emmanuel, N. P., Lydiard, R. B., & Ballenger, J. C. (1991). "Fluoxetine Treatment of Voyeurism." *American Journal of Psychiatry, 148,* 950.

Ephron, N. (1975). *Crazy Salad.* New York: Alfred Knopf.

Erikson, E. (1986). *Vital Improvements in Old Age: The Experience of Old Age in Our Time.* New York: Norton.

Erickson, P. I., & Rapkin, A. I. (1991). "Unwanted Sexual Experiences Among Middle and High School Youth." *Journal of Adolescent Youth, 12,* 319–325.

Ernster, V. L. (1975). "American Menstrual Slang." *Sex Roles, 5,* 1–13.

Espín, O. M. (1984). "Cultural and Historical Influences on Sexuality in Hispanic/Latin Women: Implications for Psychotherapy." In C. Vance (Ed.), *Pleasure and Danger: Exploring Female Sexuality.* New York: Routledge & Kegan Paul.

Essex, M., & Kanki, P. J. (1988, October). "The Origins of the AIDS Virus." *Scientific American, 259*(4), 64–71.

Ewell, M. (1993, January 9). "Anti-Gay Push in the Works." *San Jose Mercury News,* p. 3B.

Faderman, L. (1991). *Odd Girls and Twilight Lovers.* New York: Penguin Books.

Fagin, D. (1995, February 1). "DES Moms, Gay or Bisexual Daughters: Study Links Exposure to Sexual Orientation." *San Francisco Chronicle.*

Fagot, B., & Leinbach, M. (1987). "Socialization of Sex Roles Within the Family." In D. B. Carter (Ed.), *Current Conceptions of Sex Roles and Sex Typing.* New York: Praeger.

Falbo, T., & Peplau, L. A. (1980). "Power Strategies in Intimate Relationships." *Journal of Personality and Social Psychology, 38,* 618–628.

Falicov, C. (1982). "Mexican Families." In M. McGoldrick et al. (Eds.), *Ethnicity and Family Therapy.* New York: Guilford Press.

Falk, K. (1984). *How to Write a Romance and Get It Published.* New York: New American Library.

Faludi, S. (1991). *Backlash: The Undeclared War Against American Women.* New York: Crown.

Fang, R. H., Chen, C. F., & Imperato-McGinley, M. S. (1992). "A New Method for Clitoroplasty in Male-to-Female Sex Reassignment Surgery." *Plastic and Reconstructive Surgery, 89*(4), 179–182.

Farley, C. J. (1997, July 21). "Walalooza." *Time,* pp. 60–64.

Farnsworth, C. H. (1992, January 14). "Homosexual Is Granted Refugee Status in Canada." *The New York Times,* p. A5.

Fathalla, M. F. (1992). "Reproductive Health in the World: Two Decades of Progress and the Challenge Ahead." In World Health Organization, *Reproductive Health.* Biennial Report 1990–1991. Geneva, Switzerland: World Health Organization.

Fausto-Sterling, A. (1985). *Myths of Gender: Biological Theories About Women and Men.* New York: Basic Books.

Fay, R., Turner, C., Klassen, A., & Gagnon, J. (1989). "Prevalence and Patterns of Same-Gender Sexual Contact Among Men." *Science, 243*(4889), 338–348.

Fedora, O., Reddon, J. R., Morrison, J. W., & Fedora, S. T. (1992). "Sadism and Other Paraphilias in Normal Controls and Aggressive and Nonaggressive Sex Offenders." *Archives of Sexual Behavior, 21*(1), 1–15.

Fedora, O., Reddon, J. R., & Yendall, L. T. (1986). "Stimuli Eliciting Sexual Arousal in Genital Exhibitionists: A Possible Clinical Application." *Archives of Sexual Behavior, 15*(5), 417–427.

Fehr, B. (1988). "Prototype Analysis of the Concepts of Love and Commitment." *Journal of Personality and Social Psychology, 55*(4), 557–579.

Fein, R. (1980). "Research on Fathering." In A. Skolnick & J. Skolnick (Eds.), *The Family in Transition.* Boston: Little, Brown.

Feinberg, L. (1996). *Transgender Warriors: Making History from Joan of Arc to Rupaul.* Boston: Beacon Press.

Feirstein, B. (1982). *Real Men Don't Eat Quiche.* New York: Pocket Books.

Feitl, L. F. (1990, April). "My Body, My Self." *Sesame Street Magazine Parents' Guide,* pp. 20–25.

Feldman, H., Goldstein, I., Hatzichristou, D., Krane, R., & McKinlay, J. (1994). "Impotence and Its Medical and Psychosocial Correlates: Results of the Massachusetts Male Aging Study." *Journal of Urology, 151,* 54–61.

Female Condom: What Do We Know? (1996, June). *Family Health International.* Available: http://www.ama-assn.org/special/contra/support/educate/fpfaq22.htm (Last visited 1/20/98).

Feray, J. C., & Herzer, M. (1990). "Homosexual Studies and Politics in the 19th Century: Karl Maria Kertbeny." *Journal of Homosexuality, 19*(1), 23–47.

Ferree, M. M. (1991). "Beyond Separate Spheres: Feminism and Family Research." In A. Booth (Ed.), *Contemporary Families: Looking Forward, Looking Back.* Minneapolis, MN: National Council on Family Relations.

Field, M. A. (1993). "Abortion Law Today." *Journal of Legal Medicine, 14*(1), 3–24.

Findlay, H. (1992). "Freud, Fetishism, and the Lesbian Dildo Debates." *Feminist Studies, 18*(3), 563–579.

Fine, M. (1988). "Sexuality, Schooling, and Adolescent Females: The Missing Discourse of Desire." *Harvard Education Review, 58,* 29–53.

Finkelhor, D. (1984). *Child Sexual Abuse: New Theory and Research.* New York: Free Press.

Finkelhor, D. (1986a). "Prevention Approaches to Child Sexual Abuse." In M. Lystad (Ed.), *Violence in the Home: Interdisciplinary Perspectives.* New York: Brunner/Mazel.

Finkelhor, D. (1986b). "Sexual Abuse: Beyond the Family Systems Approach." *Journal of Psychotherapy and the Family, 2,* 53–65.

Finkelhor, D. (1990). "Early and Long-Term Effects of Child Sexual Abuse: An Update." *Professional Psychology: Research and Practice, 21,* 325–330.

Finkelhor, D. (1993). "Epidemiological Factors in the Clinical Identification of Child Sexual Abuse." *Child Abuse and Neglect, 17,* 67–70.

Finkelhor, D. (1994). "The International Epidemiology of Child Sexual Abuse." *Child Abuse and Neglect, 18,* 409–417.

Finkelhor, D., & Baron, L. (1986). "High-Risk Children." In D. Finkelhor (Ed.), *Sourcebook on Child Sexual Abuse.* Beverly Hills, CA: Sage Publications.

Finkelhor, D., Hotaling, G., Lewis, I. A., & Smith C. (1990). *Missing, Abducted, Runaway, and Throwaway Children in America.* Washington, DC: U.S. Department of Justice.

Finkelhor, D., Williams, L. M., & Burns, B. (1988). *Sexual Abuse in Day Care: A National Study.* Durham, NH: University of New Hampshire, Family Research Laboratory.

Finkelhor, D., & Yllo, K. (1985). *License to Rape: The Sexual Abuse of Wives.* New York: Holt Rinehart.

Finkelhor, D., et al. (1990). "Sexual Abuse in a National Survey of Adult Men and Women." *Child Abuse and Neglect, 14*(1), 19–28.

Firstman, R., & Talan, J. (1997). *The Death of Innocents.* New York: Bantam.

Fisch, H., Goluboff, E. T., Olson, J. H., Feldshuh, J., Broder, S. J., & Barad, D. H. (1996, May). "Worldwide Variations in Sperm Count." *Fertility & Sterility, 65*(5), 1009–1014.

Fisch, H., Ikeguchi, E. F., & Goluboff, E. T. (1996, December). "Worldwide Variations in Sperm Counts." *Urology 48*(6), 909–911.

Fischer, A. R., & Good, G. E. (1994). "Gender, Self, and Others: Perceptions of the Campus Environment." *Journal of Counseling Psychology, 41*(3), 343–355.

Fischhoff, B. (1992). "Giving Advice: Decision Theory Perspectives on Sexual Assault." *American Psychologist, 47,* 577–588.

Fischl, M. A., Dickinson, D. M., Scott, G. B., Klimas, N., Fletcher, M. A., & Parks, W. (1987). "Evaluation of Heterosexual Partners, Children, and Household Contacts of Adults with AIDS." *JAMA: Journal of the American Medical Association 257*(5), 640–644.

Fischl, M. A., Dickinson, D. M., Segal, Flannagan, & Rodriguez. (1987). "The Efficacy of Azidothymidine (AZT) in the Treatment of Patients with AIDS and AIDS-Related Complex." *Journal of Sex Research, 317,* 185–188.

Fishel, E. (1992, September). "Raising Sexually Healthy Kids." *Parents,* pp. 110–116.

Fisher, W. (1983, March). "Why Teenagers Get Pregnant." *Psychology Today,* 70–71.

Fisher, W. (1986). "A Psychological Approach to Human Sexuality." In D. Byrne & K. K. Kelley (Eds.), *Alternative Approaches to Human Sexuality.* Hillsdale, NJ: Erlbaum.

Fisher, W., Byrne, D., White, L., & Kelley, K. (1988). "Erotophobia-Erotophilia as a Dimension of Personality." *Journal of Sex Research, 25*(1), 123–151.

Fisher, W., & Gray, J. (1988). "Erotophobia-Erotophilia and Sexual Behavior During Pregnancy and Postpartum." *Journal of Sex Research, 25*(3), 379–396.

Fisher, W. A., & Grenier, G. (1994). "Violent Pornography, Anti-woman Thoughts, and Antiwoman Acts: In Search of Reliable Effects." *Journal of Sex Research, 31*(1), 97–113.

Fitzgerald, L. F., & Ormerod, A. J. (1991). "Perceptions of Sexual Harassment: The Influence of Gender and Academic Context." *Psychology of Women Quarterly, 15*(2), 281–294.

Flaks, D. K., Ficher, I., Masterpasqua, F., & Joseph, G. (1995). "Lesbians Choosing Motherhood: A Comparative Study of Lesbians and Heterosexual Parents and Their Children." *Developmental Psychology, 31*(1), 105–114.

Flanigan, B. J. (1990). "The Social Context of Alcohol Consumption Prior to Female Sexual Intercourse." *Journal of Alcohol and Drug Education, 36*(1), 97–113.

Flor-Henry, P., Lang, R. A., Koles, Z. J., & Frenzel, R. R. (1991). "Quantitative EEG Studies of Pedophilia." *International Journal of Psychophysiology, 10*(3), 253–258.

Foa, E. B., & Riggs, D. S. (1995, April). "Posttraumatic Stress Disorder Following Assault: Theoretical Considerations and Empirical Findings." *Current Directions in Psychological Science, 4*(2), 61–65.

Foa, U. G., Anderson, B., Converse, J., & Urbansky, W. A. (1987). "Gender-Related Sexual Attitudes: Some Cross-Cultural Similarities and Differences." *Sex Roles, 16*(19–20), 511–519.

Focus on the Family. (1993, February 11). "In Defense of a Little Virginity." *Good Times,* Santa Cruz, CA, pp. 30–31.

Foley, L. A., Evancic, C., Karnik, K., & King, J. (1995, February). "Date Rape: Effects of Race of Assailant and Victim and Gender of Subjects on Perceptions." *Journal of Black Psychology, 21*(1), 6–18.

Follingstad, D. R., Rutledge, L. L., Berg, B. J., & Hause, E. S. (1990). "The Role of Emotional Abuse in Physically Abusive Relationships." *Journal of Family Violence, 5*(2), 107–120.

Fonow, M. M., Richardson, L., & Wemmerus, V. A. (1992). "Feminist Rape Education: Does It Work?" *Gender and Society, 6*(1), 108–121.

Ford, C., & Beach, F. (1951). *Patterns of Sexual Behavior.* New York: Harper & Row.

Fordyce, E. J., Blum, S., Balanon, A., & Stoneburner, R. L. (1991). "A Method for Estimating HIV Transmission Rates Among Female Sex Partners of Male Intravenous Drug Users." *American Journal of Epidemiology, 133*(6), 590–598.

Forgey, D. G. (1975). "The Institution of Berdache Among the North American Plains Indians." *Journal of Sex Research, 11,* 1–15.

Forrest, B. (1991). "Women, HIV, and Mucosal Immunity." *The Lancet, 337,* 835–837.

Forrest, J. (1986). "The End of IUD Marketing in the United States: What Does It Mean for American Women?" *Family Planning Perspectives, 18*(2), 52–57.

Forrest, J. (1987). "Unintended Pregnancy Among American Women." *Family Planning Perspectives, 19*(2), 76–77.

Forrest, J. D., & Silverman, J. (1989). "What Public School Teachers Teach About Preventing Pregnancy, AIDS and Sexually Transmitted Diseases." *Family Planning Perspectives, 21,* 65–72.

Foucault, M. (1980). *The History of Sexuality: An Introduction. Vol. 1.* New York: Pantheon Books.

Fowler, O. S. (1878). *Amativeness: or, Evils and the Remedies of Excessive Perverted Sexuality.* New York: Fowler & Wells.

Fox, B., & Joyce, C. (1991). "Americans Compete for Control Over Sex." *New Scientist, 12,* 23.

Fox, S. I. (1987). *Human Physiology.* Dubuque, Iowa: W. C. Brown.

Frable, D. E., & Bem, S. L. (1985). "If You Are Gender Schematic, All Members of the Opposite Sex Look Alike." *Journal of Personality and Social Psychology, 49*(2), 459–468.

Frable, D. E. S., Johnson, A. E., & Kellman, H. (1997, June). "Seeing Masculine Men, Sexy Women, and Gender Differences: Exposure to Pornography and Cognitive Constructions of Gender." *Journal of Personality, 65*(2), 311–355.

Franco, E. L. (1991). "The Sexually Transmitted Disease Model for Cervical Cancer: Incoherent Epidemiologic Findings and the Role of Misclassification of Human Papillomavirus Infection." *Epidemiology, 2*(2), 98–106.

Frank, M., Poindexter, A. A., Cornin, C. M., Cox, C. A., & Bateman, L. (1993, September). "One-Year Experience with Subdermal Contraceptive Implants in the United States." *Contraception, 48*(3), 229–243.

Franklin, D. L. (1988). "The Impact of Early Childbearing on Development Outcomes: The Case of Black Adolescent Parenting." *Family Relations, 37,* 268–274.

Franz, W., & Readon, D. (1992). "Differential Impact of Abortion on Adolescents and Adults." *Adolescence, 27*(105), 161–172.

Fraser, L. (1990, February). "Nasty Girls." *Mother Jones,* pp. 32–35, 48–50.

Frayser, S. G. (1994). "Anthropology: Influence of Culture on Sex." In V. Bullough & B. B. Bullough (Eds.), *Human Sexuality: An Encyclopedia.* New York: Garland.

Frazier, P. A. (1991). "Self-Blame as a Mediator of Postrape Depressive Symptoms." *Journal of Social and Clinical Psychology, 10*(1), 47–57.

Frazier, P. A., Cochran, C. C., & Olson, A. M. (1995, March). "Social Science Research on Lay Definitions of Sexual Harassment." *Journal of Social Issues, 51*(1), 21–37.

Freeman, E. (1980). "Adolescent Contraceptive Use." *American Journal of Public Health, 70,* 790–797.

Freeman, E. W. (1996). Can Antidepressants Be Used to Tame Psychological Symptoms of PMS? Medscape, Inc. Available: http://www.medscape.com

Freeman, E. W., Rickels, K., Sondheimer, S. J., & Polansky, M. (1990, July 8). "Ineffectiveness of Progesterone Suppository Treatment for Premenstrual Syndrome." *JAMA: Journal of the American Medical Association, 264*(3), 349–353.

French, J. P., & Raven, B. (1959). "The Bases of Social Power." In I. Cartwright (Ed.), *Studies in Social Power.* Ann Arbor, MI: University of Michigan Press.

Freud, S. (1938). "Three Contributions to the Theory of Sex." A. A. Brill (Ed.), *The Basic Writings of Sigmund Freud.* New York: Modern Library.

Freund, K. (1988). "Courtship Disorder: Is This Hypothesis Valid?" In R. A. Prentky et al. (Eds.), *Human Sexual Aggression: Current Perspectives.* New York: New York Academy of Science.

Freund, K., & Blanchard, R. (1993). "Erotic Target Location Errors in Male Gender Dysphorics, Paedophiles, and Fetishists." *British Journal of Psychiatry, 162,* 558–563.

Freund, K., & Kuban, W. (1993). "Toward a Testable Developmental Model of Pedophilia: The Development of Erotic Age Preference." *Child Abuse and Neglect, 17*(2), 315–324.

Freund, K., Scher, H., & Hucker, S. (1983). "The Courtship Disorders." *Archives of Sexual Behavior, 12,* 369–379.

Freund, K., & Watson, R. J. (1993). "Gender Identity Disorder and Courtship Disorder." *Archives of Sexual Behavior, 22*(1), 13–21.

Freund, K., Watson, R., & Dickey, R. (1990). "Does Sexual Abuse in Childhood Cause Pedophilia: An Exploratory Study." *Archives of Sexual Behavior, 19*(6), 557–568.

Freund, K., Watson, R., Dickey, R., & Rienzo, D. (1991). "Erotic Gender Differentiation in Pedophilia." *Archives of Sexual Behavior, 20*(6), 555–566.

Freund, K., Watson, R., & Rienzo, D. (1988). "The Value of Self-Reports in the Study of Voyeurism and Exhibitionism." *Annals of Sex Research, 1*(2), 243–262.

Freund, M., Lee, N., & Leonard, T. L. (1991). "Sexual Behavior of Clients with Street Prostitutes in Camden, NJ." *Journal of Sex Research, 28*(4), 579–591.

Freund, M., Leonard, T. L., & Lee, N. (1989). "Sexual Behavior of Resident Street Prostitutes with Their Clients in Camden, New Jersey." *Journal of Sex Research, 26*, 460–478.

Friday, N. *Men in Love.* (1980). New York: Delacorte Press.

Friedman, J. (1992, August/September). "Cross-Cultural Perspectives on Sexuality Education." *SIECUS Report, 20*(6), 5–11.

Friedman, R. C. (1991). "Couple Therapy with Gay Couples." *Psychiatric Annals, 21*(8), 485–490.

Frisbie, W. P., Biegler, M., de Turk, P., Forbes, D., & Pullum, S. G. (1997). "Racial and Ethnic Differences in Determinants of Intrauterine Growth Retardation and Other Compromised Birth Outcomes." *American Journal of Public Health, 87*(12), 1977–1983.

Fritz, G. S., Stoll, K., & Wagner, N. N. (1981). "A Comparison of Males and Females Who Were Sexually Molested as Children." *Journal of Sex and Marital Therapy, 7*, 54–58.

Fromm, E. (1974). *The Art of Loving.* New York: Perennial Library.

Frost, P. (1992, December 7). "Artichoke." *The New Yorker,* p. 66.

Fuller, A., Jr., et al. (1980). "Toxic-Shock Syndrome." *New England Journal of Medicine, 303*(15), 880.

Furlow, F. B., & Thornhill, R. (1996, January/February). "The Orgasm Wars." *Psychology Today,* pp. 42–46.

Furstenberg, F. K., Jr., & Cherlin, A. (1991). *Divided Families.* Cambridge, MA: Harvard University Press.

Furstenberg, F. K., Jr., Lincoln, R., & Menken, J. (Eds.). (1981). *Teenage Sexuality, Pregnancy, and Childbearing.* Philadelphia: University of Pennsylvania Press.

Furstenberg, F. K., Jr., & Nord, C. (1985). "Parenting Apart: Patterns in Childrearing After Marital Disruption." *Journal of Marriage and the Family, 47*(4), 893–904.

Furstenberg, F. K., Jr., & Spanier, G. (1987). *Recycling the Family: Remarriage After Divorce* (rev. ed.). Newbury Park, CA: Sage Publications.

Furstenberg, F. K., Jr., et al. (1985). "Sex Education and Sexual Experience Among Adolescents." *American Journal of Public Health, 75*(11), 1331–1332.

Gagnon, J. (1977). *Human Sexualities.* New York: Scott, Foresman.

Gagnon, J. (1985). "Attitudes and Responses of Parents to Pre-Adolescent Masturbation." *Archives of Sexual Behavior, 14*(5), 451–466.

Gagnon, J. (1986). "Sexual Scripts: Permanence and Change." *Archives of Sexual Behavior, 15*(2), 97–120.

Gagnon, J., & Simon, W. (1973a). "Perspectives on the Sexual Scene." In J. Gagnon & W. Simon (Eds.), *The Sexual Scene* (2nd ed.). New Brunswick, NJ: Transaction Books.

Gagnon, J., & Simon, W. (1973b). *Sexual Conduct: The Social Sources of Human Sexuality.* Chicago: Aldine.

Gagnon, J., & Simon, W. (1987). "The Sexual Scripting of Oral Genital Contacts." *Archives of Sexual Behavior, 16*(1), 1–25.

Gaines, J. (1990, October 7). "A Scandal of Artificial Insemination." *The Good Health Magazine/The New York Times Magazine,* pp. 23ff.

Gallup, G. H., Jr., & Newport, F. (1990, June 4). "Parenthood: A Nearly Universal Desire." *San Francisco Chronicle,* p. 3.

Ganong, L., & Coleman, M. (1987). "Sex, Sex Roles, and Family Love." *Journal of Genetic Psychology, 148*, 45–52.

Gao, G. (1991). "Stability of Romantic Relationships in China and the United States." In S. Ting-Toomey & F. Korzenny (Eds.), *Cross-Cultural Interpersonal Communication.* Newbury Park, CA: Sage Publications.

Garber, L. (1991). *Vested Interests.* Boston: Little Brown.

Garner, D. M., Garfinkel, P. E., Schwartz, D., & Thompson, M. (1980). "Cultural Expectations of Thinness in Women." *Psychological Reports, 11*, 483–491.

Garnets, L., et al. (1990). "Violence and Victimization of Lesbians and Gay Men: Mental Health Consequences." *Journal of Interpersonal Violence, 5*, 366–383.

Garrison, J. E. (1989). "Sexual Dysfunction in the Elderly: Causes and Effects." *Journal of Psychotherapy and the Family, 5*(1–2), 149–162.

Gartner, L. M. (1997). "Breastfeeding and the Use of Human Milk." *Pediatrics, 100*(6), 1035ff.

Garza-Leal, J., & Landron, F. (1991). "Autoerotic Asphyxial Death Initially Misinterpreted as Suicide and Review of the Literature." *Journal of Forensic Science, 36*(6), 1753–1759.

Gay, P. (1986). *The Bourgeois Experience: The Tender Passion.* New York: Oxford University Press.

"Gay Teens More Likely to Take Risks, Study Finds." (1998, May 5). *San Francisco Chronicle,* p. A-3.

Gebhard, P. (1976a). "Fetishism and Sadomasochism." In P. Gebhard (Ed.), *Sex Research: Studies from the Kinsey Institute.* New York: Oxford University Press.

Gebhard, P. (Ed.). (1976b). *Sex Research: Studies from the Kinsey Institute.* New York: Oxford University Press.

Gebhard, P., Pomeroy, W. B., & Christensen, C. V. (1965). "Situational Factors Affecting Human Sexual Behavior." In F. Beach (Ed.), *Sex and Behavior.* New York: John Wiley.

Gecas, V., & Seff, M. (1991). "Families and Adolescents." In A. Booth (Ed.), *Contemporary Families: Looking Forward, Looking Back.* Minneapolis, MN: National Council on Family Relations.

Geist, C. (1980). "Violence, Passion, and Sexual Racism: The Plantation Novel." *Southern Quarterly, 18*(2), 60–72.

Gelles, R. J., & Conte, J. R. (1991). "Domestic Violence and Sexual Abuse of Children: A Review of Research in the Eighties." In A. Booth (Ed.), *Contemporary Families: Looking Forward, Looking Back.* Minneapolis, MN: National Council on Family Relations.

Gelven, P. L. (1996). "Fatal Disseminated Herpes Simplex in Pregnancy with Maternal and Neonatal Death." *Southern Medical Journal, 89*(7), 732ff.

Genevie, L., & Margolies, E. (1987). *The Motherhood Report: How Women Feel About Being Mothers.* New York: Macmillan.

Gibbs, N. (1993, May 4). "How Should We Teach Our Children About Sex?" *Time,* p. 65.

Gidyez, C. A., & Koss, M. P. (1990). "A Comparison of Group and Individual Sexual Assault Victims." *Psychology of Women Quarterly, 14*(3), 325–342.

Giles, D. (1994). "Summer Resorts: Black Resort Towns Are Enjoying a Renaissance Thanks to Buppies and Their Families." *Black Enterprise, 25*, pp. 90–91

Gillen, K., & Muncher, S. J. 1995. "Sex Differences in the Perceived Casual Structure of Date Rape: A Preliminary Report." *Aggressive Behavior, 21*(2), 101–112.

Gilligan, C. (1982). *In a Different Voice*. Cambridge, MA: Harvard University Press.

Ginsburg, F. (1989). *Contested Lives: The Abortion Debate in an American Community*. Berkeley: University of California Press.

Glascock, J., & LaRose, R. (1993, June). "Dial-a-Porn Recordings: The Role of the Female Participant in Male Sexual Fantasies." *Journal of Broadcasting and Electronic Media, 37*(3), 313–324.

Glasier, A., Thong, K. J., Dewar, M., Mackie, M., & Baird, D. T. (1992). "Mifepristone (RU-486) Compared with High-Dose Estrogen and Progesterone for Emergency Postcoital Contraception." *New England Journal of Medicine, 327*(15), 1041–1044.

Glass, R. H., & Ericsson, R. J. (1982). *Getting Pregnant in the 1980s*. Berkeley: University of California Press.

Glaus, K. O. (1988). "Alcoholism, Chemical Dependency and the Lesbian Client." Special Issue: Lesbianism: Affirming Nontraditional Roles. *Women and Therapy, 8*(1–2), 131–144.

Glazer-Malbin, N. (Ed.). (1975). *Old Family/New Family*. New York: Van Nostrand.

Glenn, J. (1981). "Penis Enlargement." *Medical Aspects of Human Sexuality, 15*(3), 23.

Glenn, N. (1991). "Quantitative Research on Marital Quality in the 1980s: A Critical Review." In A. Booth (Ed.), *Contemporary Families: Looking Forward, Looking Back*. Minneapolis, MN: National Council on Family Relations.

Glenn, N., & McLanahan, S. (1982). "Children and Marital Happiness: A Further Specification of the Relationship." *Journal of Marriage and the Family, 43*(1), 63–72.

Go, K. J. (1992). "Recent Advances in the Treatment of Male Infertility." *Naacogs Clinical Issues in Perinatal and Women's Health Nursing, 3*(2), 320–327.

Gochoros, J. S. (1989). *When Husbands Come Out of the Closet*. New York: Harrington Park Press.

Goetting, A. (1986). "The Developmental Tasks of Siblingship Over the Life Cycle." *Journal of Marriage and the Family, 48*(4), 703–714.

Gold, S. R., Balzano, F. F., & Stamey, R. (1991). "Two Studies of Females' Sexual Force Fantasies." *Journal of Sex Education and Therapy, 17*(1), 15–26.

Gold, S. R., & Gold, R. G. (1991). "Gender Differences in First Sexual Fantasies." *Journal of Sex Education and Therapy, 17*(3), 207–216.

Goldberg, L. H., Kaufman, R., Kurtz, T. O., Conant, M. A., & Eron, L. J. (1993). "Long-Term Suppression of Recurrent Genital Herpes with Acyclovir." *Archives of Dermatology, 129*(5), 582–587.

Goldberg, M. A. (1997). "It's Getting Easier for Employees to Sue You: Harassment and Discrimination Charges Against Doctors." *Medical Economics, 74*(13), 91–97.

Goldberg-Ambrose, C. (1992). "Unfinished Business in Rape Law Reform." *Journal of Social Issues, 48*(1), 173–175.

Goldman, A., & Carroll, J. L. (1990). "Educational Intervention as an Adjunct to Treatment in Erectile Dysfunction of Older Couples." *Journal of Sex and Marital Therapy, 16*(3), 127–141.

Goldmeier, D., & Hay, P. (1993). "A Review and Update on Adult Syphilis, with Particular Emphasis on Its Treatment." *International Journal of STD and AIDS, 4*(2), 70–82.

Golombok, S. (1992). "Psychological Functioning of Infertility Patients." *Human Reproduction, 7*(2), 208–212.

Golwyn, D. H., & Selvie, C. P. (1992). "Paraphilias, Nonparaphilic Sexual Addictions, and Social Phobia." *Journal of Clinical Psychiatry, 53*(9), 330.

González, E. R. (1980). "New Era in Treatment of Dysmenorrhea." *JAMA: Journal of the American Medical Association, 244*, 1885–1886.

Goode, E. (1994). *Deviant Behavior*. Englewood Cliffs, NJ: Prentice-Hall.

Goodman, E. (1985). *Keeping in Touch*. New York: Summit Books.

Goodman, W. (1992, August 4). "TV's Sexual Circus Has a Purpose." *The New York Times*, p. 2.

Gooren, L., & Cohen-Kettenis, P. T. (1991). "Development of Male Gender Identity/Role and a Sexual Orientation Towards Women in a 46,XY Subject with Incomplete Form of the Androgen Insensitivity Syndrome." *Archives of Sexual Behavior, 20*(5), 459–470.

Gordon, E. B. (1991). "Transsexual Healing: Medicaid Funding for Sex Reassignment Surgery." *Archives of Sexual Behavior, 20*(1), 61–74.

Gordon, S. (1984, March). "Parents as Sexuality Educators." *SIECUS Report*, 10–11.

Gordon, S. (1986, October). "What Kids Need to Know." *Psychology Today*, pp. 46ff.

Gorman, C. (1992, January 20). "Sizing Up the Sexes." *Time*, pp. 42–51.

Gosselin, C., & Wilson, G. (1980). *Sexual Variations*. New York: Simon & Schuster.

"Gossypol: Effective Contraceptive, But Can Side Effects Be Overcome?" (1987, January). *Contraceptive Technology Update, 8*(1), 5–6.

Gostin, L. O. (1992). "Health Law." *JAMA: Journal of the American Medical Association, 268*(3), 364–366.

Gouchie, C., & Kimura, D. (1991). "The Relationship Between Testosterone Levels and Cognitive Ability Patterns." *Psychoneuroendocrinology, 16*, 323–334.

Gould, J. B., Davey, B., & Stafford, R. S. (1989). "Socioeconomic Differences in Rates of Cesarean Section." *New England Journal of Medicine, 321*(4), 233–239.

Grady, D. (1992, June). "Sex Test of Champions: Olympic Officials Struggle to Define What Should Be Obvious—Just Who Is a Female Athlete." *Discover*, pp. 78–82.

Grafenberg, E. (1950). "The Role of Urethra in Female Orgasm." *International Journal of Sexology, 3*, 145–148.

Graham, N., & Wisch, E. D. (1994). "Drug Use Among Female Arrestees: Onset, Patterns, and Relationship to Prostitution." *Journal of Drug Issues, 24*, 315.

Graham, N. M., et al. (1992). "The Effects on Survival of Early Treatment of Human Immunodeficiency Virus Infection." *New England Journal of Medicine, 326*(16), 1032–1042.

Granberg, D. (1991). "Conformity to Religious Norms Regarding Abortion." *Sociological Quarterly, 32*(2), 267–275.

Greeley, A. (1992). "Faithful Attraction." New York: Tor Books/St. Martin's Press.

Green, R. (1987). *The "Sissy-Boy Syndrome" and the Development of Homosexuality*. New Haven, CT: Yale University Press.

Greenberg, B. S. (1994). "Content Trends in Media Sex." In D. Zillman, J. Bryant, & A. C. Huston (Eds.), *Media, Children, and the Family: Social Scientific, Psychodynamic, and Clinical Perspectives*. Hillsdale, NJ: Erlbaum.

Greenberg, J., Magder, L., & Aral, S. (1992). "Age at First Coitus: A Marker for Risky Sexual Behavior in Women." *Sexually Transmitted Diseases, 19*(6), 331–334.

Greenburg, D., & Jacobs, M. (1966). *How to Make Yourself Miserable*. New York: Random House.

Greene, B. (1993). "The View from Schools." In S. Samuels & M. Smith (Eds.). *Condoms in the Schools.* Menlo Park, CA: Henry J. Kaiser Family Foundation.

Greenfeld, L. (1997). *Sex Offenses and Offenders: An Analysis of Data on Rape and Sexual Assault.* Washington, DC: U.S. Department of Justice, Bureau of Justice Statistics.

Greensite, G. (1991). "Acquaintance Rape Clarified." *Student Guide,* Santa Cruz, CA, pp. 15, 68.

Greenwood, S. (1992). *Menopause Naturally: Preparing for the Second Half of Life.* Volcano, CA: Volcano Press.

Greer, R. A., Herkov, M. J., & Hill, L. L. (1994). "Sexuality Within a Russian Geriatric Sample: A Pilot Study." *Psychological Reports, 74*(2), 491–494.

Gregersen, E. (1986). "Human Sexuality in Cross-Cultural Perspective." In D. Byrne & K. Kelley (Eds.), *Alternative Approaches to the Study of Sexual Behavior.* Hillsdale, NJ: Erlbaum.

Gregor, T. (1985). *Anxious Pleasures: The Sexual Lives of an Amazonian People.* Chicago: University of Chicago Press.

Gressman, G. D., et al. (1992). "Female Awareness of University Sexual Harassment Policy." *Journal of College Student Development, 33*(4), 370–371.

Griffin, K., & Mason, M. (1997). "A Simple Cure for Pelvic Infections." *Health, 1,* 19.

Grimes, D. (1983). "Reversible Contraception for the 1980's." *Journal of the American Medical Association, 250,* 3081–3083.

Griswold Del Castillo, R. (1984). *La Familia: Chicano Families in the Urban Southwest, 1848 to the Present.* Notre Dame, IN: University of Notre Dame.

Gritz, E. R., Wellisch, D. K., Wang, H. J., Siau, J., Landsverk, J. A., & Cosgrove, M. D. (1989). "Long-Term Effects of Testicular Cancer on Sexual Functioning in Married Couples." *Cancer, 64*(7), 1560–1567.

Grodstein, F., Stampfer, M. J., Colditz, G. A., Willett, W. C., Manson, J. E., Jaffe, M., Rosner, B., Fuchs, C., Hankinson, S. E., Hunter, O. J., Hennekens, C. H., & Speizer, F. E. (1997, June 19). "Postmenopausal Hormone Therapy and Mortality." *New England Journal of Medicine, 336*(25), 1769–1775.

Gross, J. (1992, March 11). "Schools Are Newest Arena for Sex-Harassment Cases." *The New York Times,* pp. 1, 18.

Groth, A. N. (1979). *Men Who Rape: The Psychology of the Offender.* New York: Plenum Press.

Groth, A. N., & Burgess, A. W. (1980). "Male Rape: Offenders and Victims." *American Journal of Psychiatry, 137*(7), 806–810.

Groth, A. N., Burgess, A. W., & Holmstrom, L. L. (1977). "Rape: Power, Anger, and Sexuality." *American Journal of Psychiatry, 104*(11), 1239–1243.

Groth, A. N., Hobson, W. F., & Gary, T. (1982). "Heterosexuality, Homosexuality, and Pedophilia: Sexual Offenses Against Children." In A. Scacco (Ed.), *Male Rape: A Casebook of Sexual Aggression.* New York: AMS Press.

Gruters, R. A., et al. (1991). "Differences in Clinical Course in Zidovudine-Treated Asymptomatic HIV-Infected Men Associated with T-Cell Function at Intake." *AIDS, 5*(1), 43–47.

Gudjonsson, G. (1990). "Cognitive Distortions and Blame Attribution Among Paedophiles." *Sexual and Marital Therapy, 5*(2), 183–185.

Guerrero Pavich, E. (1986). "A Chicana Perspective on Mexican Culture and Sexuality." In L. Lister (Ed.), *Human Sexuality, Ethnoculture, and Social Work.* New York: Haworth Press.

Guidry, H. (1995). "Childhood Sexual Abuse: Role of the Family Physician." *American Family Physician, 51,* 407–414.

Gunther, A. (1995, December). "Overrating the X-Rating: The Third Person Perceptions and Support for Censorship of Pornography." *Journal of Communication, 45*(1), 27–38.

Gur, R., Mozley, L., Mozley, P., et al. (1995). "Sex Differences in Regional Cerebral Glucose Metabolism During a Resting State." *Science 267*(5197), 528–531.

Gutherie, . (1988).

Gutin, J. C. (1992, June). "Why Bother?" *Discover,* pp. 32–39.

Gutman, H. (1976). *The Black Family: From Slavery to Freedom.* New York: Pantheon.

Guttentag, M., & Secord, P. (1983). *Too Many Women.* Newbury Park, CA: Sage Publications.

Guttmacher, S., Lieberman, L., Ward, D., Freudenberg, N., Radosh, A., & des Jarlais, D. (1997). "Condom Availability in New York City Schools." *American Journal of Public Health, 87*(9), 1427–1433.

Gwartney-Gibbs, P. (1986). "The Institutionalization of Premarital Cohabitation: Estimates from Marriage License Applications." *Journal of Marriage and the Family, 48,* 423–434.

Haaga, D. A. (1991). "Homophobia?" *Journal of Behavior and Personality, 6,* 171–174.

Hack, T., Osachuk, T., & DeLuca, R. (1994, April). "Group Treatment for Sexually Abused Preadolescent Boys." *Families in Society, 75,* 217–228.

Hafner, D. W. (1992). "From Where I Sit." *Family Life Educator, 11*(2), 14–15.

Hage, J. J., Bout, C. A., Bloem, J. J., & Megens, J. A. (1993). "Phalloplasty in Female-to-Male Transsexuals: What Do Our Patients Ask For?" *Annals of Plastic Surgery, 30*(4), 323–326.

Hahn, R. A. (1992). "The State of Federal Health Statistics on Racial and Ethnic Groups." *JAMA: Journal of the American Medical Association, 267*(2), 268–271.

Hales, D. (1997). *An Invitation to Health* (7th ed.). Pacific Grove, CA: Brooks/Cole.

Halikas, J. A., Weller, R. A., & Morse, C. (1982). "Effects of Regular Marijuana Use on Sexual Performance." *Journal of Psychoactive Drugs, 14,* 59–70.

Hall, C. (1980). *A Primer of Freudian Psychology.* New York: New American Library.

Hall, G. J. (1991). "Sexual Arousal as a Function of Physiological and Cognitive Variables in a Sexual Offender Population." *Archives of Sexual Behavior, 20*(4), 359–369.

Hall, J. G., & Gilchrist, D. M. (1990). "Turner Syndrome and Its Variants." *Pediatric Clinics of North America, 37*(6), 1421–1440.

Hällström, T., & Samuelsson, S. (1990). "Changes in Women's Sexual Desire in Middle Life: The Longitudinal Study of Women in Gothenburg [Sweden]." *Archives of Sexual Behavior, 19*(3), 259–267.

Hamer, D. H., Hu, S., Magnuson, V. L., & Pattatucci, S. (1993). "A Linkage Between DNA Markers on the X-Chromosome and Male Sexual Orientation." *Science, 261*(5119), 321–327.

Haney, D. Q. (1998, May 19). "Study Backs Prostate Screening." *Monterey County Herald,* p. A-7.

Hankinson, S. E., Colditz, G. A., Hunter, D. J., Spencer, T. L., Rosner, B., & Stampflau, M. J. (1992). "A Quantitative Assessment of Oral Contraceptive Use and Risk of Ovarian Cancer." *Obstetrics and Gynecology, 80*(4), 708–714.

Hanley, R. (1988, February 4). "Surrogate Deals for Mothers Held Illegal in New Jersey." *The New York Times,* pp. 1ff.

Hansen, G. (1985). "Dating Jealousy Among College Students." *Sex Roles, 12*(7–8), 713–721.

Hansen, G. (1987). "Extradyadic Relations During Courtship." *Journal of Sex Research, 23*(3), 383–390.

Hansen, W. B., Wolkenstein, B. H., & Hahn, G. L. (1992). "Young Adult Behavior: Issues in Programming and Evaluation." *Health Education Research, 7,* 305–312.

Hanson, F. W., Happ, R. L., Tennant, F. R., Hune, S., & Peterson, A. G. (1990). "Ultrasonography—Guided Early Amniocentesis in Singleton Pregnancies." *American Journal of Obstetrics and Gynecology, 162*(6), 1381–1383.

Hare-Mustin, R. T., & Marecek, J. (1990a). "Beyond Difference." In R. T. Hare-Mustin & J. Marecek (Eds.), *Making a Difference: Psychology and the Construction of Gender.* New Haven, CT: Yale University Press.

Hare-Mustin, R. T., & Marecek, J. (1990b). "Gender and the Meaning of Difference." In R. T. Hare-Mustin & J. Marecek (Eds.), *Making a Difference: Psychology and the Construction of Gender.* New Haven, CT: Yale University Press.

Hare-Mustin, R. T., & Marecek, J. (Eds.). (1990c). *Making a Difference: Psychology and the Construction of Gender.* New Haven, CT: Yale University Press.

Hare-Mustin, R. T., & Marecek, J. (1990d). "On Making a Difference." In R. T. Hare-Mustin & J. Marecek (Eds.), *Making a Difference: Psychology and the Construction of Gender.* New Haven, CT: Yale University Press.

Hariton, E. B., & Singer, J. I. (1974). "Women's Fantasies During Sexual Intercourse." *Journal of Consulting and Clinical Psychology, 42,* 313–322.

Harlow, C. W. (1991). *Female Victims of Violent Crime.* Washington, DC: U.S. Department of Justice. (NCJ-126826).

Harmon, M. J., & Johnson, J. A. (1993). "Sex Education: Piagetian Stages and Children's Perceptions of Sexuality." *TCA Journal, 22*(2), 11–16.

Harriman, L. (1983). "Personal and Marital Changes Accompanying Parenthood." *Family Relations, 32,* 387–394.

Harris, M. B., & Turner, P. H. (1985). "Gay and Lesbian Parents." *Journal of Homosexuality, 12*(2), 101–113.

Harry, J. (1988). "Decision Making and Age Differences Among Gay Male Couples." In J. De Cecco (Ed.), *Gay Relationships.* New York: Haworth Press.

Hart, J., Cohen, E., Gingold, A., & Homburg, R. (1991). "Sexual Behavior in Pregnancy: A Study of 219 Women." *Journal of Sex Education and Therapy, 17*(2), 88–90.

Hart, L. (1994). *Fatal Women: Lesbian Sexuality and the Mark of Aggression.* Princeton, NJ: Princeton University Press.

Harvard Law Review. (1991). "Constitutional Barriers to Civil and Criminal Restrictions on Premarital and Extramarital Sex." *Harvard Law Review, 104*(7), 1660–1680.

Harvey, S. (1987). "Female Sexual Behavior: Fluctuations During the Menstrual Cycle." *Journal of Psychosomatic Research, 31,* 101–110.

Haskell, M. (1987). *From Reverence to Rape* (2nd ed.). Chicago: University of Chicago Press.

Haskell, S. G., Richardson, E. D., & Horwitz, R. I. (1997). "The Effects of Estrogen Replacement Therapy on Cognitive Function in Women: A Critical Review of the Literature." *Journal of Clinical Epidemiology, 50*(11), 1249–1264.

Hassold, T., Arnovitz, K., Jacobs, P. A., May, K., & Robinson, D. (1990). "The Parental Origin of the Missing or Additional Chromosome in 45,X and 47,XXX Females." *Birth Defects Original Article Series, 26*(4), 297–304.

Hatcher, R., Stewart, F., Trussel, J., Kowal, D., Guest, F., Stewart, G., & Cates, W. (1994). *Contraceptive Technology: 1994–1995.* New York: Irvington.

Hatchett, S. J. (1991). "Women and Men." In J. S. Jackson (Ed.), *Life in Black America.* Newbury Park, CA: Sage Publications.

Hatfield, E., & Sprecher, S. (1986). *Mirror, Mirror: The Importance of Looks in Everyday Life.* New York: State University of New York.

Hatfield, E., & Walster, G. W. (1981). *A New Look at Love.* Reading, MA: Addison-Wesley.

Hatfield, R. (1994). "Touch and Sexuality." In V. Bullough & B. B. Bullough (Eds.), *Human Sexuality: An Encyclopedia.* New York: Garland.

Hausman, B. L. (1993). "Demanding Subjectivity: Transsexualism, Medicine, and the Technologies of Gender." *Journal of the History of Sexuality, 3*(2), 270–302.

Hawkins, R. O. (1990). "The Relationship Between Culture, Personality, and Sexual Jealousy in Men in Heterosexual and Homosexual Relationships." *Journal of Homosexuality, 19*(3), 67–84.

Hawton, K., Catalan, J., & Fagg, J. (1991). "Low Sexual Desire: Sex Therapy Results and Prognostic Factors." *Behavior Research and Therapy, 29*(3), 217–224.

Hayden, N. (1991). *How to Satisfy a Woman Every Time.* New York: Dutton.

Hays, D., & Samuels, A. (1989). "Heterosexual Women's Perceptions of Their Marriages to Bisexual or Homosexual Men." *Journal of Homosexuality, 18,* 81–100.

Hazan, C., & Shaver, P. (1987). "Romantic Love Conceptualized as an Attachment Process." *Journal of Personality and Social Psychology, 52*(3), 511–524.

Hazelwood, R., Burgess, A., & Dietz, P. (1983). *Autoerotic Fatalities.* Lexington, MA: Heath.

Healy, J. M. (1988, November). "Preventing Birth Defects of the Mind." *Parents' Magazine,* pp. 176ff.

"Health & Safety." (1998, January). *Atlantic Monthly,* p. 14.

"Health Index: Condom Facts." (1994, February 14). *U.S. News and World Report, 116,* 6.

Heath, D. (1984). "An Investigation of the Origins of a Copious Vaginal Discharge During Intercourse." *Journal of Sex Research, 20,* 194–215.

Heath, R. (1972). "Pleasure and Brain Activity in Man." *Journal of Nervous and Mental Disorders, 154,* 3–18.

Hecht, M., Collier, M. J., & Ribeau, S. (1993). *African American Communication.* Newbury Park, CA: Sage Publications.

Hefner, R., Rebecca, M., & Oleshansky. (1975). "Development of Sex-Role Transcendence." *Human Development, 18,* 143–158.

Heider, K. (1979). *Grand Valley Dani: Peaceful Warriors.* New York: Holt, Rinehart & Winston.

Heilbrun, C. (1982). *Toward a Recognition of Androgyny.* New York: Norton.

Heiman, J., & LoPiccolo, J. (1988). *Becoming Orgasmic: A Sexual and Personal Growth Program for Women.* Englewood Cliffs, NJ: Prentice-Hall.

Heiman, J., LoPiccolo, L., & LoPiccolo, J. (1976). *Becoming Orgasmic: A Sexual Growth Program for Women.* Englewood Cliffs, NJ: Prentice-Hall.

Heiman, J., et al. (1986). "Historical and Current Factors Discriminating Sexually Functional from Sexually Dysfunctional Married Couples." *Journal of Marital and Family Therapy, 12*(2), 163–174.

Heins, M. (1993). *Sex, Sin and Blasphemy: A Guide to America's Censorship Wars.* New York: New Press.

Heller, L., Keren, O., Aloni, R., & Davidoff, G. (1992). "An Open Trial of Vacuum Penile Tumescence: Constriction Therapy for Neurological Impotence." *Paraplegia, 30*(8), 550–553.

Hendrick, C., & Hendrick, S. S. (1986). "A Theory and Method of Love." *Journal of Personality and Social Psychology, 50,* 392–402.

Hendrick, C., & Hendrick, S. S. (1988, May). "Lovers Wear Rose-Colored Glasses." *Journal of Social and Personal Relationships*, 5(2), 161–183.

Hendrick, S. S. (1981). "Self-Disclosure and Marital Satisfaction." *Journal of Personality and Social Psychology, 40*, 1150–1159.

Hendrick, S. S., & Hendrick, C. (1987). "Multidimensionality of Sexual Attitudes." *Journal of Sex Research, 23*(4), 502–526.

Hendrick, S. S., Hendrick, C., & Adler, N. L. (1988). "Romantic Relationships: Love, Satisfaction, and Staying Together." *Journal of Personality and Social Psychology, 54*, 980–988.

Henley, N. (1977). *Body Politics: Power, Sex, and Nonverbal Communication*. Englewood Cliffs, NJ: Prentice-Hall.

Henrick, J., & Stange, T. (1991). "Do Actions Speak Louder Than Words? An Effect of the Functional Use of Language on Dominant Sex Role Behavior in Boys and Girls." *Early Childhood Research Quarterly, 6*(4), 565–576.

Herbert, C. M. H. (1989). *Talking of Silence: The Sexual Harassment of Schoolgirls*. London: The Falmer Press.

Herdt, G. (1984). "A Comment on Cultural Attributes and Fluidity of Bisexuality." *Journal of Homosexuality, 10*(3–4), 53–61.

Herdt, G. (1987). "Transitional Objects in Sambia Initiation." Special Issue: Interpretation in Psychoanalytic Anthropology. *Ethos, 15*, 40–57.

Herdt, G., & Boxer, A. (1992). "Introduction: Culture, History, and Life Course of Gay Men." In G. Herdt (Ed.), *Gay Culture in America: Essays from the Field*. Boston: Beacon Press.

Herek, G. M. (1984). "Beyond Homophobia: A Social Psychological Perspective on Attitudes Toward Lesbians and Gay Men." *Journal of Homosexuality, 10*(1–2), 1–21.

Herek, G. M. (1985). "On Doing, Being, and Not Being: Prejudice and the Social Construction of Sexuality." *Journal of Homosexuality, 12*(1), 135–151.

Herek, G. M. (1995). "Psychological Heterosexism in the United States." In A. R. D'Augelli & C. J. Patterson (Eds.), *Lesbian, Gay, and Bisexual Identities Over the Lifespan: Psychological Perspectives*. New York: Oxford University Press.

Herek, G. M., & Berrill, K. T. (1992). *Hate Crimes: Confronting Violence Against Lesbians and Gay Men*. Newbury Park, CA: Sage Publications.

Herek, G. M., Kimmel, D. C., Amaro, H., & Melton, G. B. (1991). "Avoiding Heterosexist Bias in Psychological Research." *American Psychologist, 46*(9), 957–963.

Herman, J. (1981). *Father-Daughter Incest*. Cambridge, MA: Harvard University Press.

Herold, E. E., & Way, L. (1983). "Oral-Genital Sexual Behavior in a Sample of University Females." *Journal of Sex Research, 19*(4), 327–338.

Herzer, M. (1985). "Kertbeny and the Nameless Love." *Journal of Homosexuality, 12*(1), 1–26.

Herzog, L. (1989). "Urinary Tract Infections and Circumcision." *American Journal of Diseases of Children, 143*, 348–350.

Heslin, & Alper, .(1983).

Hetherington, S. E. (1990). "A Controlled Study of the Effect of Prepared Childbirth Classes on Obstetric Outcomes." *Birth, 17*(2), 86–90.

Hewitt, J. (1987). "Preconceptional Sex Selection." *British Journal of Hospital Medicine, 37*(2), 149ff.

Heyl, B. (1989). "Homosexuality: A Social Phenomenon." In K. McKinney & S. Sprecher (Eds.), *Human Sexuality: The Societal and Interpersonal Context*. Norwood, NJ: Ablex.

Hibbard, R. A., & Hartman, G. L. (1992). "Behavioral Problems in Alleged Sexual Abuse Victims." *Child Abuse and Neglect, 16*(5), 755–762.

Hill, I. (1987). *The Bisexual Spouse*. McLean, VA: Barlina Books.

Hilts, P. (1991, October 11). "Growing Concern Over Pelvic Infection in Women." *The New York Times*, p. B7.

Hilts, P. J. (1990, June 13). "Poorer Countries Are Hit Hardest by Spread of AIDS, U.N. Reports." *The New York Times*, p. A6.

Hines, M. (1982). "Prenatal Gonadal Hormones and Sex Differences in Human Behavior." *Psychological Bulletin, 92*, 56–80.

Hines, P. M., & Boyd-Franklin, N. (1982). "Black Families." In M. McGoldrick et al. (Eds.), *Ethnicity and Family Therapy*. New York: Guilford Press.

Hingson, R. W., Strunin, L., Berlin, B. M., & Heeren, T. (1990). "Beliefs About AIDS, Use of Alcohol and Drugs, and Unprotected Sex Among Massachusetts Adolescents." *American Journal of Public Health, 80*(3), 295–299.

Hirschfeld, M. (1978). *Research on Love Between Men*. Los Angeles: Urania Manuscripts.

Hirschfeld, M. (1991). *Transvestites: The Erotic Drive to Cross Dress*. Buffalo, NY: Prometheus Press.

Hite, S., (1976). *The Hite Report*. New York: Macmillan.

"HIV Grows Deadlier." (1997, November 30). *San Francisco Chronicle*, p. C-14.

Ho, D. D., Bredesen, D. E., Vinters, H. V., & Daar, E. S. (1989). "The Acquired Immunodeficiency Syndrome (AIDS) Dementia Complex." *Annals of Internal Medicine, 111*(5), 400–410.

Hobart, C., & Griegel, F. (1992). "Cohabitation Among Canadian Students at the End of the Eighties." *Journal of Comparative Family Studies, 23*(3), 311–338.

Hochhauser, M. (1992). "Moral Development and HIV Prevention Among Adolescents." *Family Life Educator, 10*(3), 9–12.

Hockenberry, S. L., & Billingham, R. E. (1987). "Sexual Orientation and Boyhood Gender Conformity: Development of the Boyhood Gender Conformity Scale (BGCS)." *Archives of Sexual Behavior, 16*, 475–492.

Holcomb, D. R., Holcomb, L. C., Sondag, K., & Williams, N. (1991). "Attitudes About Date Rape: Gender Differences Among College Students." *College Student Journal, 25*(4), 434–439.

Holden, C. (1994). "Teen Sex Survey Back on Track." *Science, 163*, p. 1688.

Hollander, J. B., Gonzalez, J., & Norman, T. (1992). "Patient Satisfaction with Pharmacologic Erection Program." *Urology, 39*(5), 439–441.

Holman, P. B., Jenkins, W. C., Gayle, J. A., Duncan, C., & Lindsey, B. K. (1991). "Increasing the Involvement of National and Regional Racial and Ethnic Minority Organizations in HIV Information and Education." *Public Health Reports, 106*(6), 687–694.

Holmes, K. K., et al. (1990a). "Future Directions." In K. K. Holmes et al. (Eds.), *Sexually Transmitted Diseases* (2nd ed.). New York: McGraw-Hill.

Holmes, K. K., et al. (Eds.). (1990b). *Sexually Transmitted Diseases* (2nd ed.). New York: McGraw-Hill.

Holmes, R. M. (1991). *Sex Crimes*. Newbury Park, CA: Sage Publications.

Holtzen, D. W., & Agresti, A. A. (1990). "Parental Responses to Gay and Lesbian Children." *Journal of Social and Clinical Psychology, 9*(3), 390–399.

"Home Access Health Urges Consumer Caution via Internet." (1997). *AIDS Weekly Plus*, p. 14.

"Home-Use HIV Test Kits." (1998, May 14). *FDA Backgrounder*.

Hook, E., Sondheimer, S., & Zenilman, J. (1995). "Today's Treatment for STDs." *Patient Care, 29*, 40–56.

Hook, E. W., III, et al. (1992). "Herpes Simplex Virus Infection as a Risk Factor for Human Immunodeficiency Virus Infection in Heterosexuals." *Journal of Infectious Diseases, 165*(2), 251–255.

Hooker, E. (1957). "The Adjustment of the Overt Male Homosexual." *Journal of Projective Psychology, 21,* 18–31.

Hort, B. E., Leinbach, M. D., & Fagot, B. I. (1991). "Is There Coherence Among the Cognitive Components of Gender Acquisition?" *Sex Roles, 24*(3–4), 195–207.

Houlberg, R. (1991). "The Magazine of a Sadomasochism Club—The Tie That Binds." *Journal of Homosexuality, 21*(1–2), 167–183.

Houseknecht, S. K. (1982). "Childlessness and Marital Adjustment." In J. Rosenfeld (Ed.), *Relationships: The Marriage and Family Reader.* Glencoe, IL: Scott, Foresman.

Houseknecht, S. K. (1987). "Voluntary Childlessness." In M. B. Sussman & S. K. Steinmetz (Eds.), *Handbook of Marriage and the Family.* New York: Plenum Press.

Howard, E. (1980, November). "Overcoming Rape Trauma." *Ms.,* p. 35.

Howard, J. (1988). "A Structural Approach to Interracial Patterns in Adolescent Judgments About Sexual Intimacy." *Sociological Perspectives, 31*(1), 88–121.

Howard, J. A., Blumstein, P., & Schwartz, P. (1986). "Sex, Power, and Influence Tactics in Intimate Relationships." *Journal of Personality and Social Psychology, 51*(1), 102–109.

Howard, L., et al. (1986). "Evaluation of Chlamydiazyme for the Detection of Genital Infection Caused by Chlamydia Trachomatis." *Journal of Clinical Microbiology, 23,* 329–332.

"How Reliable Are Condoms?" (1995, May). *Consumer Reports,* pp. 320–324.

"How the Public Feels." (1986, November 24). *Time,* p. 58.

"How the Public Views Abortion." (1994, November). *Family Planning Perspectives, 26*(6), 245.

Hsu, B., et al. (1994). "Gender Differences in Sexual Fantasy and Behavior in a College Population: A Ten-Year Replication. *Journal of Sex and Marital Therapy, 20*(2), 103–118.

Huang, Z., Hankinson, S. E., Colditz, G. A., Stampfer, M. J., Hunter, O. J., Manson, J. E., Hennekens, C. H., Rosner, B., Speizer, F. E., & Willet, W. C. (1997, November 5). "Dual Effects of Weight and Weight Gain on Breast Cancer Risk." *JAMA: Journal of the American Medical Association, 278*(17), 1407–1411.

Hudak, M. A. (1993, March). "Gender Schema Theory Revisited: Men's Stereotypes of American Women." *Sex Roles, 28*(5–6), 279–293.

Humm, A. J. (1992). "Homosexuality: The New Frontier in Sexuality Education." *Family Life Educator, 10*(3), 13–18.

Humphreys, L. (1975). *Tearoom Trade: Impersonal Sex in Public Places.* Chicago: Aldine.

Hunt, M. (1974). *Sexual Behavior in the 1970s.* Chicago: Playboy Press.

Hunter, A. G., & Davis, J. E. (1992). "Constructing Gender: An Exploration of Afro-American Men's Conceptualization of Manhood." *Gender and Society, 6*(3), 464–479.

Hupka, R. B. (1981). "Cultural Determinants of Jealousy." *Alternative Lifestyles, 4*(3), 310–356.

Hutchins, L., & Kaahumanu, L. (Eds.). (1990). *Any Other Name: Bisexual People Speak Out.* Boston: Alyson Publications.

Imberti, L., Sottini, A., Bettinardi, A., Puoti, M., & Primi, D. (1991). "Selective Depletion in HIV Infection of T Cells That Bear Specific T Cell Receptor V Beta Sequences." *Science, 254*(5033), 860–862.

Imperato-McGinley, J. (1979). "Steroid 5'-reductase Deficiency in Man: An Inherited Form of Male Pseudohermaphroditism." *Science, 186,* 1213–1215.

Imperato-McGinley, J. (1979). "Androgens and the Evolution of Male Gender Identity Among Male Pseudohermaphrodites with 5'-reductase Deficiency." *New England Journal of Medicine, 300,* 1233–1237.

Imperato-McGinley, J., et al. (1991). "Cognitive Abilities in Androgen-Insensitive Subjects." *Clinical Endocrinology, 34*(5), 341–347.

Inciardi, J. A. (1995, June). "Crack, Crack House Sex, and HIV Risk." *Archives of Sexual Behavior, 24*(3), 249–269.

"An Insurance Policy with Sex Appeal." (1998, March 17). *Newsweek,* p. 44.

Intersex Society of North America. (1995). Frequently Asked Questions About ISNA and Intersex. Available: http://www.isna.org/faq.html (Last visited 10/1/97).

Irvine, J. M. (1990). *Disorders of Desire.* Philadelphia: Temple University Press.

Irvine, M. (1998, June 28). "Studies Say C-Sections Can Fight AIDS." *Monterey Herald,* p. A-7.

Isensee, R. (1990). *Love Between Men: Enhancing Intimacy and Keeping Your Relationship Alive.* New York: Prentice-Hall.

Ishii-Kuntz, M. (1997a). "Chinese American Families." In M. K. DeGenova, *Families in Cultural Context.* Mountain View, CA: Mayfield.

Ishii-Kuntz, M. (1997b). "Japanese American Families." In M. K. DeGenova, *Families in Cultural Context.* Mountain View, CA: Mayfield.

Israelski, D. (1992). "Current Issues in HIV/AIDS Research: A Report from the Amsterdam Conference." Talk given at Dominican Hospital, Santa Cruz, CA.

Israelstam, S. (1986). "Alcohol and Drug Problems of Gay Males and Lesbians: Therapy, Counseling and Prevention Issues." *Journal of Drug Issues, 16*(3), 443–461.

Jackson, J. S. (Ed.). (1991). *Life in Black America.* Newbury Park, CA: Sage Publications.

Jacobs, J. (1993, February 4). "Male GIs as Sexual Prey: Welcome to the Club." *San Jose Mercury News,* p. 7b.

Jacobs, S. E., & Cromwell, J. (1992). "Visions and Revisions of Reality: Reflections on Sex, Sexuality, Gender and Gender Variance." *Journal of Homosexuality, 23*(4), 43–70.

James, C. (1992, November 22). "Dangerous Liaisons Are All the Rage." *The New York Times,* p. 13.

James, J., & Myerdling, J. (1977). "Early Sexual Experiences as a Factor in Prostitution." *American Journal of Psychiatry, 134,* 1381–1385.

Janus, S., & Janus, C. (1993). *The Janus Report on Sexual Behavior.* New York: John Wiley & Sons.

Jaschik, M. L., & Fretz, B. R. (1991). "Women's Perceptions and Labeling of Sexual Harassment." *Sex Roles, 25*(1–2), 19–23.

Jeffrey, T. B., & Jeffrey, L. K. (1991). "Psychologic Aspects of Sexual Abuse in Adolescence." *Current Opinion in Obstetrics and Gynecology, 3*(6), 825–831.

Jemmott, J. B. I., Jemmott, L. S., & Fong, G. T. (1992). "Reductions in HIV Risk–Associated Sexual Behaviors Among Black Male Adolescents: Effects of an AIDS Prevention Intervention." *American Journal of Public Health, 82*(3), 372–377.

Jenks, R. (1985). "Swinging: A Replication and Test of a Theory." *Journal of Sex Research, 21*(2), 199–210.

Jensen, M. A. (1984). *Love's Sweet Return: The Harlequin Story.* Toronto: Women's Press.

Jick, H., et al. (1981). "Vaginal Spermicides and Congenital Disorders." *JAMA: Journal of the American Medical Association, 243*(13), 1329–1332.

Joffe, G. P., et al. (1992). "Multiple Partners and Partner Choice as Risk Factors for Sexually Transmitted Disease Among Female College Students." *Sexually Transmitted Diseases, 19*(5), 272–278.

Johnson, C. (1993, June 5). "More Women-Controlled AIDS Prevention Methods Needed—WHO." *San Jose Mercury News,* p. 6.

Johnson, C. B., Stockdale, M. S., & Saal, F. E. (1991). "Persistence of Men's Misperceptions of Friendly Cues Across a Variety of Interpersonal Encounters." *Psychology of Women Quarterly, 15*(3), 463–475.

Johnston, D. (1992, April 24). "Survey Shows Number of Rapes Far Higher Than Official Figures." *The New York Times,* p. A9.

Jones, C. (1986, June). "Sharing the Childbearing Miracle." *Nurturing News, 8*(2), pp. 5, 18ff.

Jones, C. (1988). *Mind Over Labor.* New York: Penguin.

Jones, J. H. (1992). "Twenty Years After. The Legacy of the Tuskegee Syphilis Study. AIDS and the Black Community." *Hastings Center Report, 22*(6), 38–40.

Jones, J. H. (1993). *Bad Blood: The Tuskegee Syphilis Experiment* (rev. ed.). New York: Free Press.

Jones, R. W., & Bates, J. E. (1988). "Satisfaction in Male Homosexual Couples." In J. De Cecco (Ed.), *Gay Relationships.* New York: Haworth Press.

Jones, T. S., & Remland, M. S. (1992). "Sources of Variability in Perceptions of and Responses to Sexual Harassment." *Sex Roles, 27*(3–4), 121–142.

Jones, W., Chernovetz, M., & Hansson, R. (1978). "The Enigma of Androgyny: Differential Implications for Males and Females." *Journal of Consulting and Clinical Psychology, 46,* 298–313.

Jordan, W. (1968). *White Over Black: American Attitudes Toward the Negro.* Chapel Hill, NC: University of North Carolina Press.

Jumper, S. A. (1995, June). "A Meta-Analysis of the Relationship of Child Sexual Abuse to Adult Psychological Adjustment." *Child Abuse and Neglect, 19*(6), 715–728.

Jurich, A., & Polson, C. (1985). "Nonverbal Assessment of Anxiety as a Function of Intimacy of Sexual Attitude Questions." *Psychological Reports, 57*(3, Pt. 2), 1243–1247.

Kagan, J. (1976). "The Psychological Requirements for Human Development." In N. Talbot (Ed.), *Raising Children in Modern America.* Boston: Little, Brown.

Kahn, J. (1990, September 7). "Sex Education: U.S. Gets an F." *Boston Globe,* p. 32.

Kahn, Y. (1989). "Judaism and Homosexuality: The Traditionalist/Progressive Debate." *Journal of Homosexuality, 18*(3–4), 47–82.

Kalin, T. (1992, August). "Gays in Film: No Way Out." Special Issue: The Sexual Revolution in Movie, Music and TV. *US,* pp. 68–70.

Kalof, L., & Wade, B. H. (1995, August). "Sexual Attitudes and Experiences with Sexual Coercion: Exploring the Influence of Race and Gender." *Journal of Black Psychology, 21*(3), 224–238.

Kandel, D., Wu, P., & Davies, M. (1994). "Maternal Smoking During Pregnancy and Smoking by Adolescent Daughters." *American Journal of Public Health, 84*(9), 1407–1413.

Kantor, L. M. (1992). "Scared Chaste? Fear-Based Educational Curricula." *SIECUS Report, 21*(3), 1–13.

Kantor, L. (1994). "Who Decides? Parents and Comprehensive Sexuality Education." *SIECUS Report, 22*(3), 7–12.

Kantrowitz, B. (1990, February 12). "The Crack Children." *Newsweek,* pp. 62–63.

Kantrowitz, B. (1992, August 3). "Teenagers and AIDS." *Newsweek,* pp. 44–49.

Kantrowitz, B. (1996, November 4). "Gay Families Come Out." *Newsweek,* pp. 51–57.

Kantrowitz, B., Wingert, P., et al. (1992, January 13). "Breaking the Divorce Cycle." *Newsweek, 119*(2), 48.

Kaplan, A. (1979). "Clarifying the Concept of Androgyny: Implications for Therapy." *Psychology of Women, 3,* 223–230.

Kaplan, A., & Bean, J. P. (Eds.). (1979). *Beyond Sex-Role Stereotypes.* Boston: Little, Brown.

Kaplan, E. H. (1988). "Crisis? A Brief Critique of Masters, Johnson, and Kolodny." *Journal of Sex Research, 25,* 317–322.

Kaplan, H. S. (1974). *The New Sex Therapy.* New York: Brunner/Mazel.

Kaplan, H. S. (1979). *Disorders of Desire.* New York: Brunner/Mazel.

Kaplan, H. S. (1983). *The Evaluation of Sexual Disorders: Psychological and Medical Aspects.* New York: Brunner/Mazel.

Kaplan, H. S. (1987). *Sexual Aversion, Sexual Phobias, and Panic Disorders.* New York: Brunner/Mazel.

Kaplan, H. S. (1992). "A Neglected Issue: The Sexual Side Effects of Current Treatment for Breast Cancer." *Journal of Sex and Marital Therapy, 18*(1), 3–19.

Kaplan, H. S., & Owett, T. (1993). "The Female Androgen Deficiency Syndrome." *Journal of Sex and Marital Therapy, 19*(1), 3–24.

Karenga, M. (1992). "Under the Camouflage of Color and Gender: The Dread and Drama of Thomas-Hill." In R. Chrisman & R. Allen (Eds.), *Court of Appeal: The Black Community Speaks Out on the Racial and Sexual Politics of Clarence Thomas vs. Anita Hill.* New York: Ballantine.

Kassler, W. J., & Cates, W. J. (1992). "The Epidemiology and Prevention of Sexually Transmitted Diseases." *Urological Clinics of North America, 19*(1), 1–12.

Katchadourian, H. (1987). *Midlife in Perspective.* New York: W. H. Freeman.

Katz, R., Gipson, M. J., Kearl, A., & Kriskovich, M. (1989). "Assessing Sexual Aversion in College Students: The Sexual Aversion Scale." *Journal of Sex and Marital Therapy, 15*(2), 135–140.

Kaufman, D., et al. (1980). "Decreased Risk of Endometrial Cancer Among Oral Contraceptive Users." *New England Journal of Medicine, 303,* 1045–1047.

Kavich-Sharon, R. (1994). "Response to Sadomasochistic Fantasy Role Play." *Contemporary Sexuality, 28*(4), 4.

Kayal, P. M. (1992). "Healing Homophobia: Volunteerism and Sacredness in AIDS." *Journal of Religion and Health, 31*(2), 113–128.

Kaye, K., Elkind, L., Goldberg, D., & Tytan, A. (1989). "Birth Outcomes for Infants of Drug Abusing Mothers." *New York State Journal of Medicine, 144*(7), 256–261.

Kehoe, M. (1988). "Lesbians Over 60 Speak for Themselves." *Journal of Homosexuality, 16,* 1–111.

Keim, J., Woodard, M. P., & Anderson, M. K. (1992). "Screening for Chlamydia Trachomatis in College Women in Routine Gynecological Exams." *Journal of American College Health, 41*(1), 17–19, 22–23.

Keller, D., & Rosen, H. (1988). "Treating the Gay Couple Within the Context of Their Families of Origin." *Family Therapy Collections, 25,* 105–119.

Keller, S. E., Bartlett, J. A., Schleifer, S. J., Johnson, R. L., Pinner, E., & Delaney, B. (1991). "HIV-Relevant Sexual Behavior Among a Healthy Inner-City Heterosexual Adolescent Population in an Endemic Area of HIV." *Journal of Adolescent Health, 12*(1), 44–48.

Kellett, J. M. (1991). "Sexuality of the Elderly." *Sexual and Marital Therapy, 6*(2), 147–155.

Kelley, H. (1983). "Love and Commitment." In H. Kelley et al. (Eds.), *Close Relationships.* New York: W. H. Freeman.

Kellstedt, L., & Smidt, C. (1991). "Measuring Fundamentalism: An Analysis of Different Operational Strategies." *Journal for the Scientific Study of Religion, 3*(3), 259–279.

Kelly, M. P., Strassberg, D. S., & Kircher, J. R. (1990). "Attitudinal and Experiential Correlates of Anorgasmia." *Archives of Sexual Behavior, 19*(2), 165–167.

Kelly, T. E., Ferguson, J. E., & Golden, W. (1992). "Survival of Fetuses with 45,X: An Instructive Case and Hypothesis." *American Journal of Medical Genetics, 42*(6), 825–826.

Kendrick, W. (1987). *The Secret Museum: Pornography in Modern Culture.* New York: Viking Press.

Kendrick, W. (1992, May 31). "Increasing Our Dirty-Word Power: Why Yesterday's Smut Is Today's Erotica." *The New York Times Book Review,* pp. 3, 36.

Kenig, S., & Ryan, J. (1986). "Sex Differences of Tolerance and Attribution of Blame for Sexual Harassment on a University Campus." *Sex Roles, 15*(9–10), 535–549.

Kennedy, H. (1988). *Ulrichs: The Life and Works of Karl Heinrich Ulrichs, Pioneer of the Modern Gay Movement.* Boston: Alyson Publications.

Kensington, C. (1991). *Elise.* San Francisco: Spinsters Ink.

Kenyon, E. B. (1989). "The Management of Exhibitionism in the Elderly: A Case Study." *Sexual and Marital Therapy, 4*(1), 93–100.

Keuls, E. (1985). *The Reign of the Phallus: Sexual Politics in Ancient Greece.* New York: Harper & Row.

Kidder, L. H., Lafleur, R. A., & Wells, C. V. (1995, March). "Recalling Harassment, Reconstructing Experience." *Journal of Social Issues, 52*(1), 69–84.

Kilmarx, P. H., Akbar, A. Z., Thomas, J. C., Nakashima, A. K., St. Louis, M. E., Flock, M. L., & Peterman, T. A. (1997, December). "Sociodemographic Factors and the Variation in Syphilis Rates Among U.S. Counties, 1984 through 1993: An Ecological Analysis." *American Journal of Public Health, 87*(12), 1937–1943.

Kilpatrick, D., Edmunds, C., & Seymour, A. (1992). *Rape in America: A Report to the Nation.* Arlington, VA: National Victim Center and the Crime Victims Research and Treatment Center.

King, M. B. (1990). "Sneezing as a Fetishistic Stimulus." *Sexual and Marital Therapy, 5*(1), 69–72.

King, P. A. (1992). "Twenty Years After. The Legacy of the Tuskegee Syphilis Study. The Dangers of Difference." *Hastings Center Report, 22*(6), 35–38.

Kinsey, A., Pomeroy, W., & Martin, C. (1948). *Sexual Behavior in the Human Male.* Philadelphia: Saunders.

Kinsey, A., Pomeroy, W., Martin, C., & Gebhard, P. (1953). *Sexual Behavior in the Human Female.* Philadelphia: Saunders.

Kinzl, J., Traweger, C., & Biebel, W. (1995, July). "Sexual Dysfunctions: Relationship to Childhood Sexual Abuse and Early Family Experiences in a Non-Clinical Sample." *Child Abuse & Neglect, 19*(7), 785–792.

Kipnis, A. R., & Herron, E. (1993, January/February). "Ending the Battle Between the Sexes." *Utne Reader,* pp. 69–76.

Kirby, D. (1992). "School-Based Programs to Reduce Sexual Risk-Taking Behaviors." *Journal of School Health, 62*(7), 280–286.

Kirby, D. (1993a). "Research and Evaluation." In S. Samuels & M. Smith (Eds.), *Condoms in the Schools.* Menlo Park, CA: Henry J. Kaiser Family Foundation.

Kirby, D. (1993b). "Sexuality Education: It Can Reduce Unprotected Intercourse." *SIECUS Report, 21*(2), 19–25.

Kisabeth, R., Pontius, C. A., Statland, B. E., & Galper, C. (1997). "Promises and Pitfalls of Home Test Devices." *Patient Care (31)*6, 125–137.

Kisker, E. (1984). "The Effectiveness of Family Planning Clinics in Serving Adolescents." *Family Planning Perspectives, 16*(5), 212ff.

Kisker, E. (1985). "Teenagers Talk About Sex, Pregnancy and Contraception." *Family Planning Perspectives, 17*(2), 83–89.

Kissman, K., & Allen, J. A. (1993). *Single-Parent Families.* Newbury Park, CA: Sage Publications.

Kitano, H. H. (1994, November). "Recent Trends in Japanese Americans' Interracial Marriage." Paper presented at the Center for Family Studies Lecture Series, University of California, Riverside.

Kite, M. (1984). "Sex Differences in Attitudes Toward Homosexuals: A Meta-Analytic Review." *Journal of Homosexuality, 10*(1–2), 69–82.

Klassen, M. L., Jasper, C. R., & Schwartz, A. M. (1993). "Men and Women: Images of Their Relationships in Magazine Advertisements." *Journal of Advertising Research, 33*(2), 30–40.

Kleczkowska, A., et al. (1990). "Turner Syndrome: The Leuven Experience (1965–1980) in 478 Patients." *Genetic Counseling, 1*(3–4), 235–240.

Klein, M. (1991). "Why There's No Such Thing as Sexual Addiction—And Why It Really Matters." In R. T. Francoeur (Ed.), *Taking Sides: Clashing Views on Controversial Issues in Human Sexuality* (3rd ed.). Guilford, CT: Dushkin.

Klein, M. C., Gauthier, R. J., Jorgensen, S. H., Robbins, J. M., Kaczorowski, J., Johnson, B., Corriveau, M., Westreich, R., Waghorn, K., & Gelfand, M. M. (1992). "Does Episiotomy Prevent Perineal Trauma and Pelvic Floor Relaxation?" *Online Journal of Current Clinical Trials.*

Kline, A., Kline, E., & Oken, E. (1992). "Minority Women and Sexual Choice in the Age of AIDS." *Social Science and Medicine, 34*(4), 447–457.

Klinetob, N. A., & Smith, D. A. (1996, November). "Demand-Withdraw Communication in Marital Interaction: Tests of Interspousal Contingency and Gender Role Hypotheses." *Journal of Marriage and the Family, 58*(4), 945–957.

Knafo, D., & Jaffe, Y. (1984). "Sexual Fantasizing in Males and Females." *Journal of Research in Personality, 18,* 451–462.

Knapp, J., & Whitehurst, R. (1977). "Sexually Open Marriage and Relationships: Issues and Prospects." In R. Libby & R. Whitehurst (Eds.), *Marriage and Alternatives: Exploring Intimate Relationships.* Glenview, IL: Scott, Foresman.

Knopp, F. H. (1984). *Retraining Sex Offenders: Methods and Models.* Syracuse, NY: Safer Society Press.

Koblinsky, S. A., & Sugawara, A. I. (1984). "Nonsexist Curricula, Sex of Teacher and Children's Sex-Role Learning." *Sex Roles, 10,* 357–367.

Kockott, G., & Fahrner, E. M. (1998). "Male-to-Female and Female-to-Male Transsexuals: A Comparison." *Archives of Sexual Behavior, 17*(6), 539–546.

Kohl, J. V., & Francoeur, R. T. (1995). *The Scent of Eros: Mysteries of Odor in Human Sexuality.* New York: Continuum.

Kohlberg, L. (1969). "The Cognitive-Development Approach to Socialization." In A. Goslin (Ed.), *Handbook of Socialization Theory and Research.* Chicago: Rand McNally.

Kolata, G. (1990, May 31). "A Major Operation on a Fetus Works for the First Time." *The New York Times*, pp. 1ff.

Kolata, G. (1992, March 17). "How AIDS Smolders: Immune System Studies Follow the Tracks of H.I.V." *The New York Times*, pp. B5, 8.

Kolata, G. (1993). "New Pregnancy Hope: A Single Sperm Injected." *The New York Times*, p. 37.

Kolata, G. (1995, February 28). "New Picture of Who Will Get AIDS Is Dominated by Addicts." *The New York Times*, pp. 1, 3.

Kolata, G. (1995, May 28). "Will the Lawyers Kill Off Norplant?" *The New York Times*, pp. 1, 3.

Kolata, G. (1996, April 29). "Are U.S. Men Less Fertile? Latest Research Says No." *The New York Times*, p. A-8.

Kolker, A. (1989). "Advances in Prenatal Diagnosis: Social-Psychological and Policy Issues." *International Journal of Technology Assessment in Health Care, 5*(4), 601–617.

Kolodny, R., Masters, W., & Johnson, V. (1979). *Textbook of Sexual Medicine.* Boston: Little, Brown.

Konker, C. (1992). "Rethinking Child Sexual Abuse: An Anthropological Perspective." *American Journal of Orthopsychiatry, 62*(1), 147–153.

Koss, M. P. (1988). "Hidden Rape: Sexual Aggression and Victimization in a National Sample of Students in Higher Education." In A. W. Burgess (Ed.), *Rape and Sexual Assault II.* New York: Garland Press.

Kotlowitz, A. (1991). *There Are No Children Here.* New York: Doubleday.

Kowalski, K. M. (1997). "Safe Surfing on the Net." *Current Health 2, 24*(3), 28–29.

Krames, L., England, R., & Flett, G. (1988). "The Role of Masculinity and Femininity in Depression and Social Satisfaction in Elderly Years." *Sex Roles, 19*(11–12), 713–721.

Kreiger, L. M. (1996, January 21). "Foreign HIV Strains Found in California." *San Francisco Examiner*, pp. A1, A11–A12.

Kreiss, J., et al. (1992). "Efficacy of Nonoxynol-9 Contraceptive Sponge Use in Preventing Heterosexual Acquisition of HIV in Nairobi Prostitutes." *JAMA: Journal of the American Medical Association 268*(4), 477–482.

Krettek, J. E., Arkin, S. I., Chaisilwattana, P., & Monif, G. R. (1993). "Chlamydia Trachomatis in Patients Who Used Oral Contraceptives and Had Intermenstrual Spotting." *Obstetrics and Gynecology, 81*(5, Pt. 1), 728–731.

Krieger, J. N., et al. (1993). "Clinical Manifestations of Trichomoniasis in Men." *Annals of Internal Medicine, 118*(11), 844–889.

Krieger, L. M. (1992, July 19). "Global Attack on AIDS." *San Francisco Examiner*, pp. A1, 10.

Kruesi, M. J., Fine, S., Valladares, L., & Philips, R. A. (1992). "Paraphilias: A Double-Blind Crossover Comparison of Clomipramine Versus Despipramine." *Archives of Sexual Behavior, 21*(6), 587–593.

Kruks, G. (1991). "Gay and Lesbian Homeless/Street Youth: Special Issues and Concerns." Special Issue: Homeless Youth. *Journal of Adolescent Health, 12*(7), 515–518.

Kulhanjian, J. A., et al. (1992). "Identification of Women at Unsuspected Risk of Primary Infection with Herpes Simplex Virus Type 2 During Pregnancy." *New England Journal of Medicine, 326*(14), 916–920.

Kupersmid, J., & Wonderly, D. (1980). "Moral Maturity and Behavior: Failure to Find a Link." *Journal of Youth and Adolescence, 9*, 249–261.

Kurdek, L. (1988). "Relationship Quality of Gay and Lesbian Cohabiting Couples." *Journal of Homosexuality, 15*(3–4), 93–118.

Kurdek, L. (1991). "Sexuality in Homosexual and Heterosexual Couples." In K. McKinney & Susan Sprecher (Eds.), *Sexuality in Close Relationships.* Hillsdale, NJ: Erlbaum.

Kurdek, L., & Schmitt, P. (1988). "Relationship Quality of Gay Men in Closed and Open Relationships." In J. De Cecco (Ed.), *Gay Relationships.* New York: Haworth Press.

Ladas, A., Whipple, B., & Perry, J. (1982). *The G Spot.* New York: Holt, Rinehart & Winston.

La Franchi, S. (1992). "Human Growth Hormone: Who Is a Candidate for Treatment?" *Postgraduate Medicine, 91*(5), 373–374, 380–382 passim.

Lamaze, F. (1970). *Painless Childbirth* (1st ed., 1956). Chicago: H. Regnery.

Lamb, M. (1986). *The Father's Role: Cross-Cultural Perspectives.* Hillsdale, NJ: Erlbaum.

Lambert, B. (1990, September 6). "Despite Advice, Few Are Taking Drugs for AIDS." *The New York Times*, pp. A1, A18.

Lamontagne, Y., & Lesage, A. (1986). "Private Exposure and Covert Sensitization in the Treatment of Exhibitionism." *Journal of Behavior Therapy and Experimental Psychiatry, 17*(3), 197–201.

Landau, R. (1989). "Affect and Attachment: Kissing, Hugging, and Patting as Attachment Behaviors." *Infant Mental Health Journal, 10*(1), 59–69.

Landis, S. E., et al. (1992). "Results of a Randomized Trial of Partner Notification in Cases of HIV Infection in North Carolina." *New England Journal of Medicine, 326*(2), 101–106.

Laner, M. R. (1990). "Violence or Its Precipitators: Which Is More Likely to Be Identified as a Dating Problem?" *Deviant Behavior, 11*(4), 319–329.

Lang, R. (1992). Personal communication.

Lang, R., Checkley, K. L., & Pugh, G. (1987). "Genital Exhibitionism: Courtship Disorder or Narcissism?" *Canadian Journal of Behavioural Science, 19*(2), 216–232.

Lang, R., & Frenzel, R. (1988). "How Sex Offenders Lure Children." *Annals of Sex Research, 1*(2), 303–317.

Langevin, R., Wright, P., & Handy, L. (1988). "Empathy, Assertiveness, and Defensiveness Among Sex Offenders." *Annals of Sex Research, 1*, 533–547.

Langevin, R., Wright, P., & Handy, L. (1989). "Studies of Brain Damage and Dysfunction in Sex Offenders." *Annals of Sex Research, 2*(2), 163–179.

Langhoff, E., & Haseltine, W. A. (1992). "Infection of Accessory Dendritic Cells by Human Immunodeficiency Virus Type 1." *Journal of Investigative Dermatology, 99*(5), 89S–94S.

Lantz, H. (1980). "Family and Kin as Revealed in the Narratives of Ex-Slaves." *Social Science Quarterly, 60*(4), 667–674.

La Torre, R., & Wendenburg, K. (1983). "Psychological Characteristics of Bisexual, Heterosexual, and Homosexual Women." *Journal of Homosexuality, 9*(1), 87–97.

Latour, M. S., & Henthorne, T. L. (1994, September). "Ethical Judgments of Sexual Appeals in Print Advertising." *Journal of Advertising, 23*(3), 81–90.

Laube, D. (1985). "Premenstrual Syndrome." *The Female Patient, 6*, 50–61.

Laumann, E., Gagnon, J., Michael, R., & Michaels, S. (1994). *The Social Organization of Sexuality.* Chicago: University of Chicago Press.

Laurent, S. L., Thompson, S. J., Addy, C., Garrison, C. Z., & Moore, E. E. (1992). "An Epidemiologic Study of Smoking and Primary Infertility in Women." *Fertility and Sterility, 57*(3), 565–572.

Lavee, Y. (1991). "Western and Non-Western Human Sexuality: Implications for Clinical Practice." *Journal of Sex and Marital Therapy, 17*(5), 203–213.

Lavrakas, P. (1975). "Female Preferences for Male Physiques." *Journal of Research in Personality, 9*, 324–334.

Lawrence, C., III. (1992). "Cringing at the Myths of Black Sexuality." In R. Chrisman & R. Allen (Eds.), *Court of Appeal: The Black Community Speaks Out on the Racial and Sexual Politics of Clarence Thomas vs. Anita Hill.* New York: Ballantine.

Lawson, C. (1990, April 12). "Fathers, Too, Are Seeking a Balance Between Their Families and Careers." *The New York Times,* pp. 1ff.

Lazarus, A. A. (1989). "Dyspareunia: A Multimodel Psychotherapeutic Perspective." In S. R. Lieblum & R. C. Rosen (Eds.), *Principles and Practice of Sex Therapy* (2nd ed.). New York: Guilford Press.

Leary, W. (1993, May 11). "Female Condom Approved for Market." *The New York Times,* p. C5.

Leavitt, F., & Berger, J. C. (1990). "Clinical Patterns Among Male Transsexual Candidates with Erotic Interest in Males." *Archives of Sexual Behavior, 19*(5), 491–505.

Leben, L. S., & Signorella, M. L. (1993). "Gender-Schematic Processing in Children: The Role of Initial Interpretations of Stimuli." *Developmental Psychology, 29*(1), 141–150.

Ledwitz-Rigby, F. (1980). "Biochemical and Neurophysiological Influences on Human Sexual Development." In J. E. Parsons (Ed.), *The Psychobiology of Sex Differences and Sex Roles.* Washington, DC: Hemisphere.

Lee, A., & Scheurer, V. (1983). "Psychological Androgyny and Aspects of Self-Image in Women and Men." *Sex Roles, 9*, 289–306.

Lee, J. A. (1973). *The Color of Love.* Toronto: New Press.

Lee, J. A. (1988). "Love Styles." In R. Sternberg & M. Barnes (Eds.), *The Psychology of Love.* New Haven, CT: Yale University Press.

Leiblum, S. R. (1990). "Sexuality and the Midlife Woman." Special Issue: Women at Midlife and Beyond. *Psychology of Women Quarterly, 14*(4), 495–508.

Leifer, M. (1990). *Psychological Effects of Motherhood: A Study of First Pregnancy.* New York: Praeger.

Leigh, B. C. (1990). "Alcohol Expectancies and Reasons for Drinking: Comments from a Study of Sexuality." *Psychology of Addictive Behaviors, 4*(2), 91–96.

Leitenberg, H., Detzer, M. J., & Srebnik, D. (1993). "Gender Differences in Masturbation and the Relation of Masturbation Experience in Preadolescence and Early Adolescence to Sexual Behavior and Sexual Adjustment in Young Adulthood." *Archives of Sexual Behavior, 22*(2), 87–98.

Leitenberg, H., & Henning, K. (1995). "Sexual Fantasy." *Psychological Bulletin, 117*(3), 469–496.

Leland, J. (1997, November 17). "A Pill for Impotence?" *Newsweek,* pp. 62–68.

Lemkau, J. P. (1988). "Emotional Sequelae of Abortion: Implications for Clinical Practice." Special Issue: Women's Health: Our Minds, Our Bodies. *Psychology of Women Quarterly, 12,* 461–472.

Lemp, G. F., Hirozawa, A. M., Givertz, D., Nieri, G. N., Anderson, L., Lindegren, M. L., Janssen, R. S., & Katz, M. (1994). "Seroprevalence of HIV and Risk Behaviors Among Young Homosexual and Bisexual Men: The San Francisco/Berkeley Young Men's Survey." *JAMA: Journal of the American Medical Association, 272*(6), 449–454.

Lenz, R., & Chaves, B. (1981). "Becoming Active Partners: A Couple's Perspective." In D. Bullard & S. Knight (Eds.), *Sexuality and Disability: Personal Perspectives.* St. Louis, MO: Mosby.

Leo, J. (1986, November 26). "Sex and Schools." *Time,* pp. 54–63.

Leo, J. (1997, December 8). "A New Skill: Counting." *U.S. News and World Report,* p. 20.

Leonard, A. S. (1991). "From Law: Homophobia, Heterosexism and Judicial Decision Making." *Journal of Gay and Lesbian Psychotherapy, 1,* 65–91.

Lerner, H. E. (1993). *The Dance of Deception.* New York: Harper-Collins.

Lesbian, Gay, and Bisexual Youth Have Unique HIV-Prevention Needs. (1997, August 1). SIECUS. Available: http://www.siecus.org/pubs/shop/shop0011.html (Last visited 10/2/97).

"Lesbians' Cancer Risk Estimated to Be High." (1993, February 5). *San Jose Mercury News,* p. 8.

Lester, J. (1973, July). "Men: Being a Boy." *Ms.,* pp. 112–113.

Le Vay, S. (1991). "A Difference in Hypothalamic Structure Between Heterosexual and Homosexual Men." *Science, 253,* 1034–1037.

Levesque, R. J. R. (1994). "Sex Differences in the Experiences of Child Sexual Victimization." *Journal of Family Violence, 9*(4), 357–369.

Levin, R. J. (1975). "The Redbook Report on Premarital and Extramarital Sex: The End of the Double Standard?" *Redbook,* 38–44, 190–192.

Levine, L., & Barbach, L. (1983). *The Intimate Male.* New York: Signet Books.

Levine, M. P. (1987). *How Schools Can Help Combat Student Eating Disorders: Anorexia Nervosa and Bulimia.* Washington, DC: National Education Association.

Levine, M. P. (1992). "The Life and Death of Gay Clones." In G. Herdt (Ed.), *Gay Culture in America: Essays from the Field.* Boston: Beacon Press.

Levine, M. P. (1993). "The Role of Culture in Eating Disorders." In D. N. Suggs & A. W. Miracle (Eds.), *Culture and Human Sexuality.* Pacific Grove, CA: Brooks/Cole.

Levine, M. P., & Troiden, R. (1988). "The Myth of Sexual Compulsivity." *Journal of Sex Research, 25*(3), 347–363.

Levine, S. B. (1997). The Role of Psychiatry in Erectile Dysfunction: A Cautionary Essay on Emerging Treatments. Medscape, Inc. Available: http://www.medscape.com

Levine, S. B., Risen, C. B., & Althof, A. E. (1990). "Essay on the Diagnosis and Nature of Paraphilia." *Journal of Sex and Marital Therapy, 16*(2), 89–102.

Levy, S. (1997, March 31). "U.S. v. the Internet." *Newsweek,* pp. 77–79.

Lewes, K. (1992). "Homophobia and the Heterosexual Fear of AIDS." *American Imago, 49*(3), 343–356.

Lewin, T. (1997, December 21). "New Type of Early Abortions." *San Francisco Chronicle,* p. A1.

Lewis, D. (1890). *Chastity: or, Our Secret Sins.* Philadelphia: G. Maclean.

Lewis, L. (1992). "Consumer Girl Culture: How Music Video Appeals to Girls." In M. E. Brown (Ed.), *Television and Women's Culture: The Politics of the Popular.* Newbury Park, CA: Sage Publications.

Lew-Starowicz, Z. (1994, July). "Problems of Disabled Persons with a Homosexual Orientation." *International Journal of Adolescent Medicine and Health, 7*(3), 233–239.

Li, C. K. (1990). "'The Main Thing Is Being Wanted': Some Case Studies in Adult Sexual Experiences with Children." *Journal of Homosexuality, 20*(1–2), 129–143.

Liben, L. S., & Signorella, M. L. (1993). "Gender-Schematic Processing in Children: The Role of Initial Interpretations of Stimuli." *Developmental Psychology, 29*(1), 141–150.

Libman, E. (1989, July). "Sociocultural and Cognitive Factors in Aging and Sexual Expression: Conceptual and Research Issues." *Canadian Psychology, 30*(3), 560–567.

Lieberson, S., & Waters, M. (1988). *From Many Strands: Ethnic and Racial Groups in Contemporary America.* New York: Russell Sage Foundation.

Lief, H. I., & Hubschman, L. (1993). "Orgasm in the Postoperative Transsexual." *Archives of Sexual Behavior, 22*(2), 145–155.

Lifson, A. R. (1988). "Do Alternative Modes for Transmission of Human Immunodeficiency Virus Exist?" *JAMA: Journal of the American Medical Association, 152,* 1353–1357.

Lifson, A. R., et al. (1990). "HIV Seroconversion in Two Homosexual Men After Receptive Oral Intercourse with Ejaculation: Implications for Counseling Concerning Safe Sex Practices." *American Journal of Public Health, 80*(12), 1509–1511.

Lindbohm, M. L., Hietanan, M., Kyronen, P., & Sallmen, M. (1992). "Magnetic Fields of Video Display Terminals and Spontaneous Abortion." *American Journal of Epidemiology, 136,* 1041–1051.

Lindemalm, G., Korlin, D., & Uddenberg, N. (1986). "Long-Term Follow-Up of 'Sex Change' in 13 Male-to-Female Transsexuals." *Archives of Sexual Behavior, 15*(3), 187–210.

Lino, M. (1990). "Expenditures on a Child by Husband-Wife Families." *Family Economics Review, 3*(3), 2–12.

Lipman, A. (1986). "Homosexual Relationships." *Generations, 10,* 51–54.

Lipman, M. (1994, May). "Office Visit: What Do Women Need?" *Consumer Reports on Health, 6*(5), 59.

Lips, H. (1997). *Sex and Gender* (2nd ed.). Mountain View, CA: Mayfield.

Lipscomb, G. H., et al. (1992). "Male Victims of Sexual Assault." *JAMA: Journal of the American Medical Association, 267*(22), 3064–3066.

Loftus, E., & Ketcham, D. (1994). *The Myth of Repressed Memory: False Memories and Allegations of Sexual Abuse.* New York: St. Martin's Press.

Longo, R. E., & Groth, A. N. (1983). "Juvenile Sexual Offenses in the Histories of Adult Rapists and Child Molesters." *International Journal of Offender Therapy & Comparative Criminology, 27,* 150–155.

LoPresto, C., Sherman, M., & Sherman, N. (1985). "The Effects of a Masturbation Seminar on High School Males' Attitudes, False Beliefs, Guilt, and Behavior." *Journal of Sex Research, 21,* 142–156.

Lord, L. (1985, December 9). "Mortality." *U.S. News and World Report,* pp. 52–59.

Lorefice, L. (1991). "Fluoxetine Treatment of a Fetish." *Journal of Clinical Psychiatry, 52*(1), 41.

Lorenz, K. (1966). *On Aggression.* New York: Harcourt Brace Jovanovich.

Lott, B. (1990). "Dual Natures or Learned Behavior: The Challenge to Feminist Psychology." In R. T. Hare-Mustin & J. Marecek (Eds.), *Making a Difference: Psychology and the Construction of Gender.* New Haven, CT: Yale University Press.

Loulan, J. (1984). *Lesbian Sex.* San Francisco: Spinsters Book Company.

Love, P., & Robinson, J. (1994). *Hot Monogamy: Essential Steps to More Passionate, Intimate Lovemaking.* New York: Dutton.

Lowry, D., & Towles, D. (1989). "Prime-Time TV Portrayals of Sex, Contraception, and Venereal Disease." *Journalism Quarterly, 66*(2), 347–352.

Lucas, V. A. (1992). "An Investigation of the Health Care Preferences of the Lesbian Population." *Health Care for Women International, 13*(2), 221–228.

Luker, K. (1975). *Taking Chances.* Berkeley: University of California Press.

Lunneborg, P. (1992). *Abortion: The Positive Decision.* New York: Bergin & Garvy.

Lynch, F. R. (1992). "Nonghetto Gays: An Ethnography of Suburban Homosexuals." In G. Herdt (Ed.), *Gay Culture in America: Essays from the Field.* Boston: Beacon Press.

Lyon, J. (1985). *Playing God in the Nursery.* New York: Norton.

MacDonald, A., Jr. (1981). "Bisexuality: Some Comments on Research and Theory." *Journal of Homosexuality, 6,* 9–27.

Macdonald, P. T., Waldorf, D., Reinarman, C., & Murphy, S. (1988). "Heavy Cocaine Use and Sexual Behavior." *Journal of Drug Issues, 18*(3), 437–455.

Mackey, T., Sereika, S. M., Weissfeld, L. A., Hacker, S. S., Zender, J. F., & Heard, S. L. (1992). "Factors Associated with Long-Term Depressive Symptoms of Sexual Assault Victims." *Archives of Psychiatric Nursing, 6*(1), 10–25.

Macklin, E. (1987). "Nontraditional Family Forms." In M. Sussman & S. Steinmetz (Eds.), *Handbook of Marriage and the Family.* New York: Plenum Press.

Maddock, J. W., et al. (1983). "Human Sexuality and the Family." New York: Haworth Press.

Maddox, J. (1993, March 25). "Where the AIDS Virus Hides Away." *Nature, 362*(6418), 287ff.

Maden, D., Sherman, K. J., Beckmann, A. M., Hislop, T. G., Teh, C. Z., Ashley, R. L., & Daling, J. R. (1993). "History of Circumcision. Medical Conditions, and Sexual Activity and Risk of Penile Cancer." *Journal of the National Cancer Institute, 85*(1), 19–24.

Madsen, W. (1973). *Mexican-American Youth of South Texas* (2nd ed.). New York: Holt, Rinehart & Winston.

Major, B., & Cozzarelli, C. (1992). "Psychosocial Predictors of Adjustment to Abortion." *Journal of Social Issues, 48*(3), 121–142.

Malamuth, N. (1981). "Rape Fantasies as a Function of Exposure to Violent Sexual Stimuli." *Archives of Sexual Behavior, 10*(1), 33–47.

Malamuth, N. M. (1996, Summer). "Sexually Explicit Media, Gender Differences, and Evolutionary Theory." *Journal of Communication, 46*(3), 8–31.

Malamuth, N., & Spinner, B. (1980). "A Longitudinal Content Analysis of Sexual Violence in Best-Selling Erotic Magazines." *Journal of Sex Research, 16*(3), 226–237.

Malatesta, V., Chambless, D., Pollack, M., & Cantor, A. (1989). "Widowhood, Sexuality, and Aging: A Life Span Analysis." *Journal of Sex and Marital Therapy, 14*(1), 49–62.

Malcolm, S. J. (1994, October). "Was It Good For You?" *Ms.* pp. 23–25.

Mancini, J., & Bliezner, R. (1991). "Aging Parents and Adult Children Research Themes in Intergenerational Relations." In A. Booth (Ed.), *Contemporary Families: Looking Forward, Looking Back.* Minneapolis, MN: National Council on Family Relations.

Mandoki, M. W., Sumner, G. S., Hoffman, R. P., & Riconda, D. L. (1991). "A Review of Klinefelter's Syndrome in Children and Adolescents." *Journal of the American Academy of Child and Adolescence Psychiatry, 30*(2), 167–172.

Mansnerus, L. (1990, April 24). "The Cincinnati Case: What Are the Issues? What Is at Stake?" *The New York Times,* pp. B1, B3.

Marecek, J., Finn, & Cardell. (1988). "Gender Roles in the Relationships of Lesbians and Gay Men." In J. De Cecco (Ed.), *Gay Relationships.* New York: Haworth Press.

Margiglio, W. (1991). "Male Procreative Consciousness and Responsibility: A Conceptual Analysis and Research Agenda." *Journal of Family Issues, 12,* 268–290.

Margiglio, W., & Donnelly, D. (1991). "Sexual Relations in Later Life: A National Study of Married Persons." *Journal of Gerontology, 46,* S338–S344.

Margolies, L., Becher, M., & Jackson-Brewer, K. (1988). "Internalized Homophobia: Identifying and Treating the Oppressor Within." In Boston Lesbian Psychologies Collective (Eds.), *Lesbian Psychologies.* Urbana, IL: University of Illinois Press.

Margolin, L. (1992). "Sexual Abuse by Grandparents." *Child Abuse and Neglect, 16*(5), 735–742.

Margolin, L., & White, L. (1987). "The Continuing Role of Physical Attractiveness in Marriage." *Journal of Marriage and the Family, 49,* 21–27.

Margolin, M. (1978). *The Ohlone Way.* Berkeley, CA: Heyday Books.

Marieb, E. N. (1995). *Human Anatomy and Physiology* (2nd ed.). Redwood City, CA: Benjamin/Cummings.

Marijuana and Sex. (1996, April 5). Available: http://www.columbia.edu/cu/healthwise/0860.html (Last visited 1/29/98).

Marin, G., & Marin, B. V. (1989). "A Comparison of Three Interviewing Approaches for Studying Sensitive Topics with Hispanics." *Hispanic Journal of the Behavioral Sciences, 11*(4), 330–340.

Marin, G., & Marin, B. (1991). *Research with Hispanic Populations.* Newbury Park, CA: Sage Publications.

Marin, R., Hannah, D., Colin, M., Annin, P., & Gegax, T. T. (1995, February 6). "Turning in the Badges of Rebellion." *Newsweek,* p. 45.

Markman, H. (1981). "Prediction of Marital Distress: A Five-Year Follow-Up." *Journal of Consulting and Clinical Psychology, 49,* 760–761.

Markman, H., Duncan, W., Storaasli, R. D., & Howes, P. W. (1987). "The Prediction and Prevention of Marital Distress: A Longitudinal Investigation." In K. Hahlweg & M. Goldstein (Eds.), *Understanding Major Mental Disorders: The Contribution of Family Interaction Research.* New York: Family Process Press.

Markman, H., Floyd, F. J., Stanley, S. M., & Storaasli, R. D. (1988). "Prevention of Marital Distress: A Longitudinal Investigation." *Journal of Consulting and Clinical Psychology, 56*(2), 210–217.

Marmor, J. (Ed.). (1980a). *Homosexual Behavior.* New York: Basic Books.

Marmor, J. (1980b). "Homosexuality and the Issue of Mental Illness." In J. Marmor (Ed.), *Homosexual Behavior.* New York: Basic Books.

Marmor, J. (1980c). "The Multiple Roots of Homosexual Behavior." In J. Marmor (Ed.), *Homosexual Behavior.* New York: Basic Books.

Marrero, M. A., & Ory, S. J. (1991). "Unexplained Infertility." *Current Opinion in Obstetrics and Gynecology, 3*(2), 211–218.

Marshall, D. (1971). "Sexual Behavior on Mangaia." In D. Marshall & R. Suggs (Eds.), *Human Sexual Behavior.* New York: Basic Books.

Marshall, W. L. (1988). "The Use of Sexually Explicit Material by Rapists, Child Molesters, and Non-Offenders." *Journal of Sex Research, 25,* 267–268.

Marshall, W. L., Eccles, A., & Barabee, H. E. (1991). "The Treatment of Exhibitionism: A Focus on Sexual Deviance Versus Cognitive and Relationship Features." *Behaviour Research and Therapy, 29*(2), 129–135.

Marshall, W. L., Payne, K., Barabee, H. E., & Eccles, A. (1991). "Exhibitionism: Sexual Preference for Exposing." *Behaviour Research and Therapy, 29*(1), 37–40.

Marsiglio, W., & Donnelly, D. (1991). "Sexual Relations in Later Life: A National Study of Married Persons." *Journal of Gerontology, 46*(6), S338–S344.

Marsiglio, W., & Mott, F. (1986). "The Impact of Sex Education on Sexual Activity, Contraceptive Use and Premarital Pregnancy Among American Teenagers." *Family Planning Perspectives, 18*(4), 215ff.

Marsiglio, W., & Shehan, C. L. (1993). "Adolescent Males' Abortion Attitudes: Data from a National Survey." *Family Planning Perspectives 25*(4), 162–169.

Martin, G. (1989). "Relationship, Romance, and Sexual Addiction in Extramarital Affairs." *Journal of Psychology and Christianity, 8*(4), 5–25.

Martin, G. (1992, October 16). "Justify Her Love." *San Jose Mercury News,* pp. 1, 4.

Martin, P. (1981). "Happy Sexless Marriages." *Medical Aspects of Human Sexuality, 15*(1), 25.

Martin, P. M., Gresenguet, G., Massanga, M., Georges, A., & Testa, J. (1992). "Association Between HIV-1 Infection and Sexually Transmitted Disease Among Men in Central Africa." *Research in Virology, 143*(3), 205–209.

Martin, T. C., & Bumpass, L. L. (1989). "Recent Trends in Marital Disruption." *Demography, 26,* 37–51.

Martinez, F., Wright, A., Taussig, L., et al. (1994). "The Effect of Paternal Smoking on the Birthweight of Newborns Whose Mothers Did Not Smoke." *American Journal of Public Health, 84*(9), 1489–1491.

Mason, K., & Lu, Y. H. (1988). "Attitudes Toward Women's Familial Roles: Changes in the United States, 1977–1985." *Gender and Society, 2*(1), 39–57.

Massa, G., Maes, M., Heinrichs, C., Vandeweghe, M., Craen, M., & Vanderschueren-Lodeweyckx, M. (1993). "Influence of Spontaneous or Induced Puberty on the Growth Promoting Effect of Treatment with Growth Hormone in Girls with Turner's Syndrome." *Clinical Endocrinology, 38*(3), 253–260.

"Massachusetts Midwife Curb Upheld." (1987, May 25). *The New York Times,* p. 5.

Masse, M., & Rosenblum, K. (1988). "Male and Female Created They Them: The Depiction of Gender in the Advertising of Traditional Women's and Men's Magazines." *Women's Studies International Forum, 11*(2), 127–144.

Massey, F. J., et al. (1984). "Vasectomy and Health: Results from a Large Cohort Study." *JAMA: Journal of the American Medical Association, 252,* 1023–1029.

Masters, W. H., & Johnson, V. E. (1966). *Human Sexual Response.* Boston: Little, Brown.

Masters, W. H., & Johnson, V. E. (1970). *Human Sexual Inadequacy.* Boston: Little, Brown.

Masters, W. H., & Johnson, V. E. (1974). *The Pleasure Bond.* Boston: Little, Brown.

Masters, W. H., & Johnson, V. E. (1979). *Homosexuality in Perspective.* Boston: Little, Brown.

Masters, W. H., Johnson, V. E., & Kolodny, R. C. (1985). *Human Sexuality* (2nd ed.). New York: Little, Brown.

Masters, W. H., Johnson, V. E., & Kolodny, R. C. (1986). *Masters and Johnson on Sex and Human Loving.* Boston: Little, Brown.

Masters, W. H., Johnson, V. E., & Kolodny, R. C. (1988). *Crisis: AIDS and Heterosexual Behavior.* New York: Grove Press.

Masters, W. H., Johnson, V., & Kolodny, R. C. (1992). *Human Sexuality* (3rd ed.). New York: HarperCollins.

Matek, O. (1988). "Obscene Phone Callers." In D. Dailey (Ed.), *The Sexually Unusual.* New York: Harrington Park Press.

Mathur, A., Stetol, L., Schatz, D., Maclaren, N. K., Scott, M. L., & Lippe, B. (1991). "The Parental Origin of the Single X Chromosome in Turner Syndrome: Lack of Correlation with Parental Age or Clinical Phenotype." *American Journal of Human Genetics, 48*(4), 682–686.

Matsakis, A. (1991). *When the Bough Breaks.* Oakland, CA: New Harbinger Publications.

Matteo, S., & Rissman, E. (1984). "Increased Sexual Activity During Midcycle Portion of the Human Menstrual Cycle." *Hormones and Behavior, 18,* 249–255.

Mayall, A., & Russell, D. E. (1993, June). "Racism in Pornography." *Feminism & Psychology, 3*(2), 275–281.

Mays, V. M., Cochran, S. D., Bellinger, G., & Smith, R. G. (1992). "The Language of Black Gay Men's Sexual Behavior: Implications for AIDS Risk Reduction." *Journal of Sex Research, 29*(3), 425–434.

Mays, V. M., Cochran, S. D., Smith, R. G., & Daniels. (1993).

Mays, V. M., & Jackson, J. S. (1991). "AIDS Survey Methodology with Black Americans." *Social Science and Medicine, 33*(1), 47–54.

Mazel, D., & Percival, E. (1989). "Students' Experiences of Sexual Harassment at a Small University." *Sex Roles, 20,* 1–22.

Mazor, M., & Simons, H. (Eds.). (1984). *Infertility: Medical, Emotional and Social Considerations.* New York: Human Sciences Press.

Mazur, A. (1986). "U.S. Trends in Feminine Beauty and Over-adaptation." *Journal of Sex Research, 22*(3), 281–303.

McAninch, J. (1989). "Editorial Comment on the Report of the Task Force on Circumcision." *Pediatrics, 84,* 667.

McCabe, M. P. (1994). "Childhood, Adolescent and Current Psychological Factors Associated with Sexual Dysfunction." *Sexual & Marital Therapy, 9*(3), 267–276.

McCabe, M. P., & Collins, J. K. (1984). "Measurement of Depth of Desired and Experienced Sexual Involvement at Different Stages of Dating." *Journal of Sex Research, 20,* 377–390.

McCauley, E., & Ehrhardt, A. (1980). "Female Sexual Response." In D. Youngs & A. Ehrhardt (Eds.), *Psychosomatic Obstetrics and Gynecology.* New York: Appleton-Century-Crofts.

McClure, D. (1988, May). "Men with One Testicle." *Medical Aspects of Human Sexuality,* 22–32.

McConaghy, N. (1993). *Sexual Behavior: Problems and Management.* New York: Plenum Press.

McCormack, M. J., et al. (1990). "Patients' Attitudes Following Chorionic Villus Sampling." *Prenatal Diagnosis, 10*(4), 253–255.

McCormick, N. (1996). "Our Feminist Future: Women Affirming Sexuality Research in the Late Twentieth Century." *Journal of Sex Research, 33*(2), 99–102.

McEwan, K. L., Costello, C. G., & Taylor, P. J. (1987). "Adjustment to Infertility." *Journal of Abnormal Psychology, 96*(2), 108–116.

McGoldrick, M. (1982). "Normal Families: An Ethnic Perspective." In F. Walsh (Ed.), *Normal Family Processes.* New York: Guilford Press.

McGoldrick, M., Pearce, J. K., & Giordano, J. (Eds.). (1982). *Ethnicity and Family Therapy.* New York: Guilford Press.

McIntosh, E. (1989). "An Investigation of Romantic Jealousy Among Black Undergraduates." *Social Behavior and Personality, 17*(2), 135–141.

McIntyre, S. L., & Higgins, J. E. (1986). "Parity and Use-Effectiveness with the Contraceptive Sponge." *American Journal of Obstetrics and Gynecology, 155,* 796–801

McLaurin, M. (1991). *Celia: A Slave.* Athens, GA: University of Georgia Press.

McLeer, S. V., Deblinger, E. B., Henry, D., & Ovraschel, H. (1992). "Sexually Abused Children at High Risk for Post-Traumatic Stress Disorder." *Journal of the American Academy of Child and Adolescent Psychiatry, 31*(5), 875–879.

McMahon, K. (1990). "The Cosmopolitan Ideology and the Management of Desire." *Journal of Sex Research, 27*(3), 381–396.

McMullen, R. (1987). "Youth Prostitution: A Balance of Power." *Journal of Adolescence, 10,* 35–43.

McNeeley, S. G., Jr. (1992). "Pelvic Inflammatory Disease." *Current Opinion in Obstetrics and Gynecology, 4*(5), 682–686.

McNew, J., & Abell, N. "Survivors of Childhood Sexual Abuse." *Social Work, 40,* 115–126.

McWhirter, D. (1990). "Prologue." In D. McWhirter, S. A. Sanders, & J. M. Reinisch (Eds.), *Homosexuality/Heterosexuality: Concepts of Sexual Orientation.* New York: Oxford University Press.

McWhirter, D., Sanders, S. A., & Reinisch, J. M. (Eds.). (1990). *Homosexuality/Heterosexuality: Concepts of Sexual Orientation.* New York: Oxford University Press.

Meacham, R. E., & Lipshultz, L. I. (1991). "Assisted Reproductive Technologies for Male Factor Infertility." *Current Opinion in Obstetrics and Gynecology, 3*(5), 656–661.

Mead, M. (1975). *Male and Female.* New York: William Morrow.

Meek, T. D., et al. (1990). "Inhibition of HIV-1 Protease in Infected T-Lymphocytes by Synthetic Peptide Analogues." *Nature, 343*(6253), 90–92.

Meier, K. J., & McFarlane, D. R. (1993). "The Politics of Funding Abortion: State Responses to the Political Environment." *American Politics Quarterly, 21*(1), 81–101.

Metts, S., & Cupach, W. (1989). "The Role of Communication in Human Sexuality." In K. McKinney & S. Sprecher (Eds.), *Human Sexuality: The Social and Interpersonal Context.* Norwood, NJ: Ablex.

Meuwissen, I., & Over, R. (1992). "Sexual Arousal Across Phases of the Human Menstrual Cycle." *Archives of Sexual Behavior, 21,* 101–119.

Meyer, I. H. (1995, March). "Minority Stress and Mental Health in Gay Men." *Journal of Health and Social Behavior, 16*(1), 38–56.

Meyer, R. G., & Deitsch, S. E. (1996). *The Clinician's Handbook.* Needham Heights, MA: Simon & Schuster.

Michael, R., Gagnon, J., Laumann, E., & Kolata, G. (1994). *Sex in America: A Definitive Survey.* Boston: Little Brown & Co.

Milan, R., Jr., & Kilmann, P. (1987). "Interpersonal Factors in Premarital Contraception." *Journal of Sex Research, 23*(3), 321–389.

Miller, B. (1986). *Family Research Methods.* Newbury Park, CA: Sage Publications.

Miller, B. C., Christopherson, C. R., & King, P. K. (1993). "Sexual Behavior in Adolescence." In T. P. Gullotta et al. (Eds.), *Adolescent Sexuality.* Newbury Park, CA: Sage Publications.

Miller, B. C., & Dyk, P. A. (1990). "Adolescent Fertility-Related Behavior in the 1990s: Risking the Future Continued." *Journal of Family Issues, 11*(3), 235–238.

Miller, B. C., & Fox, G. L. (1987). "Theories of Adolescent Heterosexual Behavior." *Adolescent Research, 2,* 269–282.

Miller, E. M. (1986). *Street Women*. Philadelphia: Temple University Press.

Miller, J. (1995). "Gender and Power on the Streets: Street Prostitution in the Era of Crack Cocaine." *Journal of Contemporary Ethnography, 23*, 427–452.

Miller, J., & Schwartz, M. D. (1995, January). "Rape Myths and Violence Against Street Prostitutes." *Deviant Behavior, 16*(1), 1–23.

Miller, T. R., Cohen, M. A., & Wiersema, B. (1996). "Victim Costs and Consequences: A New Look." Washington, DC: U.S. Department of Justice, National Institute of Justice.

Miller, W. (1981). "Psychological Vulnerability to Unwanted Pregnancy." In F. Furstenberg et al. (Eds.), *Teenage Sexuality, Pregnancy, and Childbearing*. Philadelphia: University of Pennsylvania Press.

Mindel, C. H., Haberstein, R. W., & Wright, R., Jr. (Eds.). (1988). *Ethnic Families in America: Patterns and Variations* (3rd ed.). New York: Elsevier North Holland.

Minkoff, H. L., & Dehovitz, J. A. (1991). "Care of Women Infected with the Human Immunodeficiency Virus." *JAMA: Journal of the American Medical Association, 266*(16), 2253–2258.

Mio, J. S., & Foster, J. D. (1991). "The Effects of Rape upon Victims and Families: Implications for a Comprehensive Family Therapy." *American Journal of Family Therapy, 19*(2), 147–159.

Mishra, R. (1998, April 7). "Drug Begs Many Questions." *Monterey County Herald*, p. A-10.

Mison, R. B. (1992). "Homophobia in Manslaughter: The Homosexual Advance as Provocation." *California Law Review, 80*(1), 133–178.

Moergen, S., Merkel, W. T., & Brown, S. (1990). "The Use of Covert Sensitization and Social Skills Training in Treatment of an Obscene Phone Caller." *Journal of Behavior Therapy and Experimental Psychology, 21*(4), 269–275.

Moffatt, M. (1989). *Coming of Age in New Jersey: College and American Culture*. New Brunswick, NJ: Rutgers University Press.

Mohr, J., & Beutler, I. (1990). "Erectile Dysfunction: A Review of Diagnostic and Treatment Procedures." *Clinical Psychology Review, 10*, 123–150.

Moller, L. C., Hymel, S., & Rubin, K. H. (1992). "Sex Typing in Play and Popularity in Middle Childhood." *Sex Roles, 26*(7–8), 331–335.

Monat-Haller, R. K. (1982). *Sexuality and the Mentally Retarded: A Clinical and Therapeutic Guidebook*. San Diego, CA: College Hill Press.

Money, J. (1980). *Love and Lovesickness*. Baltimore: Johns Hopkins University Press.

Money, J. (1981). "Paraphilias: Phyletic Origins of Erotosexual Dysfunction." *International Journal of Mental Health, 10*, 75–109.

Money, J. (1986). "Statements of the Shadow Commissioners." In P. Nobile (Ed.), *United States of America vs. Sex: How the Meese Commission Lied About Pornography*. New York: Minotaur Press.

Money, J. (1988a). "Commentary: Current Status of Sex Research." *Journal of Psychology and Human Sexuality, 1*(1), 5–16.

Money, J. (1988b). *Gay, Straignt, and In-Between*. New York: Oxford University Press.

Money, J. (1990). "Forensic Sexology: Paraphilic Serial Rape (Biastophilia) and Lust Murder (Erotophonophilia)." *American Journal of Psychotherapy, 44*(1), 26–37.

Money, J., & Tucker, P. (1976). *Sexual Signatures: On Being a Man or a Woman*. London: Harrap.

Monroe, J. (1997). "'Roofies': Horror Drug of the '90s." *Current Health, 2*(1), 24–27.

Montagu, A. (1986). *Touching* (3rd ed.). New York: Columbia University Press.

Montauk, S., & Clasen, M. (1989, January). "Sex Education in Primary Care: Infancy to Puberty." *Medical Aspects of Human Sexuality*, 22–36.

Montgomery, M. J., & Sorell, G. T. (1997, January). "Differences in Love Attitudes Across Family Life Stages." *Family Relations, 46*(1), 55–61.

Moore, M. M. (1985). "Nonverbal Courtship Patterns in Women: Context and Consequences." *Ethology and Sociobiology, 6*(2), 237–247.

Mootnik, A. R., & Baker, E. (1994). "Masturbation in Captive Hylobates (Gibbons)." *Zoo Biology, 13*(4), 345–353.

Moran, J. S., Janes, H. R., Peterman, T. A., & Stone, K. M. (1990). "Increase in Condom Sales Following AIDS Education and Publicity, United States." *American Journal of Public Health, 80*(5), 607–608.

Morawski, J. G. (1990). "Toward the Unimagined: Feminism and Epistemology in Psychology." In R. T. Hare-Mustin & J. Marecek (Eds.), *Making a Difference: Psychology and the Construction of Gender*. New Haven, CT: Yale University Press.

Morgenthaler, E. (1992, January 23). "These Thieves Are Partial to Sequins, and Pretty in Pink: Gangs of Florida Transvestites Steal Millions in Dresses." *The Wall Street Journal*, p. 1.

Morin, J. (1986). *Anal Pleasure and Health: A Guide for Men and Women*. Burlingame, CA: Yes Press.

Morse, E. V., Simon, P. M., Balson, P. M., & Osofsky, H. J. (1992). "Sexual Behavior Patterns of Customers of Male Street Prostitutes." *Archives of Sexual Behavior, 21*, 347–357.

Morse, E. V., Simon, P. M., Osofsky, H. J., Balson, P. M., & Gaumer, H. R. (1991). "The Male Street Prostitute: A Vector for Transmission of HIV Infection into the Heterosexual World." *Social Science and Medicine, 32*(5), 535–539.

Moser, C. (1988). "Sadomasochism." In D. Dailey (Ed.), *The Sexually Unusual*. New York: Harrington Park Press.

Mosher, D. L., & MacIan, P. (1994). "College Men and Women Respond to X-Rated Videos Intended for Male or Female Audiences: Gender and Sexual Scripts." *Journal of Sex Research, 31*(2), 99–113.

Mosher, W. D., & McNally, J. W. (1991). "Contraceptive Use at First Premarital Intercourse: United States, 1965–1988." *Family Planning Perspectives, 23*, 108–116.

Moss, G. B., et al. (1991). "Association of Cervical Ectopy with Heterosexual Transmission of Human Immunodeficiency Virus: Results of a Study of Couples in Nairobi, Kenya." *Journal of Infectious Diseases, 164*(3), 588–591.

Mota, R. G. (1991). "Project First Hand: The Power of HIV-Infected Educators in AIDS Prevention." *Exchange: World Health Organization Global Program on AIDS, 1*, 1–12.

Mota, R. G. (1992, July). "Breast-Feeding and HIV Transmission." *I.H.P.: International Health Programs Newsletter, 1*, 1ff.

"Mothers Urged to Breast-Feed." (1997, December 3). *San Francisco Chronicle*, p. A-1.

Moultrup, D. J. (1990). *Husbands, Wives, and Lovers: The Emotional System of the Extramarital Affair*. New York: Guilford Press.

Moyer, K. E. (1974). "Sex Differences in Aggression." In R. C. Friedman, R. M. Richart, & R. L. Vande Wiele (Eds.), *Sex Differences in Behavior*. New York: John Wiley.

Muehlenhard, C. L. (1988). "Misinterpreted Dating Behaviors and the Risk of Date Rape." *Journal of Social and Clinical Psychology, 9*(1), 20–37.

Muehlenhard, C. L., & McCoy, M. L. (1991). "Double Standard/Double Bind." *Psychology of Women Quarterly, 15*, 447–461.

Muehlenhard, C. L., Ponch, I. G., Phelps, J. L., & Giusti, L. M. (1992). "Definitions of Rape: Scientific and Political Implications." *Journal of Social Issues, 48*(1), 23–44.

Muehlenhard, C. L., & Schrag, J. (1991). "Nonviolent Sexual Coercion." In A. Parrot & L. Bechhofer (Eds.), *Acquaintance Rape: The Hidden Crime.* New York: John Wiley.

Mueller, B. A., Luz-Jiminez, M., Daling, J. R., Moore, D. E., McKnight, B., & Weiss, N. S. (1992). "Risk Factors for Tubal Infertility: Influence of History of Prior Pelvic Inflammatory Disease." *Sexually Transmitted Diseases, 19*(1), 28–34.

Mulligan, T., & Moss, C. R. (1991). "Sexuality and Aging in Male Veterans: A Cross-Sectional Study of Interest, Ability, and Activity." *Archives of Sexual Behavior, 20*(1), 17–25.

Mulligan, T., & Palguta, R. (1991). "Sexual Interest, Activity, and Satisfaction Among Male Nursing Home Residents." *Archives of Sexual Behavior, 20*(2), 199–204.

Mulligan, T., Retchin, S. M., Chinchilli, V. M., & Bettinger, C. B. (1988). "The Role of Aging and Chronic Disease in Sexual Dysfunction." *Journal of the American Geriatrics Society, 36*(6), 520–524.

Mullins, L. L., Lynch, J., Orten, J., Youll, L. K., Verschraegen-Spae, Dypere, H., Speleman, F., Dhoult, M., & DePaepe, A. (1991). "Developing a Program to Assist Turner's Syndrome Patients and Families." *Social Work in Health Care, 16*(2), 69–79.

"Muppet Gender Gap." (1993). *Media Report to Women, 21*(1), 8.

Muram, D., Miller, K., & Cutler, A. (1992). "Sexual Assault of the Elderly Victim." *Journal of Interpersonal Violence, 7*(1), 70–76.

Murnen, S. K., Perot, A., & Byrne, D. (1989). "Coping with Unwanted Sexual Activity: Normative Responses, Situational Determinants, and Individual Differences." *Journal of Sex Research, 26*, 85–106.

Murrell, A., Olson, J. E., & Frieze, I. (1995, March). "Sexual Harassment and Gender Discrimination: A Longitudinal Study of Women Managers." *Journal of Social Issues, 51*(1), 139–149.

Murry, V. M. (1991). "Socio-Historical Study of Black Female Sexuality: Transition to First Coitus." In R. Staples (Ed.), *The Black Family* (4th ed.). Belmont, CA: Wadsworth.

Murstein, B. (1976). *Who Will Marry Whom: Theories and Research in Marital Choice.* New York: Springer.

Murstein, B. (1987). "A Clarification and Extension of the SVR Theory of Dyadic Pairing." *Journal of Marriage and the Family, 49*, 929–933.

Mydans, S. (1992, November 21). "Christian Conservatives Counting Hundreds of Gains in Local Votes." *The New York Times,* p. A1ff.

Nadelson, C. C. (1990). "Consequences of Rape: Clinical and Treatment Aspects." *Psychotherapy and Psychosomatics, 51*(4), 187–192.

Nadelson, C., & Sauzier, M. (1986). "Intervention Programs for Individual Victims and Their Families." In M. Lystad (Ed.), *Violence in the Home: Interdisciplinary Perspectives.* New York: Brunner/Mazel.

Nakano, M. (1990). *Japanese American Women: Three Generations, 1890–1990.* Berkeley, CA: Mina Press.

Nanda, S. (1990). *Neither Man Nor Woman: The Hijra of India.* Belmont, CA: Wadsworth.

Narod. (1995).

National Center for Environmental Health. (1995). "Smoking Men at Risk for Erectile Dysfunction." *Contemporary Sexuality, 29*(2), 8.

National Center for Health Statistics (NCHS). (1994). *Healthy People 2000 Review.* Hyattsville, MD: U.S. Public Health Service.

National Center for Health Statistics (NCHS). (1998, May). Available: http://www.cdc.gov/nchswww/fastats/

National Organization for Victim Assistance. (1992). *Community Crisis Response Team Training Manual.* Washington, DC: Author.

National Victim Center. (1995). Posttraumatic Stress Disorder (PTSD). Available: http://www.nvc.org/ns-search/infolink/INF...ch-set\35060\s7g.060c7b&NS-doc-offset+=3& (Last visited 3/10/98).

National Victim Center. (1997a). Incest. Available: http://www.nvc.org/ns-search/infolink/INF...ch-set\35060\s7g.060c7b&NS-doc-offset=1& (Last visited 3/10/98).

National Victim Center. (1997b). Male Rape. Available: http://www.nvc.org/ns-search/infolink/INF...ch-set=\35060\s7g.060c7b&NS-doc-offset=0& (Last visited 3/10/98).

National Victim Center and Crime Victims Research and Treatment Center. (1992). *Rape in America: A Report to the Nation.* Charleston, SC: Author.

National Women's Health Resource Center. (1998). Women and Sexually Transmitted Diseases (STDs). Available: http://www.healthywomen.org/qa/std.html#1 (Last visited 2/14/98).

Nava, M. (1990). *How Town.* New York: Ballantine Books.

Navarro, M. (1993, January 11). "Healthy, Gay, Guilt-Stricken: AIDS' Toll on the Virus-Free." *The New York Times,* pp. A1, A16.

NCHS. *See* National Center for Health Statistics.

Nelson, K. E., Vlahov, D., Cohn, S., Odunmbaku, M., Lindsay, A., Anthony, J. C., & Hook, E. W. (1991). "Sexually Transmitted Diseases in a Population of Intravenous Drug Users: Association with Seropositivity to the Human Immunodeficiency Virus (HIV)." *Journal of Infectious Diseases, 164*(3), 457–463.

Nelson, R. (1988). "Nonoperatic Management of Impotence." *Journal of Urology, 139*, 2–5.

Nestle, J. (1983). "The Fem Question." In C. Vance (Ed.), *Pleasure and Danger.* New York: Routledge & Kegan Paul.

Newcomb, M. (1979). "Cohabitation in America: An Assessment of Consequences." *Journal of Marriage and the Family,* 597–603.

Newcomb, M., & Bentler, P. (1980). "Assessment of Personality and Demographics Aspects of Cohabitation and Marital Success." *Journal of Personality Development, 4*(1), 11–24.

Newcomer, S., & Udry, R. (1985). "Oral Sex in an Adolescent Population." *Archives of Sexual Behavior, 14*(1), 41–46.

"New PID Treatment." (1997). *Urology Times, 25*(3), 47.

"New Pills May Ease Impotence." (1997, October 28). *Monterey Herald,* p. A-1.

"New Ratings for Content Starts Today." (1997, October 1). *San Francisco Chronicle,* p. D-3.

Newton, N. (1955). *Maternal Emotions.* New York: Basic Books.

New York City Gay and Lesbian Anti-Violence Project. (1995). "Anti-Lesbian/Gay Violence Rises in New York City and Around Country in 1994." *Stop the Violence, 6*(1), 1, 12–13.

New York State Health Department. (1992). "Methods of Personal Protection for Women to Reduce Transmission of HIV Through Vaginal Intercourse." Policy Statement, AIDS Institute.

Ng, M. (1993). "Public Responses to the Sex Education Series of Radio-Television: Hong Kong. *Journal of Sex Education and Therapy, 19*, 64–72.

NIAID/CDC. (1991). "U.S. Public Health Service National Conference: Women and HIV Infection." *Clinical Courier, 9*(6), 1–7.

Nichols, M. (1987). "Lesbian Sexuality: Issues and Developing Theory." In Boston Lesbian Psychologies Collective (Ed.), *Lesbian Psychologies: Explorations and Challenges.* Urbana, IL: University of Illinois Press.

Nichols, M. (1988). "Bisexuality in Women: Myths, Realities, and Implications for Therapy." Special Issue: Women and Sex Therapy. *Women and Therapy, 7,* 235–252.

Niebuhr, R. E., & Boyles, W. R. (1991). "Sexual Harassment of Military Personnel: An Examination of Power Differentials." Special Issue: Racial, Ethnic, and Gender Issues in the Military. *International Journal of Intercultural Relations, 15,* 445–457.

Nielson, J., & Wohlert, M. (1991). "Chromosome Abnormalities Found Among 34,910 Newborn Children: Results from a 13-Year Incidence Study in Arhus, Denmark." *Human Genetics, 87*(1), 81–83.

Nieman, L., et al. (1987). "The Progesterone Antagonist RU-486: A Potential New Contraceptive Agent." *New England Journal of Medicine, 316*(4), 187–191.

Nolin, M. J., & Petersen, K. K. (1992). "Gender Differences in Parent-Child Communication About Sexuality: An Exploratory Study. *Journal of Adolescent Research, 7,* 59–79.

Noller, P. (1984). *Nonverbal Communication and Marital Interaction.* Oxford, England: Pergamon Press.

Noller, P., & Fitzpatrick, M. A. (1991). "Marital Communication." In A. Booth (Ed.), *Contemporary Families: Looking Forward, Looking Back.* Minneapolis, MN: National Council on Family Relations.

Norris, K. (1996, September/October). "Celibate Passion." *Utne Reader,* pp. 51–53.

Norton, A. J. (1983). "Family Life Cycle: 1980." *Journal of Marriage and the Family, 45,* 267–275.

Nossiter, A. (1992, November 28). "Some Legal Experts See Intolerance as HIV and Sex Are Linked to Crime." *The New York Times,* p. 6.

Notarius, C., & Johnson, J. (1982). "Emotional Expression in Husbands and Wives." *Journal of Marriage and the Family, 44*(2), 483–489.

Notzon, F. C., et al. (1987). "Comparisons of National Cesarean-Section Rates." *New England Journal of Medicine, 316*(7), 386–389.

Nugent, R., & Gramick, J. (1989). "Homosexuality: Protestant, Catholic, and Jewish Issues: A Fishbone Tale." *Journal of Homosexuality, 18,* 7–46.

"Number of AIDS Cases Rising Faster Among Older Adults." (1998, January 23). *San Francisco Chronicle,* p. A-7.

Oakley, A. (1985). *Sex, Gender, and Society* (rev. ed.). New York: Harper & Row.

O'Carroll, R. (1989). "The Difficulty in Dealing with Deviance: An Illustrative Case Study." *Journal of Sex and Marital Therapy, 4*(2), 177–186.

Oehninger, S., & Alexander, N. J. (1991). "Male Infertility: The Focus Shifts to Sperm Manipulation." *Current Opinion in Obstetrics and Gynecology, 3*(2), 182–190.

O'Farrell, T. J., Choquette, K. A., & Birchler, G. R. (1991). "Sexual Satisfaction and Dissatisfaction in the Marital Relationships of Male Alcoholics Seeking Marital Therapy." *Journal of Studies on Alcohol, 52*(5), 441–447.

Okami, P. (1991). "Self-Reports of 'Positive' Childhood and Adolescent Sexual Contacts with Older Persons: An Exploratory Study." *Archives of Sexual Behavior, 20*(5), 437–457.

Olds, J. (1956). "Pleasure Centers in the Brain." *Scientific American, 193,* 105–116.

Olshansky, E. F. (1992). "Redefining the Concepts of Success and Failure in Infertility Treatment." *Naacogs Clinical Issues in Perinatal and Women's Health Nursing, 3*(2), 343–346.

Olson, T., & Wallace, C. (1987). "Families, Decision-Making and Human Development." *Concerned Women of America.* Washington, DC.

Orbach, S. (1982). *Fat Is a Feminist Issue II: A Program to Conquer Compulsive Eating.* New York: Berkley Books.

Orlofsky, J., & O'Heron, C. (1987). "Stereotypic and Nonstereotypic Sex Role Trait and Behavior Orientations: Implications for Personal Adjustment." *Journal of Personality and Social Psychology, 52,* 1034–1042.

Orten, J. L. (1990). "Coming Up Short: The Physical, Cognitive, and Social Effects of Turner's Syndrome." *Health and Social Work, 15*(2), 100–106.

Ortiz, M. E., & Croxatto, H. B. (1987). "The Mode of Action of IUDs." *Contraception, 36*(1), 37–53.

Osborn, J. E. (1990). "Women and HIV/AIDS: The Silent Epidemic?" *SIECUS Report, 19*(2), 1–4.

Osborn, J. E. (1996, April 7). "The Unbeliever." *The New York Times Book Review,* pp. 8–9.

Osmond, D. H., Page, K., Wiley, J., Garrett, K., Sheppard, W. H., Moss, A. R., Schrager, L., & Winkelstein, W. (1994). "HIV Infection in Homosexual and Bisexual Men 18–29 Years of Age: The San Francisco Young Men's Health Study." *American Journal of Public Health, 84*(12), 1933–1937.

Ostrow, D. G., Whitaker, R. E., Frasier, K., Cohen, C., Wan, J., Frank, C., & Fisher, E. (1991). "Racial Differences in Social Support and Mental Health in Men with HIV Infection: A Pilot Study." *AIDS Care, 3*(1), 55–62.

O'Sullivan, C. S. (1991). "Acquaintance Gang Rape on Campus." In A. Parrot & L. Bechhofer (Eds.), *Acquaintance Rape: The Hidden Crime.* New York: John Wiley.

O'Sullivan, L., & Byers, E. S. (1992). "College Students' Incorporation of Initiator and Restrictor Roles in Sexual Dating Interactions." *Journal of Sex Research, 29*(3), 435–446.

"Ovulation Cycles Linked to Ovarian Cancer." (1997, July 5). *Science News, 152,* 7.

Padgett, V. R., Brislutz, J. A., & Neal, J. A. (1989). "Pornography, Erotica, and Attitudes Toward Women: The Effects of Repeated Exposure." *Journal of Sex Research, 26,* 479–491.

Padilla, E. R., & O'Grady, K. E. (1987). "Sexuality Among Mexican Americans: A Case of Sexual Stereotyping." *Journal of Personality and Social Psychology, 52,* 5–10.

PAHO. *See* Pan American Health Organization.

Palella, F. J., Delany, K. M., Moorman, A. C., Loveless, M. O., Fuhrer, J., Satten, G. A., Aschman, D. J., Holmberg, S. D., & HIV Outpatient Study Investigators. (1998). "Declining Morbidity and Mortality Among Patients with Advanced Human Immunodeficiency Virus Infection." *New England Journal of Medicine, 338*(13), 853.

Paludi, M. A. (1990). "Sociopsychological and Structural Factors Related to Women's Vocational Development." *Annals of the New York Academy of Sciences, 602,* 157–168.

Pan, L. Z., Sheppard, H. W., Winkelstein, W., & Levy, J. A. (1991). "Lack of Detection of Human Immunodeficiency Virus in Persistently Seronegative Homosexual Men with High or Medium Risk for Infection." *Journal of Infectious Diseases, 164*(5), 962–964.

Pan American Health Organization. (1997). Adults and Children Estimated to Be Living with HIV/AIDS as of End 1997. Available: http://www.paho.org/english/aid/aidw1497.htm (Last visited 2/29/98).

Pang, S., Shlesinger, Y., Daar, E. S., Moudgil T., Ho, D. D., & Chen, I. S. (1992). "Rapid Generation of Sequence Variation During Primary HIV-1 Infection." *AIDS, 6*(5), 453–460.

Panzarine, S., & Elster, A. B. (1983). "Coping in a Group of Expectant Adolescent Fathers: An Exploratory Study." *Journal of Adolescent Health Care, 4,* 117–120.

Parachini, A. (1987, February 3). "Survivorship: A New Movement Among Cancer Patients." *Los Angeles Times,* pp. 1, 2.

Parker, H., & Parker, S. (1984). "Cultural Rules, Rituals and Behavior Regulation." *American Anthropologist, 86*(3), 584–600.

Parker, H., & Parker, S. (1986). "Father-Daughter Sexual Child Abuse: An Emerging Perspective." *American Journal of Orthopsychiatry, 56*(4), 531–549.

Parker, R. G. (1991). *Bodies, Pleasures, and Passions.* Boston: Beacon Press.

Parrinder, G. (1980). *Sex in the World's Religions.* New York: Oxford University Press.

Parsons, T. (1955). "Family Structure and the Socialization of the Child." In T. Parsons & R. F. Bales (Eds.), *Family Socialization and Interaction Process.* Glencoe, IL: Free Press.

Patterson, C. J. (1992). "Children of Lesbian and Gay Parents." *Child Development, 63,* 1025–1042.

Patton, M. (1986). "Twentieth-Century Attitudes Toward Masturbation." *Journal of Religion and Health, 25*(4), 291–302.

Paul, J. P. (1984). "The Bisexual Identity: An Idea Without Social Recognition." *Journal of Homosexuality, 9,* 45–63.

Paul, J. P. (1993). "Childhood Cross-Gender Behavior and Adult Homosexuality: The Resurgence of Biological Models of Sexuality." *Journal of Homosexuality, 24*(3–4), 41–54.

Paul, L., & Galloway, J. (1994). "Sexual Jealousy: Gender Differences in Response to Partner and Rival." *Aggressive Behavior, 20*(3), 203–211.

Paulsen, C. A., Berman, N. G., & Wang, C. (1996, May). "Data from Men in Greater Seattle Area Reveals No Downward Trend in Semen Quality: Further Evidence That Deterioration of Semen Quality Is Not Geographically Uniform." *Fertility & Sterility, 65*(5), 1015–1020.

Pauly, I., & Edgarton, M. (1986). "The Gender Identity Movement: A Growing Surgical-Psychiatric Liaison." *Archives of Sexual Behavior, 15*(4), 315–327.

Pauly, J. (1990). "Gender Identity Disorders: Evaluation and Treatment." *Journal of Sex Education and Therapy, 16*(1), 2–24.

Pavelka, M. S. M. (1995). "Sexual Nature: What Can We Learn from a Cross-Species Perspective?" In P. R. Abramson & S. D. Pinkerton (Eds.), *Sexual Nature, Sexual Culture.* Chicago: University of Chicago Press.

Peacock, N. (1982). "Contraceptive Decision-Making Among Adolescent Girls." *Journal of Sex Education and Therapy, 8,* 31–34.

Pear, R. (1992, April 22). "U.S. Reports Rise in Low-Weight Births." *The New York Times,* p. A18.

Pear, R. (1993, February 7). "As AIDS Money Is Parceled Out, Political Questions." *The New York Times,* p. E3.

Pelz, L., Sager, G., Hinkel, G. K., Kirchner, M., Kruger, C., & Verron, G. (1991). "Delayed Spontaneous Pubertal Growth Spurt in Girls with the Ullrich-Turner Syndrome." *American Journal of Medical Genetics, 40*(4), 401–405.

Peo, R. (1988). "Transvestism." In D. Dailey (Ed.), *The Sexually Unusual.* New York: Harrington Park Press.

Peplau, L. (1981). "What Homosexuals Want." *Psychology Today, 15*(3), 28–38.

Peplau, L. (1988). "Research on Homosexual Couples." In J. De Cecco (Ed.), *Gay Relationships.* New York: Haworth Press.

Peplau, L., & Cochran, S. (1988). "Value Orientations in the Intimate Relationships of Gay Men." In J. De Cecco (Ed.), *Gay Relationships.* New York: Haworth Press.

Peplau, L., & Gordon, S. (1982). "The Intimate Relationships of Lesbians and Gay Men." In E. Allgeier & N. McCormick (Eds.), *Gender Roles and Sexual Behavior.* Mountain View, CA: Mayfield.

Peplau, L., Rubin, Z., & Hill, R. (1977). "Sexual Intimacy in Dating Relationships." *Journal of Social Issues, 33*(2), 86–109.

Perez, E. (1990). "Why Women Wait to Be Tested for HIV Infection." *SIECUS Report, 19,* 6–7.

Perilstein, R., Lipper, S., & Friedman, L. J. (1991). "Three Cases of Paraphilias Responsive to Fluoxetine Treatment." *Journal of Clinical Psychology, 52*(4), 169–170.

Perlez, J. (1990, January 15). "Puberty Rite for Girls Is Bitter Issue Across Africa." *The New York Times,* p. A4.

Perlman, D. (1997, November 14). "HIV Can Hide in Cells Despite Drug Treatment, Experts Find." *San Francisco Chronicle,* p. A-1.

Perlman, D. (1997, November 22). "Infertility Treatment Not an Exact Science." *San Francisco Chronicle,* p. A-10.

Perlman, D. (1998, June 29). "Muted Hope at AIDS Conference." *San Francisco Chronicle,* p. A-6.

Perry, J. D., & Whipple, B. (1981). "Pelvic Muscle Strength of Female Ejaculators: Evidence in Support of a New Theory of Orgasm." *Journal of Sex Research, 17*(1), 22–39.

Person, E. S. (1995). *By Force of Fantasy: How We Make Our Lives.* New York: Basic Books.

Person, E. S., Terestman, N., Myers, W. A., & Goldberg, E. L. (1989). "Gender Differences in Sexual Behaviors and Fantasies in a College Population." *Journal of Sex and Marital Therapy, 15*(3), 187–214.

Persson, G., & Svanborg, A. (1992). "Marital Coital Activity in Men at the Age of 75: Relation to Somatic, Psychiatric and Social Factors at the Age of 70." *Journal of the American Geriatrics Society, 40*(5), 439–444.

Petchesky, R. P. (1990). *Abortion and Woman's Choice: The State, Sexuality, and Reproductive Freedom* (rev. ed.). Boston: Northeastern University Press.

Peters, K. (1992, October 15). "Gay Activists Denounce NAMBLA, Attempt to Highlight Differences." *Spartan Daily,* p. 1.

Peters, S., et al. (1986). "Prevalence of Child Sexual Abuse." In D. Finkelhor (Ed.), *Sourcebook on Child Sexual Abuse.* Newbury Park, CA: Sage Publications.

Peterson, H. B. (1996, April). "The Risk of Pregnancy After Tubal Sterilization: Findings from the U.S. Collaborative Review of Sterilization."

Peterson, H., et al. (1983). "Deaths Attributable to Tubal Sterilization in the United States, 1977–1981." *American Journal of Obstetrics and Gynecology, 146,* 131ff.

Peterson, J. L. (1992). "Black Men and Their Same-Sex Desires and Behaviors." In G. Herdt (Ed.), *Gay Culture in America: Essays from the Field.* Boston: Beacon Press.

Petit, C. (1992, April 2). "Why Both Parents Should Be Tested for Herpes." *San Francisco Chronicle,* p. D-7.

Peyser, M. (1997, September 29). "A Deadly Dance." *Newsweek,* pp. 76–77.

Phelps, T. M., & Winternitz, H. (1992). *Capitol Games.* New York: Hyperion Books.

Phillips, G., & Over, R. (1992). "Adult Sexual Orientation in Relation to Memories of Childhood Gender Conforming and Gender Nonconforming Behaviors." *Archives of Sexual Behavior, 21*(6), 543–558.

Pierce, P. (1994). "Sexual Harassment: Frankly, What Is It?" *Journal of Intergroup Relations, 20*, 3–12.

Piercing Exquisite: Aftercare for Navel and Nipple Piercings. (1998). Available: http://www2.ba.best.com/ardvark/ac-body.html (Last visited 1/15/98).

Pincus, S. (1988). "Sexuality in the Mentally Retarded Patient." *American Family Physician, 37*(2), 319–323.

Pines, A., & Aronson, E. (1983). "Antecedents, Correlates, and Consequences of Sexual Jealousy." *Journal of Personality, 51*(1), 108–136.

Pinker, S. (1991). *The Way the Mind Works.* New York: Norton.

Pipher, M. (1994). *Reviving Ophelia: Saving the Selves of Adolescent Girls.* New York: Ballantine.

Pistole, M. C. (1995). "College Students' Ended Love Relationships: Attachment Style and Emotion." *Journal of College Student Development, 36*(1), 53–60.

Pistole, M. C., Clark, E. M., & Tubbs, A. L. (1995, April). "Love Relationships: Attachment Style and the Investment Model." *Journal of Mental Health Counseling, 17*(2), 199–209.

Plato. (1961). "Protagoras." In E. Hamilton & H. Cairns (Eds.), *The Collected Dialogues of Plato.* New York: Bollengen Foundation.

Plummer, W., & Nelson, M. (1991, August 26). "A Mother's Priceless Gift." *People,* p. 18.

Pogrebin, L. C. (1982, February). "Are Men Discovering the Joys of Fatherhood?" *Ms.,* pp. 41–46.

Pogrebin, L. C. (1983). *Family Politics.* New York: McGraw-Hill.

Poland, R. L. (1990). "The Question of Routine Neonatal Circumcision." *New England Journal of Medicine, 322*(18), 1312–1315.

Polit-O'Hara, D., & Kahn, J. (1985). "Communication and Contraceptive Practices in Adolescent Couples." *Adolescence, 20*(77), 33–43.

Pollis, C. A. (1988). "An Assessment of the Impacts of Feminism on Sexual Science." *Journal of Sex Research, 25*(1), 85–105.

Pomeroy, W. (1972). *Dr. Kinsey and the Kinsey Institute.* New York: Harper & Row.

Pomice, E. (1990, April 2). "A Businesslike Approach to AIDS." *U.S. News & World Report,* p. 4.

Ponticas, Y. (1992). "Sexual Aversion Versus Hypoactive Sexual Desire: A Diagnostic Challenge." *Psychiatric Medicine, 10*(2), 273–281.

Popovich, P. M., Gehlauf, D. N., Jolton, J. A., & Somers, J. M. (1992). "Perceptions of Sexual Harassment as a Function of Sex of Rater and Incident Form and Consequence." *Sex Roles, 27*(11–12), 609–625.

"Positive News: Guidelines for HIV Treatment." (1997, August). San Francisco AIDS Foundation.

Potterat, J. J., Phillips, L., Rothenberg, R. B., & Darrow, W. V. (1985). "On Becoming a Prostitute: An Exploratory Case-Comparison Study." *Journal of Sex Research, 21*(3), 329–335.

Potterat, J. J., Woodhouse, D. E., Muth, J. B., & Muth, S. Q. (1990). "Estimating the Prevalence and Career Longevity of Prostitute Women." *Journal of Sex Research, 27*, 233–243.

Potterat, J. J., et al. (1985). "Gonorrhea as a Social Disease." *Sexually Transmitted Diseases, 12*, 25–32.

Power-Smith, P. (1991). "Problems in Older People's Longer Term Sexual Relationships." *Sexual & Marital Therapy, 6*(3), 287–296.

Pozo, C., et al. (1992). "Effects of Mastectomy Versus Lumpectomy on Emotional Adjustment to Breast Cancer: A Prospective Study of the First Year Postsurgery." *Journal of Clinical Oncology, 10*(8), 1292–1298.

PPFA [Planned Parenthood Federation of America]. (1985, November). "They Did It 9000 Times on Television Last Year, How Come Nobody Got Pregnant?" *San Francisco Chronicle,* p. 14.

Pratt, C., & Schmall, V. (1989). "College Students' Attitudes Toward Elderly Sexual Behavior: Implications for Family Life Education." *Family Relations, 38*, 137–141.

Prentky, R. (1985). "The Neurochemistry and Neuroendocrinology of Sexual Aggression." In D. P. Farrington and J. Gunn (Eds.), *Aggression and Dangerousness.* New York: John Wiley.

Presidential Advisory Council on HIV/AIDS. Second Progress Report. (1997, December 7). Available: http://www.cdcnac.org/exesum.html (Last visited 2/28/98).

Press, A. (1992). "Class Gender, and the Female Viewer: Women's Responses to 'Dynasty.' " In *Television and Women's Culture: The Politics of the Popular.* Newbury Park, CA: Sage Publications.

Price, D. (1993, January 14). "Twin Study Links Genetics, Gayness Closer." *San Jose Mercury News,* p. 2.

Price, J. (1982). "Who Wants to Have Children? And Why?" In J. Rosenfeld (Ed.), *Relationships: The Marriage and Family Reader.* Glenview, IL: Scott, Foresman.

Price, J. H., & Miller, P. A. (1984). "Sexual Fantasies of Black and White College Students." *Psychological Reports, 54*, 1007–1014.

Priest, R. (1992). "Child Sexual Abuse Histories Among African-American College Students: A Preliminary Study." *American Journal of Orthopsychiatry, 62*(3), 475–477.

Project Inform. (1990a, March 27). "AZT—Retrovir." *Project Inform Fact Sheet,* 1–4.

Project Inform. (1990b, June 14). "ddl—Dideoxyinosine (VIDEX)." *Project Inform Fact Sheet,* 1–2.

Project Inform. (1991, May 1). "ddC—Dideocyctidine—HIVID." *Project Inform Fact Sheet,* 1–2.

Project Inform. (1992). "The Myth of 'Too Much Spending on AIDS.' " *Project Inform Fact Sheet,* 1–2.

"Prostate Cancer Kills Blacks at Significantly Higher Rate." (1998, January 14). *San Francisco Chronicle,* p. A-2.

Pruett, K. (1987). *The Nurturing Father: Journey Toward the Complete Man.* New York: Warner Books.

Pryor, J. B., & Day, J. D. (1988). "Interpretations of Sexual Harassment: An Attributional Analysis." *Sex Roles, 18*(7–8), 405–417.

Puech-Leao, P. (1992). "Venous Surgery in Erectile Dysfunction." *Urologia Internationalis, 49*(1), 29–32.

Purvis, A. (1997, December 30, 1996–January 6, 1997). "The Global Epidemic." *Newsweek,* pp. 76–78.

Quackenbush, D. M., Strassberg, D. S., & Turner, C. (1995, February). "Gender Effects of Romantic Themes in Erotica." *Archives of Sexual Behavior, 24*(1), 21–35.

Quackenbush, R. L. (1991). "Attitudes of College Men Toward Women and Rape." *Journal of College Students Development, 32,* 376–377.

Quatrella, L., & Wentworth, K. K. (1995). "Students' Perceptions of Unequal Status Dating Relationships in Academia." *Ethics & Behavior, 5*(3), 249–259.

Raboch, J., & Raboch, J. (1992). "Infrequent Orgasms in Women." *Journal of Sex and Marital Therapy, 18*(3), 114–120.

Radway, J. A. (1984). *Reading the Romance.* Chapel Hill, NC: University of North Carolina Press.

Ramey, E. (1972). "Men's Cycles." *Ms.,* pp. 8ff.

Randolph, E. (1988, March 9). "Critics Say Medical Journals Would Have Rejected AIDS Study." *Washington Post,* p. A7.

Rangaswamy, K. (1987). "Treatment of Voyeurism by Behavior Therapy." *Child Psychiatry Quarterly, 20,* 3–4.

Rao, K., Diclemente, R. J., & Poulton, L. E. (1992). "Child Sexual Abuse of Asians Compared with Other Populations." *Journal of the American Academy of Child and Adolescent Psychiatry, 31*(5), 880–887.

Ratner, E. (1988). "A Model for the Treatment of Lesbian and Gay Alcohol Abusers." *Alcoholism Treatment Quarterly, 5*(1–2), 25–46.

Raven, B., et al. (1975). "The Bases of Conjugal Power." In R. Cromwell & D. Olson (Eds.), *Power in Families*. New York: Halstead Press.

Reece, R. (1988). "Special Issues in the Etiologies and Treatments of Sexual Problems Among Gay Men." *Journal of Homosexuality, 15*, 43–57.

Reed, D., & Weinberg, M. (1984). "Premarital Coitus: Developing and Established Sexual Scripts." *Social Psychology Quarterly, 47*(2), 129–138.

Reichel-Dolmatoff, G. (1971). *Amazonian Cosmos*. Chicago: University of Chicago Press.

Reid, P., & Comas-Diaz, L. (1990). "Gender and Ethnicity: Perspectives on Dual Status." *Sex Roles, 22*(7), 397–408.

Reilly, M. E., Lott, B., Caldwell, D., & DeLuca, L. (1992). "Tolerance for Sexual Harassment Related to Self-Reported Sexual Victimization." *Gender and Society, 6*(1), 122–138.

Reinholtz, R. K., & Muehlenhard, C. L. (1995). "Genital Perceptions and Sexual Activity in a College Population." *Journal of Sex Research, 32*(2), 155–165.

Reinisch, J. (1986, August 26). "The Kinsey Report." *San Francisco Chronicle*, p. 16.

Reinisch, J., Ziemba-Davis, M., & Saunders, S. (1991). "Hormonal Contributions to Sexually Dimorphic Behavioral Development in Humans." *Psychoneuroendocrinology, 16*, 213–278.

Reiss, I. (1967). *The Social Context of Premarital Sexual Permissiveness*. New York: Irvington.

Reiss, I. (1980). "A Multivariate Model of the Determinants of Extramarital Sexual Permissiveness." *Journal of Marriage and the Family, 42*, 395–411.

Reiss, I. (1986). *Journey into Sexuality: An Exploratory Voyage*. Englewood Cliffs, NJ: Prentice-Hall.

Reiss, I. (1989). "Society and Sexuality: A Sociological Explanation." In K. McKinney & S. Sprecher (Eds.), *Human Sexuality: The Societal and Interpersonal Context*. Norwood, NJ: Ablex.

Reiss, I. (1990). *An End to Shame: Shaping Our Next Sexual Revolution*. Buffalo, NY: Prometheus Books.

Remafedi, G. (1994). "Predictors of Unprotected Intercourse Among Gay and Bisexual Youth: Knowledge, Belief, and Behaviors." *Pediatrics, 94*, 163–168.

Remafedi, G., Resnick, M., Blum, R., & Harris, L. (1992). "Demography of Sexual Orientation in Adolescents." *Pediatrics, 89*, 714–721.

Renshaw, D. C. (1988a). "Short-Term Therapy for Sexual Dysfunction: Brief Counseling to Manage Vaginismus." *Clinical Practice in Sexuality, 6*(5), 23–39.

Renshaw, D. C. (1988b). "Young Children's Sex Play: Counseling the Parents." *Medical Aspects of Human Sexuality, 22*(12), 68–72.

Renshaw, D. (1995). *Seven Weeks to Better Sex*. New York: Random House.

Resnick, H. S. (1972). "Eroticized Repetitive Hangings: A Form of Self-Destructive Behavior." *American Journal of Psychotherapy, 26*(1), 4–21.

Resnick, M. D., Bearman, P. S., Blum, R. W., Bauman, K. E., Harris, K. M., Jones, J., Tabor, J., Beuhring, T., Fieving, R. E., Shuew, M., Ireland, M., Bearinger, L. H., & Udry, J. R. (1997, September 10). "Protecting Adolescents from Harm." *JAMA: Journal of the American Medical Association, 278*(10), 823–832.

Reuben, D. (1969). *Everything You Ever Wanted to Know About Sex—But Were Afraid to Ask*. New York: David McKay.

Reuters Health Information Services. (1997). Awareness of Emergency Contraception Increasing Slowly. Available: http://www.ama-assn.org/special/contra/newsline/reuters/12191742.htm (Last visited 1/20/98).

Rhynard, J., Krebs, M., & Glover, J. (1997). "Sexual Assault in Dating Relationships." *Journal of School Health, 67*(3), 89–94.

Rice, R. J., Roberts, P. L., Handsfield, H. H., & Holmes, K. K. (1991). "Sociodemographic Distribution of Gonorrhea Incidence: Implications for Prevention and Behavioral Research." *American Journal of Public Health, 81*(10), 1252–1258.

Rich, A. (1983). "Compulsory Heterosexuality and Lesbian Existence." In A. Snitow et al. (Eds.), *Powers of Desire: The Politics of Sexuality*. New York: Monthly Review Press.

Richards, E. P., & Bross, D. C. (1990). "Legal Aspects of STD Control: Public Duties and Private Rights." In K. K. Holmes et al. (Eds.), *Sexually Transmitted Diseases* (2nd ed.). New York: McGraw-Hill.

Richards, K. (1997). "What Is a Transgenderist?" In B. Bullough, V. L. Bullough, & J. Elias (Eds.), *Gender Blending*. New York: Prometheus Books.

Ricketts, W., & Actenberg, R. (1989). "Adoption and Foster Parenting for Lesbians and Gay Men: Creating New Traditions in Family." *Marriage and Family Review, 14*, 83–118.

Rieff, P. (1979). *Freud: The Mind of a Moralist*. Chicago: University of Chicago Press.

Rieve, J. E. (1989). "Sexuality and the Adult with Acquired Physical Disability." *Nursing Clinics of North America, 24*(1), 265–276.

Riggs, D. S. (1993). "Relationship Problems and Dating Aggression: A Potential Treatment Target." *Journal of Interpersonal Violence, 8*(1), 18–35.

Riley, A. J. (1991). "Sexuality and the Menopause." *Sexual and Marital Therapy, 6*(2), 135–146.

Rio, L. M. (1991). "Psychological and Sociological Research and the Decriminalization or Legalization of Prostitution." *Archives of Sexual Behavior, 20*(2), 205–218.

Riseden, A. D., & Hort, B. E. (1992). "A Preliminary Investigation of the Sexual Component of the Male Stereotype." Unpublished manuscript.

"Risk of Suicide and Past History of Sexual Assault." (1996). *American Family Physician, 54*(5), 1756.

Risky Sex and Non-IV Drugs. (1998). Available: http://www.columbia.edu/cu/healthwise/0399.html (Last visited 1/29/98).

Rivinus, T., & Larimer, M. (1993). "Violence, Alcohol, Other Drugs, and the College Student." *Journal of College Student Psychotherapy, 8*(1–2).

Roan, S. (1994, October 31). "Young, Active, and Infected." *San Francisco Chronicle*, p. D-8.

Roberts, E. (Ed.). (1980). *Childhood Sexual Learning: The Unwritten Curriculum*. Cambridge, MA: Ballinger.

Roberts, E. (1982). "Television and Sexual Learning in Childhood." In *National Institute of Mental Health, Television and Behavior*. Washington, DC: U.S. Government Printing Office.

Roberts, E. (1983). "Childhood Sexual Learning: The Unwritten Curriculum." In C. Davis (Ed.), *Challenges in Sexual Science*. Philadelphia: Society for the Scientific Study of Sex.

Roberts, J. (1994). "Women in U.S. Sue Makers of Norplant." *British Medical Journal, 252*, 214.

Roberts, L., & Krokoff, L. (1990). "A Time Series Analysis of Withdrawal, Hostility, and Displeasure in Satisfied and Dissatisfied Marriages." *Journal of Marriage and the Family, 52*(1), 95–105.

Roberts, M. C., Alexander, K., & Fanurik, D. (1990). "Evaluation of Commercially Available Materials to Prevent Child Sexual Abuse." *American Psychologist, 45*(6), 782–783.

Robertson, D. (1990). "Counseling Women Who Have Been Sexually Assaulted." *Issues in Criminological and Legal Psychology, 19,* 46–53.

Robertson, M. M. (1992, April). "Lesbians as an Invisible Minority in the Health Services Arena." *Health Care for Women International, 13*(2), 155–163.

Robinson, B. (1987). *Teenage Fathers.* Lexington, MA: Lexington Books.

Robinson, B. (1988). "Teenage Pregnancy from the Father's Perspective." *American Journal of Orthopsychiatry, 58*(1), 46–51.

Robinson, G. E., & Garfinkel, P. E. (1990). "Problems in the Treatment of Premenstrual Symptoms." *Canadian Journal of Psychiatry, 35*(3), 199–206.

Robinson, H. (1992, December 14). "Sex, Marriage, and Divorce." *Christianity Today, 36*(15), 29–33.

Robinson, P. (1976). *The Modernization of Sex.* New York: Harper & Row.

Robinson, P. (1983). "The Sociological Perspective." In R. Weg (Ed.), *Sexuality in the Later Years: Roles and Behavior.* New York: Academic Press.

Rodabaugh, B., & Austin, M. (1981). *Sexual Assault.* New York: Garland Press.

Roenrich, L., & Kinder, B. N. (1991). "Alcohol Expectancies and Male Sexuality: Review and Implications for Sex Therapy." *Journal of Sex and Marital Therapy, 17,* 45–54.

Rogers, M. F., White, C. R., Sanders, R., Schable, C., Ksell, T. E., Wasserman, R. L., Bellanti, J. A., Peters, S. M., & Wray, B. B. (1990). "Lack of Transmission of Human Immunodeficiency Virus from Infected Children to Their Household Contacts." *Pediatrics, 85*(2), 210–214.

Rogers, P. A., Murphy, C. R., Leeton, J., Hoise, M. J., & Beaton, L. (1992). "Turner's Syndrome Patients Lack Tight Junctions Between Uterine Epithelial Cells." *Human Reproduction, 7*(6), 883–885.

Rogers, S. M., & Turner, C. F. (1991). "Male-Male Sexual Contact in the U.S.A.: Findings from Five Sample Surveys, 1970–1990." *Journal of Sex Research, 28*(4), 491–519.

Rohypnol, "Roofie" and Rape. (1997). Available: http://www.columbia.edu/cu/healthwise/0884.html (Last visited 1/29/98).

Rome, E. (1992). "Anatomy and Physiology of Sexuality and Reproduction." In Boston Women's Health Book Collective, *The New Our Bodies, Ourselves.* New York: Simon & Schuster.

Rongen-Westelaken, C., Vanes, A., Wit, J., Otten, B. J., & Demuink Keizer-Schrama, C. (1992). "Growth Hormone Therapy in Turner's Syndrome." *American Journal of Diseases of Children, 146*(7), 817–820.

Rooks, J., Weatherby, N. L., Ernst, E. K., Stapleton, S., Rosen, D., & Rosenfield, A. (1989). "Outcomes of Care in Birth Centers." *New England Journal of Medicine, 321,* 1804–1811.

Roopnarine, J. L., & Mounts, N. S. (1987). "Current Theoretical Issues in Sex Roles and Sex Typing." In D. B. Carter (Ed.), *Current Conceptions of Sex Roles and Sex Typing: Theory and Research.* New York: Praeger.

Roos, P., & Cohen, L. (1987). "Sex Roles and Social Support as Moderates of Life Stress Adjustment." *Journal of Personality and Social Psychology, 52*(3), 576–585.

Roper, W. L., Petersen, H. B., & Curran, J. W. (1993). "Commentary: Condoms and HIV/STD Prevention—Clarifying the Message." *American Journal of Public Health, 83*(4), 501–503.

Roscoe, W. (1991). *The Zuni Man/Woman.* Albuquerque, NM: University of New Mexico Press.

Rose, S., & Sork, V. (1984). "Teaching About Female Sexuality: Putting Women on Top." *Women's Studies Quarterly, 13*(4), 19–20.

Rosegrant, J. (1986). "Contributions to Psychohistory: Fetish Symbols in *Playboy* Centerfolds." *Psychological Reports, 59*(2, Part 1), 623–631.

Rosen, R. (1982). *The Lost Sisterhood: Prostitution in America, 1900–1918.* Baltimore, MD: Johns Hopkins University Press.

Rosenberg, M. J., Davidson, A. J., Chen, J. H., Judson, F. N., & Douglas, J. M. (1992). "Barrier Contraceptives and Sexually Transmitted Diseases in Women: A Comparison of Female-Dependent Methods and Condoms." *American Journal of Public Health, 82*(5), 669–674.

Rosenberg, M. J., & Waugh, M. S. (1997, July). "Latex Condom Breakage and Slippage in a Controlled Clinical Trial." *Contraception, 56,* 17–21.

Rosenberg, P. S., Biggar, R. J., & Goedert, J. J. (1994). "Declining Age at HIV Infection in the United States." *New England Journal of Medicine, 330,* 789–790.

Rosenblum, S., & Faber, M. (1979). "The Adolescent Sexual Asphyxia Syndrome." *Journal of the American Academy of Psychiatry, 18*(3), 546–558.

Rosenfeld, R. G., Frane, J., Attie, L. M., Brasel, J. A., Bursten, S., & Clarer. (1992). "Six-Year Results of a Randomized, Prospective Trial of Human Growth Hormone and Oxandrolone in Turner Syndrome." *Journal of Pediatrics, 121*(1), 49–55.

Rosenfield, A., Peterson, H. B., & Tyler, C. W. (1997, October 17). "Editorial Note to 'Current Trends—IUD Safety: Report of a Nationwide Physician Survey,'" *Morbidity and Mortality Weekly Report, 46*(41).

Rosenstock, I. (1974). "Historical Origins of the Health Belief Model." *Health Education Monographs, 2,* 328–335.

Rosenthal, E. (1990a, February 4). "When a Pregnant Woman Drinks." *The New York Times Magazine,* pp. 30ff.

Rosenthal, E. (1990b, August 28). "The Spread of AIDS: A Mystery Unravels." *The New York Times,* pp. B5–6.

Rosenthal, E. (1992, May 26). "Cost of High-Tech Fertility: Too Many Tiny Babies." *The New York Times,* pp. B5, B7.

Rosenzweig, J. M., & Dailey, D. M. (1989). "Dyadic Adjustment/Sexual Satisfaction in Women and Men as a Function of Psychological Sex Role Self-Perception." *Journal of Sex and Marital Therapy, 15,* 42–56.

Rosman, J., & Resnick, P. J. (1989). "Sexual Attraction to Corpses: A Psychiatric Review of Necrophilia." *Bulletin of the American Academy of Psychiatry and the Law, 17*(2), 153–163.

Ross, M. (1983a). "Femininity, Masculinity, and Sexual Orientation." *Journal of Homosexuality, 9*(1), 27–36.

Ross, M. (1983b). "Homosexuality and Sex Roles: A Re-Evaluation." *Journal of Homosexuality, 9*(1), 1–6.

Ross, M. W., & Need, J. A. (1989). "Effects of Adequacy of Gender Reassignment Surgery on Psychological Adjustment: A Follow-Up of Fourteen Male-to-Female Patients." *Archives of Sexual Behavior, 18*(2), 145–153.

Ross, M. W., Wodak, A., Gold, J., & Miller, M. E. (1992). "Differences Across Sexual Orientation on HIV Risk Behaviors in Injecting Drug Users." *AIDS Care, 4*(2), 139–148.

Roth, P. (1969). *Portnoy's Complaint.* New York: Random House.

Rothblum, E. D. (1994, December). "Transforming Lesbian Sexuality." *Psychology of Women Quarterly, 18*(4), 627–641.

Rothenberg, M. (1991, April 30). "Ending Circumcision in the Jewish Community." Syllabus of Abstracts, Second International Symposium on Circumcision, San Francisco.

Rothenberg, R. (1983). "The Geography of Gonorrhea." *American Journal of Epidemiology, 117*(6), 688–694.

Rothenberg, R. B., & Potterat, J. J. (1990). "Strategies for Management of Sex Partners." In K. K. Holmes et al. (Eds.), *Sexually Transmitted Diseases* (2nd ed.). New York: McGraw-Hill.

Rotherman, M., & Weiner, N. (1983). "Androgyny, Stress, and Satisfaction." *Sex Roles, 9,* 151–158.

Rothschild, B. S., Fagan, P. J., & Woodall, C. (1991). "Sexual Functioning of Female Eating-Disordered Patients." *International Journal of Eating Disorders, 10,* 389–394.

Rotolo, J., & Lynch, J. (1991). "Penile Cancer: Curable with Early Detection." *Hospital Practice,* 131–138.

"Routine AZT Use Cuts Babies' HIV Risk, Study Finds." (1996, July 10). *San Mateo County Times,* p. A-6.

Rovet, J., & Ireland, L. (1994). "Behavioral Phenotype in Children with Turner Syndrome." *Journal of Pediatric Psychology, 19,* 779–790.

Rowan, E. L. (1988). "Pedophilia." In D. Dailey (Ed.), *The Sexually Unusual.* New York: Harrington Park Press.

Rowan, E. L. (1989). "Masturbation According to the Boy Scout Handbook." *Journal of Sex Education and Therapy, 15*(2), 77–81.

Rowland, R. (1987). "Technology and Motherhood: Reproductive Choice Reconsidered." *Signs: Journal of Women in Culture and Society, 12*(3), 512–528.

Rubenstein, C., & Tavris, C. (1987, September). "Special Survey Results: 26,000 Women Reveal the Secrets of Intimacy." *Redbook,* pp. 147–149ff.

Rubin, A. M., & Adams, J. R. (1986). "Outcomes of Sexually Open Marriages." *Journal of Sex Research, 22,* 311–319.

Rubin, L. (1976). *Worlds of Pain.* New York: Basic Books.

Rubin, L. (1990). *Erotic Wars.* New York: Farrar, Straus, & Giroux.

Rubin, R. T., Reinisch, J. M., & Haskett, R. F. (1981). "Postnatal Gonadal Steroid Effects on Human Behavior." *Science, 211,* 1318–1324.

Rubin, Z. (1973). *Liking and Loving.* New York: Holt, Rinehart & Winston.

Ruble, D. N. (1977). "Premenstrual Syndrome: A Reinterpretation." *Science, 197,* 291–292.

Rudolph, J. (1989a). "Effects of a Workshop on Mental Health Practitioners' Attitudes Toward Homosexuality and Counseling Effectiveness." *Journal of Counseling and Development, 68*(1), 81–85.

Rudolph, J. (1989b). "The Impact of Contemporary Ideology and AIDS on the Counseling of Gay Clients." *Counseling and Values, 33,* 96–108.

Rush, F. (1980). "Child Pornography." In L. Lederer (Ed.), *Take Back the Night: Women on Pornography.* New York: William Morrow.

Russell, D. (1984). *Sexual Exploitation: Rape, Child Sexual Abuse, and Workplace Harassment.* Newbury Park, CA: Sage Publications.

Russell, D. E. H. (1986). *The Secret Trauma: Incest in the Lives of Girls and Women.* New York: Basic Books.

Russell, D. E. H. (1990). *Rape in Marriage* (rev. ed.). Bloomington, IN: Indiana University Press.

Russell, S. (1991, December 3). "Women Fight Breast Cancer and the Health Care System." *San Francisco Chronicle,* pp. A1, A10.

Russell, S. (1998, April 30). "Impotence Drug Viagra Proves to Be Resounding Success." *San Francisco Chronicle,* p. A-1.

Russo, N. F., Horn, J. D., & Schwartz, R. (1992). "U.S. Abortions in Context: Selected Characteristics." *Journal of Social Issues, 48*(3), 183–202.

Russo, V. (1987). *The Celluloid Closet.* New York: Harper & Row.

"Rx for Lost Libido: Why Don't More Doctors Prescribe It?" (1996, July). *Sex Over Forty,* pp. 1–2.

Ryan, J. (1997, October 30). "A Painful Statement of Self-Identity." *San Francisco Chronicle,* p. A-1.

Sadker, M., & Sadker, D. (1994). *Failing at Fairness: How America's Schools Cheat Girls.* New York: Charles Scribner's Sons.

Safilios-Rothschild, C. (1970). "The Study of the Family Power Structure." *Journal of Marriage and the Family, 32,* 539–543.

Safilios-Rothschild, C. (1976). "Family Sociology or Wives' Sociology? A Cross-Cultural Examination of Decision-Making." *Journal of Marriage and the Family, 38,* 355–362.

Salgado de Snyder, V. N., Cervantes, R., & Padilla, A. (1990). "Gender and Ethnic Differences in Psychosocial Stress and Generalized Distress Among Hispanics." *Sex Roles, 22*(7), 441–453.

Salholz, E. (1992, August 10). "Deepening Shame." *Newsweek,* pp. 30–36.

Salovey, P., & Rodin, J. (1991). "Provoking Jealousy and Envy: Domain Relevance and Self-Esteem Threat." *Journal of Social and Clinical Psychology, 10*(4), 395–413.

Saluter, A. (1994). "Marital Status and Living Arrangements: March 1994." *Bureau of the Census Current Population Reports* (Series P20–483). Washington, DC: U.S. Government Printing Office.

"Same-Sex Harassment Ruled Illegal." (1998, March 5). *San Francisco Chronicle,* p. A-1.

(SAMHSA). (1993).

Sampson, R. (1966). *The Problem of Power.* New York: Pantheon.

Samuels, M., & Samuels, N. (1996). *The Well Pregnancy Book.* New York: Simon & Schuster.

Samuels, S., & Smith, M. (Eds.). (1993). *Condoms in the Schools.* Menlo Park, CA: Henry J. Kaiser Family Foundation.

Sanchez, Y. M. (1997). "Families of Mexican Origin." In M. K. DeGenova (Ed.), *Families in Cultural Context: Strengths and Challenges in Diversity.* Mountain View, CA: Mayfield.

Sanday, P. (1990). *Fraternity Gang Rape: Sex, Brotherhood and Privilege on Campus.* New York: New York University Press.

Sanders, J., & Robinson, W. (1979). "Talking and Not Talking About Sex: Male and Female Vocabulary." *Journal of Communication, 29*(2), 22–30.

Sanders, S. A., Reinisch, J. M., & McWhirter, D. P. (1990). "Homosexuality/Heterosexuality: An Overview." In D. P. McWhirter, S. A. Sanders, & J. M. Reinisch (Eds.), *Homosexuality/Heterosexuality: Concepts of Sexual Orientation.* New York: Oxford University Press.

Santrock, J. (1983). *Life-Span Development.* Dubuque, IA. W. C. Brown.

Sarrel, L., & Sarrel, P. (1984). *Sexual Turning Points: The Seven Stages of Adult Sexuality.* New York: Macmillan.

Sarrel, P. M. (1990). "Sexuality and Menopause." *Obstetrics and Gynecology, 75* (4 Suppl.), 26S–30S.

Sarrell, P. M., & Johnson, W. H. (1982). "Sexual Molestation of Men by Women." *Archives of Sexual Behavior, 11,* 117–131.

Sarrel, P. M., Rousseau, M., Mazure, C., & Glazer, W. (1990). "Ovarian Steroids and the Capacity to Function at Home and in the Workplace. Multidisciplinary Perspectives on Menopause." *Annals of the New York Academy of Sciences, 592,* 156–161, 185–192.

Sarton, M. (1980). *Recovering: A Journal.* New York: Norton.

Satel, S. L. (1993). "The Diagnostic Limits of 'Addiction.'" *Journal of Clinical Psychiatry, 54*(6), 237.

Satterfield, S. (1988). "Transsexualism." In D. Dailey (Ed.), *The Sexually Unusual.* New York: Harrington Park Press.

Saunders, E. (1989). "Life-Threatening Autoerotic Behavior: A Challenge for Sex Educators and Therapists." *Journal of Sex Education and Therapy, 15*(2), 77–81.

Saunders, E. B., & Awad, G. (1991). "Male Adolescent Sexual Offenders: Exhibitionism and Obscene Phone Calls." *Child Psychiatry and Human Development, 21*(3), 169–178.

Savin-Williams, R. C. (1995). "Lesbian, Gay Male, and Bisexual Adolescents." In A. R. D'Augelli & C. J. Patterson (Eds.), *Lesbian, Gay, and Bisexual Identities Over the Lifespan: Psychological Perspectives.* New York: Oxford University Press.

Savin-Williams, R., & Rodriguez, R. G. (1993). "A Developmental, Clinical Perspective on Lesbian, Gay Male, and Bisexual Youths." In T. P. Gullotta et al. (Eds.), *Adolescent Sexuality.* Newbury Park, CA: Sage Publications.

Saviteer, S. M., White, G. C., & Cohen, M. S. (1985). "HTLV-III Exposure During Cardiopulmonary Resuscitation." *New England Journal of Medicine, 313,* 1607.

Sayers, J. (1991). *Mothers of Psychoanalysis.* New York: Norton.

Scanzoni, J. (1979). "Social Processes and Power in Families." In W. Burr et al. (Eds.), *Contemporary Theories About the Family, Vol I.* New York: Free Press.

Schaap, C., Buunk, B., & Kerkstra, A. (1988). "Marital Conflict Resolutions." In P. Noller & M. A. Fitzpatrick (Eds.), *Perspectives on Marital Interaction.* Philadelphia: Multilingual Matters.

Schafer, J., & Brown, S. A. (1991). "Marijuana and Cocaine Effect Expectancies and Drug Use Patterns." *Journal of Consulting and Clinical Psychology, 59*(4), 558–565.

Schatzin, A., et al. (1987). "Alcohol Consumption and Breast Cancer in the Epidemiologic Follow-Up Study of the First National Health and Nutrition Examination Survey." *New England Journal of Medicine, 316*(19), 1169–1173.

Scherer, Y. K., Wu, Y. W., & Haughey, B. P. (1991). "AIDS and Homophobia Among Nurses." *Journal of Homosexuality, 21*(4), 17–27.

Schiavi, R. C., Schreiner-Engle, P., Mandeli, J., Schanzer, J., & Cohen, E. (1990). "Chronic Alcoholism and Male Sexual Dysfunction." *Journal of Sex and Marital Therapy, 16*(1), 23–33.

Schlesselman, J. J., et al. (1988). "Breast Cancer in Relation to Early Use of Oral Contraceptives: No Evidence of a Latent Effect." *JAMA: Journal of the American Medical Association, 259,* 1828–1833.

Schmalz, J. (1993, January 31). "Homosexuals Wake to See a Referendum: It's on Them." *The New York Times,* p. E1.

Schmidt, C. W. (1992). "Changes in Terminology for Sexual Disorders in DSM-IV." *Psychiatric Medicine, 10*(2), 247–255.

Schmitt, E. (1990, September 12). "2 Out of 3 Women in Military Study Report Sexual Harassment Incidents." *The New York Times,* p. A12.

Schneck, M. E., Sideras, K. S., Fox, R. A., & Dupuis, L. (1990). "Low-Income Adolescents and Their Infants: Dietary Findings and Health Outcomes." *Journal of the American Dietetic Association, 90*(4), 555–558.

Schover, L. R., Fife, M., & Gershenson, D. M. (1989). "Sexual Dysfunction and Treatment for Early Stage Cervical Cancer." *Cancer, 63*(1), 204–212.

Schureurs, K. M. (1993). "Sexuality in Lesbian Couples: The Importance of Gender." *Annual Review of Sex Research, 4,* 49–66.

Schwanberg, S. (1985). "Changes in Labeling Homosexuality in Health Sciences: A Preliminary Investigation." *Journal of Homosexuality, 12*(1), 51–73.

Schwartz, I. D., & Root, A. W. (1991). "The Klinefelter Syndrome of Testicular Dysgenesis." *Endocrinology and Metabolism Clinics of North America, 20*(1), 153–163.

Schwarz, P. Interview with Bryan Strong, December 20, 1992.

Scott, J. (1986). "Gender: A Useful Category of Historical Analysis." *American Historical Review, 91,* 1053–1075.

Scott, J. (1990a, December 24). "Trying to Save the Babies." *Los Angeles Times,* pp. 1, 18ff.

Scott, J. (1990b, December 31). "Low Birth Weight's High Cost." *Los Angeles Times,* p. 1.

Scott, S. G., et al. (1990). "Therapeutic Donor Insemination with Frozen Semen." *Canadian Medical Association Journal, 143*(4), 273–278.

Seachrist, L. (1995, July 15). "Nicotine Plays Deadly Role in Infant Death." *Science News, 148,* 39.

Sedlack, A. J., & Broadhurst, D. D. (1996). *Executive Summary of the Third National Incidence Study of Child Abuse and Neglect.* Washington, DC: National Center on Child Abuse and Neglect, National Committee to Prevent Child Abuse.

Seidman, S. (1989). "Constructing Sex as a Domain of Pleasure and Self-Expression: Sexual Ideology in the Sixties." *Theory, Culture, and Society, 6*(2), 293–315.

Seidman, S., & Rieder, R. O. (1994, March). "A Review of Sexual Behavior in the United States." *American Journal of Psychiatry, 151*(3), 330–341.

Selvin, B. W. (1993, June 1). "Transsexuals Are Coming to Terms with Themselves and Society." *New York Newsday,* pp. 55–59.

Senn, C., & Radtke, H. L. (1990). "Women's Evaluations of and Affective Reactions to Mainstream Violent Pornography, Nonviolent Pornography, and Erotica." *Violence and Victims, 5*(3), 143–155.

Sepah, T. (1998, January/February). "Health Notes." *Ms.,* p. 39.

Serdahely, W., & Ziemba, G. (1984). "Changing Homophobic Attitudes Through College Sexuality Education." *Journal of Homosexuality, 10*(1), 148ff.

Servi, G. (1995, July 3). "'Sexy F Seeks Hot M': A Mother's Tale." *Newsweek,* p. 51.

Severn, J., Belch, G. E., & Belch, M. A. (1990). "The Effects of Sexual and Nonsexual Advertising Appeals and Information Level on Cognitive Processing and Communication Effectiveness." *Journal of Advertising, 19,* 14–22.

"Sex Called a Big Deal on Internet." (1998, June 10). *San Francisco Chronicle,* pp. A-1, A-11.

Shah, K. V. (1997, November 6). "Human Papillomaviruses and Anogenital Cancers." *New England Journal of Medicine, 337*(19), 1386.

Shah, R., Woolley, M. M., & Costin, G. (1992). "Testicular Feminization: The Androgen Insensitivity Syndrome." *Journal of Pediatric Surgery, 27*(6), 757–760.

Shalin, D. (1990, January 23). "Glasnost and Sex." *New York Times.*

Shanis, B. S., et al. (1989). "Transmission of Sexually Transmitted Diseases by Donor Semen." *Archives of Andrology, 23*(3), 249–257.

Shannon, J. W., & Woods, W. J. (1991). "Affirmative Psychotherapy for Gay Men." *Counseling Psychologist, 19*(2), 197–215.

Shapiro, M. F., Hayward, R. A., Guillemot, D., & Jayle, D. (1992). "Residents' Experiences in, and Attitudes Toward, the Care of Persons with AIDS in Canada, France, and the United States." *JAMA: Journal of the American Medical Association, 268*(4), 510–515.

Sharpsteen, D. J. (1993). "Romantic Jealousy as an Emotion Concept: A Prototype Analysis." *Journal of Social and Personal Relationships, 10*(1), 69–82.

Shaver, P. (1984). *Emotions, Relationships, and Health.* Newbury Park, CA: Sage Publications.

Shaver, P., Hazan, C., & Bradshaw, D. (1988). "Love as Attachment: The Integration of Three Behavioral Systems." In R. Sternberg & M. Barnes (Eds.), *The Psychology of Love.* New Haven, CT: Yale University Press.

Shedler, J., & Block, J. (1990). "Adolescent Drug Use and Psychological Health: A Longitudinal Inquiry." *American Psychologist, 45,* 612–630.

Sheehan, W., & Garfinkel, B. (1988). "Adolescent Autoerotic Deaths." *American Academy of Child and Adolescent Psychiatry, 27,* 82–89.

Shelp, E. (1986). *Born to Die?* New York: Free Press.

Shenon, P. (1996, January 21). "AIDS Epidemic, Late to Arrive, Now Explodes in Populous Asia." *The New York Times,* pp. 1, 8ff.

Shepard, C. (1989). *Forgiven: The Rise and Fall of Jim Bakker and the PTL Ministry.* Boston: Atlantic Monthly Press.

Shilts, R. (1987). *And the Band Played On: Politics, People, and the AIDS Epidemic.* New York: St. Martin's Press.

Shimazaki, T. (1993–94, December/January). "A Closer Look at Sexuality Education and Japanese Youth." *SIECUS Report,* 12–15.

Shipp, E. R. (1985, December 18). "Curtailing Teen-Age Pregnancy." *The New York Times,* pp. 19, 22.

Shon, S., & Ja, D. (1982). "Asian Families." In M. McGoldrick, J. K. Pearce, & J. Giordano (Eds.), *Ethnicity and Family Therapy.* New York: Guilford Press.

Shotland, R. L., & Hunter, B. A. (1995, March). "Women's 'Token Resistant' and Compliant Sexual Behaviors as Related to Uncertain Sexual Intentions and Rape." *Personality & Social Psychology Bulletin, 21*(3), 226–236.

Simon, P. M., et al. (1992). "Psychological Characteristics of a Sample of Male Street Prostitutes." *Archives of Sexual Behavior, 21*(1), 33–44.

Simon, W., & Gagnon, J. (1986). "Sexual Scripts: Permanence and Change." *Archives of Sexual Behavior, 15*(3), 97–120.

Simon, W., & Gagnon, J. (1987). "A Sexual Scripts Approach." J. H. Geer & W. O'Donohue (Eds.), *Theories of Human Sexuality.* New York: Plenum Press.

Simons, M. (1993, January 11). "France Jails a Gambian Woman Who Had Daughters Circumcised." *The New York Times,* p. A5.

Simons, R. L., & Whitbeck, L. B. (1991). "Sexual Abuse as a Precursor to Prostitution and Victimization Among Adolescent and Adult Homeless Women." *Journal of Family Issues, 12*(3), 361–380.

Simpson, W. S., & Ramberg, J. A. (1992). "Sexual Dysfunction in Married Female Patients with Anorexia and Bulimia Nervosa." *Journal of Sex and Marital Therapy, 18*(1), 44–54.

Singh, S. (1986). "Adolescent Pregnancy in the United States: An Interstate Analysis." *Family Planning Perspectives, 18*(5), 210–220.

Skitka, L. J., & Maslach, C. (1990). "Gender Roles and the Categorization of Gender-Relevant Information." *Sex Roles, 22,* 3–4.

Skolnick, A. (1992). *The Intimate Environment: Exploring Marriage and the Family.* New York: HarperCollins.

Slade, J. (1984). "Violence in the Hard-Core Pornographic Film: A Historical Survey." *Journal of Communication, 34*(3), 148–163.

Slater, P. (1974). *The Pursuit of Loneliness.* Boston: Beacon Press.

Sluzki, C. (1982). "The Latin Lover Revisited." In M. McGoldrick et al. (Eds.), *Ethnicity and Family Therapy.* New York: Guilford Press.

Small, S. A., & Luster, T. (1994). "Adolescent Sexual Activity: An Ecological Approach." *Journal of Marriage and the Family, 56,* 181–192.

Smeltzer, S. C., & Whipple, B. (1991). "Women and HIV Infection." *IMAGE: Journal of Nursing Scholarship, 23*(4), 249–256.

Smith, C. (1991). "Sex and Gender on Prime Time." *Journal of Homosexuality, 21*(1/2), 119–138.

Smith, D. K. (1992). "HIV Disease as a Cause of Death for African Americans in 1987 and 1990." *Journal of the National Medical Association, 84*(6), 481–487.

Smith, E. A., & Udry, J. R. (1985). "Coital and Non-Coital Sexual Behaviors of White and Black Adolescents." *American Journal of Public Health, 75,* 1200–1203.

Smith, E. J. (1982). "The Black Female Adolescent: A Review of the Educational, Career, and Psychological Literature." *Psychology of Women Quarterly, 6,* 261–288.

Smith, F. (1986, June 25). "Experimental AIDS Drug May Have Led to 3 Patients' Death." *San Jose Mercury News,* pp. 1, 6.

Smith, H., & Cox, C. (1983). "Dialogue with a Dominatrix." In T. Weinberg & G. W. L. Kamel (Eds.), *S and M: Studies in Sadomasochism.* Buffalo, NY: Prometheus Books.

Smith, J. E., & Krejci, J. (1991). "Minorities Join the Majority: Eating Disturbances Among Hispanic and Native American Youth." *International Journal of Eating Disorders, 10,* 179–186.

Smith, M. W., & Kronauge, C. (1990). "The Politics of Abortion: Husband Notification Legislation." *Sociological Quarterly, 31*(4), 585–598.

Smith, R. W. (1979). "What Kind of Sex Is Natural?" In V. Bullough (Ed.), *The Frontiers of Sex Research.* Buffalo, NY: Prometheus Books.

Snitow, A. (1983). "Mass Market Romance: Pornography for Women Is Different." In A. Snitow et al. (Ed.), *Powers of Desire: The Politics of Sexuality.* New York: Monthly Review Press.

Snitow, A., Stansells, C., & Thompson, S. (Eds.). (1983). *Powers of Desire: The Politics of Sexuality.* New York: Monthly Review Press.

Snyder, P. (1974). "Prostitution in Asia." *Journal of Sex Research, 10,* 119–127.

Society for Adolescent Medicine. (1991). "Society for Adolescent Medicine Position Paper on Rreproductive Health Care for Adolescents." *Journal of Adolescent Health, 12,* 649–661.

Sollom, T. (1991). "State Legislation on Reproductive Health in 1990: What Was Proposed and Enacted." *Family Planning Perspectives, 23,* 82–94.

Sonenstein, F. L. (1986). "Rising Paternity: Sex and Contraception Among Adolescent Males." In A. B. Elster & M. E. Lamb (Eds.), *Adolescent Fatherhood.* Hillsdale, NJ: Erlbaum.

Sonenstein, F. L., et al. (1991). "Levels of Sexual Activity Among Adolescent Males in the United States." *Family Planning Perspectives, 23*(4), 162–167.

Sonenstein, F. L., & Pittman, K. (1984). "The Availability of Sex Education in Large City School Districts." *Family Planning Perspectives, 16*(1), 19–25.

Sonenstein, F. L., Pleck, J. H., & Ku, L. C. (1989). "Sexual Activity, Condom Use, and AIDS Awareness Among Adolescent Males." *Family Planning Perspectives, 21*(4), 152–158.

Sonenstein, F. L., Pleck, J. H., & Ku, L. C. (1993). "Paternity Risk Among Adolescent Males." In R. I. Lerman & T. J. Ooms (Eds.), *Changing Roles and Emerging Policies.* Philadelphia: Temple University Press.

Sorenson, S. B., & Siegel, J. M. (1992). "Gender, Ethnicity, and Sexual Assault: Findings from a Los Angeles Study." *Journal of Social Issues, 48*(1), 93–104.

South, S., & Felson, R. (1990). "The Racial Patterning of Rape." *Social Forces, 69*(1), 71–93.

Southall, D. P. (1997). "Covert Video Recordings of Life-Threatening Child Abuse: Lessons for Child Protection." *Pediatrics, 100*(5), 735ff.

Spallone, P., & Steinberg, D. L. (1987). *Made to Order: The Myth of Reproductive and Genetic Progress.* New York: Pergamon Press.

Spanier, G. B., & Thompson, L. (1987). *Parting: The Aftermath of Separation and Divorce.* Newbury Park, CA: Sage Publications.

"Special Report: Sexuality and the Cardiovascular Patient." (1980, February). *The Female Patient,* 48–54.

Specter, M. (1988, March 8). "Heterosexual AIDS Study Denounced." *The Washington Post,* p. A3.

Spector, I. P., & Carey, M. P. (1990). "Incidence and Prevalence of the Sexual Dysfunctions: A Critical Review of the Empirical Literature." *Archives of Sexual Behavior, 19*(4), 389–408.

Spence, J., & Sawin, L. L. (1985). "Images of Masculinity and Femininity." In V. O'Leary et al. (Eds.), *Sex, Gender, and Social Psychology.* Hillsdale, NJ: Erlbaum.

Spence, J., et al. (1985). "Sex Roles in Contemporary Society." In G. Lindzey & E. Aronson (Eds.), *Handbook of Social Psychology.* New York: Random House.

Spencer, S. L., & Zeiss, A. M. (1987). "Sex Roles and Sexual Dysfunction in College Students." *Journal of Sex Research, 23,* 338–347.

Spletter, M. (1982). *A Woman's Choice: New Options in the Treatment of Breast Cancer.* Boston: Beacon Press.

Spock, B., & Rothenberg, M. (1985). *Dr. Spock's Baby and Child Care.* New York: Pocket Books.

Sprecher, S. (1989). "Influences on Choice of a Partner and on Sexual Decision Making in the Relationship." In K. McKinney & S. Sprecher (Eds.), *Human Sexuality: The Social and Interpersonal Context.* Norwood, NJ: Ablex.

Sprecher, S., Hatfield, E., Cortese, A., Potapova, E., & Levitskaya, A. (1994). "Token Resistance to Sexual Intercourse and Consent in Unwanted Sexual Intercourse: College Students' Experiences in Three Countries." *Journal of Sex Research, 31*(2), 125–132.

Sprecher, S., & McKinney, K. (1993). *Sexuality.* Newbury Park, CA: Sage Publications.

Sprecher, S., McKinney, K., Walsh, R., & Anderson, C. (1988). "A Revision of the Reiss Premarital Sexual Permissiveness Scale." *Journal of Marriage and the Family, 50*(3), 821–828.

Sprecher, S., et al. (1989). "Sexual Relationships." In K. McKinney & S. Sprecher (Eds.), *Human Sexuality: The Social and Interpersonal Context.* Norwood, NJ: Ablex.

Squires, S. (1997, October 2). "Another Antidepressant Found to Ease Symptoms of PMS." *San Francisco Chronicle,* p. A-17.

Stack, C. B. (1974). *All Our Kin: Strategies for Survival in a Black Community.* New York: Harper & Row.

Stack, S., & Gundlach, J. H. (1992). "Divorce and Sex." *Archives of Sexual Behavior, 21*(4), 359–368.

Staggenborg, S. (1991). *The Pro-Choice Movement: Organization and Activism in the Abortion Conflict.* New York: Oxford University Press.

"Stanford AIDS Study Called Discouraging." (1998, June 1). *San Francisco Chronicle,* p. A-2.

Staples, R. (1988). "The Black American Family." In C. Mindel et al. (Eds.), *Ethnic Families in America: Patterns and Variations* (3rd ed.). New York: Elsevier North Holland.

Staples, R. (1991). "The Sexual Revolution and the Black Middle Class." In R. Staples (Ed.), *The Black Family* (4th ed.). Belmont, CA: Wadsworth.

Staples, R., & Johnson, L. B. (1993). *Black Families at the Crossroads: Challenges and Prospects.* San Francisco: Jossey-Bass.

Steck, L., Levitan, D., McLane, D., & Kelley, H. H. (1982). "Care, Need, and Conceptions of Love." *Journal of Personality and Social Psychology, 43,* 481–491.

Stehlin, D. (1997). Depo-Provera—The Quarterly Contraceptive. Medscape, Inc. Available: http://www.medscape.com/ govmt/FDA/patient/DepoProvera.html (Last visited 9/21/97).

Stein, J. A., Fox, S. A., & Murata, P. J. (1991). "The Influence of Ethnicity, Socioeconomic Status, and Psychological Barriers on Use of Mammography." *Journal of Health and Social Behavior, 32*(2), 101–113.

Stein, M., Chamberlin, J. W., Lerner, S. E., & Gladshteyn, M. (1993). "The Evaluation and Treatment of Sexual Dysfunction in the Neurologically Impaired Patient." *Journal of Neurologic Rehabilitation, 7*(2), 63–71.

Steiner, M., Steinberg, S., Stewart, D., Carter, D., Berger, C., Reid, R., Grover, D., & Streiner, D. (1995). "Fluoxetine in the Treatment of Premenstrual Dysphoria." *New England Journal of Medicine, 332*(23), 1529–1534.

Stelzer, C., Desmond, S. M., & Price, J. H. (1987). "Physical Attractiveness and Sexual Activity of College Students." *Psychological Reports, 60,* 567–573.

Stengel, R. (1985, December 9). "The Missing-Father Myth." *Time,* p. 90.

Stephen, T. D., & Harrison, T. M. (1985). "A Longitudinal Comparison of Couples with Sex-Typical and Non-Sex-Typical Orientation to Intimacy." *Sex Roles, 12*(1–2), 195–206.

Stephenson, P., Wagner, M., Badea, M., & Serbanescu, F. (1992). "Commentary: The Public Health Consequences of Restricted Induced Abortion—Lessons from Romania." *American Journal of Public Health, 82*(10), 1328–1331.

Stermac, L., Blanchard, R., Clemmensen, C. H., & Dickey, R. (1991). "Group Therapy for Gender-Dysphoric Heterosexual Men." *Journal of Sex and Marital Therapy, 17*(4), 252–258.

Stern, M., & Karraker, K. H. (1989). "Sex Stereotyping in Infants: A Review of Gender Labeling." *Sex Roles, 20,* 501–522.

Sternberg, R. (1986). "A Triangular Theory of Love." *Psychological Review, 93,* 119–135.

Sternberg, R. (1988). "Triangulating Love." In R. Sternberg & M. Barnes (Eds.), *The Psychology of Love.* New Haven, CT: Yale University Press.

Sternberg, R., & Grajek, S. (1984). "The Nature of Love." *Journal of Personality and Social Psychology, 47,* 312–327.

Sternberg, S. (1998, January 7). "Entrepreneur Plans to Clone Babies for Childless Couples." *USA Today,* p. 1-A.

Stets, J., & Pirog-Good, M. (1987). "Violence in Dating Relationships." *Social Psychology Quarterly, 50*(3), 237–246.

Stevens, P. E. (1992). "Lesbian Health Care Research: A Review of the Literature from 1970 to 1990." *Health Care for Women International, 13*(2), 91–120.

Stevenson, M. (1990). "Tolerance for Homosexuality and Interest in Sexuality Education." *Journal of Sex Education and Therapy, 16,* 194–197.

Stevens-Simon, C., & Beach, R. K. (1992). "School-Based Prenatal and Postpartum Care: Strategies for Meeting the Medical and Educational Needs of Pregnant and Parenting Students." *Journal of School Health, 62*(7), 304–309.

St. Lawrence, J., & Joyner, D. (1991). "The Effects of Sexually Violent Rock Music on Males' Acceptance of Violence Against Women." *Psychology of Women Quarterly, 15*(1), 49–63.

St. Lawrence, J. S., & Madakasira, S. (1992). "Evaluation and Treatment of Premature Ejaculation: A Critical Review." *International Journal of Psychiatry in Medicine, 22*(1), 77–97.

Stock, W. (1985, September 11–12). "The Effect of Pornography on Women." Paper presented at a hearing of the Attorney General's Commission on Pornography, Houston, TX.

Stockdale, M. S. (1993). "The Role of Sexual Misperceptions of Women's Friendliness in an Emerging Theory of Sexual Harassment." *Journal of Vocational Behavior, 42*(1), 84–101.

Stolberg, S. G. (1997, December 14). "Infertile Couples Try to Beat Odds." *The Herald,* pp. A1, 8.

Stoller, R. J. (1975). *Perversion: The Erotic Form of Hatred.* New York: Pantheon.

Stoller, R. J. (1977). "Sexual Deviations." In F. Beach (Ed.), *Human Sexuality in Four Perspectives.* Baltimore, MD: Johns Hopkins University Press.

Stoller, R. J. (1982). "Transvestism in Women." *Archives of Sexual Behavior, 11*(2), 99–115.

Stoller, R. J. (1991). *Pain & Passion: A Psychoanalyst Explores the World of S & M.* New York: Plenum Press.

Stone, K. M., et al. (1989). "National Surveillance for Neonatal Herpes Simplex Virus Infections." *Sexually Transmitted Diseases, 16*(3), 152–160.

Straayer, C. (1992). "Redressing the Natural—The Temporary Transvestite Film." *Wide Angle: A Quarterly Journal of Film History, Theory, and Criticism, 14*(1), 36–55.

Strage, M. (1980). *The Durable Fig Leaf.* New York: William Morrow.

Stranc, L. C. (1997). "Chorionic Villus Sampling and Amniocentesis for Prenatal Diagnosis." *Lancet, 349*(9053), 711ff.

Strasburger, V. C. (1995). *Adolescents and the Media: Medical and Psychological Impact.* Thousand Oaks, CA: Sage.

Strassberg, D. S., & Lowe, K. (1995). "Volunteer Bias in Sex Research." *Archives of Sexual Behavior, 24*(4): 369–382.

Strong, B. (1973, June). "Origins of the Sex Education Movement." *History of Education Quarterly,* 1–18.

Strong, B. (1973). "Toward a History of the Experiential Family: Sex and Incest in the 19th Century." *Journal of Marriage and the Family, 34,* 457–466.

Strong, B., & DeVault, C. (1992). *The Marriage and Family Experience.* St. Paul, MN: West.

Struckman-Johnson, D., & Struckman-Johnson, C. (1991). "Men and Women's Acceptance of Coercive Sexual Strategies Varied by Initiator Gender and Couple Intimacy." *Sex Roles, 25,* 661–676.

Studer, M., & Thornton, A. (1987). "Adolescent Religiosity and Contraceptive Use." *Journal of Marriage and the Family, 49,* 117–128.

Sue, D. (1979). "Erotic Fantasies of College Students During Coitus." *Journal of Sex Research, 15,* 299–305.

Suggs, D. N., & Miracle, A. W. (Eds.). (1993). *Culture and Human Sexuality.* Pacific Grove, CA: Brooks/Cole.

Summers, R. (1991). "Determinants of Judgments of and Responses to a Complaint of Sexual Harassment." *Sex Roles, 25*(7–8), 379–392.

Sundt, M. (1994). *Identifying the Attitudes and Beliefs That Accompany Sexual Harassment.* Unpublished doctoral dissertation, UCLA.

Surra, C. (1991). "Research and Theory on Mate Selection and Premarital Relationship in the 1980s." In A. Booth (Ed.), *Contemporary Families: Looking Forward, Looking Back.* Minneapolis, MN: National Council on Family Relations.

"Survey of 80,000 Cases Calls Birth-Defect Test Safe." (1992, August 4). *San Jose Mercury News,* p. 3F.

Susser, M. (1992). "Induced Abortion and Health as a Value." *American Journal of Public Health, 82*(10), 1323–1324.

Sward, S. (1998, June 27). "High Court Widens Employer Liability for Sex Harassment." *San Francisco Chronicle,* pp. A-1, A-15.

Swartz, J. (1998, April 16). "Surveyor of Cybersex." *San Francisco Chronicle,* p. D-3.

Sweet, J. A., & Bumpass, L. L. (1987). *American Families and Households.* New York: Russell Sage Foundation.

Swensen, C. H., Jr. (1972). "The Behavior of Love." In H. A. Otto (Ed.), *Love Today: A New Exploration."* New York: Association Press.

Symons, D. (1979). *The Evolution of Human Sexuality.* New York: Oxford University Press.

Szaz, T. (1990). *Sex by Prescription: The Startling Truth About Today's Sex Therapy.* Syracuse, NY: Syracuse University Press.

Szinovacz, M. (1987). "Family Power." In M. Sussman & S. Steinmetz (Eds.), *Handbook of Marriage and the Family.* New York: Plenum Press.

Talamini, J. T. (1982). *Boys Will Be Girls.* Washington, DC: University Press of America.

Tanfer, K. (1987). "Patterns of Premarital Cohabitation Among Never-Married Women in the United States." *Journal of Marriage and the Family, 49,* 683–697.

Tanfer, K., & Cubbins, L. A. (1992). "Coital Frequency Among Single Women: Normative Constraints and Situational Opportunities." *Journal of Sex Research, 29*(2), 221–250.

Tanfer, K., & Schoorl, J. J. (1992). "Premarital Sexual Careers and Partner Change." *Archives of Sexual Behavior, 21,* 45–68.

Tanke, E. D. (1982). "Dimensions of the Physical Attractiveness Stereotype: A Factor/Analytic Study." *Journal of Psychology, 110,* 63–74.

Tannen, D. (1990). *You Just Don't Understand: Women and Men in Conversation.* New York: Ballantine.

Tardif, G. S. (1989). "Sexual Activity After a Myocardial Infarction." *Archives of Physical Medicine and Rehabilitation, 70*(10), 763–766.

Tavris, C. (1992). *The Mismeasure of Woman.* New York: Norton.

Tavris, C., & Sadd, S. (1977). *The Redbook Report on Female Sexuality.* New York: Dell.

Taylor, E. (1989). *Prime-Time Families.* Berkeley, CA: University of California Press.

Taylor, J. R., Lockwood, A. P., & Taylor, A. J. (1996). "The Prepuce: Specialized Mucosa of the Penis and Its Loss to Circumcision." *British Journal of Urology, 77,* 291–295.

Taylor, R. J. (1994). "Black American Families." In R. J. Taylor (Ed.), *Minority Families in the United States.* Englewood Cliffs, NJ: Prentice-Hall.

Taylor, R. J., Chatters, L. M., Tucker, B., & Lewis, E. (1991). "Developments in Research on Black Families." In A. Booth (Ed.),

Contemporary Families: Looking Forward, Looking Back. Minneapolis, MN: National Council on Family Relations.

Teachman, J. D., & Polonko, K. A. (1990). "Cohabitation and Marital Stability in the United States." *Social Forces, 69*(1), 207–220.

"Teen-Age Fathers Now Getting Help." (1986, August 21). *The New York Times,* p. 24.

Teen Sex Down, New Study Shows. (1997, May 1). Available: http://www.cdc.gov/nchswww/releases/97news/97news/nsfgteen.htm (Last visited 11/21/97).

Templeman, T., & Stinnett, R. (1991). "Patterns of Sexual Arousal and History in a 'Normal' Sample of Young Men." *Archives of Sexual Behavior, 20*(2), 137–150.

Terr, L. (1994). *Unchained Memories: True Stories of Traumatic Memories.* New York: Basic Books.

Testa, R. J., Kinder, B. N., & Ironson, G. (1987). "Heterosexual Bias in the Perception of Loving Relationships of Gay Males and Lesbians." *Journal of Sex Research, 23*(2), 163–172.

Tharp, J. (1991). "The Transvestite as Monster: Gender Horror in 'The Silence of the Lambs' and 'Psycho.'" *Journal of Popular Film and Television, 19*(3), 106–113.

Thayer, L. (1986). *On Communication.* Norwood, NJ: Ablex.

Thomas, S. B., & Quinn, S. C. (1991). "The Tuskegee Syphilis Study, 1932 to 1972: Implications for HIV Education and AIDS Risk Education Programs in the Black Community." *American Journal of Public Health, 81*(11), 1498–1504.

Thompson, A. (1983). "Extramarital Sex: A Review of the Research Literature." *Journal of Sex Research, 19*(1), 1–22.

Thompson, A. (1984). "Emotional and Sexual Components of Extramarital Relations." *Journal of Marriage and the Family, 46*(1), 35–42.

Thompson, B. W. (1992). "'A Way Outa No Way': Eating Problems Among African-American, Latina, and White Women." *Gender and Society, 6*(4), 546–561.

Thompson, C. E. (1990). "Transition of the Disabled Adolescent to Adulthood." *Pediatrician, 17*(4), 308–313.

Thompson, L., & Walker, A. J. (1989). "Gender in Families: Women and Men in Marriage, Work, and Parenthood." *Journal of Marriage and the Family, 51,* 845–871.

Thompson, M. E., Chaffee, S. H., & Oshagan, H. H. (1990). "Regulating Pornography: A Public Dilemma." *Journal of Communication, 40*(3), 73–83.

Thompson, S. (1986, December 23). "Pregnant on Purpose." *The Village Voice,* pp. 28ff.

Thornberry, T. P., Smith, C. A., & Howard, G. J. (1997). "Risk Factors for Teenage Fatherhood." *Journal of Marriage & the Family 59*(3), 505–522.

Thornton, A. (1989). "Changing Attitudes Toward Family Issues in the United States." *Journal of Marriage and the Family, 51*(4), 873–893.

Thornton, A. (1990). "The Courtship Process and Adolescent Sexuality." *Journal of Family Issues, 11*(3), 239–273.

Tiefer, L. (1992). "Critique of the DSM-III-R Nosology of Sexual Dysfunctions." *Psychiatric Medicine, 10*(2), 227–245.

Tiefer, L. (1995). *Sex Is Not a Natural Act and Other Essays.* Boulder, CO: Westview Press.

Tietjen, A., & Bradley, C. F. (1985). "Social Support and Maternal Psychosocial Adjustment During the Transition to Parenthood." *Canadian Journal of Behavioural Science, 17*(2), 109–121.

Ting-Toomey, S. (1983). "An Analysis of Verbal Communication Patterns in High and Low Marital Adjustment Groups." *Human Communications Research, 9*(4), 306–319.

Ting-Toomey, S., & Korzenny, F. (Eds.). (1991). *Cross-Cultural Interpersonal Communication.* Newbury Park, CA: Sage Publications.

Toback, B. M. (1992). "Recent Advances in Female Infertility Care." *Naacogs Clinical Issues in Perinatal and Women's Health Nursing, 3*(2), 313–319.

Toback, J. (1992, august). "James Toback on 'The Hunger.'" Special Issue: The Sexual Revolution in Movie, Music & TV. *US,* pp. 56–58.

Toomey, K. E., Oberschelp, A. G., & Greenspan, J. R. (1989). "Sexually Transmitted Diseases and Native Americans: Trends in Reported Gonorrhea and Syphilis Morbidity, 1984–1988." *Public Health Reports, 104*(6), 566–572.

Torres, A., & Forrest, J. D. (1988). "Why Do Women Have Abortions?" *Family Planning Perspectives, 20,* 7–9.

Torres, A., & Singh, S. (1986). "Contraceptive Practice Among Hispanic Adolescents." *Family Planning Perspectives, 18*(4), 193–194.

Towle, L. (1993, May 24). "Making the Case for Abstinence." *Time,* p. 64.

Trafford, A. (1980, November 10). "Medical Science Discovers the Baby." *U.S. News & World Report,* pp. 59–62.

Trall, R. T. (1953). *Home Treatment of Sexual Abuse.* New York: M. L. Holbrook.

Treiman, K., & Liskin, L. (1988). "IUDs: A New Look." *Population Reports,* Series B (No. 5), 1–31.

Trent, K., & Crowder, K. (1997). "Adolescent Birth Intentions, Social Disadvantage, and Behavioral Outcomes." *Journal of Marriage and the Family 59*(3), 523–535.

Tribe, L. (1992). *Abortion: The Clash of Absolutes.* New York: Norton.

Trippet, S. E., & Bain, J. (1992, April). "Reasons American Lesbians Fail to Seek Traditional Health Care." *Health Care for Women International, 13*(2), 145–153.

Troiden, R. (1988). *Gay and Lesbian Identity: A Sociological Analysis.* New York: General Hall.

Trudel, G., Boulos, L., & Matte, B. (1994). "Dyadic Adjustment in Couples with Hypoactive Sexual Desire." *Journal of Sex Education and Therapy, 19*(1), 31–36.

True, R. H. (1990). "Psychotherapeutic Issues with Asian American Women." *Sex Roles, 22*(7), 477–485.

Trussell, C. E., & Stewart, F. (1996, March–April). "The Effectiveness of the Yuzpe Regimen of Emergency Contraception." *Family Planning Perspectives, 28*(2), 58–66.

Trussell, J., Hatcher, R. A., Cates, W., Stewart, F. H., & Kost, K. (1990). "Contraceptive Failure in the United States: An Update." *Studies in Family Planning, 21*(1), Table 1.

Trussell, J., Stewart, F., Guest, F., & Hatcher, R. A. (1992). "Emergency Contraceptive Pills: A Simple Proposal to Reduce Unintended Pregnancies." *Family Planning Perspectives, 24,* 269–273.

Tsoi, W. F. (1990). "Developmental Profile of 200 Male and 100 Female Transsexuals in Singapore." *Archives of Sexual Behavior, 19,* 595–605.

Tucker, M. B., & Taylor, R. J. (1989). "Demographic Correlates of Relationship Status Among Black Americans." *Journal of Marriage and the Family, 51,* 655–665.

Tucker, R. K., Marvin, M. G., & Vivian, B. (1991). "What Constitutes a Romantic Act?" *Psychological Reports, 89*(2), 651–654.

Tuleja, T. (1987). *Curious Customs.* New York: Harmony Books.

Tuller, N. R. (1988). "Couples: The Hidden Segment of the Gay World." In J. De Cecco (Ed.), *Gay Relationships.* New York: Haworth Press.

Turner, P. H., et al. (1985, March). "Parenting in Gay and Lesbian Families." Paper presented at the first meeting of the Future of Parenting Symposium, Chicago.

Turner, R. J., & Avison, W. R. (1985). "Assessing Risk Factors for Problem Parenting: The Significance of Social Support." *Journal of Marriage and the Family, 47*(4), 881–892.

Turque, P. (1992, September 14). "Gays Under Fire." *Newsweek,* pp. 35–40.

Tuttle, G. E., & Pillard, R. C. (1991). "Sexual Orientation and Cognitive Abilities." *Archives of Sexual Behavior, 20*(3), 307–318.

Twinam, A. (1989). "Honor, Sexuality, and Illegitimacy in Colonial Spanish America." In A. Lavrin (Ed.), *Sexuality and Marriage in Colonial Latin America.* Lincoln, NE: University of Nebraska Press.

Uba, L. (1994). *Asian Americans: Personality Patterns, Identity, and Mental Health.* New York: Guilford Press.

UCSF AIDS Health Project. (1991). "Risks of Oral Sex." *HIV Counselor Perspectives* (California Department of Health Services), *1*(2), 1–8.

Ullman, S. E., & Knight, R. A. (1991). "A Multivariate Model for Predicting Rape and Physical Injury Outcomes During Sexual Assaults." *Journal of Consulting and Clinical Psychology, 59*(5), 724–731.

Unger, R. K. (1979). "Toward a Redefinition of Sex and Gender." *American Psychologist, 34,* 1085–1094.

Uribe, V., & Harbeck, K. M. (1991). "Addressing the Needs of Lesbian, Gay, and Bisexual Youth: The Origins of Project 10 and School Based Intervention." *Journal of Homosexuality, 22,* 9–28.

Urquiza, A., & Goodlin-Jones, B. L. (1994, September). "Child Sexual Abuse and Adult Revictimization with Women of Color." *Violence & Victims, 9*(3), 223–232.

U.S. Attorney General's Commission on Pornography (AGCOP). (1986). *Final Report.* Washington, DC: U.S. Government Printing Office.

U.S. Bureau of the Census. (1996). *Statistical Abstract of the United States* (116th ed.). Washington, DC: U.S. Government Printing Office.

U.S. Bureau of the Census, International Programs Center. (1996). International Data Base: Infant Mortality. Available: http://www.census.gov/ipc/www/idpnew.html

U.S. Bureau of the Census (1997). *Statistical Abstract of the United States* (117th ed.). Washington, DC: U.S. Government Printing Office.

U.S. Department of Health and Human Services. (1997). *Vital Health Statistics: Fertility, Family Planning, and Women's Health: New Data from the 1995 National Survey of Family Growth.* Series 23, No. 19, Table 41. Washington, DC: Centers for Disease Control and Prevention.

U.S. Food and Drug Administration (USFDA). (1998). Viagra Information. Available: http://www.fda.gov/cder/news/viagra.htm (Last visited 5/14/98).

Uslander, A., et al. (1973). *Their Universe: The Story of a Unique Educational Program.* New York: Delacorte Press.

U.S. News and World Report (1996, August 19). pp. 50–51.

U.S. Surgeon General. (1996). *Physical Activity and Health: A Report of the Surgeon General* [Executive Summary]. Washington, DC: Department of Health & Human Services.

Van Buskirk. (1992, August). "Soap Opera Sex: Tuning In, Tuning Out." Special Issue: The Sexual Revolution in Movie, Music & TV. *US.,* pp. 64–67.

Vande Berg, Leah, R., & Steckfuss, D. (1992, March). "Prime-Time Television's Portrayal of Women and Work: A Demographic Profile." *Journal of Broadcasting and Electronic Media,* 195–207.

Vanderford, M. (1989). "Vilification and Social Movements: A Case Study of Pro-Life and Pro-Choice Rhetoric." *Quarterly Journal of Speech, 75*(2), 166–182.

Van der Leun, G. (1995, March). "Twilight Zone of the Id: Online Sex" (Special Issue). *Time,* pp. 36–37.

Vandewiel, H. B. M., Jaspers, J. P. M., Schultz, W. C. M. W., & Gal, J. (1990). "Treatment of Vaginismus: A Review of Concepts and Treatment Modalities." *Journal of Psychosomatic Obstetrics and Gynecology, 11,* 1–18.

Van Wyk, P. H., & Geist, C. S. (1984). "Psychosocial Development of Heterosexual, Bisexual, and Homosexual Behavior." *Archives of Sexual Behavior, 13,* 505–544.

Vasquez-Nuthall, E., Romero-Garcia, & DeLeon. (1987). "Sex Roles and Perceptions of Femininity and Masculinity of Hispanic Women: A Review of the Literature." *Psychology of Women Quarterly, 11,* 409–426.

Vaughan, D. (1986). *Uncoupling: Turning Points in Intimate Relationships.* New York: Oxford University Press.

Veevers, J. (1980). *Childless by Choice.* Toronto, Canada: Buttersworth.

Vega, W. (1991). "Hispanic Families." In A. Booth (Ed.), *Contemporary Families: Looking Forward, Looking Back.* Minneapolis, MN: National Council on Family Relations.

Ventura, J. N. (1987). "The Stresses of Parenthood Reexamined." *Family Relations, 36,* 26–29.

Verschraegen-Spae, M. R. (1992). "Familial Turner Syndrome." *Clinical Genetics, 41*(4), 218–220.

Verwoerdt, A., et al. (1969). "Sexual Behavior in Senescence." *Geriatrics, 24,* 137–157.

"A Very Sore Spot." (1997, August 25). *Newsweek,* p. 81.

Vessey, M. P., et al. (1983). "Neoplasia of the Cervix Uteri and Contraception: A Possible Adverse Effect of the Pill." *Lancet, 2,* 930–934.

"Viagra Might Help Women, Too—Test in Works." (1998, May 1). *San Francisco Chronicle,* p. A-2.

"Victims May Be Offered Anti-AIDS Drugs." (1997). *AIDS Weekly Plus,* pp. 21–23.

Vine, M., Margolin, B., Morrison, H., & Hulka, B. (1994). "Cigarette Smoking and Sperm Density: A Meta-Analysis." *Fertility and Sterility, 61*(1), 35–43.

Virga, V. (1980). *Gaywyck.* New York: Avon.

Voeller, B. (1991). "AIDS and Heterosexual Anal Intercourse." *Archives of Sexual Behavior, 20*(3), 233–276.

Vogel, D. A., Lake, M. A., & Evans, S. (1991). "Children's and Adults' Sex-Stereotyped Perceptions of Infants." *Sex Roles, 24,* 605–616.

Vonk, R., & Ashmore, R. D. (1993). "The Multifaceted Self: Androgyny Reassessed by Open-Ended Self-Descriptions." *Social Psychology Quarterly, 56*(4), 278–287.

Voydanoff, P., & Donnelly, B. (1990). *Adolescent Sexuality and Pregnancy.* Newbury Park, CA: Sage Publications.

Vredeveldt, P. (1994). *Empty Arms: Emotional Support for Those Who Have Suffered Miscarriage and Stillbirth.* Sisters, OR: Questar.

Walker, A. (1992). *Possessing the Secret of Joy.* New York: Harcourt Brace Jovanovich.

Walker, E. A., Katon, W. J., Hansom, J., & Harrop-Griffiths, J. (1992). "Medical and Psychiatric Symptoms in Women with Childhood Sexual Abuse." *Psychosomatic Medicine, 54*(6), 658–664.

Wallen, K. (1995). "The Evolution of Female Sexual Desire." In P. R. Abramson, & S. D. Pinkerton (Eds.), *Sexual Nature, Sexual Culture.* Chicago: University of Chicago Press.

Waller, W., & Hill, R. (1951). *The Family: A Dynamic Interpretation.* New York: Dryden Press.

Walling, M., Andersen, B. L., & Johnson, S. R. (1990). "Hormonal Replacement Therapy for Postmenopausal Women: A Review of Sexual Outcomes and Related Gynecologic Effects." *Archives of Sexual Behavior, 19*(2), 119–127.

Wallis, C. (1985, December 9). "Children Having Children." *Time*, pp. 78–79.

Walsh, A. (1994, December). "Homosexual and Heterosexual Child Molestation: Case Characteristics and Sentencing Differentials." *International Journal of Offender Therapy and Comparative Criminology, 38*(4), 339–353.

Walters, Andrew. (1997). Personal communication.

Wardle, F. (1989, December). "Helping Children Respect Differences." *PTA Today*, pp. 5–6.

Wardlow, G. (1997). *Contemporary Nutrition Issues and Insights.* New York: Brown Benchmark.

Washton, A. M. (1989). *Cocaine Addiction: Treatment, Recovery, and Relapse Prevention.* New York: Norton.

Waterman, C. K., Dawson, L. J., & Bologna, M. J. (1989). "Sexual Coercion in Gay Male and Lesbian Relationships: Predictors and Implications for Support Services." *Journal of Sex Research, 26*(1), 118–125.

Waterson, E. J., & Murray-Lyon, I. M. (1990). "Preventing Alcohol-Related Birth Damage: A Review." *Social Science and Medicine, 30*(3), 349–364.

Webb, P. (1983). *The Erotic Arts.* New York: Farrar, Straus & Giroux.

Webb, T. (1992, August 2). "Rural Teen Who Got AIDS Warns Others They're at Risk." *San Jose Mercury News*, p. A2.

Weeks, J. (1985). *Sexuality and Its Discontents.* London: Routledge & Kegan Paul.

Weeks, J. (1986). *Sexuality.* New York: Tavistock Publications and Ellis Horwood, Ltd.

Weeks, J. (1993, February 11). "Someone Wicked This Way Comes." *San Jose Mercury News*, pp. 1C, 6C.

Weg, R. (1983a). "Introduction: Beyond Intercourse and Orgasm." In R. Weg (Ed.), *Sexuality in the Later Years: Roles and Behavior.* New York: Academic Press.

Weg, R. (1983b). "The Physiological Perspective." In R. Weg (Ed.), *Sexuality in the Later Years: Roles and Behavior.* New York: Academic Press.

Weidner, W., Weiske, W. H., Rudnick, J., Becker, H. C., Schroeder-Printzen, J., & Brahler, E. (1992). "Venous Surgery in Veno-Occlusive Dysfunction: Long-Time Results After Dorsal Vein Resection." *Urologia Internationalis, 49*(1), 24–28.

Weinberg, M. S., & Williams, C. J. (1974). *Male Homosexuals: Their Problems and Adaptations.* New York: Oxford University Press.

Weinberg, M. S., & Williams, C. J. (1988). "Black Sexuality: A Test of Two Theories." *Journal of Sex Research, 25*(2), 197–218.

Weinberg, M. S., Williams, C. J., & Moser, C. (1984). "The Social Constituents of Sadomasochism." *Social Problems, 31*, 379–389.

Weinberg, M., Williams, C., & Pryor, D. (1994). *Dual Attraction: Understanding Bisexuality.* New York: Oxford University Press.

Weinberg, T. S. (1987). "Sadomasochism in the United States: A Review of Recent Sociological Literature." *Journal of Sex Research, 23*, 50–69.

Weinberg, T. S., & Kamel, G. W. L. (Eds.). (1983). *S and M: Studies in Sadomasochism.* Buffalo, NY: Prometheus Books.

Weir, J. (1992, March 29). "Gay-Bashing, Villany and the Oscars." *The New York Times*, p. 17.

Weis, D. (1985). "The Experience of Pain During Women's First Sexual Intercourse: Cultural Mythology About Female Sexual Initiation." *Archives of Sexual Behavior, 14*, 421–428.

Weisberg, D. K. (1990). *Children of the Night.* New York: Free Press.

Weiss, D. (1983). "Open Marriage and Multilateral Relationships: The Emergence of Nonexclusive Models of the Marital Relationship." In E. Macklin & R. Rubin (Eds.), *Contemporary Families and Alternative Lifestyles.* Newbury Park, CA: Sage Publications.

Weiss, D., & Jurich, J. (1985). "Size of Community as a Predictor of Attitudes Toward Extramarital Sexual Relations." *Journal of Marriage and the Family, 47*(1), 173–178.

Weiss, J. (1992). "Multiple Sclerosis: Will It Come Between Us? Sexual Concerns of Clients and Their Partners." *Journal of Neuroscience Nursing, 24*(4), 190–193.

Weiss, P. (1992, August 18). "The Bond of Mother's Milk." *San Jose Mercury News*, pp. 1–2E.

Weissbach, T. A., & Zagon, G. (1975). "The Effect of Deviant Group Membership upon Impression of Personality." *Journal of Social Psychology, 95*, 263–266.

Weizman, R., & Hart, J. (1987). "Sexual Behavior in Healthy Married Elderly Men." *Archives of Sexual Behavior, 16*(1), 39–44.

Wenz, P. S. (1992). *Abortion Rights as Religious Freedom.* Philadelphia: Temple University Press.

Wertz, R., & Wertz, D. (1977). *Lying-In: A History of Childbirth in America.* New York: Free Press.

Westfall, J. M., & Main, D. S. (1995). "The Contraceptive Implant and the Injectable: A Comparison of Costs." *Family Planning Perspectives, 27*(1), 34–36.

Westheimer, R. (1988). *Dr. Ruth's Guide to Good Sex.* New York: Crown.

Westheimer, R. (1993). *Dr. Ruth Talks to Kids.* New York: Simon & Schuster.

What Is Priapism? (1997, March 28). Available: http://www.columbia.edu/cu/healthwise/1133.html (Last visited 1/29/98).

Whelan, E. (1986). *Boy or Girl?* New York: Pocket Books.

Whipple, B., Ogden, G., & Komisaruk, B. R. (1992). "Physiological Correlates of Imagery-Induced Orgasm in Women." *Archives of Sexual Behavior, 21*(2), 121–133.

Whitbeck, L. B., & Hoyt, D. R. (1991). "Campus Prestige and Dating Behaviors." *College Student Journal, 25*(4), 457–469.

Whitbourne, S. K. (1990). "Sexuality in the Aging Male." *Generations, 14*(3), 28–30.

Whitbourne, S., & Ebmeyer, J. (1990). *Identity and Intimacy in Marriage: A Study of Couples.* New York: Springer-Verlag.

Whitcomb, D., et al. (1994). *The Child Victim as a Witness: Research Report.* Washington, DC: U.S. Department of Justice, Office of Juvenile Justice and Delinquency Prevention.

White, C. (1982). "Sexual Interest, Attitudes, Knowledge, and Sexual History in Relation to Sexual Behavior of the Institutionalized Aged." *Archives of Sexual Behavior, 11*, 11–21.

White, G. (1980a). "Inducing Jealousy: A Power Perspective." *Personality and Social Psychology Bulletin, 6*(2), 222–227.

White, G. (1980b, October). "Physical Attractiveness and Courtship Progress." *Journal of Personality and Social Psychology, 39*(4), 660–668.

White, G. (1981a). "Jealousy and Partner's Perceived Motives for Attraction to a Rival." *Social Psychology Quarterly, 44*(1), 24–30.

White, G. (1981b). "A Model of Romantic Jealousy." *Motivation and Education, 5*, 600–668.

White, J. W., & Farmer, R. (1992). "Research Methods: How They Shape Views of Sexual Violence." *Journal of Social Issues, 48*, 45–59.

White, J., & Parham, T. (1990). *The Psychology of Blacks: An African-American Perspective* (2nd ed.). Englewood Cliffs, NJ: Prentice-Hall.

White, P., & Rollins, J. (1981). "Rape: A Family Crisis." *Family Relations, 103*–109.

Whitehead, B. D. (1990, October 7). "How to Rebuild a 'Family Friendly' Society." *Des Moines Sunday Register*, p. 3.

Whitley, B. E., & Kite, M. E. (1995, January). "Sex Differences in Attitudes Toward Homosexuality: A Comment on Oliver and Hyde (1993)." *Psychology Bulletin, 117*(1), 146–154.

"WHO Collaborative Study of Neoplasia and Steroid Contraceptives, Breast Cancer, Cervical Cancer, and Depot Medroxyprogesterone Acetate." (1984, November 24). *Lancet, 2*(8413), 1207–1208.

Why Gal. (1992, April 17). "Male Nipples Are Good for Something." *Seattle Times*, p. 6.

Wickler, W. (1973). *The Sexual Code*. New York: Anchor Books.

Widom, C. S., & Kuhns, J. B. (1996). "Childhood Victimization and Subsequent Risk for Promiscuity, Prostitution, and Teenage Pregnancy: A Prospective Study." *American Journal of Public Health, 86*(11), 1607–1612.

Wiederman, M. W. (1997). "Extramarital Sex: Prevalence and Correlates in a National Study." *Journal of Sex Research, 34*(2), 167–175.

Wiederman, M. W., & Allgeier, E. R. (1993). "Gender Differences in Sexual Jealousy: Adaptionist or Social Learning Explanation?" *Ethnology and Sociobiology, 14*(2), 115–140.

Wiederman, M., Maynard, C., & Fretz, A. (1996, December). "Ethnicity in 25 Years of Published Sexuality Research: 1971–1995." *Journal of Sex Research 33*(4), 339–343.

Wight, D. (1992). "Impediments to Safer Heterosexual Sex: A Review of Research with Young People." *AIDS Care, 4*, 11–23.

Wilcox, A., et al. (1988). "Incidents of Early Loss of Pregnancy." *New England Journal of Medicine, 319*(4), 189–194.

Wilkerson, I. (1987, June 26). "Infant Mortality: Frightful Odds in Inner City." *The New York Times*, pp. 1ff.

Wilkinson, C. B. (Ed.). (1986). *Ethnic Psychiatry*. New York: Plenum Medical Book Company.

Wilkinson, C. B., & Spurlock, J. (1986). "The Mental Health of Black Americans: Psychiatric Diagnosis and Treatment." In C. B. Wilkinson (Ed.), *Ethnic Psychiatry*. New York: Plenum Medical Book Company.

Wilkinson, D., Zinn, M. B., & Chow, E. N. L. (1992). "Race, Class, and Gender: Introduction." *Gender and Society, 6*(3), 341–345.

Wilkinson, D., et al. (Eds.). (1992). "Transforming Social Knowledge: The Interlocking of Race, Class, and Gender." *Gender and Society*. Special Issue.

Wilkinson, D. Y. (1997). "American Families of African Descent." In M. K. DeGenova (Ed.), *Families in Cultural Context: Strengths and Challenges in Diversity*. Mountain View, CA: Mayfield.

Wilkinson, S., & Kitzinger, C. (Eds.). (1993). *Heterosexuality*. Newbury Park, CA: Sage Publications.

Willemsen, T. M. (1993). "On the Bipolarity of Androgyny: A Critical Comment on Kottke (1988)." *Psychological Reports, 72*(1), 327–332.

Willet, W. C., et al. (1987). "Moderate Alcohol Consumption and the Risk of Breast Cancer." *New England Journal of Medicine, 316*(19), 1174–1180.

Williams, D. M., Patterson, M. N., & Hughes, I. A. (1993). "Androgen Insensitivity Syndrome." *Archives of Disease in Childhood, 68*(3), 343–344.

Williams, E. A., Lam, J. A., & Shively, M. (1992). "The Impact of a University Policy on the Sexual Harassment of Female Students." *Journal of Higher Education, 63*(1), 50–64.

Williams, J. K. (1992). "School-Aged Children with Turner's Syndrome." *Journal of Pediatric Nursing, 7*(1), 14–19.

Williams, J. K., Richman, L. C., & Yarbrough, D. B. (1992). "Comparison of Visual-Spatial Performance Strategy Training in Children with Turner Syndrome and Learning Disabilities." *Journal of Learning Disabilities, 25*(10), 658–664.

Williams, J. K., et al. (1991). "A Comparison of Memory and Attention in Turner Syndrome and Learning Disability." *Journal of Pediatric Psychology, 16*(5), 585–593.

Williams, J., & Jacoby, A. (1989). "The Effects of Premarital Heterosexual and Homosexual Experience on Dating and Marriage Desirability." *Journal of Marriage and the Family, 51*, 489–497.

Williams, K. B., & Cyr, R. R. (1992). "Escalating Commitment to a Relationship: The Sexual Harassment Trap." *Sex Roles, 27*(1–2), 47–72.

Williams, L. (1994). "Recall of Childhood Trauma: A Prospective Study of Women's Memories of Child Sexual Abuse." *Journal of Consulting and Clinical Psychology, 62*, 1167–1176.

Williams, W. L. (1985). "Persistence and Change in the Berdache Tradition Among Contemporary Lakota Indians." *Journal of Homosexuality, 11*(3–4), 191–200.

Wills, G. (1989, December 21). "The Phallic Pulpit." *The New York Review of Books*, pp. 20–26.

Wills, G. (1990). *Under God*. New York: Simon & Schuster.

Wilson, G. (1978). *The Secrets of Sexual Fantasy*. London: J. M. Dent.

Wilson, M. N., et al. (1990). "Flexibility and Sharing of Childcare Duties in Black Families." *Sex Roles, 22*(7–8), 409–425.

Wilson, P. (1986). "Black Culture and Sexuality." *Journal of Social Work and Human Sexuality, 4*(3), 29–46.

Wilson, S., & Delk, J., II. (1994). "A New Treatment for Peyronie's Disease: Modeling the Penis Over an Inflatable Penile Prosthesis." *Journal of Urology, 152*, 1121–1123.

Wilson, S. M., & Medora, N. P. (1990). "Gender Comparisons of College Students' Attitudes Toward Sexual Behavior." *Adolescence, 25*(99), 615–627.

Wincze, J., Albert, A., & Bansal, S. (1993). "Sexual Arousal in Diabetic Females: Physiological and Self-Report Measures." *Archives of Sexual Behavior, 22*, 587–600.

Wincze, J., & Carey, M. (1991). *Sexual Dysfunction: A Guide for Assessment and Treatment*. New York: Guilford Press.

Winikoff, B., & Wymelenberg, S. (1997). *The Whole Truth About Contraception*. Washington, DC: National Academy of Sciences.

Wise, T. N., & Meyer, J. K. (1980). "The Border Area Between Transvestism and Gender Dysphoria: Transvestitic Applicants for Sex Reassignment." *Archives of Sexual Behavior, 9*, 327–342.

Wise, T. N., et al. (1991). "Personality and Sexual Functioning of Transvestitic Fetishists and Other Paraphilics." *Journal of Nervous and Mental Disease, 179*(11), 694–698.

Wishnietsky, D. H. (1991). "Reported and Unreported Teacher-Student Sexual Harassment." *Journal of Educational Research, 84*(3), 164–169.

Wiswell, T. E. (1990). "Routine Neonatal Circumcision: A Reappraisal." *American Family Physician, 41*(3), 859–863.

Wolberg, W. H., Romsaas, E. P., Tanner, M. A., & Malec, J. F. (1989). "Psychosexual Adaptation to Breast Cancer Surgery." *Cancer, 63*(8), 1645–1655.

Wolf, D. (1980). *The Lesbian Community*. Berkeley, CA: University of California Press.

Wolfe, L. (1981). *The Cosmos Report*. New York: Bantam.

Wolfe, S. (1996). "If You're Sexually Harassed (Legally Speaking)." *RN, 59*(2), 61–65.

Wolff, C. (1986). *Magnus Hirschfeld: A Portrait of a Pioneer in Sexology*. London: Quartet Books.

Wolinsky, S., et al. (1988, June 12). "Polymerase Chain Reaction (PCR) Detection of HIV Provirus Before HIV Seroconversion." Paper presented at the Fourth International Conference on AIDS, Stockholm, Sweden.

"Women, Coffee and Fertility." (1995, December 20). *San Francisco Chronicle*, p. A-8.

Wood, D. (1993, January 29). "Military Women Say Anti-Gay Rule Harms Heterosexuals' Careers, Too." *San Jose Mercury News*, p. 17.

Wood, F. G. (1990). *The Arrogance of Faith: Christianity and Race in America from the Colonial Era to the Twentieth Century."* New York: Knopf.

Wood, J. T. (1994). *Gendered Lives: Communication, Gender, and Culture*. Belmont, CA: Wadsworth.

Woodhouse, A. (1985). "Forgotten Women: Transvestism and Marriage." *Women's Studies International Forum, 8*(6), 583–592.

Woodhouse, A. (1989). "Breaking the Rules or Bending Them: Transvestism, Femininity, and Feminism." *Women's Studies International Forum, 12*(4), 417–423.

Woods, S. C., & Mansfield, J. G. (1981, February 11). "Ethanol and Disinhibition: Physiological and Behavioral Links." In R. Room & Collins (Eds.), *Proceedings of Alcoholism and Drug Abuse Conference, Berkeley/Oakland* (pp. 4–22). Washington, DC: U.S. Department of Health and Human Services.

Woodworth, T. W. (1996). DEA Congressional Testimony. Available: http://www.usdoj.gov/dea/ (Last visited 2/6/97).

Workman, J. E., & Johnson, K. K. (1991). "The Role of Cosmetics in Attributions About Sexual Harassment." *Sex Roles, 24*(11–12), 759–769.

World Health Organization. (1992). *Reproductive Health: A Key to a Brighter Future*. Biennial Report, 1990–1991. Geneva, Switzerland: World Health Organization.

Wright, J., Duchesne, C., Sabourin, S., Bissonnette, F., Benoit, J., & Girard, Y. (1991). "Psychosocial Distress and Infertility: Men and Women Respond Differently." *Fertility and Sterility, 55*(1), 100–108.

Wright, P., Nobrega, J., Langevin, R., & Wortzman, G. (1990). "Brain Density and Symmetry in Pedophilic and Sexually Aggressive Offenders." *Annals of Sex Research, 3*(3), 319–328.

Wyatt, G. E. (1991). "Examining Ethnicity Versus Race in AIDS Related Sex Research." *Social Science and Medicine, 33*(1), 37–45.

Wyatt, G. E. (1992). "The Sociocultural Context of African American and White American Women's Rape." *Journal of Social Issues, 48*(1), 77–91.

Wyatt, G. E., Guthrie, D., & Notgass, C. M. (1992). "Differential Effects of Women's Child Sexual Abuse and Subsequent Sexual Revictimization." *Journal of Consulting and Clinical Psychology, 60*(2), 167–174.

Wyatt, G. E., & Lyons-Rowe, S. (1990). "African American Women's Sexual Satisfaction as a Dimension of Their Sex Roles." *Sex Roles, 22*(7–8), 509–524.

Wyatt, G. E., Peters, S. D., & Guthrie, D. (1988). "Kinsey Revisited II: Comparisons of the Sexual Socialization and Sexual Behavior of Black Women Over 33 Years." *Archives of Sexual Behavior, 17*(4), 289–332.

Wyatt, G. E., & Riederle, M. (1994, September). "Sexual Harassment and Prior Sexual Trauma Among African American and White Women." *Violence and Victims, 9*(3), 233–247.

Wynn, R., & Fletcher, C. (1987). "Sex Role Development and Early Educational Experiences." In D. B. Carter (Ed.), *Current Conceptions of Sex Roles and Sex Typing*. New York: Praeger.

Yap, P. M. (1993). "Koro—A Culture-Bound Depersonalization." In D. N. Suggs & A. W. Miracle (Eds.), *Culture and Human Sexuality*. Pacific Grove, CA: Brooks/Cole.

Yapko, M. D. (1994). *Suggestions of Abuse: True and False Memories of Childhood Sexual Trauma*. New York: Simon & Schuster.

Yarber, W. L., Torabi, M. R., & Veenker, C. H. (1989). "Development of a Three-Component Sexually Transmitted Diseases Attitude Scale." *Journal of Sex Education and Therapy, 15*, 36–49.

Yawn, B. P., and Yawn, R. A. (1997). "Adolescent Pregnancy: A Preventable Consequence?" *The Prevention Researcher*. Eugene, OR: Integrated Research Services.

Yoder, J. D., & Aniakudo, P. (1995, February). "The Responses of African American Women Firefighters to Gender Harassment at Work." *Sex Roles, 32*(4–4), 125–137.

Yorke, J. A., et al. (1978). "Dynamics and Control of the Transmission of Gonorrhea." *Sexually Transmitted Diseases, 5*, 51–56.

Young, L. (1992). "Sexual Abuse and the Problem of Embodiment." *Child Abuse and Neglect, 16*(1), 89–100.

Zabin, L. S., & Clark, S. D. (1981). "Why They Delay: A Study of Teenage Family Planning Clinic Patients." *Family Planning Perspectives, 13*, 205–217.

Zabin, L. S., Hardy, J. B., Smith, E. A., & Hirsch, M. B. (1986). "Substance Use and Its Relation to Sexual Activity Among Inner-City Adolescents." *Journal of Adolescent Health Care, 7*(5), 320–331.

Zabin, L. S., Hirsch, M. B., Smith, E. A., Street, R., & Hardy, J. B. (1986). "Evaluation of a Pregnancy Prevention Program for Urban Teenagers." *Family Planning Perspectives, 18*, 119–126.

Zarit, S., et al. (1986). "Subjective Burden of Husbands and Wives as Caregivers: A Longitudinal Study." *Gerontologist, 26*, 260–266.

Zausner, M. (1986). *The Streets: A Factual Portrait of Sex Prostitutes as Told in Their Own Words*. New York: St. Martin's Press.

Zaviacic, M., et al. (1988). "Concentrations of Fructose in Female Ejaculate and Urine." *Journal of Sex Research, 24*, 319–325.

Zelnik, M. (1981). *Sex and Pregnancy in Adolescence*. Newbury Park, CA: Sage Publications.

Zelnik, M., & Kantner, J. F. (1972). "Probability of Premarital Intercourse." *Social Science Research, 1*, 335–341.

Zelnick, M., Kantner, J. F., & Ford, K. (1981). *Sex and Pregnancy in Adolescence*. Beverly Hills, CA: Sage.

Zerbe, K. J. (1992). "Why Eating-Disordered Patients Resist Sex Therapy: A Response to Simpson and Ramberg." *Journal of Sex and Marital Therapy, 18*(1), 55–64.

Zevin, D. (1992, August). "The Pleasure Principle." Special Issue: The Sexual Revolution in Movies, Music & TV. *US.*, pp. 32–36.

Zilbergeld, B. (1992). *Male Sexuality*. Boston: Little, Brown.

Zillman, D. (1994). "Erotica and Family Values." In D. Zillman, J. Bryant, & A. C. Houston (Eds.), *Media, Children, and the Family: Social Scientific, Psychodynamic, and Clinical Perspectives*. Hillsdale, NJ: Erlbaum.

Zinn, M. B. (1990). "Family, Feminism, and Race." *Gender and Society, 4*, 68–82.

Zinn, M. B., & Eitzen, D. S. (1990). *Diversity in Families* (2nd ed.). New York: HarperCollins.

Credits

Photos

Chapter 1 p. 8, © Michael Kaufman/Impact Visuals; p. 9T, © AP/Wide World Photos; p. 9B, © Christine DeVault; p. 10, © Michael Newman/PhotoEdit; p. 11, © Marc Bryan-Brown; p. 12, Everett Collection; p. 13, Everett Collection; p. 17, © Mark Seliger/Outline Press Syndicate; p. 19, Everett Collection; p. 21, © Robert Ullmann/Design Conceptions; p. 23, © John Pearson; p. 25, © Erich Lessing/Art Resource, NY; p. 26, Smithsonian Institution, National Anthropological Archives. Neg. # 85-8666; p. 31TL, © Donna Binder/Impact Visuals; p. 31TR, © Cleo/PhotoEdit; p. 31BL, © Richard Lord Ente/The Image Works; p. 31BR, © Alán Gallegos/AG Photograph **Chapter 2** p. 37T, Everett Collection; p. 42, © David Ryan/Photo 20-20; p. 47, © Irven DeVore/Anthro-Photo; p. 51, © Mary Evans Picture Library; p. 52, © Mary Evans Picture Library/Sigmund Freud Copyrights; p. 54, © Corbis-Bettmann; p. 56, © John Chiasson/Liaison Agency, Inc.; p. 57, © Bruce Powell; p. 60, © AP/Wide World Photos; p. 61, © 1978 Raymond Depardon/Magnum Photos; p. 63, © Mark E. Gibson; p. 65, © Esbin-Andersen/Photo 20-20; p. 67, © Myrleen Ferguson/PhotoEdit **Chapter 3** p. 78, Photograph by Imogen Cunningham, © 1978, 1998 The Imogen Cunningham Trust; p. 85, © C. Edelmann/La Villete/Photo Researchers, Inc.; p. 91, © Michael Newman/PhotoEdit **Chapter 4** p. 103L, © Bachmann/PhotoEdit; p. 103R, © Christie's Images; p. 104, © Shmuel Thaler/Santa Cruz Co. Sentinel; p. 109, © CNRI/Science Photo Library/Photo Researchers, Inc. **Chapter 5** p. 116, Lisa Lyon, 1981, © 1981 The Estate of Robert Mapplethorpe; p. 117, © Barbara Campbell/Liaison Agency, Inc.; p. 119, © Myrleen Ferguson/PhotoEdit; p. 128, © David Young-Wolff/PhotoEdit; p. 131, © Harvey Finkle/Impact Visuals; p. 133, © Michael Newman/PhotoEdit; p. 135, © 1985 Ken Miller; p. 141, Courtesy Dr. Donald Laub, Gender Dysphoria Program, Palo Alto **Chapter 6** p. 149, © Lisa Gallegos/AG Photograph; p. 150, © Christine DeVault; p. 155L, © David Young-Wolff/PhotoEdit; p. 155R, © Christine DeVault; p. 157, © Marilyn Humphries/Impact Visuals; p. 161, © R. Hutchings/PhotoEdit; p. 167, © Joel Gordon; p. 174, © Mary Kate Denny/PhotoEdit; p. 179, © Amy C. Etra/PhotoEdit; p. 185, © Christine DeVault; p. 188, © Lisa Gallegos/AG Photograph; p. 194, © Robert Brenner/PhotoEdit; p. 195, © Jean Mounicq/ANA, Paris; p. 197, © Rhoda Sidney/PhotoEdit **Chapter 7** p. 204, © Alice Grulich-Jones/Photo 20-20; p. 205, © David Young-Wolff/PhotoEdit; p. 209, © Michael Newman/PhotoEdit; p. 215, © Jonathan Nourok/PhotoEdit; p. 216, © Strauss/Curtis/Offshoot Stock **Chapter 8** p. 230, © Michael Newman/PhotoEdit; p. 235, © Alán Gallegos/AG Photograph; p. 239, © Suzanne Arms; p. 247, © Ron Chapple/FPG International **Chapter 9** p. 257L, © S. Vacariello/Nonstock, Inc.; p. 257R, © Joyce Tenneson/Nonstock, Inc.; p. 262, © Joel Gordon; p. 272, © Kit Hedman/Jeroboam; p. 275, © Amy Parish/Anthro-Photo; p. 263, © David Troncoso/Nonstock, Inc. **Chapter 10** p. 291, © Roberto Soncin Gerometta/Photo 20-20; p. 292, © Movie Star News; p. 295, © Markus Morianz; p. 296, © Robert Ginn/PhotoEdit; p. 298, © Porter Gifford/Liaison Agency, Inc.; p. 300, © Andrew Lichtenstein/Impact Visuals **Chapter 11** p. 311, © Joel Gordon; p. 314, © Joel Gordon; p. 318, © Jonathan A. Meyers/JAM Photography; p. 322R, © Joel Gordon; p. 322L, © Joel Gordon; p. 326, © Jonathan A. Meyers/JAM Photography; p. 328, © Joel Gordon; p. 329, © Joel Gordon; p. 330, © Joel Gordon; p. 333, © Jonathan A. Meyers/JAM Photography; p. 334, © Joel Gordon **Chapter 12** p. 358, Photos by Lennart Nillson/Bonnier Alba AB. From *Behold Man*. Little Brown and Company; p. 361, © Erika Stone; p. 367, © Mark Richards/PhotoEdit; p. 368, © Custom Medical Stock Photo. All Rights Reserved.; p. 377, © Georges DeKeerle/Liaison Agency, Inc.; p. 379, © Bob Daemmrich/Stock Boston; p. 383, © Fine Arts Museums of San Francisco, Gift of Peter F. Young, 74.21.14; p. 386, © Michael Newman/PhotoEdit; p. 387, © Myrleen Ferguson Cate/PhotoEdit **Chapter 13** p. 396, © Foto Comnet/Westlight; p. 398, © Carlos Henderson/Shooting Star; p. 401, © Christopher Brown/Stock Boston; p. 404, © Myrleen Ferguson Cate/PhotoEdit; p. 411, © Spencer Grant/The Picture Cube, Inc.; p. 417, © 1980 Hella Hammid. All rights reserved; p. 424, © Catherine Leroy/Sipa Press **Chapter 14** p. 433, © Willie L. Hill/Stock Boston; p. 435, © Roberto Soncin Gerometta/Photo 20-20; p. 445, © Chip Simons/FPG International; p. 455, © Elena Dorfman/Offshoot Stock **Chapter 15** p. 465, © Mark Richards/PhotoEdit; p. 470, 471, 474, 475, 480, Courtesy of the Center for Disease Control, Atlanta; p. 483, © Rich Frishman **Chapter 16** p. 492, © Einhorn/Liaison Agency, Inc.; p. 493, © A. Ramey/PhotoEdit; p. 497, © Custom Medical Stock Photo. All Rights Reserved.; p. 504, © Donna Binder/Impact Visuals; p. 507, © Meryl Levin/Impact Visuals; p. 510, © Grantpix/Photo Researchers, Inc.; p. 514, © Christine DeVault; p. 519, © Mark Phillips/Photo Researchers, Inc. **Chapter 17** p. 527, © Esbin-Anderson/Photo 20-20; p. 530, © Scala/Art Resource; p. 531T, © UPI/Corbis-Bettmann; p. 531B, © James D. Wilson/Liaison Agency, Inc.; p. 537, © Mark Peterson/SABA; p. 543, © Rhoda Sidney/PhotoEdit; p. 544, © Fotex/Shooting Star ; p. 550, © Custom Medical Stock Photo. All Rights Reserved. **Chapter 18** p. 560, © Bonnie Kamin; p. 561, © Fiona Hanson/Archive Photos; p. 566, © Michael Wilhoite from *Daddy's Roommate*, Alyson Publications; p. 571, © Reuters/Archive Photos; p. 572, © Eric Sander/Liaison Agency, Inc.; p. 573, Everett Collection.

Text and Illustrations

p. 48, From The Kinsey Institute New Report on Sex. Copyright ©1990 The Kinsey Institute for Research in Sex, Gender, and Reproduction. Reprinted with permission from St. Martin's Press; **p. 77,** From *The Marriage and Family Experience,* Seventh Edition by Bryan Strong, Christine DeVault, and Barbara Sayad. Copyright ©1998 Wadsworth Publishing Company. Used by permission; **p. 86,** Copyright ©1994 by Consumers Union of U.S. Inc., Yonkers, NY 10703-1057. Reprinted by permission from *Consumer Reports on Health,* May 1994; **p. 198,** Adapted from "What Doctors and Others Need to Know; Sex Facts on Human Sexuality and Aging" by R. Cross, *SIECUS Report,* June-July 1993, pp. 7-9. Reprinted by permission of SIECUS, 130 W. 42nd Street, Suite 350, New York, NY 10036-7802; **p. 210,** "The Styles of Loving: Questionnaire" by John A. Lee. Reprinted with permission from *Psychology Today* magazine. Copyright ©1974 Sussex Publishers, Inc.; **p. 220,** Adapted from "How the Tangled Web of Deception Hurts Relations" by Eric Adler from *The Kansas City Star,* August 24, 1994. Reprinted by permission of The Kansas City Star; **p. 316,** Adapted from *Contraceptive Technology* by Robert Hatcher, et al., Irvington Publishers, 1990. Reprinted by permission of Irvington Publishers, Inc.; **p. 444,** Fig. 14.4 John Leland, *Newsweek,* November 1997. Copyright ©1997 Newsweek. Used with permission; **pp. 463, 512,** Adapted with permission from William L. Yarber, Professor of Health Education, Indiana University, Bloomington; Mohammad Torabi, Professor of Health Education, Indiana University, Bloomington; L. Harold Veenker, Professor Emeritus of Health Education, Purdue University, Lafayette, IN.

Index

Boldfaced page numbers indicate pages on which key terms are defined.

Rubella, 364
Russia, 168–169

S&M. *See* Domination and submission
Sadism, sexual, 305–307, **306**
Sadistic rape, 306, 540, 542
Sadomasochism (S&M), as term, 51,
    290
    See also Domination and submission
Safer sex, 485–486
    anal intercourse and, 78, 283–284
    communication about, 236–237
    condom use in. *See* Condoms
    cunnilingus, 277–278, R-18
    dental dams and alternatives, use of,
        277, 284, R-18
    early adulthood and need for, 172
    fellatio and, 279
    HIV-positives and need for, 518–519
    kissing and, 307
    latex care, R-18
    masturbation as, 267, 563
    menstruation and, 88
    mutual disclosure and, 511
    nonoxynol-9 and, 331
    plastic wrap used in, R-18
    sex toys, 502, 503
    sexually oriented material and,
        563
    touching, erotic, 271
    vaginal intercourse and, 281
    See also HIV; STDs
Saliva, and HIV transmission, 501
Salpingectomy, 366
Salpingitis. *See* Pelvic inflammatory
        disease
Sambians, 25
Same-sex relationships. *See* Gay men;
        Homosexuality; Lesbians
Sample, **44–45**
Satyriasis, **289**
Scabies, **480**
Scat, 291
Schema, **41**
School
    condom availability in, 170–171
    gender-role learning in, 125–126
    sexual harassment in, 526
    See also College; Sex education; Teachers
Scientific method, **43**
Scripts, **130**
    See also Sexual scripts
Scrotum, **100**
Secondary sex characteristics, **105**
Secondary victimization, 544
    See also Revictimization
Secretory phase, **85**
Secure attachments, **215**
Self-awareness
    communication and, 241
    sexual enhancement and, 432–434
Self-disclosure
    Asian Americans and, 67–68
    communication and, 242, 243–244, 245,
        246
    and lasting love, **222**–223
    safer sex negotiation and, 237
    touching and, 233

Self-esteem
    ability to change and, 229
    attractiveness and, 257
    child sexual abuse and, 550, 551
    disabilities and, 409, 410
    eating disorders and, 397
    jealousy and lack of, 219
    love and, 204
    mastectomy and, 417
    prostitution and, 569–570
    psychosexual development and, 154
    sexual orientation and, 158–159
Self-help
    books, 9
    sex therapy, 453–454
Semen
    collection of, for insemination, 375
    fellatio and, 279
    production and function of, 103, **109**
    See also Ejaculation
Seminal fluid. *See* Semen
Seminal vesicles, **103**, 111–112
Seminiferous tubules, **101**, 107
Sensate focus, 435, **449**, 451, 452
Senses, and sexual response, 91
Serial monogamy, **184**
Serostatus, **498**
Servilism, 291
Sex (biological)
    defined, **116**
    differences in
        physical. *See* Physiology; Sex organs;
            Sexual response
        as slight, 127
        STD effects and transmission, 481,
            503
    gender identity and, 117–118, 139–140
    genetic selection of, 108–109
    intersexuality, 136–140
    opposite vs. other, 118–119, 122
    sociobiology and, 30
    third sex, 25–27, 59, 141
    transsexuality. *See* Transsexuality
    See also Gender; Sexuality
Sex education, 167–171
    abstinence-only programs, 168, 170
    aging and, 404
    AIDS prevention and, 168–169, 171,
        512–515
    child sexual abuse and, 553
    condom availability and, 170–171
    developmental disabilities and,
        412–413
    disability and, 410
    disagreement about curriculum,
        167–168, 513
    homosexuality and, 169
    impact of, 171
    parents and, 165, 169, 170, 513
    popular culture as source of, 9–10,
        36–39
    public support for, 513
    resource directory, R-8–R-9
    STD epidemic and, 464
    timing of, 169–170, 171
    See also Sex information; Sex therapy
Sex flush, **94**, 110, 111
Sex information

and advice genre, **36**–39
popular culture, 9–10, 36–39
sexually oriented materials, 9–10, 563
See also Sex education
Sex organs
    ambiguous (intersexed), 136–140
    assigned gender and, 116, 117
    embryonic differentiation of, 72, 73
    female
        breasts. *See* Breasts
        exercises for, R-14
        function of, 72
        internal structures, 74–78
        non-reproductive structures, 78,
            104
        self-exam of, R-12
        vulva (external structures), 72–74
    gender-dysphoria and. *See*
        Transsexuality
    language for, 151
    male
        external structures, 98–100
        function of, 98
        internal structures, 100–103
        non-reproductive structures, 103–104
        self-exam of, R-15
    STDs and, susceptibility to, 481, 503
    surgical reassignment of, 140
    See also Physiology; Sexual response;
        specific structures
Sex reassignment surgery (SRS), 140, **144**
Sex research
    of Ellis, 51, 53–54
    ethics in, 44, 47
    ethnicity and, 45, 58, 62–68
    evaluation standards for behavior,
        29–32
    fallacies affecting, 41–43
    feminist, 58–59
    of Freud, 51–53
    future of, 61–62
    on homosexuality, 54, 58, 59–61,
        158–159
    issues affecting, 43–45
    of Kaplan, 88, 90
    of Kinsey, 54–56
    of Krafft-Ebing, 51
    of Masters and Johnson, 51, 56, 88, 90,
        101
    methods, 50
        clinical, 45–46
        experimental, 50
        observational, 46–48
        survey, 46
    models, limitations of, 88
    normal/abnormal dichotomies rejected
        by, 29–32, 55–56
    normal sexual behavior, as term,
        28
    objectivity and. *See* Objectivity
    origin and themes of, 51, 53, 58–62
    popular culture and, 36–39
    sampling and, 45–46
    scientific method and, 43, 59
    and sexual response, 88, 90
    studies
        bias in, 37–39, 40, 44, 45–46, 60, 129,
            159